Contemporary Authors®
NEW REVISION SERIES

ISSN 0275-7176

Contemporary

Authors®

**A Bio-Bibliographical Guide to
Current Writers in Fiction, General Nonfiction,
Poetry, Journalism, Drama, Motion Pictures,
Television, and Other Fields**

SUSAN M. TROSKY
Editor

NEW REVISION SERIES
volume 43

 Gale Research Inc. • DETROIT • WASHINGTON, D.C. • LONDON

STAFF

Susan M. Trosky, *Editor, New Revision Series*

Elizabeth A. Des Chenes, David M. Galens, Jeff Hill, Denise E. Kasinec,
Thomas F. McMahon, Mark F. Mikula, Terrie M. Rooney, Pamela L. Shelton, Kenneth R. Shepherd,
Deborah A. Stanley, Roger M. Valade III, Polly A. Vedder, and Thomas Wiloch, *Associate Editors*

Pamela S. Dear, Margaret Mazurkiewicz, Mary L. Onorato, Scot Peacock, Anders J. Ramsey, Ken Rogers,
Geri J. Speace, Aarti Dhawan Stephens, Linda Tidrick, Brandon Trenz, and Kathleen Wilson, *Assistant Editors*

Joseph O. Aimone, Anne Blankenbaker, Ken Cuthbertson, Mindi Dickstein, Judith Farer, Elizabeth Judd,
Joan Goldsworthy, Lisa Harper, Anne Janette Johnson, Brett Lealand, Gordon Mayer, Greg Mazurkiewicz,
Jay Pederson, Tom Pendergast, Carol Was, Denise Wiloch, Michaela Swart Wilson, and Tim Winter-Damon,
Sketchwriters

James G. Lesniak, *Senior Editor, Contemporary Authors*

Victoria B. Cariappa, *Research Manager*

Mary Rose Bonk, *Research Supervisor*

Reginald A. Carlton, Frank Vincent Castronova, Andrew Guy Malonis, and Norma Sawaya,
Editorial Associates

Laurel Sprague Bowden, Dawn Marie Conzett, Eva Marie Felts, Shirley Gates, Doris Lewandowski,
Sharon McGilvray, Dana R. Schleiffers, and Amy B. Wieczorek, *Editorial Assistants*

♾ ™ This book is printed on acid-free paper that meets the minimum requirements
of American National Standard for Information Sciences-
Permanence Paper for Printed Library Materials, ANSI Z39.48-1984.

Library of Congress Catalog Card Number 81-640179

ISBN 0-8103-9137-6
ISSN 0275-7176

Printed in the United States of America.
Published simultaneously in the United Kingdom
by Gale Research International Limited
(An affiliated company of Gale Research Inc.)

I(T)P™

The trademark **ITP** is used under license.
10 9 8 7 6 5 4 3 2 1

Contents

> **Indexing note:** All *Contemporary Authors New Revision Series* entries are indexed in the *Contemporary Authors* cumulative index, which is published separately and distributed with even-numbered *Contemporary Authors* original volumes and odd-numbered *Contemporary Authors New Revison Series* volumes.
>
> **As always, the most recent *Contemporary Authors* cumulative index continues to be the user's guide to the location of an individual author's listing.**

Contemporary Authors *was named an* ***"Outstanding Reference Source"*** *by the American Library Association Reference and Adult Services Division after its 1962 inception.*
In 1985 it was listed by the same organization as one of the twenty-five most distinguished reference titles published in the past twenty-five years.

Preface

The *Contemporary Authors New Revision Series* (*CANR*) provides completely updated information on authors listed in earlier volumes of *Contemporary Authors* (*CA*). Entries for individual authors from *any* volume of *CA* may be included in a volume of the *New Revision Series*. *CANR* updates only those sketches requiring significant change.

Authors are included on the basis of specific criteria that indicate the need for significant revision. These criteria include bibliographical additions, changes in addresses or career, major awards, and personal information such as name changes or death dates. All listings in this volume have been revised or augmented in various ways. Some sketches have been extensively rewritten, and many include informative new sidelights. As always, a *CANR* listing entails no charge or obligation.

How to Get the Most out of *CA*: Use the Index

The key to locating an author's most recent entry is the *CA* cumulative index, which is published separately and distributed with even-numbered original volumes and odd-numbered revision volumes. It provides access to *all* entries in *CA* and *CANR*. Always consult the latest index to find an author's most recent entry.

For the convenience of users, the *CA* cumulative index also includes references to all entries in these Gale literary series: *Authors and Artists for Young Adults, Authors in the News, Bestsellers, Black Literature Criticism, Black Writers, Children's Literature Review, Concise Dictionary of American Literary Biography, Concise Dictionary of British Literary Biography, Contemporary Authors Autobiography Series, Contemporary Authors Bibliographical Series, Contemporary Literary Criticism, Dictionary of Literary Biography, DISCovering Authors, Drama Criticism, Hispanic Writers, Major Authors and Illustrators for Children and Young Adults, Major 20th-Century Writers, Poetry Criticism, Short Story Criticism, Something about the Author, Something about the Author Autobiography Series, Twentieth-Century Literary Criticism, World Literature Criticism,* and *Yesterday's Authors of Books for Children.*

A Sample Index Entry:

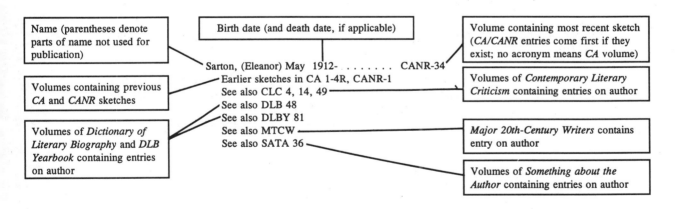

For the most recent *CA* information on Sarton, users should refer to Volume 34 of the *New Revision Series,* as designated by "CANR-34"; if that volume is unavailable, refer to CANR-1. And if CANR-1 is unavailable, refer to CA 1-4R, published in 1967, for Sarton's First Revision entry.

How Are Entries Compiled?

The editors make every effort to secure new information directly from the authors. Copies of all sketches in selected *CA* and *CANR* volumes previously published are routinely sent to listees at their last-known addresses, and returns from these authors are then assessed. For deceased writers, or those who fail to reply to requests for data, we consult other reliable biographical sources, such as those indexed in Gale's *Biography and Genealogy Master Index,* and bibliographical sources, such as *National Union Catalog, LC MARC,* and *British National Bibliography.* Further details come from published interviews, feature stories, and book reviews, and often the authors' publishers supply material.

* Indicates that a listing has been compiled from secondary sources believed to be reliable but has not been personally verified for this edition by the author sketched.

What Kinds of Information Does an Entry Provide?

Sketches in *CANR* contain the following biographical and bibliographical information:

- **Entry heading:** the most complete form of author's name, plus any pseudonyms or name variations used for writing

- **Personal information:** author's date and place of birth, family data, educational background, political and religious affiliations, and hobbies and leisure interests

- **Addresses:** author's home, office, or agent's addresses as available

- **Career summary:** name of employer, position, and dates held for each career post; résumé of other vocational achievements; military service

- **Membership information:** professional, civic, and other association memberships and any official posts held

- **Awards and honors:** military and civic citations, major prizes and nominations, fellowships, grants, and honorary degrees

- **Writings:** a comprehensive, chronological list of titles, publishers, dates of original publication and revised editions, and production information for plays, television scripts, and screenplays

- **Adaptations:** a list of films, plays, and other media which have been adapted from the author's work

- **Work in progress:** current or planned projects, with dates of completion and/or publication, and expected publisher, when known

- **Sidelights:** a biographical portrait of the author's development; information about the critical reception of the author's works; revealing comments, often by the author, on personal interests, aspirations, motivations, and thoughts on writing

- **Biographical and critical sources:** a list of books and periodicals in which additional information on an author's life and/or writings appears

Related Titles in the *CA* Series

Contemporary Authors Autobiography Series complements *CA* original and revised volumes with specially commissioned autobiographical essays by important current authors, illustrated with personal photographs they provide. Common topics include their motivations for writing, the people and experiences that shaped their careers, the rewards they derive from their work, and their impressions of the current literary scene.

Contemporary Authors Bibliographical Series surveys writings by and about important American authors since World War II. Each volume concentrates on a specific genre and features approximately ten writers; entries list works written by and about the author and contain a bibliographical essay discussing the merits and deficiencies of major critical and scholarly studies in detail.

Available in Electronic Formats

CD-ROM. Full-text bio-bibliographic entries from the entire *CA* series, covering approximately 100,000 writers, are available on CD-ROM through lease and purchase plans. The disc combines entries from the *CA, CANR,* and *Contemporary Authors Permanent Series (CAP)* print series to provide the most recent author listing. It can be searched by name, title, subject/genre, personal data, and by using boolean logic. The disc will be updated every six months. For more information, call 1-800-877-GALE.

Magnetic Tape. *CA* will be available for licensing on magnetic tape in a fielded format. Either the complete database or a custom selection of entries may be ordered. The database will be available for internal data processing and nonpublishing purposes only. For more information, call 1-800-877-GALE.

Suggestions Are Welcome

The editors welcome comments and suggestions from users on any aspects of the *CA* series. If readers would like to recommend authors whose entries should appear in future volumes of the series, they are cordially invited to write: The Editors, *Contemporary Authors,* 835 Penobscot Bldg., Detroit, MI 48226-4094; call toll-free at 1-800-347-GALE; or fax to 1-313-961-6599.

CA Numbering System and Volume Update Chart

Occasionally questions arise about the *CA* numbering system and which volumes, if any, can be discarded. Despite numbers like "29-32R," "97-100" and "142," the entire *CA* series consists of only 112 physical volumes with the publication of *CA New Revision Series* Volume 43. The following charts note changes in the numbering system and cover design, and indicate which volumes are essential for the most complete, up-to-date coverage.

CA First Revision
- 1-4R through 41-44R (11 books)
  Cover: Brown with black and gold trim.
  There will be no further First Revision volumes because revised entries are now being handled exclusively through the more efficient *New Revision Series* mentioned below.

CA Original Volumes
- 45-48 through 97-100 (14 books)
  Cover: Brown with black and gold trim.
- 101 through 142 (42 books)
  Cover: Blue and black with orange bands.
  The same as previous *CA* original volumes but with a new, simplified numbering system and new cover design.

CA Permanent Series
- *CAP*-1 and *CAP*-2 (2 books)
  Cover: Brown with red and gold trim.
  There will be no further *Permanent Series* volumes because revised entries are now being handled exclusively through the more efficient *New Revision Series* mentioned below.

CA New Revision Series
- *CANR*-1 through *CANR*-43 (43 books)
  Cover: Blue and black with green bands.
  Includes only sketches requiring extensive changes; **sketches are taken from any previously published *CA*, *CAP*, or *CANR* volume.**

If You Have: You May Discard:

If You Have:	You May Discard:
CA First Revision Volumes 1-4R through 41-44R **and** *CA Permanent Series* Volumes 1 and 2	*CA* Original Volumes 1, 2, 3, 4 Volumes 5-6 through 41-44
CA Original Volumes 45-48 through 97-100 **and** 101 through 142	**NONE:** These volumes will not be superseded by corresponding revised volumes. Individual entries from these and all other volumes appearing in the left column of this chart may be revised and included in the various volumes of the *New Revision Series*.
CA New Revision Series Volumes *CANR*-1 through *CANR*-43	**NONE:** The *New Revision Series* does not replace any single volume of *CA*. Instead, volumes of *CANR* include entries from many previous *CA* series volumes. All *New Revision Series* volumes must be retained for full coverage.

A Sampling of Authors and Media People Featured in This Volume

Robert Altman
A gifted, unconventional filmmaker, Altman served as screenwriter and director for such acclaimed movies as *M*A*S*H* and *Nashville*. He also directed *The Player*, which won a 1992 Cannes International Film Festival award.

Aime Cesaire
Cesaire, a West Indian poet and playwright, developed and promoted the idea of negritude, a philosophy that calls for blacks to reject western society and adopt the traditional values of their cultural heritage. His works include the epic poem *Return to My Native Land* and *Aime Cesaire: The Collected Poetry*.

John Leonard Clive
Clive received the 1990 National Book Critics Circle Award for criticism for *Not by Fact Alone: Essays on the Reading and Writing of History*. The renowned historian earlier wrote the widely praised *Macaulay: The Shaping of the Historian*.

Samuel R. Delaney
In his "Return to Neveryon" series, innovative science fiction writer Delaney explores creativity, politics, the power of imagination, and the boundaries of language.

Gail Godwin
Godwin's novels, including *A Southern Family, Father's Melancholy Daughter* and *The Good Husband*, examine their female protagonists' search for self-identity and their attitudes toward love, death, and relationships.

Jane Goodall
An expert on the behavior of wild chimpanzees, Goodall has spent more than thirty years living in the jungles of Tanzania studying those creatures. Her books *In the Shadow of Man* and *My Life with Chimpanzees* document her findings.

Andrew M. Greeley
Greeley, a Roman Catholic priest and sociologist whose controversial writings on religion are often at odds with Catholic theology, is also the author of such popular mystery novels as *The Cardinal Sins* and, more recently, *Fall from Grace* and *Happy Are the Peacemakers*.

Frank Herbert
Though Herbert is best remembered as the author of *Dune*, a masterpiece of modern science fiction, he also wrote *The White Plague, The Ascension Factor,* and numerous other novels of the genre.

John Jakes
Jakes incorporates both real-life and fictional characters in his best-selling "American Bicentennial" series and "North and South" trilogy.

Charles Kuralt
The folksy, affable Kuralt travels America's back roads in search of unique human interest stories. His writings include *Dateline America* and *A Life on the Road*.

P. D. James
James is the critically acclaimed author of such works as *An Unsuitable Job for a Woman, Devices and Desires,* and *The Children of Men*. This popular English mystery writer is often compared to novelists Agatha Christie and Dorothy Sayers.

Jim Lehrer
Though best known as the co-anchor of PBS-TV's Emmy Award-winning *The MacNeil/Lehrer Newshour*, Lehrer is also the author of the whimsical "One-Eyed Mack" series of novels.

Nelson Mandela
Mandela, a leader in the struggle against apartheid, became president of South Africa's African National Congress in 1991. *No Easy Walk to Freedom* and *The Struggle Is My Life* collect his speeches and other political statements.

Larry McMurtry
McMurtry, whose highly acclaimed novels and screenplays draw from the mythic past and ongoing urbanization of his native Texas, is the author of the Pulitzer Prize-winning *Lonesome Dove* and its sequel, *Streets of Laredo*.

Iris Murdoch
A former winner of the Booker Prize and James Tait Black Memorial Prize, Murdoch has earned a reputation as one of her generation's most important writers through novels such as *The Sea, The Sea* and *The Message to the Planet*.

Mary Oliver
Oliver, a celebrated poet who received the 1984 Pulitzer Prize for *American Primitive,* is also the recipient of the 1991 Christopher Award for *House of Light* and the 1992 National Book Award for *New and Selected Poems*.

Martin Cruz Smith
Smith chronicles the adventures of Russian homicide detective Arkady Renko in the bestselling suspense novel *Gorky Park* and its popular sequels, *Polar Star* and *Red Square*.

*Indicates that a listing has been compiled from secondary sources believed to be reliable
but has not been personally verified for this edition by the author sketched.*

ABRAHAMS, William (Miller) 1919-

PERSONAL: Born January 23, 1919, in Boston, MA; son
of Louis and Wilhelmina (Miller) Abrahams. *Education:*
Harvard University, B.A., 1941.

ADDRESSES: Home—375 Pinehill Rd., Burlingame, CA
94010. *Office*—E.P. Dutton, 375 Hudson St., New York,
NY 10014-3658.

CAREER: Atlantic Monthly Press, Boston, MA, editor,
1955-63, senior editor, 1963-77; West Coast Holt, Rine-
hart & Winston, New York City, senior editor, 1977-84;
E.P. Dutton/William Abrahams Books, senior editor,
1984—. *Military service:* U.S. Army, 1942-45.

AWARDS, HONORS: Fellow, Stanford University,
1949-50; nominee (with Peter Stansky), American Book
Award for biography, 1981, for *Orwell: The Transformation.*

WRITINGS:

NOVELS

Interval in Carolina, Simon & Schuster, 1945.
By the Beautiful Sea, Dial, 1947.
Imperial Waltz, Dial, 1954.
Children of Capricorn, Random House, 1963.

EDITOR

(Editor and author of introductions) *Prize Stories: The O.
 Henry Awards* (annual volumes), Doubleday,
 1967-93.
(Editor and author of introduction) *Fifty Years of the
 American Short Story, From the O. Henry Awards:
 1919-1970* (two volumes), Doubleday, 1970.
(Editor and author of introduction) *Prize Stories of the
 Seventies: From the O. Henry Awards,* Doubleday,
 1981.

Also contributing editor to *Atlantic Monthly,* 1968-1979,
and *Inquiry,* 1978-83.

BIOGRAPHIES

(With Peter Stansky) *Journey to the Frontier: Two Roads
 to the Spanish Civil War,* Little, Brown, 1966, pub-
 lished as *Journey to the Frontier: Julian Bell and John
 Cornford: Their Lives and the 1930s,* Constable, 1960.
(With Stansky) *The Unknown Orwell,* Knopf, 1970.
(With Stansky) *Orwell: The Transformation,* Knopf, 1980.

SIDELIGHTS: Author and editor William Abrahams has
served for over twenty years as the senior editor of
Doubleday's annual publication of the O. Henry Awards
short story collections, a series of books for which Abrahams has also provided introductory essays discussing the
development of American short fiction. His choices for inclusion in the O. Henry Awards collections have been
called "truly eclectic, [displaying] an editorial propensity
that enriches us all," by Andre Dubus III in the *Los Angeles Times Book Review.* In contributing to the same periodical, Don Skiles commented that Abrahams' years as
judge of the O. Henry prize stories "correspond with an
amazing renaissance in the short story—a form, like jazz,
that Americans have had a large hand in shaping. Abrahams's consistently dedicated work with the O. Henry selections has certainly helped develop and sustain that renaissance."

Abrahams is also the author of several novels, as well as
biographical works written with coauthor Peter Stansky.
Journey to the Frontier, the biography of Julian Bell and
John Conforth, and two volumes about the life of author
George Orwell, *The Unknown Orwell* and *Orwell: The
Transformation,* are generally praised for their attention
to detail. Writing for the *New York Times,* Christopher
Lehmann-Haupt observed that *Orwell: The Transforma-
tion* "is presented with considerable charm and eloquence,

and serves to give us a portrait of Orwell so vivid that we can practically picture him entering the room."

BIOGRAPHICAL/CRITICAL SOURCES:

PERIODICALS

Kenyon Review, November, 1966.
Los Angeles Times Book Review, April 27, 1986; August 9, 1987; November 29, 1990.
New York Times, November 10, 1972; May 1, 1980.
New York Times Book Review, January 3, 1971; April 27, 1986; May 21, 1989; August 12, 1990.
Times Literary Supplement, January 11, 1980.
Virginia Quarterly, summer, 1968; summer, 1981.
Washington Post Book World, May 11, 1980.*

* * *

ACKERMAN, Robert E(dwin) 1928-

PERSONAL: Born May 21, 1928, in Grand Rapids, MI; son of William Howard and Maude (DeWinter) Ackerman; married Lillian Alice Hanjian (a research anthropologist), March 30, 1952; children: Laura Lynn, Gail Ellen, James Eric. *Education:* Attended Michigan College of Mining and Technology (now Michigan Technological University), 1946-47; University of Michigan, B.A., 1950, M.A., 1951; University of Pennsylvania, Ph.D., 1961. *Politics:* Democrat. *Religion:* None.

ADDRESSES: Home—Route 3, Box 559, Pullman, WA 99163. *Office*—Department of Anthropology, Washington State University, Pullman, WA 99164-4910.

CAREER: Washington State University, Pullman, instructor, 1961-62, assistant professor, 1962-65, associate professor, 1965-73, professor of anthropology, 1973—, acting chairman of department, 1971-72, director of Museum of Anthropology, 1987—. Fellow in anthropology, Eastern Pennsylvania Psychiatric Institute, 1959-61; instructor in anthropology, Extension Division, University of Delaware, 1960-61. Has participated in numerous research archaeological expeditions and surveys in various locations in United States and abroad, including Alaska, Canada, Soviet Union, Korea, and China. Lecturer; has read papers at many scientific conferences. *Military service:* U.S. Air Force, 1952-56; Russian language specialist.

MEMBER: American Anthropological Association (fellow), American Association for the Advancement of Science (fellow), American Quaternary Association, Society for American Archaeology, Arctic Institute of North America (fellow), Society of Professional Archaeologists, American Association of University Professors, Canadian Archeological Association, Pacific Science Association,

Alaska Anthropological Association, Explorers Club (fellow), Sigma Xi.

AWARDS, HONORS: Grants from Arctic Institute of North America, 1962-63, National Park Service, 1963-65, National Science Foundation, 1966-67, 1971-72, 1992-93, National Geographic Society, 1978-81, and Alaska Geophysical and Geological Survey and Office of History and Archeology, 1993.

WRITINGS:

Prehistory in the Kuskokwim-Bristol Bay Region, Southwestern Alaska, Laboratory of Anthropology, Washington State University, 1964.
Archeological Survey: Glacier Bay National Monument, Southeastern Alaska, Laboratory of Anthropology, Washington State University, 1964.
The Archeology of the Glacier Bay Region, Southeastern Alaska, Laboratory of Anthropology, Washington State University, 1968.
Kenaitze Indians, Indian Tribal Services, 1975.
The Eskimo People of Savoonga, Indian Tribal Services, 1976.
(With Kenneth C. Reid, James D. Gallison, and Mark E. Roe) *Archaeology of Heceta Island: A Survey of 16 Timber Harvest Units in the Tongass National Forest, Southeastern Alaska,* Center for Northwest Anthropology, Washington State University, Pullman, 1985.
(With Reid, Gallison, and E. Richard Chesmore, Jr.) *Archaeology of Coffman Cove: A Survey of 15 Timber Harvest Units on Prince of Wales Island, Southeastern Alaska,* Center for Northwest Anthropology, Washington State University, Pullman, 1987.
(With Reid and Gallison) *Archaeology of Thorne Bay: A Survey of 22 Timber Harvest Units on Prince of Wales Island, Southeastern Alaska,* Center for Northwest Anthropology, Washington State University, Pullman, 1987.

Author and editor of numerous reports. Contributor to numerous books, including *Ethnohistory in Southwestern Alaska and the Southern Yukon: Method and Content,* edited by Margaret Lantis, University of Kentucky Press, 1970; *Early Native Americans: Prehistoric Demography, Economy, and Technology,* edited by D. L. Browman, Mouton, 1980; *Megaliths to Medicine Wheels: Boulder Structures in Archaeology,* edited by M. Wilson, K. L. Road, and K. J. Hardy, University of Calgary Archaeological Association, 1981; *Traditional Cultures in the Pacific Societies: Continuity and Change,* edited by Sang-bok Khan and Kwang-Ok Kim, Seoul National University Press, 1990; and *Western North America Maritime Prehistory,* edited by A. Blukia Onat, Washington State University Press, in press. Contributor to numerous periodicals, including *Current Anthropology, American Anthropologist,*

Anthropologica, American Antiquity, Ethnohistory, Current Research in the Pleistocene, Arctic, Arctic Anthropology, and *Beaver.* Associate, *Current Anthropology.*

WORK IN PROGRESS: Contributing ethnoarcheological and prehistoric archeological studies to books, journals, and conference proceedings; editing and contributing to *Prehistoric Routes into the New World: The Trek from Northeast Asia to Southern South America,* for Washington State University Press and *American Beginnings: The Archaeology and Paleoecology of Beringia*; article for *Archaeology of Prehistoric North America: An Encyclopedia.*

SIDELIGHTS: Robert E. Ackerman told *CA:* "My career in northern research really began in 1958 when I made an archeological survey of St. Lawrence in an Eskimo skin covered umiak with two Eskimo assistants. At that time Dorian Sergeev of the Institute of Ethnography in St. Petersburg, Russia was on the Chukotsk Peninsula digging a large Eskimo cemetery that dated back to the beginning of the Christian era. To see his materials it was not just a forty mile jaunt over to Cape Chaplin and then up the coast to his site, but I had to travel half-way around the world to St. Petersburg and Moscow to see his discoveries for the shores of Siberia were closed to all foreigners. In 1959 I journeyed to Russia and have made numerous trips since to Novosibirsk, Irkutsk, Khabarovsk, and Yakutsk to visit with Russian colleagues and view artifacts recovered from their excavations. The most impressive trip was in 1990 when as guest of the Institute of Archeology in Novosibirsk I traveled to the Altai Mountains to participate in an excursion led by Anatoly Derevianko to Mousterian and later to cave sites. Then as guest of the Laboratory of Archeology in Yakutsk I had the opportunity to visit the ancient site (perhaps several hundred thousand years old) of Diring Yuriak on the Lena River under excavation by Academician Yuri Mochanov.

"Years of archeological research in Alaska have led me to the Tlingit villages of the southeast, to the coastal Eskimo villages of the Bering Sea and to the interior villages of the Tanaina peoples. Studies of living peoples of Alaska and Siberia have been important to my treatment of prehistory so that where possible the lifeways of local peoples have been observed as a backdrop to my attempt to rekindle the past.

"Currently, I am trying to study from archeological remains the way people adapted to living conditions at the end of the late Pleistocene Era, some 12,000 to 11,000 years ago and adjusted to the changing environment brought about by the increased warmth of the Holocene, our present climatic interval for the last 10,000 years. As I sat in the mouth of a limestone cave in central southwestern Alaska this summer looking over the landscape, I tried to visualize how life would have been 12,000 years ago when all of the landscape was a shrub grassland with herds of bison, horse, and mammoth roaming the landscape. I almost reached for my spear, but found a trowel instead and with it returned to my own time and the excavation before me."

*   *   *

ALLEN, Gina 1918-

PERSONAL: Born July 4, 1918, in Trenton, NE; daughter of Ralph V. and Osa (Hanel) Hunkins; married Theodore W. Allen, January 28, 1939 (divorced, 1972); children: Ginita Allen Wall. *Education:* Attended University of Nebraska, 1935-37; Northwestern University, B.A., 1940. *Politics:* Democrat. *Religion:* Humanist.

ADDRESSES: Agent—Ann Elma, 52 Vanderbilt Ave., New York, NY 10017.

CAREER: Free-lance writer. Sex therapist in San Francisco and Beverly Hills, CA, 1970—; senior humanist counselor, American Humanist Association, 1971—. Executive secretary, Third Judicial District, New Mexico Youth Commission, 1955-60; state chairwoman, New Mexico Democratic Committee, 1956-59; fifth vice-president, New Mexico Congress of Parents and Teachers, beginning 1957. Lecturer on feminist issues.

MEMBER: International Association of Humanist Educators, Counselors, and Leaders (member of board of directors, 1988-92), American Humanist Association (secretary, 1973-77; founding chairwoman, Feminist Caucus, 1977-86; vice-president, 1979-83; chairwoman, Division of Humanist Counseling, 1982-86), Authors Guild, Authors League, National Organization of Women (founding member, Golden Gate chapter; member of board of directors, 1970—), Humanist Association of San Francisco (president, 1976-85).

AWARDS, HONORS: Anisfield-Wolf Award, *Saturday Review,* 1962, for *The Forbidden Man,* as the book dealing most creditably with social and group relations; merit award, American Humanist Association, 1977; named to Humanist Counselors Hall of Fame, American Humanist Association, 1989.

WRITINGS:

Prairie Children (juvenile), Row, Peterson, 1941.
(With father, Ralph V. Hunkins) *Tepee Days* (juvenile), American Book Co., 1941.
(Co-author) *Tales of the Prairies,* three books, American Book Co., 1941-45.
On the Oregon Trail (juvenile), Row, Peterson, 1942.
(With Hunkins) *Trapper Days* (juvenile), American Book Co., 1942.

(With Hunkins) *Sod-House Days* (juvenile), American Book Co., 1945.

Rustics for Keeps (autobiographical), Odyssey, 1948.

The Forbidden Man (novel), Chilton, 1961.

Gold!, Crowell, 1964.

Gold Is, Meredith, 1969.

(With Clement G. Martin) *Intimacy: Sensitivity, Sex, and the Art of Love,* Cowles, 1971.

Also author of *Party Girl,* 1962. Author of television scripts for National Broadcasting Corp. and Metromedia Television, 1966—. Contributor of short stories, articles, columns, novelettes to numerous periodicals, including *Woman's Home Companion, Ladies Home Journal, Woman's Day, Family Circle, Redbook, Family Health,* and *Humanist.* Member of editorial board, *Humanist,* 1983—.*

*   *   *

ALLWORTH, Edward A(lfred)   1920-

PERSONAL: Born December 1, 1920, in Columbia, SC; son of Edward Christopher (a college administrator) and Ethel Elaine (Walker) Allworth; married Janet Lovett, December 21, 1952; children: Clark Edward. *Education:* Oregon State University, B.S., 1948; University of Chicago, A.M., 1953; Columbia University, Ph.D., 1959.

ADDRESSES: Home—New York, NY. *Office*—Department of Middle East and Asian Languages and Culture, Columbia University, 116th & Broadway, New York, NY 10027.

CAREER: Reed College, Portland, OR, instructor in Russian and humanities, 1957-58; Ford Foundation, New York City, program assistant in international training and research, 1958-59; American Committee, Munich, Germany, assistant to director of emigrant relations, 1960-61; Columbia University, New York City, assistant professor, 1961-65, associate professor, 1965-69, professor of Turco-Soviet studies, 1970-90, emeritus professor and special lecturer, 1991—, director of Program on Soviet Nationality Problems, 1970-87, head of Central Asia Center, 1984-90. Guest scholar, Wilson Center, Smithsonian Institution, 1981. Leader, U.S. delegation of U.S.-U.S.S.R. Exchange Symposium on Literature and Nationality in Central Asia, Moscow, 1985; senior fellow, Institute for Advanced Studies, Hebrew University of Jerusalem, 1987; member of executive committee, Harriman Institute, 1992—. Consultant and advisory editor to publishers. *Military service:* U.S. Army, Airborne, 1942-47; became captain.

MEMBER: American Numismatic Society.

AWARDS, HONORS: Fellowship, Social Science Research Council, 1967-68, and American Philosophical So-

ciety, 1976; Ismail Gaspirali Award, American Association of Crimean Turks, 1985; National Endowment for the Humanities grant, 1990-93; Turkistanian-American Association award, 1991; U.S. Institute of Peace grant, 1992-94.

WRITINGS:

Uzbek Literary Politics, Mouton, 1964.

Central Asian Publishing and the Rise of Nationalism, New York Public Library, 1965.

Nationalities of the Soviet East: Publications and Writing Systems, Columbia University Press, 1971.

Soviet Asia: Bibliographies . . . and an Essay on the Soviet Asia Controversy, Praeger, 1975.

(Translator) Ibrahim Sinasi, *The Wedding of a Poet,* Griffon House, 1981.

The End of Ethnic Integration in Southern Central Asia, Kennan Institute for Advanced Russian Studies, 1982.

The Modern Uzbeks: From the Fourteenth Century to the Present, Hoover Institution Press, 1990.

EDITOR AND CONTRIBUTOR

Central Asia: A Century of Russian Rule, Columbia University Press, 1967, revised edition published as *Central Asia: 120 Years of Russian Rule,* Duke University Press, 1989.

Soviet Nationality Problems, Columbia University Press, 1971.

The Nationality Question in Soviet Central Asia, Praeger, 1973.

Nationality Group Survival in Multiethnic States, Praeger, 1977.

Ethnic Russia in the U.S.S.R.: The Dilemma of Dominance, Pergamon, 1980.

Tatars of the Crimea: Their Struggle for Survival, Duke University Press, 1988.

(And translator) *Muslim Communities Reemerge: Historical Perspective on Identity, Politics, and Opposition in the Soviet Union and Yugoslavia,* Duke University Press, 1994.

OTHER

Editor, "Central Asia" book series, Duke University Press, 1983—.

SIDELIGHTS: Edward A. Allworth told *CA:* "Nothing in intellectual life is more exciting than reading a well-written, serious book. I learn constantly from good editors and writers what I would hope to be able to emulate. An academic adviser years ago told me that no book is good if it isn't well-written. I believe it and still try to achieve it. A primary aim in my efforts is to bring the civilization and international importance of Central Asia, including Afghanistan and the former Soviet and the Chinese portions, to the attention of informed people and students everywhere. This involves human rights (free speech in particular) as well as scholarship into indigenous and borrowed ideas, culture, and technology. Readers in Central Asia itself respond to foreign writings about their world. This continues to be true because since the breakup of the USSR, the state ideology there still shapes a peculiarly one-dimensional view that sanitizes Tajik, Turkmen, Uzbek, and other histories and cultures.

"A critic commented negatively in the officially-sponsored Uzbek-Russian language journal, *Social Sciences in Uzbekistan*, 1980, on several of my books: 'Touching on the 1920s and 1930s, he [Allworth] focuses more on the works of complex or contradictory personalities (the reformers Cholpan, Fitrat, and others) and minimizes or vaguely speaks about today's attainments in the cultural life of Central Asia's people. His book, *Uzbek Literary Politics*, for example, testifies to this. . . . Allworth begins to write also [in *The Nationality Question in Soviet Central Asia*] about contemporary phenomena in the cultural life of Central Asia (regarding the younger generation, and about book publishing, for instance).' But a positive insight reached the Uzbek critic when he urged his countrymen to learn foreign languages besides Russian and to acquire disciplinary professionalism in order to win what he calls 'the ideological battle.'

"With something closer to a real exchange of ideas—one cannot speak of free press in most of contemporary Central Asia—I have faith in the chances for an informed populace. The more the Central Asians can read for themselves, rather than learning through selective translation, the better for a true understanding of themselves and of Western democracy with its liberty. My efforts to offer objective analysis are motivated not at all by political reactions to them, but it is evident that the Central Asian treatment of their own literary and cultural history has broadened as outside scrutiny has increased in penetrating scholarship. This leads Western authors in this field to surmise that we have some impact there as well as among our own readers."

*   *   *

ALTMAN, Robert 1925-

PERSONAL: Born February 20, 1925, in Kansas City, MO; married third wife, Kathryn Reed; children: (first marriage) Christine, (second marriage) Michael, Stephen, (third marriage) Bobby, Matthew (adopted). *Education:* Attended University of Missouri. *Religion:* "Hedonist."

ADDRESSES: Home—Malibu Beach, CA. *Office*—Sandcastle 5 Productions, 502 Park Avenue, Suite 156, New York, NY 10022. *Agent*—ICM, Los Angeles, CA.

CAREER: Film director and writer. Calvin Co., Kansas City, MO, writer, photographer, editor, and director of industrial films, 1950-57; television writer, producer, and director, 1957-65; director of films for various motion-picture studios, 1965—; founder, Lion's Gate Productions (film production company), Westwood Editorial Service (film post-production company), and Sandcastle 5 Productions (film production company), New York City. *Military service:* U.S. Army, 1943-47; bomber pilot.

MEMBER: Directors Guild of America.

AWARDS, HONORS: Golden Palm Award, Cannes International Film Festival, 1970, and Academy Award nomination, 1971, both for *M*A*S*H;* best film award and best director award, both from New York Film Critics Circle, both 1975, and Academy Award nominations for best picture and best director, both 1976, all for *Nashville;* Golden Bear Award, Berlin International Film Festival, 1976, for *Buffalo Bill and the Indians;* award, Cannes International Film Festival, 1993, for *The Player.*

WRITINGS:

SCREENPLAYS

(And director) *The Delinquents,* United Artists, 1955.
(And director, with George W. George) *The James Dean Story,* Warner Bros., 1957.
(With Ring Lardner, Jr.; and director) *M*A*S*H* (adapted from novel by Richard Hooker), Twentieth Century-Fox, 1970.
(And director) *Brewster McCloud,* Metro-Goldwyn-Mayer, 1970.
(With Brian McKay; and director) *McCabe and Mrs. Miller,* Warner Bros., 1971.
(And director) *Images,* Columbia, 1972.
(And director) *The Long Goodbye,* (adapted from novel by Raymond Chandler), United Artists, 1973.
(With Calder Willingham and Joan Tewkesbury; and director) *Thieves Like Us,* United Artists, 1974.
(And director) *California Split,* Columbia, 1974.
(With Tewkesbury; also director) *Nashville,* (Paramount, 1975), Bantam Books, 1976.
(With Alan Rudolph) *Buffalo Bill and the Indians; or, Sitting Bull's History Lesson* (United Artists, 1976), Bantam, 1976.
(Also director) *Three Women,* Twentieth Century-Fox, 1977.
(With John Considine, Patricia Resnick, and Allan Nicholls; also director) *A Wedding,* Twentieth Century-Fox, 1978.
(With Frank Barhydt and Resnick; and director) *Quintet,* Twentieth Century-Fox, 1979.
(With Nicholls; and director) *A Perfect Couple,* Twentieth Century-Fox, 1979.

(With Barhydt and Paul Dooley; and director) *Health,* Twentieth Century-Fox, 1982.

(With Christopher Durang; and director) *Beyond Therapy,* New World, 1987.

Also author, with Barhydt, of *L.A. Short Cuts.*

OTHER

Co-author with Arnold Weinstein, of *McTeague* (libretto), produced in Chicago, 1992.

Director of numerous films, including *The James Dean Story,* Warner Bros., 1957; *Nightmare in Chicago,* Universal, 1967; *Countdown,* Warner Bros., 1968; *That Cold Day in the Park,* Commonwealth United, 1969; *Popeye,* Paramount, 1980; *Come Back to the 5 & Dime, Jimmy Dean, Jimmy Dean,* Cinecom, 1982; *Streamers,* United Artists Classics, 1983; *Secret Honor,* Sandcastle 5, 1984; *Fool for Love,* Cannon Group, 1985; and *The Player,* Fine Line Features, 1992.

Writer, producer and director of television programs, including *The Roaring Twenties, Bonanza, Combat, Suspense Theatre, The Millionaire, Whirlybirds, The Room, The Caine Mutiny Court-Martial, Vincent and Theo,* and *Tanner '88.*

SIDELIGHTS: Robert Altman is an unconventional filmmaker. For him, a script is a launching point for improvisation; he provides his actors with an unstructured, creative atmosphere where real human behavior is valued over the contrived gestures of role playing. Altman has always been most interested in the behavior of his characters over their dialogue; he views a screenplay merely as a starting point, and as a means to gain financing; once a movie project has a producer, Altman recreates.

Altman's first major film was *M*A*S*H,* released in 1970. Already forty-five years of age, he took the job only after fourteen other directors had turned it down. His collaborator on the screenplay, Ring Lardner, Jr., was once heard to remark that "Mr. Altman does not treat a script very carefully." In *Film Quarterly,* William Johnson praised *M*A*S*H* for its strong characterization and attention to detail: "The dialogue has an almost Proustian richness, with asides and fragmentary exchanges which may easily be missed at a first viewing. In a rapid throwaway line, the general refers to 'the dark days before Pearl Harbor.'" Pauline Kael, writing in the *New Yorker,* drew attention to Altman's feel for low-keyed humor, commenting that "Altman has made a real sport of a movie which combines traditional roustabout comedy with modern attitudes."

In *McCabe and Mrs. Miller* Altman tells the story of the growth of a frontier town and the gambler McCabe's love affair with Mrs. Miller. While in *M*A*S*H* Altman makes war the backdrop and subject of satire, in *McCabe and Mrs. Miller* he plays with the quintessentially American theme of westward expansion. "Then, too," wrote Jan Dawson in *Sight and Sound,* "the West provides Altman with material for extending his satire of American attitudes. It reveals an ideology and an economic system in the making, as McCabe's route from gambler to speculator, and final extinction at the hands of big business, takes him through a capsule version of the economic history of the United States."

Altman's essentially documentary style of storytelling is revealed in *Nashville,* one of this writer/director's most important pictures. Intended loosely as a portrait of the southern town of that name, *Nashville* subordinates plot to the welter of action, light and sound that is the undisciplined nature of life. *Newsweek* called the 1975 film "everything a work of social art ought to be but seldom is, immensely moving yet terribly funny, chastening yet ultimately exhilarating. It is also that rarest thing in contemporary movies, a work of art that promises to be hugely popular." In an interview with *Film Quarterly,* Altman stated: "Well, you take from *Nashville* what you can understand. For example, my grandmother saw it and she has a totally different consciousness than I do, and she liked it."

Although the critical response to Altman's films has varied, many reviewers have heaped accolades upon him. When, in 1979, Vincent Canby was asked if there had been any American film masterpieces within the past ten years, the noted film critic responded, "I'm sure there have been, but there's only one I'm secure about—Robert Altman's *Nashville.* It's Altman at his best, which is superior to anyone else making films today."

Many of the techniques that Altman perfected in *Nashville* reappear in 1978's *A Wedding,* a comedy of manners about the clashing of classes when a Southern, nouveau riche bride marries a groom from an aristocratic midwestern family. Writing about the film, Gavin Millar observed, "Altman believes in pushing his observations on film as close to lifelike experiences as the medium will stand without boring us to tears. So he fills the screen with action and character, floods us with information, breaks up our perception of it into forgettable gobbets, buries important revelations under trivial gossip, and altogether tries to make us do the work, so he says, of making the film." *A Wedding* garnered mixed reviews. "Altman's films," wrote Colin L. Westerbeck, Jr. in *Commonweal,* "have usually been wonderful because they're one thing in our lives that doesn't just go through the motions. . . . But *A Wedding* might almost make us wonder whether Altman's own, self-invented forms haven't gone a bit dead on him. It's become too easy and automatic for him to do this kind of stuff."

Altman's next movie, *Quintet,* is the story of survivors of a nuclear holocaust who play a complicated board game as they while away their time in an end-of-the-world, arctic landscape. The movie received mostly negative reviews upon its release in 1979. Vincent Canby, while continuing to praise Altman's talent, found fault with *Quintet* in the *New York Times:* "What the rest of us see on the screen is an overproduced, undernourished screenplay . . . that bears a startling resemblance to the kind of morality play that might be written by an undergraduate who's swallowed bits and pieces of Milton, Saroyan, Ray Bradbury, and Sam Katzman without proper chewing."

In the late '80s Altman teamed up with cartoonist Gary Trudeau to create *Tanner '88,* a Home Box Office television series that satirizes the political process as it recounts the story of Jack Tanner, a fictional presidential candidate. Tanner meets up with real politicians like Gary Hart and Bob Dole; one episode was filmed at an actual fundraiser for Al Gore. In the *New Republic* Maureen Dowd called the series "the political world's answer to *Who Framed Roger Rabbit.*" "Since," she wrote, "[Altman and Trudeau] are dealing with Washington—a city that specializes in illusion—it's much harder in this show to tell the imaginary characters from the real ones."

After several more of his films met with a lukewarm critical reception, Altman was once again hailed as a gifted and original storytelling for his direction of *The Player,* based on a screenplay by novelist Michael Tolkin. Like *Tanner '88,* the film playfully juxtaposes fictional characters with their Hollywood counterparts. Terrence Rafferty described the movie in the *New Yorker* as "a brilliant dark comedy about the death of American filmmaking" and praises *The Player* for its scope: "With breathtaking assurance, the movie veers from psychological-thriller suspense to goofball comedy to icy satire." "Everything that's in there that's mean is about *me,*" Altman told Kurt Anderson in *Time.* "I mean, I talk like those guys. I get on the phone and I make those pitches the same way. I cannot tell you how many times I've said [about a proposed film], 'Well, it's kind of like *Nashville,* it's a *Nashville* kind of structure.' The film does not escape its own satire. We didn't let anybody off the hook." Indeed, *The Player* was viewed by many critics as Altman's revenge on a moviemaking industry that had rejected his idiosyncratic vision for more mainstream, commercial efforts. In a 1992 *New York* magazine interview with Altman, Jeanie Kasindorf commented: "I can suddenly see . . . studio chiefs who have told Altman that that idea is too dark, that lead character is too unsympathetic, that screenplay has no plot line, that story doesn't have a happy ending."

Altman reflected on his career to Kasindorf: "You look at the lists of the best films of the last 25 years, I've got two or three in them. . . . More people know about my films today than did when they came out. That's gratifying. And also I really do take the work seriously. I really consider it serious art and I believe in advancing and changing things. I like doing things that are dicey. Otherwise, what's the point?"

BIOGRAPHICAL/CRITICAL SOURCES:

BOOKS

Kass, Judith, *Robert Altman: American Innovator,* Popular Library, 1978.

PERIODICALS

Atlantic Monthly, April, 1974.
Chicago Tribune, February 20, 1979; April 29, 1987.
Christian Science Monitor, October 24, 1974.
Commonweal, January 19, 1979, pp. 18-19; March 27, 1987.
Esquire, September, 1975.
Film Comment, September-October, 1978.
Film Quarterly, spring, 1970, pp. 38-41; winter, 1975-76.
Globe and Mail (Toronto), February 28, 1987.
Listener, January 11, 1979, p. 57.
London Times, August 19, 1976.
Los Angeles Times, March 24, 1983; November 29, 1983; December 6, 1985; February 27, 1987.
Nation, January 11, 1986.
New Republic, March 2, 1974; May 5, 1979; January 3, 1981; December 23, 1985, p. 24; March 23, 1987; August 1, 1988; May 11, 1992.
New Statesman, October 19, 1979, p. 605; April 10, 1981; February 8, 1985, p. 36; July 4, 1986, p. 24; June 29, 1990.
Newsweek, March 11, 1974; October 26, 1981; April 26, 1982, p. 75; November 7, 1983; November 26, 1990; March 2, 1992; November 16, 1992.
New York, March 16, 1992, p. 50.
New Yorker, January 24, 1970; February 4, 1974; August 19, 1974; January 5, 1981; January 27, 1986; November 19, 1990; April 20, 1992.
New York Times, May 2, 1968, p. 57; April 15, 1977; June 13, 1977; June 19, 1977; October 28, 1977; February 4, 1979; February 9, 1979; February 18, 1979; April 6, 1979; June 10, 1979; October 11, 1981; April 7, 1982; November 12, 1982; October 9, 1983; April 4, 1985; June 7, 1985; February 27, 1987; May 21, 1988.
New York Times Magazine, June 20, 1971.
Rolling Stone, June 17, 1975; November 15, 1990.
Saturday Review, April 16, 1977.
Sight and Sound, autumn, 1971.
Time, March 2, 1987; March 2, 1992, p.74; April 20, 1992; November 23, 1992.
Times (London), February 2, 1985; February 8, 1985; October 17, 1987.

Times Educational Supplement, February 28, 1975, p. 126.

Village Voice, July 5, 1976, pp. 107-109; April 11, 1977, p. 40; February 19, 1979, p. 45; April 13, 1982, p. 51; November 23, 1982, p. 55; November 22, 1983, p. 62; April 9, 1985, p. 38; June 11, 1985, p. 60; March 22, 1988, p. 33; May 31, 1988, p. 69.

Washington Post, October 4, 1978; November 19, 1982; March 2, 1987.*

* * *

AMBROSE, Stephen E(dward) 1936-

PERSONAL: Born January 10, 1936, in Decatur, IL; son of Stephen Hedges (a physician) and Rosepha (Trippe) Ambrose; married Judith Dorlester, 1957; married Moira Buckley, 1968; children: Stephanie, Barry Halleck, Andrew, Grace, Hugh. *Education:* University of Wisconsin, B.S., 1957, Ph.D., 1963; Louisiana State University, M.A., 1958.

ADDRESSES: Office—Eisenhower Center, Metro College, University of New Orleans, Lakefront, New Orleans, LA, 70148.

CAREER: Louisiana State University in New Orleans (now University of New Orleans), 1960-64, began as instructor, became associate professor of history; Johns Hopkins University, Baltimore, MD, assistant professor, 1964-66, associate professor of history, 1966-69; U.S. Naval War College, Newport, RI, Ernest J. King Professor of Maritime History, 1969-1970; Kansas State University, Manhattan, Dwight D. Eisenhower Professor of War and Peace, 1970-71; University of New Orleans, professor of history, 1971—, and Director of the Eisenhower Center, 1983. Visiting assistant professor, Louisiana State University, Baton Rouge, 1963-64.

MEMBER: American Military Institute (member of board of directors), American Committee on the History of the Second World War (member of board of directors), Lewis and Clark Heritage Trail Foundation (member of board of directors), Big Blue Athletic Association, Chi Psi.

WRITINGS:

(Editor) *A Wisconsin Boy in Dixie,* University of Wisconsin Press, 1961.

Halleck: Lincoln's Chief of Staff, Louisiana State University Press, 1962.

Upton and the Army, Louisiana State University Press, 1964.

Duty, Honor, and Country: A History of West Point, Johns Hopkins Press, 1966.

Eisenhower and Berlin, 1945: The Decision to Halt at the Elbe, Norton, 1967.

(Editor) *Institutions in Modern America: Innovation in Structure and Process,* Johns Hopkins Press, 1967.

(Associate editor) *The Papers of Dwight D. Eisenhower: The War Years,* five volumes, Johns Hopkins Press, 1970.

The Supreme Commander: Eisenhower, Doubleday, 1970.

Rise to Globalism: American Foreign Policy since 1938, Volume 8, "Pelican History of the United States," Penguin, 1971, sixth revised edition, 1991.

(With James A. Barber, Jr.) *The Military and American Society,* Free Press, 1972.

General Ike: Abeline to Berlin (juvenile), Harper, 1973.

Crazy Horse and Custer: The Parallel Lives of Two American Warriors, illustrations by Kenneth Francis Dewey, Doubleday, 1975.

(With Richard H. Immerman) *Ike's Spies: Eisenhower and the Espionage Establishment,* Doubleday, 1981.

(With Immerman) *Milton S. Eisenhower: Educational Statesman,* Johns Hopkins Press, 1983.

Eisenhower: Soldier, General of the Army, President-Elect, 1890-1952 (also see below), Simon & Schuster, 1983.

Eisenhower: The President (also see below), Simon & Schuster, 1984.

Pegasus Bridge: 6 June, 1944, Allen & Unwin, 1984, Simon & Schuster, 1985.

Nixon: The Education of a Politician, 1913-1962, Simon & Schuster, 1987.

Nixon: The Triumph of a Politician, 1962-1972, Simon & Schuster, 1989.

Eisenhower: Soldier and President (condensed version of *Eisenhower: Soldier, General of the Army, President-Elect, 1890-1952,* and *Eisenhower: The President*), Simon & Schuster, 1990.

(Editor) Dwight D. Eisenhower, *The Wisdom of Dwight D. Eisenhower: Quotations from Ike's Speeches and Writings, 1939-1969,* Eisenhower Center, 1990.

Nixon: Ruin and Recovery, 1973-1990, Simon & Schuster, 1991.

Band of Brothers: E Company, 506th Regiment, 101st Airborne, from Normandy to Hitler's Eagle's Nest, Simon & Schuster, 1992.

(Editor) *Eisenhower and the German POWs: Facts against Falsehood,* Louisiana State University Press, 1992.

Also author of a television documentary, *Eisenhower: Supreme Commander,* British Broadcasting Corporation, 1973. Author of bi-weekly column, *Baltimore Evening Sun,* 1968—. Author of introductions for Ronald Lewin, *Hitler's Mistakes,* Morrow, 1987, and *Handbook on German Military Forces,* Louisiana State University Press, 1990. Contributor of reviews and articles to numerous journals and newspapers, including *American Historical*

Review, Harvard Magazine, American Heritage, and *New York Times Book Review.*

WORK IN PROGRESS: A long work on D-Day at Normandy.

SIDELIGHTS: Historian and biographer Stephen E. Ambrose has written about generals, presidents, major military battles, and foreign policy in his twenty-plus books, always demonstrating an uncommon ability to bring history and historical actors to vivid life. The University of New Orleans professor is best known for his multi-volume biographies of Presidents Dwight D. Eisenhower and Richard M. Nixon. Ambrose labored for nearly twenty years on the Eisenhower volumes and ten years on the Nixon volumes, both times with results that critics praised for meticulous research and balance.

Ambrose grew up in Whitewater, Wisconsin. A high-school football captain and prom king, he went to the University of Wisconsin in Madison, where he decided to major in history. After receiving his B.A. in 1957, Ambrose moved on to the Masters program at Louisiana State University, returning to the University of Wisconsin to receive his Ph.D. in history in 1963. During graduate school, Ambrose published a biography of General Henry Halleck, who had served as Chief of Staff to President Abraham Lincoln. A few years later, when Ambrose was working as an assistant professor at Louisiana State University, he received a phone call from an admirer of the book. The caller was former President Dwight D. Eisenhower.

"I was flabbergasted," Ambrose told *New York Times Book Review* contributor Herbert Mitgang. President Eisenhower told Ambrose that he liked the author's book, had thought about writing a work on Halleck himself, and wondered if the historian would come to his Gettysburg, Pennsylvania, home to talk; he also asked Ambrose if he would be interested in working on the Eisenhower papers. Ambrose recalled: "I told him, 'General, I'd prefer to write your biography.' He replied, 'I'd like to have you any way I can.' " So began Ambrose's long association with the life and reputation of President Eisenhower, an association that allowed him to produce a multi-volume set of edited papers, a biography of Milton Eisenhower (the President's brother), two books on Eisenhower's military career (*Eisenhower and Berlin, 1945: The Decision to Halt at the Elbe* and *The Supreme Commander: Eisenhower*), an analysis of Eisenhower's relationship with the espionage community, and the two-volume biography.

In the introduction to *Eisenhower: Soldier, General of the Army, President-Elect, 1890-1952,* Ambrose describes Eisenhower as "decisive, well disciplined, courageous, dedicated . . . intensely curious about people and places, often refreshingly naive, fun-loving—in short a wonderful man

to know or be around." Despite his clear liking for the former President, most reviewers found that Ambrose developed an even-handed portrait of the man who is widely perceived to have been, in the words of *Time* reviewer Donald Morrison, both a "canny leader who brilliantly outmaneuvered subordinates and statesman," and a "mediocre President . . . slow of wit and out of touch with the currents of upheaval swirling beneath the calm surface of the 1950s." In reconciling these two views, Ambrose "has provided the most complete and objective work yet on the general who became President," wrote Drew Middleton in the *New York Times Book Review. New Yorker* contributor Naomi Bliven said that the biography "offers the beguiling mixture of nostalgia and illumination we find in old newsreels, along with an abundance of themes for reflection."

Reviewers praised Ambrose's reassessment of a president who had been reviled as a bumbling, inefficient leader, a President who, in the words of *Chicago Tribune Book World* reviewer Richard Rhodes, "golfed too much, knew little and did nothing." Ambrose acknowledges such public perception, wrote Henry Brandon in the *Washington Post Book World,* but his biography portrays Eisenhower as "a man in charge if not always in control, a born leader and a deft pilot who knows how to weather storms." In volume two, *Eisenhower: The President,* Ambrose highlights the fact that "Ike," as he was affectionately known, kept his country out of war for eight turbulent years, stood up to a burgeoning military-industrial complex, and managed to maintain domestic economic prosperity.

Though most reviewers praised Ambrose for his equanimity, some thought that he failed to advance a compelling interpretation of the voluminous data he compiled. *Los Angeles Times Book Review* contributor Kenneth Reich complained that the book was too restrained. "It seems sad," he wrote, "when someone has obviously put in so much effort yet fails to go beyond evenhandedness. . . . [This] biography of Eisenhower emerges as a dull parade of data." Ivan R. Dee, writing in the *Chicago Tribune Book World,* said that the problem was that "a reader can arrive at opposite judgments about Eisenhower's performance based upon the evidence Ambrose presents," pointing to Eisenhower's handling of civil rights, the U-2 spying incident, and Middle Eastern politics as examples of failed leadership which Ambrose does not acknowledge.

After nearly twenty years of writing about one of the most loved American presidents, Ambrose turned his attention to a man he said had once been "the most hated and feared man in America," President Richard M. Nixon. A number of writers had penned psychological portraits of Nixon that attempted to account for his seeming cruelty, his terrific drive to succeed, and his failure to admit fault for the Watergate controversy and his subsequent resignation in the face of impeachment proceedings. But by 1987, no one had written a carefully-researched scholarly biography on the most controversial president of the twentieth century. With *Nixon: The Education of a Politician, 1913-1962,* the first of three volumes, Ambrose wrote that kind of biography. *Washington Post Book World* reviewer Richard Harwood echoed the praise of many critics in noting Ambrose's ability to "examine with a surgeon's neutrality all the cliches and stereotypical assumptions about the character of this strange and fascinating man." Political analyst Sidney Blumenthal wrote in the *New Republic* that "Ambrose has written the standard, a middle point of reference, around which all Nixonia may be organized."

In three volumes, Ambrose follows Nixon from his humble beginnings in Yorba Linda, California, to his academic success at Duke University, to his bitter 1950 Senate campaign, to his troubled tenure as Eisenhower's vice-president, and finally to his rise to and fall from the presidency of the United States. Along the way, Ambrose debunks many of the myths about Nixon, picturing Nixon's childhood as happy, not sad, showing that Nixon's opponents initiated the mud-slinging for which he became known, and demonstrating that the political dirty work Nixon performed while vice-president to Eisenhower was done at the President's insistence. The final volume, *Nixon: Ruin and Recovery,* follows the resuscitation of the former President's reputation throughout the 1980s. *Spectator* reviewer Anthony Howard wrote that Ambrose "has crowned the edifice of his impressive trilogy with an admirably fair-minded last volume covering easily the most controversial aspect of what was already a singularly resilient political career." Throughout the three volumes, Ambrose does not excuse Nixon for the excesses that characterized his political career nor does he attempt to provide a explanation of what motivated Nixon to behave as he did; instead, he shows what happened and lets the reader decide.

Ambrose's reluctance to offer insights into Nixon's motivations frustrated some reviewers. *New York Times* reviewer Christopher Lehmann-Haupt complained that "there is something passive about the way Mr. Ambrose tells Mr. Nixon's story. He seems always confined by context, praising his subject for this, condemning him for that. He lacks the lift of a driving thesis." Ronald Steel, writing in the *New York Times Book Review,* echoed this appraisal, suggesting that Ambrose "is better at providing information than at delving into the dark recesses of character." And Gary Wills, whose own *Nixon Agonistes* attempted to probe the dark recesses of Nixon's character, thought that Ambrose's concern for the facts made him overlook an essential undercurrent in Nixon's life.

Edward Z. Friedenberg saw Ambrose's hesitancy to pass judgment on Nixon in a slightly different light. Writing in

the Toronto *Globe and Mail,* he claimed that "Ambrose seems largely content to explain the hostility Nixon aroused in terms of his personality," but contended that "Nixon's enemies hated not merely the man but his (and his country's) policies." Thus Ambrose's equanimity led him to excuse the most sinister elements of Nixon's presidency: his policy toward Vietnam, and his willingness to do whatever it took to win. R. W. Apple, Jr. wrote in the *New York Times Book Review,* however, that "it is Mr. Ambrose's achievement to immerse himself in Mr. Nixon's life and keep his cool. . . . The result is a portrait that is all its subject is not: evenhanded and thoroughly reliable." Ambrose himself told *New York Times Book Review* contributor Alex Ward, "I make no claim to finding the key to the man—he's so complicated that it would take Shakespeare to do him justice."

Ambrose turned to less controversial material with his 1992 *Band of Brothers,* a history of the military exploits of Company E, 506th Parachute Infantry Regiment, 101st Airborne Division during their numerous engagements in World War II. Ambrose based his book on the stories he collected from the surviving members of the company as part of his work for the Eisenhower Center at the University of New Orleans. The soldiers told Ambrose of their predawn drop behind enemy lines on D-Day and of their eventual capture of German leader Adolf Hitler's beloved retreat, "Eagle Nest." The result, wrote *New York Times Book Review* contributor and combat veteran Harry G. Summers, Jr., is "a harrowing story," that captures "the true essence of a combat rifle company." *Times Literary Supplement* reviewer M. R. D. Foot wrote that the book "is full of insights into the nature of comradeship, as well as brutally frank description: noise, stench, discomfort, hunger and fear are all there, tied together in a masterly narrative flow."

BIOGRAPHICAL/CRITICAL SOURCES:

BOOKS

Ambrose, Stephen E., *Eisenhower: Soldier, General of the Army, President-Elect, 1890-1952,* Simon & Schuster, 1983.

PERIODICALS

Chicago Tribune, March 24, 1985.
Chicago Tribune Book World, October 16, 1983; October 7, 1984, pp. 1, 24; April 12, 1987, p. 3.
Globe and Mail (Toronto), March 16, 1985; July 25, 1987; November 4, 1989.
London Review of Books, July 4, 1985, pp. 5-6.
Los Angeles Times, February 13, 1981.
Los Angeles Times Book Review, November 4, 1984; June 21, 1987, p. 12; October 15, 1989; November 24, 1991, pp. 4, 11.

Nation, February 28, 1972.

New Leader, March 5, 1990, pp. 16-17.

New Republic, July 6, 1987, pp. 30-34.

Newsweek, April 27, 1987.

New Yorker, July 1, 1985, pp. 95-97.

New York Review of Books, May 6, 1971.

New York Times, April 23, 1987; November 9, 1989.

New York Times Book Review, October 4, 1970, p. 5; September 19, 1983; December 9, 1984, pp. 1, 46-47; April 28, 1985; April 26, 1987; November 12, 1989, pp. 1, 65-66; November 24, 1991, pp. 3, 25; September 6, 1992, p. 11.

Spectator, July 4, 1987, pp. 32-33; February 1, 1992, p. 32.

Time, October 3, 1983, pp. 79-80; May 4, 1987, p. 101; November 6, 1989, pp. 100-102.

Times Literary Supplement, June 1, 1967, p. 486; November 5, 1971, p. 1398; February 8, 1985, p. 135; December 25-31, 1987, p. 1424; August 21, 1992, p. 20.

Tribune Books (Chicago), July 19, 1992, p. 6.

Washington Post Book World, September 11, 1983, pp. 1, 4; September 30, 1984; May 3, 1987; November 12, 1989, pp. 1, 13; November 10, 1991, p. 5.

—*Sketch by Tom Pendergast*

*   *   *

ANDRIC, Ivo   1892-1975

PERSONAL: Born October 10, 1892, in Docu, Bosnia, Austria-Hungary (now Bosnia-Herzegovina); died March 13, 1975, in Belgrade, Yugoslavia; married Milica Babic (a painter and theatre designer), 1959 (died, 1968). *Education:* Attended University of Zagreb, Yugoslavia, Vienna University, Austria, and University of Krakow, Poland; Graz University, Austria, doctorate in philosophy, 1923. *Politics:* Communist.

CAREER: Political prisoner during World War I; Yugoslav diplomatic service, 1919-41, served in Rome, Geneva, Madrid, Bucharest, Trieste, Graz, Belgrade, and Berlin; full-time writer, 1941-49; Yugoslav Parliament, deputy and representative from Bosnia, 1949-55.

MEMBER: Federation of Writers of Yugoslavia (president, 1946-51), Serbian Academy.

AWARDS, HONORS: Prize for life work from Yugoslav Government, 1956; Nobel Prize for Literature, 1961; honorary doctorate, University of Krakow, 1964.

WRITINGS:

IN ENGLISH TRANSLATION; FICTION, EXCEPT AS NOTED

Gospodjica, [Yugoslavia], 1945, translation by Joseph Hitrec published as *The Woman from Sarajevo,* Knopf, 1965.

Travnicka hronika, [Yugoslavia], 1945, translation by Kenneth Johnstone published as *Bosnian Story,* Lincolns-Prager, 1958, British Book Center, 1959, translation by Hitrec published as *Bosnian Chronicle,* Knopf, 1963.

Na Drini cuprija, [Yugoslavia], 1945, translation by Lovett F. Edwards published as *The Bridge on the Drina,* Macmillan, 1959.

Prica o vezirovam slonu, Nakladni Zavod (Zagreb), 1948, translation by Drenka Willen published as *The Vizier's Elephant: Three Novellas,* Harcourt, 1962.

Prokleta avlija, [Yugoslavia], 1954, translation by Johnstone published as *Devil's Yard,* Grove, 1962.

Sabrana djela Ive Andrica (also see below), Mladost (Zagreb), 1963, partial translation by Hitrec published as *The Pasha's Concubine and Other Tales,* Knopf, 1968.

Most na Zepi, Svjetlost (Sarajevo), 1967, updated edition with text in Serbo-Croatian, English, German, and Italian published as *Most na Zepi/The Bridge on the Zepa/Die Bruecke ueber die Zepa/Il ponte sulla Zepa,* Oslobodenje (Sarajevo), 1971.

Letters, translation, editing, and introduction by Zelimir B. Juricic, Serbian Heritage Academy (Toronto), 1984.

The Development of Spiritual Life in Bosnia under the Influence of Turkish Rule (translation of *Die Entwicklung des geistigen Lebens in Bosnien unter der Einwirkung der turkischen Herrschaft*), edited and translated by Zelimir B. Juricic and John F. Loud, Duke University Press, 1990.

The Damned Yard and Other Stories, edited by Celia Hawkesworth, Forest Books (Boston) and Dereta (Belgrade), 1992.

The Days of the Consuls, translated by Hawkesworth with Bogdan Rakic, Forest Books, 1992.

OTHER

Ex ponto: Unruhen (prison meditations; title means "Restlessness"), Knjizevnog juga (Zagreb), 1918, reprinted, Univerzitetska biblioteka Svetozar Markovic, 1975.

Nemiri (poems; title means "Disquietudes"), Naklada S. Kugli, 1920, reprinted, Univerzitetska biblioteka Svetozar Markovic, 1975.

Put Alje Djerzeleza, [Yugoslavia], 1920.

Pripovetke (short stories), [Yugoslavia], Volume 1, 1924, Volume 2, 1931, Volume 3, 1936.

Nove pripovetka (short stories), Kultura (Zagreb), 1949.

Prica o kmetu Simanu, [Yugoslavia], 1950.

Novele, Mladinska Knjiga (Ljubljana), 1951.

Pod grabicem: Pripovetke o zivotu bosanskog sela (short stories), Seljacka knjiga (Sarajevo), 1952.

Panorama: Pripovetke (short stories), Prosveta (Belgrade), 1958.

Lica (short stories), Mladost, 1960.

Izbor, Svjetlost, 1961.

Sabrana djela Ive Andrica (title means "Collected Works of Ivo Andric"), Volumes 1-10, Mladost, 1963, Volumes 11-16, Svjetlost, 1976.

Ljubav u Kasabi (short stories), Branko Donovic (Belgrade), 1963.

Bosna hikayeleri, Varlik Yayinevi (Istanbul), 1965.

Mustafa Madzar i druge price, Svjetlost, 1965.

(Contributor) *Nouvel essai yougoslave* (essays), compiled by Aleksandar V. Stefanovic, Zalozba Obzorja, 1965.

Anikina vremena (short stories), Svjetlost, 1967.

Kula i druge pripovetke (children's stories), Veselin Maslesa (Sarajevo), 1970.

Eseji i kritike (essays), Svjetlost, 1976.

Sta sanjam i sta mi se dogada: Pesme i pesme u prozi, Prosveta, 1977.

O Vuku, Rad (Belgrade), 1977.

Wegzeichen (collection of personal impressions; title means "Road Markings"), [Munich, West Germany], 1982.

Sveske, Prosveta, 1982.

Jevrejske price, Biblioteka Narodna knjiga, 1991.

Poetry represented in *An Anthology of Modern Yugoslav Poetry,* edited by Janko Lavrin, J. Calder, 1963. Member of editorial board of *Knjizevni jug,* a literary magazine.

Some of Andric's works have been translated into German, French, Russian, Spanish, and Italian.

SIDELIGHTS: Diplomat and author Ivo Andric produced some of his most memorable writings while imprisoned for three years during World War I as a member of the revolutionary Mlada Bosna, the Bosnian organization that sought the downfall of the Hapsburg regime and the establishment of an independent state for the South Slav peoples. A member of the group shot and killed Archduke Ferdinand of Austria in 1914, an act that ignited World War I. Andric stated his philosophy in *Ex ponto: Unruhen,* a collection of his prison meditations: "There is no other truth but pain, there is no other reality but suffering, pain and suffering in every drop of water, in every blade of grass, in every grain of crystal, in every sound of living voice, in sleep and in vigil, in life, before life and perhaps also after life."

Having forged such a philosophy, Andric found his native Bosnia the perfect setting for his fiction. The people of Bosnia had been oppressed and exploited throughout their history, and the resulting torment and gloom were explored in Andric's writings. "For Andric, man, set against the vast panorama of history, is insignificant—fearful of external disaster and inwardly aware of his own insecurity in a world where everything is ephemeral, however much he may long for constancy," Konstantin Bazarov explained in *Books and Bookmen.* "The particular history of old Turkish Bosnia, with its despotism and violence, thus portrays the broader theme of man's tragic struggle against the oncoming darkness of change and death."

Following the war, Andric entered his country's diplomatic service and continued in this capacity even after the Kingdom of the Serbs, Croats, and Slovenes became Yugoslavia in 1929. The last diplomatic post Andric held was ambassador to Nazi Germany. In 1941 he fled from Berlin only a few hours before the Germans began bombing Yugoslavia. Andric's most memorable novels about Bosnia were written during World War II. When the Germans occupied Belgrade, Andric refused to leave. He holed up in his apartment and wrote what has come to be known as the Bosnian trilogy—*Gospodjica* (*The Woman from Sarajevo*), *Travnicka hronika* (*Bosnian Story* or *Bosnian Chronicle*), and *Na Drini cuprija* (*The Bridge on the Drina*).

In *The Woman from Sarajevo,* Andric portrayed the people of Sarajevo as "already burdened with the Turkish legacy of habitual indolence and with the Slavic hankering for excesses, having lately adopted the formal Austrian notions of society and social obligations, according to which one's personal prestige and the dignity of one's class were measured by a rising scale of senseless and nonproductive spending." After reading the novel in translation, William Cooper remarked that *The Woman from Sarajevo* "is so fascinating and distinguished that one feels dismayed—and ashamed—to think of the writers in lesser-known languages whose work we have never read."

Even more highly acclaimed was *Bosnian Chronicle.* Set in Travnik during the Napoleonic era, *Bosnian Chronicle* focused on the conflicts that arose between the French and Austrian consulates as they vied to win the favor of the Turkish vizier and the support of the local townspeople. In his translator's note, Joseph Hitrec declared that Andric's principal themes—"causative interplay of guilt and human suffering, the individual versus tyranny, the warping of men's destinies through historic circumstance"—were masterfully combined in *Bosnian Chronicle.* Alan Ferguson, writing in *Modern Language Review,* saw two major themes in the novel, the first being the clash between the private individual and his public image. He pointed out that the Austrian and French consuls had much in common yet were prevented from becoming friends by their official duties. The second theme that Ferguson discerned in *Bosnian Chronicle* was the clash between East and West. Bosnia epitomized the struggle between these two cultures because the Christians and Moslems had been fighting over the territory since the fourteenth century.

Bosnian Chronicle covered only seven years in the history of Bosnia, but *The Bridge on the Drina* spanned three and a half centuries. The Turks constructed the bridge over the Drina River in the sixteenth century at the town of Visegrad. The novel recorded life in Visegrad from the time of the bridge's erection to shortly before World War I. Egon Hostovsky discussed the symbolic import of the bridge in *Saturday Review:* "The ancient bridge is a piece of eternity, forged by human hands and baptized with the bold dreams of men. It has outlasted generations, invasions, wars, and peace. Everything around it was continually changing, rotting, dying, being reborn; but the bridge has stood immutable, the witness of values and efforts that do not pass."

The epic proportions of *The Bridge on the Drina* prompted many critics to liken Andric to Leo Tolstoy. Like Tolstoy, Andric was concerned with the inexorable flow of history, with the precedence that events take over the individual. Andric has also been compared to Herman Melville. Stoyan Christowe demonstrated that the elephant in the novella *The Vizier's Elephant* was similar to Melville's fictional whale, Moby Dick, because "both personify the universal, hostile forces against which man struggles." Comparisons to writers of the caliber of Tolstoy and Melville suggest that Andric was not just a regional writer, but an artist whose work had universal implications. Ferguson commented that Andric's works were not about foreign lands but "about the 'common course of all humanity'; its fundamental similarities rather than its superficial differences." The Swedish Academy attested to Andric's universality when it awarded him the Nobel Prize for Literature in 1961 "for the epic force with which he has depicted themes and human destinies drawn from the history of his country."

BIOGRAPHICAL/CRITICAL SOURCES:

BOOKS

Andric, Ivo, *Bosnian Chronicle,* translation by Joseph Hitrec, Knopf, 1963.
Contemporary Literary Criticism, Volume 8, Gale, 1978.

PERIODICALS

Books and Bookmen, November, 1974.
Book World, June 30, 1968.
Christian Century, February 15, 1967.
Christian Science Monitor, August 9, 1968.
Harvard Review, autumn, 1959.
Listener, August 11, 1966.
Literary Quarterly, summer, 1965.
Modern Language Review, October, 1975, pp. 830-838.
New York Times, October 28, 1962.
New York Times Book Review, July 28, 1968; February 23, 1969.
Saturday Review, July 11, 1959.
Slavic and East European Journal, fall, 1972.

Slavic Review, September, 1964.
Slavonic and East European Review, June, 1963; July, 1970.
Times Literary Supplement, May 20, 1965.

OBITUARIES:

PERIODICALS

AB Bookman's Weekly, April 7, 1975.
Newsweek, March 24, 1975.
New York Times, March 14, 1975.
Washington Post, March 14, 1975.*

*   *   *

ANGLADE, Jean   1915-

PERSONAL: Born March 18, 1915, in Thiers, France; son of Jean (a bricklayer) and Felistine (a servant; maiden name, Chaleron) Anglade; married Marie Ombret (a teacher), June 17, 1935; children: Michelle-Helene Anglade Vuillardot. *Education:* University of Clermont-Ferrand, agregation d'italien, 1947. *Religion:* Roman Catholic.

ADDRESSES: Home—32 avenue J. B. Marrou, Ceyrat, 631 10 Beaumont, France.

CAREER: Teacher at primary schools in Thiers, France, 1934-35, and Saint-Gervais-d'Auvergne, France, 1935-41; teacher of French at technical schools in Saint-Etienne, France, 1941-42, and Thiers, 1942-47; teacher of Italian at high schools in Tunis, Tunisia, 1947-48, and Gap, France, 1948-49; Commercial Institute, Clermont-Ferrand, France, teacher of Italian, 1949-75. *Military service:* French Air Force, 1936-38, 1939-40.

MEMBER: Societaire de la Societe des gens de lettres de France, Societe des Auteurs, Compositeurs et Editeurs de Musique, Societe des Auteurs et Compositeurs Dramatiques.

AWARDS, HONORS: Prix populiste from Cercle Populiste, 1957, for *L'Immeuble Taub;* Prix de Libraires de France, 1962, for *La Foi et la montagne;* Prix Eugene Le Roy from French Agriculture Ministry, 1970, for *Une Pomme oubliee;* Prix de l'humour noir from Cercle de l'humour noir, 1970, for *Le Point de suspension;* Prix Scarron from Cercle Scarron, 1972, for *Riez pour nous;* Grand prix de la ville de Cannes from Cannes Council, 1974, for *Un Temps pour lancer des pierres.*

WRITINGS:

NOVELS

Le Chien du Seigneur (title means "The Lord's Dog"), Plon, 1952, reprinted, Julliard, 1973.

Les Mauvais Pauvres (title means "The Bad Poor"), Plon, 1954.

Les Convoites (title means "The Coveted Town"), Gallimard, 1955.

L'Immeuble Taub (title means "Taub's House"), Gallimard, 1956.

Le Fils de Tiberio Pulci (title means "The Son of Tiberio Pulci"), R. Laffont, 1959.

Le Peche d'ecarlate (title means "The Scarlet Sin"), R. Laffont, 1960.

La Foi et la montagne (title means "The Faith and the Mountain"), R. Laffont, 1961.

La Garance (title means "The Madder"), R. Laffont, 1963.

Des Chiens vivants (novel), Julliard, 1967, translation by Robert Bullen and Rosette Letellier published as *Better a Living Dog,* Prentice-Hall, 1971.

Une Pomme oubliee (title means "A Forgotten Apple"; adaptation for television first broadcast by Antenne 2 TV, 1973), Julliard, 1969.

Le Point de suspension (title means "The Point of Suspension"), Gallimard, 1969.

Un Front de marbre (title means "A Marble Brow"), Julliard, 1970.

Le Voleur de coloquintes (title means "The Pumpkin Robber"), Julliard, 1972.

Un Temps pour lancer des pierres (title means "A Time for Throwing Stones"), Julliard, 1974.

Le Tilleul du soir (title means "The Evening Lime Tea"), Julliard, 1975.

Le Tour du doigt (title means "The Finger Round"), Julliard, 1977.

Les Ventres jaunes (title means "The Yellow Bellies"), Julliard, 1979.

La Bonne Rosee (title means "The Good Dew"), Julliard, 1980.

Les Permissions de Mai (title means "Allowances of May"), Julliard, 1981.

La Noel aux Prunes (title means "A Christmas with Plums"), Julliard, 1983.

Les Bons Dieux (title means "The Good Gods"), Julliard, 1984.

Avec flute obligee (title means "With Compulsory Flute"), Julliard, 1986.

La Dame aux ronces, Presses de la Cite, 1989.

Juste avant l'aube, Presses de la Cite, 1990.

Un parrain de cendres, Presses de la Cite, 1991.

La jardin de Mercure, Presses de la Cite, 1992.

L'impossible pendu de Toulouse, Fleuve noir, 1992.

Y a pas d'bon Dieu, Presses de la Cite, 1993.

POETRY

Chants de guerre et de paix (title means "War and Peace Songs"), Le Sol Clair, 1946.

NONFICTION

Les Greffeurs d'orties: L'Eglise et le proletariat (title means "To Graft Nettles: Church and Proletariat"), La Palatine, 1958.

Herve Bazin (title means "Herve Bazin, Writer"), Gallimard, 1962.

Sidoine Apollinaire (title means "Biography of Sidonius Apollinares"), Editions Volcans, 1963.

(With R. Baron) *Cours de composition francaise* (title means "How to Write a French Essay"), 5th edition, Dunod, 1965.

Grands Mystiques, P. Waleffe, 1967.

Celebration de la chevre, R. Morel, 1971.

Le Vie quotidienne dans le Massif Central au dix-neuvieme siecle, Hachette, 1971.

Riez pour nous (title means "Laugh for Us"), R. Morel, 1971, 2nd edition, 1972.

Solarama Auvergne (title means "Auvergne Prospects"), Solar, 1972.

La Vie quotidienne contemporaine en Italie (title means "The Contemporary Living in Italy"), Hachette, 1973.

Histoire de l'Auvergne (title means "History of Auvergne"), Hachette, 1974.

L'Auvergne que 'aime (title means "Auvergne I Like"), Sun, 1974.

Jean Anglade raconte (title means "Jean Anglade Tells"), Editions Le Cercle d'Or, 1975.

Les Singes de l'Europe (title means "The Monkeys of Europe"), Julliard, 1976.

La Vie quotidienne des immigres en France de 1919 a nos jours (title means "The Daily Living of Immigrants in France from 1919 to Now"), Hachette, 1976.

Les Grandes Heures de l'Auvergne (title means "Great Hours in Auvergne"), Librairie Academique Perrin, 1977.

Drailles et burons d'Aubrac (title means "Wandering in Aubrac"), Le Chene, 1979.

Fables omnibus (title means "Fables for Everybody"), Julliard, 1981.

L'Auvergne et le Massif Central d'hier et de demain, Editions Jean-Pierre Delarge, 1981.

Le pays oublie (title means "The Forgotten Country"), Hachette, 1982.

Mes Montagnes brulees (title means "My Burned Mountains"), A.C.E., 1985.

Confidences auvergnates, Chr. de Bartillat, 1993.

TRANSLATOR FROM ITALIAN

Niccolo Machiavelli, *Le Prince* (title means "The Prince"), Le Livre de Poche, 1972.

Giovanni Boccaccio, *Le Decameron* (title means "The Decameron"), Le Livre de Poche, 1974.

Les fioretti de Saint Francoise d'Assise (title means "The Fioretti of Saint Francis of Assisi"), Le Livre de Poche, 1983.

OTHER

Contributor to journals.

SIDELIGHTS: Jean Anglade told *CA:* "I have attempted all kinds of literary works—novels, poetry, essays, translations, biographies, history, plays, satires—but feel I am essentially a novelist because I can put in my novels all the range of literary attitudes. In France I am considered a specialist on the Auvergne area, the heart of the country, on which I have written more than a dozen books."

* * *

ANTHONY, Michael 1930-

PERSONAL: Born February 10, 1930, in Mayaro, Trinidad and Tobago; son of Nathaniel (a drain-digger) and Eva (Jones) Anthony; married Yvette Francesca (a homemaker), February 8, 1958; children: two sons, two daughters. *Education:* Attended Mayaro Roman Catholic School and Junior Technical College, San Fernando, Trinidad. *Politics:* "Uncategorized."

ADDRESSES: *Home*—99 Long Circular Rd., St. James, Port-of-Spain, Trinidad and Tobago.

CAREER: Author and lecturer. Held a number of factory jobs after immigrating to England; Reuters News Agency, London, England, sub-editor, 1964-68; lived in Brazil, 1968-70; *Texas Star,* Texaco Trinidad, Pointe-a-Pierre, Trinidad and Tobago, assistant editor, 1970-72; Ministry of Culture, Port-of-Spain, Trinidad and Tobago, researcher, 1972-88; University of Richmond, Richmond, VA, teacher of creative writing, 1992. Broadcast historical radio programs, 1975-89.

WRITINGS:

The Games Were Coming (novel), Deutsch, 1963, Houghton, 1968, expanded edition with introduction by Kenneth Ramchand, Heinemann and Deutsch, 1977.
The Year in San Fernando (novel), Deutsch, 1965, published with introduction by Paul Edwards and Ramchand, Heinemann, 1970.
Green Days by the River (novel), Houghton, 1967.
Cricket in the Road, and Other Stories, Heinemann Educational, 1973.
Sandra Street, and Other Stories, Heinemann Educational, 1973.
Glimpses of Trinidad and Tobago, with a Glance at the West Indies, Columbus (Trinidad), 1974.
King of the Masquerade, Thomas Nelson, 1974.

Profile Trinidad: A Historical Survey from the Discovery to 1900, Macmillan, 1975.
(Editor with Andrew Carr, and contributor) *David Frost Introduces Trinidad and Tobago,* Deutsch, 1975.
Folk Tales and Fantasies (short stories), illustrated by Pat Chu Foon, Columbus, 1976.
Streets of Conflict (novel), Deutsch, 1976.
The Making of Port-of-Spain, 1757-1939, Key Caribbean, 1978.
All That Glitters (novel), Deutsch, 1981.
Bright Road to El Dorado (novel), Nelson Caribbean, 1982.
Port-of-Spain in a World at War, 1939-1945, Ministry of Sports, Culture, and Youth Affairs (Port-of-Spain), 1984.
First in Trinidad, Circle Press, 1985.
Heroes of the People of Trinidad and Tobago, Circle Press, 1986.
(Editor) *The History of Aviation in Trinidad and Tobago, 1913-1962,* Paria, 1987.
A Better and Brighter Day, Circle Press, 1987.
Towns and Villages of Trinidad and Tobago, Circle Press, 1988.
Parade of the Carnivals of Trinidad, 1839-1989, Circle Press, 1989.
The Golden Quest: The Four Voyages of Christopher Columbus, Macmillan, 1992.
The Chieftain's Carnival and Other Stories, Longman, 1993.

Also contributor to periodicals.

WORK IN PROGRESS: A historical dictionary of Trinidad and Tobago, for Scarecrow Press.

SIDELIGHTS: Michael Anthony writes apparently simple tales of life on the island of Trinidad that convey deep insights into human relationships. Often told from the viewpoint of a child, these tales also give the reader a taste of Caribbean life. *New York Times* contributor Martin Levin claims, "Mr. Anthony has perfect pitch and an artist's eye for the finer shadings of the native scene he knows so intimately." Writing of Anthony's short story collection *Cricket in the Road* in *Books and Bookmen,* James Brockway finds "an evocative power I have rarely come across, a power drawn not merely from observation, but from observing *the things that matter,* and conveying them in exactly the right words and not a word too many." Brockway concludes, "Mr. Anthony reminds us that there are simpler, more essential things in life than getting and spending and he writes about them with a serenity that can only come from strength."

Daryl Cumber Dance comments in *Fifty Caribbean Writers,* "The genius of Anthony . . . is that despite the apparent simplicity of his plot, his stories are narrated with such power that not only does the reader never doubt the significance of whatever seemingly trite experience the protagonist is undergoing, but he is also irresistibly caught up in it." Dance also remarks on Anthony's treatment of women in his novels and short stories. "There are several of the strong, enduring mother figures so familiar in West Indian literature . . . ; but there are also some beautiful young Black women, whom Anthony develops with uncharacteristic sensitivity and empathy. . . . [T]here is no denying that he has created some memorable and unusual portraits of attractive, often passionate, sometimes surprisingly resilient and resourceful Black women." *Dictionary of Literary Biography* contributor Harold Barratt notes, "One of Anthony's most important contributions to the continuing development of West Indian fiction is his emphasis on strong, dour personalities. The abused or abandoned wives and mothers are particularly tenacious, and many of these women are their families' only bulwark against destitution." Anthony remarked to Dance, "The close family relationships [which appear in my works result from] a little bit of nostalgia because my father died when I was very young. I loved him very much and I really missed the fact that he wasn't there, and I thought that our relationship would have been a very meaningful one, and so I believe that I have projected this into my work."

Barratt described *The Games Were Coming,* the author's first published work, as "one of Anthony's most artistically controlled pieces of fiction." The story follows cyclist Leon Seal as he trains for the Southern Games, eschewing the pleasures of the annual carnival and neglecting his girlfriend. "Leon's rigid discipline sometimes turns him into a callous, rather rebarbative young man;" Barratt remarks, "yet there is something admirable about Leon's unswerving commitment to the rigors of his training. . . . Self-discipline, the novel implies, is essential for the achievement of excellence." In *The Year in San Fernando,* twelve-year-old Francis must work as a servant and companion for a bitter old woman to pay for his schooling. The year spent in the Chandles household proves to be pivotal in Francis' maturation. *Contemporary Novelists* contributor Jeremy Poynting finds *The Year in San Fernando* "much more than a sensitive novel about growing up" and adds, "none of Anthony's other novels quite achieves the same degree of understated but unflawed art."

Barratt notes that in both *The Year in San Fernando* and *Green Days by the River* "Anthony's skill in exploring a youngster's maturation can be seen at its most consummate." Discussing the protagonist of *Green Days by the River* Barratt comments, "Like Francis in *The Year in San Fernando,* Shellie . . . is also receptive to the changing rhythms of his world." The story follows Shellie's friendship with Mr. Gidharee, whose generosity towards the boy turns to violent rage when Shellie seduces Rosalie, Mr. Gidharee's daughter. The *New York Times*'s Levin finds that the author "makes his characters appealing without overly romanticizing them, and his ear for dialogue is magnificently accurate."

"In a more intense way than in any earlier novel, Anthony focuses on a child's attempts to discern whether people are being sincere or false" in *All That Glitters,* Poynting notes. The return of young Horace Lumpers's Aunty Roomeen to his village leads to various lessons for Horace, and he finds that "being an adult means wearing different faces," Poynting observes. The boy's discovery of his talent as a writer brings further complications, which his teacher finally resolves with the advice, " 'Make it colourful and vivid—and true' which both Horace and Michael Anthony follow," Poynting concludes.

Anthony once said, "I am essentially a novelist and since I hold that the novel tells a story I feel strongly that I should not use the medium to air my philosophies. However, I feel very strongly about the brotherhood of mankind and as a consequence abominate war. One of my main hopes is that human beings will find a way to live together without friction, and my feeling is that the most distressing thing in this world is the inhumanity of man to man on the grounds of race. I feel that if the racial problem is solved man will have found the key to peace on this planet. Although I am not hopeful about any immediate change in the Southern African situation, I think the thousands of people who are trying to solve the problem in the United States must make a great difference to the basic situation there. Yet, though I feel this way, the books I write have nothing (on the surface) to do with race or war."

Anthony also wrote that he is extremely interested in space exploration "as I sometimes find the mystery of the Universe too much to bear. I often wonder if space exploration will one day explode our present theories about God, and about the origin and formation of the matter about us. I do consider man's quest for knowledge vital and, in fact, inevitable." He also commented that he would "like to see this world of rich and poor nations, powerful and weak nations, superseded by a world of one strong nation formed out of all. In other words I am advocating World Government. I sometimes think that I am merely being idealistic, but being an optimist I am not surprised."

BIOGRAPHICAL/CRITICAL SOURCES:

BOOKS

Contemporary Authors Autobiography Series, Volume 18, Gale, 1993.

Contemporary Novelists, fifth edition, St. James Press, 1991, pp. 46-48.

Dictionary of Literary Biography, Volume 125: *Twentieth-Century Caribbean and Black African Writers,* Gale, 1993.

Fifty Caribbean Writers, Greenwood Press, 1986, pp. 19-25.

Ramchand, Kenneth, *The West Indian Novel and Its Background,* Faber, 1970.

PERIODICALS

Books and Bookmen, February, 1974.
London Magazine, April, 1967.
New York Times Book Review, August 6, 1967; April 14, 1968.
Observer, July 26, 1981.
Punch, February 22, 1967.
Spectator, February 21, 1976.
Times Literary Supplement, March 4, 1965; April 13, 1967.
World Literature Today, spring, 1984.
World Press Review, January, 1987, p. 62.

* * *

APPLEMAN, Margie
See APPLEMAN, M(arjorie) H.

* * *

APPLEMAN, M(arjorie) H. 1928-
(Margie Appleman)

PERSONAL: Born June 24, 1928, in Indiana; daughter of Theodore E. and Martha (Rathert) Haberkorn; married Philip Appleman (a professor and writer), August 19, 1950. *Education:* Sorbonne, University of Paris, Degre Superieur, 1949; Northwestern University, B.A., 1950; Indiana University, M.A., 1958.

ADDRESSES: Home—11 East 10th St., Apt. 21A, New York, NY 10009. *Office*—Department of English, New York University, New York, NY 10003.

CAREER: Indiana University-Bloomington, associate in French, 1955-66; Indiana University-Purdue University at Indianapolis, lecturer in French, 1968-72; New York University, New York City, assistant professor of English (playwriting), 1976-86; Columbia University, New York City, lecturer in English, 1977-80.

MEMBER: Dramatists Guild, Authors League of America, Academy of American Poets, International PEN (American Center), Playwrights Unit, Circle Repertory Company, League of Professional Theatre Women (member of governing board, 1990—).

AWARDS, HONORS: Fellowships from Hartford Foundation and Karolyi Foundation; Great American Play Contest finalist, Actors Theatre of Louisville, 1978; Eugene O'Neill Award finalist, National Playwrights Conference, 1979; Double Image Short Play Award from Samuel French, Inc., 1981; twelfth annual playwriting award from Jacksonville University, 1982.

WRITINGS:

PLAYS

Nice Place You Have Here, first produced in New York City at Omni Theatre, 1970.

The Best Is Yet to Be, first produced in New York City at the Manhattan Theatre Club, 1975.

The Bedroom, first produced in New York City at St. Clement's Theatre, 1978.

Crosscurrents, first produced in New York City at Open Space Theatre, 1978.

(Under name Margie Appleman) *Seduction Duet* (one-act; first produced in New York City at Circle Repertory Company, 1981), Samuel French, 1981.

Fox Trot by the Bay, first produced in Westport, CT, at White Barn Theatre, 1982.

Thirty-nine Seconds and Counting, first produced in New York City at Lucille Lortel Theatre, 1983.

Seduction Quartet, first produced in New York City at WPA Theatre, 1983.

Intermission, first produced in New York City at Circle Repertory Lab, 1985.

Happy New Year, first produced in New York City at Circle Repertory Theatre, 1987.

Where the Wind Begins, first produced in Hollywood at Circle Rep West, 1988.

The Country House, first produced in New York City at the Theatre of St. Peter's, 1988.

On the Edge, first produced in New York City at Circle Repertory Co., 1989.

Love Puzzles, first produced in East Hampton, NY, at Oddfellows Playhouse, 1992.

Also author of plays *Calliope* and *On the Brink.*

WORK IN PROGRESS: Plays, including *Radical.*

SIDELIGHTS: In *Nice Place You Have Here,* playwright M. H. Appleman examines how intimately a man's past shapes his present and his future. The play's protagonist is offered eternal life in the "here and now" by celestial visitors, but he chooses instead his finite state of being, with its memories and past experiences.

Appleman once told *CA* that her foreign travels for research, writing, study, teaching, or conferences have included France, England, Italy, Greece, Turkey, Belgium, Norway, Denmark, the Netherlands, Switzerland, Germany, Austria, Spain, Portugal, Yugoslavia, Poland, the Soviet Union, Japan, Taiwan, Hong Kong, Thailand, Cambodia, India, Iran, Israel, Lebanon, Syria, Jordan, Egypt, Algeria, Morocco, and Mexico.

BIOGRAPHICAL/CRITICAL SOURCES:

PERIODICALS

Show Business, December 24, 1970.

*   *   *

ARMSTRONG-JONES, Antony (Charles Robert) 1930-
(Tony Armstrong Jones, Snowdon)

PERSONAL: Born March 7, 1930, in London, England; son of Ronald Owen Lloyd (a barrister) and Anne (Messel) Armstrong-Jones; married Princess Margaret Rose of Great Britain, May 6, 1960 (divorced May, 1978); married Lucy Lindsay-Hogg (in television production), December, 1978; children: (first marriage) David Linley, Sarah; (second marriage) Frances. *Education:* Attended Jesus College, Cambridge, 1948-51; apprenticed with court photographer Baron Bahum, 1951.

ADDRESSES: Home—22 Launceston Pl., London W8 5RL, England.

CAREER: Free-lance photographer, 1952—; designer, 1965—; television filmmaker, 1968—. Created Earl of Snowdon, 1961. Photographic exhibitions include "Photocall," London, 1958; "Assignments," Photokina, 1972, London, 1973, Brussels, 1974, Los Angeles, St. Louis, New York, and Tokyo, 1975, Sydney, Melbourne, and Copenhagen, 1976, and Paris and Amsterdam, 1977; "Impressions of Israel," London, 1986; and "Serendipity," Brighton, Cleveland, Bradford, and Bath, 1989-90. Designs include photographic stage set for musical "Keep Your Hair On," 1957; Snowdon Aviary, London Zoo, 1965; Chairmobile (electrically powered chair for disabled), 1972; The Squirrel (with Jeremy Fry; mobile chair for disabled people), 1989. Television films include "Don't Count the Candles," Columbia Broadcasting System (CBS), 1968, "Love of a Kind," British Broadcasting Corporation (BBC), 1969, "Born to Be Small," Amateur Television (ATV), 1971, "Happy Being Happy," ATV, 1973, "Mary Kingsley," BBC, 1975, "Burke and Wills," BBC, 1975, "Peter, Tina, and Steve," ATV, 1977, and "Snowdon on Camera," BBC, 1981.

Staff member of Council of Industrial Design (London), 1961-62, consultative adviser, 1962—. Artistic adviser to London *Sunday Times* and Sunday Times Publications

Ltd., 1962-90, British *Vogue,* 1981—, and the *Telegraph Weekend Magazine,* 1990—. President of Snowdon Council; chairman of Working Party on Integrating the Disabled; president of Committee for International Year for Disabled People, England, 1981. Constable of Caernarvon Castle, Wales, 1963—.

MEMBER: Chartered Society of Designers (fellow), Royal Photographic Society of Great Britain (honorary fellow), Royal Society of the Arts (fellow), Institute of British Photographers (honorary fellow), Royal Designers for Industry (faculty member), Royal College of Art (senior fellow), British Institute of Professional Photography (fellow), Contemporary Art Society for Wales (president), Civic Trust for Wales (president), Welsh Theatre Company (president), North Wales Society of Architects (honorary member), Manchester College of Art and Design (honorary fellow), University of Bristol Photographic Society (vice-president), Royal Welsh Yacht Club (honorary member).

AWARDS, HONORS: Knight Grand Cross of Victorian Order, 1969; Emmy Award, Academy of Television Arts and Sciences for outstanding achievement in documentary programming (individual), St. George Prix, Venice Diploma, and Prague and Barcelona Film Festival awards, all 1968, all for "Don't Count the Candles"; certificate of merit, Art Directors Club of New York, 1969; Society of Publication Designers, certificate of merit, 1970, award of excellence, 1973; Chicago Hugo Award and Society of Film and Television Arts award, both 1971, both for "Born to Be Small"; Wilson Hicks Certificate of Merit for Photocommunication, 1971; Royal Photographic Society of Great Britain, Hood Award, 1979, Silver Progress Medal, 1985; doctorate from Bradford University, 1989; doctor of law, Bath University, 1989.

WRITINGS:

UNDER NAME SNOWDON, EXCEPT AS INDICATED

(Under name Antony Armstrong-Jones) *London* (photography), Weidenfeld & Nicolson, 1958, Dutton, 1959.
(With Scheverell Sitwell; under name Tony Armstrong Jones) *Malta,* Batsford, 1958.
(With Bryan Robertson and John Russell) *Private View: The Lively World of British Art,* Nelson, 1965.
Assignments (photography), Morrow, 1972.
(Photographer) *A View of Venice,* text by Derek Hart, introduction by Bruno Visentini, Conzett & Huber (Zurich), 1972.
(Under name Antony Armstrong-Jones) *The Sack of Bath: A Record and an Indictment,* Compton Russell, 1973.
The Book of the Goons, Robson Books, 1974.

Integrating the Disabled: Report of the Snowdon Working Party, National Fund for Research into Crippling Diseases, 1977.

(Photographer) John Oaksey, *Pride of the Shires: The Story of the Whitbread Horses,* Hutchinson, 1979.

Snowdon: A Photographic Autobiography, Times Books, 1979 (published in England as *Personal View,* design by Barney Wan, Weidenfeld & Nicolson, 1979).

Snowdon Tasmania Essay: A Collection of Photographs Taken by Lord Snowdon on a Visit to Tasmania, Australia, in 1980, text by Trevor Wilson, R. Banks, 1981.

(Author of foreword) Angus McBean, *Angus McBean* (photography), text by Adrian Woodhouse, Quartet Books, 1982.

Sittings: 1979-1983 (photography; introduction by John Mortimer), Harper, 1983 (published in England as *Snowdon Sittings: 1979-1983,* Weidenfeld & Nicolson, 1984).

(And photographer) *Israel: A First View,* foreword by Mortimer, captions by Gemma Levine, Little, Brown, 1986.

(Photographer) George Thomas, *My Wales,* Century, 1986.

Snowdon: Stills, 1984-1987 (photography), introduction by Harold Evans, Little, Brown, 1987.

Also author of *Inchcape Review,* 1977. Photographs represented in anthology *The Magic Image,* 1975, and have appeared in periodicals, including *Vogue, Life,* and *Look.* Editorial adviser of *Design* magazine, 1961—.

SIDELIGHTS: Photographer Antony Armstrong-Jones, who is known as Snowdon, began his career by opening his own studio shortly after an apprenticeship with a court photographer. Although successfully engaging in fashion and advertising photography for periodicals, Snowdon made his greatest mark as a theatre photographer. Displaying drive and imagination in the convention of portraiture, he was kept busy with commissions, including those of the royal family.

Snowdon met Queen Elizabeth II's sister, Princess Margaret, in 1958 and they married two years later. He was created first Earl of Snowdon in 1961, and with his new position came many official appointments to supervise government-sponsored design projects and patronage of numerous art and theatre societies; he became one of the world's most photographed photographers. Yet Snowdon also continued with his own work, producing several well-received documentaries in both book and cinematic forms. He and Princess Margaret divorced in 1978.

"I'm very much against the idea of photography as art," Snowdon once stated in a *Newsweek* interview. To Nan Robertson of the *New York Times* he elaborated: "My job is very simply that of a photojournalist. I want to stop peo-

ple's eye on the page, I want to move the viewer. . . . If you recognize a photograph by me," he continued, "I'm a failure. . . . Photographers should be chameleons."

At age forty-nine Snowdon published *Snowdon: A Photographic Autobiography,* a pictorial chronicle of his life as a photographer—from early fashion photos to portraits of the famous to serious documentary work, all accompanied by personal commentary. Reviewers like *Newsweek*'s Charles Michener and Anthony Collings noted the photographer's "chameleon" approach; "absent for the most part," they wrote, "is any reach for the grand metaphor and, indeed, any prevailing, distinctive style." Yet they added, "Snowdon's portraits . . . are all marked by a strong theatricality, a flair for *arranging* the subject and an acute sense of faces as masks that he may have inherited from his uncle, Oliver Messel, the famous British stage designer." Michener and Collings also contended that Snowdon's documentary work shows "an unflinching, sensitive, photographer" with "an extraordinarily fast set of reflexes."

Other critics were impressed by the skill and scope of Snowdon's photographs. "He is a smashingly good photographer," commented one writer for *Time,* who also remarked, "Princess Margaret's ex offers a collection dazzling in its sweep and range." "It says much for Snowdon's integrity, I think, that he emerges from this collection with his reputation enhanced, rather than diminished," applauded John Naughton in the *Listener.* "[Snowdon: A Photographic Autobiography] is really an interim report on a career well spent—an account of a photographic talent with more range and insight than one would ever have suspected from his media image."

In *Sittings: 1979-1983* Snowdon shares a collection of camera portraits taken from 1979 to 1983 in his tiny London studio; he also reveals, in the accompanying text, the philosophy that has made him one of the world's most sought-out portrait photographers. He maintains that the most important aspect of portraiture is finding out as much as possible about the subject, for he attempts not only to capture a likeness of the person, but to say something about him or her as well. Reviewing the book in the London *Times,* Michael Young observed, "There is in his work an historical Englishness and a clarity born of patient observation. Snowdon himself believes his photographs are little more than a record of people whom other people wanted to see at a particular time. . . . Rarely will these photographs be remembered for anything other than their subjects, but what subjects they are; writers, actors, philosophers, and politicians all carefully observed and recorded for posterity."

BIOGRAPHICAL/CRITICAL SOURCES:

PERIODICALS

Listener, January 3, 1980, p. 29.
New Republic, November 12, 1979.
Newsweek, November 12, 1979, p. 78.
New York Times, November 10, 1979.
Observer, December 9, 1979, p. 37.
People, November 7, 1983.
Spectator, February 2, 1980, p. 17.
Time, December 10, 1979, p. 106; December 12, 1983, p. 104.
Times (London), October 6, 1983.
Washington Post Book World, November 27, 1983, pp. 5, 9.

*   *   *

ARNEY, William Ray 1950-

PERSONAL: Born September 18, 1950, in Charlotte, NC; son of John Wilson (a retired U.S. Marine Corps officer) and Grace (in U.S. Marine Corps and a secretary; maiden name, Kuhn) Arney; married Deborah Henderson (a pharmacist), January 2, 1972; children: John Arthur. *Education:* University of Colorado at Boulder, B.A., 1971, M.A., 1972, Ph.D., 1974.

ADDRESSES: Home—2353 Crestline Blvd. N.E., Olympia, WA 98502. *Office*—Evergreen State College, Olympia, WA 98505.

CAREER: Dartmouth College, Hanover, NH, assistant professor, 1974-80, associate professor of sociology, 1980-81, adjunct assistant professor of community and family medicine, 1980-82; Evergreen State College, Olympia, WA, member of faculty, 1981—.

MEMBER: American Sociological Association, American Statistical Association.

WRITINGS:

Power and the Profession of Obstetrics, University of Chicago Press, 1982.
(With Bernard J. Bergen) *Medicine and the Management of Living: Taming the Last Great Beast,* University of Chicago Press, 1984.
Understanding Statistics in the Social Sciences, W. H. Freeman, 1989.
Experts in the Age of Systems, University of New Mexico Press, 1991.

Contributor to medical, sociology, and feminist studies journals.

WORK IN PROGRESS: Experts and Expertise in the New Age: Tickling the Tail of the Dragon.

SIDELIGHTS: William Ray Arney told *CA:* "I know why I always liked the television series *Jeopardy* with Don Pardo. I see an answer—be it a policy, a set of ethical principles, an action, a theory, an idea, or a new gadget—and I wonder what the question was that could have motivated such an answer. I don't do the usual kind of sociology where the answer to the question, 'What is the question?,' is prefabricated as another (sociological) theory which usually indicated that the people who invented the answers were pawns of power and whose words about their work are, therefore, not to be trusted. I see people as products of power, elaborate systems of power that make people both the agents and objects of plays of power. Following people like Michel Foucault, I take seriously the serious utterances of serious people and ask, 'What enabled them to say *that*?' I'm much more interested in provocative descriptions than (truthful) interpretations.

"For example, rather than interpreting the turn of modern medicine toward more humanistic approaches to patient care as a rhetorical screen for professional medicine's deepening connections to advanced capitalism, I think it is more interesting to try to understand the implications of medicine inventing the patient as a person around 1950. Medicine used to think of itself as a single combat warrior that battled against death on behalf of a relatively absent object, the ill person. Since 1950, medicine has been busy developing technologies that call the person in the patient forward. Medicine expanded its mandate into previously privileged parts of human lives. Medicine aims to tame life and to manage its vicissitudes. Death becomes, in the words of a major medical textbook, 'a special management problem.'

"As another example, much sociology and much history has been written to try to understand the motives and interests of the scientists who built the first atomic bomb. The problem is, it seems, to discover what their (rather late) protestations of moral outrage disguise. I tend to be more superficial. I am interested in the way they experienced themselves as components of a system. In my book on expertise I describe them as 'dead but real executives of the inevitable.' And I raise the possibility that their moral outrage may be more a product of the 'atomic system' than a protest against it.

"I tend to get concerned when someone tells me that there is a truth I should know, especially if the truth is announced as a 'liberation' or as being in my 'best interest.' As a teacher, I try to get students to pay attention to the rational, the reasonable, the good advice of people and of systems that support us. I want them to be able to understand what makes good advice count as such and I want them to be able to ask, 'But is that the way I want to live?' I don't want them to answer 'no' necessarily. I want them to act with some measure of commitment and, yet, I want them to sustain the question."

*   *   *

ASHE, Mary Ann
See LEWIS, Mary (Christianna Milne)

*   *   *

ASTLEY, Thea (Beatrice May) 1925-

PERSONAL: Born August 25, 1925, in Brisbane, Queensland, Australia; daughter of Cecil and Eileen (Lindsay) Astley; married Edmund John Gregson (an educational administrator), August 27, 1948; children: one son. *Education:* University of Queensland, graduated, 1947. *Avocational Interests:* Music, friends, conversation, gardening.

ADDRESSES: c/o Putnam Publishing Group, 200 Madison Ave., New York, NY 10016.

CAREER: Teacher of English in Queensland, Australia, 1944-48, and in New South Wales, Australia, 1948-67; School of English, Macquarie University, Sydney, 1968-85, began as senior tutor, became fellow.

AWARDS, HONORS: Commonwealth Literary Fund fellowship, 1961, 1964; Miles Franklin Award, 1962, for *The Well-Dressed Explorer,* 1965, for *The Slow Natives,* and 1973, for *The Acolyte;* Moomba Award, 1965, for *The Slow Natives;* Australian book of the year, 1974, and Age Newspaper book of the year, 1975, both for *A Kindness Cup;* Gold Medal Award, Australian Literature Society, 1986; Patrick White Award for lifetime achievement in literature; Steele Rudd Award, 1987, for *It's Raining in Mango;* Christina Stead Award, 1990, for *Reaching Tin River.*

WRITINGS:

NOVELS, EXCEPT AS INDICATED

Girl with a Monkey, Angus & Robertson, 1958, Penguin, 1987.
A Descant for Gossips, Angus & Robertson, 1960.
The Well-Dressed Explorer, Angus & Robertson, 1962, Penguin, 1988.
The Slow Natives, Angus & Robertson, 1965, Putnam, 1993.
A Boatload of Home Folk, Angus & Robertson, 1968.
The Acolyte (novella; also see below), Angus & Robertson, 1972, Penguin, 1991.
A Kindness Cup (novella; also see below), Thomas Nelson, 1975.
Hunting the Wild Pineapple (short stories), Thomas Nelson, 1979, Putnam, 1991.

An Item from the Late News, University of Queensland Press, 1982, Penguin, 1984.
Beachmasters, 1985, Viking, 1986.
It's Raining in Mango: Pictures from a Family Album, Putnam, 1987.
Two by Astley (includes *The Acolyte* and *The Kindness Cup*), Putnam, 1988.
Reaching Tin River, Putnam, 1990.
Vanishing Points (includes two novellas, *The Genteel Poverty Bus Company* and *Inventing the Weather*), Putnam, 1992.
Coda, Heinemann, 1994.

OTHER

(Editor) *Coast to Coast, 1969-70* (short stories), Angus & Robertson, 1971.

Also contributor of short stories to anthologies, including *Coast to Coast,* Angus & Robertson, 1961, 1963, and 1965, and *Festival and Other Stories,* Wren (Melbourne, Australia), 1974. Contributor of poems to periodicals and anthologies.

SIDELIGHTS: Prize-winning Australian novelist Thea Astley is known for her satirical portraits of small-town Australian society and for her exuberant, lyrical style. Although she has published steadily in Australia since the appearance of her first novel, *Girl with a Monkey,* in 1958, it was only in the mid-1980s that her work began to appear in the United States. In all her books, writes Sally Dawson in the *Times Literary Supplement,* "Astley has directed her satirical, sometimes moralistic gaze at the pettiness and violence of small-town philistinism." Critics praise her caustic, ironic wit, her precisely observed characters, and her poetic evocations of landscape. Judith Freeman observes in the *Los Angeles Times Book Review,* "Astley . . . is a most original writer whose sentences seem charged with incendiary power and whose insight into social mores—especially the relations between men and women—have a dead-on rightness." Noting the occurrence of "climactic physical violence" in nearly all the novelist's work, Kerryn Goldsworthy finds "something almost Gothic" in Astley's imagination, and likens her work to that of American Southern writers Flannery O'Connor and Eudora Welty. Astley, Goldsworthy adds in an article published in *Meanjin,* "seems suspended—rather than torn—between a kind of stern high-mindedness about human behavior and what seems like a wholehearted delight in the sensual qualities of the physical world. . . . Her fiction is largely about the ease with which some positive quality or experience can become its own dark shadow."

Although she has also published many full-length novels, Astley herself, in a *Publishers Weekly* interview, comments that her "favorite form is not the big long novel, it's the novella." Discussing *The Acolyte* and *A Kindness Cup,* novellas published in the early 1970s, Bret Lott writes in the *New York Times Book Review* that the two stories "take opposite tacks in their exploration of conscience muscled away by mob mentality and the resultant inevitable horror of that sacrifice: the disappearance before our very eyes of who we are, of what we love, of what our lives mean to us in the face of what may seem more important matters, whether social or artistic." *The Acolyte* is narrated by Paul Vesper, who along with several other musicians has been drawn into the orbit of a brilliant, egocentric blind pianist. Reviewing the story in the *Washington Post Book World,* Carolyn See suggests that in this novella, the author's "bursting, feverish style sets a trap for [her] that she's not quite nimble enough to escape." Given the exuberant language and unusual observations that Astley puts into her narrator's mouth, See writes, "it's hard to accept Paul as second-rate. . . . By her own energy of vision [Astley] seems incapable of creating a character who is mediocre." Judith H. McDowell, on the other hand, writing in *World Literature Today,* praises Astley's development of her characters in *The Acolyte,* including her depiction of her narrator, "a precious intellectual with a torrential vocabulary." Observes McDowell, "Astley's achievement so far has been impressive, and this book illustrates one of the main reasons why: her ability to render scenes and characters with scrupulous honesty and in dazzling detail."

See describes the second novella, *A Kindness Cup,* as "Melvillean stuff, the fiction of good-and-evil, man-and-nature, man-and-God." Based on an actual occurrence, *A Kindness Cup* concerns a massacre of aborigines by white settlers in a remote town and a self-righteous attempt by the town's schoolmaster, some twenty years after the fact, to bring the perpetrators to account. "This novel is a harsh and brutal look at the egocentricities of men, both the righteous and the guilty," writes Lott. In a *Southerly* critique, David Gilbey comments that "Astley's satirical epitomizing is deft and cruel, using characters' weaknesses, failures and roles as a frequent source of imagery." He adds that Astley's use of "angular, odd, or ugly phrases" is "dramatic" in function, "revealing the mind of the character who is using it." Anstiss Drake, reviewing *A Kindness Cup* for the *Chicago Tribune,* cites Astley's "taut, weatherbeaten style" and her ability to bring setting and characters home to the reader. "The pages are few but the scope here is enormous," writes See, "and the author's talent seemingly as limitless and scarily exuberant as her landscapes."

Vanishing Points, published in 1992, consists of two interlinked novellas set on Australia's northeastern coast near Cairns. In *The Genteel Poverty Bus Company,* reclusive, middle-aged Macintosh Hope seeks solitude on a tiny de-

sert island only to discover that a nearby island is being developed into a glitzy resort. *Inventing the Weather* is narrated by Julie, the wife of the island's developer, Clifford. Julie walks out on her unfaithful, development-obsessed husband and eventually ends up working with a group of nuns who minister to aborigines. Their sanctuary is threatened, however, when Clifford targets it for another development scheme. Jim Shepard, in the *New York Times Book Review,* finds that Astley has "romanticized" her natural settings. "The book's passionate certainty about the rightness of its cause," he adds, lends itself to "mini-screeds" that "give the narratives, despite their brevity, a slight bagginess." Nonetheless, Shepard states, "Most of the time . . . *Vanishing Points* is also shrewd, in understated ways, about some complex issues." Comments Sybil Steinberg in *Publishers Weekly,* "Astley . . . has a quicksilver prose style and a keen satirical eye that make this book a delight."

The Slow Natives, a longer novel published in 1967, demonstrates Astley's ability to create true-to-life characters. "The theme of sterility in human relationships, important in all [Astley's] novels, is a primary one again here," writes Arthur Ashworth in *Southerly.* The novel focuses on the relationship between a teen-aged boy and his middle-aged parents, a "not very bright woman," according to Ashworth, "whose life and home are run according to the notions of glossy women's magazines of the more sophisticated type," and a dull, distant father whose weakness drives his son to ever more extravagant acts of delinquency. While Ashworth finds the ending overly melodramatic and sentimental, the novel's "virtues," he writes, "are apparent: the creation of real people in real settings, the subtle exploration of anguish and despair behind the facade of personality, the astringent analysis of emotional inadequacy in human relationships." A *Time* reviewer writes that Astley's "eye and ear for . . . significant style in decor, clothes, deportment and accent make her a lively social satirist," and adds that she has created "a painfully recognizable family." "Astley's novel is remarkable for its tight structure and its verbal economy," William J. Lynch notes in *Best Sellers.* "She manipulates and interweaves the lives of several pivotal characters without losing grip on any of them."

Beachmasters, published in 1985, relates an ineffectual attempt by the native inhabitants of a tiny, fictitious South Pacific island to shake off joint French and British rule. "While that fight for independence starts out as the most decorous of rebellions—the insurgents politely knock on people's doors to inform them of the impending revolution—it will reverberate loudly, and in some cases tragically, in the lives of everyone who lives there," writes Michiko Kakutani in the *New York Times.* Astley tells her story with "comic brio," the reviewer adds, "yet, even at her most sardonic, she demonstrates a special compassion for her characters' foolishnesses and failings." Dawson describes this novel as "mature, enquiring and often verbally stunning," while Bob Halliday observes in the *Washington Post Book World:* "*Beachmasters* is a slender novel, so gracefully written that it invites reading at a single sitting. . . . Astley has infused her novel with feelings of anger and sadness that give it unusual emotional weight." "By the end of the novel," notes Kakutani, the author has produced "a gallery of portraits that combine to give us a visceral sense of [the island] as a wholly realized community, class-bound but intimate." Moreover, he adds, she has succeeded in "creating a narrative that is as remarkable for its casual epic lyricism as it is for its ability to relay private emotions."

In *It's Raining in Mango,* as in *Beachmasters,* Astley "again attempts to compress and mythologize history," Kakutani states in another *New York Times* review. Although her focus here is on family rather than national history, through her history of four generations of the Laffey family "she will also indirectly chart Australia's own entry into the modern world," the reviewer writes. Critiquing the novel in the *New York Times Book Review,* Rosellen Brown describes Astley's style as "compressed, lively, often hopped-up, sometimes mannered," and complains, "Rarely . . . does it convincingly penetrate the deeper recesses of her tormented characters." Valerie Miner, however, writing in the *Los Angeles Times Book Review,* finds that "Astley's portraits are drawn with compassionate intensity," while Kakutani praises the author's use of "her own brand of magic realism" and the way in which she "turns the violence that keeps overtaking the Laffeys . . . into a reflection of the brutalities around them: racial atrocities committed in the name of civilization; lynchings, brawls, and the simple ravages of an extreme climate."

In a *Washington Post Book World* review, Miner describes Astley's 1990 novel *Reaching Tin River* as "the raw, frantic, first-person narrative of a Queensland woman named Belle, who treads a fine line between going crazy and going on." In what Miner calls "a classic Australian search for identity," Belle, seeking a "center," becomes obsessed with a historical figure named Gaden Lockyer, a nineteenth-century Australian farmer, businessman, and politician that she comes across in an old photograph. Freeman finds the novel somewhat disappointing; it "feels hurried, as if written in a rush," she suggests, adding that "some underlying fascination with Euclidean geometry is favored over an obligation to real emotional depth in characters." Susan Whaley in the *Globe and Mail* is similarly bothered by the author's pervasive use of Euclidean metaphors and by what she discerns as "the unsettled feel of a novel-in-progress." Ursula Perrin, in the *New York*

Times Book Review, finds the novel somewhat uneven: "Much of the early writing is inflated, contorted; the ending seems . . . a sham." But she has high praise for that part of the novel that follows Belle's pursuit of Lockyer, "an excursion so eerie and hypnotic that we read on helplessly, wondering how on earth it will end." Miner, for her part, finds *Reaching Tin River* a "gripping, imaginative novel," adding that "Astley's brass and marshmallow voice offers the perfect range for Belle's furious, courageous search."

Astley is also a writer of short stories, several of which are collected in *Hunting the Wild Pineapple,* published in 1979. All of the stories in this collection have the same narrator, a cynical, one-legged, self-described "self-pitier" who runs a cheap motel in a small, remote Australian town. (The character is the adolescent of *The Slow Natives* grown to adulthood.) In these "fiercely funny, bizarre and precisely observed tales of small-town Australia," comments James Polk in a *Washington Post* review, Astley "displays a delicate hand for the precise detail and a wondrous eye for the shadings of human color, both realized in a prose that is almost poetic in its measure and intensity." He adds, "Perhaps at times the cynicism and deep ironies are too intense, verging on contempt, but most of this fine collection reads exactly right." Commenting on Astley's "spikey brand of satire," Douglas Seibold suggests in the *Chicago Tribune* that "like the wild pineapple itself, Astley's work will reward the reader hardy enough to penetrate its thorny surface."

BIOGRAPHICAL/CRITICAL SOURCES:

BOOKS

Blake, L. J., *Australian Writers,* Rigby, 1968.
Contemporary Literary Criticism, Volume 41, Gale, 1987, pp. 43-50.

PERIODICALS

Best Sellers, December 1, 1967.
Chicago Tribune, June 8, 1988; January 3, 1991.
Choice, February, 1985, pp. 810-11.
Globe & Mail (Toronto), June 23, 1990.
Kirkus Reviews, July 15, 1992, p. 863.
Los Angeles Times Book Review, August 24, 1986, p. 10; November 22, 1987, p. 13; June 19, 1988, p. 14; June 10, 1990, p. 3.
Library Journal, September 1, 1967.
Meanjin, September, 1969, pp. 416-18; April, 1980, pp. 127-33; December, 1983, pp. 478-85.
New York Times, May 28, 1986; October 28, 1987.
New York Times Book Review, June 22, 1986, p. 12; November 22, 1987, p. 14; July 31, 1988, p. 8; April 22, 1990, p. 13; December 23, 1990, p. 6; September 27, 1992, pp. 11-12; October 24, 1993, p. 26.

Publishers Weekly, March 30, 1990, pp. 42-43; July 6, 1992, p. 37.

Saturday Review, November 4, 1967.

Southerly, Volume 21, number 2, 1961, pp. 53-54; Volume 23, number 4, 1963, pp. 276-80; Volume 26, number 1, 1966, pp. 62-66; December, 1976, pp. 442-59.

Time, October 20, 1967.

Times Literary Supplement, November 15, 1985, p. 1295.

Washington Post Book World, July 1, 1984, p. 15; June 29, 1986, p. 8; August 9, 1987, p. 12; June 19, 1988, p. 11; April 29, 1990, p. 11; February 1, 1991, p. C3.

World Literature Review, Autumn, 1981, p. 724.

—*Sketch by M. L. Onorato*

*   *   *

AUMBRY, Alan
    See BAYLEY, Barrington J(ohn)

B

BARKER, Nicolas (John) 1932-

PERSONAL: Born December 6, 1932, in Cambridge, England; son of Sir Ernest and Olivia Stuart (Horner) Barker; married Joanna Mary Sophia Nyda Cotton, 1962; children: Emma, Christian, Olivia, Cecilia, Cosmo. *Education:* Received M.A. from New College, Oxford.

ADDRESSES: Home—22 Clarendon Rd., London W11, England. *Office*—British Library, Great Russell St., London WC1, England.

CAREER: Associated with Bailliere, Tindall & Cox, and Rupert Hart-Davis, 1959; National Portrait Gallery, London, England, assistant keeper, 1964; associated with Macmillan & Co., Ltd. London, 1965; Oxford University Press, Oxford, England, production manager, 1972; British Library, London, deputy keeper, 1976—.

MEMBER: Royal National Institute for the Blind (member, publications board of directors), Bibliographical Society (vice-president), Printing Historical Society, William Morris Society, Amici Thomae Mori (president), Pilgrim Trust, St. Bride's Foundation, London Library, Friends of the National Library, Roxburghe Club.

WRITINGS:

EDITOR

The Likeness of Thomas More: An Iconographical Survey of Three Centuries, Burns & Oates, 1963.
Portrait of an Obsession: The Life of Sir Thomas Phillips, the World's Greatest Book Collector, Constable, 1967.
The Early Life of James McBey: An Autobiography, 1883-1911, Oxford University Press, 1977.
Essays and Papers of A. N. L. Munby, Scolar Press, 1978.
The York Gospels, Roxburghe Club, 1988.
(And compiler, with the curatorial staff of the British Library) *Treasures of the British Library,* Abrams, 1989.

Two East Anglian Picture Books: A Facsimile of the Helmingham Herbal and Bestiary and Bodleian Library MS, Quaritch for the Roxburghe Club, 1989.
Early Italian Writing-Books: Renaissance to Baroque, British Library, 1990.

NONFICTION

The Publications of the Roxburghe Club: An Essay with a Bibliographical Table, Roxburghe Club, 1964.
(With Douglas Cleverdon) *Stanley Morison, 1889-1967: A Radio Portrait,* W. S. Cowell, 1969.
Politics and Script: Aspects of Authority and Freedom in the Development of Graeco-Latin Script from the Sixth Century B.C. to the Twentieth Century A.D., Clarendon Press, 1972.
Biobliotheca Lindesiana, Quaritch for the Roxburghe Club, 1978.
The Oxford University Press and the Spread of Learning, 1478-1978: An Illustrated History, Clarendon Press, 1978.
(Editor and author of epilogue, with John Collins) Carter, John, and Graham Pollard, *An Enquiry into the Nature of Certain Nineteenth-Century Pamphlets,* Scolar Press, 1983.
(With John Carter) *A Sequel to an Enquiry into the Nature of Certain Nineteenth-Century Pamphlets by John Carter and Graham Pollard: The Forgeries of H. Buxton Forman and T. J. Wise Re-Examined,* Scolar Press, 1983.
Aldus Manutius and the Development of Greek Script and Type in the Fifteenth Century, Chiswick Book Shop, 1985, revised edition, Fordham University Press, 1992.
The Butterfly Books: An Enquiry into the Nature of Certain Twentieth-Century Pamphlets, Bertram Rota, 1987.

(Author of introduction) *The Library of Robert Hooke: The Scientific Book Trade of Restoration England,* Modoc Press, 1989.

(Author of introduction) *Elizabethan Eccentrics: Brief Lives of English Misfits, Exploiters, Rogues and Failures, 1580-1660,* Dorset Press, 1990.

(Contributing editor) Jones, Mark, editor, *Fake? The Art of Deception,* British Museum, 1990.

OTHER

Editor of *Book Collector,* 1965—; contributor of a memoir of Arnold Fawcus to *A Sketchbook by Richard Doyle, 1824-1883: A Facsimile,* Victoria & Albert Museum, 1990.

BIOGRAPHICAL/CRITICAL SOURCES:

PERIODICALS

New York Review of Books, February 28, 1985.
Spectator, April 8, 1989.
Times Literary Supplement, March 16, 1984; November 28, 1986; June 17, 1988; August 9, 1988; June 9, 1989; June 21, 1991.*

* * *

BARRY, Herbert III 1930-

PERSONAL: Born June 2, 1930, in New York, NY; son of Herbert, Jr. (a psychiatrist) and Lucy (Brown) Barry. *Education:* Harvard University, B.A., 1952; Yale University, M.S., 1953, Ph.D., 1957. *Politics:* Democrat.

ADDRESSES: Home—522 North Neville St., Apt. 83, Pittsburgh, PA 15213. *Office*—School of Dental Medicine, University of Pittsburgh, Pittsburgh, PA 15261.

CAREER: Yale University, New Haven, CT, 1958-61, began as instructor, became assistant professor of psychology; University of Connecticut, Storrs, assistant professor of psychology, 1961-63; University of Pittsburgh, School of Pharmacy, Pittsburgh, PA, associate professor, 1963-70, professor of pharmacology, 1970-87, School of Dental Medicine, professor of physiology and pharmacology, 1987—. Yale University, National Institute of Mental Health fellow, 1957-59. Member of alcohol research review committee, National Institute on Alcohol Abuse and Alcoholism, 1972-76; member of Sociobehavioral Research Review Subcommittee (DAAR-2), National Institute on Drug Abuse, 1988-89. *Military service:* U.S. Army Reserve, 1951-57; became sergeant.

MEMBER: American Psychological Association, American Anthropological Association, American Society of Pharmacology and Experimental Therapeutics, American College of Neuropsychopharmacology, Society for Cross-Cultural Research (president, 1973-74), Society of Stimu-

lus Properties and Drugs (president, 1980-81), Phi Beta Kappa, Sigma Xi.

AWARDS, HONORS: Research Scientist Development Award, National Institute of Mental Health, 1967-77; Distinguished Scientist Award, Society of Stimulus Properties and Drugs, 1986.

WRITINGS:

(With Henrik Wallgren) *Actions of Alcohol,* two volumes, Elsevier, 1970.

(Editor with Alice Schlegel) *Cross-Cultural Samples and Codes,* University of Pittsburgh Press, 1980.

(Editor with Avraham Yacobi) *Experimental and Clinical Toxicokinetics,* American Pharmaceutical Association, 1984.

(With Schlegel) *Adolescence: An Anthropological Inquiry,* Free Press, 1991.

Contributor of more than one hundred fifty articles to scientific journals. Field editor, *Psychopharmacology,* 1974—; consulting editor to several journals on alcohol and pharmacology research, and on cross-cultural comparisons.

WORK IN PROGRESS: Research on effects of drugs, including alcohol, on behavior of rats; cross-cultural research comparing child training with other customs; studying birth order and first name as determinants of adult personality and behavior.

SIDELIGHTS: Herbert Barry III once told *CA:* "I believe that the key to successful writing is a chronic obsession with the project. With this prerequisite, the brain continually creates both the general ideas and the specific phrases, even at times when the conscious thoughts and efforts are elsewhere. Two techniques, which are helpful for most writers, are . . . thorough revisions of what has been written . . . [and] a regular schedule of several consecutive hours at the same time of day devoted to the writing."*

* * *

BARTON, Fredrick (Preston) 1948-

PERSONAL: Born January 15, 1948, in Alexandria, LA; son of V. Wayne (a pastor) and Joeddie (a teacher; maiden name, Whisenhunt) Barton. *Education:* Attended Davidson College, 1966; Valparaiso University, B.A. (with distinction), 1970; University of California, Los Angeles, M.A., 1973, C.Phil., 1975; University of Iowa, M.F.A., 1979. *Politics:* Democrat. *Avocational Interests:* Basketball, tennis, squash.

ADDRESSES: Home—63 Versailles, New Orleans, LA 70125. *Office*—Department of English, University of New Orleans, LA 70148.

CAREER: Social studies teacher at Lutheran high school in St. Louis, MO, 1970-72; *Institutions,* Chicago, IL, assistant editor, 1978; University of New Orleans, New Orleans, New Orleans, LA, professor of English, 1979—. Film editor. Producer and host of "On Film," for WWNO-Radio, 1980—, and "The Screening Room," for WDSU-TV, 1982-85; film critic, WLAE-TV, 1986-88, and WYES-TV, 1988—.

AWARDS, HONORS: Danforth fellow, 1972-76; Louisiana Division of the Arts Award for Literature, 1989; first place for a critical review, New Orleans Press Club, 1983, 1984, 1986, 1987, 1988, 1989, and 1990; Alex Waller Memorial Award, 1984, for column "Balcony Seats"; Outstanding Journalism Performance Award, 1985, for column "Balcony Seats", 1991, and 1992; American Book Award nomination, 1985, for *The El Cholo Feeling Passes*; Bronze Quill Award for editorial writing, International Association of Business Communications, 1993.

WRITINGS:

The El Cholo Feeling Passes (novel), Peachtree Publishers, 1986.
Courting Pandemonium (novel), Peachtree Publishers, 1986.
With Extreme Prejudice (novel), Villard Books, 1993.

Work represented in several anthologies, including *Something in Common,* Louisiana State University Press, 1991; and *Above Ground,* Xavier University Press, 1993. Author of column "Balcony Seats," published in *Gambit,* 1980—. Also contributor of stories, articles, and reviews to periodicals, including *Times-Picayune, Louisiana Literature, Xavier Review,* and *Cresset.* Film editor, *Gambit.*

WORK IN PROGRESS: A book of stories, *Half Past Two.*

BIOGRAPHICAL/CRITICAL SOURCES:

PERIODICALS

Los Angeles Times, December 31, 1985.
Xavier Review, spring, 1992.

*   *   *

BAUSANI, Alessandro   1921-1988

PERSONAL: Born May 29, 1921, in Rome, Italy; died March 12, 1988; son of Stefano (a bank employee) and Fulvia (Gagliardini) Bausani; married Elsa Scola, October 27, 1951. *Education:* University of Rome, Ph.D., 1943. *Religion:* Baha'i.

ADDRESSES: Home—Via F. de Grenet 91, Tre Pini, 00128 Rome, Italy. *Office*—Istituto di Studi Islamici, Scuola Orientale, University of Rome, Rome, Italy.

CAREER: University of Rome, Rome, Italy, instructor, 1944-51, assistant professor, 1951-54, associate professor, 1954-70, professor of Islamics, 1970-87.

MEMBER: National Academy ("Lincei").

AWARDS, HONORS: Sitara-e Imtiyaz (Pakistan), 1957, for studies in Urdu language and literature; award from President of Italian Republic, 1976, for work in philology; Award Hilal-i Imtiyaz (Pakistan), 1984; award from School of Culture and Art, 1984.

WRITINGS:

(Editor and translator) Muhammed Iqbal, *Il Poema celeste* (title means "The Celestial Poem"), Istituto Italiano per il Medio ed Estremo Oriente, 1952.
(Editor and translator) Omar Khayyam, *Quartine* (title means "Quatrains"), 2nd edition, G. Einaudi, 1957.
Storia delle letterature del Pakistan (title means "History of the Literatures of Pakistan"), Nuova Accademia, 1958, revised edition published as *Le Letterature del Pakistan e dell'Afghanistan* (title means "The Literatures of Pakistan and Afghanistan"), Sansoni and Accademia, 1968.
Persia religiosa da Zaratustra a Baha'u'llah (title means "The Religions of Iran: From Zarathustra to Baha'u'llah"), Saggiatore, 1959.
(With Antonio Pagliaro) *Storia della letteratura persiana* (title means "History of Persian Literature"), Nuova Accademia, 1960, new edition, Sansoni and Accademia, 1968.
(Editor) *La Religione dell'U.R.S.S.* (title means "Religion in the U.S.S.R."), Feltrinelli, 1961.
(Editor and translator) *Il Corano* (title means "The Koran"), Sansoni, 1961.
I Persiani, Sansoni, 1962, translation by J. B. Donne, published as *The Persians: From the Earliest Days to the Twentieth Century,* Elek, 1971.
Malesia: Poesie e legende (title means "Poems and Legends from Malaysia"), Nuova Accademia, 1963.
(With Felice Marie Pareja and others) *Islamologie* (title means "Islamology"), Imprimerie Catholique (Beirut), 1964.
(Translator) Omar Khayyam, *Venti Quartine di Omar Khayyam* (title means "Twenty Quatrains of Omar Khayyam"), Carlo Bestetti, Edizioni d'Arte, 1965.
(Editor) Nizami Ganjavi, *Le Sette principesse* (title means "The Seven Princesses"), Leonardo da Vinci Editrice, 1967.
(With Ahmed Ali) *Ghalib: Two Essays* (in Italian), Istituto Italiano per il Medio ed Estremo Oriente, 1969.
Geheim und Universalsprachen (title means "Secret and Universal Languages"), Kohlhammer, 1970.

Letterature de sud-est Asiatico (title means "The Litera- tures of South-East Asia"), Accademia and Sansoni, 1970.

(Editor with Ugo Bianchi and Claas Jouco Bleeker) *Prob- lems and Methods of the History of Religions,* E. J. Brill, 1972.

Le lingue inventate: Linguaggi artificiali, linguaggi segreti, linguaggi universali, Ubaldini, 1974.

L'Enciclopedia dei fratelli della purita, Istituto Universi- tario Orientale, 1978.

Notes on the Structure of the Classical Malay Hikayat, translated from Italian by Lode Brakel, Centre of Southeast Asia Studies, Monash University, 1979.

L'Islam, Garzanti, 1980.

(With others) *Iqbal und Europa: vier Vortrage,* P. Lang, 1980.

Un Filosofo "laico" del Medioevo Musulmano, Istituto di Studi Islamici, 1981.

(With Andre Guillou and Filippo Burgarella) *L'Impero bizantino e l'islamismo,* Unione Tipografico-editrice Torinese, 1981.

La Bisaccia dello Sheikh, Quaderni del Seminario di Iranistica, 1981.

Il Mondo islamico tra interazione e acculturazione, Istituto di Studi Islamic, 1981.

Il kitab 'ard miftah an-nujum attribuito a Hermes, Ac- cademia nazionale dei Lincei, 1983.

Saggi sulla fede Baha'i (title means "Essays on the Baha'i Faith"), [Rome], 1991.

La Bbona Notizzia, Recco, 1992.

WORK IN PROGRESS: Research on Islamic religion in India and Indonesia; further study of Persian literature; research on the history of Islamic science, especially as- tronomy.

SIDELIGHTS: Alessandro Bausani has traveled exten- sively in Asia, the Near East, the Pacific Islands, and South America.

*   *   *

BAUSCH, Richard (Carl) 1945-

PERSONAL: Born April 18, 1945, in Fort Benning, GA; son of Robert Carl and Helen (Simmons) Bausch; married Karen Miller (a photographer), May 3, 1969; children: Wesley, Emily, Paul. *Education:* George Mason Univer- sity, B.A., 1974; University of Iowa, M.F.A., 1975; also attended Northern Virginia Community College. *Politics:* " ' . . . only connect . . . ' E. M. Forster." *Religion:* Roman Catholic.

*ADDRESSES: Home—*Fairfax, VA. *Office—*Department of English, George Mason University, 4400 University

Dr., Fairfax, VA 22030. *Agent—*Harriet Wasserman, Russell & Volkening, Inc., 551 Fifth Ave., New York, NY 10017.

CAREER: Worked as singer-songwriter and comedian. George Mason University, Fairfax, VA, professor of En- glish, 1980—. *Military service:* U.S. Air Force, survival in- structor, 1966-69.

MEMBER: Associated Writing Programs.

AWARDS, HONORS: PEN/Faulkner Award nomina- tions, 1982, for *Take Me Back,* and 1988, for *Spirits;* Gug- genheim fellowship, 1984.

WRITINGS:

Real Presence (novel), Dial, 1980.
Take Me Back (novel), Dial, 1981.
The Last Good Time (novel), Dial, 1984.
Spirits and Other Stories (short stories), Linden Press/ Simon & Schuster, 1987.
Mr. Field's Daughter (novel), Linden Press/Simon & Schuster, 1989.
The Fireman's Wife and Other Stories (short stories), Lin- den Press, 1990.
Violence (novel), Houghton Mifflin/Seymour Lawrence, 1992.
Rebel Powers (novel), Houghton Mifflin/Seymour Law- rence, 1993.

Work represented in anthologies, including *New Writing from the South,* 1980. Contributor to *Ploughshares.*

SIDELIGHTS: "My vital subjects are family, fear, love, and anything that is irrecoverable and *missed,*" Richard Bausch once told *CA,* "but I'll dispense with all of that for a good story. . . . I grew up listening to my father tell sto- ries—he is a great story-teller, and all the Bauschs can do it." Bausch added that he has no literary creed: "My only criterion is that fiction make feeling, that it deepen feeling. If it doesn't do that it's not fiction." Bausch's works are true to his self-description: dealing with the ordinary trag- edies of American family life in our time, they spring from feeling and, at their best, create it.

Bausch's first novel, *Real Presence,* examines the crisis of faith of an aging priest, Monsignor Vincent Shepherd. Bit- ter, withdrawn, recovering from a heart attack, Shepherd is assigned to a West Virginia parish whose beloved previ- ous priest is a hard act to follow. He is shaken from his doldrums by the arrival of a down-and-out family, the Bexleys, which includes the terminally ill war veteran and ex-convict, Duck, and his wife, Elizabeth, who is pregnant with her sixth child. The Bexleys test Shepherd's ability to live up to his symbolic surname, and Elizabeth succeeds in reaching him. After Duck is killed, and while Elizabeth is in labor, Shepherd declares his desire to leave the priesthood and replace Duck as the surviving Bexleys' father figure. Thomas M. Gannon criticized the novel's ending in a review in *America,* saying, "The abrupt disregard for the emotional and physical limitations the author has previously imposed on this character is a serious defect in Bausch's otherwise careful effort." Scott Spencer, however, reviewing the novel for the *New York Times Book Review,* called the ending "moving and even satisfying" but also "a foregone conclusion." Other reviewers praised Bausch's first effort, including *Washington Post Book World*'s Doris Grumbach, who found *Real Presence* distinguished by "its distance from the customary first novel subjects." A *Critic* reviewer called it "excellently crafted," and the *Los Angeles Times Book Review*'s Dick Roraback found it an "exquisite, excruciating novel" and concluded, "Bausch has written a book that disturbs; sometimes it is good to be disturbed."

Bausch wrote his second novel, *Take Me Back,* in four months of fifteen-hour days. Set in a low-rent area of Virginia, the novel dissects the lives of Gordon Brinhart, an unsuccessful and hard-drinking insurance salesman, his wife Katherine, a former rock musician, and Katherine's illegitimate son Alex, as well as a neighboring family which includes Amy, a thirteen-year-old who is dying of leukemia. Gordon goes on a binge, loses his job, and sleeps with a seventeen-year-old neighbor; in response Katherine attempts suicide, and Alex witnesses it all. "Telling the story skillfully from the alternating points of view of the three members of the [Brinhart] family, Bausch has us suffer through the whole ordeal right along with them," wrote Bruce Cook in *Washington Post Book World.* Cook added, "*Take Me Back* isn't pretty. It is, however, as well written as any novel I have read in a while. . . . Richard Bausch has captured something essential in the quality of American life today in these pages." The *New York Times Book Review*'s Richard P. Brickner gave a nod to the novel's "uncanny skillfulness in dialogue and atmosphere" but objected to its "smallness of vision," finding in it "no evident conviction beyond the glum one that life stinks."

Bausch's third novel, *The Last Good Time,* was again the product of mere months of work. It is about two men, seventy-five-year-old Edward Cakes and eighty-nine-year-old Arthur Hagood, into whose lives the twenty-four-year-old Mary Virginia Bellini arrives by chance. Mary makes love to Edward in exchange for friendship and material support; meanwhile Arthur, bedridden in a hospital and learning of the events through Edward's visits, is jealous. On Mary's departure, Edward takes up with Ida Warren, the elderly woman upstairs whose phonograph records have been keeping him awake. "Bausch makes them all believable," wrote Art Seidenbaum in the *Los Angeles Times.* "These are little people at work here . . . ; what

stamps them as human is the novelist's gift of character." In *Washington Post Book World,* Stephen Dobyns had high praise for Bausch's style, and despite "shortcomings" of plot, structure, and character believability, called *The Last Good Time* "quite a good novel." *New York Times Book Review* critic Nancy Forbes called particular attention to the way Bausch's narrative relates the elderly's experience of time, and remarked that the book "has a way of being superlatively funny and disturbing by turns, but the experience that emerges most strongly is that of spending an interesting time getting to know the sort of people whose lives we take for granted."

While strengthening his reputation as a novelist, Bausch also wrote numerous short stories. His 1987 collection, *Spirits and Other Stories,* won considerable critical praise. Michael Dorris, in *Washington Post Book World,* called Bausch "a master of the short story," while Madison Smartt Bell in the *New York Times Book Review* termed the book a "thoughtful, honest collection" and remarked upon the absence of "superfluous stylistic flash." Thomas Cahill, writing in *Commonweal,* praised the stories' narrative magnetism and the author's ability to imagine his characters in all their details, and asserted, "It is my deep, perverse suspicion that, when I am an old man . . . all of Bausch . . . will be in print, and names like Updike, Roth, Bellow will have faded from view."

In *Mr. Field's Daughter,* Bausch's next novel, James Field, a sixtysomething widower and loan officer, leads a household that includes his widowed sister Ellen, his daughter Annie, and Annie's daughter Linda. Linda's father, the cocaine-snorting Cole Gilbertson, soon arrives, wielding a .22 pistol. Opting for realistic drama rather than melodrama, Bausch fashioned from these familiar narrative ingredients and from the conventional thoughts of his characters a work that Jonathan Yardley of *Washington Post Book World* called "exceptionally mature and satisfying" as well as "original and immensely affecting." "Strong characters sustain a family story line as a gifted novelist mines the universal in a pit of the mundane," summarized *Los Angeles Times Book Review*'s Seidenbaum. Gene Lyons, in the *New York Times Book Review,* called Bausch "an author of rare and penetrating gifts, working at the height of his powers."

Bausch published a second short story collection, *The Fireman's Wife,* in 1990. Bette Pesetsky noted in the *New York Times Book Review* that the stories "are all about relationships; they are all about redemption through understanding," and asserted, "We are fortunate to have [*The Fireman's Wife*] with which to explore and search for the meaning of how we live today." The *Los Angeles Times*'s Richard Eder found "Consolation," in which a young widow takes her baby to visit her dead husband's parents, the best story in *The Fireman's Wife,* "subtle and moving—with a fine comic turn by the widow's bossy and self-centered sister—even if the warmth at the end is a shade overinsistent."

Violence, Bausch's 1992 novel, continued the author's tradition of dealing realistically with the troubles of ordinary Americans. Charles Connally, in the grip of an emotional crisis, wanders into a Chicago convenience store where a robbery is taking place, saves the life of a woman, and is treated as a hero by the press. In the aftermath, he succumbs to depression, dropping out of college and questioning his marriage to dental hygienist Carol. "This is a sad and daring book," Carolyn See commented in *Washington Post Book World.* The *New York Times Book Review*'s Susan Kenney called the novel "masterly" for Bausch's realistic exploration of "both the public and private manifestations of violence with persistence as well as sensitivity. And he does so with a redeeming grace of language and detail that goes beyond mere witnessing, straight to the heart."

BIOGRAPHICAL/CRITICAL SOURCES:

BOOKS

Contemporary Authors Autobiography Series, Volume 14, Gale, 1992.
Contemporary Literary Criticism, Volume 51, Gale, 1989.

PERIODICALS

America, August 23, 1980, pp. 77-78.
Commonweal, October 9, 1987, pp. 568-569.
Critic, September, 1980, p. 8.
Los Angeles Times, August 20, 1980; May 14, 1981; November 9, 1984; August 16, 1990.
Los Angeles Times Book Review, August 20, 1980; July 12, 1987; May 7, 1989; September 9, 1991; January 26, 1992.
New York Times, July 18, 1987.
New York Times Book Review, April 26, 1981, p. 14; December 23, 1984; April 26, 1987; June 14, 1987, p. 16; August 27, 1989, p. 14; August 19, 1990, p. 9; January 26, 1992, p. 7.
Publishers Weekly, August 10, 1990, p. 425.
Tribune Books (Chicago), July 29, 1990.
Washington Post, March 26, 1982, pp. C1, C6.
Washington Post Book World, June 15, 1980, p. 4; May 3, 1981, p. 5; December 11, 1984; June 28, 1987, p. 6; April 30, 1989, p. 3; August 21, 1990; December 29, 1991.*

BAYLEY, Barrington J(ohn) 1937-
(Alan Aumbry, P. F. Woods)

PERSONAL: Born April 9, 1937, in Birmingham, England; son of John (a toolmaker) and Clarissa (Love) Bayley; married Joan Lucy Clarke, October 30, 1969; children: Sean, Heather.

ADDRESSES: Home—48 Turreff Ave., Donnington, Telford, Shropshire, TF2 8HE, England. *Agent*—Michael Congdon, Don Congdon Associates Inc., 156 Fifth Ave., Suite 625, New York, NY 10010.

CAREER: Writer. Has worked in civil service, in the Australian public service in London, and as a coal miner. *Military service:* Royal Air Force, 1955-57.

WRITINGS:

SCIENCE FICTION

Star Virus, Ace Books, 1970.
Annihilation Factor, Ace Books, 1972.
Empire of Two Worlds, Ace Books, 1972.
Collision Course, DAW Books, 1973, published in England as *Collision with Chronos,* Allison & Busby, 1977.
The Fall of Chronopolis, DAW Books, 1974.
The Soul of the Robot, Doubleday, 1974.
The Garments of Caean, Doubleday, 1976.
The Grand Wheel, DAW Books, 1977.
The Knights of the Limits (short stories), Allison & Busby, 1978.
Star Winds, DAW Books, 1978.
The Pillars of Eternity, DAW Books, 1979.
The Seed of Evil (short stories), Allison & Busby, 1979.
The Zen Gun, DAW Books, 1983.
The Forest of Peldain, DAW Books, 1985.
The Rod of Light, Methuen, 1985.

Contributor of articles and stories, some under pseudonyms Alan Aumbry and P. F. Woods, to British science fiction journals and popular periodicals.

SIDELIGHTS: The Pillars of Eternity is a "typical [Barrington J.] Bayley marriage of space opera and metaphysics," remarks John Clute of the *Washington Post Book World.* The *Los Angeles Times Book Review*'s Don Strachan comments, "*Pillars* exotically combines a comic-book superhero . . . with intellectually impressive science and philosophy."

Bayley once told *CA:* "My primary ambition as a science fiction writer has been to be able to inspire others as I have been inspired. A good story is one you carry on thinking about long after you have read it."

BIOGRAPHICAL/CRITICAL SOURCES:

PERIODICALS

Los Angeles Times Book Review, April 25, 1982.
Times Literary Supplement, May 30, 1980.
Washington Post Book World, April 25, 1982.

* * *

BEAUREGARD, Erving E. 1920-

PERSONAL: Born September 29, 1920, in Bondsville, MA; married wife, Caroline, April 25, 1951; children: Carolyn. *Education:* University of Chicago, A.B., 1942; University of Massachusetts, A.M., 1944; Union Graduate School, Ph.D., 1976; also attended Harvard University, Boston University, and University of Ottawa. *Politics:* Independent. *Religion:* Roman Catholic.

ADDRESSES: Home—1300 Sugar Hill Lane, Xenia, OH 45385-9317. *Office*—Department of History, University of Dayton, Dayton, OH 45469-1540.

CAREER: History teacher at private school in Monson, MA, 1944-46; Carnegie-Mellon University, Pittsburgh, PA, instructor in history, 1946-47; University of Dayton, Dayton, OH, 1947—, became professor of history. Public speaker.

MEMBER: American Association of University Professors (chairman of council of private institutions in Ohio, 1969-71; state vice-president, 1969-71; state president, 1971-72), American Historical Association, American Catholic Historical Association, African Studies Association, Southern African Research Association, Ohio Academy of History (vice-president, 1971-72; president, 1972-73), Phi Beta Kappa, Phi Kappa Phi, Phi Alpha Theta.

AWARDS, HONORS: Ford Foundation fellow, 1969; professor of the year, University of Dayton, 1972; distinguished service award, Ohio Academy of History, 1983; Robert Kennedy Award, American Association of University Professors, 1989, for contribution to academic freedom.

WRITINGS:

The History of the Ohio Conference AAUP, Ohio State University Press, 1974.
Old Franklin: The Eternal Touch; A History of Franklin College, New Athens, Harrison County, Ohio, University Press of America, 1983.
History of Academic Freedom in Ohio: Case Studies in Higher Education, 1808-1976, Peter Lang, 1988.
Bingham of the Hills: Politician and Diplomat Extraordinary, Peter Lang, 1989.

Reverend John Walker: Renaissance Man, Peter Lang, 1990.

Contributor to *New Catholic Encyclopedia, Corpus Dictionary of Western Churches,* and *Encyclopedic Dictionary of Religion.* Contributor to history and African studies journals.

WORK IN PROGRESS: The Great Cadizians.

* * *

BECKLES WILLSON, Robina (Elizabeth) 1930-

PERSONAL: Indexed in some bibliographical sources under Willson; born September 26, 1930, in London, England; daughter of Robertson (a clergyman) and Dorothy (Cuss) Ballard; married Anthony Beckles Willson (an architect); children: Mark Robert, Rachel Clare Elizabeth. *Education:* University of Liverpool, B.A. (with honors), 1948, M.A., 1952. *Religion:* Church of England.

ADDRESSES: Home—44 Popes Ave., Twickenham, Middlesex TW2 5TL, England. *Agent*—A. M. Heath & Co. Ltd., 40-42 William IV St., London WC2N 4DD, England.

CAREER: Teacher of English and music at schools in Leeds, Liverpool, and London, England.

WRITINGS:

A Reflection of Rachel, Macmillan, 1967.
Roundabout Ride, Benn, 1968.
Pendulum Quest, Macmillan, 1969.
Dancing Day, Benn, 1971.
The Shell on Your Back, Heinemann, 1972.
What a Noise, Heinemann, 1974.
Circus Parade, Macmillan, 1980.
Music Maker, Viking Kestrel, 1986.

JUVENILE

Leopards on the Loire, Gollancz, 1961.
A Time to Dance, Collins, 1962.
A Seraph in a Box, Hart-Davis, 1963.
Pineapple Palace, Hart-Davis, 1964.
Musical Instruments, Oliver & Boyd, 1964.
Anchors Wharf, Hart-Davis, 1965.
The Last Harper, Macmillan, 1972.
The Voice of Music (nonfiction), Heinemann, 1976, Atheneum, 1977.
Musical Merry-Go-Round, Heinemann, 1977, published as *Creative Drama and Musical Activities for Children,* Plays, 1979.
The Beaver Book of Ballet, Hamlyn, 1979.
Anna Pavlova: A Legend among Dancers, Hodder & Stoughton, 1981.
Eyes Wide Open, Heinemann, 1981.

Pocket Book of Ballet, Hamlyn, 1982.
Merry Christmas: Children at Christmastime around the World, Philomel Books, 1983.
Secret Witch, Hodder & Stoughton, 1983.
Square Bear, Hamish Hamilton, 1983.
Holiday Witch, Hodder & Stoughton, 1983.
Hungry Witch, Hodder & Stoughton, 1984.
Sporty Witch, Hodder & Stoughton, 1986.
Mozart's Story, A. & C. Black, 1991.
(With Lyn Gray) *Just Imagine,* Belair Publications, 1993.

Also author of *The Haunting Music,* A. & C. Black.

IN FRENCH

Le Chef de fanfare, adaptation by Ralph Sage, Benn, 1973.

OTHER

Contributor to children's programs broadcast on BBC-TV and YTV.

SIDELIGHTS: Robina Beckles Willson once wrote to *CA:* "I particularly enjoy meeting children of all ages, and I am especially pleased when my books are published as paperbacks, so that they can be bought with pocket money. Also, I am interested in the preparation of children's television, and the interaction of television and reading."

Beckles Willson recently told *CA:* "In *Just Imagine* I collaborated with an artist to produce a resource book for teachers on drama and dressing-up for younger children."

*   *   *

BENSON, Frederick William 1948-
(Ted Benson)

PERSONAL: Born September 26, 1948, in Los Angeles, CA; son of Fred S. and Bessie (Vaughn) Benson; married Elizabeth Carolyn Jones, October 23, 1970; children: Jessica Carolyn, Amy Elizabeth. *Education:* Modesto Junior College, A.A., 1968; San Jose State College (now University), B.A., 1970.

ADDRESSES: Home—P.O. Box 1164, Modesto, CA 95353.

CAREER: Modesto Bee, Modesto, CA, staff photographer, 1970—.

MEMBER: National Press Photographers Association, California Press Photographers Association.

AWARDS, HONORS: Grand prize in black and white category, American Freedom Train Photograph Contest, 1977; first place award for newspaper portrait and layout, Associated Press News Editors, 1984; Railroad History Award, Railroad and Locomotive Historical Society, 1984, for magazine article.

WRITINGS:

UNDER NAME TED BENSON; WITH OWN PHOTOGRAPHS

Mother Lode Shortline: A Sierra Railroad Pictorial, Chatham, 1970.
Sierra Railroad Film-Making: A Production Handbook, privately printed, 1976.
(With Bruce MacGregor) *Portrait of a Silver Lady,* Pruett, 1977, 2nd edition, 1979.
(With Dave Styffe) *Wheels Rolling—West,* Westrail, 1979, 2nd edition, 1981.
(With Richard Steinheimer) *Growing Up with Trains,* Interurban, 1983.
Echoes down the Canyon: A Western Pacific Journal 1968-1986, Westrail, 1987.

PHOTOGRAPHER

Harold Edmonson, *Journey to Amtrak,* Kalmbach, 1972.
Robert L. Hogan, *Mallet to Mogul,* Chatham, 1973.
William D. Middleton, *When the Steam Railroads Electrified,* Kalmbach, 1974.
Joe McMillan, *Santa Fe's Diesel Fleet,* Chatham, 1975.
Oliver Jensen, *Railroads in America,* American Heritage Books, 1975.
Bruce MacGregor, *Narrow Gauge Portrait: South Pacific Coast,* Glenwood, 1975.
Joseph A. Strapac, *Diesels of the Southern Pacific,* Chatham, 1975.
Strapac, *Cotton Belt Locomotives,* Shade Tree, 1977.
McMillan, *Route of the Warbonnets,* McMillan Publications, 1977.
Steinheimer, *The Electric Way across the Mountains,* Carbarn Press, 1980.
Strapac, *Western Pacific's Diesel Years,* Shade Tree, 1980.
George M. Craven, *Object and Image,* 2nd edition, Prentice-Hall, 1982.
MacGregor, *South Pacific Coast: A Centennial,* Pruett, 1982.
John A. Signor, *Tehachapi,* Golden West Books, 1983.
Fred A. Stindt, *Northwestern Pacific,* Volume II, privately printed, 1985.
Signor, *Donner Pass: Southern Pacific's Sierra Crossing,* Golden West Books, 1985.
Edmonson and David Goodheart, *Zephyrs through the Rockies,* Goodheart Publications, 1986.
Noel Holley, *The Milwaukee Electrics,* N. J. International, 1987.
Signor, *Los Angeles and Salt Lake Railroad,* Golden West Books, 1988.
Ken Rattenne, *The Feather River Route,* Interurban, Volume 1, 1990, Volume 2, 1991.
Signor, *Beaumont Hill,* Golden West Books, 1991.
Strapac, *Southern Pacific Historic Diesels,* Volume 1, Shade Tree, 1992.

OTHER

Also author of *Mother Lode Thunder.* Contributor to *Western Steam Spectacular,* 1981, and *New Orleans Steam Spectacular,* 1984; contributor to annuals, including *Passenger Train Annual,* 1977, 1979, 1987, and 1992, and *Rails West Annual,* 1992; contributor to Westrail calendars, 1980-88. Also photographer for *Rio Grande Diesels,* Volume 1, 1982, and Volume 2, 1984, and *Southern Pacific Motive Power,* 1968-73. Contributor of over sixty articles and more than twelve hundred photographs to periodicals, including *Trains, Passenger Train Journal, Pacific Rail News, Southern Pacific Review, Railfan and Railroad, Locomotive and Railway Preservation,* and *Union Pacific Info.*

WORK IN PROGRESS: Southern Pacific Backroads (Southern Pacific branchlines in California); *Mother Lode Thunder* (the Sierra Railroad, 1967—).

SIDELIGHTS: Frederick William Benson once told *CA:* "I consider myself very fortunate that I've been able to convert a lifelong interest in railroading into both an avocation and a profession. It was the desire to improve my fledgling snapshot approach to railroad photography that led to my involvement in high school journalism classes, and from this came the decision to major in photojournalism in college and my subsequent employment as a news photographer.

"As a rail photojournalist, my initial magazine and book contributions reflected the traditional approach to railroading, mainly the railroad as tracks and trains with heavy emphasis on mechanics. It has been my intention to expand on this rather narrow approach and deal with railroading on a broader scale and appeal to a larger audience. The railroad as a lifestyle has occupied my work with a growing frequency, beginning in earnest with *Portrait of a Silver Lady.* It was my intention to deal with the *California Zephyr* as a human experience as much as a mechanical one, and in doing so we hoped to break some new ground in rail documentation. *Portrait* met with acclaim beyond my imagination.

"Beyond *Portrait* has come an increased interest in publishing as a complete package where design and production of the publication contributes as much to the total effect as the subject matter itself. The first book to reflect this new direction, *Wheels Rolling—West,* was produced in collaboration with graphic artist and photographer Dave Styffe, and has been greeted warmly by the railfan press.

"As basic, sweeping change takes place in the railroad industry toward the end of the twentieth century, it seems much of my early innocence is being replaced with a strong sense of urgency. While it is important to develop an honest personal style with words and photographs, it is now even more important to adequately document a way of American life undergoing almost unthinkable transformation.

"Railroading has a unique place in our history, both as a cruel, baronial instrument of greed and a romantic enterprise awakening vagabond souls with lonely whistles in the night. Somewhere in the middle, truth lies in shades neither black nor white. Railroading today is a business fighting for its economic life, a smokestack industry as threatened as any of its major subscribers. In many ways, the face of the railroad industry mirrors the face of the nation. Keeping pace with industry changes is as challenging a task as any author could ask. I hope to keep up with the challenge for a long time to come."

BIOGRAPHICAL/CRITICAL SOURCES:

PERIODICALS

Railfan, October, 1977.
Trains, April, 1975; January, 1978; September, 1984.

*   *   *

BENSON, Ted
    See BENSON, Frederick William

*   *   *

BERKE, Roberta   1943-

PERSONAL: Born March 16, 1943, in Elyria, OH; daughter of Robert Sterling (in business) and Meriam Leota (in business; maiden name, Roller) Elzey; married Joseph H. Berke (a psychiatrist and writer), May 18, 1968 (divorced January, 1982); children: Joshua Damien, Deborah Melissa. *Education:* Bennington College, B.A., 1965. *Avocational Interests:* "Riding on bridlepaths through the English countryside, exploring old towns."

ADDRESSES: Office—Regent's Park College, London, OX1 2LB, England.

CAREER: Pitman College, London, England, instructor, 1966-67; Family Service Units, London, caseworker, 1967-68; Regent's Park College, Oxford, London, faculty fellow, 1986—, assistant academic dean, 1987—; writer. Regular interviewer and documentary maker for British Broadcasting Corporation Radio (BBC-Radio). Guest lecturer at University of Copenhagen and Kent State University; founding member of Arbours Association (operates crisis center and half-way houses for the emotionally distressed).

MEMBER: Society of Authors, Poetry Society.

AWARDS, HONORS: Glascock Memorial Prize for Poetry, Mount Holyoke College, 1965, for *Sphere of Light.*

WRITINGS:

Sphere of Light (poetry), Trigram Press, 1972.
Bounds Out of Bounds: A Compass for Recent American and British Poetry, Oxford University Press, 1981.

POETRY RADIO BROADCASTS

Backwards through the Funhouse, BBC-Radio 3, August 16, 1982.
The Zither Player Underground, BBC-Radio 3, November 28, 1983.
Out on the Balcony, BBC-Radio 3, October 26, 1985.
Below Grass, BBC-Radio 3, June 12, 1987.

OTHER

Contributing feature writer for BBC-Radio 3. Contributor of poems and articles to magazines in the United States and England.

SIDELIGHTS: Roberta Berke writes: "My early poems were relatively short lyrics, often nature studies, which aimed for precision and clarity. In *Sphere of Light,* eight interlocked sequences of poems reflected each other in a complex circular form which was amplified by my symbolic woodcuts. Sequences continue to attract me; the poems in *Backwards through the Funhouse* are less formal, considerably longer and almost all are concerned with human dilemmas and human speech. At the moment, I am working with actors, sound effects and music on radio, hoping to add another dimension to my poetry, as I did earlier with graphics.

"In my literary criticism, I write for literate but nonspecialist readers. My critical touchstone is: 'Does this poem intensify our experience?' I believe the critic's primary purpose is to serve the writer and the reader, not to promote esoteric theories. The aspect of criticism I find most exciting is discovering new or neglected poets. I write in a variety of forms, my choice being determined by the nature of the idea pursuing me at the time.

"I keep in close contact with the United States and many of my values and priorities are American ones, though I have lived in London since 1966."

BIOGRAPHICAL/CRITICAL SOURCES:

PERIODICALS

Booklist, April 1, 1981.
Choice, May 14, 1981.
Directions, April, 1981.
Grand Rapids Press, June 7, 1981.
Sunday Times (London), July 15, 1973.*

BERKOWITZ, William R(obby)   1939-

PERSONAL: Born September 21, 1939, in Albany, NY; son of Leon (a merchant) and Ethel (a teacher; maiden name, Strachstein) Berkowitz; married Madelon Helfer (a therapist), September 3, 1962; children: Daniel, Rachel. *Education:* Cornell University, B.A. (with honors), 1961; Stanford University, Ph.D., 1965.

ADDRESSES: Home and office—12 Pelham Ter., Arlington, MA 02174.

CAREER: Chulalongkorn University, Bangkok, Thailand, visiting lecturer in psychology, 1965-66; Lafayette College, Easton, PA, assistant professor of psychology, 1966-70; University of Massachusetts, Boston, assistant professor of psychology, 1970-72; Dr. Harry C. Solomon Mental Health Center, Lowell, MA, chief psychologist, 1973—, past chairperson of executive council and director of Consultation and Education Service and Community Extension Service. Licensed psychologist in Massachusetts. Visiting professor and lecturer, University of Lowell, 1974-78, and 1985-88. Elected member of Arlington Town Meeting, 1982—. Member of advisory board, Massachusetts Clearinghouse of Mutual Help Groups. Organizer or director of numerous local community programs. Consultant, Fall River Health and Human Service Coalition, and Massachusetts Area Health Education Center, 1988—.

MEMBER: American Psychological Association, Eastern Psychological Association, Phi Beta Kappa, Sigma Xi, Psi Chi.

WRITINGS:

Community Impact: Creating Grass-Roots Change in Hard Times, Schenkman, 1983.
Community Dreams: Ideas for Enhancing Neighborhood and Community Life, Impact Publishers, 1984.
Local Heroes, Lexington Books, 1987.
(Contributor) E. Seidman and J. Rappaport, editors, *Handbook of Community Psychology,* Plenum, 1989.

Contributor of numerous research articles to professional journals. Editor of column, "Community Action," *Community Psychologist,* 1986—; co-editor, *Neighborhood Newsletter.*

SIDELIGHTS: William R. Berkowitz told *CA:* "I continue to believe in the need for ordinary citizens to get involved in local community change, and the power of these same citizens to make real differences in local community life. More particularly, I believe that as public dollars shrink, the neighborhood will become more important for all of us in the near future. We'll all have to get better at helping and supporting one another, for there'll be few other places to turn.

"I hope soon to begin research and writing on neighborhood life, and to explore how neighborhoods can be made stronger, more vibrant, and better able to meet our needs."

* * *

BERRIGAN, Daniel 1921-

PERSONAL: Born May 9, 1921, in Virginia, MN; son of Thomas William (a railroad engineer and labor official) and Frieda (Fromhart) Berrigan. *Education:* St. Andrew on Hudson, B.A., 1946; Woodstock College, Baltimore, MD, M.A., 1952.

ADDRESSES: 220 West 98th St., #7J, New York, NY 10025.

CAREER: Entered Order of Society of Jesus (Jesuits), 1939; ordained Roman Catholic priest, 1952. St. Peter's Preparatory School, Jersey City, NJ, teacher of French, English, and Latin, 1945-49; ministerial work in Europe, 1953-54; Brooklyn Preparatory School, Brooklyn, NY, instructor in French and theology, 1954-57; Lemoyne College, Syracuse, NY, associate professor of theology, 1957-62; sabbatical in Europe, 1962-63; *Jesuit Missions,* New York City, assistant editor, 1963-65; Cornell University, Ithaca, NY, associate director of United Religious Work, 1966-68; imprisoned for anti-war activities, 1970-72; Woodstock College, New York City, professor of theology, beginning 1972. Visiting lecturer, University of Manitoba, 1973, University of Detroit, 1975, University of California-Riverside, 1976, and Yale University, 1977; has also taught at Union Seminary, Columbia University, Loyola University (New Orleans), and College of New Rochelle.

Served as auxiliary military chaplain in Germany, 1954; religious director, Walter Farrell Guild, 1954-57; staff worker, Office of Economic Opportunity, Pueblo, CO, summer, 1967; vice-chairman of American Fellowship of Reconciliation; co-founder, Catholic Peace Fellowship; adviser on film *The Mission,* directed by Roland Joffe; teacher in adult extension college in South Bronx; volunteer worker in cancer ward, Saint Rose's Hospital; New Resources AIDS volunteer, 1985-93.

AWARDS, HONORS: Lamont Poetry Selection Award, American Academy of Poets, and National Book Award nomination, 1957, for *Time without Number;* National Book Award nomination, 1967, for *No One Walks Waters;* National Book Award nomination, 1970, for *No Bars to Manhood;* Frederick G. Melcher Book Award, Unitarian Universalist Association, 1971, for *The Trial of the Catonsville Nine, No Bars to Manhood,* and *Trial Poems: A Poet, a Painter;* Thomas More Association Medal, 1971, for *The Dark Night of Resistance.*

WRITINGS:

The Bride: Essays in the Church, Macmillan, 1959.

The Bow in the Cloud: Man's Covenant with God, Coward, 1961.

They Call Us Dead Men: Reflections on Life and Conscience, Macmillan, 1966.

Consequences: Truth and . . . , Macmillan, 1967.

Go from Here: A Prison Diary, Open Space Action Committee, 1968.

(Contributor) *Delivered into Resistance,* Advocate Press, 1969.

The Trial of the Catonsville Nine (one-act play; first produced in Los Angeles at Mark Taper Forum; produced Off-Broadway at Good Shepherd-Faith Church, February 4, 1971; produced on Broadway at Lyceum Theatre, June, 1971), Beacon Press, 1970.

No Bars to Manhood, Doubleday, 1970.

(Author of introduction) Philip Berrigan, *Prison Journals of a Priest Revolutionary,* Holt, 1970.

The Dark Night of Resistance, Doubleday, 1971.

(With Robert Coles) *The Geography of Faith: Conversations between Daniel Berrigan, When Underground, and Robert Coles,* Beacon Press, 1971.

America Is Hard to Find (contains letters from Danbury Prison and writings from underground), Doubleday, 1972.

(With Lee Lockwood) *Absurd Convictions, Modest Hopes: Conversations after Prison with Lee Lockwood,* Random House, 1972.

(Author of foreword) Thich Nhat Hanh, *The Path of Return Continues the Journey,* Hoa Binh Press, 1972.

Jesus Christ, illustrations by Gregory Harris and Deborah Harris, Doubleday, 1973.

Lights On in the House of the Dead: A Prison Diary, Doubleday, 1974.

(With Thich Nhat Hanh) *The Raft Is Not the Shore: Conversations toward a Buddhist/Christian Awareness,* Beacon Press, 1975.

A Book of Parables, Seabury, 1977.

The Words Our Savior Gave Us, Templegate, 1978.

Uncommon Prayer: A Book of Psalms, illustrated by Robert McGovern, Seabury, 1978.

Beside the Sea of Glass: The Song of the Lamb, photos by Frank Kostyu, Seabury, 1978.

The Discipline of the Mountain: Dante's 'Purgatorio' in a Nuclear World, Seabury, 1979.

We Die Before We Live: Talking with the Very Ill, Seabury, 1980.

Ten Commandments for the Long Haul, Abingdon, 1981.

The Nightmare of God, illustrated by Tom Lewis, Sunburst Press, 1982.

Portraits—Of Those I Love, Crossroad Publishing, 1982.

Steadfastness of the Saints: A Journal of Peace and War in Central and North America, Orbis Books, 1985.

The Mission: A Film Journal, Harper, 1986.

To Dwell in Peace: An Autobiography, Harper, 1987.

Daniel Berrigan: Poetry, Drama, Prose, edited with an introduction by Michael True, Orbis Books, 1988.

Stations: The Way of the Cross, terra cotta reliefs by Margaret Parker, Harper, 1989.

Sorrow Built a Bridge: Friendship and AIDS, Fortkamp, 1989.

Lost and Found, illustrated by Timothy Ely, Caliban, 1989.

Jubilee!, Unicorn Press, 1990.

Whereon to Stand: The Acts of the Apostles and Ourselves, Fortkamp, 1991.

Also author of pamphlets: *The World Showed Me Its Heart,* National Sodality Service Center, 1966; (with Thich Nhat Hanh) *Contemplation and Resistance,* Hoa Binh Press, 1973; *Vietnamese Letter,* Hoa Binh Press; (with Edward W. Said and others) *Arabs and Jews: Possibility of Concord,* Association of Arab-American University Graduates, 1974; *The Hole in the Ground: A Parable for Peacemakers,* Honeywell Project, 1987; and editor of *For Swords into Plowshares, the Hammer has to Fall: The Griffiss Plowshares Action,* Plowshares Press.

POETRY

Time without Number, Macmillan, 1957.

Encounters, World Publishing, 1960, new edition, Associated Artists, 1965.

The World for Wedding Ring, Macmillan, 1962.

No One Walks Waters, Macmillan, 1966.

Love, Love at the End: Parables, Prayers, and Meditations, Macmillan, 1968.

Night Flight to Hanoi: War Diary with 11 Poems, Macmillan, 1968.

False Gods, Real Men: New Poems, Macmillan, 1969.

Crime/Trial, etchings by Robert Marx, Impressions Workshop, 1970.

Trial Poems: A Poet, A Painter, illustrated by Tom Lewis, Beacon Press, 1970.

Selected Poetry of Daniel Berrigan, S.J., Anchor-Doubleday, 1970.

Selected and New Poems, Doubleday, 1973.

Prison Poems, Unicorn Press, 1973.

Prison Poems, Viking, 1974.

Journey to Block Island, Unicorn Press, 1984.

May All Creatures Live, Berliner Press, 1984.

Homage; to Gerard Manley Hopkins, Fortkamp, 1993.

Minor Prophets, Major Themes, Fortkamp, 1993.

Poems anthologized in several volumes, including *From One Word,* Devin, 1950; *Anthology of Catholic Poets,* edited by Joyce Kilmer, with a new supplement by James Edward Tobin, Doubleday, 1955; *Sealed unto the Day,* Catholic Poetry Society of America, 1955; *Twentieth-Century American Poetry,* edited by Conrad Aiken, Modern Library, 1963; and *Against Forgetting,* edited by Caroline Forche, Norton, 1993.

RECORDINGS

Berrigan Raps, Caedmon, 1972.

The Trial of the Catonsville Nine, Caedmon, 1973.

Not Letting Me Not Let Blood: Prison Poems, National Catholic Reporter, 1976.

ADAPTATIONS: The Trial of the Catonsville Nine was filmed in 1972; *In the King of Prussia* was filmed in 1983, directed by Emile de Antonio.

SIDELIGHTS: Motivated by his radical interpretation of Roman Catholic doctrine, Daniel Berrigan has played a prominent role in the contemporary movements for peace, racial equality, and economic justice. His work as a Jesuit priest, social activist, and author of nonfiction and poetry reflects his commitment to political and spiritual activism. "Approaching Berrigan's poetry is a difficult task for those who seek to separate his sociopolitical activities or biographical data from his art," writes Alice Smith Haynes in *Dictionary of Literary Biography.* "Some critics have dismissed his later work apparently on the sole basis of its subject matter or political orientation, and those who praise his poetry often acknowledge or support his political views." Many critics, however, acknowledge Berrigan as a skillful and profound writer who successfully blends art and protest. Commenting in *Publishers Weekly* on a collection of Berrigan's work published in 1988, William Griffin remarked that "his use of words is always surprising, always pleasurable." Many of Berrigan's poems, Griffin adds, "are nearly perfect."

In his youth Berrigan was influenced by the example of Dorothy Day, leader of the pacifist Catholic Worker movement. After he entered the priesthood, his growing radicalism was fed by encounters with activist priests met while he was assigned to Lyons, France, in the early 1950s, and by church assignments in Eastern Europe and Latin America in 1964 and 1965. He was also in close contact with his brother Philip, then a priest in the Josephite Order, who was active in the civil rights movement. Berrigan's poetry of the late 1950s and early-to-mid-1960s, Haynes remarks, reveals the progress of the poet-priest towards engagement with the world. His first published volume, *Time without Number,* which earned him the Lamont Poetry Award, is "the representative work of his early years," she states, showing him to be a versatile poet comfortable with both theological and secular themes. Haynes notes technical similarities to the work of twentieth-century American poet Robert Frost and finds thematic affinities with the devotional works of seventeenth-century English poets John Donne and George Herbert. Fred Moramarco, in *Western Humanities Review,* sees in

Berrigan's verses the influence of both the nineteenth-century Jesuit poet Gerard Manley Hopkins and modern American poet e. e. cummings, "who are very clearly two sides of Berrigan, reverence and joy, the priest and the lover." Subsequent poetry, Haynes suggests, reveals a growing unity between poetic vocation, priestly calling, and social awareness: Berrigan's 1966 volume, *No One Walks Waters,* contains poems on the World War II Nazi concentration camp at Dachau, the United States' nuclear attack on the Japanese city of Hiroshima towards the end of that war, and the American bombing of North Vietnam.

During these years, Berrigan was becoming increasingly engaged in public protests against racial discrimination, urban poverty, and American political and military intervention around the world. As the United States' involvement in the Vietnam War escalated during the late 1960s, Daniel Berrigan and his brother Philip came to national attention as active, outspoken, and controversial opponents of the American role in Southeast Asia. Daniel helped found the national peace organization Clergy and Laity Concerned about Vietnam, and in February, 1968, travelled to North Vietnam with another prominent activist, Howard Zinn, to help arrange the release of three captured American airmen.

But Berrigan's most dramatic antiwar action took place in Catonsville, Maryland, on May 17, 1968. On that day Berrigan, his brother Philip, and seven other Roman Catholic activists went into a local draft board, seized hundreds of files concerning potential draftees, took the files outside, and burned the documents with homemade napalm. They then waited, praying, until federal authorities came to arrest them. A note given to reporters shortly before the raid explained: "We destroy these draft records not only because they exploit our young men but because they represent misplaced power concentrated in the ruling class of America. . . . We confront the Catholic Church, other Christian bodies, and the synagogues of America with their silence and cowardice in the face of our country's crimes." Later, at his trial for his part in the raid, Berrigan stated, "I burned some paper because I was trying to say that the burning of children was unhuman and unbearable, and . . . a cry is the only response."

The Catonsville Nine, as the group of activists came to be known, were found guilty of destroying government property and sentenced to three years in prison. The Berrigan brothers and two other defendants decided to go underground rather than go to jail, and for several months Berrigan was the focus of a massive manhunt. After finally being captured on Block Island, Rhode Island, on August 11, 1970, Berrigan served eighteen months of a reduced sentence in the federal prison in Danbury, Connecticut.

Several of Berrigan's works concern his experiences during the trial and subsequent prison term. One of these, *The Trial of the Catonsville Nine,* a courtroom drama in which Berrigan transcribed into free verse excerpts from the actual trial record, drew an enthusiastic response from audiences and generally favorable reviews from critics. Clive Barnes of the *New York Times* calls the play "a wonderfully moving testament to nine consciences. It is radical, but not at all chic, and the sincerity of its sentiments reveals the simplicity of men with many fears but no doubts." In her book *Plays, Politics, and Polemics,* Catharine Hughes finds *The Trial of the Catonsville Nine* different from most courtroom dramas: "It is more document than documentary, more personal testimony than play. . . . Yet it is surprisingly, even intensely, dramatic, more so than many more deliberately theatrical works."

Prison Poems was written during Berrigan's incarceration and contains poems on a variety of his prison observations and experiences. D. Keith Mano of *National Review* dismisses the subject matter of the poems as trivial: "Verses on: a tooth extraction, a visiting skunk, an anal search. Your average pickpocket has as much to say. . . . Jesus and Vietnam and Watergate are overwhelmed by peevish complaint." Michael True of *New Republic,* on the other hand, judges the collection to contain "the best poems of [Berrigan's] career, frequently brief lyrics, where the telling metaphor brings the events to life, tuned to the music of natural speech." True especially praises the poem "My Father," a 500-line work which he believes is "one of the most beautiful extended lyrics in contemporary poetry."

The book *Selected and New Poems* contains an overview of work from Berrigan's first book, *Time without Number,* through *Prison Poems.* Critics note a consistency of themes and concerns, particularly political concerns, in Berrigan's poems, but find a change in style from his earlier, more traditional work to tougher and more compact poems. "Those who see Berrigan as a developing poet who merges his poetic voice with his actions understand him best," writes Haynes. A reviewer for *Choice* believes that Berrigan's "earliest verse is closely allied to . . . such older poets as Emily Dickinson, G. M. Hopkins, and even Robert Frost. . . . In his later poetry he is much more open to experimentation in the use of alliteration, internal rhyme, and typography." Noting the change in Berrigan's poetry, Fred Moramarco comments in *Western Humanities Review:* "In the later poems, artifice makes way for feeling as Berrigan poet, Berrigan priest, and Berrigan public conscience become one."

Beginning in the 1970s, Berrigan increasingly turned his hand to nonfiction prose works on religious and political topics. In *The Raft Is Not the Shore,* which appeared in 1975, Berrigan and Buddhist monk Thich Nhat Hanh record their conversations about Jesus and Buddha, government, economics, war, prison, and death. The two men share a disenchantment with present society as well as a disillusionment with the alternatives that have arisen to it. D. J. O'Hanlon of *America* says that the two men "challenge us to create communities, countercultural islands of sanity, in which humanness can happen." Similarly wide-ranging is *Ten Commandments for the Long Haul,* published in 1981. Berrigan "writes of his work in a cancer ward in New York City, of befriending some workers striking at a university for fair wages, of teaching in the Bronx, of being arrested at a Lockheed plant, of his time in the Danbury prison, [and] of his alliance in the works of peace with his brother, Philip," reports Colman McCarthy of the *Washington Post.* "A tension runs through these pages. Berrigan is a citizen of fire. He writes with heat. He burns with hope." *We Die before We Live* concerns Berrigan's volunteer work among terminally ill cancer patients. "It is a spiritual book," W. W. Benjamin of *Christian Century* believes, "albeit, not a religious one. Berrigan's vignettes of those in the process of dying are neither heroic nor maudlin, yet they are unique, graphic, and particular." S. J. Curley of *Library Journal* notices several "anti-Pentagon and antibusiness digressions [which] seem out of place," but finds that "Berrigan the poet makes us see the horror and the beauty of human life and death."

Berrigan's 1987 autobiography, *To Dwell in Peace,* received mixed reviews. In the *Los Angeles Times Book Review* Thomas Cahill terms it "a bellicose book that may be the least revealing autobiography since Marcus Aurelius," and criticizes the author's style as "artificial and ethereal." Kenneth L. Woodward, on the other hand, while disturbed by what he sees as the harshness of Berrigan's judgments and the humorlessness of his self-portrayal, describes the book in the *New York Times Book Review* as "brisk" and "painfully revealing" as well as "pervasively angry." "Those readers who despised Berrigan at the peak of the Vietnam War," writes Charles Madigan in the *Chicago Tribune,* "will find him no more worthy of admiration as he reflects on the events in his life. And those who admired him, who perhaps recognized in him something of an ancient Christian ideal, will find that the fire still burns in Berrigan."

Berrigan donated the royalties from *We Die before We Live* to Saint Rose's Hospital, where for several years he did volunteer work counseling AIDS and cancer patients. Berrigan's peace efforts have turned to the antinuclear movement. In 1980, during a march at Livermore, California, to protest the arms race and the manufacture of nuclear weapons, Berrigan was one of twenty-two people arrested. On September 8, 1980, he was arrested at the General Electric plant in King of Prussia, PA, for damaging three nuclear warheads under construction there. Sen-

tenced to serve three to ten years, he appealed the case, and in 1991 the sentence was reduced to time served. Berrigan has also given classes in Christian nonviolence and counseled young men who were defying draft registration, and has worked in favor of women's rights and the abolition of capital punishment.

BIOGRAPHICAL/CRITICAL SOURCES:

BOOKS

Berrigan, Daniel, *Go from Here: A Prison Diary,* Open Space Action Committee, 1968.

Berrigan, Daniel, *Lights On in the House of the Dead: A Prison Diary,* Doubleday, 1974.

Berrigan, Daniel, *Ten Commandments for the Long Haul,* Abingdon, 1981.

Berrigan, Daniel, *To Dwell in Peace: An Autobiography,* Harper, 1987.

Berrigan, Daniel, and Robert Coles, *The Geography of Faith: Conversations between Daniel Berrigan, When Underground, and Robert Coles,* Beacon Press, 1971.

Berrigan, Daniel, and Lee Lockwood, *Absurd Convictions, Modest Hopes: Conversations after Prison with Lee Lockwood,* Random House, 1972.

Casey, William V., and Philip Nobile, editors, *The Berrigans,* Praeger, 1971.

Contemporary Authors Autobiography Series, Volume 1, Gale, 1984.

Contemporary Literary Criticism, Volume 4, Gale, 1975.

Curtis, Richard, *The Berrigan Brothers: The Story of Daniel and Philip Berrigan,* Hawthorn, 1974.

Deedy, John, *Apologies, Good Friends . . . : An Interim Biography of Daniel Berrigan,* Fides Claretian, 1981.

Dictionary of Literary Biography, Volume 5: *American Poets since World War II,* Gale, 1980.

Gray, Francine du Plessix, *Divine Disobedience: Profiles in Catholic Radicalism,* Knopf, 1970.

Hughes, Catharine, *Plays, Politics, and Polemics,* Drama Book Specialists, 1972.

Klejment, Anne, *The Berrigans: A Bibliography of Published Works by Daniel, Philip, and Elizabeth McAlister Berrigan,* Garland Publishing, 1979.

Labrie, Ross, *The Writings of Daniel Berrigan,* American University Press, 1989.

Nelson, Jack, and Ronald J. Ostrow, *The FBI and the Berrigans: The Making of a Conspiracy,* Coward, 1972.

Stringfellow, William, and Anthony Towne, *Suspect Tenderness: The Witness of the Berrigans,* Holt, 1971.

PERIODICALS

America, September 15, 1973; December 13, 1975; September 30, 1978.

Best Sellers, October 1, 1972; September 15, 1973; October 1, 1973; March, 1976.

Carleton Miscellany, fall, 1968.

Chicago Tribune, January 17, 1988, p. 6.
Choice, February, 1974.
Christian Century, May 20, 1970; June 24, 1970; April 7, 1971; December 19, 1973; July 20, 1977; October 12, 1977; February 18, 1981.
Christian Science Monitor, March 2, 1971.
Commonweal, February 18, 1972; November 25, 1977; December 22, 1978.
Detroit News, April 6, 1975.
Hudson Review, summer, 1972.
Interpretations, Number 4, 1972.
Laurel Review, Volume 9, number 1, 1969.
Library Journal, November 15, 1980.
Los Angeles Times, July 27, 1980.
Los Angeles Times Book Review, February 7, 1988.
Nation, November 18, 1968; May 4, 1970.
National Review, November 9, 1973; March 1, 1974.
New Republic, June 20, 1970; December 12, 1970; March 6, 1971; April 13, 1974.
Newsweek, October 14, 1968; February 22, 1971; February 7, 1972.
New York, February 22, 1971.
New Yorker, April 9, 1966; March 14, 1970.
New York Review of Books, November 7, 1970.
New York Times, August 12, 1970; January 31, 1971; February 8, 1971; May 30, 1971; June 16, 1971; March 11, 1988.
New York Times Book Review, July 28, 1968; February 21, 1988.
Parnassus, fall/winter, 1974.
Players, fall/winter, 1975.
Poetry, November, 1966; autumn, 1968.
Publishers Weekly, July 23, 1973.
Saturday Review, June 14, 1969.
Sewanee Review, spring, 1974.
Thoreau Society Bulletin, spring, 1974.
Time, April 15, 1985, pp. 52-57.
Virginia Quarterly Review, winter, 1969.
Washington Post, December 18, 1970; August 18, 1971; August 13, 1981.
Western Humanities Review, winter, 1974.

*   *   *

BIOY CASARES, Adolfo 1914-
(Javier Miranda, Martin Sacastru; joint pseudonyms: H[onorio] Bustos Domecq, B. Lynch Davis, B. Suarez Lynch)

PERSONAL: Surname appears in some sources as Bioy-Casares; born September 15, 1914, in Buenos Aires, Argentina; son of Adolfo and Marta (Casares) Bioy; married Silvina Ocampo (a writer); children: Marta.

ADDRESSES: Home—Posadas 1650, 1112 Buenos Aires, Argentina.

CAREER: Writer.

AWARDS, HONORS: Premio Municipal de la Ciudad de Buenos Aires, 1940, for *La invencion de Morel;* 2nd Premio Nacional de Literatura, 1963, for *El lado de la sombra;* 1st Premio Nacional de Literatura, 1969, for *El gran serafin;* Gran Premio de Honor, Argentine Society of Writers, 1975; Premio Mondello, 1984, for *Historias fantasticas;* Premio IILA (Rome), 1986, for *Historias fantasticas* and *Historias de amor;* Premio Cervantes, 1990; Premio Alfonso Reyes, 1991.

WRITINGS:

SHORT STORIES

(Under pseudonym Martin Sacastru) *17 disparos contra lo porvenir,* Tor (Buenos Aires), 1933.
Caos, Viau & Zona (Buenos Aires), 1934.
Luis Greve, muerto, Destiempo (Buenos Aires), 1937.
El perjurio de la nieve, Emece, 1944, translation by Ruth L. C. Simms published as *The Perjury of the Snow,* Vanishing Rotating Triangle (New York), 1964.
La trama celeste (title means "The Celestial Plot"), Sur, 1948, reprinted, Castalia (Madrid), 1990, translation by Simms published with her translation of *La invencion de Morel* (also see below) as *The Invention of Morel, and Other Stories from "La trama celeste,"* University of Texas Press, 1964, reprinted, 1985.
Las visperas de Fausto, Arturo J. Alvarez (Buenos Aires), 1949.
Historia prodigiosa (title means "Prodigious History"), Obregon (Mexico), 1956, augmented edition, Emece, 1961.
Guirnalda con amores: cuentos (title means "A Garland of Love: Stories"), Emece, 1959, reprinted, 1978.
El lado de la sombra, Emece, 1962.
El gran serafin, Emece, 1967.
Historias de amor, Emece, 1972.
Historias fantasticas, Alianza (Madrid), 1976.
El heroe de la mujeres, Emece, 1978.
Historias desaforadas, Emece, 1986.
Una muneca Rusa, Tusquets (Barcelona), 1991.

NOVELS

La nueva tormenta o La vida multiple de Juan Ruteno, published by author, 1935.
La invencion de Morel, prologue by Jorge Luis Borges, Losada (Buenos Aires), 1940, reprinted, Alianza, 1981, translation by Simms published with stories from *La trama celeste* as *The Invention of Morel, and Other Stories from "La trama celeste,"* University of Texas Press, 1964, reprinted, 1985.

Plan de evasion, Emece, 1945, reprinted, 1977, translation by Suzanne J. Levine published as *A Plan for Escape,* Dutton, 1975.

(With wife, Silvina Ocampo) *Los que aman, odian* (title means "Those Who Love, Hate"), Emece, 1946.

El sueno de los heroes (title means "The Dream of Heroes"), Losada, 1954, reprinted, Alianza, 1976.

Diario de la guerra del cerdo, Emece, 1969, translation by Gregory Woodruff and Donald A. Yates published as *Diary of the War of the Pig,* McGraw, 1972.

Dormir al sol, Emece, 1973, translation by Levine published as *Asleep in the Sun,* Persea, 1975.

La aventura de un fotografo en La Plata, Emece, 1985.

Also author of *Un campeon desparejo.*

OMNIBUS VOLUMES

Adolfo Bioy Casares, edited by Ofelia Kovacci, Ediciones Culturales Argentinas, Ministerio de Educacion y Justicia, Direccion General de Cultura, 1963.

Adversos milagros, prologue by Enrique Pezzoni, Monte Avila (Caracas), 1969.

Paginas de Adolfo Bioy Casares seleccionadas por el autor, preface by Alberto Lagunas, Celtia, 1985.

WITH JORGE LUIS BORGES

(Under joint pseudonym H. Bustos Domecq) *Seis problemas para don Isidro Parodi,* Sur, 1942, translation by Norman Thomas di Giovanni published under authors' real names as *Six Problems for Don Isidro Parodi,* Dutton, 1983.

(Under joint pseudonym H. Bustos Domecq) *Dos fantasias memorables,* Oportet & Haereses, 1946, reprinted under authors' real names with notes and bibliography by Horacio Jorge Becco, Edicom (Buenos Aires), 1971.

(Under joint pseudonym B. Suarez Lynch) *Un modelo para la muerte* (novel; title means "A Model for Death"), Oportet & Haereses, 1946.

Los orilleros [and] *El paraiso de los creyentes* (screenplays; titles mean "The Hoodlums" and "The Believers' Paradise"; first screenplay produced as an Argentine film directed by Ricardo Luna, 1975), Losada, 1955, reprinted, 1975.

Cronicas de Bustos Domecq, Losada, 1967, translation by di Giovanni published as *Chronicles of Bustos Domecq,* Dutton, 1976.

(And Hugo Santiago) *Les Autres; scenario original* (screenplay; produced as a French film directed by Santiago, 1974), C. Bourgois (Paris), 1974.

Contributor with Borges, under joint pseudonym B. Lynch Davis, to *Los anales de Buenos Aires,* 1946-48.

EDITOR WITH WIFE, SILVINA OCAMPO, AND BORGES

Antologia de la literatura fantastica (title means "Anthology of Fantastic Literature"), Editorial Sudamericana, 1940, reprinted, EDHASA (Barcelona), 1977.

Antologia poetica argentina (title means "Anthology of Argentine Poetry"), Editorial Sudamericana, 1941.

EDITOR OR COMPILER WITH BORGES

(And translator with Borges) *Los mejores cuentos policiales* (title means "The Best Detective Stories"), Emece, 1943, reprinted, Alianza, 1972.

(And translator with Borges) *Los mejores cuentos policiales; Segunda serie,* Emece, 1951.

Cuentos breves y extraordinarios, Raigal (Buenos Aires), 1955, revised and enlarged edition, Losada, 1973, translation by Anthony Kerrigan published as *Extraordinary Tales,* Souvenir Press, 1973.

(And author of prologue, notes, and glossary with Borges) *Poesia gauchesca* (two volumes; title means "Gaucho Poetry"), Fondo de Cultura Economica, 1955.

Libro del cielo y del infierno (anthology; title means "Book of Heaven and Hell"), Sur, 1960, reprinted, 1975.

Also editor with Borges of a series of detective novels, "The Seventh Circle," Emece, 1943-56, and of *Destiempo* (literary magazine), 1936-37.

OTHER

Prologo (miscellany), Biblos (Buenos Aires), 1929.

La estatua casera (miscellany), Jacaranda (Buenos Aires), 1936.

La otra aventura (essays), Galerna, 1968, reprinted, Emece, 1983.

Memoria sobre la pampa y los gauchos (essay), Sur, 1970, reprinted, Emece, 1986.

(Under pseudonym Javier Miranda) *Breve diccionario del argentino exquisito,* Barros Merino, 1971, augmented edition with new prologue, published under author's real name, Emece, 1978.

ADAPTATIONS: Three of the stories in *Six Problems for Don Isidro Parodi* were dramatized for radio broadcast by the British Broadcasting Corp. (BBC). Films based on Bioy Casares's work include *El crimen de Oribe,* Argentina, 1950, *L'invention de Morel,* France, 1967, *L'invenzione di Morel,* Italy, 1973, *La guerra del cerdo,* Argentina, 1975, *In memoriam,* Spain, 1977, *I problemi di don Isidro Parodi,* Italy, 1978, *El gran serafin,* Spain, 1987, *Otra esperanza,* Argentina, 1991, and *En memoria de Paulina,* Argentina, 1992.

SIDELIGHTS: A noted fiction-writer in his own right in his native Argentina, Adolfo Bioy Casares is known in the United States primarily for his collaborative work with his more famous countryman Jorge Luis Borges. The two met when Bioy Casares was seventeen and Borges nearly fifteen years older. Bioy Casares had already published his *Prologo,* and their mutual interest in books led to a friendship. Within a few years of their original meeting they began writing together.

Bioy Casares recalls that their first joint effort involved creating a commercial pamphlet about yogurt, one of the products of the Casares family's large dairy ranch. In *La otra aventura,* Bioy Casares remembers this initial endeavor: "That pamphlet was a valuable lesson to me; after writing it, I was a different writer, more experienced and skillful. Any collaboration with Borges is the equivalent of years' work."

When the two worked together on their later fiction, Emir Rodriguez Monegal suggests in *Jorge Luis Borges: A Literary Biography,* "Borges and Bioy [Casares were] replaced by their own creations. A new writer had been born, a writer who ought to be called 'Biorges' because he was neither Borges nor Bioy [Casares], and because he did not stick to one pseudonym." The two authors' various joint pseudonyms—Honorio Bustos Domecq, B. Suarez Lynch and B. Lynch Davis—were produced by combining parts of the names of two of their great-grandfathers. "In a 1964 interview," remarks Donald A. Yates in the *Washington Post Book World,* "Borges offered this insight into the nature of the collaboration. 'We wrote somewhat for each other and since everything happened in a joking mood, the stories turned out so involved, so baroque, that it was difficult to understand them. At first we made jokes, and in the end jokes on jokes. It was a kind of algebraic contest: jokes squared, jokes cubed.'"

In their work, Bioy Casares and Borges focus on social criticism of their homeland, primarily through the use of humor. Their complex exaggerations of the tragically funny Argentine society—a society in which the Peron government "elevated" an author of Borges's stature from his library position to inspector of chickens and rabbits—deal with false appearances and their acceptance in Argentina. They paint a social order which *Time*'s Paul Gray describes as "invariably monstrous: [full of] novels and poems that cannot be read, art that cannot be seen, architecture—freed from the 'demands of inhabitability'—that cannot be used."

In *Six Problems for Don Isidro Parodi,* six people visit a barber, Don Isidro Parodi, and ask for solutions to their problems. Ironically, Don Isidro himself is in jail, serving time for a murder he didn't commit; the real murderer has escaped prosecution because of his connections with the authorities. Each story defines and ridicules a particular type of Argentine personality, including what Yates identifies as "the foppish journalist" and members of the Argentine Academy of Letters. *Chronicles of Bustos Domecq*

offers a collection of tongue-in-cheek sketches of characters from Argentine literary and artistic circles. One piece deals with the poet F. J. C. Loomis, who because of his dislike of metaphors begins writing poems containing only one word. Domecq explains that the poor reception of Loomis's poem "Beret" stems from "the demands it makes on the reader of having to learn French," Gray reports. Other writers and artists Domecq praises include Adalberto Vilaseco, who repeatedly publishes the same poem with a different title each time, and artist Antarctic A. Garay, who sets up pieces of junk and invites onlookers to admire the spaces between the works—a concept he labels "concave sculpture." Gray describes Domecq as "the pure incarnation of the middleman between a world gone culturally haywire and the uncomprehending mass of mankind. . . . This inept critic is a figure of Chaplinesque pathos: a tastemaker totally lacking in taste, a perpetual target of the avant-garde's custard pies."

Initially the fruits of Borges's and Casares's collaboration were not received enthusiastically in Argentina. When Victoria Ocampo, whose magazine *Sur* published the first of the stories in 1942, realized that it was a collaborative work, she was appalled that it had appeared in her serious literary journal. Rodriguez Monegal suggests that the two authors' use of humor was lost on their original audience: "The readers [of the original works] did not realize that a joke could be serious, and that irony and parody are among the deadliest forms of criticism. The gap between readers and authors was unbridgeable. Not until Bustos Domecq's first book was reissued a quarter of a century later would it be read by readers who could see its point."

Both *Six Problems for Don Isidro Parodi* and *Chronicles of Bustos Domecq* have been well-received by U.S. reviewers. Some critics applaud the books' humor; others mention the validity of the authors' social criticism. Denis Lynn Heyck asserts in the *Chicago Tribune Book World* that *Six Problems* "is an extremely funny book. . . . [It] mercilessly exposes Argentine pretentiousness, pseudo-cosmopolitanism, and shallow nativism. . . . And it caricatures those Argentines, and others, who live life as if it were bad literature." In the *New Republic,* Clarence Brown notes the "sheer nonsensical hilarity" of *Chronicles,* while *Atlantic* reviewer Phoebe-Lou Adam finds the same book "hilariously awful and a great creation."

Plot complexity, humor, and the contradictions between appearance and reality mark the works solely written by Bioy Casares as well as his work written with Borges. *A Plan for Escape,* Robert M. Adams observes in *Review,* is "beset with complexities and ambiguities which render practically everything said in [it] subject to question." Writing in the same journal, Rodriguez Monegal refers to "the almost unbearable complexity of *A Plan for Escape* and the stories of *The Celestial Plot.*" Bizarre plots are found in others of Bioy Casares's books, as well. The narrator of *The Invention of Morel,* shipwrecked on a desert island, discovers that several people meet regularly on the island, including a woman named Faustine with whom he falls in love. Eventually he learns that the group exists merely as images projected by a machine. Propelled by love for Faustine, he attempts to become part of the film the machine is projecting. *Asleep in the Sun* tells the story of Bordenave, who sends his neurotic wife to a clinic only to have her return "inhabited" by someone else's personality.

Some critics believe these complicated plots add an element of absurd humor to Bioy Casares's work. In the *Bulletin of Hispanic Studies,* D. P. Gallagher refers to Bioy Casares's novels and short stories as "comic masterpieces whose fundamental joke is the gap that separates what his characters know from what is going on." In the *Nation,* Richard Kostelanetz labels *The Invention of Morel* "marvelously comic" because of the narrator's repeated attempts to get close to a women who does not exist. In *Asleep in the Sun,* Bordenave's efforts to remove his wife from the clinic are humorous because he succeeds in recovering her body but not her spirit.

The humor of Bioy Casares's solo work, like the parody of his works with Borges, is a double-edged humor that mixes bitterness with laughter. The bitterness is particularly evident in the theme of false appearances or perception that Rodriguez Monegal, in his *Review* article, sees as unifying Bioy Casares's work. As well as pointing out the obvious role of false appearances in *The Invention of Morel* and *Asleep in the Sun,* the critic describes less obvious occurrences of the theme. In *Diary of the War of the Pig,* for instance, in which the young people of Buenos Aires begin killing off the older people, "a political fiction masks the allegory of the corruption of the body."

The complex satire of the absurd tales written by Bioy Casares alone and in collaboration with Jorge Luis Borges exposes the senseless contradictions between reality, perception, and social acceptance in their native Argentina and in modern society in general. Comments Deborah Weinberger in *Review,* "Everything [Bioy Casares] writes offers a world or postulates the possibility of worlds different from the one we inhabit, or think we inhabit." Nathan Rosenstein concludes in the *Village Voice,* "Perhaps the most powerful theme at work . . . is the implicit and telling contrast of the intellect's great potential and the petty pursuits and intrigues of mankind."

BIOGRAPHICAL/CRITICAL SOURCES:

BOOKS

Bioy Casares, Adolfo, *The Invention of Morel, and Other Stories from "La trama celeste,"* prologue by Jorge Luis Borges, translated by Ruth L. C. Simms, University of Texas Press, 1964.

Bioy Casares, Adolfo, *La otra aventura* (essays), Galerna, 1968, reprinted, Emece, 1983.

Borinsky, Alicia, *Intersticios,* Universidad Veracruzana, 1987.

Camurati, Mireya, *Bioy Casares y el alegre trabajo de la inteligencia,* Corregidor (Buenos Aires), 1990.

Contemporary Literary Criticism, Gale, Volume 4, 1975, pp. 63-64; Volume 8, 1978, p. 94; Volume 13, 1980, pp. 83-88.

Dictionary of Literary Biography, Volume 113: *Modern Latin-American Fiction Writers, First Series,* Gale, 1992, pp. 55-66.

Gallagher, D. P., *Modern Latin American Literature,* Oxford University Press, 1973.

MacAdam, Alfred J., *Modern Latin American Narratives,* University of Chicago Press, 1977.

Martino, Daniel, *ABC de Adolfo Bioy Casares,* Emece, 1989.

Martino, Daniel, editor, *Adolfo Bioy Casares,* Ministerio de Cultura (Madrid), 1991.

Rodriguez Monegal, Emir, *Jorge Luis Borges: A Literary Biography,* Dutton, 1978.

Schwartz, Kessel, *A New History of Spanish American Fiction,* Volume 2, University of Miami Press, 1971.

Villordo, Oscar Hermes, *Genio y figura de Adolfo Bioy Casares,* Eudeba (Editorial Universitaria de Buenos Aires), 1983.

PERIODICALS

Atlantic, April, 1976; January, 1979; April, 1981.

Bulletin of Hispanic Studies, July, 1975, pp. 247-266.

Chicago Tribune Book World, April 19, 1981.

Hudson Review, summer, 1973.

Los Angeles Times, May 5, 1981.

Nation, October 11, 1965.

New Republic, June 5, 1976.

Newsweek, November 27, 1978.

New Yorker, September 19, 1970; May 25, 1981.

New York Review of Books, April 19, 1973.

New York Times Book Review, January 28, 1973; March 29, 1981.

Paris Review, winter-spring, 1967.

Review, fall, 1975.

Time, March 29, 1976, p. 74.

Times Literary Supplement, June 12, 1981; August 27, 1982.

Village Voice, November 3, 1975.

Washington Post Book World, April 19, 1981.

World Literature Today, winter, 1980.

BLACKBURN, Michael 1954-

PERSONAL: Born March 8, 1954, in County Durham, England; son of Norman Tordoff (a publican) and Joyce (a publican; maiden name, Dent) Blackburn. *Education:* University of Leeds, B.A. (with first class honors), 1976, M.A., 1977. *Politics:* Socialist.

ADDRESSES: c/o Sunk Island Publishing, P.O. Box 74, Lincoln LN1 1QG, United Kingdom.

CAREER: Full-time writer and editor; director, Artistic Licence (literature based products and services company).

WRITINGS:

The Constitution of Things (poems), Northern House, 1984.
Why Should Anyone Be Here and Singing?, Echo Room Press, 1987.
Backwards into Bedlam, Joe Soap's Canoe, 1988.
The Lean Man Shaving, Jackson's Arm, 1988.
The Prophecy of Christos, Jackson's Arm, 1992.

WORK IN PROGRESS: A second book-length collection of poems.

SIDELIGHTS: Michael Blackburn told *CA:* "Poetry is a useless art. That's why we need it."

*   *   *

BLAIR, Jessica
See SPENCE, William John Duncan

*   *   *

BLAKE, Wendon
See HOLDEN, Donald

*   *   *

BOOTH, Wayne C(layson) 1921-

PERSONAL: Born February 22, 1921, in American Fork, UT; son of Wayne Chipman and Lillian (Clayson) Booth; married Phyllis Barnes (a clinical psychologist), June 19, 1946; children: Katherine, John Richard (deceased), Alison. *Education:* Brigham Young University, B.A., 1944; University of Chicago, M.A., 1947, Ph.D., 1950. *Politics:* Democrat. *Religion:* Church of Jesus Christ of Latter-day Saints.

ADDRESSES: Home—5411 South Greenwood Ave., Chicago, IL 60615. *Office*—Department of English, University of Chicago, Chicago, IL 60637.

CAREER: University of Chicago, instructor, 1947-50; Haverford College, Haverford, PA, assistant professor, 1950-53; Earlham College, Richmond, IN, professor of English and department chairman, 1953-62; University of Chicago, Chicago, IL, George M. Pullman Professor of English, 1962-92, Distinguished Service Professor, 1970-92, dean of College, 1964-69, chairman of Committee on Ideas and Methods, 1972-75. Member of board of trustees, Earlham College, 1965-75. Princeton University, conducted Christian Gauss Seminars in Criticism, 1974; Phi Beta Kappa visiting scholar, 1977-78; University of California, Berkeley, visiting professor and Beckman lecturer, 1979; School of Criticism and Theory, University of California, Irvine, visiting professor, 1979; Princeton University, Whitney Oates visiting professor, 1984; University of Chicago, Ryerson lecturer, 1987; English Coalition Conference, lecturer, 1987; conducted seminars for high school English teachers, 1987-90. Has done consulting for South African schools and universities (with wife, 1963), Lilly Endowment, and National Endowment for the Humanities. Examiner, North Central Association of Colleges and Universities (1959-80); member of the National Advisory Council of the Danforth Foundation Associates Program, 1963-69; served on the Committee on Literature of the National Council on Religion in Higher Education, 1967-70. *Military service:* U.S. Army, infantry, 1944-46.

MEMBER: Modern Language Association of America (member of executive council, 1973-76; president, 1982; member of commission on the future of the profession, 1980-82), American Association of University Professors, National Council of Teachers of English (served on commission of literature, 1967-70), American Academy of Arts and Sciences (fellow, 1972), Academy of Literary Studies, American Philosophical Society, College Conference on Composition and Communication (member of national executive committee, 1952-56).

AWARDS, HONORS: Ford faculty fellow, 1952-53; Guggenheim fellow, 1956-57 and 1969-70; Indiana University School of Letters, fellow, summer 1962; Christian Gauss Award from Phi Beta Kappa, 1962, and David H. Russell Award for Outstanding Research from National Council of Teachers of English, 1966, both for *The Rhetoric of Fiction;* Quantrell Prize for Undergraduate Teaching, University of Chicago, 1971; Distinguished Alumnus Award from Brigham Young University, 1975; National Endowment for the Humanities fellow, 1975-76; Laing Prize, 1981, for *Critical Understanding;* Rockefeller Foundation fellow, 1981-82; award for contributions to education, American Association for Higher Education, 1986; D.Litt. from Rockford College, 1965, St. Ambrose College, 1971, University of New Hampshire, 1977, Wabash College, 1992, and Earlham College, 1994; D.H.L. (hon.) from Butler University, 1984, Lycoming College, 1985, and State University of New York, 1987.

WRITINGS:

The Rhetoric of Fiction, University of Chicago Press, 1961, expanded edition, 1983.

(Editor) *The Knowledge Most Worth Having,* University of Chicago Press, 1967.

Now Don't Try to Reason with Me: Essays and Ironies for a Credulous Age, University of Chicago Press, 1970.

A Rhetoric of Irony, University of Chicago Press, 1974.

Modern Dogma and the Rhetoric of Assent, University of Chicago Press, 1974.

Critical Understanding: The Powers and Limits of Pluralism, University of Chicago Press, 1979.

(Editor with Marshall W. Gregory) *The Harper & Row Reader: Liberal Education through Reading and Writing,* Harper, 1984, second edition, 1988, brief edition, 1990, third edition, 1992.

(With Gregory) *The Harper & Row Rhetoric: Writing as Thinking, Thinking as Writing,* Harper, 1987, second edition, 1991.

The Company We Keep: An Ethics of Fiction, University of California Press, 1988.

The Vocation of a Teacher: Rhetorical Occasions, 1967-1988, University of Chicago Press, 1988.

(Editor) *The Art of Growing Older: Writers on Living and Aging,* Poseidon, 1992.

Also author of *The Art of Deliberalizing: A Handbook for True Professionals,* 1990. Contributor to professional journals and magazines. Co-editor of *Critical Inquiry,* 1974-85, and member of editorial board, 1985—; chairman of the board of publications, University of Chicago Press, 1974-75, 1979-80, 1984-85; member of the editorial boards of *Philosophy and Literature, Philosophy and Rhetoric, Scholia Satyrica, Rhetorica,* and *Novel.*

SIDELIGHTS: Noted scholar and literary critic Wayne C. Booth is best known for his studies of literature as interaction between author and reader, for his ground-breaking contributions to the study of narrative technique, and for his defense of critical pluralism, the belief that there can be more than one valid critical approach to a work of art. He came to the writing of literary criticism relatively late, after devoting the first fourteen years of his career to university teaching, a profession which, he remarks in an article written for the *Contemporary Authors Autobiography Series,* allowed him to "be paid simply for being an intellectual." Booth reflects on the various influences that eventually led to his "vocation" of writing on "rhetorical studies," which he defines as "any inquiry that concentrates on how people get together through symbol systems, or why they so often fail to." His Mormon upbringing and subsequent grappling with the problems of religious faith, his "conversion" to "high modernism" and subsequent "deconversion," and various teachers he encountered from his high school days through his doctoral studies at the University of Chicago, all fed his "desire to think hard about what other people said and wrote." Pullman Professor of English at the University of Chicago from 1962 until his retirement in 1992, Booth has had a wide influence on literary criticism and the study of rhetoric.

In his most influential book, *The Rhetoric of Fiction,* published in 1961, Booth argues that an author's attitudes are implicitly or explicitly present in every decision he or she makes in writing a text. Consequently, as James Phelan explains in the *Dictionary of Literary Biography,* "Rather than being an art of purity and objectivity, fiction is an art in which the author attempts to shape his readers into the audience he envisions while writing, and readers attempt to join the author's implied audience." Many of the critical terms Booth developed in his study have since become part of the general critical lexicon. Booth distinguishes between the narrator of a work, the actual flesh-and-blood author of the text, and the "implied author"—the image of the author as projected by the work. Similarly, he distinguishes between the actual reader and the work's "implied" audience or reader, the audience that the author appears to imagine and works to create for his work. Narrators, the critic further points out, display differing degrees of "reliability": narrators who seem to share the author's judgments and views are "reliable," while narrators who do not are "unreliable." *The Rhetoric of Fiction* has become a basic text in the study of narrative technique.

Most of Booth's subsequent books continue his exploration of rhetoric and literature. *The Rhetoric of Irony,* published in 1974, examines the nature of irony and how it is shared by author and reader. "Booth has the good sense," remarks Philip Stevick in *Comparative Literature,* "to raise the question . . . of what the reader has to work with and how far he is entitled to go in looking for ironies where the consensus of readers has not found them before." Booth is also attuned to the psychology of the reader's response to irony, Stevick says: "Faced with a reading of an ironic work different from one's own, a reader is likely to feel threatened; having discovered to one's satisfaction the meaning of an ironic passage, one is likely to be triumphant and smug." *Modern Dogma and the Rhetoric of Assent,* which appeared the same year, deals with the problem of moral suasion, trying to show, according to Phelan, "how someone should proceed when he seeks to change someone else's mind and to indicate when someone should be willing to change his mind." "What [Booth] attempts," writes Robert Buffington in the *Sewanee Review,* "is to reestablish as intellectually respectable, roughly under the classical rhetorical heads of ethical proof and emotional proof, some of the other good reasons there are to assent to an argument besides empirical and logical proof."

In his 1979 study, *Critical Understanding: The Powers and Limits of Pluralism,* Booth pursues the view, now increasingly accepted, that there are several valid ways of defining a literary text, then tries to establish criteria for determining the legitimacy of any given critical approach to an individual text. While by his own admission he fails, as Phelan says, to "establish a firm philosophical ground from which to argue for pluralism," he nonetheless maintains that "pluralism is such a fundamental good in the critical community that no arguments can prevail against it." In the end, Phelan reports, Booth concludes that "although truth is an important value in criticism, there is no single truth that all critics can or must pursue. Furthermore, truth is less important than the kind of life we create for ourselves and our audiences as we ask and answer our literary-critical questions."

The Company We Keep, published in 1988, examines the ethical questions that, Booth asserts, inevitably come into play in the complex interaction between author and reader of a fictional work. He argues that ethics, as Anatole Broyard puts it in the *New York Times Book Review,* "is one of our kinds of meaning, and as such it becomes part of the semantics, part of the rhetoric of fiction. . . . Without an ethical frame, it might become impossible to tell a tragedy from a comedy." Summarizing Booth's conclusion, Broyard suggests that the most important ethical dimension of fiction lies in our willingness, as readers, "to think the thoughts and feel the feelings of a total stranger," the author. "This willingness of ours to entertain fictions, and of authors to create them, is a stunning proof of imagination, humanity, even faith. The process itself, independent of its results, is inspiring."

Critical response to much of Booth's work, Phelan points out, has reflected changes in the critical environment during the 1960s and 1970s, as "American criticism . . . moved from its dominant allegiance to New Criticism to its simultaneous and stormy affairs with reader-response criticism, feminism, Marxism, psychoanalysis, structuralism, and post-structuralism." A common element in all these diverse movements, Phelan suggests, is "a suspicious attitude toward one of the major assumptions of Booth's work, the importance of authorial intention in interpretation." The popular view of Booth as a "traditionalist," however, is "only partially correct," Phelan says. Moreover, Booth's influence has become evident in the work of a large number of highly diverse contemporary critics, "as their own projects lead them to engage with one or more aspects of Booth's work and as their own thinking leads them to agree or disagree with his conclusions." In the end, Phelan asserts, "Every student interested in twentieth-century rhetoric must come to terms with the body of Booth's work. The number of studies in narrative theory, rhetorical theory, the nature of interpretation, or critical methodology that are at least partially indebted to Booth is far greater than anyone would care to count."

Unlike many contemporary literary critics, Booth's writing is generally accessible and engaging, described by Stevick as "lucid, straightforward, and precise in style; witty, at times donnishly playful; rational, reasonable, and sensible; personal, at times anecdotal, almost confidential; devastating with his antagonists. Above all," Stevick adds, "it is a rhetorical manner—leading the reader, explaining, explaining again, persuading, hectoring, teaching." In addition to his scholarly writing, in the early 1970s Booth worked with Sheldon Sacks and Arthur Heiserman in founding the quarterly journal *Critical Inquiry,* described by Phelan as "one of the most important sources of lively and sophisticated debate about criticism and the arts." Booth is also known as an educator and college administrator. In the 1980s he published a college reader and a writing textbook in addition to a book about teaching, *The Vocation of a Teacher. The Art of Growing Older,* which appeared in 1992, combines Booth's commentary with a collection of essays, poems, and excerpts from works of fiction in which various authors reflect on the process of growing old. In this work, Booth has told *CA,* he "offers not only extended critical comment" on the selections in the collection "but his own views on how to join those who have turned aging into art." Of his writings, he comments, "Underlying it all has been that worrisome rhetorician's credo: 'Though the quest for *Truth* is important, it is less important than the quest for *Understanding.* It is better for two people to understand each other, even in joint error, than for one of them to hold the truth unwilling or unable to share it with the other.' "

BIOGRAPHICAL/CRITICAL SOURCES:

BOOKS

Contemporary Authors Autobiography Series, Volume 5, Gale, 1987, pp. 31-51.
Contemporary Literary Criticism, Volume 24, Gale, 1983, pp. 84-100.
Dictionary of Literary Biography, Volume 67: *Modern American Critics since 1955,* Gale, 1988, pp. 49-66.

PERIODICALS

Comparative Literature, summer, 1976, pp. 277-79.
Los Angeles Times Book Review, December 18, 1988, p.3.
New York Times Book Review, January 22, 1989, p.3; April 16, 1989, p. 20.
Sewanee Review, spring, 1975, pp. xxxiv-xl.
Times Literary Supplement, August 11, 1989, p. 865.
Tribune Books (Chicago), December 25, 1988, p. 4.

—Sketch by M. L. Onorato

BOOTY, John Everitt 1925-

PERSONAL: Born May 2, 1925, in Detroit, MI; son of George Thomas and Alma (Gamauf) Booty; married Catherine Louise Smith, June 10, 1950; children: Carol Holland, Geoffrey Rollen, Peter Thomas, Catherine Jane. *Education:* Wayne State University, B.A., 1952; Virginia Theological Seminary, B.D., 1953; Princeton University, M.A., 1957, Ph.D., 1960. *Politics:* Democrat.

ADDRESSES: Home—R.R. 1, Box 167, Center Sandwich, NH 03227. *Office*—Hamilton Hall, School of Theology, University of the South, Sewanee, TN 37375.

CAREER: Ordained Episcopal deacon, 1953, minister, 1954. Christ Episcopal Church, Dearborn, MI, curate, 1953-55; Virginia Theological Seminary, Alexandria, assistant professor, 1958-64, associate professor of church history, 1964-67; Episcopal Divinity School, Cambridge, MA, professor of church history, 1967-82; University of the South, School of Theology, Sewanee, TN, dean, 1982-85, professor of Anglican studies, 1984-90, professor emeritus, 1990—. Acting director, Institute for Theological Research, 1974-76; member of board of trustees, Boston Theological Institute, 1976-78, 1980-82. Visiting professor and research scholar, Yale Divinity School, 1985-86. Historiographer of the Episcopal Church, 1988—. Episcopal Divinity School, visiting professor, 1990-91, professor emeritus, 1991—.

MEMBER: American Historical Association, American Society of Church History, Renaissance Society of America, Society for the Promotion of Christian Knowledge/United States of America (vice-chairman, 1984-87), Modern Language Association of America.

AWARDS, HONORS: Fulbright fellow, University of London, 1957-58; award from American Philosophical Society, 1964; fellow, Folger Shakespeare Library, 1964; National Endowment for the Humanities fellowship, 1978-79; grant from Conant Fund, 1982.

WRITINGS:

John Jewel as Apologist of the Church of England, S.P.C.K., 1963.
(Editor) John Jewel, *Apology of the Church of England,* Cornell University Press, 1963.
Yearning to Be Free, Greeno-Hadden, 1974.
(Editor) *The Book of Common Prayer, 1559: The Elizabethan Prayer Book,* University Press of Virginia, 1976.
Three Anglican Divines on Prayer: Jewel, Andrewes, and Hooker (booklet), Society of St. John the Evangelist, 1978.
The Church in History, Seabury, 1979.
(Editor) Richard Hooker, *Works,* Harvard University Press, Volume 4: *Of the Laws of Ecclesiastical Polity:*

Attack and Response, 1981, Volume 6 (with W. Speed Hill), in press.
The Godly Kingdom of Tudor England: Great Books of the English Reformation, Morehouse-Barlow, 1980.
The Servant Church: Diaconal Ministry and the Episcopal Church, Morehouse- Barlow, 1982.
What Makes Us Episcopalians?, Morehouse-Barlow, 1982.
Meditating on Four Quartets, Cowley, 1983.
(Editor) *The Divine Drama in History and Liturgy* (monograph), Pickwick, 1986.
The Drama of Anglicanism, Forward Movement, 1986.
The Christ We Know, Cowley, 1987.
(Editor with Stephen Sykes) *The Study of Anglicanism,* S.P.C.K./Fortress, 1988.
The Episcopal Church in Crisis, Cowley, 1988.
Four Birthdays of the Church, Forward Movement, 1990.
The Common Book of Prayer in the Life of the Episcopal Church, Forward Movement, 1990.

Contributor to numerous books, including *Studies in Richard Hooker,* edited by Hill, Press of Case Western Reserve University, 1972; *The Spirit of Anglicanism,* edited by William J. Wolf, Morehouse-Barlow, 1979; *A Faithful Church,* edited by J. H. Westerhoff and O. C. Edwards, Morehouse-Barlow, 1981; *Caring and Curing: Health and Medicine in the Western Faith Traditions,* edited by Ronald L. Numbers and D. W. Amundsen, Macmillan, 1986.

Also contributor to *Encyclopaedia Britannica, World Book Encyclopedia,* and *Westminster Dictionary of Church History.* Contributor of many reviews and articles to theology and history journals and to newspapers. Member of editorial committee of Richard Hooker's *Works,* Harvard University Press, 1969—; member of advisory board of *Classics of Western Spirituality,* Paulist Press, 1976—. Chairman of board of editors, *St. Lukes's Journal of Theology,* 1987—.

WORK IN PROGRESS: History of the Virgina Theological Seminary; The Theology of Richard Hooker.

SIDELIGHTS: John Everitt Booty comments to *CA:* "My scholarly efforts (and writing) seem to be concentrated on sixteenth-century Anglican liturgy and piety. But my interests are broader, encompassing work on the seventeenth-century metaphysical poets and the Christian understanding of history. To further that understanding, I have recently written five short stories in sixteenth-century settings."

*   *   *

BORDEN, Lee
See DEAL, Borden

BORDEN, Leigh
   See DEAL, Borden

       *   *   *

BORETZ, Benjamin (Aaron) 1934-

PERSONAL: Born October 3, 1934, in New York, NY; son of Abraham (a mathematician) and Leah (an artist; maiden name, Yollis) Boretz; married Naomi Messinger (a painter), September 1, 1954; children: Avron Albert. *Education:* Brooklyn College (now of the City University of New York), B.A., 1950; Brandeis University, M.F.A., 1957; Princeton University, M.F.A., 1960, Ph.D., 1970.

ADDRESSES: Home—River Rd., Barrytown, Red Hook, NY 12571. *Office*—Department of Music, Bard College, Annandale-on-Hudson, NY 12504.

CAREER: Brandeis University, faculty member, 1955-57, assistant professor, 1962-63; New York University, assistant professor, 1964-69, and director of group computer synthesis; Columbia University, assistant professor, 1969-72; University of Southampton, England, Fulbright-Hays lecturer, 1971-72; Bard College, associate professor, 1973—; Avery Graduate School in Arts, faculty member and member of planning and steering committees, 1981—. Visiting faculty member, University of California, Los Angeles, 1957-59, University of California, Berkeley, and University of Chicago; visiting professor, Princeton University, 1967-68, 1970-71, 1972-74, University of Michigan, 1973. *Perspectives of New Music,* Annandale-on-Hudson, NY, co-founder with Arthur Berger and associate editor, 1961-62, editor, 1963-83, emeritus editor, 1983—. Princeton Seminar of Advanced Music Studies, composer-participant, 1959; panel participant, congress of International Musicology Society, Salzburg, Austria, 1964, Berkeley, CA, 1977, Interdisciplinary Festival Philosophy, 1970, Symposium on Philosophy, 1973, and others. Visiting composer at numerous universities.

MEMBER: International Society for Contemporary Music (member of board of governors), American Society of University Composers (co-founder; executive secretary, 1966-68), American Composers' Alliance, American Musicological Society, New York Music Critics Circle.

AWARDS, HONORS: Composition award, Fromm Foundation, 1956, for "Violin Concerto"; Ingram Merrill Foundation grant in music, 1966-67; Fulbright scholarship, 1970-71; Council of Humanities fellowship, Princeton University, 1972-73; MacDowell Colony fellowship, 1974; artist in residence, Montalvo Center for the Arts, 1975.

WRITINGS:

Meta-Variations: Studies in the Foundations of Musical Thought, Perspectives of New Music, 1969.
Language, as a Music: Six Marginal Pretexts for Composition, Lingua, 1980.
Talk: If I Am a Musical Thinker, Station Hill, 1985.
Music Columns from the Nation, 1962-1968, selected and introduced by Elaine Barkin, Open Space, 1990.

EDITOR, WITH EDWARD T. CONE

Perspectives on Schoenberg and Stravinsky, Princeton University Press, 1968, revised edition, Norton, 1972.
Perspectives on American Composers, Norton, 1971.
Perspectives on Contemporary Music Theory, Norton, 1972.
Perspectives on Notation and Performance, Norton, 1976.

Also composer of "Chamber Concerto," 1954; "Concerto Grosso," 1955; "Partita for Piano," 1955; "Wind Quintet," 1956; "Violin Concerto," 1956; "String Quartet," 1957; "Divertimento," 1957; "Donne Songs," 1959-60; "Ensemble Variations," 1962-64; "Brass Quintet," 1963-64; "Group Variations I" (for chamber orchestra), 1967; "Group Variations II" (for computer), 1973; "Liebeslied" (for pianist alone), 1976; "First Music" (for piano), 1977; "My Chart Shines High Where the Blue Milk's Upset," 1977; "Passage, for Roger Sessions," 1978; "Sound States Nos. 1-100: Unscheduled Resonances Formed in Meditation," 1980; "Real Time States, Nos. 1-120," 1980; "Real Time States, Nos. 121-204," 1981; "Authenticity: A Life in the Day" (performance-lecture piece), 1981; "Languagings, Nos. 1-75," 1981; "Midnight Music," 1982; "Formings" (collaborative sound expressions), 1982-83.

Contributor to philosophy and music journals and to *Nation.* Music critic for *Nation,* 1962-69. Member of editorial board of American Composers' Alliance, 1970-72, and *Contemporary Music Newsletter.* Member of advisory board of *Dutton's Dictionary of Twentieth Century Music.*

BIOGRAPHICAL/CRITICAL SOURCES:

PERIODICALS

Saturday Review, July 24, 1971, p. 43.
Times Literary Supplement, October 9, 1969, p. 1167.*

       *   *   *

BOSWELL
   See GORDON, Giles (Alexander Esme)

BOWDEN, Jim
See SPENCE, William John Duncan

*   *   *

BRAMANN, Jorn K(arl) 1938-

PERSONAL: Born December 21, 1938, in Wuppertal, Germany; immigrated to the United States, 1967; son of Karl (a professor of engineering) and Hanna (Benz) Bramann; divorced. *Education:* Attended University of Cologne, 1961-67; University of Wyoming, M.A., 1965; University of Oregon, Ph.D., 1971.

ADDRESSES: Office—Department of Philosophy, Frostburg State College, Frostburg, MD 21532.

CAREER: Frostburg State College, Frostburg, MD, assistant professor, 1972-76, associate professor of philosophy, 1977—. Visiting professor at University of Dortmund, 1982.

MEMBER: American Philosophical Association.

AWARDS, HONORS: Fulbright grant, 1960; fellowships from National Endowment for the Humanities, 1975-76, for study at Princeton, 1981, University of California, Irvine, and 1984, for University of California, Los Angeles.

WRITINGS:

On Location: An Anthology, Acheron, 1981.
(Editor with R. E. Pletts) Oscar Brown, *The Songs of Kicks and Co.,* Acheron, 1981.
(Translator) Wolfdietrich Schnurre, *Climb, but Downward* (poems), Acheron, 1983.
(Editor) *Self-Determination: An Anthology of Philosophy and Poetry,* Adler, 1984.
(Editor) *Unemployment and Social Values: A Collection of Literary and Philosophical Texts,* Nightsun Books, 1984.
(Translator with Jeanette Axelrod) Jochen Ziem, *Uprising in East Germany and Other Stories,* Adler, 1984.
Capital As Power: A Concise Summary of the Marxist Analysis of Capitalism, Adler, 1984.
Sunny Side Up: Industrial Strength Poetry, Nudelgrafix, 1984.
Wittgenstein's "Tractatus" and the Modern Arts, Adler, 1985.
Walden Zero: A Novella, Nightsun Books, 1988.
(Translator) Johann G. Fichte, *The Purpose of Higher Education,* Nightsun Books, 1988.
(Editor) *Higher Ed,* Nightsun Books, 1989.
(Editor with Gersham Nelson and Eira Patnaik) *From Outside of Western Civilization: A Collection of Readings,* G. Aston Nelson Books, 1991.

Camcorder Art: What to Do with Your Video Camera after You Have Read the Instruction Manual, Nightsun Books, 1992.
(Editor) *Psychoanalysis of a New Freeway,* Nightsun Books, 1992.
My Buddhist Lover: A Video Drama, Nightsun Books, 1993.

Also author of *The Water Woman: A Video Drama,* produced by Tucson Community Cable Corp., 1984. Contributor to *Austrian History Yearbook;* also contributor to numerous journals, including *Diogenes.* Editor of *Upper Potomacs.*

SIDELIGHTS: Jorn K. Bramann has produced video programs for colleges and Public Access Television, as well as slide shows on the art of the Maya in Mexico and Central America. He told *CA* that he has been inspired by the writings of Henry David Thoreau.

*   *   *

BRAND, Christianna
See LEWIS, Mary (Christianna Milne)

*   *   *

BRYAN, Ashley F. 1923-

PERSONAL: Born July 13, 1923, in New York, NY. *Education:* Attended Cooper Union and Columbia University.

ADDRESSES: Office—Dartmouth College, Department of Art, Hanover, NH 03755.

CAREER: Author and illustrator of books for children; Dartmouth College, Hanover, NH, professor of art and visual studies, then professor emeritus.

AWARDS, HONORS: American Library Association, Social Responsibilities Round Table, Coretta Scott King Award, 1980, for illustrating *Beat the Story-Drum, Pum-Pum,* and 1986, for writing *Lion and the Ostrich Chicks and Other African Folk Tales;* Coretta Scott King Honor Award, 1988, for illustrating *What a Morning! The Christmas Story in Black Spirituals.*

WRITINGS:

JUVENILES; SELF-ILLUSTRATED, EXCEPT WHERE NOTED

The Ox of the Wonderful Horns and Other African Folktales, Atheneum, 1971.
The Adventures of Aku; or, How It Came about That We Shall Always See Okra the Cat Lying on a Velvet Cushion While Okraman the Dog Sleeps among the Ashes, Atheneum, 1976.
The Dancing Granny, Macmillan, 1977.

Beat the Story-Drum, Pum-Pum (Nigerian folk tales), Atheneum, 1980.

The Cat's Drum, Atheneum, 1985.

Lion and the Ostrich Chicks and Other African Folk Tales, Atheneum, 1986.

Sh-ko and His Eight Wicked Brothers, illustrated by Fumio Yoshimura, Atheneum, 1988.

All Night, All Day, Atheneum, 1988.

Turtle Knows Your Name (a retelling), Atheneum, 1989.

Sing to the Sun, HarperCollins, 1992.

ILLUSTRATOR

Rabindranath Tagore, *Moon, for What Do You Wait?* (poems), edited by Richard Lewis, Atheneum, 1967.

Mari Evans, *Jim Flying High* (juvenile), Doubleday, 1979.

Susan Cooper, *Jethro and the Jumbie* (juvenile), Atheneum, 1979.

John Langstaff, editor, *What a Morning! The Christmas Story in Black Spirituals,* Macmillan, 1987.

OTHER

(Compiler) *Black American Spirituals, Volume I: Walk Together Children* (self-illustrated), Atheneum, 1974, *Volume II: I'm Going to Sing* (self- illustrated), Macmillan, 1982.

(Compiler and author of introduction) Paul Laurence Dunbar, *I Greet the Dawn: Poems,* Atheneum, 1978.

ADAPTATIONS: Bryan recorded *The Dancing Granny and Other African Tales* for the Caedmon record label.

SIDELIGHTS: As a folklorist, Ashley F. Bryan brings Americans to an appreciation of traditions rooted in black cultures. For example, his collection of the spirituals of American slaves *Walk Together Children* records "the brave and lonely cries of men and women forced to trust in heaven because they had no hope on earth," remarks Neil Millar in the *Christian Science Monitor.* The subject of bondage set to native African rhythms produced songs such as "Go Down Moses," "Deep River," "Mary Had a Baby," "Go Tell It on the Mountain," "Nobody Knows the Trouble I Seen," "Walk Together Children," "O Freedom," "Little David," and "Swing Low, Sweet Chariot." "With Ashley Bryan's collection," writes Virginia Hamilton in the *New York Times Book Review,* "the tradition of preserving the spiritual through teaching the young is surely enriched."

In addition to historical spirituals, several of the folklorist's collections contain stories that explain why certain animals became natural enemies. In *The Adventures of Aku,* Bryan recounts the day that the enmity between dogs and cats began. This "is a long involved magic tale that has echoes of Aladdin's lamp and Jack and the Beanstalk to mention just two familiar stories with similar motifs," says *New York Times Book Review*'s Jane Yolen. It uti-

lizes a magic ring, a stupid son, a heroic quest, and Ananse, the standard trickster figure in African folklore, to capsulize the Ashanti proverb stating, "No one knows the story of tomorrow's dawn."

The Nigerian folktales in *Beat the Story-Drum, Pum-Pum* also reveal the origins of hostilities between animals, such as that between the snake and the frog or the bush cow and the elephant. These "retellings make the stories unique, offering insight into the heart of a culture," notes M.M. Burns in *Horn Book.* Each story, the reviewer adds, "has a style and beat appropriate to the subject, the overall effect being one of musical composition with dexterously designed variations and movements."

Like *The Adventures of Aku, The Dancing Granny* continues the saga of the trickster Ananse. Originally titled "He Sings to Make the Old Woman Dance," this folktale recounts the day when a little old lady, who danced continually, foiled the Spider Ananse's plan to eat all of her food. While Granny worked, Ananse sang so that she might dance. Then, when she danced away, the spider would eat up her corn. This went on four times until Granny took Ananse to be her partner and danced him away, too.

In a departure from his usual cultural interests, Bryan ventures briefly into traditional folktales from Japan with his retelling of *Sh-Ko and His Eight Wicked Brothers.* It is a story about the sibling rivalry, the nature of true beauty, and the rewards of kindness. Sh-ko, the youngest of nine brothers, is truly ugly. He accompanies his brothers on a quest to win the hand of Princess Yakami. During the journey, he helps a rabbit in distress. In return, the grateful rabbit gives Sh-ko a magic gift and, to the dismay of his brothers, Sh-ko wins the princess' hand. "The tale," says *School Library Journal* reviewer John Philbrook, "is told in a straightforward manner, but it is not engaging; nor is sympathy aroused for the characters." While the art is traditional, in the style of Japanese picture scrolls, some critics feel that it may not appeal to young children.

Bryan's collection, *All Night, All Day: A Child's First Book of African-American Spirituals,* with his bright, abstract illustrations is generally considered more appealing to young readers. According to *Horn Book,* this volume offers "extraordinary gifts for all America's children." *Booklist* praised this collection in a special feature, "The African American Experience in Picture Books."

Bryan's next book, 1989's *Turtle Knows Your Name,* is a retelling of a folktale from the West Indies. An earlier version appeared in Elsie Clews Parson's *Folklore of the Antilles, French and English, Part II.* Word choice, language rhythm, and animal sounds contribute to the tale's festive mood. One *Horn Book* reviewer calls the work "a celebration of family love, traditional song and dance, and the ancient power of names." Inspired by the importance that black cultures attach to names, Bryan tells what happens when a young boy named UP-SILI-MANA TUM-PALERADO goes to the beach to sing and dance his name, in a time-honored tradition. A trickster turtle listens in on the ceremony, and records the name in shells on the sea floor. Because the boy's name is long, his peers tease him, so he befriends a group of animals. Later in the tale, his grandmother challenges him to find out her name, and, knowing how Turtle cataloged his own name, he asks the creature. "It's MAPASEEDO JACKALINDY EYE PIE TACKARINDY," Turtle announces. For convenience, the boy and his grandmother settle on the shorter names of Granny and Son. Contributor Marilyn Iarusso notes in *School Library Journal* that Bryan has "create[d] a rhythmic text which celebrates the pride of two people who learn to honor their names and their identities, and expect others to do the same."

Bryan's following work is a collection of poems written in rhythmic verse. Titled *Sing to the Sun,* the book celebrates nature, humanity, and life itself. All twenty-three poems are original and are considered appealing not only to children but to adults as well. A *Publishers Weekly* contributor comments that Bryan "artfully blends the traditions of African American culture with those of Western art. . . . [H]e interweaves voices that are sophisticated . . . with those that are tied to folk storytelling traditions."

BIOGRAPHICAL/CRITICAL SOURCES:

BOOKS

Bryan, Ashley F., *Turtle Knows Your Name,* Atheneum, 1989.

PERIODICALS

Booklist, September 1, 1988; October 1, 1989; February 1, 1992.
Center for Children's Books Bulletin, February, 1990.
Children's Book Review Service, December, 1988; December, 1989.
Christian Science Monitor, November 6, 1974; November 3, 1976; August 2, 1985.
Commonweal, November 22, 1974.
Horn Book, February, 1977; April, 1981; February, 1983; May, 1985; November, 1988; January, 1990; May, 1992.
Kirkus Reviews, August 1, 1988; August 15, 1992.
Language Arts, March, 1977; February, 1978; March, 1984; October, 1985.
Ms., December, 1974.
New York Times Book Review, November 3, 1974; October 10, 1976.
Publishers Weekly, July 28, 1989; July 6, 1992.
School Library Journal, October, 1989; October, 1992.

Scientific American, December, 1980.
Washington Post Book World, November 7, 1971; December 12, 1976.
Wilson Library Bulletin, February, 1986.*

*   *   *

BRYAN, Christopher 1935-

PERSONAL: Born January 24, 1935, in London, England; son of William Joseph (an engineer) and Amy (May) Bryan; married Wendy Elizabeth Smith (a social worker), July 2, 1972. *Education:* Wadham College, Oxford, B.A. (in English and theology; both with honors), 1958; Ripon Hall Theological College, M.A., 1959; University of Exeter, Ph.D., 1983. *Politics:* "Social Democrat/ Liberal."

ADDRESSES: Home—6 Park Pl., St. Leonard's, Exeter, Devonshire, England (vacations). *Office*—University of the South, Sewanee, TN (school year).

CAREER: Ordained Anglican deacon, 1960, priest, 1961; St. Mark's Church, Reigate, England, assistant curate, 1960-64; Salisbury Theological College, Salisbury, England, tutor and vice-principal, 1964-70; Virginia Theological Seminary, Alexandria, associate professor and associate director of Center for Continuing Education, 1970-74; Diocese of London, London, England, senior education officer, 1974-79; University of Exeter, Exeter, England, lecturer in religious education and St. Luke's Foundation Chaplain, 1979-83; University of the South, Sewanee, TN, professor of New Testament, 1983—. Presenter of "The Bible for Today" on Anglia Television.

WRITINGS:

Way of Freedom, Seabury, 1974.
Night of the Wolf, Harper, 1983.
Nightfall, Lion, 1986.
Christian Testamant, University of the South, 1988.
A Preface to Mark: Notes on the Gospel in Its Literary and Cultural Settings, Oxford University Press, 1993.

Contributor of articles and reviews to numerous periodicals, including *St. Luke's Journal of Theology.* Editor, *Sewanee Theological Review,* 1991—.

WORK IN PROGRESS: A sequel to *Night of the Wolf* and *Nightfall*; various theological articles, especially on Judaism and the New Testament.

SIDELIGHTS: Christopher Bryan told *CA:* "I detect three major phases in my thinking. I was initially influenced deeply by C. S. Lewis, Charles Williams, J. R. R. Tolkien, and the whole of that group known as 'The Inklings.' Secondly, I 'discovered' the theology of the Reformation and without doubt Karl Barth is the name most important to me here. Finally, I have come of late to a deeper concern about the Hebrew origins of Christian faith, and to feel the need for renewed dialogue between Christianity and Judaism. On the emotional and personal side, I owe much to the Human Relationship Training Movement, as I have experienced it both in Britain and in the United States."

*   *   *

BURANELLI, Vincent 1919-

PERSONAL: Born January 16,1919, in New York, NY; son of Prosper and Mina (Ackerman) Buranelli; married Nan Gillespie (a writer and translator), October 31, 1951. *Education:* Attended St. John's College, Annapolis, MD, 1945-46; National University of Ireland, B.A., 1947, M.A., 1948; Cambridge University, Ph.D., 1951.

ADDRESSES: Home—217 West Eden St., Edenton, NC 27932.

CAREER: United Press, Los Angeles, CA, reporter, 1941; *Business Week,* New York City, editorial writer, 1952; Lowell Thomas Newscasting, New York City, writer, 1952-65; employed with American Heritage Publishing Co., New York City, 1966-67, and Silver Burdett Publishing Co., Morristown, NJ, 1967-68; and 1984-89; free-lance writer and editor, 1968—. *Military service:* U.S. Army, 1941-45; received Purple Heart.

MEMBER: Authors Guild, Royal Dublin Society, Cambridge Union.

AWARDS, HONORS: Kaltenborn fellow in journalism, 1952-53; New Jersey Teachers award for best biography of year by a New Jersey author, 1964, for *Josiah Royce*; New Jersey Writers Conference Authors Citation, 1983, for *Spy/Counterspy: An Encyclopedia of Espionage,* and 1985, for *In the Long Run We Are All Dead: A Macroeconomics Murder Mystery*; *Edgar Allan Poe* has been selected by the U.S. Information Agency for distribution in American libraries abroad.

WRITINGS:

(Editor and author of introduction) *The Trial of Peter Zenger,* New York University Press, 1957.
Edgar Allan Poe, Twayne, 1961, 2nd edition, 1979.
The King and the Quaker: A Study of William Penn and James II, University of Pennsylvania Press, 1962.
Josiah Royce, Twayne, 1964.
Louis XIV, Twayne, 1966.
The Wizard from Vienna: Franz Anton Mesmer, Coward, 1975.
Gold: An Illustrated History, Hammond, Inc., 1979.

(Contributor) *Governing the American Democracy,* St. Martin's, 1980.
(With wife, Nan Buranelli) *Spy/Counterspy: An Encyclopedia of Espionage,* McGraw, 1982.
(With Murray Wolfson) *In the Long Run We Are All Dead: A Macroeconomics Murder Mystery,* St. Martin's, 1984.
Thomas Alva Edison, Silver Burdett, 1989.
The American Heritage History of the Bill of Rights, Volume 8: *The Eighth Amendment,* Silver Burdett, 1991.

Assistant to Lowell Thomas on writing Thomas' autobiographies, *Good Evening Everybody: From Cripple Creek to Samarkand,* Morrow, 1976, and *So Long until Tomorrow: From Quaker Hill to Kathmandu,* Morrow, 1977. Also contributor to *American Year Book,* 1984-91. Contributor of numerous articles and book reviews to periodicals, including *American Quarterly, William and Mary Quarterly, New York Historical Society Quarterly, New Scholasticism, Social Education,* and *Ethics.*

Edgar Allan Poe has been translated into Spanish, Rumanian, Arabic, Japanese, and Korean; *The Wizard from Vienna: Franz Anton Mesmer* has been translated into Japanese.

WORK IN PROGRESS: Descartes: A Biographical Introduction; Robert Louis Stevenson.

SIDELIGHTS: Vincent Buranelli told *CA:* "My decision to write history was taken while I was a graduate student at Cambridge University working under the guidance to two scholars on international reputation, Michael Oakeshott and J. P. T. Bury. From Oakeshott I learned that 'history is what the evidence obliges us to believe,' a principle that, among other things, emancipates the historian from Ranke's impossible ideal of presenting an event 'exactly as it happened.' From Bury I learned to view the differences between historians under 'the analogy of art,' where it is taken for granted that different painters will produce very different, yet all valid, interpretations of the same subject.

"The historians I remember reading before college, because we happened to have their books in the house, were Prescott, who made the conquest of Mexico a brilliant drama, and Breasted, who described the 'new past' behind Europe in Egypt and Mesopotamia. Later, three contemporaries influenced me more than any others. Hilaire Belloc taught me the virtues of closely reasoned, flowing, sinuous prose, Samuel Eliot Morison of great events expounded through high creative imagination and a grand narrative style worthy of them, and Will Durant those visions summed up in pithy lines, often Volairean irony brought up to date, that kept me thinking 'I wish I had said that.' An example: in describing the archaeological discoveries of Sir Arthur Evans on Crete, Durant says they were so remarkable that 'even the Cretans became interested.'

"My bias is therefore in favor of the artists who have increasingly been replaced by technicians. In particular, quantified history seems to me no more valid than the traditional forms (the use of statistics can be as faulty as any research, as we know from the disputed of statisticians). The loss of eloquence is not a minor matter, for it denies the reader one of the greatest pleasures of written history.

"A number of my books have been done to discover a fact or defend a position. With *The Trial of Peter Zenger,* I undertook to show that James Alexander was the journalistic genius behind the case, Zenger being merely the printer. With *The King and the Quaker,* I wanted to vindicate William Penn's loyalty to James II (which was not an attempt to validate James's rule as several critics thought). I wrote *Josiah Royce* because I could not find a biography of the subject, and *The Wizard from Vienna* because there was no American biography of Mesmer.

"*Spy/Counterspy: An Encyclopedia of Espionage* was a special case because my wife was my co-author. Nan Buranelli brought direct experience to the book, having been in ULTRA (British intelligence) in World War II. ULTRA broke the German codes and was instrumental in winning the war, a fact she described in 'ULTRA,' the longest article in our encyclopedia.

"I have two works in progress. One is a biography of Robert Louis Stevenson, aimed at the schools and therefore a comparatively minor undertaking. The other is major, a biography of Descartes I have kept at for thirty years, adding bits of research, thought and writing as time became available in between immediate demands such as office assignments and publishing deadlines.

"If I had held a professorial chair, my work would have been focused in one direction. Whether this would have been better than the freedom to pursue wayward lines of thought wherever they led, is a question impossible for me to answer. I do know, however, that the best approach to the latter vocation for nearly everyone is to cling to a secure job while breaking into history (or any other subject) on the side, always hoping for the success that will enable one to leave the job and concentrate on the writing."

*   *   *

BURNS, James MacGregor 1918-

PERSONAL: Born August 3, 1918, in Melrose, MA; son of Robert Arthur (a businessman) and Mildred (Bunce) Burns; married Janet Thompson Dismorr (a college administrator), May 23, 1942 (divorced, 1968); married Joan Simpson (a writer), September 7, 1969 (divorced, 1991); children: David MacGregor, Timothy Stewart, Deborah Edwards, Margaret Rebecca Antonia. *Education:* Williams College, B.A., 1939; attended National Institute of Public Affairs, 1939-40; Harvard University, M.A., 1947, Ph.D., 1947; postdoctoral study, London School of Economics, 1949. *Politics:* Democrat. *Religion:* Congregational.

ADDRESSES: Home—High Mowing, Bee Hill Road, Williamstown, MA 01267. *Office*—Department of Political Science, Williams College, Williamstown, MA 01267.

CAREER: Williams College, Williamstown, MA, assistant professor of political science, 1947-50, associate professor, 1950-53, professor of political science, 1953-86, Woodrow Wilson Professor of Government, 1962-86, professor emeritus, 1986—. Faculty member, Salzburg Seminar in American Studies, 1954, 1961; lecturer, Institute of History of the Soviet Academy of Sciences, Moscow and Leningrad, 1963; senior scholar, Jepson School of Leadership Studies, University of Richmond, 1990-93. Member of staff, Hoover Commission, 1948; Massachusetts delegate to Democratic National Convention, 1952, 1956, 1960, 1964; democratic candidate for Congress, 1958. Member of advisory board, Berkshire Community College, 1963-64. *Military service:* U.S. Army, 1943-45; served as combat historian in the Pacific; received four battle stars and Bronze Star.

MEMBER: International Society of Political Psychology (president, 1982-83), American Political Science Association (president, 1975-76), American Historical Association, American Philosophical Association, New England Political Science Association (president, 1960-61), American Civil Liberties Union, American Legion, Phi Beta Kappa, Delta Sigma Rho.

AWARDS, HONORS: Tamiment Institute award for best biography and Woodrow Wilson prize, both 1956, for *Roosevelt: The Lion and the Fox;* Francis Parkman Prize, Society of American Historians, Pulitzer Prize in history, and National Book Award for history and biography, all 1971, for *Roosevelt: The Soldier of Freedom;* Sarah Josepha Hale Award for general literary achievement, 1979; nominated for *Los Angeles Times* Book Prize, 1982, for *The American Experiment,* Volume I: *The Vineyard of Liberty;* Christopher Award, 1983.

WRITINGS:

POLITICAL HISTORY

Congress on Trial: The Legislative Process and the Administrative State, Harper, 1949.
Roosevelt: The Lion and the Fox, Harcourt, 1956.
John Kennedy: A Political Profile, Harcourt, 1960.

The Deadlock of Democracy: Four-Party Politics in America, Prentice-Hall, 1963.

Presidential Government: The Crucible of Leadership, Houghton, 1966.

Roosevelt: The Soldier of Freedom (sequel to *Roosevelt: The Lion and the Fox*), Harcourt, 1970.

Uncommon Sense, Harper, 1972.

Edward Kennedy and the Camelot Legacy, Norton, 1976.

State and Local Politics: Government by the People, Prentice-Hall, 1976.

Leadership, Harper, 1978.

The American Experiment, Knopf, Volume I: *The Vineyard of Liberty,* 1982, Volume II: *The Workshop of Democracy,* 1985, Volume III: *The Crosswinds of Freedom,* 1989.

The Power to Lead: The Crisis of the American Presidency, Simon & Schuster, 1984.

(With L. Marvin Overby) *Cobblestone Leadership: Majority Rule, Minority Power,* University of Oklahoma Press, 1990.

(With Stewart Burns) *A People's Charter: The Pursuit of Rights in America,* Knopf, 1991.

Also author of *Guam: Operations of the 77th Infantry Division,* 1944; co-author of *Okinawa: The Last Battle,* 1947.

WITH JACK WALTER PELTASON

Government by the People: The Dynamics of American National Government, Prentice-Hall, 1952, 12th edition, 1985.

Government by the People: The Dynamics of American State and Local Government, Prentice-Hall, 1952, 12th edition, 1985.

EDITOR

(With Peltason) *Functions and Policies of American Government,* Prentice-Hall, 1958, 3rd edition, 1967.

Lyndon Baines Johnson, *To Heal and to Build: The Programs of Lyndon B. Johnson,* McGraw, 1968.

(With Patricia Bonomi and Austin Ranney) *The American Constitutional System under Strong and Weak Parties,* Praeger, 1981.

(With others) *The Democrats Must Lead,* Westview Press, 1992.

CONTRIBUTOR

Dialogues in Americanism, Regnery, 1964.

Our American Government Today, 2nd edition, Prentice-Hall, 1966.

RECORDINGS

James MacGregor Burns Discusses Government Planning and Change, Center for Cassette Studies, c. 1975.

(With Peltason) *Resurrection of the Party System through Control of Campaign Financing,* Center for the Study of Democratic Institutions (Santa Barbara), 1976.

WORK IN PROGRESS: A reassessment of Franklin Delano Roosevelt to be published in 1995.

SIDELIGHTS: "To some historians [James MacGregor] Burns is a fine political scientist. To some political scientists he is a fine historian. In fact," wrote Walter Johnson in the *Washington Post Book World,* "he is the best of both disciplines." For more than forty years, Burns has written effective blends of history and political analysis. As Austin Ranney noted in the *Reporter,* Burns is also "the co-author of the most popular postwar college textbook in American government," *Government by the People: The Dynamics of American National Government,* and is a champion of the leadership that holds the best interests of the governed high above political gain. Gordon S. Wood commented in the *New York Review of Books* that "although [Burns] . . . is writing history, [he] is still the political scientist and has the political problems of our recent past, our present and our future very much on his mind."

Whether the subject is history, politics, or a combination of the two, Burns's books focus on the nature of political leadership. In a *New York Times* interview with Herbert Mitgang, Burns discussed his theory of leadership and its importance in *The American Experiment,* a three-volume survey of U.S. history from the New Deal to the present that includes *The Vineyard of Liberty, The Workshop of Democracy,* and *The Crosswinds of Freedom.* "What I . . . emphasize is the role of leadership," Burns said, "but I don't believe in the great-man theory of history. . . . What impresses me as I do my research is the importance of the second and third level of leaders—the staff people. It isn't just a story of Presidents and generals."

Many reviewers have commented on Burns's theory of leadership, especially as outlined in *The American Experiment.* As Pauline Maier noted in the *New York Times Book Review:* "Burns . . . has written a very different kind of history . . . in that his is much less a history of great white men. . . . He has conceived of leaders as falling into three tiers: national power-wielders, notable persons on the state and local level and what he calls 'grass roots activists'. . . . As a result of this expanded focus, women, laboring people, blacks and Indians become part of the story." And in the *New Yorker,* Naomi Bliven further observed that Burns "astutely pays particular attention to what he calls the 'third cadre' of political leadership. . . . Burns thinks of the third cadre as 'country politicians, circuit-riding lawyers, money-minded men of commerce, cracker-barrel philosophers' whose decisions about accepting or rejecting the Constitution influenced their neighbors' votes."

With the publication of *The Crosswinds of Freedom* in 1989, Burns completed *The American Experiment.* Commenting on this achievement in the *New York Times Book Review*, John A. Garraty wrote, "Mr. Burns possesses a keen eye and ear for anecdote and quotation. He is a master at summarizing clearly the most complex events, and he is capable of brilliant capsule descriptions of broad historical trends." The unifying theme of *The American Experiment* is Burns's concept of leadership. Wrote Garraty: "Again and again [in *The Crosswinds of Freedom*] . . . Mr. Burns returns to his thesis about the American experiment and to his belief in the central importance of leadership if the nation's problems are to be solved." Michael Kazin, who in the *Washington Post Book World* described Burns as "one of our most skilled interpreters of the lives of 20th-century liberal heroes," observed that social movements and cultural changes serve as briefing papers for these heroes. "For Burns," wrote Kazin, "the evolution of modern America is largely a matter of how leaders like FDR, Truman, Kennedy, Johnson, Carter and an occasional non-president like Martin Luther King, Jr. attempted to realize the lofty, yet often contradictory, vision of 'individual liberty and equality of opportunity for all.' "

According to William B. Logan in the *Saturday Review*, Burns's theory of leadership "allows him to write almost as though history were a set of linked biographies." Burns's historical narrative is complemented by short vignettes that focus on particular personalities—including relatively unknown people—involved in the shaping of U.S. history. A portrait of Mercy Warren, an influential writer of the late 1700s, appears alongside one of George Washington because Burns believes that all citizens had a hand in the shaping of America. "Burns enlivens his text," wrote Robert V. Remini in the *Chicago Tribune Book World*, "with insightful character sketches of the leading figures of his narrative. But he also includes the not-so-famous . . . whose contribution to the American experiment was nonetheless significant."

According to many reviewers these biographies make Burns's historical writing better than most. "Some may object," claimed Bernard A. Weisberger in the *Detroit News*, "to Burns' work precisely on the ground that this focus on leaders . . . and 'scenes' is outdated. . . . But such critics forget that professional historians and political scientists who have forsaken philosophy and myth in favor of 'behavioral models' . . . have produced a body of work so remote from what moves ordinary people that they have deservedly lost their audience." "Here is history as it should be written," Remini concurred. "Not the awful stuff of many academics these days who submerge the Jeffersons and Jacksons . . . beneath a sea of statistical tables, distribution curves and computer analyses. Here is history with sweep and grandeur." Mitgang

added: "Burns . . . brings an extra dimension to historical writing. [He is unlike those] who revise history by emphasizing statistical data instead of human expression."

In his two-part biography of Franklin Roosevelt, Burns's ability as a historian and a teller of tales merge to produce award-winning nonfiction. Part 1, *Roosevelt: The Lion and the Fox,* was considered "thorough, scholarly, [and] incisive in its analysis," by W. V. Shonnon in his *Commonweal* review; in the *New Republic* Richard Marshall called it "the best Roosevelt study by far." Critics were even more enthusiastic about the second part, *Roosevelt: The Soldier of Freedom,* which won the Pulitzer Prize and the National Book Award when it was published in 1971. G. W. Johnson wrote in *Book World:* "About James MacGregor Burns as a literary craftsman there can be no two opinions. . . . To style he adds the rare gift of ability to sort out from a tangled skein the significant threads that enable him to present in a consistent, coherent narrative the period he has chosen to study. There is not, and may never be a better one-volume presentation of the diplomatic and political aspects of the great war that raged in those years."

In his preface to *Roosevelt: The Soldier of Freedom,* Burns explains both the theme of the book and his personal theory of leadership: "The proposition of this work is that Franklin D. Roosevelt as a war leader was . . . divided between the man of principle of ideals, of faith . . . and . . . the man of *Real politik,* of prudence, of narrow, manageable short-run goals." This concept of leadership was expanded into a 530-page study Burns published in 1978. In *Leadership,* Burns explains that he believes there are two kinds of leaders—transactional and transformational. In democracies, most political leaders are transactional. As Richard J. Walton explained in the Chicago Tribune, "They lead by making political bargains (transactions), by serving as political brokers, giving this to gain that." What America needs are transformational leaders. "Such leadership occurs," Burns writes, "when one or more persons engage with others in such a way that leaders and followers raise one another to higher levels of motivation and morality." He cites Mao Tse-tung and Mahatma Gandhi as examples, noting of the latter that he was a leader who "aroused and elevated the hopes and demands of millions of Indians and whose life and personality were enhanced in the process."

In *Uncommon Sense* Burns lists the national goals that a transformational leader would pursue and how these goals should be accomplished. The three underlying values that all Americans and their leaders should be committed to, according to Burns, are defense of civil liberties, the abolition of poverty, and the protection of the environment. Wrote Milton R. Konvitz in the *Saturday Review*, "Burns warns . . . [that] because [these] problems are complex, many factors must be dealt with simultaneously and with equal energy. It is not, therefore, merely a question of spending more money but of reordering priorities in such a way that adequate means will be employed to achieve the desired ends." The means suggested by Burns include the strengthening of certain Presidential powers and the creation of "presidential agencies" to coordinate Executive policy decisions down through state and local levels of government.

Together with his son Stewart, Burns tackles the issue of leadership from a slightly different perspective in *A People's Charter*, published in 1991. The book explores the evolution of the rights of those who are led, following their historical development in the United States from the 18th century to the present. Alan Wolfe, writing in the *Washington Post Book World*, found the volume well-timed—*A People's Charter* was published on the 200th anniversary of the incorporation of the Bill of Rights into the U.S. Constitution—and well-intentioned. However, Wolfe faulted the Burnses for relying too heavily on their own liberal political agenda and thereby giving short shrift to the more complex and nuanced issues that a debate on rights and responsibilities should engender. "They tell the story of rights in America," he wrote, "as a simple morality play in which their own sense of morality stars." However, in the *New Republic*, Sean Wilentz described the book as "an ambitious synthesis of virtually everything connected to the pursuit of rights in America." He continued, "Taking a left-populist approach not normally associated with the senior Burns, the books shows how rights talk . . . has galvanized virtually every democratic movement in the nation's history."

In the many works he has published over his career, Burns has received accolades for his ability to combine the best lessons of the historian with those of the political scientist in forging his own view of the American reality. In the *Chicago Tribune* Walton praised Burns as an "eminent biographer . . . and superb student of American life and government." Burns's body of work, as Konvitz wrote in the *Saturday Review*, "provides a critical and provocative view of our gains and failures, and of our national goals, which as . . . Burns reminds us—always assumed not a planned but a planning society."

BIOGRAPHICAL/CRITICAL SOURCES:

BOOKS

Beschloss, Michael R. and Thomas E. Cronin, editors, *Essays in Honor of James MacGregor Burns*, Prentice-Hall, 1989.

PERIODICALS

Annals of the American Academy of Political and Social Science, November, 1949.

Atlantic Monthly, March, 1979.
Best Sellers, September 15, 1970.
Book Week, January 30, 1966.
Chicago Tribune, September 10, 1978.
Chicago Tribune Book World, February 21, 1982.
Christian Science Monitor, January 31, 1963; October 22, 1970.
Commentary, April, 1971.
Commonweal, December 7, 1956; November 24, 1978.
Critic, November 15, 1978.
Detroit News, April 4, 1982.
Harper's, January, 1971; May, 1976.
Los Angeles Times, April 11, 1984.
Los Angeles Times Book Review, November 14, 1982; April 16, 1989, p. 9.
National Review, November 3, 1970.
New Republic, January 11, 1960; February 2, 1963; February 5, 1966; May 13, 1972; July 24, 1976; December 23, 1978; December 23, 1991.
Newsweek, October 26, 1970.
New Yorker, August 18, 1956; January 9, 1971; May 17, 1982; June 25, 1984.
New York Review of Books, March 31, 1966; May 20, 1971; April 29, 1976; February 18, 1982.
New York Times, July 17, 1949; August 12, 1956; September 12, 1970; March 11, 1979; April 10, 1984; April 18, 1984; September 24, 1985; January 9, 1982; April 19, 1989; January 8, 1992.
New York Times Book Review, January 24, 1960; January 23, 1966; September 1, 1968; September 13, 1970; April 18, 1976; December 24, 1978; February 21, 1982; April 29, 1984; September 29, 1985; May 14, 1989; May 6, 1990; June 30, 1991; March 15, 1992, p. 19.
Publishers Weekly, July 26, 1985.
Reporter, March 14, 1963.
Saturday Review, August 11, 1956; January 19, 1963; February 5, 1966; September 21, 1968; September 12, 1970; February 12, 1972; May 1, 1976; February, 1982.
Time, September 28, 1970.
Times Literary Supplement, March 5, 1971.
Tribune Books (Chicago), April 29, 1990, p. 8.
Virginia Quarterly Review, autumn, 1990; summer, 1992.
Washington Post, September 9, 1970.
Washington Post Book World, June 13, 1976; September 17, 1978; February 14, 1982; May 6, 1984; April 23, 1989, p. 1; January 12, 1992.*

*   *   *

BUSTOS DOMECQ, H(onorio)
See BIOY CASARES, Adolfo

C

CALLAGHAN, Mary Rose 1944-

PERSONAL: Born January 23, 1944, in Dublin, Ireland; came to the United States in 1975; daughter of Michael Anthony (a farmer) and Sheila (a nurse; maiden name, Sullivan) Callaghan; married Robert Hogan (a writer), December 21, 1979. *Education:* National University of Ireland, University College, Dublin, B.A., 1968, teaching diploma, 1969. *Politics:* "Nonaggressive feminist." *Religion:* "Humanist."

ADDRESSES: Home—40 Seacrest, Bray, Co: Wicklow, Ireland. *Office*—Proscenium Press, P.O. Box 361, Newark, DE 19711.

CAREER: Gordon County Secondary School, Berkshire, England, high school English teacher, 1969-70; Rye St. Antony School, Oxford, England, teacher of English, 1970-73; The Arts in Ireland, assistant editor, 1973-75; Proscenium Press, Newark, DE, editorial assistant, 1975—. Dublin Institute of Adult Education, lecturer in literature, 1985-88; director of workshops and seminars, 1985—.

AWARDS, HONORS: O. Z. Whitehead competition runner-up, for *A House for Fools.*

WRITINGS:

(Assistant editor) *The Dictionary of Irish Literature,* Greenwood Press, 1979.
Mothers (novel), Arlen House, 1982, Marion Boyars, 1984.
A House for Fools (two-act play), Proscenium, 1983.
Confessions of a Prodigal Daughter (novel), Marion Boyars, 1985.
Kitty O'Shea, A Life of Katharine Parnell (biography), Pandora Press, 1989.
The Awkward Girl (novel), Attic, 1990.

Has Anyone Seen Heather? (young adult novel), Attic, 1990.

Editor of *Liquorice All-Sorts,* by Muriel Breen. Contributor to *Dictionary of Literary Biography,* edited by Jay Halio, Gale Research, 1983. Also contributor to periodicals, including *Journal of Irish Literature, Irish Times,* and *Image.* Assistant editor for *Journal of Irish Literature,* 1975-92 and guest editor of *W.E.B.*

WORK IN PROGRESS: The Imaginary Grandfather, a novel.

SIDELIGHTS: Although Mary Rose Callaghan's novels focus on women and self-awareness, Callaghan does not consider herself a feminist writer. She once told *CA:* "I am very interested in the writings of women. Still, I would not call myself a feminist writer any more than I would call someone a socialist writer or a Catholic writer, and so on. The best writing is that which illustrates the human condition. I try to do this in my own work. Women are not separate species from men. The plots of my novels are concerned with women coming to self-awareness; they try to show the connection between women. The characters are all inventions, inspired by life but remaining separate. I believe art is different from life. A good work makes a statement about life, but it is not life. My writing reflects my hope for a more humane world. I am a comic writer and, as such, deadly serious."

Confessions of a Prodigal Daughter, Callaghan's second novel, reflects her concern for a more humane world in the main character's resolution to her problems. The protagonist, the adolescent Anne, lives, often at odds, with her widowed mother and sister in Dublin, Ireland. Set in the 1960's, the tale depicts Anne's mother as a snobbish, unrealistic spendthrift—with little to spend—who expects her daughter to assume the pretenses of wealth as well. Confused by and uncomfortable with such a facade, however,

Anne retreats into the world of books, developing a passion for Italian and the works of Dante. Also figuring in the novel are the heroine's rich but stingy Aunt Allie, the wealthy, fair-weather friend Nicola, and Nicola's boyfriend, whose sexual attack upon Anne eventually lands her in a mental hospital. There she achieves peace of mind and resolves to return home and help her mother face the family's problems. "Callaghan has a light touch" and "the pace of her narrative is admirably judged," wrote Anne Haverty in her *Times Literary Supplement* assessment of *Confessions of a Prodigal Daughter*. The reviewer also added that "the perceptions of [Callaghan's] heroine are often amusing and endearing."

Callaghan adds: "I'd like to write more for young adults. Also, I'd like to write for the stage. At present I'm attempting an American novel, as I've lived there for over fifteen years."

BIOGRAPHICAL/CRITICAL SOURCES:

PERIODICALS

Guardian, November 24, 1982.
Irish Times, August 12, 1983, September 13, 1985, October 3, 1985.
New York Times Book Review, January 5, 1986.
Times Literary Supplement, September 20, 1985.

* * *

CAMERON, Kate
    See McGLAMRY, Beverly

* * *

CAMPBELL, Arthur A(ndrews) 1924-

PERSONAL: Born February 8, 1924, in Brooklyn, NY; son of Arthur Monroe and Jo Ethel (Andrews) Campbell; married Nancy Elizabeth Pyle, January 28, 1961; children: Julia, Tay. *Education:* Attended Denison University, 1943-44; Antioch College, A.B., 1948; Columbia University, post graduate studies, 1947-50.

Addresses: Office—Center for Population Research, National Institutes of Health, Bethesda, MD 20892.

CAREER: Metropolitan Life Insurance Co., New York City, editorial clerk, 1950-52; U.S. Bureau of the Census, Washington, DC, analytical statistician, 1952-56; Scripps Foundation for Research in Population Problems, Miami University, Oxford, Ohio, research associate professor, 1956-64; U.S. Department of Health, Education, and Welfare, Division of Vital Statistics, Washington, chief of Natality Statistics Branch, 1964-68; Center for Population

Research, National Institutes of Health, Bethesda, MD, deputy director, 1968—. *Military Service:* U.S. Navy, 1943-46; became lieutenant junior grade.

MEMBER: Population Association of America (president, 1973-74), International Union for the Scientific Study of Population, American Statistical Association (fellow).

AWARDS, HONORS: Department of Commerce Meritorious Service Award, 1957; Director's Award, National Institutes of Health, 1976.

WRITINGS:

(Co-author) *Family Planning, Sterility, and Population Growth,* McGraw-Hill, 1959.
(With P. K. Whelpton and John Patterson) *Fertility and Family Planning in the United States,* Princeton University Press, 1966.
(With Clyde V. Kiser and Wilson H. Grabil) *Trends and Variations in Fertility in the United States,* Harvard University Press, 1968.
Manual of Fertility Analysis, Churchill Livingstone, 1983.
(Editor) *Social, Economic, and Health Aspects of Low Fertility,* National Institutes of Health, 1980.

Also author of papers on fertility, family planning, and population.

* * *

CANNON, Lou(is S.) 1933-

PERSONAL: Born June 3, 1933, in New York, NY; son of Jack and Irene (Kohn) Cannon; married Virginia Oprian, February 2, 1953 (divorced, 1982); children: Carl, David, Judith, Jack. *Education:* Attended University of Nevada, 1950-52, and San Francisco State College (now University), 1952. *Religion:* Catholic.

ADDRESSES: Office—c/o *Washington Post,* 1150 15th Street, NW, Washington, DC 20071.

CAREER: Truck driver, 1954-56; reporter for various newspapers, 1956-59; *Contra Costa Times,* Walnut Creek, CA, managing editor, 1959-65; *San Jose Mercury-News,* San Jose, CA, copy editor, 1961-65; State Capitol bureau chief, 1965-69; Ridder Publications, Washington, DC, correspondent, 1969-72; *Washington Post,* White House correspondent, beginning 1972. *Military service:* U.S. Army, 1953-54.

MEMBER: The Newspaper Guild, Sigma Delta Chi.

AWARDS, HONORS: American Political Science Association Award, 1968, for distinguished reporting of public affairs; California Taxpayers Award, 1969, for editorial writing; Beckman Award, 1984, for best overall White House coverage; *Washington Journal Review* "Best in Business" award, 1985; Gerald R. Ford Prize, 1988, for distinguished reporting on the presidency.

WRITINGS:

Ronnie and Jesse: A Political Odyssey, Doubleday, 1969.
The McCloskey Challenge, Dutton, 1972.
Reporting an Inside View, California Journal Press, 1977.
(Compiler) *Ronald Reagan,* Political Profiles, 1980.
Reagan, Putnam, 1982.
President Reagan: The Role Of a Lifetime, Simon & Schuster, 1991.

SIDELIGHTS: A long-time journalist and White House correspondent, Lou Cannon has followed the career of former president Ronald Reagan since 1964, and has written three major books about Reagan at various stages of his career. Cannon once told *CA:* "I care a good deal, or think I do, about our political system and my intention is to write books that contribute to the understanding of that system and those who inhabit it."

Cannon's first book, *Ronnie and Jesse: A Political Odyssey,* was written at the start of Reagan's political career—he had recently been elected governor of California. In 1982, Cannon published *Reagan,* in which he traces Reagan's ascent to the presidency while only briefly examining the former president's early experiences in office. Writing in the *New York Times,* David E. Rosenbaum predicted that *Reagan* would "surely become a standard reference work for reporters and scholars. And, besides that," he added, "it's a good read."

Kevin Phillips described *Reagan* as a "well-crafted biography" in the *Washington Post Book World,* but noted that the book was short on analysis—probably because Cannon wanted future journalistic access to Reagan. Meanwhile, William E. Leuchtenburg criticized Cannon in the *New Republic* for mythologizing Reagan after having painstakingly pointed out the serious shortcomings of the man. Although Leuchtenburg praised *Reagan* for its wealth of research and for "any number of lively bits of information," the reviewer went on to fault its author for drawing conclusions inconsistent with the evidence presented.

Cannon's *President Reagan: The Role of a Lifetime* is both a biography of Reagan and an account of his two-term presidency. *Time* magazine reviewer Laurence I. Barrett described Cannon's third book on Reagan this way: "The volume's heft and density are intimidating, but *President Reagan* is essential reading for anyone who wants to understand the star of politics in the 1980s."

Praised by most major reviewers, Cannon's book is frequently described as a devastating portrait of Reagan. In the *New Republic,* Hendrik Hertzberg called *President Reagan* "devastating and superb." Hertzberg noted that Cannon has covered Reagan for more than 25 years, and "is looked upon by Reagan's friends and enemies alike as a fair witness and an impartial judge." It is for this reason, argued Hertzberg, that the criticisms leveled are so disturbing. For instance, Cannon documents how a protective staff and Reagan's ever-watchful wife, Nancy, tried to downplay the former president's failings, such as his propensity for napping during high-level meetings and his practice of watching movies during most of the 183 weekends he spent at Camp David.

Sidney Blumenthal described Cannon's book in a similar manner in the *Los Angeles Times Book Review.* "Cannon's diligent effort to understand the inner Reagan," wrote Blumenthal, "is utterly devoid of the slightest smirk. It is partly because Cannon's motives and methods are unimpeachable that his book is the most devastating of all." Blumenthal noted that Cannon's sympathy for his subject "at times crosses over into an unusual empathy," as when Cannon describes some of Reagan's shortcomings to having been raised by an alcoholic father. Finally, Michael Gartner, writing in the *Washington Post Book World,* observed that Cannon "devastates Ronald Reagan with facts, with details, with quotes, with examples and with anecdotes— tales the story-loving president would probably relish if they were not about him."

In the Chicago *Tribune Books,* Richard Norton Smith commented upon Cannon's even-handed treatment of the former president, which leads Cannon to conclude that while not a great president, Reagan was a great American. Smith observed, "Admiring Reagan's political skills more than the causes for which they were enlisted, Cannon is always thoughtful and never yields to caricature." Gartner summed up Cannon's achievement when he wrote: "This is a major work of history, of biography, of politics. Ronald Reagan, and all of us, are lucky to have had Lou Cannon taking notes."

BIOGRAPHICAL/CRITICAL SOURCES:

PERIODICALS

Commonweal, December 6, 1991.
Guardian Weekly, April 19, 1992.
Los Angeles Times, November 28, 1969.
Los Angeles Times Book Review, September 26, 1982;
    April 21, 1991, p. 1.
Nation, January 15, 1983.
National Review, February 10, 1970.
New Republic, December 6, 1982; September 9, 1991.
New Yorker, March 14, 1983; May 27, 1991.
New York Review of Books, June 13, 1991.
New York Times, November 11, 1969; November 2, 1982;
    April 24, 1991.

New York Times Book Review, October 3, 1982, p. 1; September 23, 1984; May 5, 1991, p. 3; February 23, 1992.
Observer, June 7, 1992.
Time, April 15, 1991, p. 64.
Tribune Books (Chicago), April 21, 1991, p. 1; February 16, 1992.
Washington Journalism Review, February, 1985.
Washington Post Book World, September 19, 1982, p. 1; August 19, 1984; April 21, 1991, p 1; February 9, 1992.*

* * *

CAPONIGRI, A(loysius) Robert 1915-1983

PERSONAL: Born November 16, 1915, in Chicago, IL; died March 2, 1983; son of Nicola (a journalist) and Lucia (Sorrocco) Caponigri; married Winifred Phyllis Franco (a professor), October 6, 1946; children: Victoria Marie (Mrs. John Stephan), Robert John, Lisa Marie. *Education:* Loyola University, Chicago, IL, A.B., 1935, M.A., 1936; Harvard University, postgraduate study, 1937-39; University of Chicago, Ph.D., 1942. *Religion:* Roman Catholic.

ADDRESSES: Home—317 East Napoleon Blvd., South Bend, IN 46617.

CAREER: University of Iowa, Iowa City, instructor in humanities, 1943-46; University of Notre Dame, Notre Dame, IN, assistant professor, 1946-52, associate professor, 1952-56, professor of philosophy, 1956-83, chairman of committee on humanities, 1967-83. Instructor, Luigi Sturzo Institute, Rome, Italy, 1961. Distinguished visiting professor, Loyola University, 1963; Fulbright visiting professor, University of Madrid, 1964-66; visiting lecturer, University of Padova, Bologna, spring, 1964, 1968, 1971, Luigi Sturzo Institute, 1964, 1965, 1971; visiting scholar, Center for Study of Democratic Institutions, spring, 1975, and Harvard Center for Italian Renaissance Studies in Florence, Italy, summer, 1975. Lecturer to numerous universities, including University of Oklahoma, 1976, Symposium on Religion Art in America, Vatican City, 1976, and Fordham University, 1976. Member of editorial board, University of Notre Dame Press. Fellow, Folger Shakespeare Library, 1975.

MEMBER: American Philosophical Society, Association of Philosophical Inquiry (secretary-treasurer), American Catholic Philosophical Society (member of executive board), Mediaeval Academy of America, Metaphysical Society of America.

AWARDS, HONORS: Italian Institute for Historical Studies, Fulbright research professor, 1950-51, Rockefeller Foundation fellow, 1952-53, 1974-75; research fellowships from American Philosophical Society, 1958, 1969, Grace Foundation, 1959, and American Council of Learned Societies, 1969; research grants from Italian Institute of Culture, New York, 1961, Marquette Foundation, 1961, 1964, 1969, and Instituto de Cultura Hispanica, Madrid, 1970; Fulbright lectureship in Italy, 1971; El Premio Nacional, Ministry of Culture of Spain, 1983, for work translating *On Essence.*

WRITINGS:

Time and Idea: The Theory of History in Giambattista Vico, Regnery, 1953, revised edition, University of Notre Dame Press, 1968.
History and Liberty: The Historical Writings of Benedetto Crose, Regnery, 1955.
(Translator) Pico della Mirandola, *Oration on the Dignity of Man,* Regnery, 1956.
(Editor) *Modern Catholic Thinkers,* Harper, 1960, published in two volumes, 1964.
(Translator, contributor, and author of introduction) Machiavelli, *The Prince,* Regnery, 1963.
A History of Western Philosophy, five volumes, University of Notre Dame Press, 1963-71.
(Associate editor) *Masterpieces of Catholic Literature,* two volumes, Salem Press, 1965.
(Translator and editor) *Contemporary Spanish Philosophy,* University of Notre Dame Press, 1967.
(Translator, selector, and author of introduction) Diogenes Laertius, *Lives of the Philosophers,* Regnery, 1969.
(Translator and author of introduction) Xavier Zubiri, *On Essence,* Catholic University Press, 1980.
(Translator) Ernesto Mayz Vallenilla, *The Mastery of Power,* Catholic University Press, 1981.

Contributor to numerous books, including *Studi in onore de M. F. Sciacca,* Marzorati, 1959; *The Concept of Matter,* edited by Ernan McMullin, University of Notre Dame Press, 1963; *New Themes in Christian Philosophy,* University of Notre Dame Press, 1968; and *Michele F. Sciacea: Saggi in Onore,* Marzorati, 1968. Contributor of more than fifty articles to philosophy journals in the United States and Europe.*

* * *

CARLTON, Charles Merritt 1928-

PERSONAL: Born December 12, 1928, in Poultney, VT; son of Clarence Rann (a salesman) and Margaret (Pennell) Carlton; married Mary MacDonald (a teacher), August 21, 1957; children: David, John, Stephen. *Education:* University of Vermont, B.A., 1950; Middlebury College, MA, 1951; University of Michigan, Ph.D., 1963. *Politics:* Independent. *Avocational Interests:* Photography, travel.

ADDRESSES: Home—3 Thornfield Way, Fairport, NY 14450. *Office*—Department of Linguistics, University of Rochester, Rochester, NY 14627.

CAREER: Michigan State University, East Lansing, instructor, 1958-62; University of Missouri, Columbia, assistant professor, 1962-66; University of Rochester, Rochester, NY, associate professor, 1966-78, professor of French and Romance linguistics, 1978—. Assistant director of National Defense Education Act French Institute, University of Vermont, summer, 1964; visiting lecturer, University of Kentucky summer program, Cluj, Romania, 1977. *Military service:* U.S. Army Reserve, 1950-58.

MEMBER: American Association of Teachers of French, American Association of Teachers of Spanish and Portuguese, American Association for the Advancement of Slavic Studies, American Romanian Academy, Romanian Studies Association of America, Society for Romanian Studies, Fulbright Alumni Association, Sigma Delta Pi, L'Amicale (Middlebury, VT), Rochester International Friendship Council (president, 1991-93).

AWARDS, HONORS: Fulbright fellowship in France, 1950-51; National Science Foundation Award, 1965; National Defense Education Act Title VI fellowship, 1970; Fulbright senior lecturer in Romania, 1971-72; Fulbright senior lecturer in Brazil, 1986; Fulbright faculty research awards, Romania, 1974, 1978, 1982, 1988; International Research and Exchanges Board grantee, 1982, 1991.

WRITINGS:

Studies in Romance Lexicology, University of North Carolina Press, 1965.
A Linguistic Analysis of a Collection of Late Latin Documents Composed in Ravenna Between A.D. 445-700: A Quantitative Approach, Mouton, 1973.

Contributor to *Dictionary of American Immigration History,* edited by F. Cordasco, Garland, 1989; editor of *Comparative Romance Linguistics Newsletter,* 1970-71; co-editor of *Miorita: A Journal of Romanian Studies,* 1977—; contributor of articles to journals including *Revue roumaine de linguistique, Modern Language Journal,* and *Miorita.*

*   *   *

CAROLI, Betty Boyd   1938-

PERSONAL: Born January 9, 1938, in Mount Vernon, OH; daughter of Clyde Ford (a farmer) and Edna (a teacher; maiden name, Henry) Boyd; married Livio Caroli (a musician), January 31, 1966. *Education:* Oberlin College, A.B., 1960; University of Pennsylvania, M.A., 1961; attended Salzburg Summer School and Universita per

Stranieri, both 1963; New York University, Ph.D., 1972; postdoctoral study at Columbia University, 1975, and China Institute, 1978-80.

ADDRESSES: Home—30 Fifth Ave., 15F, New York, NY 10011. *Office*—Department of Social Sciences, Kingsborough Community College of the City University of New York, Manhattan Beach, Oriental Blvd., Brooklyn, NY 11235.

CAREER: State University of New York College at Brockport, instructor in speech, 1961-63; teacher of English as a second language at British schools in Palermo, Italy, 1964, and Rome, Italy, 1964-65; Queens College of the City University of New York, Flushing, NY, lecturer in debate, 1965-66; Kingsborough Community College of the City University of New York, Brooklyn, NY, lecturer, 1966-67, instructor, 1967-70, assistant professor, 1970-73, associate professor, 1973-78, professor of history, 1978—, member of board of directors of Academy for the Humanities and Sciences, 1981-86. Member of advisory board of New Jersey Multi-Ethnic Oral History Project, 1980-82; member of Coordinating Committee for Women in the Historical Profession and Columbia University Seminar on the City. Consultant to National Congress of Neighborhood Women and Lower East Side Tenement Museum.

MEMBER: Organization of American Historians, American Italian Historical Association (member of executive board, 1975-82), Institute for Research in History (member of board of directors, 1982-83), Immigration History Society (member of executive board, 1982-85).

AWARDS, HONORS: Fulbright grant for study in Italy, 1970-71; National Endowment for the Humanities, grant for study in Italy, 1973, fellowships, 1974-75, 1981, and 1985-86.

WRITINGS:

Italian Repatriation from the United States, 1900-1914, Center for Migration Studies (Staten Island, NY), 1973.
(Editor with Robert F. Harney and Lydio Tomasi) *The Italian Immigrant Woman in North America,* Multicultural History Society, 1978.
(With Thomas Kessner) *Today's Immigrants: Their Stories; A New Look at the Newest Americans,* Oxford University Press, 1981.
(Author of introduction and contributor) Silvano M. Tomasi, editor, *Images: A Pictorial History of Italian Americans,* Center for Migration Studies, 1981.
First Ladies, Oxford University Press, 1987.
Immigrants Who Returned Home, Chelsea House, 1990.
Inside the White House, Abbeville Press, 1992.

Also contributor to books, including *The United States and Italy: The First Two Hundred Years,* edited by Humbert S. Nelli, American Italian Historical Association, 1978; *The Rhetoric of Protest and Reform, 1878-1898,* edited by Paul H. Boase, Ohio University Press, 1980; and *Ethnic and Immigration Groups: The United States, Canada, and England,* edited by Patricia Rosof, William Zeisel, Jean B. Quandt, and Miriam Maayan, Hayworth Press and Institute for Research in History, 1982. Contributor of articles and reviews to history and ethnic studies journals.

WORK IN PROGRESS: A biography of settlement leader and housing reformer Mary Kinsbury Simkhovitch; a book on four generations of Roosevelt women.

SIDELIGHTS: Betty Boyd Caroli told *CA:* "Since I was born into one of the least diverse populations in the United States (Knox County, Ohio), it is not surprising that I developed my interest in ethnicity while living in Europe. In fact, my curiosity about American history began while I was teaching English in Italy—first in Sicily and then in Rome. My return to the United States in 1965 was meant to be a temporary one, but like the Italian repatriates whom I later wrote about, the projected 'five years' stretched into many more. My own migrations and those of my Italian-born husband caused me to look more closely at the complications involved in changing one country for another, and his experiences became the subject of one chapter of *Today's Immigrants.*

"I have always been interested in women's public role—at least since the days at Oberlin when I debated at the same table Lucy Stone used—and the book *First Ladies* is an attempt to work out my own thoughts on how one group of women fit into American political history. Since the job of First Lady has no basis in the Constitution, how did it develop? And when? How did the women who held the job respond to the public's expectations, and how did those expectations change over two centuries? Who among the presidents' wives worked to change the job so that it included something more than being a submissive helper and skilled hostess?"

BIOGRAPHICAL/CRITICAL SOURCES:

PERIODICALS

American Historical Review, October, 1975.
VOYA, December, 1990, p. 310.

*   *   *

CARROLL, Robert P(eter)   1941-

PERSONAL: Born January 18, 1941, in Dublin, Ireland; son of Thomas Francis (a printer) and Kathleen (Merrick) Carroll; married Mary Anne Stevens (a primary school teacher), March 30, 1968; children: Finn Tomas, Alice Louisa, Saul Steve. *Education:* Trinity College, Dublin, B.A., 1962, M.A., 1967; University of Edinburgh, Ph.D., 1967. *Politics:* "Vaguely anarchistic." *Religion:* None.

ADDRESSES: Home—5 Marchmont Ter., Dowanhill, Glasgow G12 9LT, Scotland. *Office*—4 The Square, University of Glasgow, Glasgow G12 8QQ, Scotland.

CAREER: Worked as a bartender, bookseller, building site worker, bus conductor, and operator of a taxicab company, 1963-67; teacher of English literature and language at secondary school in Bathgate, Scotland, 1968; University of Glasgow, Glasgow, Scotland, lecturer, 1968-81, senior lecturer in Semitic studies, 1981-86, reader, 1986—, professor in Biblical studies, 1991—.

MEMBER: Association of University Teachers, Society for Biblical Literature, Society for the Study of the Old Testament, European Society for Literature and Religion.

WRITINGS:

NONFICTION

When Prophecy Failed, Seabury Press, 1979.
From Chaos to Covenant, S.C.M. Press, 1981.
Jeremiah: A Commentary, Westminster Press, 1986.
JSOT Guide to Jeremiah, Journal for the Study of the Old Testament Press, 1989.
The Bible as a Problem for Christianity, Trinity Press International, 1991.
(Editor) *Text as Pretext: Essays in Honour of Robert Davidson,* Journal for the Study of the Old Testament Press, 1992.

Contributor to *Biblical Translator, Expository Times, Journal for the Study of the Old Testament, Numen, Scottish Journal of Theology, Theology, Third World Book Review,* and other periodicals. Editor of *Transactions of the Glasgow University Oriental Society,* 1974-79.

WORK IN PROGRESS: A collection of poems; a collection of short stories; a novel; books on Jeremiah, prophecy, biblical interpretation, Jonah, metacommentary, and ideologickritik.

SIDELIGHTS: Carroll once told *CA:* "*When Prophecy Failed* is an analysis of the work of Leon Festinger's theory of cognitive dissonance as applied to the failure of biblical prophecy. It is an attempt to develop a hermeneutic of prophecy as clarified by this analysis. It is equally an attempt to look at meaning in relation to social movements. *From Chaos to Covenant* is an introduction to the study of the book of Jeremiah, stressing the creative role of the redactional construction of that book. Again questions about hermeneutic and communal responses to national disasters are to the fore in the analysis. The subtext of the biblical text is treated as a series of reflections of social movement responding to political crises of the period."

Carroll more recently added, "The *Jeremiah* commentary is a hermeneutical reading of the text as a series of social strategies responding to the catastrophe of the Babylonian destruction of Jerusalem. The text provides city and community with a voice which functions in the place of the destroyed structures and institutions of society."

Although Carroll once told *CA* that he hoped to begin writing fiction, he more recently commented, "[I am] still convinced of the truth of fiction, but still immersed in academic writing. [I] now tend to write highly imaginative books, but only in my head."

BIOGRAPHICAL/CRITICAL SOURCES:

PERIODICALS

Times Literary Supplement, May 28, 1982, p. 587.

*　　*　　*

CARTER, Nick
    See SMITH, Martin Cruz

*　　*　　*

CARTER, Roger   1939-

PERSONAL: Born January 1, 1939, in Painswick, England; son of Leslie Valentine (a decorator) and Dorothy (a housewife; maiden name, Goode) Carter; married Sandra Ann Jarvis (an editor), July 20, 1963; children: Helen Susan, Stephen David. *Education:* Victoria University of Manchester, B.Sc. (with honors), 1960; Garnett College, London, certificate in education, 1975. *Religion:* Evangelical Christian.

ADDRESSES: Home—117 Carver Hill Rd., High Wycombe, Buckinghamshire HP11 2UQ, England. *Office*—School of Business Studies, Buckinghamshire College of Higher Education, High Wycombe, Buckinghamshire, England.

CAREER: British Broadcasting Corp., London, England, studio manager, 1961-66; Northwest Metropolitan Regional Hospital Board, London, organization and methods officer, 1966-68; Overseas Civil Service, Honiara, Solomon Islands, administrative officer, 1968-71; owner and manager of a dry cleaning and laundry business in Lyme Regis, England, 1971-74; Buckinghamshire College of Higher Education, School of Business Studies, High Wyc-

ombe, England, lecturer in business studies and information technology, 1975—. Director of Good Stewarts, Ltd.

AWARDS, HONORS: Case Study of the Year Award, Case Clearing House of Great Britain and Ireland, 1980.

WRITINGS:

Quantitative Methods for Business Students, Heinemann, 1980.
Business Administration, Heinemann, 1982, Computer Science Press, 1984.
The Business of Data Processing, Pan Books, 1984.
Business Administration: A Fresh Approach, Pan Books, 1986.
Information Technology for Managers, Pan Books, 1987.
The Information Technology Handbook, Heinemann, 1987.
CBT Programming in Microtext, National Extension College, 1987.
Information Technology for Managers, Pan Books, 1987.
Using Q & A on the IBM PC and Compatibles, Heinemann-Newnes, 1988.
Students' Guide to Information Technology, Heinemann-Newnes, 1989, 2nd edition, 1992.
Students' Guide to Office Automation, Heinemann-Newnes, 1989.
Using WordPerfect Version 5 on the IBM PC and Compatibles, Heinemann-Newtech, 1989.
Using dBase IV on the IBM PC and Compatibles, Heinemann-Newtech, 1990.
Using MS Word Version 5, Heinemann-Newtech, 1990.
Information Technology Made Simple, Butterworth-Heinemann, 1991.
Using Excel Version 3, Butterworth-Heinemann, 1991.
Spreadsheet Skills with 1-2-3, Butterworth-Heinemann, 1993.
Wordprocessing Skills with WordPerfect, Butterworth-Heinemann, 1993.

Creator of educational software.

SIDELIGHTS: Roger Carter told *CA:* "I've never looked for a career, only an interesting and varied life. Currently I train college lecturers in information technology, and I develop educational courseware in this new and expanding field. Present projects include work with interactive video and authoring languages.

"I started my present job teaching business math in the School of Business Studies at Buckinghamshire College of Higher Education in 1975. My first book, which was on this subject, was commissioned in 1976. Writing it was an enormous task, for I was an inexperienced author and I did my own typing. Because of my varied business experience, I was able to add the teaching of business administration to my repertoire, and my second book was on that subject.

"I did the preparation for this book in the late 1970's, when office computing and word processing was just starting to get off the ground. As this was obviously going to be a very important development, I made it the central theme of the book. This paid off, for the book was published in the United States and then translated into Spanish—something of an achievement for a British textbook author.

"Writing that book got me interested in computing and new technology, so I diversified into teaching data processing, a subject that was just starting to be taught at my college. I wrote a book on that subject too. At about this time, I bought a microcomputer for word processing. Having purchased a computer, I couldn't resist learning to program it, and so got into educational software production. Computer programming is very time-consuming, and not very creative, so I don't do much of it now. At the time however, I learned a great deal about many aspects of computing and was able to apply this knowledge to my teaching. This coincided with a large demand for tuition in the subject, not only from students but also from college staff, and so I became involved in training staff in information technology, such as interactive video.

"I currently run training courses in computer applications such as spreadsheets and databases, and have written books on using Excel, Lotus 1-2-3, Q & A, dBase, Word, and WordPerfect."

*   *   *

CASADA, James A(llen) 1942-

PERSONAL: Born January 28, 1942, in Sylva, NC; son of Commodore Andrew and Anna Lou (Moore) Casada; married Elizabeth Ann Fox, June 3, 1967; children: Natasha Lea. *Education:* King College, Bristol, TN, B.A., 1964; Virginia Polytechnic Institute and State University, M.A., 1968; Vanderbilt University, Ph.D., 1972.

ADDRESSES: Home—1250 Yorkdale Drive, Rock Hill, SC 29730. *Office*—336 Bancroft, Winthrop University, Rock Hill, SC 29733.

CAREER: Hargrave Military Academy, Chatham, VA, teacher and soccer coach, 1964-67; Winthrop College, Rock Hill, SC, assistant professor, 1971-75, varsity soccer coach, 1975-86, associate professor, 1975-78, professor of history, 1978—; freelance writer. Regional supervisor of South Carolina high school soccer officials, 1979-87.

MEMBER: Royal Geographical Society (fellow), Outdoor Writers Association of America (secretary-

treasurer), Association for Bibliography of History (president, 1989-90), Hakluyt Society, Southern Conference on British Studies (member of executive committee, 1980-86), Southeastern Outdoor Press Association (board member, 1989—; president-elect, 1993—), Carolinas Symposium on British studies (member of executive committee, 1978-80), South Carolina Outdoor Press (board of directors, 1988—), Phi Alpha Theta, Phi Kappa Phi, Omicron Delta Kappa.

AWARDS, HONORS: American Philosophical Society grants, 1973, 1983; National Geographic Society grant, 1976; Southern Regional Education Board grant, 1981; excellence in teaching award, Phi Kappa Phi, 1976, 1977; fellowship, University of Edinburgh, 1977; district soccer coach of the year, National Association of Intercollegiate Athletics, 1979, 1982, 1984; distinguished professor, Winthrop University, 1983; Arnold Gingrich Memorial award, Federation of Fly Fishers, 1988; Harry R. E. Hampton Memorial award, South Carolina Wildlife Federation, 1993, for conservation journalism.

WRITINGS:

Dr. Livingstone and Sir Henry Morton Stanley: An Annotated Bibliography, Garland Publishing, 1977.
Sir Harry H. Johnston: A Bio-Bibliographical Study, Basler Afrika Bibliographien, 1977.
(Contributor) Helen Delpar, editor, *The Discoverers: An Encyclopedia of Exploration,* McGraw, 1980.
Africa's Great Hunters, Briar Patch, 1987.
Sir Richard F. Burton: A Bio-Bibliographical Study, G. K. Hall, 1990.
Modern Fly Fishing, North American Outdoor Group, 1993.

EDITOR

African and Afro-American History: A Review of Recent Trends, Conch, 1978.
(And contributor) *The Lion Hunter in Africa,* two volumes, Books of Rhodesia-Zimbabwe, revised edition, 1980.
A Hunter's Wanderings in Africa, Books of Zimbabwe, revised edition, 1981.
Elephant Hunting in East Equatorial Africa, Books of Zimbabwe, revised edition, 1981.
The Nile Tributaries of Abyssinia, Briar Patch, 1987.
Travels and Adventures in Southeast Africa, Briar Patch, 1987.
Richard Burton (young adult), Children's Press, 1991.
Tales of Whitetails: Archibald Rutledge's Great Deer Hunting Stories, University of South Carolina Press, 1992.
Hunting & Home in the Southern Heartland, University of South Carolina Press, 1992.

America's Greatest Game Bird: Archibald Rutledge's Turkey Hunting Tales, University of South Carolina Press, 1993.

(With C. A. Wechsler) *Last Casts and Stolen Hunts,* Live Oak Press, 1993.

Also editor of *Sporting Classics* Premier Collection revised editions of *De Shootinest Gent'man,* 1984, *Big Game Fishing,* 1986, *Ole Miss',* 1987, and *Random Cast,* 1987; senior editor, *Sporting Classics;* chief advisory editor, *Sporting Classics* Africana Sporting Series; co-editor, *Turkey & Turkey Hunting;* contributing editor, *Deer & Deer Hunting;* field editor, *Sporting Clays;* columnist, *North American Fisherman;* editor, "Outdoor Tennessee" series by University of Tennessee Press. Contributor, *Play-On Advantage: The Book of Soccer Officiating,* 1988. Correspondent, *The Herald.* Author of articles on British History in scholarly journals.

SIDELIGHTS: James Casada told *CA:* "In recent years my writing has turned increasingly to outdoor subjects. This gives me an opportunity to share with others the love of hunting, fishing, and nature which has been deeply ingrained in my soul since childhood. It is also rewarding to be able to utilize academic training to good advantage in writing on popular subjects which appeal to a broad general audience. In a sense I guess I have 'escaped' from the sometime sterility of the ivory tower; yet by the same token I realize that my work is stronger because of my years in academia. Most of all, realization has increasingly dawned that literary productions coming from an academician need not be pedantic or pedestrian."

*   *   *

CASARES, Adolfo Bioy
See BIOY CASARES, Adolfo

*   *   *

CESAIRE, Aime (Fernand) 1913-

PERSONAL: Born June 25, 1913, in Basse-Pointe, Martinique, West Indies; son of Fernand (a comptroller with the revenue service) and Marie (Hermine) Cesaire; married Suzanne Roussi (a teacher), July 10, 1937; children: Jacques, Jean-Paul, Francis, Ina, Marc, Michelle. *Education:* Attended Ecole Normale Superieure, Paris; Sorbonne, University of Paris, licencie es lettres.

ADDRESSES: Office—Assemblee Nationale, 75007 Paris, France; and La Mairie, 97200 Fort-de-France, Martinique, West Indies.

CAREER: Lycee of Fort-de-France, Martinique, teacher, 1940-45; member of the two French constituent assem-

blies, 1945-46; mayor of Fort-de-France, beginning 1945; deputy for Martinique in the French National Assembly, 1946. Conseiller general for the fourth canton (district) of Fort-de-France; president of the Parti Progressiste Martiniquais.

MEMBER: Society of African Culture (Paris; president).

AWARDS, HONORS: Aime Cesaire: The Collected Poetry was nominated for the *Los Angeles Times* Book Award, 1984.

WRITINGS:

(With Gaston Monnerville and Leopold Sedar-Senghor) *Commemoration du centenaire de l'abolition de l'esclavage: Discours pronounces a la Sorbonne le 27 avril 1948* (title means "Commemoration of the Centenary of the Abolition of Slavery: Speeches Given at the Sorbonne on April 27, 1948"), Presses Universitaires de France, 1948.

Discours sur le colonialisme, Reclame, 1950, 5th edition, Presence Africaine (Paris), 1970, translation by Joan Pinkham published as *Discourse on Colonialism,* Monthly Review Press, 1972.

Lettre a Maurice Thorez, 3rd edition, Presence Africaine, 1956, translation published as *Letter to Maurice Thorez,* 1957.

Toussaint L'Ouverture: La revolution francaise et le probleme coloniale (title means "Toussaint L'Ouverture: The French Revolution and the Colonial Problem"), Club Francais du Livre, 1960, revised edition, Presence Africaine, 1962.

Ouvres completes (title means "Complete Works"), three volumes, Editions Desormeaux, 1976.

(Contributor) *Studies in French,* William Marsh Rice University, 1977.

Culture and Colonization, University of Yaounde, 1978.

Also author of *Textes.*

POEMS

Les armes miraculeuses (title means "The Miracle Weapons"; also see below), Gallimard, 1946, reprinted, 1970.

Soleil Cou-Coupe (title means "Solar Throat Slashed"), K (Paris), 1948, reprinted (bound with *Antilles a main armee* by Charles Calixte under title *Poems from Martinique*), Kraus, 1970.

Corps perdu, illustrations by Pablo Picasso, 1949, translation by Clayton Eshleman and Annette Smith published as *Lost Body,* Braziller, 1986.

Cahier d'un retour au pays natal, Presence Africaine, 1956, 2nd edition, 1960, translation by Emil Snyders published as *Return to My Native Land,* Presence Africaine, 1968, translation by John Berger and Anna

Bostock published under same title, Penguin Books, 1969.

Ferrements (title means "Shackles"; also see below), Editions du Seuil, 1960.

Cadastre (also see below), Editions du Seuil, 1961, translation by Gregson Davis published as *Cadastre,* Third Press, 1972, translation by Snyders and Sanford Upson published under same title, Third Press, 1973.

State of the Union, translation by Eshleman and Dennis Kelly of selections from *Les armes miraculeuses, Ferrements,* and *Cadastre,* [Bloomington, IL], 1966.

Aime Cesaire: The Collected Poetry, translation and with an introduction by Eshleman and Smith, University of California Press, 1983.

Non-Vicious Circle: Twenty Poems, translation by Davis, Stanford University Press, 1985.

Lyric and Dramatic Poetry, 1946-82 (includes English translations of *Et les Chiens se taisaient* and *Moi, laminaire*), translation by Eshleman and Smith, University Press of Virginia, 1990.

Also author of *Moi, laminaire.*

PLAYS

Et les Chiens se Taisaient: Tragedie (title means "And the Dogs Were Silent: A Tragedy"), Presence Africaine, 1956.

La tragedie du roi Christophe, Presence Africaine, 1963, revised edition, 1973, translation by Ralph Manheim published as *The Tragedy of King Christophe,* Grove, 1970.

Une saison au Congo, Editions du Seuil, 1966, translation by Manheim published as *A Season in the Congo* (produced in New York at the Paperback Studio Theatre, July, 1970), Grove, 1969.

Une tempete: d'apres "le tempete" de Shakespeare. Adaptation pour un theatre negre, Editions du Seuil, 1969, translation by Richard Miller published as *A Tempest,* Ubu Repertory, 1986.

OTHER

Editor of *Tropiques,* 1941-45, and of *L'Afrique.*

SIDELIGHTS: Because of his role in creating and promoting negritude, a cultural movement which calls for black people to renounce Western society and adopt the traditional values of black civilization, Aime Cesaire is a prominent figure among blacks in the Third World. A native of the Caribbean island of Martinique, where he has served as mayor of the city of Fort-de-France since 1945, Cesaire also enjoys an international literary reputation for his poems and plays. His 1,000-line poem *Return to My Native Land,* a powerful piece written in extravagant, surreal language and dealing with the reawakening of black racial awareness, is a major work in contemporary

French-language literature. Cesaire is, Serge Gavronsky states in the *New York Times Book Review,* "one of the most powerful French poets of this century."

At the age of 18 Cesaire left his native Martinique, at that time a colony of France, to attend school in Paris. The city was the center for a number of political and cultural movements during the 1930s, several of which especially influenced the young Cesaire and his fellow black students. Marxism gave them a revolutionary perspective, while surrealism provided them with a modernist esthetic by which to express themselves. Together with Leon-Goutran Damas and Leopold Sedar Senghor, who later became president of Senegal, Cesaire founded the magazine *L'Etudiant Noir,* in which the ideology of negritude was first developed and explained. "Negritude . . . proclaimed a pride in black culture and, in turning their contemporaries' gaze away from the fascination of things French, these young students began a revolution in attitudes which was to make a profound impact after the war," Clive Wake explains in the *Times Literary Supplement.* The influence of the movement on black writers in Africa and the Caribbean was so pervasive that the term negritude has come to refer to "large areas of black African and Caribbean literature in French, roughly from the 1930s to the 1960s," Christopher Miller writes in the *Washington Post Book World.*

The first use of the word negritude occurred in Cesaire's poem *Return to My Native Land* (*Cahier d'un retour au pays natal*), first published in the magazine *Volontes* in 1939. In this poem, Cesaire combines an exuberant word-play, an encyclopedic vocabulary, and daring surreal metaphors with bits of African and Caribbean black history to create an "exorcism . . . of the poet's 'civilized' instincts, his lingering shame at belonging to a country and a race so abject, servile, petty and repressed as is his," Marjorie Perloff writes in the *American Poetry Review.* Gavronsky explains that the poem "is a concerted effort to affirm [Cesaire's] stature in French letters by a sort of poetic one-upmanship but also a determination to create a new language capable of expressing his African heritage." *Return to My Native Land,* Perloff maintains, is "a paratactic catalogue poem that piles up phrase upon phrase, image upon image, in a complex network of repetitions, its thrust is to define the threshold between sleep and waking—the sleep of oppression, the blind acceptance of the status quo, that gives way to rebirth, to a new awareness of what is and may be."

Written as Cesaire himself was leaving Paris to return to Martinique, *Return to My Native Land* reverberates with both personal and racial significance. The poet's definition of his own negritude comes to symbolize the growing self-awareness of all blacks of their cultural heritage. Judith Gleason, writing in the *Negro Digest,* believes that Cesaire's poetry is "grounded in the historical sufferings of a chosen people" and so "his is an angry, authentic vision of the promised land." Jean Paul Sartre, in an article for *The Black American Writer: Poetry and Drama,* writes that "Cesaire's words do not describe negritude, they do not designate it, they do not copy it from the outside like a painter with a model: they create it; they compose it under our very eyes."

Several critics see Cesaire as a writer who embodies the larger struggles of his people in all of his poetry. Hilary Okam of *Yale French Studies,* for example, argues that "Cesaire's poetic idiosyncrasies, especially his search for and use of uncommon vocabulary, are symptomatic of his own mental agony in the search for an exact definition of himself and, by extension, of his people and their common situation and destiny." Okam concludes that "it is clear from [Cesaire's] use of symbols and imagery, that despite years of alienation and acculturation he has continued to live in the concrete reality of his Negro-subjectivity." Writing in the *CLA Journal,* Ruth J. S. Simmons notes that although Cesaire's poetry is personal, he speaks from a perspective shared by many other blacks. "Poetry has been for him," Simmons explains, "an important vehicle of personal growth and self-revelation, [but] it has also been an important expression of the will and personality of a people. . . . [It is] impossible to consider the work of Cesaire outside of the context of the poet's personal vision and definition of his art. He defines his past as African, his present as Antillean and his condition as one of having been exploited. . . . To remove Cesaire from this context is to ignore what he was and still is as a man and as a poet."

The concerns found in *Return to My Native Land* ultimately transcend the personal or racial, addressing liberation and self-awareness in universal terms. Gleason calls *Return to My Native Land* "a masterpiece of cultural relevance, every bit as 'important' as 'The Wasteland,' its remarkable virtuosity will ensure its eloquence long after the struggle for human dignity has ceased to be viewed in racial terms." Andre Breton, writing in *What Is Surrealism?: Selected Writings,* also sees larger issues at stake in the poem. "What, in my eyes, renders this protest invaluable," Breton states, "is that it continually transcends the anguish which for a black man is inseparable from the lot of blacks in modern society, and unites with the protest of every poet, artist and thinker worthy of the name . . . to embrace the entire intolerable though amendable condition created for *man* by this society."

Cesaire's poetic language was strongly influenced by the French surrealists of the 1930s, but he uses familiar surrealist poetic techniques in a distinctive manner. Breton claims that Cesaire "is a black man who handles the French language as no white man can handle it today."

Alfred Cismaru states in *Renascence* that Cesaire's "separation from Europe makes it possible for him to break with clarity and description, and to become intimate with the fundamental essence of things. Under his powerful, poetic eye, perception knows no limits and pierces appearances without pity. Words emerge and explode like firecrackers, catching the eye and the imagination of the reader. He makes use of the entire dictionary, of artificial and vulgar words, of elegant and forgotten ones, of technical and invented vocabulary, marrying it to Antillean and African syllables, and allowing it to play freely in a sort of flaming folly that is both a challenge and a tenacious attempt at mystification."

The energy of Cesaire's poetic language is seen by some critics as a form of literary violence, with the jarring images and forceful rhythms of the poetry assaulting the reader. Perloff finds that Cesaire's "is a language so violently charged with meaning that each word falls on the ear (or hits the eye) with resounding force." Gleason explains this violence as the expression of an entire race, not just of one man: "Cesaire's is the turbulent poetry of the spiritually dislocated, of the damned. His images strike through the net. . . . Cesaire's is the Black Power of the imagination."

This violent energy is what first drew Cesaire to surrealism. The surrealist artists and writers of the 1930s saw themselves as rebels against a stale and outmoded culture. Their works were meant to revive and express unconscious, suppressed, and forbidden desires. Politically, they aligned themselves with the revolutionary left. As Gavronsky explains, "Cesaire's efforts to forge a verbal medium that would identify him with the opposition to existing political conditions and literary conventions [led him to] the same camp as the Surrealists, who had combined a new poetics that liberated the image from classical restraints with revolutionary politics influenced by Marx and his followers." Cesaire was to remain a surrealist for many years, but he eventually decided that his political concerns would best be served by more realistic forms of writing. "For decades," Karl Keller notes in the *Los Angeles Times Book Review,* "[Cesaire] found the surreal aesthetically revolutionary, but in the face of the torture and the suffering, he has pretty well abandoned it as a luxury."

In the late 1950s Cesaire began to write realistic plays for the theatre, hoping in this way to attract a larger audience to his work. These plays are more explicitly political than his poetry and focus on historical black nationalist leaders of the Third World. *The Tragedy of King Christophe (La tragedie du roi Christophe)* is a biographical drama about King Henri Christophe of Haiti, a black leader of that island nation in the early nineteenth century. After fighting in a successful revolution against the French colonists, Christophe assumed power and made himself king. But his cruelty and arbitrary use of power led to a rebellion in turn against his own rule, and Christophe committed suicide. Writing in *Studies in Black Literature,* Henry Cohen calls *The Tragedy of King Christophe* "one of French America's finest literary expressions." *A Season in the Congo* (*Une saison au Congo*) follows the political career of Patrice Lumumba, first president of the Republic of the Congo in Africa. Lumumba's career was also tragic. With the independence of the Congo in 1960, Lumumba became president of the new nation. But the resulting power struggles among black leaders led in 1961 to Lumumba's assassination by his political opponents. The reviewer for *Prairie Schooner* calls *A Season in the Congo* "a passionate and poetic drama." Wake remarks that Cesaire's plays have "greatly widened [his] audience and perhaps tempted them to read the poetry." Gavronsky claims that "in the [1960s, Cesaire] was . . . the leading black dramatist writing in French."

Despite the international acclaim he has received for his poetry and plays, Cesaire is still best known on Martinique for his political career. Since 1945 he has served as mayor of Fort-de-France and as a member of the French National Assembly. For the first decade of his career Cesaire was affiliated with the Communist bloc of the assembly, then moved to the Parti du Regroupement Africain et des Federalistes for a short time, and is now president of the Parti Progressiste Martiniquais, a leftist political organization. Cesaire's often revolutionary rhetoric is in sharp contrast to his usually moderate political actions. He opposes independence for Martinique, for example, and was instrumental in having the island declared an oversea department of France—a status similar to that of Puerto Rico to the United States. And as a chief proponent of negritude, which calls for blacks to reject Western culture, Cesaire nonetheless writes his works in French, not in his native black language of creole.

But what may seem contradictory in Cesaire's life and work is usually seen by critics as the essential tension that makes his voice uniquely important. A. James Arnold, in his *Modernism and Negritude: The Poetry and Poetics of Aime Cesaire,* examines and accepts the tension between Cesaire's European literary sources and his black subject matter and between his modernist sensibility and his black nationalist concerns. Miller explains that "Arnold poses the riddle of Cesaire with admirable clarity" and "effectively defuses . . . either a wholly African or a wholly European Cesaire." This uniting of the European and African is also noted by Clayton Eshleman and Annette Smith in their introduction to *Aime Cesaire: The Collected Poetry.* They describe Cesaire as "a bridge between the twain that, in principle, should never meet, Europe and Africa. . . . It was by borrowing European techniques that he succeeded in expressing his Africanism in its purest

form." Similarly, Sartre argues that "in Cesaire, the great surrealist tradition is realized, it takes on its definitive meaning and is destroyed: surrealism—that European movement—is taken from the Europeans by a Black man who turns it against them and gives it vigorously defined function."

It is because of his poetry that Cesaire is primarily known worldwide, while in the Third World he is usually seen as an important black nationalist theoretician. Speaking of his poetry, Gavronsky explains that Cesaire is "among the major French poets of this century." Cismaru believes that Cesaire "is a poet's poet when he stays clear of political questions, a tenacious and violent propagandist when the theme requires it. His place in contemporary French letters . . . is assured in spite of the fact that not many agree with his views on Whites in general, nor with his opinions on Europe, in particular." *Return to My Native Land* has been his most influential work, particularly in the Third World where, Wake notes, "by the 1960s it was widely known and quoted because of its ideological and political significance." To European and American critics, *Return to My Native Land* is seen as a masterpiece of surrealist literature. Cesaire's coining of the term negritude and his continued promotion of a distinctly black culture separate from Western culture has made him especially respected in the emerging black nations. Eshleman and Smith report that "although Cesaire was by no means the sole exponent of negritude, the word is now inseparable from his name, and largely responsible for his prominent position in the Third World."

BIOGRAPHICAL/CRITICAL SOURCES:

BOOKS

Aime Cesaire: The Collected Poetry, translated and with an introduction by Clayton Eshleman and Annette Smith, University of California Press, 1983.

Aime Cesaire: Ecrivain Martiniquais, Fernand Nathan, 1967.

Antoine, R., *Le Tragedie du roi Christophe d'Aime Cesaire,* Pedagogie Moderne, 1984.

Arnold, A. James, *Modernism and Negritude: The Poetry and Poetics of Aime Cesaire,* Harvard University Press, 1981.

Bigsby, C. W. E., editor, *The Black American Writer: Poetry and Drama,* Volume 2, Penguin Books, 1971.

Bouelet, Remy Sylvestre, *Espaces et dialectique du heros cesairien,* L'Harmattan, 1987.

Breton, Andre, *What Is Surrealism?: Selected Writings,* edited by Franklin Rosemont, Monad Press, 1978.

Contemporary Literary Criticism, Gale, Volume 19, 1981, Volume 32, 1985.

Kesteloot, Lilyan, *Aime Cesaire,* P. Seghers, 1962, new edition, 1970.

Leiner, Jacqueline, *Soleil eclate: Melanges offerts a Aime Cesaire a l'occasion de son soixante-dixieme anniversaire par une equipe internationale d'artiste et de chercheurs,* Gunter Narr Verlag (Tubingen), 1985.

Ngal, M., editor, *Cesaire 70,* Silex, 1985.

Owusu-Sarpong, Albert, *Le Temps historique dans l'oeuvre theatrale a'Aime Cesaire,* Naaman, 1987.

Pallister, Janis L., *Aime Cesaire,* Twayne, 1991.

Scharfman, Ronnie Leah, *Engagement and the Language of the Subject in the Poetry of Aime Cesaire,* University Presses of Florida, 1980.

Songolo, Aliko, *Aime Cesaire: Une Poetique de la decouverte,* L'Harmattan, 1985.

PERIODICALS

Afro-Hispanic Review, January, 1985, p. 1.

American Poetry Review, January-February, 1984.

Callaloo, summer, 1989, p. 612.

Choice, March, 1991, p. 1141.

CLA Journal, March, 1976; September, 1984; December, 1986.

Comparative Literature Studies, summer, 1978.

Concerning Poetry, fall, 1984.

Culture et Developpement, Volume 15, number 1, 1983, pp. 57-63.

Diagonales, October 12, 1989, pp. 5-6.

French Studies Bulletin, 1990.

Journal of Ethnic Studies, spring, 1981.

Journal of West Indian Literature, October, 1986; June, 1987.

La Licorne, number 9, 1985, pp. 153-160.

Le Monde, December, 1981.

L'Esprit Createur, spring, 1992, p. 110.

Los Angeles Times Book Review, December 4, 1983.

Negro Digest, January, 1970.

New Scholar, number 8, 1982, pp. 1-2.

New York Times Book Review, February 19, 1984.

Notre Librairie, number 74, 1984, pp. 9-13.

Prairie Schooner, spring, 1972.

Quadrant, November, 1984, pp. 50-53.

Renascence, winter, 1974.

Revue de Litterature Comparee, April/June, 1986.

Revue Francophone de Louisiane, spring, 1988, p. 1.

San Francisco Review of Books, Volume 15, number 3, 1990, p. 36.

Studies in Black Literature, winter, 1974.

Studies in the Humanities, June, 1984.

Times Literary Supplement, July 19, 1985.

Twentieth Century Literature, July, 1972.

Washington Post Book World, February 5, 1984.

Yale French Studies, number 53, 1976.*

CHRISTOPHER, Nicholas 1951-

PERSONAL: Born February 28, 1951, in New York, NY; married Constance (a writer), November 21, 1980. *Education:* Harvard College, A.B. (cum laude), 1973. *Avocational Interests:* Travel, film, ancient history.

ADDRESSES: Agent—c/o Anne Sibbald, Janklow & Nesbit Associates, 598 Madison Ave., New York, NY 10022.

CAREER: Poet and novelist. Adjunct professor of English, New York University; lecturer, Columbia University.

MEMBER: PEN.

AWARDS, HONORS: Amy Lowell Poetry travelling scholarship, 1985; fellowship, New York Foundation for the Arts, 1986; fellowship, National Endowment for the Arts, 1987; Peter I. B. Lavan Award, Academy of American Poets, 1991; Guggenheim fellowship in poetry, 1993.

WRITINGS:

On Tour With Rita (poems), Knopf, 1982.
A Short History of the Island of Butterflies (poems), Viking, 1986.
The Soloist (novel), Viking, 1986.
Desperate Characters (poems), Viking, 1988.
(Editor) *Under 35: The New Generation of American Poets,* Doubleday, 1989.
In the Year of the Comet (poems), Viking, 1992.
5 Degrees and Other Poems, Viking, 1994.
(Editor) *Walk on the Wild Side: Urban American Poetry Since 1975,* Scribner/Collier, 1994.

Work represented in anthologies, including *New York: Poems,* Avon, 1980, *The Morrow Anthology of Younger American Poets,* Morrow, 1985, and *The Grand Street Reader,* Summit, 1986. Contributor to magazines, including *New Yorker, New York Review, Nation, Grand Street, New Republic,* and *New York Times Book Review.*

SIDELIGHTS: In his first published collection of poems, *On Tour with Rita,* Nicholas Christopher presents a transcontinental nomad's fleeting glimpses of landscapes ranging from Mexico, Rome, and New Orleans to the Greek Islands. Reading like a series of postcards, according to J. D. McClatchy in *Poetry,* the poems are lucid dreams "in which Rita, the poet's muse and mirror, reflects the life around her." In his attempt to "capture the elusiveness of objects of desire," says Bruce Bennett in *Nation,* Christopher's shimmering, phantasmagorical images provide "little of substance to grasp." Richard Tillinghast in *New York Times Book Review,* however, states that though "one may experience a dizziness and exasperation" with some of the poems, "the wit and panache of passages . . . make reading Mr. Christopher a delight."

A Short History of the Island of Butterflies draws on similar themes and styles as *On Tour with Rita*. Opting for similar exotic settings—Italy and the Greek Islands—Christopher "approaches the world with a hedonist's exuberance," says David Wojahn in *New York Times Book Review*. Though Christopher's Byronic tone is "apt to become excessive and grandiloquent," claims Wojahn, "his poems are lushly textured, astutely detailed and above all sensuous," devoid of the "naive sensuality" that marked *On Tour with Rita*. J. P. White, reviewing the book in *Poetry* notes Christopher's "sensualist's eye for detail" and his "profusion of lush pictorial elements," but prefers the "grittier emotional range" of several of the poems ("Winter Night," "The Partisan," "Losing Altitude," and "Notes at Summer's End") that provide "a welcome relief from the tropical narcosis" of the other works.

Christopher trades in the lush tropical settings of his poetry for the backdrop of the classical music scene in his first novel, *The Soloist*. Max Randal is a former child prodigy who, at age 33, attempts to revive his stalled career as a concert pianist. Surrounded by all the trappings of his early success; beautiful women, eccentric friends, and excessive luxury, Max seeks solace for his tortured soul by maintaining an arduous rehearsal schedule, hoping to recover his inspiration in time for his Carnegie Hall comeback. Although Christopher Zenowich in *Chicago Tribune* characterizes Max's angst as "self-conscious soul-searching and Byronic posturing," he praises "Christopher's instinct for the power of a good tale [that] overcomes the occasional awkwardness of narration." Laura Kuhn in *Los Angeles Times* calls *The Soloist* "melodramatic . . . in a commonplace way," but asserts that the only serious flaw of this first novel "is . . . perpetuating the notion that the Romantic hero needs to be obsessed." However, "it is not character . . . that provides motive and momentum for 'The Soloist'," says Isa Kapp in *New York Times Book Review*, "but music."

In *Desperate Characters*, Christopher alters his previous poetic style and combines it with a novelistic narrative to create what *Virginia Quarterly Review* dubs "an absurdist's detective fiction." The story is summarized by Jane Mendelsohn in *Village Voice*: "The noir victim hangs out. He waits. Before he can say *Maltese Falcon*, people lie to him, the police suspect him, and women, for no apparent reason, fling themselves at him." Robert B. Shaw in *Poetry* comments that the stylized situations knowingly parody the film noir genre to create "a sense of purgatory with no exit and no redemptive purpose." Declaring the urban setting in *Desperate Characters* "vapid" but possessing an "irresistible neon intensity," *New York Times Book Review* critic Andy Brumer says the "punk-rococo imagery" is "a phantasmagorical collage reminiscent of the film 'Blade Runner'." Conversely, William Logan in *Washington Post Book World* states that "Christopher's overactive fancy . . . slides too easily into camp and trashy kitsch," while Mendelsohn lauds Christopher's "cool melancholy voice" that conveys "a remarkable mix of accessible outrageous humor with subtle psychological insight."

Reviewing the collection of poems *In the Year of the Comet, Washinton Post Book World's* Harriet Zinnes notes that Christopher's "language is always accessible, and though his internal structures can be calculating . . . he writes with a contemporary conscience." *Poetry* critic J. D. McClatchy places Christopher in good company when he summarizes that the poet "has a style in which are folded strands of Apollinaire, Frank O'Hara, James Tate, and Nanzia Nunzio." David Baker in *Poetry* further describes Christopher's style as approaching "contemporary neoclassicism" in his use of "erudition to express experience." Renowned poet Anthony Hecht as quoted in *New York Times Book Review* says, "Mr. Christopher's poetry is not merely extraordinarily good, but seems to me altogether in a class by itself."

Nicholas Christopher told *CA:* "I write daily, whether at home or traveling."

BIOGRAPHICAL/CRITICAL SOURCES:

PERIODICALS

Chicago Tribune, February 9, 1986.
Los Angeles Times, April 3, 1986.
Nation, March 26, 1983.
New York Times Book Review, May, 1 1983; April 20, 1986; June 8, 1986; February 11, 1990.
Poetry, December, 1983; December, 1986; August, 1989; November, 1992.
Village Voice, September 27, 1988.
Virginia Quarterly Review, winter, 1989.
Washington Post Book World, December 25, 1988; February 16, 1992.

* * *

CITATI, Pietro 1930-

PERSONAL: Born February 20, 1930, in Florence, Italy; son of Antonio and Andreina (Amadeo) Citati; married Elena Londini, March 21, 1953; children: Stefano. *Education:* University of Pisa, laurea in lettere, 1951. *Religion:* Roman Catholic.

ADDRESSES: Home—Via Lutezia 10, Rome, Italy. *Office*—Fondazione Lorenzo Valla, via San Godenzo 37, Rome, Italy.

CAREER: le Giorno, Mailand, Italy, literary critic, 1960-73; *le Corriere della Sera,* Mailand, literary critic,

1973-88; *la Repubblica*, Rome, Italy, literary critic, 1988—. University of Munich, lecturer in Italian, 1952-54.

AWARDS, HONORS: Premio Viareggio, 1970, for *Goethe;* Premio Bagutta, 1980, for *Vita breve di Katherine Mansfield;* Premio Strega, 1984, for *Tolstoy.*

WRITINGS:

(Compiler with Attilio Bertolucci) *Gli umoristi moderni* (title means "Modern Humorists"), Garzanti, 1956.

(Editor and translator) Leo Spitzer, *Marcel Proust e altri saggi di letteratura francese moderna* (title means "Marcel Proust and Other Essays of Modern French Literature"), Einaudi, 1960.

Goethe, Mondadori, 1970, translation by Raymond Rosenthal published under same title, Dial, 1974.

Il te del cappellaio matto (title means "The Mad Hatter's Tea-Party"), Mondadori, 1972.

(Editor) Emilio Cecchi, *La Letteratura italiana del Novecento* (title means "Italian Twentieth-Century Literature"), Mondadori, 1972.

Immagini di Alessandro Manzoni (title means "An Idea of Alessandro Manzoni"), Mondadori, 1973.

Alessandro Magno (title means "Alexander the Great"), Rizzoli (Milan), 1974.

(Translator) Athanasius, *Vita Antonii,* Fondazione Lorenzo Valla and Mondadori, 1974.

La Primavera di Cosroe, Rizzoli, 1977.

I frantumi del Mondo, Rizzoli, 1978.

Il velo nero, Rizzoli, 1979.

Vita breve di Katherine Mansfield, Rizzoli, 1980.

I racconti dei gatti e delle scimmie, Rizzoli, 1981.

Il migliore dei mondi impossibili, Rizzoli, 1982.

Tolstoy, Longanesi, 1984, translation by Rosenthal published under same title, Schocken, 1986.

Il sogno della camera rossa, Rizzoli, 1986.

Kafka, Rizzoli, 1987, translation by Rosenthal published under same title, Knopf, 1990.

Storia prima felice, poi dolentissima e funesta, Rizzoli, 1989.

Ritratti di donne, Rizzoli, 1992.

Also editor, with others, of "Scrittori greci e latini" series, published for Fondazione Lorenzo Valla by Mondadori, 1974—.

SIDELIGHTS: Kafka, Pietro Citati's biography of early twentieth-century Czech writer Franz Kafka, "should surprise even the most devoted Kafka student with its insights into the working of the writer's inner life, and its often controversial readings of individual works" states Michiko Kakutani in the *New York Times.* Kakutani adds that the book "should not, however, be read on its own as a comprehensive introduction to the writer's life and

times, for its depiction of Kafka and his writings is highly impressionistic and subjective."

Citati's biographical style, labelled "psychobiography," means "that Citati dares to write as if he knows Kafka omnisciently, as if Kafka were a character in a novel," opines John Calvin Batchelor in the *Washington Post Book World.* Kakutani, who describes the book as "half biographical sketch, half interpretive essay," also notes that "instead of meticulously chronicling the ups and downs of Kafka's life, the facts of his childhood and grown-up life, Mr. Citati attempts . . . to make an imaginative leap and show the reader what it felt like to be Franz Kafka." Joseph Coates observes in the Chicago *Tribune Books* that "Citati's approach—which is virtually a prolonged inhabitation of Kafka's mind—quarries fresh insights from most of the major works, including the three great novels *Amerika, The Trial* and *The Castle.*"

Kakutani concludes that, although one may challenge Citati's interpretations and opinions, the author's "views are both provocative and eloquently argued, and they make for a serious contribution to the ever-growing body of Kafka scholarship." Coates asserts that those familiar with Kafka's major works "will read this book with growing excitement and a transformed understanding of a profoundly religious man who had the bad luck to live in an age of bad faith."

BIOGRAPHICAL/CRITICAL SOURCES:

BOOKS

Pulce, Graziella, *Lettura d'autore: conversazioni di critica e di letteratura con Giorgio Manganelli, Pietro Citati e Alberto Arbasino,* Bulzoni (Rome), 1988.

PERIODICALS

New York Times, February 9, 1990.

New York Times Book Review, February 8, 1987, p. 25; March 4, 1990, p. 24.

Tribune Books (Chicago), February 4, 1990, p. 6.

Washington Post Book World, February 18, 1990, p. 4.

*   *   *

CLARK, Margaret Goff   1913-

PERSONAL: Born March 7, 1913, in Oklahoma City, OK; daughter of Raymond Finla and Fanny (Church) Goff; married Charles Robert Clark, 1937; children: Robert Allen, Marcia Clark Noel. *Education:* Attended Columbia University, 1934; New York State College for Teachers (now State University of New York at Buffalo), B.S., 1936. *Avocational Interests:* Archaeology, square dancing, swimming, travel, history, bridge, helping endangered animals.

ADDRESSES: Home—334 Shoreland Dr., Ft. Myers, FL 33905. *Agent*—Dorothy Markinko, McIntosh & Otis, Inc., 310 Madison Ave., New York, NY 10017.

CAREER: Elementary school teacher in Niagara, NY, 1933-34, and Buffalo, NY, 1934-39; teacher of creative writing in adult education programs, 1960-61; Georgian College Summer School of the Arts, Huntsville, Ontario, teacher of creative writing, 1974-78. Formerly deputy town clerk, Niagara.

MEMBER: National League of American Pen Women (Southwest Florida branch). Association of Professional Women Writers (president, 1960-61), Mystery Writers of America, Authors Guild, Authors League of America, Delta Sigma Epsilon, Delta Kappa Gamma (honorary member), Alpha Delta Kappa (honorary member).

AWARDS, HONORS: Distinguished alumnus award, State University of New York at Buffalo, 1979; Children's Choice Award, 1980, for *Who Stole Kathy Young?*; *The Vanishing Manatee* was named to a list of best science trade books for young readers, 1990.

WRITINGS:

The Mystery of Seneca Hill, F. Watts, 1961.
The Mystery of the Buried Indian Mask, F. Watts, 1962.
Mystery of the Marble Zoo, Funk, 1964.
Mystery at Star Lake, Funk, 1965.
Adirondack Mountain Mystery, Funk, 1966.
The Mystery of the Missing Stamps, Funk, 1967.
Danger at Niagara, Funk, 1968.
Freedom Crossing, Funk, 1969.
Benjamin Banneker, Garrard, 1971.
Mystery Horse, Dodd, 1972.
Their Eyes on the Stars: Four Black Writers, Garrard, 1973.
John Muir, Garrard, 1974.
Death at Their Heels, Dodd, 1975.
Mystery of Sebastian Island, Dodd, 1976.
Mystery in the Flooded Museum, Dodd, 1978.
Barney and the UFO, Dodd, 1979.
Who Stole Kathy Young?, Dodd, 1980.
Barney in Space, Dodd, 1981.
The Boy from the UFO, Scholastic, 1981.
Barney on Mars, Dodd, 1983.
The Latchkey Mystery, Dodd, 1985.
The Vanishing Manatee, Dutton, 1990.
The Endangered Florida Panther, Dutton, 1993.

Also author of a talking book, *The Mysterious Hole,* International Learning Co., 1975. Author of twenty-five one-act plays and numerous poems. Contributor of more than two hundred short stories to American and Canadian magazines, including *American Girl, Ingenue, Teen Talk,* and *Instructor.* Contributor to anthologies, including *The New People and Progress,* Scott, Foresman, 1955; *Let's Read,* Henry Holt, 1955; *Arrivals and Departures,* Allyn & Bacon, 1957; *Stories to Live By,* Platt, 1960; *Time of Starting Out,* F. Watts, 1962; *Acting, Acting,* F. Watts, 1962; *Pressing Onward,* Pacific Press Publishing Association, 1964; *They Loved the Land,* Garrard, 1974; *Venture,* Economy Co., 1976; *ReadAbility,* Lippincott, 1978; *Best of Aesop's Fables,* Little, Brown, 1990.

WORK IN PROGRESS: Researching and writing a nonfiction book about the Florida black bear.

SIDELIGHTS: Margaret Goff Clark began writing when her two children were young; the age level of the stories grew along with her children. Her book, *Mystery in the Flooded Museum,* was inspired by the story of "a resourceful young curator who saved the contents of the Fort Pitt Museum in Pittsburgh, Pennsylvania." Clark explains: "With only three hours warning of an impending flood, he rented a U-Haul truck, recruited some young college students and, with the help of his staff, moved the valuable artifacts to higher ground. It was a ready-made story, but how could I turn it into a flood-connected mystery for young readers? Much research and many false starts later, I completed *Mystery in the Flooded Museum.*

"My book *Who Stole Kathy Young?* was the result of a sudden idea: what if a teenaged girl saw her best friend kidnapped? On vacation on the Gulf Coast of Texas I found the background ingredients I wanted: the rich seashore life of shrimp boats and sea smells, long-legged birds in the reedy shallows, and besides all this, a mysterious old house built in the nineteenth century by a cousin of Robert Fulton. I now had appropriate places where Kathy, an attractive, profoundly deaf girl, could be held captive.

"Seeing a manatee swimming in the Caloosahatchee River behind our mobile home in Ft. Myers, Florida, sent me to the local library for information about this enormous marine animal. When the librarian said she had no books on the subject and begged that I write about it, I began a long and interesting research. I became more and more concerned about the fate of this friendly, gentle creature. *The Vanishing Manatee* was the result." Clark adds: "My interest in endangered animals [also] led to my next book, *The Endangered Florida Panther.*"

Clark explained to *CA* how she shares her love of writing and experience with young people: "I give talks to schools. My subjects are based on current books—on how the book developed, how I researched for it, how to get started in writing, and so on." She added, "I do book signings, most recently in Disney World, Niagara Falls, New York, and Ft. Myers, Florida."

In 1962, Clark was adopted by the Seneca Indians. According to Clark, she was given the Indian name, "Dehyistoesh," which means "she who writes and publishes."

BIOGRAPHICAL/CRITICAL SOURCES:

PERIODICALS

Buffalo Evening News, March 9, 1964; December 14, 1980.

Niagara Falls Gazette, July 31, 1960; March 11, 1962; April 19, 1964; August 16, 1964.

*   *   *

CLARK, Thomas Willard 1941-
(Tom Clark)

PERSONAL: Born March 1, 1941, in Chicago, IL; son of Arthur Willard (an artist) and Rita Mary (Kearin) Clark; married Angelica Louise Heinegg, March 22, 1968; children: Juliet. *Education:* Attended John Carroll University, 1959-60; University of Michigan, B.A., 1963; Cambridge University, M.A., 1965; graduate study at University of Essex, 1965-67.

ADDRESSES: Home—1740 Marin Ave., Berkeley, CA 94707. *Agent*—Glen Hartley, 25 West 19th St., New York, NY 10011.

CAREER: Poet and writer. Poetry editor, *Paris Review,* 1963-73; instructor in American poetry, University of Essex, 1966-67; senior writer, *Boulder Monthly,* 1978-79; instructor in poetics, New College of California, 1988—.

AWARDS, HONORS: Hopwood Prize, University of Michigan, 1963; Fulbright fellowship, 1963-65; Bess Hokin Prize from *Poetry,* 1966; Rockefeller fellowship, 1967-68; Poets Foundation Award, 1967; George Dillon Memorial Prize from *Poetry,* 1968; Guggenheim fellowship, 1970-71; National Endowment for the Arts grant, 1985.

WRITINGS:

POETRY

Airplanes, Once Press, 1966.
The Sand Burg: Poems, Ferry Press, 1966.
(With Ron Padgett) *Bun,* Angel Hair Books, 1968.
(With Lewis Warsh) *Chicago,* Angel Hair Books, 1969.
Stones, Harper, 1969.
Air, Harper, 1970.
Green, Black Sparrow Press, 1971.
The No Book, Ant's Forefoot, 1971.
John's Heart, Grossman, 1972.
(With Padgett and Ted Berrigan) *Back in Boston Again,* Telegraph Books, 1972.
Smack, Black Sparrow Press, 1972.

Suite, Black Sparrow Press, 1974.
Blue, Black Sparrow Press, 1974.
At Malibu, Kulchur, 1975.
Baseball, Figures, 1976.
Fan Poems, North Atlantic, 1976.
35, Poltroon Press, 1978.
How I Broke In/Six Modern Masters, Tombouctou Books, 1978
When Things Get Tough on Easy Street: Selected Poems, 1963-1978, Black Sparrow Press, 1978.
The Mutabilitie of the English Lyrick, (parodies) Poltroon Press, 1979.
The End of the Line, Little Caesar Press, 1980.
Nine Songs, Turkey Press, 1981.
A Short Guide to the High Plains, Cadmus, 1981.
Heartbreak Hotel, Toothpaste Press, 1981.
Journey to the Ulterior, Am Here/Immediate, 1981.
The Rodent Who Came to Dinner, Am Here/Immediate, 1981.
Under the Fortune Palms, Turkey Press, 1982.
Dark as Day, Smithereens Press, 1983.
Paradise Resisted: Selected Poems, 1978-1984, Black Sparrow Press, 1984.
Property, Illuminati Books, 1984.
The Border, Coffee House Press, 1984.
Easter Sunday, Coffee House Press, 1987.
Disordered Ideas, Black Sparrow Press, 1987.
Fractured Karma, Black Sparrow Press, 1990.
Sleepwalker's Fate: New and Selected Poems, 1965-1991, Black Sparrow Press, 1992.
Junkets on a Sad Planet: Scenes from the Life of John Keats, Black Sparrow Press, 1993.

BIOGRAPHIES

Neil Young, Coach House Press, 1971.
(With Mark Fidrych) *No Big Deal,* Lippincott, 1977.
The World of Damon Runyon, Harper, 1978.
Jack Kerouac: A Biography, Harcourt, 1984.
Late Returns: A Personal Memoir of Ted Berrigan, Tombouctou, 1985.
Charles Olson: The Allegory of a Poet's Life, Norton, 1991.
Robert Creeley and the Genius of the American Common Place: Together with the Poet's Own Autobiography, New Directions, 1993.

NONFICTION

Champagne and Baloney: The Rise and Fall of Finley's A's, Harper, 1976.
One Last Round for the Shuffler: A Blacklisted Ballplayer's Story, Truck Books, 1979.
The Great Naropa Poetry Wars, Cadmus Editions, 1980.
Kerouac's Last Word: Jack Kerouac in Escapade, Water Row Press, 1987.

The Poetry Beat: Reviewing the Eighties, University of Michigan Press, 1990.

FICTION

A Conversation with Hitler (stories), Black Sparrow Press, 1978.
Who Is Sylvia? (novel), Blue Wind Press, 1979.
The Last Gas Station and Other Stories, Black Sparrow Press, 1980.
The Master (novel), Harcourt, 1984.
The Exile of Celine (novelized biography), Random House, 1986.

OTHER

Also author of *The Emperor of the Animals* (three act play), first produced in London, 1966. Contributor of book reviews to the *San Francisco Chronicle, Los Angeles Times* and the *Los Angeles Herald-Examiner.*

SIDELIGHTS: Tom Clark has combined the seemingly-contradictory roles of poet, biographer, and sports writer during his writing career. Among Clark's books are a book co-written with star pitcher Mark Fidrych, numerous poems about such sports legends as Catfish Hunter, Vida Blue and Bert Campaneris, and a history of the Oakland A's baseball team. As Steven Young notes in *Contemporary Poets,* "Clark is a *Fan;* he doesn't write about baseball, he celebrates it." Speaking to *CA,* Clark easily finesses the apparent gap between his interests in poetry and sports: "I think they have a natural relationship. The best poems and the best baseball games share a dramatic tension you can't find in very many other places."

Though he is known for his poems about sports, Clark writes poems in a wide range of styles and on many subjects. He has written parodies of traditional poetry in *The Mutabilitie of the English Lyrick,* poems of tribute to such figures as Lenny Bruce, and political poems. Lewis Warsh in *Poetry* claims that Clark lets "go of all restrictions as to what goes into the poem while creating the ability to make everything come out right." He possesses, Chad Walsh writes in *Book World,* "the ability to look at the ordinary world and see it for the first time, with the freshness of a Zen Buddhist painting a landscape or composing a haiku."

Many of Clark's poems are concerned with the state of contemporary America. In *The End of the Line,* for example, Clark presents an "affecting, anguished vision of a collapsing America," as Amy Gerstler writes in *Poetry News.* "A writer known and loved for his enthusiasm, curiosity, purity and scope of imagination, and an amazing ability to blend humor and cosmic concerns, Clark has turned the considerable force of his gifts to produce a despairing book, concerned with the fate of his country." In *Paradise Resisted,* Clark examines the American West, offering "a

wide-ranging body of work examining 'the West'—a state of mind, unique geographical terrains, qualities of light, restless, boundless dreams," according to Don Skiles in the *San Francisco Chronicle.* Skiles finds the collection to be "a tough, beautiful book—a rare combination. . . . This is the real West of our time, as significant as John Ford's cinematic legends."

Clark's collection *Sleepwalker's Fate: New and Selected Poems, 1965-1991* contains an overview of his poetic work over several decades. Reviewing the book for the *San Francisco Chronicle,* Joel Lewis explains that "Clark has been one of American poetry's most consistent and constant chroniclers of our long sleepwalk to parts unknown. . . . What we have . . . in the 'Sleepwalker's Fate' is poetry's first successful X-ray of [the] American psyche as it swims through the '90s." Writing in *Small Press,* Peggy Shumaker found the collection to be "complex, alive in every line, tender, unbearable, and necessary. Clark embraces in one book twenty-five years of poems, plus baseball, classicism, jazz, physics, trout kills, popular culture, 'the smashed weirdness of the raving cadenzas of God,' and 'infinite gifts we are unable to discern.' "

In prose, Clark has made a mark as a (sometimes semi-fictional) biographer of pop musician Neil Young, and of such literary figures as Damon Runyon, Jack Kerouac, Ted Berrigan, Louis Ferdinand Celine, Charles Olson, and Robert Creeley. Clark's biography of Jack Kerouac draws on previous studies and personal accounts to give an overview of the Beat novelist's career. Clark focuses in particular on how Kerouac used the details of his life to create memorable fiction. The biography, John Montgomery notes in the Toronto *Globe and Mail,* "is readable, condensed and documented with extensive footnotes. . . . This book is an antidote and a model for academics who usually aren't able to cope with a writer like Kerouac." K. N. Richwine of *Choice* finds that *Jack Kerouac* "is written with the grace, clarity, and density of detail of one of the better *New Yorker* profiles."

In tackling the life of poet Charles Olson, Clark again provides a study of the relationship between a writer and his work. His *Charles Olson: The Allegory of a Poet's Life* is, according to Bruce Campbell in the *Review of Contemporary Fiction,* "clear, compelling, and makes Olson's life more coherent than it has ever been." "Olson," writes Thomas M. Disch in the *Los Angeles Times Book Review,* "was a pioneer in the dismantling of the college core curriculum and its replacement by a kind of autodidacticism that differed little from autointoxication. He was, in short, the high priest of high times, and Tom Clark's biography is a balefully fascinating account of both the man and the milieu he did so much to form."

With the biographical novel *The Exile of Celine,* Clark explored territory some reviewers found unnecessary. The story of French novelist Louis Ferdinand Celine's flight to Denmark after World War II, *The Exile of Celine* covers a story already told by Celine himself in a trilogy of novels written in the 1950s. "If," writes Francois Sauzey in the *New York Times Book Review,* "you have read Celine's own chronicle of the period . . ., why, you may ask in disbelief, would anyone even try to re-evoke novelistically Celine's hectic landscape?" Christopher Lehmann-Haupt of the *New York Times* admits "one finds it hard to tell what Mr. Clark is up to in his novel." But Charles Monaghan in the *Washington Post* finds much value in the novel. "The novel form," Monaghan argues, "permits Clark to make the most of the story line, to pick and choose his material as a biographer could not. . . . He has recreated the best moments of Celine's books and done it in a clean, sweet prose that displays a poet's concern for conciseness."

BIOGRAPHICAL/CRITICAL SOURCES:

BOOKS

Contemporary Poets, 5th edition, St. James Press, 1991.

PERIODICALS

America, May 19, 1979, p. 419.
American Literature, May, 1985, p. 349.
Atlantic, August, 1976, p. 88.
Best Sellers September, 1977, p. 178.
Book World, July 27, 1969.
Choice, November, 1984, p. 422.
Globe and Mail (Toronto) August 18, 1984.
Library Journal, July, 1976, p. 1547; August, 1977, p. 1670; November 15, 1978, p. 2329; July, 1984, p. 1327.
Los Angeles Times, December 26, 1980.
Los Angeles Times Book Review, February 11, 1979, p. 7; June 24, 1984, p. 3; February 22, 1987, p. 3; April 28, 1991, p. 4.
Nation, December 30, 1991, p. 851.
New York Times, May 23, 1969; January 22, 1987.
New York Times Book Review, June 17, 1984, p. 20; February 8, 1987, p. 28.
Newsweek, March 3, 1969.
Poetry, March, 1970.
Poetry News, March, 1981.
Poetry Project Newsletter, October/November, 1990.
Review of Contemporary Fiction, fall, 1991, p. 296.
San Francisco Chronicle, August 26, 1984; May 13, 1990; July 12, 1992.
Small Press, winter, 1993.
Sulfur, fall, 1991, pp. 193-198.
Washington Post, January 15, 1986; March 9, 1987.

Washington Post Book World, July 27, 1969; April 14, 1991, pp. 4, 9.
World Literature Today, spring, 1985, p. 274.

—*Sketch by Joseph O. Aimone*

*   *   *

CLARK, Tom
See CLARK, Thomas Willard

*   *   *

CLARKE, John Henrik   1915-

PERSONAL: Born January 1, 1915, in Union Springs, AL; son of John (a farmer) and Willella (Mays) Clarke; married Eugenia Evans (a teacher), December 24, 1961; children: Nzingha Marie, Sonni Kojo. *Education:* Attended New York University, 1948-52, and New School for Social Research, 1956-58; Pacific Western University, B.A.

ADDRESSES: Home—223 West 137th St., New York, NY 10030.

CAREER: New School for Social Research, New York City, occasional teacher of African and Afro-American history, 1956-58, developer of African Study Center, 1957-59, assistant to director, 1958-60; *Pittsburgh Courier,* Pittsburgh, PA, feature writer, 1957-58; *Ghana Evening News,* Accra, Ghana, feature writer, 1958; Hunter College of the City University of New York, New York City, associate professor of African and Puerto Rican studies, beginning 1970, became professor emeritus, 1985. Director, Haryou-Act (teaching program), 1964-69; lecturer in teacher training program, Columbia University, summer, 1969; Carter G. Woodson distinguished visiting professor in African history, Cornell University, 1967-70; visiting lecturer, New York University; teacher (by special license) at Malverne High School (People's College), Malverne, NY. Research director for African Heritage Exposition in New York City, 1959; coordinator and special consultant to Columbia Broadcasting System, Inc. (CBS-TV), television series, *Black Heritage,* 1968; consultant to American Heritage Press and John Wiley & Sons (publishers). Member of board of directors of Langston Hughes Center for Child Development, 1967; member of advisory board of Martin Luther King Library Center, 1969. *Military service:* U.S. Army Air Forces, 1941-45; became master sergeant.

MEMBER: International Society of African Culture, African Studies Association, American Society of African Culture, Black Academy of Arts and Letters (founding member), Association for Study of African American Life and History (executive board member, 1949-55), American Historical Society, American Academy of Political and Social Science, African Heritage Studies Association (president, 1969-73), African Scholars Council (member of board of directors), Harlem Writers Guild (founding member).

AWARDS, HONORS: Carter G. Woodson Award, 1968, for creative contribution in editing, and 1971, for excellence in teaching; National Association for Television and Radio Announcers citation for meritorious achievement in educational television, 1969; L.H.D., University of Denver, 1970; Litt.D., University of District of Columbia, 1992, and Clarke-Atlanta University, 1993.

WRITINGS:

Rebellion in Rhyme (poems), Dicker Press, 1948.

(Editor) *Harlem U.S.A.: The Story of a City within a City,* Seven Seas Books (Berlin), 1964, revised edition, Collier, 1970.

(Editor) *Harlem: A Community in Transition,* Citadel, 1965, 3rd edition, 1970.

(Editor) *American Negro Short Stories,* Hill & Wang, 1966.

(Editor) *William Styron's Nat Turner: Ten Black Writers Respond,* Beacon Press, 1968, reprinted, Greenwood Press, 1987.

(Editor and author of introduction) *Malcolm X: The Man and His Times,* Macmillan, 1969, Africa World Press, 1991.

(Editor with Vincent Harding) *Slave Trade and Slavery,* Holt, 1970.

(Editor) *Harlem: Voices from the Soul of Black America,* (short stories), New American Library, 1970.

(Editor with others) *Black Titan: W. E. B. Du Bois,* Beacon Press, 1970.

(Editor) J. A. Rogers, *World's Great Men of Color,* two volumes, Macmillan, 1972.

(Editor with Amy Jacques Garvey, and author of introduction and commentaries) *Marcus Garvey and the Vision of Africa,* Random House, 1974.

(Introduction) *Introduction to African Civilization,* Carol Publishing, 1974.

(Guest editor) *Black Families in the American Economy,* Education-Community Counselors Association (Washington, DC), 1975.

(Editor) *Dimensions of the Struggle against Apartheid: A Tribute to Paul Robeson,* African Heritage Studies Association in cooperation with United Nations Centre against Apartheid, 1979.

(Introduction) *Africa Counts,* Hill, Lawrence, 1979.

Africans at the Crossroads: Notes for an African World Revolution, Africa World Press, 1991.

Christopher Columbus and the African Holocaust, A & B Books, 1992.

An Oral Biography of Professor John Henrik Clarke, United Brothers and Sisters Communications Systems, 1992.

African People in World History, Black Classic Press, 1993.

(Editor) *Black American Short Stories,* revised edition, Hill & Wang, 1993.

Editor of *New Dimensions in African History,* Africa World Press. Contributor to books, including *Patterns of Thinking: Integrating Learning Skills in Content Teaching,* Allyn & Bacon, 1990; *Teaching Critical Thinking,* Prentice Hall, 1993. Also author of "The Lives of Great African Chiefs" published serially in *Pittsburgh Courier,* 1957-58, and of syndicated column, "African World Bookshelf." Author of numerous papers on African studies presented at international conferences. Contributor to *Negro History Bulletin, Chicago Defender, Journal of Negro Education, Phylon, Presence Africaine,* and others. Book review editor, *Negro History Bulletin,* 1947-49; co-founder and associate editor, *Harlem Quarterly,* 1949-51; editor, *African Heritage,* 1959; associate editor, *Freedomways,* 1962-83.

WORK IN PROGRESS: The Black Woman in History; an African curriculum for elementary school teachers.

SIDELIGHTS: As an editor, essayist, and educator, John Henrik Clarke has written and lectured extensively about African and Afro-American history both in the United States and West Africa. *Malcolm X: The Man and His Times,* a collection of essays about and writings by Malcolm X edited by Clarke, is described by the *New York Times*'s Christopher Lehmann-Haupt: "Malcolm is seen through different eyes at various stages of his career as Muslim, ex-Muslim, and founder of the Organization of Afro-American Unity. He is defined and redefined by friends and followers." And although Lehmann-Haupt considers the collection "overwhelmingly sympathetic," he thinks that Clarke has produced a "multifaceted picture that . . . traces his development from drifter to prophet, spells out his aims (and thereby dispels his distorted image as apostle of violent separatism) and explains why his stature among so many blacks today is heroic." Similarly, in the *New York Review of Books,* Charles V. Hamilton finds that "Clarke has done an excellent job of pulling together various stimulating sources to give the reader what the title promises, a look at the man and his time—a look at a genuine folk hero of black Americans and a master of the Politics of Sportsmanship."

BIOGRAPHICAL/CRITICAL SOURCES:

BOOKS

Authors in the News, Volume 1, Gale, 1976.

PERIODICALS

Atlanta Journal, April 8, 1973.
Black World, February, 1971; August, 1971.
Choice, February, 1969; October, 1974; June, 1975.
Essence, September, 1989.
New York Review of Books, September 12, 1968.
New York Times, May 10, 1967; August 1-2, 1968; September 29, 1969.
New York Times Book Review, March 5, 1967; August 11, 1968; September 28, 1969, p. 3.
Publishers Weekly, July 7, 1969; July 13, 1970.
Saturday Review, January 14, 1967; August 12, 1968.
Time, October 24, 1969, p. 110; February 23, 1970, p. 88.

*   *   *

CLIVE, John
See CLIVE, John Leonard

*   *   *

CLIVE, John Leonard   1924-1990
(John Clive)

PERSONAL: Born September 25, 1924, in Berlin, Germany; came to United States in 1940, naturalized citizen, 1943; died of cardiac arrest, January 7, 1990, in Cambridge, MA; son of Bruno and Rose (Rosenfeld) Clive. *Education:* University of North Carolina, A.B., 1943; Harvard University, M.A., 1947, Ph.D., 1952.

ADDRESSES: Home—38 Fernald Dr., Cambridge, MA 02138. *Office*—247 Widener Library, Harvard University, Cambridge, MA 02138.

CAREER: Harvard University, Cambridge, MA, began as teaching fellow, became assistant professor, 1948-60, professor of history and literature, 1965-75, professor of history, 1975-79, William R. Kennan, Jr., Professor of history and literature, 1979-90. University of Chicago, Chicago, IL, assistant professor, 1960-61, associate professor of history, 1961-65. Visiting fellow, All Souls College, 1977-78; Special Ford Lecturer, University of Oxford, 1978; Vernon Visiting Professor of biography, Dartmouth College, 1979. Fellow, Center for Advanced Study in the Behavioral Sciences, 1965. *Military service:* U.S. Army, 1943-46; became second lieutenant.

MEMBER: American Historical Association, Mid-West Conference of British Historical Studies (secretary,

1961-64), Massachusetts Historical Society, Phi Beta Kappa.

AWARDS, HONORS: Guggenheim fellowship, 1957-58; American Council of Learned Societies grant, 1962-63; National Book Award in history, 1974, for *Macaulay: The Shaping of the Historian;* Robert Livingston Schuyler Prize, American Historical Association, 1976; National Book Critics Circle Award for criticism, 1990, for *Not by Fact Alone: Essays on the Writing and Reading of History.*

WRITINGS:

Scotch Reviewers: The Edinburgh Review, 1802-1815, Harvard University Press, 1957.
(Editor) Thomas Carlyle, *History of Friedrich II of Prussia, Called Frederick the Great,* University of Chicago Press, 1969.
(Editor with H. J. Hanham) Henry T. Buckle, *On Scotland—The Scottish Intellect,* University of Chicago Press, 1970.
(Editor with Geoffrey Best) R. W. Church, *Oxford Movement: Twelve Years, 1833-1845,* University of Chicago Press, 1970.
(Editor with Thomas Pinney) Thomas Babington Macaulay, *Selected Writings,* University of Chicago Press, 1972.
Macaulay: The Shaping of the Historian, Knopf, 1973 (published in England as *Thomas Babington Macaulay—The Shaping of the Historian,* Secker & Warburg, 1973).
(Editor with Isaac Kramnick) *Lord Bolingbroke: Historical Writings,* University of Chicago Press, 1974.
(Editor with G. W. Bowersock and Stephen R. Graubard) *Edward Gibbon and the Decline and Fall of the Roman Empire,* Harvard University Press, 1977.
Not by Fact Alone: Essays on the Writing and Reading of History (also published as *Not by Fact Alone: Reflections on the Writing and Reading of History*), Knopf, 1989.

Also editor and translator, with O. Handlin, of *Journey to Pennsylvania* by Gottlieb Mittelberger.

NOVELS UNDER NAME JOHN CLIVE

(With J. D. Gilman) *KG 200: The Force with No Face,* Souvenir Press, 1977.
The Last Liberator, Delacorte, 1980.
Barossa, Delacorte, 1981.
(With Nicolas Head) *Ark,* Viking, 1985.

SIDELIGHTS: Nominated for the 1974 National Book Award in both history and biography, and winner of the award in the former category, John Leonard Clive's biography of the Victorian historian Thomas Babington Macaulay has drawn praise from numerous critics. Lionel Stevenson of *South Atlantic Quarterly* observed that Clive "combines expertise in history and literature" in this "major work" on Thomas Babington Macaulay. Stevenson praised Clive's scholarly efforts and cited the "large archives of unpublished letters and diaries" that were consulted for the book.

Critics from *Time* magazine and *Virginia Quarterly Review* both noted the difficulty of writing about Macaulay. As William H. Nelson of the *Quarterly* explained: "The adjectives 'common' and 'vulgar' so often used to describe [Macaulay's] appearance also regularly found their way into comments on his mind and work. . . . John Stuart Mill thought him 'an intellectual dwarf—rounded off and stunted, full grown broad and short, without a germ of principle or further growth in his whole being.' " Indeed, Queen Victoria once commented to Lord Melbourne that Macaulay was "uncouth, and not a man of the world." But Clive, according to Nelson, found "the real Macaulay under this forbidding surface . . . [and] sensibly enough, in his own early family life, from whose oppressions and joys, in Clive's view, Macaulay never escaped. . . . Cold and striving to the wider world, he was tender, solicitous, playful, charming, and flirtatious towards his adoring sisters."

Although *Time*'s Melvin Maddocks praised the "respectable case for a respectable Macaulay" that Clive was able to build, he was surprised at the popularity of the book: "Why is this potential doorstop winning such acclaim? Are readers . . . really that willing to plow through 25 pages of hearsay evidence on Macaulay's eloquence as a parliamentary orator from 1832 to 1834?" Perhaps it is because, as Maddocks proposed, "Clive . . . livens his exposition by suggesting the obligatory sinister Victorian flaw. Macaulay, a lifelong bachelor, loved his younger sisters . . . more than a brother should." He continued: "Working from this clue of psychological incest, Clive submits that Macaulay was a suppressed romantic, smoldering behind a mask of rationality. . . . A historian [however] can no more make this preacher of 'middlingness' very heroic than he can make him very wicked. . . . [Macaulay] was every inch a Victorian, and that fact finally provides the best explanation of the book's success."

Stevenson also noticed that Clive drew "a sympathetic picture of Macaulay in his social and poetical context, displaying him as more complex in his personality and more discriminating in his attitudes than is assumed by those who have not read his essays and speeches." But for Stevenson, Clive's style tended "to be wooden and repetitive, though perhaps this impression results from contrast with his subject's floridity." On the other hand, Victor Howes of the *Christian Science Monitor* stated, "It is to Clive's praise that his work reads like a great Victorian novel. . . . Macaulay looms forward from the pages of his biography like a firedrake, glittering, capacious, burning, dangerous."

Finally, almost all critics have agreed that Clive's book has simply whet their appetite for learning more about Macaulay. As Howes observed, "He leaves Macaulay at 40, on the threshold of writing his *History of England,* the book on which his modern fame most securely rests." Nelson, however, considered this one of the book's drawbacks: "If Clive is persuasive and sure in explaining Macaulay's personal life and its relationship to his career, he is less satisfying when it comes to Macaulay's importance. Partly, no doubt, this is because this volume ends when Macaulay is thirty-eight and about to begin his *History,* and Clive consequently deals with him as a historian only *en passant.* . . . Perhaps if Clive had probed and delved more, had speculated more vigorously on the relationship between Macaulay and those to and for whom he spoke, this book might have been revelational, instead of merely informative, humane, and suggestive."

To many critics, Clive's book was more than simply a biography of an important historian. For R. Rea of the *Library Journal,* it was "also a marvelous survey of the evangelical, utilitarian, middle-class milieu of pre-Victorian Britain." For Maddocks, it was a book in which "we find between all those lines an obituary on that soul of respectability that is fast fading but still not quite dead within ourselves."

Shortly before his death in 1990, Clive published *Not by Fact Alone: Essays on the Writing and Reading of History.* This compilation of essays, lectures, and articles written over the course of several decades details not only the lives of such historians as Macaulay, Edward Gibbon, and Thomas Carlyle, but also the process of researching and writing about these men, a process Clive dubs "cliography." Because it is comprised of a number of short pieces in which Clive addresses similar issues, *Washington Post Book World* critic John Kenyon notes, *Not by Fact Alone* contains a certain amount of "tiresome repetition from essay to essay." However, J. W. Burrow of the *Times Literary Supplement* claims that the essays are not just "chips from the workshop, but [rather] ruminations on favourite themes." These ruminations, Burrow continues, give the book a "relaxed, expansive and intimate" tone.

Gertrude Himmelfarb, writing in the *New York Times Book Review,* considers *Not by Fact Alone* an appropriate epilogue to Clive's work, "for in many ways [it is] more revealing of his life and work than his memorable biography of Macaulay." Describing the critical praise for *Not by Fact Alone* as "one of the most heartening developments in recent historical writing," she concludes: "At a time when professional historians have virtually given up reading the great historians, Clive's giving us reason to read them—and reason to call them great."

BIOGRAPHICAL/CRITICAL SOURCES:

PERIODICALS

Atlantic, April, 1973.
Christian Science Monitor, April 4, 1973.
Library Journal, January 15, 1973.
Listener, June 28, 1973.
New Leader, April 16, 1973.
New Republic, May 5, 1973.
New Statesman, June 29, 1973.
Newsweek, August 6, 1973.
New Yorker, April 14, 1973.
New York Times Book Review, April 1, 1973; June 10, 1973; June 2, 1974; October 23, 1977; January 27, 1980, p. 22; March 8, 1981, p. 35; March 11, 1990, p. 16; December 23, 1990, p. 20.
Observer, June 24, 1973.
South Atlantic Quarterly, spring, 1975.
Time, December 31, 1973; April 22, 1974.
Times Literary Supplement, June 29, 1973; February 2, 1990, p. 125.
Virginia Quarterly Review, winter, 1974.
Washington Post Book World, April 20, 1975; March 29, 1987, p. 12; May 14, 1989, p. 11; December 23, 1990, p. 12; December 30, 1990, p. 12.

OBITUARIES:

BOOKS

Who's Who in America, 45th edition, Marquis, 1988.

PERIODICALS

Chicago Tribune, January 14, 1990.
New York Times, January 10, 1990.
Washington Post, January 13, 1990.*

*   *   *

COGSWELL, Fred(erick William) 1917-

PERSONAL: Born November 8, 1917, in East Centreville, New Brunswick, Canada; son of Walter Scott (a farmer) and Florence (White) Cogswell; married Margaret Hynes, July 3, 1944 (died May 2, 1985); married Gail Fox, November 8, 1985; children: Carmen Patricia, Kathleen Mary. *Education:* University of New Brunswick, B.A. (with honors), 1949, M.A., 1950; University of Edinburgh, Ph.D., 1952. *Politics:* New Democratic Party. *Religion:* Christian.

ADDRESSES: Home—Comp. AG, Site 6, R.R. 4, Fredericton, New Brunswick, Canada E3B 4X5. *Office*—

University of New Brunswick, Fredericton, New Brunswick, Canada.

CAREER: University of New Brunswick, Fredericton, assistant professor, 1952-57, associate professor, 1957-61, professor of English, 1961-83, professor emeritus, 1983—. Editor and publisher, *Fiddlehead* magazine, 1952-66, and Fiddlehead Press, 1967-82. Scottish-Canadian exchange writer in residence, Edinburgh, Scotland, 1983-84. *Military service:* Canadian Army, 1940-45; became staff sergeant; was decorated.

MEMBER: Association of Canadian Publishers (honorary life member), League of Canadian Poets (honorary life member), Association of Canadian and Quebec Literatures (president, 1978-80), Atlantic Publishers Association (president, 1978-80; honorary life member).

AWARDS, HONORS: I.O.D.E. Scholar for New Brunswick, 1950-52; Nuffield fellow, 1959-60; Gold Medal of Poets Laureate International presented by Republic of the Philippines, 1965; Canada Council Senior fellowship, 1967-68; Order of Canada, 1982; L.Ld., St. Francis Xavier University, 1983, and Mount Allison University, 1987; D.C.L., King's University, 1985; 125th Anniversary Medal, government of Canada, 1992.

WRITINGS:

The Stunted Strong, Fiddlehead, 1954.
The Haloed Tree, Ryerson, 1956.
(Translator) Robert Henryson, *The Testament of Cresseid,* Ryerson, 1957.
Descent from Eden, Ryerson, 1959.
Lost Dimension, Outposts Publication, 1960.
(Editor) *A Canadian Anthology,* Fiddlehead, 1960.
(Editor and contributor) *Five New Brunswick Poets,* Fiddlehead, 1962.
(Editor with Robert Tweedie and S. W. MacNutt) *The Arts in New Brunswick,* [Fredericton], 1966.
(Editor with T. R. Lower) *The Enchanted Land,* Gage, 1967.
Star-People, Fiddlehead, 1968.
Immortal Plowman, Fiddlehead, 1969.
In Praise of Chastity, New Brunswick Chapbooks, 1970.
(Editor and translator) *One Hundred Poems of Modern Quebec,* Fiddlehead, 1970.
(Editor and translator) *A Second Hundred Poems of Modern Quebec,* Fiddlehead, 1971.
The Chains of Liliput, Fiddlehead, 1971.
The House without a Door, Fiddlehead, 1973.
Light Bird of Life: Selected Poems, Fiddlehead, 1974.
(Editor) *The Poetry of Modern Quebec,* Harvest, 1976.
Against Perspective, Fiddlehead, 1977.
The Long Apprenticeship: The Collected Poems of Fred Cogswell, Fiddlehead, 1980.
Pearls, Ragweed, 1983.

(Editor and translator) *The Complete Poems of Emile Nelligan,* Harvest, 1983.

Charles G. D. Roberts and His Works, ECW Press, 1983.

Fred Cogswell: Selected Poems, edited by Antonio D'Alfonso, Guernica, 1983.

(Editor) *The Atlantic Anthology,* Ragweed, Volume 1 (prose), 1983, Volume 2 (poetry), 1985.

(Author of introduction) Graham Adams, editor, *The Collected Poems of Sir Charles G. D. Roberts,* Wombat Press, 1985.

Meditations: Fifty Sestinas, Ragweed, 1986.

An Edge to Life, Purple Wednesday Society, 1987.

Charles Mair, ECW Press, 1988.

The Best Notes Merge, Borealis, 1988.

Black and White Tapestry, Borealis, 1989.

(Editor with JoAnne Elder) *Revos inacheves: poesie contemporaine,* Presses de'Acadie, 1990.

(Editor with Elder) *Unfinished Dreams: Contemporary Poetry of Acadie,* Grosseland, 1990.

Watching an Eagle, Borealis, 1991.

When the Right Light Shines, Borealis, 1992.

In Praise of Old Music, Borealis, 1992.

Work represented in numerous anthologies, including *A Century of Canadian Literature,* edited by Henry Green and Guy Sylvestre, Ryerson, 1967; *Made in Canada: New Poems of the Seventies,* edited by Douglas Lochhead and Raymond Souster, Oberon, 1970; *The Oxford Anthology of Canadian Literature,* Oxford University Press, 1973; and *Introduction to Literature: British, American, Canadian,* edited by G. Thomas, R. Perkyns, K. MacKinnon, and W. Katz, Holt, 1981. Contributor of poems to over one hundred periodicals, as well as articles to *Dalhouse Review, Trace, Queen's, Canadian Forum,* and other periodicals. Editor, *Humanities Association Bulletin,* 1967-72.

SIDELIGHTS: Fred Cogswell is considered by many reviewers as one of Canada's notable literary figures. Gwendolyn Davies stated in *Dictionary of Literary Biography:* "Since World War II a major force in contributing to the vitality of Canadian literature has been the poet, publisher, translator, and critic Fred Cogswell. As the guiding power behind Fiddlehead Press, he was responsible for the publication of more than three hundred titles and gave unstinting support to promising young writers." Davies added that Cogswell "has written extensively on Canadian literature . . . and he has been effective in developing an overview of Atlantic Canada's literary-cultural life in the nineteenth century. . . . His own work as a poet has earned him a place in contemporary poetry circles, while his translations of French-Canadian verse have helped to bridge the gap between the two main language groups in the country."

Cogswell once told *CA:* "I have lived, counting my wartime experience, upwards of eight years in Europe (princi-

pally Scotland). I have a fluent reading knowledge of French. I am interested quite literally in everything in the universe and I am a monist. As a poet, anthologist, critic, editor, and biographer, I have been most concerned with sincerity, accuracy, imagination, and empathy. I also prefer the plain to the ornate and feel art ought to simplify—it is a training in grasping, expressing, and communicating essentials."

BIOGRAPHICAL/CRITICAL SOURCES:

BOOKS

Directory of Literary Biography, Volume 60: *Canadian Writers since 1960, Second Series,* Gale, 1987, pp.33-41.

PERIODICALS

Quill and Quire, July, 1980.

*   *   *

COLE, W(illiam) Owen   1931-

PERSONAL: Born September 22, 1931, in Sheffield, England; son of W(illiam) Owen (a minister) and Clara (a nurse; maiden name, Coupland) Cole; married Gwynneth Georgina Bowen (a nurse), December 20, 1957; children: Eluned, Sian. *Education:* Durham University, B.A., 1954, diploma in education, 1955; University of London, diploma in theology, 1959, B.D., 1966; Leeds University, master of philosophy, 1975, Ph.D., 1979. *Religion:* Christian.

ADDRESSES: Home—134 Worcester Rd., Chichester, West Sussex PO19 4ED, England. *Office*—Department of Religious Studies, West Sussex Institute of Higher Education, Chichester, West Sussex PO19 4PE, England.

CAREER: Primary school teacher in Corsham Regis, Wiltshire, England, 1956-59; Passmores Comprehensive Secondary School, Harlow, Essex, England, head of religious studies, 1959-63; Northern Counties College, Newcastle-upon-Tyne, England, lecturer in religious studies, 1963-68; James Graham College of Education, Leeds, England, principal lecturer and head of religious studies, 1968-80; West Sussex Institute of Higher Education, Chichester, England, principal lecturer and head of religious studies, 1980-89. Part-time lecturer at Leeds University, 1976-79, and Open University, 1976-80; lecturer at Guru Nanak Foundation, New Delhi, India, 1983; visiting professor at Punjabi University, Patiala, India, 1983; honorary interfaith consultant to the Archbishops of Canterbury and York, 1981-91.

MEMBER: British Association for the History of Religions, Shap Working Party on World Religions in Education (chairman, 1979-81), British Council of Churches Committee for Relations with People of Other Faiths (moderator of religious education committee), Church of England Board of Mission Other Faiths Committee, London Diocesan Board for Schools (chairman of Education Committee, 1991—).

WRITINGS:

A Sikh Family in Britain, Religious and Moral Education Press, 1972.
(With Piara Singh Sambhi) *Sikhism,* Ward Lock, 1973.
(Editor) *World Religions: A Handbook for Teachers,* Commission for Racial Equality, 1977.
(With Sambhi) *The Sikhs,* Routledge & Kegan Paul, 1978.
(Editor) *World Faiths in Education,* Allen & Unwin, 1978.
Thinking about Sikhism, Lutterworth, 1982.
Five Religions in the Twentieth Century, Dufour, 1981, revised and expanded edition, co-authored with Peggy Morgan, published as *Six Religions in the Twentieth Century,* Hulton, 1984.
(Editor) *Comparative Religions,* Blandford, 1982.
(Editor) *Religion in the Multifaith School,* Hulton, 1983.
The Guru in Sikhism, Darton, Longman & Todd, 1984.
Sikhism and Its Indian Context, 1469-1708, Darton, Longman & Todd, 1984.
Hinduism, Longman, 1986.
Christianity, Stanley Thomas, 1989.
(With Sambhi) *Popular Dictionary of Sikhism,* Curzon Press, 1990.
(Editor) *Moral Issues in Six Religions,* Heinemann, 1991.
(With J. Lowndes) *Religious Education in the Primary Curriculum,* Chansitor/Religious and Moral Education Press, 1991.
(Editor) *Five World Faiths,* Cassell, 1991.
(With Sambhi) *Sikhism and Christianity: A Comparative Study,* Macmillan, 1993.
The Christian Bible, Heinemann, 1993.

Contributor to books, including *The Penguin Handbook of Living Religions,* edited by J. R. Hinnells, Penguin, 1984. Contributor of articles to newspapers and journals, including the *Times* (London), *Times Educational Supplement,* and the *British Journal of Religious Education.* Editor of *Shap Mailing* (1976-82), and *Sikh Bulletin* (1982—).

SIDELIGHTS: W. Owen Cole's *Sikhism and Its Indian Context, 1469-1708* discusses the influence of the major established religious traditions in India, Hinduism and Islam, on the origin and early development of the Sikh faith. Sikhism emerged from the teachings of Guru Nanak in northwestern India in the fifteenth century. In a *Times Literary Supplement* review, Christopher Shackie observed, "The consensus of Sikh feeling has tended toward the acceptance of Guru Nanak's attitude as having essentially been one of reconciliation between Hinduism and

Islam," but scholars have differed on the validity Guru Nanak ascribed to the conventional practice of these religions. "The greater part of [Cole's] book is devoted to an analysis of Guru Nanak's teachings in an effort to prove that he did indeed accord considerable value to scriptural Hinduism and Islam," noted Shackle.

Cole once told *CA:* "As a pacifist and antiracist, I consider comparative religious studies programs in schools and universities (as we have in Britain) important to creating a harmonious society. I am totally committed to the elimination of sexism, classism, racism, religious intolerance, and poverty."

BIOGRAPHICAL/CRITICAL SOURCES:

PERIODICALS

Times Literary Supplement, July 13, 1984.

*   *   *

COLEMAN, Michael C(hristopher) 1946-

PERSONAL: Born June 19, 1946, in Dublin, Ireland; son of Michael Sidney (a civil servant) and Beatrice (a housewife; maiden name, McGreevy) Coleman; married Sirkka Helina Makkonen (a teacher), September 27, 1970; children: Michael Donagh, Heli Kristiina, Markus Kevin. *Education:* University College, National University of Ireland, Dublin, B.A., 1970, Higher Diploma in Education, 1981; University of Pennsylvania, M.A., 1974, Ph.D., 1977. *Avocational Interests:* Soccer football, swimming, gardening (rockeries), miniature modelling, music (songwriting and performing locally).

ADDRESSES: Home—Auvilankuja 5 C 15, 40740 Jyvaeskylae 74, Finland. *Office*—Department of English, University of Jyvaeskylae, SF-40100 Jyvaeskylae, 10, Finland.

CAREER: Commercial artist at advertising agencies in Dublin, Ireland, 1964-67; University of Jyvaeskylae, Jyvaeskylae, Finland, lecturer in English, 1970—, docent in general history, 1985—, director of North American Studies Programme, 1991. High school teacher in Dublin, 1980-81. Visiting professor of American studies, Miami University. *Military service:* Irish National Guard, 1960's.

MEMBER: American Historical Association, Organization of American Historians, American Society of Church History, American Society for Ethnohistory, Presbyterian Historical Society, Irish Association for American Studies, Nordic Association for American Studies.

AWARDS, HONORS: Residence fellowships at Newbery Library, Chicago, IL, and National Anthropological Archives, Smithsonian Institution, Washington, DC.

WRITINGS:

Presbyterian Missionary Attitudes Toward American Indians, 1837-1893, University Press of Mississippi, 1985.
American Indian Children at School, 1850-1930, University Press of Mississippi, 1993.

Contributor of articles and reviews to scholarly journals in the United States, Canada, Scandinavia, and Ireland. Contributor of paintings and drawings to Irish, German, American, and Finnish periodicals.

WORK IN PROGRESS: A book comparing Indian and Irish educational programs in the nineteenth century.

SIDELIGHTS: Michael C. Coleman told *CA:* "I became seriously interested in American Indian history in 1970 when I first began to teach the history of the United States to Finnish students. The lectures I gave on Indian history reawakened a childhood interest in the American West, one shared and stimulated by my late father. In 1973, I was off to the University of Pennsylvania to begin my doctorate in Indian history. My advisor, Dr. Charles Rosenberg, steered me to the missionary archives at the Presbyterian Historical Society, Philadelphia—and the rest is history.

"After completing my doctorate on Presbyterian missionary attitudes toward Indians, I continued to study and write on the history of Indian and missionary confrontations, and competed my first book on the subject in 1985.

"Feeling the need to examine Indian perspectives on nineteenth century cultural confrontations, I then changed my research focus. The guest professorship in American studies at Miami University, and short term residence fellowships at the Newbery Library and National Anthropological Archives, Smithsonian Institution allowed me gather material for a new book. Utilizing about 100 written autobiographies by Indians, along with missionary and United States government records, I set out to examine the responses of Indian boys and girls to missionary and government schooling in the later nineteenth and early twentieth centuries. This book is a product of the so-called 'new social history' and 'new Indian history,' both of which have attempted to see ethnic minorities as more than merely victims of dominant cultures—such minorities were active participants in events which concerned them, and exerted influences upon those who tried to assimilate them into the dominant cultural forms. Indian children, I found, responded in mixed, ambivalent, and shifting ways to missionary and governments schools which attempted to strip them of their tribal cultures and turn them into 'civilized' and Christian Americans. Although white authorities retained a preponderance of power, these children, along with their kin and other tribal adults, to

an extent succeeded in utilizing the schools for their own personal, familial, and ethnic purposes."

Coleman also added: "My next project builds upon this study in Indian responses to school. I have already written an article comparing Indian and African motivations at missionary schools, and now intend to continue with comparative education history. My objective is to compare Indian and Irish responses to alien assimilationist educational programmes in the nineteenth century. I have already begun preliminary bibliographical searches in the educational history of my own country, Ireland—a chore made somewhat easier by the new computer bibliographical aids. But to go further with this project will require an extended research period in Ireland."

*   *   *

COLEMAN, Wanda 1946-

PERSONAL: Born November 13, 1946, in Los Angeles, CA.

ADDRESSES: Home—P.O. Box 29154, Los Angeles, CA 90029.

CAREER: Writer and performer. Worked as production editor, proofreader, magazine editor, waitress, and assistant recruiter for Peace Corps/Vista, 1968-75; staff writer for *Days of Our Lives,* National Broadcasting Co. (NBC-TV), 1975-76; medical transcriber and insurance billing clerk, 1979-84. Writer in residence at Studio Watts, 1968-69; cohost of interview program for Pacific Radio, 1981—.

MEMBER: PEN.

AWARDS, HONORS: Named to Open Door Program Hall of Fame, 1975; Emmy Award, Academy of Television Arts and Sciences, best writing in a daytime drama, 1976, for *Days of Our Lives;* fellowships from National Endowment for the Arts, 1981-82, and Guggenheim Foundation, 1984.

WRITINGS:

Art in the Court of the Blue Fag (chapbook), Black Sparrow Press, 1977.
Mad Dog Black Lady, Black Sparrow Press, 1979.
Imagoes, Black Sparrow Press, 1983, reissued, 1991.
A War of Eyes and Other Stories, Black Sparrow Press, 1988.
(Editor) *Women for All Seasons: Poetry and Prose about the Transitions in Women's Lives,* Woman's Building, 1988.
Dicksboro Hotel & Other Travels, Ambrosia Press, 1989.
(Editor) Susannah Foster, *Earthbound in Betty Grable's Shoes,* Chiron Review Press, 1990.

African Sleeping Sickness: Stories and Poems, Black Sparrow Press, 1990.

Heavy Daughter Blues: Poems and Stories, Black Sparrow Press, 1991.

Hand Dance, Black Sparrow Press, 1993.

Also author of "The Time Is Now" episode, *The Name of the Game,* NBC-TV, 1970. Contributor to periodicals, including *An Afro American and African Journal of Arts and Letters.*

SIDELIGHTS: Wanda Coleman is known in the Los Angeles area for her poetry and her poetry readings. "As a poet," she once told *CA,* "I have gained a reputation, locally, as an electrifying performer/reader, and have appeared at local rock clubs, reading the same poetry that has taken me into classrooms and community centers for over five hundred public readings since 1973." Coleman added: "Words seem inadequate in expressing the anger and outrage I feel at the persistent racism that permeates every aspect of black American life. Since words are what I am best at, I concern myself with this as an urban actuality as best I can."

Writing in *Black American Literature Forum,* Tony Magistrale explains "Coleman frequently writes to illuminate the lives of the underclass and the disenfranchised, the invisible men and woman who populate America's downtown streets after dark, the asylums and waystations, the inner city hospitals and clinics. . . . Wanda Coleman, like Gwendolyn Brooks before her, has much to tell us about what it is like to be a poor black woman in America."

Coleman's work has received considerable praise from critics. Stephen Kessler wrote in *Bachy* that Coleman "shows us scary and exciting realms of ourselves," and Holly Prado noted in the *Los Angeles Times* that Coleman's "heated and economical language and head-on sensibility take her work beyond brutality to fierce dignity." Tamar Lehrich wrote in the *Nation:* "Wanda Coleman consistently confronts her readers with images, ideas and language that threaten to offend or at least to excite." Lehrich concluded that "Wanda Coleman's poetry and prose have been inspired by her frustration and anger at her position as a black woman and by her desire to translate those feelings into action."

BIOGRAPHICAL/CRITICAL SOURCES:

PERIODICALS

African American Review, Volume 26, Summer 1992, pp. 355-57.

Bachy, Fall, 1979, Spring, 1980.

Black American Literature Forum, Volume 23, Fall 1989, pp. 539-54.

Los Angeles, April, 1983.

Los Angeles Times, September 15, 1969; November 26, 1973; January 31, 1982; November 13, 1983.

Los Angeles Times Book Review, August 14, 1988, pp. 1, 9.

Michigan Quarterly Review, Fall, 1991, pp. 717-31.

The Nation, February 20, 1988, p. 242-43.

Publishers Weekly, July 1, 1988.

Stern, May 16, 1974.

*   *   *

COLLIER, Jane
SEE COLLIER, Zena

*   *   *

COLLIER, Zena   1926- (Zena Shumsky; Jane Collier, a pseudonym)

PERSONAL: Born January 21, 1926, in London, England; married Louis Shumsky (a photographer), May 3, 1945 (divorced, 1967); married Thomas M. Hampson (a lawyer), December 30, 1969; children: (first marriage) Jeffrey (deceased), Paul. *Avocational Interests:* Books, films, theatre, jazz, and to a certain extent, politics.

ADDRESSES: Home—83 Berkeley St., Rochester, NY 14607. *Agent*—Harvey Klinger, 301 West 53rd Street, New York, NY 10019.

CAREER: Novelist and short story writer; has worked as writer of corporate communications, advertising copywriter, editorial consultant; teacher at Writer's Workshop, Nazareth College, NY, 1984—; Writers Workshop, Chautauqua Institute, NY, 1992; Aesthetic Education Institute, Eastman School of Music, artist-teacher, 1987.

MEMBER: Poets & Writers, Authors Guild, Writers & Books, National Writers Union, American Civil Liberties Union, Friends of Rochester Public Library, Friends of the University of Rochester Libraries.

AWARDS, HONORS: Resident fellow at Yaddo, MacDowell, Virginia Center for the Creative Arts and Alfred University Summer Place; Honor Roll, *Best American Short Stories,* 1972; Pushcart Prize Nominee, 1979; *Seven for the People* selected by Children's Book Council as Notable Trade Book for Children, 1979; writer-in-residence, Just Buffalo (Buffalo, NY), 1984, Southern Tier Library System (Corning, NY), 1985, Niagara-Erie Writers, (Buffalo), 1986; Hoepfner Prize, *Southern Humanities Review,* 1985, for best short story.

WRITINGS:

NOVELS

A Cooler Climate, British American Publishing, 1990.

Ghost Note, Grove Weidenfeld, 1992.

JUVENILE

(Under pseudonym Jane Collier) *The Year of the Dream,* Funk, 1962.

(Under name Zena Shumsky, with Louis Shumsky) *First Flight,* Funk, 1962.

(Under name Zena Shumsky, with Louis Shumsky) *Shutterbug,* Funk, 1963.

(Under pseudonym Jane Collier) *A Tangled Web,* Funk, 1967.

Seven for the People: Public Interest Groups at Work (nonfiction), Messner, 1979.

Next Time I'll Know, Scholastic Inc., 1981.

CONTRIBUTOR

Alfred Hitchcock Presents Stories to be Read with the Lights On, Random House, 1963.

Best Detective Stories, Dutton, 1979.

Three-Way Mirror: Reflections in Fiction and Non-fiction, Nelson Canada, 1989.

Shaking Eve's Tree: Short Stories of Jewish Women, Jewish Publication Society, 1990.

A Sound of Thunder: A Green Anthology, Addison Wesley/Rubicon, 1993.

Contributor of short stories and articles to *Alaska Quarterly Review, Alfred Hitchcock's Mystery Magazine, Family Circle, Greensboro Review, Literary Review, McCall's, Money, New Letters, Prairie Schooner, Publishers Weekly, Southern Humanities Review, Southwest Review, Upstate,* and other periodicals.

WORK IN PROGRESS: A novel, tentatively entitled *After Long Silence.*

SIDELIGHTS: When author Zena Collier's first novel, *A Cooler Climate,* came out, she was in her sixties. "This was not the first time I had seen print," she told *CA:* "I'd been writing for the past thirty years and had published short stories in periodicals and also children's books. But it was the first time I'd had a novel published." Since *A Cooler Climate* was published in 1990, Collier has gone on to publish her second novel, *Ghost Note,* and plans to continue working in the novel format. "Though I've started late as a novelist, I'm happy to have finally found my voice in the longer form, and so far as one can plan anything, I plan to mainly stay with that in the future."

A Cooler Climate, set in a Maine summer resort town, is the story of a middle-aged woman who leaves her staid, plastic surgeon husband to make her own way in the world. The protagonist, Iris Prue, accepts a position as a housekeeper, and faces a new threat to her hard-won independence when she befriends Paula, the well-to-do woman who employs her. The novel was described as a "sumptu-

ous work of courage and hope" in the *New England Review of Books;* Paul Nathan referred to Collier as a "late bloomer" in *Publishers Weekly* in praise of the work and several reviewers remarked that Collier's writing career demonstrates the value of perseverance.

Collier's next novel, *Ghost Note,* is a tale of three grown sisters' reactions to their father, who has returned to their lives after a thirty-year absence. The story is told from the varying points of view of two of the sisters and of the father. Jeffrey Richards, reviewing the work in the Raleigh, NC, *News and Observer* described the novel as "subtle and surprising," and praised Collier for treating the plot in all its complexity rather than settling for simple bromides about dead-beat dads. Jennifer Baldino said of *Ghost Note* in *Welcomat:* "While the idea of a long-lost papa coming onto the scene and whipping his three daughters into shape seems slightly far-fetched, Collier's spicy plot is plausible because of her command of the art of storytelling." The novel is semi-autobiographical; Collier's own father resurfaced after having disappeared for twenty years. " 'My father walked into my house in America when I became a mother,' " Collier told Louise Continelli in the *Buffalo News.* " 'It was traumatic.' "

Collier told *CA:* "I didn't begin to write seriously and consistently until I was close to thirty. By then, I'd been living in the U.S. for ten years, had been married for ten years, and had two children. Because I'm a native Londoner and grew up there during the Second World War, I'm occasionally asked why I haven't written a novel set in England in that era. I've set some short stories in England, but so far not a novel, though I've often used events and people from that time and place as the raw material from which to shape fiction. It's often said that the subject chooses the writer, rather than the other way around. Whether that's true or not, my subject seems to be relationships, families, the question of how we are to live. People in their infinite variety always seem to be the best and—really—only subject."

BIOGRAPHICAL/CRITICAL SOURCES:

PERIODICALS

Buffalo News, August 28, 1992.
New England Review of Books, January 1990.
News & Observer (Raleigh, NC), August 9, 1992.
Publishers Weekly, June 8, 1990.
Welcomat (Philadelphia), September 16, 1992.

*   *   *

COMER, James P(ierpont) 1934-

PERSONAL: Born September 25, 1934, in East Chicago, IN; son of Hugh (a steelworker) and Maggie (Nichols)

Comer; married Shirley Ann Arnold, June 20, 1959; children: Brian Jay, Dawn Renee. *Education:* Indiana University, B.A., 1956; Howard University, M.D., 1960, post-doctoral study, 1961-63; University of Michigan, M.P.H., 1964; Yale University, post-doctoral study, 1964-67. *Avocational Interests:* Photography, travel, sports.

ADDRESSES: Home—212 Kent Dr., North Haven, CT 06473. *Office*—Child Study Center, Yale University, 230 Southeast Rd., New Haven, CT 06519.

CAREER: St. Catherine Hospital, East Chicago, IN, intern, 1960-61; Children's Hospital of the District of Columbia, Washington, DC, fellow in child psychiatry at Hillcrest Children's Center, 1967-68; Yale University, New Haven, CT, assistant professor at Child Study Center, 1968-70, associate professor, 1970-75, professor of psychiatry, 1975-76, Maurice Falk professor of psychiatry, 1976—, director of pupil services at Baldwin-King School Program, 1968-73, associate dean of medical school, 1969—, director of Child Study Center School Unit, 1973—. National Institutes of Mental Health, member of psychiatric staff, 1967-68; Solomon Fuller Institute member, 1973—. Trustee or member of board of directors of Afro-American House, 1970-72; Children's Television Workshop, 1972-88; Wesleyan University, 1978-84; Field Foundation, 1981-88; National Council for Effective Schools, 1985—; Connecticut Energy Corp., 1986—; Black Family Roundtable of Greater New Haven, 1986—; Child Study Center School Unit, 1986—; Albertus Magnus College, 1989—; Carnegie Corp. and Carnegie Corp. of New York, both 1990; and Connecticut State University, 1991—. Has served on the advisory committees or boards of Macy Faculty Fellows of the Josiah Macy, Jr., Foundation, 1971-74, and National Board to Abolish Corporal Punishment in the Schools, 1974—. Has served on numerous panels and commissions for public and private organizations. Has appeared on radio and television. Consultant to Washington, DC, Hospitality House, National Congress of Parents and Teachers, and Institute of the Black World. Licensed to practice medicine in Maryland, 1960, Indiana, 1961, and California and Connecticut, both 1965. *Military Service:* U.S. Public Health Service, Washington, DC, lecturer, planner, and clinical psychiatrist in Commission Corps, 1961-68; became lieutenant colonel.

MEMBER: American Medical Association, National Medical Association, American Orthopsychiatric Association, American Psychiatric Association (chair of Committee of Black Psychiatrists, 1973-75), Society of Health and Human Values, Associates for Renewal in Education, Black Psychiatrists of America (co-founder), American Academy of Child and Adolescent Psychiatry, National Association for the Advancement of Colored People, National Mental Health Association, Black Coalition of New Haven, Alpha Omega Alpha, Alpha Phi Alpha.

AWARDS, HONORS: Scholarships in academic medicine from John and Mary Markle Foundation, 1969-74; special Award from Alpha Phi Alpha, 1972, for outstanding service to mankind; award from Ebony Success Library, 1973; Howard University Distinguished Alumni Award, 1975; Child Study Association/Wel-Met Family Life Book Award, 1975, for *Black Child Care;* Rockefeller Public Service Award, 1980; Media Award, NCCJ, 1981; Community Leadership Award, Greater New Haven Council of Churches, 1983; Distinguished Fellowship Award, Connecticut chapter of Phi Delta Kappa, 1984; Distinguished Educator award, Connecticut Coalition of 100 Black Women, 1985; Distinguished Service Award, Connecticut Association of Psychologists, 1985; Elm and Ivy Award, New Haven Foundation, 1985; Outstanding Leadership Award, Children's Defense Find, 1987; Lela Rowland Prevention award, National Mental Health Association, 1989; Whitney M. Young, Jr., Service Award, Boy Scouts of America, 1989; Harold W. McGraw, Jr., prize in Education, 1990; National Prudential Leadership award, Prudential Foundation, 1990; Agnes Purcell McGavin award, Solomon Carter Fuller award, and Special Presidential Commendation awards, all from American Psychiatric Association, all 1990; Vera S. Paster Award, American Orthopsychiatric Association, 1990; Charles A. Dana Prize in Education, 1991; James Bryant Conant award, Education Commission of the States, 1991; Distinguished Service award, Council of Chief State School Officers, 1991; honorary degrees from University of New Haven, 1977, Calumet College, 1978, Bank Street College, 1987, Albertus Magnus College, Quinnipiac College, and DePauw University, all 1989, and Indiana University, Wabash College, Amherst College, Northwestern University, Worcester Polytechnic Institute, State University of New York at Buffalo, New School for Social Research, John Jay College of Criminal Justice, Wesleyan University, Wheelock College, Rhode Island College, and Princeton University, all 1991.

WRITINGS:

Beyond Black and White, Quadrangle Press, 1972.

(With Alvin F. Poussaint) *Black Child Care: How to Bring Up a Healthy Black Child in America: A Guide to Emotional and Psychological Development,* Simon & Schuster, 1975.

School Power: Implications of an Intervention Project, Free Press, 1980.

Maggie's American Dream: The Life and Times of a Black Family, Plume, 1988.

(With Ronald Edmonds) *A Conversation between James Comer and Ronald Edmonds: Fundamentals of Effective School Improvement,* National Center for Effective Schools Research and Development Corp., 1989.

(With Poussaint) *Raising Black Children: Two Leading Psychiatrists Confront the Educational, Social, and Emotional Problems Facing Black Children,* Plume, 1992.

Contributor to books, including *Negroes for Medicine,* edited by Lee Cogan, Johns Hopkins Press, 1968; *Violence in America: Historical and Comparative Perspectives,* edited by Ted Gurr and Hugh Graham, New American Library, 1969; *The Rhetoric of Black Power,* edited by Robert Scott and Wayne Brockriede, Harper, 1969; *Boys No More: A Black Psychologist's View of Community,* edited by Charles W. Thomas, Glencoe Press, 1970; *To Improve Learning: An Evaluation of Instructional Technology,* Vol. II, edited by Sydney G. Tickton, Bowker, 1971; *Racism and Mental Health,* edited by Charles V. Willie, Bernard M. Kramer, and Bertram S. Brown, University of Pittsburgh Press, 1973; *The Child and His Family: Children at Psychiatric Risk,* Vol. III, edited by E. James Anthony and Cyrille Koupernik, Viley, 1974; *Education and Social Problems,* edited by Francis A. J. Ianni, Scott, Foresman, 1974; and *Common Decency,* edited by Alvin Schorr, Yale University Press, 1988.

Columnist for *Parents Magazine.* Contributor to periodicals, including *Ebony* and *Redbook.* Has served on the editorial boards of *American Journal of Orthopsychiatry,* 1970-76, *Youth and Adolescence,* 1971-87, and *Journal of Negro Education,* 1978-83; member of advisory board, *Renaissance Two: Journal of Afro-American Studies at Yale,* 1971—; editorial consultant, *Journal of the American Medical Association,* 1973—, and *Magazine of the National Association of Mental Hygiene,* 1975—; guest editor, *Journal of American Academy of Child Psychiatry,* 1985. *Beyond Black and White* was released as a sound recording, Center for Cassette Studies, c. 1974.

SIDELIGHTS: Psychiatrist and author James P. Comer theorizes that the way to improve the academic performance of children in inner-city schools is to foster a family-like atmosphere in the classroom. Comer was born into a family with strong ties of its own in East Chicago, Indiana, just south of Chicago and near the heart of the city's steel-making industry. As a young man, Comer worked in the grease pits at one of the so-called "black jobs," often the most dangerous and taxing positions. He recounts these and other memories in his book *Maggie's American Dream: The Life and Times of a Black Family,* which also features an oral history of his mother's childhood in Mississippi.

In 1966, the Baldwin-King Program of Yale's Child Study Center began a project to collaborate with two New Haven schools on improving students' performance. Comer became involved with the project and in 1980 he published a book on the experiment, *School Power: Impli-*

cations of an Intervention Project, in which he critiques ten years of attempts to reform the school. "The real value of this book," wrote a *Choice* contributor, "is in pointing out just how difficult it is to bring about change in urban schools given the complex problems of this society."

In 1972's *Beyond Black and White,* Comer meditates on the problems of race relations and discusses his experiences as a black member of the academic elite. Realizing that there wasn't a good book on black parenting, he wrote, with Alvin F. Poussaint, *Black Child Care: How to Bring Up a Healthy Black Child in American: A Guide to Emotional and Psychological Development* in 1975. *New York Times Book Review* contributor Jim Haskins noted: "The book as a whole is informative and insightful, and its bibliography is the most thorough on the subject of black emotional and psychological development I have ever found." Comer and Poussaint penned a similar title in 1992, *Raising Black Children: Two Leading Psychiatrists Confront the Educational, Social, and Emotional Problems Facing Black Children,* in which they respond to the many questions each has heard from black parents, from dealing with racism to attempting to curb violence.

BIOGRAPHICAL/CRITICAL SOURCES:

PERIODICALS

Choice, January, 1981, pp. 705-706.
Christian Science Monitor, December 9, 1988, p. D9.
Ebony, September, 1973.
Newsweek, October 2, 1989, p. 50; January 25, 1993, p. 55.
New York Times, May 30, 1975.
New York Times Book Review, July 14, 1974, p. 29; June 15, 1975, p. 28.
New York Times Magazine, April 18, 1971.
Sepia, December, 1973.
Washington Post Book World, November 16, 1980, p. 26; November 19, 1989.*

*   *   *

COOKE, John Byrne 1940-

PERSONAL: Born October 5, 1940, in New York, NY; son of Alistair (a journalist) and Ruth (an educator; maiden name, Emerson) Cooke. *Education:* Harvard University, A.B. (cum laude), 1963. *Avocational Interests:* "My principal avocation is playing traditional American music and its present-day popular offshoots. Since 1982 I have performed with the legendary Stagecoach Band in Jackson Hole, Wyoming, where I live. Other avocations include skiing and bicycling and travel."

ADDRESSES: Home—P.O. Box 7415, Jackson, WY 83001. *Agent*—Candace Lake, The Candace Lake

Agency, 822 South Robertson Boulevard, Suite 200, Los Angeles, CA 90035.

CAREER: Charles River Valley Boys (bluegrass band), Cambridge, MA, guitarist and singer, 1961-67; Leacock-Pennebaker, Inc. (filmmakers), New York City, sound and camera man, 1967; road manager for Big Brother and the Holding Company, 1968, and for entertainer Janis Joplin, 1969-70; screenwriter, 1970—; writer, 1980—.

MEMBER: Writers Guild of America (West), Western Writers of America, Authors Guild, Wyoming Writers.

AWARDS, HONORS: Spur Award for best western historical novel, and Medicine Pipe Bearer's Award for best first novel, both from Western Writers of America, 1985, for *The Snowblind Moon.*

WRITINGS:

The Snowblind Moon (novel), Simon & Schuster, 1985.
South of the Border (novel), Bantam, 1989.

WORK IN PROGRESS: The Committee of Vigilance, a historical novel set in California during the Gold Rush, scheduled for publication in 1994—"a trip in 1991 took me to the South Pacific, where I sailed on a square-rigged vessel from New Zealand to Tonga as research" for the book; *Bad Men and Lawmen,* a TV documentary series on Western outlaws and lawmen, 1865-1935. Two original screenplays in development.

SIDELIGHTS: With two recent novels John Byrne Cooke has begun carving a niche as a novelist whose work combines fiction and historical fact with grace and imagination. In *South of the Border,* published in 1989, former real-life Pinkerton detective Charles Siringo encounters Butch Cassidy in America long after he has been presumed dead. Legend (and the eyewitness account of his real-life sister) has it that Cassidy, whom Paul Newman portrayed in the 1969 film *Butch Cassidy and the Sundance Kid,* survived the famous shoot-out in South America that ended the story of that movie. Cooke imagines Cassidy in Hollywood and Mexico on the set of a feature film about the life of Pancho Villa. Grace Lichtenstein, who reviewed *South of the Border* for the *Washington Post Book World,* observed that "Like Michener, Cooke is a historian in novelist's clothing, but he is not as long-winded and his sentences are more graceful."

Lichtenstein also described *The Snowblind Moon,* which is set in late 1800s Wyoming, as a "stunning first novel." Published in 1985, Cooke's first novel concerns the relationship between a Sioux Indian tribe and a small group of white settlers. Evan S. Connell, also in the *Washington Post Book World,* noted that Cooke portrays historic events, including several U.S. military forays into Indian territory, with such skill, that "after a while we no longer

distinguish between historical and fictional incidents." "John Byrne Cooke," Connell concluded, "is a name to jot down."

Cooke told *CA:* "My professional goal is first and foremost to be a good storyteller. My motivations were a youthful love of reading and a later love of history. To the extent that all stories—except pure fantasy—take place in a historical setting, my preference is to see that time and place are rendered accurately. I'm interested in how individual lives are affected by, and in rare cases affect, the larger events of the times. Above all, I'm interested in individual responsibility and freedom.

"My greatest concern in the realm of public affairs is the steady decline in personal responsibility in the United States. We want everything and we don't want to pay for any of it. This attitude combined with an education system that fails to instill basic literacy skills and neglects geography and history completely, suggests that the prognosis for maintaining a strong, free society is not good. As Eric Severeid reminded us on the day he retired from regular commentary on CBS News, 'Democracy is not a free ride. It demands more from each of us than any other arrangement.' "

BIOGRAPHICAL/CRITICAL SOURCES:

PERIODICALS

El Paso Times, March 12, 1989.
Fort Worth Star-Telegram, April 9, 1989, sec. 8, p. 7.
Kansas City Star, March 20, 1989.
New York Times Book Review, May 7, 1989, p. 24.
Publishers Weekly, January 6, 1989, p. 92.
Washington Post Book World, February 17, 1985; March 9, 1989, p. C15.
Western American Literature, fall, 1989, p. 277.

*   *   *

COOPER, Hannah
See SPENCE, William John Duncan

*   *   *

COWASJEE, Saros   1931-

PERSONAL: Born July 12, 1931, in Secundrabad, Deccan, India; son of Dara and Meher (Bharucha) Cowasjee. *Education:* St. John's College, Agra, India, B.A., 1951; Agra University, M.A., 1955; University of Leeds, Ph.D., 1960. *Religion:* Zoroastrian.

ADDRESSES: Home—3520 Hillsdale St., No. 308, Regina, Saskatchewan, Canada S4S 5Z5. *Office*—

Department of English, University of Regina, Regina, Saskatchewan, Canada S4S 0A2.

CAREER: Agra University, Agra, India, lecturer in English, 1955-57; Times of India Press, Bombay, assistant editor, 1961-63; University of Regina, Regina, Saskatchewan, instructor, 1963-64, assistant professor, 1964-66, associate professor, 1966-71, professor of English, 1971—. University of California, Berkeley, research associate, 1970-71; University of Aarhus, Denmark, Visiting Commonwealth Professor, 1975.

MEMBER: Writers Union of Canada, Association of Canadian University Teachers of English, Association for Commonwealth Literature and Language Studies, Authors Guild of India, Cambridge Society.

AWARDS, HONORS: J. N. Tata scholarship to study for Ph.D. degree at University of Leeds, 1957-59; Canada Council and Social Sciences and Humanities Research Council leave fellowships, 1968-69, 1974-75, 1978-79, and 1986-87; Canada Council humanities research grants, 1970-71 and 1974-75; President's Research Fund special grant, 1974-75.

WRITINGS:

Sean O'Casey: The Man behind the Plays, Oliver & Boyd, 1963, St. Martin's, 1964, revised edition, Oliver & Boyd, 1965.
O'Casey, Oliver & Boyd, 1966, Barnes & Noble, 1967.
Stories and Sketches, Writers Workshop (Calcutta), 1970.
Goodbye to Elsa (novel), Bodley Head, 1974.
"Coolie": An Assessment, Oxford University Press (New Delhi), 1976.
So Many Freedoms: A Study of the Major Fiction of Mulk Raj Anand, Oxford University Press (New Delhi), 1977.
Nude Therapy (short stories), Orient Paperbacks (New Delhi), 1978.
The Last of the Maharajas (screenplay; based on novel *Private Life of an Indian Prince* by Mulk Raj Anand; also see below), Writers Workshop (Calcutta), 1980.
Suffer Little Children (novel), Allied Publishers (New Delhi), 1982.
Studies in Indian and Anglo-Indian Fiction, HarperCollins (New Delhi), 1993.

EDITOR AND AUTHOR OF INTRODUCTION

Anand, *Private Life of an Indian Prince* (novel), Bodley Head, 1970.
Anand, *Seven Summers* (novel), Cedric Chivers, 1970.
(And author of afterword) Anand, *Untouchable* (novel), preface by E. M. Forster, Bodley Head, 1970.
Anand, *Coolie* (novel), Bodley Head, 1972.

Anand, *Author to Critic: The Letters of Mulk Raj Anand to Saros Cowasjee,* Writers Workshop (Calcutta), 1973.
Anand, *The Big Heart* (novel), Arnold-Heinemann (New Delhi), 1980.

EDITOR OF ANTHOLOGIES

(With Vasant A. Shahane) *Modern Indian Fiction,* Vikas Publishing (New Delhi), 1981.
(With Shiv K. Kumar) *Modern Indian Short Stories,* Oxford University Press (New Delhi), 1982.
Stories from the Raj, Bodley Head, 1982.
More Stories from the Raj and After, Grafton Books, 1986.
(With K. S. Duggal) *When the British Left* (fiction), Arnold-Heinemann (New Delhi), 1986.
The Raj and After (fiction), Macmillan (Madras, India), 1987.
Women Writers of the Raj: Short Fiction, HarperCollins, 1990.
(With K. S. Duggal) *Orphans of the Storm: Short Fiction on the Partitioning of India,* UBS Publishers (New Delhi), 1994.

OTHER

Also author of introduction, *Hindoo Holiday* (novel), by J. R. Ackerley, Arnold-Heinemann (New Delhi), 1979; *Mulk Raj Anand: A Check-List,* by G. Packham, Literary Press (Mysore), 1980; *Durbar* (novel), by Dennis Kincaid, Arnold-Heinemann (New Delhi), 1987; *Indigo* (novel), by Christine Weston, Arnold-Heinemann (New Delhi) 1988, HarperCollins, 1993; *The Wild Sweet Witch* (novel), by Philip Mason, Penguin Books India, 1989; *Siri Ram—Revolutionist* (novel), by Edmund Candler, Arnold Publishers (New Delhi), 1990; *The Competition Wallah,* by Sir George Otto Trevelyan, HarperCollins (New Delhi), 1992.

Contributor to *The Sting and the Twinkle,* edited by E. H. Mikhail, Macmillan, 1974; *Commonwealth Writer Overseas,* edited by Alastair Niven, Didier (Brussels), 1976; *Indo-English Literature: A Collection of Critical Essays,* edited by K. K. Sharma, Vimal Prakashan (Ghaziabad, India), 1977; *Awakened Conscience: Studies in Commonwealth Literature,* edited by C. D. Narasimhaiah, Sterling Publishers (New Delhi), 1978; *Perspectives on Mulk Raj Anand,* Vimal Prakashan, 1978; *Great Writers of the English Language: Dramatists,* St. Martin's, 1979; *Encyclopedia of World Literature,* Volume 1, Ungar, 1981; *Explorations in Modern Indo-English Fiction,* edited by R. K. Dhawan, Bahri Publications (New Delhi), 1982; *Language and Literature,* edited by Satendra Nandan, University of the South Pacific (Suva, Fiji), 1983; *Modern Irish Literature,* edited by Denis Lane and Carol M. Lane, Ungar, 1987; *Studies in Contemporary Indian Fiction in English,* edited by A. N. Dwivedi, Kitab Mahal (Allahabad, India),

1987; *Subjects Worthy Fame: Essays in Commonwealth Literature in Honour of H. H. Anniah Gowda,* edited by Alan McLeod, Sterling Publishers (New Delhi), 1988; *The Novels of Mulk Raj Anand,* edited by Dhawan, Prestige Books (New Delhi), 1992.

Also general editor of "Literature of the Raj" series, Arnold-Heinemann, 1984—. Contributor of short stories and articles to numerous publications in the United Kingdom, Canada, and India, including *Dublin Review, Drama Survey, Encounter, Guardian, International Fiction Review, Irish Times, Journal of Canadian Fiction, Journal of Commonwealth Literature, Literary Criterion, Literature East and West, Review of English Literature, Thought,* and *Wascana Review.* Managing editor, *Wascana Review,* 1966-69.

WORK IN PROGRESS: A novel; editing anthologies of short fiction; critical studies on Indian literature.

SIDELIGHTS: Saros Cowasjee told *CA* that when he began his writing career, "I had all the wrong notions about writers, and seeing myself in print fired my adolescent egotism. I dreamed of the 'publishers' party' that was never given in my honor, though once a publisher's assistant in London did buy me a hamburger and a pint of beer." He also noted that when he is writing, "I waste a lot of good quality paper by tearing or discarding what I have written; I also eat more and sleep less." Adding that "there never was a set purpose" behind writing a specific book or books, he commented, "Much depended on the nature of the book I was doing. Some books came close to being pretences, others were written to unmask all pretensions—such as my best-selling novel *Goodbye to Elsa.*"

In answering the query, "What advice might you give a young writer?", Cowasjee replies, "This question interests me, for in giving advice to others I am at the same time silently acknowledging some of my own failures. First, an aspiring writer must ask himself why he wants to be a writer. If it is for fame or name, there are better and safer shortcuts to these. He must determine quickly, often with no tangible evidence at his disposal, whether he has in him the stuff that makes a writer. This is the most difficult of all, and there is no one method by which he can find out. But there is a solution to his problems if he feels he isn't cut out to be a writer. Give up writing, try something else. Better a good husband or a good father than an ever-aspiring writer.

"Where must a writer find his material? No doubt in his own life, for a creator can only explain himself in his creation. But personal sagas are of little public interest until the writer, to use T. S. Eliot's words, is able 'to transmute his personal and private agonies into something rich and strange, something universal and impersonal.' Albert Camus makes a similar demand on the artist when he says,

'There is a stage in suffering, or in any other emotion, or passion, when it belongs to what is most personal and inexpressive in man and there is a stage when it belongs to art. But in its first moments art can never do anything with it. Art is the distance that time gives to suffering. It is man's transcendence in relation to himself.'

"One last thing—be honest, desperately honest with yourself. Let your work be as intimate and soul-searching as Prufrock's colloquy of the 'you' and 'I.' Eager as the modern writer is to reveal himself, there often comes a point where he draws the line. It is beyond this line that he must take us if he is to be a true writer."

*   *   *

CREELEY, Robert (White) 1926-

PERSONAL: Born May 21, 1926, in Arlington, MA; son of Oscar Slade (a physician) and Genevieve (Jules) Creeley; married Ann McKinnon, 1946 (divorced, 1955); married Bobbie Louise Hawkins, January 27, 1957 (divorced, 1976); married Penelope Highton, 1977; children: (first marriage) David, Thomas, Charlotte; (second marriage) Kirsten (stepdaughter), Leslie (stepdaughter; deceased), Sarah, Katherine; (third marriage) William, Hannah. *Education:* Attended Harvard University, 1943-44 and 1945-46; Black Mountain College, B.A., 1955; University of New Mexico, M.A., 1960.

ADDRESSES: Home—64 Amherst St., Buffalo, NY 14207. *Office*—Department of English, State University of New York, Buffalo, NY 14260.

CAREER: Poet, novelist, short story writer, essayist, and editor. Divers Press, Palma, Mallorca, Spain, founder and publisher, 1950-54; Black Mountain College, Black Mountain, NC, instructor in English, 1954-55; instructor at school for young boys, Albuquerque, NM, beginning 1956; University of New Mexico, Albuquerque, instructor in English, 1961-62; University of British Columbia, Vancouver, instructor in English, 1962-63; University of New Mexico, lecturer in English, 1963-65; State University of New York at Buffalo, visiting professor, 1965-66, professor of English, 1967—, David Gray Professor of Poetry and Letters, 1978-89, Capen Professor of Poetry and Humanities, 1990—. Bicentennial chair of American studies at University of Helsinki, Finland, 1988. Participated in numerous poetry readings and writers' conferences. *Wartime service:* American Field Service, India and Burma, 1945-46.

MEMBER: American Academy of Arts and Letters.

AWARDS, HONORS: Levinson Prize, 1960, for group of ten poems published in *Poetry;* D. H. Lawrence fellowship (for summer writing), University of New Mexico, 1960; National Book Award nomination, 1962, for *For Love;* Leviton-Blumenthal Prize, 1964, for group of thirteen poems published in *Poetry;* Guggenheim fellowship in poetry, 1964-65 and 1971; Rockefeller Foundation grant, 1966; Union League Civic and Arts Foundation Prize, 1967; Shelley Award, 1981, and Frost Medal, 1987, both from Poetry Society of America; National Endowment for the Arts grant, 1982; Deutsche Auftauschdienst Programme (DADD) providing residency in Berlin, 1983 and 1987; Leone d'Oro Premio Speziale, Venice, 1985; Walt Whitman citation of merit, 1989; named New York State Poet, 1989.

WRITINGS:

POETRY

Le Fou, Golden Goose Press, 1952.

The Kind of Act Of, Divers Press (Palma, Mallorca, Spain), 1953.

The Immoral Proposition, Jonathan Williams, 1953.

A Snarling Garland of Xmas Verse (published anonymously), Divers Press, 1954.

All That Is Lovely in Men, Jonathan Williams, 1955.

(With others) *Ferrin and Others,* Gerhardt (Germany), 1955.

If You, Porpoise Bookshop, 1956.

The Whip, Migrant Books, 1957.

A Form of Women, Jargon Books, 1959.

For Love: Poems, 1950-1960, Scribner, 1962.

Distance, Terrence Williams, 1964.

Two Poems, Oyez, 1964.

Hi There!, Finial Press, 1965.

Words (eight poems), Perishable Press, 1965.

Poems, 1950-1965, Calder & Boyars, 1966.

About Women, Gemini, 1966.

For Joel, Perishable Press, 1966.

A Sight, Cape Coliard Press, 1967.

Words (eighty-four poems), Scribner, 1967.

Robert Creeley Reads (with recording), Turret Books, 1967.

The Finger, Black Sparrow Press, 1968, enlarged edition published as *The Finger Poems, 1966-1969,* Calder & Boyars, 1970.

5 Numbers (five poems), Poets Press, 1968, published as *Numbers* (text in English and German), translation by Klaus Reichert, Galerie Schmela (Dusseldorf, Germany), 1968.

The Charm: Early and Collected Poems, Perishable Press, 1968, expanded edition published as *The Charm,* Four Seasons Foundation, 1969.

Divisions and Other Early Poems, Perishable Press, 1968.

Pieces (fourteen poems), Black Sparrow Press, 1968.

The Boy (poem poster), Gallery Upstairs Press, 1968.

Mazatlan: Sea, Poets Press, 1969.

Pieces (seventy-two poems), Scribner, 1969.

Hero, Indianakatz, 1969.

A Wall, Bouwerie Editions, 1969.

For Betsy and Tom, Alternative Press, 1970.

For Benny and Sabrina, Samuel Charters, 1970.

America, Press of the Black Flag, 1970.

Christmas: May 10, 1970, Lockwood Memorial Library, State University of New York at Buffalo, 1970.

St. Martin's, Black Sparrow Press, 1971.

1-2-3-4-5-6-7-8-9-0, drawings by Arthur Okamura, Shambala, 1971.

Sea, Cranium Press, 1971.

For the Graduation, Cranium Press, 1971.

Change, Hermes Free Press, 1972.

One Day after Another, Alternative Press, 1972.

For My Mother: Genevieve Jules Creeley, 8 April 1887-7 October 1972 (limited edition), Sceptre Press, 1973.

His Idea, Coach House Press, 1973.

Kitchen, Wine Press, 1973.

Sitting Here, University of Connecticut Library, 1974.

Thirty Things, Black Sparrow Press, 1974.

Backwards, Sceptre Press, 1975.

Hello, Hawk Press, 1976, expanded edition published as *Hello: A Journal, February 29-May 3, 1976,* New Directions, 1978.

Away, Black Sparrow Press, 1976.

Presences (also see below), Scribner, 1976.

Selected Poems, Scribner, 1976.

Myself, Sceptre Press, 1977.

Later, Toothpaste, 1978, expanded edition, New Directions, 1979.

The Collected Poems of Robert Creeley, 1945-1975, University of California Press, 1982.

Echoes, Toothpaste, 1982.

Mirrors, New Directions, 1983.

Memories, Pig Press, 1984.

Memory Gardens, New Directions, 1986.

The Company, Burning Deck, 1988.

Places, Shuffaloff Books, 1990.

Have a Heart, Limberlost Press, 1990.

A Poetry Anthology, Edmundson Art Foundation, 1992.

EDITOR

Charles Olson, *Mayan Letters,* Divers Press, 1953.

(With Donald M. Allen, and contributor) *New American Story,* Grove, 1965.

(And author of introduction) Olson, *Selected Writings,* New Directions, 1966.

(With Allen, and contributor) *The New Writing in the U.S.A.,* Penguin, 1967.

Whitman, Penguin, 1973.

(And contributor) *The Essential Burns,* Ecco Press, 1989.

Tim Prythero, Peters Corporation, 1990.

Olson, *Selected Poems,* University of California Press, 1993.

PROSE

The Gold Diggers (short stories), Divers Press, 1954, expanded edition published as *The Gold Diggers and Other Stories,* J. Calder, 1965.

The Island (novel), Scribner, 1963.

A Day Book (poems and prose; also see below), Scribner, 1972.

Mabel: A Story, and Other Prose (includes *A Day Book* and *Presences*), Calder & Boyars, 1976.

Collected Prose, Marion Boyars, 1984, corrected edition, University of California Press, 1988.

NONFICTION

An American Sense (essay), Sigma Press, 1965.

A Quick Graph: Collected Notes and Essays, edited by Donald M. Allen, Four Seasons Foundation, 1970.

Notebook, Bouwerie Editions, 1972.

A Sense of Measure (essays), Calder & Boyars, 1972.

Inside Out (lecture), Black Sparrow Press, 1973.

The Creative (lecture), Black Sparrow Press, 1973.

Was That a Real Poem and Other Essays, Four Seasons Foundation, 1979.

Collected Essays, University of California Press, 1989.

Autobiography, Hanuman Books, 1990.

OTHER

Listen (play; produced in London, 1972), Black Sparrow Press, 1972.

Contexts of Poetry: Interviews, 1961-1971, Four Seasons Foundation, 1973.

(Author of introduction) Judson Crews, *Nolo Contendere* (poems), Wings Press, 1978.

Charles Olson and Robert Creeley: The Complete Correspondence, nine volumes, edited by George F. Butterick, Black Sparrow Press, 1980-90.

(Author of introduction) Diane Christian, *Wide-Ons* (poems), Synergistic Press, 1981.

(Author of afterword) Gilbert Sorrentino, *Splendide-Hotel,* Dalkey Archive Press, 1984.

(Author of introduction) Robert Bertholf, *Robert Duncan: A Descriptive Bibliography,* Black Sparrow Press, 1986.

(Author of introduction) Butterick, *The Collected Poems of George F. Butterick,* edited by Richard Blevins, State University of New York at Buffalo, 1988.

(Author of foreword) Gerald Burns, *A Thing about Language,* Southern Illinois University Press, 1989.

Jane Hammond, Exit Art, 1989.

Irving Layton and Robert Creeley: The Complete Correspondence, edited by Ekbert Faas and Sabrina Reed, University of Toronto Press, 1990.

(Author of afterword) Michael Rumaker, *Gringos and Other Stories: A New Edition,* North Carolina Wesleyan College Press, 1991.

(Author of introduction) Louis Zukofsky, *Complete Short Poetry,* Johns Hpokins University Press, 1991.

(Author of foreword) Diana L. Johnson, *Denny Moers: Figments of a Landscape,* Brown University, 1992.

(Contributor) Trevor Fairbrother, *Brice Marden: Boston,* Museum of Fine Arts (Boston), 1992.

(Author of preface) Jack Kerouac, *Good Blond and Others,* edited by Donald Allen, Grey Fox Press, 1993.

Work represented in numerous anthologies, including *The New American Poetry: 1945-1960,* edited by Allen, Grove, 1960; *A Controversy of Poets,* edited by Paris Leary and Robert Kelly, Doubleday, 1965; *Norton Anthology of Modern Poetry,* edited by Richard Ellmann and Robert O'Clair, Norton, 1973; *The New Oxford Book of American Verse,* edited by Ellmann, Oxford University Press, 1976; and *Poets' Encyclopedia,* edited by John Cage, Unmuzzled Ox Press, 1980. Contributor to literary periodicals, including *Paris Review, Nation, Black Mountain Review, Origin, Yugen,* and *Big Table.* Founder and editor, *Black Mountain Review,* 1954-57.

SIDELIGHTS: Once known primarily for his association with the group called the "Black Mountain Poets," Robert Creeley has become an important and influential literary figure in his own right. His poetry is noted as much for its concision as its emotional power. Albert Mobilio, writing in the *Voice Literary Supplement,* observes: "Creeley has shaped his own audience. The much imitated, often diluted minimalism, the compression of emotion into verse in which scarcely a syllable is wasted, has decisively marked a generation of poets."

Creeley first began to develop his writing talents while attending Holderness School in Plymouth, New Hampshire, on a scholarship. His articles and stories appeared regularly in the school's literary magazine, and in his senior year he became its editor in chief. Creeley was admitted to Harvard in 1943, but his academic life was disrupted when he served as an ambulance driver for the American Field Service in 1944 and 1945.

Creeley returned to Harvard after the war and became associated with such writers as John Hawkes, Mitchell Goodman, and Kenneth Koch. He began corresponding with Cid Corman and Charles Olson, two poets who were to have a substantial influence on the direction of his future work. Excited especially by Olson's ideas about literature, Creeley began to develop a distinctive and unique poetic style.

Throughout the 1950s, Creeley was associated with the "Black Mountain Poets," a group of writers including Denise Levertov, Ed Dorn, Fielding Dawson, and others who had some connection with Black Mountain College, an experimental, communal college in North Carolina that was a haven for many innovative writers and artists of the period. Creeley edited the *Black Mountain Review* and developed a close and lasting relationship with Olson, who was the rector of the college. The two engaged in a lengthy, intensive correspondence about literary matters that has been collected and published as *Charles Olson and Robert Creeley: The Complete Correspondence.* Olson and Creeley together developed the concept of "projective verse," a kind of poetry that abandoned traditional forms in favor of a freely constructed verse that took shape as the process of composing it was underway. Olson called this process "composition by field," and his famous essay on the subject, "Projective Verse," was as important for the poets of the emerging generation as T. S. Eliot's "Tradition and the Individual Talent" was to the poets of the previous generation. Olson credited Creeley with formulating one of the basic principles of this new poetry: the idea that "form is never more than an extension of content."

According to Cynthia Edelberg in *Robert Creeley's Poetry: A Critical Introduction,* another important influence on Creeley's work at this time was Paul Valery, whose book *Monsieur Teste* "was Creeley's bible from the late forties until he rejected it in the sixties." In this work Valery contends that the most significant subject for any writer is the operation of his own mind and its interaction with the world. Creeley's emphasis on charting his impressions of an immediate experience may well have been derived from his reading of Valery. But it was shaped as well by the poetic climate of the 1950s and early 1960s, which made the "chronicle of the moment" a characteristic poetic form, from the *Lunch Poems* of Frank O'Hara to the Whitmanesque catalogs of Allen Ginsberg and the harrowing confessional exposes of Sylvia Plath and Robert Lowell.

Creeley was a leader in the generational shift that veered away from history and tradition as primary poetic sources and gave new prominence to the ongoing experiences of an individual's life. Because of this emphasis, the major events of his life loom large in his literary work. Creeley's marriage to Ann McKinnon ended in divorce in 1955. The breakup of that relationship is chronicled in fictional form in his only novel, *The Island,* which drew upon his experiences on the island of Mallorca, off the coast of Spain, where he lived with Ann and their three children in 1953 and 1954. After the divorce Creeley returned to Black Mountain College for a brief time before moving west to make a new life. He was in San Francisco during the flowering of the "San Francisco Poetry Renaissance" and became associated for a time with the writers of the Beat Generation: Allen Ginsberg, Jack Kerouac, Michael McClure, and others. His work appeared in the influential

"beat" anthology *The New American Poetry: 1945-1960,* edited by Donald Allen.

In 1956 Creeley accepted a teaching position at a boys' school in Albuquerque, New Mexico, where he met his second wife, Bobbie Louise Hawkins. Though Creeley published poetry and fiction throughout the 1950s and 1960s and had even established his own imprint, the Divers Press, in 1952, his work did not receive important national recognition until Scribner published his first major collection, *For Love: Poems 1950-1960,* in 1962. This book collected work that he had been issuing in small editions and little magazines during the previous decade. When *For Love* debuted, Mibilio writes, "it was recognized at once as a pivotal contribution to the alternative poetics reshaping the American tradition. . . . The muted, delicately contrived lyrics . . . were personal and self-contained; while they drew their life from the everyday, their techniques of dislocation sprang from the mind's naturally stumbled syntax."

At this point in Creeley's career, his distinctive poetic voice gathered large numbers of followers and imitators. It was a voice that conveyed, as William Spanos declared in *Boundary*'s Creeley issue, "a music from the edge," epitomizing the poetry revolution of the period. Along with Allen Ginsberg, Lawrence Ferlinghetti, Paul Blackburn, Gary Snyder, and other poets intent on linking poetry and performance, Creeley awakened a sense of new rhythmical possibilities for the spoken word. The unforgettable sound of his voice reading poetry typified Olson's famous dictum that poetry needed to put into itself "the breathing of the man who writes." Creeley's mentors were Ezra Pound, William Carlos Williams, Louis Zukofsky, and Olson, and the odd, off-center sound of his work when read aloud is an amalgam of those influences. He writes in *A Sense of Measure,* "Williams showed me early on that rhythm was a very subtle experience, and that words might share equivalent duration even though 'formally' they seemed in no way to do so. Pound said, 'LISTEN to the sound that it makes,' and Olson . . . made it evident that we could only go 'By ear.' Finally, there was and is the fact of, what it was one had to say—in Louis Zukofsky's sense, 'Out of deep need . . . !' "

The very first poem in *For Love,* "Hart Crane," with its unorthodox, Williams-like line breaks, its nearly hidden internal rhymes, and its subtle assonance and sibilance, announces the Creeley style—a style defined by an intense concentration on the sounds and rhythms of language as well as the placement of the words on the page. This intensity produces a kind of minimal poetry, which seeks to extract the bare linguistic bones from ongoing life experiences. In his introduction to *The New Writing in the U.S.A.,* Creeley cites approvingly Herman Melville's definition of "visible truth"—"the apprehension of the absolute condition of present things"—and supplements it with William Burroughs's famous statement from *Naked Lunch* about the writer's task: "There is only one thing a writer can write about: what is in front of his senses at the moment of writing. . . . I am a recording instrument . . . I do not presume to impose 'story' 'plot' 'continuity'."

Applying Burroughs's assertion to poetry meant not imposing on the work lyricism, metaphor, paradox, irony, closure, or any other conventional elements of poetry. Creeley's most memorable early poems nearly always adopted this antipoetic stance toward both language and experience. They avoided traditional poetic devices in favor of a keen attentiveness to experience and to the ways in which a writer struggles to articulate consciousness. Characteristically, the reader is plunged into the middle of an ongoing occurrence by means of a snatch of conversation, or more usually, by an internal monologue that recreates the feeling of a fleeting moment, a sudden awareness, or a traumatic event. The poems are built around Creeley's perception of the event and the "visible truth" he garners from it. That is, he seems to be searching constantly for an absolute truth in a fleeting moment.

Creeley sharpened and developed this style throughout the 1960s and 1970s in a series of books that seemed almost designed to exemplify the principles of projective verse and the ideas about poetry he proposed in a number of critical essays and talks. A poem called "Waiting" from *Words,* Creeley's second major collection, characterizes the problems a writer encounters transforming experience into poetry. His typical stance, described in this poem, is that of a poet struggling to bring a poem into being with no resources other than the heightened attention he brings to the task. He "pushes behind the words," giving his emotions and experiences the formal contours that embody their meaning. Creeley's fear is that the words will quit coming.

Without the words that emanate from experience, life seems "a dull space of hanging actions"; the relations between things become severed and a sense of utter formlessness prevails. By discovering the appropriate form for the transitory emotional states he *needs* to write about, Creeley has always *used* poetry to take stock of both the world around him and the state of his being at any particular moment. In addition, he has always tried to write about his experiences without the stale viewpoint of habitual thought, calling instead for a clarity of vision unencumbered by preconceptions. It is Creeley's version of the advice Ezra Pound gave to all creative artists, "Make it New."

In *Pieces, A Day Book, Thirty Things,* and *Hello: A Journal, February 29-May 3, 1976,* all published between 1968 and 1978, Creeley attempted to break down the concept of a "single poem" by offering his readers sequential, associated fragments of poems with indeterminate beginnings and endings. All of these works are energized by the same heightened attention to the present that characterizes Creeley's earlier work, but in *Hello,* a book written as journal entries over a five-week period while Creeley traveled in the Orient and South Pacific, he speculates on the possibility of using memory rather than the present as a poetic source. The poetry remains stubbornly rooted in the present despite the insistent intrusion of memories, both recent and long past.

Many of the poems in *Hello* refer to the last days of Creeley's relationship with his second wife, Bobbie. That marriage ended in divorce in 1976, the same year he met Penelope Highton, his third wife, while traveling in New Zealand. In this sense, the book may be described in much the same terms as Sherman Paul, in his book *The Lost America of Love,* describes *For Love,* "Poems of two marriages, the breakup of one, the beginning of another." For all of Creeley's experimentation, he has always been in some ways an exceedingly domestic poet; his mother, children, wives, and close friends are the subjects of his best work. Because Creeley's second marriage lasted nearly twenty years, the sense of a major chunk of his life drifting away from him is very strong in *Hello.* Creeley here conveys the traumatic emotional state that almost always accompanies the breakup of long-term relationships. En route to Perth, he writes: "Sitting here in limbo, there are / people walking through my head." In Singapore he remarks on his tenuous hold on things: "Getting fainter, in the world, / fearing something's fading. . . ." Although *Hello* is superficially a record of Creeley's travels, the poems are not really about the countries he has visited, but rather about the landscape of mind he has brought with him.

It is not until Creeley's next major collection, 1979's *Later,* that the poetry seems to shift into a new phase characterized by a greater emphasis on memory, a new sense of life's discrete phases, and an intense preoccupation with aging. In "Myself," the first poem in *Later,* he writes: "I want, if older, / still to know / why, human, men / and women are / so torn, so lost / why hopes cannot / find a better world / than this." This futile but deeply human quest captures the spirit of Creeley's later work. It embodies a commonly shared realization: one becomes older but still knows very little about essential aspects of life, particularly the mysteries of human relationships. And as Alan Williamson observes in his *New York Times Book Review* assessment of *Later,* "In general, the stronger the note of elegiac bafflement and rage (the past utterly gone, the compensating wisdom not forthcoming), the better the writing."

In one of several poems in *Later* called "For Pen"—the title echoing his vocation as well as referring more apparently to the nickname of his third wife, Penelope—Creeley finds little difference between the desires of youth and age, except that age conspires with physical decline to make a mockery of desire. Ultimately, the speaker seems to come to terms with the inevitability of aging. This tone of resigned acceptance characterizes many of the poems in *Later.* He realizes, in "After," that "I'll not write again / things a young man / thinks, not the words / of that feeling." But there are other words he can and does make poetry of—the words of present feelings that both incorporate and reflect upon the past. These words are the "measure" of a life—what one is and has been capable of. "Measure is my testament," Creeley writes in *A Sense of Measure.* "What uses me is what I use and in that complex measure is the issue. I cannot cut down trees with my bare hand, which is measure of both tree and hand. In that way I feel that poetry, in the very subtlety of its relation to image and rhythm, offers an intensely various record of such things. It is equally one of them." Creeley continues to adhere to this testament in *Later,* where the poems seem to be a part of his continuing effort to discover the measure of things—the worth of any of life's singular episodes to the whole of that life.

This effort culminates in the ten-part title poem, "Later," written over a period of ten days in September of 1977. The poem presents a kaleidoscopic view of various times and events important to Creeley's life, beginning with an evocation of lost youth. Youth, in later life, can only become a palpable part of the present through the evocative power of memory. Another section of the poem comments on how certain empirical sensations are repositories of memory. A taste, a smell, a touch, can evoke a lost world. "Later" continues to present a flood of childhood memories: a lost childhood dog that Creeley fantasizes running into again after all these years; memories of his mother and friends and neighbors; sights and sounds of his early days all evoked and made a part of the poetry he is composing in an attic room in Buffalo, September, 1977.

The poem's final lines reveal the most affirmative and optimistic aspects of Creeley's later work: "the wonder of life is / that *it is* at all. . . ." This acceptance of things as they are is tempered in the later work by a nostalgia for things as they were. One feels, in *Later,* a longing for the excitement and turmoil of the Black Mountain-Beat Generation days when poetry seemed much more central to American life and culture than it does in the technology-dominated society of the later twentieth century.

In the work produced after the material included in his *Collected Poems, 1945-1975* there is an increasing tendency to derive poetry from what the English Romantic poet William Wordsworth called "emotion recollected in

tranquility." It is a poetry that remembers and reflects and seems much less tied to the exigencies of the present than the earlier work. In *Mirrors,* published in 1984, the commitment to identifying and reconstructing those moments from the past that have most shaped his life deepens. The collection bears an epigraph from Francis Bacon: "In Mirrours, there is the like / Angle of Incidence, from the Object / to the Glasse, and from the Glasse / to the Eye." Poetry, in this sense, is the mirror which deflects the memory of past experience into our awareness in the present. Creeley reaches into early childhood in a poem called "Memory 1930" to illuminate the moment he learned of his father's death at a time when he was obviously too young to comprehend the impact it would have on his entire life. Here he presents it as a major fissure in his early life, viewed from an "angle of incidence" over fifty years later. He creates a picture of himself as a child, witnessing what appears as a surreal scene—that of his dying father being driven away in an ambulance. It is as if Creeley, who has written about the death of his father more obliquely in earlier work, can now bring that momentous event clearly into focus so that he observes the impact it had on his young self, who sits intently observing its occurrence. The older Creeley watches the young Creeley watching his father being driven away in an ambulance to die. In this way, "Memory 1930" and other poems in *Mirrors* are attempts at recovering those pieces of the past that best reflect Creeley's life.

Mirrors reveals how much a part of our characters memories become with each passing year, so that as we age we accumulate the mannerisms of our parents and reexperience past situations. This theme of the present incorporating the past is most literal in "Prospect," one of the most memorable poems in *Mirrors.* It is an atypical Creeley poem because it utilizes conventional elements of poetry—symbolism, metaphor, and imagery—in a surprisingly traditional manner. In fact, the poem has a remarkably unique resonance because Creeley's physical description of nature conveys both present and past psychological states. It takes no deep looking into the poem to see the landscape as emblematic of the state of Creeley's later life, invigorated by a new marriage and the birth of a new child, his son William. The poem concludes with the reflections awakened by a contemplation of the landscape, which is described as peaceful and beautiful, yet in the end "faintly painful." The final phrase surprises, coming at the end of an otherwise tranquil and nearly celebratory poem. It reminds the reader that although embarking on a new life can create the illusion that it is possible to exist in an Edenic landscape apart from time, in reality the past remains an integral part of the present. "Faintly painful," with its echoing first syllable rhyme, is exactly right to convey the contrary feelings of both relief and regret that the poem ultimately leaves the reader with—relief that the thoughtfulness the landscape provokes is not more painful, regret that there is any pain at all.

But pain has been one of the most constant elements in Creeley's work, and this later poetry continues to search for words to express it with sensitivity and exactness and without the sometimes maudlin excesses of "confessional" verse. Though these poems are more rooted in memory than the earlier work, Creeley remains committed to the poetic task of getting things exactly right. This has been the task of his writing throughout his career, and as readers look into the "mirror" of Creeley's work, they can see not only his aging, but their own.

BIOGRAPHICAL/CRITICAL SOURCES:

BOOKS

Allen, Donald, editor, *The New American Poetry: 1945-1960,* Grove, 1960.

Allen, editor, *Robert Creeley, Contexts of Poetry: Interviews, 1961-1971,* Four Seasons Foundation, 1973.

Allen and Warren Tallman, editors, *The Poetics of the New American Poetry,* Grove, 1973.

Butterick, George F., editor, *Charles Olson and Robert Creeley: The Complete Correspondence,* Black Sparrow Press, 1980.

Contemporary Authors Autobiography Series, Volume 10, Gale, 1989.

Contemporary Literary Criticism, Gale, Volume 1, 1973, Volume 2, 1974, Volume 4, 1975, Volume 8, 1978, Volume 11, 1979, Volume 15, 1980, Volume 36, 1986.

Corman, Cid, editor, *The Gist of Origin,* Viking, 1975.

Creeley, Robert, *A Sense of Measure,* Calder & Boyars, 1972.

Creeley, *Hello,* Hawk Press, 1976, expanded edition published as *Hello: A Journal, February 29-May 3, 1976,* New Directions, 1978.

Creeley, *Later,* Toothpaste, 1978, expanded edition, New Directions, 1979.

Creeley, *Mirrors,* New Directions, 1983.

Creeley and Allen, editors, *New American Story,* Grove, 1965.

Creeley and Allen, editors, *The New Writing in the U.S.A.,* Penguin, 1967.

Dictionary of Literary Biography, Gale, Volume 5: *American Poets since World War II,* 1980, Volume 16: *The Beats: Literary Bohemians in Postwar America,* 1983.

Edelberg, Cynthia Dubin, *Robert Creeley's Poetry: A Critical Introduction,* University of New Mexico Press, 1978.

Ford, Arthur L., *Robert Creeley,* Twayne, 1978.

Novik, Mary, *Robert Creeley: An Inventory, 1945-1970,* Kent State University Press, 1973.

Olson, Charles, *Mayan Letters,* edited by Creeley, Divers Press, 1953, Grossman, 1968.

Olson, *The Human Universe,* Auerhan, 1965.

Paul, Sherman, *The Lost America of Love,* Louisiana State University Press, 1981.

Sheffler, Ronald Anthony, *The Development of Robert Creeley's Poetry,* University of Massachusetts, 1971.

Wilson, John, editor, *Robert Creeley's Life and Work: A Sense of Increment,* University of Michigan Press, 1987.

PERIODICALS

American Book Review, May/June, 1984.

American Poetry Review, November/December, 1976.

Atlantic, November, 1962; February, 1968; October, 1977.

Books Abroad, autumn, 1967.

Book Week, June 4, 1967.

Boundary 2, spring, 1975; spring and fall (special two-volume issue on Creeley), 1978.

Cambridge Quarterly, summer, 1969.

Canadian Forum, August, 1967; September, 1970.

Christian Science Monitor, October 9, 1969.

Commonweal, December 10, 1965.

Contemporary Literature, spring, 1972.

Critique, spring, 1964.

Encounter, February, 1969.

Fifties, Volume 2, 1959.

Harper's, August, 1967; September, 1983.

Hudson Review, summer, 1963; summer, 1967; spring, 1970; summer, 1977.

Iowa Review, spring, 1982.

Kenyon Review, spring, 1970.

Kulchur, Number 3, 1961.

Library Journal, September 1, 1979.

Listener, March 23, 1967.

London Magazine, June/July, 1973.

Los Angeles Times Book Review, April 17, 1983; October 30, 1983; March 4, 1984; June 24, 1984; June 23, 1991, p. 8.

Minnesota Review, Volume 8, number 2, 1968; Volume 9, number 1, 1969.

Modern Poetry Studies, winter, 1977.

Nation, August 25, 1962.

National Observer, October 30, 1967.

National Review, November 19, 1960.

New Leader, October 27, 1969.

New Republic, October 11, 1969; December 18, 1976.

New Statesman, August 6, 1965; March 10, 1987.

New York Review of Books, January 20, 1966; August 1, 1968.

New York Times, June 27, 1967.

New York Times Book Review, November 4, 1962; September 22, 1963; November 19, 1967; October 27, 1968; January 7, 1973; May 1, 1977; March 9, 1980; August 7, 1983; June 24, 1984; September 23, 1984.

Observer (London), September 6, 1970.

Open Letter, winter, 1976-77.
Paris Review, fall, 1968.
Parnassus, fall/winter, 1984.
Partisan Review, summer, 1968.
Poetry, March, 1954; May, 1958; September, 1958; March, 1963; April, 1964; August, 1966; January, 1968; March, 1968; August, 1968; May, 1970; December, 1970; September, 1984.
Publishers Weekly, March 18, 1968.
Sagetreib, Volume 1, number 3, 1982; Volume 3, number 2, 1984.
Saturday Review, August 4, 1962; December 11, 1965; June 3, 1967.
Sewanee Review, winter, 1961.
Southwest Review, winter, 1964.
Time, July 12, 1971.
Times Literary Supplement, March 16, 1967; August 7, 1970; November 12, 1970; December 11, 1970; May 20, 1977; May 30, 1980; February 20, 1981; November 4, 1983; May 10, 1991, p. 22.
Village Voice, October 22, 1958; December 10, 1979; November 25, 1981.
Voice Literary Supplement, September, 1991, p. 14.
Virginia Quarterly Review, summer, 1968; winter, 1972; spring, 1973.
Washington Post Book World, August 11, 1991, p. 13.
Western Humanities Review, spring, 1970.
World Literature Today, autumn, 1984.
Yale Review, October, 1962; December, 1969; spring, 1970.

* * *

CRIM, Keith R(enn) 1924-
(Casey Renn)

PERSONAL: Born September 30, 1924, in Winchester, VA; son of Harry Marshall (a clergyman) and Grace (Renn) Crim; married Evelyn Ritchie (a teacher), August 26, 1947 (divorced); married Julia Firr Hickson, June 29, 1979; children: (first marriage) Deborah Ann, Gregory Marshall (deceased), Edward McDonald, Julia Ruth, Martin Ritchie; (second marriage) Laura Renn. *Education:* Bridgewater College, B.A., 1947; Union Theological Seminary, B.D., 1950, Th.M., 1951, Th.D., 1959; University of Basel, graduate study, 1951-52. *Politics:* Democrat.

ADDRESSES: Office—Department of Philo-Religious Studies, Virginia Commonwealth University, 901 West Franklin St., Richmond, VA 23220.

CAREER: Clergyman of Presbyterian Church, ordained 1950; Taejon, Korea, missionary, 1952-66; Taejon College, Taejon, Korea, assistant professor, 1956-59, associate professor, 1959-62, professor of English, 1962-65,

acting president, 1958-59, 1964-65; John Knox Press, Richmond, VA, senior book editor, 1967-69; American Bible Society, New York City, Bible translator, 1969-73; Virginia Commonwealth University, Richmond, professor of religious studies, 1973-83; Westminster Press, Philadelphia, PA, editorial director, 1983-89; New Concord Presbyterian Church, New Concord, VA, pastor, 1991—. Visiting professor of world religions, Austin Presbyterian Seminary, 1962-63. Teacher in seminars for translators in Asia, North America, and Europe; consultant on translation projects in Korea and Curacao, and in Amerindian languages. *Military Service:* U.S. Army, Military Intelligence, 1943-46; served in Europe; became staff sergeant.

MEMBER: American Academy of Religion, Society of Biblical Literature, Catholic Bible Association, Virginia Writers' Club (president 1977-78).

WRITINGS:

The Royal Psalms, John Knox, 1962.
(Under pseudonym Casey Renn) *Limericks—Lay and Clerical,* line drawing by Jeanne Meinke, John Knox, 1969.
(With George A. Buttrick and others) *The Interpreter's Dictionary of the Bible,* Abingdon, 1976.
(Editor) *Interpreter's Dictionary of the Bible,* supplementary volume, Abingdon, 1978.
(Editor) *Abingdon Dictionary of Living Religions,* Abingdon, 1981, published as *Perennial Dictionary of World Religions,* Abingdon, 1989.

TRANSLATOR FROM GERMAN

The Praise of God in the Psalms, John Knox, 1964.
Dietrich Bonhoefer, *I Loved This People,* John Knox, 1965.
Karl Barth, *Selected Prayers,* John Knox, 1966.
K. Barth, *Ad Limina Apostolorum,* John Knox, 1968.
Hans W. Wolff, *The Old Testament: A Guide to It's Writings,* Fortress, 1973.
Hans Kraus, *Theology of the Psalms,* Augsburg Publishing House, 1986.

OTHER

Contributor of news reports from Korea to *Christian Century,* 1959-62, 1964-66. *Journal of Bible Literature,* editorial board, 1975-78; Old Testament, *Good News Bible,* translation team, 1978; *Quarterly Review,* editorial board, 1980-84.

WORK IN PROGRESS: A novel dealing with tensions between Americans and Koreans on an army base in South Korea.

SIDELIGHTS: In addition to fluency in German and Korean, Keith Crim reads French, and has some ability in

Japanese, Dutch, Italian, and the classical European languages.*

*   *   *

CROSSMAN, Richard (Howard Stafford) 1907-1974

PERSONAL: Born December 15, 1907, in London, England; died of liver cancer, April 5, 1974; son of Stafford (a justice) and Helen (Howard) Crossman; married second wife, Inezita Hilda Baker, 1937; married third wife, Anne Patricia McDougall, June 2, 1954; children: Patrick, Virginia. *Education:* New College, Oxford, B.A.; University of Berlin, graduate study, 1930-31. *Politics:* Labour.

CAREER: Oxford University, Oxford, England, fellow of New College and tutor, 1930-37; lecturer, Oxford University Delegacy for Extra Mural Studies and Worker's Educational Association, 1938-40; British Foreign Office, Political Intelligence Department, London, England, director of German section, 1940-43; Allied Forces Headquarters, Algiers, deputy director of psychological warfare, 1943; Supreme Headquarters of the Allied Expeditionary Forces, London, assistant chief of psychological warfare, 1944-45; Labour Member of Parliament from Coventry East, 1945-74, served as Minister of Housing and Local Government, 1964-66, leader of House of Commons and Lord President of the Council, 1966-68; Secretary of State for Social Services in charge of Department of Health and Social Security, 1968-70. Member of Labour Party executive committee, 1952-67. Leader of Labour group on Oxford City Council, 1934-40; member of Malta Round Table Conference, 1945, Anglo-American Palestine Commission, 1946; chairman of working party on National Superannuation, 1956, and working party on science, 1963.

MEMBER: Athenaeum Club, Farmers' Club, Garrick Club.

AWARDS, HONORS: Order of the British Empire, 1945; Privy Councillor, 1964.

WRITINGS:

(Editor) *Oxford and the Groups,* Blackwell, 1934.
Plato Today, Allen & Unwin, 1937, revised edition, Oxford University Press, 1959.
Government and the Governed, Christopher, 1939, 5th edition, Pica Press, 1969.
How Britain is Governed, Labour Book Service, 1939.
Palestine Mission: A Personal Record, Harper, 1947.
(Editor and author of introduction) *The God That Failed,* Harper, 1950.

(Editor and contributor) *New Fabian Essays,* Praeger, 1952, reprinted with new introduction by Crossman, Dent, 1970.
The Charm of Politics and Other Essays in Political Criticism, Harper, 1958.
A Nation Reborn: A Personal Report on the Roles Played by Weizmann, Bevin, and Ben-Gurion in the Story of Israel, Atheneum, 1960 (published in England as *A Nation Reborn: The Israel of Weizmann, Bevin, and Ben-Gurion,* Hamish Hamilton, 1960).
Planning for Freedom, Hamish Hamilton, 1965.
The Politics of Socialism, Atheneum, 1965.
(With Lawrence Alloway and Paul Chambers) *Three Studies in Modern Communication,* Panther, 1969.
The Myths of Cabinet Government, Harvard University Press, 1972 (published in England as *Inside View: Three Lectures on Prime Ministerial Government,* J. Cape, 1972).
The Diaries of a Cabinet Minister (also see below), Volume I: *Minister of Housing, 1964-1966,* Hamish Hamilton, 1975, Holt, 1976, Volume II: *Lord President of the Council and Leader of the House of Commons, 1966-68,* Hamish Hamilton, 1976, Holt, 1977, Volume III: *Secretary of State for Social Services, 1968-70,* Hamish Hamilton, 1977, Holt, 1978.
The Crossman Diaries: Selections from the Diaries of a Cabinet Minister, 1964-1970, edited with an introduction by Anthony Howard, Hamish Hamilton, 1979.
The Backbench Diaries of Richard Crossman, edited by Janet Morgan, Holmes & Meier, 1981 (published in England as *The Backbench Diaries,* Hamish Hamilton, 1981).

Also author of pamphlets, including *A Palestine Munich?,* with Michael Foot, Gollancz, 1946; *Socialism and the New Despotism,* Fabian Society, 1956; *Labour in the Affluent Society,* Fabian Society, 1960; *Socialism and Planning,* Fabian Society, 1967; *Paying for the Social Services,* Fabian Society, 1969; and *The Role of the Volunteer in the Modern Social Service,* University of Oxford, 1974. Contributor to Jacob Peter Mayer's *Political Thought: The European Tradition,* J. M. Dent, 1939, and to Daniel Lerner's *Sykewar: Psychological Warfare against Germany, D-Day to VE-Day,* G. W. Stewart, 1949. Also contributor of articles and reviews to *New Statesman and Nation, Spectator, New York Times Magazine, New Republic, Observer Review,* and other periodicals. Assistant editor, *New Statesman and Nation,* 1938-55; editor, *New Statesman,* 1970-72.

SIDELIGHTS: "A bubbling, brilliant and provocative man, Richard Crossman was one of the rallying points for the left wing of the British Labour Party," writes Alden Whitman of the *New York Times.* Crossman represented his party in Parliament for nearly thirty years, dubbing himself the keeper of "Britain's Socialist conscience." His manner with other politicians was polemical and adversarial, and he was not afraid to challenge them on the floor of Parliament or in the pages of *New Statesman,* which he edited for several years. "I am an intellectual," Crossman once wrote, "which means that though I have warm personal feelings, my loyalty is primarily to ideas and to chasing ideas in argument, which is the only way I can think." Whitman recalls: "He was rarely out of the news, either owing to the trenchancy of remarks about the Conservatives or to criticisms directed at him."

In the months shortly before his death, Crossman dictated to his secretary several thousand pages worth of memoirs, which were edited and published posthumously as *The Diaries of a Cabinet Minister.* The *New York Times Book Review*'s Anthony Sampson observes: "It was Crossman's ambition to be able to describe the true workings of British government, both from outside and from inside, with the accuracy and honesty of an academic who was also a participant." Because the memoirs were, like their author, acerbic and opinionated, many politicians were appalled that they had been published at all; with the passage of time, however, the controversy over the diaries has settled a bit, and it is possible to measure their contribution to modern British history.

In *The Diaries of a Cabinet Minister,* Crossman showed an unexpected flair for the role of the diarist. David Watt, writing in the *Times Literary Supplement,* explains: "What distinguishes Crossman from all rivals and imitators is not so much that he gives more information to the listener, or that his political observations are acuter, or even that he possessed the authentic diarist's mixture of extreme egocentricity and insatiable curiosity, though all that is true: it is that he was . . . a born teacher." Though *Washington Post Book World* critic Godfrey Hodgson warns, "for American readers, much of the subject matter [in the diaries] will be obscure and even trivial," he stresses that, "for those who have the curiosity to try it, and the patience to persevere, Crossman has written an extraordinarily rich book about how politics and government actually work, anywhere, and especially about the human ambitions, irritations, rivalries and manipulations with which politicians . . . make a system work. Or rather, in this case, make it not work." In a review of Crossman's memoirs, *Listener* contributor Barbara Castle proclaims: "I am now more than ever convinced that every serious politician should keep a diary and, if it is readable, publish it."

In addition to their importance as an insider's view of British Parliament, most reviewers found *The Diaries of a Cabinet Minister* and their companion, *The Backbench Diaries,* to be, through the sheer audacity of the author's views, very entertaining books. Sampson admits that Crossman's pompous philosophizing made him "a caricature of the intellectual in politics." However, he continues, "it is as a diarist, not as a practical politician, that we must judge Crossman in this book, and the more outrageous his arrogance, the more engaging are his entries." Watt notes that "there are inevitably moments where his skill or his vitality flags. But [Crossman's] anecdotes are as hilarious, his judgments as provocative, and the force of his personality as strongly communicated as ever."

Two decades after their controversial publication, the impact of Crossman's diaries is still being felt. Patrick Brogan of the *Washington Post Book World* calls the collected diaries "unquestionably the most important personal document to come out of British politics in the 1960s," while Sampson feels that Crossman's career as a politician has been superseded by his legacy as a diarist, for "in that role he will have few rivals." Sydney Jacobson relates in the *Listener* that a colleague of Crossman's once said to him, " 'You have an irresistible temptation to say what people don't like to hear.' This was true, and it may be that this striving for intellectual honesty by voicing the unpalatable opinion and asking the awkward question was Crossman's finest contribution to politics."

BIOGRAPHICAL/CRITICAL SOURCES:

BOOKS

Crossman, Richard, *Palestine Mission: A Personal Record,* Harper, 1947.

PERIODICALS

Books and Bookmen, July, 1972, p. 37; April, 1976, pp. 6-8; May, 1977, pp. 38-41; April, 1978, pp. 8-10; May, 1978, pp. 12-14; May, 1979, pp. 8-9.
Commentary, July, 1990, p. 32.
Economist, March 14, 1981, pp. 91-92.
Listener, December 11, 1975, pp. 802-804; November 4, 1976, pp. 587-588; April 5, 1979, pp. 496-497; March 5, 1981, pp. 298-299.
New Republic, June 18, 1977, pp. 31-32.
New Statesman, July 26, 1968; December 12, 1975, pp. 758-759; November 4, 1977, p. 622; April 6, 1979; March 6, 1981, p. 19.
Newsweek, July 6, 1970; June 14, 1971.
New Yorker, May 9, 1977, p. 143; October 2, 1978, pp. 142, 144-147.
New York Herald Tribune, November 3, 1946.
New York Review of Books, November 9, 1978, pp. 41-44; July 16, 1981, pp. 3-4.
New York Times, April 6, 1974, p. 34.
New York Times Book Review, September 12, 1976; August 21, 1977, pp. 10-11; July 16, 1978; June 14, 1981, pp. 1, 22-23.
Pathfinder, December 18, 1946.

Saturday Evening Post, January 3, 1948.

Spectator, October 7, 1955; December 13, 1975, p. 760; November 5, 1977, pp. 19-20; April 7, 1979, pp. 20-21; March 28, 1981, pp. 19-20.

Times Literary Supplement, May 19, 1972; January 30, 1976, pp. 105-106; December 2, 1977, p. 1421; March 6, 1981, p. 245.

Washington Post Book World, September 12, 1976; June 11, 1978.

OBITUARIES:

PERIODICALS

Current Biography, June, 1974.*

—*Sketch by Brandon Trenz*

* * *

CROWLEY, John 1942-

PERSONAL: Born December 1, 1942, in Presque Isle, ME; son of Joseph B. (a doctor) and Patience (Lyon) Crowley. *Education:* Indiana University, B.A., 1964.

ADDRESSES: Home—Box 395, Conway, MA 01341.

CAREER: Photographer and commercial artist, 1964-66; fiction writer and free-lance writer for films and television, 1966—.

AWARDS, HONORS: American Book Award nominee, 1980, for *Engine Summer;* Hugo Award nominee, Nebula Award nominee, World Fantasy Award, all 1982, all for *Little, Big;* American Film Festival Award, 1982, for *America Lost and Found.*

WRITINGS:

NOVELS

The Deep, Doubleday, 1975.
Beasts, Doubleday, 1976.
Engine Summer, Doubleday, 1979.
Little, Big, Bantam, 1981.
Aegypt, Bantam, 1987.
Great Work of Time, Bantam, 1991.

SHORT STORIES

(Contributor) *Shadows,* Doubleday, 1977.
(Contributor) *Elsewhere,* Ace Books, 1981.
Novelty, Bantam, 1989.

OTHER

Author of television scripts for *America Lost and Found* and *No Place to Hide,* Public Broadcasting System. Contributor to periodicals, including *Omni.*

SIDELIGHTS: Author John Crowley is praised by critics for his thoughtful, finely-wrought works of science fiction and fantasy. Reviewing Crowley's first novel, *The Deep,* for the *New York Times Book Review,* Gerald Jonas found that "paraphrase is useless to convey the intensity of Crowley's prose; anyone interested in the risk-taking side of modern science fiction will want to experience it first-hand." Some critics observed that with his third novel, *Engine Summer,* Crowley had begun developing more complex plots and characters, and his themes reflected the influence of the fantasy genre. Of *Engine Summer,* Charles Nicol wrote in *Saturday Review:* "A lyric adventure as concerned with the meaning of actions as with the actions themselves, it presents a meditative world that should appeal to lovers of the great fantasies. Crowley has published some science fiction previously; here he has gone beyond his genre into that hilly country on the borderlands of literature." Similarly, Nebula and Hugo Award winner *Little, Big* was described as a "dense, marvelous, magic-realist family chronicle about the end of time and the new world to come," by John Clute in *Book World.*

Novelist Carolyn See, in a review for the *Los Angeles Times,* found Crowley's fifth novel, *Aegypt,* to contain "some extraordinary storytelling." Incorporating fantasy, satire, and philosophical romance, the novel centers on Pierce Moffat, a professor of Renaissance history whose desire to write a book about finding the meaning in life leads him to a mythical area and a mysterious woman. *Washington Post Book World* contributor Michael Dirda remarked that *Aegypt* "is clearly a novel where thought speaks louder than action, where people, places and events are at once actual and allegorical. . . . Crowley wants readers to appreciate his foreshadowings, echoes, bits of odd lore, multiple voices—in the evolution of complex pattern is his art." Dirda also notes, however, that Crowley's narrative is so complex that it can occasionally be confusing. Commenting on this complexity, John Clute, in a review for the *New York Times Book Review,* suggested that the novel provides "a dizzying experience."

BIOGRAPHICAL/CRITICAL SOURCES:

BOOKS

Contemporary Literary Criticism, Volume 57, Gale, 1990, pp. 155-164.
Dictionary of Literary Biography Yearbook 1982, Gale, 1983, p. 240-244.

PERIODICALS

Analog: Science Fiction/Science Fact, June, 1977; August, 1987; December, 1989.
Berkshire Sampler, September 13, 1981.
Chicago Tribune Book World, October 18, 1981.
Extrapolation, spring, 1990.
Locus, August, 1991; September, 1991.

Los Angeles Times, May 4, 1987.

Magazine of Fantasy and Science Fiction, April, 1980; December, 1987; January, 1992.

New Statesman, November 20, 1987.

New York Times Book Review, November 21, 1976; March 27, 1977; May 20, 1979; March 2, 1986; October 12, 1986; May 3, 1987, pp. 9, 11; August 14, 1988; May 21, 1989; July 5, 1992.

Publishers Weekly, February 20, 1987; April 14, 1989.

Saturday Review, April 14, 1979.

Science Fiction and Fantasy Book Review, January-February, 1982.

Times Literary Supplement, May 28, 1982; November 20-26, 1987.

Washington Post Book World, March 23, 1980; July 26, 1981; October 4, 1981; April 19, 1987, pp. 1, 7; March 19, 1989.

D

DANZIGER, Sheldon H. 1948-

PERSONAL: Born September 30, 1948, in Houston, TX; son of Calman and Sarah (Rosenbaum) Danziger; married Sandra Klein (a sociologist), January 3, 1971; children: Jacob Klein, Anna Klein. *Education:* Columbia University, B.A. (magna cum laude), 1970; Massachusetts Institute of Technology, Ph.D., 1975.

ADDRESSES: Office—Institute for Public Policy Studies, 457B Lorch Hall, University of Michigan, Ann Arbor, MI 48109-1220.

CAREER: University of Wisconsin—Madison, assistant professor, 1976-79, associate professor, 1979-83, professor of social work, 1983-88, Romnes Faculty Fellow, 1984-88; University of Michigan, Ann Arbor, professor of social work and public policy, 1988—. Institute for Research on Poverty, University of Wisconsin, fellow, 1974-76, research economist, 1974-83, director, 1983-88.

MEMBER: Phi Beta Kappa.

AWARDS, HONORS: Woodrow Wilson fellow, 1970; National Science Foundation fellow, 1970-72.

WRITINGS:

(Editor with Daniel H. Weinberg) *Fighting Poverty: What Works and What Doesn't,* Harvard University Press, 1986.
(Editor with Kent Portney) *Distributional Aspects of Public Policies,* St. Martin's, 1987.
(Editor with John Witte) *Setting Wisconsin Priorities,* University of Wisconsin, 1987.
(Editor with Peter Gottschalk) *Uneven Tides: Rising Inequality in America,* Russell Sage Foundation, 1993.

Contributor of more than seventy articles to social science and economic journals.

DAVIDSON, Lionel 1922-
(David Line)

PERSONAL: Born March 31, 1922, in Hull, Yorkshire, England; married Fay Jacobs, 1949 (died 1988); married Frances Ullman, 1989; children: (first marriage) two sons.

ADDRESSES: Agent—Curtis Brown Ltd., 162 Regent St., London W1R 5TB, England.

CAREER: Writer and editor for several British magazines, 1946-59; novelist and screenwriter, 1959—. *Military service:* Royal Navy, Submarine Service, 1941-46.

AWARDS, HONORS: Silver Quill Award, Authors' Club, for most promising first novel, 1960, for *The Night of Wenceslas;* Gold Dagger Award, Crime Writers' Association, for best crime novel, 1960, for *The Night of Wenceslas,* 1967, for *The Menorah Men,* and 1978, for *The Chelsea Murders;* President's Prize for Literature, Israel, for *Smith's Gazelle.*

WRITINGS:

NOVELS

The Night of Wenceslas, Harper, 1961.
The Rose of Tibet, Harper, 1962.
The Menorah Men, Harper, 1966 (published in England as *A Long Way to Shiloh,* Gollancz, 1966).
Making Good Again, Harper, 1968.
Smith's Gazelle, Knopf, 1971.
The Sun Chemist, Knopf, 1976.
Murder Games, Coward, 1978 (published in England as *The Chelsea Murders,* J. Cape, 1978).
Under Plum Lake (juvenile), Knopf, 1980.

JUVENILE; UNDER PSEUDONYM DAVID LINE

Soldier and Me, Harper, 1965, (published in England as *Run for Your Life,* J. Cape, 1966).

Mike and Me, J. Cape, 1974.
Screaming High, Little, Brown, 1985.

Also author of screenplays. Contributor of short stories to *Alfred Hitchcock's Mystery Magazine* and *Suspense,* and to the anthologies *Winter's Crimes 13,* Macmillan, 1981, and *Winter's Crimes 16,* Macmillan, 1984.

SIDELIGHTS: Lionel Davidson is a writer of thrillers and adventure novels which draw upon his own travels around the world for their settings and backgrounds. "His books," Rosemarie Mroz writes in the *Dictionary of Literary Biography,* "are both original and entertaining; he expertly combines dialogue and descriptive prose to produce convincing, lively fiction with memorable characters and settings."

Davidson's first novel, *The Night of Wenceslas,* was the product of his knowledge of Eastern Europe, gained during postwar visits as a journalist. The complex plot concerns a phony inheritance, smuggling, and a chase; the tone is sometimes comic as well as exciting; the historical background is that of Prague both before and after its takeover by the Communists. The novel was a critical and commercial success in Britain and the United States. The *New York Times Book Review*'s Anthony Boucher called the novel's chase scene "one of the most colorful" he'd seen in years.

For his second novel, Davidson switched scenes to Tibet. *The Rose of Tibet* concerns the search for a missing Englishman in that mountainous Central Asian land. Charles Houston, the missing man's half-brother, searches for him, and encounters monks, villagers, prophecies, winter storms, and a beautiful, emerald-bedecked abbess with whom he escapes from a Chinese invasion. In a dust-jacket quote, the great suspense novelist Daphne du Maurier compared the novel favorably to *She* and *King Solomon's Mines,* by H. Rider Haggard. Like Davidson's first novel, his second was a commercial as well as a critical success.

Davidson's third novel, *The Menorah Men* (published in England as *A Long Way To Shiloh*), introduced his readers to the author's concern for Israel. Casper Laing, a British archeologist, is searching for an old, precious menorah, or Jewish ritual candelabrum, before it can be found by Arab rivals. The book was a bestseller in England, but according to Mroz, Davidson's "ability to blend fact and fiction smoothly, as well as his ability to capture the spirit of people and place, makes the book more than simply a commercial success."

Davidson's next novel, *Making Good Again,* represented something of a departure for the author, an attempt to write a serious novel about postwar Germany and the ethical questions relating to the Nazi legacy. (The title refers to the German Federal Indemnification Law, a complex network of legal provisions by which the government made amends for war crimes against German Jews.) The plot revolves around the efforts of three lawyers—an Englishman, a German, and an Israeli—to discover the fate of a missing German-Jewish banker in order to determine what should be done with his fortune. Many reviewers, accustomed to Davidson's earlier, more light-hearted work, did not seem to know quite how to approach *Making Good Again.* For example, a *Punch* reviewer wrote: "Before reading *Making Good Again* I'd have made Lionel Davidson my choice for the title of best thriller writer in the business. This present books alters that position. For better? For worse?—it's hard to be sure. . . . [He] has great talent. His dialogue is supple, subtle and tempts you on. He can rise to high comedy and even to high seriousness. But to the very end of this one I remained in doubt whether he had wholly made up his mind about the kind of novel he meant to write." A *Jewish Quarterly* critic noted: "This book has all the qualities which have distinguished Lionel Davidson's earlier books—a crackling tale told at a crackling pace; vivid characterisation; humour—but on this occasion he has attempted to do more, and one wishes he hadn't. On one level, *Making Good Again* is a thriller. . . . On another level it is a parable about guilt and reparation. . . . Mr. Davidson raises the questions [about German guilt] but does not come near to providing an answer. . . . It may be ungracious to complain of this in a book which offers so much, but one has a right to expect more of Mr. Davidson."

More comfortable with the book's mixture of tones and levels, a *Time* reviewer wrote, "[*Making Good Again* is] an odd, quiet novel that contemplates the limits of private responsibility and public guilt. This moral terrain, though fascinating, is often overwrought in literature. And Davidson's low-key philosophic inquiry, conducted in a wonderfully conversational tone and decked out with the trappings of an international suspense tale, runs the risk of seeming schematic or frivolous. . . . [But] cleverly, wisely, Davidson . . . turns the book into a rueful seminar on the possibilities that men have of ever 'making good again' after various sorts of failure." Both the *New York Times Book Review*'s Martin Levin and a *New Yorker* reviewer saw Davidson's exploration of the human element as one of the most successful parts of the book. "With the legal machinery as a *modus operandi,*" wrote Levin, "Mr. Davidson proceeds to explore a variety of exclusive human situations. . . . The denouement . . . is a bit anticlimactic, but [the] journey is nonetheless rewarding for the reader." The *New Yorker* concluded: "[*Making Good Again*] is essentially a story of suspense, but Mr. Davidson is in manner, tempo, and tone an apt and interesting pupil of Graham Greene, and he has given his entertainment a bottom of human doubt and human certitude."

After the ambiguous response to *Making Good Again,* Davidson followed up with two Israeli novels, *Smith's Gazelle* and *The Sun Chemist.* Smith's gazelle is the name of a rare gazelle found in Israel. A Bedouin shepherd, Hamud, finds a pregnant member of the species in a ravine where Hamud is hiding after avenging the murder of his wife. Hamud turns the ravine into a rough-and-ready nature refuge for the gazelle species; he is joined in this task by Musallem and Jonathan, an Arab and Israeli boy respectively. During the Six-Day War, the herd is destroyed by land mines, except for one male and one female, who apparently escape to become the new Adam and Eve of their species.

Contrasting in tone to the natural beauty present in *Smith's Gazelle, The Sun Chemist* is a suspense novel based on historical facts. The plot involves the research of Dr. Chaim Weizmann, the scientist who was also the founder of the state of Israel, into an alternative energy source based on fermented sweet potatoes—a source that would free the West from dependence on Arab oil. In Davidson's treatment, the narrator, Igor Druyanov, has stumbled upon Weizmann's researches in the course of editing the late scientist's papers. Druyanov is harassed by a rival scientist, Ham Wyke, in a chase that ends in a ruined fortress.

Davidson's next novel, *The Chelsea Murders,* is a puzzle-mystery that contains parodies and literary allusions. In the plot's seven murders, as summarized in *Contemporary Novelists,* "Each of the seven victims has the initials of one of the luminaries who lived in Chelsea, figures like Dante Gabriel Rossetti, Oscar Wilde, and Algernon Charles Swinburne. . . . In addition, the clues, mailed to the police through different ingenious guises, are quotations from the writers, emphasizing the novel's resemblance to an intricate game."

With *Under Plum Lake,* Davidson turned from the thriller genre to write a utopian fantasy for children. The novel tells of the underwater world of Egon, where people live ten times the normal human span, are enormously intelligent and have solved such everyday problems of life as illness and injury. The protagonist, Barry Gordon, is a British youth who discovers Egon while exploring seaside caves. He is befriended by Dido, an Egon youth who guides Barry through the magical land. Reviewer Anstiss Drake, in the *Chicago Tribune Book World,* compared Davidson's literary fantasy to Coleridge's poem "Kubla Khan," adding, "Egon thus joins the ranks of literature's ideal worlds such as Utopia, Shangri-la, and Islandia," and called the book "a work of superb imagination." Paul Zweig, writing in the *New York Times Book Review,* was less enthusiastic, praising *Under Plum Lake* as "a swift, lean tale" but claiming that the utopian nature of Egon detracted from the novel's dramatic potential. "Egon is such

a happy place, its people are so light-hearted, its scientists so benignly brilliant, that it finally defeats the story-teller. . . . In Egon, nothing happens next, and so there is no story to tell. . . . Happiness, it seems, does not love the story form." Edward Blishen, in the *Times Literary Supplement,* however, found that the novel was "kept in movement as a story by the urgent sadness that blows, as it were, backwards from its ending." At book's end, Barry must return to his own world, with his memories of Egon incompletely erased, and with the lifelong knowledge that the reality of human life is far inferior to something he has known and lost.

BIOGRAPHICAL/CRITICAL SOURCES:

BOOKS

Contemporary Novelists, Gale, 1991, pp. 226-27.
Dictionary of Literary Biography, Volume 14: *British Novelists since 1960,* Gale, 1983, pp. 244-48.

PERIODICALS

Best Sellers, December 1, 1968.
Chicago Tribune Book World, November 11, 1980, p. 7.
Jewish Quarterly, winter, 1968-69.
Los Angeles Times, October 29, 1980.
New Yorker, December 7, 1968.
New York Times, October 16, 1976.
New York Times Book Review, December 7, 1970, p. 12.
Punch, October 9, 1968.
Time, October 11, 1968.
Times Literary Supplement, October 17, 1968; November 21, 1980, p. 1325.

*   *   *

DAVIS, B. Lynch
See BIOY CASARES, Adolfo

*   *   *

DAVISON, Peter (Hubert)   1928-

PERSONAL: Born June 27, 1928, in New York, NY; son of Edward (a poet) and Natalie (Weiner) Davison; married Jane Auchincloss Truslow (a writer), March 7, 1959 (died July 4, 1981); married Joan Edelman Goody (an architect), August 11, 1984; children: (first marriage) Edward Angus, Lesley Truslow. *Education:* Harvard University, A.B. (magna cum laude), 1949.

ADDRESSES: Home and office—70 River St., Boston, MA 02108.

CAREER: Poet, editor and lecturer. Harcourt, Brace, and Co. (publishers), New York City, editorial assistant,

1950-51, assistant editor, 1953-55; Harvard University Press, Cambridge, MA, assistant to director, 1955-56; Atlantic Monthly Press, Boston, MA, associate editor, 1956-59, executive editor, 1959-64, director, 1964-79, senior editor, 1979-85; consulting editor at Houghton Mifflin Co. (publishers), Boston, MA, 1985—; poetry editor, *Atlantic Monthly*, 1972—. Member of literature panel, National Endowment for the Arts, 1980-83. *Military service:* U.S. Army, 1951-53.

MEMBER: National Translation Center, Yaddo (member of corporation), Phi Beta Kappa; Harvard Club (New York City); Examiner Club, St. Botolph Club, Signet Society (all Boston).

AWARDS, HONORS: Fulbright Scholar, St. John's College, Cambridge University, 1949-50; Yale Series of Younger Poets Prize, 1963, for *The Breaking of the Day and Other Poems;* National Institute of Arts and Letters Award, 1972; National Book Critics Circle Award in poetry, 1979, for *Hello, Darkness: The Collected Poems of L. E. Sissman;* James Michener Award, Academy of American Poets, 1980 and 1984.

WRITINGS:

POETRY

The Breaking of the Day and Other Poems, Yale University Press, 1964.
The City and the Island, Atheneum, 1966.
Pretending to Be Asleep, Atheneum, 1970.
Dark Houses (1870-1898), Halty Ferguson (Cambridge, MA), 1971.
Walking the Boundaries: Poems, 1957-1974, Atheneum, 1974.
A Voice in the Mountain, Atheneum, 1977.
Barn Fever and Other Poems, Atheneum, 1981.
Praying Wrong: New and Selected Poems, 1957-1984, Atheneum, 1984.
The Great Ledge, Knopf, 1989.
Collected Poems, Knopf, 1994.

OTHER

Half Remembered: A Personal History (autobiography), Harper, 1973, revised edition, Story Line Press, 1991.
(Editor) L. E. Sissman, *Hello, Darkness: The Collected Poems of L. E. Sissman,* Atlantic-Little, Brown, 1978.
(Editor) *The World of Farley Mowat: A Selection from His Work,* Atlantic-Little, Brown, 1980.
One of the Dangerous Trades: Essays on the Work and Workings of Poetry, University of Michigan Press, 1991.
The Fading Smile: From Beauty to Truth in Boston, 1955-1960, Knopf, 1994.

Work included in numerous anthologies, including *A Controversy of Poets,* Doubleday/Anchor, 1965, *Twentieth Century Poetry: American and British,* McGraw, 1970, *Understanding Poetry,* Harcourt, 1976, *A Green Place: Modern Poems,* Delacorte, 1982, *Western Wind: An Introduction to Poetry,* Random House, *The New Yorker Book of Poetry,* and several volumes of *Borestone Mountain Poetry Awards* and *The Best American Poetry.* Contributor of poems and critical essays to *Encounter, Kenyon Review, Partisan Review, Atlantic, New Yorker, Hudson Review, American Scholar, Harper's, Antioch Review, Ploughshares, Iowa Review, New Republic, Poetry, American Poetry Review,* and other publications.

ADAPTATIONS: A recording of Davison's verse, *Paradise as a Garden,* has been issued by Watershed.

WORK IN PROGRESS: Poems, criticism, and travel essays.

SIDELIGHTS: "Peter Davison's greatest asset," William C. Rice maintains in *Chronicles of Culture,* "may be the fact that, unlike most contemporary American poets, he's spent his adult life outside the academic world. . . . Davison writes not of sabbaticals and professional ennui, nor of vacations on Cape Cod and brief sexuo-intellectual entanglements. Instead, he writes about animals, friendship, religious faith, marriage, children, death, and the passage of time." The son of poet Edward Davison, who ran the University of Colorado's Writers Conference, the young Peter Davison met such prominent writers as Robert Frost, Robert Penn Warren, Carl Sandburg, Ford Madox Ford, and John Crowe Ransom. His own work—especially those poems concerned with rural life, the work ethic, and family—closely resembles that of Robert Frost, who served as Davison's mentor. "An accomplished poet of unquestionable importance," Hugh M. Ruppersburg writes in the *Dictionary of Literary Biography,* "Peter Davison has worked diligently to forge an authentic voice."

Like his mentor Robert Frost, Davison employs a natural voice in his poems and speaks of common concerns. *Washington Post Book World* reviewer Vernon Young explains that Davison writes "a poetry of reminiscence and conservation" on such timeless subjects as youth, aging, and women. "Davison writes in what I suppose might be called the middle register of diction," Young states. "[His poems] are about illumination and endurance and sufferance, and the rhetoric that animates them is far from being merely conventional." Davison, James Finn Cotter notes in *America,* is "a reporter of life fashioned close to the land and the thoughts that arise from such a life." Jay Parini, writing in the *Virginia Quarterly Review,* sees in Davison's poems "a civilized wit, and this contributes to the profound sense of balance, of equilibrium." Davison, Parini concludes, "is one of our truest poets, one whose fundamental sanity and intelligence are more than welcome in a time of cultural disarray."

In 1985, Davison issued a major retrospective volume, *Praying Wrong: New and Selected Poems, 1957-1984.* Containing selections from his previous seven volumes as well as twenty poems new at the time, *Praying Wrong* scanned the poet's entire oeuvre. James Dickey, assessing the collection for the *Boston Sunday Globe,* regretted a weakness for generalizations which he found in Davison's work, but offered high approbation to offset it. Davison, according to Dickey, "understands, as few poets do, for example, the true nature of work, and particularly of farming. He knows how to do something with land besides look at it." R. W. Flint of the *New York Times Book Review* notes that *Praying Wrong* is a "strong oblique debt to Frost." Comparing Davison to Frost, Dickey finds that "Davison's poems on some of the same subjects [such as the New England work ethic] are not only quite different from Frost's but in my opinion are superior to them." Dickey concludes that Davison's "voice is his; he has earned it and can use it, and as a result is surely one of our better poets." Observing that Davison had selected from among his own work "with a connoisseur's detachment," Flint concludes: "This will unquestionably be the Davison volume to own for a long time to come."

Speaking of his own career, Davison told *CA:* "I must be one of the few poets of my generation who has never either taken or given a creative writing class, but I cannot suggest what to make of that fact. I have seldom found my editorial career in conflict with my writing except at UNFATHOMABLE depths. Poetry for me is not work but pleasure, not a career but a second life—a play within a play."

BIOGRAPHICAL/CRITICAL SOURCES:

BOOKS

Contemporary Authors Autobiography Series, Volume 4, Gale, 1986, pp. 127-141.
Contemporary Literary Criticism, Volume 28, Gale, 1984, pp. 99-104.
Contemporary Poets, St. James Press, 1991, pp. 216-217.
Dictionary of Literary Biography, Volume 5: *American Poets since World War II,* Gale, 1980.
Rotella, Guy, *Three Contemporary Poets of New England: Meredith, Booth, and Davison,* Twayne, 1983.

PERIODICALS

America, July 18-25, 1981, pp. 36-37.
Atlantic, May, 1970.
Boston Sunday Globe, December 30, 1984, pp. A12, A14.
Christian Science Monitor, June 4, 1970.
Chronicles of Culture, August, 1985, p. 28.

Contemporary Literature, winter, 1968.
Detroit News, March 3, 1985.
New York Times Book Review, December 11, 1966; September 13, 1981, pp. 14, 32; January 27, 1985, pp. 18-19.
Parnassus: Poetry in Review, spring-summer, 1975, pp. 75-89.
Poetry, August, 1982, pp. 293-305.
Publishers Weekly, October 12, 1984, p. 49.
Virginia Quarterly Review, autumn, 1978, pp. 762-68; summer, 1985, p. 98.
Washington Post Book World, May 3, 1981, p. 8.

*   *   *

DEAL, Borden 1922-1985
(Lee Borden, Leigh Borden)

PERSONAL: Original name, Loyse Youth Deal; born October 12, 1922, in Pontotoc, MS; died of a heart attack, January 22, 1985, in Sarasota, FL; son of Borden Lee and Jimmie Anne (Smith) Deal; married second wife, Babs Hodges (a writer), 1952 (divorced, 1975); married; wife's name, Patricia; children: (second marriage) Ashley and Shane (daughters), Brett. *Education:* University of Alabama, B.A., 1949; Mexico City College, graduate study, 1950. *Politics:* Democrat. *Avocational Interests:* Fishing, golf, guitar playing.

CAREER: U.S. Department of Labor, Washington, DC, auditor, 1941-42; Association Films, New York City, correspondent; worked variously as a skip tracer, telephone solicitor, and copywriter, 1950-55; free-lance writer. Lecturer. *Military service:* U.S. Navy, 1942-45.

MEMBER: Authors Guild, American PEN, Tennessee Squire Association, Sarasota Writers' Roundtable.

AWARDS, HONORS: Guggenheim fellow, 1957; honorable mention, American Library Association Liberty and Justice Awards, for *Walk through the Valley;* Alabama Library Association Literary Award, 1963; John H. McGinnis Memorial Award.

WRITINGS:

Walk through the Valley, Scribner, 1956.
Dunbar's Cove, Scribner, 1957.
Search for Surrender, Gold Medal, 1957.
Killer in the House, New American Library, 1957.
(Under pseudonym Lee Borden) *Secret of Sylvia,* Gold Medal, 1958.
The Insolent Breed, Scribner, 1959.
Dragon's Wine, Scribner, 1960.
(Under pseudonym Lee Borden) *Devil's Whispers,* Avon, 1961.
The Spangled Road, Scribner, 1962.

The Tobacco Men (based on notes by Theodore Dreiser), Holt, 1965.
A Long Way to Go, Doubleday, 1965.
Interstate, Doubleday, 1970.
A Neo-Socratic Dialogue on the Reluctant Empire, Outlaw Press, 1971.
Bluegrass, Doubleday, 1976.
(Under pseudonym Leigh Borden) *Legend of the Bluegrass,* Doubleday, 1977.
Adventure, Doubleday, 1978.
Antaeus, Learning Corp., 1982.
There Were also Strangers; A Novel, New Horizon Press, 1985.
The Platinum Man; A Novel, New Horizon Press, 1986.

"BOOKMAN SAGA"

The Loser, Doubleday, 1964.
The Advocate, Doubleday, 1968.
The Winner, Doubleday, 1973.

"OLDEN TIMES" SERIES

The Least One, introduced by Sara de Saussure Davis, Doubleday, 1967.
. . . The Other Room, Doubleday, 1974.

OTHER

Also author of short stories anthologized in *Best American Short Stories of 1949, Best Detective Stories of the Year, The Wonderful World of Dogs, Best American Short Stories of 1962,* and in numerous high school and college textbooks. Contributor of more than one hundred stories, poems, and reviews to *New York Times Book Review, Saturday Review,* and other periodicals. Deal's books have been translated into over twenty languages.

ADAPTATIONS: The Insolent Breed is the basis for the Broadway musical *A Joyful Noise.*

SIDELIGHTS: Borden Deal, a prolific Southern writer, recreated the South and black culture with a certainty born of experience. A Mississippi native, son of a farming family, Deal returned again and again in his fiction to places and people that he knew. The cites of farming ventures from his youth became the basis for communities written about in *The Least One* and *. . . The Other Room,* and the quest for land, identity, and personal ambition figure strongly in much of his work.

Deal's first novel, *Walk through the Valley,* and subsequent works such as *Dunbar's Cove* and *Interstate,* all deal in one way or another with man's attachment to the land. Deal's characters not only draw their livelihood from the land, but often appear to have an almost mystical union with the very earth. In *Walk through the Valley,* Fate Laird searches for fertile and prosperous country; in the latter two novels, the characters are dedicated to the pres-

ervation of their homes in the face of encroaching civilization, the federal government, and overzealous engineers. *Dunbar's Cove* pits protagonist Matthew Dunbar against the Tennessee Valley Authority (TVA) while *Interstate* intertwines the lives of the people attempting, respectively, to protect and to invade Blackwater Swamp, the last refuge for the ivory-billed woodpecker and the planned route for a new interstate highway.

A search for self and the celebration of life weave into Deal's writing as well. *A Long Way to Go, The Least One,* its sequel *. . . The Other Room,* and *There Were also Strangers* all concern themselves with youthful protagonists and their struggle with emerging selfhood. In all of these, Deal used what some critics considered provocative symbolism to represent not only the development of the young characters but also the adult world into which they were moving. *There Were also Strangers* is an autobiographical novel where thirteen-year-old Borden Deal is confronted by his alter ego who leads him to view the steamy nightlife of his Southern village. In *. . . The Other Room,* the young protagonist explores sex with his schoolteacher, and religion with a con man. "With humor and poignance, Deal describes growing up poor in the rural South of the Depression," comments a reviewer in *Publishers Weekly.*

Adult themes of sexual infidelity, lust, greed, and sociopolitical ambition did not escape Deal's attention. Deal's *Bookman* series as well as the suspenseful *Adventure* and *Dragon's Wine* all address concerns of this nature. Jungian overtones, seen in many of Deal's works are, according to James R. Waddell, writing in the *Dictionary of Literary Biography,* especially strong in the latter. Deal once commented in *CA* that the theories of psychologist C. J. Jung were a major element in his work and credited Jung's idea of "ancient myths embedded so deeply in the human psyche they recur over and over again throughout the history of mankind" as being a "primary influence" in his writing. Many critics agreed that Deal succeeded not only in representing "real" characters in believable situations—in and out of history—but also managed to craft harrowing, dark tales of human fallibility.

Borden Deal once told *CA* that he wished his books to be a "panorama of the New South." He noted that his characters "live and work in real time in real places: raising horses, building highways and TVA dams, running for public office, farming the Southern earth. The drama of their individual lives embodies the important story of the years since about 1890, when the South began gradually to emerge from the shadow of a losing war in the wrong cause, to regain at last, with the election of the first Southern president in over a hundred years, its original position as a prime mover in the destiny of the nation."

BIOGRAPHICAL/CRITICAL SOURCES:

BOOKS

Dictionary of Literary Biography, Volume 6: *American Novelists since World War II, Second Series,* Gale, 1980, pp. 69-72.
The Rising South, Volume 2, University of Alabama Press, 1976.

PERIODICALS

Best Sellers, June 1, 1970.
Booklist, March 15, 1973, p. 672.
Kirkus Reviews, March 1, 1970, p. 270; September 15, 1978, p. 1026; October 15, 1985, p. 1096.
National Review, April 13, 1973.
New Yorker, January 4, 1969.
New York Times Book Review, October 27, 1974, p. 57; February 13, 1977, p. 26.
Publishers Weekly, November 24, 1969, p. 43; February 23, 1970, p. 150; November 20, 1972, p. 62; June 3, 1974, p. 151; November 8, 1976, p. 42; May 29, 1978, p. 50; October 16, 1978, p. 107; November 1, 1985, p. 54.
Southwest Review, summer, 1966.
Washington Post Book World, January 14, 1973, p. 15; March 24, 1974, p. 4.*

*   *   *

de BONO, Edward 1933-

PERSONAL: Born May 19, 1933, in Malta; son of Joseph Edward (a physician) and Josephine (maiden name, Burns) de Bono; married Josephine Hall-White, 1971; children: two sons. *Education:* St. Edward's College, Malta; Royal University of Malta, B.Sc., 1953, M.D., 1955; Oxford University, M.A., 1957, D.Phil., 1961; Cambridge University, Ph.D., 1963. *Avocational Interests:* Polo, canoeing (paddled 112 miles from Oxford to London non-stop while at Oxford University), games design.

ADDRESSES: Home—11 Warkworth St., Cambridge, England. *Agent*—Michael Horniman, A. P. Watt, 26/28 Bedford Row, London WC1R 4HL, England.

CAREER: Oxford University, Oxford, England, research assistant, 1957-60, lecturer, 1960-61; University of London, London, England, lecturer, 1961-63; Cambridge University, Cambridge, England, assistant director of research, 1963-76, lecturer in medicine, 1976-83. Research associate and honorary registrar, St. Thomas Hospital Medical School, University of London; research associate, Harvard Medical School; honorary consultant, Boston City Hospital, 1965-66. Honorary director and founding member of Cognitive Research Trust, 1971—; secretary-

general of Supranational Independent Thinking Organisation (SITO), 1983—. Lecturer to industry and education groups on research cognitive processes. Inventor; designer of the L-game.

MEMBER: Medical Research Society; Athenaeum Club.

AWARDS, HONORS: Rhodes Scholar.

WRITINGS:

The Use of Lateral Thinking, J. Cape, 1967, published as *New Think: The Use of Lateral Thinking in the Generation of Ideas,* Basic Books, 1967.
The Five-Day Course in Thinking, Basic Books, 1967, reprinted with a foreword by Isaac Asimov, International Center for Creative Thinking, 1990.
The Mechanism of Mind, Simon & Schuster, 1969.
Lateral Thinking: Creation Step by Step, Harper, 1970 (published in England as *Lateral Thinking: A Textbook of Creativity,* Ward, Lock, 1970).
The Dog Exercising Machine, J. Cape, 1970, Simon & Schuster, 1971.
(Editor) *Technology Today,* Routledge & Kegan Paul, 1971.
Lateral Thinking for Management: A Handbook of Creativity, American Management Association, 1971.
Practical Thinking: Four Ways to Be Right, Five Ways to Be Wrong, Five Ways to Understand, J. Cape, 1971.
Children Solve Problems, Penguin, 1972, Harper, 1974.
PO: A Device for Successful Thinking, Simon & Schuster, 1972 (published in England as *PO: Beyond Yes & No,* Penguin Education, 1973).
Think Tank, Think Tank Corp., 1973.
(Editor) *Eureka: A History of Inventions,* Holt, 1974.
Teaching Thinking, Maurice Temple Smith, 1976.
The Greatest Thinkers, Putnam, 1976.
Wordpower: An Illustrated Dictionary of Vital Words, Harper, 1977.
The Case of the Disappearing Elephant (juvenile; illustrated by George Craig), Dent, 1977.
Opportunities: A Handbook of Business Opportunity Search, Associated Business Programmes (London), 1978.
The Happiness Purpose, Maurice Temple Smith, 1978.
Future Positive, Maurice Temple Smith, 1979, Viking, 1993.
Atlas of Management Thinking, Maurice Temple Smith, 1981.
De Bono's Thinking Course, B.B.C. Publications, 1982, Facts on File, 1986.
Learn-to-Think, Capra/New, 1982.
Tactics: The Art and Science of Success, Little, Brown, 1984.
Conflicts: A Better Way to Resolve Them, Harrap, 1985.

Six Thinking Hats: An Essential Approach to Business Management from the Creator of Lateral Thinking, Penguin, 1985, Little, Brown, 1985, Viking, 1986, published as *The Power of Focused Thinking: Six Thinking Hats,* International Center for Creative Thinking, 1990.

CoRT Thinking Program: CoRT 1-Breadth, Pergamon, 1987.

Letters to Thinkers: Further Thoughts on Lateral Thinking, Harrap, 1987.

Masterthinker II: Six Thinking Hats, International Center for Creative Thinking, 1988.

Masterthinker, International Center for Creative Thinking, 1990.

Masterthinker's Handbook, International Center for Creative Thinking, 1990.

Thinking Skills for Success, Paradigm (Eden Prairie, MN), 1990.

I Am Right, You Are Wrong: From This to the New Renaissance: From Rock Logic to Water Logic, Viking (London), 1990, Viking (New York), 1991.

Handbook for the Positive Revolution, Viking, 1991.

Six Action Shoes, Harper Business, 1991.

Serious Creativity: Using the Power of Lateral Thinking to Create New Ideas, Harper Business, 1992.

Surpetition: Creating Value Monopolies When Everyone Else Is Merely Competing, Harper Business, 1992.

Practical Thinking, Viking, 1992.

Teach Your Child How to Think, Viking, 1993.

Future Positive, Viking, 1993.

Also author of *Decision Mate,* International Center for Creative Thinking, and *Positive Revolution for Brazil,* 1990.

OTHER

The Greatest Thinkers (thirteen-part television series), WDR (Germany), 1980.

De Bono's Thinking Course (ten-part television series), British Broadcasting Corporation, 1982.

Sixty Minutes to Super Thinking (cassette recording), Audio Renaissance, 1988.

Also author of *How to Change Ideas: Your Own* (recording), J. Norton Publishers. Writer of television items and of feature stories for *Sunday Mirror, Telegraph Machine, Nova, Oz, Mind Alive, Science Journal, Sunday Times, Fashion,* and *Honey.* Contributor of articles to professional journals, including *Nature, Lancet, Clinical Science,* and *American Journal of Physiology.*

SIDELIGHTS: After beginning his career as a medical doctor, Edward de Bono turned his attention to the study of thinking, eventually writing several books on the subject. He has applied his core theory of "lateral thinking" to other fields, such as business management, education,

and conflict resolution. A prolific writer, de Bono has also authored a children's book as well as an illustrated book on how children learn.

The concept of "lateral thinking," or creative thinking, is central to de Bono's work and was first put forth in *The Use of Lateral Thinking,* also known as *New Think.* In the work, de Bono contrasts "lateral thinking" with "vertical thinking," which is habitual thinking that explores only the most obvious solutions to a problem. "Lateral thinking" does not accept the obvious premises of the problem, but instead looks for ways to go around them; de Bono believes that this creative method of thinking can be learned. Clarence Petersen, reviewing *New Think* in the *Chicago Tribune,* reports that the book includes "useful exercises on thinking 'laterally' " and that through those exercises, de Bono "shows how to break with habitual thinking."

The author turned his "lateral thinking" method into a thinking course, which was the basis for a ten-part television series aired by the British Broadcasting Company. *De Bono's Thinking Course,* a work based on the series, was hailed by Petersen in the Chicago *Tribune Books* as "a startling book for people who think they know how to think." Claiming that the book's many exercises are fun as well as frustrating, Petersen attested that de Bono "shows how thinking works, . . . and how it can be unleashed to run in new directions." De Bono has elaborated the original principle of "lateral thinking" through several other metaphorically-labeled types of thinking. In *Serious Creativity,* for example, de Bono discusses his "Six Thinking Hats" method and introduces the concept of "creative pause." A *Los Angeles Times Book Review* writer, although expressing mixed feelings about the whimsy of the "Six Hats" image, states that the tool "actually makes a lot of sense. You just have to suspend your disbelief and try it."

De Bono has also explored the question of how children think. In *Children Solve Problems,* he wrote up the results of a study in which he gave children six creative tasks. The children were asked to design a sleep machine, an elephant-weighing machine, a system for constructing a house, and a system for building a rocket. They were also asked to think of ways to improve the human body and to help the police in their work. The book is illustrated with two hundred drawings made by the children themselves, showing how they solved these problems. De Bono compares the children's problem-solving techniques with adult approaches, and he also expresses the opinion that schools discourage children's creativity when they should be encouraging it.

BIOGRAPHICAL/CRITICAL SOURCES:

PERIODICALS

Chicago Tribune, February 24, 1985.
Library Journal, May 1, 1974, p. 1297.
Los Angeles Times Book Review, June 7, 1992, p. 6.
Realities (France), August, 1967.
Realities (United States), November, 1967.
Times Literary Supplement, March 30, 1973; August 9, 1985, p. 886.
Tribune Books (Chicago), May 1, 1988, p. 8.*

*   *   *

DEBRAY, (Jules) Regis   1940-

PERSONAL: Born September 2, 1940, in Paris, France; son of Georges (a lawyer) and Janine Alexandre (a city councilwoman) Debray; married Elizabeth Burgos, February 12, 1968 (divorced); children: one daughter. *Education:* Ecole Normale Superieure, Agrege de Philosophie; former student of Louis Althusser.

CAREER: Writer and philosopher. Went to Bolivia as a journalist to interview Che Guevara, 1967, and was arrested and later convicted for taking part in the guerrilla movement; began serving a thirty-year prison sentence in Casino Militar, Bolivia, November 17, 1967; released from prison, 1970. Adviser on foreign affairs to French President Francois Mitterand; responsible for Third World affairs, office of Secretary-General of Presidency of the Republic, 1981-84; served in office of President of the Republic, 1984-85, 1987-88; member, Conseil d'Etat, 1985-92; maitre des requetes, Conseil d'Etat, 1985.

AWARDS, HONORS: Prix Femina, 1977.

WRITINGS:

Revolution dans la Revolution?: Lutte Armee et Lutte Politique en Amerique Latine, F. Maspero, 1967, translation by Bobbye Ortiz published as *Revolution in the Revolution?: Armed Struggle and Political Struggle in Latin America,* Monthly Review Press, 1967, Greenwood Press, 1980.
La Frontiere [et] *Un jeune homme a la page* (two stories), Editions du Seuil, 1967, translation by Helen R. Lane published as *The Border* [and] *Young Man in the Know,* Grove, 1968, translation by Louis Allen published as *The Frontier* [and] *A With-It Young Man,* Sheed & Ward, 1968.
Essais sur l'Amerique latine, F. Maspero, 1967.
(With Fidel Castro) *On Trial,* translation by Marianne Alexander, Lorrimer, 1968.
Defensa en Camiri, Siglo Ilustrado, 1968, translation published as *Declaration at the Court Martial, Camiri,*

Bolivia, 1968, published as *Che Lives: Regis Debray's Declaration at Camiri,* Iskra Communications (Goleta, CA), 1968.
Strategy for Revolution: Essays on Latin America, edited by Robin Blackburn, J. Cape, 1970.
Entretiens avec Allende sur la situation au Chili, F. Maspero, 1971, translation by Ben Brewster and others published as *The Chilean Revolution: Conversations with Allende,* postscript by Salvador Allende, Random House, 1971, translation by Peter Beglan published as *Conversation with Allende: Socialism in Chile,* New Left Books, 1971.
Apprendre d'eux [and] *Nous les Tupamaros,* translated from the Spanish by Elisabeth Chopard Lallier, F. Maspero, 1971.
Prison Writings of Regis Debray, translation by Rosemary Sheed, Random House, 1973, Allen Lane (London), 1973.
La Critique des armes, Editions du Seuil, 1974, translation by Rosemary Sheed published as *A Critique of Arms,* Penguin, 1977.
La Guerrilla du Che, Editions du Seuil, 1974, translation published as *Che's Guerrilla War,* Penguin, 1976.
L'epreuve du feu (Volume 2 of *La Critique des armes*), Editions du Seuil, 1974, translation by Rosemary Sheed published as *The Revolution on Trial,* Penguin, 1978.
(With Santiago Carillo and Max Gallo) *Demain l'Espagne,* Editions du Seuil, 1974.
L'Indesirable (novel), 1975, translation by Rosemary Sheed as *The Undesirable Alien,* Viking, 1978, Allen Lane, 1978.
Journal d'un petit bourgeois entre deux feux et quatre murs, Editions du Seuil, 1976.
La neige brule, B. Grasset, 1977.
Lettre aux communistes francais et a quelques autres, Editions du Seuil, 1978.
Modeste contribution aux discours et ceremonies officielles du dixieme anniversaire de mai 68, F. Maspero, 1978.
Le Pouvoir intellectuel en France, Ramsay (Paris), 1979, translation by David Macey published as *Teachers, Writers, Celebrities: The Intellectuals of Modern France,* introduction by Francis Mulhern, Routledge, Chapman & Hall, 1985.
Le Scribe: Genese du politique, B. Grasset, 1980.
Critique de la raison politique, 1984, abridged translation by David Macey published as *Critique of Political Reason,* New Left Books, 1983, Schocken, 1984.
Le Puissance et les reves, Gallimard, 1984.
Les Empires contre l'Europe, Gallimard, 1985.
Comete, ma comete, Gallimard, 1986.
Eloges, Gallimard, 1986.
Masques, Gallimard, 1987.
Que vive la Republique, Editions O. Jacob, 1988.

Tous azimuts, Editions O. Jacob, 1989.

A demain, de Gaulle, Gallimard, 1990.

Christophe Colomb, le visiteur de l'aube [suivi de] *Traites de Tordesilla* ("Les Voies du Sud series"), translation from the Spanish by Bernard Lefargues, with an introduction by Bartolome Bennassar, La Difference (Paris), 1991.

Cours de mediologie generale, Gallimard, 1991.

La France a l'Exposition universelle, Seville 1992: Facettes d'une nation, Exposicion Universal de 1992 (Seville, Spain), 1992.

Vie et mort de l'image: Une histoire de regard en Occident, Gallimard, 1992.

Also author of *L'Anniversaire* (two long essays on the continental strategy of revolution plus a third essay), 1967, and (with Barbara Deming) *Revolution, Violent and Nonviolent: Two Documents,* reprinted from February, 1968 *Liberation.* Contributor to *Evergreen Review, New Left Review, Marcha, Harper's, New Perspectives Quarterly,* and *Economist.*

SIDELIGHTS: Regis Debray had already made his mark as a young European intellectual, and had influenced the evolving political thought of Fidel Castro, with the publication of *Revolution in the Revolution?: Armed Struggle and Political Struggle in Latin America,* when he decided to see first-hand the kind of guerrilla activity he had dealt with abstractly in the book. He journeyed to Bolivia as a correspondent for a Mexican magazine, fell—with two others—into the hands of troops searching for guerrillas, and had the fabulous luck of not being killed. "According to some reports," wrote Elliott Anderson later in *Chicago Tribune Book World,* "only the immediate presence of two Spanish-speaking CIA agents saved him from execution." Jean-Paul Sartre, who deeply influenced Debray, said that Debray was jailed for having written *Revolution in the Revolution?*; however, Debray could well have remained alive *because* he wrote the book. "It gave him worldwide notoriety, and by the time the Bolivian military leaders realized whom they held prisoner, the scandal produced in Europe and America was such that it would have been dangerous to eliminate the young writer," wrote Juan Bosch. At the time the book's English translation appeared in print, Debray was on trial, soon to receive a thirty-year sentence for crimes he may not have committed.

The series of essays entitled *Revolution in the Revolution?* was written after a stay in Havana, where Debray had extensive conversations with leaders of revolutionary and communist movements from every Latin American country. Robin Blackburn notes that "the passion and revolutionary romanticism which infuse Debray's writing remind one more of the young Malraux." Blackburn continues: "His essay does not explore conceivable scenarios of revolution . . . nor does he provide a learned 'Marxist' ac-

count of the relationship of class forces and the continent's economic future. He addresses himself to the predicament of the lonely, hunted guerrilla, the embattled miners of Bolivia, the desperate inhabitants of the Caracas slums and the bitter peasantry of the under-developed, over-exploited interior—in these he sees the truth and the future of the South American continent." In the book, Debray analyzed the characteristic mistakes revolutionary groups made in their estimation of their own strength, and recommended that guerrillas be a roving force with, initially, modest social objectives. Debray also described Latin America's thirst for freedom from United States domination and the need for Latin American countries to adopt tactics suited to their unique conditions. Debray believed that the study of European and Asian communist revolutions would be misleading for South American countries because each revolution must be effected in accord with its regional and national peculiarities. He commented that "one may consider it a stroke of good luck that Fidel had not read the military writings of Mao Tse-Tung before disembarking on the coast to Oriente." For Debray at that time, as T. Richard Snyder pointed out, violence was "an essential ingredient of revolution." Later, in a two-volume opus published in 1974, Debray was to issue a "critique" of the use of arms.

In a letter from his Bolivian cell entitled "A Message to My Friends," Debray claimed that he was not being accused personally, but that Castro's Cuba was being indicted through him. He stated: "Over the two month period [before my trial], I was not once accused of being a guerrilla," although he admitted that for a long time he had "planned and intended to join the guerrillas. . . . Che decided that the time was not yet ripe for that . . . and that for the moment it was better I served by keeping the outside world informed." Debray added that although *Revolution in the Revolution?* "does express many of Che's ideas, it did not play any part in the organization of the guerrilla movement in Bolivia."

Debray's imprisonment became a *cause celebre* in intellectual circles in Europe and North America, with writers and professors such as Sartre, Francois Mauriac, Herbert Marcuse, Noam Chomsky, Graham Greene, Bertrand Russell, and others protesting the incarceration. Yet in "A Message to My Friends," Debray condemned the "vile publicity which the bourgeois press and the mass-circulation magazines gave to my situation, deforming and dissimulating its real meaning." He was appalled by "[t]he circus they were staging with me in the role of the clown" and detested the "sentiment" displayed and especially the active support of his family, who presented him to the public as "a decent young man."

Prior to his release from prison, Debray said, as noted by John L. Hess, that his " 'greatest joy' would be 'to recover the anonymity from which I emerged for reasons independent of my will.' " Hess commented that "for the author of *Revolution in the Revolution?* the wish seems rather optimistic." Indeed, although not retaining all the glamour of a political prisoner, Debray traveled to Cuba and to Chile after his release from prison, where he met with socialist President Salvador Allende, then returned to his native France to establish an enduring career as a writer and political figure. A volume of early fiction, *The Frontier* [and] *A With-It Young Man,* was published in 1968, while the author was still in prison. Stanley Reynolds, reviewing the two-story volume, stated that "Debray is a writer of power, already accomplished with the short story and holding great promise as a novelist" and that "Debray has an objectivity that would be impressive in any writer so politically committed."

In 1975, Debray's first novel, *Undesirable Alien,* appeared. The book is a fictional examination of questions arising from Debray's experiences as a Western European involved in Latin American revolutionary movements. The main character, Frank, is a Trotskyist Swiss intellectual who faces the question of what a man like himself is doing "trying to use the works of Karl Marx to help one make revolution on the shores of the Orinoco." He has a Latin-American girlfriend, Celia, and a passion for Bogart and Bond movies—attributes which highlight for the reader the romantic overtones of Frank's ventures. At the novel's end, however, he opts for urban terrorism as a strategy. According to reviewer Valentine Cunningham of the *Times Literary Supplement,* Debray raises the issue of "leftist disillusionments . . . : the Party's dirty machiavellianism, its heartless switches of policy that condemn brave guerrillas to death . . . above all, the denial of life before and after the desired apocalypse." Praising Debray for the seriousness and political experience he brings to the novel, Cunningham also mentions approvingly Debray's use of a variety of narrative devices.

Robert Maurer, in *Saturday Review,* was less sanguine about Debray's novelistic craftsmanship, but admired *Undesirable Alien* as "a telling exploration of revolutionary motives" and "a revealing document." Mary Hope, reviewing the novel for the *Spectator,* pronounced herself "agreeably surprised," calling it "a deeply pessimistic book with more humanity beneath the rhetoric than you might expect." In *Chicago Tribune Book World,* Elliott Anderson categorized the novel as "a curious mix of romantic self-yearning and revolutionary theory, plus a simple and at times engaging story." Thomas R. Edwards, in the *New Republic,* wondered, however, whether fiction was the best medium for Debray, saying, "one hears in this novel the voice of the theoretician." In Edwards's opinion, "If Debray could have stood a little farther back from his ideological position—which needn't be the same thing as

rejecting it—*Undesirable Alien* could have been a fascinating study in the ambiguities of duty and desire." Edwards added that the book was "intelligent and deeply felt, and for such virtues one can put up with a certain amount of lecturing."

Debray's output since *Undesirable Alien* has consisted largely of nonfiction and journalism, often produced in tandem with his career as a foreign-affairs official in the government of Francois Mitterand. His book *Teachers, Writers, Celebrities: The Intellectuals of Modern France,* attempts to analyze twentieth-century French intellectual history in a systematic way. In the *Times Literary Supplement,* Patrick McCarthy claimed that Debray was "exaggerating his case" for systematic analysis and that Debray was wrong in attributing the post-1960 decline of the French left wing to the rise of the mass media, but that nevertheless "one may perceive real merits in his book. . . . Debray laments rather than analyses this [historical situation in contemporary France] but he has written a lively book." Eugen Weber, in a *New York Times Book Review* treatment of Debray's *Critique of Political Reason,* called *Teachers, Writers, Celebrities* "a very readable denunciation from the inside of a complicated machine that runs on hot air."

Critique of Political Reason appeared in English in 1984. The book analyzes Marxist ideology as a belief, a subjective phenomenon akin to religion. Subjective belief, which was not dwelled upon by Marx or his early followers, is necessary for revolution, in Debray's view. Reviewer Weber found Debray's analysis "obvious," and expressed the opinion that in not seeing its obviousness, Debray had risked discrediting the very ideology he supported. Weber also accused Debray of verbosity and banal, sentimental rhetoric.

Debray's *Les Empires contre l'Europe,* whose title means "The Empires Against Europe," was published in 1985, a time when debate raged in France over the reality, or lack of it, of the Soviet threat, and the wisdom, or lack of it, of siding with the United States. Debray saw the Soviet threat as mythical, and opposed such American moves as the installation of Cruise missiles in France. McCarthy, reviewing the French edition of the book for the *Times Literary Supplement,* echoed Weber in calling Debray's prose "flowery" and "prone to rhetoric"; he also, however, claimed that Debray could be "extremely funny" when satirizing, for instance, European dignitaries.

As time went on, Debray moved to a more centrist political position. In 1990, his book *A demain, de Gaulle* was issued. The book was published, as were many others on the same subject, for the centennial year of the birth of Charles de Gaulle. Assessing it for the *Times Literary Supplement,* Tony Judt called it "a paean of praise to de

Gaulle and his political ideas," and commented that Debray's books always reflect fashionable political and intellectual currents in the France of the moment. Referring to de Gaulle as "now the idol of erstwhile radical intellectuals, who combine the urge to atone for past errors with a loss of faith in the contemporary French political scene," Judt felt that Debray and others like him had gone overboard in switching to the neo-Gaullist view, overlooking some of de Gaulle's flaws, such as a tendency toward anti-semitism and toward government by charisma. Said Judt: "If Debray and the other newly minted philo-Gaullists would only moderate their enthusiasms a little, it might be easier to take them seriously."

Like all serious thinkers and writers in a changing world, Regis Debray continues to evolve. The continuing trajectory of his career has provided both an inspiring model for his admirers, and a document of changes in French intellectual history since 1960.

BIOGRAPHICAL/CRITICAL SOURCES:

BOOKS

Gutierrez, Carlos Maria, *Note sulla situazione politica boliviana*, Edizioni della Liberia, 1970.
Huberman, Leo, and Paul M. Sweeney, editors, *Regis Debray and the Latin American Revolution*, Monthly Review Press, 1968.

PERIODICALS

Chicago Tribune Book World, November 26, 1978, p. 16.
Christian Century, January 17, 1968.
Evergreen Review, February, 1968.
Nation, January 29, 1968.
New Republic, December 23 & 30, 1978, pp. 30-32.
New Statesman, April 28, 1967; August 9, 1968.
New York Times, July 21, 1967; July 3, 1968; December 12, 1969; December 25, 1970; February 17, 1971.
New York Times Book Review, January 29, 1984, p. 12.
Observer, August 27, 1967.
Ramparts, September, 1967.
Saturday Review, June 24, 1978, p. 35.
Spectator, July 29, 1978, p. 24.
Times Literary Supplement, August 11, 1978, p. 905; July 10, 1981, p. 772; December 13, 1985, p. 1418; September 28, 1990, pp. 1018, 1020.
Washington Post, May 4, 1969.

*   *   *

de GRAFT, J. C.
See de GRAFT, Joe (Coleman)

de GRAFT, Joe (Coleman)   1924-1978
(J. C. de Graft)

PERSONAL: Born April 2, 1924, in Ghana; died November 1, 1978; son of Joseph (in business) and Janet (a homemaker; maiden name, Acquaye) de Graft; married Leone Buckle (a professional accountant), 1953; children: Carol, Joseph, Dave. *Education:* Attended Mfantsipim School, 1939-43; Achimota College, 1944-46; and University College of the Gold Coast, 1950-53.

CAREER: Playwright, poet, novelist, and educator. Mfantsipim School, teacher of English and developer of Mfantsipim Drama Laboratory, 1955-60; University of Ghana, Legon, founder of drama and theatre studies division; Ghana Drama Studio, Accra, director, beginning in 1961; UNESCO, Nairobi, Kenya, teacher of English, 1970s; University of Ghana, associate professor and director of the School of Performing Arts, 1977-78.

WRITINGS:

NOVELS

Sons and Daughters, Oxford University Press, 1964.
The Secret of Opokuwa: The Success Story of the Girl with a Big State Secret, Anowuo Educational Publications, 1967.
Visitor from the Past, Anowuo, 1968.
Muntu, Heinemann, 1977.

STAGE PLAYS

Village Investment, first produced at Ghana Drama Studio, Accra, 1962.
Visitor from the Past, first produced at Ghana Drama Studio, 1962.
Ananse and the Gum Man, produced at Ghana Drama Studio, 1965.
(As J. C. de Graft) *Through a Film Darkly* (adapted from *Visitor from the Past*), Oxford University Press, 1970.
Muntu, first produced at University of Nairobi Free Travelling Theatre, 1975.
Mambo (adapted from *Macbeth* by William Shakespeare), produced at School of Performing Arts, Legon, Ghana, 1978.

SCREENPLAYS

No Tears for Ananse (adapted from his stage play *Ananse and the Gum Man*), Ghana Film Production, 1965.
Hamile (adapted from *Hamlet* by Shakespeare), Ghana Film Production, 1965.

OTHER

(As J. C. de Graft) *Beneath the Jazz and Brass* (poems), Heinemann, 1975.

Contributor to anthologies, including *Messages: Poems from Ghana,* edited by Kofi Awoonor and G. Adali-Mortty, Heinemann, 1970. Contributor to periodicals, including *African Literature Today* and *Okyeame.*

SIDELIGHTS: After his death Joe de Graft received the title of "elder statesman of Ghanaian letters" from a writer for *West Africa* magazine who noted that de Graft's younger colleagues "look[ed] up to him as a monumental figure, teacher and practitioner in one." In his plays, novels, and poetry, de Graft employed uniquely African themes, incorporated pieces of myth, and used aspects of Western literature. He produced numerous Shakespearean plays for radio and theatre and adapted two works with new titles. De Graft was instrumental in the development of Ghanaian theatre and spent a number of years affiliated with the Ghana Drama Studio, where several of his plays were produced. In his *West Africa* obituary, it was noted that de Graft was suited to be an elder statesman by his own background: "De Graft was a creature of the old world—in his case the settled Cape Coast oligarchy of his youth—and of the new urban jet-set."

De Graft was born into Ghana's upper class in 1932. His businessman father gave the youth a privileged education at some of the best schools of his country, including the University of the Gold Coast, from which de Graft was among the first to graduate. He then became an English teacher at the school of his childhood and helped with school theatre productions as founder of its Mfantsipim Drama Laboratory. He left Africa for a year on a fellowship that allowed him to observe the theatres of the United Kingdom and the United States.

While de Graft was pursuing his career in the 1950s, local politics in Ghana were evolving, causing the country's theatre to change as well. "De Graft appeared completely unaffected by the strong nationalist aspirations of the popular theater," writes Kofi Ermeleh Agovi in the *Dictionary of Literary Biography.* "Later, in the early 1960s, he started to develop a sympathy for the aspirations of cultural nationalism in Africa." But Agovi writes that even as de Graft warmed to the idea that African writers must concentrate on uniquely African subjects, the author balked. De Graft wrote, in a book review in *Okyeame* in 1966, of one author's "almost paranoiac search for distinctively Ghanaian forms of expression," Agovi notes.

But if de Graft had worries about the direction in which Ghana was headed, he also profited from cultural nationalism. The country's new leader, Kwame Nkrumah, opened numerous cultural institutions and sought to create a National Theatre Movement. De Graft became the first director of the Ghana Drama Studio, founded by playwright Efua Sutherland. His first play, *Village Invest-* *ment,* about a boy who leaves his village to gain useful wisdom in the city never to return, appeared there in 1961.

Other plays followed soon after: A work about an African who encounters a white woman from his student days in Britain (*Visitor from the Past,* adapted and later made into a film as *Through a Film Darkly,*) and another based on a traditional folktale (*Ananse and the Gum Man*). Meanwhile, he helped to build up the country's resources for teaching drama. He carried that project from Ghana to Egypt in 1970, working for UNESCO.

Of de Graft's last two works, one was the most wholly African play he wrote, the modern classic *Muntu,* which treated African history from Creation to modern days. The other, *Mambo,* was an adaptation of Shakespeare's *Macbeth,* which was produced in 1978, the year of the playwright's death. Agovi wrote that *Muntu* was "a culmination of de Graft's consistent admiration for his roots in African culture and his desire to mold it effectively for artistic purposes." *Mambo,* on the other hand, was a political treatment of African politics as what de Graft called the "latest political murders and military coups."

Discussions of de Graft present a dichotomy in his work between old and new, Western and African influences. The writer himself was quoted in *West Africa* as saying that he was less concerned with the source of inspiration than its quality: "My imaginative life is like a fire that feeds on more than charcoal: butane gas, electricity, palm-oil, petrol as well as dry cow-dung and faggots have kept it burning."

BIOGRAPHICAL/CRITICAL SOURCES:

BOOKS

Dictionary of Literary Biography: Volume 117, *Twentieth-Century Caribbean and Black African Writers,* First Series, Gale, 1992.
Echkardt, Ulrich, editor, *Horizonte-Magazin 79,* Berliner Festspiele GmbH, 1979, pp. 28-29.
Fraser, Robert, *West African Poetry: A Critical History,* Cambridge University Press, 1986, pp. 139-146.
Ogunba, Oyin and Abiola Irele, editors, *Theatre in Africa,* Ibadan University Press, 1978, pp. 55-72.
Ogungbesan, Kolawole, editor, *New West African Literature,* Heinemann, 1989, pp. 31-44.
Zell, Hans M. and others, *A New Reader's Guide to African Literature,* Holmes & Meier, 1983, pp. 388-389.

PERIODICALS

Cultural Events in Africa, Number 46, 1968.
Greenfield Review, fall, 1972, pp. 23-30.
Okike, September, 1981, pp. 70-79.
World Literature Written in English, November, 1979, pp. 314-331.

OBITUARIES:

PERIODICALS

West Africa, January 1, 1979, pp. 16-19.*

—*Sketch by Gordon Mayer*

*   *   *

de GRAZIA, Sebastian 1917-

PERSONAL: Born August 11, 1917, in Chicago, IL; son of Alfred Joseph and Catherine Cardinale (Lupo) de Grazia; married Miriam Lund Carlson (divorced); married Anna Maria d'Annunzio di Montenevoso (divorced); married Lucia Peavey Heffelfinger; children: (first marriage) Alfred Joseph III, Margreta, Sebastian, Jr.; (second marriage) Marco, Tancredi. *Education:* University of Chicago, A.B., 1939, Ph.D., 1947.

ADDRESSES: Home—914 The Great Rd., Princeton, NJ 08540.

CAREER: Federal Communications Commission, Washington, DC, member of research staff, 1941-43; University of Chicago, Chicago, IL, assistant professor of political science, 1945-50; consultant for business firms and for state and U.S. government, 1947—; University of Florence, Florence, Italy, visiting research professor, 1950-52; George Washington University, Washington, DC, senior research scientist, 1952-55; Twentieth Century Fund, New York City, director of research, 1957-62; Rutgers University, New Brunswick, NJ, professor of political philosophy at Eagleton Institute, 1962-85. Visiting professor at University of Florence, 1950-52, Princeton University, 1957, University of Madrid, 1963, John Jay College of Criminal Justice of the City University of New York, 1967-73, Institute for Advanced Study, Princeton, NJ, 1982-83, and Princeton University, 1991-92. *Military service:* Office of Strategic Services (OSS), 1943-45.

MEMBER: Institut International de Philosophie Politique, Association Internationale de Science Politique, American Political Science Association, American Society for Political and Legal Philosophy, Quadrangle Club (Chicago), Century Club (New York), Cosmos Club (Washington, DC), Nassau Club (Princeton), Prettybook Club (Princeton).

AWARDS, HONORS: Research grants from American Philosophical Society, Social Science Research Council, and American Council of Learned Societies; Pulitzer Prize, 1990, for *Machiavelli in Hell.*

WRITINGS:

The Political Community, University of Chicago Press, 1948.
Errors of Psychotherapy, Doubleday, 1952.

Of Time, Work, and Leisure, Twentieth Century Fund, 1962.
Time and the Machine, Pratt Adlib Press, 1963.
(With Livio C. Stecchini) *The Coup d'Etat: Past Significance and Modern Technique,* U.S. Naval Ordnance Test Station, 1965.
(Editor) *Masters of Chinese Political Thought: From the Beginnings to the Han Dynasty,* Viking, 1973.
Machiavelli in Hell (biography), Princeton University Press, 1989.

SIDELIGHTS: Machiavelli in Hell, for which Sebastian de Grazia won the Pulitzer Prize for biography in 1990, does not approach the Florentine Renaissance political philosopher "from a directly historical perspective," writes Charles Trinkhaus in *Renaissance Quarterly.* Instead, de Grazia treats the author of *The Prince* "from the vision of political philosophy in the very broad sense, which would include theology, metaphysics, and ethics as fundamental ingredients." Nonetheless, the critic continues, de Grazia's approach "is historical in fixing Machiavelli as very much a part of his own time, a figure whose values and views were those of the profounder type of Renaissance humanist." Trinkhaus lauds de Grazia's "near-total intimacy" with the writings of Machiavelli, and concludes that his portrayal of the Florentine is not only "more convincing" than other recent books about him, but is also "the most beautifully conceived and executed one."

Writing in the *Times Literary Supplement,* reviewer Nicolai Rubinstein expresses "reservations about de Grazia's use of evidence." However, these concerns "should not obscure [de Grazia's] real achievement in presenting a singularly rounded picture of Machiavelli, even if we are not always convinced of the accuracy of its details and shades," Rubinstein continues, adding that "by skilfully interweaving the various strands of [Machiavelli's] life and writings, Sebastian de Grazia succeeds in presenting an arresting image of the man through his work." Thomas D'Evelyn, reviewing *Machiavelli in Hell* for the *Christian Science Monitor,* praises de Grazia's style as "pithy, sinewy, vigorous—taut and relaxed by turns: not unlike [Machiavelli's]." De Grazia's book is "both monumental and intimate, provocative and winning," D'Evelyn states, suggesting that it "should help restore Machiavelli to his rightful place among the sages," and "help restore wisdom and common sense to our political climate of ideas."

BIOGRAPHICAL/CRITICAL SOURCES:

PERIODICALS

Christian Science Monitor, August 9, 1989.
New York Times Book Review, November 5, 1989, p. 25.
Renaissance Quarterly, winter, 1990.
Times Literary Supplement, January 19, 1990, p. 70.

DELANY, Samuel R(ay, Jr.) 1942-
(K. Leslie Steiner)

PERSONAL: Born April 1, 1942, in New York, NY; son of Samuel R. (a funeral director) and Margaret Carey (a library clerk; maiden name, Boyd) Delany; married Marilyn Hacker (a poet), August 24, 1961 (divorced, 1980); children: Iva Alyxander. *Education:* Attended City College (now of the City University of New York), 1960 and 1962-63.

ADDRESSES: Agent—Henry Morrison, Inc., Box 235, Bedford Hills, NY 10507.

CAREER: Writer. Butler Professor of English, State University of New York at Buffalo, 1975; senior fellow at the Center for Twentieth Century Studies, University of Wisconsin—Milwaukee, 1977; senior fellow at the Society for the Humanities, Cornell University, 1987; professor of comparative literature, University of Massachusetts—Amherst, 1988.

AWARDS, HONORS: Science Fiction Writers of America, Nebula Awards for best novel in 1966 for *Babel-17* and in 1967 for *The Einstein Intersection,* for best short story in 1967 for "Aye and Gomorrah," and for best novelette in 1969 for "Time Considered as a Helix of Semi-Precious Stones"; Hugo Award for best short story, Science Fiction Convention, 1970, for "Time Considered as a Helix of Semi-Precious Stones"; American Book Award nomination, 1980, for *Tales of Neveryon;* Pilgrim Award, Science Fiction Research Association, 1985.

WRITINGS:

SCIENCE FICTION

The Jewels of Aptor (abridged edition bound with *Second Ending* by James White), Ace Books, 1962, hardcover edition, Gollancz, 1968, complete edition published with an introduction by Don Hausdorff, Gregg Press, 1976.

Captives of the Flame (first novel in trilogy; bound with *The Psionic Menace* by Keith Woodcott), Ace Books, 1963, revised edition published under author's original title *Out of the Dead City* (also see below), Sphere Books, 1968.

The Towers of Toron (second novel in trilogy; also see below; bound with *The Lunar Eye* by Robert Moore Williams), Ace Books, 1964.

City of a Thousand Suns (third novel in trilogy; also see below), Ace Books, 1965.

The Ballad of Beta-2 (also see below; bound with *Alpha Yes, Terra No!* by Emil Petaja), Ace Books, 1965, hardcover edition published with an introduction by David G. Hartwell, Gregg Press, 1977.

Empire Star (also see below; bound with *The Three Lords of Imeten* by Tom Purdom), Ace Books, 1966, hard-

cover edition published with an introduction by Hartwell, Gregg Press, 1977.

Babel-17, Ace Books, 1966, hardcover edition, Gollancz, 1967, published with an introduction by Robert Scholes, 1976.

The Einstein Intersection, slightly abridged edition, Ace Books, 1967, hardcover edition, Gollancz, 1968, complete edition, Ace Books, 1972.

Nova, Doubleday, 1968.

The Fall of the Towers (trilogy; contains *Out of the Dead City, The Towers of Toron,* and *City of a Thousand Suns*), Ace Books, 1970, hardcover edition published with introduction by Joseph Milicia, Gregg Press, 1977.

Driftglass: Ten Tales of Speculative Fiction, Doubleday, 1971.

The Tides of Lust, Lancer Books, 1973.

Dhalgren, Bantam, 1975, hardcover edition published with introduction by Jean Mark Gawron, Gregg Press, 1978.

The Ballad of Beta-2 [and] *Empire Star,* Ace Books, 1975.

Triton, Bantam, 1976.

Empire: A Visual Novel, illustrations by Howard V. Chaykin, Berkley Books, 1978.

Distant Stars, Bantam, 1981.

Stars in My Pocket Like Grains of Sand, Bantam, 1984.

The Complete Nebula Award-Winning Fiction, Bantam, 1986.

The Star Pits (bound with *Tango Charlie and Foxtrot Romeo* by John Varley), Tor Books, 1989.

They Fly at Ciron, Incunabula, 1992.

"RETURN TO NEVERYON" SERIES; SWORD AND SORCERY NOVELS

Tales of Neveryon, Bantam, 1979.

Neveryona; or, The Tale of Signs and Cities, Bantam, 1983.

Flight from Neveryon, Bantam, 1985.

The Bridge of Lost Desire, Arbor House, 1987.

OTHER

The Jewel-Hinged Jaw: Notes on the Language of Science Fiction, Dragon Press, 1977, revised edition, Berkley Publishing, 1978.

The American Shore: Meditations on a Tale of Science Fiction by Thomas M. Disch—"Angouleme" (criticism), Dragon Press, 1978.

Heavenly Breakfast: An Essay on the Winter of Love (memoir), Bantam, 1979.

Starboard Wine: More Notes on the Language of Science Fiction, Dragon Press, 1984.

The Motion of Light in Water: Sex and Science Fiction Writing in the East Village, 1957-1965, Arbor House, 1988.

Wagner/Artaud: A Play of Nineteenth and Twentieth Century Critical Fictions, Ansatz Press, 1988.

Straits of Messina (essays; originally published in magazines under pseudonym K. Leslie Steiner), Serconia Press, 1989.

Also author of scripts, director, and editor for two short films, *Tiresias,* 1970, and *The Orchid,* 1971; author of two scripts for the *Wonder Woman Comic Series,* 1972, and of the radio play *The Star Pit,* based on his short story of the same title. Editor, *Quark,* 1970-71.

SIDELIGHTS: "Samuel R. Delany is one of today's most innovative and imaginative writers of science-fiction," comments Jane Branham Weedman in her study of the author, *Samuel R. Delany.* In his science fiction, which includes over fifteen novels and two collections of short stories, the author "has explored what happens when alien world views intersect, collide, or mesh," writes Greg Tate in the *Voice Literary Supplement.* Delany first appeared on the science fiction horizon in the early 1960s, and in the decade that followed he established himself as one of the stars of the genre. Like many of his contemporaries who entered science fiction in the 1960s, he is less concerned with the conventions of the genre, more interested in science fiction as literature, literature which offers a wide range of artistic opportunities. As a result, maintains Weedman, "Delany's works are excellent examples of modern science-fiction as it has developed from the earlier and more limited science-fiction tradition, especially because of his manipulation of cultural theories, his detailed futuristic or alternate settings, and his stylistic innovations."

"One is drawn into Delany's stories because they have a complexity," observes Sandra Y. Govan in the *Black American Literature Forum,* "an acute consciousness of language, structure, and form; a dexterous ability to weave together mythology and anthropology, linguistic theory and cultural history, gestalt psychology and sociology as well as philosophy, structuralism, and the adventure story." At the center of the complex web of personal, cultural, artistic, and intellectual concerns that provides the framework for all of his work is Delany's examination of how language and myth influence reality. "According to [the author]," writes Govan in the *Dictionary of Literary Biography,* "language identifies or negates the self. It is self-reflective; it shapes perceptions." By shaping perceptions, language in turn has the capacity to shape reality. Myths can exercise much the same power. In his science fiction, Delany "creates new myths, or inversions of old ones, by which his protagonists measure themselves and their societies against the traditional myths that Delany includes," Weedman observes. In this way, as Peter S. Alterman comments in the *Dictionary of Literary Biography,* the author confronts "the question of the extent to which myths and archetypes create reality."

In societies in which language and myth are recognized as determinants of reality, the artist—one who works in language and myth—plays a crucial part. For this reason, the protagonist of a Delany novel is often an artist of some sort. "The role which Delany defines for the artist is to observe, record, transmit, and question paradigms in society," explains Weedman. But Delany's artists do more than chronicle and critique the societies of which they are a part. His artists are always among those at the margin of society; they are outcasts and often criminals. "The criminal and the artist both operate outside the normal standards of society," observes Alterman, "according to their own self-centered value systems." The artist/criminal goes beyond observation and commentary. His actions at the margin push society's values to their limits and beyond, providing the experimentation necessary to prepare for eventual change.

Delany entered the world of science fiction in 1962 with the publication of his novel *The Jewels of Aptor.* Over the next six years, he published eight more, including *Babel-17, The Einstein Intersection,* and *Nova,* his first printed originally in hardcover. Douglas Barbour, writing in *Science Fiction Writers,* describes these early novels as "colorful, exciting, entertaining, and intellectually provocative to a degree not found in most genre science fiction." Barbour adds that although they do adhere to science fiction conventions, they "begin the exploration of those literary obsessions that define [Delany's] oeuvre: problems of communication and community; new kinds of sexual/love/family relationships; the artist as social outsider . . . ; cultural interactions and the exploration of human social possibilities these allow; archetypal and mythic structures in the imagination."

With the publication of *Babel-17* in 1966, Delany began to gain recognition in the science fiction world. The novel, which earned its author his first Nebula Award, is a story of galactic warfare between the forces of the Alliance, which includes the Earth, and the forces of the Invaders. The poet Rydra Wong is enlisted by Alliance intelligence to decipher communications intercepted from its enemy. When she discovers that these dispatches contain not a code but rather an unknown language, her quest becomes one of learning this mysterious tongue labeled *Babel-17.* While leading an interstellar mission in search of clues, Rydra gains insights into the nature of language and, in the process, discovers the unique character of the enigmatic new language of the Invaders.

Babel-17 itself becomes an exploration of language and its ability to structure experience. A central image in the novel, as George Edgar Slusser points out in his study *The Delany Intersection: Samuel R. Delany Considered as a Writer of Semi-Precious Words,* is that of "the web and its weaver or breaker." The web, continues Slusser, "stands, simultaneously, for unity and isolation, interconnectedness and entanglement." And, as Alterman points out in *Science-Fiction Studies,* "the web is an image of the effect of language on the mind and of the mind as shaper of reality." Weedman elaborates in her essay on the novel: "The language one learns necessarily constrains and structures what it is that one says." In its ability to connect and constrain is the power of the language/web. "Language . . . has a direct effect on how one thinks," explains Weedman, "since the structure of the language influences the processes by which one formulates ideas." At the center of the language as web "is one who joins and cuts—the artist-hero," comments Slusser. And, in *Babel-17,* the poet Rydra Wong demonstrates that only she is able to master this new language weapon and turn it against its creators.

Delany followed *Babel-17* with another Nebula winner, *The Einstein Intersection.* This novel represents a "move from a consideration of the relationship among language, thought, action and time to an analytic and imaginative investigation of the patterns of myths and archetypes and their interaction with the conscious mind," writes Alterman. Slusser sees this development in themes as part of a logical progression: "[Myths] too are seen essentially as language constructs: verbal scenarios for human action sanctioned by tradition or authority." Comparing this novel to *Babel-17,* he adds that "Delany's sense of the language act, in this novel, has a broader social valence."

The Einstein Intersection relates the story of a strange race of beings that occupies a post-apocalyptic Earth. This race assumes the traditions—economic, political, and religious—of the extinct humans in an attempt to make sense of the remnant world in which they find themselves. "While they try to live by the myths of man," writes Barbour in *Foundation,* "they cannot create a viable culture of their own. . . . Their more profound hope is to recognize that they do not have to live out the old myths at all, that the 'difference' they seek to hide or dissemble is the key to their cultural and racial salvation."

"Difference is a key word in this novel," Weedman explains, "for it designates the importance of the individual and his ability to make choices, on the basis of being different from others, which affect his life, thus enabling him to question the paradigms of his society." The artist is the embodiment of this difference and in *The Einstein Intersection* the artist is Lobey, a musician. The power of Lobey's music is its ability to create order, to destroy the old myths and usher in the new. At its core, then, *"The Einstein Intersection* is . . . a novel about experiments in culture," Weedman comments.

Delany's next novel, *Nova,* "stands as the summation of [his] career up to that time," writes Barbour in *Science Fiction Writers: Critical Studies of the Major Authors from*

the Early Nineteenth Century to the Present Day. "Packing his story full of color and incident, violent action and tender introspective moments, he has created one of the grandest space operas ever written." In this novel, Delany presents a galaxy divided into three camps, all embroiled in a bitter conflict caused by a shortage of the fuel illyrion on which they all depend. In chronicling one group's quest for a new source of the fuel, the author examines, according to Weedman, "how technology changes the world and philosophies for world survival. Delany also explores conflicts between and within societies, as well as the problems created by people's different perceptions and different reality models."

"In developing this tale," notes Slusser, "Delany has inverted the traditional epic relationship, in which the human subject (the quest) dominates the 'form.' Here instead is a 'subjunctive epic.' Men do not struggle against an inhuman system so much as inside an unhuman one." The system inside which these societies struggle is economic; the goal of the quester, who is driven by selfishness, is a commodity. Whether the commodity is abundant or scarce, as Jeanne Murray Walker points out in *Extrapolation,* this "is a world where groups are out of alignment, off balance, where some suffer while others prosper, where the object of exchange is used to divide rather than to unite." Walker concludes in her essay that "by ordering the action of *Nova* in the quest pattern, but assuming a value system quite different from that assumed by medieval romance writers, Delany shows that neither pattern nor action operate as they once did. Both fail." Even so, as she continues, "individuals must continue to quest. Through their quests they find meaning for themselves."

After the publication of *Nova,* Delany turned his creative urges to forms other than the novel, writing a number of short stories, editing four quarterlies of speculative fiction, and dabbling in such diverse media as film and comic books. Also at this time, he engaged himself in conceiving, writing, and polishing what would become his longest, most complex, and most controversial novel, *Dhalgren*—a work that would earn him national recognition. On its shifting surface, this novel represents the experience of a nameless amnesiac, an artist/criminal, during the period of time he spends in a temporally and spatially isolated city scarred by destruction and decay. As Alterman relates in the *Dictionary of Literary Biography,* "it begins with the genesis of a protagonist, one so unformed that he has no name, no identity, the quest for which is the novel's central theme." The critic goes on to explain that "at the end Kid has a name and a life, both of which are the novel itself; he is a persona whose experience in *Dhalgren* defines him."

Dhalgren's length and complexity provide a significant challenge to readers, but as Gerald Jonas observes in the *New York Times Book Review,* "the most important fact about Delany's novel . . . is that nothing in it is clear. Nothing is meant to be clear." He adds: "An event may be described two or three times, and each recounting is slightly disconcertingly different from the one before." What is more, continues the reviewer, "the nameless narrator experiences time discontinuously; whole days seem to be excised from his memory." According to Weedman, "Delany creates disorientation in *Dhalgren* to explore the problems which occur when reality models differ from reality." And in Jonas's estimation, "If the book can be said to be *about* anything, it is about nothing less than the nature of reality."

"*Dhalgren* has drawn more widely divergent critical response than any other Delany novel," comments Govan in her *Dictionary of Literary Biography* essay. "Some reviewers deny that it is science fiction, while others praise it for its daring and experimental form." For instance, *Magazine of Fantasy and Science Fiction* book reviewer Algis Budrys contends that "this book is not science fiction, or science fantasy, but allegorical quasi-fantasy on the [James Gould] Cozzens model. Thus, although it demonstrates the breadth of Delany's education, and many of its passages are excellent prose, it presents no new literary inventions." In his *Science Fiction Writers* essay, Barbour describes the same novel as "the very stuff of science fiction but lacking the usual structural emblems of the genre." "One thing is certain," offers Jonas, " 'Dhalgren' is not a conventional novel, whether considered in terms of S.F. or the mainstream."

Following the exhaustive involvement with Kid necessary to complete *Dhalgren,* Delany chose to do a novel in which he distanced himself from his protagonist, giving him a chance to look at the relationship between an individual and his society in a new light. "I wanted to do a psychological analysis of someone with whom you're just not in sympathy, someone whom you watch making all the wrong choices, even though his plight itself is sympathetic," Delany explained in an interview with Larry McCaffery and Sinda Gregory published in their book *Alive and Writing: Interviews with American Authors of the 1980s.* The novel is *Triton;* its main character is Bron.

"*Triton* is set in a sort of sexual utopia, where every form of sexual behavior is accepted, and sex-change operations (not to mention 'refixations,' to alter sexual preference) are common," observes Michael Goodwin in *Mother Jones.* In this world of freedom lives Bron, whom Govan describes in *Black American Literature Forum* as "a narrow-minded, isolated man, so self-serving that he is incapable of reaching outside himself to love another or even understand another despite his best intentions." In an at-

tempt to solve his problems, he undergoes a sex-change operation, but finds no happiness. "Bron is finally trapped in total social and psychological stasis, lost in isolation beyond any help her society can offer its citizens," comments Barbour in *Science Fiction Writers.*

In this novel, once again Delany creates an exotic new world, having values and conventions that differ from ours. In exploring this fictional world, he can set up a critique of our present-day society. In *Triton,* he casts a critical eye, as Weedman points out, on "sexual persecution against women, ambisexuals, and homosexuals." She concludes that the work is "on the necessity of knowing one's self despite sexual identification, knowing one's sexual identity is not one's total identity."

In the 1980s, Delany continued to experiment in his fiction writing. In his "Neveryon" series, which includes *Tales of Neveryon, Neveryona; or, The Tale of Signs and Cities, Flight from Neveryon,* and *The Bridge of Lost Desire,* he chooses a different setting. "Instead of being set in some imagined future, [they] are set in some magical, distant past, just as civilization is being created," observes McCaffery in a *Science-Fiction Studies* interview with Delany. Their focus, suggests Gregory in the same interview, is "power—all kinds of power: sexual, economic, even racial power via the issue of slavery."

Throughout these tales of a world of dragons, treasures, and fabulous cities Delany weaves the story of Gorgik, a slave who rises to power and abolishes slavery. In one story, the novel-length "Tale of Plagues and Carnivals," he shifts in time from his primitive world to present-day New York and back to examine the devastating effects of a disease such as acquired immune deficiency syndrome (AIDS). And, in the appendices that accompany each of these books, he reflects on the creative process itself. Of the four, it is *Neveryona,* the story of Pryn—a girl who flees her mountain home on a journey of discovery—that has received the most attention from reviewers. *Science Fiction and Fantasy Book Review* contributor Michael R. Collings calls it "a stirring fable of adventure and education, of heroic action and even more heroic normality in a world where survival itself is constantly threatened." Faren C. Miller finds the book groundbreaking; she writes in *Locus:* "Combining differing perspectives with extraordinary talent for the *details* of a world—its smells, its shadows, workaday furnishings, and playful frills— Delany has produced a sourcebook for a new generation of fantasy writers." The book also "presents a new manifestation of Delany's continuing concern for language and the magic of fiction, whereby words become symbols for other, larger things," Collings observes.

In *Stars in My Pocket Like Grains of Sand,* Delany returns to distant worlds of the future. The book is "a densely textured, intricately worked out novelistic structure which delights and astonishes even as it forces a confrontation with a wide range of thought-provoking issues," writes McCaffery in *Fantasy Review*. Included are "an examination of interstellar politics among thousands of far flung worlds, a love story, a meandering essay on the variety of human relationships and the inexplicability of sexual attractiveness, and a hypnotic crash-course on a fascinating body of literature which does not yet exist," notes H. J. Kirchhoff in the Toronto *Globe and Mail*.

Beneath the surface features, as Jonas suggests in the *New York Times Book Review*, the reader can discover the fullness of this Delany novel. The reviewer writes: "To unpack the layers of meaning in seemingly offhand remarks or exchanges of social pleasantries, the reader must be alert to small shifts in emphasis, repeated phrases or gestures that assume new significance in new contexts, patterns of behavior that only become apparent when the author supplies a crucial piece of information at just the proper moment." Here in the words and gestures of the characters and the subtle way in which the author fashions his work is the fundamental concern of the novel. "I take the most basic subject here to be the nature of information itself," McCaffery explains, "the way it is processed, stored and decoded symbolically, the way it is distorted by the present and the past, the way it has become a commodity . . . the way that the play of textualities defines our perception of the universe."

"This is an astonishing new Delany," according to Somtow Sucharitkul in the *Washington Post Book World*, "more richly textured, smoother, more colorful than ever before." Jonas commends the novel because of the interaction it encourages with the reader. "Sentence by sentence, phrase by phrase, it invites the reader to collaborate in the process of creation, in a way that few novels do," writes the reviewer. "The reader who accepts this invitation has an extraordinarily satisfying experience in store for him/her." "*Stars in My Pocket Like Grains of Sand* . . . confirms that [Delany] is American SF's most consistently brilliant and inventive writer," McCaffery claims.

Critics often comment on Delany's use of fiction as a forum to call for greater acceptance of women's rights and gay rights; yet, as Govan maintains in her *Dictionary of Literary Biography* contribution, "a recurring motif frequently overlooked in Delany's fiction is his subtle emphasis on race. Black and mixed-blood characters cross the spectrum of his speculative futures, both as a testimony to a future Delany believes will change to reflect human diversity honestly and as a commentary on the racial politics of the present."

In novels such as *Babel-17*, Delany demonstrates how language can be used to rob the black man of his identity.

"White culture exerts a great influence because it can force stereotypic definitions on the black person," writes Weedman. She adds that "if the black person capitulates to the definition imposed on him by a force outside of his culture, then he is in danger of losing his identity." In his other novels, Govan points out, "Delany utilizes existing negative racial mythologies about blacks, but, in all his works, he twists the commonplace images and stereotypes to his own ends." In using his fiction to promote awareness of the race issue, he and other black writers like him "have mastered the dominant culture's language and turned it against its formulators in protest," writes Weedman.

"Delany is not only a gifted writer," claims Barbour in his *Foundation* article, "he is one of the most articulate theorists of sf to have emerged from the ranks of its writers." In such critical works as *The Jewel-Hinged Jaw, The American Shore,* and *Starboard Wine,* "he has done much to open up critical discussion of sf as a genre, forcefully arguing its great potential as art," adds the reviewer. In his nonfiction, Delany offers a functional description of science fiction and contrasts it with other genres such as naturalistic fiction and fantasy. He also attempts to expand "the domain of his chosen genre by claiming it the modern mode of fiction *par excellence,*" comments Slusser, "the one most suited to deal with the complexities of paradox and probability, chaos, irrationality, and the need for logic and order."

With the publication of *The Motion of Light in Water,* Delany turned to writing about himself. This memoir of his early days as a writer in New York's East Village is "an extraordinary account of life experienced by a precocious black artist of the 1960s," as E. Guereschi writes in *Choice*. The book reveals much of Delany's sexual adventures, with partners of both sexes at the time, his nervous breakdown, and the general sense of living on the edge in an exciting and innovative period. Moreover, the book tells of Delany's realization and eventual acceptance of his homosexuality. Thomas M. Disch, writing in the *American Book Review,* finds that Delany "can't help creating legends and elaborating myths. Indeed, it is his forte, the open secret of his success as an SF writer. [Delany's] SF heroes are variations of an archetype he calls The Kid. . . . In his memoir, the author himself [is] finally assuming the role in which his fictive alter-egos have enjoyed their success. That is the book's strength even more than its weakness." Guereschi believes that the memoir "defines an arduous search for identity," while Disch concludes that *The Motion of Light in Water* "has the potential of being as popular, as representative of its era, as *On the Road.*"

Samuel R. Delany is not a simple man: a black man in a white society, a writer who suffers from dyslexia, an artist who is also a critic. His race, lifestyle, chosen profession, and chosen genre keep him far from the mainstream. "His own term 'multiplex' probably best describes his work (attitudes, ideas, themes, craftsmanship, all their interrelations, as well as his relation as artist, to them all)," Barbour suggests. And, adds the reviewer, "His great perseverance in continually developing his craft and never resting on his past achievements is revealed in the steady growth in [his] artistry." In Weedman's estimation, "Few writers approach the lyricism, the command of language, the powerful combination of style and content that distinguishes Delany's works. More importantly," she concludes, "few writers, whether in science fiction or mundane fiction, so successfully create works which make us question ourselves, our actions, our beliefs, and our society as Delany has helped us do." Writing in the *Washington Post Book World,* John Clute places Delany in a central position in modern science fiction. In his best work, Clute believes, Delany "treated the interstellar venues of space opera as analogues of urban life in the decaying hearts of the great American cities. As a black gay New Yorker much too well educated for his own good, Delany . . . illuminated the world the way a torch might cast light in a cellar."

BIOGRAPHICAL/CRITICAL SOURCES:

BOOKS

Bleiler, E. F., editor, *Science Fiction Writers: Critical Studies of the Major Authors from the Early Nineteenth Century to the Present Day,* Scribner, 1982.

Contemporary Literary Criticism, Gale, Volume 8, 1978, Volume 14, 1980, Volume 38, 1986.

Delany, Samuel R., *The Jewel-Hinged Jaw: Notes on the Language of Science Fiction,* Dragon Press, 1977, revised edition, Berkley Publishing, 1978.

Delany, Samuel R., *Heavenly Breakfast: An Essay on the Winter of Love,* Bantam, 1979.

Delany, Samuel R., *The Motion of Light in Water: Sex and Science Fiction Writing in the East Village, 1957-1965,* Arbor House, 1988.

Dictionary of Literary Biography, Gale, Volume 8: *Twentieth-Century American Science Fiction Writers,* 1981, Volume 33: *Afro-American Fiction Writers after 1955,* 1984.

Kostelanetz, Richard, editor, *American Writing Today,* Whitston, 1991.

McCaffery, Larry, and Sinda Gregory, editors, *Alive and Writing: Interviews with American Authors of the 1980s,* University of Illinois Press, 1987.

McEvoy, Seth, *Samuel R. Delany,* Ungar, 1984.

Peplow, Michael W., and Robert S. Bravard, *Samuel R. Delany: A Primary and Secondary Bibliography, 1962-1979,* G. K. Hall, 1980.

Platt, Charles, editor, *Dream Makers: The Uncommon People Who Write Science Fiction,* Berkley Books, 1980.

Slusser, George Edgar, *The Delany Intersection: Samuel R. Delany Considered as a Writer of Semi-Precious Words,* Borgo, 1977.

Smith, Nicholas D., editor, *Philosophers Look at Science Fiction,* Nelson-Hall, 1982.

Weedman, Jane Branham, *Samuel R. Delany,* Starmont House, 1982.

PERIODICALS

American Book Review, January, 1989.

Analog Science Fiction/Science Fact, April, 1985.

Black American Literature Forum, summer, 1984.

Choice, February, 1989.

Commonweal, December 5, 1975.

Extrapolation, fall, 1982; winter, 1989; fall, 1989.

Fantasy Review, December, 1984.

Foundation, March, 1975.

Globe and Mail (Toronto), February 9, 1985.

Locus, summer, 1983; October, 1989.

Los Angeles Times Book Review, March 13, 1988.

Magazine of Fantasy and Science Fiction, November, 1975; June, 1980; May, 1989.

Mother Jones, August, 1976.

New York Review of Books, January 29, 1991.

New York Times Book Review, February 16, 1975; March 28, 1976; October 28, 1979; February 10, 1985.

Publishers Weekly, January 29, 1988; October 19, 1992.

Science Fiction and Fantasy Book Review, July/August, 1983.

Science Fiction Chronicle, November, 1987; February, 1990.

Science-Fiction Studies, November, 1981; July, 1987; November, 1990.

Voice Literary Supplement, February, 1985.

Washington Post Book World, January 27, 1985; August 25, 1991.*

*   *   *

DEVERELL, William H(erbert) 1937-

PERSONAL: Born March 4, 1937, in Regina, Saskatchewan, Canada; son of Robert J. (a journalist) and Grace Amy (Barber) Deverell; married Tekla Melnyk (a Jungian psychologist); children: Daniel Mark, Tamara Lise. *Education:* University of Saskatchewan, B.A., LL.B., 1962.

ADDRESSES: Home—Razor Point Rd., Rural Route 1, North Pender Island, British Columbia, Canada V0N 2M0.

CAREER: Saskatoon Star-Phoenix, Saskatoon, Saskatchewan, 1956-60, began as reporter, became night editor; associated with Canadian Press, Montreal, Quebec, 1960-62; *Vancouver Sun,* Vancouver, British Columbia, transportation editor, 1963; partner and trial attorney with firm in Vancouver, 1964-79; writer, 1979—.

MEMBER: Writers Union of Canada, British Crime Writers Association, Crime Writers of Canada, Canadian Bar Association (past chair, criminal justice section), British Columbia Bar Association, British Columbia Civil Liberties Association (founding member; past president).

AWARDS, HONORS: McClelland & Stewart/Seal First Novel Award, 1979, and book of the year award from Periodical Distributors Association of Canada, 1980, both for *Needles.*

WRITINGS:

NOVELS

Needles, Little, Brown, 1979.
High Crimes, McClelland & Stewart, 1979, St. Martin's, 1981.
Mecca, McClelland & Stewart, 1983, Bantam, 1985.
Dance of Shiva, McClelland & Stewart, 1984, Bantam, 1985.
Platinum Blues, McClelland & Stewart, 1988, British American, 1990.
Mindfield, McClelland & Stewart, 1989, British American, 1990.

NONFICTION

Fatal Cruise: The Trial of Robert Frisbee, McClelland & Stewart, 1991.

Also author of *The Button Man,* a Canadian Broadcasting Company (CBC) television pilot for the CBC-TV series *Street Legal.*

SIDELIGHTS: In the late 1970s, William H. Deverell fulfilled a lifelong ambition by taking a sabbatical from his successful criminal law practice in order to write a novel. "I'd read lots of thrillers, and lawyers being naturally competitive, thought I could do better," he told Eleanor Wachtel of *Western Living.* Tackling the project with determination, Deverell often spent up to fifteen hours a day at his manual typewriter. His efforts ultimately paid off when his psychological thriller *Needles* won a $50,000 McClelland & Stewart/Seal First Novel Award.

Upon returning to his law partnership after one year, Deverell became the target of office banter. Colleagues greeted him exclaiming, "What a scam you pulled off," said Wachtel. It was "as if there were some sort of trickery" involved in Deverell's success. For a short time Deverell attempted to juggle a writing career with his practice of law, but he eventually decided to write full time. His 1988 novel, *Platinum Blues,* offers "hilariously

pointed observations on the legal chicanery and artistic horn-swoggling that goes on in the record industry," commented Marilyn Stasio in the *New York Times Book Review.* Frederick Busch in *Tribune Books* noted that "Deverell writes with a snappy pace and a fine sense of humor," and Margaret Cannon of the Toronto *Globe and Mail* stated that *Platinum Blues* is Deverell's "best work so far," adding, "The trial scenes are good and not too long, the romance is believable, and the dialogue is as crisp as a new $20 bill."

Deverell's first nonfiction work, *Fatal Cruise,* concerns the case of Robert Frisbee, a man accused of murdering his elderly female employer, Muriel Barnett, while on a luxury cruise ship. Deverell, Frisbee's defense attorney, provides the setting and circumstances of the killing as well as the legal events which follow. Cannon asserted that *Fatal Cruise* "is as compelling as any novel," and continued, "In Deverell's clear prose and with his novelist's gift for characterization, the tangled lives of Robert and Muriel come back to life."

BIOGRAPHICAL/CRITICAL SOURCES:

PERIODICALS

Globe and Mail (Toronto), October 1, 1988; October 28, 1989; October 26, 1991, p. C7.
New York Times Book Review, September 30, 1990, p. 32.
Tribune Books (Chicago), August 26, 1990, Section 14, p. 6.
Western Living, November, 1979.

*   *   *

DICKINSON, Patric Thomas   1914-

PERSONAL: Born December 26, 1914, in Nasirabad, India; son of Arthur Thomas (an army officer) and Eileen (Kirwan) Dickinson; married Sheila Dunbar Shannon (an editor and anthologist), December 19, 1947; children: David Dunbar, Virginia Kirwan. *Education:* St. Catharine's College, Cambridge, B.A. (with honors), 1936. *Avocational Interests:* Collecting Sunderland lustre pottery and watching golf.

ADDRESSES: Home—38 Church Square, Rye, East Sussex, England.

CAREER: Schoolmaster, 1936-39; British Broadcasting Corp., London, England, producer, Transcription Service, 1942-45, poetry editor, Home Service and Third Programme, 1945-48; free-lance writer, broadcaster, and critic, 1948—. City University, London, Gresham Professor of Rhetoric, 1964-67; lecturer and reader. Poetry Festival Royal Court Theater, director, 1963.

MEMBER: Savile Club.

AWARDS, HONORS: Atlantic Award in literature, 1948; Cholmondeley Award for Poets, 1973.

WRITINGS:

POETRY

The Seven Days of Jericho, Andrew Dakers, 1944.
Theseus and the Minotaur, and Poems, J. Cape, 1946.
Stone in the Midst, and Poems (also see below), Methuen, 1948.
The Sailing Race, and Other Poems, Chatto & Windus, 1952.
The Scale of Things, Chatto & Windus, 1955.
The World I See, Chatto & Windus, 1960.
This Cold Universe, Chatto & Windus, 1964.
The Good Minute: An Autobiographical Study, Gollancz, 1965.
Selected Poems, Chatto & Windus, 1968.
More than Time, Chatto & Windus, 1971.
A Wintering Tree, Chatto & Windus, 1973.
The Bearing Beast, Chatto & Windus, 1976.
Our Living John, Chatto & Windus, 1979.
Poems from Rye, Martellow Bookshop, 1980.
To Go Hidden, Mandeville Press, 1980.
Winter Hostages, Mandeville Press, 1981.
A Rift in Time, Chatto & Windus, 1983.
To Go Hidden, Mandeville Press, 1984.
Not Hereafter, Mandeville Press, 1991.

Also author of *A Sun Dog,* 1988, and *Two Into One,* 1989.

EDITOR

Soldier's Verse, Muller, 1945.
Byron, *Poems,* Grey Walls Press, 1949.
(With Sheila Shannon) *Poems to Remember: A Book for Children,* Harvill, 1958.
(With Shannon) *Poets' Choice: An Anthology of English Poetry from Spenser to the Present Day,* Evans Brothers, 1967.

PLAYS

Stone in the Midst (produced in London, 1951), published in *Stone in the Midst, and Poems,* Methuen, 1948.
(Adaptor) Jules Supervielle, *Robinson,* produced in London, 1953.
The Golden Touch, produced in Wolverhampton, England, 1956.
(Translator) Aristophanes, *Aristophanes against War: Three Plays* (includes *The Acharnians, The Peace,* and *Lysistrata*), Oxford University Press, 1957.
A Durable Fire (produced in Canterbury, England, 1962), Chatto & Windus, 1962.
(Adaptor) Plautus, *Pseudous,* produced in Stoke-on-Trent, England, 1966.

(Translator) Aristophanes, *The Complete Plays,* Oxford University Press, 1970.
(Adaptor and translator) Plautus, *Mercator,* produced in Stoke-on-Trent as *The Business Man,* 1982.

Author of *The First Family,* 1960, *Wilfred Own,* 1970, and *The Pensive Prisoner,* 1970; author of television adaptation of *Lysistrata,* 1964.

LIBRETTOS

(With Bernard Rose) *Ode to St. Catharine,* produced in Cambridge, England, 1973.
(With Alan Ridout) *Creation,* produced in Ely, England, 1973.
(With Stephen Dodgson) *The Miller's Secret,* produced in Cookham, England, 1973.

Author of librettos *The Return of Odysseus,* with Malcolm Arnold, and *Good King Wenceslaus,* with Alan Ridout.

OTHER

A Round of Golf Courses: A Selection of the Best Eighteen (guidebook), Evans Brothers, 1951.
(Translator) Virgil, *The Aeneid,* New American Library, 1962.
(Author of introduction and notes) C. Day Lewis, *C. Day Lewis: Selections from His Poetry,* Chatto & Windus, 1967.

SIDELIGHTS: Commenting on the work of poet Patric Thomas Dickinson in the *Times Literary Supplement,* George Szirtes wrote of the author's ability to hear "the still small voice in nature. What impresses most in [*A Rift in Time*] is its sense of the intensity of certain moments, caught sometimes as a child would catch it . . .or celebrated and cherished . . . . Dickinson's speech, which is slightly clipped, is given its lyricism by his sense of the *mot juste.*"

BIOGRAPHICAL/CRITICAL SOURCES:

PERIODICALS

London Magazine, October, 1969.
New Statesman, February 28, 1969.
Poetry, September, 1969.
Times Literary Supplement, August 24, 1967; April 4, 1980; December 11, 1981; July 15, 1983.*

*   *   *

DILLARD, Annie 1945-

PERSONAL: Born April 30, 1945, in Pittsburgh, PA; daughter of Frank and Pam (Lambert) Doak; married Richard Dillard (a professor and writer), June 4, 1964 (divorced); married Gary Clevidence (a writer), April 12,

1980 (divorced); married Robert D. Richardson, Jr. (a professor and writer), c. 1988; children: (with Clevidence) Cody Rose; Carin, Shelly (stepchildren). *Education:* Hollins College, B.A., 1967, M.A., 1968.

ADDRESSES: Home—158 Mt. Vernon, Middletown, CT 06457; (summer) South Wellfleet, MA. *Office*—Wesleyan University, Middletown, CT. *Agent*—Timothy Seldes, Russell & Volkening, 50 West 29th St., New York, NY 10001.

CAREER: Writer. Western Washington University, Bellingham, scholar in residence, 1975-79; Wesleyan University, Middletown, CT, distinguished visiting professor, beginning in 1979, full adjunct professor, beginning in 1983, writer in residence, beginning in 1987. Member of U.S. cultural delegation to China, 1982. Board member, Western States Arts Foundation, Milton Centre, and Key West Literary Seminar; board member and chairman (1991—), Wesleyan Writers' Conference. Member, New York Public Library National Literacy Committee, National Committee for U.S.-China relations, and Catholic Commission on Intellectual and Cultural Affairs. Member of usage panel, *American Heritage Dictionary.*

MEMBER: International PEN, Century Association, Poetry Society of America, Western Writers of America, Phi Beta Kappa.

AWARDS, HONORS: Pulitzer Prize (general nonfiction), 1975, for *Pilgrim at Tinker Creek;* New York Press Club Award for Excellence, 1975; Washington State Governor's Award for Literature, 1978; grants from National Endowment for the Arts, 1980-81, and Guggenheim Foundation, 1985-86; *Los Angeles Times* Book Prize nomination, 1982, for *Living by Fiction;* honorary degrees from Boston College, 1986, Connecticut College, and University of Hartford, both 1993; National Book Critics Circle award nomination, 1987, for *An American Childhood;* Appalachian Gold Medallion, University of Charleston, 1989; St. Botolph's Club Foundation Award, Boston, 1989; English-speaking Union Ambassador Book Award, 1990, for *The Writing Life;* History Maker Award, Historical Society of Western Pennsylvania, 1993.

WRITINGS:

Tickets for a Prayer Wheel (poems), University of Missouri Press, 1974.
Pilgrim at Tinker Creek (also see below), Harper's Magazine Press, 1974.
Holy the Firm (also see below), Harper, 1978.
Living by Fiction (also see below), Harper, 1982.
Teaching a Stone to Talk: Expeditions and Encounters (also see below), Harper, 1982.
Encounters with Chinese Writers, Wesleyan University Press, 1984.

(Contributor) *Inventing the Truth: The Art and Craft of Memoir,* edited by William Zinsser, Houghton, 1987.
An American Childhood (also see below), Harper, 1987.
(Editor with Robert Atwan) *The Best American Essays, 1988,* Ticknor & Fields, 1988.
The Annie Dillard Library (contains *Living by Fiction, An American Childhood, Holy the Firm, Pilgrim at Tinker Creek,* and *Teaching a Stone to Talk*), Harper, 1989.
The Writing Life, Harper, 1989.
Three by Annie Dillard (contains *Pilgrim at Tinker Creek, An American Childhood,* and *The Writing Life*), Harper, 1990.
The Living (novel), HarperCollins, 1992.

Columnist, *Living Wilderness,* 1973-75. Contributing editor, *Harper's,* 1974-81, and 1983-85. Contributor of fiction, essays, and poetry to numerous periodicals, including *Atlantic Monthly, American Scholar, Poetry,* and *Chicago Review.*

SIDELIGHTS: Annie Dillard has carved a unique niche for herself in the world of American letters. Over the course of her career, Dillard has written essays, poetry, memoirs, literary criticism—even a western novel. In whatever genre she works, Dillard distinguishes herself with her carefully wrought language, keen observations, and original metaphysical insights. Her first significant publication, *Pilgrim at Tinker Creek,* drew numerous comparisons to Thoreau's *Walden;* in the years since *Pilgrim* appeared, Dillard's name has come to stand for excellence in writing.

Tickets for a Prayer Wheel was Dillard's first publication. This slim volume of poetry—which expressed the author's yearning to sense a hidden God—was praised by reviewers. Within months of *Tickets*'s appearance, however, the book was completely overshadowed by the release of *Pilgrim at Tinker Creek.* Dillard lived quietly on Tinker Creek in Virginia's Roanoke Valley, observing the natural world, taking notes, and reading voluminously in a wide variety of disciplines, including theology, philosophy, natural science, and physics. Following the progression of seasons, *Pilgrim* probes the cosmic significance of the beauty and violence coexisting in the natural world.

The book met with immediate popular and critical success. "One of the most pleasing traits of the book is the graceful harmony between scrutiny of real phenomena and the reflections to which that gives rise," noted a *Commentary* reviewer. "Anecdotes of animal behavior become so effortlessly enlarged into symbols by the deepened insight of meditation. Like a true transcendentalist, Miss Dillard understands her task to be that of full alertness." Other critics found fault Dillard's work, however, calling it self-absorbed or overwritten. Charles Deemer of the

New Leader, for example, claimed that "if Annie Dillard had not spelled out what she was up to in this book, I don't think I would have guessed. . . . Her observations are typically described in overstatement reaching toward hysteria." A more charitable assessment came from Muriel Haynes of *Ms.* While finding Dillard to be "susceptible to fits of rapture," Haynes asserted that the author's "imaginative flights have the special beauty of surprise."

The author's next book delved into the metaphysical aspects of pain. *Holy the Firm* was inspired by the plight of one of Dillard's neighbors, a seven-year-old child badly burned in a plane crash. As Dillard reflects on the maimed child and on a moth consumed by flame, she struggles with the problem of reconciling faith in a loving god with the reality of a violent world. Only seventy-six pages long, the book overflows with "great richness, beauty and power," according to Frederick Buechner in the *New York Times Book Review. Atlantic* reviewer C. Michael Curtis concurred, adding that "Dillard writes about the ferocity and beauty of natural order with . . . grace."

Elegant writing also distinguishes *Living by Fiction,* Dillard's fourth book, in which the author analyzes the differences between modernist and traditional fiction. "Everyone who timidly, bombastically, reverently, scholastically—even fraudulently—essays to live 'the life of the mind' should read this book," advised Carolyn See in the *Los Angeles Times.* See went on to describe *Living by Fiction* as "somewhere between scholarship, metaphysics, an acid trip and a wonderful conversation with a most smart person." "Whether the field of investigation is nature or fiction, Annie Dillard digs for ultimate meanings as instinctively and as determinedly as hogs for truffles," remarked *Washington Post Book World* contributor John Breslin. "The resulting upheaval can be disconcerting . . . still, uncovered morsels are rich and tasty."

Dillard returned to reflections on nature and religion in a book of essays entitled *Teaching a Stone to Talk: Expeditions and Encounters.* In minutely detailed descriptions of a solar eclipse, visits to South America and the Galapagos Islands, and other, more commonplace events and locations, Dillard continues "the pilgrimage begun at Tinker Creek with an acuity of eye and ear that is matched by an ability to communicate a sense of wonder," stated Beaufort Cranford in the *Detroit News. Washington Post Book World* contributor Douglas Bauer was similarly pleased with the collection, judging the essays to be "almost uniformly splendid." In his estimation, Dillard's "art as an essayist is to move with the scrutinous eye through events and receptions that are random on their surfaces and to find, with grace and always-redeeming wit, the connections."

Dillard later chronicled her experiences as a member of a Chinese-American cultural exchange in a short, straightforward volume entitled *Encounters with Chinese Writers;* she then looked deeply into her past to produce another best-seller, *An American Childhood.* On one level, *An American Childhood* details Dillard's upbringing in an idiosyncratic, wealthy family; in another sense, the memoir tells the story of a young person's awakening to the world. In the words of *Washington Post* writer Charles Trueheart, Dillard's "memories of childhood are like her observations of nature: they feed her acrobatic thinking, and drive the free verse of her prose." Critics also applauded Dillard's keen insight into the unique perceptions of youth, as well as her exuberant spirit. "Loving and lyrical, nostalgic without being wistful, this is a book about the capacity for joy," said *Los Angeles Times Book Review* contributor Cyra McFadden, while Noel Perrin of the *New York Times Book Review* observed that "Ms. Dillard has written an autobiography in semimystical prose about the growth of her own mind, and it's an exceptionally interesting account."

The activity that had occupied most of Dillard's adulthood was the subject of her next book, *The Writing Life.* With regard to content, *The Writing Life* is not a manual on craft nor a guide to getting published; rather, it is a study of a writer at work and the processes involved in that work. Among critics, the book drew mixed reaction. "Annie Dillard is one of my favorite contemporary authors," Sara Maitland acknowledged in the *New York Times Book Review.* "Dillard is a wonderful writer and *The Writing Life* is full of joys. These are clearest to me when she comes at her subject tangentially, talking not of herself at her desk but of other parallel cases—the last chapter, a story about a stunt pilot who was an artist of air, is, quite simply, breathtaking. There are so many bits like this. . . . Unfortunately, the bits do not add up to a book." *Washington Post Book World* contributor Wendy Law-Yone voiced similar sentiments, finding the book "intriguing but not entirely satisfying" and "a sketch rather than a finished portrait." Nevertheless, she wondered, "Can anyone who has ever read Annie Dillard resist hearing what she has to say about writing? Her authority has been clear since *Pilgrim at Tinker Creek*—a mystic's wonder at the physical world expressed in beautiful, near-biblical prose."

Dillard ventured into new territory with her 1992 publication, *The Living,* a sprawling historical novel set in the Pacific Northwest. Reviewers hailed the author's first novel as masterful. "Her triumph is that this panoramic evocation of a very specific landscape and people might as well have been settled upon any other time and place—for this is, above all, a novel about the reiterant, precarious, wondrous, solitary, terrifying, utterly common condition of human life," wrote Molly Gloss in *Washington Post Book World*. Dillard's celebrated skill with words was also much in evidence here, according to Gloss, who noted that Dillard "uses language gracefully, releasing at times a vivid, startling imagery." Carol Anshaw concurred in the *Los Angeles Times Book Review:* "The many readers who have been drawn in the past to Dillard's work for its elegant and muscular language won't be disappointed in these pages."

BIOGRAPHICAL/CRITICAL SOURCES:

BOOKS

Contemporary Literary Criticism, Gale, Volume 9, 1978, Volume 60, 1990.
Dictionary of Literary Biography Yearbook: 1980, Gale, 1981.
Ihab, Hassan, *Selves at Risk: Patterns of Quest in Contemporary American Letters,* University of Wisconsin Press, 1991.
Johnson, Sandra Humble, *The Space Between: Literary Epiphany in the Works of Annie Dillard,* Kent State University Press, 1992.
Smith, Linda, *Annie Dillard,* Twayne, 1991.

PERIODICALS

America, April 20, 1974; February 11, 1978, pp. 363-364; May 6, 1978.
American Literature, March, 1987.
Atlantic, December, 1977.
Best Sellers, December, 1977.
Chicago Tribune, October 1, 1987.
Chicago Tribune Book World, September 12, 1982, p. 7; November 21, 1982, p. 5.
Commentary, October, 1974.
Commonweal, October 24, 1975, pp. 495-496; February 3, 1978.
Detroit News, October 31, 1982, p. 2H.
Globe and Mail (Toronto), November 28, 1987.
Los Angeles Times, April 27, 1982; November 19, 1982.
Los Angeles Times Book Review, November 18, 1984, p. 11; September 20, 1987, pp. 1, 14; October 31, 1982, p. 2; November 18, 1984, p. 11; July 6, 1986, p. 10; September 20, 1987, pp. 1, 14; May 31, 1992, pp. 1, 7.
Ms., August, 1974.
Nation, November 20, 1982, pp. 535-536; October 16, 1989, pp. 435-436.
New Leader, June 24, 1974.
New Republic, April 6, 1974.
New York Times, September 21, 1977; March 12, 1982, p. C18; November 25, 1982.
New York Times Book Review, March 24, 1974 pp. 4-5; September 25, 1977, pp. 12, 40; May 9, 1982, pp. 10, 22-23; July 1, 1979, p. 21; November 28, 1982, pp. 13,

19; January 1, 1984, p. 32; September 23, 1984, p. 29; September 27, 1987, p. 7; September 17, 1989, p. 15.
People, October 19, 1987, p. 99.
Publishers Weekly, September 1, 1989, pp. 67-68.
South Atlantic Quarterly, spring, 1986, pp. 111-122.
Time, March 18, 1974; October 10, 1977.
Tribune Books (Chicago), September 13, 1987, pp. 1, 12; December 18, 1988, p. 3; August 27, 1989, p. 6.
Village Voice, July 13, 1982, pp. 40-41.
Virginia Quarterly Review, autumn, 1974, pp. 637-640.
Washington Post, October 28, 1987.
Washington Post Book World, October 16, 1977, p. E6; April 4, 1982, p. 4; January 2, 1983, p. 6; September 9, 1984, p. 6; July 6, 1986, p. 13; September 6, 1987, p. 11; August 14, 1988, p. 12; August 27, 1989, p. 6; September 24, 1989, p. 4, May 3, 1992, pp. 1-2.

—*Sketch by Joan Goldsworthy*

*   *   *

DIXON, Rosie
See WOOD, Christopher (Hovelle)

*   *   *

DOENECKE, Justus Drew   1938-

PERSONAL: Surname is pronounced "don-a-key"; born March 5, 1938, in Brooklyn, NY; son of Justus Christian (a building estimator) and Eleanor (a former elementary school teacher; maiden name, Smith) Doenecke; married Carol Anne Soukup (an artist), March 21, 1970. *Education:* Colgate University, A.B., 1960; Princeton University, M.A., 1962, Ph.D., 1966. *Religion:* Episcopal.

ADDRESSES: Home—3943 Riverview Blvd. W., Bradenton, FL 34209. *Office*—Division of Social Science, New College, University of South Florida, Sarasota, FL 34243-2197.

CAREER: Colgate University, Hamilton, NY, instructor in history, 1963-64; Ohio Wesleyan University, Delaware, OH, instructor, 1965-66, assistant professor of history, 1966-69; University of South Florida, New College, Sarasota, assistant professor, 1969-71, associate professor, 1971-77, professor of history, 1977—. Visiting fellow, New College, Oxford University, 1991.

MEMBER: American Historical Association, Organization of American Historians, Conference on Peace Research in History (member of council, 1975-89), Society for Historians of American Foreign Relations (program co-chairman, 1986; member of Arthur S. Link Award committee, 1992—), Phi Beta Kappa.

AWARDS, HONORS: Woodrow Wilson fellowship, 1960-61; Danforth fellowship, 1960-65; Institute for Humane Studies, Menlo Park, CA, fellow, summers, 1970-71, 1975-76, 1981, senior research fellow, 1977-78; National Endowment for the Humanities fellow, summer, 1971; grants from John Anson Kittredge Educational Fund, 1973, 1980, Harry S Truman Library Institute, 1973, and Shell Oil Co., 1975; Arthur L. Link Prize for documentary editing, Society for Historians of American Foreign Relations, 1991.

WRITINGS:

The Literature of Isolationism: A Guide to Non-Interventionist Scholarship, 1930-1972, Ralph Myles, 1972.
Not to the Swift: The Old Isolationists in the Cold War Era, Bucknell University Press, 1978.
The Presidencies of James A. Garfield and Chester A. Arthur, Regents Press of Kansas, 1981.
The Diplomacy of Frustration: The Manchurian Crisis of 1931-1933 as Revealed in the Papers of Stanley K. Hornbeck, Hoover Institution, 1981.
When the Wicked Rise: American Opinion-Makers and the Manchurian Crisis of 1931-1933, Bucknell University Press, 1984.
Anti-Intervention: A Bibliographical Introduction to Isolationism and Pacifism from World War I to the Early Cold War, Garland Publishing, 1987.
In Danger Undaunted: The Isolationist Movement of 1940-1941 as Revealed through the Papers of the America First Committee, Hoover Institution, 1990.
(With John E. Wilzas) *From Isolation to War, 1931-1941,* 2nd edition, Harland Davidson, 1991.

Contributor to *Dictionary of the History of American Foreign Policy,* and *Dictionary of American Biography.* Contributor to history journals. Member of editorial board, *Anglican and Episcopal History,* 1987—.

SIDELIGHTS: Justus Drew Doenecke once told *CA:* "Much of my work has focused on alternatives to the foreign policies of Franklin D. Roosevelt, Truman, and Eisenhower. In venturing into such topics as isolationism, pacifism, and anti-interventionism, I hope to put anti-interventionist thought in the context of its own time and thereby reveal the hopes and fears of its proponents. My interpretation is revisionist only in the sense that I see the anti-interventionist heritage, like that of the administrations they so passionately criticized, containing wisdom as well as folly. The warnings of anti-interventionists against presidential duplicity remain timely. So does their critique of messianic foreign policy pronouncements. It is never the purpose of my work to plead their case or to justify their beliefs and behavior. It is very much my purpose to delineate who the isolationists were, what they believed, and what they did, and—so far as possible—to correct the one-sided and unequivocally negative picture that has

come down in so much of our popular rhetoric and culture."

*   *   *

DOMECQ, H(onorio) Bustos
See BIOY CASARES, Adolfo

*   *   *

DRAKE, Albert (Dee) 1935-

PERSONAL: Born March 26, 1935, in Portland, OR; son of Albert Howard and Hildah (Lotten) Drake; married Barbara Robertson (a writer), December 28, 1960 (divorced); children: Moss Christopher, Monica Durrell, Barbara Ellen. *Education:* Attended Portland State College (now University), 1956-59; University of Oregon, B.A., 1962, M.F.A., 1966. *Politics:* None. *Religion:* Christian.

ADDRESSES: Home—9727 Southeast Reedway, Portland, OR 97266.

CAREER: Has worked as a laborer, mechanic, gravedigger, and in warehouses; Oregon Research Institute, Eugene, OR, medical research assistant, 1963-64; University of Oregon, Eugene, OR, research assistant, 1965, teaching assistant, 1965-66; Michigan State University, East Lansing, MI, assistant professor, 1966-70, associate professor, 1970-79, professor of English, 1979-91, professor emeritus, 1991—. Director, Clarion Science Fiction and Fantasy Writing Workshop, 1983, 1988, 1989, 1990; poet-in-the-schools, 1974—. Consultant, Breitenbush Press, 1979-80. *Military service:* National Guard, 1953-60.

AWARDS, HONORS: Ernest Haycox fiction award, 1961, 1962; Coordinating Council of Literary Magazines grant, 1972, 1974, 1978; National Endowment for the Arts grants, 1974, 1983; Michigan State University summer humanities grant, 1979; Michigan Council for the Arts grant, 1981-82. Also recipient of prizes from periodicals, including *St. Andrew's Review,* 1974, *Writer's Digest,* 1979, and *Fresh Weekly,* 1980.

WRITINGS:

POETRY

Crap Game, Stone Press, 1968.
(Editor and contributor) *Michigan Signatures: An Anthology of Current Michigan Poetry,* Quixote Press, 1969.
(With Lawson Inada and Doug Lawder) *Three Northwest Poets,* Quixote Press, 1970.
Riding Bike, Stone Press, 1973.
By Breathing In and Out, Three Rivers, 1974.
Cheap Thrills, Peaceweed Press, 1975.

Returning to Oregon, Cider Press, 1975.

Roadsalt, Bieler, 1976.

Reaching for the Sun, Laughing Bear Press, 1979.

Garage, Mudborn, 1980.

Homesick, Canoe Press, 1988.

FICTION

The Postcard Mysteries and Other Stories, Red Cedar, 1976.

Tillamook Burn (fiction and poetry), Fault, 1977.

In the Time of Surveys, White Ewe, 1978.

One Summer, White Ewe, 1979.

Beyond the Pavement, White Ewe, 1981.

I Remember the Day James Dean Died and Other Stories, White Ewe, 1983.

NONFICTION

The Big "Little GTO" Book, Motorbooks, 1982.

Street Was Fun in '51, Flat Out Press, 1982.

A 1950's Rod & Custom Builder's Wishbook, Flat Out Press, 1985.

Herding Goats, Flat Out Press, 1989.

Hot Rodder!, Flat Out Press, 1993.

Contributor of fiction to *Best American Short Stories 1971* and to magazines, including *Northwest Review, Redbook,* and *Chicago Review*; contributor of poetry, articles, and reviews to anthologies and to more than two hundred fifty magazines, including *Western Humanities Review, New York Quarterly, Poetry Now, Poetry Northwest, Rod Action, Street Rodder, Rodder's Digest,* and *Super Ford.* Assistant editor, *Northwest Review,* 1964-66; editor, Stone Press, 1968—, and *Happiness Holding Tank* (poetry magazine), 1970-92; contributing editor, *Popular Culture,* 1977-78.

SIDELIGHTS: "I have been writing steadily for thirty-three years now, long enough to be able to see where I've been," Albert Drake told *CA.* "It took five years to learn how to write, and another five to understand what I wanted to write about. I'm still interested in short fiction, but these days find myself thinking more in terms of books. That's not the same as thinking in terms of money, however. The patterns seem larger, or perhaps I've learned to extend my vision, or perhaps I've suddenly realized that time is running out. In that summing-up mood, two recent events have given me pleasure: the publication of *Rockbottom 9* which features sixty pages of my work as well as critical essays about my work, and the completion of a doctoral dissertation which examines the process of revision in my work."

DRAPER, Jo 1949-

PERSONAL: Born February 21, 1949, in Winchester, England; daughter of John Kenneth (a farmer) and Betty (a telephonist; maiden name, Taylor) Draper; married Christopher Chaplin (a data base manager), June 7, 1971. *Education:* Educated in England.

ADDRESSES: c/o Dovecote Press, Stanbridge, Wimborne, Dorset, England.

CAREER: Has held various archaeological jobs, 1967—. Conservator for Northampton Museum, Northampton, England, c. 1971-72.

MEMBER: Dorset Natural History and Archaeological Society (editor, 1981—).

WRITINGS:

(With husband, Christopher Chaplin) *Dorchester Excavations* (monographs), Volume 1, Dorset Natural History and Archaeology Society, 1982.

Excavations on Roman Sites at Gestingthorpe, Essex (monograph), East Anglian Archaeology, 1984.

Postmedieval Pottery, 1650-1800, Shire Publications, 1984.

A Dorchester Camera (photographs), Dovecote Press, 1984.

Thomas Hardy's England (photograph album), introduced and edited by John Fowles, Little, Brown, 1984.

(With Chaplin) *Dorset From the Air,* Dovecote Press, 1985.

Dorset: A Complete Guide, Dovecote Press, 1986, new edition, 1992.

Dorset Food, Dovecote Press, 1988.

Dorchester: An illustrated History, Dovecote Press, 1992.

Contributor of articles and reports to local history and archaeological journals, including *Post Medieval Archaeology, Popular Archaeology,* and *Northamptonshire.*

WORK IN PROGRESS: An exhibition for the Dorset County Museum on life in Dorset during World War II.

SIDELIGHTS: Thomas Hardy's England is a collection of photographs depicting the English novelist's native Dorset near the turn of the century; in the accompanying text, local historian and archaeologist Jo Draper presents a short biography of Hardy and an account of life in Hardyesque Dorset. Reviewing the book for the *Washington Post,* Michele Slung expressed keen disappointment that the chronology and attributions of the photographs were sparse and unclear, seeking particularly the pictures taken by Hardy's associate and frequent walking companion, photographer Hermann Lea. Still, the reviewer acknowledged that the selection gives "a wide, if not deep, portrait of Victorian Dorset," and added that "one feels not only the pull of Hardy's England but of all his fiction-writing peers." Commending Draper and editor John Fowles for avoiding "nostalgia's insidious distortions," Slung called *Thomas Hardy's England* "a worthwhile tour guide."

BIOGRAPHICAL/CRITICAL SOURCES:

PERIODICALS

Washington Post, February 25, 1985.

*　　*　　*

DUNN, James Taylor 1912-

PERSONAL: Born February 28, 1912, in St. Paul, MN; son of John W. G. (in the insurance and loan business) and Alice (Monfort) Dunn; married Marie-Catherine Bach, December 23, 1946. *Education:* Hamilton College, A.B., 1936; Syracuse University, B.S. (magna cum laude), 1939.

ADDRESSES: Home—7039 San Pedro, No. 907, San Antonio, TX (winter); and Box 227, Marine on St. Croix, MN 55047 (summer).

CAREER: Globe magazine, St. Paul, MN, assistant editor, 1936-38; Chemung County Library, Elmira, NY, librarian, 1940; Olean Public Library, Olean, NY, head librarian, 1941-48; New York State Historical Association, Cooperstown, librarian, 1948-55; Minnesota Historical Society, St. Paul, chief librarian, 1955-72, retired as research associate. *Military service:* U.S. Army, Anti-Aircraft Artillery, 1942-46; served in European Theater; became first lieutenant; awarded four battle stars.

MEMBER: American Association for Retired Persons, Minnesota Historical Society (honorary life member), St. Croix River Association (honorary life member), San Antonio Museum Association, Ramsey County Historical Society (patron), Washington County Historical Society (life member).

AWARDS, HONORS: John Cotton Dana Award, Olean New York Public Library, 1948; Certificate of Commendation, American Association for State and Local History, 1990; Lifetime Achievement Award, St. Croix Valley Heritage Coalition, 1991.

WRITINGS:

(Editor) James W. Taylor, *A Choice Nook of Memory: The Diary of a Cincinnati Law Clerk, 1842-1844,* Ohio Archaeological and Historical Society, 1950.

(Editor with A. Hermina Poatgieter) *The Gopher Reader, Books I and II,* Minnesota Historical Society, 1958, 2nd edition, 1975.

The St. Croix: Midwest Border River, Holt, 1965, new edition, Minnesota Historical Society, 1979.

Marine on St. Croix: From Lumber Village to Summer Haven, 1838-1968, Women's Civic Club, Marine on St. Croix (MN), 1968.

State Parks of the St. Croix Valley, Minnesota Parks Foundation, 1982.

Saint Paul's Schubert Club: A Century of Music, Schubert Club, 1983.

Saving a River: The Story of the St. Croix River Association, 1911-1986, St. Croix River Association, 1986.

Marine on St. Croix: 150 Years of Village Life, Marine Restoration Society, 1989.

Contributor of articles and books reviews to *American Heritage, Vermont Life, Beaver, Minnesota History, New York History, Alaska Life,* and *Wisconsin Magazine of History.*

WORK IN PROGRESS: Pounding the "Globe": Letters of Ezra Pound to James Taylor Dunn, 1936-1959; editing *Elizabeth and the Far Islands: Ten Years on the Faroes, 1895-1919* by Elizabeth Taylor.

SIDELIGHTS: James Taylor Dunn told *CA:* "Local history in all its aspects has been the guiding force in all my writings. The story of the street where one lives leads to the important part of all history, be it village, county, state, or country."

*　　*　　*

DUNNETT, Dorothy 1923-
(Dorothy Halliday)

PERSONAL: Born August 25, 1923, in Dunfermline, Scotland; daughter of Alexander and Dorothy E. (Millard) Halliday; married Alastair M. Dunnett, LL.D. (an editor, author, playwright, and company chairman), September 17, 1946; children: two sons, Ninian M. and Mungo H. *Avocational Interests:* Travel ("abroad a good deal, often in the United States"), sailing ("have done a lot around Hebridean Islands off Scotland"), opera, orchestral music, ballet ("keen supporter of Scottish opera and the Edinburgh International Festival of Music and the Arts.")

ADDRESSES: Home—87 Colinton Rd., Edinburgh, EH10 5DF, Scotland. *Agent*—Curtis Brown, 162-168 Regent St., London W1R 5TB, England.

CAREER: Historical novelist and writer of thrillers. British Civil Service, Scottish Government Departments, Edinburgh, assistant press officer, 1940-46; executive officer, Board of Trade, Glasgow, Scotland, 1946-55; professional portrait painter, 1950—; non-executive director, Scottish Television, 1979-92. Trustee, Scottish National War Memorial, 1962—; trustee, National Library of Scotland, 1986—; director, Edinburgh Book Festival, 1990—. Fellow, Royal Society of Arts, 1986.

AWARDS, HONORS: Scottish Arts Council Award, 1976, for *Checkmate;* member, Order of the British Empire, 1992; award for services to literature, St. Andrews Presbyterian College (Laurinburg, NC), 1993, for services to literature.

WRITINGS:

"LYMOND SAGA"; HISTORICAL FICTION NOVELS

The Game of Kings, Putnam, 1961.
Queens' Play, Putnam, 1964.
The Disorderly Knights, Putnam, 1966.
Pawn in Frankincense, Putnam, 1969.
The Ringed Castle, Cassell, 1971, Putnam, 1972.
Checkmate, Putnam, 1975.

"JOHNSON JOHNSON" SERIES; SUSPENSE NOVELS

(Under name Dorothy Halliday) *Dolly and the Singing Bird,* Cassell, 1968, published under name Dorothy Dunnett as *The Photogenic Soprano,* Houghton, 1968.
(Under name Dorothy Halliday) *Dolly and the Cookie Bird,* Cassell, 1970, published under name Dorothy Dunnett as *Murder in the Round,* Houghton, 1970.
(Under name Dorothy Halliday) *Dolly and the Doctor Bird,* Cassell, 1971, published under name Dorothy Dunnett as *Match for a Murderer,* Houghton, 1971.
(Under name Dorothy Halliday) *Dolly and the Starry Bird,* Cassell, 1973, published under name Dorothy Dunnett as *Murder in Focus,* Houghton, 1973.
Dolly and the Nanny Bird, Michael Joseph, 1976, Knopf, 1982.
Dolly and the Bird of Paradise, Michael Joseph, 1983.
Moroccan Traffic, Chatto & Windus, 1991, published as *Send a Fax to the Kasbah,* Harcourt, 1992.

"HOUSE OF NICCOLO" SERIES; HISTORICAL FICTION NOVELS

Niccolo Rising, Knopf, 1986.
The Spring of the Ram, Michael Joseph, 1987, Knopf, 1988.
Race of Scorpions, Michael Joseph, 1989, Knopf, 1990.
Scales of Gold, Michael Joseph, 1991, Knopf, 1992.
The Unicorn Hunt, Michael Joseph, 1993, Knopf, 1994.

OTHER

(Contributor) *Scottish Short Stories* (anthology), Collins, 1973.
King Hereafter, Knopf, 1982.
(With husband, Alastair M. Dunnett) *The Scottish Highlands* (nonfiction), photographs by David Paterson, Mainstream (Edinburgh), 1988.

WORK IN PROGRESS: New novels in "House of Niccolo" series and "Johnson Johnson" series.

SIDELIGHTS: After a career as a successful portrait painter, Dorothy Dunnett became a published novelist at the age of thirty-eight with her first historical novel, *The Game of Kings.* It quickly established her as a popular and critically successful contributor to the genre of historical fiction. *The Game of Kings* was the first in a six-volume series called the Lymond Saga, which deals with power struggles in the Scotland of the 16th century. The protagonist of the entire series, Francis Crawford of Lymond, is sent into exile as a rebel during the tumultuous period when the throne of Scotland was being disputed between Scottish Catholics, represented by Mary, Queen of Scots, and English Protestants, represented by Henry VIII and his daughter Elizabeth. Not only is Francis Crawford of Lymond an exiled rebel, he is a man whose birth and inheritance are the subject of a mystery plot; the six-volume saga sweeps through France, Russia, and Turkey as well as Scotland until the time when the hero is able to return to his homeland in safety, with the mystery of his background cleared up.

The noted historical novelist Cecilia Holland, reviewing Dunnett's 1989 novel *Race of Scorpions* for *Washington Post Book World,* looked back at *The Game of Kings* as "a masterpiece of historical fiction, a pyrotechnic blend of passionate scholarship and high-speed storytelling soaked with the scents and colors and sounds and combustible emotions of the 16th-century feudal Scotland that is its ultimate hero." Analyzing the character of Francis Crawford of Lymond, Holland described him as a charming rogue of an outlaw with a bitter, biting wit. Holland also noted Dunnett's witty prose, her eye for detail and the wealth of historical detail that filled out her work. The same qualities were noted by Stewart Sanderson in *Contemporary Novelists.* Remarking on the large number of subplots in the Lymond novels, Sanderson expressed gratitude for the lists of major characters the novelist supplied in each volume. Sanderson also noted that Dunnett's historical research was so well-grounded and so detailed that a reader could use the novels as guides to the real-life Scottish settings where the action took place. "Dunnett's stamina in historical and topographical research is indefatigable; and she seemingly cannot bear to throw anything away unused," Sanderson wrote, reassuring readers that despite the density of detail, "the author has such energy, such narrative pace, such inventiveness, wit and vitality, that the story is driven forward at breath-taking speed." An incidental fact about the Lymond Saga, noted by Lawrence Block in a review of a Dunnett thriller in *Washington Post Book World,* is that all six of the novels' titles refer to the game of chess.

Dunnett began to publish a second series of historical novels in 1986, with *Niccolo Rising*. This series moves us to the Mediterranean world—France, Venice, and Cyprus—and Flanders during the period in the fifteenth century when the merchant class was rising, through trade and banking, to take its place alongside the nobles at the top of European society. The hero of the series is an apprentice named Claes who, during the course of the series' first volume, *Niccolo Rising*, acquires the new name Niccolo and ascends to the position of husband of a wealthy widow, Marian de Charetty. Like Francis Crawford of Lymond, Niccolo faces a mystery about his parentage, which helps keep the plot going at a swift pace; and like the Lymond saga, the Niccolo series is packed with exhaustively researched, realistic historical detail. Calling *Niccolo Rising* "an excellent read" and calling attention to Dunnett's gift for wit, irony, characterization, and dialogue, H. J. Kirchhoff of the Toronto *Globe and Mail* described the character of Niccolo as "brilliant, mysterious and charismatic, a hell-raiser and a lover." However, Holland, in her review of the third novel in the Niccolo series, *Race of Scorpions*, presented a different opinion, calling Niccolo "nice," lacking in moral complexity, simple in his actions, and therefore uninteresting. Holland found as much to enjoy in Dunnett's "House of Niccolo" series as in the "Lymond" saga, but felt that in *Race of Scorpions*, the historical details were cluttered and threatened to overwhelm the plot.

A considerably more positive note was struck by Joan Aiken in a long review of *Niccolo Rising* in *Washington Post Book World*. Aiken's first response after reading the book, she told readers, was "simple awestruck admiration at the sheer volume of knowledge deployed in its construction and at the energy and power of organization required to create and manipulate such a complicated plot." Aiken's response to the character of Claes/Niccolo was as follows: "In the course of the action Claes, the easygoing simpleton, is totally transformed into a shrewd, subtle, far-seeing negotiator. . . . Can we quite believe that such a startling change could take place in this simple fellow, all during just one year? Well—such is the persuasiveness and knowledgeability of Dunnett's writing—that, yes, we almost can. . . . Claes, with all his contrarieties, is a solid figure, full of possibility—to me, much more interesting than Francis Crawford of Lymond." Aiken also praised Dunnett's ability to portray character relationships, expressed a fondness for the descriptions of Renaissance clothing in *Niccolo Rising*, and found fault only with the novel's villain, Simon, and with the rendering of the scenes of violent action, which she termed "over-excited." Asserting a resemblance in atmosphere, though not in plot, between *Niccolo Rising* and Alexandre Dumas's *The Count of Monte Cristo*, Aiken wrote, "But Dunnett, of course, is more subtle than Dumas and probably a far better historian."

Dunnett's other major historical novel, *King Hereafter*, was written between the Lymond saga and the House of Niccolo series. (The title is also, Dunnett told *CA*, "Pure Shakespeare.") The subject of the book is Macbeth, the 11th-century Scottish king whom Shakespeare immortalized. Dunnett calls the character Thorfinn, which she claims is Macbeth's Old Norse name, and gives Lady Macbeth the Norse name Ingeborg and the baptismal name Groa. Thomas Flanagan, a National Book Critics Circle Award-winning historical novelist, reviewed the novel for *Washington Post Book World* and, like reviewers of Dunnett's other novels, was impressed by the complexity of plot and of historical detail. "Dunnett has done a splendid job of restoring [Macbeth's] world, its colors, textures, sounds, the look of its seacoasts and mountains, the ways in which men measured their wills and strengths and their booty, one against another," Flanagan wrote. He was less impressed by the characterization of Thorfinn/Macbeth, however, and expressed doubts about Dunnett's premise that Thorfinn and Macbeth were one and the same person. "It was Thorfinn, the Norwegian earl of Orkney, who defeated King Duncan in battle, but it was Macbeth who killed Duncan, later, and then claimed the throne," Flanagan wrote. "[C]onventional history tells us that Thorfinn had a wife named Ingeborg, and Macbeth a wife named Grua." Flanagan concluded his historical musing with the wish that Dunnett had added a note making the facts clear for readers. "In fact," Dunnett told *CA*, "the book presents in ficitonal form a historical theory based on several years of original research."

In intervals between historical novels, Dunnett has written thrillers. Her first seven thrillers constitute the "Johnson Johnson" series, in which the major continuing character is a bifocal-wearing American portrait painter named Johnson Johnson, who owns a yacht named the Dolly. Each book in the series is narrated by a woman, and each book's title refers to a bird which symbolizes the narrator. Thus, in *Dolly and the Bird of Paradise*, the sixth volume in the series, published in 1983, the "bird of paradise" is Rita Geddes, a Scottish makeup artist. In recent years, however, all the volumes have been retitled and the name Dolly has been dropped. The most recent volume was published in 1991, with the title *Moroccan Traffic*.

Although feeling that the first half of *Dolly and the Bird of Paradise* was slow-paced, Lawrence Block, writing in the *Washington Post Book World*, commended Dunnett's depiction of settings such as the Caribbean islands of Martinique and St. Lucia, and enjoyed later aspects of the plot, which, he claimed, "has enough twists and turns to disorient almost anyone." Summing up the series in his *Contemporary Novelists* assessment of Dunnett, Sanderson wrote, "The thrillers with their different narrators' voices are great fun, substituting for the classic car chase some hard sailing in foul weather."

An enthusiast of sailing in her own life, Dunnett has transmuted this personal interest into fiction with the "Johnson Johnson" series. Her background as a painter appears in expert references to Renaissance painting in the House of Niccolo series, and more generally in the word-portraiture of characters such as Francis Crawford of Lymond and Claes/Niccolo the upwardly mobile apprentice. Her love for the landscape of Scotland is apparent throughout the Lymond Saga, and her keenness for travel appears in virtually all of her books. Dunnett's many readers have responded with enthusiasm to the many strengths of her work, to the extent that an international correspondence magazine on her work was launched in Chicago in 1984, and it now has an additional base in Edinburgh. Contributors and readers meet regularly on both sides of the Atlantic.

BIOGRAPHICAL/CRITICAL SOURCES:

BOOKS

Contemporary Novelists, 5th edition, St. James Press, 1991.
Hart, Russell, *The Scottish Novel: From Smollett to Spark,* Harvard University Press, 1978, pp. 193-197.

PERIODICALS

Alliance of Literary Societies, April, 1992.
Birmingham Post, April 7, 1990.
Book and Magazine Collector 53, (Dunnett bibliography edition) August, 1988.
Capetown Librarian, September, 1982.
Globe and Mail (Toronto), January 10, 1987.
Harper's, October, 1971.
Independent (London), April 13, 1990.
Million, November/December, 1991.
New York Times Book Review, December 8, 1968; July 25, 1982; October 19, 1986.
Observer, March 25, 1990.
Scotland on Sunday, October 22, 1989.
Scots Magazine, August, 1986.
Sunday Telegraph, November 10, 1991; June 13, 1993.
Sunday Times, April 1, 1990.
Times (London), May 15, 1986; November 29, 1986.
Times Literary Supplement, October 23, 1969.
Today's Seniors, February, 1990.
Washington Post Book World, August 8, 1982, pp. 3-4; March 18, 1984, pp. 5, 14; May 18, 1990; September 21, 1986, pp. 1, 10.

Woman and Home, September, 1989.

*   *   *

DUSKIN, Ruthie
See FELDMAN, Ruth Duskin

*   *   *

DZIECH, Billie Wright   1941-

PERSONAL: Born September 25, 1941, in Dayton, KY; daughter of William James and Virginia (Vogt) Wright; married Robert William Dziech (an architect and engineer), November 28, 1964; children: Robert William II. *Education:* Attended Agnes Scott College, 1959-60; University of Cincinnati, B.A., 1963, M.A., 1965, Ed.D., 1975.

ADDRESSES: Home—7190 Fair Oaks Dr., Cincinnati, OH 45237. *Office*—Office of the Dean, University of Cincinnati, M.L. U47, Cincinnati, OH 45221-0105.

CAREER: University of Cincinnati, Cincinnati, OH, instructor, 1965-70, assistant professor, 1970-72, associate professor, 1972-83, professor of English, 1983—, assistant to the dean, 1985—.

WRITINGS:

(With Linda Weiner) *The Lecherous Professor: Sexual Harassment on Campus,* Beacon Press, 1984, 2nd edition, University of Illinois Press, 1990.
(With Charles B. Schudson) *On Trial: American Courts and Their Treatment of Sexually Abused Children,* Beacon Press, 1989, 2nd edition, 1991.
(Editor) *Prisoners of Elitism: The Community College's Struggle for Stature,* Jossey-Bass, 1992.

Also contributor to *Issues for Community College Leaders in a New Era,* edited by George B. Vaughan and others, Jossey-Bass, 1984. Contributor to academic journals.

WORK IN PROGRESS: The Greeks, a book about the fraternity and sorority system in higher education.

BIOGRAPHICAL/CRITICAL SOURCES:

PERIODICALS

Chicago Tribune Book World, July 21, 1985, p. 26.
New York Times Book Review, July 16, 1989, p. 21.

E

EBY, Cecil D(eGrotte) 1927-

PERSONAL: Born August 1, 1927, in Charles Town, WV; son of Cecil DeGrotte and Ellen (Turner) Eby; married Patricia McGuire, 1956 (marriage ended); married Eleonora Arato; children (first marriage): Clare Virginia, Lillian Turner. *Education:* Shepherd College, A.B., 1950; Northwestern University, M.A., 1951; University of Pennsylvania, Ph.D., 1958. *Religion:* Episcopalian.

ADDRESSES: Home—Ann Arbor, MI and Deer Isle, ME (summer). *Office*—Department of English Language and Literature, 7609 Haven Hall, University of Michigan, Ann Arbor, MI 48109-1045.

CAREER: High Point College, High Point, NC, 1955-57, began as instructor, became assistant professor of English; Madison College, Harrisonburg, VA, assistant professor of English, 1957-60; Washington and Lee University, Lexington, VA, associate professor of English, 1960-65; University of Michigan, Ann Arbor, 1965—, became professor of English and American studies; University of Mississippi, chair of English department, 1975-76; University of Szeged (Hungary), professor, 1988-89. Fulbright lecturer in American studies, University of Salamanca (Spain), 1962-63; Fulbright Chair of American Studies, University of Valencia (Spain), 1967-68; Fulbright lecturer in American literature, University of Budapest (Hungary), 1982. *Military service:* U.S. Naval Reserve, 1945-46.

AWARDS, HONORS: Rackham research awards, University of Michigan, 1966, 1971, 1977, 1979, and 1990.

WRITINGS:

Porte Crayon: The Life of David H. Strother, University of North Carolina Press, 1960.
The Siege of the Alcazar, Random House, 1965.
Between the Bullet and the Lie: American Volunteers in the Spanish Civil War, Holt, 1969.

That Disgraceful Affair: The Black Hawk War, Norton, 1973.
The Road to Armageddon: The Martial Spirit in English Popular Literature, 1870-1914, Duke University Press, 1987.

EDITOR

The Old South Illustrated, University of North Carolina Press, 1959.
A Virginia Yankee in the Civil War, University of North Carolina Press, 1961.

OTHER

Contributor to *American Heritage, American Literature, American Quarterly, Connoisseur, Der Spiegel, New England Quarterly, Southwest Review,* and other professional publications. *Shenandoah,* member of editorial board, 1960-65, editor, 1962.

Between the Bullet and the Lie: American Volunteers in the Spanish Civil War has been translated into Spanish, and *The Siege of the Alcazar* has been translated into Dutch, Finnish, German, Italian, and Portuguese.

WORK IN PROGRESS: A nonfiction book, *City at War: Budapest 1944-45.*

SIDELIGHTS: Cecil D. Eby told *CA:* "My best work, a Civil War novel titled *The Man Who Lost the War,* remains unpublished. Although based upon extensive research into historical accounts of the war, it appears to be unsuitable as a publishing venture in this particular epoch because it creates a character who is neither super-hero nor wimp, does not interrupt battle scenes with torrid sexual forays, and holds that historical fiction should treat the probable rather than the fantastic or the ridiculous. It is probably unique in dealing with a young Confederate soldier who is not especially a rough-as-a-cob good-ole-boy, that staple of contemporary Civil War fiction."

BIOGRAPHICAL/CRITICAL SOURCES:

PERIODICALS

Nation, April 6, 1970.
New York Review, September 25, 1969.
New York Times, July 25, 1969.
Times Literary Supplement, April 18, 1966.
Washington Post, August 17, 1969.

* * *

ENGEL, Herbert M.   1918-

PERSONAL: Born June 20, 1918, in Gloversville, NY; son of Eugene I. (a glove worker) and Laura (a glove worker; maiden name, Joffe) Engel; married Rose Helen Fink, January 16, 1944; children: Jean Engel Hecht, Renee Engel Krosner, David, Thomas, Laura Engel Sahr. *Education:* New York State College for Teachers (now State University of New York at Albany), A.B., 1941; University of Wisconsin—Madison, M.A., 1942.

ADDRESSES: Home—11 Ormond St., Albany, NY 12203.

CAREER: Personnel assistant at men's clothing manufacturing plant in Philadelphia, PA, 1946; New York State Department of Labor, Albany, NY, on-the-job training program evaluator, 1946-52, director of Bureau of On-the-Job-Training, 1952-57; New York State Department of Civil Service, Albany, training supervisor, 1957-61, assistant director of public employee training, 1961-68, director of training, 1968-76; Pennsylvania Governor's Office of Budget and Administration, Harrisburg, Commonwealth training coordinator, 1976-79. Member of faculty at State University of New York College of Technology at Utica-Rome, 1967-74, College of St. Rose, 1968-69, Russell Sage College, 1970-75, St. Lawrence University, and Hudson Valley Community College; visiting lecturer at State University of New York at Albany, 1975-76. Director of Division of Personnel Programs and Training, New York State Office for Local Government, 1972-73; consultant to public and private organizations, including the United Nations, 1976; executive secretary of New York State Personnel Council; founder and past member of board of directors of New York State Training Council; co-organizer of Federal Training Council, Harrisburg. *Military service:* U.S. Army Air Forces, occupational counselor, classification specialist, and public relations specialist, 1942-45.

MEMBER: American Society for Public Administration, Hudson-Mohawk Training Directors Society (co-founder; past president).

AWARDS, HONORS: Professionalism Award from International Personnel Management Association, 1971.

WRITINGS:

(Contributor) K. T. Byers, editor, *Employee Training and Development in the Public Service,* Public Personnel Administration, 1970.
Handbook of Creative Learning Exercises, Gulf Publishing, 1973.
How to Delegate: Getting Things Done, Gulf Publishing, 1983.
Shtetl in the Adirondacks: The Story of Gloversville and Its Jews, Purple Mountain Press, 1992.

Contributor to magazines, including *Catholic World, Training in Business and Industry, Bureaucrat, Occupations, Public Personnel Review, ASTD Journal,* and *Office Automation.*

WORK IN PROGRESS: Jesse and Bessie, Sam and Blanche, the story of the coming together of Jesse Lasky and Sam Goldfish (later Goldwyn), and their future wives in the Adirondacks in 1909; *Why Screw Up,* a book on learning to distinguish between facts and inferences and the impact on one's decisions.

* * *

ENRICK, Norbert Lloyd   1920-

PERSONAL: Born April 11, 1920, in Berlin, Germany; son of Max M. (a medical doctor) and Elfe (Wilkiser) Enrick; married Mary Lynch, May 17, 1952; children: Ellen Marguerite, Robert Neal. *Education:* City College (now City College of the City University of New York), B.A., 1941; Columbia University, M.S., 1945, additional study, 1948-50; University of Virginia, Ph.D., 1963.

ADDRESSES: Home—1577 Morris Rd., Kent, OH 44240. *Office*—Administrative Sciences Department, Kent State University, Kent, OH 44242.

CAREER: Werner Management Consultants, New York City, management consulting engineer, 1948-53; Institute of Textile Technology, Charlottesville, VA, director of operations research and computer laboratory, 1953-60; University of Virginia, Charlottesville, VA, associate professor, 1960-65; Stevens Institute of Technology, Hoboken, NJ, professor of management science, 1965-66; Kent State University, Kent, OH, professor of administrative sciences, 1966—. Consultant to National Aeronautics and Space Administration and to business firms. Professor and chief, College of Research Statistics, American Academy of Neurological and Orthopaedic Surgeons.

MEMBER: American Society for Quality Control (fellow), American Statistical Association (president of Virginia section, 1956-58), Operations Research Society of America, American Society for Testing and Materials, Fiber Society, Academy of Marketing Science, Scientific Society, Sigma Xi.

AWARDS, HONORS: Best Paper award, American Society for Quality Control, 1960; distinguished paper award, International College of Physicians and Surgeons, London.

WRITINGS:

Quality Control, Industrial Press, 1948, 7th edition published as *Quality Control and Reliability,* 1977.
Cases in Management Statistics, Holt, 1963.
Management Control Manual, Rayon Publishing, 1964.
Sales and Production Management Manual, Wiley, 1964.
Management Operations Research, Holt, 1965.
Management Planning, McGraw, 1967.
Market and Sales Forecasting, Intext, 1969.
Decision Oriented Statistics, Mason & Lipscomb, 1970.
Statistical Functions, Kent State University Press, 1970.
Effective Graphic Communication, Mason & Lipscomb, 1972.
Quality Control for Profit, Industrial Press, 1978.
Market and Sales Forecasting, Robert E. Krieger, 1980.
Handbook of Effective Graphic and Tabular Communication, Robert E. Krieger, 1980.
Management Handbook of Decision-Oriented Statistics, Robert E. Krieger, 1980.
Statistical Functions and Formulas, Robert E. Krieger, 1981.
(Editor) *Time Study Manual for the Textile Industry,* Robert E. Krieger, 1982.
(With Harry E. Mottley, Jr.) *Manufacturing Analysis for Productivity and Quality/Cost Enhancement,* Industrial Press, 1983.
Experimentation and Statistical Validation: A Practical Working Guide Using Illustrations from the Health and Related Sciences, Robert E. Krieger, 1983.
Quality, Reliability and Process Improvement, Industrial Press, 1985.
(With Ronald H. Lester and Mottley) *Quality Control for Profit,* Dekker, 1985.

Author of articles on quality assurance, reliability, operations research and statistics for academic journals.*

*   *   *

ERDMAN, Paul E(mil) 1932-

PERSONAL: Born May 19, 1932, in Stratford, Ontario, Canada; son of Horace Herman (a clergyman) and Helen (Bertram) Erdman; married Helly Elizabeth Boeglin, September 11, 1954; children: Constance Ann Catherine, Jen-

nifer Michele. *Education:* Concordia College, St. Louis, MO, B.A., 1954; Georgetown University, B.Sc., 1955; University of Basel, M.A., 1956, Ph.D., 1958. *Religion:* Lutheran.

ADDRESSES: Home—1817 Lytton Springs Rd., Healdsburg, CA 95448.

CAREER: Writer. European Coal and Steel Community, Luxembourg, economist, 1958-59; Stanford Research Institute, Menlo Park, CA, and Zurich, Switzerland, international economist, 1959-62; Electronics International Capital Ltd., Hamilton, Bermuda, executive vice-president, 1962-65; Salik Bank of Basel, Basel, Switzerland, vice-chairman, 1965-69; United California Bank of Basel, Basel, vice-chairman, 1969-70. KGO-TV, San Francisco, CA, host of "Moneytalk," 1983-86, commentator, 1987—.

MEMBER: Mystery Writers of America, Authors Guild, Authors League of America.

AWARDS, HONORS: Edgar Award, Mystery Writers of America, 1974, for *The Billion Dollar Sure Thing.*

WRITINGS:

NOVELS

The Billion Dollar Sure Thing, Scribner, 1973, published in England as *The Billion Dollar Killing,* Arrow Books, 1974.
The Silver Bears, Scribner, 1974.
The Crash of '79, Simon & Schuster, 1976.
The Last Days of America, Simon & Schuster, 1981.
The Panic of '89, Doubleday, 1987.
The Palace, Doubleday, 1988.
The Swiss Account, Tor/St. Martin's, 1992.
Zero Coupon, Forge/St. Martin's, 1993.

NONFICTION

Swiss-American Economic Relations, J. C. B. Mohr, 1958.
Die Europaeische Wirtschaftsgemeinschaft unde die Drittlaender (title means "The European Economic Community and Third Countries"), J. C. B. Mohr, 1960.
Paul Erdman's Money Book: An Investors Guide to Economics and Finance, Random House, 1984, published in England as *Paul Erdman's Money Guide,* Secker & Warburg, 1985.
What's Next: How to Prepare Yourself for the Crash of '89 and Profit in the 1990's, Doubleday, 1988.

OTHER

Author of column, *Nihon Kezai Shimbun* (The "Nikkei"); author of column and contributing editor, *Manhattan, Inc.,* 1987—.

ADAPTATIONS: The Billion Dollar Sure Thing was adapted for film by Allen J. Trustman; *The Silver Bears* was adapted for film by Peter Stone and released by Columbia, 1978.

SIDELIGHTS: "A banker who can write is unusual enough," declares a *Time* writer about Paul E. Erdman, "[but] a banker who starts writing novels in jail, and transmutes global finance and oil politics into plausible thrillers about world economic collapse—well, there is only one." As a best-selling author on the subject of international finance and intrigue, Erdman is credited by many observers with the introduction of realistic financial details and an insider's knowledge of world banking into popular fiction. Oliver Hancock, writing in the *Gold Coast Pictorial,* espouses the idea that Erdman is responsible for "having invented a whole new mode of fiction—finance fiction which as fi-fi will take its place in library catalogues along with sci-fi."

Erdman's career as a writer of fiction began within the confines of a Swiss prison. Edwin McDowell outlines in the *New York Times Book Review* the circumstances that led to the future author's incarceration: "The United California Bank of Basel, of which he was chief executive, collapsed in 1970 with losses of some $65 million because of unauthorized speculation in silver and cocoa futures. [Erdman] was . . . a guest of the Swiss government for nine months in a 17th-century dungeon in Basel, until he was freed in June 1971 on $125,000 bail" and ordered to stand trial. Though a prisoner, according to Stephen Leiper in the *Washington Post,* Erdman "languished . . . in relative comfort. He was allowed to order dinner and wine sent in to his cell." A number of bank employees were jailed as a result of investigations by the Swiss government. When the case came to trial in 1973, Erdman was fined and given an eight-year sentence. Switzerland, however, had ceased to be his place of residence, the United States having been his home for some time. He was uncomfortable with the Swiss system of justice, and explained to Hancock: "I did not exactly intend to attend the trial."

During the period of his confinement, Erdman had begun what was to have been a nonfiction work on economics, but as he observes to McDowell, "I had no research facilities, so I decided to try it in novel form." The result, the bulk of which was completed out of jail, became *The Billion Dollar Sure Thing,* published in 1973. The roots of the novel lay in Erdman's financial expertise and his perceptions of the world economic situation. "I had just come off the excitement of international banking," he recalls in *Time,* "and I was full of theories. Primarily I was convinced that the world was facing the first cataclysmic financial events since World War II, a massive increase in the price of gold and the devaluation of the dollar." The

release of *The Billion Dollar Sure Thing,* whose plot concerns an international intrigue surrounding the attempts of various individuals and countries to manipulate both the value of the dollar and the price of gold, coincided in a startling way with what was actually taking place on the world financial scene. As Hancock points out: "When published in the summer of 1973, it contained more truth than fiction. The price of gold had just hit the top and the dollar, the bottom, in the world market. It was all in headlines on the front pages of newspapers here and abroad."

The strangely prophetic quality of *The Billion Dollar Sure Thing* set a pattern for subsequent works by Erdman: novels in which the elements of international monetary power, politics, and espionage combine to provide not only fictional thrills, but in the words of *New York Times* critic Christopher Lehmann-Haupt, "the dividend of feeling right on top of the news." Indeed, Lehmann-Haupt finds Erdman's store of economic lore not only entertaining, but also useful. *The Billion Dollar Sure Thing,* he insists, "really does teach you a thing or two—if you never understood before—about international exchange rates, the gold standard, and the importance of worldwide confidence in the dollar."

Erdman followed *The Billion Dollar Sure Thing* with his 1974 novel, *The Silver Bears.* Noting the dearth of "first-class [novels] of contemporary American business," R. Z. Sheppard of *Time* finds Erdman an exception. "His plots and characters tend to be simple, but he combines a zest for the intricate poetry of the big deal with the ability and cheerful willingness to explain it," declares Sheppard. "*The Silver Bears* deals in a baser metal [than *The Billion Dollar Sure Thing*], but it is just as entertaining and instructive as the first novel. Although names and places have been somewhat altered, the plot is built on the manic-depressive 1968 fluctuations in the price of silver." Newgate Callendar reports in the *New York Times Book Review* that "Erdman, who [has an] ingenious mind, fulfills his duty as a novelist by keeping interest sustained and by giving the ending a double twist that satisfies the novelistic proprieties as well as the inner man."

Erdman's next foray into fiction, *The Crash of '79,* once again struck both readers and critics as uncannily lifelike and current. Henry Allen states in the *Washington Post* that "there's just enough truth in [Erdman's novels] that when the projected date for *The Crash of '79* came and went (March 20) the Wall Street Journal ran a piece saying it hadn't happened." The plot of Erdman's third novel concerns what a *Times Literary Supplement* critic calls "a catastrophe brought about by a fatal combination of European weakness, American inefficiency, Iranian aggressiveness, Israeli self-delusion, and Swiss greed." Dealing with the interrelated dangers of Western dependence on Middle Eastern oil, nuclear and conventional arms proliferation, and the enormous deposits of Arab dollars held in American banks, the novel seemed to one reader quoted by Daniel Yergin in *Esquire* "like fact, like an article in *Foreign Affairs*—only with a plot."

Discussing *The Crash of '79* with Yergin in 1978, Erdman said, "The book is not a forecast. It's based on vague projections made a couple of years ago. I didn't take it too seriously for 1979. But if you move it up to '81 or '83, even I start to take some of that stuff seriously—unfortunately. What I do is write anticipatory novels, and I would say that the issues discussed in the novel have surfaced since the book was published. . . . I regard *The Crash of '79* as a teaching tool. This novel has done something that newspapers, magazines, and television have not done, and I suppose that is why a lot of people are reading it."

Erdman's reflection on the size of the book's readership is borne out by sales of over three million copies, but as a number of reviewers took pains to point out, *The Crash of '79* enjoyed an influential as well as a large audience, one that studied the book with a seriousness not normally accorded to thrillers. Michael M. Thomas, for example, speaks in the *Saturday Review* of the "novel's apocalyptic title and awesome topicality." He goes on to add, "Parts of the business community hailed it as a fifth gospel." Yergin reports that "an astonishing number of people professionally involved with foreign policy, energy, finance, and arms have been reading the book. . . . Erdman, the wildcatter working beyond the borders of government officials, the press, consultants, and research institutes, hit a deep and rich reservoir of anxiety that others had missed—or wanted to miss."

According to Charles Wheeler in the *Times Literary Supplement*, Erdman's next book, *The Last Days of America*, reports on "the decline of America's will to lead the West and the opportunities this presents to its more irresponsible allies to take the world to the brink of disaster." The plot involves the attempts of a newly rearmed, ultraconservative West Germany to separate itself from NATO, take position as a world power, and acquire cruise missiles from a corrupt and failing American firm. Capturing the quality that critics have consistently identified as central to the novelist's appeal, Wheeler remarks that *The Last Days of America* "appears here just as German conservatives have scored their first electoral victory in West Berlin, as Britain considers reducing its forces in Germany, and as Herr Schmidt . . . struggles to head off a revolt among his fellow Social Democrats against the stationing of medium-range nuclear missiles in Europe." Wheeler concludes that Erdman "is a master of timing. . . . Readers . . . should find Mr. Erdman's predictions diverting."

Erdman returned to nonfiction with his 1984 work *Paul Erdman's Money Book: An Investor's Guide to Economics*

and Finance. An introduction to such basic subjects as the bond market and real estate, its tone was decidedly more moderate than that of his novels. Erdman warns fledgling investors against the commodities and gold markets, and spices his rather conservative recommendations with tales of contemporary high finance. A *New York Times Book Review* critic states: "It comes as something of a surprise that the same man who so successfully concocts financial thrillers . . . could write such a measured explanation of economics and finance for the neophyte. But maybe it's not so surprising if one recalls that his novels are remarkable for what they teach readers about the international financial markets."

As if to end each decade with a bang, Erdman in 1987 offered the public his next novel, *The Panic of '89*. This time the crash would occur through international debt collapse, as a result of shaky loans made by U.S. banks to Third World nations. *Time* reviewer Sheppard notes the rickety nature of Erdman's craftsmanship, but explains, "Fussy readers should put their aesthetics on hold and allow Erdman to teach them a thing or two about how the world runs." In a similar vein, Jeffrey E. Garten in the *New York Times Book Review* writes: "If Mr. Erdman has stretched credibility just a little, he has used the right ingredients. Let's hope this one *is* fiction." In a *Chicago Tribune* review of *The Panic of '89*, Terry Brown offers the observation: "Fortunately, Erdman is best known as a successful novelist, not as an accurate prognosticator." Still, the book "explain[s] some of the complex world of international finance." Brown summarizes that the novel serves to "remind readers of the continued vulnerability of the global financial system. Similarly, the book underscores the fact that this nation has come to live primarily for today."

The Palace, Erdman's sixth novel, ventured into new territory, with results that displeased some reviewers. The book tells the story of Danny Lehman, who rises to the top in the world of Las Vegas and Atlantic City casino ownership. Patricia Lush, writing in the Toronto *Globe & Mail*, prefers Lehman to Paul Meyer, the Teutonic hero of *The Panic of '89*, and calls the book "a fairly rollicking, fast-paced tale." However, John Haslett Cuff, in a later *Globe & Mail* review, remarks, "It is to be hoped that whatever contractual arrangements Erdman has that forced him to concoct this literary equivalent of the phony stock issue has now ended, and that he will retire to the Cayman Islands and confine his writing to postcards." Rudy Maxa in the *Washington Post* compares *The Palace* unfavorably to Erdman's financial thrillers, noting that "for Erdman fans this time around, *The Palace* is about as entertaining as a bear market."

Returning to economic nonfiction in 1988 with *What's Next?: How to Prepare Yourself for the Crash of '89 and*

Profit in the 1990s, Erdman forecast an "inevitable" recession following a stock crash around the summer of 1989. Less apocalyptic than Erdman's thrillers, however, *What's Next?* predicted a recovery after about ten months of recession. In a 1988 *Washington Post* interview with Cris Oppenheimer, Erdman stood by his prediction, but also reminded readers that he is not infallible: "There's nothing I would change [about the predictions in *What's Next?*]. Although two months from now, who knows? People ought to take it for what it is: one guy's view."

BIOGRAPHICAL/CRITICAL SOURCES:

BOOKS

Authors in the News, Volume 1, Gale, 1976.
Contemporary Literary Criticism, Volume 25, Gale, 1983.

PERIODICALS

Business Week, March 9, 1987.
Chicago Tribune, July 25, 1982; February 13, 1987; July 18, 1988.
Esquire, April 11, 1978.
Globe & Mail (Toronto), August 15, 1987; March 5, 1988; March 26, 1988.

Gold Coast Pictorial, December, 1973.
Los Angeles Times, February 7, 1988.
Los Angeles Times Book Review, February 15, 1987, p. 4.
National Review, October 27, 1978.
New York Times, July 23, 1973.
New York Times Book Review, August 5, 1973, p. 10; August 18, 1974, p. 23; January 11, 1987, p. 9; March 6, 1988, p. 20; August 26, 1989, p. 19.
Time, July 29, 1974, p. 65; November 1, 1979; February 2, 1987, p. 70.
Times Literary Supplement, April 29, 1977; June 12, 1981, p. 672; March 22, 1985, p. 328.
Wall Street Journal, July 11, 1973, p. 12.
Washington Post, April 21, 1979; February 9, 1988; April 8, 1988.

*   *   *

EVANS, Jonathan
See FREEMANTLE, Brian (Harry)

F

FALLOWS, James M(ackenzie) 1949-

PERSONAL: Born August 2, 1949, in Philadelphia, PA; son of James Albert (a physician) and Jean (Mackenzie) Fallows; married Deborah Jean Zerad, June 22, 1971; children: Thomas Mackenzie, Tad Andrew. *Education:* Harvard University, B.A., 1970; Queen's College, Oxford, diploma in economic development, 1972.

ADDRESSES: Home—Washington, DC. *Office*— *Atlantic Monthly,* 745 Boylston St., Boston, MA 02116-2636.

CAREER: Harvard Crimson, president, 1969; *Washington Monthly,* Washington, DC, editor, 1972-74; *Texas Monthly,* Austin, TX, editor, 1974-76; chief speechwriter for President Carter, Washington, DC, 1977-79; *Atlantic Monthly,* Boston, MA, Washington editor, 1979—; national commentator, National Public Radio, 1987—.

MEMBER: Phi Beta Kappa.

AWARDS,HONORS: Rhodes scholar, 1970-72; American Book Award in general non-fiction, 1983, and one of five finalists for National Book Critics Circle Award, general non-fiction, 1982, both for National Defense.

WRITINGS:

NON-FICTION

The Water Lords, Grossman, 1971.
(With Mark J. Green and David Zwick) *Who Runs Congress?,* Bantam, 1972.
National Defense, Random House, 1981.
More Like Us: Making America Great Again, Houghton, 1989.
Japanese Education: What Can It Teach American Schools?, Educational Research Service, 1990.
Looking at the Sun, Pantheon, 1994.

EDITOR

(With Charles Peters) *The System,* Praeger, 1976.
(With Peters) *Inside the System,* Praeger, 1976.

SIDELIGHTS: James Fallows, an editor at the *Atlantic Monthly* and a former speechwriter for President Carter, is known for his insightful analysis of socio-political issues. His first book, a report of the findings Ralph Nader's study group disclosed on an environmental crisis in Savannah, Georgia titled *The Water Lords,* earned critical praise for its objectivity and thorough research. In a *Library Journal* review, H. T. Armistead called Fallows' book "a well-researched account of corporate indifference and cynicism towards the considerable filth discharged into water, land, and air." Since publication of *The Water Lords* in 1971, Fallows has continued to explore both social and political issues in his works of nonfiction, achieving critical praise due to his fluid prose and balanced perspective.

Fallows received a great deal of attention for his timely analysis of defense spending in *National Defense,* published in 1981. Christopher Lehmann-Haupt wrote in the *New York Times:* "I wish everyone who knows the alphabet would read James Fallows's *National Defense,* a succinct analysis of the United States' present military status." The critic praised Fallows for having "pitched an emotional subject on such an unusually commonsensical level." Fallows argues that the issue of national defense in the U.S. revolves around how much is spent, rather than the quality and effectiveness of the weapons purchased. It could well be the case, asserts Fallows, that spending less might produce a stronger arsenal if defense dollars were allocated along more practical, and less theoretical, lines. Fallows explains his conclusions in terms of the checkered histories of two U.S. weapons systems—the M-16 rifle and the F-16 fighter plane. In *Saturday Review* Robert R. Harris summarized the central thesis of the book this way: "With no malice or rancor toward the military, Fallows calmly demonstrates how the Pentagon's 'culture of procurement' is attracted to expensive weapons that are so overladen with costly sophisticated hardware that they often malfunction in combat."

National Defense garnered praise from a wide-range of reviewers, many of whom complimented Fallows on having re-shaped the terms of the defense-spending debate. In the *Nation,* Thomas Powers commented, "Fallows has managed to transcend the standard alternatives in debate on military matters—more, bigger and better to keep the Russians at bay; or universal disarmament, the abolition of war and the brotherhood of man." Powers called the book "sane, sensible, thoroughly balanced and profoundly original." Most critics praised the reasonable tone with which Fallows made his case. Martin F. Nolan, writing in the *New York Times Book Review,* described the prose as spare and controlled, "unencumbered by liberal cant." In the *New York Review of Books,* Herbert Scoville, Jr. asserted that Fallows' observations are "so full of common sense, a quality which he finds badly lacking within the Pentagon, that it is unfortunate that his wisdom was not used in the past and not available earlier to the new administration."

Fallows moved his family to Japan to witness the economic success of that country, and he also visited Malaysia, Korea, Taiwan, the Philippines, and Indochina in order to gain several different perspectives on Japanese culture before writing 1989's *More Like Us: Making America Great Again.* He believes that Americans should not imitate Japan, as many economists and other experts have suggested, but should instead reinforce native cultural strengths like rugged individualism and a commitment to democratic ideals. To support this claim, Fallows tells three uniquely American success stories in which individuals triumph through personal effort and perseverance. A reviewer in the *Los Angeles Times Book Review* summed up Fallows' argument this way: "We should not try to become more like the Japanese, he argues; more orderly and self-denying. We should become more like ourselves—hence, the title—more free-swinging, democratic and risky." Wrote Dennis H. Wrong in the *New York Times Book Review,* "All this sounds a bit boosterish and even chauvinistic, as does the book's unfortunate subtitle. But Mr. Fallows's assessment is a balanced and judicious one."

Although reviewers tended to find the discussion of the problem persuasive, several faulted Fallows on the conclusions he draws. Fallows argues against the privileging of I.Q. tests and grades, which, he believes, create an educational meritocracy that erodes the sense of possibility in American students. Many of his ideas have political coun-

terparts or consequences; for instance, Fallows proposes that the draft should be restored so that minorities and the poor will no longer have to fight wars like Vietnam, while the more affluent and educated members of their generation obtain draft deferments. Robert B. Reich described *More Like Us* as "a provocative, puzzling, and faintly jingoistic book" in his *New Republic* review. According to Reich, Fallows begins with a strong argument for the mobility and opportunity of American culture, only to backtrack when he examines the class barriers and educational problems that plague this country.

The *Los Angeles Times* reviewer reached a similar conclusion, noting that while Fallows probes "good, even radical questions," his remedies are hollow and commonplace. Reviewing *More Like Us* in *Tribune Books,* William Neikirk sympathized with Fallows' argument, but he ultimately found it naive. He wrote, "While Fallows' call for a renewal of American culture and a return to America's individualistic roots is touching, I am not sure it suffices as a real solution to the nation's economic problems."

Whether or not an individual reviewer agreed with his conclusions, most acknowledged that Fallows makes a clear and provocative case for his views. Neikirk noted, "Fallows writes with ease and grace, crucial for serious nonfiction work, and there is much good sense here." In the *Washington Post Book World,* Jonathan Yardley described Fallows' strengths as a writer and thinker this way: "It is the particular talent of James Fallows to be able to take complex, nettlesome situations and boil them down to their essentials, often in the process revealing those essentials to be so simple and obvious that the rest of us are left to wonder why we never perceived them ourselves."

BIOGRAPHICAL/CRITICAL SOURCES:

PERIODICALS

Christian Century, December 1, 1971.
Commonweal, December 15, 1989.
Guardian Weekly, June 28, 1981.
Library Journal, October 15, 1971.
Los Angeles Times Book Review, March 26, 1989.
Nation, June 6, 1981; April 9, 1983.
New Republic, May 2, 1981; April 3, 1989.
Newsweek, April 3, 1989, p. 45.
New Yorker, July 13, 1981.
New York Review of Books, June 11, 1981; March 30, 1989.
New York Times, June 9, 1981.
New York Times Book Review, August 8, 1971; June 28, 1981; March 26, 1989, p. 7; March 11, 1990.
Saturday Review, June, 1981; July, 1981; August, 1981; December, 1981.
Tribune Books (Chicago), March 26, 1989.

Village Voice, June 15, 1982.
Virginia Quarterly Review, summer, 1982.
Washington Post Book World, May 31, 1981; April 25,
   1982, p. 16; March 5, 1989, p. 3.

—*Sketch by Elizabeth Judd*

*   *   *

FATHER XAVIER
See HURWOOD, Bernhardt J.

*   *   *

FAX, Elton Clay 1909-

PERSONAL: Born October 9, 1909, in Baltimore, MD;
son of Mark Oakland (a clerk) and Willie Estelle (Smith)
Fax; married Grace Elizabeth Turner, March 12, 1929
(deceased); children: Betty Louise (Mrs. James Evans),
Virginia Mae (deceased), Leon. *Education:* Attended Claflin College; Syracuse University, B.F.A., 1931. *Religion:*
Protestant.

ADDRESSES: Home—51-28 30th Ave., Woodside, NY
11377. *Office*—P.O. Box 2188, Astoria Station, Long Island City, NY 11102-0004.

CAREER: Writer, illustrator, and lecturer. Claflin College, Orangeburg, SC, teacher of art, art history, and history, 1935-36; Harlem Art Center, New York City,
teacher of life drawing, 1936-41; City College (now of the
City University of New York), New York City, teacher of
watercolor painting and art history, 1957-58. Lecturer in
high schools and community centers; artist in residence at
and consultant to many universities, including Purdue
University, Princeton University, Fisk University, Western Michigan University, University of Hartford, and
Texas Southern University. Specialist-grantee for U.S.
Department of State in international cultural exchange
program to South America and the Caribbean, 1955; delegate to Second International Congress of Society of African Culture in Rome, Italy, 1959; State Department lec-
turer in East Africa, 1963; guest writer of Soviet Writers
Union to U.S.S.R., 1971, 1973; participant in Union of
Bulgarian Writers Conference in Sofia, Bulgaria, 1977.
Exhibitions include those at National Gallery of Art and
Corcoran Gallery of Art, Washington, DC, Kerlan Collection, University of Minnesota, and National Museum,
Tashkent, Uzbekistan.

MEMBER: Authors Guild of America, National Writers
Union, PEN, Syracuse University Alumni Association.

AWARDS, HONORS: Gold medal, Women's Civic
League Contest, 1932; MacDowell Colony fellow, 1968;
Coretta Scott King Award, American Library Associa-
tion, 1972, for *Seventeen Black Artists;* Louis E. Seley
NACAL gold medal, 1972, for painting, "Machinists
Board U.S.S. *Hunley,* Charleston, SC, March 1969";
Arena Players award, 1972; Rockefeller Foundation fel-
low, 1976; chancellor's medal, Syracuse University, 1990.

WRITINGS:

West Africa Vignettes, self-illustrated, American Society
   of African Culture, 1960, enlarged edition, 1963.
Contemporary Black Leaders, Dodd, 1970.
Seventeen Black Artists, Dodd, 1971.
Garvey: The Story of a Pioneer Black Nationalist, foreword
   by John Henrik Clarke, Dodd, 1972.
*Through Black Eyes: Journeys of a Black Artist in East Af-
   rica and Russia,* self-illustrated, Dodd, 1974.
Black Artists of the New Generation, foreword by Romare
   Bearden, Dodd, 1977.
Hashar (title means "Working Together"), self-
   illustrated, Progress Publishers (Moscow), 1980.
Elyuchin (title means "For the People"), Progress Pub-
   lishers, 1983.
Soviet People as I Knew Them, Progress Publishers, 1988.

Also author and illustrator of *Black and Beautiful,* privately printed. Contributor to *Harlem, U.S.A.,* and *Dictionary of American Negro Biography.*

ILLUSTRATOR

Robert N. McClean, *Tommy Two Wheels,* Friendship
   Press, 1943.
Shirley Graham and George D. Lipscomb, *Dr. George
   Washington Carver: Scientist,* Messner, 1944.
Georgene Faulkner and John Becker, *Melindy's Medal,*
   Messner, 1945.
Clifford B. Upton, *Upton Arithmetic—Grade 4,* American
   Book Co., 1945.
Shannon Garst, *Sitting Bull: Champion of His People,*
   Messner, 1946.
Story Parade Treasure Book (includes *Susie's Story,* by
   Aileen Fisher, and *The Haunted Skyscraper,* by Jan
   Flory), John C. Winston, 1946.
Florence Hayes, *Skid,* Houghton, 1948.
Garst, *Buffalo Bill,* Messner, 1948.
Faulkner, *Melindy's Happy Summer,* Messner, 1949.
Montgomery M. Atwater, *Avalanche Patrol,* Random
   House, 1951.
Celeste Edell, *A Present from Rosita,* Messner, 1952.
Atwater, *Rustlers on the High Range,* Random House,
   1952.
Eugene F. Moran, Sr., *Famous Harbours of the World,*
   Random House, 1953.
Regina Woody, *Almena's Dogs,* Farrar, Straus, 1954.
Clara Baldwin, *Cotton for Jim,* Abingdon, 1954.

Harold Lamb, *Genghis Khan and the Mongol Horde,* Random House, 1954.

Jeanette Eaton, *Trumpeter's Tale: The Story of Young Louis Armstrong,* Morrow, 1955.

James H. Robinson, editor, *Love of This Land,* Christian Education Press, 1956.

Harold Courlander, *Terrapin's Pot of Sense,* Holt, 1957.

Ella Huff Kepple, *Mateo of Mexico,* Friendship Press, 1958.

Verna Aardema, *Otwe,* Coward, 1960.

Aardema, *The Na of Wa,* Coward, 1960.

Aardema, *The Sky God Stories,* Coward, 1960.

Aardema, *Tales from the Story Hat,* Coward, 1960.

Letta Schatz, *Taiwo and Her Twin,* McGraw-Hill, 1964.

Aardema, *More Tales from the Story Hat,* Coward, 1966.

Johanna Johnston, *Paul Cuffee: America's First Black Captain,* Dodd, 1970.

Genevieve Gray, *The Seven Wishes of Joanna Peabody,* Lothrop, 1972.

Glennette Tilley Turner, *Take a Walk in Their Shoes,* Cobblehill Books, 1989.

SIDELIGHTS: An award-winning artist and essayist, Elton Clay Fax is well known for both his paintings and his children's book illustrations. His writing in books such as *Contemporary Black Leaders, Seventeen Black Artists,* and *Black Artists of the New Generation* profiles the diversity of black Americans while maintaining the common thread of a proud African American legacy. In each case, the author is conscious of the black experience and how it has molded the individual.

In his book *Garvey,* Fax provides a detailed narrative on the life of the charismatic black Jamaican nationalist Marcus Garvey. He explores events from the late nineteenth century, when the Panama Canal was being built by black laborers, to the 1920s, when Garvey gained prominence as a black leader with his Universal Negro Improvement Association. Fax also recounts the ambitious steamship venture, Black Star Line, which ultimately led to Garvey's imprisonment and exile. John Ralph Willis, writing in the *New York Times Book Review,* commends the author for having "succeeded in rescuing Garvey from the oblivion to which he had been consigned in the 1950s and 60s."

Fax's interest in black culture has led him to travel in black countries in East Africa as well as Soviet Central Asia. His volume *Through Black Eyes* combines text and drawings in what critics deemed a sensitive portrayal of the people and places he visited. Likewise, in *Hashar* and *Elyuchin,* Fax provides illustrations and descriptions of his journeys. Of his extensive traveling experience Fax told *CA:* "If I have learned anything at all from my travels and contacts with peoples whose lands and cultures seem so remote to ours it is this: as an American of African descent I find that I hold much in common with many of our overseas neighbors whose experiences with exploitation and racism parallel my own. And I am convinced that the humanity of the world's peoples (and, I fear, their inhumanity too) are of far more significance to me than are the differences of race, color, language, and custom."

BIOGRAPHICAL/CRITICAL SOURCES:

BOOKS

Driskell, David C., *Elton Fax: Drawings from Africa,* Fisk University, 1968.

PERIODICALS

Best Sellers, May 15, 1972, p. 78.
New York Times Book Review, August 20, 1972, pp. 5, 18.
Saturday Review, July 1, 1972, p. 52.*

*   *   *

FEDERMAN, Raymond   1928-

PERSONAL: Born May 15, 1928, in Paris, France; immigrated to United States, 1948, naturalized citizen, 1953; son of Simon (a painter) and Marguerite (Epstein) Federman; married Erica Hubscher, September 14, 1960; children: Simone Juliette. *Education:* Columbia University, B.A. (cum laude), 1957; University of California, Los Angeles, M.A., 1959, Ph.D., 1963. *Avocational Interests:* Cinema, theater, jazz.

ADDRESSES: Home—46 Four Seasons W., Eggertsville, NY 14226. *Office*—State University of New York at Buffalo, Buffalo, NY 14260.

CAREER: University of California, Santa Barbara, assistant professor, 1962-64; State University of New York at Buffalo, Buffalo, associate professor of French, 1964-68, professor of English and comparative literature, 1968-73, distinguished professor of English and comparative literature, 1990—. Visiting professor, University of Montreal, 1970, and Hebrew University, Jerusalem, 1982-83. Jazz saxophonist, 1947-50. Member of board of directors, Coordinating Council of Literary Magazines, 1976-79, and of Hallwalls, 1980—. Co-director, Fiction Collective, 1977-80. Fiction judge for CAPS, 1980. *Military service:* U.S. Army, 82nd Airborne Division, 1951-54; served in Korea and Japan; became sergeant.

MEMBER: Modern Language Association of America, American Association for the Studies of Dada and Surrealism, PEN American Center, Samuel Beckett Society (honorary trustee), Phi Beta Kappa.

AWARDS, HONORS: Grants from State University of New York, New York State Research Foundation, and the Asia Foundation; Guggenheim fellowship, 1966-67;

Frances Steloff prize, 1971, and *Panache* Experimental Fiction Prize, 1972, both for *Double or Nothing;* Pushcart anthology prize, 1977; Camargo Foundation fellowship, 1977; Fulbright fellowship to Israel, 1982-83; National Endowment for the Arts fellowship, 1985; New York State Foundation for the Arts fellowship, 1986; American Book Award, 1986, for *Smiles on Washington Square;* DAAD fellowship (Berlin Artist Program), 1989-90, in residence in Berlin Germany.

WRITINGS:

POETRY

(Translator) F. J. Temples, *Postal Cards,* Noel Young, 1964.
Among the Beasts/Parmi les Monstres (bilingual), Editions Millas-Martin (Paris), 1967.
Me Too, West Coast Poetry Review, 1975.
Duel, Stopover Press, 1991.
Nowthen, Editions Isele, 1992.

NOVELS

Double or Nothing, Swallow Press, 1971.
Amer Eldorado, Editions Stock (Paris), 1974.
Take It or Leave It, Fiction Collective, 1976.
The Voice in the Closet/La Voix dans le cabinet de Debarras (bilingual), Coda, 1979.
The Twofold Vibration, Indiana University Press, 1982.
Smiles on Washington Square, Thunder's Mouth, 1985.
To Whom It May Concern, Fiction Collective, 1990.
A Version of My Life, Maro Verlag, 1993.

OTHER

Journey to Chaos: Samuel Beckett's Early Fiction, University of California Press, 1965.
(Editor and translator) Yvonne Caroutch, *Paysages provisoires/Temporary Landscapes* (bilingual), Stamperia di Venizia, 1965.
(With John Fletcher) *Samuel Beckett: His Work and His Critics,* University of California Press, 1970.
(Editor) *Cinq Nouvelles* (collected fiction), Appleton-Century-Crofts, 1970.
(Editor) *Surfiction: Fiction Now and Tomorrow* (essays), Swallow Press, 1975, revised edition, 1981.
(Editor with Tom Bishop) *Samuel Beckett: Cahier de L'Herne,* Editions de L'Herne, 1976.
(Editor with Lawrence Graver) *Samuel Beckett: The Critical Heritage,* Routledge & Kegan Paul, 1979.
(Translator with Genevieve James) Michel Serres, *Detachment,* Ohio University Press, 1989.
Critifiction: The Way of Literature (essays), State University of New York Press, 1993.

Contributor to numerous books and anthologies, including *On Contemporary Literature, Samuel Beckett Now, Essaying Essays, Pushcart Prize Anthology II, The Wake of the Wake, Bright Moments,* and *Imaged Words and Worded Images.* Also contributor of fiction and poetry to numerous periodicals, including *Partisan Review, Chicago Review, Tri-Quarterly, Paris Review,* and *North American Review.* Contributor of articles and essays to *French Review, Modern Drama, Film Quarterly, Comparative Literature,* and many other periodicals. Co-editor of *MICA* (literary magazine), 1960-63; contributing editor of *American Book Review;* member of editorial board of *Jewish Publication Society* and *Buff.*

ADAPTATIONS: The Voice in the Closet was adapted into a full-length modern ballet under the title *Project X.* All of Federman's novels have been adapted into radio plays and broadcast in German by the Bayerischer Rundfunk (Bavarian Radio) in Munich.

SIDELIGHTS: A bilingual novelist, poet, critic, and translator, Raymond Federman attempts in his novels to redefine fiction, calling the developing form "surfiction." "Building on the work of Joyce, Celine, Beckett, and other twentieth-century masters, his fictions are fascinating constructs that combine a brilliant style, unorthodox typography, and a masterful new approach to the development of characters and literary structure," declares Welch D. Everman in the *Dictionary of Literary Biography Yearbook: 1980.* "Unlike the traditional novel, these works are not intended to be representations of events; they are events in their own right, language events that reflect on their own mode of becoming and that, in effect, critique themselves. . . . Federman questions the very nature of fiction, the fiction writer, and the reality that the writer's language is supposed to represent."

The reality that affected Federman's life most strongly was the Nazi Holocaust. In the summer of 1942, the Gestapo entered his family's apartment, taking his parents and his two sisters to the death camps; Raymond, whom his parents hid in a closet, escaped. Although Federman's fiction is experimental in form, its contents grapple with the experience of death and survival that marked the author while he was young. Questioning the validity of autobiography and fiction alike, Federman creates autobiographical fictions, and does so in a language, English, that he learned as an adult. Federman's first book of poems, *Among the Beasts/Parmi les Monstres,* is a crucial text in his canon, the earliest literary version of his Holocaust experience. His subsequent fictions, according to Everman, rewrite this "original text."

Federman's first novel, *Double or Nothing,* is a multilayered, bleakly comic work whose plot focuses on a young French immigrant who lost his family in the concentration camps. The immigrant's story is told by a would-be author who narrates his own life as well as that of the young immigrant. Comments on the writing process are intertwined with the narrative. At least two additional voices are added to the layering, producing a potentially infinite regression of narrators. Typography is of central importance to the novel, for each page is a complete visual unit. "Humor is one of Federman's key tools," Everman points out. "The style is frantic and purposely paradoxical, and often the reader laughs not so much at the antics of the characters as at his own confusion in the face of this convoluted text."

Take It or Leave It, Federman's second novel in English, is an extended reworking of his French novel *Amer Eldorado.* A note on the title page calls it an "exaggerated second-hand tale." The plot concerns a young French immigrant in the American Army, Frenchy, who has thirty days to travel from Fort Bragg, North Carolina, to a ship that will take him to Korea, but who must first travel north to upstate New York to retrieve some crucial papers. The digressive story is told by a nameless narrator who is interrupted by faceless audience members and literary critics. "*Take It or Leave It* is a text which constitutes, contradicts, and erases itself, as it constitutes, contradicts, and erases the voices which it produces and by which it is produced," Everman says.

The Voice in the Closet/La Voix dans le cabinet Debarras, Federman's bilingual novel of 1979, marks a shift in the author's work while preserving his preoccupation with form. Federman sets himself a strict form, consisting of twenty pages with eighteen lines per page and sixty-eight characters per line. From this constricted form—which parallels the physical constriction of a closet—emerges the voice of a boy hiding in a closet while the Nazis take away his family. The voice speaks to a writer named federman (with a lowercase f), who has repeatedly tried and failed to tell the boy's story. Critic Peter Quartermain, writing in the *Chicago Review,* calls *The Voice in the Closet* "a compelling book indeed. . . . [It] astonishes partly because nothing in Federman's previous work . . . prepares us for the obsessive immediacy of this. This book may be a one-shot, perhaps, but in it Federman has come to do what over a generation ago D. H. Lawrence enjoined readers as well as writers to do: trust the tale."

The English version of *The Voice in the Closet* is part of Federman's 1982 novel, *The Twofold Vibration.* Here, typography and style are more traditional than in most of Federman's earlier work. The novel's setting is New Year's Eve, 1999. In a persistently self-reflexive style, the narrator, an old man whose history contains many parallels with Federman's, tells the story of his life. Meanwhile, two characters named Namredef and Moinous, who serve as doubles for the narrator, argue about the way the story ought to be told. Reviewing the book for the *Times Literary Supplement,* Brian Morton comments: "For the first

time with any success, Federman . . . combines a sense of time and consequence with the spatial concerns of radical postmodernist fiction. . . . If this is not what John Gardner called 'metaphiction for the millions,' it is at least an entertaining and salutary journey through the darker and more troubled outlands of contemporary history and fiction."

Smiles on Washington Square was published in 1985, and once again features a character named Moinous who bears resemblances to Federman. Moinous, a French-born naturalized American who has served in Korea, is out of work in New York City. At a political rally, he meets—or perhaps does not meet—Sucette, the leftist daughter of a wealthy New England family. Sucette, who is studying creative writing at Columbia University, begins to write stories about a man named Moinous. Two weeks later, they may or may not meet again; indeed, the whole love story may belong to Sucette's creative writing efforts. Reviewing the book for the *Los Angeles Times Book Review,* Allen Boyer terms it "more of a teasing exercise than a novel—long on intellect, but short on flesh and bone. . . . The book could be called subdued or spare, but precious would be a better term. Instead of sensation, passion, or plot, it offers a suggestion that life and art are necessarily related, competitive and tentative—and this idea is hardly new." Alan Cheuse, in the *New York Times Book Review,* was more appreciative, saying, "In this new work of fiction [Federman] appears intent on compressing and compacting his story. . . . The result is much more charming and readable than anything else of his in English. . . . Basically, the novel succeeds because of its appealing voice, something resembling Moinous's 'English with a French Accent.' "

Federman once told *CA:* "I write to gain my freedom and hopefully to liberate my readers from all conventions. Anything goes because meaning does not precede language, language produces meaning. There is as much value in making nonsense as there is in making sense; it's simply a question of direction." Of his work, Federman once commented, "My entire writing career has been a Journey to Chaos."

Several of Federman's books have been translated into Polish, German, French, Portuguese, Italian, Spanish, Japanese, Chinese, Hungarian, Romanian, Hebrew, and Dutch.

BIOGRAPHICAL/CRITICAL SOURCES:

BOOKS

Contemporary Authors Autobiography Series, Volume 8, Gale, 1989.
Contemporary Literary Criticism, Gale, Volume 6, 1976, Volume 47, 1988.

Dictionary of Literary Biography Yearbook: 1980, Gale, 1981.

Federman, Raymond, *Take It or Leave It,* Fiction Collective, 1976.

Pearce, Richard, *The Novel in Motion: An Approach to Modern Fiction,* Ohio State University Press, 1983, pp. 118-130.

PERIODICALS

American Book Review, March-April, 1981, pp. 10-12; January-February, 1982, pp. 2-3; November-December, 1983, p. 7; September-October, 1986, pp. 22-23.

boundary 2, fall, 1976, pp. 153-165.

Chicago Review, summer, 1977, pp. 145-149; autumn, 1980, pp. 65-74.

Chicago Tribune Book World, September 2, 1982.

fiction international, numbers 2-3, 1974, pp. 147-150.

Los Angeles Times Book Review, February 9, 1986, p. 4.

Michigan Quarterly Review, winter, 1974.

New Republic, July 11, 1970, p. 23.

New York Times Book Review, January 23, 1966, p. 4; October 1, 1972, pp. 40-41; September 15, 1974, p. 47; November 7, 1982, pp. 12, 26; November 24, 1985, p. 24.

North American Review, March, 1986, pp. 67-69.

Saturday Review, January 22, 1972, p. 67.

Times Literary Supplement, May 5, 1966, p. 388; October 12, 1973, p. 1217; December 3, 1982, p. 1344.

Yale Review, spring, 1983, pp. 12-13.

*　　　*　　　*

FELDMAN, Ruth Duskin 1934-
(Ruthie Duskin)

PERSONAL: Born June 13, 1934, in Chicago, IL; daughter of Boris (a teacher) and Rita (a writer and teacher; maiden name, Schayer) Duskin; married Gilbert Feldman (a lawyer), June 14, 1953; children: Steven, Laurie, Heidi. *Education:* Northwestern University, B.S. (magna cum laude), 1954; attended Loyola University, 1954.

ADDRESSES: Home and office—935 Fairview Rd., Highland Park, IL 60035.

CAREER: Teacher in Evanston, IL, 1954-55; Lerner Newspapers, Highland Park, IL, correspondent and staff writer, 1973-81; free-lance writer and photographer, 1981—. Quiz show contestant, 1941-50; coordinator of Junior Great Books reading program in Highland Park, 1962-74; lecturer.

MEMBER: American Society of Journalists and Authors, Authors Guild, Authors League of America, Society of Professional Journalists, National Writers Union, Independent Writers of Chicago, Society of Midland Authors.

AWARDS, HONORS: Awards for best educational filmstrip scripts from *Previews,* 1977, for "The Middle East," and 1980, for "Study Skills"; awards for best column from Lerner Newspapers, 1978 and 1979, and honorable mention for best feature, 1979 and 1980; Certificate of Creative Excellence from United States Industrial Film Festival, 1980, for filmstrip script "How Cultures Change"; Bronze Award from Houston International Film Festival, 1981, for filmstrip script "A Serious Injury"; award from Independent Writers of Chicago, 1983, for *Whatever Happened to the Quiz Kids?—Perils and Profits of Growing Up Gifted;* Benjamin Fine Award for outstanding educational reporting from National Association of Secondary School Principals, 1983; runner-up, Society of American Travel Writers' Lowell Thomas Award, *US* magazine, 1986; finalist, American Society of Journalists and Authors award for articles, 1992.

WRITINGS:

(With father, Boris Duskin; under name Ruthie Duskin) *Chemi the Magician* (children's science fiction), Dodd, 1947.

Whatever Happened to the Quiz Kids?—Perils and Profits of Growing Up Gifted, Chicago Review Press, 1982.

(With Steven R. Lake) *Rematch: Winning Legal Battles with Your Ex,* Chicago Review Press, 1989.

(With Marcia B. Cherney and Susan A. Tynan) *Communicoding,* Donald I. Fine, 1989.

(With Diane E. Papalia and Sally Wendkos Olds) *Human Development,* 4th edition, McGraw, 1989.

PLAYS

The Elves and the Shoemaker (one-act), produced in Milwaukee, WI, at North Lake Mall, 1982.

OTHER

Also author of study guides to *A Child's World,* McGraw, 1990, 1993, and *Human Development,* McGraw, 1992. Author of scripts for educational and industrial filmstrips, slide shows, and video tapes. Author of column in *Prism,* 1983-84, and of series of columns in *Free Spirit* newsletter, 1987-88. Education columnist for *Chicago Parent,* 1984-86. Contributor to periodicals, including *Better Homes and Gardens, Chicago Sun-Times, Chicago Tribune, Instructor, New Choices, Relax, USAir, Vista USA, Travel and Leisure,* and *Woman's Day.* Creative editor of *Humanistic Judaism,* 1983—.

WORK IN PROGRESS: Adult Development and Aging, with Diane E. Papalia and Cameron Camp.

SIDELIGHTS: Ruth Duskin Feldman gained childhood fame as Ruthie Duskin on the 1940s radio show "The

Quiz Kids." "We made films, records, and front-page headlines," Feldman later explained in *G/C/T.* "I even got to play with a paper doll of myself!" At age thirteen Feldman, as Ruthie Duskin, had already written her first book, *Chemi the Magician,* and by the time she left the quiz show she had met and appeared with such celebrities as Bing Crosby and Judy Garland. She later attended Northwestern University, where she graduated with honors in 1954, and then began raising her family. Meanwhile, she did free-lance writing and later joined the staff of a community newspaper.

Her interest in quiz shows was revived when fellow "quiz kid" Harve Bennett produced a new version of the children's program for cable television. Feldman then began tracing the lives of several people who had once appeared on the old show. The result was *Whatever Happened to the Quiz Kids?—Perils and Profits of Growing Up Gifted,* in which she documents the successes and failures of "prodigies" from the 1940s and 1950s. She told *People* that one of her many discoveries was that the ex-contestants were still idealists. "Answering my question about life goals," she noted, "most of them spoke of wanting to make a contribution to society."

Feldman told *CA:* "My decision to write *Whatever Happened to the Quiz Kids?* followed three decades of silence on that subject. I 'came out of the closet' when the show was revived on cable TV. Part of my motivation was to help today's gifted youngsters and their parents and teachers gain insight into the promise and the pain of growing up gifted in America—as well as to examine the relationship between childhood intelligence and adult success. I am continuing to do that in lectures for parents, teachers, and students throughout the country. As a free-lance writer, my current specialties are education, travel, and human interest articles."

Feldman recently told *CA,* "And, now that I'm a grandmother of three, I am (appropriately) coauthoring a college textbook on adult development and aging."

BIOGRAPHICAL/CRITICAL SOURCES:

PERIODICALS

G/C/T, May/June, 1985.
Los Angeles Times Book Review, February 27, 1983.
Miami Herald, March 11, 1983.
People, December 20, 1982.
Village Voice, March 29, 1983.

*   *   *

FENNELLY, Tony 1945-

PERSONAL: Born November 25, 1945, in Orange, NJ; daughter of Thomas Richard and Mary V. (a librarian; maiden name, Lynch) Fennelly; married Richard Catoire, December 24, 1972. *Education:* University of New Orleans, B.A., 1976; additional study at Fricke School of Music.

ADDRESSES: Home—921 Clouet St., New Orleans, LA 70117.

CAREER: Clerk, barmaid, and waitress, 1967-69; exotic dancer and free-lance writer, 1969-85; welfare caseworker in Gretna, LA, 1985-86; actress and public speaker.

MEMBER: International Association of Crime Writers, Mystery Writers of America, Authors Guild, American Federation of Astrologers.

AWARDS, HONORS: Edgar Award nomination, Mystery Writers of America, 1985, for *The Glory Hole Murders;* Arthur Award for acting, Barn Theater.

WRITINGS:

The Theology of Time Travel, Ellipsis, 1976.
The Glory Hole Murders (novel), Carroll & Graf, 1985.
The Closet Hanging (novel), Carroll & Graf, 1987.
Kiss Yourself Goodbye, Arlington, 1989.
The Hippie in the Wall, St. Martin's, in press.
Cherry, Rotbuch, in press.

Also contributor of material to *Bob Orban's Current Comedy.*

WORK IN PROGRESS: One—900 DEAD: A Margo Fortier Mystery.

SIDELIGHTS: Tony Fennelly once told *CA:* "Talent is genetic. My father (who kissed the Blarney Stone, literally) had published fiction. My mother was a published poet and a very good one—so I was born a writer. But I was not born a professional writer. I spent ten years learning my craft, writing full time without making a nickel. I wrote eight full-length books before one was published. I never got discouraged for long or thought of quitting. I was put on this earth to entertain people with my writing."

Fennelly recently wrote *CA:* "I love to go on personal appearance tours and travel every chance I get, but my characters can never leave the Mississippi Delta. This policy isn't a limitation, as anything that can be found anywhere else can be found here, distilled and more vibrant than life. We have ballet, opera, art galleries, every variety of cultural expression, industry, and politics, power brokers on every level, premium hotels, restaurants, race tracks and cruise ships, all within a ten-minute drive of anywhere.

"We meet up with high society on St. Charles Avenue and homeless winos on Camp Street. And we see every kind of crime and criminal from the Ninth Ward to City Hall.

"New Orleans is the foremost character in all of my books and the easiest to present. My readers already know this city and have long been drawn to its ambiance and intrigue.

"My next U.S. publication, *The Hippie in the Wall,* takes place in a Bourbon Street night club, actually the same one in which I tossed tassels during the summer of 1970."

BIOGRAPHICAL/CRITICAL SOURCES:

PERIODICALS

Der Speigel, December 8, 1991.
Impact, November 15, 1985.
Mandate, February, 1987.
New Orleans Times-Picayune, April 20, 1986.
Sonntags Zeitung, July 29, 1990.

*   *   *

FIELDING, Joy   1945-

PERSONAL: Born March 18, 1945, in Toronto, Ontario, Canada; daughter of Leo H. and Anne Tepperman; married Warren (a lawyer), January 11, 1974; children: Shannon, Anne. *Education:* University of Toronto, B.A., 1966. *Avocational Interests:* Reading, tennis, swimming, movies, travel, bridge, golf.

ADDRESSES: Home—Toronto, Ontario, Canada. *Office*—c/o Writer's Union of Canada, 24 Ryerson Ave., Toronto, Ontario M5T 2P3, Canada.

CAREER: Writer. Previously worked as an actress, assistant social worker, substitute teacher, and bank teller.

AWARDS, HONORS: Book of the Year award, Periodical Distributors of Canada, 1981, for *Kiss Mommy Goodbye.*

WRITINGS:

The Best of Friends, Putnam, 1972.
The Transformation, Playboy Press, 1976.
Trance, Playboy Press, 1977.
Kiss Mommy Goodbye, Doubleday, 1981.
The Other Woman, Doubleday, 1983.
Life Penalty, Doubleday, 1984.
The Deep End, Doubleday, 1986.
Good Intentions, Doubleday, 1989.
See Jane Run, Morrow, 1991.
Tell Me No Secrets, Morrow, 1993.

Also writer of two television plays, *Drifters* and *Open House,* for the Canadian Broadcasting Company (CBC); former book reviewer for *Toronto Star, Globe and Mail,* and CBC's *The Journal* and *The Radio Show with Jack Faar;* contributor of articles and short stories to publications in Canada, the United States, and England.

SIDELIGHTS: Joy Fielding told *CA:* "I played with cutout dolls until I was fourteen years old, long past the age my friends played with theirs. That's what I still feel like I'm doing when I'm writing—playing with my cut-outs. Everybody says what I tell them to say, and does what I want them to do, unlike life, which is not so easily constructed."

*   *   *

FONTENOT, Chester J.   1950-

PERSONAL: Born February 5, 1950, in Los Angeles, CA; son of Chester and Bertha (Lee) Fontenot; married wife, Melody, March 26, 1988; children: Jeremy, Camara, Jasmine, Rick, Chester III. *Education:* Whittier College, B.A., 1972; University of California, Irvine, Ph.D., 1975.

ADDRESSES: Office—Department of English, University of Illinois at Urbana, 608 S. Wright St., Urbana, IL 61801-3613.

CAREER: University of Nebraska, Lincoln, assistant professor of English, 1975-77; Cornell University, Ithaca, NY, assistant professor of English, 1977-79; University of Illinois, Urbana-Champaign, associate professor of American and Afro-American literature, 1979—. Ordained Baptist minister, 1982; pastor, United Church of Christ interfaith ministry; pastor, Mt. Zion Baptist Church, Connersville, IN. Visiting scholar at State University of New York at Binghamton, 1978, and Colgate University, 1978; visiting artist at Purdue University, 1980—.

MEMBER: Modern Language Association of America, Association for the Study of Afro-American Life and History, Association for the Study of Multi-Ethnic Literature in the United States, United Church Foundation and National Baptist Convention, College Language Association, Midwest Modern Language Association.

AWARDS, HONORS: Maude Hammond Fling fellow, 1977.

WRITINGS:

(Editor) *Writing about Black Literature,* University of Nebraska Curriculum Development Center, 1976.
Franz Fanon: Language as the God Gone Astray in the Flesh, University of Nebraska Press, 1979.
(Editor with Joe Weilmann) *Studies in Black Literature: Black American Prose Theory,* Penkeville Publishing, 1983.
(Editor with Weilmann) *Studies in Black Literature's Belief vs. Theory in Black American Literature,* Penkeville Publishing, 1985.

Also author of *Warring Selves: Black Fiction, 1918-1980,* University of Illinois Press.

PLAYS

Stalemate (one-act), first produced in Los Angeles, CA at the Afro-American Repertory Theatre, March, 1973.
The Seventh Son (one-act), first produced in New York City at the Frank Silvera Writers Workshop, 1978.

OTHER

Author of *Black Literature in Midwest,* a television series for Nebraska Educational Television Council for Higher Education; contributor to literature and black studies journals; advisory editor of *Black America Literature Forum.*

SIDELIGHTS: Chester J. Fontenot once told *CA:* "My vocational interests are black culture, black literature, black religion, and black theatre. I am motivated by my belief in God, the creator and sustainer of all things.

"My calling as a minister has intensified my study of black culture. It is through my study of black culture that I have been able to maintain a dialectic between scholarship and direct ministry. As a playwright, I am interested in creating a vision of black life that is holistic, focusing on the black family. All of my writings are an attempt to reconcile the sufferings of black people with the humanity evident in the black culture. Black religion, literary theory, and such are all attempts to make sense out of a culture that dares to hope against hope.

"I have become less interested in literary theory, and more interested in the sociology of religion. My book on black religion will evaluate the black Baptist church and its ministry. In particular it will analyze the declining status of the church in the black community."*

*   *   *

FORD, Kirk
   See SPENCE, William John Duncan

*   *   *

FRANKLAND, Mark   1934-

PERSONAL: Born April 19, 1934, in London, England; son of Roger and Elizabeth (Sanday) Frankland. *Education:* Cambridge University, B.A., 1957.

ADDRESSES: Office—Observer, 8 St. Andrew's Hill, London EC4, England.

CAREER: Observer, London, England, foreign correspondent, 1961—. Foreign correspondent for *Economist,* London, 1967-75. Has reported from Moscow, Saigon, Tokyo, and Washington, DC.

WRITINGS:

Krushchev: A Political Biography, Stein & Day, 1967.
The Mother-of-Pearl Men (novel), J. Murray, 1985.
Richard Robertovich (novel), Beaufort Books, 1987.
The Sixth Continent: Russia and the Making of Mikhail Gorbachev, Harper, 1987.
The Patriots' Revolution: How Eastern Europe Toppled Communism and Won Its Freedom, Sinclair Stevenson, 1990, Ivan R. Dee, 1992.

SIDELIGHTS: Mark Frankland's writings show a deep fascination with Russian culture and society, developed as a foreign correspondent for British newspapers since the 1960s. Harrison E. Salisbury, writing for the *New York Times Book Review,* notes that Frankland's first-hand observation of Krushchev allowed him to draw a realistic portrait of the Soviet premier in his 1967 biography. *Times Literary Supplement* contributor Alastair McAuley found Frankland's analysis of the rise of Gorbachev, *The Sixth Continent,* to be "a marvelous evocation of Russia. . . . He has managed to capture the depth of feeling that Russians have for their country." Craig R. Whitney praised the same title in *New York Times Book Review* as "a well-informed, colorful account of a skeptical, experienced observer's theory of how we got from Brezhnev's gerontocracy to Mr. Gorbachev's glasnost." *The Patriots' Revolution,* Frankland's analysis of the collapse of communism in Eastern Europe, was described by Steven Lukes in *Times Literary Supplement* as "exemplary . . . both as journalism and contemporary history."

Frankland's novels have also drawn on his experiences as a journalist in Moscow and Saigon. Although some reviewers have criticized his fiction for weakness in characterization, his novels have been praised for imparting a rich sense of a foreign culture. Isabel Raphael, writing for the London *Times,* found Frankland's portrait of Moscow in *Richard Robertovich* "brilliantly detailed." *The Mother-of-Pearl Men* was described by Stewart Dalby in the *Times Literary Supplement* as "a compelling portrait of Saigon in the early 1970s." He comments that Frankland's novel, unlike many recent dramatizations of the Vietnam conflict, "is not about the agony of the American entanglement . . . but the torments of the Vietnamese themselves."

BIOGRAPHICAL/CRITICAL SOURCES:

PERIODICALS

Los Angeles Times Book Review, November 8, 1987, p. 4.
New York Times Book Review, September 17, 1967, p. 28; November 22, 1987, p. 18.
Spectator, July 18, 1987, pp. 28-29.
Time, June 16, 1967; August 22, 1985; January 8, 1987.
Times (London), August 22, 1985; January 8, 1987.

Times Literary Supplement, February 6, 1987, p. 134; August 14, 1987, p. 883; November 8, 1985, p. 1266; February 6, 1987; August 23, 1991, p. 9.*

* * *

FREEMAN, Gillian 1929-
(Eliot George, Elaine Jackson)

PERSONAL: Born December 5, 1929, in England; daughter of Jack (a dental surgeon) and Freda (Davids) Freeman; married Edward Thorpe, September 12, 1955; children: Harriet Amelia, Matilda Helen Rachel. *Education:* University of Reading, B.A. (with honors), 1951. *Avocational Interests:* Theatre, ballet, and cinema techniques.

ADDRESSES: Home—42 Jacksons Lane, London N6, England. *Agent*—Richard Scott Simon, Sheil Landes Associates, 43 Doughty St., London WC1N 2LF, England.

CAREER: C. J. Lytle Ltd., London, England, copywriter, 1951-52; London County Council, London, teacher, 1952-53; *North London Observer,* London, reporter, 1953; Louis Golding, London, literary secretary, 1953-55; author, 1955—.

WRITINGS:

The Liberty Man, Longmans, Green, 1955.
Fall of Innocence, Longmans, Green, 1956.
Jack Would Be a Gentleman, Longmans, Green, 1959.
The Story of Albert Einstein (juvenile), Vallentine, Mitchell, 1960.
(Under pseudonym Eliot George) *The Leather Boys* (also see below), Anthony Blond, 1961.
The Campaign, Longmans, Green, 1963.
The Leader (novel), Anthony Blond, 1965, Lippincott, 1966.
The Undergrowth of Literature (nonfiction), Thomas Nelson, 1967.
The Alabaster Egg (novel), Viking, 1970.
The Marriage Machine (novel), Stein and Day, 1975.
The Schoolgirl Ethic: The Life and Work of Angela Brazil (biography), Penguin, 1976.
The Confessions of Elisabeth Von S. (novel), Dutton, 1978, published in England as *Nazi Lady,* Anthony Blond, 1978.
An Easter Egg Hunt (novel), Congdon & Lattes, 1981.
(Under pseudonym Elaine Jackson) *Love Child* (novel), W. H. Allen, 1984.
(With husband, Edward Thorpe) *Ballet Genius,* Equation, 1989.
Termination Rock (novel), Unwin Hyman, 1989.

PLAYS

Pursuit (one-act), produced by the National Theatre Co., 1969.

Mayerling (scenario), produced by the Royal Ballet, 1978.
Isadora (scenario), produced by the Royal Ballet, 1981.

OTHER

Author of screenplays, including "The Leather Boys" (based on Freeman's novel of same title), 1963; "That Cold Day in the Park" (based on a novel by Richard Miles), 1965; "I Want What I Want" (based on a novel by Geoff Brown), 1973; "Day after the Fair" (based on a short story by Thomas Hardy), 1987; and "Girl on a Motorcycle." Contributor to anthologies, including *Women Writing,* W. H. Allen, 1979. Also contributor of stories and fiction reviews to *Spectator, London Magazine, Courier, Books and Bookmen, Sunday Times, Times Literary Supplement,* and other publications.

SIDELIGHTS: Literary critic and novelist Gillian Freeman began writing novels about the contemporary class structure in Britain, gradually using more complex structures, multiple narrative voices, and an interest in mysteries of the past to create her later fiction. Her novel *An Easter Egg Hunt* draws on her knowledge of "schoolgirl fiction" and Edwardian Britain (she is the biographer of Angela Brazil, a giant of early twentieth-century juvenile fiction). This intricately constructed novel tells of the disappearance of a girl from a British "school for young ladies" in 1915. The story is told from three points of view, at three different points in time. Stuart Evans, in the London *Times,* found the multiple levels of story-telling in the novel "ingenious" and "extremely artful."

Several reviewers noted Freeman's gift for social comedy and her detailed knowledge of the Edwardian period. Patricia Craig observed in *Times Literary Supplement* that while *An Easter Egg Hunt* reflects the conventions of "schoolgirl fiction"—the uniforms, the sports, the loved and unloved teachers—it does so in a self-conscious and restrained style. Craig wrote, "Her subject is violent feeling, betrayal, desperation—all dispassionately expressed," noting of Freeman that, "as always, she is adept at selecting the most striking details of social custom and behavior." Jean Strouse also praised *An Easter Egg Hunt* as an "ingenious little period piece mystery" where "the girls say wonderfully Edwardian things." Strouse concluded that Freeman's novel makes what "might have [been] called jolly good reading."

Like *An Easter Egg Hunt, Termination Rock* also uses multiple narrative voices and plays with the conventions of popular fiction. In *Termination Rock,* a nineteenth-century ghost intrudes into the life and thoughts of a present-day woman named Joanna. Freeman combines elements of the historical romance with the narrative style of the protagonist as Joanna seeks to understand the ghost's presence. Jane O'Grady suggested in *Times Literary Supplement* that Freeman may have intended the novel as a psychological exploration, but concluded that ultimately, the separate story lines are not satisfyingly integrated.

BIOGRAPHICAL/CRITICAL SOURCES:

BOOKS

Brophy, Brigid, *Don't Never Forget,* J. Cape, 1966.

PERIODICALS

Books and Bookmen, May, 1963.
Listener, November 2, 1967.
London Magazine, May, 1963; December 1967.
Los Angeles Times, October 5, 1979.
Newsweek, October 12, 1921, p. 106.
New York, June 9, 1969.
New York Times, February 26, 1972.
Observer (London), October 29, 1967.
Times (London), May 28, 1981.
Times Literary Supplement, October 16, 1970; May 22, 1981, p. 561; August 25, 1989, p. 918.

*   *   *

FREEMANTLE, Brian (Harry) 1936-
   (Jonathan Evans, Richard Gant, John Maxwell, Jack Winchester)

PERSONAL: Born June 10, 1936, in Southampton, England; son of Harold (a seaman) and Violet (Street) Freemantle; married Maureen Hazel Tipney (a television make-up artist), December 8, 1957; children: Victoria, Emma, Charlotte. *Education:* Attended secondary school in Southampton, England. *Politics:* Liberal. *Religion:* Church of England.

ADDRESSES: Agent—Jonathan Clowes, 10 Iron Bridge House, Bridge Approach, London NW1 8BD, England.

CAREER: Reporter for the *New Milton Advertiser,* 1953-58, and the *Bristol Evening World,* 1958; *Evening News,* London, England, reporter, 1959-61; *Daily Express,* London, reporter, 1961-63, assistant foreign editor, 1963-69; *Daily Sketch,* London, foreign editor, 1969-70; *Daily Mail,* London, foreign editor, 1971-75, writer, 1975—.

WRITINGS:

NOVELS

The Touchables (novelization of film), Hodder & Stoughton, 1968.
Goodbye to an Old Friend, Putnam, 1973.
Face Me When You Walk Away, Putnam, 1974.
The Man Who Wanted Tomorrow, Stein & Day, 1975.
The November Man, J. Cape, 1976.
Deaken's War, Hutchinson, 1982, Tor Books, 1985.
Rules of Engagement, Century, 1984.

Vietnam Legacy, Tor Books, 1984.
The Lost American, Tor Books, 1984.
Dirty White (published in England as *The Laundryman*), Tor Books, 1986.
The Kremlin Kiss, Century, 1986.
The Bearpit, Century, 1988.
O'Farrell's Law, Tor Books, 1990.
The Factory, Century, 1990.
The Choice of Eddie Franks, Tor Books, 1990.
Betrayals, Tor Books, 1991.
Little Grey Mice, St. Martin's, 1992.
The Button Man, St. Martin's, 1993.

"CHARLIE MUFFIN" MYSTERIES

Charlie M., Doubleday, 1977, published in England as *Charlie Muffin,* J. Cape, 1977.
Here Comes Charlie M., Doubleday, 1978, published in England as *Clap Hands, Here Comes Charlie,* J. Cape, 1978.
The Inscrutable Charlie Muffin, Doubleday, 1979.
Charlie Muffin U.S.A., Doubleday, 1980, published in England as *Charlie Muffin's Uncle Sam,* J. Cape, 1980.
Madrigal for Charlie Muffin, Hutchinson, 1981.
The Blind Run, Bantam, 1986.
Charlie Muffin and Russian Rose, Century, 1987.
See Charlie Run (published in England as *Charlie Muffin San*), Bantam, 1989.
The Run Around, Bantam, 1989.
Comrade Charlie, St. Martin's, 1992.
Charlie's Apprentice, Random House, 1993.

NONFICTION

KGB, Holt, 1982.
CIA, Stein & Day, 1983.
The Fix: Inside the World Drug Trade, Tor Books, 1985.
The Steal: Counterfeiting and Industrial Espionage, M. Joseph, 1987.

UNDER PSEUDONYM JONATHAN EVANS

The Solitary Man (also published under pseudonym Jack Winchester), Hamish Hamilton, 1980.
The Midas Men, M. Joseph, 1981, published as *Sagomi Gambit,* Tor Books, 1988.
Takeover, Tor Books, 1982, published in England as *Chairman of the Board,* M. Joseph, 1982.
Misfire, Futura, 1982.
Monopoly, M. Joseph, 1984.
The Kremlin Correction, Tor Books, 1984.

UNDER PSEUDONYM RICHARD GANT

Sean Connery: Gilt-Edged Bond, Mayflower, 1967.

UNDER PSEUDONYM JOHN MAXWELL

The Mary Celeste, J. Cape, 1979.

HMS Bounty, J. Cape, 1979.

SIDELIGHTS: The espionage novels of Brian Freemantle have been compared to those of John le Carre, for they feature heroes who do not quite fit the mold of the cool, smooth superspy. Freemantle's spies are fallible and emotional, relying upon their wits—and, often, sheer luck—to get through each calamitous adventure. Though Freemantle has created many such characters, none has earned such widespread popularity as has Charlie Muffin, the aging British agent who is the star of a dozen of Freemantle's thrillers.

Charlie Muffin, as described by *New York Times Book Review* mystery critic Newgate Callendar, "is a slob who all but sleeps in his clothes, fudges expense accounts, breaks all the rules, [and] is held in disdain by [his superiors]." However, Callendar continues, he is also "the best in the business, a man who can synthesize tiny facts and see the big picture and who is held in great respect even by his KGB adversaries." Charlie is an expert in Russian affairs, and his adventures usually take him behind the Iron Curtain; he is particularly adept at transporting defectors to and from the Soviet Union. Too often, however, Charlie is too smart for his own good, discovering prematurely the seedy machinations behind his missions. For this reason, he has several times been jailed, exiled, and marked for death by his own government. Charlie always bounces back, though—usually with a vengeance.

Critics have identified several reasons for the popularity of the Charlie Muffin novels. The first, of course, is Charlie himself. Freemantle's hero is a likeable, sympathetic, three-dimensional character; though he describes Charlie as "rich in tradecraft, afraid of no one and tough in the scrum," Frederick Busch of the Chicago *Tribune Books* notes that the British spy is "always battling deep feelings: anger at his bosses, sadness for his dead wife and for his Russian lover, trapped in the service of the KGB." Nearly as important as his character is Freemantle's skill as a storyteller. "The reader is captured by the narrative," praises Jim Stinson in the *Los Angeles Times Book Review.* "Except for the flawed, ruefully attractive Charlie, the characters are only as round as they need to be. . . . [Freemantle] handles story, logic, tension, pace and surprise with sure control. He hauls you aboard and won't let you off until the roller coaster stops."

An interesting feature of the Charlie Muffin books is Freemantle's near-fanatical avoidance of the words "he said." "There is something almost poetic about the way Freemantle ignores the demands of transitive verbs," Callendar writes, "sometimes going through extraordinary contortions to achieve his end." Some examples include: " 'And?' lured Charlie," " 'Sir Henry,' he placated," and " 'Everyone will know,' undertook Santana heavily." Cal-

lendar lists the author's idiosyncratic style as "one of the charms" of Freemantle's novels. "One waits with fascination for the next verbal mix-up, and there are many."

In addition to the Charlie Muffin stories, Freemantle has written a number of other spy thrillers, under a variety of names. Many of the plots and settings for these novels are the product of Freemantle's thirty years as a foreign press correspondent for several British publications. His experience as both an investigator and a world traveler lends an air of believability to his books. "What Freemantle writes does not seem exaggerated," says Callendar in a review of *Face Me When You Walk Away,* "even if he uses his license as a novelist to arrange matters thus and so." Still, he will probably remain best known as the creator of Charlie Muffin—and, according to Busch, rightly so. "Certain writers seem to be at their best with only certain of their characters," he explains. "[Sir Arthur] Conan Doyle's Professor Challenger never came close to the electricity of Sherlock Holmes. Muffin is Brian Freemantle's Holmes."

BIOGRAPHICAL/CRITICAL SOURCES:

BOOKS

Freemantle, Brian, *Charlie M.,* Doubleday, 1977.
Freemantle, Brian, *Charlie Muffin, U.S.A.,* Doubleday, 1980.
Freemantle, Brian, *The Run Around,* Bantam, 1989.

PERIODICALS

Economist, November 27, 1982, p. 105; March 2, 1985, p. 88.
Listener, July 3, 1986.
Los Angeles Times, July 24, 1980.
Los Angeles Times Book Review, May 13, 1984, p. 13; December 14, 1986, p. 4; August 23, 1987, p. 4.
New Statesman, February 22, 1985, p. 30.
New Yorker, July 21, 1986, p. 95; September 14, 1987, p. 136.
New York Times Book Review, February 23, 1973, p. 49; January 19, 1975, p. 36; December 14, 1975, p. 31; November 27, 1977, p. 36; December 9, 1979, p. 20; December 7, 1980, p. 45; September 7, 1986, p. 17; November 1, 1987, p. 34; June 25, 1989, p. 31; February 25, 1990, p. 35.
Times Literary Supplement, July 12, 1974, p. 741.
Tribune Books (Chicago), June 11, 1989, p. 8; March 11, 1990, p. 7.
West Coast Review of Books, July/August, 1984, p. 42; September/October, 1984, p. 57; number 4, 1986, p. 38; number 2, 1987, p. 32.

FRIEDMAN, Lawrence Meir 1930-

PERSONAL: Born April 2, 1930, in Chicago, IL; son of I. M. and Ethel (Shapiro) Friedman; married Leah Feigenbaum, March 27, 1955; children: Jane, Amy. *Education:* University of Chicago, A.B., 1948, J.D. 1951, M.LL., 1953. *Religion:* Jewish. *Avocational Interests:* Music, literature, history, Bible studies.

ADDRESSES: Home—724 Frenchman's Rd., Stanford, CA 94305.

CAREER: D'Ancona, Pflaum, Wyatt & Riskind (law firm), Chicago, IL, associate, 1955-57; St. Louis University, Law School, St. Louis, MO, 1957-61, began as assistant professor, became associate professor; University of Wisconsin—Madison, Law School, 1961-68, began as associate professor, became professor of law; Stanford University, Stanford, CA, professor of law, 1968-76, Marion Rice Kirkwood Professor of Law, 1976—. David Stouffer Memorial Lecturer, Rutgers University Law School, 1969; fellow, Center for Advanced Study in the Behavioral Sciences, 1973-74; Sibley lecturer, University of Georgia Law School, 1976; Wayne Morse lecturer, University of Oregon, 1985; fellow, Institute for Advanced Study, Berlin, Germany, 1985; Childress memorial lecturer, St. Louis University, 1987. *Military service:* U.S. Army, 1953-54; became sergeant.

MEMBER: American Academy of Arts and Sciences, Law and Society Association (president, 1979-81), American Society for Legal History (vice-president, 1987-89; president, 1990—).

AWARDS, HONORS: Scribes Award, 1974, for *A History of the American Law;* Triennial award from the Order of Coif, 1976; Willard Hurst prize, 1982.

WRITINGS:

Contract Law in America, University of Wisconsin Press, 1965.
Government and Slum Housing: A Century of Frustration, Rand McNally, 1968.
(With Stewart Macaulay) *Law and the Behavioral Sciences,* Bobbs-Merrill, 1969, 2nd edition, 1977.
A History of American Law, Simon & Schuster, 1973, 2nd edition, 1985.
The Legal System: A Social Science Perspective, Russell Sage, 1975.
Law and Society: An Introduction, Prentice-Hall, 1978.
(With Robert V. Percival) *The Roots of Justice: Crime and Punishment in Alameda County, California, 1870-1910,* University of North Carolina Press, 1981.
(With Curt D. Furberg and David L. DeMets) *Fundamentals of Clinical Trials,* J. Wright/PSG Inc., 1982.
American Law, Norton, 1984.

Total Justice: What Americans Want from the Legal System and Why, Russell Sage, 1985.
Your Time Will Come: The Law of Age Discrimination and Mandatory Retirement, Russell Sage, 1985.
(Editor with Harry N. Scheiber) *American Law and the Constitutional Order: Historical Perspectives,* Harvard University Press, 1988.
The Republic of Choice: Law, Authority, and Culture, Harvard University Press, 1990.
Crime and Punishment in American History, Basic Books, 1993.

SIDELIGHTS: Noted Stanford law professor Lawrence Meir Friedman has written and edited scholarly works on the laws and legal system of the United States. Two works in particular, *American Law* and *A History of American Law* have earned praise for their depth, attention to detail, and coherency.

In his 1984 work *American Law* Friedman analyzes the social forces that have shaped and are shaped by legal doctrine. The text spans the roots of American law through contemporary concerns with First Amendment rights and the problems of racial relations and equality, as dealt with under such landmark mandates as the 1954 "Brown vs. Board of Education" Supreme Court decision outlawing segregation in public schools, the Civil Rights Act of 1964, and the Voting Rights Act of 1965. Regarding *American Law,* Francis A. Allen stated that Friedman "achieves the considerable feat of raising interesting points in the discussions of almost every topic he addresses" and has the "admirable capacity of bringing together knowledge and insights gleaned from scores, perhaps hundreds," of sources, "integrating the information into a generally coherent whole." Allen concludes that the author "has proved himself a perceptive and knowledgeable guide." In the *Los Angeles Times Book Review,* Merton Kamins asserted: "The organization is logical and clearheaded. The prose is lucid, clean, laced with wit and arresting images. Simplifying but never simple-minded, this is a remarkable book."

Friedman has also written a legal reference book, the widely-acclaimed *A History of the American Law.* This overview assesses the highly complex subject of multijurisdictional American law, including sociological and anthropological subtexts, an area of special concern and expertise for the author. Calvin A. Woodward, in a review of the 1985 edition of *A History of the American Law* in the *New York Times Book Review,* stated that the new version is both richer and more balanced than the earlier volume because of Friedman's decision to place "slightly more emphasis on noneconomic factors. Crime (and criminology and penology) and family law are given rather more, certainly more sensitive, attention than earlier." Assessing Friedman's book, Woodward declared, "Every law student must be in his debt, and every historian may find in his example the model for his own future work. The very least we can say is that he has provided us with the best single, coherent history of American law that now exists." He concluded: "It will surely provide the introduction to the history of American law taught and learned in universities and law schools throughout this country for many years to come."

BIOGRAPHICAL/CRITICAL SOURCES:

PERIODICALS

Ethics, January, 1987, p. 505.
Journal of American History, December, 1983, p. 688; December, 1986, p. 724.
Los Angeles Times Book Review, January 6, 1985, p. 9; March 23, 1986, p. 14.
New York Times Book Review, December 2, 1984, p. 73; January 19, 1986, p. 32; February 16, 1986, p. 31.
Political Science Quarterly, winter, 1991, p. 746.
Tribune Books (Chicago), October 4, 1987, p. 23.

*   *   *

FRYKMAN, John H(arvey) 1932-

PERSONAL: First syllable of surname rhymes with "lick"; born April 19, 1932, in Boston, MA; son of Albion Helmer (a carpenter) and Ruth Maria Elizabeth (Kindberg) Frykman; married Nancy Alice Willock (a bookkeeper), June 7, 1957; married second wife, Cheryl Corinne Arnold (a teacher), December 22, 1968; children: (first marriage) Kristin Linnea, Lars Andrew, Erik John. *Education:* Attended University of Massachusetts, 1950-51; Wentworth Institute, Boston, Certificate in Architectural Construction, 1955; Bethany College, B.A., 1957; Lutheran Theological Seminary at Philadelphia, M.Div., 1960; additional study at University of California Medical Center, San Francisco, 1968-69, and Mental Research Institute, Palo Alto, CA, 1970-71. *Avocational In-*

terests: Music, photography, art, building, crafts, hiking, boating, a variety of sports.

ADDRESSES: Office—Cypress Institute, 24730 Lower Trail, Carmel, CA 93923.

CAREER: Part-time work while student included dairy hand, janitor, singer with jazz combo, and carpenter; ordained to Lutheran ministry, 1960; associate pastor of church in Sacramento, CA, 1960-62; pastor of church in Oakland, CA, 1962-68; Haight-Ashbury Medical Clinic, San Francisco, CA, director of drug treatment program, 1968-70; Carmel Unified School District, Carmel, CA, community counselor, 1970-72; Cypress Institute, Carmel, president and executive director, 1972—. Instructor in departments of criminology, sociology, and education, University of California Extension, 1970-74; associate staff member of National Drug Abuse Training Center, California State University, Hayward, 1970—. Consultant to Youth Office, City of Oslo, Norway, 1971. *Military service:* U.S. Army, 1952-54; served in Korea. California Army National Guard, chaplain, 1964-67.

WRITINGS:

It's Happening (poems), C/J Press (Oakland, CA), 1967.
A New Connection: An Approach to Persons Involved in Compulsive Drug Use, C/J Press (San Francisco), 1970, revised and enlarged edition, Scrimshaw Press (San Francisco), 1971, revised and enlarged edition published as *A New Connection: A Problem-Solving Approach to Chemical Dependency,* Regent Press, 1992.
Teenage Survival Handbook, Palo Colorado Press, 1978.
The Hassle Handbook, Regent Street Books, 1984.

Contributor to *A Drug Abuse Anthology,* Holt, 1970. Contributor to drug treatment program symposia proceedings.

WORK IN PROGRESS: A guide to family counseling, *Making the Impossible Difficult.**

G

GANT, Richard
   See FREEMANTLE, Brian (Harry)

* * *

GARD, (Sanford) Wayne   1899-1986

PERSONAL: Born June 21, 1899, in Brocton, IL; died of pneumonia, September 24, 1986, in Dallas, TX; son of Guy William and Winnie (Sanford) Gard; married Hazel Anna Dell, 1925; children: Christopher. *Education:* Illinois College, A.B., 1921; Northwestern University, M.A., 1925; Columbia University, postgraduate study, 1928. *Avocational Interests:* tennis.

CAREER: Associated Press, Chicago, news writer, 1925-26; Grinnell College, Grinnell, IA, teacher, 1925-30; *Chicago Daily News,* editorial writer, 1929; *Des Moines Register and Tribune,* editorial writer, 1930-32; *Vanity Fair,* New York City, assistant editor, 1932; *Dallas Morning News,* editorial writer, 1933-64. Writer, 1927-86. *Military service:* U.S. Army, 1918; served in World War I.

MEMBER: Texas State Historical Association (former president), Organization of American Historians, Western History Association, Texas Folklore Society, Sigma Delta Chi (past president, Dallas chapter; former member, national executive council), Phi Beta Kappa (past president, Dallas association).

AWARDS, HONORS: Research awards from Texas State Historical Association and American Philosophical Society; Litt.D., Illinois College, 1959; Summerfield G. Roberts Award of the Sons of the Republic of Texas, 1965, for *Rawhide Texas.*

WRITINGS:

Book Reviewing, Knopf, 1927.
Sam Bass, Houghton, 1936.
Frontier Justice, University of Oklahoma Press, 1949.
The Chisholm Trail, University of Oklahoma Press, 1954.
Fabulous Quarter Horse: Steel Dust, Duell, 1958.
The Great Buffalo Hunt, Knopf, 1959.
Rawhide Texas, University of Oklahoma Press, 1965.
(Editor and author of introduction) *Up the Trail in Seventy-Nine,* University of Oklahoma Press, 1968.
Reminiscences of Range Life, Steck-Vaughn, 1970.
Unitarianism in Dallas: An Outline History of the First Unitarian Church of Dallas, Texas in its First Seventy Years, 1899-1968, First Unitarian Church (Dallas, TX), 1973.

Contributor to *The Book of the American West,* Messner, 1963; *Along the Early Trails of the Southwest,* Pemberton, 1969; and to encyclopedias and magazines, including *American Heritage, American West, American Mercury, House and Garden,* and *Nation's Business.*

SIDELIGHTS: Wayne Gard began his newspaper reporting career as a part-time Associated Press correspondent in Burma, India, from 1921 to 1924 where he was also teaching high school English. In 1933, after several years of dividing his time between teaching and reporting duties in Iowa and Chicago, he became an editorial writer for the *Dallas Morning News* where he remained until his retirement in 1964. During these years, he became increasingly interested in the history of the American West and documented the Texas frontier life in several historical books, including *Sam Bass, Frontier Justice,* and the best-selling *Chisholm Trail.*

In *Wayne Gard, Historian of the West,* Ramon F. Adams calls Gard "an accurate and meticulous historian. Through his careful research and sound scholarship, he has brought to light phases of the history of the American West neglected by other historians. He has helped rescue from distorted Hollywood images, and to show in their true light, such frontier figures as the cowboy, the buffalo hunter, the gunman, the vigilante, and the peace officer."

BIOGRAPHICAL/CRITICAL SOURCES:

BOOKS

Adams, Ramon Frederick, *Wayne Gard, Historian of the West*, Steck-Vaughn, 1970.

OBITUARIES:

PERIODICALS

Dallas Morning News, September 27, 1986.
Dallas Times Herald, September 27, 1986.*

*　　*　　*

GAREFFA, Peter M(ichael) 1952-

PERSONAL: Born August 1, 1952, in Detroit, MI; son of Emil Anthony (a truck driver and union official) and Anne (a waitress; maiden name, Ganoff) Gareffa; divorced; children: Jennifer Ann. *Education:* Wayne State University, B.S.Ed., 1975, graduate study, 1975; certificate from Publishing Institute, University of Denver, 1983; certificate from Graduate School of Business, University of Michigan, 1986. *Politics:* Independent. *Religion:* Roman Catholic. *Avocational Interests:* Collecting P. G. Wodehouse first editions, golf, movies, music, sailing, softball, volleyball.

ADDRESSES: Home—St. Clair Shores, MI. *Office*—Contemporary Biographies, Gale Research Inc., 835 Penobscot Bldg., Detroit, MI 48226.

CAREER: Busboy, waiter, and cook in a small restaurant in East Detroit, MI, 1966; supermarket stock clerk in St. Clair Shores, MI, 1968-75; substitute teacher of social studies and English at junior high school and high school in Mt. Clemens, MI, 1975-76; Gale Research Inc., Detroit, MI, *Contemporary Authors* series, assistant editor, 1976-80, associate editor, 1980-84, *Contemporary Newsmakers* series, coeditor, 1985, editor, 1985-86, editor-supervisor, 1986-89, Biography Division, senior editor, 1990—. Free-lance photographer, 1973-75.

WRITINGS:

(Assistant editor) *Contemporary Authors*, Revised Volumes, Volume 25-28 through New Revision Series, Volume 1, Gale, 1976-81.

(Assistant editor) *Contemporary Authors*, Permanent Series, Volume 2, Gale, 1978.

(Associate editor) *Contemporary Authors*, New Revisions Series, Volume 2-14, Gale, 1981-85.

(Co-editor) *Contemporary Newsmakers, 1985*, Issues 1-4, Gale, 1985-86, annual cumulation, Gale, 1986.

(Editor) *Contemporary Newsmakers, 1986*, Issues 1-4, Gale, 1986-87.

(Editor) *Contemporary Newsmakers, 1987*, Issues 1-4, Gale, 1987-88.

(Editor) *Contemporary Newsmakers, 1988*, Issues 1-4, Gale, 1988-89.

(Editor) *Contemporary Newsmakers, 1989*, Issue 1, Gale, 1989.

Senior editor of *Contemporary Musicians, Contemporary Black Biography, Who's Who Among Hispanic Americans, Who's Who Among Asian Americans, Twentieth Century Young Adult Writers, Ethnic Genealogy Sourcebook Series, Encyclopedia of Consumer Brands, Encyclopedia of American Industries, Small Business Profiles, Professional Sports Team Histories, World Encyclopedia of Soccer, Science Fiction and Fantasy Literature, 1975-1991, Biography and Genealogy Master Index, Passenger and Immigration Lists Index, Contemporary Authors Autobiography Series, Who's Who Among Black Americans, Who's Who in Technology, Newsmakers, International Directory of Company Histories, Annual Obituary, Writers Directory,* and *Awards Almanac.* Contributor of stories, articles, and cartoons to "a couple of totally insignificant magazines."

WORK IN PROGRESS: "Currently the only editorial employee of Gale Research not working on a novel."

SIDELIGHTS: Peter M. Gareffa began his work at Gale Research in 1976 as an assistant editor on *Contemporary Authors* Revision Series, writing and editing biographical sketches on authors. Beginning with his promotion to associate editor in 1980, his editorial responsibilities focused on training new assistant editors and coordinating the *CA* Revision series' interviews with authors. In 1982, when the decision was made to initiate a new series to be entitled *Contemporary Newsmakers*—based on the highly successful *CA* format, but profiling non-writers in the news—Gareffa and Gale senior editor Ann Evory became co-editors. *CN* proved very successful, and at the end of its first year of publication Gareffa was promoted to sole editor of the series and supervisor of the *CN* staff.

In 1988, *CN*'s title was simplified to *Newsmakers* and, to reflect the series' expanded coverage and popular focus, sported a new, cleaner page design and cover. The department grew, and the staff increased its efforts to bring to market other series in the area of popular culture, including such titles as *Contemporary Musicians* and *Contemporary Black Biography.*

Then, in 1990, Gareffa was promoted to senior editor within Gale's Biography Division, eventually becoming the supervisor of three supervisors and twelve editors of both Gale and St. James Press projects. Titles within his area of responsibility include directories, indexes, business publications, and a great many biographical and autobiographical books and electronic products. The thirty-five people in his area work on such diverse titles as *Biography and Genealogy Master Index, Contemporary Authors Autobiography Series, International Directory of Company Histories, Who's Who Among Black Americans, Annual Obituary, World Encyclopedia of Soccer, Twentieth Century Young Adult Writers, Science Fiction and Fantasy Literature,* and *Encyclopedia of Consumer Brands,* in addition to the three titles originally started in the *Newsmakers* department.

Gareffa explains his vision of his current responsibilities to *CA:* "My job is to get stuff off my desk. You see, other people have the job of putting stuff *on* my desk—paperwork, problems, questions, conflicts—and my job is to remove these obstacles so they can do their work. I have no real work of my own; ideally, I create an impediment-free environment so other people can get their jobs done while I goof off."

An avid sportsman, Gareffa has served at various times as player-manager of Gale's men's softball team, co-ed softball team, and one of the teams in the company's volleyball league. And although plans for a Gale polo league failed to materialize, he has been of some help organizing a number of company golf outings.

*   *   *

GEORGE, Eliot
  See FREEMAN, Gillian

*   *   *

GILLIAN, Kay
  See SMITH, Kay Nolte

*   *   *

GITTINGS, Robert (William Victor) 1911-1992

PERSONAL: Born February 1, 1911, in Portsmouth, Hampshire, England; died February 18, 1992, in Chichester, West Sussex, England; son of Claude Bromley (a surgeon) and Dora (Brayshaw) Gittings; married Katherine Edith Campbell (a teacher), 1934; married Joan Grenville Manton (an author, writing as Jo Manton), 1949; children: (first marriage) Robert Jr., John; (second marriage) Clare. *Education:* Jesus College, Cambridge, B.A., 1933, M.A., 1936. *Avocational Interests:* Music, the English countryside, and "traditional sports, *but not* blood sports."

ADDRESSES: Home—The Stables, East Dean, Chichester, West Sussex, England.

CAREER: Cambridge University, Jesus College, Cambridge, England, supervisor in history, 1933-40; British Broadcasting Corporation, London, England, writer and producer of literary and historical features, 1940-63; poet and biographer. Visiting professor of English literature, Vanderbilt University, summer, 1966, Boston University, 1970, and University of Washington, Seattle, 1972, 1974.

MEMBER: Royal Society of Literature (fellow).

AWARDS, HONORS: Royal Society of Literature award, 1955, for *John Keats: The Living Year, 21 September, 1818, to 21 September, 1819;* W. H. Smith and Son Literary Award, 1969, for *John Keats;* Litt.D. Cambridge University, 1970; Commander of the Order of the British Empire, 1970; Phi Beta Kappa Christian Gauss Award, 1975, for *Young Thomas Hardy;* James Tait Black Memorial Prize, for *The Older Hardy.*

WRITINGS:

NONFICTION

John Keats: The Living Year, 21 September, 1818, to 21 September, 1819, Heinemann, 1954.
The Mask of Keats: A Study of Problems, Harvard University Press, 1956.
(With wife, Jo Manton) *Windows on History,* four books, Hulton, 1959-61.
Shakespeare's Rival: A Study in Three Parts, Heinemann, 1960.
(With Jo Manton) *The Story of John Keats* (juvenile), Dutton, 1962.
The Keats Inheritance, Heinemann, 1964.
(With Jo Manton) *Makers of the Twentieth Century,* Longacre Press, 1966.
John Keats, Little, Brown, 1968.
Young Thomas Hardy, Little, Brown, 1975.
The Older Hardy (sequel to *Young Thomas Hardy*), Heinemann, 1978, published in U.S. as *Thomas Hardy's Later Years,* Little, Brown, 1978.
The Nature of Biography, University of Washington Press, 1978.
(With Jo Manton) *The Second Mrs. Hardy,* University of Washington Press, 1979.
(With Jo Manton) *Dorothy Wordsworth,* Oxford University Press, 1985.
People, Places, Personal, Secker & Warburg, 1985.
(With Jo Manton) *Claire Clairmont and the Shelleys 1798-1879,* Oxford University Press, 1992.

EDITOR

The Living Shakespeare, Heinemann, 1960, Barnes & Noble, 1968.
(With Evelyn Hardy) *Some Recollections by Emma Hardy,* Oxford University Press, 1961.

(And author of introduction and commentary) *Selected Poems and Letters of John Keats,* Barnes & Noble, 1966.

Robert Southey and Samuel Taylor Coleridge, *Omniana; or, Horae otiosiores,* Centaur Press, 1969.

The Odes of Keats and Their Earliest Known Manuscripts in Facsimile, Kent State University Press, 1970.

Letters of John Keats: A New Selection, Oxford University Press, 1970.

Also editor with James Reeves of *Selected Poems of Thomas Hardy,* 1981.

POETRY

The Roman Road and Other Poems, Oxford University Press, 1932.

The Story of Psyche, Cambridge University Press, 1936.

Wentworth Place, Heinemann, 1950.

Famous Meeting: Poems, Narrative and Lyric, Heinemann, 1953.

This Tower My Prison and Other Poems, Heinemann, 1961.

Matters of Love and Death, Heinemann, 1968.

American Journey: Twenty-five Sonnets, Heinemann, 1972.

Collected Poems, Heinemann, 1976.

(With Jo Manton) *The Flying Horses: Tales from China,* with verses in Chinese style by Gittings, illustrated by Derek Collard, Holt, 1977.

PLAYS

The Makers of Violence (verse play), Heinemann, 1951.

Through a Glass, Lightly, Heinemann, 1952.

"Man's Estate: A Play of Saint Richard of Chichester," published with a play by Leo Lehman, *Two Saint's Plays,* Heinemann, 1954.

Out of this Wood: A Country Sequence of Five Plays (contains "The Bronte Sisters," "Our Clouded Hills," "Parson Herrick's Parishioners," "Thomas Tusser's Wife," and "William Cowper's Muse,"), Heinemann, 1955.

Also author of *The Seven Sleepers,* 1950.

OTHER

Author with Jo Manton of *The Peach Blossom Forest and Other Chinese Legends,* 1951; and of *Love's a Gamble: A Ballad Opera,* 1961. Also author of *son et lumiere* scripts for St. Paul's and Canterbury Cathedrals, including *Conflict at Canterbury: An Entertainment in Sound and Light,* 1970. Author of introduction to several books, including *The Old Playgoer,* by William Robson, Centaur Press, 1969; and *Recollections of Writers,* by Charles Cowden Clarke and Mary Cowden Clarke, Centaur Press, 1969.

SIDELIGHTS: Beginning his literary career as a poet, Gittings turned to literary biography in middle age, winning his greatest acclaim. His award-winning book, *John Keats,* "is a book both judicious and vivid, . . . a scrupulously exact and moving biography," writes Paul West in *Book World.* Uncluttered with "the minutiae of inquiry, it flows on above its contentious footnotes, bringing Keats more physically alive for us . . . than any other scholarly account." *New York Review of Books* contributor G. M. Matthews notes that it was Gittings' aim to "find the factual basis for almost every reported incident or event of Keats' life." Explaining his reasoning, Gittings writes: "The vital force behind all his verse was his power to apply imagination to every aspect of life, so that the result far transcended its origins. This is why no part of Keats' life should be neglected, and every incident, once truly recorded, may have an immense value in interpreting the poetry."

Another major biographical achievement of Gittings' later life was his "masterly" two-volume biography of Thomas Hardy, as John Bayley deemed it in the *New York Review of Books.* The first volume, *Young Thomas Hardy,* took the well-known Victorian novelist-poet from his birth till after the success of *Far from the Madding Crowd.* Reviewing the volume for the *New Republic,* Richard Ellmann interpreted Gittings to say that "Hardy's sensitivity about class, both before and after he changed social classes, was the mainspring of his talent." Ellmann continued, "On certain controversial subjects of Hardy's life he [Gittings] appears to offer conclusive verdicts." These subjects included the sanity of Hardy's first wife and the relationship of Hardy to his beloved cousin Tryphena Sparks. Irving Howe, in the *New York Times Book Review,* called the first volume "solid in construction, if somewhat phlegmatic in voice" and "the richest account thus far of Hardy's childhood, youth and literary beginnings." Howe also termed the portrait of Hardy "curiously elusive," partly because of Hardy's own secretiveness about his life.

Howe, reviewing Gittings' second volume, found the work "first-rate" in its treatment of Hardy's sense of class inferiority, and called Gittings "a superb researcher." *The Older Hardy,* published in the U.S. as *Thomas Hardy's Later Years,* focused on the subject's years as a respected author. Howe found that the Hardy of Gittings' portrait was "an egocentric, withdrawn, chilly man, tight with his money and far more interested in writing poems upstairs than living in any other room." Samuel Hynes, reviewing *The Older Hardy* for the *Times Literary Supplement,* claimed that Gittings' "greatest gift as a biographer" was "his tireless and ingenious pursuit of hidden facts in the subject's background." Assessing both Gittings' volumes in the *New York Review of Books,* Stephen Spender called the effort "scrupulous" and "detailed."

In 1978, Gittings collected several essays on the biographer's craft in *The Nature of Biography.* The work focuses on the history of the biography form rather than on theory or on Gittings' personal methods. In *Book World,* Michael Dirda commented that the essays were "suggestive and tentative, not to say tantalizing. Nearly all are written with charm, several offer intimate biographical glances into the biographical process, and each makes clear the variety of pleasure and instruction available from life-writing." *Times Literary Supplement* contributor Michael Holroyd called the volume, "knowledgable, wise and charming," but regretted its slightness. "Mr. Gittings is an optimist," Holroyd observed, "perhaps every biographer needs to be."

BIOGRAPHICAL/CRITICAL SOURCES:

PERIODICALS

Book World, July 28, 1968, p. 1.
Christian Science Monitor, July 25, 1968.
Globe & Mail (Toronto), January 11, 1986; October 8, 1988.
New Republic, September 7, 1968; November 29, 1975, pp. 28-29; May 27, 1978, pp. 27-29.
New Statesman, March 22, 1968.
New Yorker, August 25, 1975, p. 87; July 10, 1978, p. 90; December 24, 1979, p. 102.
New York Review of Books, November 7, 1968; November 27, 1975, pp. 11-16; June 15, 1978, pp. 12-15; October 7, 1982, pp. 9-13.
New York Times, July 17, 1968.
New York Times Book Review, July 6, 1975; May 7, 1978, pp. 11, 14.
Observer (London), March 17, 1968.
Punch, April 10, 1968.
Saturday Review, July 22, 1978, pp. 40-41, 43.
Spectator, April 25, 1992, pp. 38-39.
Times (London), May 16, 1985.
Times Literary Supplement, August 4, 1972, pp. 910-11; April 18, 1975, pp. 414-15; April 8, 1977, p. 428; March 10, 1978; November 24, 1978, p. 136; December 7, 1979, pp. 90-91; April 17, 1992, p. 5.
Washington Post Book World, February 10, 1979, p. 12; July 1, 1979, p. F3; September 1, 1985, p. 5.

OBITUARIES:

PERIODICALS

Times (London), February 21, 1992, p. 17.*

*   *   *

GLASS, Joanna (McClelland) 1936-

PERSONAL: Original name, Joan McClelland; born October 7, 1936, in Saskatoon, Saskatchewan, Canada;

daughter of Morrell MacKenzie and Katharine (Switzer) McClelland; married Alexander Glass, 1959 (divorced, 1974); children: Jennifer, Mavis, Lawrence. *Education:* Attended Saskatoon Collegiate, Saskatoon, Saskatchewan.

ADDRESSES: Home—Toronto, Canada. *Agent*—Lucy Kroll Agency, 390 West End Ave., New York, NY 10024; (screenplays) David Wirtschafter, International Creative Management, 8899 Beverly Blvd., Los Angeles, CA 90048.

AWARDS, HONORS: National Endowment grant, 1980; Guggenheim Fellowship, 1981; Antoinette Perry Award nomination, best play, 1984, for Play Memory; Rockefeller grant, 1985.

CAREER: Writer. Yale University, New Haven, CT, playwright-in-residence, 1987.

WRITINGS:

NOVELS

Reflections on a Mountain Summer, Knopf, 1974.
Woman Wanted, St. Martin's, 1985.

PLAYS

Santacqua, produced in New York, NY, at Herbert Berghof Studio workshop, 1969.
Trying (one-act), produced in Detroit, MI, at Hilberry Theatre, Wayne State University, 1971.
Jewish Strawberries (one-act), produced at Hilberry Theatre, 1971.
Canadian Gothic [and] *American Modern* (one-act; produced at Manhattan Theatre Club, 1972), Dramatists Play Service, 1977.
Artichoke (two-act; produced at Long Wharf Theatre, 1975), Dramatists Play Service, 1979.
The Last Chalice, produced in Winnipeg, Manitoba, by the Manitoba Theatre Centre, 1977, extensively revised as *Play Memory* (produced on Broadway, 1984), Samuel French, c. 1984.
To Grandmother's House We Go (two-act; produced on Broadway, 1981), Samuel French, 1981.
Yesteryear, produced in Toronto, Canada, at St. Lawrence Centre, 1989.
If We Are Women, produced in Williamstown, MA, at Williamstown Theatre Festival, 1993.

Also author of *Towering Babble,* 1987.

OTHER

Contributor to anthologies, including *Winter's Tales, 22* (includes the short story, "At the King Edward Hotel"), edited by James Wright, St. Martin's, 1976; and *Best Short Plays, 1978,* edited by Stanley Richards, Chilton, 1978.

ADAPTATIONS: Artichoke was adapted for television and broadcast by Canadian Broadcasting Corp.

(CBC-TV), 1977; film rights for *Woman Wanted* were purchased by Zanuck, Brown, and for *Reflections on a Mountain Summer* by Lorimar.

SIDELIGHTS: Canadian-born playwright Joanna Glass began her career as an actress, training for the stage in Canada and California. She started to devote more time to her writing, however, and saw several of her short plays produced in workshops. In 1972 her two one-act plays, *Canadian Gothic* and *American Modern,* became her professional breakthrough by way of a New York production. Productions of *Artichoke* in the United States in 1975 and in Canada in 1976 "drew critical attention . . . to Glass's talent for piquant dialogue and her facility for countering the expectations of established literary norms," according to Diane Bessai in *The Oxford Companion to Canadian Theatre.* The play is a comic work about family conflict, infidelity, and love set in Saskatchewan. Featuring a lonely farm wife and her unfaithful husband, the play focuses on the wife's love affair with a visiting poetry professor—the exotic "artichoke," as David Richards explains in the *Washington Post,* "in the eyes of the others, who view themselves more as turnips." Richard Eder, reviewing the play for the *New York Times,* comments, "It has the feel of a comic ballad, and in many respects a delightful one."

Glass moved up to Broadway with her next two plays. *To Grandmother's House We Go* was produced in 1981 and starred the legendary actress Eva LeGallienne. A play of intergenerational conflict, *To Grandmother's House We Go* explores the relationships among family members as they gather together in New England to celebrate Thanksgiving at Grandmother's house. *New York Times* reviewer Frank Rich praised the roles of the older members of the household and family, but called the younger characters stereotypical, noting that "Grandie's grandchildren are mopey, casebook neurotics." The *Los Angeles Times*'s Sylvie Drake, however, declared: "Glass writes with grace. Her perceptions are incisive, her characters whole and her dialogue sharp and laced with understated wit."

Another of Glass's works, *Play Memory,* was also produced on Broadway. According to Rich, this piece was "about the emotional legacy that parents bequeath to their children; it invokes such grave matters as poverty, alcoholism, child abuse and mental illness." *New York Times* contributor Mel Gussow, reviewing an out-of-town preview of *Play Memory,* called the climactic confrontation between the mother and father "the play's most moving encounter. . . . By the end of the family journey, one is touched by the pitiable, unpaternal father who, in desolation, has a single selfless moment."

Also a novelist, Glass published her second novel, *Woman Wanted,* in 1985. It is the story of Emma Riley, a brash young Irish woman who answers an ad to be a housekeeper for Richard Goddard, a widowed Yale professor, and his 23-year-old son, Wendell, a temperamental poet. Emma and Richard have an affair, but their relationship is threatened by the love between Emma and Wendell. Elissa Rabellino, writing in the *Los Angeles Times Book Review,* noted that "Emma is an engaging narrator, funny and passionate," but remarked that the novel's stylistic devices—such as breaking the dialogue into play script form—were distracting. *New York Times Book Review* contributor Carolyn See wrote, "The universal problem Emma exemplifies, of always being 'indispensable' but never loved, is well worth consideration. Mrs. Glass's solution, Emma's solution, is both audacious and traditional, and completely rooted in character."

BIOGRAPHICAL/CRITICAL SOURCES:

BOOKS

Benson, Eugene, and L. W. Conolly, editors, *The Oxford Companion to Canadian Theatre,* Oxford University Press, 1989, pp. 234-35.

PERIODICALS

Atlantic Monthly, August, 1985, p. 91.
Atlantis, autumn, 1978.
Chicago Tribune, April 20, 1981.
Los Angeles Times, October 4, 1983.
Los Angeles Times Book Review, November 24, 1985, p. 6.
New York Times, February 26, 1979; January 16, 1981; February 15, 1981; October 22, 1983; April 27, 1984; June 17, 1987.
New York Times Book Review, August 25, 1985, p. 10.
Publishers Weekly, April 12, 1985, p. 89.
Washington Post, August 7, 1986.

*   *   *

GLUBOK, Shirley (Astor)

PERSONAL: Surname is pronounced "*Glue*-bach"; born in St. Louis, MO; daughter of Yale I. (a merchant) and Ann (a merchant; maiden name, Astor) Glubok; married Alfred H. Tamarin (an author and photographer), February 25, 1968 (died August 19, 1980). *Education:* Washington University, A.B.; Columbia University, M.A., 1958; graduate study at Hunter College of the City University of New York and New York University. *Religion:* Jewish.

ADDRESSES: Home—50 East 72nd St., New York, NY 10021.

CAREER: Writer. Teacher in St. Louis, MO, and New York City, 1955-64; lecturer in art history at the Metropolitan Museum of Art in New York City, 1958—, for the National Humanities Series, 1972, at America's Society in New York City, 1988-90, at the Cooper Hewitt Museum in New York City, 1989-90, and at the Spanish Institute in New York City, 1992—; author-in-residence at Greenhill School in Dallas, TX, 1977; taught graduate course at Boston University, 1987; lecturer in Boston schools on private grant, 1981—; lecturer to classes on art and children's literature, to various professional educators' and librarians' associations, and to university groups.

MEMBER: Authors League of America, Archaeological Institute of America, College Art Association, Coffee House, Racquet Club of Palm Springs.

AWARDS, HONORS: Lewis Carroll Shelf Award, 1963, for *The Art of Ancient Egypt;* Spur Award, Western Writers of America, 1971, for *The Art of the Southwest Indians* and *The Art of the Old West; Boston Globe-Horn Book* award for best nonfiction book, 1976, for *Voyaging to Cathay;* Author of the Year Award, Children's Book Guild of Washington, D.C., 1980; Central Missouri State University award, 1987, for outstanding contribution to children's literature; American Library Association notable book citations for *The Art of Ancient Greece, The Art of the Eskimo, Discovering Tut-ankh-Amen's Tomb, The Art of Ancient Egypt, The Art of Ancient Peru,* and *Voyaging to Cathay;* Children's Book Showcase award for *The Art of the Northwest Coast Indians;* American Institute of Graphic Arts award, for *The Art of Lands in the Bible, The Art of Africa, The Art of Ancient Peru, Fall of the Aztecs,* and *Voyaging to Cathay:Americans in the China Trade;* Mark Twain Award for *Knights in Armor;* Library of Congress citation for *The Art of the Eskimo, The Art of Africa,* and *The Art of Ancient Peru.*

WRITINGS:

CHILDREN'S NONFICTION

The Art of Ancient Egypt, Atheneum, 1962.
The Art of Lands in the Bible, Atheneum, 1963.
The Art of Ancient Greece, Atheneum, 1963.
The Art of the North American Indian, Harper, 1964.
The Art of the Eskimo, photographs by husband, Alfred H. Tamarin, Harper, 1964.
The Art of Ancient Rome, Harper, 1965.
The Art of Africa, photographs by Tamarin, Harper, 1965.
Art and Archaeology, Harper, 1966.
The Art of Ancient Peru, photographs by Tamarin, Harper, 1966.
The Art of the Etruscans, photographs by Tamarin, Harper, 1967.
The Art of Ancient Mexico, photographs by Tamarin, Harper, 1968.
Knights in Armor, Harper, 1969.

The Art of India, photographs by Tamarin, Macmillan, 1969.
The Art of Colonial America, Macmillan, 1970.
The Art of Japan, photographs by Tamarin, Macmillan, 1970.
The Art of the Old West, Macmillan, 1971.
The Art of the Southwest Indians, Macmillan, 1971.
The Art of the New American Nation, Macmillan, 1972.
The Art of the Spanish in the United States and Puerto Rico, photographs by Tamarin, Macmillan, 1972.
The Art of America from Jackson to Lincoln, Macmillan, 1973.
The Art of China, Macmillan, 1973.
The Art of America in the Early Twentieth Century, Macmillan, 1974.
The Art of America in the Gilded Age, Macmillan, 1974.
The Art of the Northwest Coast Indians, Macmillan, 1975.
The Art of the Plains Indians, photographs by Tamarin, Macmillan, 1975.
Dolls, Dolls, Dolls, photographs by Tamarin, Follett, 1975.
(With Tamarin) *Ancient Indians of the Southwest,* Doubleday, 1975.
(With Tamarin) *Voyaging to Cathay: Americans in the China Trade,* Viking, 1976.
(With Tamarin) *Olympic Games in Ancient Greece,* Harper, 1976.
The Art of America since World War II, Macmillan, 1976.
The Art of the Woodland Indians, photographs by Tamarin, Macmillan, 1976.
The Art of Photography, Macmillan, 1977.
The Art of the Vikings, Macmillan, 1978.
The Art of the Southeastern Indians, photographs by Tamarin, Macmillan, 1978.
(With Tamarin) *The Mummy of Ramose: The Life and Death of an Ancient Egyptian Nobleman,* Harper, 1978.
The Art of the Comic Strip, Macmillan, 1979.
The Art of Ancient Egypt under the Pharaohs, Macmillan, 1980.
Dolls' Houses: Life in Miniature, Harper, 1984.
Great Lives: Painting, Scribner, 1994.

EDITOR

Bernal Diaz del Castillo, *The Fall of the Aztecs,* St. Martin's, 1965.
Garcilaso de la Vega, and Pedro Pizarro, *The Fall of the Incas,* Macmillan, 1967.
Howard Carter, *Discovering Tut-ankh-Amen's Tomb,* Macmillan, 1968.
Leonard Woolley, *Discovering the Royal Tombs at Ur,* Macmillan, 1969.
Alice Morse Earle, *Home and Child Life in Colonial Days,* photographs by Tamarin, Macmillan, 1969.

Austin Henry Layard, *Digging in Assyria,* Macmillan, 1970.

OTHER

Contributor to "Basic Reading Textbook" series, Holt/ Silver Burdett; contributor of articles to various magazines and journals, including *Teacher, Scanorama, Scholastic, Connoisseur, Antiques, Review, Columbia Museum News, Art and Antiques, Auction Forum, Miniature Collector, Oasis, Art and Auction,* and *House and Garden.*

SIDELIGHTS: Shirley Glubok's books introduce children to the art of numerous cultures through a blend of photographs and simple text. Glubok has examined the art of Japan, India, and Africa, and of such people as the North American Indians and the Vikings. May Hill Arbuthnot and Zena Sutherland maintain in their *Children and Books* that Glubok's works "are impressive because of the combination of authoritative knowledge, simple presentation, dignified format, and a recurrent emphasis on the relationship between an art form and the culture in which it was created."

While Glubok was a second-grade teacher in a suburb of St. Louis, she arranged for her class to visit the St. Louis Art Museum. She prepared her students for the trip by going through a catalog of the museum's pieces. "Without consciously setting out to do so," Glubok recalls in her *Something about the Author Autobiography Series* essay, "I was developing a technique of introducing works of art to school children." The next time the class went to the museum, Glubok took the children through the exhibits herself, having each child choose a favorite painting and explain what they liked about it. The other children then expressed their opinions before moving on to the next painting. Glubok explains the reasoning behind this method: "I thought it was important for the children to know that they did not have to like a work of art just because they thought they were supposed to; they should form their own opinions. I also thought it was important for them to learn to express their ideas in spoken words as well as in writing, and to learn to listen to each other attentively."

After graduate school at Columbia University, Glubok was hired to give lectures to children at the Metropolitan Museum of Art on Saturdays. "The children and I explored the galleries together. I urged them to look at a work and try to react personally before I gave them information about the materials, the artist who created it, when and how it was made, and what it stood for," relates Glubok in her essay. During the week she taught at a private school and worked on rewriting a picture book she had begun in St. Louis. A literary agent showed some interest in her writing ability, telling her that Atheneum's new children's department was looking for art books. Glubok

submitted a proposal and *The Art of Ancient Egypt* was published in 1962.

Speaking of that first book, Glubok maintains that "one of the most demanding aspects was cutting down the text to fit the page and balancing the pictures with the text. I had to make every single word count." As soon as the book was complete, the next one was begun. Glubok's editor and agent originally decided that they did not want a series, but as soon as the reviews of *The Art of Ancient Egypt* came out they changed their minds, and thirty books with "The Art of" as the first words of their title have followed.

All of the books in the series maintain a similar format, containing large photographs, usually black and white, with limited but clear and simple text. Such books as *The Art of the Lands in the Bible, The Art of Ancient Rome, The Art of Japan,* and *The Art of the Southwest Indian* all introduce children to a variety of cultures and customs through the art. "In each book [Glubok] writes she continues her marriage between children and art," asserts Lee B. Hopkins in his *More Books by More People: Interviews with Sixty-five Authors of Books for Children,* adding: "For each one she recruits one or more 'junior literary advisors' who read over her manuscript and help her select the works of art to be photographed. And she listens to them!" In addition to collaborating with young people on her many books, Glubok also worked with her husband, Alfred Tamarin, before his death in 1980.

Critics often praise the clear prose style, carefully selected artwork, and remarkable photographs of Glubok's books, although a *Kirkus Service* contributor points out that Glubok's "approach gives primacy to experiencing art over studying art, which is not inappropriate for the age level, but it also has a built-in limitation: the author tells only what *she* thinks the child wants to know or should know." Hopkins, however, believes that Glubok's books "open the door to the world of art and history to readers of all ages. Leafing through [the books] is almost as good as going to the best museum, for they impart tremendous understanding and appreciation of the art world."

Glubok once commented on what she wishes her writing to achieve: "My aim is to introduce young readers to the great art treasures of the world and to try and understand the people who made them. By appreciating the beauty of other cultures, we can all make our own lives more beautiful and understand ourselves a little bit better."

BIOGRAPHICAL/CRITICAL SOURCES:

BOOKS

Arbuthnot, May Hill, and Zena Sutherland, *Children and Books,* 4th edition, Scott, Foresman, 1972, pp. 598-599.

Children's Literature Review, Volume 1, Gale, 1976.
Hopkins, Lee B., *More Books by More People: Interviews with Sixty-five Authors of Books for Children,* Citation, 1974, pp. 187-193.
Something about the Author Autobiography Series, Volume 7, Gale, 1989, pp. 59-73.

PERIODICALS

Booklist, September 1, 1970; July 1, 1972; January 1, 1973; July 1, 1973.
Bulletin of the Center for Children's Books, July-August, 1970; December, 1970; November, 1972; March, 1973; September, 1973; April, 1974; September, 1974; July-August, 1975; May, 1976; January, 1977; May, 1977; February, 1978; September, 1978; October, 1978; April, 1979; October, 1979; June, 1980; October, 1984.
Childhood Education, January, 1974.
Cricket, May, 1978.
Horn Book, February, 1970; February, 1973; August, 1973; April, 1974; April, 1976; June, 1976; August, 1976; December, 1976; December, 1977; June, 1978; August, 1979; January-February, 1985.
Kirkus Reviews, May 1, 1968, p. 514; April 1, 1970; May 1, 1972; October 1, 1972; April 15, 1973; November 1, 1973; April 1, 1974; April 15, 1975.
Library Journal, January 15, 1974.
New York Times Book Review, June 2, 1974; April 9, 1978; April 14, 1978; April 30, 1978.
Publishers Weekly, January 15, 1973; May 6, 1974; April 28, 1975; January 5, 1976; August 15, 1977.
School Library Journal, September, 1970; September, 1975; December, 1976; January, 1978; September, 1979; September, 1980; February, 1985; May, 1989; May, 1990.
Science Books, May, 1970.

*   *   *

GODWIN, Gail (Kathleen) 1937-

PERSONAL: Born June 18, 1937, in Birmingham, AL; daughter of Mose Winston and Kathleen (a teacher and writer; maiden name, Krahenbuhl) Godwin; married Douglas Kennedy (a photographer), 1960 (divorced, 1961); married Ian Marshall (a psychiatrist), 1965 (divorced, 1966). *Education:* Attended Peace Junior College, 1955-57; University of North Carolina, B.A., 1959; University of Iowa, M.A., 1968, Ph.D. in English, 1971.

ADDRESSES: Home—P.O. Box 946, Woodstock, NY 12498. *Agent*—John Hawkins, Paul R. Reynolds, Inc., 71 West 23rd St., New York, NY 10010.

CAREER: Miami Herald, Miami, FL, reporter, 1959-60; U.S. Embassy, London, England, travel consultant in U.S.

Travel Service, 1962-65; University of Iowa, Iowa City, instructor in English literature, 1967-71, instructor in Writer's Workshop, 1972-73; University of Illinois, Center for Advanced Studies, Urbana-Champaign, fellow, 1971-72; writer. Special lecturer in Brazil for United States Information Service, State Department Cultural Program, spring, 1976; lecturer in English and creative writing at colleges and universities, including Vassar College, spring, 1977, and Columbia University, beginning fall, 1978.

MEMBER: PEN, Authors Guild, American Society of Composers, Authors, and Publishers (ASCAP).

AWARDS, HONORS: National Endowment for the Arts grant in creative writing, 1974-75; nominated for a National Book Award, 1974, for *The Odd Woman;* Guggenheim fellowship in creative writing, 1975-76; National Endowment for the Arts grant for librettists, 1977-78; nominated for American Book Awards, 1980, for *Violet Clay,* and 1982, for *A Mother and Two Daughters;* Award in Literature, American Institute and Academy of Arts and Letters, 1981.

WRITINGS:

NOVELS

The Perfectionists, Harper, 1970.
Glass People, Knopf, 1972.
The Odd Woman, Knopf, 1974.
Violet Clay, Knopf, 1978.
A Mother and Two Daughters, Viking, 1982.
The Finishing School, Viking, 1985.
A Southern Family, Morrow, 1987.
Father Melancholy's Daughter, Morrow, 1991.
The Good Husband, Ballantine, 1994.

OTHER

Dream Children (short stories), Knopf, 1976.
Mr. Bedford and the Muses (a novella and short stories), Viking, 1983.
(Editor with Shannon Ravenel) *The Best American Short Stories, 1985,* Houghton, 1985.

Contributor to books, including *The Writer on Her Work* (essays), edited by Janet Sternburg, Norton, 1980; and *Real Life* (short stories), Doubleday, 1981. Also contributor of essays and short stories to periodicals, including *Atlantic, Antaeus, Ms., Harper's, Writer, McCall's, Cosmopolitan, North American Review, Paris Review,* and *Esquire.* Reviewer for *North American Review, New York Times Book Review, Chicago Tribune Book World,* and *New Republic.* Member of editorial board of *Writer.*

Librettist of musical works by Robert Starer, *The Last Lover,* produced in Katonah, NY, 1975; *Journals of a Songmaker,* produced in Pittsburgh, PA, with Pittsburgh Symphony Orchestra, 1976; *Apollonia,* produced in Minneapolis, MN, 1979; *Anna Margarita's Will,* recorded by C.R.I., 1980; and *Remembering Felix,* 1987, recorded by Spectrum, 1989.

SIDELIGHTS: "More than any other contemporary writer, Gail Godwin reminds me of 19th century pleasures, civilized, passionate about ideas, ironic about passions," states Carol Sternhell in a *Village Voice* review of *The Finishing School.* "Her characters—sensible, intelligent women all—have houses, histories, ghosts; they comfortably inhabit worlds both real and literary, equally at home in North Carolina, Greenwich Village and the England of *Middlemarch.*" Godwin's protagonists are modern women, though, often creative and frequently Southern. And like many other writers of her era, she tends to focus "sharply on the relationships of men and women who find their roles no longer clearly delineated by tradition and their freedom yet strange and not entirely comfortable," as Carl Solana Weeks says in *Dictionary of Literary Biography.* "Godwin's great topic," notes Lee Smith, reviewing *Father Melancholy's Daughter* in the *Los Angeles Times Book Review,* "is woman's search for identity: A death in the family frequently precipitates this search. The tension between art and real life (many of her women are artists or would-be artists) is another thematic constant in her work. Her literate, smart women characters possess the free will to make choices, to take responsibility for their lives."

Literature has figured in Godwin's life from an early age. She grew up in Asheville, North Carolina, in the shadow of another writer, Thomas Wolfe. During the war her mother was a reporter, and Godwin recalls in an essay in *The Writer on Her Work* that "whenever Mrs. Wolfe called up the paper to announce, 'I have just remembered something else about Tom,' " her mother "was sent off immediately to the dead novelist's home on Spruce Street." Godwin's parents were divorced, and while Godwin was growing up, her mother taught writing and wrote love stories on the weekend to support her daughter while Godwin's grandmother ran the house. And although her mother never sold any of her novels, Godwin writes in the essay, "already, at five, I had allied myself with the typewriter rather than the stove. The person at the stove usually had the thankless task of fueling. Whereas, if you were faithful to your vision at the typewriter, by lunchtime you could make two more characters happy—even if you weren't so happy yourself. What is more, if you retyped your story neatly in the afternoon and sent it off in a manila envelope to New York, you'd get a check back for $100 within two or three weeks (300 words to the page, 16-17 pages, 2 cents a word: in 1942, $100 went a long way)." Godwin told *CA* that her mother was her first teacher, saying, "She was doing things with her mind, using her imagination and making something out of nothing, really. I remember when she would read to me at night. My favorite book that she read was a little empty address book—it had a picture of some faraway place on the front—and she would read stories out of this blank book. It was just fascinating."

Not that her grandmother was dispensable. Godwin indicates in *The Writer on Her Work* that "in our manless little family, she also played the mother and could be counted on to cook, sew on buttons, polish the piano, and give encouragement to creative endeavors. She was my mother's first reader, while the stories were still in their morning draft; 'It moves a little slowly here,' she'd say, or 'I didn't understand why the girl did this.' And the tempo would be stepped up, the heroine's ambiguous action sharpened in the afternoon draft; for if my grandmother didn't follow tempo and motive, how would all those other women who would buy the magazines?"

Godwin didn't meet her father until he showed up many years later at her high school graduation when, she recalls in the essay, he introduced himself and she flung herself, "weeping," into his arms. He invited her to come and live with him, which she did, briefly, before he shot and killed himself like the lovable ne'er-do-well Uncle Ambrose in *Violet Clay.*

After graduating from the University of North Carolina, Godwin was hired as a reporter for the *Miami Herald* and was reluctantly fired a year later by a bureau chief who had failed to make a good reporter out of her. She married her first husband, newspaper photographer Douglas Kennedy, around that time. After her divorce, she completed her first novel, *Gull Key,* the story of "a young wife left alone all day on a Florida island while her husband slogs away at his job on the mainland," according to Godwin in *The Writer on Her Work.* (She worked on the book during her slow hours at the U.S. Travel Service in London.) Having submitted the manuscript to several English publishers without good results, she relates that she even sent a copy to a fly-by-night agency that advertised in a magazine, "WANTED: UNPUBLISHED NOVELS IN WHICH WOMEN'S PROBLEMS AND LOVE INTERESTS ARE PREDOMINANT. ATTRACTIVE TERMS." She was never able to track down the agency or anyone associated with it.

Not satisfied with her work at the time, Godwin found focussing on characters and themes outside of herself to be helpful. She got the idea for one of her most highly-regarded short stories, "An Intermediate Stop" (now included in her collection *Dream Children*), in a writing class at the London City Literary Institute after the teacher instructed the students to write a 450-word story beginning with the sentence, " '*Run away,' he muttered to himself, sitting up and biting his nails.*" Godwin writes in

The Writer on Her Work that "when that must be your first sentence, it sort of excludes a story about a woman in her late twenties, adrift among the options of wifehood, career, vocation, a story that I had begun too many times already—both in fiction and reality—and could not resolve. My teacher wisely understood Gide's maxim for himself as writer: 'The best means of learning to know oneself is seeking to understand others.' "

Godwin describes "An Intermediate Stop" as a story "about an English vicar who has seen God, who writes a small book about his experience, and becomes famous. He gets caught up in the international lecture-tour circuit. My story shows him winding up his exhausting American tour at a small Episcopal college for women in the South. He is at his lowest point, having parroted back his own written words until he has lost touch with their meaning." *New York Times* critic Anatole Broyard indicates that, here, "another kind of epiphany—in the form of a [young woman]—restores his faith. The brilliance with which this girl is evoked reminds us that love and religion both partake of the numinous." A draft of the story also got the author accepted into the University of Iowa Writer's Workshop.

Godwin's novel, *The Perfectionists,* a draft of which was her Ph.D. thesis at Iowa, was published in 1970. It relates the story of the disintegrating "perfect" marriage of a psychiatrist and his wife while they are vacationing in Majorca with the man's son. Robert Scholes in *Saturday Review* writes that "the eerie tension that marks this complex relationship is the great achievement of the novel. It is an extraordinary accomplishment, which is bound to attract and hold many readers." Scholes describes the book as "too good, too clever, and too finished a product to be patronized as a 'first novel.' " Joyce Carol Oates in the *New York Times Book Review* calls it "a most intelligent and engrossing novel" and "the paranoid tragedy of our contemporary worship of self-consciousness, of constant analysis."

In Godwin's *Glass People,* Francesca Bolt, pampered and adored wife in a flawless but sterile marital environment, leaves her husband in a brief bid for freedom. This book, too, is praised as "a formally executed, precise, and altogether professional short novel" by Oates in *Book World.* Weeks indicates, however, that in *Glass People,* Godwin is exploring "a theme introduced in *The Perfectionists,* that of a resolution of woman's dilemma through complete self-abnegation; but the author, already suspicious of this alternative in her first novel, presents it here as neither fully convincing nor ironic." As the *New York Times Book Review* critic asks: "Are we really to root for blankminded Francesca to break free, when her author has promised us throughout that she's totally incapable of doing so?" Genevieve Stuttaford, though, in *Saturday Re-*

view, argues that "the characters in *Glass People* are meticulously drawn and effectively realized, the facets of their personalities subtly, yet precisely, laid bare. The author is cooly neutral, and she makes no judgements. This is the way it is, Godwin is saying, and you must decide who the villains are."

"Marking a major advance in Godwin's development as a novelist," reports Weeks in *Dictionary of Literary Biography,* "her third book, *The Odd Woman,* is twice as long as either of her previous novels, not from extension of plot but from a wealth of incidents told in flashback and in fantasy and a more thorough realization of present action." The odd woman of the book, "odd" in this case meaning not paired with another person, is Jane Clifford, a thirty-two-year-old teacher of Romantic and Victorian literature at a midwestern college, who is engaged in a sporadic love affair with an art historian who teaches at another school. For Jane, Susan E. Lorsch point out in *Critique,* "the worlds of fiction and the 'real' world are one." Not only does Jane experience "literary worlds as real," continues Lorsch, "she treats the actual world as if it were an aesthetic creation." Lorsch further notes that "the entire book moves toward the climax and the completion of Jane's perception that the worlds of life and art are far from identical."

The Odd Woman's major theme, Anne Z. Mickelson suggests in *Reaching Out: Sensitivity and Order in Recent American Fiction by Women,* is "how to achieve freedom while in union with another person, and impose one's own order on life so as to find self-fulfillment." Because literature is explored in the novel as one means of giving shape to life, the book is generally regarded as cerebral and allusive. In *Times Literary Supplement* critic Victoria Glendinning's words, the book is "too closely or specifically tied to its culture" to be considered universal. Lore Dickstein, however, in the *New York Times Book Review,* calls the novel "a pleasure to read. Godwin's prose is elegant, full of nuance and feeling, and sparkling with ironic humor."

Violet Clay, Weeks comments, confirms Godwin's "mastery of the full, free narrative technique of *The Odd Woman*—the integration of fantasy and flashback into the narrative line—while also recalling the clean, classic structure of her two earlier novels." Weeks continues, "In *Violet Clay* Godwin raises a question that is central to understanding her work as a whole: what is the relationship between the artist and her art? The answer implied in Violet Clay's achievement as a painter reflects directly Godwin's ideals as a writer."

The title character of the novel, Violet Clay, leaves the South for New York at age twenty-four to become an artist, but "nine years later," John Leonard explains in the

New York Times, "all that she paints are covers on Gothic romances for a paperback publishing house." Violet finally loses her job at Harrow House because the new art director wants to use photographs of terrorized women on the jackets of the romances rather than the idealized paintings Violet creates. When Violet finds out that her only living relative, Uncle Ambrose, a failed writer, has shot himself, she journeys to the Plommet Falls, New York, cabin in which he died to claim his body and bury him. And, in *Washington Post Book World* critic Susan Shreve's words, "she decides to stay on and face the demons with her paint and brush."

Violet Clay reflects "the old-fashioned assumption that character develops and is good for something besides the daily recital to one's analyst," points out a *Harper's* critic. In Leonard's opinion, however, *Violet Clay* is "too intelligent for its own good. It is overgrown with ideas. You can't see the feelings for the ideas." Katha Pollitt in the *New York Times Book Review* comments that *Violet Clay* "has the pep-talk quality of so many recent novels in which the heroine strides off the last page, her own woman at last." As Sternhell argues, though, Godwin's novels "are not about book-ness, not about the *idea* of literature, but about human beings who take ideas seriously. Clever abstracts are not her medium: her 'vital artistic subject,' like Violet Clay's is, will always be the 'living human figure.'"

Godwin's next novel, *A Mother and Two Daughters,* is a comedy of manners which portrays women who "are able to achieve a kind of balance, to find ways of fully becoming themselves that don't necessitate a rejection of everything in their heritage," Susan Wood relates in *Washington Post Book World*. Set against a current-events background of the Iranian revolution, Three Mile Island, and Skylab, the novel opens in the changing town of Mountain City, North Carolina (a fictional city), with the death of Leonard Strickland of a heart attack as he is driving home with his wife from a party. The book records "the reactions and relationships of his wife Nell and daughters Cate and Lydia, both in their late thirties, as the bereavement forces each of them to evaluate the achievement and purpose of their own lives," Jennifer Uglow writes in the *Times Literary Supplement*. Josephine Hendin writes in the *New York Times Book Review,* "As each woman exerts her claims on the others, as each confronts the envy and anger the others can inspire, Gail Godwin orchestrates their entanglements with great skill." And "for the first time," according to John F. Baker in *Publishers Weekly,* "Godwin enters several very different minds and personalities, those of her three protagonists."

Godwin once told Baker that she thinks of *A Mother and Two Daughters* as "a broadening of my canvas," remarking, "It most surprised me that I could get into the head

of an elderly woman, but in fact it was easy. Nell's state of calm acceptance, her ability to sense the stillness at the center of things, is what I most aspire to." Nell, Lisa Schwarzbaum comments in the *Detroit News,* "raised to be a gracious gentlewoman—albeit sharper, more direct, less genteel, more 'North-thinking' than the other good ladies of Mountain City, N.C.—faces her future without the philosophical, steadying man on whom she had relied so thoroughly for support and definition." Here, according to Anne Tyler in the *New Republic,* Godwin provides the reader with a "meticulous" documentation of small-town life with its "rituals of Christmas party and book club meeting."

Not content to focus only on the three main characters, though, Godwin portrays "one great enormous pot of people," declares Caroline Moorhead in *Spectator,* a whole "series of characters in all their intertwined relationships with each other, each other's lovers, children, parents, acquaintances." According to Uglow, the cast of *A Mother and Two Daughters* includes "a Southern *grande dame* with a pregnant teenage protege; a pesticide baron with two sons, one retarded, the other gay; a hillbilly relative whose nose was bitten off in a brawl; [and] a one-legged Vietnam veteran whose wife runs a local nursery school." Christopher Lehmann-Haupt, in the *New York Times,* says that these characters are amazingly vivid, citing "the sense one gets that their lives are actually unfolding in the same world as yours." Tyler indicates that "there's an observant, amused, but kindly eye at work here, and not a single cheap shot is taken at these people who might so easily have been caricatures in someone else's hands."

A Mother and Two Daughters is "the richest, and most universal" of Godwin's books, "with a wholeness about its encompassing view of a large Southern family," according to Louise Sweeney in *Christian Science Monitor,* and is widely regarded as an unusually artful bestseller, appealing not only to the general public but also to Godwin's longtime followers. *Washington Post Book World* reviewer Jonathan Yardley finds *A Mother and Two Daughters* "a work of complete maturity and artistic control, one that I'm fully confident will find a permanent and substantial place in our national literature." He further comments that Godwin "turns out—this was not really evident in her four previous books—to be a stunningly gifted novelist of manners."

In *The Finishing School,* Godwin uses a first-person voice to create "a narrative of humanly impressive energies, as happy-sad in its texture as life itself may be said to be," according to William H. Pritchard in the *New Republic*. Shifting from one age perspective to another, Justin Stokes, a successful forty-year-old actress, tells the story of the summer she turns fourteen and her life is changed forever when she undergoes what *Time* reviewer Paul

Gray calls "a brief but harrowing rite of passage toward maturity." After her father and grandparents die in quick succession, the young Justin, her mother, and her brother leave Fredericksburg, Virginia, to live with her aunt in an upstate New York industrial town. There she makes friends with the local bohemian, Ursula DeVane, a forty-four-year-old failed actress who lives with her brother Julian, a talented musician of little consequence, in an old rundown home.

Ursula takes Justin on as her protegee, and they begin to meet in an old stone hut in the woods, the "Finishing School," in which Ursula "enthralls Justin with tales of her past and encourages her artistic aspirations," as Susan Wood puts it in the *Washington Post Book World.* The novel "charts the exhilaration, the enchantment, the transformation, then the inevitable disillusionment and loss inherent in such a friendship and self-discovery," according to Frances Taliaferro in the *New York Times Book Review.* And, as Sternhell relates, it is essentially "the tale of a daughter with two mothers." Where *A Mother and Two Daughters* "was symphonic—many movements, many instruments—*The Finishing School* plays a gentle, chilling theme with variations." Sternhell further comments that the book, despite its realistic form, "often reads like a fable, a contemporary myth; daughters love mothers, and—variations on a theme—daughters betray mothers, repeatedly, inevitably."

The Finishing School may be "old fashioned," according to Lehmann-Haupt, "in its preoccupation with such Aristotelian verities as plot, reversal, discovery, and the tragic flaw. But Miss Godwin's power to isolate and elevate subtle feelings makes her traditional story seem almost innovative." Although it doesn't quite meet the definition of true tragedy, the book is "a finely nuanced, compassionate psychological novel, subtler and more concentrated" than *A Mother and Two Daughters,* Taliaferro maintains. And Lehmann-Haupt points out that Godwin's characters serve to lend the novel a variety "as well as to distinguish the two worlds that Justin Stokes inhabits—the two dimensional world of the [industrial] lookalikes and the rich, mysterious kingdom where 'art's redemptive power' is supposed to prevail." The characterization of Justin "is one of the most trustworthy portraits of an adolescent in current literature" says Taliaferro, and the book itself, she concludes, is "a wise contribution to the literature of growing up."

With her seventh novel, *A Southern Family,* published in 1987, Godwin returns to the setting of Mountain City first found in *A Mother and Two Daughters.* Another novel of manners in the Victorian tradition, this work revolves around the death of a member of the Quick family. Theo, a twenty-eight-year-old divorced father of a young son, is found dead after he apparently killed his girlfriend and

committed suicide. The novel focusses on reactions from family members, including novelist Clare, her quirky mother Lily, and Clare's alcoholic half-brother Rafe. *A Southern Family,* according to Susan Heeger in the *Los Angeles Times Book Review,* "takes off from Theo's death on a discursive exploration of family history and relationships as the Quicks struggle to measure their blame and—belatedly—to know the brother and son they failed in life." Several reviewers consider *A Southern Family* to be one of Godwin's most accomplished works. "Suffice it to say that *A Southern Family* is an ambitious book that entirely fulfills its ambitions," declares Yardley in *Washington Post Book World.* "Not merely is it psychologically acute, it is dense with closely observed social and physical detail that in every instance is exactly right." Likewise, Beverly Lowry, writing in the *New York Times Book Review,* proclaims that Godwin's *A Southern Family* "is the best she's written," concluding that Godwin's works "all give evidence of a supple intelligence working on the page."

Father Melancholy's Daughter, published in 1991, is the story of Margaret Gower, whose mother Ruth, when Margaret is six years old, leaves the family and is killed in a car crash a year later. Margaret and her father, Walter, an Episcopal priest, are thrust into an especially close father-daughter relationship in which much of their time is devoted to puzzling over Ruth's absence. The narrative switches time tracks from twenty-two-year-old Margaret, who is in love with a fortyish counselor named Adrian Bonner, to the younger Margaret of Ruth's disappearance. Calling the novel "a penetrating study of a child's coming to terms with her world," Nancy Wigston in the Toronto *Globe and Mail* writes in her conclusion that "The real achievement here is Margaret herself: Gail Godwin has created that rarity in fiction, a character who evolves, believably." *New York Times Book Review* contributor Richard Bausch, however, expresses dissatisfaction with Margaret's lack of self-awareness, but he attests that the novel has "a number of real satisfactions, namely the characters that surround Margaret and her father—the parishioners of St. Cuthbert's. . . . Gail Godwin is almost Chaucerian in her delivery of these people, with their small distinguishing characteristics and their vibrant physicality." Gray writes in *Time,* "Born in the South, Godwin appears to be one of those writers who inherited a subject for life; then she developed the wisdom and talent to make her birthright seem constantly fresh and enthralling."

BIOGRAPHICAL/CRITICAL SOURCES:

BOOKS

Contemporary Literary Criticism, Gale, Volume 5, 1976, Volume 8, 1978, Volume 31, 1985, Volume 69, 1992.

Dictionary of Literary Biography, Volume 6: *American Novelists since World War II,* Gale, 1981.

Godwin, Gail, *Violet Clay,* Knopf, 1978.

Godwin, Gail, *The Finishing School,* Viking, 1985.

Mickelson, Anne Z., *Reaching Out: Sensitivity and Order in Recent American Fiction by Women,* Scarecrow, 1979.

Sternburg, Janet, editor, *The Writer on Her Work,* Norton, 1980.

PERIODICALS

America, December 21, 1974; April 17, 1982.

Atlantic, May, 1976; October, 1979.

Book World, October 1, 1972.

Boston Globe, February 21, 1982.

Chicago Tribune Book World, January 10, 1982; October 16, 1983; January 27, 1984; October 25, 1987.

Christian Science Monitor, November 20, 1974; April 1, 1976; June 23, 1978; July 21, 1983; September 2, 1983.

Commonweal, June 1, 1984.

Critique, winter, 1978.

Critique: Studies in Modern Fiction, number 3, 1980.

Detroit Free Press, March 10, 1985.

Detroit News, April 11, 1982; October 16, 1983; February 10, 1985.

Globe and Mail (Toronto), April 13, 1991, p. C6.

Harper's, July, 1978.

Listener, June 9, 1977.

Los Angeles Times, November 13, 1981.

Los Angeles Times Book Review, September 11, 1983; February 24, 1985; February 9, 1986; October 4, 1987; March 3, 1991, pp. 2, 11.

Miami Herald, February 29, 1976.

Ms., January, 1982.

National Review, September 15, 1978.

New Republic, January 25, 1975; July 8, 1978; February 17, 1982; December 19, 1983; February 25, 1985.

New Statesman, August 15, 1975.

Newsweek, February 23, 1976; January 11, 1982; September 12, 1983; February 25, 1985.

New Yorker, November 18, 1974; January 18, 1982.

New York Review of Books, February 20, 1975; April 1, 1976; July 20, 1978.

New York Times, September 21, 1972; September 30, 1974; February 16, 1976; May 18, 1978; December 22, 1981; September 6, 1983; October 4, 1983; January 24, 1985; December 15, 1985; September 21, 1987.

New York Times Book Review, June 7, 1970; October 15, 1972; October 20, 1974; February 22, 1976; May 21, 1978; January 10, 1982; September 18, 1983; January 27, 1985; August 10, 1986; October 11, 1987; March 3, 1991, p. 7.

New York Times Magazine, December 15, 1985.

Observer, February 5, 1984.

Pacific Sun, September 23-29, 1983.

Progressive, October, 1978.

Publishers Weekly, January 15, 1982.

Saturday Review, August 8, 1970; October 28, 1972; February 21, 1976; June 10, 1978; January, 1982.

Spectator, January 15, 1977; September 2, 1978; February 6, 1982.

Sunday Star-Telegram (Ft. Worth), February 14, 1982.

Time, January 25, 1982; February 11, 1985; October 5, 1987, p. 82.

Times (London), February 18, 1982; March 28, 1985.

Times Literary Supplement, July 23, 1971; July 4, 1975; September 15, 1978; March 5, 1982; February 17, 1984; November 20, 1987, p. 1274; May 24, 1991, p. 21.

Village Voice, March 30, 1982; February 26, 1985.

Washington Post, February 7, 1983; March 7, 1991, p. D1.

Washington Post Book World, May 21, 1978; December 13, 1981; September 11, 1983; February 3, 1985; September 13, 1987; March 17, 1991, p. 4.

Writer, September, 1975; December, 1976.

*   *   *

GOOCH, Steve 1945-

PERSONAL: Born July 22, 1945, in Surrey, England. *Education:* Trinity College, Cambridge, B.A. (with honors), 1967; graduate study at St. John's College, Cambridge, 1967-68, and University of Birmingham, 1968-69.

ADDRESSES: Home—7 Winterbourne Road, Thornton Heath, Surrey CR7 7QX, England. *Agent*—Casarotto Ramsay Ltd., National House, 60-66 Wardour St., London W1V 3HP, England.

CAREER: Free-lance writer and theatrical director, 1969-72; *Plays and Players,* London, England, assistant editor, 1972-73; Half Moon Theatre, London, resident dramatist, 1973-74; Greenwich Theatre, London, resident dramatist, 1974-75; director, lecturer, and writer, 1975-81; *Platform* magazine, co-editor, 1979-1982; Solent Peoples Theatre, Southampton, England, resident dramatist, 1981-82; Theatre Venture, London, resident dramatist, 1983-84; writer, 1984—; Warehouse Theatre, Croydon, resident dramatist, 1986-87; Gate Theatre, London, resident dramatist, 1990-91. Also worked as teacher and translator; served on Arts Council of Great Britain's Theatre Writing Committee, 1983-87.

MEMBER: Theatre Writers Union (member of negotiating team).

AWARDS, HONORS: Arts Council scholarship, 1973; award from Thames Television, 1974, for *The Women-Pirates Ann Bonney and Mary Read.*

WRITINGS:

(Translator) Wolf Biermann, *Poems and Ballads,* Pluto Press, 1977.

(Translator) Guenther Wallraff, *Walraff, the Undesirable Journalist,* Pluto Press, 1978.

All Together Now, Methuen, 1984.

Writing a Play, A & C Black, 1988.

PUBLISHED PLAYS

Big Wolf (two-act; translation and adaptation of play by Harald Mueller; first produced on the West End at Royal Court Theatre, April, 1972), Davis Poynter, 1972.

Will Wat: If Not, What Will? (two-act; first produced in London at Half Moon Theatre, May, 1972), Pluto Press, 1975.

Female Transport (two-act; first produced in London at Half Moon Theatre, November, 1973; produced in New York City, 1976; produced in Paris, 1987), Pluto Press, 1975.

(With Paul Thompson) *The Motor Show* (two-act; first produced in Dagenham, England, March, 1974; produced in London at Half Moon Theatre, March, 1974), Pluto Press, 1975.

The Mother (two-act; translation and adaptation of play by Bertolt Brecht; first produced in London at Half Moon Theatre, May, 1972), Eyre Methuen, 1978.

The Women-Pirates Ann Bonney and Mary Read (two-act; first produced on the West End at Aldwych Theatre, August, 1978), Pluto Press, 1978.

Cock-Artist (one-act; translation of play by R. W. Fassbinder; first produced in London at Almost Free Theatre, November, 1974), published in *Gambit 39/40,* J. Calder, 1982.

Landmark (also see below; two-act; first produced in Essex, England at Essex University, December, 1980), Theatre Action Press, 1982.

Fast One (two-act; first produced in England at Solent Peoples Theatre, February, 1982), Solent Peoples Theatre, 1982.

Home Work (one-act; translation of play by F. X. Kroetz; produced at Battersea Arts Centre, London, 1990), published in *Gambit 39/40,* John Calder, 1982.

Taking Liberties (two-act; first produced in London at Theatre Venture, 1984), Theatre Venture, 1984.

Massa (two-act; first produced at Central School of Speech and Drama, 1989) New Cross Publications, 1990.

Lulu (two-act; translation of plays by Frank Wedekind; first produced by Red Shift Theatre Co., 1990), Absolute Press, 1990.

The Marquis of Keith (two-act; translation of play by Frank Wedekind; first produced by Gate Theatre, 1990), Absolute Press, 1990.

Also author of *Mister Fun* (two-act; first produced by Metro Theatre Co. in Sheffield, 1986; produced in Paris, 1987), published by Metro.

UNPUBLISHED PLAYS

Great Expectations (two-act; adaptation of novel by Charles Dickens), first produced in Liverpool, England, at Liverpool Playhouse, December, 1970.

Man Is Man (two-act; translation and adaptation of play by Brecht), first produced on the West End at Royal Court Theatre, March, 1971.

It's All for the Best (two-act; adaptation of Voltaire's *Candide*), first produced in Stoke-on-Trent, England, at Victoria Theatre, May, 1972.

Nick (one-act), first produced in Exeter, England, at Northcott Theatre, November, 1972.

Dick (two-act), first produced in London at Half Moon Theatre, December, 1973.

(Co-author) *Strike '26* (two-act), first produced on tour by Popular Theatre, May, 1975.

(Co-author) *Made in Britain* (two-act), first produced in Oxford, England, at Oxford Playhouse, May, 1976.

Our Land Our Lives (two-act; earlier version of *Landmark*), first produced on tour by 7:84 Touring Theatre Company, October, 1976.

Back Street Romeo (two-act), first produced in London at Half Moon Theatre, February, 1977.

Rosie (one-act; translation of play by Mueller), first produced in London at Half Moon Theatre, June, 1977.

(With Paul Thompson and Michelene Wandor) *Future Perfect,* first produced in England, 1980.

Fuente Ovejuna (two-act; adaptation of play by Lope de Vega), first produced by Theatre Venture, 1983.

Good for You (two-act), first produced in Leicester, England, March, 1985.

Star Turns (two-act), first produced by Warehouse Theatre, Croydon, 1987.

St. Joan of the Stockyards (two-act; translation of a work by Brecht), first produced at Derby Playhouse, 1988.

Our Say (two-act), first produced in Wednesbury, England, 1989.

OTHER

Translator of radio plays, including "The Kiosk" by Askenazy, 1970; "Delinquent" by Mueller, 1978; and "Santis" by Martin Walser, 1980. Author of original radio plays, including "What They Want" (based on Terence's *The Brothers*), 1983; and *Bill of Health,* 1987. Unproduced and unpublished plays include "How the Peace Was Lost," "Passed On," "Trumpets and Drums" (translation of play by Brecht), "In the Club," "Fatzer" (reconstruction of play by Brecht), "Running Wild" and "Free Time."

WORK IN PROGRESS: Volume of adaptations for New Cross Press, including *Back Street Romeo, What They Want,* and *Fuente Ovejuna;* "Dark Glory," a play about the early life of Alfred Lord Tennyson; "Loving Me," a play about "Red Emma" Goldman and the "Hobo King" Doc Reitman.

SIDELIGHTS: Steve Gooch told *CA:* "From *Female Transport* in 1973 (which has now received over 250 productions around the world) to *Dark Glory* in 1993, my plays have set themselves outside both the social and aesthetic values of established, mainstream theatre. Whether intended for performance to a specific community, or written for a more general audience, they have attempted to articulate the collective dynamic of life for those who—by virtue of class, gender or both—find themselves on the receiving end of governing policy.

"This is a world of differing languages, where not so much the reality of the characters' situation but their conflicting views of it are the main source of tension. It is also a world of multiple relationships, where the one-to-one confrontations of traditional drama are replaced by the group dynamics of modern life. In pursuing these ends, the plays have moved towards a distinct dramatic principle, in which those listening are as important as those speaking."

*   *   *

GOODALL, Jane   1934-
(Jane van Lawick-Goodall)

PERSONAL: Born April 3, 1934, in London, England; daughter of Mortimer Herbert (a businessman and motor car racer) and Myfanwe (an author under name Vanne Goodall; maiden name Joseph) Goodall; married Hugo van Lawick (a nature photographer), March 28, 1964 (divorced); married Derek Bryceson (a member of Parliament and director of Tanzania National Parks), 1973 (deceased); children: (first marriage) Hugo Eric Louis. *Education:* Attended Uplands School, England; Cambridge University, Ph.D., 1965. *Religion:* Church of England. *Avocational Interests:* Riding, photography, reading, classical music.

ADDRESSES: Home and office—Gombe Stream Research Centre, P.O. Box 185, Kigoma, Tanzania, East Africa.

CAREER: Gombe Stream Research Centre, Tanzania, East Africa, ethologist, 1960—; writer, 1965—. Assistant secretary to Dr. Louis S. B. Leakey, 1960; assistant curator of National Museum of Natural History, Nairobi, Kenya, 1960. Visiting professor of psychiatry and human biology, Stanford University, 1970-75; honorary visiting professor of zoology, University of Dar Es Salaam, Tanzania, 1972—.

MEMBER: American Academy of Arts and Sciences (honorary foreign member, 1972—).

AWARDS, HONORS: Wilkie Brothers Foundation grant, 1960; two Franklin Burr prizes from National Geographic Society; gold medal for conservation from San Diego Zoological Society; conservation award from New York Zoological Society; J. Paul Getty Wildlife Conservation Prize, 1984; R. R. Hawkins Award from Association of American Publishers, 1987, for *The Chimpanzees of Gombe: Patterns of Behavior.*

WRITINGS:

UNDER NAME JANE van LAWICK-GOODALL

(Contributor) Irven De Vore, editor, *Primate Behavior,* Holt, 1965.

My Friends the Wild Chimpanzees, with photographs by Hugo van Lawick, National Geographic Society, 1967.

(Contributor) Desmond Morris, editor, *Primate Ethology,* Aldine, 1967.

The Behavior of Free-Living Chimpanzees in the Gombe Stream Reserve (monograph), Tindall & Cassell, 1968.

(With Hugo van Lawick) *Innocent Killers,* Collins, 1970, Houghton, 1971.

In the Shadow of Man, with photographs by Hugo van Lawick, Houghton, 1971, revised edition published under name Jane Goodall, 1988, abbreviated edition published as *Selected from In the Shadow of Man,* Literacy Volunteers of New York City, 1992.

(With Hugo van Lawick) *Grub:·The Bush Baby* (story of authors' son), Houghton, 1972.

UNDER NAME JANE GOODALL

The Chimpanzees of Gombe: Patterns of Behavior, Harvard University Press, 1986.

My Life with Chimpanzees, Simon & Schuster, 1988.

The Chimpanzee Family Book, Picture Book Studio, 1989.

Through a Window: My Thirty Years with the Chimpanzees of Gombe, Houghton, 1990.

The Chimpanzee: The Living Link between 'Man' and 'Beast,' Edinburgh University Press, 1992.

EDITOR; "JANE GOODALL'S ANIMAL WORLD" SERIES

Jane Goodall's Animal World: Chimpanzees, Macmillan, 1989.

Jane Goodall's Animal World: Lions, Macmillan, 1989.

Jane Goodall's Animal World: Hippos, Macmillan, 1989.

Jane Goodall's Animal World: Pandas, Macmillan, 1989.

Jane Goodall's Animal World: Elephants, Macmillan, 1990.

Jane Goodall's Animal World: Gorillas, Macmillan, 1990.
Jane Goodall's Animal World: Sea Otters, Macmillan, 1990.
Jane Goodall's Animal World: Tigers, Macmillan, 1990.

OTHER

Contributor to *National Geographic, Nature, Annals of the New York Academy of Science,* and other journals.

ADAPTATIONS: Several television specials have featured Goodall and her work, including *Miss Goodall and the Wild Chimpanzees,* Columbia Broadcasting System, 1965; *Through a Window* has been adapted for an audio cassette.

WORK IN PROGRESS: Continued research and teaching on chimpanzee behavior.

SIDELIGHTS: Naturalist Jane Goodall has spent more than three decades in the jungles of Tanzania studying the behavior of wild chimpanzees. An animal lover since birth, the gentle Goodall has devoted herself to a quest for deeper understanding of the rich social, biological, and cultural interaction among the species most closely related to man. *New York Times* contributor John Noble Wilford calls Goodall "something of a celebrity: the young Englishwoman who plunges into Africa, spends the days and years in communion with chimpanzees, . . . dispatches occasional learned reports and keeps right on studying the animals she finds so fascinating." Wilford concludes that by virtue of her tenacious and inspiring work, Goodall has become "an authority of the first rank in the study of animal behavior."

Many youngsters dream of becoming wildlife biologists in the wilds of Africa. Goodall was one such child—she spent hours observing the animals in or near her London home and delighted in a toy chimpanzee someone had given her. Soon after graduating from high school, Goodall took an extended trip to Kenya in East Africa. There she became acquainted with Louis S. B. Leakey, a noted naturalist and paleontologist. Leakey was so impressed with Goodall's devotion to wildlife that he gave her a job so she could stay in Africa. Goodall served as an assistant secretary, accompanied the Leakeys on fossil-hunting trips to the remote Olduvai Gorge region, and helped to improve the National Museum of Natural History in Nairobi. In 1960, Leakey proposed a project that proved irresistible to Goodall: a six-month field study of the wild chimpanzees on a reserve in Tanzania.

Goodall had no formal training in ethology (the study of animal behavior) when she began her duties in the Gombe Stream Chimpanzee Reserve. What she did have was a fierce curiosity about her subject and a high tolerance for primitive living conditions in rugged, inhospitable terrain. Fighting malaria and the constant intrusion of cobras, centipedes, and thieving baboons, Goodall attempted to

follow the activities of an elusive band of chimps that lived in the Gombe area. For months she observed the animals through binoculars, slowly moving closer as they became accustomed to her presence. After six months she realized that her task, if done properly, would take years and years. The Leakey family helped to find further funding for the project, and Goodall patiently and painstakingly began to compile a wealth of original observations of wild chimpanzee behavior.

Goodall's many fascinating discoveries are documented in the books she has written, most notably *In the Shadow of Man* and *The Chimpanzees of Gombe: Patterns of Behavior.* Goodall has also been featured in several *National Geographic* television specials. As John H. Crook notes in the *New York Times Book Review,* Goodall's "careful documentation puts the necessary flesh on much that has been merely speculation and corrects earlier accounts of chimpanzee behavior." Among other things, Goodall has observed wild chimps making and using simple tools, stalking and killing small animals for food, battling rival troops of chimps for terrain, and cooperating in such group activities as hunting and defending territory. Most critics agree that the value of Goodall's research lies in the longevity of the project—her unbroken observation of individual animals for a decade or more has led to a number of important discoveries about chimpanzee child rearing, aggression, and personality development. "Jane Goodall's popular books on chimpanzees have the family lines of Tolstoy and the addictive intrigue of a soap opera—the 'Dynasty' of chimps," writes *Washington Post* correspondent Carla Hall.

Goodall did not seek to become a celebrity. Her earliest work—and much of her subsequent writing—is scholarly, aimed at the university-trained specialist. She does realize, however, that lay readers, especially children, are fascinated by primates. According to Denise R. Majkut in *Best Sellers,* throughout Goodall's work the author "comes across as a great lover of nature—loving the beauty of the wild jungles of Africa, the continuing struggle for survival there of the chimps, and man's typical behavior." Indeed, Goodall has taken numerous leaves from her field studies in recent years in order to become a spokesperson for conservation of chimpanzee habitat as well as for humane treatment of captive primates. Goodall especially likes to impart these ideas to children. "I feel it's something I want to spend more time telling children: that animals are like us," she told *Publishers Weekly.* "They feel pain like we do. We want to make people understand that every chimp is an individual, with the same kinds of intellectual abilities."

Goodall is only the eighth person in the history of Cambridge University to have received a Ph.D. without first earning a baccalaureate. The honor was based on a thesis she produced after her first five years in the Gombe Stream Reserve. Bettyann Kevles claims in the *Los Angeles Times Book Review* that Goodall has done more than any other scientist to enlighten humankind about the rich life of chimpanzees. Kevles writes: "Thanks to the painstaking efforts of Goodall and her colleagues, we admire the chimpanzees of Gombe because we understand the complexity of their lives." Now an international traveller who lectures and writes in addition to her field work, Goodall hopes her work will help win new respect for members of the animal kingdom. "I want to make [people] aware that animals have their own needs, emotions, and feelings—they matter," she told *Publishers Weekly*. " . . . I want to give kids a passion, an understanding and awareness of the wonder of animals."

BIOGRAPHICAL/CRITICAL SOURCES:

BOOKS

Coerr, Eleanor B., *Jane Goodall,* Putnam, 1976.
Fox, Mary Virginia, *Jane Goodall: Living Chimp Style,* Dillon, 1981.
Goodall, Jane van Lawick, *In the Shadow of Man,* Houghton, 1971, revised edition, 1988.
Goodall, Jane, and Hugo van Lawick, *Grub: The Bush Baby,* Houghton, 1972.
Goodall, Jane, *My Life with the Chimpanzees,* Simon & Schuster, 1988.
Green, Timothy, *The Restless Spirit: Profiles in Adventure,* Walker & Co., 1970 (published in England as *The Adventurers,* M. Joseph, 1970).

PERIODICALS

American Biology Teacher, May, 1985, pp. 267-269.
American Scientist, May, 1992, p. 290.
Belles Lettres, winter, 1991, p. 59.
Best Sellers, November 15, 1971.
Chicago Tribune, August 24, 1986; February 15, 1987.
Chicago Tribune Book World, October 17, 1971.
Choice, January, 1972.
Christian Science Monitor, October 14, 1971; May 5, 1989, p. 12; October 25, 1990, p. 12.
Economist, October 30, 1971; September 22, 1990, p. 100.
Ladies' Home Journal, October, 1971; February, 1975.
Listener, November 25, 1971.
Los Angeles Times Book Review, December 28, 1986.
McCall's, August, 1970.
Ms., March, 1992, p. 61.
Nation, January 17, 1972.
Natural History, December, 1967.
Nature, November 22, 1990, p. 371.
New Age Journal, November, 1989, p. 68.
New Statesman, December 4, 1970; December 3, 1971.
Newsweek, June 2, 1975; October 1, 1990, p. 69.
New York, September 10, 1990, p. 116.

New Yorker, November 27, 1989, p. 144; December 10, 1990, p. 160.
New York Review of Books, May 30, 1991, p. 43.
New York Times, November 26, 1971; August 19, 1986.
New York Times Book Review, August 24, 1986, p. 1; October 1, 1989, p. 35; October 28, 1990, p. 7.
New York Times Magazine, February 18, 1973.
Observer, September 9, 1990, p. 54; September 22, 1991, p. 59.
Publishers Weekly, November 22, 1970; August 9, 1971; October 2, 1972; January 29, 1988, p. 396.
Saturday Review of Science, February, 1973.
Science Teacher, December, 1990, p. 14.
Small Press, April, 1990, p. 31.
Time, November 30, 1970; November 8, 1971.
Times Literary Supplement, November 20, 1970; November 19, 1971; May 1, 1987, p. 473; November 30, 1990, p. 1299.
Tribune Books (Chicago), November 9, 1986; June 5, 1988, p. 4; October 28, 1990, p. 6; February 9, 1992, p. 8.
U.S. News and World Report, November 5, 1984, p. 81.
Voice Literary Supplement, September, 1986, p. 9.
Washington Post, September 18, 1984; January 24, 1987.
Washington Post Book World, March 13, 1988, p. 10.
World and I, November, 1990, p. 396.

* * *

GOODLAD, John I. 1920-

PERSONAL: Born August 19, 1920, in North Vancouver, British Columbia, Canada; married Evalene M. Pearson, August 23, 1945; children: Stephen John, Mary Paula. *Education:* Vancouver Normal School, teaching certificate, 1939; University of British Columbia, B.A. (first class honors), M.A., 1945; University of Chicago, Ph.D., 1949.

ADDRESSES: Office—Center for Educational Renewal, College of Education, DQ-12, University of Washington, Seattle, WA 98195.

CAREER: Teacher and principal at schools in Surrey, British Columbia, Canada, and director of education at British Columbia Provincial Industrial School for Boys; Emory University, Atlanta, GA, associate professor, 1949-50, professor, director of division of teacher education, and director of Agnes Scott College-Emory University teacher education program, 1950-56; University of Chicago, Chicago, IL, professor and director of Center for Teacher Education, 1956-60; University of California, Los Angeles, professor of education and director of University Elementary School, 1960-85, dean of Graduate School of Education, 1967-83; University of Washington, Seattle, currently professor and director, Center for Educational

Renewal. Director of research and development division, Institute for Development of Educational Activities, 1966-81; first Distinguished Visiting Scholar in Educational Policy, Hoover Institution, 1993.

Council for the Study of Mankind board of directors, member, 1965-71, chairman, 1969-71; member of board of directors, National Foundation for the Improvement of Education, 1970-74, Longview Foundation, 1972—, and Global Perspectives in Education, Inc. (founding member), 1974-86; National Humanities Faculty, member of board of trustees, 1972-76, vice-chairman, 1973-74; UNESCO Institute for Education, member of governing board, 1972-79, vice-chairman, 1974-75. Encyclopaedia Britannica Educational Corp., chairman of educational advisory board, 1966-69, member of board of directors, 1984—; International Learning Cooperative, chairman of professional advisory council and member of governing board, 1978—. Member of President's Task Force on Early Education, 1966-67, and President's Task Force on Education of the Gifted, 1967-68.

MEMBER: American Association of Colleges for Teacher Education (president, 1989-90), National Society for the Study of Education (member of board, 1961-89; chairman, 1972-73), Association for Supervision and Curriculum Development (chairman of publications committee, 1955-57), American Council on Education (chairman of Council on Cooperation in Teacher Education, 1959-62), National Society of College Teachers of Education (president, 1962-63), American Educational Research Association (president, 1967-68), National Academy of Education (founding member; secretary-treasurer, 1971-77).

AWARDS, HONORS: Fellow, Kappa Phi Kappa, 1946-47, Ford Foundation, 1952-53, International Institute of Arts and Letters; *The Nongraded Elementary School* was selected as one of the best education books of 1959 by the Enoch Pratt Library; L.H.D., National College of Education, 1967, University of Louisville, 1968, Southern Illinois University, 1982, Bank Street College of Education, 1984, Niagara University, 1989, State University of New York, College at Brockport, 1991, Miami University, 1991; Phi Lambda Theta selection as one of the outstanding educational books of the year for *Behind the Classroom Door* in 1970-71 and for *The Elementary School in the United States* in 1972-73; LL.D., Kent State University, 1974, Pepperdine University, 1976, Simon Fraser University, 1983, University of Manitoba, 1992; First Award, Phi Delta Kappa, for meritorious contributions to education through research, evaluation, and development, 1975; D.Ed., Eastern Michigan University, 1982; Medal for Distinguished Service, Teachers College, Columbia University, 1983; Distinguished Contribution to Curriculum Award, American Educational Research Association, 1983; Kappa Delta Pi Distinguished Book Award,

1984, and American Educational Research Association Outstanding Book Award, 1985, both for *A Place Called School: Prospects for the Future;* Award for Outstanding Leadership in Educational Reform, California Educational Partnership Consortium, 1986; Crystal Apple Award, California Council on the Education of Teachers, 1989; Litt.D., Montclair State College, 1992; *The Moral Dimensions of Teaching* was selected by the Critic's Choice Panel of the American Educational Studies Association as one of the outstanding recent books in the area of Educational Studies; fund for the Advancement of Education postdoctoral fellow.

WRITINGS:

(With Herrick, Estvan, and Eberman) *The Elementary School,* Prentice-Hall, 1956.

(With Spain and Drummond) *Educational Leadership and the Elementary School Principal,* Holt, 1956.

(With Robert H. Anderson) *The Nongraded Elementary School,* Harcourt, 1959, revised edition, 1963, reprinted, Teachers College Press, 1987.

Planning and Organizing for Teaching, National Education Association, 1963.

School Curriculum Reform in the United States, Fund for the Advancement of Education, 1964.

(Editor) *The Changing American School,* National Society for the Study of Education, 1966.

The Development of a Conceptual System for Dealing with Problems of Curriculum and Instruction, University of California Press, 1966.

(With others) *The Changing School Curriculum,* Fund for the Advancement of Education, 1966.

(With O'Toole and Tyler) *Computers and Information Systems in Education,* Harcourt, 1966.

School, Curriculum, and the Individual, Blaisdell, 1966.

(With Klein and others) *Behind the Classroom Door,* Charles A. Jones Publishing, 1970, revised edition published as *Looking behind the Classroom Door,* 1974.

(Editor and contributor) *Schooling for the Future: Toward Quality and Equality in American Precollgiate Education,* President's Commission on School Finance, 1971.

(Editor with Harold G. Shane) *The Elementary School in the United States,* University of Chicago Press, 1973.

(With Klein, Novotney, and others) *Early Schooling in the United States,* McGraw, 1973.

(With Feshbach and Lombard) *Early Schooling in England and Israel,* McGraw, 1973.

(Editor) Carmen Culver and Gary J. Hoban, *Power to Change: Issues for the Innovative Educator,* McGraw, 1973.

(With Klein, Novotney, Tye, and others) *Toward a Mankind School: An Adventure in Humanistic Education,* McGraw, 1974.

(With others) *The Conventional and the Alternative in Education,* McCutcheon, 1975.

The Dynamics of Educational Change: Toward Responsive Schools, McGraw, 1975.

Facing the Future: Issues in Education and Schooling, McGraw, 1976.

(With others) *Curriculum Inquiry: The Study of Curriculum Practice,* McGraw, 1979.

(Editor with Gary Fenstermacher) *Individual Differences and the Common Curriculum,* University of Chicago Press, 1983.

A Place Called School: Prospects for the Future, McGraw, 1984.

(Editor) *The Ecology of School Renewal,* University of Chicago Press, 1987.

(Co-editor) *School-University Partnerships in Action: Concepts, Cases, and Concerns,* Teachers College Press, 1988.

(Co-editor) *Access to Knowledge: An Agenda for Our Nation's Schools,* College Entrance Examination Board, 1990.

(Co-editor) *The Moral Dimensions of Teaching,* Jossey-Bass, 1990.

(Co-editor) *Places Where Teachers Are Taught,* Jossey-Bass, 1990.

Teachers for Our Nation's Schools, Jossey-Bass, 1990.

(Co-editor) *Integrating General and Special Education,* Macmillan, 1992.

OTHER

Author of *The Uses of Alternative Theories of Educational Change,* 1976. Contributor to almost 100 books including *The Education of Teachers: New Perspectives,* National Commission on Teacher Education and Professional Standards, 1958; *Education Parks,* U.S. Commission on Civil Rights, 1967; *Schooling for a Global Age,* edited by James Becker, McGraw, 1979; *Arts and the Schools,* edited by Jerome J. Hausman, McGraw, 1980; and *Teaching Thinking: An Agenda for the 21st Century,* edited by Cathy Collins and John N. Mangieri, Erlbaum, 1992.

Contributor to *Encyclopaedia Britannica* and *Encyclopedia of Educational Research;* contributor of more than 150 articles to education journals and yearbooks. Contributing editor, *Progressive Education,* 1955-58. Member of editorial advisory board, *Child's World,* 1952-75, *Education Digest,* 1968-70, *Educational Forum,* 1969-71, *Educational Technology,* 1970-72, *International Review of Education,* 1972-79, *Learning,* 1972-75, *Tech Journal of Education,* 1974-77, *Review of Education,* 1974—, *Journal of Aesthetic Education,* 1976-78, *Educational Horizons,* 1978-83, and *Consultation,* 1982—; chairman of editorial

advisory board, *New Standard Encyclopedia,* 1953—; member of board of editors, *School Review,* 1956-58, *Journal of Teacher Education,* 1958-60, *American Educational Research Journal,* 1964-66, and *Metropolitan Universities,* 1989—; editorial consultant, *Journal of Curriculum Studies,* 1967-75; international consultant, *New Education* (Australia), 1990—; member of board of reviewers, *Journal of Research and Development in Education,* 1979-90.

Several of Goodlad's books have been translated into Japanese, Hebrew, Italian, and Spanish.

WORK IN PROGRESS: Developing and implementing an agenda for teacher education in a democracy.

SIDELIGHTS: A Place Called School: Prospects for the Future is the culmination of an eight-year study of thirty-eight public schools conducted by the author, John I. Goodlad, and his assistants. The study, described by *Washington Post Book World* contributor Robert Fancher as Goodlad's "personal magnum opus," involved classroom observation and lengthy interviews with thousands of teachers, students, and parents. The book reveals "in short, that schools provide limited avenues to very limited parts of the domain of human understanding, and that they do not even provide all students with access to these routes of learning," observes Fancher.

One of Goodlad's main concerns is the failure of teachers to cultivate students' analytical skills. " 'Not even 1%' of instructional time, he found, was devoted to discussions that 'required some kind of open response involving reasoning or perhaps an opinion from students," reports Walter Karp in *Harper's.* The teachers are not entirely to blame, however. As Fred M. Hechinger explains in the *New York Times,* "The message teachers get from outside the school is 'back-to-basics and more discipline,' a message that does little to stimulate imaginative planning by teachers and leaves even less room for change." Even those teachers who want to encourage their students' intellectual development are inhibited by overcrowded classrooms. "Goodlad warns that 'talk of securing and maintaining a stable corps of understanding teachers is empty rhetoric' unless we lighten their classroom load," writes Andrew Hacker in the *New York Review of Books.*

Other targets of Goodlad's criticism include ability grouping and tracking. While these programs were originally implemented to assist all students, Goodlad finds that for the most part, only the academically gifted students benefit from them. He observes that in ability grouping, for example, the slow students often fall progressively behind the better ones, a process that is accelerated, according to Karp, "by giving the best students the best teachers and struggling students the worst ones." In addition, Goodlad assesses vocational education, a program designed to train students for future employment, as " 'virtually irrelevant to job fate,' " reports Karp.

Reviewing *A Place Called School: Prospects for the Future,* Thomas P. O'Malley of *America* remarks, "Of the books I have read on education, this is the best because it is based on solid evidence." Fancher, on the other hand, maintains that while the book is informative, it "cannot exercise its due influence because it is a drearily-written, cumbersome tome." Despite these reservations, Fancher concedes that "one would be hard pressed to imagine a better study within the realm of reasonable human effort."

BIOGRAPHICAL/CRITICAL SOURCES:

BOOKS

Goodlad, John I., *A Place Called School: Prospects for the Future,* McGraw, 1984.

PERIODICALS

America, November 10, 1984.
Harper's, June, 1985.
New York Review of Books, April 12, 1984.
New York Times, March 29, 1983.
Washington Post Book World, September 18, 1983.

*   *   *

GORDON, Giles (Alexander Esme) 1940- (Boswell)

PERSONAL: Born May 23, 1940, in Edinburgh, Scotland; son of Alexander Esme and Betsy Ballmont (McCurry) Gordon; married Margaret Anna Eastoe (a book illustrator), March 21, 1964, divorced, December 31, 1989; married Margaret Ann McKernan (a publisher), May 5, 1990; children: (first marriage) Callum Giles, Gareth Alexander, Harriet Miranda; (second marriage) Lucy Frances McKernan, Clare Esme McKernan. *Education:* Attended Edinburgh Academy, 1952-58.

ADDRESSES: Home—9 St. Ann's Gardens, Queen's Crescent, London NW5 4ER, England. *Office*—Sheil Land Associates, 43 Doughty St., London WC1N 2LF, England.

CAREER: Writer and theater critic. Oliver & Boyd (book publishers), Edinburgh, Scotland, trainee, 1959-63; Secker & Warburg (book publishers), London, England, advertising manager, 1963-64; Hutchinson & Co. (book publishers), London, editor, 1964-66; Penguin Books, Harmondsworth, Middlesex, England, editor, 1966-67; Victor Gollancz (book publishers), London, editorial director, 1967-72; Anthony Sheil Associates (literary agents), London, partner, 1972-90; Sheil Land Associates (literary agents), London, 1990—; lecturer in creative writing,

Tufts University-in-London, 1972-1977; C. Day Lewis fellow in creative writing, King's College, London, 1974-75; lecturer in English drama, Hollins University-in-London, 1984-86.

MEMBER: Royal Society of Literature (fellow; councilmember, 1992—), Arts Council of Great Britain (member of literature panel, 1966-70), Society of Young Publishers (past secretary and chairman), Society of Authors (member of committee of management, 1973-76), Authors' Club (councilmember, 1992—), Writers' Guild of Great Britain, Garrick Club.

WRITINGS:

POETRY

Landscape Any Date, Macdonald, 1963.
Two and Two Make One, Akros, 1966.
Two Elegies, Turret Books, 1968.
Twelve Poems for Callum, Akros, 1970.
Eight Poems for Gareth, Sceptre Press, 1970.
Between Appointments, Sceptre Press, 1971.
One Man, Two Women: A Sequence of Thirteen Poems, Sheep Press, 1974.
The Egyptian Room, Metropolitan Museum of Art, Sceptre Press, 1974.
The Oban Poems, Sceptre Press, 1977.

SHORT STORY COLLECTIONS

Pictures from an Exhibition, Dial Press, 1970.
Farewell, Fond Dreams: Fictions, Hutchinson, 1975.
The Illusionist, and Other Fictions, Harvester Press, 1978.

NOVELS

The Umbrella Man, Allison & Busby, 1971.
About a Marriage, Stein & Day, 1972.
Girl with Red Hair, Hutchinson, 1973, Wildwood House, 1974.
100 Scenes from Married Life: A Selection (sequel to *About a Marriage*), Hutchinson, 1976.
Enemies: A Novel about Friendship, Harvester Press, 1977.
Couple, Sceptre Press, 1978.
Ambrose's Vision: Sketches Towards the Creation of a Cathedral, Harvester Press, 1980.

JUVENILE

Walter and the Balloon (illustrated by Margaret Anna Gordon), Heinemann, 1975.

EDITOR

(With Alex Hamilton, and contributor) *Factions,* M. Joseph, 1974.
(And author of introduction) *Beyond the Words: Eleven Writers in Search of a New Fiction,* Hutchinson, 1975.

(With B. S. Johnson and Michael Bakewell) *You Always Remember the First Time,* Quartet Books, 1975.

(With Dulan Barber, and contributor) *Members of the Jury,* Wildwood House, 1975.

Prevailing Spirits: A Book of Scottish Ghost Stories, Hamish Hamilton, 1976.

A Book of Contemporary Nightmares, M. Joseph, 1977.

(With Fred Urquhart) *Modern Scottish Short Stories,* Hamish Hamilton, 1978.

(And author of introduction) *Shakespeare Stories,* Hamish Hamilton, 1982.

(And author of introduction) *Modern Short Stories 2: 1940-1980* (Gordon not associated with previous edition), Dent, 1982.

(And author of introduction) *English Short Stories: 1900 to the Present,* Dent, 1988.

(And author of introduction) *The Twentieth-Century Short Story in England* (bibliography), British Council, 1989.

Also co-editor, with David Hughes, of Heinemann's *Best Short Stories* series, 1986—, Norton's *Best English Short Stories* series, 1989—, and of Minerva's *The Minerva Book of Short Stories* series, 1990—.

OTHER

Books 2000: Some Likely Trends in Publishing, Association of Assistant Librarians, 1969.

(Contributor) Trevor Royle, editor, *Jock Tamson's Bairns,* Hamish Hamilton, 1977.

Aren't We Due a Royalty Statement? A Stern Account of Literary, Publishing and Theatrical Folk (autobiography), Chatto & Windus, 1993.

Contributor to *Transatlantic Review, New Review, New Statesman, Guardian, Times* (London), *Plays and Players, Drama, Tatler,* and to *The Scotsman,* under pseudonym Boswell. Co-editor and founder, *New Saltire* (Scottish literary magazine), 1960-62. Editor, *Drama,* 1981-83. Theater critic for *Spectator,* 1983-84, *Punch,* 1985-87, and *London Daily News,* 1988. Columnist on publishing, *Times Weekend Review,* 1993—.

WORK IN PROGRESS: The Obituarist, "a comic novel," for Chatto & Windus.

SIDELIGHTS: The title of experimental writer is a dangerous and unpopular one to carry, particularly in British literary circles. Yet it is this title with which Giles Gordon is most often labeled. He has earned his reputation on the strength—or, according to his critics, weakness—of his novels and short stories, many of which explore the power of words and language, and which challenge the reader to take a more active role in literature. Seldom has Gordon consecutively published two novels or collections in the same vein, choosing rather to seek new directions with each new book. Randall Stevenson, writing in the *Dictionary of Literary Biography,* lauds Gordon's "enthusiasm for innovation at a time when such experimental fiction has not been much in vogue among British writers."

In literary reviews, Gordon's work is often described as vague, convoluted, repetitive, and tedious—reflections of his penchant for describing the minute details of action and setting while almost completely ignoring character, plot, and structure. For this he has often been compared to Alain Robbe-Grillet and other practitioners of the complex literary style known as the *nouveau roman.* "There is even a case to be made for Giles Gordon being the only true inheritor of the late B. S. Johnson's mantle," argues Valentine Cunningham in the *Times Literary Supplement.* Because of the complexity of his writing, Gordon has never enjoyed much critical or financial success, and praise for his work is grudging and rare. This has not affected his determination, however, for he is quoted as saying: "There's only one thing better than being understood and that's not being understood. Then there is still something to strive for."

Gordon began his writing career as a poet, privately publishing several collections of his works while serving as a free-lance columnist. At the same time he was composing works of short fiction, some of which were published in local journals. His first short story collection, *Pictures from an Exhibition,* was released in 1970, and it quickly established Gordon as a skillful—if frustrating—author of experimental fiction. Many of the stories in *Pictures from an Exhibition* deal with minutiae: a word, an image. Others seems to waver back and forth between the realms of fiction and poetry, both in content and structure. In retrospect, Stevenson cites *Pictures from an Exhibition* as "an early example of Gordon's creation of fictions which do not directly invite the reader to enter an imagined world, but draw his attention instead to the raw materials and processes of construction involved in the creation of such fictional worlds." Reviewers of the time, however, were not so generous: one *Times Literary Supplement* reviewer called Gordon's prose "tiresomely profligate with words repeating, twisting, worrying the impression he wants, like a director going over and over the same shot. . . . Only when he is also able to clear the air with a definite, brief—and often very eloquently phrased—statement or descriptive punch-line does [this] method really seem justified."

Just a year after the publication of *Pictures from an Exhibition* Gordon produced his first novel, *The Umbrella Man.* This work picks up where the short stories left off, integrating Gordon's use of striking imagery with his fascination with life's forgettable details, all the while telling the somewhat odd story of Felix, the eponymous umbrella man, and his desire to have a relationship with Delia, a woman he sees through a window. The novel is punctuated by dream-like scenes, unbelievable circumstances, and mysteries which ultimately go unresolved. These techniques irked one *Times Literary Supplement* critic, who called them "simply examples of bad writing, despite Giles Gordon's mildly radical intentions." Another reviewer, writing in the *Listener,* was pleased by Gordon's refusal to give the people what they want: "Cliches of our time are undermined: sleeping together (Felix and Delia did) doesn't mean making love (they didn't); and older notions are reinstated: Eros is all there is, maybe, but marriage was made to contain it. The effect is eerie, . . . but it's also rather cheering."

Much of the dissatisfaction expressed by critics over *The Umbrella Man* can be attributed to Gordon's use of three different narrational viewpoints: the first-person accounts of Felix and Delia, as well as the omniscient third-person narration. Gordon freely intermingles these voices—often several times in a single chapter—so that the reader is never quite sure, at first, who is speaking, and when the change-over occurred. Furthermore, there is often a question as to the reliability of each narrator's account. "The distinction between what is subjective or imagined and what is objective or actual is one which becomes thoroughly blurred," says Stevenson. "The reader is obliged to wonder how much of the novel's action exists only in the imaginations of its characters." In the end, Felix and Delia consummate their relationship; the three viewpoints are unified, the cloud of confusion swept away.

In Gordon's second novel, *About a Marriage,* there is little resemblance to the experimental fiction that had defined his previous works. Instead, Gordon relies upon his ability to render the activities of life, from courtship to marriage to the raising of children, in the smallest detail. One *Times Literary Supplement* reviewer compared this treatment to a dissection, noting that this is "a dangerous enough task at the best of times, since the likelihood is that the dissecter will be left with the component parts strewn about his narrative." Stevenson, however, proclaims this same dissection to be "the principal strength of *About a Marriage,*" facilitating the "closeness and intimacy with which Gordon presents . . . the day-to-day banalities of an evolving relationship and marriage." Oswell Blakeston, reviewing the novel for *Books and Bookmen,* is impressed with the earnestness with which the story is told: "Mr. Gordon tells his cautionary tale with great honesty and never pushes argument to the peripheries where it might contradict itself."

About a Marriage is, to no small extent, autobiographical: the main character, Edward, is a writer who left Scotland to work in London, just as Gordon did; his wife, Ann, is an illustrator of children's books—a vocation shared by Gordon's own wife, Margaret Anna; Edward and Ann's children are born in the same years as Gordon's two sons.

This "tendency toward autobiography, with an accompanying realistic style meticulously attentive to the details of everyday domestic life," according to Stevenson, forms one of the two major aspects of Gordon's writing. The other, of course, is his use of experimental style and structure. Though not always equally represented, these two techniques appear in most of Gordon's writing the publication of *About a Marriage* in 1972.

Stevenson describes Gordon's next novel, *Girl with Red Hair,* as "an emphatic return to [his] experimental idiom. It is his most unconventional novel and the one which demonstrates most clearly the influence of the French writers of the *nouveau roman.*" It is loosely structured around a mystery story, wherein the narrator might be the witness, suspect, or investigator in a murder that may or may not have actually occurred. In an apparent parody of the crime-story genre, Gordon deliberately illuminates the details of completely irrelevant events while staunchly refusing to address the clues. "The novel has no clear story or plot," explains Stevenson, "or at any rate none that the reader can follow with any confidence." And, as if *Girl with Red Hair* were not challenging enough, it is written entirely using the second person "you"—a technique that many readers find difficult, if not completely frustrating.

Despite (or perhaps in response to) the obfuscating nature of *Girl with Red Hair,* many critics of the novel welcomed Gordon's return to the genre of experimental fiction. Writing in the *Listener,* Valentine Cunningham calls the use of distracting description and second-person narration "a roundabout way of tackling the nature of reality and reality in the novel, of challenging fiction's and novelists' claims to evidence about their people, and the reader's status as honorary witness." Still, it is not surprising that many reviewers disliked *Girl with Red Hair.* One critic for the *Times Literary Supplement* laments that Gordon's application of experimental methods to the thriller genre "baffles without reward. . . . When he is not pretentious, he is flat; sometimes . . . he manages to be both."

In 1977, Gordon published *Enemies: A Novel about Friendship,* his most critically acclaimed novel to date. It presents the story of two married couples who vacation together at a country house in an anonymous European locale. While there, they partake in leisurely walks, extramarital affairs, petty spats, and relaxed dinners in the garden. In the end, the garden is mysteriously destroyed, the country is thrown into revolution, and the vacationers (presumably) go home. "I found considerable narrative power in *Enemies,*" writes John Mellors in the *Listener,* "even though the narrative is concerned more with what goes on in the mind than with events in the material world." Stevenson credits this power to Gordon's successful synthesis of experimentation and detailed realism, noting how he "risks failure in seeking a strength for his fiction." And the risks paid off: the *Spectator*'s Peter Ackroyd hails *Enemies* as Gordon's "best book so far," demonstrating that " 'modern' fiction needn't be silly or laughable, that it can be written with the same expertise and considerably more subtlety than the 'straight' novel, and that it needn't lose any ground in doing so." Ackroyd concludes by calling Gordon "a perfectly straightforward and accessible writer. And that's as it should be."

Riding upon the wave of critical acceptance that surrounded *Enemies,* Gordon wrote another realism-meets-experimentation novel entitled *Ambrose's Vision: Sketches Toward the Creation of a Cathedral.* Like *The Umbrella Man* and *Girl with Red Hair, Ambrose's Vision* has a dream-like quality to it, straddling the line between poetry and prose. Yet, it is meticulously detailed in its description of a young boy's dream of building a cathedral and his life-long execution of that dream. The underlying theme of the novel, according to the *Spectator*'s Francis King, is an examination of the exhaustive and often obsessive nature of artistic creation, questioning why an artist should "pour out so much blood, sweat and tears to produce something so seemingly useless" as a cathedral. Ambrose's cathedral, too, is more than it seems: it is described in the novel as "his symphony (Ambrose the composer), his epic poem (Ambrose the poet), his canvas (Ambrose the painter)." Though describing Gordon as "a difficult and sometimes even enigmatic writer," King recommends *Ambrose's Vision* as a work which "amply repays not merely a visit but careful scrutiny." However, Stevenson finds this novel a less successful combination of experiment and detail than *Enemies,* claiming "the two aspects seem to coexist rather than cohere," resulting in "a rather unsatisfactory novel."

Since the 1980 publication of *Ambrose's Vision,* Gordon has concentrated his efforts upon collections of short stories (both as an editor and contributor) as well as contributing theater reviews to the *Spectator, Observer, Punch, London Daily News,* and other publications, all the while maintaining a position as a respected literary agent. Many of Gordon's experiences as a British literary "insider" have been compiled in his 1993 memoirs, *Aren't We Due a Royalty Statement? A Stern Account of Literary, Publishing and Theatrical Folk.* In it, Gordon recalls at length his days in London's exclusive Garrick Club, rubbing shoulders with Kingsley Amis, Saul Bellow, and Yukio Mishima, and describes his connections with the infamous satirical publications *Private Eye* and *Spycatcher.*

"Having decided to reveal the secrets of his life as a literary agent," writes Robyn Sisman, reviewing *Aren't We Due a Royalty Statement?* in the *Observer,* "Gordon does not go about it too seriously." "There are two ways of reading this book," explains the *Spectator*'s Julie Burchill. "One is to read it straight. . . . Reading it this way, you may expect it to be 'scurrilous, uproarious and gloriously

indiscreet,' as promised. You will know dismay. But if you read it as a spoof autobiography . . . it really works." Though Burchill considers Gordon's collection to be "a bit depressing," with each anecdote "a comfy, creaking cliche simply not worthy of Mr. Gordon's gilded flourishes," she stresses that the book contains "pearls of wisdom that I would risk my last tooth prising open an oyster-shell to get at."

"Twenty years ago I was mildly confident that I'd write the great novel," Gordon once told *CA.* "I now realise, having published six, that I won't. This comes as a shock to the system." He is currently at work on a comic novel entitled *The Obituarist.* "I can pretend that it will be the great novel," he told *CA,* "at least until the first sentence is written. As to poetry, the muse has gone forever, which is probably as well."

BIOGRAPHICAL/CRITICAL SOURCES:

BOOKS

Dictionary of Literary Biography, Volume 14: *British Novelists Since 1960,* Gale, 1982.
Gordon, Giles, *Ambrose's Vision: Sketches Towards the Creation of a Cathedral,* Harvester Press, 1980.
Gordon, Giles, *Aren't We Due a Royalty Statement? A Stern Account of Literary, Publishing and Theatrical Folk,* Chatto & Windus, 1993.
Gordon, Giles, editor, *Beyond the Words,* Hutchinson, 1975.

PERIODICALS

Books and Bookmen, September, 1972, p. 82.
Guardian Weekly, September 12, 1976, p. 22.
Listener, April 9, 1970, p. 488; December 2, 1971, p. 773; June 29, 1972, p. 874; January 24, 1974, p. 120; July 31, 1975, p. 158; September 16, 1976, p. 350; October 27, 1977, p. 550; January 4, 1979, p. 30; July 3, 1980, p. 25; January 13, 1983, p. 23.
New Statesman, November 12, 1971, p. 658; June 30, 1972, p. 914; February 1, 1974, p. 159; March 7, 1975, p. 315; September 3, 1976, p. 313; February 18, 1977, p. 227; September 16, 1977, p. 375; November 3, 1978, p. 590; June 13, 1980, p. 904; August 13, 1993, p. 41.
New Yorker, August 22, 1983, p. 93.
New York Times Book Review, August 13, 1972, p. 32.
Observer, June 21, 1970, p. 30; November 14, 1971, p. 33; June 25, 1972, p. 30; January 20, 1974, p. 26; March 9, 1975, p. 30; September 19, 1976, p. 27; March 13, 1977, p. 29; September 18, 1977, p. 24; December 10, 1978, p. 35; June 8, 1980, p. 29; August 15, 1993, p. 49.
Spectator, December 4, 1971, p. 811; July 8, 1972, p. 54; March 1, 1975, p. 244; September 4, 1976, p. 16; Octo-

ber 8, 1977, p. 23; November 18, 1978, p. 23; June 7, 1980, p. 21; August 7, 1993, p. 24.

Times (London), October 30, 1986; July 27, 1989; August 2, 1990.

Times Educational Supplement, December 30, 1983, p. 22.

Times Literary Supplement, April 23, 1970, p. 445; December 24, 1971, p. 1597; July 28, 1972, p. 865; January 25, 1974, p. 69; April 26, 1974, p. 433; December 6, 1974, p. 1378; February 28, 1975, p. 213; April 30, 1976, p. 507; September 3, 1976, p. 1069; February 18, 1977, p. 173; July 13, 1980, p. 664; November 12, 1982, p. 1243; January 21, 1986, p. 1324; December 1, 1989, p. 1337.

—Sketch by Brandon Trenz

*   *   *

GRAPE, Oliver
See WOOD, Christopher (Hovelle)

*   *   *

GREELEY, Andrew M(oran) 1928-

PERSONAL: Born February 5, 1928, in Oak Park, IL; son of Andrew T. (a corporation executive) and Grace (McNichols) Greeley. *Education:* St. Mary of the Lake Seminary, A.B., 1950, S.T.B., 1952, S.T.L., 1954; University of Chicago, M.A., 1961, Ph.D., 1962. *Politics:* Democrat.

ADDRESSES: Home—1012 East 47th St., Chicago, IL 60653. *Office*—National Opinion Research Center, University of Chicago, 1155 East 60th St., Chicago, IL 60637; and Department of Sociology, University of Arizona, Tucson, AZ 85721.

CAREER: Ordained Roman Catholic priest, 1954. Church of Christ the King, Chicago, IL, assistant pastor, 1954-64; University of Chicago, National Opinion Research Center, Chicago, IL, senior study director, 1961-68, program director for higher education, 1968-70, director of Center for the Study of American Pluralism, 1971-85, research associate, 1985—; University of Arizona, Tucson, professor of sociology, 1978—; University of Chicago, Chicago, IL, professor of social science, 1991—. Lecturer in sociology of religion, University of Chicago, 1962-72; professor of sociology of education, University of Illinois at Chicago. Member of planning committee, National Conference on Higher Education, 1969; member of board of advisers on student unrest, National Institute of Mental Health. Has made a number of appearances on radio and television programs.

MEMBER: American Sociological Association, American Catholic Sociological Society (former president), Soci-

ety for the Scientific Study of Religion, Religious Research Association.

AWARDS, HONORS: Thomas Alva Edison Award, 1962, for *Catholic Hour* radio broadcasts; Catholic Press Association award for best book for young people, 1965; C. Albert Kobb award, National Catholic Education Association, 1977; Mark Twain Award, Society for the Study of Midwestern Literature, 1987; Popular Culture Award, Center for the Study of Popular Culture (Bowling Green State University), 1986; Freedom to Read Award, Friends of the Chicago Public Library, 1989; LL.D., St. Joseph's College (Rensselaer, IN), 1967; Litt.D., St. Mary's College (Winona, MN), 1967; honorary Doctor of Humane Letters, Bowling Green State University (Bowling Green, OH), 1986; honorary Doctorate of Humanities, St. Louis University (St. Louis, MO), 1991; honorary Doctorate, Northern Michigan University.

WRITINGS:

RELIGION

The Church and the Suburbs, Sheed, 1959.

Strangers in the House: Catholic Youth in America, Sheed, 1961, revised edition, Doubleday, 1967.

(Editor with Michael E. Schlitz) *Catholics in the Archdiocese of Chicago,* Chicago Archdiocesan Conservation Council, 1962.

Religion and Career: A Study of College Graduates, Sheed, 1963.

Letters to a Young Man, Sheed, 1964.

Letters to Nancy, from Andrew M. Greeley, Sheed, 1964.

Priests for Tomorrow, Ave Maria Press, 1964.

And Young Men Shall See Visions: Letters from Andrew M. Greeley, Sheed, 1964.

(With Peter H. Rossi) *The Education of Catholic Americans,* Aldine, 1966.

The Hesitant Pilgrim: American Catholicism after the Council, Sheed, 1966.

The Catholic Experience: An Interpretation of the History of American Catholicism, Doubleday, 1967.

(With William Van Cleve and Grace Ann Carroll) *The Changing Catholic College,* Aldine, 1967.

The Crucible of Change: The Social Dynamics of Pastoral Practice, Sheed, 1968.

Uncertain Trumpet: The Priest in Modern America, Sheed, 1968.

Youth Asks, "Does God Talk?," Nelson, 1968, published as *Youth Asks, "Does God Still Speak?,"* 1970.

(With Martin E. Marty and Stuart E. Rosenberg) *What Do We Believe? The Stance of Religion in America,* Meredith, 1968.

From Backwater to Mainstream: A Profile of Catholic Higher Education, McGraw, 1969.

A Future to Hope In: Socio-Religious Speculations, Doubleday, 1969.

Life for a Wanderer: A New Look at Christian Spirituality, Doubleday, 1969.

Religion in the Year 2000, Sheed, 1969.

New Horizons for the Priesthood, Sheed, 1970.

The Life of the Spirit (also the Mind, the Heart, the Libido), National Catholic Reporter, 1970.

(With William E. Brown) *Can Catholic Schools Survive?,* Sheed, 1970.

The Jesus Myth, Doubleday, 1971.

The Touch of the Spirit, Herder & Herder, 1971.

What a Modern Catholic Believes about God, Thomas More Press, 1971.

Priests in the United States: Reflections on a Survey, Doubleday, 1972.

The Sinai Myth, Doubleday, 1972.

The Unsecular Man: The Persistence of Religion, Schocken, 1972.

What a Modern Catholic Believes about the Church, Thomas More Press, 1972.

The Catholic Priest in the United States: Sociological Investigations, United States Catholic Conference, 1972.

(Editor with Gregory Baum) *The Persistence of Religion,* Seabury, 1973.

The Devil, You Say! Man and His Personal Devils and Angels, Doubleday, 1974.

(With Baum) *The Church as Institution,* Herder & Herder, 1974.

May the Wind Be at Your Back: The Prayer of St. Patrick, Seabury, 1975.

(With William C. McCready and Kathleen McCourt) *Catholic Schools in a Declining Church,* Sheed, 1976.

The Communal Catholic: A Personal Manifesto, Seabury, 1976.

Death and Beyond, Thomas More Press, 1976.

The American Catholic: A Social Portrait, Basic Books, 1977.

The Mary Myth: On the Femininity of God, Seabury, 1977.

An Ugly Little Secret: Anti-Catholicism in North America, Sheed, 1977.

Everything You Wanted to Know about the Catholic Church but Were Too Pious to Ask, Thomas More Press, 1978.

(Editor with Baum) *Communication in the Church Concilium,* Seabury, 1978.

Crisis in the Church: A Study of Religion in America, Thomas More Press, 1979.

The Making of the Popes, 1978: The Politics of Intrigue in the Vatican, Sheed, 1979.

Catholic High Schools and Minority Students, Transaction Publications, 1982.

The Bottom Line Catechism for Contemporary Catholics, Thomas More Press, 1982.

Religion: A Secular Theory, Free Press, 1982.

The Catholic WHY? Book, Thomas More Press, 1983.

How to Save the Catholic Church, Penguin, 1984.

(With Mary G. Durka) *Angry Catholic Women,* Thomas More Press, 1984.

American Catholics since the Council: An Unauthorized Report, Thomas More Press, 1985.

Patience of a Saint, Warner Books, 1986.

Catholic Contributions: Sociology and Policy, Thomas More Press, 1987.

When Life Hurts: Healing Themes from the Gospels, Thomas More Press, 1988.

Religious Indicators, 1940-1985, Harvard University Press, 1989.

God in Popular Culture, Thomas More Press, 1989.

Myths of Religion, Warner Books, 1989.

Religious Change in America, Harvard University Press, 1989.

Complaints against God, Thomas More Press, 1989.

Year of Grace: A Spiritual Journal, Thomas More Press, 1990.

(With Jacob Neusner) *The Bible and Us: A Priest and a Rabbi Read Scripture Together,* Warner Books, 1990.

The Book of Irish American Prayers and Blessings, Thomas More, 1991.

(Contributor) *The Seven Deadly Sins: Stories on Human Weakness and Virtue,* Liguori Publications, 1992.

Love Affair: A Prayer Journal, Crossroad, 1992.

Also author of *Teenage World: Its Crises and Anxieties,* Divine Word Publications, and of a number of shorter works. Author of syndicated column "People and Values," appearing in approximately eighty newspapers. Contributor to Catholic magazines.

SOCIOLOGY

Why Can't They Be Like Us?: Facts and Fallacies about Ethnic Differences and Group Conflicts in America (also see below), Institute of Human Relations Press, 1969.

A Fresh Look at Vocations, Clarentian, 1969.

(With Joe L. Spaeth) *Recent Alumni and Higher Education,* McGraw, 1970.

Why Can't They Be Like Us?: America's White Ethnic Groups (includes portions of *Why Can't They Be Like Us?: Facts and Fallacies about Ethnic Differences and Group Conflicts in America*), Dutton, 1971.

The Denominational Society: A Sociological Approach to Religion in America, Scott, Foresman, 1972.

That Most Distressful Nation: The Taming of the American Irish, Quadrangle, 1972.

The New Agenda, Doubleday, 1973.

Building Coalitions: American Politics in the 1970s, New Viewpoints, 1974.

Ethnicity in the United States: A Preliminary Reconnaissance, Wiley, 1974.

MEDIA: Ethnic Media in the United States, Project IMPRESS (Hanover, N.H.), 1974.

The Sociology of the Paranormal: A Reconnaissance, Sage Publications, 1975.

Ethnicity, Denomination, and Inequality, Sage Publications, 1976.

The Great Mysteries: An Essential Catechism, Seabury, 1976.

(With McCready) *The Ultimate Values of the American Population,* Sage Publications, 1976.

Neighborhood (photographs by Greeley), Seabury, 1977.

No Bigger Than Necessary: An Alternative to Socialism, Capitalism, and Anarchism, New American Library, 1977.

(Editor) *The Family in Crisis or in Transition: A Sociological and Theological Perspective,* Seabury, 1979.

The Irish Americans: The Rise to Money and Power, Times Books, 1980.

(With McCready) *Ethnic Drinking Subcultures,* Praeger, 1980.

Editor, *Ethnicity.* Contributor to sociology and education journals.

RELATIONSHIPS

The Friendship Game, Doubleday, 1970.
Sexual Intimacy, Thomas More Press, 1973.
Ecstasy: A Way of Knowing, Prentice-Hall, 1974.
Love and Play, Thomas More Press, 1975.
Faithful Attraction: Discovering Intimacy, Love and Fidelity in American Marriage, Tor, 1991.
The Sense of Love, Ashland Poetry Press, 1992.

NOVELS

Nora Maeve and Sebi (illustrated by Diane Dawson), Paulist/Newman, 1976.
The Magic Cup: An Irish Legend, McGraw, 1979.
Death in April, McGraw, 1980.
The Cardinal Sins, Warner Books, 1981.
Thy Brother's Wife (book one of the "Passover Trilogy"), Warner Books, 1982.
Ascent into Hell (book two of the "Passover Trilogy"), Warner Books, 1984.
Lord of the Dance (book three of the "Passover Trilogy"), Warner Books, 1987.
Love Song, Warner Books, 1988.
All about Women, Tor, 1989.
The Search for Maggie Ward, Warner Books, 1991.
The Cardinal Virtues, Warner Books, 1991.
An Occasion of Sin, Jove, 1992.
Wages of Sin, Putnam, 1992.
Fall from Grace, Putnam, 1993.

MYSTERY NOVELS FEATURING FATHER "BLACKIE" RYAN

Virgin and Martyr, Warner Books, 1985.
Happy Are the Meek, Warner Books, 1985.
Happy Are Those Who Thirst for Justice, Mysterious Press, 1987.
Rite of Spring, Warner Books, 1987.
Happy Are the Clean of Heart, Warner Books, 1988.
St. Valentine's Night, Warner Books, 1989.
Happy Are the Merciful, Jove, 1992.
Happy Are the Peacemakers, Jove, 1993.

SCIENCE FICTION NOVELS

Angels of September, G. K. Hall, 1986.
God Game, Warner Books, 1986.
The Final Planet, Warner Books, 1987.
Angel Fire, Random House, 1988.

OTHER

Come Blow Your Mind with Me (essays), Doubleday, 1971.
(With J. N. Kotre) *The Best of Times, the Worst of Times* (biography), Nelson Hall, 1978.
Women I've Met (poetry), Sheed, 1979.
A Piece of My Mind . . . on Just about Everything (selection of newspaper columns), Doubleday, 1983.
Confessions of a Parish Priest: An Autobiography, Simon & Schuster, 1986.
An Andrew Greeley Reader (essays), edited by John Sprague, Thomas More Press, 1987.
Andrew Greeley's Chicago, Contemporary Books, 1989.
(Author of introduction) John Appel, *Pat-Riots to Patriots: American Irish in Caricature and Comic Art,* Michigan State University Museum, 1990.
Andrew Greeley (autobiography), Tor, 1990.
(Editor with Michael Cassutt) *Sacred Visions* (science fiction anthology), Tor, 1991.
(Author of foreword) Mary E. Andereck, *Ethnic Awareness and the School: An Ethnographic Study,* Sage, 1992.

SIDELIGHTS: Andrew Greeley is, according to a *Time* writer, "a Roman Catholic priest, a sociologist, a theologian, a weekly columnist, the author of [numerous] books, and a celibate sex expert. He is an informational machine gun who can fire off an article on Jesus to the *New York Times Magazine,* on ethnic groups to the *Antioch Review,* and on war to *Dissent.*" *Time* reports that Greeley's friend, psychologist-priest Eugene Kennedy, calls him "obsessive, compulsive, a workaholic. . . . He's a natural resource. He should be protected under an ecological act." While dividing his time between the National Opinion Research Center at the University of Chicago, where he has been involved in sociological research since 1961, and the University of Arizona, where he holds a professorship,

Greeley has also published scores of books and hundreds of popular and scholarly articles, making him one of the nation's leading authorities on the sociology of religion.

The adjective "controversial" arises often in articles on Greeley and in reviews of his many books. Much of the controversy surrounding Greeley stems from the difficulty critics have experienced in trying to label him. As another *Time* reporter explains: "On practically any topic, Greeley manages to strike some readers as outrageously unfair and others as eminently fair, as left wing and right wing, as wise and wrong-headed." Greeley advocates a great many changes within the Catholic church, including the ordination of women, liberalized policies on birth control and divorce, and a more democratic process for selecting popes, cardinals, and bishops; as a result, he is often at odds with church leaders. On the other hand, he feels that priests are most effective in serving the people when they remain celibate and that the church has taken the correct stand on abortion; he is, therefore, open to criticism from his more liberal colleagues. He maintains, *Time* continues, that "the present leadership of the church is morally, intellectually, and religiously bankrupt" and has referred to the hierarchy as "mitred pinheads." At the same time, he feels no affinity for the more radical element within the church and has said of activist Jesuit Daniel Berrigan, "As a political strategist, he's a great poet."

Greeley has further fueled the fires of controversy by writing more than a dozen bestselling mystery, fantasy, and science fiction novels, often filled with corruption, murder and lurid sex. Because many of these novels—such as *The Cardinal Sins* and *Thy Brother's Wife*—feature priests and other members of the clergy as principle characters, they are regarded by critics as a forum in which Greeley can air the church's dirty laundry. Other critics have simply dismissed him as a pulp writer. Greeley writes in *Contemporary Authors Autobiography Series (CAAS):* "I became in the minds of many the renegade priest who wrote 'steamy' novels to make money." Furthermore, he has been ostracized from the Archdiocese of Chicago, refused a parish, and treated as a "non-person" by the Catholic church. (He relates in *CAAS:* "When I tried to pledge a million dollars from my book royalties for the inner-city Catholic schools, [Chicago's] Cardinal Bernardin bluntly turned down the pledge without giving a reason—arguably the first time in history the Catholic Church has turned down money from anyone.")

Despite his marginal status within the church, Greeley still considers himself a man of the cloth first. "I am not a novelist or a sociologist or a writer or any of those things, not primarily, not essentially, not in the core of my being," he tells *CAAS.* "I'm a priest who happens to do these other things as a way of being a priest. . . . I will never leave the priesthood. If ecclesiastical authorities try to throw me

out—a serious danger in these days of Thermidor against the Vatican Council—I won't go." As to his novels, and their subject matter, he explains in the *New York Times Magazine* that he attempts in his fiction to address those religious issues closest to him: "Stories have always been the best way to talk about religion because stories appeal to the emotions and the whole personality and not just to the mind."

As a young man in Catholic school, Greeley was enthralled by the works of such Catholic poets and novelists as G. K. Chesterton and Evelyn Waugh. "It seemed to me that fiction was a brilliant way of passing on religion," he recalls in *CAAS.* "I thought that it must be challenging and rewarding to write 'Catholic fiction,' even if I never expected to do it myself." Still, within a few years Greeley was contributing articles and essays to Catholic magazines and conferences; the first of these were written pseudonymously, but later he grew bold enough to use his own name. In 1958 an editor at the Catholic publishers Sheed and Ward offered to expand two of Greeley's articles into a book entitled *The Church and the Suburbs.* He writes in *CAAS:* "This was a big step, much bigger, it would turn out, than I had expected. For a priest to set a word on paper in those days was a dangerous move (it still is). To write a book was to cut oneself off from most of the rest of the priesthood."

Though *The Church and the Suburbs* was, in the author's own words, "not exactly a best-seller," it awakened in Greeley a desire not only to express his controversial viewpoints, but to express them in print. Within twenty-five years he would produce more than sixty works of religious and sociological study. "It would be many years [after the publication of *The Church and the Suburbs*] before I would think of myself as a writer," he tells *CAAS,* "but in fact the writer in me was out of the box and would not go back into it ever again."

Greeley's writings have covered myriad topics, many of which deal with the role of religion in modern life. His subjects have included ethnicity, religious education, church politics, secular politics, the family, death and dying, vocations, history, and the future. His opinions in most of these areas have proven controversial to some extent, but when he tackles the subject of sex—particularly as it relates to religion today—he stirs up more than the usual amount of critical commentary. A good example is his book *Sexual Intimacy,* which the *Time* writer calls "a priest's enthusiastic endorsement of inventive marital sex play," and which J. W. Gartland of *Library Journal* recommends to Catholics who "seek a 'sexier' sexual relationship with their spouse and need supportive religious sanctions." In a much-quoted chapter entitled "How to Be Sexy," Greeley portrays a wife greeting her husband "wearing only panties and a martini pitcher—or maybe only the martini pitcher." According to *Time:* "One right-wing Catholic columnist declared that even discussing the book would be an occasion of sin." But, Greeley explains to Pamela Porvaznik in an interview for the *Detroit News Sunday Magazine,* "a vigorous sexual life is one of the biggest problems confronting married couples. How can people grow in intimacy? How can they consistently reassure themselves and each other of their own worth? These are real issues, and it's time the Church put them into perspective."

In a review of *Sexual Intimacy* for *America,* T. F. Driver writes: "Whatever scholarship may lie behind the book's judgments has been carefully (or do I mean carelessly) hidden. Though the book contains precious little theological reflection, it is based, I think, on an erroneous theological assumption namely, that the God we have known all along as Yahweh is the same who presides over the modern sexual revolution. It sounds to me like the old game of baptizing everything in sight." However, Charles Dollen of *Best Sellers* calls it "by far one of the best books on marriage and sexuality that has been published in many, many years. . . . [Greeley's] style is witty, charming and far above average. But it is the content that sets this book apart. He has some vital insights into what sex and sexuality are all about." *Commentary*'s John Garvey finds *Sexual Intimacy* to be "a mixed thing. At its worst it offers incredibly bad taste ('it is no exaggeration . . . to say that the wife clad in panties and martini pitcher is imitating Yahweh's behavior'). . . . But Greeley is often very good. [His] comparisons of erotic and divine love are often to the point, especially the relationship between divine and human vulnerability."

One of Greeley's best-known nonfiction works is *The Making of the Popes, 1978: The Politics of Intrigue in the Vatican.* In this book he details the series of startling events that took place in Rome beginning in the summer of 1978: the death of Pope Paul VI in July; the subsequent election of John Paul I, who died after only thirty-three days in office; and the election of John Paul II, the first non-Italian pope since 1522. The book is particularly noteworthy for its inclusion of little-known "inside information" on the process of electing a new pope, much of it supplied by an informant that Greeley calls "Deep Purple." The title of the book and the use of stylistic devices such as a diary format are intentionally reminiscent of Theodore H. White's *Making of the President* books, reinforcing Greeley's thesis that papal elections have all of the mystery, the jockeying for power, and the behind-the-scenes intrigue of an American presidential election. Several reviewers, including R. A. Schroth of the *New York Times Book Review,* note that Greeley's choice of the name "Deep Purple" for his unnamed source suggests that "he clearly identifies with Woodward and Bernstein."

Thus, although the author sees himself as a journalist covering what is, essentially, a political event, he still leaves himself the option of injecting personal comments (as White is known to do) on the various candidates, the election process, and the diverse political powers that subtly influence the voting. "The White model works pretty well," writes Robert Blair Kaiser of the *New York Times,* "freeing the author to present an account of [the] doings in Rome, which, for all its ambiguous partisanship, tells us more about the election of two popes (and the future of the church) than less knowing reporters ever could."

Greeley's partisanship leads him to offer in *The Making of the Popes* the opinion that the church did not need another leader like Paul VI, "a grim, stern, pessimistic, solemn-faced pope who did not appeal to the world as a man who is really possessed by the 'good news' he claims to be teaching." He would prefer, Kaiser says, "a hopeful holy man who smiles," a man "whose faith makes him happy and whose hope makes him joyful." Greeley was satisfied with the choice of John Paul I and just as happy with his successor, John Paul II, but his approval of the cardinals' choices has not altered his view of papal elections. He told Linda Witt of *People:* "The cardinals are a closed group of men who have spent their whole lives strictly in ecclesiastical activities. Their average age is over sixty, and they are extremely cautious and conservative. In many cases they are totally out of touch with the world. There were between thirty and thirty-five cardinals—about one-third of those voting—who had no notion of what was going on, and who drifted from candidate to candidate depending on who seemed likely to win." Asked what kind of election process he would prefer, Greeley replied: "In the early church, the Pope and all the bishops were elected by the people of their diocese. The cardinals would go into St. Peter's and pick a man and bring him out. If the faithful applauded, he was the Pope. If they booed, the cardinals went back inside and tried again. I'm not suggesting we revert to that, but I would like to see a gradual sharing of power with the rest of the church." J. J. Hughes of *America,* while expressing a few misgivings about Greeley's reportage, concludes that "the book is a remarkable achievement. We are fools, and guilty fools, if we dismiss it as unworthy of serious consideration."

Though the research Greeley conducts at Chicago's National Opinion Research Center is not officially opposed by the Catholic church, each of Greeley's many sociological and religious studies inevitably sparks at least some discussion among church leaders; on more than one occasion, this discussion has turned quickly to open hostility toward the author. "My colleagues and I soon became accustomed to the pattern of reaction to our work," he relates in *CAAS.* "First of all it would be distorted, ridiculed, rejected. The attacks would never touch the work itself (with which no competent scholar has ever found serious fault) but would rather concentrate on my character and personality and on distortions of what the research actually reported. Then, sometimes in a year or two, certainly in five years, our findings would be accepted as what everyone knew to be true, rarely with credit to those who originally reported it." Even liberal Catholics, such as the editors of *Commonweal*, have railed Greeley's research, accusing him of aspiring to bishophood. "I was astonished at the hostility of Catholic 'liberals'," he continues in *CAAS*. "In their world . . . there was no such thing as objective evidence if it seemed to go against their biases. To disagree with them on the basis of evidence was grounds for character assassination."

The gap between Greeley and the rest of the Catholic Church was further widened in 1981 with the publication of *The Cardinal Sins*. Though not his first work of fiction, *The Cardinal Sins* was attacked by church officials for its unflattering portrayal of Cardinal Patrick Donohue, a fictional character who swiftly ascends to the top of Chicago's religious hierarchy despite his penchant for brutal sex. The church accused Greeley of using this character to slander the late John Cardinal Cody, then Archbishop of Chicago and longtime rival of Greeley's. These accusations are not unsubstantiated: *The Cardinal Sins*'s Patrick Donahue funnels church funds to his mistress sister-in-law in South America; at the time of the novel's publication, coincidentally, Cardinal Cody was under investigation for allegedly channeling close to one million dollars to a female companion who also happened to be his stepcousin. Greeley denies any connection between the fictional cardinal and Chicago's Archbishop. "Patrick Donahue is a much better bishop than Cody and a much better human being [than Cardinal Cody]," he explains in the *New York Times*.

In general, Greeley's novels have not received much critical praise. Christine B. Vogel of the *Washington Post Book World* describes them as "distinctly unscholarly and unpriestly," bearing "dubious literary merit." *America*'s Sean O'Faolain observes that the author is "all too visible" in his novels, "constantly manipulating both character and plot and infusing everybody, most notably the women, with his own often silly romantic notions." The novels' protagonists are, according to Elaine Kendall of the *Los Angeles Times Book Review*, "so tormented by temptations of the flesh that a questioning reader wonders whatever made them take the vow of celibacy in the first place." And the *New York Times Book Review*'s Sheila Paulos proclaims: "Andrew M. Greeley may be a great priest, a great sociologist, even a great fellow. But . . . a great novelist he is not."

If not a great novelist, Greeley is undeniably a popular one. His novels consistently reach the bestseller lists and

linger there for weeks or months. Even his critics have admitted, at times, to his novels' appeal. "To give credit where it's due," *Washington Post Book World* reviewer Maude McDaniel writes, "anybody who reads Andrew Greeley's fiction gets involved." Webster Schott supports this claim in the *New York Times Book Review*: "He is never dull, he spins wondrous romances and he has an admirable ideal for what his church should become." Toronto *Globe and Mail* critic John Doyle attributes the author's popularity to the mystique of the clergy: "Greeley's novels have all been bestsellers because they help satisfy a natural need to know about the private lives of powerful, celibate men. Ecclesiastical power is as much an aphrodisiac as any other type." Abigail McCarthy of the *Chicago Tribune* agrees, noting Greeley's ability to combine "an apparently inside view of Catholic Church politics" with "a judicious mixture of money and clinically detailed sex."

"In recent years," Greeley tells *CAAS*, "critical writers have begun to understand the themes of my fiction and to attribute considerable value to the books." However, this has had little impact on the Catholic church's determination to treat him as a peripheral member; although Greeley has since made peace with Chicago's Cardinal Bernardin, his "celebrity" status keeps him outside the fold. It is this continuing marginality that is hardest for Greeley to endure. He once told a *CA* interviewer: "I have to say in fairness to the Catholic hierarchy that, off the record and privately, many of them are very friendly and encouraging. . . . The thing I find hard in the church . . . is the criticism from other priests who define me as a success because I have published a lot of books, do a lot of traveling, and get my name in the paper. Their resentment is, first of all, a big surprise, and it is also very hard to bear."

Still, Greeley has no plans to stop writing novels; rather, he defends both his fiction and nonfiction writing as portraying the church and clergy as real people. "I'm saying here's my church, made up of human beings with all the weaknesses and frailties and yet with the capacity to transcend those limitations and to produce great people, great art, great mysticism and great missionaries," Greeley explains in the *New York Times*. "If it shocks people to hear a priest say we're not perfect, then it's high time they be disabused of wrong notions about us." As for his reputation as a greedy author of "steamy" novels, he contends in *CAAS*: "The books were not 'steamy' (and research on the readers indicates that they don't think so) and I gave most of the money away. . . . My stories of God's love and the presence of Grace in the universe were vilified and denounced without being understood and often without being read (many of the bishops who complained had only read passages torn out of context). . . . The objections seemed to be that (1) a priest ought not to know anything about sex and (2) a priest ought not to write novels that millions of people read. But there is nothing wrong with sex. And a priest would not 'know' about sex only if he were not human."

Greeley once said: "I never courted controversy, but I also never walked away from it." That willingness to create and confront controversy, Jacob Neusner claims in *America,* makes Greeley exactly what the Catholic Church has needed: a catalyst. "He has defined the issues, set forth the propositions for analysis and argument and brought public discourse to the public at large. . . . He has taught us what it means to be religious in the United States in our time." Neusner concludes: "Had Greeley not lived and done his work, I may fairly claim that we religious people in the United States—Christians and Jews alike—should understand ourselves less perspicaciously than we do."

BIOGRAPHICAL/CRITICAL SOURCES:

BOOKS

Contemporary Authors Autobiograpy Series, Volume 7, Gale, 1988.
Contemporary Literary Criticism, Volume 28, Gale, 1984.
Shafer, Ingrid, *The Womanliness of God: Andrew Greeley's Romances of Renewal,* Loyola University Press, 1986.
Shafer, Ingrid, editor, *Andrew Greeley's World: A Collection of Critical Essays, 1986-1988,* Warner Books, 1989.

PERIODICALS

America, February 10, 1968, p. 196; March 2, 1968, p. 297; May 4, 1968, p. 617; September 11, 1971, p. 153; November 20, 1971, p. 438; October 7, 1972, p. 270; December 8, 1973; November 30, 1974, p. 352; April 26, 1975, p. 326; May 15, 1976, p. 425; November 13, 1976, p. 326; April 9, 1977; May 26, 1979; September 15, 1979, p. 117; June 4, 1982, p. 342; October 22, 1983, p. 236; October 4, 1986, p. 170; May 13, 1989, p. 459; May 12, 1990, p. 481; June 16, 1990, p. 611; August 25, 1990, p. 113; June 1, 1991, p. 604; August 14, 1992, p. 18.
Best Sellers, November 15, 1973.
Chicago Tribune, March 3, 1985; August 22, 1989.
Chicago Tribune Book World, May 24, 1981; May 2, 1982; June 26, 1983; November 25, 1984; August 31, 1986.
Christian Century, February 20, 1985, p. 196; September 30, 1987, p. 836; April 18, 1990, p. 410; March 20, 1991, p. 345.
Commonweal, December 14, 1973; June 18, 1976; August 31, 1979; July 17, 1987, pp. 412-417; January 23, 1988, pp. 63-66; May 18, 1990, p. 323; December 7, 1990, p. 727; August 14, 1992, pp. 18-21.
Detroit News, September 7, 1980; May 20, 1984; February 23, 1986.
Detroit News Sunday Magazine, February 2, 1975.

Economist, April 7, 1990, p. 102.
Globe and Mail (Toronto), March 2, 1985; August 20, 1988; July 13, 1991, p. C6.
Library Journal, November 15, 1973.
Los Angeles Times, May 6, 1982.
Los Angeles Times Book Review, March 28, 1982; September 4, 1983, p. 6; December 9, 1984, p. 16; April 7, 1985, p. 4; March 16, 1986, p. 4; September 14, 1986, p. 3; February 15, 1987, p. 4; April 30, 1989, p. 6; April 15, 1990, p. 8; September 16, 1990, p. 10; April 28, 1991, p. 14.
National Catholic Reporter, January 15, 1988, p. 7.
National Review, April 15, 1977; February 22, 1985, p. 42; December 5, 1986, p. 48; April 16, 1990, p. 51.
New Republic, December 17, 1984, p. 35; September 24, 1990, p. 33.
New York Review of Books, March 4, 1976.
New York Times, March 13, 1972; March 6, 1977; September 21, 1979; March 22, 1981; October 31, 1985; March 24, 1993, p. B2.
New York Times Book Review, June 24, 1979; July 26, 1981; April 11, 1982; July 3, 1983, p. 8; January 6, 1985, p. 18; March 10, 1985, p. 13; September 29, 1985, p. 46; March 30, 1986, p. 10; September 14, 1986, p. 14; September 21, 1986, p. 31; February 8, 1987, p. 31; July 31, 1988, p. 32; August 14, 1988, p. 16; January 22, 1989, p. 23; September 17, 1989, p. 24; January 7, 1990, p. 18; April 22, 1990, p. 9; September 2, 1990, p. 9; December 30, 1990, p. 14; June 23, 1991, p. 28; June 30, 1991, p. 20; October 6, 1991, p. 32.
New York Times Magazine, May 6, 1984, p. 34.
People, July 9, 1979; May 3, 1993, p. 36.
Publishers Weekly, April 10, 1987, p. 78.
Time, January 7, 1974; July 16, 1978; August 10, 1981; July 1, 1991, p. 71.
Times Literary Supplement, August 31, 1984.
Tribune Books (Chicago), January 27, 1991, p. 6.
Village Voice, January 29, 1985, p. 47.
Virginia Quarterly Review, winter, 1990, p. 27.
Wall Street Journal, March 4, 1986, p. 28.
Washington Post, June 11, 1981; January 24, 1984; April 6, 1984, p. D8; June 27, 1986; July 21, 1986; August 19, 1986; June 13, 1987; November 16, 1987.
Washington Post Book World, February 24, 1985, p. 1; March 24, 1985, p. 6; January 27, 1986; March 11, 1990, p. 13.
West Coast Review of Books, May, 1985, p. 32; Number 4, 1986, p. 33; Number 6, 1988, p. 44; Number 2, 1989, p. 26; Number 2, 1991, p. 35.

—Sketch by Brandon Trenz

GREELEY, Valerie 1953-

PERSONAL: Born September 29, 1953, in Bury, Lancashire, England; daughter of John (an engineer) and Dorothy Vernon (Waterson) Greeley; married Anthony Richard Corrigan (a teacher), August 14, 1976; children: Patrick Richard, James John. *Education:* Manchester Polytechnic, B.A. (with first class honors), 1975. *Religion:* Church of England.

ADDRESSES: Home—89 Audley Rd., Alsager, Stoke-on-Trent ST7 2QW, England. *Agent*—Rosemary Sandberg, 44 Bowerdean St., London SW6 3TW, England.

CAREER: Free-lance fashion textile and wallpaper designer, 1975—, and illustrator, 1980—; worked on commissioned greeting card designs for Camden Graphics, 1977-87. Guest lecturer at Manchester Polytechnic and North Staffordshire Polytechnic. Work exhibited in "Illustrators," London, England, 1992. Consultant to Design Council.

AWARDS, HONORS: White Is the Moon was voted one of top ten picture books for children by *Redbook* magazine.

WRITINGS:

SELF-ILLUSTRATED CHILDREN'S BOOKS

Farm Animals, Blackie & Son, 1981.
Field Animals, Blackie & Son, 1981.
Zoo Animals, Blackie & Son, 1981.
Pets, Blackie & Son, 1981.
A Book of Days, Blackie & Son, 1984.
An Illustrated Address Book, Blackie & Son, 1989.
Where's My Share?, Blackie & Son, 1989.
White Is the Moon, Blackie & Son, 1989, Macmillan, 1991.
Animals at Home, Blackie & Son, 1992.
A Year of Prayers, World International Enterprises, 1992.

Also author of a series of decorative books. Illustrator, with M. Tempest, of *Little Grey Rabbit's Country Book* by G. Duff, Collins, 1990.

Where's My Share? has been translated into French and German.

WORK IN PROGRESS: A Baby Album, for World International Enterprises; *Acorn's Story,* based on the life cycle of an oak tree.

SIDELIGHTS: Valerie Greeley once told *CA:* "I have always loved the unspoiled countryside and all things natural—birds, wildflowers, butterflies, et cetera. I love tiny details and enjoy the decorative element in nature.

"At art college I studied fabric design and produced detailed and decorative work for fabrics and wallpapers. After graduation I was offered a sponsored exhibition at the Design Centre in London. As a result of the Texprint design exhibition I was able to establish myself as a free-lance designer.

"My work was suitable for reproduction by greeting card manufacturers and publishers of children's books. I was invited to produce a range of four wordless board books for the very young, and these were published in 1981.

"I have always loved poetry, especially nature poetry, and I decided to produce a book on the natural year. I illustrated each month with its natural beauties, supplementing the illustration with a carefully chosen anthology of relevant poetry. *A Book of Days* was the result."

She added: "Whilst researching material for nursery rhymes I came across a rhyme called 'What's in There—Gold, Money?' I felt that this would lend itself to a more naturalistic and rhythmic interpretation. *Where's My Share?* was the result." A different poem played a part in another Greeley work. She explained: "I wrote and illustrated *White Is the Moon* using a similar simple rhyme based on the concept of night and day and color." The work includes Greeley's depictions of a green frog at dawn and a gray seal at dusk.

Greeley's series of animal picture board books for infants and toddlers (*Farm Animals, Field Animals, Zoo Animals,* and *Pets*) features "painstakingly painted" illustrations, according to Lucy Micklethwait in the *Times Literary Supplement,* and Carrie Carmichael noted in the *New York Times Book Review* that the "drawings of the animals and their habitats are lovely and realistic."

BIOGRAPHICAL/CRITICAL SOURCES:

PERIODICALS

Books for Keeps, July, 1992, p. 8.
New York Times Book Review, November 11, 1984, p. 57.
Times Literary Supplement, July 24, 1981, p. 840.

*   *   *

GREENFIELD, Eloise 1929-

PERSONAL: Born May 17, 1929, in Parmele, NC; daughter of Weston W. and Lessie (Jones) Little; married Robert J. Greenfield (a procurement specialist), April 29, 1950; children: Steven, Monica. *Education:* Attended Miner Teachers College, 1946-49.

ADDRESSES: Office—Honey Productions, Inc., P.O. Box 29077, Washington, DC 20017. *Agent*—Marie Brown, Marie Brown Associates, 412 West 154th St., New York, NY 10032.

CAREER: U.S. Patent Office, Washington, DC, clerk-typist, 1949-56, supervisory patent assistant, 1956-60;

worked as a secretary, case-control technician, and an administrative assistant in Washington, DC from 1964-68. District of Columbia Black Writers' Workshop, co-director of adult fiction, 1971-73, director of children's literature, 1973-74; District of Columbia Commission on the Arts and Humanities, writer-in-residence, 1973, 1985-86. Participant in numerous school and library programs and workshops for children and adults.

AWARDS, HONORS: Carter G. Woodson Book Award, National Council for the Social Studies, 1974, for *Rosa Parks;* Irma Simonton Black Award, Bank Street College of Education, 1974, for *She Come Bringing Me That Little Baby Girl; New York Times* Outstanding Book of the Year citation, 1974, for *Sister;* Jane Addams Children's Book Award, Women's International League for Peace and Freedom, 1976, for *Paul Robeson;* American Library Association Notable Book citations, 1976, for *Me and Neesie,* 1979, for *Honey, I Love, and Other Love Poems,* 1982, for *Daydreamers;* Council on Interracial Books for Children award, 1977, for body of work; Coretta Scott King Award, 1978, for *Africa Dream;* Classroom Choice Book citation, 1978, for *Honey, I Love, and Other Love Poems;* Children's Book of the Year citation, Child Study Book Committee, 1979, for *I Can Do It by Myself;* Notable Trade Book in the Field of Social Studies citations, 1980, for *Childtimes: A Three-Generation Memoir,* 1982, for *Alesia;* New York Public Library recommended list, 1981, for *Alesia;* National Black Child Development Institute award, 1981, for body of work; Mills College award, 1983, for body of work; Washington, DC Mayor's Art Award in Literature, 1983; honored at Ninth Annual Celebration of Black Writing, Philadelphia, PA, 1993, for lifetime achievement.

WRITINGS:

Sister (novel), illustrated by Moneta Barnett, Crowell, 1974.
Honey, I Love, and Other Love Poems, illustrated by Diane and Leo Dillon, Crowell, 1978.
Talk about a Family (novel), illustrated by James Calvin, Lippincott, 1978.
Nathaniel Talking (poems), Writers & Readers, 1988.
Night on Neighborhood Street (poems), illustrated by Jan Spivey Gilchrist, Dial, 1991.
Koya DeLaney and the Good Girl Blues, Scholastic, 1992.
Talk About a Family, HarperCollins, 1993.

PICTURE BOOKS

Bubbles, illustrated by Eric Marlow, Drum & Spear, 1972, published with illustrations by Pat Cummings as *Good News,* Coward, 1977.
She Come Bringing Me That Little Baby Girl, illustrated by John Steptoe, Lippincott, 1974.
Me and Neesie, illustrated by Barnett, Crowell, 1975.
First Pink Light, illustrated by Barnett, Crowell, 1976.

Africa Dream, illustrated by Carole Byard, John Day, 1977.
(With mother, Lessie Jones Little) *I Can Do It by Myself,* illustrated by Byard, Crowell, 1978.
Darlene, illustrated by George Ford, Methuen, 1980.
Grandmama's Joy, illustrated by Byard, Collins, 1980.
Daydreamers, with pictures by Tom Feelings, Dial, 1981.
Grandpa's Face, illustrated by Floyd Cooper, Putnam, 1988.
Under the Sunday Tree, illustrated by Amos Ferguson, HarperCollins, 1988.
My Doll, Keshia, illustrated by Gilchrist, Writers & Readers, 1991.
My Daddy and I, illustrated by Gilchrist, Writers & Readers, 1991.
I Make Music, illustrated by Gilchrist, Writers & Readers, 1991.
First Pink Light, illustrated by Gilchrist, Writers & Readers, 1991.
Big Friend, Little Friend, illustrated by Gilchrist, Writers & Readers, 1991.
Aaron and Gayla's Alphabet Book, illustrated by Gilchrist, Writers & Readers, 1992.

BIOGRAPHIES

Rosa Parks, illustrated by Marlow, Crowell, 1973.
Paul Robeson, illustrated by Ford, Crowell, 1975.
Mary McLeod Bethune, illustrated by Jerry Pinkney, Crowell, 1977.
(With Little) *Childtimes: A Three-Generation Memoir* (autobiography), illustrated by Pinkney, Crowell, 1979.
(With Alesia Revis) *Alesia,* illustrated by Ford, with photographs by Sandra Turner Bond, Philomel Books, 1981.

CONTRIBUTOR TO ANTHOLOGIES

Alma Murray and Robert Thomas, editors, *The Journey: Scholastic Black Literature,* Scholastic Book Services, 1970.
Karen S. Kleiman and Mel Cebulash, editors, *Double Action Short Stories,* Scholastic Book Services, 1973.
Love, Scholastic Book Services, 1975.
Encore (textbook), Houghton, 1978.
Daystreaming, Economy Company, 1978.
Forerunners, Economy Company, 1978.
Burning Bright, Open Court, 1979.
Friends Are Like That, Crowell, 1979.
Language Activity Kit: Teachers' Edition, Harcourt, 1979.
Building Reading Skills, McDougal, Littell, 1980.
New Routes to English: Book 5, Collier Books, 1980.
New Routes to English: Advanced Skills One, Collier Books, 1980.
Jumping Up, Lippincott, 1981.
Emblems, Houghton, 1981.

Listen, Children, Bantam, 1982.
Bonus Book, Gateways, Level K, Houghton, 1983.
New Treasury of Children's Poetry, Doubleday, 1984.
Scott, Foresman Anthology of Children's Literature, Scott, Foresman, 1984.

OTHER

Contributor to *World Book Encyclopedia;* author of 1979 bookmark poem for Children's Book Council. Also contributor to magazines and newspapers, including *Black World, Cricket, Ebony, Jr.!, Horn Book, Interracial Books for Children Bulletin, Ms., Negro History Bulletin, Scholastic Scope,* and *Washington Post.*

ADAPTATIONS: Daydreamers was dramatized for the Public Broadcasting System (PBS) Reading Rainbow Television Series.

SIDELIGHTS: Eloise Greenfield stated that her goal in writing is "to give children words to love, to grow on." The author of more than a dozen prize-winning books for children, Greenfield admits that, since her own childhood, she has loved the sounds and rhythms of words. In her stories and poetry she tries to produce what she calls "word-madness," a creative, joyous response brought on by reading. As she explains in *Horn Book:* "I want to be one of those who can choose and order words that children will want to celebrate. I want to make them shout and laugh and blink back tears and care about themselves."

Greenfield also lists as a priority of her writing the communication of "a true knowledge of Black heritage, including both the African and American experiences." Through her easy-to-read biographies of famous black Americans, such as *Rosa Parks, Paul Robeson,* and *Mary McLeod Bethune,* she seeks to inform young readers about the historical contributions of blacks in this nation. "A true history must be the concern of every Black writer," she states in *Horn Book.* "It is necessary for Black children to have a true knowledge of their past and present, in order that they may develop an informed sense of direction for their future."

This concern for a personal past as well as a public one has prompted Greenfield to team with her mother for *Childtimes: A Three-Generation Memoir.* The autobiographical work describes the childhood memories of Greenfield, her mother, and her maternal grandmother. According to Rosalie Black Kiah in *Language Arts,* each experience in *Childtimes,* "though set in a different time, is rich in human feeling and strong family love." *Washington Post Book World* contributor Mary Helen Washington writes: "I recognize the significance of *Childtimes* as a document of black life because . . . it unlocked personal recollections of my own past, which I do not want to lose." In the *Interracial Books for Children Bulletin,* Geraldine L. Wil-

son calls the book "carefully considered and thoughtful, . . . moving deliberately, constructed with loving care." M. R. Singer concludes in the *School Library Journal:* "The intimate details of loving and growing up and the honesty with which they are told . . . will involve all readers . . . and broaden their understanding of this country's recent past."

Much of Greenfield's fiction concerns family bonding, a subject the author finds as important as black history. Noting in *Horn Book* that "love is a staple in most Black families," she writes repeatedly of the changing patterns of parental and sibling involvement, stressing the child's ability to cope with novelties both positive and negative. In her Irma Simonton Black Award-winning picture book, *She Come Bringing Me That Little Baby Girl,* for instance, a young character named Kevin must learn to share his parents' love with his new sister. A novel entitled *Sister,* which received a *New York Times* Outstanding Book of the Year citation, concerns a girl caught in the family stress following a parent's death. Greenfield explains the point of *Sister* in *Horn Book:* "Sister . . . discovers that she can use her good times as stepping stones, as bridges, to get over the hard times. . . . My hope is that children in trouble will not view themselves as blades of wheat caught in countervailing winds but will seek solutions, even partial or temporary solutions, to their problems."

Unsatisfied with network television's portrayal of black families, which she calls "a funhouse mirror, reflecting misshapen images" in *Horn Book,* Greenfield seeks to reinforce positive and realistic aspects of black family life. While she tells *Language Arts* that she looks back on her own childhood with pleasure, she remains aware of the modern dynamics of family structure. She states: "Families come in various shapes. There is no one shape that carries with it more legitimacy than any other. . . . In the case of divorce and separation—the problems that parents have—the children can go on and build their own lives regardless of the problems of the parents. Children *have* to go on and build their own lives." Kiah notes that Greenfield does not construct her fiction from personal incidents but rather looks for themes from a more universal background. "She draws from those things she has experienced, observed, heard about, and read about. Then she combines them, changes them and finally develops them into her stories." The resulting work has a wide appeal, according to Betty Valdes in the *Interracial Books for Children Bulletin.* Valdes feels that Greenfield "consistently . . . illuminates key aspects of the Black experience in a way that underlines both its uniqueness and its universality."

This is proven out in *Grandpa's Face,* in which Greenfield constructs a story about a young girl and her relationship with her grandfather, who she loves dearly. One day, according to Jeanne Fox-Alston in *Washington Post Book World,* little Tomika sees her grandfather, who frequently acts in community theater productions, rehearsing. "The cold, mean look on his face scares her," Fox-Alston recounts, and she worries that she might do something that will cause him to regard her with the same angry countenance. In her poetry as well as her prose, Greenfield attempts to involve children in their own worlds. In *Under the Sunday Tree* and *Night on Neighborhood Street,* Greenfield brings her young readers into the happenings around them. *Night on Neighborhood Street* examines "realistic" life an urban community, according to *Tribune Books.* The volume's seventeen poems show children in typical situations, including attending church, avoiding drug pushers, and playing games with their families.

Greenfield has resided in Washington, DC, since childhood and has participated in numerous writing workshops and conferences on literature there. She explains in *Language Arts* that her work with the District of Columbia Black Writers' Workshop convinced her of the need to build a collection of "good black books" for children. "It has been inspiring to me to be a part of this struggle," she affirms. "I would like to have time to write an occasional short story, . . . but I don't feel any urgency about them. It seems that I am always being pushed from inside to do children's books; those are more important." Stating another aim of hers in *Horn Book,* Greenfield claims: "Through the written word I want to give children a love for the arts that will provoke creative thought and activity. . . . A strong love for the arts can enhance and direct their creativity as well as provide satisfying moments throughout their lives."

BIOGRAPHICAL/CRITICAL SOURCES:

BOOKS

Children's Literature Review, Volume 4, Gale, 1982.
Greenfield, Eloise, and Lessie Jones Little, *Childtimes: A Three-Generation Memoir,* illustrated by Jerry Pinkney, Crowell, 1979.
Sims, Rudine, *Shadow and Substance: Afro-American Experience in Contemporary Children's Literature,* National Council of Teachers of English, 1982.

PERIODICALS

Africa Woman, March-April, 1980.
Christian Science Monitor, February 21, 1990, p. 13; May 1, 1992, p. 10.
Encore, December 6, 1976.
Freedomways, Volume 21, number 1, 1981; Volume 22, number 2, 1982.
HCA Companion, first quarter, 1984.

Horn Book, December, 1975; April, 1977; November-December, 1991, p. 750; January-February, 1992, p. 59.
Instructor, March, 1990, p. 23.
Interracial Books for Children Bulletin, Volume 11, number 5, 1980; Volume 11, number 8, 1980.
Language Arts, September, 1980.
Metropolitan Washington, August, 1982.
Negro History Bulletin, April-May, 1975; September-October, 1978.
New York Times Book Review, May 5, 1974; November 3, 1974; March 26, 1989.
Parents Magazine, December, 1991, p. 178.
School Library Journal, December, 1979; September, 1991, p. 245; December, 1991, p. 92; January, 1992, p. 90; March, 1992, p. 237.
Top of the News, winter, 1980.
Tribune Books (Chicago), February 26, 1989; February 9, 1992.
Washington Post Book World, May 1, 1977; January 13, 1980; May 10, 1981; November 5, 1989; December 9, 1990; December 1, 1991.*

*   *   *

GREER, Ann Lennarson 1944-

PERSONAL: Born December 3, 1944, in Chicago, IL; daughter of Vernon E. C. (a physician) and Dee Ellen (a teacher; maiden name, Wing) Lennarson; married Scott Greer (a professor), December 22, 1969; children: Scott Edward Lennarson. *Education:* Lake Forest College, B.A., 1967; Northwestern University, M.A., 1968, Ph.D., 1970.

ADDRESSES: Home—9430 North Upper River Rd., River Hills, WI 53217. *Office*—University of Wisconsin—Milwaukee, Department of Sociology, Bolton Hall, P.O. Box 413, Milwaukee, WI 53201.

CAREER: Lake Forest College, Lake Forest, IL, assistant professor of sociology, 1969-72; University of Wisconsin—Milwaukee, assistant professor, 1972-76, associate professor of urban affairs and sociology, 1976-83, professor of sociology and urban studies, 1983—, director of Urban Research Center, 1976-82; Brunel Institute for Organizational and Social Studies, Brunel University, London, England, senior research associate, 1984-85; Health Policy Institute, Medical College of Wisconsin, adjunct professor of sociology, 1992—.

MEMBER: International Society for Technology Assessment in Health Care, American Sociological Association, Association for Health Services Research, Society for

Knowledge Utilization and Planned Change (board member), Milwaukee Academy of Medicine, Phi Beta Kappa.

AWARDS, HONORS: National Association of Schools of Public Affairs and Administration, fellow, 1974-75; National Institutes of Health, fellow, 1984-85.

WRITINGS:

The Mayor's Mandate: Municipal Statecraft and Political Trust, Schenkman, 1974.
(Editor with husband, Scott Greer) *Neighborhood and Ghetto: The Local Area in Large–Scale Society,* Basic Books, 1974.
(With S. Greer) *Understanding Sociology,* W. C. Brown, 1974.
(Editor with David Nachmias) *Self Governance in the Interpenetrated Society* (special issue of *Policy Sciences,* Volume 14, number 2), Elsevier, 1982.
(Senior editor with S. Greer) *Cities and Sickness: Health Care in Urban America,* Sage Publications, 1983.
(Co-author) *Health Care for the Urban Poor,* Rowman & Allanheld, 1983.
(Co-author with Eli Ginzberg and others) *Health Policy in Action: The Municipal Health Service Program,* Rowman & Allanheld, 1983.

Also co-editor of *Brown Reprints* and the series *Elements of Sociology,* both for W. C. Brown. Contributor of chapters to books and of articles to periodicals.

WORK IN PROGRESS: A book on the hospital and the culture of medicine, tentatively titled *Suspended Judgment.*

*   *   *

GREER, Scott (Allen) 1922-

PERSONAL: Born October 25, 1922, in Sweetwater, TX; son of Azzie Allen and Mary Lee (Scott) Greer; married Dorothy Marion Dewey, 1945 (divorced, 1969); married Ann Louise Lennarson (a professor of sociology), December 22, 1969; children: (first marriage) Eve Shannon, (second marriage) Scott Edward Lennarson. *Education:* Baylor University, A.B., 1946; University of California, Los Angeles, M.A., 1951, Ph.D., 1952.

ADDRESSES: Home—9430 North Upper River Rd., River Hills, WI 53217. *Office*—University of Wisconsin—Milwaukee, Department of Sociology, Bolton Hall, P.O. Box 413, Milwaukee, WI 53201.

CAREER: University of California, Santa Barbara, assistant professor of political science, 1951-52; Occidental College, Los Angeles, CA, assistant professor of political science, 1952-56; Metropolitan St. Louis Survey, St.

Louis, MO, chief sociologist, 1956-57; Northwestern University, Evanston, IL, associate professor, 1957-62, professor of political science and sociology, 1962-64, director of Center for Metropolitan Studies, 1960-66; University of Wisconsin, Milwaukee, faculty member, 1974—, acting director of Urban Social Institutions, 1977—.

MEMBER: American Sociological Association (fellow), American Political Science Association, Sociological Research Association, Midwest Sociological Society (president, 1978).

AWARDS, HONORS: Arizona Quarterly poetry award, 1961.

WRITINGS:

The Landscape Has Voices (poetry), Waco, 1946.
Social Organization, Random House, 1955.
Last Man In: Racial Access to Union Power, Free Press, 1959.
The Emerging City: Myth and Reality, Free Press, 1962.
Governing the Metropolis, Wiley, 1962.
Metropolitics: A Study of Political Culture, Wiley, 1963.
Via Urbana and Other Poems, Swallow Press, 1963.
Urban Renewal and American Cities, Bobbs-Merrill, 1965.
(With David Minar) *The Concept of Community,* Aldine, 1969.
The Logic of Social Inquiry, Aldine, 1969, published with new author introduction, Transaction Books, 1989.
The Urbane View, Oxford University Press, 1972.
(Editor with wife, Ann Lennarson Greer) *Neighborhood and Ghetto: The Local Area in Large-Scale Society,* Basic Books, 1974.
(With A. L. Greer) *Understanding Sociology,* W. C. Brown, 1974.
(Editor with Ronald D. Hedlund and James L. Gibson) *Accountability in Urban Society: Public Agencies under Fire,* Sage, 1978.
(Editor) *Ethics, Machines, and the American Urban Future,* Schenkman, 1981.
(Editor with A. L. Greer) *Cities and Sickness: Health Care in Urban America,* Sage, 1983.

WORK IN PROGRESS: Research on governance by citizens' boards; a study of community mental health centers.

*   *   *

GREY, Jerry 1926-

PERSONAL: Born October 25, 1926, in New York, NY; son of Abraham and Lillian (Danowitz) Grey; married Vivian Hoffman, June 27, 1948 (divorced); married Florence Maier (a fashion artist), 1974; children: (first marriage) Leslie Ann, Jacquelyn Eve (deceased). *Education:*

Cornell University, B.M.E., 1947, M.S., 1949; California Institute of Technology, Ph.D., 1952. *Politics:* Independent. *Religion:* Hebrew. *Avocational Interests:* Tennis, sailing, ice skating, and other sports.

ADDRESSES: Home—360 Dune Road, Box 428, Bridgehampton, NY 11932. *Office*—American Institute of Aeronautics and Astronautics, 370 L'Enfant Promenade SW, Washington, DC 20024.

CAREER: Cornell University, Ithaca, NY, instructor in thermodynamics, 1947-49; Fairchild Corp., Engine Division, Farmingdale, NY, development engineer, 1949-50; California Institute of Technology, Pasadena, hypersonic aerodynamicist at Guggenheim Aerospace Laboratory, 1950-51; Marquardt Aircraft Co., Van Nuys, CA, senior engineer, 1951-52; Princeton University, School of Engineering and Applied Science, Princeton, NJ, research associate, 1952-56, assistant professor, 1956-59, associate professor of aerospace science, 1960-67, director of Nuclear Propulsion Research Laboratory, 1962-67; Greyrad Corp., Princeton, president, 1959-71; American Institute of Aeronautics and Astronautics (AAIA), New York City, administrator for technical activities and communications, 1971-82; Calprobe Corp. (high-temperature instrumentation), New York City, president, 1972-83; Applied Solar Energy Corp., director, 1978-92; *Aerospace America,* New York City, publisher, 1982-87; AIAA, Washington, DC, director of Science and Technology Policy, 1987—.

Chairman of solar power advisory council, Office of Technology Assessment, U.S. Congress, 1974-80. Member of Commercial Space Transportation Advisory Committee, U.S. Department of Transportation, 1985-90. Member, Secretary of Energy Advisory Board, 1992—. Visiting professor of mechanical and aerospace engineering, Princeton University, 1990—. Holds nine U.S. patents and foreign patents. Former consultant to Los Alamos Scientific Laboratory, Atomic Industrial Forum, National Aeronautics and Space Administration, Princeton University (on nuclear fusion and space power), Radio Corp. of America, General Electric Co., Boeing Airplane Co., and other firms and laboratories. *Military Service:* U.S. Naval Reserve, active duty, 1943-46.

MEMBER: International Astronautical Federation (president), American Institute of Aeronautics and Astronautics (fellow; vice president, 1966-71), American Astronautical Society (member of board of directors), American Association of Engineering Societies (chairman, 1979-80), Scientists' Institute for Public Information (member of board of directors), American Association for the Advancement of Science, American Nuclear Society, National Space Society (director), Institute of Electrical and Electronics Engineers, American Society of Electrical Engineers, Aviation/Space Writers Association, New York Academy of Sciences, Sigma Xi, Phi Kappa Phi, Tau Beta Phi, Explorers Club, Cosmos Club, Bridgehampton Tennis and Surf Club, Key Biscayne Tennis Association.

AWARDS, HONORS: National Award, Aviation/Space Writers Association, 1987.

WRITINGS:

(Contributor) Angelo Miele, *Flight Mechanics: Theory of Flight Paths,* Volume 1, Addison-Wesley, 1962.
(Contributor) C. W. Watson, editor, *Nuclear Rocket Propulsion,* College of Engineering, University of Florida, 1964.
Nuclear Propulsion (audiovisual book), Educom, 1970.
The Race for Electric Power (juvenile), Westminster, 1972.
The Facts of Flight (juvenile), Westminster, 1973.
Noise! Noise! Noise! (juvenile), Westminster, 1975.
Enterprise, Morrow, 1979.
Aeronautics in China, American Institute of Aeronautics and Astronautics, 1981.
Beachheads in Space: A Blueprint for the Future, Macmillan, 1983.

EDITOR

(With Vivian Grey) *Space Flight Report to the Nation,* Basic Books, 1962.
(With J. Preston Layton) *New Space Transportation Systems,* American Institute of Aeronautics and Astronautics, 1973.
(With Arthur Henderson) *Exploration of the Solar System,* American Institute of Aeronautics and Astronautics, 1974.
Aircraft Fuel Conservation, American Institute of Aeronautics and Astronautics, 1974.
(With H. Killian and G. L. Dugger) *Solar Energy for Earth,* American Institute of Aeronautics and Astronautics, 1975.
Advanced Energy Technology, American Institute of Aeronautics and Astronautics, 1976.
The Technical Basis for a National Civil Aviation Research, Technology and Development Program, American Institute of Aeronautics and Astronautics, 1976.
(With Peter Downey and Bruce Davis) *Space: A Resource for Earth,* American Institute of Aeronautics and Astronautics, 1977.
Space Manufacturing Facilities, American Institute of Aeronautics and Astronautics, 1977.
Space Manufacturing II, American Institute of Aeronautics and Astronautics, 1977.
(With Robert L. Salkeld and Donald W. Patterson) *Space Transportation Systems: 1980-2000,* American Institute of Aeronautics and Astronautics, 1978.

(With Martin Newman) *Utilization of Alternative Fuels for Transportation,* American Institute of Aeronautics and Astronautics, 1979.

Space Manufacturing III, American Institute of Aeronautics and Astronautics, 1979.

Aerospace Technology and Marine Transport, American Institute of Aeronautics and Astronautics, 1979.

Working in Space, American Institute of Aeronautics and Astronautics, 1981.

Space Tracking and Data Systems, American Institute of Aeronautics and Astronautics, 1981.

Space Manufacturing 4, American Institute of Aeronautics and Astronautics, 1982.

Global Implications of Space Technology, American Institute of Aeronautics and Astronautics, 1982.

Aerospace Technology and Commercial Nuclear Power, American Institute of Aeronautics and Astronautics, 1982.

The U.S. Civil Space Program: An Investment in America, American Institute of Aeronautics and Astronautics, 1987.

Strategic Planning for Commercial Space Growth, American Institute of Aeronautics and Astronautics, 1989.

(With Emily Pelton) *Assessment of Strategic Missile Defense Technologies,* American Institute of Aeronautics and Astronautics, 1989.

(With Cynthia Womack) *The Role of Technology in Revitalizing U.S. General Aviation,* American Institute of Aeronautics and Astronautics, 1990.

Assessment of New Technologies for the Space Exploration Initiative, American Institute of Aeronautics and Astronautics, 1990.

Atmospheric Effects of Chemical Rocket Propulsion, American Institute of Aeronautics and Astronautics, 1991.

Assessment of Ballistic Missile Defense Technologies, American Institute of Aeronautics and Astronautics, 1993.

OTHER

Author of more than thirty proprietary technical reports and collaborator on others; also author of monographs. Contributor to *Encyclopedia of Science and Technology.* Contributor of popular articles to periodicals, including *Journal of Spacecraft and Rockets, Times* (London), *L'Aerotecnica, Penthouse, Omni, Science, Technology Review, Discover, Science 83, Environment, Leaders, New York Times, Aerospace America,* and *Disarmament.*

SIDELIGHTS: Jerry Gold once told *CA* that he is "highly optimistic about man's ability to ensure his own survival and, indeed, his continued movement toward maturity, despite the apparent difficulties he keeps generating."

BIOGRAPHICAL/CRITICAL SOURCES:

PERIODICALS

New York Times, July 3, 1979.
Saturday Review, June 23, 1979.
Spectrum, September, 1984.

*   *   *

GROSS, Johannes Heinrich   1916-

PERSONAL: Born September 13, 1916, in Bonn, Germany; son of Michael (a farmer) and Anna Maria (Pung) Gross. *Education:* Attended Theological Faculty of Trier, 1937-39, 1945-48, Habilitation in Old Testament, 1955; University of Bonn, Dr.Theol., 1951; Biblical Institute, Rome, Italy, Lic.Bibl., 1953.

ADDRESSES: Home—Agnesstrasse 13, 8400 Regensburg, Germany. *Office*—University of Regensburg, 8400 Regensburg, Germany.

CAREER: Secular priest; Theological Faculty of Trier, Trier, Germany, assistant professor, 1953-57, ordinary professor of theology, 1957-68; University of Saarbruecken, Saarbruecken, Germany, assistant professor of theology, 1957-68; University of Regensburg, Regensburg, Germany, professor, 1968—, dean of theological faculty, 1968-69. *Military service:* German Army, 1939-45.

MEMBER: Society of Biblical Literature, Organisation Beirat der Goerresgesellschaft.

WRITINGS:

Weltherrschaft als religioese Idee, Hanstein, 1953.
Weltfrieden im Alten Testament und Alten Orient, Paulinus-Verlag, 1956, 2nd edition, 1967.
Kleine Bibelkunde zum Alten Testament, Koesel, 1967, translation published as *Biblical Introduction to the Old Testament,* University of Notre Dame Press, 1968.
Umkehr aus ganzem Herzen, Verl. Kath. Bibelwerk, 1972.
Kernfragen des Alten Testaments, Pustet-Verlag, 1977.
(Contributor) *Geistliche Schriftlesung,* Patmos-Verlag, 1978-80.

WORK IN PROGRESS: Commentaries.

*   *   *

GRUENBAUM, Adolf   1923-

PERSONAL: Born May 15, 1923, in Cologne, Germany; naturalized U.S. citizen; son of Benjamin (a businessman) and Hannah (Freiwillig) Gruenbaum; married Thelma Braverman, June 16, 1949; children: Barbara Susan. *Education:* Wesleyan University, B.A., 1943; Yale University, M.S. (physics), 1948, Ph.D. (philosophy), 1951.

ADDRESSES: Home—7141 Roycrest Pl., Pittsburgh, PA 15208. *Office*—2510 Cathedral of Learning, University of Pittsburgh, Pittsburgh, PA 15260-6125.

CAREER: Lehigh University, Bethlehem, PA, instructor, 1950-51, assistant professor, 1951-53, associate professor, 1953-55, professor of philosophy, 1955-56, William Wilson Selfridge Professor of Philosophy, 1956-60; University of Pittsburgh, Pittsburgh, PA, Andrew Mellon Professor of Philosophy, 1960—, research professor of psychiatry, 1979—, Center for Philosophy of Science, director, 1960-78, chairman, 1978—.

Visiting research professor, Center for Philosophy of Science, University of Minnesota, 1956 and 1959; Arnold Isenberg Memorial Lecturer, Michigan State University, 1965; Matchette Lecturer, Wesleyan University, 1966; Louis Clark Vanuxem Lecturer, Princeton University, 1967; Monday Lecturer, University of Chicago, and Mahlon Powell Lecturer, Indiana University at Bloomington, both 1968; Thalheimer Lecturer, Johns Hopkins University, 1969; Everett W. Hall Lecturer, University of Iowa, 1973; Einstein Centennial Lecturer, Institute of Advanced Study, 1979-80; Konstanz Lecturer, University of Konstanz, 1983; Werner Heisenberg Lecturer, Bavarian Academy of Sciences, 1985; Gifford Lecturer, University of St. Andrews, 1985; Alberto J. Coffa Memorial Lecturer, Indiana University at Bloomington, 1986; visiting Mellon Professor, California Institute of Technology, 1990; and Gustav Bergmann Memorial Lecturer and Bean Visiting Professor, University of Iowa, both 1993. Visiting professor, Summer Institute for College Teachers in Philosophy and the Sciences, Stanford University, 1967; visiting distinguished professor, University of Alberta, 1988. Visiting lecturer in philosophy at University of Notre Dame, and University of Duesseldorf, both 1976. Lecturer at research management seminars conducted by E. I. DuPont Co., 1965-69. Visiting fellow, Center for Advanced Study in the Behavioral Sciences, Stanford University, summer, 1967; visiting scholar, Southern Methodist University, 1972. Chairman or member of committees and panels on philosophy for National Science Foundation, International Congress of Logic, Methodology, Philosophy of Science, and others. *Military service:* U.S. Army, Military Intelligence, 1944-46.

MEMBER: American Academy of Arts and Sciences (fellow), American Philosophical Association (president of eastern division, 1982-83; member of advisory committee of the program committee, 1986-89), Philosophy of Science Association (president, 1965-67 and 1968-70), Phi-

losophy of the Physical Sciences, American Association for the Advancement of Science (fellow; vice-president, 1963), Academy of Humanism, British Society for the Philosophy of Science, Hellenic Society for Philosophical Studies (Greece), Phi Beta Kappa, Omicron Delta Kappa (honorary member), Sigma Xi.

AWARDS, HONORS: Alfred Noble Robinson Award for teaching, Lehigh University, 1953; Ford Foundation faculty fellow, 1954-55; J. Walker Tomb Prize, Princeton University, 1958; alumni honor citation, Wesleyan University, 1959; chosen "great professor" by the student yearbook, University of Pittsburgh *OWL*, 1967; Senior U.S. Scientist Award, Alexander von Humboldt Foundation, 1985, for research accomplishments; Freguene Prize for Philosophy of Science, Italian Parliament, 1989; Wilbur Lucius Cross Medal, Yale University, 1990; recipient of National Science Foundation research grants; Fritz Thyssen Stiftung grants; laureate, Academy of Humanism.

WRITINGS:

Philosophical Problems of Space and Time, Knopf, 1963, 2nd edition, Reidel, 1973.

Modern Science and Zeno's Paradoxes, Wesleyan University Press, 1967, 2nd revised edition, Allen & Unwin, 1968.

Geometry and Chronometry in Philosophical Perspective, University of Minnesota Press, 1968.

The Foundations of Psychoanalysis: A Philosophical Critique, University of California Press, 1984.

Psychoanalyse in Wissenschafts-theoretischer sicht—Zum werk Sigmund Freuds und seiner rezeption, Universitaetsverlag Konstanz, 1987.

Psicoanalisi: Obiezioni E Risposte, Armando Editore, 1988.

(Editor with Wesley C. Salmon) *The Limitations of Deductivism,* University of California Press, 1988.

(Editor) *Kritische Betrachtungen zur Psychoanalyse,* Springer Verlag, 1991.

Freud e il Teismo, Edizioni Scientifiche Italiani, 1991.

Validation in Clinical Theory of Psychoanalysis: A Study in the Philosophy of Psychoanalysis, International Universities Press, 1993.

La Psychanalyse a l'Epreuve, Editions de l'Eclat, 1993.

Contributor to many books, including *Readings in the Philosophy of Science,* edited by Herbert Feigel and M. Brodbeck, Appleton-Century-Crofts, 1953; *Psychoanalysis, Scientific Method, and Philosophy,* New York University Press, 1959; *Philosophy of Science,* edited by B. Baumrin, Wiley, 1963; *Relativity Theory,* L. P. Williams, Wiley, 1968; *Foundations of Space-Time Theories,* edited by Glymour Earman and Stachel, University of Minnesota Press, 1977; and *Placebo: Theory, Research, and Mechanism,*

Guilford, 1985. Also contributor to proceedings. General editor, with Larry Lauden, of "Pittsburgh Series in the Philosophy and History of Science," University of California Press. Contributor to *Encyclopedia of Philosophy* and of about 250 articles to professional journals. Member of editorial board, *Encyclopedia of Philosophy*; member of board of editors, *International Forum for Psychoanalysis, Philosophy of Science, Philosopher's Index, American Philosophical Quarterly, Studies in History and Philosophy of Science, Humanities in Society, Erkenntnis, Iride, Cognitive Science Reports, Epistemologia, Al-Kindi,* and *Psychoanalysis and Contemporary Thought;* member of editorial advisory board, *Boston Studies in the Philosophy of Science.*

*   *   *

GRUTZMACHER, Harold M(artin) Jr. 1930-

PERSONAL: Born November 17, 1930, in Chicago, IL; son of Harold Martin and Irene Evelyn (Kowalski) Grutzmacher; married Marjorie Sharlene Anderson, November 5, 1955; children: Stephen Robert, Sharon Lynn, Alison. *Education:* Beloit College, B.A., 1952; Northwestern University, M.A., 1953, Ph.D., 1962. *Avocational Interests:* Reading, sports reporting.

ADDRESSES: Home—Box 153, Ephraim, WI 54211. *Office*—Pasttimes Books, Box 153, Ephraim, WI 54211.

CAREER: Carthage College, Carthage, IL, assistant professor of English, 1958-60; Knox College, Galesburg, IL, instructor in English, 1960-65; Parsons College, Fairfield, IA, chairman of rhetoric, 1965-67; University of Tampa, Tampa, FL, vice president of academic affairs, 1967-70; Beloit College, WI, dean of students, 1970-75; Pastimes Books, Ephraim and Sister Bay, WI, owner and manager, 1978—. *Chicago Tribune,* Chicago, IL, book reviewer, 1962-73; *Tampa Tribune,* book reviewer, 1967-70; *Door County Advocate,* political reporter, 1976-85; *Milwaukee Journal,* Milwaukee, WI, poetry reviewer, 1980—. Has given poetry readings and served as judge in poetry competitions. *Military service:* U.S. Army, 1956-68.

MEMBER: American Association of University Professors, Peninsula Arts Association, Wisconsin Academy Republican, Tau Kappa Epsilon.

WRITINGS:

A Giant of My World, Golden Quill, 1960.
Generations, Spoon River Poetry Press, 1983.
(Editor) *A Grace Samuelson Sampler,* 1985.
(Editor) *Young with Ephraim,* 1985.

Contributor to a number of literary periodicals, including *Cornucopia, American Weave, Approach, Epos, Wormwood Review, Northwestern Tri-Quarterly,* and *Door County Advocate.**

H

HALLIDAY, Dorothy
See DUNNETT, Dorothy

*   *   *

HANNAH, Barry 1942-

PERSONAL: Born April 23, 1942, in Meridian, MS; son of William (an insurance agent) and Elizabeth (King) Hannah; divorced; children: Barry, Jr., Ted, Lee. *Education:* Mississippi College, Clinton, B.A. in pre-med, 1964; University of Arkansas, M.A., 1966, M.F.A. in creative writing, 1967.

CAREER: Writer. Clemson University, Clemson, SC, teacher of literature and fiction, 1967-73; Middlebury College, Middlebury, VT, writer in residence, 1974-75; University of Alabama, Tuscaloosa, AL, teacher of literature and fiction, 1975-80; worked as writer with filmmaker Robert Altman in Hollywood, CA, 1980; University of Iowa, Iowa City, writer in residence, 1981; University of Mississippi, University, writer in residence, 1982, 1984-85; University of Montana, Missoula, writer in residence, 1982-83.

AWARDS, HONORS: Bellaman Foundation award in fiction, 1970; Atherton fellowship from Bread Loaf Writers Conference, 1971; nomination for National Book Award, 1972, for *Geronimo Rex;* Arnold Gingrich Award for short fiction from *Esquire,* 1978, for *Airships;* special award from American Academy of Arts and Letters, 1978.

WRITINGS:

NOVELS

Geronimo Rex, Knopf, 1972.
Nightwatchmen, Viking, 1973.
Ray, Knopf, 1981.

The Tennis Handsome, Knopf, 1983.
Hey Jack!, Dutton, 1987.
Boomerang, Houghton/Seymour Lawrence, 1989.
Never Die, Houghton/Seymour Lawrence, 1991.
Bats Out of Hell, Houghton/Seymour Lawrence, 1993.

OTHER

Airships (short stories), Knopf, 1978.
Two Stories (short stories), Nouveau Press, 1982.
Black Butterfly (short stories), Palaemon Press, 1982.
Power and Light (novella), Palaemon Press, 1983.
Captain Maximus (short stories), Knopf, 1985.

Contributor to periodicals, including *Esquire.*

SIDELIGHTS: Barry Hannah is among the most prominent writers to emerge from the American South since World War II. His novels and short stories reveal a preoccupation with violence and sex that marks him as a disturbing and often demanding author. His first novel, *Geronimo Rex,* details the struggles and adventures of Harry Monroe, a romantic youth with literary aspirations in Louisiana. Amid the turbulent racial struggle of the early 1960s, Monroe abandons his plans to write and begins a period of disappointment and depravity with a succession of local whores. At his spiritual nadir, he desperately adopts the legendary Indian warrior Geronimo as his inspiration. "What I especially liked about Geronimo," Monroe declares, "was that he had cheated, lied, stolen, usurped, killed, burned, raped. . . . I thought I would like to get into that line of work." At college, Monroe befriends Bobby Dove Fleece, a pallid youth cowed by domineering parents. The two students eventually oppose an avid racist, Whitfield Peter, in a wild shootout culminating in the bigot's defeat. Monroe then marries and enrolls in graduate school.

Geronimo Rex was greeted with great enthusiasm by most critics and was nominated for a National Book Award. Jim Harrison, writing in the *New York Times Book Review,* called it "almost a totally successful book" and declared, "The writing is intricate enough to make it hard to believe that it's really a first novel." Although John Skow, in the *Washington Post,* protested that the book's momentum was disrupted by its subplots, he agreed that the language was "raucously good" and anticipated Hannah's next work.

Hannah returned to Harry Monroe in the following novel, *Nightwatchmen.* While studying for his doctorate, Monroe meets Thorpe Trove, a rich but strange figure whose estate functions as a meeting place for several of Monroe's fellow students. Thorpe is obsessed with the Knocker, a mysterious killer plaguing the academic community of Southern Mississippi University. *Nightwatchmen* focuses on Thorpe's efforts to expose the Knocker, for which purpose he recruits an equally eccentric detective, the elderly Howard Hunter. *Nightwatchmen* abounds in scenes or speeches of mutilation and death. In taped accounts, provided by acquaintances of the Knocker's victims, gruesome acts are related in a manner that both reinforces the notion of society as violent and underscores its callous acceptance of mayhem. In addition, Hurricane Camille wreaks havoc on the area, accounting for more grisly death and chaos. Perhaps because of these sensational aspects, *Nightwatchmen* failed to entice critics and was ultimately ignored.

In 1978 Hannah produced his first collection of short stories, *Airships.* Equally comprising new work and stories previously featured in *Esquire,* the volume served to confirm Hannah's standing as a unique Southern writer. Several stories in *Airships* were culled from Hannah's abandoned novel on the adventures of Confederate General Jeb Stuart. Centering on the recollections of maimed survivors of Stuart's campaigns, these stories range in subject from the brutality of war to the obsessive love for Stuart harbored by a homosexual Confederate. Other tales show a similar preoccupation with violence and deviant behavior in events ranging from tennis tournaments to the apocalypse. In the particularly unsettling "Eating Wives and Friends," Hannah portrays an impending world in which the 1930s are referred to as the "Mild Depression." It is a nightmare of ghoulish depravity, however humorously represented, in which trespassers on private property are shot and eaten, and in which impoverished wanderers are compelled to eat grass and even poison ivy to survive. Writing in the *New York Times Book Review,* Michael Wood hailed the collection's longer works for their "careful, sympathetic wit [in depicting] the string of unlikely shocks and half-hearted enthusiasmms that often make up a life." *Time*'s Paul Gray noted that most of the tales "are

artfully rounded-off vignettes humping with humor and menace."

Hannah's third novel, *Ray,* recounts the experiences of an apparently immortal, and slightly unhinged, protagonist who served in both the Civil War and the Vietnam War and who also worked in Alabama as a doctor. Like the preceding novels and *Airships, Ray* emphasizes violence and death as its title character recalls a gruesome event in Vietnam, contemplates suicide, and reflects on a defeat suffered in Virginia during the Civil War. *Newsweek*'s Walter Clemons described Ray as "a griper, but also an accepter," adding that "he wakes up every morning voracious for more sex, more fights, more disappointments." Clemons characterized the novel as a work "of brilliant particulars, dizzying juxtapositions and no reassuring narrative transitions." Benjamin DeMott was exuberant in praising *Ray* as "the funniest, weirdest, soul-happiest work by a genuinely young American writer that I've read in a long while."

In *The Tennis Handsome,* Hannah further pursued his interest in graphic, and often absurd, violence. Ostensibly concerned with the exploits of an incredibly attractive tennis player, French Edward, and his twisted mentor, Baby Levaster, *The Tennis Handsome* abounds in scenes of perverse mayhem—including a woman raped by a walrus—and absurdist humor. Reviewer Jack Beatty, in the *New Republic,* complained that the overwhelmingly violent nature of the novel resulted in "a lurid gumbo of inconsequence," lacking in plot, character growth, or logic of development. Ivan Gold, writing in the *New York Times Book Review,* was less critical, conceding that *The Tennis Handsome* might not be Hannah's best book, but that "it's as good a place to start as any." Gold was impressed with the bizarre tone of the novel, and noting that it was partially derived from works first featured in *Airships,* said that "the stories are worth repeating." But Christopher Lehmann-Haupt in the *New York Times* was exhausted by the novel's frantic pace. Observing that Hannah's flamboyant language "palls eventually" and that the book lacked credible characterrs, Lehmann-Haupt added, "Finally, the only living thing in 'The Tennis Handsome' is the author's fierce determination to stun us with his zaniness."

Hannah's 1985 story collection, *Captain Maximus,* represented for some reviewers a powerful step forward from the failings of *The Tennis Handsome.* One widely noticed story in the collection, "Idaho," is a semiautobiographical work about Hannah's meeting with the late Montana poet Richard Hugo, and features such other well-known writers as Thomas McGuane. Another story, "Power and Light," is an assemblage of "quick camera cuts," in the words of *Washington Post Book World* critic Doris Betts, among a cast of Seattle characters. George Stade, in the

New York Times Book Review, claimed that "Power and Light" "is evidence that Mr. Hannah has more than one way of writing like no one else. The prose now is cool, distant, mostly without personal inflection. . . . Anything written by Mr. Hannah is well worth having." While reprising some of the violence of earlier books and once again showcasing Hannah's "vital" prose, *Captain Maximus* also features "more narrative movement" than *Ray* and *The Tennis Handsome,* according to Lehmann-Haupt. Placing Hannah "at the forefront of America's latest crop of experimental writers" alongside Raymond Carver and Frederick Barthelme, Peter Ross in the *Detroit News* felt that Hannah "serves up an unimpeachably original imagination, a mature sense of self-mockery and an abundance of technical and pyrotechnic skill."

In 1987, Hannah emerged with a new novel, *Hey Jack!* Featuring an antiheroic character named Homer, who goes nameless until the last page, the novel showed "in graphic detail," according to Michiko Kakutani in the *New York Times,* "just how short, brutish and nasty life in a small Southern town can be." In this fictional town—which strongly resembles the university community of Oxford, Mississippi—"there are exactly five topics of conversation," Kakutani observed, "money, Negroes, women, religion, and Elvis Presley." Kakutani opined that the novel was made up of rehashed versions of previous Hannah characters, adding up to a set of misfits without meaning. Jonathan Yardley, in the *Washington Post,* felt that Hannah had "dug himself into a rut" with the book. Thomas R. Edwards, in the *New York Times Book Review,* suggested that "geography, culture, and a sense of his precursors—especially Faulkner—seem to be interfering with [Hannah's] performance." However, Richard Eder in the *Los Angeles Times Book Review* called *Hey Jack!* a "compelling novella," finding that "Homer's wandering cogitations, his tales, his pleasures and his anguish all ramble to a purpose. They test and reveal the tensile strength of a cord that is never really loosed . . . that binds his Southern community and perhaps all communities to their own."

The 1989 *Boomerang* was termed a "brief, minor but brilliant autobiographical novel" by *New York Times Book Review* critic Joanne Kennedy. In this book, the narrator ruminates about his life in a series of episodes which are "held together by three boomerang-throwing sessions." Southern boyhood, failed marriages, drinking, and dogs feature prominently, as do celebrities such as film director Robert Altman, actor Jack Nicholson, and singer-writer Jimmy Buffett. Stating that the book broke no new ground, Kennedy observed, "what we get from Mr. Hannah is instinct and impact over plot, as always. And in clean, spare prose and a distinctive raconteur's voice that could only be Southern, there is originality, power, pain

and deadpan humor." Alex Raskin, in the *Los Angeles Times Book Review,* singled out Hannah's satirical characterizations for praise, calling *Boomerang* "a fortuitous blend of novel and autobiography."

Hannah's next novel, *Never Die,* is set in Nitburg, Texas, in 1910, and presents "a surreal version" of the old West, in the words of *Washington Post Book World* reviewer Richard Gehr. Calling the book "entertaining," Gehr raised serious reservations about its "static" characters and its many narrative quirks. Janet Kaye, in the *New York Times Book Review,* was unsettled by the book's combination of violence and parody, as well as its "undeveloped" characters and its plot's lack of conviction.

Describing his own work for *CA,* Hannah admitted its autobiographical bent, saying, "The main part of my stories always comes out of life. I'm terribly affected by something, obsessed with it, or find a situation I can't forget, and then the rest is imagination. . . . I have to do quite a bit of life or I just don't feel I've anything to say. . . . I don't come in at eight o'clock and hit the typewriter till two every day like some writers. I have to feel something." He has expressed admiration for other writers, such as Ernest Hemingway and Walker Percy, and gratitude to his teachers and literary friends at the University of Arkansas, Bill Harrison, Ben Kimpel, and Jim Whitehead. Hannah credits his graduate school experience with helping make him a writer: "I found my 'soul' in the writing classes I took . . . it turned my whole life around. Even if you just get self-educated around a university, it's good to have a few props and know some good books."

BIOGRAPHICAL/CRITICAL SOURCES:

BOOKS

Contemporary Literary Criticism, Gale, Volume 23, 1983, Volume 38, 1986.
Dictionary of Literary Biography, Volume 6: *American Novelists since World War II,* Second Series, Gale, 1980.

PERIODICALS

Chicago Tribune Book World, November 23, 1980; July 3, 1983.
Detroit News, August 4, 1985.
Los Angeles Times Book Review, September 6, 1987, p. 3; September 13, 1987; May 7, 1989, p. 6.
Nation, November 29, 1980; June 1, 1985, pp. 677-79.
New Republic, December 13, 1980; April 18, 1983, p. 39.
Newsweek, May 8, 1978; December 15, 1980.
New York, May 16, 1983, p. 66.
New Yorker, September 9, 1972.
New York Review of Books, April 23, 1978; June 27, 1985, pp. 33-34.

New York Times, April 15, 1978; April 18, 1983, p. C15; April 29, 1985, p. C18; November 18, 1987.
New York Times Book Review, May 14, 1972, April 23, 1978; May 21, 1978; November 16, 1980; December 21, 1981; May 1, 1983, pp. 11, 19; June 9, 1985, p. 14; November 1, 1987; May 14, 1989, p. 19, July 7, 1991, p. 18.
Saturday Review, June 10, 1978; November, 1980.
Time, May 15, 1978; January 12, 1981; July 22, 1985, p. 70.
Washington Post, April 19, 1972; August 26, 1987.
Washington Post Book World, June 23, 1985, p. 11; March 16, 1986; August 17, 1986, June 2, 1991, p. 3.*

* * *

HANSEN, Joyce (Viola) 1942-

PERSONAL: Born October 18, 1942, in New York, NY; daughter of Austin Victor (a photographer) and Lillian (Dancy) Hansen; married Matthew Nelson (a musician), December 18, 1982. *Education:* Pace University, B.A., 1972; New York University, M.A., 1978.

ADDRESSES: Home—19 Dongan Pl., New York, NY 10040. *Office*—c/o Walker and Co., 720 Fifth Ave., New York, NY 10019.

CAREER: Board of Education, New York City, teacher of reading and English, 1973—; Empire State College, Brooklyn, NY, mentor, 1987—.

MEMBER: Harlem Writers Guild, Society of Children's Book Writers, PEN.

AWARDS, HONORS: Parents Choice literature citation, 1986, for *Yellow Bird and Me;* honorable mention in literature, Coretta Scott King Award, 1987, for *Which Way Freedom?*

WRITINGS:

CHILDREN'S FICTION

The Gift-Giver, Houghton, 1980.
Home Boy, Houghton, 1982.
Yellow Bird and Me (sequel to *The Gift-Giver*), Houghton, 1986.
Which Way Freedom?, Walker, 1986, published as *Which Way to Freedom,* 1991.

CHILDREN'S NONFICTION

Out from This Place (part of history series for young adults), Walker, 1988.
Between Two Fires: Black Soldiers in the Civil War (part of "African-American Experience" series), F. Watts, 1993.

OTHER

(Contributor) David E. Nelson, *Utah Education Quality Indicators,* Utah State Office of Education, 1983.

SIDELIGHTS: Joyce Hansen is the author of children's novels that have been praised for their convincing depiction of black children in both contemporary and historical settings. Her first three novels, *The Gift-Giver, Yellow Bird and Me,* and *Home Boy* feature the lives of inner-city children in New York, while *Which Way Freedom?* and *Out from This Place* dramatize the experiences of young blacks during the time of Civil War, slavery and afterwards. An English teacher in New York City schools, Hansen strives for realistic settings in her books, in addition to authentic dialect and lively storytelling, as a way to reach out to young readers with positive messages of support and guidance. "I take writing for children very seriously," she once stated. "So many children need direction—so many are floundering. I write for all children who need and can relate to the things I write about—the importance of family, maintaining a sense of hope, and responsibility for oneself and other living things."

Hansen was born in 1942 in New York City, and grew up in a Bronx neighborhood which provides many of the experiences in her first novel, *The Gift-Giver.* During her girlhood, as she recalled, "New York City neighborhoods were thriving urban villages that children could grow and develop in." In the *Gift-Giver,* which describes a foster child who positively influences others with his caring nature, Hansen attempted to recreate the secure atmosphere of immediate and extended family that she knew as a young girl. In doing so, she also emphasized the positive forces at work within inner cities to counter such perils as poverty, violence, and drugs. "We forget that there are many people in our so-called slums or ghettos that manage to raise whole and healthy families under extreme conditions," Hansen once commented. "Not every story coming out of the black communities of New York City are horror stories."

Hansen was influenced to become a writer by both her mother and father who provided, as she once described, an atmosphere "rich in family love and caring." Her mother, who had aspirations to become a journalist at one time, passed on to Hansen an appreciation for books and reading. "She grew up in a large family during the depression and though she was intelligent and literate she couldn't even finish high school because she had to work," Hansen remembered. "She was my first teacher." From her father, a photographer from the Caribbean, Hansen learned the art of storytelling. "He entertained my brothers and me with stories about his boyhood in the West Indies and his experiences as a young man in the Harlem of the 20s and 30s," she once commented. "I also learned from him to see the beauty and poetry in the everyday scenes and 'just plain folks' he captured in his photographs."

Hansen received a bachelor's degree from Pace University in 1972, followed several years later by a master's degree from New York University. In 1973, she began a career teaching in New York City schools, where she worked at one time as a special education instructor for adolescents with reading disabilities. Through her teaching work, which predominantly involves black and Hispanic students, Hansen became aware of the positive results to be gained by providing students with literature they could identify with. "Literature can be a great teacher, yet large numbers of Black and other youngsters of color never have a chance to explore themselves or their lives through the literary process . . . ," she stated in *Interracial Books for Children Bulletin*. "*All* children need sound, solid literature that relates to their own experiences and interests," she added, especially those "children who, for whatever reason, have learning difficulties."

Hansen's own work as a children's novelist has been greatly influenced by her students. "Though I often complain that I don't have enough time to write because I teach, if I didn't teach, I wouldn't have been moved to write some of the stories I've created thus far," she stated in *Horn Book*. Describing her students as her "muse," Hansen commented in *Horn Book* that, as is the case with the innovative nicknames derived by her students, she is "influenced by their creativity—the way they twist, bend, enliven, deconstruct, and sometimes even destroy language; their loves, hates, fears, feelings, and needs filter into my writing." While Hansen's objectives as a reading teacher propel a major part of her writing, she maintains the necessity of relating stories that students like her own would respond to. Hansen tests her writing by asking, as she recounted in *Horn Book*, "what I am going to do . . . to make a reluctant reader want to read [a story]. . . . I imagine I hear Tatoo whispering in my ear, 'Miss Hansen, you know I'm not going to read all of that description'; or Milk Crate muttering, 'Boring, boring, boring'; or Skeletal yelling, 'This ain't like us.'"

As a result, Hansen's novels have been praised by critics for their convincingly-drawn characters and accurate depictions of atmosphere and black dialect. Regarding *The Gift-Giver*, which is told through the language and observations of a fifth-grade girl (Doris), Hansen "paints an effective, inside picture of childhood in a New York ghetto," commented Judith Goldberger in *Booklist*. The novel tells the story of Doris's friendship with Amir, her shy and quiet classmate, from whom she learns valuable lessons in friendship and caring for others. According to Zena Sutherland in the *Bulletin of the Center for Children's Books*, the novel's strengths are "well-developed plot threads that

are nicely knit, a memorable depiction of a person whose understanding and compassion are gifts to his friends, and a poignantly realistic ending." In *Yellow Bird and Me*, the sequel to *The Gift-Giver*, Hansen relates the story of Doris as she, in turn, helps a troubled classmate overcome a learning disability and discover his talents as a theatrical performer. "Smoothly written and easy to read," according to a contributor to *Kirkus Reviews*, the novel utilizes colloquial black English with "strength and vitality." Furthermore, the contributor continues, the novel is "rich with the distinctive personalities in Doris's world . . . [and] is particularly valuable for its emphasis on friendship, generosity of spirit, and seeing what's below the surface."

In her novel *Home Boy*, likewise set in New York's inner city, Hansen relates the life of a troubled teenaged boy (Marcus) from the Caribbean who stabs another boy in a fight. Alternating between scenes of New York and Marcus's native Caribbean, the novel reveals the damaging influences of the boy's family, his involvement with selling drugs, and the pressures of adjusting to life in a foreign city. Inspired by an actual newspaper account of a Jamaican boy who stabbed and killed another youth in a New York City high school, Hansen modeled Marcus as "a composite of the many young men I've met through teaching," she commented. Despite its tragic overtones, the novel finds positives in the efforts of Marcus's girlfriend to get him on track, in addition to the affirming support of his reconciled parents and Marcus's own will to reform. The novel "revolves around Blacks and inner city life," wrote Kevin Kenny in *Voice of Youth Advocates*, yet holds appeal for many readers in its exploration of such universal themes as "quests for dignity, pursuits of familial and personal love, and the search for individual understanding."

After writing three works set in New York City, Hansen made a notable departure with two historical novels that take place during the American Civil War and postwar Reconstruction period. Again influenced by her students, Hansen evolved into historical fiction after she "began to think about how much drama there is in the black experience that is unknown to our youth and how historical fiction is a good way to make history come alive for young people," she wrote in *Horn Book*. Although vastly different in location and time period than her previous fiction, Hansen's historical novels similarly offer strong characterizations, in addition to authentic depictions of atmosphere and dialect. *Which Way Freedom?* tells the story of a young slave (Obi) who escapes from South Carolina and joins a black Union regiment during the Civil War, while the sequel, *Out from This Place*, tells the story of Obi's female friend (Easter) as she moves forward with her life after the Civil War. In both books, Hansen intersperses authentic black Gullah Island dialect with documented and little-known details of everyday life for slaves in their struggles before and after freedom.

Initially, Hansen had some difficulty making the transition to this type of writing: "Not being an historian, and deciding to write an historical novel, I felt like a trespasser on someone else's property who was tampering with a story that was not my own," she explained in *The New Advocate.* "I was an explorer in a strange land without a map or compass." Hansen did extensive research and read numerous histories of the period, including a collection of interviews with former slaves, for over a year before she began to write. She was surprised to find that the facts she uncovered during this period reshaped her view of history and her ideas about the way history should be presented to young readers: "My problem was that not all [the historic facts discovered through research] were compatible with the images that I wanted to create—images of a people bravely struggling to be free," she remembered in *The New Advocate.* "As I continued my reading and research, I came across still more conflicting and contradictory information. As a result, I had to reassess my purposes. Was I trying merely to confirm my own beliefs, or was I attempting to understand what those times might have been like? What I was, in fact, learning was that history is made up of individual stories shaded by individual perceptions and experiences . . . I was beginning to understand just how complex history is and that it defies any grand, simplistic interpretations."

Hansen also commented in *The New Advocate* on the responsibility involved in writing books for a young audience. "As [children] seek to understand an increasingly confusing world, their minds are malleable and vulnerable. Because of this, the responsibility of writers is enormous. Our job is to arrest the spread of ignorance, to inform, to provide insight and perspective, to entertain. Our words are powerful and those of us who are fortunate enough to have our words read must not abuse that power and privilege." Hansen added comments which give insight into the motivation behind her work: "I think the ultimate aim in any book we write for young people should be to show the heights to which humanity can reach even as we expose the depths to which we can sink. The word is powerful. We must use our words to help our children acquire a richness of soul and spirit so that maybe one fine day we will learn to live with ourselves and each other in love and harmony."

BIOGRAPHICAL/CRITICAL SOURCES:

BOOKS

Children's Literature Review, Volume 21, Gale, 1990.
Twentieth-Century Children's Writers, 3rd edition, St. James Press, 1989.

PERIODICALS

Booklist, January 1, 1981, p. 624; January 15, 1989, p. 871.
Bulletin of the Center for Children's Books, January, 1981, p. 94; April, 1986; July-August, 1986.
Horn Book, December, 1980, p. 641; November, 1986, p.745; September/October, 1987, pp. 644-646.
Interracial Books for Children Bulletin, Volume 15, Number 4, 1984, pp. 9-11.
Kirkus Reviews, April 1, 1986, p. 545.
Language Arts, December, 1986, p. 823.
Los Angeles Times Book Review, July 13, 1986, p. 6.
New Advocate, Volume 3, number 3, summer 1990, pp. 167-173.
Publishers Weekly, October 24, 1980, p. 49.
Voice of Youth Advocates, February, 1983, p. 36; February, 1989, p. 285.*

*   *   *

HARTER, Eugene C(laudius) 1926-

PERSONAL: Born August 11, 1926, in Rio de Janeiro, Brazil; immigrated to United States, 1935; son of Eugene C. (a U.S. State Department consul and businessman) and Maglin (a teacher; maiden name, Harris) Harter; married Dorothy Bierly (a literary agent and editor), August 27, 1949; children: Eugene C. III, Dorothy Ann Harter Tucker, David, Melissa. *Education:* Wittenberg University, B.A., 1949; graduate study at George Washington University, 1973-74, and University of Virginia, 1976. *Religion:* Deist. *Avocational Interests:* Professional baseball, politics, newspaper history, religious absurdism studies, advocating free press, travel.

ADDRESSES: Agent—Dorothy Harter, 416 High St., Chestertown, MD 21620.

CAREER: Ansonia Times, Ansonia, OH, editor, 1951; *Garrett Clipper,* Garrett, IN, business manager, 1953-56; *Des Plaines Journal,* Des Plaines, IL, advertising manager, 1956-60; *Mundelein News,* Mundelein, IL, publisher, 1960; *Libertyville News,* Libertyville, IL, publisher, 1960; *News Journal,* Campbellsville, KY, publisher and editor, 1962-66; U.S. Department of State, Washington, DC, 1969-82, publication specialist and served as attache to Beirut, Lebanon, 1969-70, and Mexico City, 1970, U.S. consul to Brazil, 1971-73, cultural and economic specialist with International Communication Agency, 1973-78, U.S. consul to Ecuador, 1979-80, appointed career member of Senior Foreign Service with rank of counselor, 1981, member of policy planning staff, International Communication Agency, 1981-82. Lecturer, Civil War Institute, Gettysburg College, 1988. Newspaper consultant and sales representative for Harris-Intertype Co., 1960-62;

nominee of Democratic Party, U.S. House of Representatives, 1966. Member of Fulbright Commission to Ecuador. *Military service:* U.S. Navy, 1944-46; served in Atlantic theater.

MEMBER: International Association of Weekly Newspaper Editors, American Foreign Service Association, Diplomat and Consular Officers Retired, Illinois Press Association, Ohio Press Association, Kentucky Press Association, Indiana Press Association, Mensa, Delta Sigma Phi, Washington Economic Club.

AWARDS, HONORS: Davis Medal for outstanding research in U.S. Southern history.

WRITINGS:

The Lost Colony of the Confederacy, University Press of Mississippi, 1986.
Boilerplating America: The Hidden Newspaper, University Press of America, 1991.
(Contributor) J. Dawsey and C. Dawsey, editors, *Confederados: Old South Immigrants in Brazil,* University of Alabama Press, 1993.

Contributor of articles and book reviews to magazines, including *Lithopinion, Graphic Arts Monthly,* and *World.*

WORK IN PROGRESS: Mountain Editor, an account of Harter's experiences as an editor in Kentucky; *The Amazon Trail,* jungle adventures of the Confederates who migrated to Brazil; *Grass Roots,* the story of the "rather odd" beginnings of America's free press; a film adaptation of *The Lost Colony of the Confederacy.*

SIDELIGHTS: Eugene C. Harter told *CA:* "Thank God for my international wanderlust and itchy feet! How difficult it is for writers to undertake projects that are outside of their living experience. I choose subjects that I have been accidentally thrust against: kidnappers and bombings in Beirut (I lived there), my membership in a colony of Confederate refugees living in southern Brazil and along the Amazon river, the secret history of the survival of small grass roots newspapers in America, and the mysterious and artificial ways blacks and whites in America contrive to get along without actually touching. These subjects were not only 'researched' but also display the intense focus of autobiographical narrative.

"My first book was well received, and I was most grateful. Five printings including a foreign language edition. However, if things had turned out differently I would still be on the bridge of my 48 foot motor yacht, mindlessly, happily cruising the Chesapeake Bay, out of sight of a writing keyboard.

"My second book, *Boilerplating America: The Hidden Newspaper,* is a history of the unique American free press so blithely distorted and ignored by historians. The 'free press' began in the post-Civil War period, not in the nervous big cities but in country press serving the quiet, smaller towns and farms across this vast country."

Harter continued: "It was the wanderlust of my grandfather who migrated to Brazil following the Civil War that brought about my book *The Lost Colony of the Confederacy.* I was born and raised in this colony. I was surprised to learn that very little has been written in American history about emigration from the South. My book is a sampling rather than an inventory of the episode. I am content to seed this little-plowed ground." Remarked Bob Roesler in the *New Orleans Times-Picayune:* "Harter's fast-moving story . . . reads like a Hollywood novel . . . an exciting adventure tale almost everyone should enjoy."

Harter also informed *CA* that his research formed a part of the Public Broadcasting System documentary *The Last Confederates,* in which he appeared as a narrator. This film, which was distributed in 1986, tells the story of some twenty thousand members of the Confederacy who fled to Brazil.

BIOGRAPHICAL/CRITICAL SOURCES:

PERIODICALS

Baltimore Sun, December 31, 1985; January 5, 1986.
Columbia Journalism Review, February, 1976.
Detroit News, November 24, 1985.
Journalism Quarterly, spring, 1992.
New Orleans Times-Picayune, December 22, 1985.

*   *   *

HAVENS, Leston Laycock 1924-

PERSONAL: Born July 31, 1924, in Brooklyn, NY; son of Valentine Britton (a lawyer) and Nellie Falk (a housewife; maiden name, Laycock) Havens; married Susan Elizabeth Miller (a painter, therapist, and adoption researcher), May 19, 1973; children: Emily E.; (from previous marriage) Christopher W., Jeffrey B., Jennifer F., Sarah B. *Education:* Williams College, B.A. (magna cum laude), 1947; Cornell University, M.D., 1952.

ADDRESSES: Home—151 Brattle St., Cambridge, MA 02138. *Office*—Department of Psychiatry, Harvard Medical School, Cambridge Hospital, Cambridge, MA 02139.

CAREER: New York Hospital, New York City, intern, 1952-53, assistant resident in internal medicine, 1953-54; Massachusetts Mental Health Center, Boston Psychopathic Hospital, Boston, resident and chief of service,

1954-58, staff visitor and assistant clinical director, 1958-62, principal investigator of studies in visual word perception, 1960-66, program director of Psychiatric Rehabilitation Internship Program, 1962-68; Harvard University, Harvard Medical School, Boston, assistant professor, 1963-64, associate clinical professor, 1965-71, psychoanalyst, 1967—, professor of psychiatry, 1971—. Carnegie visiting professor, Massachusetts Institute of Technology, 1968; H.B. Williams traveling professor, Australian and New Zealand College of Psychiatrists. Chief psychiatric consultant, Massachusetts Rehabilitation Commission, 1959-65; regional mental health administrator, Massachusetts Department of Mental Health, 1968-69. Director of Residency Training, Cambridge Hospital, 1987—. *Military service:* U.S. Army, 1944-46; became second lieutenant.

AWARDS, HONORS: A. E. Bennett Award, Society for Biological Psychiatry, 1958; McCurdy Prize, Massachusetts Society for Research in Psychiatry, 1962; H. C. Solomon Award, Massachusetts Mental Health Center, 1977, for research; recipient of several teaching awards from Harvard Medical School.

WRITINGS:

Approaches to the Mind: Movement of the Psychiatric Schools From Sects Toward Science, Little, Brown, 1973.
Participant Observation, Jason Aronson, 1976.
Making Contact: Uses of Language in Psychotherapy, Harvard University Press, 1986.
A Safe Place, Harvard University Press, 1989.
Coming to Life, Harvard University Press, 1993.

WORK IN PROGRESS: The Human Ground: A Traveller's Guide.

*　　　*　　　*

HELWIG, David (Gordon)　1938-

PERSONAL: Born April 5, 1938, in Toronto, Ontario, Canada; son of William Gordon (a cabinetmaker) and Ivy (Abbott) Helwig; married Nancy Keeling, September 19, 1959; children: Sarah Magdalen, Kathleen Rebecca. *Education:* University of Toronto, B.A., 1960; University of Liverpool, M.A., 1962. *Avocational Interests:* Singing.

ADDRESSES: 4380 avenue de Chateaubriand, Montreal, Quebec, Canada, H2J 2T8.

CAREER: Queen's University, Kingston, Ontario, assistant professor of English, 1962-74, member of English faculty, 1976-80; Canadian Broadcasting Corp., television drama department, literary manager and story editor for crime series *Sidestreet,* 1974-76.

AWARDS, HONORS: Centennial Award, for *A Time of Winter;* first prize in an annual Canadian Broadcasting Corporation poetry competition, 1983, for *Catchpenny Poems.*

WRITINGS:

NOVELS

The Day before Tomorrow, Oberon, 1971, published as *Message from a Spy,* Paperjacks, 1975.
The Glass Knight (first volume in Kingston tetralogy), Oberon, 1976.
Jennifer (second volume in Kingston tetralogy) Oberon, 1979, Beaufort, 1983.
The King's Evil, Oberon, 1981, Beaufort, 1984.
It Is Always Summer (fourth volume of Kingston tetralogy), Stoddart, 1982, Beaufort, 1982.
A Sound Like Laughter (third volume in Kingston tetralogy), Stoddart,1983, Beaufort, 1983.
The Only Son, Stoddart, 1984, Beaufort, 1984.
The Bishop, Viking, 1986, Penguin, 1986.
A Postcard from Rome, Penguin, 1988.
Old Wars, Penguin, 1990.
Of Desire, Viking, 1990.

POETRY

The Sign of the Gunman, Oberon, 1969.
The Best Name of Silence, Oberon, 1972.
Atlantic Crossings, Oberon, 1974.
A Book of the Hours, Oberon, 1979.
The Rain Falls Like Rain, Oberon, 1982.
Catchpenny Poems, Oberon, 1983.
The Hundred Old Names, Oberon, 1988.
The Beloved, Oberon, 1992.

EDITOR

(With Tom Marshall) *Fourteen Stories High: Best Canadian Stories of 71,* Oberon, 1971.
(With Joan Harcourt) *New Canadian Stories,* annual volumes, Oberon, 1972-75.
The Human Elements (critical essays), Oberon, 1978.
Love and Money: The Politics of Culture, Oberon, 1980.
The Human Elements, Second Series, Oberon, 1981.
(With Sandra Martin) *Coming Attractions* (short stories), annual volumes, 1983-1985.
(With Martin) *Best Canadian Stories,* annual series, Oberon, 1983-1986.
(With daughter, Maggie Helwig) *Coming Attractions 5,* Oberon, 1987.
(With M. Helwig) *Best Canadian Stories,* annual series, Oberon, 1988-1990.

OTHER

Figures in a Landscape (poems and three plays: *A Time of Winter,* produced in Kingston, Ontario, by Domino

Theatre, 1967, *The Dreambook,* and *The Dancers of Kolbek*), Oberon, 1968.

The Streets of Summer (short stories), Oberon, 1969.

(By Billie Miller as told to Helwig) *A Book About Billie* (documentary), Oberon, 1972.

Work represented in numerous anthologies, including *Canadian Short Stories,* edited by Robert Weaver, Oxford University Press, 1968, and *Canadian Poetry: The Modern Era,* edited by Newlove, McClelland & Stewart, 1977. Co-editor of *Quarry,* 1962-74; editor-at-large, Oberon Press, 1973-74.

SIDELIGHTS: Versatile and prolific, David Helwig has produced realistic and dreamlike novels, spy fiction, short stories, plays, radio and television scripts, and poetry collections, and has edited numerous books. His career has placed him among the more prominent Canadian men of letters of the generation that includes former classmate Margaret Atwood and former colleague Michael Ondaatje.

Helwig's "most substantial achievement in fiction," according to Tom Marshall in the *Dictionary of Literary Biography,* is his tetralogy of novels set in Kingston, Ontario, which "provide[s] an impressive panorama of contemporary life in this unique eastern Ontario city." The first, *The Glass Knight,* says Gary Draper in *Books in Canada,* "tells the story of Robert Mallen's not-very-successful affair with the exotic Elizabeth Ross." Robert's ex-wife is the title character of the second volume, *Jennifer.* Both these novels, Draper says, "are novels of character. Robert and Jennifer are ordinary people, caught in the ordinary confusions of growing older and falling in and out of love."

It Is Always Summer, the third in the tetralogy to be published, is fourth in its fictive chronological sequence. "It has the virtues of its predecessors and more," declares Draper. Taking place ten years after *The Glass Knight,* the work is more ambitious than the first two books, with a larger cast of characters. "Helwig shows the different faces (or facets) that each character reveals in different social contexts," Draper writes. "In addition, . . . the six central characters reveal their private, inner spaces. . . . Some of the most successful passages in the book are those in which Helwig orchestrates a conversation of many voices. There are some real virtuoso pieces here, drawing power from a sub-surface of sexuality." *Publishers Weekly* reviewer Barbara A. Bannon calls the book "a sophisticated novel of manners."

A Sound Like Laughter, which completes the tetralogy, is Helwig's first comic novel. The laughter is dark, however; Jim Moore, writing in the *Los Angeles Times Book Review,* draws from the novel this moral: "Better let the gods do the laughing." This book, says I. M. Owen in *Books in Canada,* "is about the disastrous messes we can get our-

selves into in the pursuit of what seem to us reasonable goals." Marianne, a middle-aged mental health center administrator, is having an affair with Ernest, a hapless college voice coach. In the course of the novel, she makes love to a drug dealer who burglarizes her home; Ernest makes love to the babysitter who has helped the burglar. "Helwig writes in a laconic, limpid style," Moore comments, "he keeps lines of action sublimely straight." Describing the novel as "exuberant comedy" as well as "very sad," Owen praises Helwig's "beautiful prose."

Helwig's first novel after completing the tetralogy, *The Only Son,* is a study of Canadian society. The main character, Walter, is a young Torontonian whose British parents are servants in a wealthy household; the plot follows Walter's successful attempt to escape from the servant class and attain social respectability by becoming a philosophy professor. Reviewing the book for the Toronto *Globe and Mail,* William French calls it "compelling" and "a rare example of Canadian fiction that deals with our class structure."

An earlier novel that shows Helwig's versatility, the 1981 *The King's Evil,* stands out for its poetic, fairy-tale atmosphere. The novel is a narrative within a narrative. The frame device shows us a CBC radio producer who has suffered a nervous breakdown and who, during his convalescence, does research into Canadian Loyalist history. The dreamlike tale within the tale postulates that King Charles I of England was not beheaded, but was taken to Virginia. Praising Helwig's handling of archetypal symbols, Hilda Kirkwood claims in *Canadian Forum,* "It is a strange and very beautiful dream, the work of a poet casting his spell upon us." D. W. Nichol, in *Books in Canada,* finds the novel as a whole "diffuse," but commends "its exploration of fakes within fakes."

The 1986 novel *The Bishop* is a character study of an Anglican bishop who, after suffering a paralytic stroke, lies in bed remembering his life. Stating that the novel contains "passages of great beauty," *Globe and Mail* contributor Douglas Hill adds, "Helwig has gifts of making much out of the ordinary and unspectacular." In his 1989 novel, *Old Wars,* Helwig switches both genre and locale. A spy novel set partly in Greece, *Old Wars* is "moody, suspenseful, and very well written," comments Newgate Callendar in the *New York Times Book Review.*

If *The King's Evil* is poetry in prose, Helwig has produced a large amount of poetry in verse as well. From Helwig's early work, Tom Marshall singles out the long poem *Atlantic Crossings* as the finest. The four-part poem concerns the New World explorations of St. Brendan, Columbus, the Norsemen, and a slave trader. *The Rain Falls Like Rain,* published in 1982, is an omnibus volume containing poems from Helwig's five previous collections as well as newer work. In *Books in Canada,* reviewer Peter O'Brien comments: "There is a marvelously complex simplicity in Helwig's finest work. . . . Helwig's poems are not only understated, they are poems of breath, with all the mystery and strength that breathing implies." Helwig's *Catchpenny Poems* of 1983 won first prize in an annual competition sponsored by the Canadian Broadcasting Corporation.

BIOGRAPHICAL/CRITICAL SOURCES:

BOOKS

Dictionary of Literary Biography, Volume 60: *Canadian Writers since 1960,* Second Series, Gale, 1987, pp. 114-117.
Marshall, Tom, *Harsh and Lovely Land,* University of British Columbia Press, 1979, pp. 162-170.
Moss, John, editor, *Present Tense,* NC Press, 1985, pp. 112-121.
Pearce, John, editor, *Twelve Voices: Interviews with Canadian Poets,* Borealis, 1981, pp. 25-41.

PERIODICALS

Books in Canada, November, 1979, p. 8; October, 1981, pp. 13, 15; May, 1982, p. 12; June, 1982, p. 30; March, 1983, pp. 22-23; April, 1983, pp. 20-21; March, 1984, p. 14; August, 1986, p. 18; March, 1987, p. 29; April, 1988, p. 25; August, 1989, p. 6; October, 1990, p. 46.
Canadian Forum, January, 1969; March, 1970; February, 1982, p. 44; June-July, 1982, p. 38.
Fiddlehead, January-February, 1969.
Globe & Mail (Toronto), March 10, 1984; May 26, 1984; September 29, 1984; December 14, 1985; November 29, 1986; September 12, 1987, November 14, 1987; December 17, 1988; October 21, 1989.
Los Angeles Times Book Review, October 30, 1983, p. 9; January 13, 1985, p. 7.
Maclean's, October 22, 1979, p. 58; March 1, 1982, p. 56; April 25, 1983, p. 56.
New York Times Book Review, July 8, 1984, p. 20; January 11, 1987, p. 23; October 22, 1989, p. 37.
Poetry, August, 1984, p. 307.
Publishers Weekly, June 18, 1982, p. 59; May 27, 1983, p. 60; November 30, 1990, p. 56.
Queen's Quarterly, Volume 81, number 2, 1974, pp. 202-214.
Quill and Quire, March, 1982.
Saturday Night, December, 1971, pp. 38-39, 43.
Times Literary Supplement, May 14, 1976; May, 1983, p. 64.

HENRY, Laurin L(uther) 1921-

PERSONAL: Born May 23, 1921, in Kankakee, IL; son of Laurimer L. and Jeanette (Wagner) Henry; married Kathleen Jane Stephan, 1946; children: Stephanie J., Robin L. *Education:* DePauw University, B.A. (with honors), 1942; University of Chicago, M.A., 1948, Ph.D., 1960.

ADDRESSES: Home—1364 Hilltop Rd., Charlottesville, VA 22903-1225. *Office*—Center for Public Service, 918 Emmet St., Charlottesville, VA 22903.

CAREER: Public Administration Clearing House, Washington, DC, staff assistant, 1952-55; Brookings Institution, Washington, DC, research associate, 1955-61, senior staff member, 1961-64; University of Virginia, Charlottesville, Professor of Government, 1964-78; Virginia Commonwealth University, dean of School of Community Services, 1978-86, professor 1986-87, professor emeritus, 1987—; guest scholar, University of Virginia, 1988—; visiting professor, Johns Hopkins University; consultant to Alaska Statehood Commission, National Aeronautics and Space Administration, U.S. Bureau of the Budget, U.S. General Accounting Office, and U.S. Civil Service Commission. *Military service:* U.S. Navy, 1942-46; became chief petty officer as personnel classification specialist.

MEMBER: American Society for Public Administration, National Association of Schools of Public Affairs and Administration (president, 1971-72), Phi Beta Kappa, Phi Kappa Phi.

AWARDS, HONORS: L. D. White Prize, American Political Science Association; fellow, National Academy of Public Administration.

WRITINGS:

(Contributor) *Administrative Aspects of U.S. Foreign Assistance Programs,* Brookings Institution, 1957.
(Contributor) *Government and Politics in Latin America,* Ronald, 1958.
Presidential Transitions, Brookings Institution, 1960.
(With P. T. David) *The Presidential Election and Transition, 1960-61,* Brookings Institution, 1961.

Also author of *The NASA-University Memorandum of Understanding,* 1967. Contributor to professional publications.*

*   *   *

HERBERT, Frank (Patrick) 1920-1986

PERSONAL: Born October 8, 1920, in Tacoma, WA; died of complications following cancer surgery, February 11 (some sources say February 12), 1986, in Madison, WI;

son of Frank and Eileen Marie (McCarthy) Herbert; married Flora Parkinson, March, 1941 (divorced, 1945); married Beverly Ann Stuart, June 23, 1946; marriage ended; married third wife, Theresa; children: Penny (Mrs. D. R. Merritt), Brian Patrick, Bruce Calvin. *Education:* Attended University of Washington, 1946-47.

ADDRESSES: Home—Port Townsend, WA. *Agent*—Lurton Blassingame, 60 East 42nd St., New York, NY 10017; and Ned Brown, P.O. Box 5020, Beverly Hills, CA 90210.

CAREER: Novelist. Reporter, photographer, and editor for west coast newspapers, including the *Glendale Star* (California), the *Oregon Statesman,* the *Seattle Star,* and the *San Francisco Examiner,* 1939-69; educational writer, *Seattle Post-Intelligence,* Seattle, WA, 1969-72; lecturer in general and interdisciplinary studies, University of Washington, Seattle, 1970-72; consultant in social and ecological studies, Lincoln Foundation, and to countries of Vietnam and Pakistan, 1971; director and photographer of television show, *The Tillers,* 1973.

MEMBER: World without War Council (member of national council, 1970-73; member of Seattle council, 1972-86).

AWARDS, HONORS: Nebula Award, Science Fiction Writers of America, 1965, and Hugo Award, World Science Fiction Convention, 1966, both for *Dune;* Prix Apollo, 1978; Doctor of Humanities, Seattle University, 1980.

WRITINGS:

SCIENCE FICTION NOVELS

The Dragon in the Sea (originally serialized in *Amazing Science Fiction* as "Under Pressure"), Doubleday, 1956, published as *Twenty-first Century Sub,* Avon, 1956, published as *Under Pressure,* Ballantine, 1974.
The Green Brain (originally serialized in *Amazing Stories*), Berkley Publishing, 1966.
Destination: Void (originally serialized in *Galaxy;* also see below), Berkley Publishing, 1966, revised edition, 1978.
The Eyes of Heisenberg (originally serialized in *Galaxy*), Berkley Publishing, 1966.
The Heaven Makers (originally serialized in *Amazing Stories*), Avon, 1968.
The Santaroga Barrier (originally serialized in *Amazing Stories*), Berkley Publishing, 1968.
Whipping Star (originally serialized in *If;* also see below), Berkley Publishing, 1970.
The God Makers (also see below), Berkley Publishing, 1971.

Hellstrom's Hive (based on the film *The Hellstrom Chronicle;* originally serialized in *Galaxy* as "Project 40"), Doubleday, 1973.
The Dosadi Experiment (sequel to *Whipping Star;* also see below), Berkley Publishing, 1977.
(With Bill Ransom) *The Jesus Incident* (also see below), Berkley Publishing, 1979.
Direct Descent, Ace Books, 1980.
Priests of Psi (also see below), Gollancz, 1980.
The White Plague, Putnam, 1982.
(With Ransom) *The Lazarus Effect,* Putnam, 1983.
Worlds beyond Dune: The Best of Frank Herbert (contains *The Jesus Incident, Whipping Star, Destination: Void, The God Makers,* and *The Dosadi Experiment*), Berkley Publishing, 1987.
(With son, Brian Herbert) *Man of Two Worlds,* Ace Books, 1987.
(With Ransom) *The Ascension Factor,* Ace Books, 1989.

"THE DUNE CHRONICLES" SERIES

Dune (originally serialized in *Analog;* also see below), Chilton, 1965, twenty-fifth anniversary edition, Ace Books, 1990.
Dune Messiah (originally serialized in *Galaxy;* also see below), Berkley Publishing, 1970.
Children of Dune (also see below), Berkley Publishing, 1976.
The Illustrated Dune, Berkley Publishing, 1978.
The Great Dune Trilogy (contains *Dune, Dune Messiah,* and *Children of Dune*), Gollancz, 1979.
God Emperor of Dune (Literary Guild selection; excerpt appeared in *Playboy*), Berkley Publishing, 1981.
Heretics of Dune, Putnam, 1984.
Chapterhouse: Dune, Putnam, 1985.

SHORT STORIES

(With others) *Five Fates,* Doubleday, 1970.
The Worlds of Frank Herbert, Ace Books, 1970.
The Book of Frank Herbert, DAW Books, 1972.
The Best of Frank Herbert, Sphere Books, 1974.
The Priests of Psi, and Other Stories, Gollancz, 1980.
Eye ("Masterworks of Science Fiction and Fantasy" series), edited by Byron Preiss, illustrated by Jim Burns, Berkley Publishing, 1985.

OTHER

(Editor) *New World or No World* (interviews), Ace Books, 1970.
Soul Catcher (fiction), Berkley Publishing, 1972.
Threshold: The Blue Angels Experience (nonfiction), Ballantine, 1973.
(Editor with others) *Tomorrow, and Tomorrow, and Tomorrow . . . .,* Holt, 1974.
Sandworms of Dune (recording), Caedmon, 1978.

The Truths of Dune (recording), Caedmon, 1979.
The Battles of Dune (recording), Caedmon, 1979.
(With Max Barnard) *Without Me You're Nothing: The Essential Guide to Home Computers* (nonfiction), Simon & Schuster, 1981.
(Editor) *Nebula Awards Fifteen* (anthology), Harper, 1981.
The Dune Encyclopedia, edited by Willis E. McNelly, Putnam, 1984.
The Maker of Dune, edited by Timothy O'Reilly, Berkeley Publishing, 1987.
(Author of foreword) Bryan Brewer, editor, *Eclipse*, second edition, Earth View, 1991.
The Songs of Muad'Dib: The Poetry of Frank Herbert, edited by B. Herbert, Ace Books, 1992.

Also author of *The Dune Coloring Book* (fourteen volumes), Putnam. Contributor of fiction to *Esquire, Galaxy, Amazing Stories, Analog,* and other magazines. *Dune* has been translated into over fourteen languages.

ADAPTATIONS: Dune was adapted for the screen by David Lynch and filmed by Universal in 1984.

SIDELIGHTS: Frank Herbert is most often remembered as the creator of the tremendously popular "Dune Chronicles." The first volume, 1965's *Dune,* instantly placed him among such preeminent authors as J. R. R. Tolkien, C. S. Lewis, Robert Heinlein, and Isaac Asimov as a brilliant creator of imagined worlds. The novel first became a cult favorite and then a full-blown bestseller; it has never been out of print, selling tens of millions of copies and spawning five sequels and a film adaptation in the more than twenty-five years since it was first published. *Dune* is considered by many to be among the most influential novels in its genre and is described by Robert A. Foster in the *Dictionary of Literary Biography* as "one of the unquestioned masterpieces of modern science fiction."

The popularity of *Dune* has been built around Herbert's portrayal of the desert planet Arrakis and its inhabitants—a portrayal which Joseph McClellan of the *Washington Post Book World* considers to be "more complete and deeply detailed than any author in the [science fiction] field had ever managed or attempted before." The novel takes place twenty-five centuries hence, when the known universe is controlled by two political powers, the Imperium and the Great Houses. These forces maintain a delicate and uneasy peace, occasionally punctuated by espionage, collusion, and infighting. The balance is further complicated by the presence of powerful independent organizations, such as the Spacing Guild and the cultish Bene Gesserit. As the novel opens, Duke Leto Atreides has been asked to abandon the throne of his home world of Caladan for that of Arrakis, known to its natives as Dune. This planet is a burning desert—quite unlike the

watery paradise of Caladan—but is also the only source for the spice melange, an addictive narcotic which imparts to its user limited prescient abilities. The spice is highly valued by the Spacing Guild (whose navigators use the drug to help them traverse the cosmos), among others, making Arrakis a source of power to whoever controls it.

Leto takes his wife, Jessica, his son, Paul, and their entourage to Dune. Before they can assume control, however, they are ambushed by the forces of the Harkonnen family, arch rivals of House Atreides. Duke Leto is killed, but Paul and his mother escape to the desert wastes where they encounter the indigenous people known as the Fremen. Years of living in the sands have forced the Fremen to adapt: they have constructed special suits to conserve and re-use their body's fluids; they have designed machinery to draw precious moisture from the atmosphere; and, most importantly, they have perfected methods by which melange can be harvested and distilled. The Fremen have learned the secret of the "spice cycle"—that the production of melange is intrinsic to the life cycle of Dune's most frightening creatures, the monstrous sandworms.

Paul and Jessica are introduced to the ways of Fremen culture. In a Fremen rite of passage, Paul ingests a near-lethal dose of spice, awakening within him the ability to see the future—and, to some extent, to alter it. He is hailed by the Fremen as their messiah, Muad'Dib. With them as his army, Paul struggles to wrest his father's usurped throne away from the Harkonnens; however, deep within the "network of probability" that makes up the future, Paul glimpses a terrible holy war drawing ever closer—a bloody jihad that he is destined to bring about.

While the plot of *Dune* is typical of heroic fantasy and science fiction, the world and culture of Arrakis set the novel apart from standard fare. Foster credits Herbert with establishing the science fiction tradition of "the invented-world novel, in which details of history, languages, customs, geography, and ecology . . . are combined with a rich complexity that pleases the reader by its verisimilitude and imaginative scope." While *New York Times* reviewer John Leonard admits that *Dune* was not the first science fiction novel to create a self-consistent and logical alien world (Tolkien had already done so with his "Lord of the Rings" trilogy, as had Lewis in his tales of Narnia), he considers Herbert's work to be more ambitious than that of his predecessors. "J. R. R. Tolkien and C. S. Lewis, with their readymade Christian moralizing to fall back on, are not in Mr. Herbert's inventive league," Leonard writes. "For *Dune,* [Herbert] dreamed up several complete religions, and alien ecology and technology, entire histories and cultures and black arts."

Lending an additional air of believability to the novel is Herbert's detailed account of Arrakis's ecosystem; for instance, Foster cites the spice cycle as "one of the best examples of true scientific imagination in science fiction." *Dune* represented the first time a fiction writer had addressed these issues so effectively, and the result was dramatic. Gerald Jonas explains in the *New York Times Book Review:* "So completely did Mr. Herbert work out the interactions of man and beast and geography and climate that [*Dune*] became the standard for a new subgenre of 'ecological' science fiction." As popularity of *Dune* rose, Herbert embarked on a lecture tour of college campuses, explaining how the environmental concerns of Dune's inhabitants were analogous to our own. In this way, he has often been credited as contributing to the birth of America's environmental movement. *America*'s Willis E. McNelly sees Herbert's message in the *Dune* novels as: "We need to understand what we are doing to our own environment . . . because some of the things we've done . . . may already be beyond redemption with disastrous consequences for the earth and for human life."

Dune was soon followed by 1970's *Dune Messiah* and 1976's *Children of Dune.* Each novel continues the account of Paul-Muad'Dib's rise to power, his attempts to unify Arrakis's people and to control its harsh climate, and the destructive results that follow. Paul's failure illustrates a motif that appears throughout Herbert's fiction: the false, or flawed, messiah. He elaborated in *Critical Encounters:* "[*Dune*] began with a concept: to do a long novel about the messianic convulsions which periodically inflict themselves on human societies. I had this theory that superheroes were disastrous for humans, that even if you postulated an infallible hero, the things this hero set in motion fell eventually into the hands of fallible mortals. What better way to destroy a civilization, a society or a race than to set people into the wild oscillations which follow their turning over their judgement and decision-making faculties to a superhero?" Herbert further commented in *Dream Makers:* "The bottom line in the *Dune* [series] is: beware of heroes. [It is] much better to rely on your own judgement, and your own mistakes."

At the end of *Children of Dune,* Paul has been replaced by his son, Leto II, as ruler of Arrakis and the Galactic Empire to which it belongs. A powerful prescient, Leto has guided his people down the "Golden Path" that will ultimately lead to three millennia of peace; furthermore, he has merged his body with larval sandtrout, and as they develop he will be transformed over thousands of years into a giant half-human, half-sandworm—the ultimate fusion of man and environment. Though he had planned to close his Dune Chronicles here, Herbert returned to Arrakis with *God Emperor of Dune, Heretics of Dune,* and *Chapterhouse: Dune.* While these later novels take place

long after the rule of Paul-Muad'Dib, they continue to explore the themes first introduced in *Dune.* Although many critics echoed Leonard's complaint that "Frank Herbert should never have written a sequel to *Dune,* much less [five] of them," it is only when viewing the completed series that the importance of Herbert's work can be understood. As a writer for the *West Coast Review of Books* points out: "It's inevitable that sequels to a book as important as *Dune* would generate considerable controversy. The subjectivity of readers, measuring each new volume against their memory of the original, prevents them from properly appreciating the overall complexity and beauty of the series."

Recently, many reviewers have, indeed, begun to recognize the significance of Herbert's "Dune *Chronicles.*" "In a very strict and limited way," comments Joseph M. Lenz in *Coordinates,* "the Dune books can be called classics. . . . I mean that they are classical, reminiscent of and belonging to a literary tradition that originates with Rome and *The Aeneid.*" Jonas cites Herbert's refusal to treat the science fiction genre lightly as a source of the series' power and popularity. "The conspiratorial characters of Dune deal only with issues of transcendent importance—the fate of mankind, the possibility of free will, the existence of evil," he points out. "The strength of [Herbert's] series comes from its utter seriousness. There is not a trace of irony, not a whiff of self-mocking doubt." Jonas continues: "Whatever else the characters in Herbert's books have to worry about, none suffers from that common malady of our day: a sense of meaninglessness. Virtually every page in the trilogy contains a sentence that hints at the momentousness of the events being described."

Foster observes that, "with its emphasis on intrigue, consciousness, supernormal mental powers, and the functional meaning of abstractions such as peace," most of the "action" in the Dune series takes place on an intellectual level. The contemplative nature of Herbert's fiction makes it an ideal forum for many of Herbert's philosophical beliefs, and nowhere are those beliefs better represented than in the "Dune Chronicles." "Herbert's work is informed by an evolving body of concepts to which the Dune [series] holds the key," claims Timothy O'Reilly in *Frank Herbert.* Herbert's work "shows the possibilities for good and evil of factors present, but unnoticed, in our culture. He gives his readers ideals and dreams, but not as an excuse for avoiding the realities of the present. . . . Most of all, he offers a chance to practice in fiction the lessons that are increasingly demanded by our lives: how to live with the pressure of changing times." O'Reilly concludes: "The end result of all this art is a novel packed with ideas that cannot easily be shaken from the mind, but which is never overburdened by their weight."

By infusing his fiction with philosophical and theological discussion, Herbert successfully transcends the limitations common to the science fiction genre. "Although *Dune* possesses a broad popular appeal which is often denied to the 'highbrow' novel, it reveals itself to formal literary analysis as a subtle, complex, and carefully crafted work of art," maintains John Ower in *Extrapolation.* "It thus constitutes an eloquent comment on the increasing maturity of science fiction as a form." O'Reilly, too, sees *Dune* as a step in the evolution of the genre. He writes in *Critical Encounters:* "When [a science fiction novel] reaches the subconscious levels . . . , as *Dune* so clearly does, it goes beyond being even a cautionary fable and becomes, in Herbert's own words, a 'training manual for consciousness.' "

Because of the tremendous success of the "Dune Chronicles," it has been the tendency of some reviewers to dismiss Herbert's other works of short and long fiction as inferior. However, these works often reveal to the reader a number of motifs only hinted at in the Dune books. Three such works are *The Dragon in the Sea, Destination: Void,* and *The White Plague. The Dragon in the Sea* is set in the foreseeable future, near the end of the next world war. Because the superpowers have fought for sixteen years, they have nearly depleted their supplies of natural resources, and must send submarine wolf packs to steal crude oil from ocean wells. The action and dialogue take place entirely within the confines of a four-man subtug, the Fenian Ram, whose crew acts as a microcosmic representation of the dangerous and paranoid world above the waves; as the tension in the subtug increases, each crew member must adapt to his environment or be destroyed by it. "The subtug crew responds to these pressures with adaptations which are insane when judged by outside standards," Foster notes, adding that "as Captain Sparrow explains, 'I'm nuts in a way which fits me perfectly to my world. That makes my world nuts and me normal. Not sane. Normal. Adapted.' "

Many critics consider *The Dragon in the Sea* to be vastly underrated, for it succeeds as both an action novel and a psychological thriller. "It all works," according to Foster, "because the conceptual unfolding is matched step by step in the action of the plot. The ideas never interrupt the action; they are tightly woven into it." J. Frances McComas, writing in the *New York Times Book Review,* feels that Herbert's account of a future war "comes very close to matching—in suspense, action and psychic strain—any chronicle of real war." The drama played out within the cramped space of the Fenian Ram is the same one Paul Atreides is forced to play out in the deserts of Arrakis: adapt or die. "All of Herbert's books portray and test the human ability to consciously adapt," contends O'Reilly. "He sets his characters in the most stressful situations imaginable [because] there is no test so powerfully able to bring out latent adaptability as one in which the stakes are survival."

The concept of forced adaptation is also the basis for Herbert's 1967 novel, *Destination: Void.* In the future, scientists are desperate to develop artificial intelligence, or thinking machines. In order to bring about this breakthrough, a series of spaceships are launched, each manned by a four-man skeleton crew. Unbeknownst to the crew, the ship has been designed to fail halfway into their long journey; the only way to ensure survival is to somehow raise the ship's computer to a level of human consciousness before the ship's systems fail. Each of the four crew members is expert in a single discipline—psychology, biology, chemistry, and computer science—and approaches the problem through that discipline; however, each one also represents an aspect of humanity—intelligence, sensation, intuition, and religious devotion—the sum of which are secretly fed to the computer. The computer learns from both the crew's methods and their emotions, and eventually evolves to full consciousness. It repairs itself and delivers the crew to a habitable planet; salvation does not come cheap, however, for the ship demands that it be worshipped as a saviour.

David M. Miller, writing in his book *Frank Herbert,* calls *Destination: Void* "an essay rather than an entertainment [wherein] the 'hero' is really the idea, and the novel is a 'lab-report.' " Patricia S. Warrick concurs, though she stresses in *The Cybernectic Imagination in Science Fiction* that the novel "never sacrifices plot to philosophical discussion; it is uniquely successful in dramatizing the issues rather than merely talking about them." Though Miller admits that *Destination: Void* resembles *The Dragon in the Sea* and *Dune* in that it explores the concept of growth through forced adaptation, "the reader may discover that it reveals some facets of Herbert's vision more explicitly" than his previous novels. Warrick concludes: "[*Destination: Void*] is a unique literary accomplishment."

In 1982's *The White Plague,* Herbert yet again explores the ability of humans to overcome incredible changes in their environment. Described by Jonas as "a brilliant, brooding meditation on the war between man's tendencies toward self-destruction and his instinct for self-preservation," the novel tells the story of a biologist, John O'Neill, who is driven mad by the death of his wife and children, victims of an Irish Republican Army bomb. Bent on revenge, he develops a DNA-based plague virus that affects only females; when his demands are ignored by the government O'Neill unleashes his creation, killing hundreds of thousands of women and girls. Their world in a shambles, scientists and governments must unite to protect the surviving women and find a cure for the plague.

Although *Los Angeles Times Book Review* contributor Mark Rose calls *The White Plague* "engaging entertainment, intriguing, wholly believable and even important," fellow critic Craig Shaw Gardner found certain flaws, particularly in Herbert's choice of narrator. Gardner comments in the *Washington Post Book World:* "By writing most of the novel from the point of view of a mad man incapable of feeling . . . Herbert robs the reader of the opportunity for empathy, and the book falls flat." Still, *Fantasy Newsletter*'s William Coyle maintains that "the basic situation is vintage Herbert: catastrophe averted or mitigated by man's willingness to discard traditional behavior patterns."

Though Herbert will largely be remembered as the author of *Dune,* he left behind a greater legacy than of his fiction. "The commercial success of *Dune* paved the way for large advances, bigger printings, best-seller status, and heavy subsidiary sales for many other writers," explains McNelly. "Every member of the [Science Fiction Writers Association] owes Frank Herbert and *Dune* considerable gratitude." Don D'Ammassa, writing in the *Science Fiction Chronicle,* agrees that *Dune* opened the door for many other writers, for it "introduced science fiction to readers outside the normal science fiction spectrum." He concludes: "[Herbert's] departure deprives us of one of the most significant voices in the field, as well as one of the more talented writers."

For an interview with this author, see *Contemporary Authors New Revision Series,* Volume 5.

BIOGRAPHICAL/CRITICAL SOURCES:

BOOKS

Aldiss, Brian W., *Billion Year Spree: The True History of Science Fiction,* Doubleday, 1973.
Berger, Harold L., *Science Fiction and the New Dark Age,* Popular Press, 1976.
Contemporary Literary Criticism, Gale, Volume 12, 1980, Volume 23, 1983, Volume 35, 1985, Volume 44, 1987.
Dictionary of Literary Biography, Volume 8: *Twentieth-Century Science Fiction Writers,* Gale, 1981.
McNelly, Willis E., *The Dune Encyclopedia,* Putnam, 1984.
Miller, David M., *Frank Herbert,* Starmont House, 1980.
O'Reilly, Timothy, *Frank Herbert,* Ungar, 1981.
Platt, Charles, *Dream Makers: The Uncommon People Who Write Science Fiction,* Berkley Publishing, 1980.
Riley, Dick, editor, *Critical Encounters: Writers and Themes in Science Fiction,* Ungar, 1978.
Scholes, Robert, *Structural Fabulation: An Essay on Fiction of the Future,* University of Notre Dame Press, 1975.
Scholes, Robert and Eric S. Rabkin, *Science Fiction: History, Science, Vision,* Oxford University Press, 1977.
Slusser, George E., Eric S. Rabkin, and Robert Scholes, editors, *Coordinates: Placing Science Fiction and Fantasy,* Southern Illinois University Press, 1983.
Warrick, Patricia S., *The Cybernetic Imagination in Science Fiction,* Massachusetts Institute of Technology Press, 1980.
Yoke, Carl B., and Donald M. Hassler, editors, *Death and the Serpent: Immortality in Science Fiction and Fantasy,* Greenwood Press, 1985.

PERIODICALS

Amazing Stories, July, 1956.
America, June 10, 1972; June 26, 1976.
Analog, July, 1956; April, 1966; June, 1970; August, 1981; February, 1984; September, 1984; August, 1985.
Booklist, May 1, 1976.
Commonweal, September 7, 1984, p. 475.
English Journal, February, 1974.
Extrapolation, December, 1971; May, 1974; December, 1974; May, 1976; winter, 1983, pp. 340-355.
Fantasy Newsletter, November, 1982, p. 32.
Future Life, Number 14, 1979.
Galaxy, April, 1966; September, 1976; August, 1977.
Los Angeles Times, August 31, 1984.
Los Angeles Times Book Review, September 29, 1982, p. 2; August 28, 1983, p. 4; May 5, 1985, p. 7.
Maclean's, May 21, 1984, p. 62.
Magazine of Fantasy and Science Fiction, March, 1966; April, 1969; May, 1971; February, 1977.
National Observer, May 23, 1977.
Newsweek, April 30, 1984, p. 73.
New Worlds, October, 1966.
New York Times, September 2, 1977; June 1, 1979; April 27, 1981.
New York Times Book Review, March 11, 1956; September 8, 1974; August 1, 1976; November 27, 1977; May 17, 1981, p. 15; September 26, 1983, p. 15; June 10, 1984, p. 24; June 16, 1985, p. 18.
Observer, October 3, 1976.
Psychology Today, August, 1974.
School Library Journal, March, 1973.
Science Fiction & Fantasy Book Review, September, 1983, p. 30.
Science Fiction Chronicle, June, 1985, p. 42.
Science Fiction Review, August, 1970; August, 1979; November, 1983.
Science Fiction Studies, July, 1981, pp. 149-155.
Spectator, August 26, 1978; January 12, 1980.
Time, March 29, 1971.
Times (London), November 7, 1984.
Times Literary Supplement, January 14, 1977.
Tribune Books (Chicago), June 14, 1981; April 22, 1984, p. 11; June 30, 1985, p. 24.
Washington Post, December 14, 1984.

Washington Post Book World, May 9, 1976; May 24, 1981, p. 8; August 29, 1982, p. 7; May 26, 1985, p. 11; October 27, 1985, p. 17.
West Coast Review of Books, July/August, 1985, p. 28.

OBITUARIES:

PERIODICALS

Chicago Tribune, February 14, 1986.
Detroit Free Press, February 13, 1986.
Extrapolation, winter, 1986, pp. 352-355.
Fantasy Review, February, 1986, p. 6.
Los Angeles Times, February 13, 1986.
Newsweek, February 24, 1986.
New York Times, February 13, 1986.
Publishers Weekly, February 28, 1986.
Science Fiction Chronicle, April, 1986, p. 24.
Time, February 24, 1986.
Washington Post, February 13, 1986.*

—*Sketch by Brandon Trenz*

* * *

HERRICK, Neal Q(uentin) 1927-

PERSONAL: Born September 22, 1927, in Lynn, MA; son of Neal D. and Irma (Carr) Herrick; married Jeanne P. Morrissey, April 5, 1952 (divorced, 1972); children: Peter F., Kenneth M., Julia A., Elizabeth K. *Education:* University of New Hampshire, B.A., 1953. *Politics:* Democrat.

CAREER: Has worked as railroad lineman, salesman, construction worker, clerk, automobile worker, reporter, workmen's compensation claims examiner, personnel specialist, auditor and management analyst; W. E. Upjohn Institute for Employment Research, Washington, DC, visiting fellow, 1970-71; U.S. Department of Labor, Washington, DC, director of planning, 1972-73; Academy for Contemporary Problems, Columbus, OH, senior fellow, 1973-74; Governor's Business and Employment Council, Columbus, consultant, 1974-76; former adjunct professor at Ohio State University; director, Ohio Quality of Work Project; consultant, National Center for Productivity and Quality of Working Life, 1976-77; University of Arizona, Tucson, lecturer. *Military service:* U.S. Navy, 1945-47; became first lieutenant.

MEMBER: Industrial Relations Research Association, Ohio Citizens Council.

WRITINGS:

(With Harold Sheppard) *Where Have All the Robots Gone?,* Free Press, 1972.
The Quality of Work and Its Outcomes: Estimating Potential Increases in Labor Productivity, Academy for Contemporary Problems, 1975.

Improving Government: Experiments with Quality of Working Life Systems, Issues and Approaches, Praeger, 1983.
Joint Management and Employee Participation: Labor and Management at the Crossroads, Jossey-Bass, 1990.

OTHER

Contributor to *Monthly Labor Review, Manpower, Worker Alienation, Employee Relations* and *Working Papers.**

* * *

HOGENDORN, Jan S(tafford) 1937-

PERSONAL: Born October 27, 1937, in Lahaina, HI; son of Paul Earl and Helen (Stafford) Hogendorn; married Dianne Hodet (a librarian), September 6, 1960; children: Christiaan Paul. *Education:* Wesleyan University, Middletown, CT, B.A., 1960; London School of Economics and Political Science, M.Sc., 1962, Ph.D., 1966; additional study at Harvard University, 1962-63. *Politics:* Democrat. *Religion:* Unitarian Universalist.

ADDRESSES: Home—R.F.D. 1, North Vassalboro, ME 04962. *Office*—Department of Economics, Colby College, Mayflower Hill, Waterville, ME 04901.

CAREER: Boston University, Boston, MA, instructor in economics, 1963; Colby College, Waterville, ME, assistant professor, 1966-69, associate professor of economics, 1969-76, Grossman Professor of Economics, 1976, chairman of department, 1972-80, 1988-90. Ford Foundation Professor of Development Economics, Robert College, Istanbul, Turkey, 1971-72; Fulbright professor of economic history, Ahmadu Bello University, 1975. Associate, Columbia University, 1977—; research associate, University of Birmingham, 1980; visiting senior member, Linacre College, Oxford University, 1987.

MEMBER: American Economic Association, Royal Economic Society, African Studies Association, Society for Religion in Higher Education (fellow), American Association of University Professors, Phi Beta Kappa.

AWARDS, HONORS: Fulbright fellow in England, 1960-61, and Nigeria, 1975; Danforth fellow, 1965-66; Guggenheim fellow, 1987; recipient of grants from the Mellon Foundation and the Social Science Research Council.

WRITINGS:

Managing the Modern Economy, Winthrop, 1972.
Markets in the Modern Economy, Winthrop, 1975.
Modern Economics, Winthrop, 1975.
Nigerian Groundnut Exports, Oxford University Press, 1978.

(With Henry Gemery) *The Uncommon Market: Essays in the Economic History of the Atlantic Slave Trade,* Academic Press, 1979.

(With Wilson Brown) *The New International Economics,* Addison-Wesley, 1979.

The Grossman Lectures at Colby College, Colby College Press, 1984.

(With Marion Johnson) *The Shell Money of the Slave Trade,* Cambridge University Press, 1986.

Economic Development, Harper, 1987.

(With Paul Lovejoy) *Slow Death for Slavery: The Course of Abolition in Northern Nigeria, 1897-1936,* Cambridge University Press, 1993.

(With Wilson Brown) *International Finance, Trade, and Business,* Addison-Wesley, in press.

SIDELIGHTS: Jan S. Hogendorn explained to *CA* that he "specializes in African economic history, development economics, and international trade."

*   *   *

HOKE, Helen L.
  See WATTS, Helen L. Hoke

*   *   *

HOLBROOK, David (Kenneth)   1923-

PERSONAL: Born January 9, 1923, in Norwich, Norfolk, England; son of Kenneth Redvers and Elsie Eleanor (Grimmer) Holbrook; married Margot Davies-Jones, April 23, 1949; children: Susan Magdalen, Kate Cressida, Jonathan Benedict, Thomas Simeon David. *Education:* Downing College, Cambridge, B.A., 1947, M.A., 1952. *Politics:* "Existentialist, follower of Polanyi and the existentialist movement in psychotherapy." *Religion:* Agnostic. *Avocational Interests:* Painting, music, cooking.

ADDRESSES: Home—Denmore Lodge, Bruswick Gardens, Cambridge CB5 8DQ, England.

CAREER: Author, poet, and critic. Bureau of Current Affairs, London, England, assistant editor, 1947-51; Workers' Educational Association, East Anglia, England, tutor, 1951-54; Cambridgeshire Village College, Bassingbourn, England, tutor, 1954-61; Cambridge University, Cambridge, England, fellow at King's College, 1961-65, fellow and director of English studies at Downing College, 1981-88, emeritus fellow, 1988—. Hooker Distinguished Visiting Professor, MacMaster University, Hamilton, Ontario, 1984. Consultant on National Defense Education Act English programs in United States, 1966. *Military ser-*

vice: British Army, Tank Regiment, 1942-45; served in Normandy invasion; became lieutenant.

AWARDS, HONORS: First writer to receive fellowship from Cambridge University Press (in collaboration with King's College) to write poetry and educational books, 1961-65; Leverhulme senior research fellowship, 1965 and 1988-90; Arts Council Writer's grants, 1970, 1976, and 1979.

WRITINGS:

English for Maturity, Cambridge University Press, 1961, 2nd edition, 1967.

Llareggub Revisited: Dylan Thomas and the State of Modern Poetry (criticism), Bowes, 1962, published with an introduction by Harry T. Moore as *Dylan Thomas and Poetic Dissociation,* Southern Illinois University Press, 1964.

Lights in the Sky (short stories), Putnam, 1962.

The Secret Places, preface by Naomi Mitchison, Methuen, 1964, University of Alabama Press, 1965.

(With Raymond O'Malley and others) *English in the C.S.E.,* Cambridge University Press, 1964.

English for the Rejected, Cambridge University Press, 1964.

The Quest for Love (criticism), Methuen, 1964, University of Alabama Press, 1965.

The Exploring Word: Creative Disciplines in the Education of Teachers of English, Cambridge University Press, 1967.

Children's Writing: Problems of Sincerity and Realism, Cambridge University Press, 1967.

(Author of introduction) T. F. Powys, *Mr. Weston's Good Wine,* Heinemann, 1967.

Human Hope and the Death Instinct, Pergamon, 1971.

Sex and Dehumanization in Art, Thought, and Life in Our Time, Pitman, 1972.

The Masks of Hate: The Problem of False Solutions in the Culture of an Acquisitive Society, Pergamon, 1972.

Dylan Thomas: The Code of Night, Athlone Press, 1972.

The Pseudo-Revolution, Tom Stacey, 1972.

English in Australia Now, Cambridge University Press, 1972.

Changing Attitudes to the Nature of Man: A Working Bibliography, Hertis, 1973.

Gustav Mahler and the Courage to Be, Vision Press, 1975.

Sylvia Plath: Poetry and Existence, Athlone Press, 1976.

(Co-author) *The Apple Tree,* Cambridge University Press, 1976.

Lost Bearings in English Poetry, Barnes & Noble, 1977.

Education, Nihilism, and Survival, Darton, Longman & Todd, 1977.

English for Meaning, National Foundation for Educational Research, 1980.

Education and Philosophical Anthropology: Toward a New View of Man for the Humanities and English, Associated University Presses, 1986.

Evolution and the Humanities, Ewer Press, 1986.

The Novel and Authenticity, Barnes & Noble, 1987.

Further Studies in Philosophical Anthropology, Avebury, 1988.

Images of Woman in Literature, New York University Press, 1989.

What Is It to Be Human?: New Perspectives in Philosophy, Gower, 1990.

Edith Wharton and the Unsatisfactory Man, St. Martin's, 1991.

The Skeleton in the Wardrobe: C. S. Lewis's Fantasies: A Phenomenological Study, Associated University Presses, 1991.

Where D. H. Lawrence Was Wrong about Woman, Bucknell University Press, 1992.

Charles Dickens and the Image of Woman, New York University Press, 1993.

Creativity and Popular Culture, Associated University Presses, 1994.

POETRY

Imaginings, Putnam, 1961.

Against the Cruel Frost, Putnam, 1963.

Object Relations, Methuen, 1967.

Old World, New World, Rapp & Whiting, 1969.

A Chance of a Lifetime, Anvil Press, 1978.

Moments in Italy: Poems and Sketches, Keepsake Press, 1978.

Selected Poems, 1961-1978, Anvil Press, 1980.

NOVELS

Flesh Wounds, Methuen, 1966.

A Play of Passion, W. H. Allen, 1978.

Nothing Larger than Life, R. Hale, 1987.

Worlds Apart, R. Hale, 1988.

A Little Athens, R. Hale, 1990.

Jennifer, R. Hale, 1991.

The Gold in Father's Heart, R. Hale, 1992.

Even If They Fail, Martin Breese International, 1994.

EDITOR OF COMPILATIONS

Children's Games, Gordon Fraser, 1957.

Iron, Honey, Gold (verse anthology), Cambridge University Press, 1961, published in four volumes under same title, 1965.

People and Diamonds (short story anthology), Cambridge University Press, 1962.

Thieves and Angels (anthology of dramatic pieces), Cambridge University Press, 1963.

Visions of Life (prose anthology), Cambridge University Press, 1964.

I've Got to Use Words (four texts in creative English for less able children), Cambridge University Press, 1966.

(With Elizabeth Poston) *The Cambridge Hymnal,* Cambridge University Press, 1966.

Plucking the Rushes: An Anthology of Chinese Poetry, translated by Arthur Waley, Heinemann, 1968.

The Case against Pornography, Open Court, 1972.

The Honey of Man, Thomas Nelson, 1973.

CONTRIBUTOR

Denys Thompson, editor, *Discrimination and Popular Culture,* Pelican, 1965.

Thomas Blackburn, editor, *Understanding Poetry,* Methuen, 1966.

Edward Blishen, *The World of the Child,* Hamlyn, 1966.

Also contributor to numerous books, including *The Black Rainbow,* edited by Peter Abbs, 1975; *New Stories 1,* edited by Margaret Drabble, Arts Council of Great Britain, 1976; *Human Needs and Politics,* edited by Ross Fitzgerald, 1977; *Writers of East Anglia,* edited by Angus Wilson, 1977; *What it Means to be Woman,* edited by Fitzgerald, 1978; and *The Sources of Hope,* edited by Fitzgerald, 1979.

OTHER

The Borderline (opera for children), music by Wilfred Mellers, produced in London, 1959.

(Editor) "The Broadstream Books" series (shortened editions of literary works for school use, with first series including *Oliver Twist, My Childhood, Roughing It,* and *Pudd'nhead Wilson*), Cambridge University Press, 1965.

(With John Joubert) *The Quarry* (opera for children), Novello, 1967.

Has also written librettos for a dramatic cantata, play-in-music, and songs. Contributor to *Penguin New Poets No. 4, Pelican Guide to English Literature,* and to numerous journals and newspapers. Member of editorial board, *New Universities Quarterly,* 1982-86.

SIDELIGHTS: David Holbrook is a prolific author who has proven his literary ability in many genres, including fiction, poetry, criticism, and philosophy. *Dictionary of Literary Biography* contributor John Fletcher feels that Holbrook's finest work is in the field of educational theory, where the writer has produced pioneering books on the teaching of English. His special concern is children who are not academically oriented. He believes that such students are capable of expressing themselves in very sophisticated ways, if only they are encouraged to do so. Fletcher comments: "In trying to contribute to reform in English teaching, Holbrook has aimed always to bear in mind the primary need in all human beings, whether clever or not, to make sense of their lives."

Another *Dictionary of Literary Biography* contributor, John Ferns, rates Holbrook as "an important, contemporary poet." Although strongly rooted in everyday life, Holbrook's poetry frequently touches on philosophical issues. In a *Times Literary Supplement* review of *Selected Poems, 1961-1978,* Tom Disch states that Holbrook "writes warm, rambling accounts of a country life so ideal and so enviable one might be tempted to doubt its existence, had not Holbrook documented it so amply. He loves his wife, worries about and dotes on his children, tends his garden, and inspects the changing of the seasons like a drill-master. . . . His lapses are few, and his successes preponderate and form together [a] richly varied landscape" marked by "grace, geniality, [and] unusual dignity." Ferns lauds the poet for "reasserting goodness and truth, celebrating life and reality, in what he views as a technologically dominated society devoted to dehumanization, hate and false solutions. . . . Holbrook's poetry is important because of his honest and open wrestling with such basic human realities as love and death, family life, the love of animal and natural life and with such other fundamental experiences as ordinary human beings normally encounter."

While Holbrook has not achieved quite the same level of success with his fiction as he has with his writing in other fields, he is nevertheless respected as a capable novelist and short story stylist. His fiction tends to be largely drawn from his own experiences, and, in the view of Fletcher, "the more direct and uncensored the reporting, the more vivid the writing tends to be. At its best, his fiction about his childhood . . . has a vividness which occasionally approaches that of James Joyce in *A Portrait of the Artist as a Young Man.*" Fletcher praises the novel *Flesh Wounds* for its fine passages "on the confusion of battle and the appalling taste of war," and singles out *A Play of Passion* as being "strong on atmosphere, setting, and characterization." He concludes: "Ultimately, perhaps, Holbrook is not . . . really interested in fiction at all; but, rather, in illustrating in thinly-veiled autobiography the theories about life, spontaneity, wholeness, and so on, which he pursues in his . . . polemical writing." Discussing Holbrook's role as novelist, Geoffrey Strickland suggests in *London Magazine* that "Holbrook is still waiting to be found, in that his rightful place would be among the nation's best-selling novelists and the few who, in the post-war period, can be said to belong to English literature."

Writing in the *Times Higher Educational Supplement,* David Hamilton-Eddy states: "To build a substantial reputation in one literary field is a signal achievement; but Holbrook's name is known and respected in the domains of educational theory and practice, in literary criticism and as a novelist and poet. . . . For David Holbrook, literature and the arts are important insofar as they illuminate the quest for creativity, love and life, as against destruction, hate and death. He views with horror the tendencies towards decadence in modern culture, the contemporary morbid fascination with violence and pornography."

BIOGRAPHICAL/CRITICAL SOURCES:

BOOKS

Dictionary of Literary Biography, Gale, Volume 14: *British Novelists since 1960,* 1983, Volume 40: *Poets of Great Britain and Ireland since 1960,* 1985.

PERIODICALS

Books and Bookmen, September, 1973.
Guardian, March 28, 1963.
Haltwhistle Quarterly, spring, 1979.
Human World, May, 1973.
Journal of Moral Education, February, 1973.
Listener, July 6, 1967.
London Magazine, October/November, 1993.
Observer, May 14, 1967.
Punch, July 5, 1967.
Time, August 14, 1964.
Times Higher Educational Supplement, April 30, 1993.
Times Literary Supplement, April 6, 1967; May 25, 1967; June 22, 1967; July 13, 1967; April 3, 1981, p. 389; March 4, 1988, p. 253.
Words, 1986.

*   *   *

HOLDEN, Donald 1931-
(Wendon Blake)

PERSONAL: Born April 22, 1931, in Los Angeles, CA; son of Mack (a salesman) and Miriam (Epstein) Holden; married Wilma Shaffer, January 10, 1954; children: Wendy, Blake. *Education:* Columbia University, B.A., 1951; Ohio State University, M.A., 1952.

ADDRESSES: Home and office—128 Deertrack Lane, Irvington-on-Hudson, NY 10533.

CAREER: Philadelphia College of Art, Philadelphia, PA, director of public relations, 1953-55; Henry Dreyfuss Associated (industrial designers), New York City, director of public relations, 1956-60; Metropolitan Museum of Art, New York City, associate manager of public relations, 1960-61; *Fortune,* New York City, art consultant, 1961-62; Watson-Guptill Publications, New York City, editorial director, 1962-79, editorial consultant, 1979-87; artist specializing in watercolor and drawing. Art exhibited in one-man exhibitions and group shows; art also represented in collections at Metropolitan Museum of Art, New York City, Victoria and Albert Museum, London, and Corcoran Gallery, Washington, DC, and at numerous galleries in New York City, Philadelphia, San Francisco, Boston, Scottsdale, and Washington, DC. Member of faculty and member of artist advisory board, Scottsdale Artists School. Lecturer on art at museums and universities.

MEMBER: National Art Education Association, Authors Guild, Authors League of America, Artist Equity Association (member of advisory board, 1989—), Century Association, Phi Beta Kappa.

AWARDS, HONORS: LL.D., Portland School of Art, 1986; New York artists fellowship, Drawing Society.

WRITINGS:

Art Career Guide, Watson-Guptill, 1961, 4th edition, 1983.
Whistler Landscapes and Seascapes, Watson-Guptill, 1969.

UNDER PSEUDONYM WENDON BLAKE

Acrylic Watercolor Painting, Watson-Guptill, 1970.
Complete Guide to Acrylic Painting, Watson-Guptill, 1971.
Creative Color: A Practical Guide for Oil Painters, Watson-Guptill, 1972, revised edition published as *Creative Color for the Oil Painter,* 1983.
Landscape Painting in Oil, Watson-Guptill, 1976, revised and enlarged edition published as *Complete Guide to Landscape Painting in Oil,* 1981.
The Watercolor Painting Book (also see below), Watson-Guptill, 1976, revised edition published as *The Complete Watercolor Book,* North Light, 1989.
The Acrylic Painting Book (also see below), Watson-Guptill, 1979, revised edition published as *The Complete Acrylic Painting Book,* North Light, 1989.
The Oil Painting Book (also see below), Watson-Guptill, 1979, published as *The Complete Oil Painting Book,* North Light, 1989.
The Portrait and Figure Painting Book (also see below), Watson-Guptill, 1979.
Acrylic Painting (originally published as part of *The Acrylic Painting Book*), Watson-Guptill, 1979.
Landscapes in Oil (originally published as part of *The Oil Painting Book*), Watson-Guptill, 1979.
Landscapes in Watercolor (originally published as part of *The Watercolor Painting Book*), Watson-Guptill, 1979.
Oil Painting (originally published as part of *The Oil Painting Book*), Watson-Guptill, 1979.
Seascapes in Acrylic (originally published as part of *The Acrylic Painting Book*), Watson-Guptill, 1979.

Watercolor Painting (originally published as part of *The Watercolor Painting Book*), Watson-Guptill, 1979.
The Drawing Book (also see below), Watson-Guptill, 1980.
Children's Portraits in Oil (originally published as part of *The Portrait and Figure Painting Book*), Watson-Guptill, 1980.
Figures in Oil (originally published as part of *The Portrait and Figure Painting Book*), Watson-Guptill, 1980.
Landscapes in Acrylic (originally published as part of *The Acrylic Painting Book*), Watson-Guptill, 1980.
Portraits in Oil (originally published as part of *The Portrait and Figure Painting Book*), Watson-Guptill, 1980.
Seascapes in Oil (originally published as part of *The Oil Painting Book*), Watson-Guptill, 1980.
Seascapes in Watercolor (originally published as part of *The Drawing Book*), Watson-Guptill, 1980.
The Color Book (also see below), Watson-Guptill, 1981, revised edition published as *The Artist's Guide to Using Color,* North Light, 1992.
Figure Drawing (originally published as part of *The Drawing Book*), Watson-Guptill, 1981.
Landscape Drawing (originally published as part of *The Drawing Book*), Watson-Guptill, 1981.
Portrait Drawing (originally published as part of *The Drawing Book*), Watson-Guptill, 1981.
Starting to Draw (originally published as part of *The Drawing Book*), Watson-Guptill, 1981.
Painting in Alkyd, Watson-Guptill, 1982.
Color in Acrylic (originally published as part of *The Color Book*), Watson-Guptill, 1982.
Color in Oil (originally published as part of *The Color Book*), Watson-Guptill, 1982.
Color in Watercolor (originally published as part of *The Color Book*), Watson-Guptill, 1982.
The Complete Painting Course, Bonanza, 1984.
Getting Started in Drawing (originally published as part of *The Drawing Book*), North Light, 1991.

OTHER

Contributor of articles to periodicals, including *American Artist, Fortune, McCall's, Arts, American Institute of Graphic Arts Journal, Intellectual Digest, New York Times, Penthouse, Art/World, Artist's Magazine,* and *Drawing.*

BIOGRAPHICAL/CRITICAL SOURCES:

PERIODICALS

American Artist, April, 1989.
Los Angeles Times Book Review, July 31, 1983.

HOLLAND, Harrison M(elsher) 1921-

PERSONAL: Born June 4, 1921, in Tacoma, WA; son of Roy M. (a newspaper journalist) and Florence M. (a housewife) Holland; married Esther Rykkea (a housewife), December 14, 1947; children: Mark, Suzanne Holland Alouzi, Mary Holland Leonard, Christopher, Scott. *Education:* University of Washington, Seattle, B.A., 1944; Columbia University, M.A., 1949; George Washington University, Ph.D., 1958.

ADDRESSES: Home—2967 Frontera Way, Burlingame, CA 94305-6055. *Office*—Asia/Pacific Research Center, Stanford University, Stanford, CA 94305-6055.

CAREER: U.S. Department of State, Washington, DC, international relations officer, 1947-54, officer of U.S.Foreign Service in Japan, 1954-66, American consul in Amsterdam, Netherlands, 1956-58, embassy officer responsible for all matters concerning the U.S. Japan Security Treaty, 1962-66; U.S. Department of Defense, International Security Affairs, Pentagon, Washington, DC, deputy director of Far East region, 1966-68; U.S. Department of State, officer in charge of East Asian personnel, 1968-71, diplomat in residence at California State University, San Francisco (now San Francisco State University), 1971-73; San Francisco State University, professor of Japanese studies and foreign relations and founder and director of U.S.-Japan Institute, 1973-80; Keio University, Tokyo, Japan, visiting professor of American politics and foreign policy, 1980-81, 1989-91; Stanford University, Stanford, CA, visiting scholar at Hoover Institution on War, Revolution, and Peace, 1981-86, research scholar at Asia/Pacific Research Center, 1981—. Advisor to Sano Foundation, 1988-91; consultant to Kanda International University, 1988-91. *Military service:* Officer in U.S. Navy during World War II.

MEMBER: International House of Japan, Association for Asian Studies, Asiatic Society of Japan, Japan Society of Northern California.

AWARDS, HONORS: Grants from Kajima Foundation, 1980-81, and U.S.-Japan Friendship Commission, 1984-87.

WRITINGS:

Managing Diplomacy: The United States and Japan, Hoover Institution, 1984.
Managing Defense: Japan's Dilemma, University Press of America, 1988.
(With John Emmerson) *The Eagle and the Rising Sun: America and Japan in the 20th Century,* Addison-Wesley, 1988.
Japan Challenges America: Managing an Alliance in Crisis, Westview, 1992.

Contributor of articles and reviews to political science journals and Japanese newspapers, including *Foreign Service Journal, Sekai Shuho,* and *Pacific Community.*

SIDELIGHTS: Harrison M. Holland told *CA:* "My academic work is devoted to improving understanding between Japan and the United States. My writing and lecturing is also devoted to this end.

"My interest in Japan has been sustained over the years by my experiences as a naval officer in World War II in the Pacific. The need to better understand Japan and vice versa has been the main inspiration for my research, writing, and teaching. As the world shrinks and as the challenge from Japan grows ever more real, the United States must discard emotion and look at our Pacific neighbor with growing realism and objectivity. This is what has provoked my writing and teaching and channeled my energies. It is important for Americans to understand what motivates the Japanese to export, export, export, and to curtail their defense buildup. Unless greater understanding is brought to these two major issues in U.S.-Japan relations, these two great countries will begin to drift apart at terrible cost to both."

* * *

HOPE, Bob 1903-

PERSONAL: Birth-given name, Leslie Townes Hope; born May 29, 1903, in Eltham, England; came to United States in 1907, naturalized citizen, 1920; son of William Henry (a stonemason) and Avis (a concert singer; maiden name, Townes) Hope; married Dolores Reade (a singer; president of Eisenhower Medical Center), February 19, 1934; children: Linda Hope Lande, Anthony Reade, William Kelly Francis, Honorah Hope McCullagh. *Education:* Attended primary and secondary schools in Cleveland, OH.

ADDRESSES: Office—3808 Riverside Dr., Burbank, CA 91505.

CAREER: Comedian and actor. Former dance instructor, amateur boxer (under name Packy East) and newspaper reporter. Made show business debut in Fatty Arbuckle Revue as partner of vaudeville dancing act; made Broadway debut in *Sidewalks of New York,* 1922, and subsequently appeared in *Ballyhoo,* 1932, *Roberta,* 1933, *Say When,* 1934, *Ziegfeld's Follies,* 1935, and *Red, Hot and Blue,* 1936. As motion picture actor, appeared in more than fifty films, including: *The Big Broadcast of 1938,* Paramount, 1938; *Road to Singapore,* Paramount, 1940; *Road to Morocco,* Paramount, 1942; *The Paleface,* Paramount, 1948; *Fancy Pants,* Paramount, 1950; *The Seven Little Foys,* Paramount, 1955; *Call Me Bwana,* United Artists,

963; and *Cancel My Reservation,* Warner Brothers, 1972. Host of radio program, "Pepsodent Show," National Broadcasting Co., beginning 1938; made television debut in *Star Spangled Revue,* 1950 and has appeared in and hosted more than three hundred television specials, including *The Bob Hope Christmas Special,* 1987; *The Bob Hope Birthday Special,* 1988; *Bob Hope's Yellow Ribbon Party,* 1990. Entertainer for United Service Organizations (USO) shows throughout the world, 1941— . Producer of *Paris Holiday,* United Artists, 1958, and *Alias Jesse James,* United Artists, 1959.

MEMBER: American Guild of Variety Artists (former president), Friars Club.

AWARDS, HONORS: Received more than one thousand awards and citations for professional and humanitarian endeavors, including People to People Award from President Dwight D. Eisenhower; Congressional Gold Medal from President John F. Kennedy; Medal of Freedom from President Lyndon B. Johnson; Peabody Award in recognition of three decades in broadcasting, 1968; Jean Herholdt Humanitarian Award; Distinguished Service Medals from all branches of U.S. armed forces; honorary Commander of the Order of the British Empire; four Special Academy Awards from Academy of Motion Picture Arts and Sciences; Emmy Award from National Academy of Television Arts and Sciences; three People's Choice Awards for best male entertainer, 1975-76; Kennedy Center honors, 1985; opening of Bob Hope Cultural Center, 1988.

Received more than forty honorary degrees, including D.H.L. from Georgetown University, Southern Methodist University, Ohio State University, and Indiana University; L.L.D. from University of Wyoming, Northwestern University, University of Scranton, St. Bonaventure University, and Pace College; D.F.A. from Brown University and Jacksonville University; D.H. from Bowling Green University and Norwich University; Doctor of Humane Service from Drury College; Doctor of Humane Humor from Benedictine College.

WRITINGS:

I Never Left Home, Simon & Schuster, 1944.
So This is Peace, Simon & Schuster, 1946.
(With Pete Martin) *Have Tux, Will Travel: Bob Hope's Own Story,* Simon & Schuster, 1954.
I Owe Russia $1,200, Doubleday, 1963.
Five Women I Love, Doubleday, 1966.
(With Martin) *The Last Christmas Show,* Doubleday, 1974.
(With Bob Thomas) *The Road to Hollywood: My Forty-Year Love Affair With the Movies,* Doubleday, 1977.

(With Dwayne Netland; introduction by Gerald R. Ford) *Confessions of a Hooker: My Lifelong Love Affair with Golf,* Doubleday, 1985.
(With Melville Shavelson) *Don't Shoot, It's Only Me: Bob Hope's Comedy History of the United States,* Putnam, 1990.
We Could've Finished Last Without You: An Irreverent Look at the Atlanta Braves, the Losingest Team in Baseball for the Past 25 Years, Longstreet Press, 1991.

Also author of *They've Got Me Covered,* 1941.

SIDELIGHTS: Bob Hope's worldwide popularity as a comedic entertainer has spanned several decades, and he has been hailed as the "King of Comedy" by millions. Presenting him with the Congressional Gold Medal in 1963, then-President John F. Kennedy praised Hope as "America's most prized ambassador of goodwill throughout the world."

Hope has also received acclaim from his colleagues and fellow performers. In an interview with Dick Cavett in *New Times,* comic actor Woody Allen called Hope "a very, very gifted comedian. . . . I think if someone put together a compendium of his pictures . . . it would become apparent how talented he is." Nonetheless, critics have not been unanimous in their assessment of Hope's talent as a performer. While praising his rapid-fire technique and his encyclopedic memory for jokes, some maintain that Hope's reliance on prepared verbal gags limits his effectiveness as a comedian. Hope also suffered criticism of a different sort during the 1970s due to his fervent support of the U.S. war effort in Vietnam.

Hope's energy and stamina have made his name legendary, however. In 1978, at the age of seventy five, he appeared in 131 stage shows, thirty television programs, and played golf for charity twenty-five times. "I just can't sit back and play golf," Hope told *People* interviewer Martha Smilgis. "I want to keep going." Part of Hope's motivation comes from his childhood. "There were seven boys in my family and we were poor. . . . There was a time when I couldn't get a job. I was $400 in debt just for coffee and doughnuts." But most of his love of performing comes from his reaction to the audience, he explained to Smilgis. "I've never met a comedian who didn't get therapy out of a good audience. I love it. I don't consider it work." Hope sounded a similar note in the last lines of *Don't Shoot, It's Only Me: Bob Hope's Comedy History of the United States:* "People ask me why I don't retire and go fishing. I have one answer that sums it all up. Fish don't applaud."

Despite its subtitle, *Don't Shoot* is more accurately a memoir of Hope's sixty-plus-year-career as a comic performer. The book contains reminiscences of Hope's many tours overseas to entertain troops during wartime, and is filled with anecdotes about fellow entertainers, politicians, and studio heads who number among his many friends. Although treating Hope's contributions as a public figure with respect and admiration, Lawrence Christon noted "a stale, second-hand quality" to the book in his review in the *Los Angeles Times Book Review*. The reviewer also commented on an apparent lack of introspection on the part of the book's author. However, a *Publishers Weekly* critic praised *Don't Shoot, It's Only Me* as "an odds-on crowd pleaser, funny and touching."

The Road to Hollywood: My Forty-Year Love Affair with the Movies, published in 1977, also received a mixed reception from critics. J. Anthony Lukas, reviewing the work in the *New York Times Book Review,* called Hope's sense of comic timing "astonishing" and "devastatingly effective," but faulted the entertainer for his excessive piety toward some American institutions. In the *New York Times,* A. H. Weiler complimented Hope's humorous, often ghost-written, one-liners, but felt that in print such jokes fell flat, a testimony to the power of Hope's comic delivery.

A pastime that has occupied Hope nearly as much as show business is golf—Hope is a co-sponsor of the Professional Golf Association's "Bob Hope Chrysler Classic." "It's my favorite thing in the world," he told E. M. Swift in *Sports Illustrated.* Hope made his favorite sport the subject of his 1985 book, *Confessions of a Hooker: My Lifelong Love Affair with Golf,* which was coauthored with Dwayne Netland. In it, Hope recounts favorite jokes and anecdotes from his own golfing experience and analyzes the golfing styles of a host of celebrities that includes Jack Nicklaus, Humphrey Bogart, Babe Ruth, Joe Louis, Richard Nixon, Ronald Reagan, and King Baudoin of Belgium. *Confessions of a Hooker* contains one hundred photos and an introduction by fellow-golfer and former U.S. President Gerald R. Ford. According to *Publishers Weekly* reviewer Genevieve Stutta Ford, the book is "enormously entertaining" and "there is a laugh line in virtually every paragraph."

BIOGRAPHICAL/CRITICAL SOURCES:

BOOKS

Hope, Bob, *Don't Shoot, It's Only Me: Bob Hope's Comedy History of the United States,* Putnam, 1990.
Morella, Epstein, and Clark, *The Amazing Careers of Bob Hope,* Arlington House, 1973.

PERIODICALS

Chicago Tribune, December 13, 1987; June 1, 1990, Section 2, pp. 1-2.
Library Journal, July, 1977; April 1, 1990, pp. 121-22.
Los Angeles Times, May 14, 1988.
Los Angeles Times Book Review, May 27, 1990, p. 9.
New Times, August 7, 1978.

New York Times, September 12, 1977; September 28, 1989.
New York Times Book Review, July 17, 1977, pp. 13, 30; June 10, 1990.
People, January 15, 1979; January 18, 1988.
Publishers Weekly, October 23, 1967, p. 53; March 1, 1985, p. 75; March 23, 1990, p. 71.
Sports Illustrated, January 23, 1989, pp. 20-23.
Time, August 19, 1985.
Washington Post Book World, July 8, 1990, p. 8.*

*   *   *

HOWSE, Ernest Marshall (Frazer) 1902-

PERSONAL: Born September 29, 1902, in Newfoundland, Canada; son of Charles (a clergyman) and Elfreda (Palmer) Howse; married Esther Lilian Black, September 17, 1932; children: Margery, Joan Dyer, David C. N., George A. *Education:* Dalhousie University, B.A., 1929; Pine Hill Divinity Hall, graduate (with honors), 1931; Union Theological Seminary, S.T.M., 1932; University of Edinburgh, Ph.D., 1934. *Politics:* Independent. *Religion:* United Church of Canada. *Avocational Interests:* Carpentry, boating, fishing.

ADDRESSES: Home—Chester Village, 717 Broadview Ave., Toronto, Ontario M5P 2E8, Canada.

CAREER: Ordained minister of United Church of Canada, 1931; minister in Beverly Hills, CA, 1934-35, Winnipeg, Manitoba, 1935-48, and Toronto, Ontario, 1948-70. Co-president, Continuing Committee of Muslim-Christian Cooperation, Cairo, Egypt, 1955; moderator, United Church of Canada, 1964-66; Canadian delegate to First World Conference on Religion and Peace, Kyoto, Japan, 1970. Commissioner of the general council, United Church of Canada, Belleville, 1942, Montreal, 1946, Toronto, 1950, Sackville, 1954, Windsor, 1956, Edmonton, 1960, London, 1962, Newfoundland, 1964, and Waterloo, 1966.

Special correspondent for the Winnipeg *Free Press,* 1948, 1954, and 1961; correspondent for the Toronto *Star,* 1954; syndicated columnist in Canadian newspapers, 1957-64; columnist for Toronto *Telegram,* 1964-70, and Toronto *Star,* 1970—.

MEMBER: Empire Club of Canada (director, 1956-70; honorary officer, 1970—).

AWARDS, HONORS: Received key to city and made honorary citizen of Seoul, Korea, 1965; D.D., United College, 1948, Huntington College (now University; Sudbury, Ontario), 1964, Pine Hill Divinity Hall, 1966, and Victoria University (Toronto), 1967; D.Litt., University of Newfoundland, 1965; award of merit, City of Toronto, 1980, for "having attained distinction and renown in various fields of endeavour."

WRITINGS:

Our Prophetic Heritage, Ryerson Press, 1945.
The Law and the Prophets, Ryerson Press, 1947.
Saints in Politics: The 'Clapham Sect' and the Growth of Freedom, University of Toronto Press, 1952, third edition, Allen & Unwin, 1971.
Spiritual Values in Shakespeare, Abingdon, 1955.
The Lively Oracles, Allen & Unwin, 1956.
People and Provocations, Ryerson, 1965.

Also author of the autobiography *Roses in December,* 1982. Contributor to journals and newspapers.*

*   *   *

HUANG, Ray (Jen-yu)   1918-

PERSONAL: Born June 25, 1918, in Changsha, China; son of Cheng-pai and Chang-shun (Li) Huang; married Gayle Bates, September 20, 1966; children: Jefferson. *Education:* Attended U.S. Command and General Staff College, 1947; University of Michigan, B.A., 1954, M.A., 1957, Ph.D., 1964.

ADDRESSES: Home—10 Bonticou View Dr., New Paltz, NY 12561.

CAREER: Southern Illinois University, Edwardsville, assistant professor of history, 1964-66; Columbia University, New York City, visiting associate professor of history, 1966-67; State University College at New Paltz, New Paltz, NY, associate professor, 1967-71, professor of Chinese history, 1971-80. Research fellow at Harvard University, 1970-71. *Military service:* Chinese National Army, served in India, Burma, and Manchuria, 1941-50; became major.

MEMBER: PEN.

AWARDS, HONORS: American Council of Learned Societies fellowship, 1966 and 1972; National Science Foundation grant, 1973; Guggenheim fellowship, 1975-76; nomination for American Book Awards, history category, 1982, for *1587, A Year of No Significance: The Ming Dynasty in Decline.*

WRITINGS:

Taxation and Governmental Finance in Sixteenth-Century Ming China, Cambridge University Press, 1974.
(With Joseph Needham) *The Nature of Chinese Society: A Technical Interpretation,* East & West Library, 1974.
1587, A Year of No Significance: The Ming Dynasty in Decline, Yale University Press, 1981.

Wan-li Shih-wu-nian, Chung-hua Book Co. (Peking), 1982.
China, A Macro History, M. E. Sharpe, 1988.

Also author of *Military Expenditures in Sixteenth-Century Ming China, Oriens Extremus,* 1970. Contributor to *Government in Ming Times: Seven Studies,* 1969; *Self and Society in Ming Thought,* 1970; and *Cambridge History of China.*

BIOGRAPHICAL/CRITICAL SOURCES:

PERIODICALS

New York Times Book Review, June 21, 1981.*

*   *   *

HUCHEL, Peter   1903-1981

PERSONAL: Born April 3, 1903, in Lichterfelde, Berlin, Germany; died in 1981 (one source says 1980); son of Friedrich (a civil servant) and Marie (Zimmermann) Huchel; married Monica Nora Rosenthal, 1953; children: one son, one daughter. *Education:* Attended Humboldt University, University of Freiburg, and University of Vienna.

CAREER: Freelance writer and translator, 1925-40; Berliner Rundfunk (East Berlin Radio service), 1945-48, began as editor and producer of radio plays, became artistic director; *Sinn und Form* (magazine), chief editor, 1949-62; freelance writer and translator, 1962-81. *Military service:* German Army, 1940-45.

MEMBER: German Academy of Arts, Free Academy of Arts (honorary member), Gruppe 47 ("Group 47").

AWARDS, HONORS: Die Kolonne prize for lyric poetry, 1932; National Prize, 1951; Theodor Fontane Prize of Mark Brandenburg, 1955; plaquette of the Free Academy of Arts, Hamburg, 1959; Theodor Fontane Prize for literature, 1963; Young Generation's Prize, Hamburg, 1965; Nordrhein-Westfalen Grand Prize for Art, 1968.

WRITINGS:

POETRY

Gedichte (title means "Poems") Aufbau Verlag, 1948.
Chausseen, Chausseen: Gedichte (title means "Roads, Roads: Poems"), S. Fischer, 1963.
Die Sternenreuse: Gedichte, 1925-1947 (title means "Grid of Stars: Poems, 1925-1947"), Piper, 1967.
Gezaehlte Tage: Gedichte (title means "Numbered Days: Poems"), Suhrkamp, 1972.
Ausgewaehlte Gedichte (title means "Selected Poems"), Suhrkamp, 1973.
Selected Poems, translated by Michael Hamburger, Carcanet Press, 1974.

(Editor) *Gedichte: Marie Luise Kaschnitz* (title means "Poems of Marie Luise Kaschnitz"), Suhrkamp, 1975.

Der Tod des Buedners (title means "The Death of the Cottager"), Erker-Presse, 1976.

Unbewohnbar die Trauer: Gedichte (sound recording; title means "Unbearable the Sorrow: Poems"), St. Gallen, 1978.

Die neunte Stunde: Gedichte (title means "The Ninth Hour: Poems"), Suhrkamp, 1979.

The Garden of Theophrastus and Other Poems, translated by Hamburger, Carcanet Press, 1983.

Gesammelte Werke in zwei Banden (title means "Collected Works in Two Volumes;" includes *Der Knabenteich*), edited by Axel Vieregg, Suhrkamp, 1984.

Margarethe Minde: Eine Dichtung fuer den Rundfunk (title means "Margarethe Minde: A Poem for the Radio"), Suhrkamp, 1984.

A Thistle in His Mouth, translated by Henry Beissel, Cormorant Books, 1988.

Contributor to *Das innere Reich* and other periodicals.

OTHER

(With Hans Henny Jahnn) *Ein Briefwechsel: 1951-1959* (title means "A Correspondence: 1951-1959"), Hase & Koehler, 1974.

Peter Huchel (essays and criticism), edited by Vieregg, Suhrkamp, 1986.

(Editor) *Sinn und Form: Beitrage zur Literatur, 1949-1958* (title means "Meaning and Form: Contributions to Literature, 1949-1958"), eleven volumes, Rutten and Loening, 1989.

SIDELIGHTS: Peter Huchel is often considered the most important poet of World War II-era Germany. His style, particularly in his earlier verse, echoes his love for the German countryside—inspired by the years he spent as a child on his grandfather's farm in Mark Brandenburg. As an adult, Huchel was the editor of *Sinn und Form*, a German literary magazine that provided a forum for many of Europe's most talented and influential writers. Though his work and ideas were suppressed by the East German government in later years, Huchel continued to write and comment about his homeland. Today, he holds a place alongside such masters as Bertolt Brecht as one of the favorite sons of German literature.

The poems Huchel wrote as a young man began to appear in periodicals in the mid-1920's. Rich in language and traditional in form, they revealed from the beginning a mastery of rhythm. These early poems, concerned mostly with the rural scenes and peasant life of Mark Brandenburg, are seen by some West German critics as examples of modern "Naturlyrik," whose exponents seek to deal both lovingly and knowledgeably with the concrete details of nature.

Many of these poems also reflect Huchel's concern for the poor of Brandenburg, the exploited farm laborers and migrant workers, the servants and the vagrants. As he wrote many years later, "I wanted to make visible in the poem a deliberately ignored, suppressed class, the class of the people." This element in his work has been castigated by East German critics as evidence of his socialist leanings, even though Huchel had always refused to affiliate himself with any political party.

John Flores found some justification for both the East and the West German views of Huchel's work, but maintained in his book *Poetry in East Germany* that Huchel's early verse expresses "a class-consciousness which is at the same time consciousness of a more fundamental relationship between man and his environment" and "a 'version of pastoral,' a kind of personal idyll." Flores continues to list the two major components of Huchel's verse as "the sense of continuity . . . between past, present and future activity . . . and the seemingly magical harmony between productive human activity and the processes of nature."

Though Huchel's first poetry collection, entitled *Der Knabenteich* ("The Boy's Pond"), won a prize from the literary journal *Die Kolonne* in 1932, it was never actually published until after his death: Huchel withdrew it when the Nazis came to power, fearing that it would be confused with the kind of nature poetry associated with National Socialism. Between 1933 and 1945, Huchel wrote a number of apolitical radio plays but, apart from a few verses appearing in the periodical *Das innere Reich*, published virtually no poetry. He did continue to write, however—grim and wintry verse written in reaction to Nazism and the war. Most of Huchel's work from this period was destroyed during the Allied bombing of Germany, though some of it was later reconstructed and published posthumously.

From 1940 to 1945, Huchel served as a conscript in the German army. He was sent to the Eastern Front where he was eventually captured by the Russians. In 1945, he was taken to the Soviet Zone of Berlin, where for the next three years he worked for the local radio station. His first published volume of verse, which appeared in 1948, consisted mainly of earlier work, with only a few of the generally inferior poems written during the Nazi years included.

In the years just after the war Huchel's poetry took on a more optimistic tone, reflecting his hope that the Communist government of East Germany might achieve a more just society there. His verse at this time approached the "socialist realism" urged upon East European writers by the government. "Das Gesetz" ("The Law"), the best-known product of this phase of Huchel's work, is a never-completed and generally rather uninspired verse chronicle in praise of the land reform program announced in 1945.

This hopeful interlude ended with the government's decision in 1952 to collectivize the land which had been given to the peasants; Huchel's subsequent poetry was, for the most part, a somber meditation on the pain and uncertainty of human existence, with no suggestion that this condition might be alleviated by any kind of political development. His style seemed to change as well, becoming more cryptic and abstract.

In 1949, Huchel became editor of the East German quarterly *Sinn und Form* ("Meaning and Form"). With the support of Johannes R. Becher, a powerful figure in German politics, Huchel quickly turned *Sinn und Form* into one of the best—and most controversial—cultural periodicals in Europe. Huchel published work that he admired for its literary quality alone and frequently offended the East German literary establishment by ignoring every other consideration, including the nationality, political views, and literary orthodoxy of its author. His contributors included such illustrious writers as Pablo Neruda, Bertolt Brecht, Thomas Mann, Nathalie Sarraute, Johannes Bobrowski, and Jean-Paul Sartre, to name only a few. All the while, Huchel and Becher withstood tremendous pressure from the Socialist government of the new German Democratic Republic, which sought to use *Sinn und Form* as its own personal sounding board.

"For the West German critic Marcel Reich-Ranicki *Sinn und Form* came to signify 'a quiet enclave of liberalism in a loud world of dogmatism,' " Philip Brady relates in the *Times Literary Supplement.* Huchel was ultimately ousted from his position as general editor, and the magazine eventually became something of a political organ. Brady stresses, though, that for a decade "*Sinn und Form* was the sole meeting-place for a unique community of writers, thinkers and critics who had returned from exile [during the war]." Huchel described in a 1971 interview the difficulty of keeping control of *Sinn und Form* for even that long: "*Kulturpolitik* [the cultural standards deemed acceptable by the Socialist government] never stood still: what was acceptable one day, was no longer so the next day and then back again the day after that. I steered a straight course: but I knew that my rowing was at times desperate and cramped and against the tide." The first ten years of *Sinn und Form* have been recently bound and reprinted as an eleven volume set entitled *Sinn und Form: Beitrage zur Literatur, 1949-1958* ("Meaning and Form: Contributions to Literature, 1949-1958").

Huchel's disenchantment with socialism and his eschewal of socialist realism did not, of course, pass unnoticed in East Germany. His refusal to toe the party line either as a poet or as an editor brought him increasingly into conflict with the authorities. In 1962, Huchel was dismissed from the editorship of *Sinn und Form* and publicly disgraced. Unable to publish in East Germany (though he

was by then widely regarded as his country's most eminent poet), he retired into complete seclusion in his house near Potsdam. There he remained, under unofficial house arrest, until 1971, when he was allowed to leave East Germany with his family. He went first to Italy and then to West Germany, where he remained until his death in 1981.

Meanwhile, in 1963, Huchel's second volume of poetry appeared in West Germany as *Chausseen, Chausseen.* "This poetry of disenchantment," Flores wrote, "is dominated by embittered reflections; an abstract, fragmented style; and images of an icy, static landscape. . . . Nature itself is dead . . . leaving only silence, blindness, and icy treachery." This hopeless mood of tired aloofness is persistent in Huchel's later work. A *Times Literary Supplement* reviewer contrasted his 1972 collection *Gezaehlte Tage* ("Numbered Days") to the work of Robert Frost: "Unlike Frost, Huchel has become alienated from nature by his experience of man's inhumanity and his subsequent creative isolation; he finds himself cast into a spiritual winter from which nature has withdrawn into itself and refuses to reveal itself to him any more." The reviewer felt that *Gezaehlte Tage* reaffirmed Huchel's status as "a major poet," and proclaimed that it "may well be the most important volume of poetry to emerge from Germany for some time." Another critic in the same journal once described Huchel as "certainly one of the most courageous and humane of living contemplative poets."

Many of Huchel's works have been recently published as compilations; these include *The Garden of Theophrastus and Other Poems* and *Die neunte Stunde* ("The Ninth Hour"). In each Huchel continued to share his bleak but enigmatic view of man and nature. "[Huchel's verse] recreates an autumnal landscape haunted by death and replete with blackness, isolation and decline," writes Brady. "It is peopled with lonely figures, the gypsy, the old peasant woman, [and] the poet himself." When once asked how to approach the meaning of his poems, Brady relates, "Huchel replied 'with caution,' adding, in a memorable phrase, that to prise 'meaning' from a poem is 'like taking a scythe to the sunset.' "

BIOGRAPHICAL/CRITICAL SOURCES:

BOOKS

Deutsche Dichter der Gegenwart, Erich Schmidt Verlag, 1973.

Flores, John, *Poetry in East Germany,* Yale University Press, 1971.

Huchel, Peter, *Selected Poems,* translated and introduced by Michael Hamburger, Carcanet Press, 1974.

Hummage fuer Peter Huchel, Piper, 1968.

Keith-Smith, Brian, editor, *Essays on Contemporary German Literature* (Volume 4 of "German Men of Letters"), Oswald Wolff, 1966.

Mayer, Hans, editor, *Ueber Peter Huchel,* Suhrkamp, 1973.

PERIODICALS

Akzente, XII, 1965.
Globe & Mail (Toronto), June 18, 1988.
Neue Deutsche Literatur 1, 1953.
Times Literary Supplement, September 28, 1967; December 29, 1972, p. 1572; April 11, 1980, p. 422; October 14, 1983, p. 1136; January 10, 1986, p. 33; June 30-July 6, 1989, p. 721.*

*   *   *

HULSE, Michael (William) 1955-

PERSONAL: Surname rhymes with "pulse"; born June 12, 1955, in Stoke-on-Trent, England; son of William Ernest (a schoolteacher) and Adelheid Elisabeth Theresia (Gebhard) Hulse. *Education:* University of St. Andrews, M.A. (with first class honors), 1977.

ADDRESSES: c/o Harvill, 77-85 Fulham Palace Rd., Hammersmith, London W6 8JB, England.

CAREER: University of Erlangen-Nuernberg, Erlangen, West Germany, lecturer in English language and drama, 1977-79; Catholic University of Eichstaett, Eichstaett, West Germany, lecturer in English language and literature, American history and literature, and drama, 1981-83; University of Cologne, Cologne, Germany, part-time lecturer, 1985—; Deutsche Welle TV, Cologne, Germany, translator, 1986—; writer. Director of Cologne International Literature Festival, 1994.

MEMBER: Poetry Society, Society of Authors, PEN.

AWARDS, HONORS: First prize, National Poetry Competition (England), 1978, for "Dole Queue"; second prize, *New Poetry* competition, 1978; West Midlands Arts Writer's Bursary grant, 1979; Eric Gregory Award, Society of Authors, 1980, for unpublished typescript of *Knowing and Forgetting;* third prize, Tate Gallery poetry competition, 1985; second prize, *Times Literary Supplement/* Cheltenham Literature Festival poetry competition, 1987; first prize, Bridport poetry competition, 1988; Hawthornden Castle Fellowship, 1991; Cholmondeley Award, Society of Authors, 1991.

WRITINGS:

POETRY

Monochrome Blood, Oasis Books, 1980.
Dole Queue, White Friar Press, 1981.

Knowing and Forgetting, Secker & Warburg, 1981.
Propaganda, Secker & Warburg, 1985.
Eating Strawberries in the Necropolis, Harvill, 1991.
Mother of Battles (pamphlet), Littlewood Arc, 1991.
(Editor, with David Kennedy and David Morley) *The New Poetry,* Bloodaxe, 1993.
Monteverdi's Photographs, Folio, 1993.

TRANSLATOR

Botho Strauss, *Tumult,* Carcanet, 1984.
Essays in Honor of Elias Canetti, Farrar, Straus, 1987.
Volkmar Essers, *Matisse,* Taschen, 1987.
Matthias Arnold, *Toulouse-Lautrec,* Taschen, 1987.
Ingo F. Walther and Rainer Metzger, *Chagall,* Taschen, 1987.
Walther, *Gauguin,* Taschen, 1988.
Luise Rinser, *Prison Journal,* Macmillan, 1987, Schocken Books, 1988.
Johann Wolfgang Goethe, *The Sorrows of Young Werther,* Penguin, 1989.
Ulrich Bischoff, *Munch,* Taschen, 1989.
Hajo Duechting, *Cezanne,* Taschen, 1989.
Karl Lagerfeld (photography and design), Taschen, 1990.
Chargesheimer (photography and design), Taschen, 1990.
Dahmane (photography and design), Taschen, 1990.
Walther and Metzger, *The Complete Paintings of van Gogh,* two volumes, Taschen, 1990.
Robert Descharnes and Gilles Neret, *Salvador Dali,* Taschen, 1990.
Elfriede Jelinek, *Wonderful Wonderful Times,* Serpent's Tail, 1990.
Rinser, *Jan Lobel from Warsaw,* Polygon, 1991.
Rulf Guenter Renner, *Edward Hopper,* Taschen, 1991.
Reinhard Steiner, *Egon Schiele,* Taschen, 1991.
Bernd Growe, *Degas,* Taschen, 1992.
Walther, *Picasso,* two volumes, Taschen, 1992.
Guenter Metken, *Gauguin in Tahiti,* Norton, 1992.
Andreas Maeckler, *Helnwein,* Taschen, 1992.
Matthias Dietz and Michael Moenninger, *Japan Design,* 1992.
Jakob Wassermann, *Caspar Hauser,* Penguin, 1992.
Jelinek, *Lust,* Serpent's Tail, 1992.
Selected Poems of Rainer Maria Rilke, Anvil Press, in press.

Also translator for galleries, artists, and periodicals in Germany, Switzerland, Britain, and the U.S. Has adapted and translated material for television.

OTHER

(Translator) Ingeborg Bachmann, librettist, *The Idiot: Paraphrases of Dostoyevsky* (ballet-pantomime), by Hans Werner Henze, performed in London, Barbican Theatre, 1991.

Work represented in several anthologies, including *Germany in British Poetry since 1945: An Anthology,* edited by Guenther Blaicher, Verlag Friedrich Pustet, 1987, and *Earth Against Heaven: A Tiananmen Square Anthology,* edited by Walter Tonetto, Five Islands Press, 1990. Contributor of essays and reviews to periodicals in Great Britain, Australia, Canada, New Zealand and Germany, including *Times Literary Supplement, Guardian,* and *Spectator.* Associate editor, Littlewood Arc, Todmorden, England, 1992—. Hulse's poems have been translated into German, French, Greek, and Arabic.

WORK IN PROGRESS: Translations: *Vincent van Gogh: The Reed Pen Drawings,* by Fritz Erpel, for Norton; *Written in the West,* by Wim Wenders, for Norton; and *Impressionist Painting,* two volumes, by Peter H. Feist et al., for Taschen. Also in progress: a novel; an anthology of contemporary German poetry in English translation; a book on Kuching (Sarawak); essays on contemporary British poetry.

SIDELIGHTS: Michael Hulse once told *CA:* "Critics emphasize the abstraction in my poetry, so as a counterbalance I'd like to say that I'm happiest living in my instincts, not in my intellect. Still, the two can't really be separated, and the penalty (if penalty it is) of being a rational animal is that no experience enters the awareness unattended. This is intensely liberating, since it is liberating to sense one's connections with a culture and so to sense oneself, but at the same time it is stifling, since some half-forgotten directness of experience (known in childhood? in love and sex? in birth or death?) seems mostly inaccessible. For me, poetry has always been a way for the whole man to express equally his noble, trivial, beautiful, ugly, original, and humdrum selves. Poetry which admits Greek myth but not James Bond, Claude-ish landscape but not backstreets, highmindedness but not smallness, has always seemed to me to be untrue to the human animal. Life isn't simple, clean, or tidy—fortunately.

"I grew up with one English and one German parent, and that has been an advantage since I have never dreamt that either Britain or Germany was the entire known world. But it has been a disadvantage in leaving me homeless, somehow an exile, no matter which of the two countries I live in. So I feel split, culturally, politically, linguistically, emotionally—even in details like the look and smell of city streets, the different ways landscapes have evolved, food and drink. My favorite beer is Schlenkerla Rauchbier from Bamberg. My favorite cheese is an applewood smoked that I could buy in Oxford. My poetry hasn't yet found a place for that beer and that cheese, but I wish it would."

BIOGRAPHICAL/CRITICAL SOURCES:

PERIODICALS

Poetry Canada Review, autumn, 1985.

*   *   *

HUMPHREY, Hubert H(oratio)   1911-1978

PERSONAL: Born May 27, 1911, in Wallace, SD; died January 13, 1978, in Waverly, MN; son of Hubert (a pharmacist) and Christine (Sannes) Humphrey; married Muriel Fay Buck, September 3, 1936; children: Nancy, Hubert, Robert, Douglas. *Education:* Denver College of Pharmacy, received degree, 1933; University of Minnesota, B.A. (magna cum laude), 1939; Louisiana State University, M.A., 1940.

CAREER: University of Minnesota, Minneapolis, instructor in political science, 1940-41; War Production Administration, head of Minnesota branch and state director of training re-employment division, 1941-42; War Manpower Progress Commission, assistant regional director, 1943; Macalester College, St. Paul, MN, professor for Army Air Force Training Program, 1943-44; Franklin D. Roosevelt for President campaign, Minneapolis manager, 1944; Mayor of Minneapolis, 1945-48; member of U.S. Senate from Minnesota, 1948-64; U.S. Delegate to the United Nations, 1956-57; 38th Vice-President of the United States, 1964-68; Democratic candidate for President of United States, 1968; University of Minnesota, professor of social science, 1969-70; member of U.S. Senate, 1970-1978; Deputy President pro tem of the Senate, 1977-1978.

Co-founder of Americans for Democratic Action, 1947; U.S. Delegate to UNESCO Conference in Paris and the Nuclear Test Suspension Conference in Geneva, 1958; contended for U.S. Presidential nomination, Democratic Party, 1960; Assistant Majority Leader (Whip), U.S. Senate, 1961-64; floor manager of Civil Rights Act of 1964; chairman, Board of Consultants, Encyclopaedia Britannica Education Corporation, and member of board, Encyclopaedia Britannica, Inc., 1969-70; contended for Democratic Presidential nomination, 1972; chairman of Board of Trustees, Woodrow Wilson International Center for Scholars, 1970-72; chairman, Vice-Presidential Selection Commission, Democratic Party, 1972-74. Has served as chairman of the Congressional joint economic committee; chairman of the Senate agriculture and forestry committee; member of Senate foreign relations committee; select committee on nutrition and human needs; Technology Assessment Board; and National Ocean Policy Study Group. Member of twelve Senate subcommittees.

WRITINGS:

The Cause Is Mankind: A Liberal Program for Modern America, Praeger, 1964.

War on Poverty, McGraw, 1964.

(Editor) *Integration Versus Segregation,* Crowell, 1964.

(Co-author) *Moral Crisis: The Case for Civil Rights,* Gilbert Publishing, 1964.

Beyond Civil Rights: A New Day of Equality, Random House, 1964.

The Political Philosophy of the New Deal, Louisiana State University Press, 1970.

The Education of a Public Man: My Life and Politics, Doubleday, 1976.

Hubert Humphrey: The Man and His Dream (collected works), compiled by Sheldon D. Engelmayer and Robert J. Wagman, Methuen, 1978.

Also author of a regular newspaper column distributed by the Register and Tribune Syndicate, 1969-70.

SIDELIGHTS: When Hubert Humphrey died of cancer in January, 1978, a saddened President Jimmy Carter released the following statement: "From time to time our nation is blessed by the presence of men and women who bear the marks of greatness and who help us see a better vision of what we can become. Hubert Humphrey was such a man." Humphrey's funeral was attended by three presidents: Carter, Richard Nixon, and Gerald Ford. Indeed, it marked Nixon's first appearance in Washington, D.C. following his resignation as President of the United States.

When he died, Humphrey had been in public service for thirty-two years. His service to the U.S. government included his election as Vice President of the United States under President Lyndon Johnson—during which time he acted as a member of the Cabinet and National Security Council and chairman of the National Aeronautics and Space Council, Peace Corps Advisory Council, National Advisory Council to the Office of Economic Opportunity, the President's Council on Youth Opportunity, and National Council on Indian Opportunities. At the request of President Johnson Humphrey undertook numerous overseas assignments, most notable of which were the Nuclear Proliferation Treaty, the Kennedy Round of Trade Negotiations, and the North Atlantic Treaty Organization.

Senator Humphrey's distinguished record of accomplishment in Congress included work on such projects as Medicare, Project Headstart, Peace Corps, Department of Housing and Urban Development, the U.S. Arms Control and Disarmament Agency, the 1964 Civil Rights Act, Vista, the Nuclear Test Ban Treaty of 1963, the Federal Scholarship Program, the Council of Youth Opportunity, and Job Corps. He wrote forty-two bills, co-wrote an additional 135, introduced eleven resolutions, and made eighteen amendments during his time of service. "In my years of public life," he wrote, "I have tried to serve as a voice and worker for the cause of equal justice and equal opportunity, for the general welfare, and for the common defense of our country." On January 5, 1977, Humphrey was unanimously elected Deputy President pro tem of the Senate by Democratic members of the Senate. He died one year later.

Upon his death, Edwin Warner wrote in *Time* magazine that Humphrey "preached not only the politics of joy but the politics of plenty. He was the quintessential, unrepentant New Dealer." Mel Elfin eulogized him in *Newsweek* as "indisputably the best orator of his generation, but he spoke in a voice that was a trifle too reedy and perhaps an octave too high. It was a voice that seemed forever poised between the lachrymose and the eloquent, yet it was a voice that could electrify." Humphrey was a politician known as much for his eloquence as for the depth of his emotion. In countless speeches, in his writings, and in his life he was a man of passion who, as Senator Robert Dole once observed, brought "out the best in everyone." He was, as Humphrey said it himself, "a public man."

BIOGRAPHICAL/CRITICAL SOURCES:

PERIODICALS

New Republic, July 24, 1976, pp. 28-30.
New York Times Book Review, June 6, 1976, pp. 6, 22; July 23, 1978, p. 16.
Perspectives on Political Science, winter, 1992, p. 36.
Saturday Review, July 31, 1965, p. 27.
Times Literary Supplement, January 15, 1971, p. 63.

OBITUARIES:

PERIODICALS

Newsweek, January 23, 1978, pp. 16-24.
New York Times, January 14, 1978; January 16, 1978.
Time, January 23, 1978, pp. 21-22, 24-26.
Washington Post, January 16, 1978.*

*   *   *

HURWOOD, Bernhardt J. 1926-1987
(Father Xavier, Mallory T. Knight, D. Gunther Wilde)

PERSONAL: Born July 22, 1926, in New York, NY; died of cancer, January 23, 1987; son of Abraham (an accountant) and Jeanette (Jackson) Hurwood; married Laura Fenga, April 26, 1958 (marriage ended); married Marci Vitous. *Education:* Northwestern University, B.S., 1949. *Avocational Interests:* Photography, art, conversation.

ADDRESSES: Home—New York City.

CAREER: U.S. Merchant Marine, seaman, 1945-47; film editor with Television Arts Productions, Berkeley, CA, 1949, Chicago Film Laboratory, Chicago, IL, 1949-50, and National Broadcasting Co. (news and special events), New York City, 1951-52; free-lance film editor, 1955-61; free-lance writer, 1961-87.

WRITINGS:

Terror by Night, Lancer, 1963.
(With F. S. Klaf) *A Psychiatrist Looks at Erotica,* Ace Books, 1964.
(Translator, with Klaf) *The Hundred Merry Tales,* Citadel, 1964.
Monsters Galore, Fawcett, 1965.
Golden Age of Erotica, Sherbourne, 1965.
Strange Lives, Popular Library, 1966.
Monsters and Nightmares, Belmont Books, 1967.
Strange Talents, Ace Books, 1967.
(Translator) *The Facetiae of Poggio Bracciolini,* Award Books, 1968.
(Editor) *The First Occult Review Reader,* Award Books, 1968.
Vampires, Werewolves and Ghouls, Ace Books, 1968.
Torture through the Ages, Paperback Library, 1969.
(Editor) *The Second Occult Review Reader,* Award Books, 1969.
(With Frank Grosfield) *Korea: Land of the 38th Parallel,* Parents' Magazine Press, 1969.
Society and the Assassin, Parents' Magazine Press, 1970.
The Two Sided Triangle, Ace Books, 1970.
Ghosts, Ghouls, and Other Horrors, Scholastic, Inc., 1971.
(Editor) *The Hag of the Dribble and Other True Ghosts from the Files of Elliot O'Donnell,* Taplinger, 1971.
The Invisibles, Fawcett, 1971.
Life, the Unknown, Ace Books, 1971.
Haunted Houses, Scholastic Inc., 1972.
Passport to the Supernatural, Taplinger, 1972.
Rip Off!, Fawcett, 1972.
Vampires, Werewolves, and Other Demons, Scholastic Inc., 1972.
Chilling Ghost Stories, Scholastic Inc., 1973.
Eerie Tales of Terror and Dread, Scholastic Inc., 1973.
The Mindmaster, Fawcett, 1973.
The Girls, the Massage and Everything, Fawcett, 1973.
The Sensuous New Yorker, Award Books, 1973.
The Bisexuals, Fawcett, 1974.
Born Innocent (novelization of the teleplay by Gerald Di Pego), Ace Books, 1975.
Strange Curses, Scholastic Inc., 1975.
The Whole Sex Catalogue, Pinnacle Books, 1975.
(Editor) *Joys of Oral Love,* Carlyle Communications, 1975.
Confessions of a Sex Researcher, Pocket Books, 1976.

(With Bernard Korman) *Hands: The Power of Hand Awareness,* Sunridge Press, 1978.
Burt Reynolds, Quick Fox, 1979.
My Savage Muse: The Story of My Life—Edgar Allan Poe, Everest House, 1980.
Vampires, Quick Fox, 1981.
Writing Becomes Electronic, Congdon & Weed, 1986.

UNDER PSEUDONYM FATHER XAVIER

Casebook: Exorcism and Possession, New American Library, 1974.

UNDER PSEUDONYM MALLORY T. KNIGHT; "THE MAN FROM T.O.M.C.A.T." SERIES

The Deadly Dozen Dragons of Joy, Award Books, 1967.
The Million Missing Maidens, Award Books, 1967.
The Terrible Ten, Award Books, 1967.
The Dirty Rotten Depriving Ray, Award Books, 1967.
Tsimmis in Tangier, Award Books, 1968.
The Malignant Metaphysical Menace, Award Books, 1968.
The Ominous Orgy, Award Books, 1969.
The Return of Alexander Graham Wang, Award Books, 1969.
Peking Pornographer, Award Books, 1969.
The Bra Burners' Brigade, Award Books, 1971.

UNDER PSEUDONYM D. GUNTHER WILDE

Deviation, Macfadden, 1966.
(Compiler) *When Maidens Were Deflowered and Knightly Lost Their Heads* (anthology), Belmont Books, 1967.
Claws, Dorchester Publishing, 1978.

OTHER

Wrote screenplay for *The Creatures from the Negative,* produced by Ram Films; author of approximately two hundred short motion picture scripts for animated cartoons. Columnist for *Writer's World;* entertainment editor for *Gallery* and *Genesis* magazines during their first year of publication; contributor of articles and film reviews for magazines.

SIDELIGHTS: Bernhardt J. Hurwood once told *CA:* "I earn my living as a writer because the thought of wearing another man's collar is abhorrent to me. . . . I do not believe that poverty enriches, ennobles, or strengthens character. It destroys the body and the spirit. . . . The things that bother me the most are hypocrisy and the growing impersonalization or dehumanization of our society. The thing I value most is freedom to be an individual and to express myself as I see fit. If all writers would remember to attack hypocrisy and defend individuality and freedom, not only would they be able to sleep nights, they might in the long run be extending that gift to millions of others. . . . For the record I have been in all of the states except Alaska and Hawaii. I have been to England, France, Germany, Holland, Italy, Ireland, Iceland, Canada, Nova Scotia, Newfoundland, Bermuda, Cuba, Chile, Curacao, Panama, Spain, Trinidad, and Tobago (where I was once shipwrecked)."

OBITUARIES:

PERIODICALS

New York Daily News, January 27, 1987.
New York Times, January 26, 1987.*

I

IBBOTSON, Eva 1925-

PERSONAL: Born January 21, 1925, in Vienna, Austria; daughter of B. P. (a physiologist) and Anna (a writer; maiden name, Gmeyner) Wiesner; married Alan Ibbotson (a university lecturer), June 21, 1948; children: Lalage Ann, Tobias John, Piers David, Justin Paul. *Education:* Bedford College, London, B.Sc., 1945; attended Cambridge University, 1946-47; University of Durham, diploma in education, 1965. *Politics:* "Wavering." *Religion:* None. *Avocational Interests:* Ecology and environmental preservation, music, continental literature, history ("My favorite year is 1904!").

ADDRESSES: Home—2 Collingwood Ter., Jesmond, Newcastle-upon-Tyne NE2 2JP, England. *Agent*—Curtis Brown, 162-168 Regent St., London W1R 5TA, England; John Cushman Associates Inc., 25 West 43rd St., New York, NY 10036.

CAREER: Writer. Former research worker, university teacher, and school teacher.

AWARDS, HONORS: Award for best romantic novel of the year published in England, Romantic Novelists Association, 1983, for *Magic Flutes.*

WRITINGS:

NOVELS

A Countess Below Stairs, Macdonald, 1981.
Magic Flutes, Century, 1982.
A Company of Swans, St. Martin's, 1985.
Madensky Square, St. Martin's, 1988.
The Morning Gift, St. Martin's, 1993.

JUVENILE

The Great Ghost Rescue, Walck, 1975.
Which Witch, Pan Books, 1982.

The Worm and the Toffee-Nosed Princess, and Other Stories of Monsters (folklore), illustrated by Margaret Chamberlain, Macmillan, 1983.
The Haunting of Hiram C. Hopgood, Macmillan, 1987.
Not Just a Witch, illustrated by Alice Englander, Macmillan, 1989.

OTHER

Linda Came Today (television drama), ATV, 1965.
A Glove Shop in Vienna, and Other Stories, Century, 1984, St. Martin's, 1992.

Contributor to *Yearbook of the American Short Story.* Also contributor of over one hundred articles and stories to periodicals.

SIDELIGHTS: Eva Ibbotson once told *CA:* "After years of writing magazine stories and books for children, I am trying hard to break down the barrier between 'romantic novels' and 'serious novels' which are respectfully reviewed. My aim is to produce books that are light, humorous, even a little erudite but secure in their happy endings. One could call it an attempt to write, in words, a good Viennese waltz!"

BIOGRAPHICAL/CRITICAL SOURCES:

PERIODICALS

Books for Keeps, November, 1988, p. 9; January, 1992, p. 9.
New York Times Book Review, January 15, 1989, p. 22; August 25, 1991, p. 22.
Times Educational Supplement, July 22, 1983, p. 780; November 8, 1991, p. 42.
Washington Post Book World, January 6, 1985, p. 11.

INGRAHAM, Barton L(ee) 1930-

PERSONAL: Born June 10, 1930, in Paterson, NJ; son of Lee G. and Margie (maiden name, Olson) Ingraham. *Education:* Harvard University, A.B., 1952, J.D., 1957; University of California, Berkeley, D.Crim., 1972.

ADDRESSES: Home—2830 Calle de Oriente, Santa Fe, NM 87505.

CAREER: Private practice of law in New Jersey, 1958-59, New York, 1959-60, New Mexico, 1960-67, and California, 1967-70; University of Maryland, College Park, associate professor at Institute of Criminal Justice and Criminology, 1970-92; retired.

MEMBER: American Society of Criminology, American Judicature Society, Academy of Criminal Justice Sciences, California Bar Association.

WRITINGS:

Political Crime in Europe: A Comparative Study of France, Germany, and England, University of California Press, 1979.
The Structure of Criminal Procedure: China, the Soviet Union, France, and the United States, Greenwood Press, 1987.
(With Thomas P. Mauriello) *Police Investigation Handbook,* Matthew Bender, 1990.

Contributor to books on law and criminology; contributor to professional journals.

SIDELIGHTS: In *Political Crime in Europe: A Comparative Study of France, Germany, and England* Barton L. Ingraham examines political crime policies in France, Germany, and England during the last two hundred years. Recognizing that the definition of political crime varies with time and place, Ingraham interprets it to be "acts which officials treat as if they were political and criminal regardless of their real nature and the motivation of their perpetrators." According to Nigel Cross in the *New Statesman,* "Ingraham . . . concludes that failure to employ limited measures of repression during a period of weakness is most likely to lead to dictatorship." Writing in the *American Academy of Political and Social Science Annals,* Jacques Fomerand determined that while Ingraham's interpretations of historical and legal data need further clarification, "*Political Crime in Europe* reveals an impressive degree of careful research and scholarship and yields considerable valuable empirical information." The critic added: "The subject is both timely and significant, and its treatment has, unquestionably, great heuristic value. As such, *Political Crime in Europe* is a useful contribution to a generally neglected field of comparative public policy."

In two subsequent volumes on criminal law, Ingraham continues his investigation of legal procedures. In *The Structure of Criminal Procedure: China, the Soviet Union, France, and the United States* he analyzes criminal procedural systems and concepts of legality in diverse sociopolitical systems, and concludes that all legal systems perform six basic procedural "tasks": intake; screening; charging and defending (i.e., guaranteeing some rights and protections for those charged with crimes); trial; sentencing; and appeal. His third volume, *Police Investigation Handbook,* co-authored with Thomas Mauriello, an experienced investigator with a police background, provides a comprehensive look at modern criminal investigation practices in the United States. *Police Investigation Handbook* has sold widely and is in use in many police departments across the country.

Ingraham told *CA:* "I have not done enough yet to engage in retrospectives. Maybe when I'm eighty."

BIOGRAPHICAL/CRITICAL SOURCES:

PERIODICALS

American Academy of Political and Social Science Annals, July, 1980.
New Statesman, July 25, 1980.

*   *   *

ISAACSON, Walter (Seff) 1952-

PERSONAL: Born May 20, 1952, in New Orleans, LA; son of Irwin, Jr., and Betsy (Seff) Isaacson; married Cathy Wright, September 15, 1984; children: Elizabeth Carter. *Education:* Harvard University, B.A., 1974; Pembroke College, Oxford, M.A., 1976.

ADDRESSES: Home—76 Dellwood Rd., Bronxville, NY 10708. *Office*—*Time,* Time and Life Building, Rockefeller Center, New York, NY 10020. *Agent*—Amanda Urban, International Creative Management, 40 West 57th St., New York, NY 10019.

CAREER: Sunday Times, London, England, reporter, 1976-77; *States-Item,* New Orleans, LA, reporter, 1977-78; *Time,* New York City, staff writer, 1978-79, Washington, DC, correspondent, 1979-81, associate editor, 1981-84, senior editor, then assistant managing editor, 1984—.

MEMBER: Council on Foreign Relations, Century Club, Harvard Club.

AWARDS, HONORS: Mary Hemingway Award, Overseas Press Club of America, 1979, for article "The Colombian Connection"; Overseas Press Club Award for foreign news interpretation, 1982, for article "Arming the

World"; Harry Truman Book Prize, 1987, for *The Wise Men.*

WRITINGS:

NONFICTION

Pro and Con, Putnam, 1983.
(With Evan Thomas) *The Wise Men: Six Friends and the World They Made,* Simon & Schuster, 1986.
Kissinger: A Biography, Simon & Schuster, 1992.

SIDELIGHTS: Walter Isaacson is a journalist who rose through the ranks of *Time* to become that magazine's senior editor in 1984. In addition to his work at *Time,* Isaacson has written several works of nonfiction, including *Pro and Con,* published in 1983, and *The Wise Men: Six Friends and the World They Made,* a biographical study of men influential in shaping mid-twentieth-century international affairs. He is also the author of a 1992 biography of Henry Kissinger, a former national security advisor who served as Secretary of State under President Richard Nixon.

George F. Kennan, Dean Acheson, Charles Bohlen, Robert A. Lovett, W. Averell Harriman, and John J. McCloy are the politicians and policymakers Isaacson and his co-author, *Newsweek* editor Evan Thomas, profile in *The Wise Men.* The study is "a richly textured account of a class, and of a historical period, that is now in eclipse," according to Ronald Steel in the *New York Times Book Review.* Steel found the authors' research "thorough and their narrative smooth-flowing. They see the flaws of the men they write about, but make us aware of their virtues as well." Although depicting their subjects as an integral part of a bureaucratic "establishment" that prompted

Americans to view Russia and Communism as a serious threat—with both the arms race and, ultimately, U.S. involvement in the Vietnam War as a consequence—Isaacson and Evans admit in their conclusion that "there certainly does not now exist, and may never again, a breed of statesmen with the same synergism, the talent to work together in a way that transcends their contribution as individuals."

Isaacson's biography of statesman Henry Kissinger is widely regarded as a balanced, intriguing, and well-written study of the personal and political life of the former U.S. Secretary of State. In the words of Pricilla Johnson McMillan, reviewing the book for the *Chicago Tribune,* Isaacson's work provides an opportunity "for reassessing the high-wire act by which Kissinger riveted world attention." Godfrey Hodgson, in a review for *Book World,* referred to *Kissinger: A Biography* as a "meticulously researched, intelligent and fair book" that "lets the reader know the worst." And, although Hodgson personally considered the author's portrayal perhaps "too kind," he credited Isaacson for his "compassionate understanding of the roots of [Kissinger's] shortcomings, and a generous . . . estimate of his positive achievements."

BIOGRAPHICAL/CRITICAL SOURCES:

PERIODICALS

Chicago Tribune, August 30, 1992.

New York Times Book Review, November 2, 1986; September 6, 1992.

Times Literary Supplement, May 8, 1987.

The Wall Street Journal, September 16, 1992.

Washington Post Book World, October 19, 1986; September 6, 1992.

J

JABLOW, Martha M(oraghan) 1944-

PERSONAL: Born November 23, 1944, in Midland, TX; daughter of Martin John and Jane (Pratt) Moraghan; married Paul John Jablow (an editor), April 25, 1970; children: Cara Kathleen, David H. *Education:* Manhattanville College, B.A., 1966.

ADDRESSES: Home and office—6604 Wayne Ave., Philadelphia, PA 19119. *Agent*—Philippa Brophy, Sterling Lord Literistic Agency, Inc., One Madison Ave., New York, NY 10010.

CAREER: New York Times, New York City, news assistant, 1966-69; *Raleigh Times,* Raleigh, NC, reporter, 1969-71; *Baltimore Sun,* Baltimore, MD, reporter, 1972-73; free-lance writer in Philadelphia, PA, 1974—.

WRITINGS:

Cara: Growing with a Retarded Child, Temple University Press, 1982.
(With Nancy Samalin) *Loving Your Child is Not Enough,* Viking, 1987.
(With Harry A. Cole) *One in a Million,* Little, Brown, 1990.
A Parent's Guide to Eating Disorders and Obesity (foreword by C. Everett Koop), Delta, 1992.
(With Gail B. Slap, M.D.) *Teenage Health Care,* Pocket Books, 1994.

Contributor to magazines and newspapers, including *Parents' Magazine, New York Times,* and *Publishers Weekly.*

SIDELIGHTS: Martha M. Jablow once told *CA:* "As a newspaper reporter, I often wrote stories on medicine and education. When our first child was born with L.C. Syndrome in 1974, my journalistic background was a natural gateway for writing a book about her experiences.

"*Cara* was written for parents and professionals because I found, at the time of Cara's birth, very little useful information about raising a retarded child or the advantages of early intervention programs. Cara and her contemporaries were pioneers in this field. As longitudinal studies have finally shown, early intervention helps a 'delayed' baby reach developmental milestones (like dressing, feeding herself, talking) far earlier than if the child is left alone; the child becomes more independent and requires fewer special education services later.

"Two subsequent books (both collaborations) were quite different. The child-rearing book was a lively how-to, and *One in a Million* gave me the opportunity to stretch, to take basic reporting of a medical story and shape it into a novelistic narrative. The eating disorders and obesity book provided another writing challenge: to shape medical information into accessible, useful guidance for parents. The latest book, *Teenage Health Care,* was the greatest challenge yet—a mammoth project that we hope will be regarded as the 'Spock of adolescence.' "

*   *   *

JACKSON, Elaine
See FREEMAN, Gillian

*   *   *

JAKES, John (William) 1932-
(Alan Payne, Jay Scotland)

PERSONAL: Born March 31, 1932, in Chicago, IL; son of John Adrian (a Railway Express general manager) and Bertha (Retz) Jakes; married Rachel Ann Payne (a teacher), June 15, 1951; children: Andrea, Ellen, John Michael, Victoria. *Education:* DePauw University, A.B., 1953; Ohio State University, M.A., 1954. *Politics:* Independent. *Religion:* Protestant. *Avocational Interests:* Swimming, running, bowling, golf, acting and directing in community theater.

ADDRESSES: Agent—Rembar & Curtis, 19 West 44th St., New York, NY 10036.

CAREER: Abbott Laboratories, North Chicago, IL, 1954-60, began as copywriter, became product promotion manager; Rumrill Co. (advertising agency), Rochester, NY, copywriter, 1960-61; free-lance writer, 1961-65; Kircher Helton & Collet, Inc. (advertising agency), Dayton, OH, senior copywriter, 1965-68; Oppenheim, Herminghausen, Clarke, Inc. (advertising agency), Dayton, 1968-70, began as copy chief, became vice-president; Dancer-Fitzgerald-Sample, Inc. (advertising agency), Dayton, creative director, 1970-71; freelance writer, 1971—.

MEMBER: Authors Guild, Authors League of America, Dramatists Guild, Science Fiction Writers of America.

AWARDS, HONORS: L.L.D., Wright State University, 1976; Litt.D., DePauw University, 1977; Porgie Award, 1977, for best books in a series; Ohioana Book Award for fiction, 1978, for "American Bicentennial" series; Friends of the Rochester Library Literary Award, 1983.

WRITINGS:

The Texans Ride North: The Story of the Cattle Trails (juvenile), John C. Winston, 1952.

Wear a Fast Gun, Arcadia House, 1956.

A Night for Treason, Bouregy & Curl, 1956.

(Under pseudonym Alan Payne) *Murder, He Says,* Ace Books, 1958.

The Devil Has Four Faces, Bouregy, 1959.

Johnny Havoc, Belmont Books, 1960.

Johnny Havoc Meets Zelda, Belmont Books, 1962, published as *Havoc for Sale,* Armchair Detective Library, 1990.

Johnny Havoc and the Doll Who Had "It," Belmont Books, 1963, published as *Holiday for Havoc,* Armchair Detective Library, 1991.

G.I. Girls, Monarch, 1963.

Tiros: Weather Eye in Space, Messner, 1966.

When the Star Kings Die, Ace Books, 1967.

Great War Correspondents, Putnam, 1967.

Famous Firsts in Sports, Putnam, 1967.

Making It Big, Belmont Books, 1968, published as *Johnny Havoc and the Siren in Red,* Armchair Detective Library, 1991.

Great Women Reporters, Putnam, 1969.

Tonight We Steal the Stars (bound with *The Wagered World* by Laurence M. Janifer and S. J. Treibich), Ace Books, 1969.

The Hybrid, Paperback Library, 1969.

The Last Magicians, Signet, 1969.

Secrets of Stardeep, Westminster, 1969, published with *Time Gate* (also see below), New American Library, 1982.

The Planet Wizard, Ace Books, 1969.

The Asylum World, Paperback Library, 1969.

Mohawk: The Life of Joseph Brant, Crowell, 1969.

Black in Time, Paperback Library, 1970.

Six Gun Planet, Paperback Library, 1970.

Mask of Chaos (bound with *The Star Virus* by Barrington T. Bayler), Ace Books, 1970.

Monte Cristo 99, Modern Library, 1970.

Master of the Dark Gate, Lancer Books, 1970.

Conquest of the Planet of the Apes (novelization of film of the same title), Award Books, 1972.

Time Gate, Westminster, 1972.

Witch of the Dark Gate, Lancer Books, 1972.

Mention My Name in Atlantis: Being, at Last, the True Account of the Calamitous Destruction of the Great Island Kingdom, Together with a Narrative of Its Wondrous Intercourses with a Superior Race of Other-Worldlings, as Transcribed from the Ms. of a Survivor, Hopter the Vintner, for the Enlightenment of a Dubious Posterity, DAW Books, 1972.

On Wheels, Paperback Library, 1973.

The Best of John Jakes (science fiction), edited by Martin H. Greenberg and Joseph D. Olander, DAW Books, 1977.

The Bastard Photostory, Jove, 1980.

North and South (first volume in "North and South" trilogy), Harcourt, 1982.

Love and War (second volume in "North and South" trilogy), Harcourt, 1984.

Susanna of the Alamo: A True Story (juvenile), Harcourt, 1986.

Heaven and Hell (third volume in "North and South" trilogy), Dell, 1988.

California Gold, Random House, 1989.

The Best Western Stories of John Jakes, Ohio University Press, 1991.

Homeland, Doubleday, 1993.

In the Big Country: The Best Western Stories of John Jakes, G. K. Hall, 1993.

"BRAK THE BARBARIAN" SERIES

Brak the Barbarian, Avon, 1968.

Brak the Barbarian versus the Sorceress, Paperback Library, 1969.

Brak versus the Mark of the Demons, Paperback Library, 1969.

Brak: When the Idols Walked, Tower, 1978.
Fortunes of Brak, Dell, 1980.

*"AMERICAN BICENTENNIAL" SERIES PUBLISHED BY
PYRAMID; ALSO PUBLISHED AS "KENT FAMILY
CHRONICLES" SERIES BY JOVE*

The Bastard (also see below), Pyramid, 1974, Jove, 1978,
    published in England in two volumes, Volume 1: *For-
    tune's Whirlwind,* Volume 2: *To an Unknown Shore,*
    Corgi, 1975.
The Rebels (also see below), Pyramid, 1975, Jove, 1979.
The Seekers (also see below), Pyramid, 1975, Jove, 1979.
The Titans, Pyramid, 1976, Jove, 1976.
The Furies (also see below), Pyramid, 1976, Jove, 1978.
The Patriots (contains *The Bastard* and *The Rebels*),
    Landfall Press, 1976.
The Pioneers (contains *The Seekers* and *The Furies*),
    Landfall Press, 1976.
The Warriors, Pyramid, 1977, Jove, 1977.
The Lawless, Jove, 1978.
The Americans, Jove, 1980.

PLAYS

(Author of lyrics) *Dracula, Baby* (musical comedy), Dra-
    matic Publishing, 1970.
(Author of book and lyrics) *Wind in the Willows* (musical
    comedy), Performance Publishing, 1972.
A Spell of Evil (three-act melodrama), Performance Pub-
    lishing, 1972.
Violence (two one-acts), Performance Publishing, 1972.
Stranger with Roses (one-act), Dramatic Publishing, 1972.
(Author of book and lyrics) *Gaslight Girl* (musical), Dra-
    matic Publishing, 1973.
(Author of book and lyrics) *Doctor, Doctor!* (musical),
    McAfee Music Corp., 1973.
(Author of book and lyrics) *Shepherd Song* (musical),
    McAfee Music Corp., 1974.

UNDER PSEUDONYM JAY SCOTLAND

The Seventh Man, Mystery House, 1958, published under
    name John Jakes, Pinnacle, 1981.
I, Barbarian, Avon, 1959, published under name John
    Jakes, Pinnacle, 1979.
Strike the Black Flag, Ace Books, 1961.
Sir Scoundrel, Ace Books, 1962.
Veils of Salmoe, Avon, 1962, published under name John
    Jakes as *King's Crusader,* Pinnacle, 1976.
Arena, Ace Books, 1963.
Traitors' Legion, Ace Books, 1963, published under name
    John Jakes as *The Man From Cannae,* Pinnacle, 1977.

OTHER

Also author, under pseudonym Alan Payne, of *This Will
Slay You,* 1958. Contributor of short stories to magazines.

ADAPTATIONS: Three of the "American Bicentennial"
books, *The Bastard, The Rebels,* and *The Seekers,* were
adapted for television by Operation Prime Time and Universal Studios; *North and South* was filmed for television,
ABC, 1985.

SIDELIGHTS: John Jakes was a prolific but obscure
writer for some twenty years, until his "American Bicentennial" series of historical novels captured the public's
imagination and made him famous. Jakes had published
his first work while he was still a high school student, and
throughout the 1950s and 1960s he turned out more than
fifty books in various genres, including science fiction,
mystery, children's literature, and suspense. Most of his
early works were written in his spare time while he held
down full-time positions in the advertising industry; the
resounding success of the "American Bicentennial" series
finally enabled him to devote himself to writing full time.
Jakes followed his landmark series with other bestselling
novels based on American history, including *North and
South, Love and War,* and *California Gold.*

While Jakes's books are phenomenally popular, few critics
have called his prose style anything more than workman-
like. The author himself has no pretensions on his writing.
"Sue me for not being Flaubert," Jakes told *People* contributor Susan Schindehette. "I've given it the best shot I
can." But Martin H. Greenberg and Walter Herrscher,
writing in the *Dictionary of Literary Biography Yearbook:
1983,* laud Jakes as "a natural storyteller" whose body of
work is consistently characterized by "attention to detail,
careful plotting, epic sweep, and—where required, strong
historical research." Discussing his early work, Greenberg
and Herrscher state: "Jakes was much more than simply
a pedestrian science fiction writer. He did some outstanding work in this demanding popular genre, and his collection, *The Best of John Jakes,* contains excellent work, most
notably the novella *Here Is Thy Sting,* which focuses on
the meaning of death, and 'The Sellers of the Dream,' a
moving and devastating attack on our consumer society."
Greenberg and Herrscher also praise Jakes's "Brak the
Barbarian" series, which lampoons the "Sword and Sorcery" genre; his sci-fi/western *Six-Gun Planet*; and his futuristic novel *On Wheels,* which both men judge to be "a
minor masterpiece of social speculation."

Whatever the merits of Jakes's early work, it brought him
little recognition and only a modest secondary income. He
felt he'd bottomed out as a writer in 1973, when he accepted an assignment to write a novelization of the last
film in the "Planet of the Apes" movie series. He remembers the job—which took him three weeks and earned him
a quick $1,500—with bitterness. "When that *Planet of the
Apes* thing came along, I said to [my wife], 'I've been wasting the last 20 years.' I finally began to think I couldn't
cut it as a writer,' " he recalls in a *Publishers Weekly* inter-

view with Robert Dahlin. Fortunately for Jakes, his fellow writer Don Moffit had a higher opinion of his work.

Moffit had been approached by Lyle Kenyon Engel, a leader of the paperback trade industry, to write a series of historical novels for publication around the time of the Bicentennial of the United States. The books would follow several generations of the fictional Kent family through the first hundred years of the country's history. Moffit was unavailable for the job, but he suggested that Engel review Jakes's early historical fiction (much of which had been published under the pseudonym Jay Scotland). These "solidly researched, well-plotted commercial novels with believable characters," as they are described in the *Dictionary of Literary Biography Yearbook: 1983,* convinced Engel that Jakes was the man to pen the Kent family chronicles.

The series was originally intended to total five books, but its success was so great that Engel was eager to extend Jakes's contract. Eight titles were eventually published, beginning with *The Bastard* in 1974 and concluding with *The Americans* in 1980. None of the titles sold less than 3.5 million copies, and the series as a whole sold over forty million copies. Marked by vivid plots and memorable, simply drawn characters, the saga took readers through seven generations of the Kent family history. Engel would have continued the series for as long as it remained profitable, but after *The Americans,* Jakes rebelled. That act opened a professional rift between the two men, but Jakes stood firm in his decision. "I'll always be grateful to [Engel]," he explains in *Publishers Weekly,* "because he gave me the chance that made all the difference, but I believe in the theater principle. You should end something leaving the audience wanting more, rather than taking the television route where the story drags on and on week after week."

Following his triumph in the realm of paperback publishing, Jakes was approached by the Harcourt Brace Jovanovich publishing house to produce a trio of hardcover novels covering the Civil War era. The "North and South" trilogy—*North and South, Love and War,* and *Heaven and Hell*—intertwined fictional and real-life characters much as the "American Bicentennial" series had, and proved to be as successful. The central characters were two men who, after becoming friends at West Point, found themselves enemies in war. Their descendants' adventures continue through the Reconstruction period and the taming of the American frontier. Rory Quirk, writing in the *Washington Post,* credits Jakes with creating "a graphic, fast-paced amalgam of good, evil, love, lust, war, violence and Americana." He further comments: "The imposition and ultimate failure of Reconstruction in the South covers some well-traveled ground but Jakes manages to resift the historical information, meld it with his

fictional characters and produce an informative and nicely crafted narrative. . . . Jakes is particularly adept at capturing the splendid desolation of the untamed West, the mind-numbing isolation of duty with the frontier Army, and the unremitting brutality of the subjugation of the American Indian."

Discussing his work with Elizabeth Venant, staff writer for the *Los Angeles Times,* Jakes notes that his early inspiration came from the swashbuckling adventure films of the 1930s and 1940s. "I have this gigantic cinemascope screen in my head," he comments. "I always see what I'm writing about in terms of the colors of the clothes, the weather, the sky." Responding to the charge that his work has little literary merit, Jakes states: "There's an unfortunate lack in American letters. You have either very literary material or the trash end of the spectrum." He defends his own contribution to the reading public, saying: "One thing I'll never apologize for is my success. I paid my dues for 25 years. I worked my fingers down to the bone."

Greenberg and Herrscher summarize: "Jakes's historical novels cannot be judged by usual literary standards. They are unabashedly fiction for the mass market, and it cannot be expected that they display the virtues of interpretive fiction. . . . Jakes's novels do not provide that main quality we expect from interpretive fiction: a sharper and deeper awareness of life, often in memorable prose. But Jakes has not claimed to be this kind of writer. In an afterword to *North and South* he says that his primary purpose is to entertain; and if a writer is to be judged solely on the success of his intentions, then John Jakes is without doubt one of the most successful and important writers in the history of commercial fiction."

BIOGRAPHICAL/CRITICAL SOURCES:

BOOKS

Contemporary Literary Criticism, Volume 29, Gale, 1984.
Dictionary of Literary Biography Yearbook: 1983, Gale, 1984.
Hawkins, R., *The Kent Family Chronicles Encyclopedia,* Bantam, 1979.

PERIODICALS

Chicago Tribune Book World, February 21, 1982.
Christian Science Monitor, April 7, 1982, p. 17.
Detroit News, February 23, 1982.
Los Angeles Times, September 18, 1989.
Los Angeles Times Book Review, March 21, 1982; December 2, 1984; September 27, 1987; August 20, 1989, p. 5.
New York Times, May 2, 1986.
New York Times Book Review, March 7, 1982, p. 24; October 8, 1989, p. 24.
People, November 12, 1984, pp. 63-64.

Publishers Weekly, April 5, 1976; November 30, 1984, pp. 99-100.

Washington Post, March 7, 1976, p. F10; February 3, 1982, p. E3; February 28, 1982; November 3, 1984, p. 3.

Washington Post Book World, April 3, 1977; October 18, 1987; September 17, 1989.*

—*Sidelights by Joan Goldsworthy*

* * *

JAMES, (David) John

PERSONAL: Born in Wales; married Helen Mary Norman; children: Helen Sarah, David Owen. *Education:* Selwyn College, Cambridge, M.A., 1950. *Religion:* Church in Wales (Episcopalian).

ADDRESSES: Agent—Hope Leresche & Steele, 11 Jubilee Pl., London SW3 3TE, England.

CAREER: Civil servant, England, 1949—.

MEMBER: British Psychological Society, PEN, East Anglia Writers Association.

WRITINGS:

Votan, Cassell, 1966, Bantam, 1987.
Not for All the Gold in Ireland, Cassell, 1967, Bantam, 1988.
Men Went to Cattraeth, Cassell, 1969, Bantam, 1988.
Seventeen of Leyden: A Frolic through This Vale of Tears, Cassell, 1970.
The Lords of Loone, Cassell, 1972.
The Bridge of Sand, Hutchinson, 1976.
Talleyman, Gollancz, 1986.
Talleyman in the Ice, Futura, 1989.
The Paladins: A Social History of the RAF up to the Outbreak of World War II, Macdonald, 1990.

SIDELIGHTS: "John James has a quality as scarce among historical novelists as soap among the Vandals: a sense of fun," Martin Levin wrote in a *New York Times Book Review* of *Votan.* In his story of a second-century adventurer who changes his name to Votan after an encounter with a Norse god, James mixes history with an often bloody, sometimes humorous account of the hero's quest to fulfill his mission. *Best Sellers* reviewer Eugene A. Dooley noted the paganism of the story's principals, remarking that "the pages seem to drip with blood many times." Despite this objection, however, Dooley deemed *Votan* "fascinating and nevertheless a mystifying book, one that undoubtedly portrays the plunging enthusiasm of its author."

James told *CA:* "As a Welshman, with English as a learned language, I concern myself more and more with the matter of Britain and the unity of the Island, in prose and verse."

BIOGRAPHICAL/CRITICAL SOURCES:

PERIODICALS

Best Sellers, June 15, 1967.
New York Times Book Review, July 30, 1967, p. 26.*

* * *

JAMES, P. D.
See WHITE, Phyllis Dorothy James

* * *

JENSEN, Julie
See McDONALD, Julie

* * *

JOHNSON, Lemuel A. 1941-

PERSONAL: Born December 15, 1941, in Northern Nigeria; son of Thomas Ishelu and Daisy (a teacher; maiden name, Williams) Johnson; married Marian Yankson (a dental hygienist), August 28, 1965; children: Yma, Yshely. *Education:* Oberlin College, B.A., 1965; Pennsylvania State University, M.A., 1966; University of Michigan, Ph.D., 1969; also studied at Middlebury College, Universite d'Aix-Marseille II, and University of Paris.

ADDRESSES: Home—415 Ventura Court, Ann Arbor, MI 48163. *Office*—Department of English, University of Michigan, Ann Arbor, MI 48164.

CAREER: Pennsylvania State University, University Park, faculty member in department of Spanish, Italian, and Portuguese, 1966; University of Michigan, Ann Arbor, faculty member in department of Romance languages and literature, 1967-68, faculty member in department of English, 1968-70, associate professor of English, 1972—; University of Sierra Leone, Fourah Bay College, Freetown, faculty member in department of English, 1970-72. Peace Corps, training program instructor, 1964; West African Examinations Council, examiner in English oral literature, 1970-72; Sierra Leone Broadcasting Service, host for "Radio Forum Series," 1971-72; has given poetry readings at University of Michigan, 1973 and 1974.

MEMBER: African Studies Association, Midwest Modern Language Association, African Literature Association (president, 1977-78).

AWARDS, HONORS: Avery Hopwood Awards, University of Michigan, 1967, for essay "Piano and Drum" and short story collection *The Voice of the Turtle;* Bredvold-Thorpe prize for scholarly publication, University of Michigan, 1972, for *The Devil, the Gargoyle and the Buffoon: The Negro as Metaphor in Western Literature.*

WRITINGS:

(Contributor of translation) *Modern Spanish Theatre,* Dutton, 1968.

The Devil, the Gargoyle and the Buffoon: The Negro as Metaphor in Western Literature (revision of the author's thesis), Kennikat, 1971.

Highlife for Caliban (poetry), Ardis, 1973.

Hand on the Navel (poetry), Ardis, 1978.

Toward Defining the African Aesthetic (selected papers of the African Literature Association), Three Continents Press, 1983.

Also author of the short story collection *The Voice of the Turtle* and the essay "Piano and Drum." Contributor to anthologies, including *African Writing Today,* Manyland Books, 1970; *New African Literature and the Arts,* edited by Joseph Okpaku, Crowell, 1970; and *Blacks in Hispanic Literature,* edited by Miriam DeCosta. Contributor to *Literary Review* and *Journal of New African Literature and the Arts.*

BIOGRAPHICAL/CRITICAL SOURCES:

BOOKS

African Authors: A Companion to Black African Writing: Volume 1, *1300-1973,* Black Orpheus Press, 1973, p. 167.

PERIODICALS

Choice, September, 1972, p. 806; June, 1974, p. 609; December, 1978, p. 1379.

Library Journal, May 1, 1974, p. 1307; September 1, 1978, p. 1641.*

*   *   *

JONES, Annabel
See LEWIS, Mary (Christianna Milne)

*   *   *

JONES, Frank 1937-

PERSONAL: Born December 10, 1937, in Luton, Bedfordshire, England; son of Daniel Brynmore (in business) and Margaret (a housewife; maiden name, Hopkins) Jones; married Ayesha Bibi Faheza Rahim (a property manager), November 30, 1959; children: Frank, Farida,

Bryn, Ivor, Yasmin, Fazia. *Education:* Attended University of Toronto, 1976.

ADDRESSES: Home—58 Rose Park Dr., Toronto, Ontario M4T 1R1, Canada. *Office*— *Toronto Star,* 1 Yonge St., Toronto, Ontario M5E 1E6, Canada.

CAREER: Apprentice reporter for Hastings and St. Leonards *Observer* (weekly newspaper), beginning c. 1954; *Winnipeg Tribune,* Winnipeg, Manitoba, journalist, 1959-60; *Toronto Telegram,* Toronto, Ontario, journalist, 1960-66; *Toronto Star,* Toronto, journalist, 1966—, columnist, 1982—.

MEMBER: Canadian Crime Writers Association.

AWARDS, HONORS: National Newspaper Award, Toronto Press Club, 1973, for coverage of war in the Middle East; Southam fellow, University of Toronto, 1976-77.

WRITINGS:

Trail of Blood: A Canadian Murder Odyssey, McGraw, 1981.

Master and Maid: The Charles Massey Murder (fiction), Irwin, 1985.

Murderous Women, Key Porter, 1991.

Beyond Suspicion, Key Porter, 1992, published as *White-Collar Killers,* Headline, 1992.

Murderous Innocents, Headline, in press.

Writer for "Scales of Justice" series, Canadian Broadcasting Corporation (CBC-Radio).

SIDELIGHTS: Frank Jones once told *CA:* "I rebelled against school and was looking for the earliest opportunity to leave. At the age of twelve I had a letter accepted by a national newspaper in London for which I was paid a guinea (about two dollars). This was the first notion I had that you could actually receive money for writing, which was about the only thing I enjoyed doing at school. So I left school at sixteen and secured a job on a weekly newspaper, the Hastings and St. Leonards *Observer,* as an apprentice reporter—which means I have been a journalist for the unimaginable period of thirty-two years.

"Being a journalist had, if anything, steered me away from writing books. Partly it was a question of time, but it was also my interviewing people day in and day out and hearing how well they could express their predicaments as they were living them that certainly put me off of writing fiction—I felt could never invent dialogue that was anywhere near as good as the real thing.

"So I moved into authorship backwards. My first book, *Trail of Blood,* stemmed from a series of articles I wrote for the *Toronto Star* on murder cases. I found murder a fascinating subject because many murders reveal much about social conditions. My second book, *Master and*

Maid, explored the same subject area, although this time it was a fictionalized version of a society murder that took place in Toronto in 1915."

Jones recently added, "Since acquiring a home in Wales, where my wife and I now spend part of each year, my interest has moved to the fertile British murder scene. I am now working on my second book written exclusively for Headline, a British publisher with a substantial true crime list.

"My method, as it was from the beginning, is to explore murder as a mirror, perhaps a snapshot of society at a particular moment in time. In addition to reading everything I can about a case, I try to visit the scene of the crime, and contact lawyers, police officers, people involved in the case and journalists who covered it. These contacts, I hope, give depth to the stories but, as a bonus, have also provided me with an eccentric and fascinating circle of friends."

*   *   *

JONES, Tony Armstrong
    See ARMSTRONG-JONES, Antony

K

KAISER, Walter Christian, Jr. 1933-

PERSONAL: Born April 11, 1933, in Folcroft, PA; son of Walter Christian (a farmer) and Estelle Evelyn (a housewife; maiden name, Jaworsky) Kaiser; married Margaret Ruth Burk (a homemaker), August 24, 1957; children: Walter Christian III, Brian Addison, Kathleen Elise, Jonathan Kevin. *Education:* Wheaton College, Wheaton, IL, B.A., 1955 B.D., 1958; Brandeis University, M.A., 1962, Ph.D., 1973. *Avocational Interests:* Gardening, woodcutting, international travel, studies in management and administration.

ADDRESSES: Home—Kerith Farm, N1138 Sauk Trail Rd., Cedar Grove, WI 53013. *Office*—Gordon-Conwell Theological Seminary, 130 Essex St., South Hamilton, MA 01982.

CAREER: Ordained Evangelical Protestant minister, 1966. Assistant pastor of Evangelical Protestant church in Geneva, IL, 1957-58; Wheaton College, Wheaton IL, instructor, 1958-61, assistant professor of Bible, 1961-65, acting director of archaeology and Near Eastern studies, 1965-66; Trinity Evangelical Divinity School, Deerfield, IL, associate professor, 1966-73, professor of Semitics and Old Testament and chairman of department 1973-80, academic dean and vice-president of education, 1980—, senior vice president of education, 1989-93; Gordon-Conwell Theological Seminary, South Hamilton, MA, distinguished professor, 1993—. Member of board of trustees of Wheaton College, 1981—.

MEMBER: Near East Archaeological Society (member of board of directors), Society of Biblical Literature, Evangelical Theological Society (national president, 1977), Institute of Biblical Research, Wheaton College Honors Society.

AWARDS, HONORS: Danforth Foundation grant, 1961-63.

WRITINGS:

The Old Testament in Contemporary Preaching, Baker Book, 1973.
Toward an Old Testament Theology, Zondervan, 1977.
Ecclesiastes: Total Life, Moody, 1979.
Toward an Exegetical Theology: Biblical Exegesis for Preaching and Teaching, Baker Book, 1981.
A Biblical Approach to Personal Suffering, Moody, 1983.
Toward Old Testament Ethics, Zondervan, 1983.
Malachi: God's Unchanging Love, Baker Book, 1984.
The Uses of the Old Testament in the New, Moody, 1985.
Quest for Renewal: Personal Revival in the Old Testament, Moody, 1986.
Have You Seen the Power of God Lately?: Studies in the Life of Elijah, Here's Life Publishers, 1987.
Toward Rediscovering the Old Testament, Zondervan, 1987.
Hard Sayings of the Old Testament, InterVarsity Press, 1988.
Back Toward the Future: Hints for Interpreting Biblical Prophecy, Baker Book, 1989.
More Hard Sayings of the Old Testament, InterVarsity Press, 1992.
The Journey Isn't Over: The Pilgrim Psalms for Life's Challenges and Joys, Baker Book, 1993.
(With Moises Silva) *An Introduction to Hermeneutics,* Zondervan, 1994.

EDITOR

Classical Evangelical Essays in Old Testament Interpretation, Baker Book, 1972.
(Co-editor) *A Tribute to Gleason Archer: Essays in Old Testament Studies,* Moody, 1986.

(Co-editor) *Expositor's Bible Commentary,* Zondervan, 1990.

OTHER

Also author of foreword, E. W. Hengstenberg, *Christology of the Old Testament,* Kregel; author of "Commentary on Exodus" in *Expositor's Bible Commentary,* Zondervan, 1990; author of "Commentary on Leviticus" in *The New Interpreter's Bible,* Abingdon, 1994; translator of *New International Version.* Contributor to religious journals.

SIDELIGHTS: Walter Christian Kaiser, Jr. once told *CA:* "My interest in the study of the Old Testament began during my high school days when discussions in biology, history, and literature classes turned to the topics of man's origins and the roots of Western civilization. Added impetus was supplied by the sensational discoveries reported from the field of ancient Near Eastern archaeology.

"In spite of the advances made by archaeology in understanding the Old Testament backgrounds, the text of the Old Testament still remained a closed book as far as most Christian and Western readers were concerned. The tendency was to read the New Testament back into the text and message of the Old Testament rather than to allow it to stand on its own terms. In this sense, my approach to the Old Testament will differ from that of many other interpreters—especially of conservative Protestant and Catholic readers of the Old Testament.

"The effect of this approach has been to open up the Old Testament for Christian readers rather than inhibiting them from finding personal relevance and unifying themes with the thought and message of the New Testament. We have argued that there is a unifying theme which does carry through both testaments and that the ethical and moral demands of the former testament are not foreign or basically antithetical to those of the later testament, when proper allowance is made for the presence of conscious obsolescence or features that were deliberately limited in their duration and application. In both of these areas, our thesis is somewhat unique. Few on the contemporary scene have explored the question of a unifying theme or center for Old Testament theology; most prefer to stress diversity and pluralism today. But in the area of Old Testament ethics we pioneered, no other book on this subject in any European language or in English appeared in this century until 1991.

"One other theme runs through my books: the hermeneutical problem of bridging the gap between the 'then' (or B.C. status of the Old Testament text) and the 'now' (or 1990s position and needs of the contemporary reader, listener, and interpreter of that B.C. text). This problem I tackle in my second 'Toward' book, *Toward an Exegetical Theology.* I have attempted to give a practical demonstra-

tion of my theoretical conclusions in my three books written on three 'little orphan' Old Testament books: *Ecclesiastes: Total Life, Malachi: God's Unchanging Love* and *A Biblical Approach to Personal Suffering* (a study on the Old Testament book of Lamentations)."*

* * *

KALLIFATIDES, Theodor 1938-

PERSONAL: Born March 12, 1938, in Molai, Greece; emigrated to Sweden in 1964; son of Dimitrios (a teacher) and Antonia (maiden name, Kiriazakou) Kallifatides; married Gunilla Ander (a sociologist); children: Markus, Johanna. *Education:* University of Stockholm, B.A., 1967. *Avocational Interests:* Chess, prize fighting.

ADDRESSES: Home—Bjoerkvaegen 12., Huddinge 141 44, Sweden. *Office*—Svenska Dagbladet, Raalambsvaegen 7, Stockholm, Sweden.

CAREER: University of Stockholm, Stockholm, Sweden, lecturer in philosophy, 1969-72; *Bonniers Litteraera Magazin,* Stockholm, editor-in-chief, 1972-76; *Svenska Dagbladet,* Stockholm, critic, 1976—. *Military service:* Greek Army, 1960-62.

MEMBER: International PEN, Union of Swedish Writers.

AWARDS, HONORS: Novel award, 1981, for *En Fallen Angel;* Stina Ekdahl-Eld Prize, Swedish Academy, 1987, for lifetime work; City of Stockholm Award, 1992, for *The King's Medallion.*

WRITINGS:

Minnet i exil (title means "Memory in Exile"), Bonniers, 1969.
Utlaenningar (title means "Foreigners"), Bonniers, 1970.
Tiden aer inte oskyldig (title means "Time Is Not Innocent"), Bonniers, 1971.
Vad haender sedan, Ali? (play; title means "What Happened Then, Ali?"), Radio Sweden, 1971.
(Editor, with Tobias Berggren) *Dikten finns overallt* (title means "Poetry Is Everywhere"), Prisma, 1973.
Jag heter Stelios (screenplay; title means "My Name Is Stelios"), Swedish Filminstitute, 1973.
Plogen och Svaerdet (title means "The Plough and The Sword"), Bonniers, 1975.
(With Henrik Tikkanen) *Den sena hemkomsten: skisser fran Grekland,* Bonniers, 1976.
Boender och Herrar, Bonniers, 1973, translation by Thomas Teal published as *Masters and Peasants,* Doubleday, 1977.
Den Grymma Freden (title means "The Atrocious Peace"), Bonniers, 1977.

Kaerleken (also see below; title means "Love") Bonniers, 1978.

En Fallen Angel (title means "A Fallen Angel"), Bonniers, 1981.

Brannvin och rosor (title means "Wine and Roses"), Bonniers, 1983.

Hustaznas hezze (title means "The Master of Desires"), Bonniers, 1986.

En lang dag i Athen (title means "A Long Delay in Athens"), Bonniers, 1989.

Vem vaz Gabriella Orlova? Bonniers, 1992.

Marias frihet (play), produced at Uppialos Tower Theatre, 1993.

Also author of a full-length movie based on his novel *Kaerleken.*

SIDELIGHTS: Theodor Kallifatides told *CA:* "I emigrated to Sweden from Greece in 1964. I decided to write in Swedish instead of Greek, and that had a very significant impact on my work. I speak English, French, Greek, Swedish, Danish, and Norwegian. I have written more about my childhood and early youth in Greece than my adult life in Sweden. I have tried to understand the Greek way of thinking and living which, among other things, produced so many saints, heroes, torture experts, and dictators. I have had the dubious benefit of experiencing a world war, a civil war, and a couple of dictatorships. Writing in a language other than my mother tongue was for me a means to greater freedom emotionally and to intellectual objectivity and, of course, it was, too, a kind of intellectual challenge, I suppose."

*   *   *

KAMEN, Betty 1925-

PERSONAL: Born June 23, 1925, in New York, NY; daughter of Louis (a baker) and Claire (a photographic laboratory technician; maiden name, Moss) Banoff; married Si Kamen (a writer), December 29, 1946; children: Kathi Kamen Goldmark, Paul, Michael. *Education:* Brooklyn College (now of the City University of New York), B.A., 1946; Goddard College, M.A., 1979; Columbia Pacific University, Ph.D., 1983. *Politics:* Democrat. *Religion:* Jewish.

ADDRESSES: Home and office—Nutrition Encounter, 61 Bahama Reef, Box 5847, Novato, CA 94949.

CAREER: Homemaker in Hempstead, NY, 1946-60; photojournalist in Cold Spring Harbor, NY, 1960-80; national lecturer, producer of filmstrips, and writer, 1980—. Host, "Nutrition 57," WHLI-Radio, 1977-78, and WMCA-Radio, 1979-83; host, "Nutrition Dialogue," Satellite Program Network (SPN) Cable Television, 1982; Stress Cen-

ter, Huntington, NY, director of nutrition, 1982-83; consultant to Japanese health business, 1984—; host, "Nutrition Dialogue," KNBR-Radio, 1989.

MEMBER: International College of Applied Nutrition, International Association of Preventative Medicine, National Health Federation, American Federation of Television and Radio Artists, La Leche League, Northwest Academy of Medical Prevention, New York State Coalition Against Fluoridation.

AWARDS, HONORS: Kids Are What They Eat, voted among 10 best by *Ms.* magazine, 1984; honorary member of Indonesian Medical Society, 1993.

WRITINGS:

(With husband, Si Kamen) *The Kamen Plan for Total Nutrition During Pregnancy,* Appleton, 1981.

Kids are What They Eat: What Every Parent Needs to Know About Nutrition, Arco, 1983.

In Pursuit of Youth: Everyday Nutrition for Everyone over Thirty-five, Dodd, 1984.

Osteoporosis: What It Is, How to Prevent It, How to Stop It, Pinnacle Books, 1984.

Total Nutrition During Pregnancy: How to Be Sure You and Your Baby Are Eating the Right Stuff, Keats, 1986.

The Breastfeeding Bible, 1986.

Total Nutrition for Breast-Feeding Mothers, Little, Brown, 1986.

Nutrition in Nursing: A Handbook of Nursing Science, Keats, 1987.

Sesame: Superfood Seed, Keats, 1987.

Germanium: A New Approach to Immunity, Nutrition Encounter, Inc., 1987.

Siberian Ginseng: Fabled Oriental Tonic Herb, Keats, 1988.

Startling New Facts about Osteoporosis, 1989.

Chromium: Diet, Supplement & Exercise Strategy, Nutrition Encounter, 1990.

New Facts about Fiber, Nutrition Encounter, 1991.

Everything You Wanted to Know about Potassium, But Were Too Tired to Ask, Nutrition Encounter, 1992.

Hormone Replacement Therapy: Yes or No? How to Make An Informed Decision, Nutrition Encounter, 1992.

Contributing editor of *Let's Live, Health Foods Business, Health Freedom News, Health World,* and *Your Good Health.* Articles have appeared in *Chicago Tribune, Detroit News, New York Times,* and *Orlando Sentinel.* Columnist for *Pacific Sun,* 1985-88.

WORK IN PROGRESS: Cholesterol: New Facts, New Solutions, and *55 Simple, Easy, Inexpensive Ways to Stay Healthy.*

SIDELIGHTS: Betty Kamen told *CA:* "Degenerative disease is increasing. Lifestyle changes can halt its progression. My mission is to motivate people to initiate change.

"I became aware of the relationship between nutrition and good health in 1948 (I am the oldest health food nut) when my first child had a bad cold. My learning process was not one of trial and error. The answers were clear-cut right from the start: Only real food would engender good health.

BIOGRAPHICAL/CRITICAL SOURCES:

PERIODICALS

New York Times, January 9, 1983.
Prevention, February, 1983.

*   *   *

KATZMAN, Allen   1937-

PERSONAL: Born April 27, 1937, in Brooklyn, NY; died of injuries sustained in an automobile accident, June 9, 1985, in Saugerties, NY; son of Benjamin and Ruth (Greenhouse) Katzman; married Estelle Halpern, November 24, 1973; children: Ivy (died June 9, 1985). *Education:* City College (now of the City University of New York), B.A., 1958.

ADDRESSES: Home—105 Riverside Dr., No. 2F, New York, NY 10024.

CAREER: Poet, teacher, journalist, producer, and publisher for the American underground; *East Village Other* (EVO), New York City, co-founder, 1965, became publisher; Underground Press Syndicate, founder, 1966; Swift Comics, Bantam, producer; Bell-McClure Syndicate, North American Newspaper Alliance, Inc., columnist. Minister of Information for the Yippie Party and key witness in Chicago Conspiracy Trial, 1969-70. Instructor in underground journalism at the Columbia University Graduate School of Journalism and New School for Social Research, both in New York City; created the first closed circuit community television station, Westbeth TV, 1971; lecturer on U.S. college campuses. *Military service:* U.S. Army, 1958-60; became sergeant.

AWARDS, HONORS: New York State Council on the Arts poetry grant, 1971.

WRITINGS:

POETRY

Poems from Oklahoma, and Other Poems, Hesperidian Press, 1962.
The Bloodletting, Renegade Press, 1964.
The Comanche Cantos, Sign of the Gun Press, 1966.
The Immaculate: Poems, Doubleday, 1970.

Paracelsus' Walk, Hesperidian Press, 1978.
Passing Through, Hesperidian Press, 1982.

EDITOR

Jerry Rubin, *We Are Everywhere,* Harper, 1971.
Our Time: An Anthology of Interviews from "The East Village Other," Dial, 1972.

Also editor for and contributor to *Intrepid.* Poems represented in several anthologies, including *Notes from the Underground,* edited by Jesse Kornbluth, Viking, 1968; *The Hippie Papers,* edited by Jerry Hopkins, New American Library, 1968; and *The Open Conspiracy: What America's Angry Generation Is Saying,* edited by Ethel G. Romm, Giniger, 1970. Contributor of poetry, essays, and articles to numerous underground publications, including *Los Angeles Free Press.*

WORK IN PROGRESS: An Autobiography of the '60s (autobiography); *Along the Way* (poetry).

SIDELIGHTS: A leader in the alternative print media movement of the 1960s, Allen Katzman helped to organize the Underground Press Syndicate, a fraternal group of over two hundred newspapers with the purpose of pulling together like-minded counter-culture writers, editors, and artists. Abe Peck in *Uncovering the Sixties: The Life and Times of the Underground Press* writes, "Katzman foresaw a hip Associated Press, and more—income-pooling and article-sharing, joint advertising and typesetting resources." A contemporary of William Burroughs, Ishmael Reed, Allen Ginsberg, Ed Sanders, Tuli Kupferberg, and Diane DiPrima, Peck says, Katzman would frequent the same New York haunts as these poets, many of whom were published in the alternative presses of the era. Peck quotes Katzman as saying, "We weren't journalists. We were revolutionaries."

Katzman was also a pioneer publisher of the New Comic Art, presenting the work of Kim Deitch, Art Spiegelman, Trina Robbins, and Allan Shenker in the *East Village Other* and later in Swift Comics. In 1966 he produced the first *Electric Newspaper,* now a collector's item, for ESP records. A recognized authority on underground journalism, Katzman said that his paper, the *East Village Other,* "has been an active force in the creation of alternate solutions to the military/industrial complex of American 'hypocracy.' "

Katzman and his daughter, Ivy, were killed in an automobile accident in 1985. Before his death, he had finished two manuscripts, an autobiography and a book of poetry.

BIOGRAPHICAL/CRITICAL SOURCES:

BOOKS

Uncovering the Sixties: The Life and Times of the Underground Press, Citadel Underground, 1985, pp. 14, 15, 39, 40, 157.

PERIODICALS

New Republic, May 20, 1972, p. 26.
New York Times Book Review, April 9, 1972, p. 34.
Washington Post, April 5, 1972.

[Sketch reviewed by wife, Estelle Halpern]

*   *   *

KAUFFMAN, Janet   1945-

PERSONAL: Born June 10, 1945, in Lancaster, PA; daughter of Chester and Thelma (Hershey) Kauffman. *Education:* Juniata College, B.A., 1967; University of Chicago, M.A., 1968, Ph.D., 1972.

ADDRESSES: Office—Department of English, Eastern Michigan University, Ypsilanti, MI 48197. *Agent*—Liz Darhansoff, 1220 Park Ave., New York, NY 10128.

CAREER: Jackson Community College, Jackson, MI, teacher of English, 1977-88; Eastern Michigan University, Ypsilanti, MI, professor of English, 1988—. Visiting associate professor at University of Michigan, 1984-85.

AWARDS, HONORS: National Endowment for the Arts Fellowship, 1984; Rosenthal Award from the American Academy and Institute of Arts and Letters, 1985; PEN/Faulkner Award nomination, 1986.

WRITINGS:

POETRY

(Contributor) James Tipton, Herbert Scott, and Conrad Hillberry, editors, *The Third Coast: Contemporary Michigan Poetry,* Wayne State University Press, 1976.
(With Jerome J. McGann) *Writing Home,* Coldwater Press, 1978.
The Weather Book, Texas Tech University Press, 1981.
Where the World Is, Montparnasse Editions, 1988.

FICTION

Places in the World a Woman Could Walk (short stories), Knopf, 1984.
Collaborators (novel), Knopf, 1986.
Obscene Gestures for Women (short stories), Knopf, 1989.
The Body in Four Parts (novel), Graywolf Press, 1993.

Contributor to periodicals, including *New Yorker, Antaeus, Southern Poetry Review,* and *Beloit Poetry Journal.*

SIDELIGHTS: Poet and fiction-writer Janet Kauffman grew up in Pennsylvania and now lives on a farm in Michigan; these familiar settings frequently figure in her stories and verse. Her work is often described as minimalist: focusing on limited numbers of characters and employing the slightest of plots, it reaches the reader through precisely observed detail, a strong sense of place, and an intense, poetic style that is at once spare and richly imagistic. While her protagonists are most typically resilient, intelligent women struggling with harsh circumstances, Kauffman's deft portrayals of both male and female characters have won critical praise. Kauffman has been described by the *Detroit Free Press* as "Michigan's most famous short story writer," and has been greeted as an important new voice in American fiction.

Her first book of prose, *Places in the World a Woman Could Walk,* is a collection of short stories about rural women who, says Wendy Lesser in the *New York Times Book Review,* "are strong without being self-sufficient, knowing yet not sophisticated, accustomed to long silences but delighted at the least chance for conversation." The narrator of "Patriotic" works her farm with the assistance of two neighbors because her husband is off on a construction job; Lady Fretts, of the book's title story, decides to go to Greece after twelve years spent sitting at home and mourning her husband's death. In "Isn't It Something," Celia Dollop flees from her husband to live in the woods, and in "The Alvordton Spa and Sweat Shop," Marabelle the beautician lives in the basement of a house left unfinished when the builder, her lover, deserted her. Writing "elliptically, sometimes quirkily," according to Robert Towers in the *New York Review of Books,* Kauffman is praised by *Queen's Quarterly* reviewer Judith Russell for her "taut and complex syntax, poetic rhythm and beautifully observed detail."

In her second collection of short stories, *Obscene Gestures for Women,* Kauffman broadens her landscape to encompass urban and suburban America. "Many of these," Robert Kelly writes in the *New York Times Book Review,* "are angry stories, stabbed through with beauty and delight." A hypnotherapist tells the female protagonist of the title story that rather than grinding her teeth she ought to direct her tension outward by making an obscene gesture. Relating the incident, the protagonist wonders "if he's ever given thought to obscene gestures for women. Specifically for women. Could he see that women, physiologically, do not screw the world? I said, Give me an obscene gesture for women, and sure, I'd use it." The women in these stories, Julia Lisella suggests in a *Village Voice* review, resist male power structures through the "obscene gesture" of rejecting traditional roles as "wives and nurturers." Assessing the author as a "skilled and perceptive storyteller," Linda Barrett Osborne comments in the

Washington Post Book World that "Kauffman's fiction makes political statements that are not subtle, but which nevertheless are deft and well-aimed."

Kauffman's first novel, published in 1986, develops a short story that appeared in her collection *Places in the World a Woman Could Walk.* Set on a Pennsylvania tobacco farm wedged between a prison and the sea, *Collaborators* deals with the relationship between a daughter and her strong, unconventional, and overwhelming mother as the girl grows into adulthood. "The story goes to the heart not only of mother-daughter relationships, but of the negotiations between body and mind, character and culture, identity and loss," Stacey D'Erasmo reports in the *Village Voice.* Like Kauffman's short fiction, *Collaborators* displays the author's allusive, poetic prose style. "*Collaborators* is essentially a long tone poem, a dreamlike montage of images describing the exchanges of mind that take place between members of a family," writes Michiko Kakutani in the *New York Times.* Discussing the novel in the *Los Angeles Times Book Review,* Laura Kalpakian comments: "Kauffman spurns the novelist's clunky tools of conventionally rendered dialogue, action, scenic depiction in favor of the poet's reliance on brilliant, sustained metaphor, conduits of expression, emotion distilled into succinct expression." While Kakutani complains that Kauffman's writing sometimes overpowers the novel's relatively slight plot, many reviewers find Kauffman's style highly effective. "*Collaborators* is a novel that needs to be read slowly, word by word, image by image," states Ursula Hegi in the *New York Times Book Review,* "to allow Janet Kauffman's extraordinary gift for language and character development to unfold."

In her second novel, *The Body in Four Parts,* published in 1993, Kauffman continues her experimentation with innovative narrative forms. This "multivocal, multimodal" novel, as Sybil Steinberg describes it in *Publishers Weekly,* is narrated by the body speaking in the voice of one of its elements, earth. The book is divided into four sections, one for each of the elements (earth, water, air, and fire), which also figure as characters. Ron Antonucci, reviewing the novel for the *Library Journal,* finds it "eloquently written" but "needlessly abstruse." Steinberg, on the other hand, finds the novel "rewarding." Kauffman, she writes, "has a way of re-envisioning what prose is able to be, casting toward an expanded consciousness that can take in almost any human element; as a writer, she is a convinced democrat, evoking characters, metaphors, physical things and relationships in an inclusively imaginative assortment of words."

BIOGRAPHICAL/CRITICAL SOURCES:

BOOKS

Contemporary Literary Criticism, Volume 42, Gale, 1987.

Dictionary of Literary Biography Yearbook: 1986, Gale, 1987.
Kauffman, Janet, *Obscene Gestures for Women,* Knopf, 1989.

PERIODICALS

Detroit Free Press, March 26, 1985.
Detroit News, January 16, 1984.
Globe & Mail, March 28, 1987.
Library Journal, April 1, 1993, pp. 131-32.
Los Angeles Times Book Review, May 11, 1986, pp. 1, 8.
Ms., May 31, 1984.
New York Review of Books, May 31, 1984, pp. 35-36.
New York Times, February 19, 1986, p. C20.
New York Times Book Review, January 8, 1984; April 20, 1986, p. 17; September 24, 1989, p. 3.
Publishers Weekly, February 15, 1993, pp. 200, 204.
Queen's Quarterly, spring, 1987, pp. 191-192.
Saturday Review, January 10, 1984.
Village Voice, April 29, 1986, pp. 50-51; January 9, 1990, pp. 57-58.
Washington Post Book World, January 28, 1990, p. 6.

*   *   *

KEENE, James A(llen) 1932-

PERSONAL: Born October 27, 1932, in Detroit, MI; son of Samuel B. (a lawyer) and Bernice F. (Frazer) Keene; married Mary Bloom (in publishing), August 12, 1956; children: Karen Keene Gamow, Judith Ann. *Education:* Eastman School of Music, B.M., 1954; Wayne State University, M.M.Ed., 1959; University of Michigan, Ph.D., 1969.

CAREER: Montana State University, Bozeman, instructor in music, 1959-62; University of Vermont, Burlington, assistant professor of music, 1963-67; Mansfield State College, Mansfield, PA, associate professor, 1967-69, professor of music, 1969-80, chairman of department, 1975-80; Western Illinois University, Macomb, professor of music and chairman of department, beginning 1980.

WRITINGS:

A History of Music Education in the United States, University Press of New England, 1982.
Music and Education in Vermont, 1700-1900, Glenbridge Publishing, 1987.
(Compiler) *Manual of Archival Reprography,* K. G. Saur, 1989.

Contributor to music journals, including *American Music Teacher, Instrumentalist,* and *Journal of Research in Music Education.*

SIDELIGHTS: James A. Keene once told *CA:* "I was prompted to write [*A History of Music Education in the United States*] because no one had written a history of music education in this country since the 1920s. It was a long subject and getting bigger all the time with the increasing interest of doctoral students from America's colleges and universities. The book took a long time to write and could have been written six more times from six different points of view.

"I was taken with the cyclic nature of educational methodology. In each period the educational status quo was criticized and reform was called for. In time, that very reform became suspect and we returned again to a previous philosophy. Yet, in every period, groups of talented young people grew up to take their places as intelligent, social, political, and business leaders, as well as creative artists. They looked back and identified individual teachers who cared and made a difference."*

*   *   *

KEENER, Frederick M(ichael) 1937-

PERSONAL: Born December 28, 1937, in New York, NY; son of Frederick J. (an accountant) and Anne (Doran) Keener; married Ann R. Monahan (a teacher), September 2, 1961; children: Thomas, David. *Education:* St. John's University, Jamaica, NY, B.A., 1959; Columbia University, M.A., 1960, Ph.D., 1965.

ADDRESSES: Home—380 Yale Road, Garden City South, NY 11530. *Office*—Department of English, Hofstra University, 1000 Fulton Ave., Hempstead, NY 11550.

CAREER: St. John's University, Jamaica, NY, assistant professor of English, 1961-65; Columbia University, New York City, assistant professor, 1966-72, associate professor of English and dean of summer session, 1972-74; Hofstra University, Hempstead, NY, associate professor, 1974-77, professor of English, 1977—.

MEMBER: Modern Language Association of America (member of Shaughnessy Prize committee, 1986-89), American Society for Eighteenth-Century Studies (member of committee on teaching, 1985-87, chair 1987-89), Columbia University Seminar on Eighteenth-Century European Culture.

AWARDS, HONORS: National Endowment for the Humanities fellow, 1976-77.

WRITINGS:

English Dialogues of the Dead: A Critical History, an Anthology, and a Checklist, Columbia University Press, 1973.
An Essay on Pope, Columbia University Press, 1974.

(Contributor) Ronald C. Rosbottom, editor, *Studies in Eighteenth-Century Culture,* Volume VI, University of Wisconsin Press, 1977.
(Contributor) Roseann Runte, editor, *Studies in Eighteenth-Century Culture,* Volume IX, University of Wisconsin Press, 1979.
The Chain of Becoming: The Philosophical Tale, the Novel, and a Neglected Realism of Enlightenment: Swift, Montesquieu, Voltaire, Johnson, and Austen, Columbia University Press, 1983.
(Editor, with Susan Lorsch) *Eighteenth-Century Women and the Arts,* Greenwood Press, 1988.

Contributor to *Twentieth-Century Literature, Modern Language Quarterly, Modern Language Review, Essays in Criticism,* and other publications. Comparative literature editor, *Eighteenth-Century Studies,* 1989-92.

SIDELIGHTS: Frederick M. Keener's studies of eighteenth-century literature have been well received by critics. Claude Rawson, for example, judged *An Essay on Pope* to be "a sharp, intelligent and humane little book" in his review for the *Times Literary Supplement.* Rawson also stated that "it deserves to be read, studied, agreed with, disagreed with, and, above all, welcomed for the centrality and integrity of its purposes." In similar terms, Ronald Paulson, reviewing Keener's 1983 book *The Chain of Becoming: The Philosophical Tale, the Novel, and a Neglected Realism of Enlightenment* in *Studies in English Literature* found the work to be a "sensitive study of the philosophical tale" and "essential reading for students of the novel."

BIOGRAPHICAL/CRITICAL SOURCES:

PERIODICALS

Studies in English Literature, summer, 1983.
Times Literary Supplement, March 14, 1975; August 5, 1983.

*   *   *

KEEPING, Charles (William James) 1924-1988

PERSONAL: Born September 22, 1924, in Lambeth, London, England; died May 16, 1988; son of Charles (a professional boxer, under name Charles Clark, and newspaperman) and Eliza Ann (Trodd) Keeping; married Renate Meyer (an artist and illustrator), September 20, 1952; children: Jonathan, Vicki, Sean, Frank. *Education:* Polytechnic of Central London, National Diploma in Design, 1952.

Politics: "Individualist." *Religion:* None. *Avocational Interests:* Walking, good conversation over a pint of beer in a pub, modern jazz, folksinging.

ADDRESSES: *Home*—16 Church Rd., Shortlands, Bromley BR2 0HP, England. *Office*—Camberwell School of Art and Crafts, London, England. *Agent*—B. L. Kearley Ltd., 59 George St. London W1, England.

CAREER: Apprenticed to printing trade, 1938; after war service, worked as engineer and rent collector before starting full-time art studies in 1949; Polytechnic of Central London, London, England, visiting lecturer in lithography, 1956-63; Croydon College of Art, Croydon, England, visiting lecturer in lithography, 1963-78; Camberwell School of Art and Crafts, London, visiting lecturer in print making, 1979-88. Book illustrator, advertising artist, and designer of wall murals, posters, and book jackets. Lithographs exhibited in London, Italy, Australia, and United States, including International Exhibition of Lithography, Cincinnati, OH, 1958; prints in many collections, including the Victoria and Albert Museum, London. *Military service:* Royal Navy, 1942-46; served as telegraphist.

MEMBER: Society of Industrial Artists.

AWARDS, HONORS: Carnegie Medal commendation, British Library Association, 1957, for *The Silver Branch,* 1958, for *Warrior Scarlet,* 1963, for *The Latchkey Children,* 1965, for *Elidor,* 1967, for *The Dream Time,* and 1978, for *A Kind of Wild Justice;* Carnegie Medal, 1959, for *The Lantern Bearers,* and 1970, for *The God Beneath the Sea;* Spring Book Festival older honor, *New York Herald Tribune,* 1958, for *The Silver Branch,* and 1962, for *Dawn Wind;* International Board on Books for Young People (IBBY) honour list, 1960, for *Warrior Scarlet;* Certificate of Merit, British Library Association, 1966, for *Shaun and the Cart-Horse,* and 1970, for *The God Beneath the Sea;* Certificate of Merit, Leipzig Book Fair, 1966, for *Black Dolly: The Story of a Junk Cart Pony;* Kate Greenaway Medal, British Library Association, 1967, for *Charley, Charlotte and the Golden Canary,* and 1981, for *The Highwayman;* Kate Greenaway honour, 1969, for *Joseph's Yard,* commendations, 1970, for *The God Beneath the Sea,* and 1974, for *The Railway Passage;* W. H. Smith Illustration Award, Victoria and Albert Museum, 1972, for *Tinker, Tailor: Folk Song Tales,* and 1977, for *The Wildman;* Bratislava Biennale, honorable mention, 1973, for *The Spider's Web,* golden apple award, 1976, for *The Railway Passage;* Hans Christian Andersen highly commended illustrator award, IBBY, 1974; Kurt Maschler Award runner-up, 1985, for *The Wedding Ghost.*

WRITINGS:

SELF-ILLUSTRATED CHILDREN'S BOOKS

Shaun and the Cart-Horse, F. Watts, 1966.
Molly o' the Moors: The Story of a Pony, World Publishing, 1966, published as *Black Dolly: The Story of a Junk Cart Pony,* Brockhampton Press, 1966.
Charley, Charlotte and the Golden Canary, F. Watts, 1967.
Alfie Finds the Other Side of the World, F. Watts, 1968, published as *Alfie and the Ferryboat,* Oxford University Press, 1968.
(Compiler) *Tinker, Tailor: Folk Song Tales,* Brockhampton Press, 1968.
(Reteller) *The Christmas Story, as Told on "Play School,"* British Broadcasting Corporation, 1968, published as *The Christmas Story,* F. Watts, 1969.
Joseph's Yard (also see below), Oxford University Press, 1969, F. Watts, 1970.
Through the Window (also see below), F. Watts, 1970.
The Garden Shed, Oxford University Press, 1971.
The Spider's Web, Oxford University Press, 1972.
Richard, Oxford University Press, 1973.
The Nanny Goat and the Fierce Dog, Abelard, 1973, S. G. Phillips, 1974.
(Compiler of words and music) *Cockney Ding Dong,* Kestrel Books, 1973.
The Railway Passage, Oxford University Press, 1974.
Wasteground Circus, Oxford University Press, 1975.
Inter-City, Oxford University Press, 1977.
Miss Emily and the Bird of Make-Believe, Hutchinson, 1978.
River, Oxford University Press, 1978.
Willie's Fire-Engine, Oxford University Press, 1980.
(With Kevin Crossley-Holland) *Beowulf,* Oxford University Press, 1982.
Sammy Streetsinger, Oxford University Press(England), 1984, Oxford University Press (U.S.), 1987.
(Compiler) *Charles Keeping's Book of Classic Ghost Stories,* Peter Bedrick, 1986.
(Compiler) *Charles Keeping's Classic Tales of the Macabre,* Peter Bedrick, 1987.
Adam and Paradise Island, Oxford University Press, 1989.

Adapted *Joseph's Yard* and *Through the Window* for television.

ILLUSTRATOR

Nicholas Stuart Gray, *Over the Hills to Babylon,* Oxford University Press, 1954, Hawthorn, 1970.
Rosemary Sutcliff, *The Silver Branch,* Oxford University Press, 1957, Walck, 1959.
Sutcliff, *Warrior Scarlet,* Walck, 1958, 2nd edition, 1966.

John Stewart Murphy, *Bridges,* Oxford University Press, 1958.

Murphy, *Ships,* Oxford University Press, 1959.

Sutcliff, *The Lantern-Bearers,* 1959.

Sutcliff, *Knight's Fee,* Oxford University Press, 1960, Walck, 1961.

Murphy, *Roads,* Oxford University Press, 1960.

Ira Nesdale, *Riverbend Bricky,* Blackie, 1960.

Kathleen Fidler, *Tales of Pirates and Castaways,* Lutterworth, 1960.

Fidler, *Tales of the West Country,* Lutterworth, 1961.

Charles Kingsley, *The Heroes,* Hutchinson, 1961.

Mitchell Dawson, *The Queen of Trent,* Abelard, 1961.

Sir Henry Rider Haggard, *King Solomon's Mines,* Blackie, 1961.

Sutcliff, *Dawn Wind,* Oxford University Press, 1961, Walck, 1962.

Murphy, *Canals,* Oxford University Press, 1961.

Sutcliff, reteller, *Dragon Slayer,* Bodley Head, 1961, published as *Beowulf,* Dutton, 1962, published as *Dragon Slayer: The Story of Beowulf,* Macmillan, 1980.

Ruth Chandler, *Three Trumpets,* Abelard, 1962.

Kenneth Grahame, *The Golden Age* [and] *Dream Days,* Bodley Head, 1962, Dufour, 1965.

Barbara Leonie Picard, *Lost John,* Oxford University Press, 1962, Criterion, 1963.

Murphy, *Dams,* Oxford University Press, 1963.

Clare Compton, *Harriet and the Cherry Pie,* Bodley Head, 1963.

E. M. Almedingen, *The Knights of the Golden Table,* Bodley Head, 1963, Lippincott, 1964.

Philip Rush, *The Castle and the Harp,* Collins, 1963.

Paul Berna, *Flood Warning,* Pantheon, 1963.

Eric Allen, *The Latchkey Children,* Oxford University Press, 1963.

Wilkie Collins, *The Moonstone,* Oxford University Press, 1963.

Mollie Hunter, *Patrick Kentigern Keenan,* Blackie, 1963, published as *The Smartest Man in Ireland,* Funk, 1965.

James Holding, *The King's Contest and Other North African Tales,* Abelard, 1964.

Henry Treece, *The Children's Crusade,* Longmans, 1964.

Nesdale, *Bricky and the Hobo,* Blackie, 1964.

Murphy, *Railways,* Oxford University Press, 1964.

Treece, *The Last of the Vikings,* Brockhampton Press, 1964, published as *The Last Viking,* Pantheon, 1966.

Elizabeth Grove, *Whitsun Warpath,* Jonathan Cape, 1964.

Jacoba Tadema-Sporry, *The Story of Egypt,* translated by Elsa Hammond, Thomas Nelson, 1964.

Hunter, *The Kelpie's Pearls,* Blackie & Son, 1964, Funk, 1966.

Almedingen, *The Treasure of Siegfried,* Bodley Head, 1964, Lippincott, 1965.

Treece, *Horned Helmet,* Puffin, 1965.

Murphy, *Wells,* Oxford University Press, 1965.

Gray, *The Apple Stone,* Dobson, 1965, Hawthorn, 1969.

Alan Garner, *Elidor,* Collins, 1965.

Henry Daniel-Rops, *The Life of Our Lord,* Hawthorn, 1965.

Sutcliff, *The Mark of the Horse Lord,* Walck, 1965.

Sutcliff, *Heroes and History,* Putnam, 1965.

Treece, *Splintered Sword,* Brockhampton Press, 1965, Duell, Sloan & Pearce, 1966.

John Reginald Milsome, *Damien the Leper's Friend,* Burns & Oates, 1965.

Kevin Crossley-Holland, *King Horn,* Macmillan, 1965, Dutton, 1966.

Walter Macken, *Island of the Great Yellow Ox,* Macmillan, 1966.

Richard Potts, *An Owl for His Birthday,* Lutterworth, 1966.

Erich Maria Remarque, *All Quiet on the Western Front,* translated by A. W. Wheen, Folio Society, 1966.

Eric and Nancy Protter, editors and adapters, *Celtic Folk and Fairy Tales,* Duell, Sloan & Pearce, 1966.

Holding, *The Sky-Eater and Other South Sea Tales,* Abelard, 1966.

Edna Walker Chandler, *With Books on Her Head,* Meredith Press, 1967.

Geoffrey Trease, *Bent is the Bow,* Nelson, 1967.

Trease, *The Red Towers of Granada,* Vanguard Press, 1967.

James Reeves, *The Cold Flame,* Hamish Hamilton, 1967, Meredith, 1969.

Treece, *Swords from the North,* Pantheon, 1967.

Gray, *Mainly in Moonlight: Ten Stories of Sorcery and the Supernatural,* Meredith Press, 1967.

Treece, *The Dream Time,* Brockhampton Press, 1967, Hawthorn, 1968.

Gray, *Grimbold's Other World,* Meredith Press, 1968.

W. Somerset Maugham, *The Mixture as Before,* Heron, 1968.

Kenneth McLeish, *The Story of Aeneas,* Longmans, 1968.

Potts, *The Haunted Mine,* Lutterworth, 1968.

Reeves, compiler, *An Anthology of Free Verse,* Basil Blackwell, 1968.

Macken, *The Flight of the Doves,* Macmillan, 1968.

Holding, *Poko and the Golden Demon,* Abelard, 1968.

(With Sweithlan Kraczyna) Kenneth Cavander, *The 'Iliad' and 'Odyssey' of Homer: Radio Plays,* British Broadcasting Company, 1969.

Aldous Huxley, *After Many a Summer,* Heron, 1969.

Nevil Shute, *Ruined City* [and] *Landfall: A Channel Story,* Heron, 1969.

Margaret Jessy Miller editor, *Knights, Beasts and Wonders: Tales and Legends from Mediaeval Britain,* David White, 1969.

Roger Lancelyn Green, reteller, *The Tale of Ancient Israel,* Dent, 1969, Dutton, 1970.

Robert Elliot Rogerson, *Enjoy Reading!,* edited by Rogerson and C. M. Smith, W. & R. Chambers, Book 4, 1970, Book 5, 1971.

John Watts, *Early Encounters: An Introductory Stage,* Longmans, 1970.

Lee Cooper, *Five Fables from France,* Abelard, 1970.

Leon Garfield and Edward Blishen, *The God Beneath the Sea,* Kestrel Books, 1970, Pantheon, 1971.

Nigel Grimshaw, *The Angry Valley,* Longman, 1970.

Pamela L. Travers, *Friend Monkey,* Harcourt, 1971.

William Cole, compiler, *The Poet's Tales: A New Book of Story Poems,* World Publishing, 1971.

Fedor Dostoyevski, *The Idiot,* Folio Society, 1971.

Mary Shura Craig, *The Valley of the Frost Giants,* Lothrop, 1971.

Treece, *The Invaders: Three Stories,* Crowell, 1972.

Robert Newman, *The Twelve Labors of Hercules,* Crowell, 1972.

Roger Squire, reteller, *Wizards and Wampum: Legends of the Iroquois,* Abelard, 1972.

Garfield and Blishen, *The Golden Shadow,* Kestrel Books, 1972, Pantheon, 1973.

Ursula Synge, *Weland: Smith of the Gods,* Bodley Head, 1972, S. G. Phillips, 1973.

Montague Rhodes James, *Ghost Stories of M. R. James,* selected by Nigel Kneale, Folio Society, 1973.

Ian Serraillier, *I'll Tell You a Tale: A Collection of Poems and Ballads,* Longman, 1973.

Sutcliff, *The Capricorn Bracelet,* Oxford University Press, 1973.

Cooper, *The Strange Feathery Beast and Other French Fables,* Carousel, 1973.

Helen L. Hoke, *Weirdies: A Horrifying Concatenation of the Super-Sur-Real or Almost or Not-Quite Real,* Franklin Watts (London), 1973, published as *Weirdies, Weirdies, Weirdies: A Horrifying Concatenation of the Super-Sur-Real or Almost Not-Quite Real,* F. Watts (New York), 1975.

Daphne du Maurier, *The Birds, and Other Stories,* abridged and simplified by Lewis Jones, Longman, 1973.

Hoke, *Monsters, Monsters, Monsters,* F. Watts, 1974.

Forbes Stuart, reteller, *The Magic Horns: Folk Tales from Africa,* Abelard, 1974, Addison-Wesley, 1976.

Travers, *About the Sleeping Beauty,* McGraw, 1975.

Marian Lines, *Tower Blocks: Poems of the City,* F. Watts, 1975.

Bernard Ashley, *Terry on the Fence,* Oxford University Press, 1975, S. G. Phillips, 1977.

Robert Swindells, *When Darkness Comes,* Morrow, 1975.

David Kossoff, *The Little Book of Sylvanus (died 41 A.D.),* St. Martin's, 1975.

Sutcliff, *Blood Feud,* Oxford University Press, 1976, Dutton, 1977.

Potts, *A Boy and His Bike,* Dobson, 1976.

Crossley-Holland, *The Wildman,* Deutsch, 1976.

Horace Walpole, *The Castle of Otranto: A Gothic Story,* Folio Society, 1976.

Victor Hugo, *Les Miserables,* translated by Norman Denny, Folio Press, 1976.

Rene Guillot, *Tipiti, The Robin,* translated by Gwen Marsh, published with *Pascal and the Lioness,* illustrated by Barry Wilkinson, translated and adapted by Christina Holyoak, Bodley Head, 1976.

Hoke, compiler, *Haunts, Haunts, Haunts,* F. Watts, 1977, published as *Spectres, Spooks, and Shuddery Shades,* 1977.

Ashley, *A Kind of Wild Justice,* S. G. Phillips, 1979.

Stuart, *The Mermaids' Revenge: Folk Tales from Britain and Ireland,* Abelard, 1979.

Leonard Clark, *The Tale of Prince Igor,* Dobson, 1979.

Nina Bawden, *The Robbers,* Gollancz, 1979.

Charles Causley, editor, *The Batsford Book of Stories in Verse for Children,* Batsford, 1979.

Tony Drake, *Breakback Alley,* Collins, 1979.

Ashley, *Break in the Sun: A Novel,* S. G. Phillips, 1980.

Alfred Noyes, *The Highwayman,* Oxford University Press, 1981.

(With Derek Collard and Jeroo Roy) John Bailey, McLeish, and David Spearman, retellers, *Gods and Men: Myths and Legends from the World's Religions,* Oxford University Press, 1981.

Charles Dickens, *The Posthumous Papers of the Pickwick Club,* Folio Society, 1981.

Dickens, *Great Expectations,* Folio Society, 1981.

Dickens, *Our Mutual Friend,* Folio Society, 1982.

Rudyard Kipling, *The Beginning of the Armadilloes,* Macmillan, 1982, Peter Bedrick, 1983.

Dickens, *The Mystery of Edwin Drood,* edited by Arthur J. Cox, Folio Society, 1983.

Dickens, *The Personal History of David Copperfield,* Folio Society, 1983.

Causley, compiler, *The Sun Dancing: Christian Verse,* Puffin, 1984.

Kipling, *Rikki-Tikki-Tavi and Other Animal Stories,* Macmillan, 1984.

Garfield, *The Wedding Ghost,* Oxford University Press, 1985.

Alfred Tennyson, *The Lady of Shalott,* Oxford University Press, 1985.

Dickens, *The Life and Adventures of Nicholas Nickleby,* Folio Society, 1986.

Edgar Allan Poe, *Two Tales,* Chimaera Press, 1986.

Neil Philip, reteller, *The Tale of Sir Gawain,* Philomel Books, 1987.

Crossley-Holland, reteller, *Beowulf,* Oxford University Press, 1988.

Bram Stoker, *Dracula,* Blackie, 1988.

Mary Shelley, *Frankenstein,* Blackie, 1988.

Anna Sewell, *Black Beauty,* Gollancz, 1989.

Also illustrator of Ted Kavanaugh's *Man Must Measure,* 1955; Martha Freudenberger and Magda Kelber's *Heute Morgen,* 2 and 3, 1956-57; Guthrie Foote's *Merrily on High,* 1959; Joseph Conrad's *The Shadow-Line* [and] *Within the Tides,* 1962; Frank Knight's *They Told Mr. Hakluyt,* 1964; Emily Bronte's *Wuthering Heights,* 1964; Joan Tate's *Jenny,* 1964, *The Next-Doors,* 1964, and *Mrs. Jenny,* 1965; Lace Kendall's *The Rain Boat,* 1965; Denys Thompson and R. J. Harris's *Your English,* 1965, Harold Keith's *Komantcia,* 1966; Murphy's *Harbours and Docks,* 1967; Marie Butts's *Champion of Charlemagne,* 1967; Frederic Westcott's *Bach,* 1967; Hunter's *Thomas and the Warlock,* 1967; H. G. Welles's *Mr. Britling Sees It Through,* 1969; Huxley's *Time Must Have a Stop,* 1969; Shute's *On the Beach,* 1970; Potts's *The Story of Tod;* Maugham's *Of Human Bondage;* and Robert Louis Stevenson's *Stumpy, Dr. Jekyll and Mr. Hyde, The Wrecker, New Arabian Nights,* and *More New Arabian Nights.*

ADAPTATIONS: Charley, Charlotte and the Golden Canary, Alfie Finds the Other Side of the World, and *Through the Window* were adapted for filmstrips by Weston Woods.

SIDELIGHTS: Author of more than twenty self-illustrated children's books and illustrator of more than two hundred other books for children and adults, Charles Keeping was one of the most productive illustrators of his time. As M. S. Crouch put it in *Junior Bookshelf,* Keeping's "capacity for work was phenomenal. He met each challenge with enormous creative energy." Crouch added, "No illustrator in this century has worked harder. . . ." More than merely prolific, Keeping had a distinctive individual style, which evolved from his use of dark browns and blacks during his early days to brighter colors in middle-period works such as *Charley, Charlotte and the Golden Canary,* to greater delicacy in later years. Anne Carter, in *Twentieth-Century Children's Writers,* found a somberness in Keeping's imagination, adding, "in later years he could become truly frightening. . . . He can be violent, gloomy, and difficult. He was undoubtedly one of the outstanding figures of his times."

Keeping's maternal ancestors were seafarers; he was descended from street traders on his father's side. He was born in Lambeth Walk in South London and grew up in the docks and market area, and his work was mainly concerned with the people and animals in the work streets of London. As a child he would look through his backyard fence to a stable and, as he said in an interview with Cor-

nelia Jones and Olivia R. Way for *British Children's Authors,* "I was always looking at this isolated situation or image moving across. I started to create stories around these things so that the horse, the people, the chickens, the dogs, all became sort of symbols. . . . Certainly these early impressions were the strongest I experienced. They were so strong that I never thought of anything else than writing about them and drawing them." Because of his family's financial need after his father's death, Keeping became apprentice to a printer at the age of fourteen. Wartime service in the Royal Navy followed, and then part-time schooling supplemented by work as a gas meter collector in the North Paddington section of London. "I never stopped drawing," he told Jones and Way of those years. A grant in 1949 freed him to become a full-time student. After graduating, he turned to book illustration as a better source of income than painting or lithography. His success as a children's book illustrator came about partly because of the encouragement of children's book editor Mabel George at Oxford University Press, who commissioned him to illustrate several novels by Rosemary Sutcliff, beginning with *The Silver Branch* in 1957. Keeping's pictures for that book, according to a London *Times* obituary, "marked the arrival of a highly original talent."

Like many children's illustrators, Keeping began writing his own stories after several years' success as an illustrator. His literary style was unadorned, and as time went on he learned to simplify his texts so that they sometimes became virtual captions for his richly detailed pictures. *Richard,* the story of a day in the life of a London police horse, was an example of this style. *Joseph's Yard,* which *Books* reviewer Jessica Jenkins summarized as "a recreation of the myth of Adonis in a bleak backyard," was another example, for "with a brief text and a combination of resist-work techniques (wax and scratch, wax and watercolor, water and waterproof ink), Charles Keeping creates page after page of visual stimulus and an extraordinary range and depth of emotion." In a *Books* review of *Through the Window,* Anne Wood stated that Keeping draws "upon the background of his own childhood, he seeks to show the effect of a child's closeness to a particular environment upon his developing understanding of the texture of life. . . . Keeping sets out the truth about feelings in the uncompromising context of his wonderfully beautiful art, and we owe him a debt for his courage in widening the scope of the picture book in this way."

Keeping's final work as a writer, *Adam and Paradise Island,* was published in 1989. The narrative recounts how young Adam and some old and young friends construct a playground out of junk on urban Paradise Island after the borough council has bulldozed the place for use as part of a new toll road. Calling Keeping "one of our most powerful illustrators . . . a writer with a wholly distinctive voice," London *Times* critic Brian Alderson commented on Keeping's drily humorous style, "even-handed" satire and "buoyant acceptance of the world as it is."

BIOGRAPHICAL/CRITICAL SOURCES:

BOOKS

Chevalier, Tracy, editor, *Twentieth-Century Children's Writers,* 3rd edition, St. James Press, 1989, pp. 511-513.
Illustrators of Children's Books: 1957-1966, Horn Book, 1968.
Jones, Cornelia, and Olivia R. Way, *British Children's Authors: Interviews at Home,* American Library Association, 1976, pp. 101-113.
Wintle and Fisher, *The Pied Pipers,* Paddington Press, 1975.

PERIODICALS

Books, March, 1970; November, 1970.
Horn Book, October, 1974; April, 1981, p. 181.
Junior Bookshelf, December, 1984, p. 245; December, 1986, p. 235; August, 1988, pp. 173-75; August, 1989, p. 158.
Publishers Weekly, May 20, 1988, p. 94.
School Library Journal, January, 1981, p. 51.
Times (London), June 10, 1989.
Times Educational Supplement, May 27, 1983, p. 29; November 27, 1987, p. 47.
Times Literary Supplement, September 19, 1980, p. 1028; November 30, 1984, p. 1379; July 7, 1989, p. 757.
Voice of Youth Advocates, June, 1988, p. 84.
Washington Post Book World, December 27, 1987, p. 8.

OBITUARIES:

PERIODICALS

School Library Journal, August, 1988.
Times (London), May 20, 1988.*

*   *   *

KELLER, Charles 1942-

PERSONAL: Born March 30, 1942, in New York, NY.

ADDRESSES: Home—162 19th St., Union City, NJ 07087.

WRITINGS:

Ballpoint Bananas, and Other Jokes for Kids, Prentice-Hall, 1973.
Too Funny for Words: Gesture Jokes for Children, Prentice-Hall, 1973.
Laugh Lines, Prentice-Hall, 1974.

The Star-Spangled Banana, and Other Revolutionary Riddles, Prentice-Hall, 1974.
Going Bananas, Prentice-Hall, 1975.
Punch Lines, Prentice-Hall, 1975.
Daffynitions, Prentice-Hall, 1976.
(With Linda Glovach) *The Little Witch Presents a Monster Joke Book,* Prentice-Hall, 1976.
Giggle Puss: Pet Jokes for Kids, Prentice-Hall, 1977.
Llama Beans, Prentice-Hall, 1977.
Laughing: A Historical Collection of American Humor, Prentice-Hall, 1977.
More Ballpoint Bananas, Prentice-Hall, 1977.
The Nutty Joke Book, Prentice-Hall, 1978.
School Daze, Prentice-Hall, 1978.
The Wizard of Gauze, and Other Gags for Kids, Prentice-Hall, 1979.
The Best of Rube Goldberg, Prentice-Hall, 1979.
Still Going Bananas, Prentice-Hall, 1980.
News Breaks, Prentice-Hall, 1980.
Growing Up Laughing, Prentice-Hall, 1981.
What's the Score?: Sports Jokes, Prentice-Hall, 1981.
Smokey the Shark, and Other Fishy Tales, Prentice-Hall, 1981.
Ohm on the Range: Robot and Computer Jokes, Prentice-Hall, 1982.
Oh, Brother!: Family Jokes, Prentice-Hall, 1982.
Alexander the Grape: Fruit and Vegetable Jokes, Prentice-Hall, 1982.
Remember the Ala Mode: Riddles and Puns, Prentice-Hall, 1983.
Norma Lee I Don't Knock on Doors: Knock, Knock Jokes, Prentice-Hall, 1983.
What's Up, Doc? Doctor and Dentist Jokes, Prentice-Hall, 1984.
Grime Doesn't Pay: Law and Order Jokes, Prentice-Hall, 1984.
Astronuts: Space Jokes and Riddles, Prentice-Hall, 1985.
Swine Lake: Music and Dance Riddles, Prentice-Hall, 1985.
Waiter, There's a Fly in My Soup!: Restaurant Jokes, Prentice-Hall, 1986.
Count Draculations!: Monster Riddles, Prentice-Hall, 1986.
Colossal Fossils: Dinosaur Riddles, Prentice-Hall, 1987.
It's Raining Cats and Dogs: Cat and Dog Jokes, Pippin, 1988.
King Henry the Ape: Animal Jokes, Pippin, 1989.
Driving Me Crazy: Fun-on-Wheels Jokes, Pippin, 1989.
Tongue Twisters, Simon & Schuster, 1989.
Belly Laughs: Food Jokes and Riddles, Simon & Schuster, 1990.
Take Me to Your Liter: Science and Math Jokes, Pippin, 1991.

The Planet of the Grapes: Show Biz Jokes and Riddles, Pippin, 1992.

Also author of *Glory, Glory, How Peculiar* and *The Silly Song Book.* Author of the syndicated newspaper column "Corn on the Cob."

*　　*　　*

KELLY, George A(nthony) 1916-

PERSONAL: Born September 17, 1916, in New York, NY. *Education:* Catholic University of America, M.A., 1943, Ph.D., 1946.

ADDRESSES: Office—St. John's University, Grand Central and Utopia Parkways, Jamaica, NY 11439.

CAREER: Ordained Roman Catholic priest, 1942, elevated to right reverend monsignor, 1964. Parish priest, 1945-59; Archdiocese of New York City, director of Family Life Bureau, 1955-65, Family Consultation Service, 1955-65, secretary for education, 1966-70; St. John's University, Jamaica, NY, John A. Flynn Professor of Contemporary Catholic Problems, 1970—, director of Institute for Advanced Studies in Catholic Doctrine, 1975-81. Co-chair, Archdiocesan Parish Councils, 1966-70; consultor, Archdiocese of New York, Congregation for the Clergy, Rome, 1984. Lecturer, St. Joseph's Seminary, Yonkers, NY, 1946-49, and Catholic University of America, 1952. Associate chaplain, Catholic Trade Unionists Association, 1945-52; conductor, Family Life Institutes, U.S. Army and U.S. Air Force, 1960-61. Member, Papal Birth Control Commission, 1965; member of advisory board, National Catholic Welfare Conference, 1965; secretary of the board of trustees, St. Joseph's Seminary; secretary of the advisory board, Pastoral Life Conference.

MEMBER: American Association of University Professors, American Sociological Association, Association for the Sociology of Religion, American Catholic Historical Association, American Catholic Theological Society, American Catholic Sociological Society, Fellowship of Catholic Scholars (executive secretary, 1976-81; president, 1985-87), National Catholic Education Association.

AWARDS, HONORS: Cardinal Wright Award, Friends of the Fellowship of Catholic Scholars, 1979, for *The Battle for the American Church;* Faith and Family award, Women for Faith and Family, 1988.

WRITINGS:

Primer on the Taft-Hartley Act, Christopher, 1948.
The Story of St. Monica's Parish, Monica Press, 1954.
Catholic Marriage Manual, Random House, 1958.
Catholic Family Handbook, Random House, 1959.

Catholic Youth's Guide to Life and Love, Random House, 1960.
Overpopulation—A Catholic View, Paulist Press, 1960.
Catholic Guide to Expectant Motherhood, Random House, 1961.
Dating for Young Catholics, Doubleday, 1963.
Birth Control and Catholics, Doubleday, 1963.
Your Child and Sex, Random House, 1966.
Who Is My Neighbor?, Random House, 1966.
The Christian Role in Today's Society, Random House, 1966.
Catholics and the Practice of the Faith, St. John's University Press, Volume 1: *Catholic Youth,* 1967, Volume 2: *Catholic Parents,* 1971.
Why Should the Catholic University Survive?, St. John's University Press, 1975.
The Catholic Church and the American Poor, Alba House, 1976.
Sacrament of Penance and Reconciliation, Franciscan Herald Press, 1976.
Who Should Run the Catholic Church?, Our Sunday Visitor, 1976.
The Battle for the American Church, Doubleday, 1979.
The Crisis of Authority, Regnery-Gateway, 1980.
The New Biblical Theorists, Servant Books, 1983.
The Church's Problem with Bible Scholars, Franciscan Herald Press, 1985.
Inside My Father's House, Doubleday, 1989.
Keeping the Church Catholic with John Paul II, Doubleday, 1990.

Also author of *Catholics and the Practice of Faith,* 1946. Contributor to periodicals, including *Catholic Digest* and *Homiletic and Pastoral Review.*

EDITOR

Government Aid to Nonpublic Schools: Yes or No?, St. John's University Press, 1972.
The Parish, St. John's University Press, 1973.
The Sacrament of Penance in Our Time, Daughters of St. Paul, 1976.
The Sacrament of the Eucharist in Our Time, Daughters of St. Paul, 1978.
The Teaching Church in Our Time, Daughters of St. Paul, 1978.
Human Sexuality in Our Time, Daughters of St. Paul, 1979.
Catechetical Instruction and the Catholic Faithful, Daughters of St. Paul, 1982.

SIDELIGHTS: George A. Kelly opens his book *The Battle for the American Church* by stating: "A guerilla-type warfare is going on inside the Church and its outcome is clearly doubtful. The Pope and the Roman Curia are fending off with mixed success the attacks of their theologians who, in the name of scholarship, demand more radical accommodation with Protestant and secular thought. The issues at stake are the correctness of Catholic doctrine and the survival of the Catholic Church as a significant influence in the life of her own communicants." In a *Washington Post* review of the book, Colman McCarthy comments that although he doesn't agree with Kelly's thesis, he nevertheless "enjoyed nearly every page of [the author's work]. His intelligence is forceful and he is able to be angry without being mean. He loves his church and thrives on its teachings, ancient and modern."

BIOGRAPHICAL/CRITICAL SOURCES:

BOOKS

Kelly, George A., *The Battle for the American Church*, Doubleday, 1979.

PERIODICALS

Washington Post, October 5, 1979.*

*   *   *

KELLY, M(ilton) T(erry)   1947-

PERSONAL: Born November 30, 1947, in Toronto, Ontario, Canada; son of Milton Thomas and Sybil Lucy Preston (Vores) Kelly; children: Jonah Preston. *Education:* York University, B.A., 1970; University of Toronto, B.Ed., 1976. *Avocational Interests:* Canoeing, cross-country skiing.

ADDRESSES: Home—60 Kendal Ave., Toronto, Ontario M5R 1L9, Canada. *Office*—c/o Stoddart Publishing Co. Ltd., 34 Lesmill Rd., Don Mills, Ontario M3B 2T6, Canada.

CAREER: Maclean-Hunter Ltd. (publishers), Toronto, Ontario, business journalist, 1970-71; International Press, Toronto, assistant editor of *Ski Canada* and *Racquets Canada,* and associate editor of *Who's Who in Canada,* 1972-73; *Scotsman,* Edinburgh, Scotland, general reporter, 1973-74; *Moose Jaw Times Herald,* Moose Jaw, Saskatchewan, city hall reporter, 1974-75; McClelland & Stewart (publishers), Toronto, manuscripts editor, 1975; Levack District High School, Sudbury, Ontario, teacher of English and creative writing, 1976-77; novelist, playwright, and free-lance writer, 1977—. Contributing interviewer, *Imprint,* T.V. Ontario, 1989—. Coordinator of public relations for the Jeux Canada Games, Ministry of Culture and Recreation, Government of Ontario, 1981.

MEMBER: International PEN, Writers Union of Canada, Playwrights Canada, Alliance of Canadian Cinema, Television and Radio Artists, Pollution Probe, Champlain Society, Canadian Association in Solidarity with Native Peo-

ples, Wilderness Canoe Association, Federation of Ontario Naturalists.

AWARDS, HONORS: Grants from Ontario Trackers Association, 1971, Canada Council, 1976, 1978, 1980, 1983-87, and 1989, and Ontario Arts Council, 1990 and 1991; Ontario Arts Council Awards, 1977-88; finalist in Best First Novel of the Year Competition, *Books in Canada,* 1978, for *I Do Remember the Fall;* nomination for best short story, fiction category, National Magazine Awards, 1983, for "Unbodied Souls" in *Toronto Life;* Award for Poetry, Toronto Arts Council, 1986; Governor General's Award for Literature, fiction category, 1987, for *A Dream like Mine;* President's Prize for Fiction, York University, 1989, 1990.

WRITINGS:

I Do Remember the Fall (novel), Simon & Pierre, 1978.
Country You Can't Walk In (poetry), Penumbra Press, 1979, published as *Country You Can't Walk In and Other Poems,* 1984.
The More Loving One (novel and three short stories), Black Moss Press, 1980.
The Ruined Season (novel), Black Moss Press, 1982.
The Green Dolphin (play; produced at Theatre Pass Muraille, 1982), Playwrights Canada, 1982.
Wildfire: The Legend of Tom Longboat (screenplay), Canadian Broadcasting Corp. (CBC-TV), 1983.
A Dream like Mine (novel), Stoddard/General Publishing, 1987.
(Editor and author of introduction) Walter Kenyon, *Arctic Argonauts,* Penumbra Press, 1990.
Breath Dances between Them (short stories), Stoddart, 1991.

Also author of play *McClusky and O'Sullivan,* 1983, and a filmscript for *Young Canadians and the Law,* CBC-TV. Contributor to anthologies, including *The Saturday Night Traveller,* HarperCollins, 1990; *Best Canadian Essays,* edited by George Galt, Quarry Press, 1991; *Canadian Literary Landmarks,* edited by John Robert Colombo; *Un Dozen: 13 Canadian Poets,* edited by Judith Fitzgerald; *The Northern Ontario Anthology,* edited by Fred Mason; and *Whale Sound* and *Whales: A Celebration,* both edited by Greg Gatenby. Author of column "Between the Sexes" in Toronto *Globe & Mail,* 1979-81. Contributor to periodicals, including *Canadian Forum, Antigonish Review, Poetry, Scotsman, Performing Arts in Canada, Northern Journey,* and *Toronto Life.*

A Dream like Mine was translated into French.

ADAPTATIONS: A Dream like Mine was released as the movie *Clearcut,* Famous Players/Cinexus, 1991.

SIDELIGHTS: M. T. Kelly once told *CA:* "My major interest is literature, because I find it is 'the best way there is of breaking bread with the dead'—and the living. It makes me feel less lonely. In my work I would like to do what a favorite poet of mine, W. B. Yeats, described: 'Those images seek / that constitute the wild / the lion and the virgin / the harlot and the child.' "

BIOGRAPHICAL/CRITICAL SOURCES:

PERIODICALS

Books in Canada, December, 1980; November, 1987, p. 30; June, 1991, p. 46.
Canadian Forum, June-July, 1981.
Maclean's, March 6, 1978; February 23, 1981.
Quill & Quire, January, 1981; August, 1983; December, 1987, p. 24; August, 1991, p. 17.

*   *   *

KENNEDY, Susan Estabrook   1942-

PERSONAL: Born June 8, 1942, in New York, NY; daughter of Austin Lovell and Dorothy (Ogden) Estabrook; married E. Craig Kennedy, Jr. (a data processing management consultant), November 28, 1970. *Education:* Marymount Manhattan College, B.A. (summa cum laude), 1964; Columbia University, M.A., 1965, Ph.D., 1971.

ADDRESSES: Office—College of Humanities and Sciences, Virginia Commonwealth University, Richmond, VA 23284.

CAREER: Hunter College of the City University of New York, New York City, lecturer in history, 1966-67; Temple University, Philadelphia, PA, instructor, 1967-72, assistant professor of history, 1972-73; Virginia Commonwealth University, Richmond, assistant professor, 1973-76, associate professor, 1976-81, professor of history, 1981—, associate dean, 1993—.

MEMBER: American Historical Association, Organization of American Historians, American Association of University Professors, Oral History Association, Intertel.

AWARDS, HONORS: Guggenheim fellowship, 1978-79; Herbert Hoover scholar, 1980, 1982, 1993; American Council of Learned Societies grant, 1980; Perrine fellow, 1982-83, 1993; Danforth associate, 1980-86.

WRITINGS:

The Banking Crisis of 1933, University Press of Kentucky, 1973.
If All We Did Was to Weep at Home: A History of White Working-Class Women in America, Indiana University Press, 1979.
America's White Working Class Women: A Historical Bibliography, Garland, 1981.

Contributor to *Michigan History, Nevada Historical Society Quarterly, Prospects, Dictionary of American Biography, American National Biography, European Immigrant Woman,* and *International Journal of Women's Studies.*

*   *   *

KHOMAINI, Ayatollah Sayyed Ruholla Mousavi
See KHOMEINI, Ruhollah (Mussavi)

*   *   *

KHOMEINI, Ayatollah
See KHOMEINI, Ruhollah (Mussavi)

*   *   *

KHOMEINI, Ayatollah Ruhollah
See KHOMEINI, Ruhollah (Mussavi)

*   *   *

KHOMEINI, Imam
See KHOMEINI, Ruhollah (Mussavi)

*   *   *

KHOMEINI, Ruhollah (Mussavi)   1900(?)-1989
(Ayatollah Sayyed Ruholla Mousavi Khomaini, Ayatollah Khomeini, Ayatollah Ruhollah Khomeini, Imam Khomeini, Ruhollah Khumeini)

PERSONAL: Birth-given name, Ruhollah Hendi; name changed c. 1930; some sources transliterate given name as Ruh Allah; adopted surname variously transliterated as Khomeini, Khomaini, Khomeyni, Khumeini, and Khumayni; born May 17, 1900 (some sources say 1901 or 1902), in Khomein (some sources transliterate name as Khumain), Persia (now Iran); died June 3, 1989, of a heart attack following surgery for stomach cancer in Teheran, Iran; son of Sayyed Mustafa Mussavi (a Muslim clergyman) and Hajar (Saghafi) Hendi; married c. 1930, wife's name Batoul (deceased); remarried, wife's name Khadijeh; children: (first marriage) Mustafa (son; deceased); (second marriage) Ahmad (son), Zahra (daughter), three other daughters. *Education:* Attended religious schools in Qom, Iran. *Religion:* Shi'ite Muslim.

CAREER: Muslim clergyman; secular and religious leader of Iran, 1979-89.

AWARDS, HONORS: Named *Time* magazine's "Man of the Year," 1979.

WRITINGS:

A Concise Commandments of Islam, Chehel-Sotoon Madrasah & Library, 1980.

The Revolutionary Line of Action, Great Islamic Library, 1980.

Light of the Path, Jihad for Construction, External Liaison Section, 1982.

UNDER NAME AYATOLLAH KHOMEINI

Sayings of the Ayatollah Khomeini: Political, Philosophical, Social, and Religious, selected and translated from Farsi into French by Jean-Marie Xaviere, translated from French into English by Harold J. Salemson, English edition edited by Tony Hendra, introduction by Clive Irving, Bantam, 1980.

UNDER NAME AYATOLLAH RUHOLLAH KHOMEINI

Islamic Government, translated by Joint Publications Research Service, Manor Books, 1979.

The Sparks that Lit the Recent Islamic Movement: June 5, 1963, Adjad Book Designers & Builders, 1989.

UNDER NAME AYATOLLAH SAYYED RUHOLLA MOUSAVI KHOMAINI

A Clarification of Questions: An Unabridged Translation of Rezaleh Towzih Al-Masael, translated by J. Borujerdi, Westview, 1984.

UNDER NAME IMAM KHOMEINI

Islam and Revolution: Writings and Declarations of Imam Khomeini, translated and annotated by Hamid Algar, Mizan Press, 1981.

Imam Khomeini and November 4th, Ministry of Islamic Guidance, 1982.

Selected Messages and Speeches of Imam Khomeini, Ministry of Islamic Guidance, 1982.

Practical Laws of Islam, Tahrike Tarsile Quran, 1983.

Imam Khomeini, the Pope, and Christianity, Islamic Propagation Organization, 1984.

UNDER NAME RUHOLLAH KHUMEINI

Khumeini Speaks Revolution, compiled by Mohiuddin Ayyubi, translated by N. M. Shaikh, International Islamic Publishers, 1981.

Also author of *Kasf' ol-Assraar* (title means "Unveiling the Mysteries"), 1941.

SOUND RECORDINGS:

Turmoil in Iran: Ayatollah Khomeini Faces the Nation (cassette recording of speech from Ponchartrain, France, broadcast January 14, 1979), Encyclopedia Americana/CBS News Audio Resource Library, 1979.

SIDELIGHTS: In naming Ruhollah Khomeini (more popularly known by his religious titles Imam Khomeini, Ayatollah Khomeini, or simply the Ayatollah) 1979's "Man of the Year" as the person who has "done the most to change the news, for better or for worse," the editors of *Time* magazine observed: "Khomeini's importance far transcends the nightmare of the embassy seizure, transcends indeed the overthrow of the Shah of Iran. The revolution that he led to triumph threatens to upset the world balance of power more than any political event since Hitler's conquest of Europe."

The apparent suddenness of Khomeini's arrival on the world political scene in 1979 caught most Westerners by surprise, but as John Renard noted in *America:* "One embarrassingly obvious lapse was the almost universal refusal to pay attention to what Khomeini was saying and writing. Of all the prominent dramatis personae, Khomeini turned out to be the most consistent. He knew exactly what he wanted, and he began saying so forty years ago."

As early as 1941 Khomeini, in his book *Kasf' ol-Assraar* ("Unveiling the Mysteries"), stated his conviction that religion, politics, and culture are inseparable, and he strongly denounced the civil leadership of Iran for its efforts to modernize and Westernize the country—a trend Khomeini viewed as an evil threat to Islamic culture. This view was both a personal one and one that reflected his position as a member of the Shi'ite Muslim clergy.

Khomeini's formative years were set against a backdrop of religious devotion and violence. His father, a Muslim clergyman and community leader, was murdered while on a religious pilgrimage to Iraq when Khomeini was a small child. Raised in an atmosphere of religious militance by his mother and an aunt, Khomeini eventually came to study Islamic theology under one of the leading teachers of the time, Ayatollah Abdul Karim Haeri. Khomeini also studied Islamic law and mysticism, as well as the writings of Plato (whose concept of a philosopher-king he would ultimately aspire to personify), eventually becoming a religious scholar and teacher at the Islamic institute of Madresseh Faizieh in Qom.

As a Shi'ite fundamentalist, Khomeini stressed strict adherence to and interpretation of the Koran for all, including the government. His criticism of secular authorities brought him into increasing conflict with Shah Mohammed Reza Pahlavi, Iran's monarch since 1941. Khomeini remained neutral in the events that brought Mohammed Mossadegh's National Front to power in 1951, but when the United States returned the Shah to the throne Khomeini's opposition increased, further fueled by his perception of the United States as being the real power behind the Iranian government.

Khomeini's struggles with the Shah led to his becoming recognized in 1962 as the acclaimed leader of the Shi'ites. The following year the Shah proposed sweeping social changes unacceptable to Khomeini, including female suffrage and agrarian reform that stripped the Shi'ite clergy of much of its considerable property holdings. Following a series of bloody riots for which he was believed responsible, Khomeini was placed under house arrest for nearly a year. In November, 1964, when Khomeini opposed an agreement between the Shah and the United States that removed U.S. military personnel from the jurisdiction of Iranian courts, he was exiled by the Shah to Turkey. Eager to avoid rioting by Iranian students in Turkey, authorities permitted Khomeini to travel to nearby Iraq in 1965.

Khomeini increased his invective against the Shah while in exile, sending tape-recorded sermons to his followers in Iran, who would then copy and distribute them nationwide. His influence in Iran diminished slightly over the next decade as ever increasing oil wealth poured into the country, bringing with it Western technology, popular culture, and attitudes. But with Iran's financial gains came political corruption, inequality of distribution of the new-found wealth, and brutally repressive treatment of the Shah's political opposition, all of which precipitated a spirit of revolution, with Khomeini as the popularly acknowledged leader.

The Shah, through his secret police, the SAVAK, escalated the level of repression, which only served to feed the intensifying call for revolt. After Khomeini's son Mustafa died in 1977 under suspicious circumstances believed to have been orchestrated by SAVAK, the Ayatollah began calling for open rebellion through strikes, riots, and appeals to the military to turn against the Shah.

The Shah pressured Iraq to expel Khomeini in October, 1978, forcing Khomeini to relocate to France. There he attracted the attention of the international press, and through the media called for the support of Muslims worldwide in the overthrow of the Shah. Realizing that his own political position was rapidly becoming untenable, but not wanting Khomeini to control the political future of Iran, the Shah on December 29, 1978, appointed Shahpur Bakhtiar to head a civilian government. On January 16, 1979, ten days after Bakhtiar's government was in place, the Shah left Iran for Egypt for what was described as a "vacation."

Khomeini returned to Iran on February 1, 1979, and demanded that the Bakhtiar government turn over power to him, which it did in ten days. On March 31st Khomeini received a plebiscite from the Iranian people establishing an Islamic republic—a theocracy—in Iran, marking the end of the Shah's thirty-seven-year reign, as well as 2,500 years of monarchy. Khomeini immediately began to erase all vestiges of Western culture from Iran, with the notable exception of weapons technology. Crushing his opposition (which included many moderates who had also opposed the Shah) with a level of violence that equalled or exceeded that of the Shah, he began enforcing edicts concerning all facets of Iranian life, including dress, personal hygiene, and sexual activity of all descriptions. These edicts are detailed in the book *A Clarification of Questions,* which lists Khomeini as author.

In a Toronto *Globe & Mail* review of *A Clarification of Questions,* Zuhair Kashmeri described the book as "a tangled behavior code of 2,897 proscriptions formalized in the fifties to which each current grand ayatollah automatically lends his authorship." Donald Shojai, in a review for the *Los Angeles Times Book Review,* wrote: "Despite glaring drawbacks, the book has value. . . . [It] reveals the extent to which the purity code can dominate thinking in Shi'ite Islam." Shojai concluded his review with the observation that "the last section, in Khomeini's own words, drives the nail home: A priest can preach hatred while pointing the way to heaven."

During the period when Khomeini was consolidating his power, the United States, fearful of a cutoff of Iranian oil, observed the developments with caution. Lowered oil revenues for Iran—the result of strikes among oil workers, which had helped to topple the Shah—and the general chaos resulting from the revolution had virtually crippled the Iranian economy. Khomeini's dislike of the United States was real enough, but labeling the West as "the Great Satan" also benefited Khomeini by serving as a rallying point to unify the Iranians against a common enemy.

The full extent of Khomeini's hatred for the United States became apparent on November 4, 1979—precisely fifteen years after his exile to Turkey—when a large mob led by an armed group of "student militants" stormed the U.S. Embassy in Teheran. The embassy was ransacked and the bound, blindfolded embassy personnel were paraded through the jeering crowd before the astonished eyes of American television viewers. When horrified Western diplomats appealed to Khomeini to observe international convention and release the embassy personnel, the Ayatollah claimed to have no control over the acts of the students.

Undaunted by U.S. diplomatic appeals and threats, the Iranians hinted that they might put on trial and execute the hostages as spies. They also demanded that the United States assist in returning the terminally ill Shah to Iran to stand trial. When it became apparent that the United States would not, or could not, comply, Khomeini declared that no further progress on the release of the hostages could be made until the American people voted President Jimmy Carter out of office and replaced him with a president more "suitable to" Iran.

Following a failed rescue attempt by the U.S. military, the frustration and sense of helplessness felt by the United States seemed nearly complete. This, along with other factors, was believed by many political observers to contribute to Carter's defeat by Ronald Reagan in the 1980 presidential election. Finally, on the day Reagan was sworn into office in January, 1981, it was announced that after 444 days in captivity the hostages would be released.

Following the return of the fifty-two Americans, Khomeini's attention turned to other methods of spreading his Islamic revolution. He started a protracted, bloody war with neighboring Iraq, a war which saw poorly equipped Iranian forces decimated in human-wave assaults against the outnumbered but better-equipped troops of Iraq. Westerners recognized the effort as suicidal, but the Iranians perceived their fallen as heroes, martyrs to the cause of Islam, inspiring even more support for the *jihad,* or holy war. Khomeini also offered aid to others engaged in state-sponsored terrorism against the West—most notably the Palestinian Liberation Organization and Shi'ite rebels in Lebanon—by providing weapons and training.

By 1988, the war with Iraq had claimed nearly one million Iranian lives and had all but toppled the nation's economy. In August of that year, Khomeini agreed to the terms of a United Nations-sponsored peace treaty with Iraq—a decision he described as "more deadly than drinking poison." The two countries maintained an uneasy peace thereafter; during 1991's Gulf War, in fact, several Iraqi planes fled to Iran to seek refuge.

Khomeini once again made headlines in February, 1989, when he issued a *fatwa,* a religious edict calling for the death of British author Salman Rushdie, who had written the novel *The Satanic Verses* containing what many believed to be blasphemous depictions of the prophet Muhammed. "It is incumbent on every Muslim to do everything possible to send him to hell," he announced. Not only did this declaration further sour most foreigners' perceptions of the Ayatollah, it led to Britain all but severing its political ties with Iran.

Khomeini's writings reflected not only the political differences between the Islamic fundamentalists and the West, but also pointed out the basic philosophical and cultural differences that resulted in years of war and hatred, opening a gap in understanding between the West and the Middle East. In a *Village Voice* review of *Sayings of the Ayatollah Khomeini,* Eliot Fremont-Smith cautioned Westerners that misunderstanding and misperception existed on both sides of the conflict; in particular, he suspected the translators, editors, and publishers of the book of taking liberties

with the text, deliberately twisting Khomeini's religious writings ridiculously out of context: "Of course, for the sophisticated soul, the book is a barrel (or teacup) of laughs; but it's very hard to accept that Bantam [the book's publisher], [Tony] Hendra [the English-language edition editor], et al. didn't intend the book as an American *amusement*—even calling it 'The Little Green Book'—which makes those of us with a secular ethic (beginning with honesty and diffusing, if we're nervous enough, into empathy and certain practical moratoriums) squirm. And I resent it. I resent the messiness in France [where the original selection and translation of the book took place] and now at Bantam that seems to take advantage of every ignorance, and present a probably authentic selection of fundamentalist rules as a possible parody. It smacks of a marketing decision: Insight for citizens (however belatedly, we *are* interested) takes second place to continuing dumb exclamation."

However hated or mistrusted by the rest of the world, at the time of his death in June, 1989, Khomeini was worshipped by the people of Iran, as evidenced by the one million citizens who attended the Ayatollah's funeral. Wild with grief, thousands of people stormed the gravesite, surging through a protective barrier to seize the leader's casket, sending the body tumbling into the crowd. Several people were crushed in the ensuing riot, more than 11,000 were injured (many falling into the open grave) and thousands more succumbed to the hundred-degree heat. "People love him too much to let him go," a young student explained in the London *Times,* "everyone wanted a piece of him."

Political pundits were divided as to the effect of Khomeini's rule. A London *Times* obituary described the Ayatollah's reign as, "in all significant respects, a disaster. For Iran it was comparable to the Mongolian invasion of the 13th Century. For neighbouring Islamic nations his effect was to frighten moderate leadership and paralyse reform." *Newsweek*'s Harry Anderson observed that, since Khomeini did not choose a successor, his death "leaves behind a country demoralized and devoid of a charismatic figure capable of fulfilling [Khomeini's] dual religious and political roles." A writer for *Time,* however, compared Khomeini to other great twentieth-century revolutionaries: "Like the Soviet Union's Vladimir Lenin, he fomented a revolution from distant exile, then returned to try to bend it to his will. Like India's Mohandas Gandhi, he mobilized spiritual forces for political ends. Like China's Mao Zedong, he attempted to push beyond nationalism to ideological and cultural revolution, believing that by destroying the old order, he could create the conditions for the emergence of a utopia."

BIOGRAPHICAL/CRITICAL SOURCES:

BOOKS

Gordon, Matthew, *Ayatollah Khomeini*, Chelsea House, 1987.

Taheri, Amir, *The Spirit of Allah*, Hutchinson, 1988.

PERIODICALS

America, March 20, 1982.

American Spectator, August, 1989, p. 12; October, 1989, p. 8.

Economist, April 2, 1988, p. 81; June 10, 1989, p. 35; September 9, 1989, p. 109.

Globe & Mail (Toronto), May 11, 1985.

Los Angeles Times Book Review, December 2, 1984.

Maclean's, June 19, 1989.

Middle East Journal, spring, 1983.

National Review, June 30, 1989, p. 15.

New Republic, June 18, 1984; September 4, 1989, p. 35.

Newsweek, January 29, 1979; February 12, 1979; March 12, 1979; March 19, 1979; April 30, 1979; June 11, 1979; August 6, 1979; August 13, 1979; August 27, 1979; September 3, 1979; November 26, 1979; December 3, 1979; December 10, 1979; December 24, 1979; December 31, 1979; June 12, 1989, p. 40.

New York Review of Books, July 20, 1989, p. 16.

New York Times, December 11, 1979.

New York Times Magazine, October 7, 1979.

People, March 5, 1979.

Time, January 29, 1979; February 5, 1979; February 12, 1979; February 19, 1979; February 26, 1979; March 12, 1979; March 19, 1979; April 30, 1979; June 18, 1979; July 16, 1979; August 27, 1979; September 3, 1979; October 1, 1979; October 22, 1979; November 26, 1979; December 3, 1979; December 10, 1979; December 17, 1979; December 24, 1979; December 31, 1979; January 7, 1980; June 12, 1989, p. 36.

Times (London), January 1, 1985; June 7, 1989.

Times Literary Supplement, March 21, 1986, p. 293.

Village Voice, April 7, 1980.

OBITUARIES:

PERIODICALS

Los Angeles Times, June 4, 1989.

Times (London), June 5, 1989.

Washington Post, June 12, 1989.*

*   *   *

KHUMEINI, Ruhollah
   See KHOMEINI, Ruhollah (Mussavi)

KITUOMBA
   See ODAGA, Asenath (Bole)

*   *   *

KNIGHT, Mallory T.
   See HURWOOD, Bernhardt J.

*   *   *

KNIGHTS, L(ionel) C(harles) 1906-

PERSONAL: Born May 15, 1906, in Grantham, Lincolnshire, England; son of C. E. and Lois M. (Kenney) Knights; married Elizabeth Mary Barnes, October 31, 1936; children: Charles Benjamin, Christine Frances. *Education:* Cambridge University, B.A., 1928, M.A., 1931, Ph.D., 1936.

ADDRESSES: Home—11 Summerville, Durham DM1 4QH, England.

CAREER: University of Manchester, Manchester, England, assistant lecturer in English, 1933-34, senior lecturer in English, 1935-47; University of Sheffield, Sheffield, England, professor of English literature, 1947-52; University of Bristol, Bristol, England, Winterstoke Professor of English, 1953-64; Cambridge University, Cambridge, England, fellow of Queen's College, 1965-73, King Edward VII Professor of English Literature, 1965-73, professor emeritus, 1973—. Visiting Andrew Mellon Professor of English, University of Pittsburgh, 1961-62; Beckman Visiting Professor, University of California, Berkeley, 1970. Fellow, Kenyon School of Letters, 1950; lecturer, British Council in Germany, Austria, Italy, and India.

MEMBER: American Academy of Arts and Sciences (honorary member).

AWARDS, HONORS: Docteur de l'univ., University of Bordeaux, 1964; honorary doctorates from University of York, 1969, University of Manchester, 1974, University of Sheffield, 1978, University of Warwich, 1979, and University of Bristol, 1984; honorary fellow, Selwyn College, Cambridge University, 1974.

WRITINGS:

How Many Children Had Lady Macbeth, Minority Press, 1933.

Drama and Society in the Age of Jonson, Chatto & Windus, 1937, Norton, 1968.

Explorations: Essays in Criticism, Chatto & Windus, 1946.

Shakespeare's Politics (annual Shakespeare lecture), British Academy, 1957.

Some Shakespearean Themes, Chatto & Windus, 1959.

An Approach to Hamlet, Chatto & Windus, 1960.

(Editor with Basil Cottle) *Metaphor and Symbol,* Butterworth & Co., 1960.

Further Explorations, Stanford University Press, 1965.

Public Voices: Literature and Politics, Chatto & Windus, 1971, Rowman & Littlefield, 1972.

Explorations III, University of Pittsburgh Press, 1976.

Hamlet and Other Shakespearean Essays, Cambridge University Press, 1979.

Selected Essays in Criticism, Cambridge University Press, 1981.

Contributor to periodicals, including *Southern Review, Kenyon Review,* and *New York Review of Books.* Member of editorial board, *Scrutiny,* 1932-53.

*   *   *

KOLIN, Philip C(harles) 1945-

PERSONAL: Born November 21, 1945, in Chicago, IL; married Janeen L. Cufaude (a registered nurse), 1968 (divorced); children: Eric, Kristen. *Education:* Illinois State Teachers College, Chicago-South (now Chicago State University), B.S. (with highest honors), 1966; University of Chicago, M.A., 1967; Northwestern University, Ph.D., 1973. *Religion:* Roman Catholic.

ADDRESSES: Home—3004 Mesa Dr., Hattiesburg, MS 39402. *Office*—Department of English, University of Southern Mississippi, Hattiesburg, MS 39406-8395.

CAREER: Western Illinois University, Macomb, instructor in English, 1967-68; Illinois State University, Normal, instructor in English, 1968-70; Milton College, Milton, WI, assistant professor of English, 1973-74; University of Southern Mississippi, Hattiesburg, assistant professor, 1974-78, associate professor, 1978-83, professor of English, 1983—; Charles W. Moorman Alumni Distinguished Professor in the Humanities, 1991—. Institutions of Higher Learning, State of Mississippi, co-chairman of mindpower scholarship committee, 1984, and Mindpower Scholarship Contest, 1985.

MEMBER: South Central Modern Language Association, South Atlantic Modern Language Association, Mississippi Folklore Society, American Society for Theatre Research.

AWARDS, HONORS: Book-of-the Year Award, *American Journal of Nursing,* 1981, for *Professional Writing for Nurses in Education, Practice, and Research;* award for editing "best new journal," Council of Editors of Learned Journals, 1986, for *Studies in American Drama, 1945-Present;* summer research award and research grants, University of Southern Mississippi, 1986; nominated for

Hewitt Award in Theatre History, 1989, for *David Rabe: A Stage History and a Primary and Secondary Bibliography.*

WRITINGS:

The Elizabethan Stage Doctor as a Dramatic Convention, Salzburg Studies in English (Salzburg, Austria), 1975.

(With Janeen L. Kolin) *Professional Writing for Nurses in Education, Practice, and Research,* Mosby, 1980.

Successful Writing at Work, Heath, 1982, 4th edition, 1994.

(Editor) *Shakespeare in the South: Essays on Performance,* University Press of Mississippi, 1983.

(With Kolin) *Models for Technical Writing,* St. Martin's, 1985.

(Editor) *Shakespeare and Southern Writers: A Study in Influence,* University Press of Mississippi, 1985.

(Editor, with J. Madison Davis) *Critical Essays on Edward Albee,* University Press of Mississippi, 1986.

David Rabe: A Stage History and a Primary and Secondary Bibliography, Garland, 1988.

Conversations with Edward Albee, University Press of Mississippi, 1988.

American Playwrights since 1945: A Guide to Scholarship, Criticism, and Performance, Greenwood Press, 1989.

Feminist Criticism of Shakespeare's Plays: An Annotated Bibliography and a Commentary, Garland Publishing, 1991.

Confronting Tennessee Williams's A Streetcar Named Desire: Essays in Critical Pluralism, Greenwood Press, 1992.

Roses for Sharron: Poems, Colonial Press, 1993.

Critical Essays on Titus Andronicus (part of "Garland Shakespeare Criticism" series), Garland Publishing, 1994.

Also author of *Instructor's Guide to Successful Writing at Work,* Heath, 1982, 4th edition, 1994, and *Instructor's Manual to Accompany Models for Technical Writing,* St. Martin's, 1985. Contributor of more than one hundred articles and reviews to literature, linguistic, theatre, and folklore journals. Co-founder and co-editor, with Colby H. Kullman, of *Studies in American Drama, 1945-Present;* co-editor of *Mississippi Folklore Register,* 1976-89; assistant editor of *Seventeenth-Century News;* member of editorial board of *Theatre Symposium;* general editor of "Garland Shakespeare Criticism" series, 1992—.

WORK IN PROGRESS: Twenty-three Interviews with Contemporary American Playwrights, Tennessee Williams as a Political Thinker, and *A Streetcar Named Desire on the World Stage.*

SIDELIGHTS: Philip C. Kolin told *CA:* "I have eclectic interests as the titles of my publications and the journals I have edited demonstrate: technical and business writing,

Shakespeare, popular culture, modern and contemporary American drama, especially the reputation and production of the plays of Tennessee Williams. I reap a great deal of satisfaction from writing and revising my works and from my editing and bibliographic work. These, for me, are complementary activities. In fact, editing others' works helps me to sharpen my own. I am proudest of winning a Book-of-the-Year Award for *Professional Writing for Nurses* (co-authored with Janeen L. Kolin, R.N.), doing the editions of *Successful Writing at Work,* and establishing (with Collby H. Kullman, my best friend) *Studies in American Drama, 1945-Present.* This journal, the only scholarly one exclusively devoted to American drama and theatre since World War II, has been needed for some time. My co-editor and I strive to publish the best scholarly articles we can find on theatre history, dramatic technique, performance theory, biography, and interpretation. *Studies* also publishes original theatre documents, reviews, and author/theme bibliographies. Few journals offer readers such variety. But then variety in subject matter and rhetorical approach is what I have sought.

"In the last few years I have sought to combine my research in theatre history and cultural studies by extensively publishing works on the reception of Tennessee Williams's plays, especially *A Streetcar Named Desire,* overseas and on multicultural interpretations of Williams's plays. My books in progress—on *Streetcar* on the world stage and on Williams as a political thinker—further my commitment to eclecticism. I am very grateful to God and to all those friends and family who have believed in me and my work."

*   *   *

KURALT, Charles (Bishop) 1934-

PERSONAL: Born September 10, 1934, in Wilmington, NC; son of Wallace Hamilton (a social worker) and Ina (a teacher; maiden name, Bishop) Kuralt; married Sory Guthery, 1957 (divorced); married Suzanna Folsom Baird, June 1, 1962; children (first marriage): Lisa Catherine, Susan Guthery. *Education:* University of North Carolina, B.A., 1955.

ADDRESSES: Office—CBS News, 524 West 57th St., New York, NY 10019.

CAREER: Charlotte News, Charlotte, NC, reporter and columnist, 1955-57; CBS News, Columbia Broadcasting System, New York, NY, writer, 1957-59, host of *Eyewitness to History,* 1959, correspondent for Latin American bureau, 1960-63, chief correspondent for U.S. West Coast, 1963, overseas correspondent until 1967, feature reporter

for "On the Road" segments, 1967—, anchor of *CBS News Sunday Morning,* 1979—.

MEMBER: Players Club (New York City).

AWARDS, HONORS: Ernie Pyle Memorial Award, Scripps-Howard Foundation, 1959; nine Emmy Awards, National Academy of Television Arts and Sciences, between 1969-92; George Foster Peabody Broadcasting Awards, the University of Georgia, 1969, 1976, and 1979; Media Award, Odyssey Institute, 1979; named Broadcaster of the Year, International Radio and Television Society, 1985.

WRITINGS:

To the Top of the World: The Adventures and Misadventures of the Plaisted Polar Expedition, March 28-May 4, 1967, Holt, 1968.
Dateline America, Harcourt, 1979.
On the Road with Charles Kuralt, Putnam, 1985.
Southerners: Portrait of a People, Oxmoor House, 1986.
(With Louis McGlohan) *North Carolina Is My Home,* East Woods, 1986.
A Life on the Road, Putnam, 1990.

Contributor to periodicals, including *Saturday Review, Field and Stream, TV Guide,* and *Reader's Digest.*

SIDELIGHTS: Charles Kuralt is known nationwide as the CBS News correspondent who combs the back roads of America in search of off-beat human interest stories. Kuralt's "On the Road" feature has been a part of the *CBS Nightly News* since 1967 and has offered "for many the unexpected, cheerful footnote to the evening news," to quote *Saturday Review* correspondent Peter Quinn Hackes. The affable Kuralt took to the road to find an antidote to the invariably grim fare that comprises most nightly newscasts. Margaret Engel notes in the *Washington Post Book World* that, in the process of compiling his "On the Road" sketches, Kuralt became "a reporter who devised a whole genre of journalism. He helped spawn a fascination with roadside America that one sees in newly issued books about diners, movie houses, gas stations, motels, rural artists and down-home restaurants."

The stories Kuralt reports translate easily into the print medium as well. Such books as *On the Road with Charles Kuralt* and *A Life on the Road* chronicle Kuralt's methods of obtaining his film vignettes and offer profiles of some of the interesting people he has met in his travels. Engel writes of *A Life on the Road:* "Armchair travelers should be grateful that for 33 years, their pioneer has been someone with the discipline, intelligence and compassion of Charles Kuralt. . . . This book is a welcome lift, an episodic discovery of the strengths and resourcefulness of people who achieved greatness in large and small ways." Both *On the Road with Charles Kuralt* and *A Life on the*

Road spent numerous weeks on the bestseller lists in 1985 and 1990, respectively.

Kuralt was born and raised in North Carolina. He spent most of his childhood on his grandparents' tobacco farm, and there he satisfied his yen for travel by reading *National Geographic* magazine. As a high school student he won a national essay award from the American Legion in its "Voice of Democracy" contest. The award included a visit to the White House to meet then-president Harry S. Truman as well as the honor of hearing Edward R. Murrow read the essay over the radio.

In college at the University of North Carolina, Kuralt served as editor of the campus newspaper, the *Daily Tar Heel.* He earned a bachelor's degree in 1955 and took a job as a reporter at the *Charlotte News* in North Carolina. It was there that he began his lifelong pursuit of human interest stories, in this case for a daily column in the newspaper.

At the tender age of twenty-three Kuralt became a news writer for the Columbia Broadcasting System (CBS) in New York City. He joined CBS in 1957 as a copywriter for the radio division, but the following year he moved into television as a writer for the fifteen-minute CBS evening news show. By 1959 he was promoted to correspondent, and after covering the 1960 presidential campaigns he was sent to the Latin America bureau. After three years based in Rio de Janeiro, he returned to America as manager of the Los Angeles news bureau. Kuralt reported news from all over the globe, including Cuba, Vietnam, Asia, Africa, and Europe. He also prepared pieces for a documentary series called *CBS Reports.*

Eventually Kuralt began to question his own dedication to "hard news." He once told Arthur Unger of the *Christian Science Monitor:* "I was always worried that some NBC man was sneaking around behind my back getting better stories." A major career change came in 1967. Kuralt said: "I got the idea . . . one night in an airplane as I looked down at the lights in the countryside and wondered . . . what was going on down there. There are a lot of Americans who don't live in cities and don't make headlines. I was interested in finding out about them." From that idea "On the Road" was born. Kuralt convinced CBS management that he could find off-beat tales in America's back waters and small towns. He was given use of a second-hand motor home and the services of a cameraman and a sound technician. Together the three men set out to explore the country.

In *A Life on the Road,* reports Willie Morris of the Chicago *Tribune Books,* Kuralt wrote, " 'On the Road' seemed to work best when I went slow and took it easy. I found that while it helped to have a story in mind up the road somewhere . . . I might find something more interesting along the way. When I finally shook off the tempo of daily journalism and fell into the rhythms of the countryside, I didn't have to worry about finding stories any longer. They found me." Kuralt celebrated the ordinary from all over America in segments that "manage to charm and move the viewer without stooping to tricks or pressing the CUTE button," to quote *Washington Post Book World* contributor Dennis Drabelle. Over time, Kuralt's "On the Road" segments won several Emmy Awards and three George Foster Peabody awards for broadcast news reporting.

In the *Christian Science Monitor,* Kuralt said: "I have come to believe that it is useful to just once in awhile acknowledge that the whole country is not in flames and that everything going on in America is not represented by those big black headlines on page one." In the course of his travels, Kuralt has interviewed lumberjacks and cowpokes, fishermen and inventors, free spirits and philanthropists—many of whom have helped him confirm America's strengths as a nation. Quinn Hackes calls Kuralt simply "the bard of the byways."

Kuralt's best-known books are companions to his television pieces. *On the Road with Charles Kuralt* collects some of the more intriguing "On the Road" segments from the 1970s and 1980s. *A Life on the Road* is Kuralt's memoir of his discoveries great and small through two decades of almost constant travel. In a *Chicago Tribune* review of *A Life on the Road,* Morris writes: "Charles Kuralt's prose is clean, flexible and incisive, its context his own generous humanity. He himself is the best testimony to the quiet civilization that lies beneath our many layers."

Since 1979 Kuralt has also served as anchorman for the *CBS News Sunday Morning,* a program that offers his human interest topics as well as the breaking stories of the day. Reflecting on his four-decade career with CBS—and the success of "On the Road"—Kuralt told Charles Champlin of the *Los Angeles Times:* "Covering Congress is a life-absorbing job. But I'd rather do the small things. . . . Kids, cops, dogs, that kind of thing." He concluded: "I get to choose all my own stories. It's still the best job in television."

BIOGRAPHICAL/CRITICAL SOURCES:

PERIODICALS

Chicago Tribune, June 18, 1987; November 4, 1990.
Christian Science Monitor, July 24, 1974.
Los Angeles Times, June 17, 1987; October 14, 1988.
Newsweek, July 4, 1983.
New York Times, January 7, 1986.
New York Times Book Review, October 28, 1990.
Saturday Review, September/October, 1985.
Time, April 2, 1984.

Washington Post, August 25, 1979; April 28, 1981; June
   26, 1983.
Washington Post Book World, October 13, 1985; October
   28, 1990.*

—Sketch by Anne Janette Johnson

L

LACEY, Robert 1944-

PERSONAL: Born January 3, 1944, in Guildford, Surrey, England; son of Leonard John (a banker) and Vida (Winch) Lacey; married Alexandra Jane Avrach (a graphic designer), April 3, 1971; children: Sasha (son), Scarlett, Bruno. *Education:* Selwyn College, Cambridge, B.A., 1966, diploma of education, 1967, M.A., 1970.

ADDRESSES: Agent—Janklow & Nesbit Associates, 598 Madison Ave., New York, NY 10022-1614.

CAREER: Writer. *Illustrated London News,* London, England, writer, 1968; *Sunday Times,* London, assistant editor of *Sunday Times Magazine,* 1969-73, "Look!" page, editor, 1973-74.

WRITINGS:

Robert, Earl of Essex, Atheneum, 1971, published in England as *Robert, Earl of Essex: An Elizabethan Icarus,* Weidenfeld & Nicolson, 1971.
The Life and Times of Henry VIII, Weidenfeld & Nicolson, 1972, Abbeville Press, 1992.
The Queens of the North Atlantic, Sidgwick & Jackson, 1973.
Sir Walter Ralegh, Weidenfeld & Nicolson, 1973, Atheneum, 1973.
Majesty: Elizabeth II and the House of Windsor, Harcourt, 1977, revised edition, Sphere, 1978.
The Kingdom, Hutchinson, 1981, Avon, 1983.
Princess, Times Books, 1982.
Aristocrats (based on television series of same name; also see below), BBC Publications/Hutchinson, 1983.
Ford: The Men and the Machine, Little, Brown, 1986.
God Bless Her!, Century, 1987.
Little Man: Meyer Lansky and the Gangster Life, Little, Brown, 1991.

EDITOR AND CONTRIBUTOR

The French Revolution: A Collection of Contemporary Documents, Grossman, Volume 1: *The Fall of the Bastille,* 1968, Volume 2: *The Terror,* 1968, revised edition published in one volume as *The French Revolution,* Jackdaw, 1976.
The Rise of Napoleon, Grossman, 1971.
The Pallisers: A Full Guide to the Serial, BBC Publications, 1971.
The Peninsular War, Grossman, 1971.
The Retreat from Moscow, 1812, Grossman, 1971.
War and Peace: A Full Guide to the Serial, British Broadcasting Corp., 1972.
Drake and the "Golden Hinde": A Collection of Contemporary Documents, Jackdaw, 1975.
Elizabeth II: The Work of the Queen; A Collection of Documents, Jackdaw, 1977.

OTHER

Also author of documentary series *Aristocrats,* broadcast on BBC-TV. Contributor to periodicals.

SIDELIGHTS: British historian, journalist, and biographer Robert Lacey specializes in a particular type of "anthropological" biography that analyzes its subject—usually an elite family or a representative individual—in order to illuminate the customs, beliefs, and rituals of an entire segment of society. To get inside his subjects—which have included the British Royal Family, the founding chieftain of Saudi Arabia, and Henry Ford and his automobile company—Lacey has gone to great lengths to gain their trust. For example, he learned Arabic and moved to Saudia Arabia for eighteen months in order to research his history of that country, entitled *The Kingdom.* "I feel it's one of the duties of a biographer to go through a stage of seeing the world exactly as his subject sees or saw it," Robert Lacey once told *CA.* "I just don't understand people who write books which are dismissive of their subjects. I can't imagine myself devoting three or four years to studying something for which I have no respect or interest."

Lacey completed two biographies, *Robert, Earl of Essex* and *Sir Walter Ralegh,* while on the editorial staff of the London *Sunday Times.* On the strength of those critically acclaimed books, he was commissioned to write a history of the reign of Queen Elizabeth II, which he commenced in 1974. Published three years later to coincide with the queen's Silver Jubilee, *Majesty: Elizabeth II and the House of Windsor* became an international bestseller that established Lacey's reputation for accuracy, fairness, thorough scholarship, and a lively prose style.

"If Elizabeth II were not a queen, no one would write a book about her," Lacey observed in *Majesty,* pinpointing one of the primary difficulties he had in enlivening his subject, who was an ordinary woman in extraordinary circumstances, for his readers. He overcame that obstacle in part by emphasizing the queen's role in the public's imagination and her function as a *tabula rasa* onto which people project their fantasies and opinions of royalty. As the symbol of British nationalism, the queen is almost universally revered in her own country, where people's admiration for her presented Lacey with yet another problem in writing his book. "It was very difficult to get people to say anything uncomplimentary about her," he remarked to *CA.* "The British royal head of state is almost an icon," he continued. "It is one of her valuable functions to stand for everything that people agree upon, while politicians concentrate on what people disagree about. . . . So one is dealing there with a very precious part of the way the country runs."

In researching his next book, *The Kingdom,* Lacey faced almost the opposite set of circumstances, in which the Arab people would criticize their ruler bluntly on a face-to-face basis but would strenuously avoid putting their complaints in writing. Lacey explained to *CA* that in Saudi Arabia "there are two sorts of truth: the spoken truth and the written truth. The spoken truth is close to the Western idea of the truth. If you are talking, you can gossip and you can criticize. . . . But when it came to writing, which was my job, writing is like carving out the tablets in marble. This is something which is preserved forever and where you don't have any criticism." Indeed, *The Kingdom* was banned in Saudi Arabia because of its unflattering depictions of the bedouins and its impartial treatment of Abdul Aziz Ibn Sa'ud, the country's founding ruler. In the West, however, the book was very well received. In his review for *Chicago Tribune Book World,* Milton Viorst described Lacey's tone as "fair without being bland, understanding without being apologetic. His sense of balance keeps him to the essentials of the story, preserving him

from such labyrinths as international economics and intra-Arab relations. His sure hand makes a forbidding culture intelligible. *The Kingdom* must be ranked as a model work of popular history."

Lacey turned to lighter subjects for his next two publications, *Princess,* a handsome pictorial biography of Diana, Princess of Wales, and *Aristocrats,* a survey of European nobility produced in conjunction with his BBC-TV documentary series of the same name. Neither book received serious critical attention, but both were judged competent treatments of their themes. London *Times* contributor Tim Heald described *Aristocrats* as "an imaginative attempt to make a book out of a TV series." Reviewing *Princess* for the *Times Literary Supplement,* Victoria Glendinning wrote that Lacey "knows more than he has space to write, so within his fairy-story framework every sentence makes its point, and he still finds room for anecdote and dialogue."

Turning to the United States for inspiration for his next project, an examination of four generations of the Ford family and their automotive empire, Lacey, in typical fashion, moved to Michigan in 1984 to conduct research, which included working on an assembly line in a Detroit auto plant. The result of his labor, *Ford: The Men and the Machine,* was published two years later to enthusiastic reviews. Writing in the *New York Times Book Review,* biographer Ted Morgan found that "*Ford* is really two books in one, in which Robert Lacey has indefatigably combed the archives and beguiled 100 birds of various plumage to sing. The first is an Alger-ish account of Henry Ford's triumph. . . . The second book is like a television serial. It is as rich in incident and character as the prime-time soaps and requires no suspension of disbelief, being true." Morgan concluded that "Robert Lacey has made the transition to the American industrial monarch with no loss of panache." "Lacey's research is prodigious," Ruth Clements noted in her review for the Toronto *Globe and Mail,* "but the impressive accumulation of facts and anecdotes does not in itself account for the book's appeal. It is Lacey's insights into the American psyche—restless, driven, and teeming with unresolved tensions—that give this book its depth and dynamic edge."

Lacey investigated another realm of American mythology—the glamorization of organized crime—in his well-received 1991 biography of the Mafia's accountant Meyer Lansky, on whose life the character of Hyman Roth in the first two *Godfather* movies was based. "Americans cherish their gangsters," Lacey stated in *Little Man: Meyer Lansky and the Gangster Life.* "They delight in the myths of cleverness, power, and wealth which they wreath around these defective outlaws." Evaluating the biography for the *New York Times Book Review,* one critic deemed *Little Man* to be "a useful and informative corrective, an exercise in demythologizing that we do well to take to heart. It does not have the narrative sweep of Lacey's exemplary history of the Ford family and it is longer than need be, but it is sober, balanced and persuasive." Describing Lacey's technique in his review for *Newsweek*, Malcolm Jones, Jr., commended the author for cleverly using "the minutiae of Lansky's existence—what he ate, what he wore, the inscription on his dog's tombstone—not to bring the legend to life but to show that behind the myths there wasn't much life there to start with. Dour and wittily deflating, *Little Man* is a scrupulous, scathing indictment of the gangster life."

For a previously published interview, see entry in *Contemporary Authors New Revision Series,* Volume 16, Gale, 1986, pp. 208-214.

BIOGRAPHICAL/CRITICAL SOURCES:

BOOKS

Lacey, Robert, *Majesty: Elizabeth II and the House of Windsor,* Harcourt, 1977, revised edition, Sphere, 1978.
Lacey, Robert, *Little Man: Meyer Lansky and the Gangster Life,* Little, Brown, 1991.

PERIODICALS

Chicago Tribune, July 3, 1986, p. 3.
Chicago Tribune Book World, March 7, 1982.
Detroit Free Press, May 4, 1986.
Globe and Mail (Toronto), August 2, 1986; August 22, 1987; November 30, 1991.
Los Angeles Times Book Review, August 3, 1986, p. 4; November 10, 1991, p. 1.
Newsweek, November 11, 1991, p. 71.
New Yorker, September 8, 1986, p. 137.
New York Times, June 9, 1971; February 23, 1977; June 26, 1986.
New York Times Book Review, July 13, 1986, pp. 1, 36-37; October 20, 1991, p. 29; October 13, 1993, p. 3.
Spectator, October 26, 1991, p. 37.
Time, November 4, 1991, p. 93.
Times (London), October 20, 1983.
Times Literary Supplement, September 19, 1968, p. 1023; June 25, 1982; February 7, 1992, p. 6.

*   *   *

LACOUTURE, Jean Marie Gerard   1921-

PERSONAL: Born June 9, 1921, in Bordeaux, France; son of Antoine Joseph (a surgeon) and Anne-Marie (Servantie) Lacouture; married Simonne Gresillon (a writer), August 28, 1951. *Education:* Free School of Political Science, diploma, 1941; attended University of Paris, 1942; re-

ceived doctorate in sociology, Sorbonne, 1960s. *Religion:* Roman Catholic.

ADDRESSES: Home—143 rue d'Alesia, 75014 Paris, France.

CAREER: Headquarters of General Leclerc, press attache in Indochina, 1945-47, member of French general staff in Morocco, 1947-49; diplomatic editor of *Combat,* 1950-51; *Le Monde,* diplomatic editor, 1951-53, head of overseas service, 1957, then chief reporter; Egyptian correspondent for *France-Soir,* 1954-56. Professor at Institute of Political Studies, Paris, 1964-78; lecturer, Universite de Vincennes. Editor, *Etudes mediterraneennes,* 1957-62; general editor, Editions du Seuil, 1961-77. *Military service:* Army, 1944-46.

AWARDS, HONORS: Fellow, Harvard University.

WRITINGS:

IN ENGLISH TRANSLATION

(With wife, Simonne Lacouture) *L'Egypte en mouvement,* Editions du Seuil, 1956, revised edition, 1962, translation by Francis Scarfe published as *Egypt in Transition,* Criterion, 1958.
(With Philippe Devillers) *La Fin d'une guerre: Indochine, 1954,* Editions du Seuil, 1960, revised translation by Alexander Lieven and Adam Roberts published as *End of a War: Indochina, 1954,* Praeger, 1969.
Le Vietnam entre deux paix, Editions du Seuil, 1965, translation by Konrad Kellen and Joel Carmichael published as *Vietnam: Between Two Truces,* Random House, 1966.
De Gaulle, Editions du Seuil, 1965, new edition, 1969, translation by Francis K. Price published as *De Gaulle,* New American Library, 1966, revised edition translated by Price and John Skeffington, Hutchinson, 1970.
Ho Chi Minh, Editions du Seuil, 1967, revised edition, 1977, translation by Peter Wiles published as *Ho Chi Minh: A Political Biography,* edited by Jane Clark Seitz, Random House, 1968.
Quatre Hommes et leurs peuples: Sur-pouvoir et sous-developpement, Editions du Seuil, 1969, translation by Patricia Wolf published as *The Demigods: Charismatic Leadership in the Third World,* Knopf, 1970.
Nasser, Editions du Seuil, 1971, translation by Daniel Hofstadter published as *Nasser: A Biography,* Random House, 1973.
Andre Malraux: Une Vie dans le siecle, Editions du Seuil, 1973, new edition, 1976, translation by Alan Sheridan published as *Andre Malraux,* Pantheon, 1975.
(With Mahmoud Hussein and Saul Friedlaender) *Arabes et Israeliens: Un Premier Dialogue,* Editions du Seuil,

1974, translation published as *Arabs and Israelis,* Holmes & Meier, 1975.

Leon Blum, Editions du Seuil, 1977, translation by George Holoch published as *Leon Blum,* Holmes & Meier, 1982.

Pierre Mendes France, Editions du Seuil, 1981, translation by Holoch published as *Pierre Mendes France,* Holmes & Meier, 1984.

Charles de Gaulle (three volumes), Editions du Seuil, 1984-86, translation published as *De Gaulle* (two volumes), Volume 1: translation by Patrick O'Brian as *De Gaulle, the Rebel, 1890-1944,* Volume 2: translation by Alan Sheridan as *De Gaulle, the Ruler, 1945-1970,* Norton, 1990-92.

(Author of introduction) *Robert Capa,* Centre national de la photographie, translation by Abigail Pollak published as *Robert Capa,* Pantheon Books, 1989.

(Contributor) William Manchester, *In Our Time: The World as Seen by Magnum Photographers,* American Federation of Arts/Norton, 1989.

Also author with S. Lacouture of *Israel and Arabs: The Third Combat,* 1967.

IN FRENCH

(With S. Lacouture) *Le Maroc a l'epreuve* (title means "Morocco's Ordeal"), Editions du Seuil, 1958.

Cinq Hommes et la France (title means "Five Men and France"), Editions du Seuil, 1961.

(With Jean Baumier) *Le Poids du tiers monde: Un Milliard d'hommes* (title means "The Weight of the Third World"), Arthaud, 1962.

(Editor) Charles de Gaulle, *Les citations du President de Gaulle,* (title means "Quotations of President de Gaulle"), Editions du Seuil, 1968.

(With Philippe Devillers) *Vietnam,* Editions du Seuil, 1969.

Un Sang d'encre: Conversations avec Claude Glayman, Stock, 1974.

(With Gabriel Dardaud) *Les Emirats mirages,* Editions du Seuil, 1975.

(Author of introduction) Georges Buis, *Les Fanfares perdues,* Editions du Seuil, 1975.

(Author of introduction) Alexandre Minkowski, *Le Mandarin aux pieds nues,* Editions du Seuil, 1975.

(With S. Lacouture) *Vietnam: Voyage a travers une victoire,* Editions du Seuil, 1976.

(Co-author of introduction) Haroun Tazieff, *Jouer avec le feu,* Editions du Seuil, 1976.

Survive le peuple cambodgien!, Editions du Seuil, 1978.

Le Rugby: C'est un monde, Editions du Seuil, 1979.

Francois Mauriac, Editions du Seuil, 1980.

Le pieton de Bordeaux, photography by Michel Guillard, ACE, 1981.

(With S. Lacouture) *En passant par la France; journal de voyage,* Editions du Seuil, 1982.

(Author of introduction) Y Phandara, *Retour a Phnom Penh; le Cambodge du genocide a la colonisation,* Editions A. M. Metailie, 1982.

Profils perdus; 53 portraits de notre temps, Editions A. M. Metailie, 1983.

(Interviewer) Miguel Angel Estrella, *Musique pour l'esperance,* Cana/J. Offredo (Paris), 1983.

(Co-author of introduction) Francois Mauriac, *L'imitation des bourreaux de Jesus Christ,* Desclee de Brouwer (Paris), 1984.

Champollion, une view de lumieres, B. Grasset (Paris), 1988.

(With Roland Mehl) *De Gaulle, ou, L'eternel defi; 56 temoignages,* Editions du Seuil, 1988.

Enquete sur l'auteur; reponse tardive a Andre Malraux sur quelques questions relatives a la condition de journaliste, Arlea, 1989.

(Contributor) *De Gaulle et les ecrivains,* edited by Jean Serroy, Presses universitaires de Grenoble, 1991.

Jesuites; une multibiographie, Editions du Seuil, 1991.

(With Marc Riboud) *Angkor, serenite bouddhique,* Impr. nationale editions, 1992.

Also author with Sihanouk of *L'Indochine vue de Pekin,* 1972.

SIDELIGHTS: Renowned political biographer Jean Marie Gerard Lacouture has written several books of breadth and complexity in depicting the careers of major twentieth-century leaders in the Middle East, Indochina and his native France. In *Ho Chi Minh,* Lacouture draws upon records of the French Surete, interviews with Ho Chi Minh's earlier Communist acquaintances, and his own experience in Vietnam as a correspondent for *Le Monde,* to write this political biography of the leader who organized the Vietnamese Communist party. Published in the United States in the midst of the Vietnam war, *Ho Chi Minh* offers insight into an ambiguous and often underestimated figure. Peter Arnett, reviewing the work in *Book World,* noted, "This frankly admiring political biography of North Vietnamese President Ho Chi Minh . . . shows to what degree the wispy-bearded leader influences and motivates his people, and—particularly significant at this time—how, throughout his life up to and including this second Vietnamese war, Ho has deliberately sought the propitious moment to negotiate or act."

Writing in the *New York Times Book Review,* George McT. Kahin observed, "This is a sympathetic biography, but Lacouture has made a clear effort to be objective, incorporating even Trotskyite criticism and emphasizing Ho's willingness to apply ruthless measures when he considered them politically necessary." Saul Maloff reached a similar conclusion in *Newsweek:* "Lacouture . . . has written a political biography of immense sophistication, especially in tracing and analyzing the convolutions of inner-party disputes and shifts of 'line.' He makes no bones about where his sympathies lie. He admires and respects Ho, though as a non-Communist he is also critical." In *Leon Blum,* Lacouture depicts the life of another physically frail and temperamentally self-effacing man of action. Leon Blum was the lawyer who assisted in the defense of Emile Zola when he was prosecuted for writing his "J'accuse" article denouncing Anti-Semitism and demanding justice during the Dreyfus Affair at the turn of the century; Blum later became the first Jew and the first Socialist to govern France as Prime Minister of the Popular Front Government. Jim Hoagland, in the *Washington Post Book World,* describes Lacouture's book as "a dazzling, complex work that appears in the guise of a biography of Leon Blum. But this book is far more. It is a biography of a social movement and its time."

According to Herbert R. Lottman, reviewing this biography in the *New York Times Book Review,* "The book contains a formidable quantity of first-hand material, and there is no pretense at objectivity; occasionally the text reads like campaign biography. Certainly Leon Blum deserves all the passionate admiration he gets here. . . ." Although Lacouture's stance towards Blum is sympathetic, he is also, at times, critical. In the *New York Review of Books,* Robert O. Paxton writes: "Lacouture is sufficiently immersed in post-Gaullist perspectives to deplore Blum's preoccupation with British approval and his admiration for Roosevelt's America—the subjects of Lacouture's harshest criticism, along with Blum's 'absurd' belief up to 1936 that one could simultaneously disarm and oppose Hitler." Paxton concludes, "The life of Leon Blum is well suited to the traditional political biography at which Jean Lacouture excels: a life fully integrated around reasonable discussion of public choices."

Lacouture's biography of Charles de Gaulle, hailed as his most ambitious work to date and published in the United States in two volumes as *De Gaulle,* is praised as a "magnificent biography" and as "a feast, robust, subtle, joyful, complex, a celebration to be savored" by Stephen E. Ambrose, who reviewed the first volume, *The Rebel, 1890-1944,* in the *New York Times Book Review.* "Lacouture draws a portrait of the leader of Free (later Fighting) France," writes Douglas Porch in the *Washington Post Book World,* "which places his actions in the context of his conservative upbringing, his brilliant but iconoclastic career in the French army prior to 1940, and an unswerving vision of France's great power role which he maintained through defeat, occupation and exile." Porch concludes, "After one reads this fair, well-researched and entertaining biography, de Gaulle may not become a more

sympathetic character. But he certainly emerges as a more comprehensible one."

In the *Times Literary Supplement,* Vincent Wright observes, "It is not difficult to see why *De Gaulle: The Ruler,* [the second of two volumes] was so well received. It tells a wonderful story wonderfully well. It is magnificently well informed, for Lacouture has read everything, knows many of the people he cites and has interviewed many he did not know personally. . . . And, no mean achievement, it is fair." On the other hand, Ambrose, in what is otherwise a highly positive review, argues: "This superb biography has a flaw, one that is consistent with the subject. It is an ignorance—really a willful ignorance—of the United States, its history, its politicians, its soldiers. . . . [Lacouture] describes Theodore Roosevelt as the conqueror of Cuba and inexcusably misplaces the locale of the American landings in Normandy on D-day."

Despite his praise for the breadth of the biography, Wright denies that it should necessarily be hailed as a "masterpiece." "Indeed," he contends, "*De Gaulle: The Ruler* suffers from two quite serious defects: it is too heavy on details and too light on sustained analysis." Viewing Lacouture's achievement differently, John Campbell in the London *Times* declares, "There have been many biographies of de Gaulle, but Jean Lacouture's is *the* biography. Both the scale and the style of his book match his subject."

BIOGRAPHICAL/CRITICAL SOURCES:

BOOKS

Guillemin, Henri, *Une certaine esperance; conversations avec Jean Lacouture,* Arlea, 1992.

PERIODICALS

Antioch Review, winter, 1969-70.
Book World, July 7, 1968.
Globe & Mail (Toronto), March 23, 1991.
Los Angeles Times Book Review, November 18, 1990, p. 4.
Nation, May 2, 1966; February 14, 1976.
New Republic, April 16, 1966; February 21, 1976; February 7, 1983, p. 35; April 8, 1985; December 17, 1990.
Newsweek, March 14, 1966; July 15, 1968; November 23, 1970; December 29, 1975.
New Yorker, November 15, 1958; June 11, 1966; September 3, 1973; March 22, 1976; February 11, 1991.
New York Review of Books, November 17, 1966; September 11, 1969; March 4, 1976; January 20, 1983, p. 16; June 13, 1985; April 23, 1992, p. 6.
New York Times, July 9, 1968.
New York Times Book Review, December 14, 1958; May 13, 1966; December 18, 1966; August 4, 1968; August 24, 1969; August 19, 1973; January 11, 1976; Decem-

ber 26, 1982, p. 4; April 21, 1985, p. 10; December 11, 1988, p. 38; November 11, 1990, p. 1; May 10, 1992, p. 3; May 31, 1992, p. 19.

Observer, November 18, 1990, p. 62; January 5, 1992, p. 42.

Saturday Review, December 27, 1958; April 9, 1966; November 12, 1966; January 30, 1971; January 24, 1976.

Spectator, May 10, 1968; May 16, 1970.

Time, July 19, 1968.

Times (London), January 19, 1991.

Times Educational Supplement, December 7, 1990, p. 28; January 31, 1992, p. 27.

Times Literary Supplement, February 20, 1959; February 9, 1967; May 2, 1968; November 13, 1969; July 7, 1971; May 30, 1980; July 10, 1981; August 16, 1985; February 1, 1991, p. 20; April 24, 1992, p. 23; August 7, 1992, p. 23.

Tribune Books (Chicago), December 9, 1990, p. 1; December 29, 1991, p. 6; April 12, 1992, p. 6.

Virginia Quarterly Review, spring, 1976.

Voice Literary Supplement, December, 1990, p. 29.

Washington Post Book World, March 6, 1983, p. 1; March 10, 1985, p. 7; December 30, 1990, p. 1; April 19, 1992, p. 4.*

*   *   *

LAUER, Jeanette C(arol) 1935-

PERSONAL: Born July 14, 1935, in St. Louis, MO; daughter of Clinton J. (an automobile worker) and Blanche A. (a bookkeeper; maiden name, Gideon) Pentecost; married Robert H. Lauer (a professor), July 2, 1954; children: Jon Robert, Julie Anne, Jeffrey David. *Education:* University of Missouri—St. Louis, B.S. (summa cum laude), 1970; Washington University, M.A., 1972, Ph.D., 1975. *Religion:* Presbyterian.

ADDRESSES: Home—13949 Davenport Ave., San Diego, CA 92129. *Office*—College of Liberal Studies, United States International University, 10455 Pomerado Rd., San Diego, CA 92131.

CAREER: Washington University, St. Louis, MO, instructor in history, 1972-73, summer, 1974; St. Louis Community College at Florissant Valley, Florissant, MO, assistant professor of history, 1974-82; United States International University, San Diego, CA, associate professor, 1983-89, professor of history, 1990—, dean of College of Liberal Studies, 1990—. Has presented numerous papers at conferences, conventions, and national meetings, 1976—.

MEMBER: American Historical Association, Organization of American Historians, American Studies Association, Association for Couples in Marriage Enrichment.

AWARDS, HONORS: Woodrow Wilson fellowship, 1970-71.

WRITINGS:

(With husband, Robert H. Lauer) *Fashion Power: The Meaning of Fashion in American Society,* Prentice-Hall, 1981.

(With R. H. Lauer) *The Spirit and the Flesh: Sex in Utopian Communities,* Scarecrow, 1983.

(With R. H. Lauer) *Til Death Do Us Part: How Couples Stay Together,* Haworth Press, 1986.

(With R. H. Lauer) *Watersheds: Mastering Life's Unpredictable Crises,* Little, Brown, 1988.

(With R. H. Lauer) *Marriage and Family: The Quest for Intimacy,* W. C. Brown, 1991, 2nd edition, 1993.

(With R. H. Lauer) *No Secrets: How Much Honesty Is Good for Your Marriage?,* Zondervan, 1993.

(With R. H. Lauer) *The Joy Ride: Everyday Ways to Lasting Happiness,* Abingdon, 1994.

Also contributor to books, including *Social Change: Conjectures, Explorations, and Diagnoses,* edited by George K. Zollschan and Walter Hirsh, Schenkman, 1976; *Biographical Dictionary of American Mayors, 1820-1980,* edited by Melvin G. Holli and Peter d'A. Jones, Greenwood Press, 1981; and *Encyclopedia of Southern Culture,* 1989. Co-editor of "Teaching History Today" column in *American Historical Association Newsletter,* 1980-89. Contributor to periodicals, including *International Review of History and Political Science, Canadian Review of American Studies, Journal of Family Issues, Journal of Popular Culture, Missouri Historical Review, Journal of Sociology and Social Welfare,* and *Psychology Today. Watersheds: Mastering Life's Unpredictable Crises* has been produced on audiotape by Nightingale-Conant.

Watersheds: Mastering Life's Unpredictable Crises has been translated into French and Portuguese.

WORK IN PROGRESS: Research on leadership in nineteenth- and twentieth-century communitarian groups, peak experiences, and a variety of topics concerning relationships.

SIDELIGHTS: Jeanette C. Lauer once told *CA:* "My research and writing have led me into diverse areas of study. For example, *Fashion Power* examines the meaning of fashion in America over the past two centuries. This meaning is explored by looking at clothing as nonverbal communication and at the perceived causes of fashion. It also looks at what fashion is believed to say about human nature and the nature of society, at how fashion relates to national identity, and at the consequences of fashion for health, the economy, family life, and personal growth. Fashion plays a vital role in our lives; this study furnishes insight into the nature of its role.

"Stress and change, like fashion, are constants of everyday experience. My current research centers on a sociohistorical examination of the relationship of stress and change in St. Louis from 1879 to 1929. I am examining numerous indicators of change and stress and considering their relationship to each other. Hopefully, this study will provide a better understanding of the impact change has on individuals and society as a whole."

*   *   *

LAUER, Robert H(arold)   1933-

PERSONAL: Born June 28, 1933, in St. Louis, MO; son of Earl Ervin and Frances P. (Bushen) Lauer; married Jeanette C. Pentecost, July 2, 1954; children: Jon Robert, Julie Anne, Jeffrey David. *Education:* Washington University, St. Louis, B.S. (magna cum laude), 1954, Ph.D., 1970; Southern Seminary, B.D., 1958; Southern Illinois University at Edwardsville, M.A., 1969.

ADDRESSES: Home—13949 Davenport Ave., San Diego, CA 92129. *Office*—School of Human Behavior, United States International University, San Diego, CA 92131.

CAREER: Orville Baptist Church, Orville, KY, pastor, 1956-58; Salem Baptist Church, Florissant, MO, pastor, 1958-68; Southern Illinois University at Edwardsville, lecturer, 1968-69, instructor, 1969-70, assistant professor, 1970-73, associate professor, 1973-75, professor of sociology, 1975-82, chairman of department, 1972-76; United States International University, San Diego, CA, dean of School of Human Behavior, 1983-87; La Jolla Presbyterian Church, La Jolla, CA, minister of Christian education, 1991—. Affiliate professor, United States International University, 1992—. Former vice-chairman of Florissant (MO) Charter Commission. Has conducted seminars and workshops in the United States, Indonesia, Thailand, and Costa Rica.

MEMBER: American Sociological Association, National Council on Family Relations, Association for Couples in Marriage Enrichment, Pacific Sociological Society, Tau Beta Pi.

AWARDS, HONORS: First Prize paper, Institute of Radio Engineers; selected as Outstanding Teacher by sociology students, Southern Illinois University, ten different years.

WRITINGS:

Science Object Lessons, Zondervan, 1968.
Perspectives on Social Change, Allyn & Bacon, 1973, 4th edition, 1991.
Social Problems, W. C. Brown, 1976.

(Editor) *Social Movements and Social Change,* Southern Illinois University Press, 1976.
(With Warren Handel) *Social Psychology: The Theory and Application of Symbolic Interaction,* Houghton, 1977, 2nd edition, Prentice-Hall, 1983.
Social Problems and the Quality of Life, W. C. Brown, 1978, 6th edition, 1994.
(With Bill R. Hampton) *Solving Problems in Secondary School Administration: A Human Organization Approach,* Allyn & Bacon, 1981.
(With wife, Jeanette C. Lauer) *Fashion Power: The Meaning of Fashion in American Society,* Prentice-Hall, 1981.
Temporal Man: The Meaning and Uses of Social Time, Praeger, 1981.
(With J. C. Lauer) *The Spirit and the Flesh: Sex in Utopian Communities,* Scarecrow, 1983.
(With J. C. Lauer) *Til Death Do Us Part: How Couples Stay Together,* Haworth Press, 1986.
(With J. C. Lauer) *Watersheds: Mastering Life's Unpredictable Crises,* Little, Brown, 1988.
(With J. C. Lauer) *Marriage and Family: The Quest for Intimacy,* W. C. Brown, 1991, 2nd edition, 1993.
(With J. C. Lauer) *No Secrets: How Much Honesty Is Good for Your Marriage?,* Zondervan, 1993.
(With J. C. Lauer) *The Joy Ride: Everyday Ways to Lasting Happiness,* Abingdon, 1994.

Also contributor to *Social Change: Conjectures, Explorations, and Diagnoses,* edited by George K. Zollschan and Walter Hirsh, Schenkman, 1976; and *Encyclopedia of Southern Culture,* 1989. Contributor of more than two hundred articles to periodicals, including *International Review of History and Political Science, Journal of Popular Culture, Canadian Review of American Studies, Missouri Historical Review, Journal of Sociology and Social Welfare, Journal of Family Issues,* and *Psychology Today. Watersheds: Mastering Life's Unpredictable Crises* has been produced on audiotape by Nightingale-Conant.

Watersheds: Mastering Life's Unpredictable Crises has been translated into French and Portuguese.

WORK IN PROGRESS: Research on marital relationships and leadership styles.

*   *   *

LAYTON, Irving (Peter)   1912-

PERSONAL: Original surname, Lasarovitch; name legally changed; born March 12, 1912, in Neamts, Rumania; immigrated to Canada, 1913; son of Moses and Keine (Moscovitch) Lasarovitch; married Faye Lynch, September 13, 1938 (divorced, 1946); married Frances Sutherland, September 13, 1946 (divorced, 1961); married Aviva Cantor (a writer of children's stories), September 13, 1961 (marriage dissolved); married Harriet Bernstein (a publicist; divorced, March 19, 1984); married Anna Pottier; children: (with Sutherland) Max Rubin, Naomi Parker; (with Cantor) David Herschel; (with Bernstein) Samantha Clara. *Education:* Macdonald College, B.Sc., 1939; McGill University, M.A., 1946.

ADDRESSES: Home—6879 Monkland Ave., Montreal, Quebec H4B 1J5, Canada.

CAREER: Jewish Public Library, Montreal, Quebec, lecturer, 1943-58; high school teacher in Montreal, 1945-60; Sir George Williams University (now Sir George Williams Campus of Concordia University), Montreal, lecturer, 1949-65, poet in residence, 1965-69; University of Guelph, Guelph, Ontario, poet in residence, 1969-70; York University, Toronto, Ontario, professor of English literature, 1970-78; Concordia University, Sir George Williams Campus, Montreal poet in residence 1978—. *Military service:* Canadian Army, Artillery, 1942-43; became lieutenant.

MEMBER: PEN.

AWARDS, HONORS: Canada Foundation fellow, 1957; Canada Council awards, 1959 and 1960; Governor-General's Award, 1959, for *A Red Carpet for the Sun;* President's Medal, University of Western Ontario, 1961, for poem "Keine Lasarovitch 1870-1959"; Prix Litteraire de Quebec, 1963, for *Balls for a One-Armed Juggler;* Canada Council Special Arts Award, 1963 and 1968; Centennial Medal, 1967; D.C.L., Bishops University, 1972, and Concordia University, 1975; Canada Council Senior Arts Fellowship and travel grant, 1973 and 1979; Order of Canada, 1976; *Encyclopedia Britannica* Life Achievement Award, 1978; Canada Council long term arts award, 1979-81.

WRITINGS:

POETRY, EXCEPT AS INDICATED

Here and Now, First Statement, 1945.
Now Is the Place (poems and stories), First Statement, 1948.
The Black Huntsmen, privately printed, 1951.
Love the Conqueror Worm, Contact, 1951.
(With Louis Dudek and Raymond Souster) *Cerberus,* Contact, 1952.
In the Midst of My Fever, Divers, 1954.
The Long Peashooter, Laocoon, 1954.
The Cold Green Element, Contact, 1955.
The Blue Propeller, Contact, 1955.
The Blue Calf, Contact, 1956.
Music on a Kazoo, Contact, 1956.

The Improved Binoculars (selected poems), introduction by William Carlos Williams, Jargon, 1956.
A Laughter in the Mind, Jargon, 1958.
A Red Carpet for the Sun (collected poems), McClelland & Stewart, 1959.
The Swinging Flesh (poems and short stories), McClelland & Stewart, 1961.
Balls for a One-Armed Juggler, McClelland & Stewart, 1963.
The Laughing Rooster, McClelland & Stewart, 1964.
Collected Poems, McClelland & Stewart, 1965.
Periods of the Moon, McClelland & Stewart, 1967.
The Shattered Plinths, McClelland & Stewart, 1968.
Selected Poems, McClelland & Stewart, 1969.
The Whole Bloody Bird: Obs, Aphs, and Pomes, McClelland & Stewart, 1969.
Nail Polish, McClelland & Stewart, 1971.
The Collected Poems of Irving Layton, McClelland & Stewart, 1971.
Lovers and Lesser Men, McClelland & Stewart, 1973.
The Pole-Vaulter, McClelland & Stewart, 1974.
Seventy-five Greek Poems, McClelland & Stewart, 1974.
The Darkening Fire: Selected Poems, 1945-1968, McClelland & Stewart, 1975.
The Unwavering Eye: Selected Poems, 1969-1975, McClelland & Stewart, 1975.
For My Brother Jesus, McClelland & Stewart, 1976.
The Covenant, McClelland & Stewart, 1977.
The Collected Poems of Irving Layton, McClelland & Stewart, 1977.
The Uncollected Poems of Irving Layton, 1936-1959, Mosaic Press, 1977.
The Selected Poems of Irving Layton, New Directions, 1977.
The Tightrope Dancer, McClelland & Stewart, 1978.
(With Carlo Mattioli) *Irving Layton, Carlo Mattioli,* Edizioni (Milan, Italy), 1978.
The Love Poems of Irving Layton, McClelland & Stewart, 1979.
Droppings from Heaven, McClelland & Stewart, 1979.
For My Neighbors in Hell, Mosaic Press, 1980.
Europe and Other Bad News, McClelland & Stewart, 1981.
A Wild Peculiar Joy, McClelland & Stewart, 1982.
Shadows on the Ground, Mosaic/Valley Editions, 1982.
The Gucci Bag, Mosaic Press, 1983.
The Love Poems of Irving Layton, with Reverence & Delight, Mosaic/Valley Editions, 1984.
A Spider Danced a Cozy Jig, Stoddart, 1984.
Dance with Desire: Love Poems, McClelland & Stewart, 1986.
Final Reckoning: Poems 1982-1986, Mosaic/Valley Editions, 1987.
Fortunate Exile, McClelland & Stewart, 1987.
Rawprint, The Workshop, 1989.

Fornalutx: Selected Poems, 1928-1990, University of Toronto Press, 1992.

Also author of *In un'eta di ghiaccio* (title means "In an Ice Age"; bilingual selected poems), 1981; (with Salvatore Fiume) *A Tall Man Executes a Jig* (portfolio), 1985; *Selected Poems,* [Seoul, South Korea], 1985; *Where Burning Sappho Loved,* [Athens, Greece], 1985; *A Wild Peculiar Joy: Selected Poems 1945-1989,* 1989; *Tutto Sommato Poesie 1945-88* (a bilingual Italian- English edition of selected poems), 1989.

Work represented in numerous anthologies, including *Book of Canadian Poetry,* edited by A. J. M. Smith, Gage, 1948; *Book of Canadian Stories,* edited by D. Pacey, Ryerson, 1950; *Canadian Short Stories,* edited by R. Weaver and H. James, Oxford University Press, 1952; *Oxford Book of Canadian Verse,* edited by Smith, Oxford University Press, 1960; *How Do I Love Thee: Sixty Poets of Canada (and Quebec) Select and Introduce Their Favourite Poems from Their Own Work,* edited by John Robert Colombo, M. G. Hurtig, 1970; *Il Freddo Verde,* edited by Giulio Einaudi, 1974; *Irving Layton/Aligi Sassu Portfolio,* 1978. Contributor of poetry and stories to various periodicals, including *Poetry, Canadian Forum,* and *Sail.*

EDITOR

(With Louis Dudek) *Canadian Poems, 1850-1952,* Contact, 1952, 2nd edition, 1953.
Pan-ic: A Selection of Contemporary Canadian Poems, Alan Brilliant, 1958.
Love Where the Nights Are Long: Canadian Love Poems, McClelland & Stewart, 1962.

Also editor and author of introduction, *Poems for Twenty-seven Cents,* [Montreal], 1961; and *Anvil Blood: A Selection of Workshop Poems,* [Toronto], 1973; editor of *Anvil: A Selection of Workshop Poems,* [Montreal], 1966; and *Shark Tank,* [Toronto], 1977. Cofounder and editor, *First Statement and Northern Review,* 1941-43; former associate editor, *Contact, Black Mountain Review,* and several other magazines.

OTHER

(Author of introduction) *Poems to Colour: A Selection of Workshop Poems,* York University, 1970.
Engagements: The Prose of Irving Layton, edited by Seymour Mayne, McClelland & Stewart, 1972.
Taking Sides (prose), McClelland & Stewart, 1977.
(With Dorothy Rath) *An Unlikely Affair: The Irving Layton-Dorothy Rath Correspondence,* Mosaic/Valley Editions, 1980.
(With David O'Rourke) *Waiting for the Messiah: A Memoir,* McClelland & Stewart, 1985.

Wild Gooseberries: Selected Letters of Irving Layton, 1939-89, edited by Francis Mansbridge, Macmillan, 1989.
(With Robert Creeley) *Irving Layton & Robert Creeley: The Complete Correspondence,* University of Toronto Press, 1990.

Layton's writings have been translated into more than ten languages, including Italian and Spanish. His papers are housed at the library of Concordia University.

ADAPTATIONS: Layton's poetry has been released on several audio recordings.

SIDELIGHTS: Irving Layton is considered one of Canada's most prolific and controversial poets. While critics have praised several of the most distinctive aspects of his work: the fact that his best poems can be read and reread without becoming tiresome, and second, that Layton's verse can withstand academic scrutiny, his proclamations of self-worth have irritated some reviewers. Ira Bruce Nadel notes in the *Dictionary of Literary Biography:* "Layton embodies his own idea of the poet as one who should 'disturb and discomfort' society as well as the universe," and later adds that "His rapturous style, blunt criticisms, and flaunting sensuality have influenced several younger poets, notably Leonard Cohen and Seymour Mayne. Despite objections to his bombast and egotism, Layton's writing opened the eyes of Canadian poets to the spiritual energy and visionary force attainable from uniting romantic ideas with an ironic point of view."

Layton once commented: "One of my sisters thought I should be a plumber or an electrician; another saw in me the ability to become a peddlar; my third and oldest sister was sure I was devious and slippery enough to make a fine lawyer or politician. My mother, presiding over these three witches, pointed to the fly-spotted ceiling, indicating God by that gesture, and said, 'He will be what the Almighty wants him to be.' My devout mother turned out to be right. From earliest childhood I longed to match sounds with sense; and when I was older, to make music out of words. Everywhere I went, mystery dogged my steps. The skinny dead rat in the lane, the fire that broke out in our house on Sabbath eve, the energy that went with cruelty and the power that went with hate. The empty sky had no answers for my queries and the stars at night only winked and said nothing.

"I wrote my first poem for a teacher who was astonishingly beautiful. For weeks I mentally drooled over the white cleavage she had carelessly exposed to a precocious eleven-year-old. So there it was: the two grand mysteries of sexuality and death. I write because I'm driven to say something about them, to celebrate what my limited brain cannot comprehend. To rejoice in my more arrogant moods to think the Creator Himself doesn't comprehend

His handiwork. I write because the only solace He has in His immense and eternal solitude are the poems and stories that tell Him—like all creators, He too is hungry for praise—how exciting and beautiful, how majestic and terrible are His works and to give Him an honest, up-to-date report on His most baffling creation, Man. I know whenever I put in a good word for the strange biped He made, God's despair is lessened. Ultimately, I write because I am less cruel than He is."

BIOGRAPHICAL/CRITICAL SOURCES:

BOOKS

Bennet, Joy, and James Polson, *Irving Layton: A Bibliography: 1934-1977,* Concordia University Libraries, 1979.
Burgess, G. C. Ian, *Irving Layton's Poetry: A Catalogue and Chronology,* McGill University, 1974.
Cameron, Elspeth, *Irving Layton: A Portrait,* Stoddart, 1985.
Contemporary Literary Criticism, Gale, Volume 2, 1974, Volume 15, 1980.
Francis, Wynne, *Irving Layton and His Works,* ECW, 1984.
Mandel, Eli, *Irving Layton,* Forum House, 1969, revised edition, 1981.
Mayne, Seymour, editor, *Irving Layton: The Poet and His Critics,* McGraw Hill/Ryerson Press, 1978.
Meyer, Bruce, and Brian O'Riordan, *In Their Words: Interviews with Fourteen Canadian Writers,* Anasi, 1984, pp. 10-25.
Nadel, Ira Bruce, "Irving Layton," in *Dictionary of Literary Biography,* Volume 88: *Canadian Writers, 1920-1959: Second Series,* Gale, 1989.
Rizzardi, Alfredo, editor, *Italian Critics on Irving Layton,* Editore Piovan (Albano, Italy), 1988.
Woodstock, George, *Odysseus Ever Returning: Essays on Canadian Writers and Writing,* McClelland & Stewart, 1970, pp. 76-92.

PERIODICALS

Canadian Forum, June, 1969.
Canadian Literature, autumn, 1962, pp. 21-34; spring, 1972, pp. 102-04; autumn, 1972, pp. 70-83; winter, 1973, pp. 12-13, 18; winter, 1980, pp. 52- 65.
Fiddlehead, spring, 1967; summer, 1967.
Mosaic, January, 1968, pp. 103-11.
New Republic, July 2, 1977.
New York Times Book Review, October 9, 1977.
Queen's Quarterly, winter, 1955-1956, pp. 587-591.
The Record (Sherbrooke, Quebec), November 2, 1984.
Village Voice, March 31, 1966.

LEA, Timothy
See WOOD, Christopher (Hovelle)

* * *

LeCLAIR, Thomas 1944-
(Tom LeClair)

PERSONAL: Born March 25, 1944, in Rutland, VT; son of C. E. and Florence (Spaulding) LeClair; children: Thomas, Mary, Casey. *Education:* Boston College, B.A., 1965; University of Vermont, M.A., 1967; Duke University, Ph.D., 1972.

ADDRESSES: Home—357 Howell Ave., Cincinnati, OH 45220. *Office*—Department of English, University of Cincinnati, Cincinnati, OH 45221.

CAREER: University of Cincinnati, Cincinnati, OH, instructor, 1970-72, assistant professor, 1973-75, associate professor, 1976-79, professor of English, 1980—. Fulbright lecturer at University of Athens, Greece, 1981-82.

AWARDS, HONORS: Pushcart Prize, Pushcart Press, 1983-84, for "Avant-Garde Mastery," an essay on contemporary fiction.

WRITINGS:

(Editor with Larry McCaffery) *Anything Can Happen: Interviews with Contemporary American Novelists,* University of Illinois Press, 1983.
In the Loop: Don DeLillo and the Systems Novel, University of Illinois Press, 1987.
The Art of Excess: Mastery in Contemporary Fiction, University of Illinois Press, 1989.

Fiction reviewer for *New York Times Book Review, New Republic, Washington Post,* and *USA Today.*

SIDELIGHTS: Tom LeClair and Larry McCaffery conduct and edit interviews with eighteen domestic writers in *Anything Can Happen: Interviews with Contemporary American Novelists.* The book includes conversations with lesser-known artists like Raymond Federman and Steve Katz, as well as established masters of the genre, such as John Barth, Donald Barthelme, and Toni Morrison. David Montrose, writing in the *Times Literary Supplement,* noted that "LeClair and McCaffery should be complimented . . . for paying attention to some relatively new authors." "The canon of Modern American Literature could do with some expansion," he added.

Los Angeles Times Book Review critic Brian Stonehill observed that one recurrent question the interviewees address, "How true should fiction be?," split the novelists into two camps: those "who want to represent reality versus those who want to create it." The reviewer found this timeless debate between Truth and Beauty particularly apt in a world where "most popular storytelling is done by film and video." Stonehill also deemed the interview format generally effective. "LeClair and McCaffery don't always ask the questions one would like," he wrote, "but they often receive quality answers anyway."

LeClair told *CA:* "My ambition is to not write about literature and to write a decent book about Greece."

BIOGRAPHICAL/CRITICAL SOURCES:

PERIODICALS

Los Angeles Times Book Review, April 17, 1983.
Times Literary Supplement, September 23, 1983.

*   *   *

LeCLAIR, Tom
    See LeCLAIR, Thomas

*   *   *

LEE, Larry
    See LEE, Lawrence

*   *   *

LEE, Lawrence   1941-1990
    (Larry Lee)

PERSONAL: Born in Fort Worth, TX; died of complications from acquired immune deficiency syndrome (AIDS), April 5, 1990, in San Francisco, CA. *Education:* Graduated from University of Texas.

CAREER: Writer and television documentary producer, 1971-90. Worked as a copy boy, *Star-Telegram,* Fort Worth, TX, as a reporter, United Press International, as executive producer of "Target 4 Investigative Team," KRON-TV, and as founder of KPTF-FM (radio), Houston, TX.

AWARDS, HONORS: Received Peabody Award, Dupont Award and Emmy Award for television documentaries.

WRITINGS:

UNDER NAME LARRY LEE

(With Barry Gifford) *Jack's Book: An Oral Biography of Jack Kerouac,* St. Martin's, 1978.
(With Gifford) *Saroyan: A Biography,* Harper, 1984.

Contributor to *Village Voice* and *Rolling Stone.*

SIDELIGHTS: Known professionally as Larry Lee, Lawrence Lee was an award-winning radio and television pro-

ducer, a print journalist, and a biographer of the American writers Jack Kerouac and William Saroyan. Among the most successful television documentaries Lee produced were *Climate of Death,* about the war in El Salvador, *In the Midst of Life,* the first television documentary about AIDS, and *Shattered Dreams,* about a Belgian boys' home that sheltered Jewish children during the Second World War. He also conducted a popular San Francisco radio interview program.

In 1978, Lee and *San Francisco Review of Books* editor and poet Barry Gifford published a biography of Beat novelist Jack Kerouac. To assemble the book, the two writers traveled across the country taping interviews with over one hundred people who had known Kerouac. The list of interviewees included fellow Beats, relatives, and friends, including Gary Snyder, Allen Ginsburg, Peter Orlovsky, Michael McClure, Stella Sampas (Kerouac's widow), William Burroughs, Gore Vidal, Gregory Corso, and Philip Whalen. Organized into six chapters, the interviews give a variety of reminiscent perspectives on Kerouac the writer and the man, which the authors stitch loosely together with their own comments.

Not all critics found the authors' commentary to be accurate. John Coyne in *National Review* deplored "the inability, for instance, to offer a satisfactory explanation of Kerouac's swing to *National Review* conservatism in the late Sixties" and the "glaring error" of asserting that Kerouac had met William Buckley at Columbia University in the 1940s. Yet he described the book as "generally splendid." Russell Davies in the *New Statesman* thought the biography appropriate for an author known for a spontaneous stream-of-consciousness writing style. "It is fitting," Davies wrote, "that an author whose garrulity became his guiding literary principle should be commemorated by a book in which his friends shoot their mouths off into a tape-recorder." And while *Commonweal* reviewer Eleanor Wymard acknowledges a serious effort in the book to separate "Kerouac the man from Kerouac the cult figure," *Book World*'s Vivian Gornick complains of "mythicizing." Richard Kostelanetz, in the *New York Times Book Review,* describes the authors' own commentary as being "modest, circumspect," while complaining that the interviewees' "descriptions tend to be prosaic—quite ordinary in perception and language." Kostelanetz points out with favor the "elaborate, cross-referenced index in which the real-life models for Kerouac's characters are identified by name and vice-versa."

In his second joint venture with Gifford, Lee wrote a biography of the American playwright and fiction writer William Saroyan. Like *Jack's Book, Saroyan* is a biography based on interviews with people close to the subject. This method provokes mixed responses from reviewers—mixed in their assessment of what the book is trying to do as much as of whether it is successful or even a good idea. A critic for *Publishers Weekly* called it a "sympathetic biography," while a *Chicago Tribune* reviewer dismissed it as a portrait of Saroyan as a "consummate boor." The sheer volume of anecdote led Richard Lillard in the *Los Angeles Times Book Review* to call it a "sprightly volume, rich in journalistic gossip and name dropping," which Marsha Norman in the *New York Times Book Review* attacked as being "not so much a biography [of Saroyan] as a chronicle of failure."

The structure of the book, unorthodox for a biography, seems to work particularly well for sympathetic readers. The book begins with Saroyan at the apex of his career—successful, happy, famous—then flashes back to his early career and forward to the decline that followed. A critic for *Kirkus Reviews* called this strategy a "hapless, bewildering, downright perverse structure." Lillard, though, says the book "moves with particular ease" through Saroyan's life.

BIOGRAPHICAL/CRITICAL SOURCES:

PERIODICALS

Best Sellers, January, 1985, p. 380.
Booklist, November 1, 1982, p. 332.
Book World, October 22, 1978, p. E5.
Chicago Tribune, March 24, 1985.
Commonweal, March 24, 1980, pp. 157-158.
Kirkus Reviews, October 1, 1984, pp. 953-954.
Los Angeles Times Book Review, November 25, 1984, pp. 3-6.
National Review, March 2, 1979, p. 311.
New Statesman, March 23, 1979, pp. 399-400.
New York Times Book Review, December 31, 1978, p. 16; November 25, 1984, p. 14.
Publishers Weekly, September 28, 1984, p. 105.
Saturday Review, August, 1978, p. 50.
Theater Crafts, February, 1988.
Western American Literature, winter, 1986, pp. 370-371.
World Literature Today, winter, 1986, p. 114.

OBITUARIES:

PERIODICALS

Chicago Tribune, April 8, 1990.
New York Times, April 7, 1990.*

—*Sketch by Joseph O. Aimone*

*   *   *

LEGER, Alexis
See LEGER, (Marie-Rene Auguste) Alexis Saint-Leger

LEGER, (Marie-Rene Auguste) Alexis Saint-Leger 1887-1975
(Alexis Leger, Saintleger Leger, St.-John Perse)

PERSONAL: Born May 31, 1887, in Saint-Leger-les-Feuilles, French West Indies; brought to France at age of eleven; died September 20, 1975, in Giens, France; son of Amedee (a lawyer) and Mme. Leger (*nee* Dormoy); married Dorothy Milburn Russell, 1958. *Education:* Attended Universities of Bordeaux and Paris, studied medicine, law, and literature, licencie en Droit; held a diploma from the Ecole des Hautes Etudes Commerciales.

CAREER: French Foreign Office, deputy diplomat in the political and commercial division, 1914-16, served as secretary of the French Embassy in Peking, China, 1916-21; collaborator with French Foreign Minister, Aristide Briand, 1921-32; chef de cabinet, Ministry of Foreign Affairs, 1925-32, counsellor, 1925, minister, 1927; secretary-general of Ministry of Foreign Affairs, and Ambassador of France, 1932-40, removed from this post as a result of his firm stand against the appeasement of Germany; lost his French citizenship, October 29, 1940; fled to Arachon (France), to England, Canada, and finally arrived in Washington, DC, in January, 1941; consultant on French poetry at the Library of Congress, 1941-45; his French citizenship was restored in 1945; he returned to France, 1957, and maintained homes in Washington and Giens until his death.

MEMBER: American Academy of Arts and Sciences (honorary), American Academy of Arts and Letters, National Institute of Arts and Letters of America, Modern Language Association of America (honorary fellow), Bayerischen Akademie der Schoenen Kuenste.

AWARDS, HONORS: Knight Commander of Royal Victorian Order; Grand Officer of Legion of Honor; Knight Commander of the Bath; Knight of the Grand Cross of the British Empire; Commander des Arts et des Lettres; honorary degree from Yale University; American Academy and Institute of Arts and Letters Award of Merit, 1950; Grand Prix National des Letters, 1959; Grand Prix International de Poesie (Belgium), 1959; Nobel Prize for Literature, 1960.

WRITINGS:

(Under name Saintleger Leger) *Eloges* (poetry; title means "Eulogies"; also see below), Gallimard, 1911, published under pseudonym St.-John Perse, Gallimard, 1925, translation by Louise Varese published as *Eloges, and Other Poems,* introduction by Archibald MacLeish, Norton, 1944, revised bilingual edition, without introduction, Pantheon Books, 1956.

UNDER PSEUDONYM ST.-JOHN PERSE

Anabase (poem), Gallimard, 1924, bilingual edition with English translation by T. S. Eliot published as *Anabasis*, Faber, 1930, 2nd edition, revised and corrected, Harcourt, 1949.

Amitie du prince (originally published as part of *Eloges*), R. Davis, 1924, critical edition, Gallimard, 1979.

Exil: Poeme, Cahiers du Sud, 1942, critical edition edited by Roger Little published as *Exil,* Athlone Press, 1973.

Pluies (poetry), Editions des Lettres Francaises (Buenos Aires), 1944.

Quatre Poemes (1941-1944), Editions des Lettres Francaises, 1944, published as *Exil, suivi de Poemes a l'etrangere, Pluies, Neiges,* Gallimard, 1945, revised and corrected edition, Gallimard, 1946, bilingual edition with English translation by Denis Devlin published as *Exile, and Other Poems,* Pantheon Books, 1949, 2nd bilingual edition, Pantheon Books, 1953.

Vents (epic poem; also see below), Gallimard, 1946, bilingual edition with English translation by Hugh Chisholm published as *Winds,* Pantheon Books, 1952, 2nd bilingual edition, 1961.

Oeuvre poetique de Saint-John Perse, two volumes, Gallimard, 1953, revised edition, 1960.

Amers (poetry; also see below), NRF, 1953, bilingual edition with English translation by Wallace Fowlie published as *Seamarks,* Pantheon Books, 1958.

Etroits sont les vaisseaux (also published as part of *Amers*), NRF, 1956.

Chronique (poem; also see below), Gallimard, 1960, bilingual edition with English translation by Robert Fitzerald, Pantheon Books, 1960.

On Poetry (Nobel Prize acceptance speech; also see below), bilingual edition with English translation by W. H. Auden, Pantheon Books, 1961.

L'ordre des oiseaux (poems), Au vent d'Arles, 1962, published as *Oiseaux,* Gallimard, 1963, bilingual edition with translation by Robert Fitzgerald published as *Birds,* Pantheon Books, 1966.

Pour Dante (address; also see below), Gallimard, 1965.

Two Addresses: On Poetry [and] *Dante* (includes Auden's translation of *On Poetry* and Fitzgerald's translation of *Pour Dante*), Pantheon Books, 1966.

Eloges [and] *La gloire des rois* [and] *Exil* [and] *Anabase,* Gallimard, 1967.

Vents [and] *Chronique,* Gallimard, 1968.

Chante par celle qui fut la . . . (bilingual edition), translation by Richard Howard, Princeton University Press, 1970.

Collected Poems, translations by W. H. Auden and others, Princeton University Press, 1971.

Oeuvres completes, Gallimard, 1972.

Chant pour un equinoxe, Gallimard, 1975, translation by Richard Howard published as *Song for an Equinox,* Princeton University Press, 1977.

Letters of St.-John Perse, translated and edited by Arthur J. Knodel, Princeton University Press, 1979.

OTHER

(Under name Alexis Leger) *La Publication francaise pendant la guerre, bibliographie restreinte (1940-1945),* four volumes, 1940s.

(Under name Alexis Leger) *Briand,* Wells College Press, 1943.

(Under name Alexis Saintleger Leger) *A Selection of Works for an Understanding of World Affairs since 1914,* [Washington], 1943.

Contributor to *Nouvelle Revue Francaise, Poetry, Transition, Commerce, Mesa, Partisan Review, Intentions, Sewanee Review, Briarcliff Quarterly, Atlantic, Berkeley Review,* and other publications.

SIDELIGHTS: Diplomatic service and the writing of poetry were dual preoccupations during the greater part of Alexis Saint-Leger's life. It was the poet Paul Claudel, whom Leger met in 1905, who first suggested that Leger enter government service. For twenty-six years he served as a highly distinguished diplomat. At the same time he was writing poetry in secret in his spare time. His early writings were for the most part ignored, though *Anabase* was translated into German by Rainer Maria Rilke (1925), into English by T. S. Eliot (1930), and into Italian by Giuseppe Ungaretti (1931). (Wallace Fowlie recalls the story of Leger's recognition by Marcel Proust, who, in *Cities of the Plain,* published in 1922, includes an episode wherein he mentions a book of poems by a Saintleger Leger.)

From 1924 until 1942 Leger published no poetry, but he continued to write, accumulating five volumes of poems. When he fled Paris in 1940 he left his manuscripts (fifteen years of work) behind. The poems were destroyed by the Nazi police, and today the bulk of his work is by many standards small. He wrote carefully and was reluctant to publish in haste. He has, however, as Wallace Fowlie maintained, "taken his place beside the four or five major poets of modern France: Baudelaire, Mallarme, Rimbaud, Valery, Claudel." Fowlie considers *Anabase* to be "one of the key poems of our age. It represents the poet as conqueror of the word. . . ." Eliot thought it as important as James Joyce's later work.

To conceal his diplomat's identity Leger published his poetry under the pseudonym St.-John Perse. Some of the very early poems, however, were published without his consent (especially in *Nouvelle Revue Francaise* and *Commerce,* 1909-10) under the name Saintleger Leger. The name St.-John Perse, perhaps chosen because of Leger's admiration for the Roman poet Persius, was first used for the publication of "Anabase" in *Nouvelle Revue Francaise,* January, 1924.

Solitude and exile were Perse's themes. He was interested in the unity and totality of things. Fowlie wrote: "To man and to every aspiration of man he ascribes some eternal meaning. Everything precarious and ephemeral appears less so in the condition of his poetry." Fowlie added, "[Perse] is the contemporary poet who comes perhaps closest to considering himself the instrument of superior revelation." His poems praised and celebrated the entire cosmos. His style was dazzling, opulent, set forth in non-traditional stanzas in which, as Fowlie wrote, one finds "language brought back, almost by force, to its essential rhythm, language which uses myths and symbols, language which does not describe but which suggests." Transition between images was often nonexistent. Perse believed that the poet relies on his subconscious, but a subconscious that has been mastered by reason. His literary forebears included Persius, Tacitus, Racine, and Claudel.

Perse was also noted for his brilliant and spellbinding conversations. His knowledge of botany, zoology, geology—anything concerned with nature—was considered encyclopedic, and he avowed passions for horses and boats. His childhood and youth (indeed his entire life) gave his name an almost legendary quality: his nurse on the island of his birth was a secret priestess of Shira; his friends in China were the philosophers of the East; in his spare time he traveled to the Gobi Desert and the South Sea Islands; and he was at one time one of the most powerful officials in France. He recalled his diverse experiences with ease, wrote Pierre Geurre, and spoke "a language of surprising diversity and exactitude, occasionally stopping to find an even more precise word to accurately define his thought. While listening to him, one gets the impression that something in the flow of time or being becomes immobilized and that the magic of word and thought creates a pause around itself."

Perse said he was not a professional writer, and he could hardly be considered bookish. Guerre noted Leger's "instinctive" distrust of books, and recalled an anecdote: "When during the war he worked at the Library of Congress in Washington, American critics, curious about the books he himself read, vainly ransacked the card files trying to find what he had taken out. But for five years Perse had not borrowed one book from the famous national library. As he wrote to a poet friend: 'My hostility to culture springs from homeopathy. I believe that culture should be carried to the utmost limit, at which point it disclaims itself, and ungrateful to itself, cancels itself out.' "

Although Perse spent much of his life after 1941 in America, his allegiance belonged entirely to France. In 1942 he wrote to Archibald MacLeish: "I have nothing to say about France: it is myself and all of myself. . . . For me it is the holy kind, and the only one, in which I can communicate with anything universal, anything essential. Even were I not an essentially French animal, an essentially French clay (and my last breath, as my first, will chemically be French), the French language would still be my only imaginable refuge, the shelter and retreat par excellence, the only locus in this world where I can remain in order to understand, desire, or renounce anything at all."

In 1960, Perse was awarded the Nobel Prize for literature. The *Washington Post's* Joseph McLellan recalls that "his acceptance speech was a tribute to the art of poetry, an assertion of its continuing value in an age of technology. 'It is enough,' the speech concluded, 'for the poet to be the guilty conscience of his time.' "

BIOGRAPHICAL/CRITICAL SOURCES:

BOOKS

Bosquet, Alain, *Saint-John Perse,* Seghers, 1953, revised edition, 1967.
Contemporary Literary Criticism, Gale, Volume 11, 1979, Volume 46, 1988.
Saillet, Maurice, *Saint-John Perse: Poete de Gloire,* Mercure de France, 1952.

PERIODICALS

Christian Science Monitor, October 26, 1960.
Contemporary Review, March, 1961.
Poetry, January, 1961.
Reporter, February 2, 1961.
Washington Post, September 2, 1987.
Yale Review, December 2, 1960.

OBITUARIES:

PERIODICALS

Newsweek, October 6, 1975.
New York Times, September 22, 1975.
Time, October 6, 1975.
Washington Post, September 24, 1975.*

* * *

LEGER, Saintleger
  See LEGER, (Marie-Rene Auguste) Alexis Saint-Leger

LEHRER, James (Charles) 1934-
(Jim Lehrer)

PERSONAL: Born May 19, 1934, in Wichita, KS; son of Harry Frederick (a bus station manager) and Lois Catherine (a bank clerk; maiden name, Chapman) Lehrer; married Kate Staples (a writer), June 4, 1960; children: Jamie, Lucy, Amanda. *Education:* Victoria College, A.A., 1954; University of Missouri, B.J., 1956. *Avocational Interests:* Collecting bus depot signs and other memorabilia.

ADDRESSES: Home—3356 Macomb, Washington, DC 20016. *Office*—WETA-TV, P.O. Box 2626, Washington, DC 20013; and *MacNeil/Lehrer NewsHour,* 3620 27th St. S., Arlington, VA 22206.

CAREER: Dallas Morning News, Dallas, TX, reporter, 1959-61; *Dallas Times Herald,* Dallas, reporter, columnist, and city editor, 1961-70; KERA-TV, Dallas, executive producer and correspondent, and executive director of public affairs, 1970-72; Public Broadcasting Service (PBS-TV), Washington, DC, public affairs coordinator, 1972-73, co-anchor of the *Robert MacNeil Report,* 1975, associate editor and co-anchor of the *MacNeil/Lehrer Report,* 1975-83, and the *MacNeil/Lehrer NewsHour,* 1983—; NPACT-WETA-TV, Washington, DC, correspondent, 1973—. Co-partner, MacNeil-Lehrer Productions. Instructor in creative writing at Dallas College and Southern Methodist University, 1967-68. Moderator for *U.S. Chronicle,* a thirteen-week series of half-hour public affairs programs for PBS-TV, 1980. *Military service:* U.S. Marine Corps, 1956-59.

MEMBER: Texas Institute of Letters, Council of Foreign Relations.

AWARDS, HONORS: National Academy of Television Arts and Sciences, Emmy Award for journalism, 1973, for coverage of the Senate Watergate Committee's investigation, Emmy Award for outstanding background and analysis of a single current story, 1984, for the *MacNeil/Lehrer NewsHour* coverage of U.S. Marines in Beirut, and Emmy Award for outstanding coverage of a single breaking news story, 1984, for the *MacNeil/Lehrer NewsHour* report on the U.S. invasion of Grenada; George Polk Award for journalism, 1974, for coverage of the Senate Watergate Committee's investigation; Columbia-Dupont Award for excellence in broadcast journalism, 1976-77, for the *MacNeil/Lehrer Report;* George Foster Peabody Award for meritorious service in broadcasting, 1977, for the *MacNeil/Lehrer Report;* leadership award, Association for Continuing Higher Education, 1981, for the *MacNeil/Lehrer Report.*

WRITINGS:

Viva Max (novel), Duell, Sloan & Pierce, 1966.
We Were Dreamers (memoirs), Atheneum, 1975.

Silversides Thruliner (two-act play), produced at New Stage Theater in Jackson, MS, 1986.
Cedar Chest (two-act play), produced at New Stage Theater in Jackson, MS, 1986.
Chili Queen (two-act play), produced in New York City at Hartley House Theater, 1986.

UNDER NAME JIM LEHRER

Kick the Can, Putnam, 1988.
Crown Oklahoma, Putnam, 1989.
The Sooner Spy, Putnam, 1990.
Lost and Found, Putnam, 1991.
A Bus of My Own, Putnam, 1992, published as *A Bus of My Own: A Memoir,* Plume Books, 1992.
Short List, Putnam, 1992.
Blue Hearts: A Novel, Random House, 1993.

Also author of column "Politics: Dallas" in the *Dallas Times Herald. MED*

ADAPTATIONS: Lehrer's first novel, *Viva Max,* was adapted for a film of the same title starring Peter Ustinov, released by Commonwealth United in 1969.

SIDELIGHTS: Jim Lehrer is best known as co-anchor of public television's Emmy Award-winning *MacNeil/Lehrer Report* and *MacNeil/Lehrer NewsHour.* In 1975, Lehrer teamed up with Robert MacNeil to host the *Report,* a nightly half-hour television news program broadcast on Public Television Service (PBS-TV). The show quickly earned critical acclaim for its in-depth coverage of stories which contrasted with the brief synopses of events provided by commercial network news. The format of the *Report* allowed it to focus comprehensively on one topic per nightly segment instead of the gamut of daily news. The show also utilized interviews and analysis rather than the visual effects employed by the networks.

The *Report,* aimed at the news "connoisseur" rather than the general public, did not attempt to compete with popular network news productions. Rather, it followed the network shows as a supplement for the serious news viewer. Pronounced by *Time*'s Thomas Griffith as the provider of "TV's best discussion of public affairs," the *Report* was nevertheless not known for its public appeal. As Alexander Cockburn of *Harper's* commented, "Admirers of the *MacNeil/Lehrer Report*—and there are many of them—often talk about it in terms normally reserved for unpalatable but nutritious breakfast foods: unalluring, perhaps, to the frivolous new consumer, but packed full of fiber."

In 1983, the *Report* altered its format. Now titled the *MacNeil/Lehrer NewsHour,* it was expanded to an hour-long show featuring a new multi-issue format with a broadcast time opposite the networks' news programming. These changes met with criticism from reviewers who felt that the solemn, nonsensational style of the *Report* could not sustain viewer interest for an entire hour, particularly in competition with the networks' faster-paced, high-visibility programs. As the *NewsHour* continued, however, the show regained much of its credibility. Alex Raksin wrote in the *Los Angeles Times Book Review* that "America's political leaders have come to see the *NewsHour* as a haven where they can chuck PR and confess at least some of their real stands on the issues." Another *Los Angeles Times Book Review* critic, Mark Harris, attested that "Lehrer on my TV screen these recent nights remains as I have always known him, rational, reasonable, straightforward and unemotional, respectful of the newsworthy people with whom he converses, and responsible to the facts insofar as they can be known."

In addition to his journalism career, Lehrer has written novels, plays, and memoirs. Ed Weiner stated in the *New York Times Book Review* that Lehrer exhibits "an enviable knack for telling a story as though he were truly telling it: natural, relaxed and written for the ear." Five of his novels—*Kick the Can, Crown Oklahoma, The Sooner Spy, Lost and Found,* and *Short List*—feature The One-Eyed Mack, a protagonist who evolves from a sixteen-year-old Kansas teenager (who lost his left eye thanks to the sharp edge of a kicked tin can) on a wanderer's path across the South to become a husband, father, and Lieutenant Governor of Oklahoma. As Lieutenant Governor, he encounters quirky characters and humorously bizarre situations: he tracks down an ostensible Mafia crime ring based in Oklahoma, investigates a Russian spy relocated to the Sooner State, searches for citizens with unexplained disappearances, and, through a series of unplanned circumstances, finds himself on the short list of suggested names for Vice-President of the United States.

In the series' first novel, *Kick the Can,* Mack, realizing that his limited eyesight will prevent him from following his father's footsteps into a career with the Kansas Highway Patrol, tries for a job with his second love, the local bus company. When the bus company won't hire him because of his partial blindness, he decides to don an eyepatch and head south to Texas to become a pirate. His adventures and relationships along the way comprise the bulk of the story. Reviewing the novel in the *Chicago Tribune,* Kenneth R. Clark stated, "It's hard to think of Jim Lehrer . . . as a novelist of eccentric whimsy, but *Kick the Can* will enshrine him in that category forever." Other critics noted the work's shortcomings; Robert Day, for instance, writing in the *Washington Post Book World,* opined that "the problem is that not much of the novel seems organic to it. It is all one device after another spread onto the narrative, which itself lurches like one of the old buses the characters drive."

Crown Oklahoma, the next novel in the One-Eyed Mack series, "is a darling book, and Jim Lehrer, under his preoc-

cupied frown of the White Protestant news-mogul must be a terminally Big Silly," remarked Carolyn See in the *Los Angeles Times.* Set in the 1970s, *Crown Oklahoma* follows Mack, now Lieutenant Governor of Oklahoma, as he attempts to crack a supposed Mafia infiltration into the Sooner State. The Mob's presence in the state has been falsely concocted by a national television news anchor and reported on the *CBS Evening News;* the story unfolds as One-Eyed Mack tries to uncover information about the Oklahoma members of the so-called crime ring. As Karen Ray observed in the *New York Times Book Review,* "The Okie crime organization scheme is meant to sound far-fetched, and Mr. Lehrer uses it to get in his licks about responsibility, and the lack thereof, in television journalism." See noted that the author "has taken the whole solemn concept of the news, and tickled it, poked it in the ribs, jabbed and punched it into giggling submission." In the *Washington Post,* Gene Lyons found *Crown Oklahoma* "such an amiable, unpretentious little novel that it's hard to dislike."

The next One-Eyed Mack novel, *The Sooner Spy,* deals with Mack's discovery that a retired Soviet defector has been living in Oklahoma. As Mack investigates the situation, he stumbles across a Russian spy sent to track down the retired defector. Newgate Callendar of the *New York Times Book Review* labelled the book "pleasantly wacky and sentimental," and Charles Champlin claimed in the *Los Angeles Times Book Review* that "Lehrer is most blessedly adroit and light-handed. His glimpses of the political process . . . are so amusing that the tale in all its improbabilities is a taste treat."

Lehrer's plays comprise an important part of his body of fiction. A heart attack and double bypass surgery in 1983 prompted Lehrer to return to fiction writing, but he felt overwhelmed by the thought of attempting a novel. At his wife's suggestion, he tried writing a play, which he had last done thirty years earlier in college. About his efforts, Lehrer explained in an article for the *Washington Post,* "There are some risks in all of this. I have set myself up to fail in public, to be loudly told to stick to journalism and leave play writing to those who already know how. But I am having pure, eye-watering pleasure watching and listening as professional actors come alive on stage as people I created. . . . I love it all—the talk, the smells, the process, the make-believe, the magic." In the *New York Times,* Jay Sharbutt summarized Lehrer's play *Chili Queen* as a "black but warm four-character comedy." Loosely based on a real-life experience at a Texas Dairy Queen in which Lehrer witnessed a heated argument between a waitress and a customer over the exact amount of money the customer had paid, the play is a "reasonably well-constructed seriocomic vignette with dialogue and performances that transcend the stereotypical," according to Stephen Holden, also of the *New York Times.* He further characterized it as a "small dark comedy that reserves its sharpest satirical jabs for the way television packages daily events while coolly manipulating the hapless participants."

Lehrer's first book of memoirs, *We Were Dreamers,* details his family's experiences in 1946, when he was twelve years old. Fulfilling a lifelong dream, his father bought an intercity bus service which the family named the Kansas Central Lines. Financing the purchase meant selling the family home; Lehrer, his parents, and older brother devoted much of their time and energy to creating a successful bus line. Inexperience and financial difficulties defeated the family, however, and they declared bankruptcy after only a year in business. But Lehrer gleaned enough impressions from that year of hardship and family togetherness to compile what John K. Andrews, Jr., of *National Review* described as a "rich stew of boyhood memories," in which the elder Mr. Lehrer "emerges under his son's loving pen as a particularly memorable man," despite his failure as a businessman. *A Bus of My Own,* Lehrer's second book of memoirs, addresses both his earlier life and anecdotes pertaining to politics, government, and the *MacNeil/Lehrer NewsHour.* Raksin believed that the various elements which comprise Lehrer's personal history, from his happy childhood to his health concerns in middle age "all seem to have gifted him with an unusual ability to laugh at the everyday problems he encounters in his work at the *NewsHour.*"

BIOGRAPHICAL/CRITICAL SOURCES:

BOOKS

Lehrer, Jim, *We Were Dreamers,* Atheneum, 1975.
Lehrer, Jim, *A Bus of My Own,* Putnam, 1992, published as *A Bus of My Own: A Memoir,* Plume, 1992.

PERIODICALS

Harper's, August, 1982.
Los Angeles Times, November 18, 1986; August 7, 1989.
Los Angeles Times Book Review, May 22, 1988, p. 8; March 11, 1990, p. 8; August 23, 1992, p. 6.
National Observer, February 2, 1970.
National Review, October 15, 1976.
New Leader, October 17, 1983.
New York Times, November 7, 1986; November 26, 1986.
New York Times Book Review, June 25, 1989, p. 24; March 11, 1990, p. 33; July 14, 1991, p. 20; February 23, 1992, p. 20.
Saturday Review, July, 1980.
Smithsonian, May, 1981.
Time, September 6, 1982; September 19, 1983.
Tribune Books (Chicago), April 30, 1989, p. 6.
TV Guide, October 8, 1977; January 23, 1982.

Variety, October 15, 1969; December 24, 1969.
Washington Post, November 9, 1986; July 17, 1987; May 22, 1989.
Washington Post Book World, May 15, 1988, p. 7; March 11, 1990, p. 5.

—Sketch by Michaela Swart Wilson

*   *   *

LEHRER, Jim
    See LEHRER, James (Charles)

*   *   *

LEON, Pierre R.   1926-

PERSONAL: Born March 12, 1926, in Ligre, France; son of Roger and Marie Louise (Cosson) Leon; married Monique Maury (a university professor), April 18, 1949; children: Francoise. *Education:* University of Paris, Licence es Lettres, 1951; University of Besancon, Doctorat, 1960; Sorbonne, University of Paris, Doctorat es Lettres, 1972.

ADDRESSES: Home—150 Farnham Ave., No. 504, Toronto, Ontario M4V 1H5, Canada. *Office*—Department of French, University of Toronto, Ontario M5S 1A8, Canada.

CAREER: University of Paris, Sorbonne, Paris, France, attache at Institute of Phonetics, 1950-58; Ohio State University, Columbus, assistant professor of French, 1958-60; University of Besancon, Besancon, France, director of language laboratory at Center for Applied Linguistics, 1960-63; Ohio State University, associate professor of French, 1963-64; University of Toronto, Toronto, Ontario, associate professor, 1964-65, professor of French, 1965—, director of Experimental Phonetics Laboratory, 1966—. University de Pau, maitre de conferences, 1978—, professor titulaire, 1980. *Military service:* French Army, 1948-49; French Army Reserve, beginning 1949; became lieutenant.

MEMBER: International Phonetic Association, Internationale des Sciences Phonetiques (fellow), Speech Association of America, Modern Language Association of America, Societe Royale du Canada, Association Canadienne Francaise pour l'Avancement des Sciences, Societe Linguistique (Paris), Union des Ecrivains Quebecois, Conseil Permanent de la Societe, l'Academie des Sciences et des Lettres de la Societe.

AWARDS, HONORS: Canada Council grants, 1965-85; Prize of the French Academy, 1966, for *Introduction a la phonetique corrective a l'usage des professeurs de francais* l'etranger; Palmes academiques, chevalier, 1978, officier, 1987; Prix Loisirs Jeunes, 1981, for *Grepotame*; doctorat honoris causa, Universite de Nancy, 1982.

WRITINGS:

Aide-memoire d'orthoepie, Didier, 1961, revised edition published as *Prononciation du francais standard: Aide-memoire d'orthoepie*, 1966, 2nd edition, 1972.

Laboratoire de langues et correction phonetique: Essai methodologique, Didier, 1962, 2nd edition, 1976.

(With wife, Monique Leon) *Introduction a la phonetique corrective a l'usage des professeurs de francais a l'etranger*, Hachette-Larousse, 1964, 4th edition, 1971.

(With others) *Le Francais international*, two volumes, Centre Educatif et Culture (Montreal), 1967.

(With Philippe Martin) *Prolegomenes a l'etude des structures intonatives*, Didier, 1970.

(With Allan Grundstrom) *Interrogation et intonation en francais standard et en francais canadien*, Didier, 1973.

(Editor with Henri Mitterand) *L'Analyse du discours*, Centre Educatif et Culturel, 1976.

Applied and Experimental Linguistics, Didier, 1979.

(With Martin) *Toronto English*, Didier, 1979.

(With Ivan Fonagy) *L'Accent en francais contemporain*, Didier, 1980.

Animots croises, Nathan (Paris), 1980.

Grepotame (collection of drawings and nursery rhymes), Nathan, 1981.

(With Mario Rossi) *Problemes de prosodie*, Didier, Volume 1: *Approached theoriques*, 1981, Volume 2: *Experimentations, modeles et fonctions*, 1982.

Les Voleurs d'etoiles de St. Arbroussepoil, Lemeac (Montreal), 1982.

(With Jack Yashinsky) *Options nouvelles en didactique des langues*, Didier, 1982.

(With Bieler, Haac, and M. Leon) *Perspectives de France*, Prentice-Hall, 1982.

(With F. Carton and Rossi) *Les Accents des francais*, Hachette-Larousse, 1983.

Les Mots d'Arlequin (poems), Naaman, Sherbrooke, 1983.

(With R. Baligand and C. Tatilon) *Interpretations orales*, Hachette-Larousse, 1984.

(With P. Perron) *Le Dialogue*, Didier, 1985.

(Translator) *Chants de la toundra* (poems), La Decouverte/Maspero (Paris), 1985.

EDITOR AND CONTRIBUTOR

Applied Linguistics and the Teaching of French/ Linguistique appliquee et enseignement du francais, Centre Educatif et Culture, 1967.

Recherches sur la structure phonique du francais canadien, Didier, 1969.

(With Georges Faure and Andre Rigault) *Prosodic Feature Analysis/Analyse des faits prosodiques*, Didier, 1970.

(With others) *Problemes de l'analyse textuelle/Problems of Textual Analysis*, Didier, 1971.

(With others) *Hommages a Pierre Delattre*, Mouton, 1972.

(With Henry Schogt and Edward Burstynsky) *La Phonologie*, Klincsieck (Paris), 1976.

Crocogouron, Editions du soleil, 1990.

Phonetisme et prononciations du francais, Nathan, 1992.

Traite de phonostylistique, Nathan, 1993.

Pigore et compagnie, Editions des Plaines, 1993.

Sur la piste des Jolicoeur, VLB, 1993.

OTHER

Also contributor of articles to linguistic journals and art reviews to *L'Express* (Toronto).

SIDELIGHTS: Pierre R. Leon once told *CA:* "As a university professor, I write articles and books in order to share my research findings with colleagues in the same fields. I have written on many different subjects, because I don't like to stay with the same problems for very long.

"As a creative writer, I started to write titles for paintings I used to do as a hobby. My paintings were highly stylized or somewhat abstract and one of my colleague at the university, also a good friend—the late Marshall McLuhan—suggested that I write a few lines of poetry for each of my visual works. I enjoyed this kind of language play and some of my lines became small poems. One day a publisher noted these small pieces of poetry in a gallery where I was exhibiting banners (made of applique on large pieces of material). He asked me to give him my poems, demanding eighty pieces within three months. I accepted the challenge and published my first booklet of poems, *Les Mots d'Arlequin*."

*   *   *

LESTER, Julius (Bernard) 1939-

PERSONAL: Born January 27, 1939, in St. Louis, MO; son of W. D. (a minister) and Julia (Smith) Lester; married Joan Steinau (a researcher), 1962 (divorced, 1970); married Alida Carolyn Fechner, March 21, 1979; children: (first marriage) Jody Simone, Malcolm Coltrane; (second marriage) Elena Milad (stepdaughter), David Julius. *Education:* Fisk University, B.A., 1960.

ADDRESSES: Office—University of Massachusetts—Amherst, Amherst, MA 01002.

CAREER: Newport Folk Festival, Newport, RI, director, 1966-68; New School for Social Research, New York City, lecturer, 1968-70; WBAI-FM, New York City, producer and host of live radio show "The Great Proletarian Cultural Revolution," 1968-75; University of Massachusetts—Amherst, professor of Afro-American studies, 1971-88, professor of Near Eastern and Judaic Studies, 1982—, acting director and associate director of Institute for Advanced Studies in Humanities, 1982-84; Vanderbilt University, Nashville, TN, writer-in-residence, 1985. Professional musician and singer. Host of live television show "Free Time," WNET-TV, New York City, 1971-73. Lester's photographs of the 1960s civil rights movement have been exhibited at the Smithsonian Institution and are on permanent display at Howard University.

AWARDS, HONORS: Distinguished Teacher's Award, 1983-84; Faculty Fellowship Award for Distinguished Research and Scholarship, 1985; National Professor of the Year Silver Medal Award, from Council for Advancement and Support of Education, 1985; Massachusetts State Professor of the Year and Gold Medal Award for National Professor of the Year, both from Council for Advancement and Support of Education, both 1986; chosen distinguished faculty lecturer, 1986-87; *To Be a Slave* was nominated for the Newbery Award; *The Long Journey Home: Stories from Black History* was a National Book Award finalist.

WRITINGS:

(With Pete Seeger) *The 12-String Guitar as Played by Leadbelly,* Oak, 1965.
Look Out Whitey! Black Power's Gon' Get Your Mama!, Dial, 1968.
To Be a Slave, Dial, 1969.
Black Folktales, Baron, 1969.
Search for the New Land: History as Subjective Experience, Dial, 1969.
Revolutionary Notes, Baron, 1969.
(Editor) *The Seventh Son: The Thoughts and Writings of W. E. B. Du Bois,* two volumes, Random House, 1971.
(Compiler with Rae Pace Alexander) *Young and Black in America,* Random House, 1971.
The Long Journey Home: Stories from Black History, Dial, 1972.
The Knee-High Man and Other Tales, Dial, 1972.
Two Love Stories, Dial, 1972.
(Editor) Stanley Couch, *Ain't No Ambulances for No Nigguhs Tonight* (poems), Baron, 1972.
Who I Am (poems), Dial, 1974.
All Is Well: An Autobiography, Morrow, 1976.
This Strange New Feeling, Dial, 1982.
Do Lord Remember Me (novel), Holt, 1984.
The Tales of Uncle Remus: The Adventures of Brer Rabbit, Dial, 1987.

More Tales of Uncle Remus: The Further Adventures of Brer Rabbit, His Friends, Enemies, and Others, Dial, 1988.
Lovesong: Becoming a Jew (autobiography), Holt, 1988.
How Many Spots Does a Leopard Have? and Other Tales, illustrations by David Shannon, Scholastic, Inc., 1989.
Falling Pieces of the Broken Sky (essays), Arcade, 1990.
Further Tales of Uncle Remus: The Misadventures of Brer Rabbit, Brer Fox, Brer Wolf, the Doodang, and Other Creatures, illustrations by Jerry Pinkney, Dial, 1990.

Contributor of essays and reviews to numerous magazines and newspapers, including *New York Times Book Review, New York Times, Nation, Katallagete, Democracy,* and *Village Voice.* Associate editor, *Sing Out,* 1964-70; contributing editor, *Broadside of New York,* 1964-70. Lester's books have been translated into seven languages.

SIDELIGHTS: Julius Lester is "foremost among young black writers who produce their work from a position of historical strength," writes critic John A. Williams in the *New York Times Book Review.* Drawing on old documents and folktales, Lester fashions stories that proclaim the heritage of black Americans and "attempt to recreate the social life of the past," note Eric and Naomi Foner in the *New York Review of Books.* Lester's tales are more than simple reportage. Their purpose, as the Foners point out, is "not merely to impart historical information, but to teach moral and political lessons." Because he feels that the history of minority groups has been largely ignored, Lester intends to furnish his young readers with what he calls "a usable past" and with what the Foners call "a sense of history which will help shape their lives and politics." Lester has also retold the traditional Uncle Remus tales for children, while in *How Many Spots Does a Leopard Have?* he combines folktales from the African and Jewish cultures.

Lester's characters fall into two categories: those drawn from Afro-American folklore and those drawn from black history. The former are imaginary creatures, or sometimes animals, such as *The Knee-High Man's* Mr. Bear and Mr. Rabbit; the latter are real people, "ordinary men and women who might appear only in . . . a neglected manuscript at the Library of Congress," according to William Loren Katz in the *Washington Post Book World.* Critics find that Lester uses both types of characters to reveal the black individual's struggle against slavery.

Black Folktales, Lester's first collection of folk stories, features larger- than-life heroes (including a cigar-smoking black God), shrewd animals, and cunning human beings. While some of the characters are taken from African legends and others from American slave tales, they all demonstrate that "black resistance to white oppression is as old as the confrontation between the two groups," says Williams. Most reviewers applaud Lester's view of Afro-American folklore and praise his storytelling skills, but a few object to what they perceive as the anti-white tone of the book. Zena Sutherland, writing in *Bulletin of the Center for Children's Books,* calls *Black Folktales* "a vehicle for hostility. . . . There is no story that concerns white people in which they are not pictured as venal or stupid or both."

Lester also deals with white oppression in his second collection of folktales, *The Knee-High Man and Other Tales.* Although these six animal stories are funny, *New York Times Book Review* critic Ethel Richards suggests that "powerfully important lessons ride the humor. In 'The Farmer and the Snake,' the lesson is that kindness will not change the nature of a thing—in this case, the nature of a poisonous snake to bite." A *Junior Bookshelf* reviewer points out that this story—as well as others in the book—reflects the relationship between owner and slave. While pursuing the same theme, Lester moves into the realm of nonfiction with *The Long Journey Home: Stories from Black History,* a documentary collection of slave narratives, and *To Be a Slave,* a collection of six stories based on historical fact. Both books showcase ordinary people in adverse circumstances and provide the reader with a look at what Lester calls "history from the bottom up." *Black Like Me* author John Howard Griffin, writing in the *New York Times Book Review,* commends Lester's approach, saying that the stories "help destroy the delusion that black men did not suffer as another man would in similar circumstances," and the Foners applaud the fact that "Lester does not feel it is necessary to make every black man and woman a super-hero." *New York Times Book Review* contributor Rosalind K. Goddard recommends Lester's writing as both lesson and entertainment: "These stories point the way for young blacks to find their roots, so important to the realization of their identities, as well as offer a stimulating and informative experience for all."

In *Lovesong: Becoming a Jew* Lester presents the autobiographical story of his conversion to the Jewish faith. Beginning with his southern childhood as the son of a Methodist minister, following his years of atheism and civil rights activity, and ending with his exploration of many faiths, *Lovesong* concludes with Lester's embrace of Judaism in 1983. Discussing the book in a *Partisan Review* article, David Lehman remarked that the author relates his experiences with "conviction and passion."

With *How Many Spots Does a Leopard Have?* Lester drew from folktales of both the African and Jewish traditions to write new stories in a modern language. "Although I am of African and Jewish ancestry," Lester writes in his introduction to the collection, "I am also an Ameri-

can. . . . I have fitted the story to my mouth and tongue." Assessing the collection in the *Los Angeles Times Book Review,* Sonja Bolle called the stories "so lively they positively dance."

BIOGRAPHICAL/CRITICAL SOURCES:

BOOKS

Children's Literature Review, Volume 2, Gale, 1976.
Krim, Seymour, *You and Me,* Holt, 1972.
Lester, Julius, *All Is Well: An Autobiography,* Morrow, 1976.
Lester, *Lovesong: Becoming a Jew,* Holt, 1988.
Lester, *How Many Spots Does a Leopard Have? and Other Stories,* Scholastic, Inc., 1989.

PERIODICALS

Bulletin of the Center for Children's Books, February, 1970.
Dissent, winter, 1989, p. 116.
Essence, August, 1989, p. 98; July, 1991, p. 100.
Junior Bookshelf, February, 1975.
Los Angeles Times Book Review, January 31, 1988; January 27, 1991, p. 8.
Nation, June 22, 1970.
New Advocate, summer, 1990, p. 206.
New York Review of Books, April 20, 1972.
New York Times Book Review, November 3, 1968; November 9, 1969; July 23, 1972; February 4, 1973; September 5, 1982; February 17, 1985; May 17, 1987, p. 32; January 14, 1990, p. 17; August 12, 1990, p. 29.
Partisan Review, Volume 57, number 2, 1990, pp. 321-25.
Publishers Weekly, February 12, 1988.
Quill and Quire, December, 1989, p. 24.
Times Literary Supplement, April 3, 1987.
Tribune Books (Chicago), February 26, 1989, p. 8; February 11, 1990, p. 6.
Washington Post, March 12, 1985.
Washington Post Book World, September 3, 1972; February 14, 1988.*

*   *   *

LEVERING, Frank (Graham) 1952-

PERSONAL: Born July 5, 1952, in Mt. Airy, NC; son of Samuel Ralph (an orchardist) and Miriam (an orchardist; maiden name, Lindsey) Levering; married Wanda Marie Urbanski (an orchardist and writer), October 1, 1983. *Education:* Wesleyan University, B.A. (magna cum laude), 1974; Harvard University, M.Th., 1978.

ADDRESSES: Home—Route 2, Ararat, VA 24053.

CAREER: Writer. Has worked as a cabdriver and airport security guard; orchardist at Levering Orchard, Orchard Gap, VA, 1985—. Active in Amnesty International.

MEMBER: Writers Guild of America, Sierra Club, Phi Beta Kappa.

WRITINGS:

Chest Pains (two-act play), first produced in Middletown, CT, at Wesleyan University, December, 1973.
Parasite (screenplay), Embassy Pictures, 1982.
(With Alton A. Lindsey, Mary Durant, Michael Harwood, Robert Aaron Petty, Robert Owen Petty, and Scott Russell Sanders) *The Bicentennial of John James Audubon* (essays), Indiana University, 1985.
(With wife, Wanda Urbanski) *Simple Living: One Couple's Search for a Better Life,* Viking, 1992.

Also author of *It's Your Life* (a stage play about the prevention of teen pregnancy), produced in North Carolina through Surry County Health Department and Surry Arts Council from a grant from the March of Dimes. Author of numerous screenplays, as yet neither published nor produced. Regular contributor to *Los Angeles Herald* column "First Person"; contributor of book reviews to the *Los Angeles Times* and of poems to *Thoreau Journal Quarterly.*

SIDELIGHTS: The Bicentennial of John James Audubon, written by Alton A. Lindsey, Mary Durant, Michael Harwood, Frank Levering, Robert Aaron Petty, Robert Owen Petty, and Scott Russell Sanders, is an essay collection commemorating the two hundredth birthday of America's foremost ornithologist. Expressing the "different perspectives" of biologists, conservationists, historians, and professional writers, the book "modestly shape[s] into an informal biography," related David Graber in the *Los Angeles Times Book Review;* contributor Levering, for instance, investigates Audubon's notorious penchant for reinventing the truth. "What rings clear from all the contributors to this volume is the rare and marvelous coincidence of the man Audubon with his place and time. For very few, it seems, was the American wilderness a place of personal, physical delight," the critic observed. "The writing in this collection is good, the content . . . is pleasant, satisfying and useful. . . . The book works."

Levering told *CA:* "I grew up on a fruit orchard in the Virginia Blue Ridge and have often written about the Blue Ridge Mountains. Combined with my Quaker background, my primary interests as a writer have been Appalachian culture, natural history, and religion. I also lived for six years in Los Angeles, and as a screenwriter focused primarily on family dramas."

BIOGRAPHICAL/CRITICAL SOURCES:

PERIODICALS

Los Angeles Times Book Review, May 26, 1985.

*   *   *

LEVI, Maurice (David) 1945-

PERSONAL: Surname is pronounced *"lee*-vye"; born September 28, 1945, in London, England; son of Karl (in sales) and Louise Hannah (Magson) Levi; married Kate Birkinshaw, January 14, 1979; children: Adam Julian, Naomi Anne, Jonathan Karl. *Education:* Victoria University of Manchester, B.A. (with first class honors), 1967; University of Chicago, M.A., 1968, Ph.D., 1972. *Religion:* Jewish. *Avocational Interests:* Astronomy, salmon fishing.

ADDRESSES: Home—1832 Allison Rd., Vancouver, British Columbia, Canada. *Office*—Faculty of Commerce, University of British Columbia, Vancouver, British Columbia V6T 1Z2, Canada.

CAREER: University of British Columbia, Vancouver, Killam Fellow, 1972-73, assistant professor, 1974-79, associate professor, 1979-82, Bank of Montreal Professor of Business and Commerce, 1982—. Visiting professor at Hebrew University of Jerusalem, 1976; visiting associate professor at University of California, Berkeley, 1979; visiting scholar at Massachusetts Institute of Technology, 1980; visiting professor at London Business School, 1985; Nomura fellow, University of Exeter, 1990. Intern at Citibank; member of Vancouver Economic Advisory Commission; consultant to Shell Oil.

MEMBER: Canadian Economic Association, American Economic Association.

AWARDS, HONORS: T. S. Ashton Prize, University of Manchester, 1966, for top undergraduate; Cobden Prize, University of Manchester, 1967, for top undergraduate; Ford Foundation grant, 1969-70; J. S. Perry Award, J. S. Perry Foundation, 1970; Bronfman Award, Samuel Bronfman Foundation, 1978, for research on international finance; Seagram award, 1978; Canada Council fellow, 1978, 1980, and 1985.

WRITINGS:

(With Martin Jay Kupferman) *Slowth,* Wiley, 1980.
Economics Deciphered: A Layman's Survival Guide, Basic Books, 1981.
International Finance, McGraw-Hill, 1983.
Thinking Economically: How Economic Principles Can Contribute to Clear Thinking, Basic Books, 1985.
International Finance: The Markets and Financial Management of Multinational Business, McGraw-Hill, 1990.

Economics and the Modern World, Heath, 1994.

Also contributor of articles to professional journals.

*   *   *

LEVITT, Morton P(aul) 1936-

PERSONAL: Born December 22, 1936, in Brooklyn, NY; son of Nathan (a painting contractor) and Winnie (Maslow) Levitt; married Annette Shandler (a critic). *Education:* Dickinson College, A.B., 1958; Columbia University, M.A., 1960; Pennsylvania State University, Ph.D., 1965.

ADDRESSES: Home—Philadelphia, PA. *Office*—Department of English, Temple University, Broad St. and Montgomery Ave., Philadelphia, PA 19122.

CAREER: Temple University, Philadelphia, PA, assistant professor, 1965-71, associate professor, 1971-80, professor of English, 1980—. Fulbright professor at University of Zagreb, 1974-75; visiting professor at University of Granada, 1983, Concordia University, 1983, and University of British Columbia, 1988.

MEMBER: James Joyce Foundation, Modern Greek Studies Association.

WRITINGS:

Bloomsday: An Interpretation of James Joyce's "Ulysses," New York Graphic Society, 1972.
The Cretan Glance: The World and Art of Kikos Kazantzakis, Ohio State University Press, 1980.
Modernist Survivors: The Contemporary Novel in England, the United States, France, and Latin America, Ohio State University Press, 1987.

Also editor of *Journal of Modern Literature,* 1986—.

WORK IN PROGRESS: James Joyce, Modernism, Myth and the Jews: Collected Essays.

SIDELIGHTS: Morton P. Levitt once told *CA:* "I think of myself as an unreconstructed New Critic, understanding that term to mean the freedom to use any sources—mythic, political, even biographical—so long as they manifest a basic respect for the primacy of the text. All of my work follows this principle, although in recent years it has become more directly judgmental and personal. The text of *Bloomsday* is intended as an introduction to literate non-Joyceans. I have always thought of *Ulysses* as an accessible novel, not at all arcane or destined for a privileged few, and my book attempts to demonstrate that principle. The glorious engravings by Saul Field make the same point. My book on Kazantzakis, which took nine years to complete, deals with a writer from the opposite end of the Modernist spectrum, the least appreciated, I think, of the

major figures of his generation. My title comes from a metaphor of Kazantzakis's and suggests the uniquely Cretan inheritance which forms all of his life and work and which works in uneasy tension with his Western European intellectuality. *The Cretan Glance* endeavors to establish Kazantzakis as a novelist and epic poet worthy of consideration alongside James Joyce—even more heretically, alongside Homer as well. It remains, so far as I know, the only critical study, in any language, of Kazantzakis's fiction.

"*Modernist Survivors* is a more ambitious book still, a study of contemporary fiction in England, France, the United States, and Latin America. Its basic premise is that Modernism in the novel survives, even thrives, if one is willing to discard the critical cliches and look beyond the English language and conventional wisdom; the idea of post-Modernism in the novel seems to me to be as inaccurate as it is inelegant. I discuss the works of some two dozen novelists, among them Thomas Pynchon, Robert Coover, E. L. Doctorow, and John Barth in the United States; Alain Robbe-Grillet, Butor, and Simon in France; Drabble, Cooper, and B. S. Johnson in England; and Cortazar, Puig, Cabrera Infante, Arenas, Callado, Donoso, Vargas Llosa, Garcia Marquez, and Carlos Fuentes in Latin America. And I use Joyce as a metaphor to elucidate the nature of Modernism and what I see—from this date, after the most self-destructive half-century in human history—as a profoundly humanistic movement. It is an argumentative but, I hope, balanced approach.

Levitt added, "Although I had literally never spent a moment thinking that I might someday be an editor, now that I am one, it seems both natural and inevitable, as if I had spent my entire career in preparation."

*   *   *

LEWIS, Mary (Christianna) 1907(?)-1988
(Mary Ann Ashe, Christianna Brand, Annabel Jones, Mary Roland, China Thompson)

PERSONAL: Born December 17, 1907 (one source indicates 1909), in Malaya; died March 11, 1988; daughter of Alexander Brand (a rubber planter) and Nancy (Irving) Milne; married Roland Swaine Lewis (a surgeon), 1939; children: Victoria. *Education:* Educated in India and at a Franciscan convent, Taunton, Somerset, England. *Politics:* Conservative.

ADDRESSES: Home—88 Maida Vale, London W.9, England. *Agent*—A.M. Heath & Co. Ltd., 40-42 William IV St., London WC2N 4DD, England; and Otto Penzler, Mysterious Agency, 129 West 56th St., New York, NY 10019.

CAREER: Novelist and free-lance writer. Worked variously as a salesperson, governess, dancer, model, receptionist, and secretary.

MEMBER: Crime Writers Association (chairperson, 1972-73), Mystery Writers of America, Detection Club.

AWARDS, HONORS: Received two awards for best short story from Mystery Writers of America; named Grand Master in Sweden.

WRITINGS:

(Under pseudonym Mary Roland) *The Single Pilgrim,* Crowell, 1946.

(Under pseudonym China Thompson) *Starrbelow* (mystery romance), Scribner, 1958, published under pseudonym Christianna Brand, Brooke House, 1977.

(Under pseudonym Annabel Jones) *The Radiant Dove* (romance fiction), St. Martin's, 1974.

(Under pseudonym Mary Ann Ashe) *Alas, for Her That Met Me!,* Star Books, 1976.

(Under pseudonym Mary Ann Ashe) *A Ring of Roses,* Star Books, 1976, published under pseudonym Christianna Brand, W. H. Allen, 1977.

UNDER PSEUDONYM CHRISTIANNA BRAND

Death in High Heels (mystery novel), Bodley Head, 1941, Scribner, 1954, reprinted, Carroll & Graf, 1989.

Heads You Lose (mystery novel), Bodley Head, 1942, Dodd, 1943, reprinted, Ian Henry, 1981.

Green for Danger (mystery novel), Dodd, 1945, reprinted, M. Joseph, 1973, new edition, Hamlyn, 1982.

The Crooked Wreath (mystery novel), Dodd, 1947, published in England as *Suddenly at His Residence,* Bodley Head, 1947, reprinted, M. Joseph, 1973.

Welcome to Danger (children's novel), Dodd, 1948, published in England as *Danger Unlimited,* Foley House, 1949.

Death of Jezebel (mystery novel), Dodd, 1948, reprinted, Ian Henry, 1977.

Cat and Mouse (mystery novel), Knopf, 1950, reprinted, Avon, 1976, new edition, Ian Henry, 1982.

London Particular (mystery novel), M. Joseph, 1952, published as *Fog of Doubt,* Scribner, 1953, reprinted, Carroll & Graf, 1984.

Tour de Force (mystery novel), Scribner, 1955, new edition, Hamlyn, 1980.

The Three-Cornered Halo (mystery novel), Scribner, 1957.

Heaven Knows Who (nonfiction), Scribner, 1960.

(Compiler) *Naughty Children: An Anthology* (juvenile), illustrated by Edward Ardizzone, Gollancz, 1962, Dutton, 1963.

Nurse Matilda (juvenile), illustrated by Ardizzone, Brockhampton Press, 1963, Dutton, 1964.

What Dread Hand? (short stories), M. Joseph, 1964.

Nurse Matilda Goes to Town (juvenile), illustrated by Ardizzone, Brockhampton Press, 1966, Dutton, 1967.

Nurse Matilda Goes to Hospital (juvenile), illustrated by Ardizzone, Brockhampton Press, 1969.

Court of Foxes, M. Joseph, 1969, Brooke House, 1977.

Brand X (short stories), M. Joseph, 1974.

The Honey Harlot (mystery novel), W. H. Allen, 1978.

The Rose in Darkness (mystery novel), Brand, 1979.

The Brides of Aberdar (romance fiction), St. Martin's, 1982.

Buffet for Unwelcome Guests: The Best Short Mysteries of Christianna Brand, edited by Francis M. Nevins, Jr., and Martin H. Greenberg, Southern Illinois University Press, 1983.

(With others) *Crime on the Coast, and No Flowers by Request,* Gollancz, 1984.

OTHER

Also author, under pseudonym Christianna Brand, of screenplays *Death in High Heels,* 1947, (with W. P. Lipscomb and Francis Cowdry) *The Mark of Cain,* 1948, and (with others) *Secret People,* 1952. Contributor, under pseudonym Christianna Brand, to *The Great Detectives,* edited by Otto Penzler, Little, Brown, 1978; and, with others, to *Making a Film,* edited by Lindsay Anderson, Macmillan, 1952. Contributor, under pseudonym Christianna Brand, to anthologies, including *Best Police Stories,* edited by Roy Vickers, Faber, 1966; and *Verdict of Thirteen,* edited by Julian Symons, Harper, 1979. Contributor to periodicals, including *Chicago Tribune, Saturday Evening Post, Woman, Saint,* and *Ellery Queen's Mystery Magazine. Death in High Heels* has been released in an audio version.

ADAPTATIONS: Green for Danger was filmed starring Alastair Sim as Inspector Cockrill.

SIDELIGHTS: Best known for her mystery stories as author Christianna Brand, Mary Lewis focused on three detectives through her suspense work. Inspector Cockrill of the Kent County Police, Inspector Chucky, and Inspector Charlesworth comprise the series detectives of more than ten of her books and many of her short stories. Her mysteries feature intricate plot twists and numerous clues cleverly planted to engage and mislead the unwary reader. In addition to her detective novels and short stories, she also penned several romance novels and the humorous "Nurse Matilda" children's series, illustrated by her cousin Edward Ardizzone. Based on recollections of stories told by her grandfather, the series depicts the many adventures of the Brown children and Nurse Matilda, their repulsive-looking nanny who becomes more beautiful as her unruly charges gradually benefit from her wisdom and eccentric teaching methods.

Mary Lewis once told *CA:* "What is my aim? To write good, readable (saleable) entertainment books and above all to write them well. I detest illiterate writing. I detest bad style, bad grammar, bad punctuation. At four years of age, I read fluently; and I was brought up on the classics, and I hope I may say that I really can't write other than in good style.

"I write in a sort of rat's nest of papers all over two desks; and a book is for some time a sort of rat's nest of ideas in my mind, until it slowly and painfully clears to what is a strong plot, highly involved, but, one hopes, easy to read and understand. I write largely crime stories, and these I believe may be brought to a very highly skilled craft; but I don't claim as some do that they are an art form.

"My pet loves are good literature, painting, and Siamese cats. My hates are sloppy work, dirt in any form (mental or physical), and noise.

"As a girl I was very poor, cold, and hungry, and I have known a great deal of suffering—for many years, for personal family reasons I was able to write hardly at all so that there has been a long gap in my work. It was a bitter sacrifice—of money, of recognition, above all of talent wasted; but people are more important than anything else, and that's the end of it. Compassion is all—and everything adds up to being a writer. We are what we remember, and as writers, we become a sort of sponge that soaks up our experience and emerges in what we have to say."

BIOGRAPHICAL/CRITICAL SOURCES:

BOOKS

Symons, Julian, editor, *The Hundred Best Crime Stories,* London Sunday Times, 1959.
Twentieth-Century Crime and Mystery Writers, 2nd edition, St. Martin's, 1985.

PERIODICALS

Armchair Detective, summer, 1988, p. 228; winter, 1989, p. 76; summer, 1990, p. 319.
Christian Science Monitor, May 2, 1968, p. 85.
New York Times Book Review, August 4, 1968, p. 20; January 3, 1982, p. 19; July 11, 1982, p. 31; August 4, 1985, p. 28; January 15, 1989, p. 34.
Saturday Review, May 11, 1968, p. 38.
Times (London), April 8, 1982.
Times Literary Supplement, November 30, 1967, p. 1149.

OBITUARIES:

PERIODICALS

Times (London), March 14, 1988.*

LIDDY, James (Daniel Reeves) 1934-

PERSONAL: Born July 1, 1934, in Kilkee, Ireland; son of James (a doctor) and Clare (Reeves) Liddy. *Education:* University College, Dublin, M.A., 1959; King's Inns, Dublin, barrister, 1959. *Politics:* Fine Gael. *Religion:* Catholic.

ADDRESSES: Home—Coolgreany, Gorey, County Wexford, Ireland. *Office*—Department of English, University of Wisconsin—Milwaukee, Milwaukee, WI 53201.

CAREER: Poet, writer. University of Wisconsin—Milwaukee, professor of English, 1976—. Poet-in-residence at San Francisco State University, 1967-68, and at Harpur College; visiting professor at State University of New York, Lewis and Clark College, Dennison University, and University College of Galway. Literature director of Gorey Arts Festival.

WRITINGS:

Esau, My Kingdom for a Drink: Homage to James Joyce on His Eightieth Birthday (booklet), Dolmen Press, 1962.
(Contributor) Donald Carroll, editor, *New Poets of Ireland,* Alan Swallow, 1963.
In a Blue Smoke (poems), Dufour, 1968.
Blue Mountain (poems), Dufour, 1968.
(With Jim Chapson and Thomas Hill) *Blue House: Poems in the Chinese Manner,* White Rabbit Press, 1968.
A Life of Stephen Dedalus (booklet), White Rabbit Press, 1969.
A Munster Song of Love and War (booklet), White Rabbit Press, 1971.
(Editor) *Nine Queen Bees,* White Rabbit Press, 1971.
Baudelaire's Bar Flowers, Capra Press, 1974.
Corca Bascin, Dolmen Press, 1977.
Comyn's Lay, Hit & Run Press, 1978.
At the Grave of Fr. Sweetman, Malton Press, 1984.
Young Men Go out Walking (novel), Wolfhound Press, 1986.
A White Thought in a White Shade: New and Selected Poems, Kerr's Pink Press, 1987.
In the Slovak Bowling Alley, Blue Canary Press, 1990.
Notes Towards a Video of Avondale House, International University Press, 1991.

Also contributor to *New York Times, Dublin Magazine, Irish Times,* and *Milwaukee Journal.*

SIDELIGHTS: James Liddy, a native of Ireland, gave up practicing law in 1966 to become a full-time writer and editor. Since then he has travelled widely in the United States and the United Kingdom, giving poetry readings and teaching English and creative writing. "If you are an Irish poet of my generation," he told the *Milwaukee Journal,* "you simply had to have divine figures, like Yeats and

Joyce. And there's Patrick Kavanagh. You definitely have to go for style." *Milwaukee Journal* book editor Leslie Cross feels that despite these national influences, Liddy's idiom "is distinctly his own and definitely contemporary, with a lusty candor that must endear him to his students."

Liddy told *CA:* "I believe that literature is the religion and politics of the imagination. Therefore a writer never grows too old. He only gets tired on fame—he gets his adolescence back from obscurity."

BIOGRAPHICAL/CRITICAL SOURCES:

BOOKS

Authors in the News, Volume II, Gale, 1976.

PERIODICALS

Milwaukee Journal, February 8, 1976.
Poetry, December, 1971.
Times Literary Supplement, July 28, 1978.

*   *   *

LINE, David
   See DAVIDSON, Lionel

*   *   *

LOGAN, Jake
   See SMITH, Martin Cruz

*   *   *

LOWRY, Lois   1937-

PERSONAL: Born March 20, 1937, in Honolulu, HI; daughter of Robert E. (a dentist) and Katharine (Landis) Hammersberg; married Donald Grey Lowry (an attorney), June 11, 1956 (divorced, 1977); children: Alix, Grey, Kristin, Benjamin. *Education:* Attended Brown University, 1954-56; University of Southern Maine, B.A., 1972, also graduate study. *Religion:* Episcopalian.

ADDRESSES: Home—8 Lexington Avenue, Cambridge, MA 02138; and Sanbornton, NH.

CAREER: Free-lance writer and photographer, 1972—.

AWARDS, HONORS: Children's Literature Award, International Reading Association, 1978, for *A Summer to Die;* American Library Association Notable Book citation, 1980 for *Autumn Street;* American Book Award nomination (juvenile paperback category), 1983, for *Anastasia Again!; Boston Globe-Horn Book* award, Golden

Kite Award, and Child Study Award, Children's Book Committee of Bank Street College, all 1987, all for *Rabble Starkey;* Newbery Medal, National Jewish Book Award, and Sidney Taylor Award, National Jewish Libraries, all 1990, all for *Number the Stars;* Newbery Medal, 1994 for *The Giver.*

WRITINGS:

JUVENILE NOVELS

A Summer to Die, Houghton, 1977.
Find a Stranger, Say Goodbye, Houghton, 1978.
Anastasia Krupnik, Houghton, 1979.
Autumn Street, Houghton, 1979.
Anastasia Again!, Houghton, 1981.
Anastasia at Your Service, Houghton, 1982.
Taking Care of Terrific, Houghton, 1983.
Anastasia Ask Your Analyst, Houghton, 1984.
Us and Uncle Fraud, Houghton, 1984.
One Hundredth Thing About Caroline, Houghton, 1985.
Anastasia on Her Own, Houghton, 1985.
Switcharound, Houghton, 1985.
Anastasia Has the Answers, Houghton, 1986.
Rabble Starkey, Houghton, 1987.
Anastasia's Chosen Career, Houghton, 1987.
All about Sam, Houghton, 1988.
Number the Stars, Houghton, 1989.
Your Move J.P.!, Houghton, 1990.
Anastasia at This Address, Houghton, 1991.
Attaboy, Sam!, Hougton, 1992.
The Giver, Houghton, 1993.

OTHER

Black American Literature (textbook), J. Weston Walsh, 1973.
Literature of the American Revolution (textbook), J. Weston Walsh, 1974.
Values and the Family, Walsh, 1977.
(Photographer) Frederick H. Lewis, *Here in Kennebunkport,* Durrell, 1978.

Author of introduction, Frances H. Burnett, *The Secret Garden,* Bantam, 1987. Contributor of stories, articles, and photographs to periodicals.

SIDELIGHTS: Lois Lowry is a children's writer whose books have broad appeal. She "writes well in different modes and for all ages," according to a reviewer in *Language Arts,* and her novels frequently explore topical themes, such as an adopted child's search for her real mother or the loneliness facing the elderly. She once told *CA* that she gauges her success as a writer by her ability to "help adolescents answer their own questions about life, identity, and human relationships." In a *Publishers Weekly* interview, Lowry says that "kids are too sophisticated nowadays to enjoy a completely idealized view of human existence," noting that when she was a child certain books, such as *Catcher in the Rye,* were off-limits to readers her age because "there was a feeling that kids should be protected from—what?—real life." Lowry strives to create realistic characters who suffer some of the same problems as her readers and with whom they can identify; in *Publishers Weekly* she says that "when I'm writing I always think about that kid who lives inside me."

Born the daughter of an army dentist stationed at Pearl Harbor, Hawaii, Lowry moved to Pennsylvania at the outbreak of World War II to live with her mother's family. She lived in Japan briefly following the war before returning to the United States to attend boarding school and college. She left Brown University her sophomore year to get married. Lowry explained to *CA:* "That was the '50's, and that's what you did when somebody asked you to marry him; immediately you gave up your academic aspirations. Then I had four children by the time I was twenty-five." Eventually Lowry returned to college and began writing textbooks while she was a graduate student. For a while she was a professional photographer of children, and it did not occur to her to write children's books until she impressed an editor with a short story she had written for a magazine.

Her first novel, *A Summer to Die,* involves thirteen-year-old Meg Chalmers' adjustment to living in the country for a year while her English-professor father is on sabbatical. Meg's older sister, Molly, inspires in her both feelings of jealously and inferiority, until Molly is stricken with leukemia. Through her sister's fatal illness Meg matures and discovers strength. She befriends a young couple who invite her to witness the birth of their baby, and it is through these events Meg comes to understand cycles of life and death. The book is autobiographical from the standpoint that Lowry's own sister died from cancer while they were both in their twenties, but she says that "very little [of *A Summer to Die*] was factual, except the emotions."

Well-received by critics, *A Summer to Die* garners praise for both its form and content. "The author skillfully integrates the subplot—the natural, home birth of Ben and Maria's baby—with Molly's death, and explores the meaning of mourning, loss and sorrow without being too heavy handed or obvious," according to a reviewer in *Kliatt.* A *Horn Book* contributor calls the novel "not simply another story on a subject currently in vogue," but rather "a well-crafted reaffirmation of universal values." The writing is "beautifully unobtrusive, yet bracing and compelling" in a *Junior Bookshelf* reviewer's eyes, and a *Publishers Weekly* contributor proclaims *A Summer to Die* "a marvelous book and a help in understanding loss."

Memories of childhood, as well as experiences as a parent, have inspired some of Lowry's most popular characters,

especially the adolescent Anastasia Krupnik. "Until I was about twelve I thought my parents were terrific, wise, and wonderful, beautiful, loving, and well-dressed," she confesses to *CA,* "By age twelve and a half they turned into stupid boring people with whom I did not want to be seen in public. . . . That happens to all kids, and to the kids in my books as well." The precocious Anastasia is confronted with crises ranging from dealing with her weird parents (her father keeps his poetry manuscripts in the refrigerator crisper in case the house burns down) to being the only one in her class who cannot climb the rope in gym; with each volume of the series she reaches a new level of maturity.

Originally written as a short story for a magazine, Lowry decided to expand the devilish Anastasia character after growing so fond of her. As Lowry tells *CA:* "I did not intend to make [her] into a series . . . [but] I have the feeling that she's going to go on forever—or until I get quite sick of her, which hasn't happened yet. I'm still very fond of her and her whole family." As a ten-year-old in the first installment of the series, Anastasia deals with the impending birth of a sibling and her anguish over her name. In *Anastasia Again!* she must adjust to her parents' decision to move from Cambridge, Massachusetts to a large Victorian house in the suburbs—a move she originally protests. Subsequent volumes address such pressing issues as Anastasia's belief that she needs psychotherapy because of all the "different personalities seething inside," and her concern over her raging hormones. Carrie Carmichael sums up the focus of the Anastasia series in *New York Times Book Review,* "Lois Lowry addresses every teenager's fear: being weird."

Lowry confronts more serious topics in several of her other works. In *Find a Stranger, Say Goodbye,* Lowry tells the story of Natalie Armstrong, an adopted girl who is searching for her natural parents. *Rabble Starkey* is about a twelve-year-old girl who grows up without a father and watches her best friend's mother go insane. In *Switcharound* Caroline and her brother J.P. are sent, against their will, to spend the summer in Des Moines with their father and his new wife, and are duped into babysitting and baseball coaching duties much to their dismay. "Young readers are bound to identify with these injustices of childhood," says Kristiana Gregory, writing in *Los Angeles Times Book Review,* "and also the warmth within a caring family." *Publishers Weekly* contributor Amanda Smith states that Lowry's "conviction that teenagers must be prepared to live in a sophisticated world is a major influence on her work," which is "elegant and witty . . . tempered with compassion and often with humor."

Autumn Street, one of Lowry's darker visions of childhood, is partly autobiographical. In it, Elizabeth Lorimer recounts the year she was six and moved to her grandfather's house in Pennsylvania at the start of World War II, just as Lowry had herself. Elizabeth recalls her guilt over the death of her sadistic neighbor, Noah Hoffman, and the murder of the housekeeper's grandson. Elizabeth contracts a serious case of pneumonia and falls into a coma; she regains consciousness on her birthday, the first day of spring. A reviewer in the *New Yorker* characterizes the work as "a fine novel about the twilight zone between early childhood and the first dawning of adult understanding." Though these dark themes suggest a work that is more suitable for adults than juveniles, Lowry does not object to the publisher's decision to market it as a children's book. "Publishers, for whatever reason, feel that they have to put an age level on a book," Lowry tells *CA.* "It does cross those boundaries. . . . I'm glad special people come along and find *Autumn Street* and it becomes special to them."

Lowry won the prestigious Newbery Medal in 1990 for *Number the Stars,* a historical account of Nazi-occupied Denmark during World War II. Ten-year-old Annemarie Johansen's family becomes involved in the resistance movement by shuttling Denmark's Jews into neutral Sweden, thereby saving them from imprisonment in concentration camps. Annemarie's best friend, Ellen Rosen, is Jewish, and poses as her sister to avoid detection by the Germans during their journey to safety. Though Edith Milton, writing in *New York Times Book Review,* states that "the book fails to offer . . . any sense of the horror that is the alternative if the Johansens' efforts to save Ellen and her family fail," Newbery Committee Chair Caroline Ward notes in *School Library Journal,* "Lowry creates suspense and tension without wavering from the viewpoint of Annemarie, a child who shows the true meaning of courage." *Los Angeles Times Book Review* contributor Carolyn Meyer regards the book as "poignant because it may have happened just this way."

Lowry explains to *CA* that writing children's books is not as easy as it looks. "An awful lot of people believe the myth that it's easy to write for kids, so they think they can sit down and do it on Sunday afternoon after the dishes are done. People who think that are wrong. They should spend their time *reading* books for young people. A lot of them think they can write for young people but they haven't read what's being written, so they aren't familiar with it. I think, in general, anybody who wants to write anything should *a,* read a lot and *b,* write a lot, and quit

worrying about who's going to buy it. It seems to be a part of the current generation, which is very impatient, to want to sit down and write something and sell it. If they'd concentrate on the writing instead of the selling, they'd probably end up a lot better off. But it's tough to convince them of that. Instant gratification seems to be very important these days."

BIOGRAPHICAL/CRITICAL SOURCES:

BOOKS

Children's Literature Review, Volume 6, Gale, 1984.
Dictionary of Literary Biography, Volume 52: *American Writers for Children since 1960: Fiction,* Gale, 1986.

PERIODICALS

Horn Book, August, 1977; June, 1978; December, 1979; August, 1980; October, 1981; December, 1982; June, 1983.
Junior Bookshelf, August, 1979; August, 1980.
Kirkus Review, March 1, 1978; December 15, 1979; June 15, 1980.
Kliatt, April, 1979; April, 1982.
Language Arts, October, 1977; May, 1982; March, 1983.
Los Angeles Times Book Review, August 27, 1989.
New Yorker, December 1, 1980.
New York Times Book Review, September 18, 1977; February 28, 1982; April 11, 1982; September 14, 1986; May 21, 1989.
Publishers Weekly, June 29, 1977; May 15, 1978; March 26, 1979; September 24, 1979; April 11, 1980; July 27, 1984; February 21, 1986.
School Library Journal, May, 1977; May, 1978; October, 1979; April, 1980; October, 1981; November, 1982.
Times Literary Supplement, March 28, 1980.

—*Sketch by Kathleen Wilson*

*   *   *

LYNCH, B. Suarez
See BIOY CASARES, Adolfo

*   *   *

LYNCH DAVIS, B.
See BIOY CASARES, Adolfo

M

Mac LAVERTY, Bernard 1942-

PERSONAL: Born September 14, 1942, in Belfast, Northern Ireland; son of John (a commercial artist) and Molly (Boyd) Mac Laverty; married Madeline McGuckin, March 30, 1967; children: Ciara, Claire, John, Judith. *Education:* Queens University (Belfast), B.A., 1970, education diploma, 1975.

ADDRESSES: Home—26 Roxburgh St., Hillhead, Glasgow G12 9AP, Scotland.

CAREER: Writer. Medical laboratory technician, Belfast, Northern Ireland, 1960-70; teacher, Edinburgh, Scotland, 1975-78, and Isle of Islay, Scotland, 1978-81. Writer-in-residence at Aberdeen University, 1983-85.

AWARDS, HONORS: Northern Ireland Arts Council award, 1975, for stories contributed to periodicals; Scottish Arts Council award, 1978, for *Secrets and Other Stories;* Pharic McLaren Award, Radio Industries of Scotland, for best radio play, and second place for Pye Radio Award, both 1981, both for *My Dear Palestrina;* Scottish Arts Council award, and second place for fiction from *Guardian,* both 1981, both for *Lamb;* Jacobs Award for best play, Radio Telefis Eireann, for *My Dear Palestrina* (television production); Scottish Arts Council award, 1982, and arts award, Irish *Sunday Independent,* 1983, both for *A Time to Dance and Other Stories;* best screenplay award from the London *Evening Standard,* 1984, for *Cal; Lamb* voted best film by the youth jury and ecumenical jury at Lucarno Film Festival, 1987; Scottish Arts Council award, 1988, for *The Great Profundo and Other Stories;* Scottish Writer of the Year (McVities prize; joint winner), 1988; Irish Post Award, 1989.

WRITINGS:

Secrets and Other Stories, Blackstaff Press, 1977, Viking, 1984.

A Man in Search of a Pet (for children), Blackstaff Press, 1978.

Lamb (novel; also see below), Braziller, 1980.

A Time to Dance and Other Stories, Braziller, 1982.

Cal (novel; also see below), Braziller, 1983.

The Great Profundo and Other Stories, Cape/Blackstaff Press, 1987.

Andrew McAndrew (for children), Walker Books, 1988, Candlewick Press, 1993.

RADIO PLAYS

My Dear Palestrina (adapted by Mac Laverty from his own short story; also see below), British Broadcasting Corporation (BBC), November, 1980.

Secrets, BBC, 1981.

No Joke, BBC, 1983.

The Break, BBC, 1988.

Some Surrender, BBC, 1988.

TELEPLAYS

My Dear Palestrina (adapted by Mac Laverty from his own radio play), BBC, December, 1980.

Phonefun Limited, BBC, 1982.

The Daily Woman, BBC, 1986.

Sometime in August, BBC, 1989.

SCREENPLAYS

Cal (adapted by Mac Laverty from his own novel), Warner Bros., 1984.

Lamb (adapted by Mac Laverty from his own novel), Flickers/Limehouse, 1986.

OTHER

Hostages (drama documentary), Granada, 1992, and Home Box Office (HBO), 1993.

Also author of television adaptation *The Real Charlotte,* by Somerville & Ross, Granada/Gandon, 1989. Work anthologized in *Scottish Short Stories 1977, 1978, 1980,* and *1982.* Contributor to periodicals, including the *New Statesman* and *GQ.*

WORK IN PROGRESS: Walking the Dog and Other Stories; a screenplay tentatively titled *Perugia.*

SIDELIGHTS: Bernard Mac Laverty is an acclaimed Irish writer who began earning praise with his first book, *Secrets and Other Stories,* which contains poignant and sometimes somber tales of Irish life. Kate Cruise O'Brien in the *Times Literary Supplement* deemed them "fine stories describing with surprising tenderness the atmosphere and realities of modern Ireland," and, discussing the story "Between Two Shores," cited Mac Laverty's ability "to convey vividly a sense of the squalor of loneliness." O'Brien called the story, which concerns one man's qualms about returning home to his wife after an affair and consequent venereal infection, "the finest story in this remarkably good collection."

Other reviewers were similarly impressed with Mac Laverty's depictions of Irish life. Writing in *Books and Bookmen,* Patricia Craig declared that the stories in *Secrets* are "completely without affectation or self-indulgence." William DeMeritt, in his review for *Eire-Ireland,* acknowledged Mac Laverty's skillful handling of the coming-of-age theme, and wrote that "several of the better stories . . . deal with a boy's loss of innocence or his initiation into a corrupted world." DeMeritt found particularly noteworthy "The Exercise," in which a schoolboy is thrashed by his Latin instructor for insisting that his homework was actually completed by his barman father, and "The Deep End," where a boy witnesses a public drowning and is subsequently comforted by his mother. DeMeritt added that Mac Laverty's rendering of the loss of innocence "is usually comically ironic" and that "the loss seems to matter less than the innocence itself."

Mac Laverty's first novel, *Lamb,* is set in an Irish reformatory and concerns a naive instructor's affection for an epileptic student. The *Listener*'s John Naughton praised Mac Laverty's skill in evoking the "casual, almost cheerful, brutality" of the reformatory as well as his ability in avoiding schmaltz while fashioning "an ending which, though predictably tragic and moving, is in no way sentimental." Julia O'Faolain, in a review for the *New York Times Book Review,* commended the author's "tactfully and movingly graphed" handling of the protagonists' gradual friendship and called the work "an impressive book."

Citing the title story of *A Time to Dance and Other Stories,* in which a boy discovers that his mother is a stripper, and "The Beginnings of a Sin," where an altar boy learns that the priest he admires is a drunk, Deirdre Donahue wrote in the *Washington Post Book World* that Mac Laverty's "best stories map out a frightening terrain where the inhabitants smash up against reality." Alison Weir of *British Book News* wrote that *A Time to Dance* "observes the human race with love and heaps loving detail on each story."

Mac Laverty continued to explore the nuances of human emotion and behavior in his second novel, *Cal,* which is set amid the Catholic-Protestant conflict in Northern Ireland. The novel's title character is a young man who falls in love with the widow of a murdered policeman. Although haunted by his complicity—he drove the getaway car after the policeman was shot—Cal is drawn to the widow and eventually earns her love, whereupon he is further overwhelmed by guilt for his misdeed. Valentine Cunningham, reviewing *Cal* for the *Observer,* called it "a formidable fictional triumph" and described the lovers as "characters with a Shakespearean largeness of moral scope." Michael Gorra, writing in the *New York Times Book Review,* declared that *Cal* "opens into a world larger than itself with a confidence that makes one take that world on the novel's terms." Gorra added that Cal "begins in the conscience, where ideology ends, and its meditation on human suffering and responsibility carries the complexity and amplitude of the very finest novels."

In a review of *The Great Profundo and Other Stories, New Statesman*'s Christina Koning noted that Mac Laverty's stories "offer vignettes of real life, in almost all of which an ironic point is made which undermines the narrator's (and the reader's) assumptions. . . . Mac Laverty is a writer who deals in understatement in order to reveal the disturbing truth beneath the commonplace fact." *The Great Profundo* includes "End of Season," which deals with a man who returns to his honeymoon site years after his wife's death, and the title story, about a sword swallower whose act becomes fatal. Although Patricia Craig in the *Times Literary Supplement* maintained that in *The Great Profundo* "the briskness or exuberance which marked his earlier collections seems to have been toned down," she also complimented Mac Laverty's "faculty for close observation and . . . telling way with detail" and added, "The stories in his new collection show, by and large, what the Great Profundo claims for his act: genuineness and a lack of trickery."

Mac Laverty once told *CA:* "If I've learned anything, it's to underwrite as much as possible and to rewrite. I think you reach a stage where instead of rewriting, you just don't bother writing the bad stuff down. But at the beginning, I wrote and rewrote and hacked it about and crossed out words. I don't do so much rewriting now; I think because you have a pre-edit in your head before you put it down." He added, "I'm a very disorganized person. I can only refer to what has happened in the past, that if I do start a piece of work like *Lamb* or *Cal,* I'll work at it almost solidly, all day and at night, until I get it into some sort of shape. And then I might work regular hours on rewriting it. I think both the novels were written in about two-and-a-half to three months, and then each of them I worked on for about a year rewriting. I think it's a bit like being a sculptor in a way, in that you can't sculpt anything if you don't have a block of stone. For the writer, that block of stone is the basic first draft of fifty to sixty thousand words or whatever. Once he's got that, then he can begin to work the material."

For a previously published interview, see entry in *Contemporary Authors,* Gale, Volume 118, 1986, pp. 301-305.

BIOGRAPHICAL/CRITICAL SOURCES:

BOOKS

Contemporary Literary Criticism, Volume 31, Gale, 1985.

PERIODICALS

Books and Bookmen, April 8, 1978; January, 1983.
British Book News, October, 1982.
Eire-Ireland, summer, 1978; spring, 1981.
Film Comment, August, 1984.
Listener, April 3, 1980.
New Statesman, December 4, 1987, p. 33.
Newsweek, September 5, 1983.
New Yorker, September 20, 1983.
New York Times, August 20, 1983.
New York Times Book Review, November 2, 1980; August 21, 1983; June 26, 1988, p. 38.
Observer, January 16, 1983; December 13, 1987, p. 22; July 15, 1990, p. 53.
Time, September 3, 1984.
Times Educational Supplement, May 25, 1990, p. B6; May 24, 1991, p. 24.
Times Literary Supplement, December 11, 1987, p. 1375.

*   *   *

MANDEL, Eli(as Wolf) 1922-

PERSONAL: Born in 1922, in Estevan, Saskatchewan, Canada; married; wife's name, Ann; children: three. *Education:* University of Saskatchewan, B.A., 1949, M.A., 1950; University of Toronto, Ph.D., 1957.

ADDRESSES: Office—Division of Humanities, York University, Toronto, Ontario, Canada.

CAREER: College Militaire Royal de Saint-Jean, St. Jean, Quebec, assistant professor, 1953-55, associate professor, 1955-57; University of Alberta, Edmonton, assistant professor, 1957-59, associate professor of English, 1959-63; York University, Toronto, Ontario, associate professor,

1963-64; University of Alberta, professor of English, 1964-67; York University, professor of English, 1967-80, professor of English and humanities, 1980—. Guest instructor, Banff Centre, 1970, 1973-77, 1983, Art Board, Fort San, Saskatchewan, 1977-78, and San Francisco University, 1980; writer-in-residence, Regina, Saskatchewan, 1978-79, and University of Rome, 1983; visiting professor, University of Victoria, 1970-80. Has given poetry readings and professional lectures at institutions throughout Canada and the United States. Host of Canadian television and radio broadcasts. York University, member of Humanities Research Council, 1959-61, member of board of governors, 1970-71. Member of board of governors, Canada Council Arts Award, 1972-80. *Military service:* Canadian Army; served in medical corps.

MEMBER: Modern Language Association of America, Canadian Ethic Studies Association, League of Canadian Poets, Canadian Association of University Teachers, Association of Canadian Radio and Television Artists, Association of Canadian University Teachers of English (member of executive committee, 1962-64), Association for Canadian and Quebec Literatures, Canadian Association for Commonwealth Literature and Language Studies, Royal Society of Canada (fellow).

AWARDS, HONORS: Canada Foundation fellowship, 1959-60; Canada Council Award, 1961, for *Fuseli Poems;* President's Medal in Poetry, University of Western Ontario, 1963; Governor General's Award in Poetry, 1967; Centennial Medal, 1967; Canada Council Senior Arts Award, 1971-72; Ontario Art Council awards, 1973, 1976, 1977, 1979, 1980; Silver Jubilee Medal, 1977.

WRITINGS:

POETRY

(With Gael Turnbull and Phyllis Webb) *Trio,* Contact Press, 1954.
Fuseli Poems, Contact Press, 1960.
Black and Secret Man, Ryerson Press, 1964.
An Idiot Joy, Hurtig, 1967.
Crusoe: Poems Selected and New, Anansi, 1973.
Stony Plain, Porcepic, 1973.
(With wife, Ann Mandel) *Out of Place,* Porcepic, 1977.
Mary Midnight, Coach House, 1979.
Dreaming Backwards: The Selected Poetry of Eli Mandel, 1954-1981, General Publishing, 1981.
Life Sentence: Poems and Journals, 1976-1980, Porcepic, 1981.
The Family Romance, Turnstone Press, 1986.

OTHER

(Editor with Jean-Guy Pilon) *Poetry 62,* Ryerson Press, 1961.

Criticism: The Silent Speaking Words, C.B.C. Publications, 1966, 2nd edition, 1983.

Irving Layton, Forum House, 1969.

(Editor) *Five Modern Canadian Poets,* Holt, 1970.

(Editor with Desmond Maxwell) *English Poems of the Twentieth Century,* Macmillan, 1971.

(Editor) *Contexts of Canadian Criticism,* University of Chicago Press, 1971.

(Editor) *Poets of Contemporary Canada, 1960-1970,* McClelland & Stewart, 1972.

(Editor) *Eight More Canadian Poets,* Holt, 1972.

(Author of introduction) *Three,* Summer Thought Press, 1972.

(Author of introduction) *The Unwavering Eye: Selected Poems, 1969-1975* by Irving Layton, McClelland & Stewart, 1975.

(Editor and author of introduction) *The Poetry of Irving Layton,* McClelland & Stewart, 1977, 2nd revised edition, Coles, 1981.

Another Time, Porcepic, 1977.

(With Phyllis Schwartz) *Teaching Poetry,* Concept Press, 1979.

(Author of preface) *Field Notes: The Complete Poetry of Robert Kroetsch,* General Publishing, 1981.

(Author of preface) Frank Davey, *Surviving the Paraphrase,* Turnstone Press, 1983.

(Editor with David Taras) *A Passion for Identity: Introduction to Canadian Studies,* Turnstone Press, 1986.

Also contributor to numerous books, including *Of Several Branches,* University of Toronto Press, 1968; *Fearful Joy,* edited by James Downey and Ben Jones, McGill-Queens, 1974; and *Margaret Atwood: Language, Text, and System,* edited by Sherrill E. Grace and Lorraine Weir, University of British Columbia Press, 1983. Work represented in many anthologies, including *Blasted Pine,* Macmillan, 1957; *Penguin Book of Canadian Verse,* Penguin, 1958; *Oxford Book of Canadian Verse,* Oxford University Press, 1960; and *Canadian Poetry: The Modern Era,* McClelland & Stewart, 1977.

Contributor to proceedings. Contributor of poetry and reviews to numerous journals, including *Queen's Quarterly, Arts Canada, Canadian Literature, Canadian Forum, Tamarack Review,* and *Fiddlehead.* Member of editorial board, *Boundary 2,* 1973-77, *Canadian Ethnic Studies,* 1974-77, and *Canadian Journal of Sociological and Political Theory,* 1980—.

*   *   *

MANDELA, Nelson R(olihlahla) 1918-

PERSONAL: Born 1918 in Umtata, Transkei, South Africa; son of Henry Mandela (a Tembu tribal chief); married Edith Ntoko (a nurse; divorced); married Nomzamo Winnie Madikileza (a social worker and political activist), June 14, 1958; children: (first marriage) Makgatho, Thembi (deceased), Makaziwe Phumla Mandela; (second marriage) Zenani (married to Prince Thumbumuzi Dhlamini of Swaziland), Zindziswa. *Education:* Attended University College of Fort Hare and Witwatersrand University; University of South Africa, law degree, 1942.

ADDRESSES: Office—c/o African National Congress of South Africa, 801 Second Avenue, New York, NY 10017.

CAREER: Mandela & Tambo law firm, Johannesburg, South Africa, partner, 1952- c. 1960; political organizer and leader of the African National Congress (ANC), Johannesburg, South Africa, 1944—, held successive posts as secretary and president of the Congress Youth League, deputy national president of the ANC, and commander of the Umkonto we Sizwe ("Spear of the Nation") paramilitary organization; sentenced to five years in prison for inciting Africans to strike and for leaving South Africa without a valid travel document, 1962; sentenced to life imprisonment for sabotage and treason, 1964; incarcerated in various penal institutions, including Robben Island and Pollsmoor prisons, South Africa, 1962-90. President of African National Congress, 1991—.

AWARDS, HONORS: Honorary doctor of law degrees from the National University of Lesotho, 1979, and City College of the City University of New York, 1983; Jawaharlal Nehru Award for International Understanding from the government of India, 1980; Bruno Kreisky Prize for Human Rights from the government of Austria, 1981; named honorary citizen of Glasgow, 1981, and Rome, 1983; Simon Bolivar International Prize from UNESCO, 1983; nominated for 1987 Nobel Peace Prize; human rights award, American Jewish Committee, 1993.

WRITINGS:

NONFICTION

No Easy Walk to Freedom, Basic Books, 1965.

Nelson Mandela Speaks, African National Congress Publicity and Information Bureau (London), c. 1970.

The Struggle Is My Life, International Defence and Aid Fund (London), 1978, revised and updated edition, Pathfinder Press, 1986, further revised and updated edition published as *Nelson Mandela: The Struggle Is My Life: His Speeches and Writings Brought Together with Historical Documents and Accounts of Mandela in Prison by Fellow-prisoners,* International Defence and Aid Fund, 1990.

Nelson Mandela, Symbol of Resistance and Hope for a Free South Africa: Selected Speeches since His Release, edited by E. S. Reddy, Sterling, 1990.

Nelson Mandela, Speeches 1990: "Intensify the Struggle to Abolish Apartheid," edited by Greg McCartan, photographs by Margrethe Siem, Pathfinder Press, 1990.

(With Fidel Castro) *How Far We Slaves Have Come! South Africa and Cuba in Today's World,* Pathfinder Press, 1991.

OTHER

Contributor of articles to the South African political journal *Liberation,* 1953-59; author of introduction to *Oliver Tambo Speaks: Preparing for Power,* Braziller, 1988.

SIDELIGHTS: Nelson Mandela has been called both "the world's most famous political prisoner" and "South Africa's Great Black Hope," by journalist Tom Mathews in *Newsweek.* A leader of the banned African National Congress (ANC) insurgent movement during the 1950s and 60s, Mandela had been jailed by white governments for a quarter of a century for his efforts to enfranchise his fellow blacks. Through his leadership and personal sacrifices, Mandela has come to symbolize the struggle against apartheid, the system of enforced racial inequality that denied political rights to South Africa's black majority. Mandela's release from prison in February, 1990, was followed by a triumphant world tour that included eight major cities in the United States. Strong admiration for the former political prisoner provided a common bond for many Americans who were at odds over how to defeat racial injustice. "No leader since the Reverend Martin Luther King, Jr., has brought together such a diverse coalition in the fight against racial injustice," noted a writer for *Time.*

Upon his release, Mandela commended his wife, Winnie, for her steadfast support during his long confinement. Carrying her husband's political torch, she endured repeated jailings, banishment and house arrest to emerge as a formidable leader in her own right. Although Winnie's disputed involvement with the kidnappings, assaults and murder perpetrated by her bodyguards has tarnished her image as "Mother of the Nation," her husband has lost none of his political charisma. Since his release from prison, Mandela has been engaged in negotiations on behalf of the ANC with South African president F. W. de Klerk over a settlement of power that would result in democratic-styled elections. Among the challenges endangering Mandela's efforts, however, is the bloody feud between the Zulu organization Inkatha and the ANC over who speaks for black South Africans, and threats from the South African right wing, which vows to take up arms if the ANC comes to power.

Both Nelson and Winnie Mandela are descended from Xhosa-speaking tribal chieftains from the Transkei region of South Africa. Mandela left his ancestral home at a young age to avoid an arranged marriage and pursue a professional career in the commercial capital of Johannes-

burg. Obtaining his law degree from the University of South Africa in 1942, Mandela joined the ANC two years later at the age of twenty-six and helped found the Congress Youth League (CYL) with Walter Sisulu, Oliver Tambo, and others. With Mandela as its secretary, the CYL urged its parent organization, the ANC, to abandon the strictly constitutional approach to reform that it had fruitlessly pursued with successive white minority governments since its founding in 1912 in favor of a more militant and confrontational strategy.

Under strong youth pressure, the ANC adopted a new program of action in 1949 that recognized such nonviolent—but sometimes illegal—tactics as electoral boycotts, "stay-at-homes" (general strikes), student demonstrations, and civil disobedience. In June, 1952, Mandela mounted the first major test of the new ANC program by organizing the Defiance Against Unjust Laws campaign, a coordinated civil disobedience of six selected apartheid laws by a multiracial group of some eighty-six hundred volunteers. The government's violent response to the Defiance Campaign generated a backlash of popular support for the ANC that helped thrust Nelson Mandela to national prominence; it also brought him a nine-month suspended jail sentence, a two-year government "banning" order that confined him to Johannesburg and prohibited him from attending public gatherings, and an order to resign his ANC leadership posts as deputy president of the national organization, president of the Transvaal branch, and president of the CYL. Mandela refused to do so, and as a result he was obliged to conduct most of his political organizing work under the cover of his Johannesburg law partnership with Oliver Tambo and to limit his public profile to writing articles for the pro-ANC journal *Liberation.*

In December, 1956, following a year of ANC-led mass protests against the Nationalists' proposal to create seven tiny tribal "homelands" in which to segregate South Africa's black population, the government brought charges against Mandela and 155 other anti-apartheid leaders under anti-Communist and treason statutes. During most of the four-and-one-half years that the "Treason Trial" lasted, Mandela remained free on bail, continuing to work at his law office during the evenings and discreetly engaging in political activities within the limitations of a new five-year banning order leveled on him in February, 1956.

In March of 1960, an action occurred that marked a historical watershed in the struggle for black rights in South Africa. Responding to a demonstration against "pass laws," which required black South Africans to carry government identification documents, the police in the Johannesburg suburb of Sharpeville turned their weapons on a group of unarmed protesters, killing sixty-nine people. The massacre sparked a wave of angry new protests and public pass-book burnings, to which Pretoria (the seat of the South African government) responded by declaring a state of national emergency. The government banned the ANC and PAC, and detained some eighteen hundred political activists without charges, including Mandela and the other "Treason Trial" defendants. This crackdown prompted the trial lawyers to withdraw from the case, declaring that the emergency restrictions prevented them from mounting an effective defense, and left Mandela, Duma Nokwe, Walter Sisulu, and several others to represent their sizable group of ANC leaders.

As an advocate for his group, Mandela distinguished himself with his legal ability and eloquent statements of the ANC's political and social philosophy. He defended the 1949 Programme of Action and the Defiance Campaign as necessary disruptive tactics when the government was indifferent to legal pressure; he also sought to assuage white fears of a black political takeover by insisting that the ANC's form of nationalism recognized the right of all South African racial groups to enjoy political freedom and nondiscrimination together in the same country. In a unique legal victory for South African black activists, the trial judge acquitted all the defendants for insufficient evidence in March, 1961, finding that the ANC did not have a policy of violence.

Among those anxiously awaiting the verdict was Nomzamo Winnie Madikileza, who had married Mandela during the early stages of the trial. The government's ban of the ANC meant an end to any normal home life for the Mandelas, however. Immediately after his release, Mandela went underground to avoid new government banning orders. He surfaced in late March to deliver the keynote speech at the All-In African Conference held in Pietermaritzburg, which had been organized by the ANC and other opposition political organizations to address the Nationalists' plan to declare a racialist South African republic in May of that year. The All-In Conference opposed this proposal with a demand that the government hold elections for a fully representative national convention empowered to draft a new and democratic constitution for all South Africans. Meeting no response to the assembly's demands from the H. F. Verwoerd government, Mandela helped organize a three-day general strike for the end of May to press for the convention. Verwoerd's security forces mobilized heavily against the strike by suspending civil liberties, making massive preemptive arrests, and deploying heavy military equipment, which succeeded in limiting public support for the action (although hundreds of thousands of Africans nationwide still stayed away from work).

Facing arrest, Mandela once again disappeared underground, this time for seventeen months, assuming numerous disguises in a cat-and-mouse game with the police during which he became popularly known as the "Black Pim-

pernel." The ANC leader was finally captured disguised as a chauffeur in the province of Natal by police acting on an informer's tip in August, 1962. Brought to trial in October on charges of inciting Africans to strike and leaving the country without a valid travel document, Mandela turned his defense into an indictment of the apartheid system. In an eloquent statement to the presiding judge, the ANC leader rejected the right of the court to hear the case on the grounds that—as a black man—he could not be given a fair trial under a judicial system intended to enforce white domination, and, furthermore, that he considered himself neither legally nor morally bound to obey laws created by a parliament in which he had no representation. Despite his impressive courtroom performance, Mandela was convicted of both charges and sentenced to five years in prison.

Unknown to the authorities at the time of his trial, Mandela and other ANC leaders had reluctantly decided to launch an underground paramilitary movement in 1961 for the first time in the ANC's history. In November of 1961, Mandela helped organize and assumed command of the Umkonto we Sizwe ("Spear of the Nation") guerrilla organization and began planning a sabotage campaign directed against government installations and the economic infrastructure. Umkonto's first military action occurred on December 16, 1961, when the organization simultaneously attacked government buildings in Johannesburg, Port Elizabeth, and Durban. The group went on to engage in many more acts of sabotage over the next year while Mandela traveled surreptitiously to England, Ethiopia, Algeria, and other African countries to meet political leaders, seek arms for the movement, and undergo military training.

Mandela's role in leading Umkonto came to light in June, 1963, when police raided the ANC's underground headquarters in the Johannesburg suburb of Rivonia and discovered documents relating to the armed movement. Nine top ANC leaders, including Mandela, were arrested and brought to trial in early 1964 on charges of committing sabotage and conspiring to overthrow the government by revolution with the help of foreign troops. Mandela once again conducted his own defense, using the courtroom as a platform to explain and justify the ANC's turn to armed struggle and to condemn the apartheid regime. Mandela declared at the trial, "It would be unrealistic and wrong for African leaders to continue preaching peace and nonviolence at a time when the Government met our peaceful demands with force." He fully acknowledged helping to found Umkonto and planning acts of sabotage, but he denied the government's contention that the ANC and Umkonto intended to subject the antiapartheid struggle to revolutionary control, either foreign or domestic.

While he acknowledged being strongly influenced by Marxist thought, Mandela denied ever having been a member of the Communist party, insisting that he held a deep and abiding admiration for Western legal and political institutions and wished to "borrow the best from both East and West" to reshape South African society. As elaborated in the ANC's Freedom Charter (a 1955 manifesto that Mandela helped to draft that remains the basic statement of the group's political purpose), the ANC looked forward to a democratic, pluralist society with certain mildly socialistic reforms—including land redistribution, nationalization of the country's mines, and a progressive tax and incomes policy—intended to dilute the economic power of the white minority and raise the country's black majority out of poverty.

Mandela's trial ended in June, 1964, when he and eight other defendants were convicted of sabotage and treason and sentenced to life imprisonment. Confined to the Robben Island fortress for political prisoners seven miles offshore from Cape Town, the ANC leaders were kept rigidly isolated from the outside world. They were denied access to radio, television, and newspapers, and prohibited from publishing articles, giving public interviews, or even discussing politics with visitors. All Mandela's past speeches and published works were banned, and merely possessing his writings in South Africa was made a criminal offense. Despite these restrictions, two book-length collections of Mandela's best known political statements were published abroad and have since circulated widely among South African anti-apartheid activists.

No Easy Walk to Freedom, published in 1965, includes Mandela's 1953 presidential address to the Transvaal province ANC (in which he discusses the Defiance Campaign), his speech at the 1961 All-In African Conference, and excerpts from his testimony at his three political trials. A second collection, *The Struggle Is My Life,* contains material from 1944 to 1985, including four prison statements from Mandela; and a revised 1986 edition of the title incorporates the memoirs of two of Mandela's fellow prisoners from Robben Island prison who had been released. Six speeches made by Mandela between February and May, 1990, during his first months of freedom, are collected in *Nelson Mandela, Speeches 1990: "Intensify the Struggle to Abolish Apartheid."* Published in 1990, the volume also includes Mandela's 1989 letter to South African president P. W. Botha stressing the need for negotiations between the government and the ANC.

Shortly after her husband's 1962 conviction, Winnie Mandela received her first government banning order restricting her to Johannesburg and preventing her from attending public or private meetings of any kind. In 1965, the government forced her out of her job with the Child Welfare Society by further restricting her to her home town-

ship of Orlando West and preventing her from engaging in essential fieldwork elsewhere in the Soweto district. She was then fired from a succession of low-paying jobs in the white commercial district after the security police pressured her employers, and she finally found herself reduced to supporting her two young daughters on the charity of friends and political associates. Despite this hardship, Winnie Mandela continued to work surreptitiously with the ANC during the 1960s by helping produce banned political pamphlets and newsletters in her home. During this period, the suspicious police ransacked the Mandela house repeatedly, but prosecutors could never find enough evidence to bring a court case against her.

In May, 1969, however, Winnie Mandela was arrested with other suspected ANC sympathizers under a new law that allowed the government to detain "terrorist" suspects indefinitely without charges. Taken to Pretoria Prison, she was interrogated virtually nonstop for five days and nights about her supposed links to ANC saboteurs. She was then jailed without charges for seventeen months, spending the first two hundred days of this period incommunicado and in solitary confinement. Finally, under pressure from Nelson Mandela's lawyers, the authorities improved Winnie's confinement conditions and brought her to trial on twenty-one political charges in September, 1970. The trial judge dismissed the case against her and all but one of her co-defendants for insufficient evidence, and Winnie Mandela was released that month.

Though freed from prison, Winnie Mandela was still subjected to close police vigilance in the early 1970s as South Africa's white minority government reacted to new challenges from a growing world anti-apartheid movement and the anti-colonial wars in nearby Mozambique and Angola. Immediately upon her release, she was placed under a new five-year banning order that confined her to her home during the evenings and on weekends. She was subjected to frequent police home searches in ensuing years and was arrested and sentenced to six months in prison for talking to another banned person in 1974. The authorities eventually allowed her banning order to expire in October, 1975, and over the next ten months she was able to enjoy the rights of free association and movement for the first time in many years.

This period of relative freedom for Winnie Mandela coincided with the birth of a militant "Black Consciousness" youth movement led by Stephen Biko and other students in Soweto. The student revolt had as its immediate aim the annulment of the Bantu Education Act, which consigned blacks to inferior education and obliged them to learn Afrikaans, the language of South African whites of Dutch descent, instead of English. When police shot down a number of unarmed demonstrators in Soweto in June, 1976, however, the township's youth erupted in a fury of uncontrolled rioting and clashes with the security forces that left at least six hundred people dead. Many of the participants in the Soweto uprising who escaped being killed or imprisoned fled the country and made contact with ANC exile headquarters in Lusaka, Zambia. This militant young cadre helped to radicalize the Congress and substantially strengthen its military wing, allowing the ANC to reestablish both a political and military presence inside South Africa by the end of the decade.

The ebb in the popular struggle after the Soweto uprising lasted until 1984, when the townships exploded again over the adoption of a new South African constitution that gave parliamentary representation to "Coloureds" and Indians but not to blacks. The townships remained in a state of near-continuous political turmoil in succeeding years as anti-government youth clashed violently with the security forces and other blacks accused of collaborating with the regime. But, unlike the situation a decade earlier, when the township civilians stood unorganized and alone against the apartheid government, a number of powerful social and political forces joined the fray in the mid-1980s to mount the greatest challenge to white minority rule in South African history. The United Democratic Front (UDF), a coalition of some 680 anti-apartheid organizations that supports the political line of the ANC, organized large street demonstrations and protests by township squatters facing eviction that were harshly repressed by the government in 1985. Meanwhile, the ANC itself stepped up its guerrilla campaign in South Africa and began targeting white residential areas and causing civilian casualties for the first time. The Nationalist government of P. W. Botha also came under mounting attack from abroad as the United States and other Western countries imposed limited trade and investment sanctions on South Africa in a bid to force reform. Finally, in 1987, the one-million-strong black trade union movement began to flex its powerful muscles with strikes by workers in the strategic transport and mining sectors.

A common demand voiced throughout the previous decade by the diverse forces seeking to change the apartheid system was that Nelson Mandela be released immediately. In 1985, Winnie Mandela managed to break her government restrictions and return to Soweto to join the fight for her husband's freedom (this turn of events occurred after her Brandfort house was firebombed and burned to the ground in August of that year while she was in Johannesburg for medical treatment). Accusing the security police of the attack and saying that she feared for her life, Winnie Mandela insisted on moving back to her Soweto house; amid much local and international publicity, the Botha government permitted her to do so. In succeeding months, Winnie Mandela took advantage of the government's weakened position to openly flout her banning orders by

giving press interviews and speaking out militantly at public demonstrations and at the funerals of young township victims of government repression.

Speaking at a funeral on a return visit to Brandfort in April, 1986, for example, Winnie Mandela denounced the authorities as "terrorists" and called on blacks to take "direct action" against the government to free the imprisoned nationalist leaders. "The time has come where we must show that we are disciplined and trained warriors," she added in what some observers interpreted as a call to insurrection. In a bid to improve its international image and deflect criticism of a new state of emergency it had imposed the previous month, the Botha regime, in July, 1986, chose not to prosecute Winnie Mandela and instead lifted all banning restrictions on her. Among Winnie Mandela's first public actions once her right to free speech had been restored was to call for international economic sanctions against the apartheid government.

The Botha government met the current crisis with a "divide and rule" strategy combining harsh repression and isolated reforms that did not fundamentally alter the structure of apartheid. While repealing such symbols of apartheid as pass laws and long-standing bans on interracial sex and marriage, the government violently crushed the township uprisings and detained tens of thousands of antiapartheid protestors without trial under sweeping state-of-emergency powers. Fearing the popular reaction if Mandela were to die in prison, previous South African governments sought to find a way to free him as early as 1973, but the confined ANC leader had always rejected conditions that he accept exile abroad or in the Transkei "homeland" and that he renounce violence by the insurgent organization. In late 1987, the Botha regime began hinting at the possibility that it might finally release Nelson Mandela unconditionally in an attempt to mollify domestic and international public opinion. The advisability of releasing the ANC leader in terms of domestic politics reportedly stimulated a hot debate in the Botha cabinet, with those in favor of the move arguing that Mandela was now more conservative than much of the current ANC leadership and could therefore effect a split in the organization. Detractors contended that freeing South Africa's best-known political prisoner could further alienate hardline whites and possibly stimulate a black insurrection. Reform-minded South Africans, on the other hand, believed Mandela was the only political leader prestigious enough to win the confidence of both liberal whites and the increasingly alienated black township youth, thereby delivering the country from the specter of race war.

In November, 1987, the authorities unconditionally freed Mandela's long-time comrade-in-arms Govan Mbeki (a top ANC and South African Communist party leader who was convicted at the Rivonia Trial and served twenty-four years on Robben Island), as a way of testing the political waters for Mandela's possible release. In August, 1988, Mandela was diagnosed with tuberculosis, and the announcement prompted a new round of demands from the international community that he should be set free. The next year brought the release of Walter Sisulu—considered by some to be the second most important figure in South Africa's fight against apartheid—along with the rest of the Rivonia prisoners with the exception of Mandela himself. South African president F. W. de Klerk, who succeeded Botha in 1989, came into power on a reform platform; with the Rivonia amnesties, de Klerk initiated the first conciliatory measures which soon included unconditional freedom for Mandela and the lifting of the ban on the ANC (the government had delayed Mandela's pardon with the stipulation that he formally renounce violence, but it finally relented, granting his freedom February 11, 1990). De Klerk was quoted in *Time* as saying, "I came to the conclusion that [Mandela] is committed to a peaceful solution and a peaceful process." Bruce W. Nelan of *Time* suggested that de Klerk intended to demystify Mandela and the antiapartheid movement by setting its "spiritual leader" free: "By legalizing the ANC, [de Klerk] removes its cloak of underground heroism and turns it into an ordinary political party. Both Mandela and his organization will then be forced by circumstance and expectation to make compromises. And compromises are expected to anger and disillusion segments of the black majority, giving the government opportunities to divide the opposition." Nelan further conjectured that the South African president looked for the end of international sanctions against South Africa by beginning talks with black leaders—and the longer the government dragged out negotiations, the more likely momentum behind the antiapartheid movement would falter.

Embarking on a thirteen country tour in June and July, 1990, Mandela was received in the United States as—in the words of Nelan—a "heroic superstar." His mission, however, was political; he wanted both assurances from governments that sanctions would remain in place until South Africa was committed to peaceful change, and donations to revitalize the ANC. In New York City, people jammed the streets to catch a glimpse of Mandela passing by in a ticker tape parade. Speaking at a crossroads in Harlem, Mandela told a crowd nearing 100,000, "I am here to claim you because . . . you have claimed our struggle." Mandela also appeared at rallies in seven other American cities, including Boston, Miami, Detroit, and Los Angeles. In Washington, DC, President George Bush—who, as vice-president under Ronald Reagan, fought against the Comprehensive Anti-Apartheid Act of 1986—agreed to keep economic sanctions in place, at least for the short term. "I want to find a way to show our appreciation to

de Klerk, and yet I don't want to pull the rug out from under Mr. Mandela," Bush was quoted as saying in *Time*.

Upon his return to South Africa, Mandela was faced with serious obstacles which threatened to disrupt any progress he made negotiating with the government. Bloody clashes between the ANC and its backers, and Inkatha, a Zulu organization of about 1.5 million members, had been flaring up since 1987 in Natal Province. Led by Chief Mangosuthu Buthelezi, who "opposes strikes, armed struggle and foreign sanctions against the country's white government," according to Jeffrey Bartholet in *Newsweek*, Inkatha had been targeting the United Democratic Front, an organization comprised of Zulus who support the ANC. While still in prison, Mandela had hoped for a reconciliation with Buthelezi, but his very release sparked two days of violence in Natal that killed fifty people. In March, 1990, Mandela agreed to hold a joint rally with Buthelezi in Durban, but cancelled out when the venue appeared too potentially explosive. Two weeks after the ANC announced an end to armed struggle against apartheid in August, 1990, a raid by Inkatha supporters on train passengers at Soweto's Inhlazane Station resulted in a wave of violence that spread to other townships around Johannesburg, leaving more than two hundred people dead. Right-wing politicians exploited the turmoil, attempting to use the ethnic strife as proof of the unviability of a black South African government. "The rivalry plays on white fears that tribalism could rip apart a post-apartheid South Africa. While de Klerk's National Party ties its future to the ANC, the right-wing Conservative Party has seized on Buthelezi's demands for a role equal to Mandela's," commented Joseph Contreras in *Newsweek*. While de Klerk pressed Mandela to help quell the violence by meeting with Buthelezi, Mandela blamed Pretoria. "Under the noses of the police, Inkatha *impis* go places fully armed and attack and kill people," he reportedly said.

Black-on-black violence continued unabated, with the ANC withdrawing from talks in May, 1991, after the government refused to outlaw tribal weapons carried by Inkatha party members. In the same month, Winnie Mandela was convicted of kidnapping and being an accessory to assault and sentenced to six years in prison. The conviction stemmed from the actions of her bodyguards, who called themselves the Mandela United Football Club although—as John Bierman reported in *Maclean's*—"they never played a single organized game of soccer." In 1988, members of the club kidnapped four black youths from a hostel. According to Bierman, "evidence showed that [Winnie] Mandela's bodyguards took the victims to her Soweto home, where they tied them up and savagely beat them. One of the youths, fourteen year-old James (Stompie) Moeketsi Seipei, was later found dead." Winnie Mandela denied any involvement in the crime, stating in court she was in the Orange Free State—three hundred kilometers away—when it occurred; she has since appealed the decision. Mandela supported his wife throughout her trial. He appeared to observers to be devoted to the woman who supported him through the many years of his imprisonment with her visits and letters, who endured jail and police mistreatment on his behalf. "There have been moments when conscience and a sense of guilt have ravaged every part of my being," Mandela once wrote his wife, agonized by separation from his family.

Mandela insisted that the negative publicity surrounding Winnie's court case had no effect on his negotiations with Pretoria. Although far from fully enfranchising the black population, the government did institute further reforms, including the repeal of the Population Registration Act in June, 1991, which required every South African baby to be documented by race. Although international response was positive, the South African government was far from eradicating apartheid; blacks still didn't have the right to vote. Mandela, whom political experts considered outmaneuvered by de Klerk, had become increasingly cynical of the president, stating, "What he has done is merely to bring about changes which maintain the status quo."

The ANC addressed their setbacks at a national conference in Durban during July, 1991—the first such gathering in South Africa in thirty years. The party had been splitting between young radicals who favored a more militant approach toward immediate change, and older, conservative leaders who recommended negotiating gradually with the government. The Durban conference reaffirmed the moderate philosophy within the ANC by electing Mandela president, Walter Sisulu deputy president, and Cyril Ramaphosa secretary general. "This is an overwhelming victory for the moderates and a crushing blow to the militants who were outpolled two-to-one," commented South African political expert Donald Simpson in *Maclean's*.

Mandela struggled to balance his group's objectives with assurances to white South Africans that the ANC did not wish to turn the country into a socialist state. "We would nationalize the mines, the banks and other monopolies, but the rest of the economy is based on private enterprise," Mandela informed *Newsweek* in an interview. "Not even the land is nationalized, which is normally the first sector of the economy which socialist [governments] nationalize."

A growing distrust of de Klerk among blacks soured into seething resentment in June, 1992, when about two hundred Inkatha supporters rampaged through the township of Boipatong with guns, machetes and spears, killing at least forty people. Witnesses claimed the Zulu attackers

had been assisted by the police. Rejecting calls among militant members to reengage in armed struggle, ANC leaders instead displayed their frustration with the government's inability to control the violence—and the seeming insincerity within de Klerk's National Party in negotiating a new, nonracial constitution—by withdrawing from the talks. A campaign of mass-action (boycotts, strikes and sit-ins) was instituted while the ANC pressed Pretoria with a list of demands, including a full investigation of the Boipatong massacre.

Addressing a Pretoria rally comprised of 70,000 peaceful marchers in August, 1992, Mandela responded to the crowd's calls of "De Klerk must go!" with a statement indicating the true purpose of the march: not to overthrow de Klerk, but to prompt him into faster action towards creating a democratic government. Mandela and de Klerk finally met on September 26, 1992, for the first time since May, agreeing to resume negotiations on the constitution and to accelerate efforts in forging an interim government. Several conditions laid down by the ANC for the resumption of talks were met by de Klerk, namely the erection of fences around single-sex workers' hostels (often the origination point of Inkatha-inspired violence), a ban on carrying tribal weapons in public, and the release of close to five hundred blacks, deemed political prisoners by the ANC. In exchange for the amnesty, the ANC agreed to a general amnesty for white governmental officials accused of crimes during the years of apartheid. One day after Mandela's summit with de Klerk, Buthelezi walked out of negotiations, angered over the deals struck between the two leaders. Buthelezi made it clear that Inkatha would not participate in postapartheid elections, even though political experts suggested de Klerk's Nationalist Party was counting on Buthelezi's (and Inkatha's) support to bolster their showings at the polls against the ANC. De Klerk denied Buthelezi's charges of striking "illegitimate" deals and claimed the real impediment to progress was due to factionalism between the blacks. Addressing this setback on television, de Klerk said, "It appears to me more and more that we won't have peace until Mr. Mandela and Chief Buthelezi make their peace."

Despite his long imprisonment and personal suffering, political setbacks and the unrelenting strife between Inkatha and the ANC, Mandela's efforts to end institutional apartheid were finally realized in June, 1993, when South Africa's first free elections were announced. Scheduled for April 27, 1994, the election was agreed upon by a majority of the country's twenty-six parties as a measure to reassure blacks that change is coming. "And the voters will almost certainly reward Mandela's stoic struggle by conferring on him the leadership of his country," declared Scott MacLeod in *Time*. The populace is expected to elect a bicameral legislature, with the party winning the most seats selecting the next president of South Africa. During the transition period, the legislature will serve a term of five years and also be given the duty of drafting a new constitution. De Klerk is insisting, on behalf of his party, on a power-sharing clause in the constitution which will prevent the ANC from assuming absolute control of the government. "We must ensure that there will never be domination again in South Africa. I'm not talking about minority vetoes but about preventing the misuse of power to the detriment of minorities," de Klerk told *Time.* However, Mandela commented to interviewers in *Time* that the National Party's definition of power sharing "means the party that loses the elections should continue to govern," adding, "we have moved them away from that."

Apartheid's official demise signals a turbulent period of adjustment for South Africa; for Mandela, it means a difficult role at the forefront of the healing process. While the announcement of elections will result in the lifting of remaining sanctions against South Africa, the economy has been in recession, staggered by millions of dollars in lost investments. Educational opportunities among black children are very poor, and the country's black majority—who have had so little for so long—are now beginning to expect an immediate redistribution of resources. Bloodshed continues to rip apart the black community, in spite of Buthelezi's pledge to join Mandela in quelling the violence (more than one hundred people were killed in factional fighting in July, 1993, in the townships of Tokoza and Katlehong, which observers linked to the ongoing feud between Inkatha and ANC supporters). And a Mandela-led government faces the additional threat from white rightists who have declared they will take up arms in insurrection.

Mandela looks forward to the future, however. He has stated that he will be looking to Western nations, led by the United States, to provide substantial assistance to South Africa along the lines of the Marshall Plan (the blueprint for the rebuilding of Europe at the end of World War II). While Mandela does not discount the threats from the right-wing, he believes that a reorganized police force will protect the new society from those who wish to sabotage it. Despite the many hardships Mandela has endured at the behest of the state—most notably his bleak confinement in Robben Island and Pollsmoor Prisons, and the forced estrangement from his family—he has remained remarkably free of bitterness. In an interview with *Time,* Mandela described his struggle for racial equality as just one among many: "There are countless people who went to jail and aren't bitter at all, because they can see that their sacrifices were not in vain, and the ideas for which we lived and sacrificed are about to come to fruition. And that removes the bitterness from their hearts."

BIOGRAPHICAL/CRITICAL SOURCES:

BOOKS

Benson, Mary, *Nelson Mandela: The Man and the Movement,* Norton, 1986.

Harrison, Nancy, *Winnie Mandela* (biography), Braziller, 1986.

Mandela, Nelson R., *No Easy Walk to Freedom,* Basic Books, 1965.

Mandela, Nelson R., *The Struggle Is My Life,* Pathfinder Press, 1986.

Mandela, Winnie, *Part of My Soul Went with Him* (autobiography), edited by Anne Benjamin and Mary Benson, Norton, 1985.

Newsmakers: 1990, Gale, 1990.

PERIODICALS

Crisis, February, 1983.

Detroit News, July 6, 1993, p. 2A.

Ebony, December, 1985; September, 1986.

Globe and Mail (Toronto), December 14, 1985.

Library Journal, December, 1986, p. 117; September 15, 1990, p. 61.

Maclean's, May 27, 1991, pp. 22-23; July 15, 1991, p. 23.

Ms., November, 1985; January, 1987.

Nation, July 1, 1991, pp. 15-18.

National Review, April 30, 1990, pp. 37-39.

New Republic, October 19, 1992, pp. 16-19.

New Statesman, June 7, 1985; September 25, 1992, pp. 26-27.

Newsweek, September 9, 1985; February 24, 1986; February 19, 1990, pp. 44-51; March 5, 1990, p. 31; July 2, 1990, pp. 16-20; August 27, 1990, pp. 41-42; May 27, 1991, p. 33; July 1, 1991, p. 37; March 2, 1992, p. 42; July 6, 1992, p. 47.

New York Review of Books, May 8, 1986.

New York Times, July 19, 1978; July 7, 1985; July 29, 1986; June 21, 1992, sec. 1, pp. 1, 14; October 25, 1992, p. E5; July 7, 1993, p. A3.

New York Times Book Review, December 8, 1985.

People, February 26, 1990, p. 77-79.

Time, January 5, 1987; August 29, 1988, p. 43; May 29, 1989, p. 77; October 23, 1989, p. 49; December 25, 1989, p. 28; January 29, 1990, p. 49; February 19, 1990, p. 42-44; June 25, 1990, pp. 20-21; December 17, 1990, p. 25; July 1, 1991, pp. 38-39; August 17, 1992, p. 15; June 14, 1993, pp. 34-38.

U.S. News & World Report, February 27, 1989, p. 13; April 9, 1990, p. 15.*

—Sketch by Scot Peacock

MANDELKER, Daniel Robert   1926-

PERSONAL: Born July 18, 1926, in Milwaukee, WI; son of Adolph Irwin and Marie (Manner) Mandelker; divorced, 1966; children: Amy, John. *Education:* University of Wisconsin, B.A., 1947, LL.B., 1949; Yale University, J.S.D., 1956.

ADDRESSES: Office—School of Law, Washington University, St. Louis, MO 63130.

CAREER: Drake University, School of Law, Des Moines, IA, assistant professor, 1949-51; U.S. Housing and Home Finance Agency, Washington, DC, attorney and advisor, 1952-53; Indiana University, School of Law, Indianapolis, assistant professor, 1953-57, associate professor of law, 1957-62; Washington University, School of Law, St. Louis, MO, associate professor, 1962-63, professor of law, 1963-74, Howard A. Stamper Professor of Law, 1974—. Visiting professor, University of Washington, 1968-69; Walter E. Meyer Visiting Research Professor of Law and Social Problems, School of Law, Columbia University, 1971-72; Will E. Orgain Lecturer, School of Law, University of Texas, 1977; visiting distinguished lecturer, Urban Studies Center, Florida Atlantic University, 1989; First Journal of Planning Literature Lecturer, College of Law and School of Planning, Ohio State University, 1989; Fifth Annual Rita C. Davidson Memorial Lecturer, Maryland Land Use Roundtable, 1991; Fifteenth Denman Lecturer, Department of Land Economy, Cambridge University, 1992; national distinguished lecturer, Florida State University, 1992-93; university lecturer, University of Wisconsin—Madison, 1993. Member of faculty, Brookings Institution Urban Program, 1965-73, Salzburg Seminar in American Studies, 1977, and American Planning Association, 1981-90. Visiting instructor at University of Oklahoma, summer, 1958, University of Puerto Rico, summer, 1968, Summer School for Law Teachers, New York University, 1969, Wayne State University, summer, 1969, University of Utah, summer, 1975, and University of Texas, summer, 1976. Visiting scholar, Institute of State and Law, Moscow, 1978, and Department of Urban Planning, Israel, 1983; visiting fellow, University of Copenhagen, and University College, London, 1989, and University College, University of Law, 1989. Lecturer, workshops and conference on Land Use Law for Planners and Lawyers, 1982—.

Legal advisor, Indiana legislative study committee on town incorporation and annexation, 1958-59. Transportation Research Board, chairman of committee on urban-metropolitan transportation law, 1964-70, member of legal task force on joint development, 1971-73, member of committee on transportation and land development policy, 1973-82; Urban Land Institute, member of Development Policies and Regulations Council, 1980—, member

of research committee, 1981-82. Director of National Coalition to Preserve Scenic Beauty, 1981-84. Consultant on national housing policy, Committee on Banking and Currency, U.S. House of Representatives, 1970-71; consultant to federal government and several cities, states, foundations, and corporations on land use and zoning policies.

MEMBER: American Bar Association (chairman of committee on education and curriculum, 1965-70; member of special committee on housing and urban development law, 1980-82), National Academy of Sciences, Association of American Law Schools (chairman of section on local government law), American Planning Association (chairman of Planning and Law Division, 1979-82; member of board of directors, 1981-84; chairman of division council, 1981-84), American Institute of Certified Planners, Phi Kappa Phi, Phi Beta Kappa, Order of the Coif.

AWARDS, HONORS: Ford Foundation fellow, Yale University, 1951-55; Ford Foundation law faculty fellow (London), 1959-60; Urban Land Institute research fellow, 1976—, senior fellow, 1989—; John C. Vance Award cowinner, 1988, for most outstanding paper on transportation law submitted to Transportation Research Board.

WRITINGS:

Green Belts and Urban Growth: English Town and Country Planning in Action, University of Wisconsin Press, 1962.

Inverse Condemnation: The Constitutional Limits of Public Responsibility, School of Law, Washington University, 1964.

Managing Our Urban Environment: Cases, Text and Problems, Bobbs-Merrill, 1966, 2nd edition, 1971.

Supplementary Case Studies in Land Planning and Development, School of Law, Washington University, 1968.

The Zoning Dilemma, Bobbs-Merrill, 1970, 2nd edition, 1971.

(With William Ewald) *Street Graphics,* American Society of Landscape Architects Foundation, 1971, 3rd edition, Planners Press, 1988.

(With Roger Montgomery) *Housing in America: Problems and Perspectives,* Bobbs-Merrill, 1973, 2nd edition, 1979.

Housing Subsidies in the United States and England, Bobbs-Merrill, 1973.

(With G. Hagevik and R. Brail) *Air Quality Management and Land Use Planning,* Praeger, 1974.

New Developments in Land and Environmental Controls, Bobbs-Merrill, 1974.

Environmental and Land Controls Legislation, Bobbs-Merrill, 1976, supplement, 1982.

(With Dawn C. Netsch) *State and Local Government in a Federal System: Cases and Materials,* Michie Co., 1977, 3rd edition (with Netsch, P. Salsich, and J. Wegner), 1990, and supplement, 1992.

(With Roger A. Cunningham) *Planning and Control of Land Development: Cases and Materials,* Bobbs-Merrill, 1979, 3rd edition, 1990.

(With G. Feder and M. Collins) *Reviving Cities through Tax Abatement,* Center for Urban Policy Research, 1980.

Environment and Equity: A Regulatory Challenge, McGraw, 1981.

(With others) *Housing and Community Development: Cases and Materials,* Michie Co., 1981, 2nd edition, 1989.

(With F. Anderson and D. Tarlock) *Environmental Protection: Law and Policy,* Little, Brown, 1984, 3rd edition, 1990, supplement, 1991.

(With J. Gerard and T. Sullivan) *Federal Land Use Law: Limitations, Procedures, Remedies,* Michie Co., 1986, 2nd edition 1992.

(With W. Ewald) *Street Graphics and the Law,* Planners Press, 1988.

NEPA Law and Litigation: The National Environmental Policy Act, Clark Boardman, 1990, 2nd edition, 1992.

Also author of monographs, including *Controlling Planned Residential Development,* 1966; *1974 Five Year Boundary Review Report: An Evaluation of the Hawaii Land Use Law,* with S. Spiegel, 1974; *Legal Techniques for Reserving Right-of-Way for Future Projects including Corridor Protection,* with A. Kolis, 1987; and *The Application of the National Environmental Policy Act to Highway Projects,* with G. Feder, 1990. Editor of monograph *The Capacity of the Legal System to Facilitate the Urban Development Process: Korea and the Philippines,* 1972.

Contributor to numerous books, including *Planning for a Nation of Cities,* edited by S. Warner, MIT Press, 1966; *Frontiers of Planned Unit Development,* edited by R. Burchell, Center for Urban Policy Research, Rutgers University, 1973; *Land Use: Planning, Politics, and Policy,* edited by R. Coward, 1976; *A Planner's Guide to Land Use Law,* 1983; *Land Use and the Constitution: Principles for Planning Practice,* 1989; and *Intergovernmental Decisionmaking for Environmental Protection and Public Works,* 1992. Also contributor of articles to legal and planning journals, including *Urban Land, Journal of Planning Literature, Urban Law and Policy, Land Use Law and Zoning Digest, Journal of Urban Law,* and *Journal of American Institute of Planners.* Member of editorial boards, *Land Use Law and Zoning Digest,* beginning 1967, *Land Economics,* 1972-77, *Real Estate Law Journal,* 1972—, *Sage Urban Studies Abstracts,* 1973—, *Journal of the American Planning Association,* 1975-85, *Urban Law and Policy,*

1977-92, *Land Use and Environmental Law Review,* 1981—, *Journal of Planning Literature,* 1984—, *Urban Affairs Quarterly,* 1985-89, and *Florida State University Journal of Land Use and Environmental Law,* 1985—; note editor, *Wisconsin Law Review.* Member of the board of consulting editors, *Encyclopedia of Housing,* 1991—.

*   *   *

MANN, Josephine
   See PULLEIN-THOMPSON, Josephine (Mary Wedderburn)

*   *   *

MARCUS, Alfred A(llen) 1950-

PERSONAL: Born January 21, 1950, in Pittsburgh, PA; son of Marcus James (a manager) and Alice (a beautician; maiden name, Freed) Marcus; married Judith Davis (a social worker), July 1, 1973; children: David Isaac, Ariel Jonathan. *Education:* Attended Hebrew University of Jerusalem, 1969-70; University of Chicago, B.A., 1971, M.A., 1973; Harvard University, Ph.D., 1977. *Religion:* Jewish.

ADDRESSES: Home—2820 Monterey Parkway, St. Louis Park, MN 55416. *Office*—Carlson School of Management, Strategic Management Department, University of Minnesota, Minneapolis, MN 55456.

CAREER: University of Pittsburgh, Pittsburgh, PA, assistant professor of business, 1977-79; Battelle Memorial Institute, Human Affairs Research Center, Seattle, research scientist, 1979-84; University of Washington, Seattle, adjunct professor of business, 1980-81; University of Minnesota, Minneapolis, assistant professor, 1984-88, associate professor, 1987-92, professor of management, 1993—, director of Strategic Management Research Center. Lecturer, Massachusetts Institute of Technology. Consultant to National Academy of Sciences, 1975-76.

WRITINGS:

Promise and Performance: Choosing and Implementing an Environmental Policy, Greenwood Press, 1980.
The Adversary Economy: Business Responses to Changing Government Requirements, Quorum Books, 1984.
(Editor with Al Kaufman and David Beam) *Business Strategy and Public Policy,* Quorum Books, 1986.
(With R. Buchholz and J. Post) *Managing the Environment: Business Cases,* Prentice-Hall, 1992.
Controversial Issues in Energy Policy, Sage Publications, 1992.
Business and Society: Ethics, Government, and the World Economy, Irwin, 1993.

Also contributor to periodicals, including *Academy of Management Review, Administrative Law Review, Human Resources Management, Harvard Environmental Law Review, Energy, Energy Policy,* and *Policy Studies Journal.*

WORK IN PROGRESS: Research on the compensation policy in the United States and Japan for victims of pollution and toxic substances; research on the response of the nuclear power industry to reforms initiated after the Three Mile Island incident.

SIDELIGHTS: Alfred A. Marcus once told *CA:* "My first book, *Promise and Performance: Choosing and Implementing an Environmental Policy,* is an outgrowth of my Ph.D. dissertation. At the time of my Ph.D. I was serving as a consultant to the National Academy of Sciences, which was studying decision making at the Environmental Protection Agency (EPA). I did open-ended interviews with nearly one hundred officials at the agency. *Promise and Performance: Choosing and Implementing an Environmental Policy* deals with the origins of the EPA, its unique structure, and its divisions; it takes a policy, research, and program perspective. The book is useful in explaining why the EPA does not treat pollution as would an economist—as an externality—but rather treats it in political terms in terms of conflicts reflected in its organization between the White House and Congress.

"My second book, *The Adversary Economy: Business Responses to Changing Government Requirements,* was written while I was a research scientist at the Battelle Memorial Institute's Human Affairs Research Center in Seattle, Washington. I worked in the Science and Government Study Center with attorneys, economists, and other political scientists on programs of vital concern to the nation's future—synfuels, emergency response in the case of nuclear accidents, solar power and conservation, management and organization issues in nuclear power, and so on. My interest in the impact of government on business and in regulation was stimulated by my earlier teaching experience, but at Battelle I could see some of the nation's important regulatory issues being handled first hand. So I started to write about the conflict between business and government. I looked at the growth and decline of regulation; at the synfuels program as an example of industrial policy; at deregulation in the airlines, natural gas, and communications industry; at the rise and importance of public interest groups which challenged business authority; at the different responses businesses were making to the challenge of a growing regulatory burden; and at regulatory reform. My idea was to try to see these issues from the perspective of the practicing public affairs officer in a large corporation. I saw the increasing importance of the public affairs function and business politics as the 1980's wore on and tried to put these trends in perspective.

"My interests remain in the area of business-government relations, regulation, energy, and environmental policy. I have done research on the effects of politics on the economic cycle, nuclear safety organization and management, and toxic torts. I have edited a book with Al Kaufman of the University of New Hampshire and David Beam of Illinois Institute of Technology on business strategy and public policy. There are three major issues that concerned us: the conflict within the firm between profit-making and broader values; the conflict between the firm and the politics of the industry of which it is part; and business's need to promote larger values that are in the public interest. *Business Strategy and Public Policy* has various contributions from academics and practitioners that deal with these issues in a concrete, case specific way."

Marcus recently told *CA:* "My last three books came out in 1992 and 1993. *Managing the Environment: Business Cases* is a result of a three year collaboration with the National Wildlife Federation/Corporate Conservation Council to develop curriculum material on business and the environment for business schools. *Controversial Issues in Energy Policy* places United States policies in a comparative perspective. It has chapters on energy policies in other major consuming nations like Japan and on the major producing nations in OPEC as well as chapters on specific energy forms, such as nuclear. *Business and Society: Ethics, Government, and the World Economy* is a compilation of conceptual and case material I have written for use in the course I teach at the University of Minnesota.

"Writing *Business and Society: Ethics, Government, and the World Economy* was a major undertaking. It is over 600 pages long. People ask, 'How long did it take?' From the actual start of the drafting of chapters to the appearance of the book in published form took under three years, but really much longer, as material in the book comes from the teaching I have done at University of Minnesota for the last eight years. The book covers a wide variety of topics from business ethics to global competitiveness, energy and environmental issues, and technology and its impacts.

"As well as the text (eighteen chapters), there are fifteen cases on such infamous figures [and situations] as Dennis Levine, and the Chrysler bailout, Bhopal, and the Ford Pinto problem. I used the book in draft form in a course I taught at MIT's Sloan School during the year of my sabbatical and had two students who worked for Chrysler and did for Lee Iacocca the hypothetical job I presented in a case of investigating Honda's rise and the lessons for the U.S. auto manufacturers. They were in charge of applying some of these lessons to Chrysler."

MARSHALL, John 1922-

PERSONAL: Born in 1922, in Nottingham, England; son of Thomas and Doris (Mayhew) Marshall; married Ann Simm, 1950; children: Simon, Andrew, Jennifer. *Education:* Attended college in Loughborough, England. *Avocational Interests:* History of music, playing flute (amateur orchestra and chamber music groups), photography, travel, walking.

ADDRESSES: Home—24 Maypole Close, Bewdley, Worcestershire DY12 1BZ, England.

CAREER: Writer. Teacher in Bolton, Bewdley, Worcestershire, England.

MEMBER: Railway and Canal Historical Society, Stephenson Locomotive Society.

WRITINGS:

The Lancashire and Yorkshire Railway, three volumes, David & Charles, 1969-72.
The Guinness Book of Rail Facts and Feats, Guinness Superlatives, 1972, 3rd edition, 1979.
Metre Gauge Railways in South and East Switzerland, David & Charles, 1974.
Rail Facts and Feats, Two Continents Publishing, 1974.
Railway History in Pictures: Lancashire and Yorkshire Railway, David & Charles, 1977.
A Biographical Dictionary of Railway Engineers, David & Charles, 1978.
Forgotten Railways: Northwest England, David & Charles, 1981.
The Cromford and High Peak Railway, David & Charles, 1982.
Guinness Fact Book: Rail, Guinness Books, 1985.
Rail: The Records, Guinness Books, 1985.
Guinness Railway Book, Guinness Books, 1989.
The Severn Valley Railway, David & Charles, 1989.

Contributor to magazines, including *Railway Magazine, Railway World,* and *British Railway Journal.*

SIDELIGHTS: John Marshall once told *CA:* "Writing railway history is an exacting and time-consuming process. Every detail must be correct; this involves many hours of painstaking research. One is writing for a readership that will pounce on the smallest error. Mountains of correspondence comes in, but out of it all emerge some wonderful friendships. The Guinness books have provided an outlet for my fascination with some strange and extraordinary facts of railway history which emerge during research."

MARTIN, Jane Roland 1929-

PERSONAL: Born July 20, 1929, in New York, NY; daughter of Charles (a journalist) and Sarah (a teacher; maiden name, Starr) Roland; married Michael Martin (a professor), June 15, 1962; children: Timothy, Thomas. *Education:* Radcliffe College, A.B., 1951, Ph.D., 1961; Harvard University, Ed.M., 1956.

ADDRESSES: Home—389 Central St., Newton, MA 02166. *Office*—Department of Philosophy, University of Massachusetts, Harbor Campus, Boston, MA 02125.

CAREER: University of Massachusetts, Harbor Campus, Boston, associate professor, 1972-81, professor of philosophy, 1981-93, professor emeritus, 1993—.

MEMBER: American Philosophical Association, Society for Women in Philosophy, Philosophy of Education Society (president, 1980-81).

AWARDS, HONORS: Bunting Institute fellow, 1980-81; National Science Foundation fellow, 1984-85; Guggenheim fellow, 1987-88; Distinguished Woman Philosopher Award, Society for Women in Philosophy, 1991; Award for Distinguished Contribution to Education, Harvard Graduate School of Education, 1992; Doctor of Humane Letters, Salem State College, 1993; Award for Distinguished Contributions to Curriculum, American Educational Research Association.

WRITINGS:

Readings in the Philosophy of Education, Allyn & Bacon, 1970.
Explaining, Understanding, and Teaching, McGraw, 1970.
Reclaiming a Conversation: The Ideal of the Educated Woman, Yale University Press, 1985.
The Schoolhome: Rethinking Schools for Changing Families, Harvard University Press, 1992.
Changing the Educational Landscape: Philosophy, Women and Curriculum, Routledge, 1994.

WORK IN PROGRESS: Culture and Curriculum: Superabundance in an Age of Scarcity.

SIDELIGHTS: Jane Roland Martin once told *CA:* "The parties to the conversation about women's education reclaimed in my book *Reclaiming a Conversation* are Plato, Rousseau, Mary Wollstonecraft, Catharine Beecher, and Charlotte Perkins Gilman. The point of reclaiming this conversation is to shed light on the education of both sexes today." Martin describing her later work, states: "*The Schoolhome* explicitly takes up that question in relation to America's changed and changing realities: in particular, the transformation of 'the' American home and family, the changed composition of the U.S. population, and the increase in violence in both our private homes and our public spaces."

* * *

MARTINDALE, Patrick Victor
See WHITE, Patrick (Victor Martindale)

* * *

MASTERS, Brian 1939-

PERSONAL: Born May 25, 1939, in London, England; son of Geoffrey Howard (a merchant) and Mabel (Ingledew) Masters. *Education:* University College, Cardiff, Wales, B.A. (with first class honors), 1961; University of Montpellier, Licencie es lettres, 1962.

ADDRESSES: Home—47 Caithness Rd., London W.14, England. *Agent*—Jacintha Alexander, 47 Emperor's Gate, London S.W.7, England.

CAREER: Worldways Ltd. (tour organizers), London, England, incoming tours manager, 1962-79, managing director, 1979—.

MEMBER: International PEN, Society of Authors, Royal Society of Arts (fellow), Garrick Club, Beefsteak Club, Pratt's Club, Academy Club, Aspinall's.

WRITINGS:

Sartre, Heinemann Educational, 1969.
Camus, Heinemann Educational, 1970.
A Student's Guide to Moliere, Heinemann Educational, 1970.
A Student's Guide to Rabelais, Heinemann Educational, 1971.
Saint-Exupery, Heinemann Educational, 1973.
The Dukes, Blond & Briggs, 1975, revised edition, 1980.
Now Barabbas Was a Rotter: The Extraordinary Life of Marie Corelli, Hamish Hamilton, 1978.
The Mistresses of Charles II, Blond & Briggs, 1979.
Georgiana, Duchess of Devonshire, Hamish Hamilton, 1981.
Great Hostesses, Constable, 1982.
Killing for Company: The Case of Dennis Nilsen, J. Cape, 1985, Stein & Day, 1986.
The Swinging Sixties, Constable, 1985.
The Passion of John Aspinall, J. Cape, 1988.
Gary, J. Cape, 1990.
The Life of E. F. Benson, Chatto & Windus, 1991.

Also author of *Maharana: The Udaipur Dynasty,* 1990, and *The Shrine of Jeffrey Dahmer,* 1993. Contributor to

periodicals, including *Spectator, Standard, Times* (London), and *Literary Review.*

WORK IN PROGRESS: A translation of Voltaire's *Traite sur la Tolerance;* an anthology, *Masters on Murder.*

SIDELIGHTS: "The best writing must be enthusiastic and this quality is encouraged by variety," Brian Masters once told *CA.* Masters's own varied bibliography includes biographical studies on the British aristocracy, Victorian novelist Marie Corelli and Edwardian novelist E. F. Benson, and mass murderers Dennis Nilsen and Jeffrey Dahmer, a survey of famous British socialites, student guides to several French authors, and a popular history of the 1960s. He has also published an account of John Aspinall's world contribution to the breeding of wild animals in captivity.

Times Literary Supplement reviewer J. I. M. Stewart labels Masters's book *Now Barabbas Was a Rotter: The Extraordinary Life of Marie Corelli* "at once amusing and the issue of much painstaking research." Stewart observes that Corelli's novels using Christian themes were among the most popular of turn-of-the-century Britain, but that the literary world scorned the author. According to the critic, Masters shows that Corelli's "devouring egoism . . . made her indeed unbearable to cultivated people and at the same time a figure of awe to the unsophisticated." Stewart concludes that Masters exhibits "a fair-minded perception of [Corelli's] dilemmas and predicament which in the end establishes her as the protagonist of a humane and compassionate comedy."

In *Georgiana, Duchess of Devonshire,* Masters recounts life at the center of late eighteenth-century high-society Britain, basing his account on unpublished family papers and an extensive reading of the diaries, journals, and letters of the period. Among other topics, Masters explores the tangled sexual relationships of Georgiana and her husband, the fifth duke of Devonshire—particularly their menage-a-trois with Lady Elizabeth Foster—and offers evidence in favor of the long-questioned legitimacy of the sixth duke, Lord Hartington. The author also discusses the duchess's political activism and ability, her friendship with most of the great men and women of the day, and her tragic addiction to gambling. "With a wealth of new manuscript material and with a brilliant 'feel' for the period, [Masters] superbly depicts the warmth of heart as well as the social brilliance of Georgiana," explains A. N. Wilson in the *Times Literary Supplement,* adding, "She could not have hoped for a more elegantly made biography in our day; nor one more punctilious in its genealogical grasp, more solid in its historical truth, more incisive in its human sympathy."

Times Literary Supplement critic Mary Amory applauds Masters's book *Great Hostesses,* which deals with enter-

aining the upper stratum of twentieth-century London
ociety: "Brian Masters is a sane guide to a giddy world
and gives his heroines their due, a chapter not a book. If
he result is like dining entirely on mille feuilles, they have
been whisked up from the best cream and served with a
light touch." *Spectator* reviewer Hugh Montgomery-
Massingberd describes *Great Hostesses* as "a highly enter-
aining and deceptively well done study." Montgomery-
Massingberd further notes that Masters "is living up to his
name as one of the ablest operatives in the upper-class industry."

BIOGRAPHICAL/CRITICAL SOURCES:

PERIODICALS

New Statesman, February 22, 1985.
Spectator, November 20, 1982; February 23, 1985.
Times (London), December 23, 1981.
Times Literary Supplement, January 13, 1978; September
    25, 1981; November 19, 1982; March 29, 1985.

*   *   *

MAXWELL, John
    See FREEMANTLE, Brian (Harry)

*   *   *

MAYERS, Marvin K(eene) 1927-

PERSONAL: Born October 25, 1927, in Canton, OH; son
of Homer Douglas (a salesman) and Irma Hope (Kean)
Mayers; married Marilyn Ann Peipgrass (a secretary),
May 24, 1952; children: Margaret Lynn (Mrs. Richard A.
New), Donna Grace. *Education:* Wheaton College, Whea-
ton, IL, B.A., 1949; Fuller Theological Seminary, B.D.,
1952; University of Chicago, M.A., 1958, Ph.D., 1960.
Religion: Evangelical.

ADDRESSES: Home—14718 Mansa, La Mirada, CA
90638. *Office*—School of Intercultural Studies and World
Missions, Biola University, La Mirada, CA 90639.

CAREER: Wycliffe Bible Translators, Huntington Beach,
CA, translator, 1952—, dean, 1989—; Summer Institute
of Linguistics, Santa Ana, CA, field researcher and translator, 1952-65; Wheaton College, Wheaton, IL, associate
professor, 1965-70, professor of anthropology, 1970-74;
University of Texas at Arlington, professor of linguistics,
1974-82; Biola University, La Mirada, CA, professor and
dean of School of Intercultural Studies and World Missions, 1982-89. Director, Texas Summer Institute of Linguistics, Dallas, 1976-82. Visiting professor of linguistics,
University of Washington, summers, 1958-67, 1974-82.

MEMBER: American Anthropological Association (fellow).

AWARDS, HONORS: Organization of American States
fellowship, 1958-59; Tyndale Foundation fellowship for
Philippine studies, 1969.

WRITINGS:

(Editor) *Pocomchi Texts,* University of Oklahoma Press,
    1958.
(Editor) *Languages of Guatemala,* Mouton, 1966.
(With others) *Reshaping Evangelical Higher Education,*
    Zondervan, 1972.
(Compiler with David D. Koechel, and designer) *Love
    Goes On Forever,* Zondervan, 1972.
*Christianity Confronts Culture: A Strategy for Crosscul-
    tural Evangelism,* Zondervan, 1973, revised edition,
    1987.
A Look at Latin American Lifestyles, Summer Institute of
    Linguistics, 1976.
(With Stephen A. Grunlan) *Cultural Anthropology: A
    Christian Perspective,* Zondervan, 1978, 2nd edition,
    1988.
A Look at Filipino Lifestyles, Summer Institute of Linguis-
    tics, 1980.
(Contributor) Clifford A. Wilson and Donald W. McK-
    eon, *The Language Gap,* Zondervan, 1984.
(With Sherwood G. Lingenfelter) *Ministering Cross-
    Culturally: An Incarnational Model for Personal Rela-
    tionships,* Baker Book, 1986.
(Editor with Daniel D. Rath) *Nucleation in Papua New
    Guinea Cultures,* International Museum of Cultures,
    1988.

Contributor to *Anthropological Linguistics, International
Journal of Applied Linguistics,* and *Linguistics.*

*WORK IN PROGRESS: Latin American Culture; Bicul-
tural Evangelism: Philippine Focus; Crosscultural Education: Crosscultural Perspectives on Marriage and Family.*

*   *   *

McCALL, Edith (Sansom) 1911-

PERSONAL: Born September 5, 1911, in Charles City,
IA; daughter of William John and Mary (May) Sansom;
married Merle R. McCall, 1935 (divorced, 1963); married
Howard C. Worley, 1971 (died, 1974); children: (first
marriage) Constance McCall Johnston, Mary McCall.
Education: Attended Stevens Point State Teachers College
(now University of Wisconsin—Stevens Point), 1928-30;
University of Chicago, M.A., 1949. *Avocational Interests:*
Gardening, wood carving, traveling.

ADDRESSES: Home—Box 255, Hollister, MO 65672.

CAREER: Elementary school teacher in Elmhurst, IL,
1930-35; and in Western Springs, IL, 1943-47; La Grange

Public Schools, La Grange, IL, reading consultant, 1947-55; full-time writer, 1953—.

MEMBER: Authors League of America, Society of Children's Book Writers and Illustrators, Western Writers of America, Missouri Writers Guild (president, Springfield chapter, 1961; president of state guild, 1971), White River Valley Historical Society (secretary, 1961-62), Pi Lambda Theta.

AWARDS, HONORS: Missouri Writers Guild Award, 1960, for *Hunters Blaze the Trails,* and 1984, for *Conquering the Rivers: Henry Miller Shreve and the Navigation of America's Inland Waterways;* Spur Award nomination, Western Writers of America, 1985; Distinguished Alumnus Award, University of Wisconsin—Stevens Point, 1988, for her writing career; honor book selection, Children's Reading Round Table of Chicago, 1989, for *Better Than a Brother;* Captain Donald T. Wright Award in Maritime Journalism, 1992, for *Conquering the Rivers: Henry Miller Shreve and the Navigation of America's Inland Waterways.*

WRITINGS:

(With Charlotte E. Wilcox) *Come On,* Benefic, 1955.
(With Wilcox) *Here We Go,* Benefic, 1955.
(With Wilcox) *Step Lively,* Benefic, 1955.
(With Marjorie Ann Banks) *Where Rivers Meet,* Benefic, 1958, revised edition, 1973.
(With George Crout) *Where the Ohio Flows,* Benefic, 1960, revised edition, 1964.
English Village in the Ozarks, privately printed, 1969, new edition, 1985.
(With Crout) *You and Ohio,* Benefic, 1971.
(With Muriel Stanek) *People and Our Country,* Benefic, 1976, revised edition published as part of "People in a World of Change" series (also see below), 1978.
Conquering the Rivers: Henry Miller Shreve and the Navigation of America's Inland Waterways, Louisiana State University Press, 1984.
Message from the Mountains (juvenile historical novel), Walker & Co., 1985.
Mississippi Steamboatman: The Story of Henry Miller Shreve (juvenile biography), Walker & Co., 1986.
Better Than a Brother (juvenile historical novel), Walker & Co., 1988.
Biography of a River: The Living Mississippi, Walker & Co., 1990.
Sometimes We Dance Alone (autobiographical/inspirational), Barton & Brett, 1993.

"BUTTON FAMILY" SERIES; REVISED EDITIONS PUBLISHED IN 1960-61

Bucky Button, Benefic, 1953.
The Buttons at the Zoo, Benefic, 1954.
The Buttons and the Pet Parade, Benefic, 1954.

The Buttons at the Farm, Benefic, 1955.
The Buttons Go Camping, Benefic, 1956.
The Buttons at the Soap Box Derby, Benefic, 1957.
The Buttons Take a Boat Ride, Benefic, 1957.
The Buttons and Mr. Pete, Benefic, 1957.
The Buttons and the Boy Scouts, Benefic, 1958.
The Buttons and the Little League, Benefic, 1958.
The Buttons and the Whirlybird, Benefic, 1959.
The Buttons See Things That Go, Benefic, 1959.

"FRONTIERS OF AMERICA" SERIES

Log Fort Adventures, Children's Press, 1958.
Steamboats to the West, Children's Press, 1959.
Hunters Blaze the Trail, Children's Press, 1959.
Explorers in a New World, Children's Press, 1960.
Men on Iron Horses, Children's Press, 1960.
Settlers on a Strange Shore, Children's Press, 1960.
Heroes of the Western Outposts, Children's Press, 1960.
Pioneers of the Early Waterways, Children's Press, 1961.
Wagons over the Mountains, Children's Press, 1961.
Cumberland Gap and Trails West, Children's Press, 1961.
Mail Riders, Children's Press, 1961.
Gold Rush Adventures, Children's Press, 1962.
Pioneering on the Plains, Children's Press, 1962.
Pirates and Privateers, Children's Press, 1963.
Pioneer Show Folk, Children's Press, 1963.
Pioneer Traders, Children's Press, 1964.
Cowboys and Cattle Drives, Children's Press, 1964.
Fort in the Wilderness, Children's Press, 1968.
Stalwart Men of Early Texas, Children's Press, 1970.

Also author of teacher's guide to "Frontiers of America" series, 1980.

"HOW" SERIES

How We Get Our Mail, Benefic, 1961.
How Airplanes Help Us, Benefic, 1961.
How We Get Our Clothing, Benefic, 1961.
How We Get Cloth, Benefic, 1961.

"LEARNING FOR LIVING IN TODAY'S WORLD" SERIES

(With Clarence Samford and Ruth Gue) *You Are Here,* Benefic, 1963.
(With Samford and Gue) *You and the Neighborhood,* Benefic, 1963.
(With Samford and Gue) *You and the Community,* Benefic, 1963.
(With Samford and Floyd Cunningham) *You and Regions Far and Near,* Benefic, 1963.
(With Samford and Cunningham) *You and the United States,* Benefic, 1964.
(With Samford and Cunningham) *You and the Americas,* Benefic, 1965.
(With Samford and Cunningham) *You and the World,* Benefic, 1966.

(With Mark M. Krug) *You and the Nation,* Benefic, 1968.

"BUTTERNUT BILL" SERIES

Butternut Bill, Benefic, 1965.
Butternut Bill and the Bee Tree, Benefic, 1965.
Butternut Bill and the Big Cash, Benefic, 1965.
Butternut Bill and the Bear, Benefic, 1965.
Butternut Bill and Little River, Benefic, 1966.
Butternut Bill and the Big Pumpkin, Benefic, 1966.
Butternut Bill and His Friends, Benefic, 1968.
Butternut Bill and the Train, Benefic, 1969.

"MAN IN A WORLD OF CHANGE" SERIES

(With Muriel Stanek and Evalyn Rapparlie) *Man and His Families,* Benefic, 1971.
(With Stanek and Rapparlie) *Man and His Community,* Benefic, 1971.
(With Stanek and Rapparlie) *Man and His Cities,* Benefic, 1971.
(With Stanek and Rapparlie) *Man and the Regions of the World,* Benefic, 1971.
(With Rapparlie and Jack B. Spatafora) *Man—United States and Americas,* Benefic, 1972.
(With Rapparlie and Spatafora) *Man—His World and Cultures,* Benefic, 1972.

"PEOPLE IN A WORLD OF CHANGE" SERIES; BASIC SOCIAL STUDIES TEXTS

(With Robert A. Carter and Vernon Prinzing) *You: Family and School,* Benefic, 1978.
(With Carter and Prinzing) *You: People and Places,* Benefic, 1978.
(With Carter and Prinzing) *You: Communities and Change,* Benefic, 1978.
(With Carter and Prinzing) *You: Earth and Its Regions,* Benefic, 1978.
(With Carter and Prinzing) *You: United States and Americas,* Benefic, 1978.
(With Carter and Prinzing) *You: World and Cultures,* Benefic, 1978.
(With Stanek) *People and Our Country,* Benefic, 1978.

OTHER

Also author of "Health Action" series, three books, Benefic, 1954-55, revised editions, 1963.

ADAPTATIONS: Recordings for each of the "Butternut Bill" series books were made in 1969.

WORK IN PROGRESS: An adult historical novel set west of the Appalachians in the early 1800s.

SIDELIGHTS: Edith McCall once told *CA:* "When I was in college, I took courses under an American history professor who saw influential people of the past as distinct personalities and not just names. He permanently changed my attitude toward American history. I thought it a shame that my childhood instruction had left me unaware of the fascinating details and failed to bring the story of my nation to life. That professor opened my eyes and gave birth to my love of the subject. I became especially fascinated by our westward growth and the courage of the people responsible for it. Most of my published writing reflects this interest. I'd like to have children and adults, too, see American history as the greatest drama of all time. I find it most fascinating to learn the stories of almost unknown people who make important contributions. I try to retell their histories in a manner that won't 'turn people off,' whether I'm writing for the young child or the adult."

BIOGRAPHICAL/CRITICAL SOURCES:

BOOKS

McCall, Edith, *Sometimes We Dance Alone* (autobiographical/inspirational), Barton & Brett, 1993.

*   *   *

McCANN, Francis Daniel, Jr. 1938-
(Frank D. McCann, Jr.)

PERSONAL: Born December 15, 1938, in Lackawanna, NY; son of Francis Daniel (a teacher) and Catherine L. (a teacher; maiden name, Moran) McCann; married Diane Marie Sankis (a nurse practitioner), 1962; children: Teresa Bernadette, Katherine Diane. *Education:* Niagara University, A.B., 1960; Kent State University, M.A., 1962; attended Pontifical Catholic University of Rio de Janeiro, 1965; Indiana University at Bloomington, Ph.D., 1967. *Politics:* Democrat. *Religion:* Roman Catholic.

ADDRESSES: Office—Department of History, University of New Hampshire, Durham, NH 03824.

CAREER: Wisconsin State University (now University of Wisconsin—River Falls), assistant professor of history, 1966-68; University of New Hampshire, Durham, assistant professor, 1971-73, associate professor, 1973-82, professor of history 1982—, director, Center for International Perspectives, 1982-90. Research fellow at Princeton University, 1970-71; Fulbright Professor at Universidade de Brasilia, 1976-77, and Universidade Federal do Rio de Janeiro, 1991. Visiting professor at New York University, 1978, and University of New Mexico, 1983. *Military service:* U.S. Army Reserve, 1960-75; active duty as assistant professor at U.S. Military Academy, West Point, NY, 1968-70; became captain.

MEMBER: American Historical Association, Conference on Latin American History (chairman of Committee on Brazilian Studies, 1979-80), Latin American Studies Association, Society for Historians of American Foreign Relations, New England Council on Latin American Studies (president, 1975-76), Northeast Association of Brazilianists (vice-president, 1987-89; president, 1989-91), Conference on Latin American History (chairperson, International Scholarly Relations Committee, 1988-91).

AWARDS, HONORS: Fulbright grants for Brazil, 1965-66, 1974, 1976-77, and 1991; fellow, National Historical Publications Commission, 1970-71; grants, American Philosophical Society, 1970, 1971, 1973, and 1991; Stuart L. Bemath Memorial Prize, Society for Historians of American Foreign Relations, 1975, for *The Brazilian-American Alliance, 1937-1945;* grant, Social Science Research Council and American Council of Learned Societies, 1976-77; named guest scholar, Woodrow Wilson International Center for Scholars, 1978; elected corresponding member, Instituto de Geografia e Historia Militar do Brasil, 1979; New England Council on Latin American Studies Prize, 1985, for "Formative Period of Twentieth-Century Brazilian Army Thought"; Heinz Endowment grant, 1985-87; faculty scholar award, University of New Hampshire, 1987; decorated by Brazilian government, rank of Comendador, Order of Rio Branco, 1987; Creative Programming Award, National University Continuing Education Association, 1989, for EXPERIENCE BRAZIL! (a cultural training workshop); American Council of Learned Societies travel grant (Poland), 1990.

WRITINGS:

(Under name Frank D. McCann, Jr.) *The Brazilian-American Alliance, 1937-1945,* Princeton University Press, 1973.
(Under name Frank D. McCann, Jr.) *A nacao armada: Ensaios sobre a historia do exercito brasileiro* (title means "The Nation in Arms: Essays on the History of the Brazilian Army"), Editora Guararapes, 1982.
(Editor and contributor, under name Frank D. McCann, Jr., with Michael Conniff) *Modern Brazil: Elites and Masses in Historical Perspective,* University of Nebraska Press, 1989.

Also contributor to books, including *Religious and Cultural Factors in Latin America,* Charles J. Fleener and Harry J. Cargas, editors, St. Louis University Press, 1970; *Cultural Change in Brazil,* Merrill Rippy, editor, Ball State University Press, 1969; *Essays Concerning the Socio-Economic History of Brazil,* Duaril Alden and Warren Dean, editors, University Presses of Florida, 1977; *Brazil in the International System,* Wayne A. Selcher, editor, Westview, 1981; *War, Business and World Military-Industrial Complexes,* B. Franklin Cooling, editor, Kennikat Press, 1981; *Biographical Dictionary of Internationalists,* Warren F. Kuehl, editor, Greenwood Press, 1983; *A Revolutao de 30: Seminario Internacional,* Editora Universidade de Brasilia, 1983; *Encyclopedia of World Biogra-*

phy, David Eggenberger, editor, McGraw-Hill, 1987; and *The Politics of Antipolitics: The Military in Latin America,* Brian Loveman and Thomas Davies, editors, University of Nebraska Press, 1989. Contributor of approximately seventy-five articles, reviews and opinion pieces to Latin American studies, history and military journals, including *A Defesa Nacional,* and newspapers.

WORK IN PROGRESS: Brazil and the United States: Western Hemisphere Giants, for University of Georgia Press; "Historical Setting," Chapter 1 of *Brazil: A Country Study,* for Federal Research Division, Library of Congress; *The Brazilian Army, A History 1889-1930; The Brazilian Army, A History 1930-1992; Gies Monteiro: Biography of a Brazilian General,* with Peter S. Smith.

SIDELIGHTS: Francis David McCann, Jr., once told *CA:* "The liveliness of Brazilians first attracted me to Brazil and to the Portuguese language. The result has been an active career of research and teaching that has taken me to Latin America twenty-one times. I had the extraordinary good luck to find previously unused documents in the research for my first book, and I take pride in being one of the pioneers in the United States in Brazilian studies.

"When researching *The Brazilian-American Alliance,* the two most important sets of documents were the private papers of President Getulio Vargas and his foreign minister, Oswaldo Aranha. At the time (between 1965 and 1969), the papers were in the hands of two families. This meant working at the dining room table of Getulio's daughter, Alzira Vargas do Amaral Peixoto, and in dimly lit rooms over the Aranha garage. It was an exciting experience to have the inner workings of the Brazilian Government open before me. It allowed me to be more exact and more personal in treating the process of policy formation and execution. In addition, Alzira Vargas and Aranha's son, Euclides, explained a great deal about the personal relationships of people in the documents. Today these records are housed in a marvelous archive in the Centro de Pesquisa e Documentacao de Historia Contemporanea do Brasil (CPDOC) in Rio de Janeiro. In crafting the essays and book that came out of that research, I was most fortunate to have the criticism and advice of two excellent historians, Robert H. Ferrell and Robert E. Quirk. Their work was the standard against which I measured mine. They taught me that the secret to good writing is rewriting.

"As a historian, I believe it is important to see the places where the history I write is set. As a result my studies of the army have taken me to archives in Brasilia and Rio de Janeiro, and to army posts from Manuas to Rosario do Sul in Rio Grande do Sul. I've had lengthy, seminar-style discussions with officers in the Command and General Staff School in Rio, and lectured to officers on my research in

Brasilia and Rio de Janeiro. Studying a closed, secretive institution such as an army is a slow business, requiring access to many people. It takes years, especially for a foreigner, to build up sufficient confidence and reputation. I have become particularly fascinated with the role of ideas and how they are shaped and transmitted. My articles that have appeared in the Brazilian Army's journal, *A Defesa Nacional*, have helped shape the way the officer corps thinks about its history.

"My current writings on Brazilian-American relations shows a history of Brazilians wanting a special friendship with the United States, and Americans repeatedly holding them at arm's length, if not rejecting completely their advances. It is a curious, imbalanced relationship.

"My preoccupation is to help people in the United States better understand the realities of Latin America. Many of the problems of the region are the results of policies formulated in Washington, DC. I have come to believe that it is not merely a matter of understanding Brazilians or Mexicans better, but of understanding ourselves and the system in which we live and how it affects the rest of the world.

"In historical writing I try to show the role of individuals as much as possible, because I believe that it is the individual act that shapes the whole, rather than the reverse."

BIOGRAPHICAL/CRITICAL SOURCES:

PERIODICALS

American Historical Review, December, 1975.
Hispanic American Historical Review, May, 1979; November, 1979; February, 1984.
Latin American Research Review, spring, 1979.

*   *   *

McCANN, Frank D., Jr.
See McCANN, Francis Daniel, Jr.

*   *   *

MCCUNN, Ruthanne Lum 1946-

PERSONAL: Born February 21, 1946, in San Francisco, CA; married Don McCunn (a writer, theater director, and actor). *Education:* University of Texas at Austin, B.A., 1968; San Francisco State College (now University), Teaching Credential, 1969. *Politics:* Independent.

ADDRESSES: Home—1007 Castro, San Francisco, CA 94114. *Agent*—Peter Ginsburg, President, Curtis Brown, Ltd., 1750 Montgomery Street, San Francisco, CA 94111.

CAREER: Librarian at public schools in Santa Barbara, CA, 1969-70, teacher, 1970-73; teacher in San Francisco

Unified School District, CA, 1974-78; writer, 1979—. Member of California State Committee for Evaluation and Selection of Texts for State Adoption, Committee for Library Services, and Committee for Legal Compliance; member of advisory board of Asian Women United and Chinese Culture Center; consultant on bilingual and bicultural education and on teaching English as a second language. Guest lecturer at University of California at Santa Cruz, 1988, Cornell University, 1989, and University of San Francisco, 1993.

MEMBER: Amnesty International, American Civil Liberties Union, Chinese Historical Society, Chinese for Affirmative Action, International Institute of San Francisco.

AWARDS, HONORS: American Book Award, Before Columbus Foundation, 1984, for *Pie-Biter;* Best Nonfiction Adventure Book, Southwestern Booksellers Association, 1985, for *Sole Survivor; Chinese American Portraits* was named one of the best nonfiction books of 1989, *Choice Magazine;* Distinguished Achievement Award, National Women's Political Caucus, 1991.

WRITINGS:

An Illustrated History of the Chinese in America, Design Enterprises of San Francisco, 1979.
Thousand Pieces of Gold (biographical novel), Design Enterprises of San Francisco, 1981.
Pie-Biter (picture book), Design Enterprises of San Francisco, 1983.
Sole Survivor (nonfiction), Design Associates of San Francisco, 1985.
Chinese American Portraits: Personal Histories 1828-1888 (nonfiction), Chronicle Books, 1988.
Chinese Proverbs (nonfiction), Chronicle Books, 1991.

Also contributor of articles to *Yihai, School Library Journal, Chinese America: History and Perspectives.*

WORK IN PROGRESS: Double Brilliance (historical novel).

SIDELIGHTS: For Ruthanne Lum McCunn the Asian-American experience is a personal reality. Born in San Francisco to a father of Scottish descent and a mother of Chinese descent, she was raised in Hong Kong until the age of sixteen. At that time McCunn returned to the United States to attend college and live with her father's family in Boise, Idaho. After experiencing what she described as culture shock, McCunn fled from the Northwest back to San Francisco. Recalling her past episodes with rejection and discrimination as a "foreign devil" and a "hybrid" to Mildred Hamilton in the *San Francisco Examiner*, McCunn explained that she had since resolved to "work . . . against the stereotype in America that Asians are somehow less human than Caucasians" by revealing "the rich Chinese-American history that is totally unmined."

Fulfilling that commitment, McCunn writes about various true-to-life experiences of Asian-Americans. In her book *Thousand Pieces of Gold,* for example, readers discover the multiple hardships overcome by a Chinese woman sold into slavery in the United States during the 1870s. The American Book Award-winning *Pie-Biter* features heroism in a folktale about an Asian-American youth who has a penchant for American pies. And in *Sole Survivor* McCunn spotlights a Chinese sailor who was shipwrecked on a raft in the Atlantic Ocean for 133 days. Collectively, the author's stories reflect what Hamilton observed as the "determined struggle for survival of earlier Asians" who, like McCunn, became caught between different cultures.

BIOGRAPHICAL/CRITICAL SOURCES:

PERIODICALS

Examiner (San Francisco), December 8, 1985.
Los Angeles Times, September 25, 1983.
Sampan, January, 1982.
San Francisco Chronicle, September 21, 1983.
Womanews, November, 1985.

* * *

McDONALD, Julie   1929-
(Julie Jensen; Julie Jensen McDonald)

PERSONAL: Born June 22, 1929, in Audubon County, IA; daughter of Alfred J. (a farmer) and Myrtle (Faurschou) Jensen; married Elliott R. McDonald, Jr. (an attorney), May 6, 1952; children: Beth Pearson, Elliott R. III. *Education:* University of Iowa, B.A. and Certificate in Journalism, 1951. *Politics:* Republican (moderate). *Religion:* Presbyterian. *Avocational Interests:* Paintings, drawings, and prints ("collect modestly"), travel, Scottish Deerhounds, and Friends of the Public Library projects.

ADDRESSES: Home—2802 East Locust St., Davenport, IA 52803.

CAREER: Rockford Register-Republic and Morning Star, Rockford, IL, women's editor, 1951-52; *Quad-City Times,* Davenport, IA, feature writer and fine arts critic, 1962-82; *Rock Island Argus,* Rock Island, IL, arts writer, 1983—. Iowa Arts Council, chair, 1969-73, writer-in-the-schools, 1974—; Lecturer in English, Black Hawk College, Moline, IL, 1965; lecturer in journalism, St. Ambrose University, Davenport, IA, 1974—. Clarinetist, formerly performing with Rockford Symphony Orchestra, now with Bettendorf Community Band. Liaison director, Scott County Association for Mental Health, 1956-58; secre-

tary, Scott County Republican Central Committee, 1957-74. Also author of monthly column "Artswise," for *The Gold Book.*

MEMBER: P.E.O. Sisterhood, Davenport Museum of Art (trustee), Phi Beta Kappa.

AWARDS, HONORS: Quad-City Writer of the Year, 1969; doctorate of letters, St. Ambrose University, 1972; Governor's Media in the Arts Award, 1975; Friends of American Writers Award, 1979, for *Petra;* first place in state and national competitions for fiction, National Federation of Press Women, and Johnson Brigham Award, Iowa Library Association, both 1983, both for *The Sailing Out;* National Federation of Press Women, first place awards, 1988, for *The Heather and the Rose,* and 1991, for *Young Rakes,* third place awards, 1990, for *Nils Discovers America,* and 1992, for *The Odyssey of a Museum.*

WRITINGS:

NOVELS

Amalie's Story, Simon & Schuster, 1970.
Petra, Iowa State University Press, 1978.
The Sailing Out, Iowa State University Press, 1982.
The Heather and the Rose, Sutherland, 1985.
The Ballad of Bishop Hill, Sutherland, 1986.
Reaching: A Novel, Sutherland, 1988.
Young Rakes, East Hall Press, 1991.

OTHER

Baby Black, Angus Journal, 1960.
Pathways to the Present (originally published as a fifty-part historical series in the *Quad-City Times*), Boyar Books, 1977.
(Contributor) Clarence Andrews, editor, *Growing Up in Iowa,* Iowa State University Press, 1978.
(Contributor) C. Andrews, editor, *Christmas in Iowa,* Midwest Heritage, 1979.
Ruth Buxton Sayre: First Lady of the Farms (biography), Iowa State University Press, 1980.
Delectably Danish: Recipes and Reflections, Penfield Press, 1982.
(Compiler with Lynn Hattery-Beyer and Joan Liffring-Zug) John Zug, editor, *German Proverbs,* Penfield Press, 1988.
(Under name Julie Jensen McDonald) *Nils Discovers America: Adventures with Erik* (for children), illustrated by Norma Wangsness, Penfield Press, 1990.
Danish Proverbs, Penfield Press, 1993.

Also author of *The Odyssey of a Museum: A History of the Putnam Museum,* (Davenport, IA), 1992, and *Definitely Danish* (essays), in press; author of unpublished novel *Emporium;* author of three-act play, *High Rise,* produced by Playcrafters, Moline, IL; historical play, *Time and the*

River, produced by Quad-City Center for Performing Arts; and two three-act plays for Davenport Junior Theatre. Adapter of *My Brother Corant Wood* by Nan Wood Graham, in press. Contributor of essay to the *Time-Life Book of Christmas,* 1987. Contributor of articles to newspapers under name Julie Jensen.

WORK IN PROGRESS: Trio (former working title, *We Three*) and *North of the Heart,* both novels.

SIDELIGHTS: Julie McDonald once told *CA:* "Working with children in the State Arts Council's Writers-in-the-Schools Program has helped me sort out why and how I function as a writer. Trying to transmit a vision always makes it much more one's own."

McDonald also noted that "as a lifelong midwesterner, I have spent my writing life sifting midwestern experience for fictional truth. That truth in its quiet solidity is not destined for best-sellerdom, but I am satisfied to attempt its expression with all the honesty and craft I can muster. I believe that attention must be paid to this life in this place because there is value in it for people everywhere. . . . I am astonished by letters from readers who think my novels are true stories, but I shouldn't be, as I do a great deal of research to make them seem real."

*   *   *

McDONALD, Julie Jensen
See McDONALD, Julie

*   *   *

McGLAMRY, Beverly 1932-
(Kate Cameron)

PERSONAL: Born August 1, 1932, in Somerset, MA; daughter of Charles Bradford (a public utility employee) and Dorothy (a homemaker; maiden name, Dodge) Grime; married Charles McGlamry (a utility company supervisor), August 26, 1961; children: Charles, Richard, Mary Ann. *Education:* Attended high school in Somerset, MA.

ADDRESSES: Home and office—7910 Northwest 171st St., Hialeah, FL 33015.

CAREER: Worked at various clerical and secretarial jobs, 1950-73; Palm Springs Elementary School, Hialeah, FL, teacher's aide, 1973-81; writer, 1981—.

MEMBER: Author's Guild, Romance Writers of America, Florida State Poetry Association, Writers Support Group, Florida Center for the Book.

AWARDS, HONORS: Numerous poetry awards, including prizes from New York Poetry Forum, 1982, for "Evo-

lution"; Poets and Patrons International, 1982, for "The Unicorn in the Garden"; World Order of Narrative Poets (New York), 1982, for "Art Gallery", 1983, for "Picture Me Then," and 1985, for "Olympic Games"; World Order of Narrative Poets (California), 1983, for "Saga of the Sword"; Florida State Poetry Association, 1985, for "1001 Delights"; and Space Coast Poetry Club, 1985, for "Master Plan" and "On Visiting an Art Exhibit."

WRITINGS:

Family Bible (historical romance), Ballantine, 1985.
Goodly Heritage (historical romance), Ballantine, 1986.
(Under pseudonym Kate Cameron) *As If They were Gods* (historical novel), Ballantine, 1987.
(Under pseudonym Kate Cameron) *Orenda* (historical novel), Ballantine, 1991.

Contributor of an article and poems to magazines, including *Pudding, Tempest, Manna, Earthwise, Writer,* and *Women's Circle.* Also contributor to *Woman Sleuth Anthology,* Crossing Press, 1988.

WORK IN PROGRESS: The Legend Makers, a novel "about the Native Americans of early Florida at the time of European contact," for Ballantine, 1995.

SIDELIGHTS: Beverly McGlamry told *CA:* "I came late trying my hand at writing, and I consider myself fortunate that my efforts thus far have met with a certain amount of success. I am having a wonderful time doing what I have always longed to do. I write about what interests me most—people, and because history also intrigues me, I enjoy setting my stories in eras other than the present. With *Orenda,* a story about the Seventeenth Century Iroquois Nation, and *The Legend Makers,* I went from writing about the aborigines of the British Isles (*As If They were Gods*) to writing stories featuring the native peoples of my own country.

"I try hard to make all the background details authentic, whatever the era or ethnic group, yet my characters are rarely involved with what are commonly known as 'great moments in history'; they are ordinary people, living ordinary lives which are affected by these 'great moments' only to the degree that your life or mine is affected by the momentous happenings of today. Bertrand Russell once said that there are two motives for reading a book—to enjoy it, or to boast about it. My novels are meant to entertain.

"Ten years ago I doubt if I could have described with any degree of certainty the personal views and values that are reflected in my fictional characters. But it occurs to me now that what I've been trying to say all along is that the greatest gift humankind is born with is the capacity to feel—to love or hate, to be happy or sad. I'm not denigrating man's ability to reason, but this is a talent all of us make use of, whether we think we do or not. Emotion, however, can be wantonly splurged, dealt out stingily, or spent with discretion, and it's how the individual chooses to make use of this precious gift that largely molds his character."

* * *

McMURTRY, Larry (Jeff) 1936-

PERSONAL: Born June 3, 1936, in Wichita Falls, TX; son of William Jefferson (a rancher) and Hazel Ruth (McIver) McMurtry; married Josephine Ballard, July 15, 1959 (divorced, 1966); children: James Lawrence. *Education:* North Texas State College (now University), B.A., 1958; Rice University, M.A., 1960; additional study at Stanford University, 1960.

ADDRESSES: Office—Booked Up Book Store, 1209 31st St. N.W., Washington, DC 20007. *Agent*—Irving Paul Lazar, The Irving Paul Lazar Agency, 120 El Camino, Beverly Hills, CA 90212.

CAREER: Texas Christian University, Fort Worth, instructor, 1961-62; Rice University, Houston, TX, lecturer in English and creative writing, 1963-69; Booked Up Book Store, Washington, DC, co-owner, 1970—. Visiting professor at George Mason College, 1970, and at American University, 1970-71. Has worked as a rare book scout and dealer for book stores in Texas and California.

MEMBER: PEN American Center (president, 1989), Texas Institute of Letters.

AWARDS, HONORS: Wallace Stegner fellowship, 1960; Jesse H. Jones Award from Texas Institute of Letters, 1962, for *Horseman, Pass By;* Guggenheim fellowship, 1964; Academy of Motion Picture Arts and Sciences Award (Oscar) for best screenplay based on material from another medium, 1972, for *The Last Picture Show;* Barbara McCombs/Lon Tinkle Award for continuing excellence in Texas letters from Texas Institute of Letters, 1986; Pulitzer Prize for fiction, Spur Award from Western Writers of America, and Texas Literary Award from Southwestern Booksellers Association, all 1986, all for *Lonesome Dove.*

WRITINGS:

NOVELS

Horseman, Pass By, Harper, 1961, Texas A & M University Press, 1988, published as *Hud,* Popular Library, 1961.
Leaving Cheyenne, Harper, 1963, Texas A & M University Press, 1986.
The Last Picture Show (also see below), Dial, 1966, Simon & Schuster, 1989.

Moving On, Simon & Schuster, 1970, Pocket Books, 1988.
All My Friends Are Going to Be Strangers, Simon & Schuster, 1972.
Terms of Endearment, Simon & Schuster, 1975.
Somebody's Darling, Simon & Schuster, 1978.
Cadillac Jack, Simon & Schuster, 1982.
The Desert Rose, Simon & Schuster, 1983.
Lonesome Dove, Simon & Schuster, 1985.
Texasville (sequel to *The Last Picture Show;* also see below), Simon & Schuster, 1987.
Anything for Billy, Simon & Schuster, 1988.
Some Can Whistle (sequel to *All My Friends Are Going to Be Strangers*), Simon & Schuster, 1989.
Buffalo Girls, Simon & Schuster, 1990.
The Evening Star (sequel to *Terms of Endearment*), Simon & Schuster, 1992.
Streets of Laredo (sequel to *Lonesome Dove*), Simon & Schuster, 1993.

ESSAYS

In a Narrow Grave: Essays on Texas, Encino Press, 1968, Simon & Schuster, 1989.
It's Always We Rambled: An Essay on Rodeo, Hallman, 1974.
Film Flam: Essays on Hollywood, Simon & Schuster, 1987.

SCRIPTS

(With Peter Bogdanovich) *The Last Picture Show* (screenplay; based on McMurtry's novel of same title; produced by Columbia Pictures, 1971), B.B.S. Productions, 1970.
Texasville (screenplay; based on McMurtry's novel of the same title), Columbia Pictures, 1990.
Montana (teleplay), Turner Network Television (TNT), 1990.
Falling from Grace (screenplay), Columbia Pictures, 1992.
(With Cybill Shepherd) *Memphis* (teleplay; based on a novel by Shelby Foote), Turner Home Entertainment, 1992.

OTHER

(Author of foreword) Frederick L. Olmsted, *Journey through Texas: or, A Saddle-Trip on the Southwestern Frontier,* University of Texas Press, 1978.
(Author of foreword) John R. Erickson, *Panhandle Cowboy,* University of Nebraska Press, 1980.
(Contributor) *Texas in Transition,* Lyndon Baines Johnson School of Public Affairs, 1986.
(Author of introduction) Dan Flores, *Canyon Visions: Photographs & Pastels of the Texas Plains,* Texas Tech University Press, 1989.
(Author of introduction) Donna A. Demac, *Liberty Denied: The Current Rise of Censorship in America,* Rutgers University Press, 1990.

(Author of foreword) Clarus Backes, editor, *Growing Up Western,* Knopf, 1990.

Contributor of numerous articles, essays, and book reviews for magazines and newspapers, including *Atlantic, Gentleman's Quarterly, New York Times, Saturday Review,* and *Washington Post.* Contributing editor of *American Film,* 1975—.

ADAPTATIONS: Hud, based on *Horseman, Pass By,* was produced by Paramount in 1962, and won two Academy Awards from the Academy of Motion Picture Arts and Sciences; *Lovin' Molly,* based on *Leaving Cheyenne,* was produced by Columbia Pictures in 1974; *Terms of Endearment,* based on the novel of the same title, was produced by Paramount in 1983, and won four Golden Globe Awards, the "best picture" award from the New York Film Critics Circle, and five Academy Awards from the Academy of Motion Picture Arts and Sciences, including "best picture of the year"; *Lonesome Dove,* based on the novel of the same title, was produced as a television miniseries for Columbia Broadcasting System (CBS) in 1989; *Return to Lonesome Dove,* based on characters from *Lonesome Dove,* was produced as a television miniseries for CBS in 1993.

SIDELIGHTS: In the more than thirty years since he published his first novel, Larry McMurtry has emerged as one of Texas's most prominent fiction writers. Though he has lived outside Texas for two decades, McMurtry has drawn themes for many of his novels from the uneasy interaction between his native state's mythic past and its problematic, ongoing urbanization. His earliest works, such as the critically acclaimed *Horseman, Pass By* and *The Last Picture Show,* expose the bleak prospects for adolescents on the rural ranches or in the small towns of west Texas, while his novels written in the 1970s, including *Terms of Endearment,* trace Texas characters drawn into the urban milieus of Houston, Hollywood, and Washington, DC. More recently, his 1986 Pulitzer Prize-winning novel *Lonesome Dove* has received high praise for its realistic detailing of a cattle drive from the last century, a transformation into fiction of a part of Texas history the author previously approached in his essays on cowboys, ranching, and rodeos. As Si Dunn notes in the *Dallas News,* McMurtry's readers find him "a writer who has made living in Texas a literary experience."

As a spokesman for the status of modern Texas letters, McMurtry has been known to criticize some Texas writers for their tendency to overlook the potentially rich material to be found in the present-day experience of Texas's new industries and burgeoning urban areas. In a piece from *In a Narrow Grave: Essays on Texas,* he concludes: "Texas writers are sometimes so anxious to avoid the accusation of provincialism that they will hardly condescend to render the particularities of their own place, though it ought to be clear that literature thrives on particulars. The material is here, and it has barely been touched. If this is truly the era of the Absurd, then all the better for the Texas writer, for where else except California can one find a richer mixture of absurdities? Literature has coped fairly well with the physical circumstances of life in Texas, but our emotional experience remains largely unexplored, and therein lie the drama, poems, and novels."

In *The Ghost Country: A Study of the Novels of Larry McMurtry,* Raymond L. Neinstein expresses the belief that McMurtry "has journeyed from an old-fashioned regionalism to a kind of 'neo-regionalism,' his characters, and the novels themselves, turning from the land as the locus of their values to an imaginary, fictive 'place.' But they, characters and novels both, are finally not able to manage there, at least not comfortably. McMurtry clearly does not trust 'living in the head'; the pull of the old myth is still strong." McMurtry himself is aware of this dichotomy, as he writes in *Holiday:* "A part of my generation may keep something of the frontier spirit even though the frontier is lost. What they may keep is a sense of daring and independence, transferred from the life of action to the life of the mind."

In McMurtry's case, this description is particularly apt. The son and grandson of cattle ranchers, he grew up in sparsely populated Archer County in north central Texas. From childhood he was more interested in reading than ranching, but the family stories he heard as a youth exerted an enormous influence on his sense of identity. He writes in *In a Narrow Grave:* "It is indeed a complex distance from those traildrivers who made my father and my uncles determined to be cowboys to the mechanical horse that helps convince my son that he is a cowboy, as he takes a vertical ride in front of a laundrymat." If he felt pride and nostalgia for the ranching way of life, which was vanishing even as he came of age, McMurtry was far less enthusiastic about tiny Archer City, where he attended high school as an honor student. McMurtry found little with which to nourish his imagination within the confines of the town, as he notes in *In a Narrow Grave:* "I grew up in a bookless town, in a bookless part of the state—when I stepped into a university library, at age eighteen, the whole of the world's literature lay before me unread, a country as vast, as promising, and, so far as I knew, as trackless as the West must have seemed to the first white men who looked upon it."

In creating his own fiction, however, McMurtry has drawn many of his themes from his "blood's country" of Texas. His early works portray a fictional town and countryside with a strong resemblance to Archer County. In *Horseman, Pass By,* his first novel, McMurtry introduces an adolescent narrator named Lonnie Bannon, who describes a series of tragic events that occur on his grandfather's ranch when an epidemic of hoof-and-mouth disease is discovered. Nearing manhood himself, the orphaned Lonnie is confronted with several role models whose behavior he must evaluate: his step-uncle Hud, an egotistic and ruthless hedonist; his grandfather's hired hand Jesse, a storytelling drifter; and his grandfather Homer, who, Charles D. Peavy states in his book *Larry McMurtry,* "epitomizes all the rugged virtues of a pioneer ethic." Lonnie's frustration is additionally fanned by the presence of Halmea, the black housekeeper who Peavy suggests is both "love object and mother surrogate" to the young man. John Gerlach notes in the *Dictionary of Literary Biography* that the relationship between Lonnie and Halmea, based on "tenderness, lack of fulfillment, and separation due here to differences in age and race" marks "the beginning of what becomes an essential theme in [McMurtry's] later works—people's needs do not match their circumstances." Peavy sees *Horseman, Pass By* as the first chronicle of another recurring McMurtry theme: "the initiation into manhood and its inevitable corollaries—loneliness and loss of innocence."

Horseman, Pass By was published in 1961, when its author was twenty-five. While not an immediate commercial success, it established a reputation for McMurtry among critics of Western literature. In an article in *Regional Perspectives: An Examination of America's Literary Heritage,* Larry Goodwyn calls McMurtry "one of the most interesting young novelists in the Southwest—and certainly the most embattled in terms of frontier heritage." While McMurtry claims in *In a Narrow Grave* that "the world quietly overlooked" *Horseman, Pass By,* and that he himself has come to consider it an immature work, the book was not only significant enough to warrant an Academy Award-winning movie adaptation, but also of sufficient literary merit to garner McMurtry a 1964 Guggenheim award for creative writing. Peavy quotes a letter that critic John Howard Griffin wrote to McMurtry's agent after reading *Horseman, Pass By:* "This is probably the starkest, most truthful, most terrible and yet beautiful treatment of [ranching country] I've seen. It will offend many, who prefer the glamour treatment—but it is a true portrait of the loneliness and pervading melancholy of cowboying; and of its compensations in nature, in human relationships."

Leaving Cheyenne, McMurtry's second novel, was published in 1963. Also set in ranching country, the story revolves around a character named Molly Taylor and the two men she loves throughout a lifetime, Gid, a rancher, and Johnny, a cowboy. Each of the three central characters narrates a section of the book; their intertwined lives are traced from youth to death. "McMurtry is psychologically precise in tracing this three-sided relationship," writes Walter Clemons in the *New York Times Book Re-*

view. "Odd as the roots of this friendship may seem, there's enduring consideration and feeling in it. The story takes so many years to tell because feelings that last a lifetime are the subject." Gerlach notes that *Leaving Cheyenne* explores a new aspect of the theme of "mismatching and the isolation it brings. . . . The expanded time scheme and number of narrators enrich the themes of the novel." Clemons, who calls McMurtry "one of the two best writers to come out of Texas in the [1960s]," claims that *Leaving Cheyenne* is "a rarity among second novels in its exhilarating ease, assurance and openness of feeling."

When evaluating McMurtry's early works, critics tend to group *Horseman, Pass By* and *Leaving Cheyenne* due to their similarities of setting and theme. In a 1974 *New York* magazine discussion of his writings, McMurtry himself analyzes the two novels together, with pointed remarks about his attitude concerning them: "It is perhaps worth pointing out that both [*Leaving Cheyenne*] and my first novel were written in the same year—my twenty-third. I revised around on both books for a while, but essentially both incorporate, at best, a 22-year-old's vision. . . . I don't want that vision back, nor am I overjoyed to see the literary results of it applauded." Others praise the young author's efforts. Goodwyn, for one, writes: "McMurtry's first two novels . . . were promising efforts to put the materials of frontier culture to serious literary use. . . . [Both books] are in-the-grain novels of people striving to live by the cultural values of the legend. . . . McMurtry speaks through a narrator who is frontiersman enough to move with ease through the tall-in-the-saddle milieu, but sensitive enough to note the ritualized energy and directionless fury surrounding him. . . . Relying . . . on the literary device of the provincial narrator, McMurtry found a voice that seemed to serve well as a strengthening connection between himself and his sources."

The fictional town of Thalia figures peripherally in both *Horseman, Pass By* and *Leaving Cheyenne.* In *The Last Picture Show,* McMurtry's third novel, Thalia becomes the primary setting and the debilitating monotony of small town life one of the primary themes. Thomas Lask in the *New York Times* describes McMurtry's rendering of Thalia: "A sorrier place would be hard to find. It is desiccated and shabby physically, mean and small-minded spiritually. Mr. McMurtry is expert in anatomizing its suffocating and dead-end character." The novel's action once again revolves around a group of late adolescents who are struggling to achieve adulthood in the town's confining atmosphere. Peavy writes of McMurtry: "He examines the town's inhabitants—the oil rich, the roughnecks, the religious fanatics, the high school football stars, the love-starved women—with an eye that is at once sociological and satiric. For the first time he abandons the first-person narrative in his fiction, and the result is a dispassionate, cold look at the sordidness and hypocrisy that characterize the town."

First published in 1966, *The Last Picture Show* raised some controversy in McMurtry's home town of Archer City and elsewhere for its graphic detailing of teenage sexuality—including exhibitionism, bestiality, petting, masturbation, and homosexuality. "On the surface," Peavy notes, "McMurtry's treatment of small-town sexuality may seem quite sensational; actually, it is accurate. In the cloying confines of Thalia, the only outlet for frustrations, loneliness, boredom, even hatred—for both adolescents and adults—is sex. . . . Some of McMurtry's sexual scenes are highly symbolic, all are important thematically, and none should be taken as sensationalism." W. T. Jack expresses the same opinion in the *New York Times Book Review:* "Offensive? Miraculously, no. McMurtry is an alchemist who converts the basest materials to gold. The sexual encounters are sad, funny, touching, sometimes horrifying, but always honest, always human." Peavy feels, in fact, that "neither Updike nor Salinger has been successful as McMurtry in describing the gnawing ache that accompanies adolescent sexuality."

Some critics have felt that the characterization in *The Last Picture Show* approaches stereotype in certain instances. Peavy states: "McMurtry has said that part of the concern of *The Last Picture Show* is to portray how the town is emotionally centered in high school—in adolescence. As a result, the protagonist of the book is somewhat inadequately developed." In an essay for *Colonial Times,* McMurtry admits that his approach to the material in *The Last Picture Show* was "too bitter." He writes that Archer City "had not been cruel to me, only honestly indifferent, and my handling of many of the characters in the book represented a failure of generosity for which I blame no one but myself."

According to Peavy, some of the difficulties in McMurtry's novel have been surmounted in the film script of *The Last Picture Show* through the added perspective of director and co-writer Peter Bogdanovich. "The film script . . . is a much more sympathetic portrait of McMurtry's hometown than is the novel," Peavy suggests. "The combination of the two young writers [McMurtry and Bogdanovich] was fortunate." Filmed in black and white on location in Archer City, *The Last Picture Show* was a commercial and critical success. It won three Academy Awards from the Academy of Motion Picture Arts and Sciences, including an award for best screenplay based on material from another medium. In an *Atlantic* review, David Denby states that the movie "reverses many of the sentimental assumptions about small towns that were prevalent in the movies of the forties, but it never becomes a cinematic expose. It's a tough-minded, humorous, and

delicate film—a rare combination in an American movie." Writing for *Newsweek,* Paul D. Zimmerman calls the film "a masterpiece" with "a finely tuned screenplay." Zimmerman also claims that *The Last Picture Show* "is not merely the best American movie of a rather dreary year; it is the most impressive work by a young American director since *Citizen Kane.*"

McMurtry followed *The Last Picture Show* with what some have called his "urban trilogy" of novels: *Moving On, All My Friends Are Going to Be Strangers,* and *Terms of Endearment.* The books represent a radical departure in setting and tone from the author's earlier works as they detail the lives of Houston urbanites, some of whom travel across the country in various, seemingly aimless pursuits. In her *Western American Literature* study on McMurtry's work, Janis P. Stout writes of *Moving On* and *All My Friends:* "None of the characters in these two novels has any sense of a usable past, and none is purposefully directed toward the future. They inhabit the burgeoning cities of Texas with no apparent means of orienting themselves and nothing to engage them but endless, unsatisfying motion—as the title *Moving On* well indicates." McMurtry uses a revolving set of characters as the cast for all three books. The supporting troupe in one novel may evolve to primary importance in another volume, as is the case with Emma Horton, who appears briefly in *Moving On* and *All My Friends* before becoming the protagonist in *Terms of Endearment.* R. C. Reynolds notes in the *Southwest Review:* "Though time sequences often fall out of order in the three novels, key events and characters are repeated often enough to maintain a continuous theme which, not surprisingly, has three parts: sex and its frustrations, academics and its frustrations, and something like culture and its frustrations which McMurtry has branded *Ecch-Texas.*"

Considered as a group, *Moving On, All My Friends,* and *Terms of Endearment* have not achieved the favorable critical response that followed McMurtry's earlier publications. Stout claims, for instance, that "the journey pattern so insistent in McMurtry's first three novels has in [*Moving On* and *All My Friends*] become dominant, as the characters drive endlessly and pointlessly around the country chiefly between Texas and California. Not surprisingly, novels so constituted lack cohesive form; or rather, their forms may be described as being imitative to a radical and destructive degree. Similarly, McMurtry's construction of novels by no apparent principle but random accretion appears to be a self-defeating enterprise. The pattern of transient involvement . . . is brilliantly indicative of the cultural shortcoming McMurtry indicts . . . ; unfortunately, this expressive form, by its very nature, is destructive of the overall novelistic structure and renders the work a chronicle of tedium." Goodwyn senses an ambiguity at work in the novels: "The frontier ethos, removed from the center of [McMurtry's] work, continues to hover around the edges—it surfaces in minor characters who move with purpose through novels that do not."

Reviewers have not been unanimously disappointed with McMurtry's efforts in the "urban trilogy," however. In a review of *Moving On* for the *New York Times,* John Leonard writes: "McMurtry has a good ear: [the characters] talk the way people actually talk in Houston, at rodeos, in Hollywood. Mr. McMurtry also has a marvelous eye for locale: the Southwest is superbly evoked. It is a pleasure . . . to escape claustrophobic novels that rely on the excitation of the verbal glands instead of the exploration of social reality." "It is difficult to characterize a talent as outsized as McMurtry's," suggests Jim Harrison in the *New York Times Book Review.* "Often his work seems disproportionately violent, but these qualities in *All My Friends Are Going to Be Strangers* are tempered by his comic genius, his ability to render a sense of landscape and place, and an interior intellectual tension that resembles in intensity that of Saul Bellow's *Mr. Sammler's Planet.* McMurtry . . . has a sense of construction and proper velocity that always saves him." A *Times Literary Supplement* reviewer likewise concludes: "There are few books one remembers with a real sense of affection, but *All My Friends* is indisputably one of them. Mr. McMurtry's talent for characterization and the evocation of place— together with his ability to blend them convincingly, so that they seem almost to interdepend—makes [the protagonist's] near-indefinable yearnings for a past which seems close enough to grab at wholly understandable."

Terms of Endearment, first published in 1975, has since become the most popular segment of the "urban trilogy." The story concerns Aurora Greenway, a New England-born widow who lives in Houston, and her married daughter, Emma. The greater portion of the novel deals with Aurora's relationship with her several "suitors," including a retired armored corps commander and an oil millionaire, but the final chapter in the book follows Emma through a deteriorating marriage to her ultimate death from cancer. *New York Times* critic Christopher Lehmann-Haupt observes that "maybe what keeps one entertained [with the book] is the sympathy with which Mr. McMurtry writes about these people. . . . One laughs at the slapstick, one weeps at the maudlin, and one likes all of Mr. McMurtry's characters, no matter how delicately or broadly they are drawn." Gerlach finds Aurora "loveable because she can turn a phrase. . . . Her story has endless permutations but no motion; she is timeless." Though some critics feel that the tragic ending strikes a jarring note, following as it does the light comic adventures of Aurora, they nonetheless find the section moving. Robert Towers notes: "The final scenes between the dying

Emma and her stricken boys are the most affecting in the book."

At least one critical comment on the "urban trilogy" has been proven erroneous. In 1976, R. C. Reynolds claimed: "One cannot help but feel that McMurtry wrote all three novels with an eye toward Hollywood's acceptance of them for film [but] one must doubt the possibility of film adaptation for any of the three." Whether or not McMurtry intended to attract the attention of film producers, one of the books was eventually made into a highly successful movie. The film version of *Terms of Endearment* won the coveted Academy Award for best picture of the year in 1983. Though the film adaptation by James L. Brooks created a major character not found in the novel and eliminated numerous other characters, its plot remained faithful to McMurtry's work. Calling the movie "a funny, touching, beautifully acted film," *New York Times* critic Janet Maslin has suggested that despite the changes from novel to screenplay, the finished product "does echo the book's arch dialogue and its considerable sprawl."

Terms of Endearment, according to McMurtry, marked a turning point in his fiction writing. "I was halfway through my sixth Texas novel," he explained in the *Atlantic,* "when I suddenly began to notice that where place was concerned, I was sucking air. The book is set in Houston, but none of the characters are Texans." Having himself moved from Houston to Washington, DC, in 1970, McMurtry began to seek new regional settings for his novels. In 1976 he told the *Dallas News:* "I lived in Texas quite a while, and for my own creative purposes had kind of exhausted it. Texas is not an inexhaustible region." He elaborated on this point in the *Atlantic,* concluding: "The move off the land is now virtually completed, and that was the great subject that Texas offered writers of my generation. The one basic subject it offers us now is loneliness, and one can only ring the changes on that so many times."

The three novels McMurtry published between 1978 and 1983 all have primary settings outside of Texas. *Somebody's Darling* centers on the Hollywood career of a young female film director, *Cadillac Jack* follows the cross-country ramblings of an aging antiques dealer, and *The Desert Rose* provides a fictional portrait of a goodhearted Las Vegas showgirl. Critical appraisals of these works concentrate on McMurtry's ability to create appealing characters who are independent of his traditional regional setting. In a *Dictionary of Literary Biography Yearbook* essay, Brooks Landon suggests that *Somebody's Darling* contains "two of [McMurtry's] most mature and most fully realized characters." *Washington Post Book World* contributor Jonathan Yardley similarly states of *Somebody's Darling:* "Mr. McMurtry's characters are real, believable and touching, his prose has life and immediacy and he is a very funny writer." Less successful, according to reviewers, is *Cadillac Jack,* a novel based in Washington, DC. Peter Prince writes in the *Nation* that the principal character "is the man to squelch everything down to the level of his own deep ordinariness," while Yardley states in the *Washington Post* that "the city as it emerges in the novel is a mere caricature, like too many of the characters in it." Of the three books, *The Desert Rose* has received the most commendation for its sympathetic characterization. Yardley claims in the *Washington Post Book World:* "In her innocent, plucky, unaffected way [the protagonist] is as courageous a character as one could hope to meet." As Larry McCaffery observes in the *Los Angeles Times Book Review,* McMurtry "flirts with being unbearably cute . . . but his lack of condescension toward characters and situation makes his depictions ring true."

McMurtry's ability to transcend caricature and present his characters as real, living people has given him a reputation as something of a mythbreaker. Nowhere is this reputation better supported than in his triptych of historical westerns, *Lonesome Dove, Anything for Billy,* and *Buffalo Girls.* Together, they successfully debunk the myths of the Old West—with its hardy cowboys, ruthless gunslingers, and savage Indians—recasting them as the sad inhabitants of a dying era.

Lonesome Dove, McMurtry's eight-hundred-page 1985 release, not only returns to the author's native state for its setting—a locale he had consciously avoided for five years—but also concerns the brief cattle drive era that has proven the focus of much of the Western romantic mystique. McMurtry told the *New York Times Book Review* that the novel "grew out of my sense of having heard my uncles talk about the extraordinary days when the range was open," a subject the author had previously addressed only in his nonfiction. According to the reviewers, a strong advantage to the book is the author's objective presentation of frontier life. As George Garrett explains in the *Chicago Tribune Book World, Lonesome Dove* contains "the authority of exact authenticity. You can easily believe that this is how it really was to be there, to live, to suffer and rejoice, then and there. And thus, the reader is most subtly led to see where the literary conventions of the Western came from, how they came to be in the first place, and which are true and which are false." *New York Times Book Review* contributor Nicholas Lemann also writes of *Lonesome Dove:* "Everything about the book feels true; being anti-mythic is a great aid to accuracy about the lonely, ignorant, violent West." This anti-mythic foundation in the novel, according to Lemann, "works to reinforce the strength of the traditionally mythic parts . . . by making it far more credible than the old familiar horse operas."

Lonesome Dove achieved best-seller status within weeks of its release and was a critical success as well. "McMurtry is a storyteller who works hard to satisfy his audience's yearning for the familiar," states R. Z. Sheppard in *Time.* "What, after all, are legends made of? The secret of his success is embellishment, the odd detail or colorful phrase that keeps the tale from slipping into a rut." *Newsweek*'s Walter Clemons claims that the novel "shows, early on, just about every symptom of American Epic except pretentiousness." Clemons concludes: "It's a pleasure . . . to be able to recommend a big popular novel that's amply imagined and crisply, lovingly written. I haven't enjoyed a book more this year." "The aspects of cowboying that we have found stirring for so long are, inevitably, the aspects that are stirring when given full-dress treatment by a first-rate novelist," explains Lemann. *Lonesome Dove* was awarded the Pulitzer Prize for fiction in April of 1986.

McMurtry's contrasting of the "popular" Old West to the "real" Old West is more heavy-handed in his 1988 novel *Anything for Billy.* Cast in the role of narrator is Benjamin Sippy, a depressed Easterner fascinated by the cowboy adventures he reads and writes about in such dime novels as "Orson Oxx, Man of Iron" and "Solemn Sam, the Sad Man from San Saba." Fed up with his oppressive wife and his nine horrible daughters, Sippy heads west to live the life of an outlaw. The western plains that await him, though, are not those of his precious dime novels; there are more bugs than buffalo. After a disastrous attempt at train robbery, Sippy meets a buck-toothed simpleton named Billy Bone who, though never having pulled a trigger, has somehow built a reputation as a gunfighter—a reputation he is determined to live up to. With the help of Sippy's writing and a sawed-off shotgun, Billy Bone transforms himself into Billy the Kid.

McMurtry's retelling of the story of Billy the Kid is far different from that of authors preceding him, and it is a portrayal that Julian Loose of the *Times Literary Supplement* warns "will certainly upset anyone nostalgic for Hollywood's version of the boy who never grew old." Missing from its pages is the Lincoln County war, mentor-turned-adversary John Chisum, or the traitorous Pat Garrett. The Kid himself is ugly, crude, and ignorant; he is afraid of thunder and lightning; possessing poor vision and bad aim, he compensates by shooting his victims at close range with an oversized gun, often without provocation. "There is nothing heroic or even accomplished about this Billy," laments Loose, "yet he exudes an irresistible boyish charm" that "attracts followers and lovers who will do 'anything for Billy' but [who] cannot stop him wandering on to his premature and pointless doom."

The theme of *Anything for Billy* is age-old: Don't believe everything you read. Like *Lonesome Dove,* Mervyn Rothstein says in the *New York Times,* "*Anything for Billy* is constantly reminding the reader of the disparity between the mythic West of pulp fiction and the considerably less romantic reality of day-to-day life on the frontier." "The book's greatest strength," adds *Village Voice*'s M. George Stevenson, "is in Sippy's accounts of how his dime novelist's expectations of the West were either too grand or too mundane." By making Sippy both a writer and reader of pulp fictions, McMurtry points his finger at all those people who perpetuate the myths of the Old West. Robert Gish, reviewing *Anything for Billy* in the *Los Angeles Times Book Review*, proclaims the novel "a tall tale that outdoes any previous telling about Billy the *bandito* boy of old New Mexico," and which forces readers to "think again about the real and the imagined West and the rendering of them in words."

As with *Anything for Billy*, the 1990 novel *Buffalo Girls* features a cast of historical characters: Calamity Jane, Wild Bill Hickok, Buffalo Bill Cody, and Sitting Bull. Unlike young Billy Bone, though, the characters in *Buffalo Girls* are depicted at the end of their careers; tired, old and drunk, they travel together now in Buffalo Bill's Wild West Show, emulating the adventures that made them into legends. The dwindling lives of McMurtry's characters mirror the approaching demise of the Wild West itself: the once-untamable land has been settled, the animals slaughtered, the bloodthirsty Indians relegated to small parcels of land. "Almost everyone in *Buffalo Girls* knows himself and his world to be on the verge of extinction," Susan Fromberg Schaeffer observes in the *New York Times Book Review*. "They begin to understand that they have outlived their time. The question then becomes whether they can find a new way to live, or at least a new meaning that will justify their lives. That most of them fail to do so should be no surprise, because the Wild West, as Mr. McMurtry seems to conceive it [is] the childhood of our country and, like all childhoods, it must pass."

In his three historical Westerns, says Jack Butler of the *New York Times Book Review*, McMurtry "has been alternating the Old Wild West with the West of the present or near-present" in order to counterpoint the overly-romanticized myths that permeate American literature. "I'm a critic of the myth of the cowboy," McMurtry explains in the *New York Times*. "I don't feel that it's a myth that pertains, and since it's a part of my heritage I feel it's a legitimate task to criticize it." The reason for the popularity of the cowboy myth, that of the tough-but-fair rogue who adheres to the "code of the West," is, the author believes, rooted in the American psyche. McMurtry continues: "If you actually read the biography of any of the famous gunfighters . . . they led very drab, mostly very repetitive, not very exciting lives. But people cherish a certain vision, because it fulfills psychological needs. People need to believe that cowboys are simple, strong and

free, and not twisted, fascistic and dumb, as many cowboys I've known have been."

Though McMurtry claims in the *New York Times* that he is "simply having fun reinventing" the myth of the Wild West, critics see greater significance in his historical novels. Schaeffer describes *Buffalo Girls* as "a work of resurrection, a book that rescues an important era of our country's saga both from that taxidermist, the history book, and from that waxwork beautifier, the myth machine." Butler, too, praises McMurtry's efforts: "I think Larry McMurtry may be a great writer. He's doing something with the American West that is very much like what William Faulkner did with Mississippi. He is re- (not de-) mythologizing it. . . . None of this would matter if he were not a poet, a resonant scene-setter and a master of voice, but he is; and since the West figures so strongly in our vision of what it means to be American, Mr. McMurtry's labor is, I think, essential literature."

Somewhere during the late 1980s McMurtry's reputation underwent a transformation. Perhaps because of the successes of such films as *The Last Picture Show* and *Terms of Endearment*, as well as the television miniseries *Lonesome Dove*, McMurtry began to be known, to the general public, more for his screenplays and for the cinematic adaptations of his novels than for the novels themselves. Reviewers would often criticize his books in Hollywood terms, as if they had already been translated to the screen; *The Evening Star*, for example, is panned by Mark Starr of *Newsweek* as "more script than novel," and Robert Plunkett of the *New York Times Book Review* attributes the popularity of its main character, Aurora Greenway, in no small part to the performance of Shirley MacLaine in *Terms of Endearment*. "It is damning praise to be termed a 'cinematic' writer," concludes Julia Cameron in the *Los Angeles Times Book Review*, "and McMurtry most certainly is."

Coupled with his growing reputation as a "Hollywood writer" is the fact that four of McMurtry's most recent novels, *Texasville*, *Some Can Whistle*, *The Evening Star*, and *The Streets of Laredo*, are all sequels to earlier novels (*The Last Picture Show*, *All My Friends are Going to be Strangers*, *Terms of Endearment*, and *Lonesome Dove*, respectively). "More than any other writer I know of, McMurtry is inclined to return to his earlier books and spin off sequels," observes H. H. Harriman in the *Detroit News*. "It is hard to say exactly what the motivation is here—genuine and fond nostalgia, what could pass for a genuine preoccupation with unfinished business, or more darkly, the less than genuine and never gentle persuasion of a publisher's greed."

Of his sequels, the one that has best weathered the critical storm is 1987's *Texasville*. Though it reintroduces the city of Thalia, Texas, and the characters first visited in *The Last Picture Show*, its tone is far different from that of its predecessor. Set thirty years after the events of the first novel, *Texasville* shows Thalia's residents as middle-aged men and women who, having made their fortunes during the oil boom of the 1970s, are now systematically going bankrupt. The town is as stifling and monotonous as ever, but the once-idealistic adolescents of *The Last Picture Show* have ceased to struggle against it. "They have stopped having thoughts," writes Louise Erdrich in the *New York Times Book Review*. "They simply act out their emotions by destroying things. . . . Waste is celebrated." While the observations of *Texasville*'s main character render the decline of Thalia in a humorous light, it is humor of the darkest, most cynical variety. "If Thalia . . . can stand for modern America," John Clute opines in the *Times Literary Supplement*, "then for Larry McMurtry modern America is terrifyingly like hell."

As the town goes rapidly insane, the inhabitants once again turn to sex—and lots of it—to keep their minds off their moral and financial deterioration. "But there's something sadder and more irrevocable" about the promiscuity in *Texasville*, according to Michiko Kakutani of the *New York Times*. "Everyone is older now, sinking into the disappointments and weariness of middle age, and for most of them, familial security and enduring love are no longer dreamed-of possibilities but lost opportunities, consigned to a receding past." Erdrich, too, notes the difference between the two novels' use of frequent sex: "In *The Last Picture Show*, the quest was not only for sex, but sex linked to tenderness and mystery, to love. In *Texasville*, sex is just sex. It happens everywhere and often."

Though *Texasville* is universally regarded as a very different book from its predecessor, it is still considered by many critics to be a literary success. "While [*Texasville*] lacks the ambition and epic resonance of *Lonesome Dove*, it shows off the author at his popular storytelling best, and it attests, again, to his sure feeling for people and place," lauds Kakutani, and while Yardley describes the novel as "a big ol' mess of a book," he ultimately praises *Texasville* as "a novel that transcends its shortcomings . . . it is of a piece with all McMurtry's best work."

More prey to poor and mixed reviews were the novels *Some Can Whistle* and *The Evening Star*, two more sequels. Each reprises a popular set of characters who, now much older, attempt to reconcile with their families and, eventually, themselves. Unlike the sprawling books in his "urban trilogy", McMurtry's sequels are more static, his characters less prone to travel and relationships. Both novels are rife with absurd humor and sudden, jarring tragedy—a combination which, Kakutani admits, seems "contrived and melodramatic," but is executed successfully through the author's "fluency and poise as a writer."

Although his recent penchant for sequels has led to McMurtry being further pigeonholed as a "cinematic writer" by some critics (*Time*'s Paul Gray, for instance, said of *Some Can Whistle*: "Everything and everyone in the tale reeks of Hollywood"), his books remain popular among loyal readers. Kakutani explains: "While utterly satisfying on their own, [these sequels] also give the longtime reader the pleasure of seeing a character mature through the decades. The result is not unlike growing old in the company of a favorite relative or friend."

If *Texasville* has fared the best among McMurtry's sequels, 1993's *Streets of Laredo* has probably fared the worst. Several critics have discussed the dangers of continuing a tale as well-constructed as *Lonesome Dove*. "Part of the very bittersweet pleasure of finishing reading a great book is that its story and characters are *finite*," Harriman comments. "In that respect, they 'die,' only to live on in our memories. Sequels than are a kind of exhumation, a dishonor to the memory of the dead." In *Streets of Laredo*, Harriman concludes, "the tried and true caveats about the built-in, inevitable disappointments of sequels have been overlooked, and a Pulitzer Prize-winner has been reduced to pandering."

Still, not all reviewers disliked *Streets of Laredo*. The *Detroit Free Press*'s Martin F. Kohn lauds the way McMurtry "depicts the wild West on its last legs—more vicious than ever, as if enraged by its own coming demise at the hands of railroads, growing towns and other constructs of civilization." Kohn calls the novel "a delicious, though vividly violent, read" wherein "verbal stands of color are planted at many a turn . . . relieving the brutal landscape of the main narrative. . . . As a purveyor of time, place, plot and character [McMurtry] remains our novelist laureate of the old West." *New York Times Book Review* critic Noel Perrin also notes that, on many pages, *Streets of Laredo* "is the full equal of *Lonesome Dove*"—in the end, however, Perrin admits that "there are also many on which Mr. McMurtry makes you wish he had left the characters of *Lonesome Dove* in peace."

In addition to his writing, McMurtry divides his time between the Washington, D.C., book store he has owned since 1970, a ranch in Texas that he bought several years ago, and coast-to-coast driving trips behind the wheel of a Cadillac. He explains in *Time*: "Having a bookstore is a good balance to writing. . . . Writing is solitary. Bookselling is social." In 1989 he was chosen president of the PEN American Center, a prestigious writers' organization with affiliates around the world. He was the first non-New Yorker to head the American branch since Indiana's Booth Tarkington, who founded it in 1922.

Though McMurtry no longer wears the sweatshirt with "Minor Regional Novelist" emblazoned on its front, he still describes his approach to his craft in peculiarly Texan terms. Writing, he claims in the *Los Angeles Times,* is "the ultimate analogue to my herding tradition. I herd words, I herd them into sentences and then I herd them into paragraphs and then I herd these paragraphs into books." As Raymond Neinstein indicates, the region McMurtry has written about with such success is "a ghost country . . . a country of love and of blood-ties. When those ties break down, when the love is gone, when the inheritance or inheritability of that country is somehow thwarted and its traditions are no longer viable, then the poignancy of the country's neglected beauty, of the tradition's unusable force, and of the human life left to survive without that beauty, that tradition, that center, becomes the subject of McMurtry's powerful and nostalgic novels." These novels, McMurtry tells the *Los Angeles Times,* are not based on mere "notes of scandals of the neighborhood," but rather are built by essential flights of imagination. "I am more and more convinced," he says, "that the essential reward of writing fiction is in the delight of seeing what you can make out of the sole tools of your imagination and your experience."

BIOGRAPHICAL/CRITICAL SOURCES:

BOOKS

Authors in the News, Volume 2, Gale, 1976.

Bennett, Patrick, *Talking with Texas Writers: Twelve Interviews,* Texas A & M University Press, 1980.

Bestsellers 89, Issue 2, Gale, 1989.

Burke, John Gordon, editor, *Regional Perspectives: An Examination of America's Literary Heritage,* American Library Association, 1971, reprinted, 1973.

Contemporary Literary Criticism, Gale, Volume 2, 1974, Volume 3, 1975, Volume 7, 1977, Volume 11, 1979, Volume 27, 1984, Volume 44, 1987.

Dictionary of Literary Biography, Volume II: *American Novelists since World War II,* Gale, 1978.

Dictionary of Literary Biography Yearbook, Gale, *1980, 1981, 1987,* 1988.

Landess, Thomas, *Larry McMurtry,* Steck-Vaughn, 1969.

McCullough, David W., *People Books and Book People,* Harmony Books, 1981.

McMurtry, Larry, *In a Narrow Grave: Essays on Texas,* Encino Press, 1968, Simon & Schuster, 1971.

Neinstein, Raymond L., *The Ghost Country: A Study of the Novels of Larry McMurtry,* Creative Arts Book Company, 1976.

Pages: The World of Books, Writers, and Writing, Gale, 1976.

Peavy, Charles D., *Larry McMurtry,* Twayne, 1977.

Schmidt, Dorey, editor, *Larry McMurtry: Unredeemed Dreams,* School of Humanities, Pan American University, 1978.

PERIODICALS

America, March 5, 1983.

American Film, November, 1975; December, 1975; January-February, 1976; March, 1976; April, 1976; May, 1976; June, 1976.

Arlington Quarterly, winter, 1969-70.

Atlantic, December, 1971; March, 1975.

Best Sellers, July 1, 1970.

Books and Bookmen, November, 1973.

Book Week, October 23, 1966.

Book World, June 21, 1970.

Chicago Tribune, June 9, 1987; November 14, 1989; July 15, 1990, p. 1; October 21, 1990.

Chicago Tribune Book World, October 17, 1982; December 25, 1983; June 9, 1985.

Christian Science Monitor, February 6, 1976.

Colonial Times, December 21-January 12, 1972.

Commentary, January, 1972.

Commonweal, November 5, 1971; October 20, 1972.

Daily Rag, October, 1972.

Dallas News, January 18, 1976.

Detroit Free Press, November 13, 1988; February 5, 1989; July 25, 1993, p. J6.

Detroit News, February 27, 1972; April 26, 1987; November 13, 1988; July 31, 1993, p. D14.

Film Quarterly, summer, 1964.

Forum, summer-fall, 1972.

Globe & Mail (Toronto), August 10, 1985; June 20, 1987; January 20, 1990.

Holiday, September, 1965.

Houston Post, October 30, 1966; August 23, 1968.

Literature/Film Quarterly, April, 1973.

Los Angeles Times, May 27, 1984; January 31, 1989; July 3, 1989; September 28, 1990, p. F1.

Los Angeles Times Book Review, November 14, 1982; September 4, 1983; June 9, 1985; August 16, 1987; October 30, 1988, p. 1; October 22, 1989, p. 2; October 21, 1990, p. 2; June 7, 1992, p. 4.

Maclean's, December 25, 1978.

Nation, February 3, 1979; November 20, 1982.

National Review, November 26, 1982; November 25, 1983.

New Republic, October 16, 1971; April 1, 1972; November 29, 1975; September 2, 1985.

Newsweek, October 1, 1971; June 3, 1985; September 26, 1988, p. 76; June 8, 1992, p. 58.

New York, February 5, 1973; April 29, 1974; October 3, 1988, p. 70.

New Yorker, October 9, 1971; June 14, 1976; August 26, 1985; November 11, 1985.

New York Review of Books, August 13, 1992.

New York Times, December 3, 1966; June 10, 1970; October 22, 1975; December 20, 1978; December 28, 1981; January 23, 1983; June 3, 1985; April 8, 1987; June 27, 1987; February 28, 1988, p. 34; September 28,

1988; November 1, 1988, p. C17; September 5, 1990; October 16, 1990; May 12, 1992, p. C17.

New York Times Book Review, November 13, 1966; July 26, 1970; August 15, 1971; March 19, 1972; October 19, 1975; November 19, 1978; November 21, 1982; October 23, 1983; June 2, 1985; June 9, 1985; September 15, 1985; April 19, 1987, p. 7; May 31, 1987; October 16, 1988, p. 3; October 22, 1989, p. 8; October 7, 1990, p. 3; June 21, 1992, p. 12; July 25, 1993, p. 9.

People, May 4, 1987.

Prairie Schooner, summer, 1979.

Re: Arts and Letters, fall, 1969.

Saturday Review, October 17, 1970; October 16, 1971; January 10, 1976.

South Dakota Review, summer, 1966; Volume XIII, number 2, 1975.

Southwest Review, winter, 1976.

Southwestern American Literature, January, 1971.

Texas Observer, February 26, 1971.

Time, October 11, 1971; June 10, 1985; April 20, 1987, p. 71; October 24, 1988, p. 92; October 16, 1989, p. 89; May 25, 1992, p. 73; August 9, 1993.

Times (London), March 8, 1990.

Times Literary Supplement, March 23, 1973; September 11, 1987; November 3, 1989, p. 1217.

Tribune Books (Chicago), April 5, 1987; October 9, 1988, p. 1; October 15, 1989, p. 4; May 17, 1992, p. 1.

Variety, February 14, 1990, p. 58; February 24, 1992, p. 247.

Village Voice, October 30, 1988, p. 63.

Village Voice Literary Supplement, October, 1982.

Vogue, March, 1984.

Washington Post, December 2, 1971; March 4, 1972; June 23, 1974; October 13, 1982; January 13, 1987; February 5, 1989.

Washington Post Book World, November 12, 1978; August 28, 1983; June 9, 1985; April 12, 1987; July 26, 1987; October 9, 1988, p. 1; October 22, 1989, p. 5; October 7, 1990, p. 6.

Washington Post Magazine, December 5, 1982.

Western American Literature, fall, 1967; fall, 1969; Number 7, 1972; spring, 1976; November, 1986.

Western Humanities Review, autumn, 1970; winter, 1975.

—*Sketch by Brandon Trenz*

*   *   *

MEIER, Matt S(ebastian) 1917-

PERSONAL: Born on June 4, 1917, in Covington, KY; son of Matthias John (a barber) and Mary (Berberich) Meier; married Bettie C. Beckman (a secretary), September 21, 1946; children: Gary Peter, Guy Patrick, G. Paul, G. Philip, Pepe. *Education:* University of Miami, A.B. (magna cum laude), 1948; University of the Americas, Mexico City, Mexico, M.A. (magna cum laude), 1949; University of California, Berkeley, Ph.D., 1954. *Politics:* Democrat. *Religion:* Roman Catholic.

ADDRESSES: Home—688 Picasso Terrace, Sunnyvale, CA 94087-2809. *Office*—Department of History, Santa Clara University, Santa Clara, CA 95053.

CAREER: High school teacher in Oroville, CA, 1954-55; Bakersfield College, Bakersfield, CA, instructor in Latin American history, 1955-63; University of Santa Clara, Santa Clara, CA, assistant professor of history, 1963-66, chairman of department of history, 1968-71 and 1976-79, Patrick A. Donohue, S. J. Professor of the College of Arts and Sciences, 1983-89, professor emeritus, 1989. Fulbright professor, National University Tucuman and Instituto Nacional de Profesorado Secundario, Buenos Aires, Argentina, 1958-59; visiting professor, San Jose State College, 1968. *Military service:* U.S. Army, Signal Corps, 1943-46; became technical sergeant.

MEMBER: American Historical Association, American Association of University Professors (local president, 1962-63, 1970-71), Pacific Coast Council on Latin American Studies (president, 1964-65 and 1976-77).

WRITINGS:

(Compiler) *Bibliography of Mexican American History,* Greenwood Press, 1984.

Mexican American Biographies: A Historical Dictionary, 1836-1987, Greenwood Press, 1988.

(Reviser) Carey McWilliams, *North from Mexico: The Spanish-Speaking People of the United States,* Greenwood Press, 1990.

Also contributor to *Borderlands Sourcebook,* edited by Ellwyn R. Stoddard, University of Oklahoma Press, 1983, and *Catholics in America: 1776-1976,* edited by Robert Trisco, National Conference of Catholic Bishops, 1976.

WITH FELICIANO RIVERA

The Chicanos: A History of Mexican Americans, Hill & Wang, 1972, revised edition published as *Mexican Americans/American Mexicans: From Conquistadors to Chicanos,* 1993.

A Bibliography for Chicano History, R. & E. Research Associates, 1972.

(Editors) *Readings on La Raza: The Twentieth Century,* Hill & Wang, 1973.

Dictionary of Mexican American History, Greenwood Press, 1981.

WORK IN PROGRESS: Editor-in-chief, *Notable Latino Americans: A Biographical Dictionary,* Greenwood Press.

SIDELIGHTS: "I believe strongly," Matt S. Meier once told *CA,* "in the importance of a maximum number of Americans, both Anglo and Chicano, expanding their understanding of the historical reasons for the current position of Mexican Americans, social, political, and economic. Only with knowledge and deeper understanding can progress come."

A *New Republic* reviewer calls *The Chicanos: A History of Mexican Americans* "especially good; it is not long or pretentious, nor is it especially polemical. Rather the authors in a quiet but determined way want to educate their readers, presumably the Anglos. . . . It would be nice if a few Texas Rangers, so exclusively Anglo, so powerful and sure of themselves, so willing to use force to keep 'them' in line, were to read what Meier and Rivera have to say, and even nicer if senators like John Tower and Barry Goldwater, or Peter Dominick, who represent so many Chicanos, also dipped into these pages."

BIOGRAPHICAL/CRITICAL SOURCES:

PERIODICALS

New Republic, August 19, 1972.
New York Review of Books, August 31, 1972.
Congressional Record, October 25, 1972.
California Historical Quarterly, summer, 1973.

*   *   *

MENDES FRANCE, Pierre   1907-1982

PERSONAL: Born January 11, 1907, in Paris, France; died of a heart attack, October 18, 1982, in Paris, France; son of Cerf (a merchant) and Palmyre (Cahn) Mendes-France; married Lily Cicurel (a portrait painter), December 26, 1933 (deceased); married Marie-Claire Servan-Schrieber, January 2, 1971; children: (first marriage) Bernard, Michel. *Education:* University of Paris, Docteur en droit, 1928, diploma in political science, 1928.

ADDRESSES: Home—53 rue Mon Laigne, Paris, 75008, France.

CAREER: Admitted to the Bar, 1927; lawyer in France, 1927-67. Deputy from Eure in French National Assembly, 1932-40; mayor of Louviers, France, 1934-58; undersecretary of state for Department of the Treasury, 1938; commissioner of finance for Committee of National Liberation, 1943-44; minister of national economy, 1944-45; deputy from Eure in National Assembly, 1945-58; governor for France of the International Monetary Fund and International Bank for reconstruction and Development, 1946-58; permanent French representative to the Economic and Social Council of the United Nations (ECOSOC), 1947-50; minister of foreign affairs and prime min-

ister of France, 1954-55; minister without portfolio, 1956; president of editorial committee of *Cahiers de la Republique* until 1963; deputy from Isere in National Assembly, 1967-68; Visiting professor at Ecole National d'Administration. *Military service:* French Air Force, 1939-40; entered as lieutenant, tried by Vichy government for desertion; escaped to serve with Charles De Gaulle's Free French forces in London, 1940-43; received Legion of Honor, War Cross, Medal of the Resistance, Medal of Escaped Prisoners; named Grand Officer of the Order of Leopold.

WRITINGS:

ENGLISH TRANSLATIONS

Liberte, liberte cherie, Didier, 1934, translation by Terence Kilmartin published as *The Pursuit of Freedom,* Longmans, Green, 1956.
(With Gabriel Ardant) *La Science economique et l'action,* Unesco-Julliard, 1954, translation published as *Economics in Action,* Columbia University Press, 1955.
La Republique moderne: Propositions, Gallimard, 1962, translation by Anne Carter published as *A Modern French Republic,* Hill & Wang, 1963, revised French edition, 1966.
Dialogues avec l'Asie d'aujord'hui, Gallimard, 1972, translation by Susan Danon published as *Face to Face with Asia,* Liveright, 1974.

OTHER

La Banque internationale (title means "The International Bank"), Librairie Valois, 1930.
Dire la verite; causeries du samedi, juin 1954-fevrier 1955, Julliard, 1955.
Gouverner, c'est choisir (title means "To Govern Is to Choose"), Julliard, Volume 1: *Discours d'investiture et responses aux interpellateurs* (title means "Investiture Discourse and Responses to Interpellators"), 1953, Volume 2: *Sept mois et dix-sept jours* (title means "Seven Months and Seventeen Days"), 1955, Volume 3: *La Politique et la verite* (title means "Politics and the Truth"), 1958.
(With Pietro Nenni and Aneurin Bevan) *Recontres: Nenni, Bevan, Mendes France* (discussions organized by *L'Express),* Julliard, 1959.
(Contributor) *Le Plan Sauvy,* Calmann-Levy, 1960.
(Author of introduction) *Servir la Republique* (title means "To Serve the Republic"), Julliard, 1963.
(With Michel Debre) *Le Grand Debat* (title means "The Great Debate"), Gonthier, 1966.
L'Experience economique du Front populaire sous la direction de MM. Pierre Mendes-France, Jean-Marcel Jeanneney. avec la participation de MM. Georges Dupeux, Georges Lefranc, Simon Nora, edited by

Jean-Marcel Jeanneney, Ecole normale superieure, 1966.

Pour preparer l'avenir (title means "Preparing for the Future"), Denoel, 1968.

(With Ardant) *Science economique et lucidite politique* (title means "Economic Science and Political Lucidity"), Gallimard, 1973.

Choisir (title means "To Choose"), Stock, 1974.

La Verite guidait leurs pas (title means "The Truth Guided Their Steps"), Gallimard, 1976.

(Contributor) *Solutions socialistes; a propos de "La transition socialiste"*, Ramsay, 1978.

Hommage a Pierre Mendes France, Club socialiste du livre, 1982.

(With Francois Lanzenberg) *Regard sur la Ve Republique; 1958-1978*, Fayard, 1983.

Oeuvres completes (title means "Complete Works"), six volumes, Gallimard, 1984-90.

Lettres a une citoyenne ordinaire, 1965-1982, Syros/ Alternatives, 1988.

Also author of *L'Oeuvre financiere du gouvernement Poincare* (title means "The Fiscal Accomplishment of the Poincare Government"), 1928; *Histoire de la stabilisation du franc* (title means "History of the Stabilization of the Franc"), 1928; *Roissy-en-France* (memoirs), 1946. Contributor to periodicals. Editor in chief of *Le Courrier de la Republique*.

SIDELIGHTS: For over fifty years Pierre Mendes France was a key proponent of the Socialist movement in France. From the time he joined the Radical Socialist party at age sixteen, to his short term as premier of France in 1954-55, to his support for student anarchists in the 1968 riots, Mendes France never wavered in his support of liberal democracy. His writings document how his staunch philosophy guided his turbulent political career and provide a detailed account of the major figures and events of twentieth-century French history. Douglas Johnson in the *Times Literary Supplement* summarizes Mendes France's influence on French politics by noting that "generations have recognized . . . him with a respect which has varied from the grudging to the wildly enthusiastic, but which has always been real."

Born in Paris to a middle-class Jewish family of both Portuguese and French heritage, Mendes France established himself as a political intellectual at an early age. He became the youngest lawyer in France at the age of twenty-one and was elected the youngest member of the National Assembly when he was twenty-five. He interrupted his promising political career to join the French Air Force at the start of World War II. When he relocated to Casablanca in 1940, he was arrested for desertion and sentenced to six years in prison by the Vichy government. He escaped and fought with the Resistance until he reached

London and joined the Free French forces, where he quickly aligned himself with its charismatic leader, Charles de Gaulle.

In 1944 de Gaulle named Mendes France Minister of National Economy in the first of many post-war governments in France, but he left the position the following year and permanently parted ways with de Gaulle. Mendes France subsequently remained active in a number of political positions and solidified his reputation for being a principled politician who never relinquished his beliefs despite their unpopularity with French citizens. Among his controversial stands were his beliefs that the president should not be chosen by popular election and that alcoholism among the French should be curtailed by increasing milk consumption.

However, Mendes France was propelled into national favor by his promise to end France's involvement in Vietnam and was elected premier of France on June 18, 1954. One month later he had successfully negotiated a peace treaty with Vietnam, and France's troops soon left the region (paving the way for the United States to take their place). Riding on a wave of new-found popularity, Mendes France proceeded to grant autonomy to the French-controlled province of Tunisia in northern Africa. However, his support quickly withered when he advocated Germany's rearmament and entrance into the North American Treaty Organization (NATO) and insisted on maintaining control of the province of Algeria in Africa. On February 6, 1955, after only seven months as premier, Mendes France's opponents in the National Assembly united to oust him with a vote of no confidence.

Mendes France remained an active spokesperson for the French left for the next twenty-five years, constantly urging for change and radical reforms through his writings and speeches. In his last public appearance in 1982, he attempted to negotiate peace between Israel and Palestine. His former interior minister and protege, Francois Mitterrand, won the 1981 presidential election and acknowledged his debt to Mendes France at his inauguration: "Without you this would not have been possible," according to *Annual Obituaries*. Upon learning of Mendes France's death in 1982, Mitterrand remarked, "France has just lost one of its greatest sons. For me, he was a companion, a friend, and example," the *New York Times* notes.

In his review of Mendes France's collection of essays on prominent political leaders, entitled *La Verite guidait leurs pas*, Johnson suggests that "Pierre Mendes France is the best Prime Minister that France never had." Johnson further explains that Mendes France's short tenure as premier "has assumed the proportions of a legend," and that his popularity is due to the "integrity and the moral ascendancy [he] exerted over many of [his] contemporaries"— traits that eventually excluded him from power and created animosity among other factions. Johnson draws a comparison in his review between Mendes France's glory days and those of his American contemporary, Franklin Roosevelt: "The deliberate use of the initials PMF appeared as an ostentatious reference to FDR." Likewise, during his tenure as premier, Mendes France held weekly radio broadcasts known as "Saturday chats," a concept similar to Roosevelt's popular "fireside chats." These were collected and published in 1955 as *Dire la verite; causeries du samedi, june 1954-fevrier 1955.* One of Mendes France's more popular collections is the diary of his 1972 trip to Asia, published in English as *Face to Face with Asia,* an informal account of his meetings with the heads of state of Japan, Hong Kong, China, Burma, and India in a time before these countries were open to many Westerners. A contributor to *Choice* characterizes the book as an account "about men and nations caught in international events of great significance" and notes that Mendes France's observations are "candid" and "quite revealing."

Mendes France summarized his political philosophy in a 1969 article for *Saturday Review:* "In my opinion, politics is not what one calls a vocation or a profession. . . . It is a mission, with its greatness and with its demands, which can be burdensome." Even towards the end of his long career, his idealism remained intact: "I remain, in spite of everything, an optimist, because I believe that truth and justice always have, eventually, the last word." He believed in a participatory democracy in which "all elected leaders . . . awaken everywhere the feeling of solidarity that gets citizens involved in the great issues that concern everyone. In turn, a sense of civic responsibility and citizens' involvement should make it possible for public officials to fight [for] what is good for the public as a whole." Johnson recognizes Mendes France's integrity: "When he writes . . . that he has never taken a decision by calculating how it would effect his personal position and career, then we believe him."

Pierre Mendes France once told *CA:* "I wish with all my heart that those in positions of responsibility —in the administration, the political parties, the unions, cultural organizations and others—will occupy themselves in bringing the necessary improvements [to France's political system] to fruition. If not, they risk condemning many, especially young people, to becoming discouraged, pouring themselves into skepticism, and renouncing their best aspirations, while others, even only a minority, will seek in violence the means of achieving a new sort of life better adapted to their impatience. The duty of the politician is to work without respite for that which can make a better future, in order to spare his country from the most dangerous tensions and convulsions. For that, he must be capable of devoting himself to the projects of the future and, little by little, of assuring their success, in spite of the resistance from routines, vested interests, privilege, and selfishness."

BIOGRAPHICAL/CRITICAL SOURCES:

BOOKS

Annual Obituaries, St. Martin's Press, 1982.
de Tarr, Francis, *The French Radical Party from Herriot to Mendes France,* Oxford University Press, 1961, Greenwood Press, 1980.
Lacouture, Jean, *Pierre Mendes France,* Seuil, 1981.
McCormick, Donald, *Mr. France,* Jarrolds, 1955.
Werth, Alexander, *Lost Statesman: The Strange Story of Pierre Mendes France,* Abelard, 1958.

PERIODICALS

Choice, September, 1974.
Saturday Review, May 31, 1969.
Times Literary Supplement, March 5, 1976; January 10, 1992.
Virginia Quarterly Review, summer, 1974.

OBITUARIES:

PERIODICALS

Newsweek, November 1, 1982.
New York Times, October 19, 1982.
Time, November 1, 1982.*

—*Sketch by Kathleen Wilson*

*   *   *

MEYER, Ben F(ranklin)   1927-

PERSONAL: Born November 5, 1927, in Chicago, IL; son of Ben F. (a banker) and Mary (Connor) Meyer; married Denise Oppliger, March 27, 1969. *Education:* University of Santa Clara, S.T.M., 1958; Biblical Institute, Rome, Italy, S.S.L., 1961; Gregorian University, Rome, Italy, S.T.D. (summa cum laude), 1965. *Politics:* Democrat. *Religion:* Roman Catholic.

ADDRESSES: Home—2160 Lakeshore Rd., Apt. 1008, Burlington, Ontario, Canada. *Office*—Department of Religious Studies, McMaster University, Hamilton, Ontario, Canada.

CAREER: Graduate Theological Union, Berkeley, CA, assistant professor of religion, 1965-68; McMaster University, Hamilton, Ontario, Canada, associate professor, 1969-74, professor of religious studies, 1974—.

MEMBER: Society of Biblical Literature, Catholic Biblical Association, Studorum Novi Testamenti Societas, Canadian Society of Biblical Studies (president, 1988-89).

AWARDS, HONORS: Fulbright fellow, Germany, 1964-65; Canada Council fellowships in Greece and Switzerland, 1976-77, 1983-84.

WRITINGS:

The Man for Others, Bruce, 1970.
The Church in Three Tenses, Doubleday, 1971.
The Aims of Jesus, S. C. M. Press, 1979.
Early Christian Self-Definition, Center for Hermeneutical Studies (Berkeley), 1980.
(Editor with E. P. Sanders) *Jewish and Christian Self-Definition: Self-Definition in the Greco-Roman World,* Fortress, 1983.
Critical Realism and the New Testament, Pickwick, 1989.
(Editor with Sean McEvenue) *Lonergan's Hermeneutics; Its Development and Application,* Catholic University of America Press, 1989.
Christus Faber: The Master Builder and the House of God, Pickwick, 1992.
(Editor and author of introduction) Otto Knoch and others, *One Loaf, One Cup: Ecumenical Studies of 1 Corinthians 11 and Other Eucharistic Texts: The Cambridge Conference on the Eucharist, August 1988,* Mercer University Press, 1993.

Also author of television documentary, *Christianity,* Ontario Educational Authority, 1973.

SIDELIGHTS: Ben F. Meyer has traveled throughout the Near East, Europe, and South America, and has a secondary residence in Switzerland.

BIOGRAPHICAL/CRITICAL SOURCES:

BOOKS

Hawkin, David J. and Tom Robinson, editors, *Self-Definition and Self-Discovery in Early Christianity: A Study in Changing Horizons; Essays in Appreciation of Ben F. Meyer from Former Students,* E. Mellen Press, 1990.

*   *   *

MIDGLEY, Mary   1919-

PERSONAL: Born September 13, 1919, in London, England; daughter of Tom Burton (a canon) and Evelyn Lesley (Hay) Scrutton; married Geoffrey Midgley (a university lecturer), December 18, 1950; children: Thomas, David, Martin. *Education:* Somerville College, Oxford, M.A. (with first class honors), 1942.

ADDRESSES: Home—1A Collingwood Terrace, Newcastle on Tyne NE2 2JP, England.

CAREER: Civil servant, 1942-43; high school teacher of classics in Berkshire, England, 1943-44, and in Bedford,

England, 1944-45; University of Reading, Reading, England, lecturer in philosophy, 1949-50; University of Newcastle upon Tyne, Newcastle upon Tyne, England, part-time lecturer, 1965-70, full-time lecturer, 1970-75, senior lecturer in philosophy, 1975-80. Broadcaster.

WRITINGS:

Beast and Man: The Roots of Human Nature, Cornell University Press, 1978.
Heart and Mind: The Varieties of Moral Experience, St. Martin's, 1981.
Animals and Why They Matter: A Journey round the Species Barrier, University of Georgia Press, 1983.
Women's Choices: Philosophical Problems Facing Feminism, St. Martin's, 1983.
Wickedness: A Philosophical Essay, Routledge & Kegan Paul, 1984.
Evolution as a Religion, Methuen, 1985.
Biological and Cultural Evolution, Institute for Cultural Research, 1985.
Wisdom, Information & Wonder. What is Knowledge For?, Routledge, Chapman & Hall, 1989.
Can't We Make Moral Judgments?, St. Martin's, 1991.
Science & Salvation; A Modern Myth & Its Meaning, Routledge, Chapman & Hall, 1992.

Also contributor of articles and reviews to philosophy journals and newspapers.

WORK IN PROGRESS: "Continuing research on human nature, with a view to using the wide range of animal comparisons to correct the constrictions and prejudices which have dogged enquiry into the psychology of motive and sterilized much English speaking moral philosophy in this century."

SIDELIGHTS: British philosopher Mary Midgley draws from the sciences of psychology, anthropology, and ethology to form conceptual schemes of human nature, moral experience, and the problem of evil. She is perhaps best known for her books that delve into the relationship between humans and animals, including *Beast and Man: The Roots of Human Nature* and *Why They Matter: A Journey round the Species Barrier.* In an assessment of the latter for the *New York Review of Books,* Peter Singer writes: "Midgley's aim is to explore the way we think and about the differences between ourselves and other animals, and she does this in a wonderfully readable and entertaining way. She is also a very effective critic, demolishing some of the most frequently heard arguments against the protection of animals." *Beast and Man,* notes James Grant in *New Statesman* review, "explores and criticizes . . . ways in which misconceptions about animals have underlain misunderstandings about ourselves. . . . Midgley shows how ethology, the study of animal behavior, can aid social science by helping it to criticize these myths in terms of which we think about ourselves."

Midgley, who was until 1980 a senior lecturer in philosophy at the University of Newcastle upon Tyne, has received praise for her lucid discussions of complex philosophical issues. In a *Washington Post Book World* essay about *Beast and Man,* William McPherson suggests that Midgley began the studies that led to the book "by thinking about human nature and the problem of evil." The resulting work, writes McPherson, "is a modest, wise, beautifully written and learned book, as simple as possible—she detests jargon of all kinds—and stunningly intelligent." Grant likewise notes that Midgley is "a professional philosopher, but unlike some of her academic colleagues, she discusses philosophical issues in a way that makes clear how they relate to one another, and why they are important."

BIOGRAPHICAL/CRITICAL SOURCES:

PERIODICALS

New Statesman, August 10, 1979.
New York Review of Books, January 17, 1985.
New York Times Book Review, August 4, 1991.
Observer, October 7, 1984.
Spectator, April 21, 1979; September 15, 1984.
Times (London), April 16, 1992.
Times Educational Supplement, February 17, 1984.
Times Literary Supplement, April 25, 1980; January 15, 1982; June 1, 1984; June 8, 1984; December 21, 1984.
Washington Post Book World, October 8, 1978; October 15, 1978.

*   *   *

MILLETT, John (Antill) 1922-

PERSONAL: Born February 3, 1922, in Niangla, New South Wales, Australia; son of John (a farmer) and Doris (Antill) Millett; married Marion Moss (a secretary), July 28, 1960; children: Scott, Shelley. *Education:* University of Sydney, L.L.B., 1952. *Avocational Interests:* Travelling to the United States and Europe, especially Provence, France.

ADDRESSES: Home and office—The Magistrates House, Market Pl., Berrima 2577, New South Wales, Australia.

CAREER: Called to the Bar in Australia, 1952; solicitor in New South Wales, Victoria, and Queensland, Australia, 1952—. Partner in law firm, J. Antill Millett & Partners, Sydney, Australia. Feature poet, Terrace du Forum, Paris, France, 1989. Member of judging panel for New South Wales Government Ministry for the Arts Literary Award, 1993. Has read poetry at poetry festivals. *Military service:*

Royal Australian Air Force; air gunner in Britain during World War II.

MEMBER: Australian Society of Accountants, Australian Institute of Valuers, Chartered Institute of Secretaries.

AWARDS, HONORS: Annual award for best book of poetry, Australian Poetry Society, 1974, for *The Silences;* Australia Council Literary Board awards, 1975 and 1980.

WRITINGS:

POETRY

Calendar Adam, South Head Press, 1971.
The Silences, South Head Press, 1973.
Love Tree of the Coomera, South Head Press, 1975.
West of the Cunderang, South Head Press, 1977.
Tail Arse Charlie (based on Millett's radio play of same title; also see below), South Head Press, 1982, Samsidat, 1984.
Come Down Cunderang, South Head Press, 1985.
Blue Dynamite, South Head Press, 1986.
Voyeur from Australia, Samsisdat, 1988.
The Nine Lives of Big Meg O'Shannessy, Story Line Press, 1989.
The World Faces Johnny Tripod, Story Line Press, 1990.

OTHER

Also author of radio play, *Tail Arse Charlie,* broadcast by Australian Broadcasting Corp., 1981. Translator of work of Swiss poet Pierre Etienne. Contributor to numerous periodicals in Australia, United States, England, Canada, Ireland, France, and New Zealand including *Aspect, Canberra Times, Compass, Greenfield Review, Maryland Poetry Review, Samisdat, Fiddlehead, Bogg, Poetry Ireland, Sud, Pacific Moana Quarterly,* and *Overland.* Guest editor of *Issue,* 1974-75; managing editor of *Poetry Australia,* New South Wales, 1970-86, editor, 1987—.

Many of Millet's poems have been translated into French and Russian.

ADAPTATIONS: Millett read poetry from *Tail Arse Charlie* on a thirty-minute radio feature for ABC Radio (Australia), April, 1982, and 1983.

SIDELIGHTS: John Millett's poetry collections have drawn critical praise in Australia, Great Britain, and the United States. In a *Hudson Review* piece about *Come Down Cunderang,* Robert McDowell writes: "Many Americans, especially urban Americans, might find it difficult to enter imaginatively a sprawling narrative in which people, animals, and the land itself are so intricately and essentially bound together. The condition is . . . in the past. And gone for good. The best we can do is keep it alive in memory. Accomplishing this, John Millett has created a dramatic world I did not know before I read his book." Millett, who served in England as an air gunner attached to the Royal Australian Air Force during World War II, has written a book of poems on his war experience, *Tail Arse Charlie*. Reviewing the work for *Overland*, Frank Kellaway claims: "I believe this is amongst the best poetry about war written in English in this century. . . . There is still torment here, even thirty-five years after the event, but there is also poise and understanding, a sort of acceptance which has a strong, unsentimental dignity."

BIOGRAPHICAL/CRITICAL SOURCES:

PERIODICALS

Hudson Review, winter, 1986.
Overland (Australia), Volume 89, 1982.
Weekend Australia, April 24-25, 1982.

*   *   *

MILLINGTON, Barry   1951-

PERSONAL: Born November 1, 1951, in Essex, England; son of Arthur Leonard and Joan Audrey (Barlow) Millington. *Education:* Clare College, Cambridge, B.A., 1974. *Politics:* "Armchair Marxist." *Religion:* Agnostic.

ADDRESSES: Office—c/o *BBC Music Magazine,* Woodlands, 80 Wood Lane, London W12 0TT, England.

CAREER: Thames & Hudson Ltd. (book publishers), London, senior editor, 1977-88; freelance writer on music.

MEMBER: Royal Musical Association, National Union of Journalists, Critics Circle.

WRITINGS:

Wagner, Dent, 1984, revised edition, Princeton University Press, 1992.
(With Stewart Spencer) *Selected Letters of Richard Wagner* (critical edition), Norton, 1987.
(General editor) *The Wagner Compendium: A Guide to Wagner's Life and Music,* Schirmer, 1992.
(Editor with Spencer) *Wagner in Performance,* Yale University Press, 1992.
(Editor with Spencer) *Wagner's "Ring of the Nibelung": A Companion,* Thames & Hudson, 1993.

Contributor to *The Wagner Companion,* edited by Raymond Mander and Joe Mitchenson, W. H. Allen, 1977, and *New Grove Dictionary of Opera*. Reviews editor, *BBC Music Magazine,* London, 1992—. Also contributor to magazines and newspapers, including *London Times* and *Opera.*

BIOGRAPHICAL/CRITICAL SOURCES:

PERIODICALS

Times Literary Supplement, February 1, 1985.

*   *   *

MIRANDA, Javier
See BIOY CASARES, Adolfo

*   *   *

MITCHELL, P(hilip) M(arshall)   1916-

PERSONAL: Born September 23, 1916; married, 1941; children: three; foster daughter. *Education:* Cornell University, B.A., 1938; University of Illinois, Ph.D., 1942.

ADDRESSES: Office—Morrill Hall, Cornell University, Ithaca, NY 14853.

CAREER: Harvard University, Cambridge, MA, instructor in German, 1946-49; University of Kansas, Lawrence, assistant professor, 1950-54, associate professor of German, 1954-58; University of Illinois at Urbana-Champaign, Urbana, professor of German, 1958-86; Cornell University Library, Ithaca, NY, curator of Fiske Icelandic Collection, 1986-93. Managing editor of *Journal of English and Germanic Philosophy,* 1959-81.

MEMBER: Danish Academy of Arts and Sciences.

AWARDS, HONORS: Knight's Cross, Order of Dannabrog; Knight's Cross, Order of the Icelandic Falcon.

WRITINGS:

A Bibliographical Guide to Danish Literature, Munksgaard, 1951.
A History of Danish Literature, Gyldendal, 1957, American-Scandinavian Foundation, 1958, 2nd edition, Kraus-Thomson Organization, 1971.
A Bibliography of English Imprints in Denmark through 1900, Libraries, University of Kansas, 1960.
A Bibliography of Seventeenth-Century German Imprints in Denmark and the Duchies of Schleswig-Holstein, three volumes, Libraries, University of Kansas, 1969-76.
Vilhelm Groenbech: En indfoering, Gyldendal, 1970.
Halldor Hermannsson, Cornell University Press, 1978.
Vilhelm Goenbech, Twayne, 1978.
Henrik Pontoppidan, Twayne, 1979.
Willard Fiske in Iceland, Cornell University Library, 1989.

EDITOR

(With Frederick Julius Billeskov-Jansen) *Anthology of Danish Literature* (bilingual), Southern Illinois University Press, 1971, published in two volumes, Volume 1: *Middle Ages to Romanticism,* 1972, Volume 2: *Realism to the Present,* 1972.

Johann Christoph Gottsched, *Ausgewaehlte Werke,* De Gruyter, Volume 7: *Ausfuehrliche Redekunst,* Part 3: *Anhang und Variantverzeichnis,* 1975, Volume 6: *Versuch Einer Critischen Dichtkunst: Kommentar,* 1978, Volume 5: *Weltweisheit,* 1983, Volume 11: *Kommentar zu I-IV,* 1983, Volume 12: *Gottechad Bibliographic,* 1983.

(With Kenneth H. Ober) *Bibliography of Modern Icelandic Literature in Translation, Including Works Written by Icelanders in Other Languages,* Cornell University Press, 1975.

(With Marianne E. Kalinke) *A Bibliography of Old Noerse-Icelandic Romances,* Cornell University Press, 1985.

Friedrich Nicelai, *Saemt liche Werke,* Volume 3-4, Peter Lang, 1991.

TRANSLATOR

Selected Essays of Ludvig Holberg, University of Kansas Press, 1955.

(With W. D. Paden) Vilhelm Groenbech, *Religious Currents in the Nineteenth Century,* Southern Illinois University Press, 1973.

(With K. H. Ober) *The Royal Guest and Other Classical Danish Narratives,* University of Chicago Press, 1977.

(With Paden) Isak Dinesen, *Carnival: Entertainments and Posthumous Tales,* University of Chicago Press, 1977.

(With Paden) Dinesen, *Daguerrotypes and Other Essays,* University of Chicago Press, 1979.

Ludvig Holberg, *Moral Reflections and Epistles,* Norvik Press, 1991.

OTHER

Editor of *Scandinavian Studies,* 1981-83.

BIOGRAPHICAL/CRITICAL SOURCES:

PERIODICALS

Times Literary Supplement, October 27, 1978.

*   *   *

MITCHELL, W(illiam) O(rmond) 1914-

PERSONAL: Born March 13, 1914, in Weyburn, Saskatchewan, Canada; son of Ormond S. and Margaret Letitia (MacMurray) Mitchell; married Merna Lynne Hirtle, August 15, 1942; children: Ormond Skinner, Hugh Hirtle, Willa Lynne. *Education:* Attended University of Manitoba, 1932-34; University of Alberta, B.A., 1942. *Politics:*

Liberal. *Religion:* Presbyterian. *Avocational Interests:* Angling, orchid culture, dramatics.

ADDRESSES: Home—Calgary, Alberta, Canada.

CAREER: Author. High school principal in Castor, Alberta, and in New Dayton, Alberta, 1942-44; *Maclean's,* Toronto, Ontario, fiction editor, 1948-51; writer-in-residence at University of Calgary, 1968-71, University of Windsor, 1979-87, University of Alberta, York University, and University of Toronto. Instructor in creative writing at the Banff Centre. Actor, appearing in *Anne of Green Gables Sequel: Road to Avonlea.*

MEMBER: Delta Kappa Epsilon.

AWARDS, HONORS: Eugene Field Award, 1947, for *Who Has Seen the Wind;* President's medal from University of Western Ontario, 1953; *Maclean's* Novel Award, 1953; Stephen Leacock Memorial Medal, 1962, for *Jake and the Kid;* received the Order of Canada, 1972; Chambers Award, 1975, for "Back to Beulah"; Drama Award from Canadian Authors Association, 1984, for "Back to Beulah"; Sir Frederic Haltaine Award, 1989; Stephen Leacock Memorial Medal, 1990.

WRITINGS:

Who Has Seen the Wind, Little, Brown, 1947.
Jake and the Kid (story collection), Macmillan, 1961.
The Kite, Macmillan, 1962.
The Black Bonspiel of Wullie MacCrimmon (novella), Frontiers Unlimited, 1965.
The Vanishing Point, Macmillan, 1973.
How I Spent My Summer Holidays, Macmillan, 1982.
Since Daisy Creek (novel), Macmillan, 1984.
Ladybug, Ladybug (novel), McClelland & Stewart, 1988.
According to Jake and the Kid (short stories), McClelland & Stewart, 1989.
Roses Are Difficult Here (novel), McClelland & Stewart, 1990.
For Art's Sake (novel), McClelland & Stewart, 1992.

PLAYS

The Devil's Instrument (first produced in Ottawa at the National Arts Centre, 1972), Simon & Pierre, 1973.
Back to Beulah, first produced in Calgary, 1974.
Sacrament (film script), produced by the Canadian Broadcasting Co. (CBC), 1978.
The Day Jake Made 'er Rain, first produced in Winnipeg, 1979.
The Dramatic W. O. Mitchell (includes *The Devil's Instrument, The Kite,* and *The Black Bonspiel of Wullie MacCrimmon* [first produced in Calgary, 1979]), Macmillan, 1982.

OTHER

Work appears in anthologies, including *The Best American Short Stories: 1946,* edited by Martha Foley, Houghton, 1946; *Book of Canadian Stories,* edited by Desmond Pacey, Ryerson Press, 1950; *Calvacade of the North,* edited by G. E. Nelson, Doubleday, 1958; *Three Worlds of Drama,* edited by J. P. Livesley, Macmillan, 1966; *Wild Rose Country: Stories from Alberta,* edited by David Carpenter, Oberon Press, 1977. Work also appears in *Canadian Short Stories,* 1960.

Also author of weekly radio series "Jake and the Kid," for CBC, 1950-58. Contributor to *Maclean's, Atlantic, Queen's Quarterly, Liberty, Canadian Forum, Ladies' Home Journal,* and *Imperial Oil Review.*

ADAPTATIONS: Who Has Seen the Wind and *According to Jake and the Kid* have been adapted into audiocassettes, McClelland & Stewart, 1990.

WORK IN PROGRESS: Brotherhood True or False, The Black Bonspiel, and *The Devil's Instrument,* all novels; *Wild Rose,* a feature film, for Meadow Lark Films.

SIDELIGHTS: One of Canada's most well-respected writers, W. O. Mitchell is known for his humor and nostalgic re-creation of small town Canadian life as well as for his love for the people and places of his native Saskatchewan. In addition to "Jake and the Kid," a popular radio series aired by the Canadian Broadcasting Company (CBC), Mitchell has also penned novels, short stories, and plays. In all of these genres, Michael Peterman writes in *Profiles in Canadian Literature,* Mitchell "has developed his talents with admirable agility and energy."

"Jake and the Kid" was first broadcast on June 27, 1950, and ran until 1958. Set in the imaginary small town of Crocus, Saskatchewan, the series concerned a young boy, "the Kid," and his friendship with Jake, the hired man on his mother's farm. Told from the Kid's perspective, Mitchell's gentle satire of small town life and his skillfully created characters were extremely popular with Canadian radio listeners. "We experience again," Catherine McLay writes in the *Journal of Popular Culture,* "our own childhood and our own pastoral roots." Part of the reason for the show's popularity was the character of Jake, who seems to embody something of the Canadian pioneering past. "Jake's appeal," McLay believes, "is that of the original frontier hero: he is physically strong, self-reliant, practical, free, unburdened by wife and child, illiterate and uncultured but optimistic in his outlook on life." Mitchell uses the same characters in a series of short stories first published in *Maclean's* and later collected as *Jake and the Kid.* Winner of the Stephen Leacock Memorial Medal, the collection contains stories that "were among the first," Margaret Laurence states in *Canadian Literature,* "that

many of us who lived on the prairies had ever read concerning our own people, our own place and our time."

A young boy in the Canadian west is also the focus for Mitchell's first novel, *Who Has Seen the Wind.* Described by Richard Sullivan of the *New York Times Book Review* as "a piece of brilliantly sustained prose, a very beautiful, keen, perceptive rendering of human beings engaged in the ordinary yet profoundly—almost mysteriously—meaningful drama of every day," *Who Has Seen the Wind* enjoys a reputation as a Canadian classic. Peterman calls the work "a remarkable novel," while S. Gingell of *Canadian Studies in Literature* notes that "in studies of Canadian Prairie literature and in surveys of the development and outstanding achievements of Canadian fiction, W. O. Mitchell's novel *Who Has Seen the Wind* has been uniformly praised for its evocative style."

The novel is, William H. New explains in *Articulating West: Essays on Purpose and Form in Modern Canadian Literature,* "a study of Brian O'Connal's transition from the perfection of sensitive childhood, through conflict, to a balance that is achieved in early maturity." Along the way, the boy is influenced by many adult characters who live in his small Saskatchewan town. Although these other characters are carefully developed and the events they share with O'Connal are vividly presented, "Brian's growth to responsibility always remains central," New writes. The novel achieves, Peterman judges, "an extraordinary power and charm. Its success, I would argue, lies in its focussing so precisely upon Brian's growth; all the events . . . serve that purpose."

In contrast to *Who Has Seen the Wind,* Mitchell's novel *The Kite* focuses on adult characters, although it again depicts a learning relationship between a younger and an older male. David Lang is a middle-aged reporter who comes to interview Daddy Sherry, reputed to be the world's oldest living man. The relationship that develops between the two men becomes the central focus of the novel, echoing the earlier relationships between Jake and the Kid and between Brian O'Connal and the adult characters he meets. However, "the educative relationship," Peterman writes, "between a boy and his older guide is less effective when the boy becomes a middle-aged man." Nonetheless, the passive Lang is transformed by the example of Daddy Sherry's wisecracking vitality. As New believes, both Lang and O'Connal "undergo a process of growth and development that results in their increased awareness of realities beyond the physical."

A similar concern is central to *The Vanishing Point,* Mitchell's next novel. First published as a serial in *Maclean's* under the title "The Alien," it concerns Carlyle Sinclair, a white man on a Canadian Indian reservation who serves as school teacher and Indian agent. The vanishing point is the point in artistic perspective where "parallel lines" meet to give the illusion of three-dimensional depth. The relationship between illusion and reality is constantly examined as Sinclair, according to New in a review of the book for *Canadian Forum,* discovers "the extent to which illusion confuses the real world in which he must live." Herbert Rosengarten makes the same point in *Canadian Literature.* The vanishing point of the title, he notes, is a metaphor for "the lines men draw for themselves and for others in their desire to impose order, purpose, direction, on human life." The results of this recurring discrepancy between reality and illusion are, New states, "often very funny."

Mitchell experiments in *The Vanishing Point* with stream-of-consciousness techniques and a nonchronological structure. Peterman judges this to be adventurous, but Rosengarten does not believe the approach works. Mitchell's oblique creation of his characters, Rosengarten argues, "takes a long time, and in Carlyle's case doesn't seem complete—he remains flat and featureless."

The familiar Saskatchewan small town setting is returned to in *How I Spent My Summer Holidays,* the reminiscences of the narrator about his boyhood. Although similar to Mitchell's earlier treatments of such material, *Summer Holidays* differs "in the discordant note set at the beginning—bizarre, darkly sexual," Paul Roberts writes in *Saturday Night.* The worst characters in previous Mitchell novels are, if not entirely honorable, at least harmless. But in *Summer Holidays,* one character, King Motherwell, is an alcoholic and bootlegger who murders his wife and lands in an insane asylum. Mark Abley of *Maclean's* notes that "these pages are liberally sprinkled with madmen, whores, religious fanatics, prigs, bigots, and drunkards." Arguing that Mitchell has consistently dealt with the theme of innocence, Guy Hamel sees Motherwell as "a tragic catalyst who brings about for Hugh [the young boy of the novel] the end of his childhood." Thus, *Summer Holidays,* although less gentle than previous works, presents Mitchell's familiar themes of transition into manhood. Hamel, writing in *Fiddlehead,* describes the book as Mitchell's "most sophisticated novel formally."

With *Summer Holidays,* Candas Jane Dorsey ventures in a review of *Roses Are Difficult Here* in the Toronto *Globe and Mail,* Mitchell "tunnelled, not for the first time but for the first sustained journey, down below that calm, deceptively flat surface to the great depths and layers beneath the strata of human frailty and complexity and astonishing variety. And since then his books have never completely returned to the sunny summer." *Since Daisy Creek,* Mitchell's first novel after *Summer Holidays,* looks at the regeneration of Colin Dobbs, a middle-aged creative writing instructor who for the past decade has been unable to write successfully. To offset his problem, he undertakes

a new avocation as a grizzly-bear hunter, until an adult female bear nearly batters him to death. His ensuing, painful recovery—both physical and emotional—is eased by the aid of his daughter, who has returned after running away years earlier. At least one commentator, Patrick O'Flaherty of *Canadian Forum,* claims that *Since Daisy Creek* contains excessive profanities and that the work becomes mawkish, especially toward its conclusion: "Whatever is the root cause of all the cusswords," the critic writes, "it has not quite driven sentimentality out of the picture." Conversely, Jamie Conklin of *Quill and Quire* applauds Mitchell's effort, calling *Since Daisy Creek* "a wonderful novel, packed with action, emotion, and insight." The reviewer concludes that the author has "dodged the dangers of cliche and imitation, and in doing so has once again achieved the high standard of storytelling for which he is known."

A retired English professor figures as the protagonist in Mitchell's 1988 thriller *Ladybug, Ladybug,* a novel that combines both comedy and tragedy. Aging and widowed Kenneth Lyon, divested of his status as emeritus professor—and consequently ousted from his office—places a newspaper ad for domestic help, so he can write his biography of Mark Twain from his home. Nadya, a twenty-seven-year-old aspiring actress and single mother, answers his ad, bringing into Lyon's life not only her young daughter, Rosemary, but her spurned former lover, a psychotic who is bent on revenge. Although Toronto *Globe and Mail* reviewer William French believes that *Ladybug, Ladybug* is overly sentimental—"Mitchell builds the doom-laden tension to the breaking point, and shamelessly manipulates our emotions"—the commentator acknowledges that Mitchell's characteristic humor surfaces as well. In one scene, French points out, the author chronicles an argument over which academic candidate should receive an honorary degree. Among the nominees is a pioneering psychologist who has overseen an investigation entitled "Phallometric Study of Erotic Preferences of Deviate and Non-Deviate Males through Measurement of Changes in Penis Volume."

A multitude of offbeat characters populate Mitchell's 1990 *Roses Are Difficult Here,* a novel that explores the structure of a small prairie town through the eyes of a university scholar. Set in the 1950s in the fictional community of Shelby, the work turns on June Melquist, an attractive sociologist who arrives from a neighboring institute to conduct an intense study of Shelby's social makeup. For assistance, she enlists the aid of Matt Stanley, editor of the *Shelby Chinook,* who introduces her to colorful town locals ranging from Mame Napoleon, wife of Shelby's septic-tank cleaner, to Nettie Fitzgerald, arrogant wife of the town doctor who snubs June in the fear "that the sociologist will trumpet the cultural backwardness of Shelby to a world that is just waiting for an excuse to ridicule the town," maintains Victor Dwyer in *Maclean's.*

Although Mitchell is sometimes classified as a regional humorist, Dick Harrison sees him as a writer who uses humor to explores serious issues. Writing in *Unnamed Country: The Struggle for a Canadian Prairie Fiction,* Harrison notes that Mitchell's "sensibility enlivens fairly traditional comic forms to a breadth and depth of human comedy never approached by [other Canadian western writers]. . . . He faces seriously the questions of man's relationship to the prairie [and] is the only major writer in the period of 'prairie realism' to present a reconciliation of the human spirit with the prairie." Mitchell himself might not agree with such an academic analysis of his literary technique: "It's a very uncerebral process," he told H. J. Kirchhoff in the Toronto *Globe and Mail.* "If the reader is giggling or moved to tears, that's the criticism that counts."

Mitchell commented: "The use of humor by a fiction writer is dangerous. Critically so. I say this because if laughter is an ingredient in his fiction recipe, the writer will get no respect from the either-or people, and there are a lot of those folks out there, the sturm und drangers, who have never noticed that life does not sound only the low notes of storm and stress, but chords of both high and low. So too must the fiction illusions of actuality. Geoffrey Chaucer knew that. So did Charles Dickens and John Steinbeck and Mark Twain. Henry James did not, nor did Thomas Mann. William Shakespeare did though. He called it comic relief, which causes the emotional pendulum to swing higher and lower, through contrast between tears and laughter.

"I take humor to be a very serious matter. Its main quality has to be logical surprise, unpredictable as life itself. Its use must be responsible. If not, then satire becomes simply invective, directed against undeserving targets. Comedy turns into one-liner slapstick. No space given to irony."

BIOGRAPHICAL/CRITICAL SOURCES:

BOOKS

Cameron, Donald, *Conversations with Canadian Novelists,* Part 2, Macmillan (Toronto), 1973.
Contemporary Literary Criticism, Volume 25, Gale, 1983.
Harrison, Dick, *Unnamed Country: The Struggle for a Canadian Prairie Fiction,* University of Alberta Press, 1977.
Heath, Jeffrey M., editor, *Profiles in Canadian Literature,* Volume 2, Dundurn Press, 1980.
McCourt, Edward A., *The Canadian West in Fiction,* Ryerson Press, 1970.

New, William H., *Articulating West: Essays on Purpose and Form in Modern Canadian Literature,* New Press, 1972.
Vertical Man/Horizontal World: Man and Landscape in Canadian Prairie Fiction, University of British Columbia Press, 1973.

PERIODICALS

Booklist, March 15, 1947.
Books in Canada, November, 1981; April, 1983.
Canadian Forum, April, 1947; Mary/June, 1974; November, 1984, p. 36.
Canadian Literature, autumn, 1962; winter, 1962; summer, 1963; winter, 1963; summer, 1974; summer, 1978.
Canadian Studies in Literature, Volume 6, number 2, 1981.
Chicago Sun Book Week, August 17, 1947.
Fiddlehead, July, 1982.
Globe and Mail (Toronto), October 27, 1984; October 29, 1988; October 21, 1989; November 25, 1989; October 13, 1990.
Journal of Canadian Fiction, spring, 1973; spring, 1974.
Journal of Canadian Studies, November, 1970; November, 1975.
Journal of Popular Culture, fall, 1980.
Maclean's, November 2, 1981; November 5, 1990, p. 82.
New York Herald Tribune Weekly Book Review, March 2, 1947.
New York Times Book Review, February 23, 1947.
Publishers Weekly, October 18, 1985, p. 48.
Quill and Quire, November, 1984, p. 35; February, 1989, p. 24.
San Francisco Chronicle, March 13, 1947.
Saturday Night, October, 1981; November, 1981.
Tamarack Review, winter, 1963.

*   *   *

MOL, Hans
See MOL, J(ohannis) J(acob)

*   *   *

MOL, J(ohannis) J(acob) 1922-
(Hans Mol)

PERSONAL: Born February 14, 1922, in Rozenburg, Netherlands; naturalized U.S. citizen; son of Johannis Jacob (a farmer) and Jacoba Jobbina (de Koster) Mol; married Lavelette Ruth McIntyre, February 14, 1953; children: Ian, David, Gillian, Margery. *Education:* United Theological Faculty, Sydney, Australia, certificate, 1951;

Union Theological Seminary, New York, NY, B.Div., 1955; Columbia University, M.A., 1956, Ph.D., 1960.

ADDRESSES: Home—31 Tempe Crescent, Queanbeyan 2620, Australia. *Office*—Department of Religious Studies, McMaster University, Hamilton, Ontario, Canada L8S 4K1.

CAREER: Deputy administrator of sugar beet industry in Netherlands, 1946-48; ordained Presbyterian minister, 1952; chaplain to immigrants in Bonegilla, Australia, 1952-54; Bethel Presbyterian Church, White Hall, MD, pastor, 1956-60; University of Canterbury, Christchurch, New Zealand, lecturer in sociology, 1961-63; Australian National University, Canberra, fellow in sociology at Institute of Advanced Studies, 1963-70; McMaster University, Hamilton, Ontario, professor of religious studies, 1970—. Visiting professor at University of Arizona, summer, 1967, University of California, Santa Barbara, autumn, 1969, and Marquette University, winter, 1970; Paine Lecturer, University of Missouri—Columbia, 1978. Delegate and section chairman, Eighth World Congress of Sociology, Varna, Bulgaria, 1970. Presented keynote opening address at 15th World Congress of the History of Religion, Sydney, Australia, 1985.

MEMBER: International Sociological Association (president of committee on the sociology of religion, 1974-78), Conference Internationale de Sociologie Religieuse (member of executive committee, 1971-78), Religious Research Association (member of board of directors, 1972-74), Sociological Association of Australia and New Zealand (secretary-treasurer, 1963-69), Canberra Sociological Society (president, 1967-68).

AWARDS, HONORS: Canada Council fellowship, 1977, 1984.

WRITINGS:

The Relevance of a Shackled Vision: A Sociologist's Interpretation of the Churches' Dilemma in a Secular World, A.C.T., 1965.
The Breaking of Traditions: Theological Convictions in Colonial America, Glendessary Press, 1968.

Also author of monographs, including *Churches and Immigrants: A Sociological Study of the Mutual Effect of Religion and Emigrant Adjustment,* Research Group for European Migration Problems, 1961; *Church Attendance in Christchurch, New Zealand,* Department of Psychology and Sociology, University of Canterbury, 1962; and *Changes in Religious Behaviour of Dutch Immigrants,* Research Group for European Migration Problems, 1965. Contributor to books, including *Australian Society,* edited by Alan Davies and Solomon Encel, F. W. Cheshire, 1965; *The Challenge,* edited by Ivan Southall, Landesdowne Press (Melbourne), 1966; *The Pattern of New Zealand*

Culture, edited by A. L. McLeod, Cornell University Press, 1968; *Australia, New Zealand and the South Pacific,* edited by Charles Osborne, Praeger, 1970; *Social Demography,* edited by Thomas R. Ford and Gordon F. de Jong, Prentice-Hall, 1970; (with M. T. V. Reidy) *New Zealand Society,* edited by Stephen D. Webb and John Colette, Wiley (Sydney), 1973; *Social Change in Australia,* edited by Don Edgar, F. W. Cheshire, 1974; *The Family in Australia: Social, Demographic and Psychological Aspects,* edited by Jerzy Krupinski and Alan Stoller, Pergamon, 1974; *Current Research in Sociology,* edited by Margaret S. Archer, Mouton, 1974; and *Religion in Canadian Society,* edited by Stewart Crysdale and Les Wheatcroft, Macmillan (Toronto), 1976.

UNDER NAME HANS MOL

Race and Religion in New Zealand: A Critical Review of the Policies and Practices of the Churches in New Zealand Relevant to Racial Integration, National Council of Churches in New Zealand, 1966.
Christianity in Chains: A Sociologist's Interpretation of the Churches' Dilemma in a Secular World, Nelson (Melbourne), 1969.
Religion in Australia: A Sociological Investigation, Nelson, 1971.
(Editor with Margaret Hetherton and Margaret Henty and contributor) *Western Religion: A Country by Country Sociological Inquiry,* Mouton, 1972.
Identity and the Sacred: A Sketch for a New Social Scientific Theory of Religion, Blackwell, 1976, Free Press, 1977.
(Editor and contributor) *Identity and Religion: International, Cross-Cultural Approaches,* Sage Publications (London), 1978.
Wholeness and Breakdown: A Model for the Interpretation of Nature and Society, University of Madras Press, 1978.
The Fixed and the Fickle: Religion and Identity in New Zealand, Wilfrid Laurier University Press, 1982.
The Firm and the Formless: Religion and Identity in Aboriginal Australia, Wilfrid Laurier University Press, 1982.
Meaning and Place: An Introduction to the Social Scientific Study of Religion, Pilgrim Press (New York), 1983.
The Faith of Australians, Allen & Unwin, 1985.
Faith and Fragility: Religion and Identity in Canada, Trinity Press (Burlington, Ontario), 1985.

OTHER

How God Hoodwinked Hitler, Albatross Press (Sydney, Australia), 1989.

Contributor of numerous articles to professional journals, including *Sociological Analysis, American Sociologist, In-*

ternational Migration Review, Australian and New Zealand Journal of Sociology, and *Review of Religious Research.*

SIDELIGHTS: J. J. Mol spent the years 1943 to 1945 in German prisons and concentration camps.

* * *

MORGAN, Edwin (George) 1920-

PERSONAL: Born April 27, 1920, in Glasgow, Scotland; son of Stanley Lawrence and Margaret McKillop (Arnott) Morgan. *Education:* University of Glasgow, M.A., 1947. *Avocational Interests:* Photography, scrapbooks, walking in cities.

ADDRESSES: Home—19 Whittingehame Ct., Glasgow G12 0BG, Scotland.

CAREER: University of Glasgow, Glasgow, Scotland, assistant lecturer, 1947-50, lecturer, 1950-65, senior lecturer, 1965-71, reader, 1971-75, titular professor of English, 1975-80, professor emeritus, 1980—; visiting professor, Strathclyde University, 1987-90. Visual and concrete poems have been exhibited internationally. *Military service:* Royal Army Medical Corps, 1940-46.

AWARDS, HONORS: Cholmondeley Award, 1968; Scottish Arts Council award, 1969, 1973, 1975, 1978, 1983, 1984, and 1991; Hungarian PEN Memorial Medal, 1972; Royal Bank of Scotland Book of the Year Award, 1983; Soros Translation Award, Columbia University Translation Center, 1985; Officer, Order of the British Empire, 1983; D.Litt., Loughborough University, 1981, University of Glasgow, 1990, and University of Edinburgh, 1991; D.Univ., Stirling University, 1989, and University of Waikato, 1992; named honorary professor, University of Central Wales, 1991; M. Univ., Open University, 1992.

WRITINGS:

POETRY

The Vision of Cathkin Braes and Other Poems, Maclellan, 1952.
The Cape of Good Hope, Peter Russell, 1955.
Scotch Mist, Renegade Press, 1965.
Starryveldt, Eugen Gomringer Press (Frauenfeld, Switzerland), 1965.
Sealwear, Gold Seal Press (Glasgow), 1966.
Emergent Poems, Hansjoerg Mayer (Stuttgart), 1967.
The Second Life, Edinburgh University Press, 1968.
Gnomes, Akros Publications, 1968.
Proverbfolder, Openings Press, 1969.
(With Alan Bold and Edward Brathwaite) *Penguin Modern Poets 15,* Penguin, 1969.

The Horseman's Word: A Sequence of Concrete Poems, Akros Publications, 1970.
Twelve Songs, Castlelaw Press, 1970.
The Dolphin's Song, School of English Press (Leeds), 1971.
Glasgow Sonnets, Castlelaw Press, 1972.
Instamatic Poems, Ian McKelvie, 1972.
The Whittrick: A Poem in Eight Dialogues. . . 1955-1961, Akros Publications, 1973.
From Glasgow to Saturn (British Poetry Book Club choice), Dufour, 1973.
!?,. Nuspeak 8, being a visual poem, Scottish Arts Council, 1973.
The New Divan, Carcanet New Press, 1977.
Colour Poems, Third Eye Centre, 1978.
Star Gate: Science Fiction Poems, Third Eye Centre, 1979.
Poems of Thirty Years, Carcanet New Press, 1982.
Grafts/Takes, Mariscat Press (Glasgow), 1983.
4 Glasgow Subway Poems, National Book League, 1983.
Sonnets from Scotland, Mariscat Press, 1984.
Selected Poems, Carcanet Press, 1985.
From the Video Box, Mariscat Press, 1986.
Newspoems, Wacy! (London), 1987.
Themes on a Variation, Carcanet Press, 1988.
Tales from Limerick Zoo, Mariscat Press, 1988.
Collected Poems, Carcanet Press, 1990.
Hold Hands among the Atoms, Mariscat Press, 1991.
(With Norma MacCaig and Liz Lochhead) *Three Scottish Poets,* Canongate, 1992.

TRANSLATIONS

Beowulf: A Verse Translation into Modern English, Hand & Flower Press, 1952, University of California Press, 1962.
Poems from Eugenio Montale, University of Reading School of Art, 1959.
Sovpoems: Brecht, Neruda, Pasternak, Tsvetayeva, Mayakovsky, Martynov, Yevtushenko, Migrant Press, 1961.
Selected Poems: Sandor Weores, Penguin, 1970.
Wi the Haill Voice: 25 Poems by Vladimir Mayakovsky, Carcanet Press, 1972.
Fifty Renascence Love-Poems, Whiteknights Press, 1975.
Rites of Passage: Translations, Carcanet Press, 1976.
August Graf von Platen-Hallermuende, *Selected Poems,* Castlelaw Press, 1978.
The Apple-tree: A Medieval Dutch Play in a Version by Edwin Morgan, Third Eye Centre, 1982.
Master Peter Pathelin, Third Eye Centre, 1983.
(With others) Sandor Weores, *Eternal Moment: Selected Poems,* Anvil Press, 1988.
Edmond Rostand, *Cyrano de Bergerac,* Carcanet Press, 1992.

NONFICTION

Essays, Carcanet Press, 1974, Dufour, 1975.

Hugh MacDiarmid, Longman, 1976.

East European Poets, Open University Press, 1976.

Provenance and Problematics of "Sublime and Alarming Images" in Poetry, British Academy, 1977.

Edwin Morgan: An Interview, Akros Publications, 1977.

Twentieth-Century Scottish Classics, Book Trust Scotland, 1987.

Crossing the Border: Essays on Scottish Literature, Carcanet Press, 1990.

Nothing Not Giving Messages: Reflections on His Work and Life (interviews), edited by Hamish Whyte, Polygon, 1990.

Also author of *Language, Poetry and Language Poetry,* 1990, and *Evening Will Come They Will Sew the Blue Sail,* 1991.

EDITOR

Collins Albatross Book of Longer Poems: English And American Poetry from the Fourteenth Century to the Present Day, Collins, 1963.

(With George Bruce and Marice Lindsay) *Scottish Poetry, Volumes I-VI,* Edinburgh University Press, 1966-1972.

New English Dramatists 14, Penguin, 1970.

Scottish Satirical Verse, Carcanet Press, 1980.

David Anderson and David MacLennan, *Roadworks: Song Lyrics for Wildcat,* Third Eye Centre, 1987.

(With Carl Macdougall) *New Writing Scotland, Volumes 5-6,* Association for Scottish Literary Studies, 1987-88.

(With Hamish Whyte) *New Writing Scotland, Volume 7,* Association for Scottish Literary Studies, 1989.

RECORDINGS

Selected Poems, Canto, 1987.

Seventeen Poems of Edwin Morgan, Scotsoun, 1987.

OPERA LIBRETTOS

Composer of *The Charcoal-Burner,* 1969; *Valentine,* 1976; *Columba,* 1976; *Spell,* 1979.

OTHER

Contributor of essays, poems and translations to periodicals.

Collections of Morgan's manuscripts are located at Glasgow University Library, Mitchell Library, Glasgow, the National Library of Scotland, Edinburgh, Brynmoor Jones Library at the University of Hull, John Rylands University Library of Manchester, Reading University Library, Lockwood Library, and the State University of New York at Buffalo.

SIDELIGHTS: Edwin Morgan works in a variety of poetic forms. His principal achievement in poetry, Alan Young remarks in the *Dictionary of Literary Biography,* "has been to revive some of the modernist spirit of linguistic adventure and play, otherwise mostly defunct in Britain for several decades. His poems and translations demonstrate an excitement about the possibilities of poetic innovation, an excitement that has taken him into unusual experimental idioms." Carol Rumens, reviewing *Poems of Thirty Years* for the *Times Literary Supplement,* summed up Morgan's varied career: "A poet's poet, with a wide knowledge of many languages and cultures, his modernist roots reach into eastern Europe and Latin America. The many forms of expression his talent has sought include concrete and sound poetry, free verse, narratives and dialogues as well as traditional metrics. His subjects range, as the title of his 1973 volume suggests, from Glasgow to Saturn." Morgan justifies the variety of his work, George Szirtes notes in *Literary Review,* with this explanation: "The poet, I think, is entitled to set up his camp on other worlds than this and to bring back what he can in the way of human relevance."

Morgan's varied approaches and styles unnerve some critics. John Matthias, writing in *Poetry,* claims that "the trouble with being versatile and working in many forms is that readers (and especially critics) will want one thing or another, this sort of poem or that." Morgan has written concrete poems, visual poems (some of these dependent on colors to make their point), parodies, dialogues, science fiction, comedy, and personal poems. This variety of work is a key to understanding Morgan's career as a poet. "Morgan's poetry," Alan Munton writes in *British Book News,* "is serious, playful, generous, and open." In addition to writing poetry, Morgan has translated work from a variety of languages and edited collections of new writing.

Though Morgan's poems rarely repeat themselves in form, they do display several consistent themes. An unconventional use of typography and grammar, a frequent wit, and a socialist political sensibility are among the most commonly cited characteristics of his work. In his experimental poems, for example, Morgan has turned a handful of typical Scottish words into a visual map of Scotland, written a sonnet based on the fourteen words found in a John Cage sentence, and used words that sound like pomander to create a visual representation of that fruit. As Richard Kostelanetz notes in his *A Dictionary of the Avant-Gardes,* "One virtue of Morgan's experimental poems is that each invention is unique to one poem; none of his devices are repeated." Desmond Graham, writing in *Stand,* finds that Morgan's "wit has done as much as anything to make the 'Concrete' and 'Sound' poem respectable and accessible."

When Morgan has turned to more conventional poetic forms, the results have garnered critical praise as well. His *Glasgow Sonnets,* a ten-poem sequence providing a realistic look at that city's poorest districts, has been called "well made and moving" by Matthias and "remarkable" by Dabney Stuart in *Library Journal.* Writing in *London Magazine,* John Wain finds that "the tightness and elegance of the sonnet form is itself an ironic comment on the disordered, sprawling dilapidation of the city."

"In terms of technical variety," Robin Fulton claims in *World Literature Today,* "it seems that Morgan can carry off, with panache, whatever task he sets himself, and on that score alone he has few peers. . . . He is one of the few writers in Britain today whose poems are able to celebrate not just life in general but the small things that often make life in particular joyful and touching." "Back and forth across time and space, the connexions [Morgan] forges between known worlds of experience and those previously unexplored have extended the territory of scripted English in quite spectacular ways," Colin Nicholson writes in his *Poem, Purpose and Place: Shaping Identity in Contemporary Scottish Verse.* In *Lines Review,* Robin Hamilton concludes that Morgan is "a poetic talent of the first order. Already his work is considered to be one of the finest imaginative achievements of writing in English in the twentieth century."

BIOGRAPHICAL/CRITICAL SOURCES:

BOOKS

Contemporary Literary Criticism, Volume 31, Gale, 1985.

Crawford, Robert and Hamish Whyte, editors, *About Edwin Morgan,* University of Edinburgh Press, 1990.

Dictionary of Literary Biography, Volume 27: Poets of Great Britain and Ireland, 1945-1960, Gale, 1984.

Fulton, Robin, *Contemporary Scottish Poetry: Individuals and Contexts,* M. Macdonald, 1974, pp. 13-40.

Jones, Peter and Michael Schmidt, editors, *British Poetry since 1970: A Critical Survey,* Persea Books, 1980.

Kostelanetz, Richard, *A Dictionary of the Avant-Gardes,* A Cappella Books, 1993.

Nicholson, Colin, *Poem, Purpose and Place: Shaping Identity in Contemporary Scottish Verse,* Polygon (Edinburgh), 1992, pp. 57-79.

Schmidt, Michael, *A Reader's Guide to Fifty Modern British Poets,* Barnes & Noble, 1979, pp. 314-320.

Thomson, Geddes, *The Poetry of Edwin Morgan,* Association for Scottish Literary Studies, 1986.

Whyte, Hamish, *Edwin Morgan: A Selected Bibliography, 1950-1980,* Mitchell Library, 1980.

Worlds: Seven Modern Poets, Penguin, 1974.

PERIODICALS

Akros, December, 1976, pp. 3-23; April, 1980, pp. 23-39.

Ambit, Number 93, 1983, p. 67.

British Book News, January, 1983, pp. 51-52; July, 1985.

Choice, December, 1975.

Dalhousie Review, winter, 1982-83.

Encounter, October, 1977, p. 89; January, 1983, p. 60.

English Ayr, March, 1982, pp. 22-39.

Library Journal, August, 1968, p. 2882; November 15, 1973, p. 3381.

Lines Review, June, 1983, pp. 41-44.

Listener, March 28, 1968, pp. 413-415; December 24, 1970; August 11, 1977; December 16, 1982, pp. 23-24.

Literary Review, March, 1983, pp. 42-43.

London Magazine, July, 1968; July, 1983, pp. 74-78.

Nation, March 16, 1974.

New Statesman, July 20, 1973; September 30, 1977; December 17, 1982, p. 45.

New Statesman and Nation, February 9, 1968, pp. 178-179; July 20, 1973, pp. 93-94.

Observer, May 12, 1968; February 27, 1977.

Poetry, October, 1968; July, 1969; April, 1974, pp. 45-55; January, 1978.

Scottish International, August, 1968.

Spectator, June 1, 1991, p. 31.

Stand, Volume 10, number 4, 1969, pp. 60-68; Volume 14, number 3, 1973, pp.70-73; Volume 19, number 1, 1977-78, pp.74-80; spring, 1989, pp. 76-84.

Times (London), August 8, 1991, p. 12.

Times Literary Supplement, February 15, 1968; October 14, 1977; December 10, 1982, p. 1376; April 26, 1985, p. 470; June 10, 1988, p. 650; June 1, 1990, p. 584; November 15, 1991, p. 10.

World Literature Today, autumn, 1978; summer, 1983, p. 460.

—*Sketch by Joseph O. Aimone*

*   *   *

MORRELL, David   1943-

PERSONAL: Born April 24, 1943, in Kitchener, Ontario, Canada; son of George Morrell (a Royal Air Force bombardier) and Beatrice (an upholsterer; maiden name, Markle) Morrell Bamberger; married Donna Maziarz (an editorial assistant), October 10, 1965; children: Sarie, Matthew (deceased). *Education:* University of Waterloo, B.A., 1966; Pennsylvania State University, M.A., 1967, Ph.D., 1970; graduate of National Outdoor Leadership School, WY. *Politics:* "Common sense." *Religion:* Roman Catholic.

ADDRESSES: Office—c/o Warner Books, Inc., 1271 Avenue of the Americas, New York, NY 10020. *Agent*—Henry Morrison, P.O. Box 235, Bedford Hills, NY 10507.

CAREER: University of Iowa, Iowa City, assistant professor, 1970-74, associate professor, 1974-77, professor of American literature, 1977-86.

MEMBER: Horror Writers of America, Mystery Writers of America, Writers Guild of America.

AWARDS, HONORS: Distinguished Recognition award, Friends of American Writers, 1972, for *First Blood;* best novella awards, Horror Writers of America, 1989, for "Orange Is for Anguish, Blue for Insanity," and 1991, for "The Beautiful Uncut Hair of Graves;" twice nominated for World Fantasy Award for best novella.

WRITINGS:

NOVELS

First Blood, M. Evans, 1972.
Testament, M. Evans, 1975.
Last Reveille (western), M. Evans, 1977.
The Totem (horror), M. Evans, 1979.
Blood Oath, St. Martin's, 1982.
The Brotherhood of the Rose, St. Martin's, 1984.
Rambo: First Blood, Part II (novelization of film of the same title), Berkley, 1985.
The Fraternity of the Stone, St. Martin's, 1985.
The League of Night and Fog, Dutton, 1987.
The Fifth Profession, Warner, 1990.
The Covenant of the Flame, Warner, 1991.
Assumed Identity, Warner, 1993.

Also author of *Rambo III* (novelization of film of the same title).

OTHER

John Barth: An Introduction, Pennsylvania State University Press, 1976.
The Hundred-Year Christmas (fantasy), Donald M. Grant, 1983.
Fireflies (nonfiction), Dutton, 1988.

Contributor to *Ellery Queen's Mystery Magazine, Alfred Hitchcock's Mystery Magazine, Rod Serling's Twilight Zone Magazine, Journal of General Education, Bulletin of the Midwest Modern Language Association,* and *Philological Quarterly.*

ADAPTATIONS: First Blood was adapted for the screen by Michael Kozoll, William Sakheim, and Q. Moonblood and released by Orion Pictures in 1982; *Rambo: First Blood, Part II* and *Rambo III,* based on characters created by Morrell, were filmed in 1985 and 1988, respectively; *The Brotherhood of the Rose* was broadcast as a miniseries by the National Broadcasting Corporation in 1989. Several of Morrell's novels have been released on audio tape.

SIDELIGHTS: With his debut novel, *First Blood,* David Morrell garnered critical attention as a skilled author of action stories. Two decades and more than a dozen novels later he is still best known as the "father" of John Rambo, the protagonist of *First Blood* who was later played by Sylvester Stallone in a wildly successful series of motion pictures.

The novel *First Blood* deals with Rambo's return to America after a long and grueling tour of duty in Vietnam. As the young vet hitchhikes through Kentucky, he attracts the attention of local police chief Wilfred Teasle, who gives him a lift outside the city limits. Teasle's message is polite but firm: Stay out of town. When Rambo re-enters the city not once but twice, he is finally arrested. Wishing to teach the scruffy young man, who is assumed to be just another drifter, a lesson about Southern hospitality, Teasle instructs a deputy to shave Rambo and cut his hair. Pushed too far, Rambo lashes out: using the shaving razor to kill one officer and wound another, he breaks out of jail, steals a police motorcycle, and rides naked into the rainy night.

The rest of *First Blood* is a headlong chase through the mountains of Kentucky, pitting Teasle—himself a decorated veteran of the Korean War—and his men against ex-green beret Rambo. As they scour the vast hills, police and national guard manhunters find themselves easy targets for Rambo's traps and ambushes. Ultimately, the two former soldiers must face each other man-to-man. Reviewer Michael Gassaniga, writing in the *National Review,* hails *First Blood* as "the best American suspense novel of [the year], and perhaps one of the best ever."

Critics often pointed to Morrell's no-frills writing style as the strongest element in *First Blood.* "From the first sentence, the reader knows that a born storyteller is talking," *Saturday Review*'s Joseph Catinella asserts, while a *Washington Post Book World* critic dubs *First Blood* "the best chase thriller since [Geoffrey Household's] *Rogue Male*" (a work which Morrell lists among his major influences). Published in 1972, at a time when many returning Vietnam vets were greeted with animosity or open hostility, Morrell's novel makes a statement about war, and what happens to soldiers when the war is over. "Rambo may be the boldest embodiment of a system that trains men to kill," observes Catinella, and *New York Times Book Review* critic John Deck concurs: "[*First Blood*] contains its warning: When Johnny comes marching home this time, watch out."

In 1982, ten years after its publication, *First Blood* was translated to the screen. Though it was a tremendous success, sparking two sequels, Morrell was dissatisfied with the way John Rambo was perceived by audiences. Inspired in part by Morrell's father, a Royal Air Force bombardier, and named after 19th-century French poet Arthur Rimbaud, the Rambo that Morrell had hoped to create was more than just a machine-gun toting superhero. "[He] is not a he-man who goes looking for trouble," the author explains in *People*. "Rambo is a person who wants desperately to be left alone. Eventually he is forced to fight back, but he would never do so unless he is in a corner. He is not a warmonger."

During the years between the publication of *First Blood* and the Rambo movies, Morrell began writing mystery-adventure novels—thrillers on a grand scale, filled with espionage, assassination, and worldwide terrorism. Among these is the 1984 bestseller *The Brotherhood of the Rose,* the first in a series of books that feature a revolving cast of characters, both heroic and villainous. "*The Brotherhood of the Rose* has everything, every ingredient necessary for a first-class thriller," James Kaufman hails in the *Christian Science Monitor*. "It is obvious that [Morrell] is talking intrigue novelist Robert Ludlum." The *Washington Post Book World*'s Michael Dirda ranked Morrell above Ludlum, saying: "By comparison to any Ludlum, *The Brotherhood of the Rose* really *moves.*"

The principle players in *The Brotherhood of the Rose* are Chris Kilmoonie and Saul Grisman, orphans adopted together and raised as brothers, educated at a private academy for boys and trained in warfare and martial arts. Their mentor and father figure, Eliot, has sent them through Army special forces training and Israeli "assassination school", so they now work together as the perfect hit team. But Eliot turns against the brothers, who soon discover that they are not the only killing team their mentor has created. Chris and Saul band together—first in defense, then to attack.

Morrell's use of spare, utilitarian language and "normal" characters in abnormal situations has drawn both positive and negative reviews from critics. "David Morrell invests the characters in this spy thriller with a high degree of normalcy, but, ironically, that only makes them less credible," remarks Mason Buck in the *New York Times Book Review*. "For a trio caught up in such a murderous vortex, these people are just too nice and reasonable." Dirda also notes that the author's prose is rather plain, and that the plot is, at times, "improbable even for the semi-fantasy world of the thriller. . . . But none of these cavils matter once *The Brotherhood of the Rose* begins: all any reader will want to do is turn the next page and the one after that until it's way past bedtime."

Morrell has followed *The Brotherhood of the Rose* with a string of bestselling thrillers that include *The Fraternity of the Stone, The League of Night and Fog,* and *The Covenant of the Flame.* Though he is occasionally chided for constructing flat characters or over-complicated plots, the consensus of reviewers agree upon one thing: he is a born storyteller. "He's a master of violence and of who, how

and why—in short, suspense," writes a *Publishers Weekly* critic, while George C. Chesbro of the *Washington Post Book World* calls Morrell "a wildflower of a writer, durable and tenacious, producing flat, foot-in-the-face sentences which do their job, which is to keep the reader turning the pages." Dirda concludes: "In none of [his books] does the action ever flag. As Morrell has memorably said of his work—but in words that should become the motto of any storyteller—'If you're writing a book, by God, let's move that sucker along.' "

Morrell told *CA:* "I became a writer because of the influence of Stirling Silliphant's writing for the TV series *Route 66.* I write high-action thrillers that try to communicate important issues to a broad audience—issues such as professionalism, discipline, religion, the relationship between parents and children, and the effects of grief."

BIOGRAPHICAL/CRITICAL SOURCES:

PERIODICALS

Christian Science Monitor, June 13, 1984, p. 27; October 23, 1985, p. 22.
Fantasy Review, January, 1984, p. 26; March, 1984, p. 8.
Los Angeles Times Book Review, December 22, 1985, p. 8; May 10, 1987, p. 8.
National Review, February 16, 1973, p. 222; May 28, 1976, p. 574; January 19, 1979, p. 111.
Newsweek, July 10, 1972, p. 92.
New York Times Book Review, June 18, 1972, p. 6; December 12, 1982, p. 37; May 13, 1984, p. 22; November 3, 1985, p. 26; August 16, 1987, p. 16; May 26, 1991, p. 22.
New Yorker, July 16, 1984, p. 93.
Observer, February 4, 1973, p. 36.
Publishers Weekly, September 13, 1985, p. 123.
Saturday Review, May 27, 1972, p. 68; December 2, 1972, p. 80.
Time, May 29, 1972, p. 82; July 11, 1988, p. 103.
Times Literary Supplement, November 10, 1972, p. 1375.
Tribune Books (Chicago), May 26, 1991, p. 7.
Washington Post Book World, July 2, 1972, p. 9; May 13, 1984, p. 6; February 3, 1985, p. 12; October 6, 1985, p. 195; June 21, 1987, p. 9; September 11, 1988, p. 3; May 5, 1991, p. 12; May 19, 1991, p. 12.

—Sketch by Brandon Trenz

*   *   *

MORRIS, Leon (Lamb) 1914-

PERSONAL: Born March 15, 1914, in Lithgow, New South Wales, Australia; son of George Coleman and Ivy (Lamb) Morris; married Mildred Dann, January 4, 1941. *Education:* University of Sydney, B.Sc., 1934; Australian

College of Theology, Licentiate in Theology (first class), 1938; University of London, B.D. (first class), 1943, Master of Theology, 1946; Cambridge University, Ph.D., 1952; University of Melbourne, M.Sc., 1966.

ADDRESSES: Home and office—17 Queens Ave., Doncaster, Victoria 3108, Australia.

CAREER: Clergyman, Church of England; Ridley College, Melbourne, Australia, vice-principal, 1945-60; Cambridge University, Cambridge, England, warden of Tyndale House, 1961-63; Ridley College, principal, 1964-79.

MEMBER: Studiorum Novi Testamenti Societas.

WRITINGS:

The Apostolic Preaching of the Cross, Eerdmans, 1955, 3rd edition, 1965.
The Wages of Sin: An Examination of the New Testament Teaching on Death, Tyndale Press, 1955.
The Story of the Cross: A Devotional Study of St. Matthew, Chapters 26-28, Eerdmans, 1957.
The First Epistle of Paul to the Corinthians: An Introduction and Commentary, Eerdmans, 1958, 2nd edition, 1985.
The Lord from Heaven: A Study of the New Testament Teaching on the Deity and Humanity of Jesus Christ, Eerdmans, 1958.
The First and Second Epistles to the Thessalonians, Eerdmans, 1959.
Spirit of the Living God, Inter-Varsity Press, 1960.
The Story of the Christ Child: A Devotional Study of the Nativity Stories in St. Luke and St. Matthew, Marshall, Morgan & Scott, 1960, Eerdmans, 1961.
The Biblical Doctrine of Judgment, Eerdmans, 1960.
The Dead Sea Scrolls and St. John's Gospel, The Bookroom, 1960.
Christian Worship, Church Pastoral Aid Society, 1962.
Good Enough?, Inter-Varsity Fellowship, 1962.
Ministers of God, Inter-Varsity Press, 1964.
The Abolition of Religion: A Study in Religionless Christianity, Inter-Varsity Press, 1964.
The New Testament and the Jewish Lectionaries, Tyndale Press, 1964.
The Cross in the New Testament, Eerdmans, 1965.
Glory in the Cross: A Study in Atonement, Hodder & Stoughton, 1966.
Ruth (bound with *Judges,* by Arthur E. Cundall), Inter-Varsity Press, 1968.
The Revelation of St. John: An Introduction and Commentary, Eerdmans, 1969.
Studies in the Fourth Gospel, Eerdmans, 1969.
Bible Study Books: Timothy-James, Scripture Union, 1969.
This Is the Testimony, Ridley College, 1970.

Gospel of John, Eerdmans, 1971, published in England as *The Gospel according to John: The English Text with Introduction, Exposition, and Notes,* Marshall, Morgan & Scott, 1972.
Apocalyptic, Eerdmans, 1972, 2nd edition, Inter-Varsity Press, 1973.
The Gospel according to St. Luke: An Introduction and Commentary, Inter-Varsity Press, 1974.
The Holy Spirit, Scripture Union, 1974.
I Believe in Revelation, Hodder & Stoughton, 1976.
The Authority and Relevance of the Bible in the Modern World, Bible Society in Australia, 1980.
Testaments of Love, Eerdmans, 1981.
Hebrews (expositor's Bible commentary), Zondervan, 1981.
What's a Nice Church Like Ours Doing in a World Like This?, Anglican Information Office, 1983.
Hebrews (Bible study commentary), Zondervan, 1983.
The Atonement, Inter-Varsity Press, 1983.
Reflections on the Gospel of John, Baker Book, Volume 1: *The Word Was Made Flesh,* 1986, Volume 2: *The Bread of Life,* 1987, Volume 3: *The True Vine,* 1988, Volume 4: *Crucified and Risen,* 1988.
New Testament Theology, Zondervan, 1986.
The Cross of Jesus, Eerdmans, 1988.
The Epistle to the Romans, Eerdmans, 1988.
Work Biblical Themes 1 and 2: Thessalonians, Word Publishing, 1989.
Jesus Is the Christ, Eerdmans, 1989.
The Gospel according to Matthew, Eerdmans, 1992.
(With D. A. Carson and D. Moo) *An Introduction to the New Testament,* Zondervan, 1992.

General editor, "Great Doctrines of the Bible," Inter-Varsity Fellowship, 1960—, and Tyndale New Testament Commentaries. Contributor of articles to religious journals.

WORK IN PROGRESS: Commentary on the Epistle to the Galatians.

SIDELIGHTS: Leon Morris once told *CA:* "I write in the hope that what I write will be of interest and help to those who read. I write on biblical topics for they seem to me far and away the most significant. I hope that writing on these topics will bring both writer and reader a little nearer to God."

*   *   *

MORTON, Frederic 1924-

PERSONAL: Born October 5, 1924, in Vienna, Austria; came to the United States in 1943; son of Frank (a manufacturer of metal goods) and Rose (Ungvary) Morton;

married Marcia Colman, March 28, 1957; children: Rebecca. *Education:* College of the City of New York (now City College of the City University of New York), B.S., 1947; New School for Social Research, M.A., 1949.

ADDRESSES: Home—110 Riverside Dr., New York, NY 10024. *Agent*—The Lantz Office, 888 Seventh Ave., New York, NY 10106.

CAREER: Lecturer in English and creative writing at University of Utah, New York University, University of Southern California, Johns Hopkins University, and New School for Social Research, 1951-59; University of Nebraska, Tom Osborn Distinguished Lecturer, 1989; freelance writer, 1959—.

MEMBER: Authors Guild, Authors League of America, PEN (executive board member).

AWARDS, HONORS: Breadloaf Writers' Conference fellowship, 1947; Yaddo residence fellowship, 1951; Columbia University fellowship, 1955; National Book Award nomination, National Institute of Arts and Letters, 1962, and Author of the Year award, National Anti-Defamation League of B'nai B'rith, 1963, both for *The Rothschilds;* American Book Award nomination in general nonfiction, 1980, for *A Nervous Splendor: Vienna, 1888-1889;* honorary professorship, President of the Austrian Republic, 1980; Golden Merit Award, City of Vienna, 1986.

WRITINGS:

NOVELS

The Hound, Dodd, 1947.
The Darkness Below, Crown, 1949.
Asphalt and Desire, Harcourt, 1952.
The Witching Ship, Random House, 1960.
The Schatten Affair, Atheneum, 1965.
Snow Gods, World Publishing, 1968.
An Unknown Woman, Atlantic-Little, Brown, 1976.
The Forever Street, Doubleday, 1984.
Crosstown Sabbath, Grove, 1987.
Sacred Lies, Scribner, 1994.

NONFICTION

The Rothschilds (biography), Atheneum, 1962.
A Nervous Splendor: Vienna, 1888-1889 (history), Atlantic Little, Brown, 1979.
Thunder at Twilight: Vienna, 1913-1914, Scribner, 1989.

OTHER

Work anthologized in *Best American Short Stories of 1965.* Contributor of articles and short stories to numerous periodicals, including *Holiday, Atlantic, Esquire, Reporter, Nation, Playboy,* and *New York Times Book Review.*

ADAPTATIONS: Frederick Morton's Vienna, a personal documentary, was produced and broadcast by Austrian State Television in 1992.

SIDELIGHTS: Fleeing Austria after its annexation by Hitler, Frederic Morton lived first in England and then in America. He worked in a bakery and took a B.A. in chemistry with the idea of some day running a bakery. When his first novel won the Dodd Mead Intercollegiate Literary Prize, Morton abandoned a baking career in favor of an academic and literary one. During the 1950s, he taught at various colleges while selling his free-lance writing to magazines. In the late 1950s, he decided to devote himself full-time to writing. His first nonfiction work, *The Rothschilds,* has been translated into nineteen languages and made into a successful Broadway musical.

Morton remarked on his writing talents to an interviewer for *Book Week,* "I'm always amazed when I see another book come out." He explained that he belonged to the "Teutonic school of peripatetic procrastination" and, when the weather is nice, he takes "work walks," always remembering pad and pencil "to prove that I'm working." "I have a good alternative for when it rains," he said; "again it's physical, always with the Teutonic school. Somersaults. I do somersaults on the theory I can stimulate myself to greater mental activity. And I chin myself on the molding over my door. It tires me out. To simmer down I nap or clean the typewriter."

Morton fictionalized his family history to create *The Forever Street.* Set in his native Austria, the novel follows three generations of the Spiegelglass family from the close of the Austro-Hungarian Empire through World War I, and finally to the Nazi invasion of 1938. "Morton has chosen to weave a novel out of his memories, experiences, imagination and family folklore. The combination gives it, at times, the surreal quality of being refracted through a dream frozen in time," observes *Washington Post* reviewer Faiga Levine. Much of the book takes place in Vienna, "which [the author] conjures up in Surrealist detail only to expose its unwavering though often elegant malevolence," notes Richard Plant in the *New York Times Book Review.*

Levine and Plant both noted that many of *The Forever Street*'s characters and events, while vividly evoked, are inadequately explained. Because of this, maintains Levine, "too much of this rather bizarre fiction becomes a confusing blur much too soon." Plant, however, compares Morton's language to Vladimir Nabokov's and concludes: "Mr. Morton has brought off a remarkable coup; he has psychologized a legend, yet never lost the punch of an energetic story. This is a novel of Vienna, old and very new, Jewish and gentile, rendered into seductive English by a transplanted Viennese, thus creating a confluence of multinational streams."

BIOGRAPHICAL/CRITICAL SOURCES:

PERIODICALS

Best Sellers, January 1, 1969.
Books and Bookmen, December, 1966.
Book Week, February 6, 1966.
Book World, February 23, 1969.
Christian Science Monitor, August 4, 1976.
Harper's, December, 1965.
Hudson Review, spring, 1966.
Life, September 3, 1965.
Nation, March 3, 1969.
National Observer, February 3, 1969.
Newsweek, June 21, 1976; November 2, 1976.
New Yorker, January 11, 1969.
New York Times, January 21, 1966; November 5, 1971; July 13, 1976; October 25, 1979; June 10, 1984.
New York Times Book Review, January 5, 1969; September 12, 1976; November 18, 1979.
Saturday Review, October 16, 1965; December 28, 1968.
Time, September 19, 1965.
Variety, October 21, 1970.
Washington Post, June 11, 1984.

*   *   *

MOSES, Claire Goldberg 1941-

PERSONAL: Born June 22, 1941, in Hartford, CT; daughter of Abraham R. and Pauline (Hurwich) Goldberg; married Arnold Moses (a certified public accountant), 1966; children: Lisa, Leslie. *Education:* Attended Institut de Sciences Politiques, Paris, France, 1960-61, and Columbia University, 1963-64; Smith College, A.B. (magna cum laude), 1963; George Washington University, M.Phil., 1972, Ph.D., 1978.

ADDRESSES: Home—11658 Mediterranean Ct., Reston, VA 22090. *Office*— Women's Studies Program, University of Maryland at College Park, College Park, MD 20742.

CAREER: Business International, New York, NY, associate European editor, 1965-67; American Historical Association, Washington, DC, staff associate, 1976; University of Maryland at College Park, professor and director of women's studies, 1977—. Editor and manager of *Feminist Studies,* 1977—; group organizer and lobbyist for Reston Women's Center, 1970-75.

MEMBER: American Historical Association, National Women's Studies Association, Society for French Historical Studies, Coordinating Committee of Women in Histor-

ical Profession/Conference Group on Women's History (co-president), Phi Beta Kappa.

AWARDS, HONORS: Joan Kelly Prize, American Historical Association, 1985, for *French Feminism in the Nineteenth Century;* named Maryland Woman of Letters by women legislators of Maryland.

WRITINGS:

French Feminism in the Nineteenth Century, State University of New York Press, 1984.
(Contributor) Samia Spencer, editor, *French Women and the Age of Enlightenment,* Indiana University Press, 1984.
(With Leslie Wahl Rabine) *Feminism, Socialism, and French Romanticism,* Indiana University Press, 1993.
Women and Collective Struggle, University of Illinois Press, in press.

Contributor of articles and reviews to magazines, including *Journal of Modern History.* Editor of *Feminist Studies.*

*   *   *

MOYNIHAN, Daniel P(atrick) 1927-

PERSONAL: Born March 16, 1927, in Tulsa, OK; son of John Henry (a journalist) and Margaret Ann (Phipps) Moynihan; married Elizabeth Therese Brennan (a painter and sculptor), May 29, 1955; children: Timothy Patrick, Maura Russell, John McCloskey. *Education:* Attended City College (now City College of the City University of New York) and Middlebury College; Tufts University, B.N.S., 1946, B.A. (cum laude), 1948; Fletcher School of Law and Diplomacy, M.A., 1949, Ph.D., 1961; graduate study at London School of Economics and Political Science, London, 1950-51. *Politics:* Democrat. *Religion:* Roman Catholic.

ADDRESSES: Home—West Davenport, NY. *Office*— Dirken Senate Office Building, Washington, DC 20510.

CAREER: Budget assistant at U.S. Air Force base, Ruislip, England, 1951-53; International Rescue Committee, New York City, director of public relations, 1954; Office of the Governor, Albany, NY, 1955-58, began as special assistant to the secretary to the governor, became assistant secretary, then acting secretary to the governor; Syracuse University, Maxwell School of Citizenship and Public Affairs, Syracuse, NY, director of New York State Government Research Project, 1959-60, assistant professor of political science, 1960-61; U.S. Department of Labor, Washington, DC, special assistant to secretary of labor, 1961-62, executive assistant to secretary of labor, 1962-63, assistant secretary of labor for policy planning and research, 1963-65; Democratic primary candidate for president of New York City Council, 1965; codirector of policy and planning for mayoral campaign of Abraham Beame, New York City, 1965; Wesleyan University, Center for Advanced Studies, Middletown, CT, fellow, 1965-66; Massachusetts Institute of Technology and Harvard University Joint Center for Urban Studies, Cambridge, MA, director, 1966-69, senior member, 1966-77, professor of government, 1972-77; Harvard University, Cambridge, professor of education and urban politics, Graduate School of Education, 1966-73, professor of government, Kennedy School of Government, 1973—; U.S. Government, Washington, DC, assistant to the president for urban affairs, counsellor to the president, and executive secretary of Urban Affairs Council, 1969-70; U.S. ambassador to India, New Delhi, 1973-75; United Nations, New York City, U.S. ambassador and member of cabinet, 1975-76; U.S. Senate, Washington, DC, New York state senator, 1977—.

Worker for mayoral campaign of Robert F. Wagner, New York City, 1953; secretary of public affairs committee, New York State Democratic Committee, 1958-60; member of New York State Tenure Commission, 1959-60; delegate to Democratic National Convention, 1960 and 1976; member of President's Council on Pennsylvania Avenue, 1962-64; vice-chairman of President's Temporary Commission on Pennsylvania Avenue, 1964-73; member of Massachusetts advisory committee, U.S. Commission on Civil Rights, 1967; member of Massachusetts Democratic Advisory Council, 1967; member of U.S. delegation, 26th General Assembly of United Nations, 1971; member of President's Science Advisory Committee, 1971-73; chairman of advisory committee on traffic safety, Department of Health, Education, and Welfare. Consultant to U.S. president, 1971-73, to Congressional committees, and to numerous government agencies. Member of U.S. Senate Select Committee on Finance, Senate Environment and Public Works Committee, and Senate Finance Committee, 1977—. Lecturer at Russell Sage College, 1957-58, Cornell University, 1959, and at other colleges and universities in the eastern United States. Director of University of Maryland Overseas Program, 1962-63; senior member of Institute of Politics, Kennedy School of Government, Harvard University, 1966—; vice-chairman, Woodrow Wilson International Center for Scholars, 1971—. Chairman of board of trustees, Joseph H. Hirsshorn Museum and Sculpture Garden, 1971—. Consultant to businesses and political organizations. *Military service:* U.S. Navy, 1944-47; became gunnery officer.

MEMBER: American Political Science Association, American Society for Public Administration, American Irish Historical Society, American Philosophical Society, American Association for the Advancement of Science (vice-chairman, 1971; director, 1972-73), American Academy of Arts and Sciences (fellow; chairman of seminar on poverty), National Academy of Public Administration, Catholic Association for International Peace, National Council on Aging, Federal City Club (Washington, DC), Century Club (New York City), Harvard Club (New York City).

AWARDS, HONORS: National Book Award nomination, and Anisfield-Wolf Award in Race Relations from *Saturday Review,* both 1964, for *Beyond the Melting Pot: The Negroes, Puerto Ricans, Jews, Italians, and Irish of New York City;* Meritorious Service Award, U.S. Department of Labor, 1964; Arthur S. Fleming Award as one of ten outstanding young men in federal government, 1965; International League for Human Rights award, 1975; John LaFarge Award for Interracial Justice, 1980; Hubert Humphrey Award, American Political Science Association, 1983; medallion, State University of New York at Albany, 1984; Henry Medal, Smithsonian Institution, 1985; Seal Medallion, Central Intelligence Agency, 1986; Memorial Sloan-Kettering Cancer Center Medal, 1986; Britannica Award, 1986. Honorary A.M., Harvard University, 1966; honorary LL.D., La Salle College, 1966, Catholic University of America, 1968, New School of Social Research, 1968, University of California, 1969, University of Notre Dame, 1969, St. Bonaventure University, 1972, St. Anselm's College, 1976, Adelphi University, 1976, and Hebrew University, 1976; honorary Doctorate of Public Administration, Providence College, 1967; honorary L.H.D., University of Akron, 1967, and Hamilton College, 1968; honorary D.S.Sc., Villanova University, 1968; honorary D.H., Bridgewater State College, 1972; honorary D.Sc., Michigan Technological University, 1972.

WRITINGS:

(With Nathan Glazer) *Beyond the Melting Pot: The Negroes, Puerto Ricans, Jews, Italians, and Irish of New York City,* M.I.T. Press, 1963, 2nd edition, 1970.
(With Eli Ginzberg and others) *The Negro Challenge to the Business Community,* McGraw, 1964.
The Assault on Poverty, Harper, 1965.
(With Margaret S. Gordon and others) *Poverty in America,* Chandler Publishing, 1965.
(With Paul Barton and Ellen Broderick) *The Negro Family: The Case for National Action,* U.S. Department of Labor, 1965.
Traffic Safety and the Health of the Body Politic, Center for Advanced Studies, Wesleyan University, 1966.
Maximum Feasible Misunderstanding: Community Action in the War on Poverty, Free Press, 1969.
(With others) *Violent Crime: Homicide, Assault, Rape, Robbery—A Report,* Braziller, 1970.
The Politics of a Guaranteed Income: The Nixon Administration and the Family Assistance Plan, Random House, 1973.

Coping: Essays on the Practice of Government, Random
House, 1973, published as *Coping: On the Practice of
Government,* 1974.
(With others) *Business and Society in Change,* American
Telephone and Telegraph, 1975.
(Author of foreword) Jeffrey O'Connell, *Ending Insult to
Injury: No-Fault Insurance for Products and Services,*
University of Illinois Press, 1975.
(With others) *Materials Related to Welfare Research and
Experimentation,* U.S. Government Printing Office,
1978.
(With Suzanne Weaver) *A Dangerous Place,* Little,
Brown, 1978.
(Author of foreword) Charles Brooks, *Best Editorial Car-
toons of the Year: 1980 Edition,* Pelican, 1980.
*Counting Our Blessings: Reflections on the Future of Amer-
ica,* Little, Brown, 1980.
(Author of foreword) Philip Van Slyck, *Strategies for the
Nineteen Eighties: Lessons of Cuba, Vietnam, and Af-
ghanistan,* Greenwood Publishing, 1981.
Loyalties, Harcourt, 1984.
*Family and a Nation: The Godkin Lectures, Harvard Uni-
versity,* Harcourt, 1986.
Came the Revolution: Argument in the Reagan Era, Har-
court, 1988.
Welfare Reform: Consensus or Conflict?, edited by James
S. Denton, University Press of America, 1988.
On the Law of Nations, Harvard University Press, 1992.
Pandaemonium: Ethnicity in International Politics, Ox-
ford University Press, 1993.

EDITOR

Arthur J. Goldberg, *The Defenses of Freedom: The Public
Papers of Arthur J. Goldberg,* Harper, 1966.
(With Corinne Saposs Schelling) *On Understanding Pov-
erty: Perspectives from the Social Sciences,* Basic
Books, 1969.
Toward a National Urban Policy, Basic Books, 1970.
Urban America: The Expert Looks at the City, [Washing-
ton], 1970.
(With Frederick Mostella) *On Equality of Educational
Opportunity,* Random House, 1972.
(With Glazer and Schelling) *Ethnicity: Theory and Experi-
ence,* Harvard University Press, 1975.

OTHER

Also author of numerous papers and reports for government agencies and political organizations; author of sound
recording "The Uses and Abuses of United States-Soviet
Union Detente." Author of introductions to over forty-
five books, including *A Cartoon History of United States
Foreign Policy, 1776-1976,* Foreign Policy Association,
1976; *No Margin for Error: America in the Eighties,* Random House, 1980; and *Within the System: My Half Cen-

tury in Social Security,* Aetex Publications, 1992; contributor to *Encyclopedia Britannica;* also contributor of numerous articles and reviews to periodicals, including
*Commentary, New Republic, Harvard Review, America,
National Jewish Monthly, Reporter, American Political
Science Review,* and *Commonweal.* Member of editorial
board, *American Scholar* and *Public Interest.*

SIDELIGHTS: Daniel P. Moynihan has achieved two
major roles as an academic scholar and public servant
within his career. As a professor and specialist in urban
politics and education at Harvard University, an advisor
to four U.S. presidents, a U.S. ambassador to India and
the United Nations, and a U.S. senator, his effect on
American politics has been profound and at times controversial. In his role as an author, Moynihan became nation-
ally known for *Beyond the Melting Pot: The Negroes,
Puerto Ricans, Jews, Italians, and Irish of New York City,*
written in 1963 with Nathan Glazer, and *The Negro Family: The Case for National Action,* published in 1965.

"Everything that Senator Daniel Patrick Moynihan of
New York writes is of interest because he combines a restless and iconoclastic mind with a temperament that is essentially conservative," stated William V. Shannon in the
New York Times Book Review. "This interplay produces
insights and convictions that are surprising. Mr. Moynihan expresses them in prose that is always stylish and is
variously elegant, ironic or engagingly discursive." Shannon described "this idiosyncratic mix" in Moynihan's collection of essays, *Loyalties,* noting that "the essays discuss
Mr. Moynihan's opposition to the MX missile, his outrage
at the campaign in the United States against Israel and his
devotion to the ideal of international law in the conduct
of foreign affairs. As the mere listing of them makes them
clear, these three topics are unrelated and only tenuously
held together by the idea of loyalty. Mr. Moynihan does
not press this common theme very vigorously, but it does
not greatly matter since each of the essays is freshly written and has its own intrinsic interest." Moynihan's arguments against the MX missile and B-1 bomber and his
views on international law and foreign politics led Morton
Kondracke to remark in *New Republic:* "It should be said
that Moynihan can explain and defend each of his actions
and positions with his customary intellectual agility. His
arguments deserve respect, but aren't really convincing."
However, Kondracke concluded, "Moynihan surely has
many of the talents required for national political leadership. He has thunderous powers of expression. He is a man
of stunning insight and considerable and intellectual courage." According to Richard Berstein in the *New York
Times Book Review,* "The mind of Daniel Patrick Moynihan has ranged so nimbly over so many subjects that the
senior senator of New York may well be the foremost
scholar-politician of the land." However, Berstein wrote

in regard to *Loyalties* that the fact that "Mr. Moynihan refuses to allow certain principles, such as those of international law, to be sacrificed under any circumstances is intellectually and morally consistent. Yet the senator's final recommendation to face our very dangerous world by renouncing certain types of actions seems, at least to this reader, inadequate."

Family and a Nation is a compilation of Moynihan's 1985 Godkin lectures at Harvard University. It was described by Walter Goodman in the *New York Times* as "a tale of the inability of politicians and social scientists to do something about the continuing destruction of the two-parent family, particularly in the nation's black ghettos, with its accompanying school failure, drug addiction, crime and general disorder." It is an issue that Moynihan has been battling over the past decades. According to Bryce Nelson in the *Los Angeles Times Book Review,* "Moynihan made his living as a Harvard social scientist before entering political life; his arguments are strengthened by constant use of census and demographic data." "The main strength of Moynihan's work," Nelson continued, "is not as a systematic analysis of the cures and causes of childhood poverty and family disintegration. . . . He is at his best when he leaves his statistics-stuffed notes on the lectern and talks to us from the heart."

Came the Revolution: Argument in the Reagan Era reflects Moynihan's view of the first eight years of the Reagan administration. Hendrik Hertzberg remarked in a critique of *Came the Revolution* for the *New York Times Book Review:* "[Moynihan's] work as a writer complements his work as a politician. The combination has made him one of the nation's most influential voices on public policy, especially on the issues of welfare and national security." Although Hertzberg found Moynihan's writing to have "some of the human interest of a picaresque political detective story," *Washington Post Book World*'s Richard J. Walton wrote, "For all his pungent, commonsense criticism of Reaganomics, Moynihan doesn't see the inescapable connection between the deficits and reckless military spending. But since it is the reviewer's conviction that the Reagan administration's most pernicious legacy will be the economic state of the union, I think it is only responsible to concentrate on that aspect of Moynihan's book."

On the Law of Nations was published shortly after the Iraqi invasion of Kuwait. "It is an elegant and persuasive history-cum-argument about international law," summarized Roger Rosenblatt in the *New York Times Book Review.* Rosenblatt added, "Senator Moynihan demonstrates convincingly that since the 18th century, American leaders and thinkers have honored the ideals of international law, conduct to the contrary notwithstanding. In the modern presidential era, however, even the pretense of reverence has been dropped." "The burden of his message," commented David Fromkin of the *Washington Post Book World,* "is that we ought to play the game by the rules, not so much because we owe it to others as because we owe it to ourselves."

BIOGRAPHICAL/CRITICAL SOURCES:

BOOKS

Rather, Dan, and Gary Paul Gates, *The Palace Guard,* Harper, 1974.

PERIODICALS

Book World, February 2, 1986, p. 3.
Chicago Tribune, September 3, 1986, pp. 1, 3.
Commentary, May, 1969, pp. 87, 89; March, 1971, pp. 41-52; April, 1973, pp. 84, 86-87; March, 1975.
Commonweal, May 16, 1969, pp. 267-269; April, 1975, pp. 227-228.
Detroit Free Press, August 18, 1982; April 16, 1984, pp. 1A, 11A.
Harper's, June, 1973, pp. 86, 88-89.
L'Express, June 30-July 6, 1969.
Los Angeles Times Book Review, January 28, 1979, p. 4; August 31, 1980, p. 1; March 23, 1986, p. 7; March 13, 1988, pp. 2, 11; September 2, 1990, p. 15.
Nation, July 5, 1975, pp. 8-13; December 20, 1975, pp. 654-658; February 9, 1976, pp. 21-22; February 14, 1976, pp. 163-164; September 22, 1979, pp. 245-246; July 12, 1980, pp. 38, 40.
National Review, May 19, 1970, pp. 519-520; March 1, 1974, p. 269; January 23, 1976, pp. 20-21; August 3, 1979, pp. 962-966.
New Republic, February 22, 1969, pp. 23-24; April 10, 1976, pp. 17-19; August 16, 1980, pp. 17-19; July 9, 1984, pp. 27-31.
Newsweek, February 10, 1969; October 20, 1975, pp. 50-51; November 20, 1978, pp. 125-126.
New Yorker, June 7, 1969, pp. 143-151; August 23, 1969, p. 96; April 22, 1974, p. 151.
New York Review of Books, March 22, 1973, pp. 9-12; May 3, 1979, pp. 8-11.
New York Times, February 1, 1969; February 2, 1969; October 22, 1969; February 26, 1985; November 3, 1985, pp. 70, 89, 91-92; January 31, 1986, p. 22; November 30, 1987; December 20, 1987; January 1, 1988; January 18, 1988; April 4, 1988, p. C22.
New York Times Book Review, January 27, 1974, pp. 2-4; December 10, 1978, pp. 3, 45; November 30, 1980, p. 9; March 5, 1984; April 8, 1984, p. 17; March 2, 1986, p. 9; April 17, 1988, p. 11; August 26, 1990, pp. 1, 16; May 10, 1992, p. 28.
New York Times Magazine, November 3, 1984.
Saturday Review, March 8, 1969.
Time, December 1, 1975, pp. 8-10; January 26, 1976, pp. 26-34; February 16, 1976, p. 11.

Times Educational Supplement, August 21, 1981, p. 18.
Village Voice, April 3, 1969, pp. 7-8, 17-20.
Virginia Quarterly Review, summer, 1969.
Washington Post, February 6, 1969; July 7, 1980; December 5, 1987; March 30, 1988; April 24, 1988; May 8, 1988; March 18, 1989; March 24, 1989.
Washington Post Book World, May 30, 1970; September 7, 1980, p. 6; March 11, 1984, p. 7; February 2, 1986, p. 3; December 5, 1987; October 7, 1990, p. 1.*

—*Sidelights by Cynthia Walker*

*   *   *

MURDOCH, (Jean) Iris   1919-

PERSONAL: Born July 15, 1919, in Dublin, Ireland; daughter of Wills John Hughes (a British civil servant) and Irene Alice (Richardson) Murdoch; married John Oliver Bayley (a professor, novelist, critic), 1956. *Education:* Somerville College, Oxford, B.A. (first-class honours), 1942; Newnham College, Cambridge, Sarah Smithson studentship in philosophy, 1947-48. *Religion:* Christian. *Avocational Interests:* Learning languages.

ADDRESSES: Home—30 Charlbury Rd., Oxford OX2 6UU, England.

CAREER: Writer. British Treasury, London, England, assistant principal, 1942-44; United National Relief and Rehabilitation Administration (UNRRA), administrative officer in London, Belgium, and Austria, 1944-46; Oxford University, St. Anne's College, Oxford, England, fellow and university lecturer in philosophy, 1948-63, honorary fellow, 1963—; Royal College of Art, London, lecturer, 1963-67. Member of Formentor Prize Committee.

AWARDS, HONORS: Book of the Year award, *Yorkshire Post,* 1969, for *Bruno's Dream;* Whitehead Literary Award for fiction, 1974, for *The Sacred and Profane Love Machine;* James Tait Black Memorial Prize, 1974, for *The Black Prince;* named Commander, Order of the British Empire, 1976, Dame Commander, 1986; Booker Prize, 1978, for *The Sea, The Sea;* medal of honor for literature, National Arts Club, 1990.

WRITINGS:

NOVELS

Under the Net, Viking, 1954, published with introduction and notes by Dorothy Jones, Longmans, Green, 1966, Penguin, 1977.
The Flight from the Enchanter, Viking, 1956, Penguin, 1987.
The Sandcastle, Viking, 1957, Penguin, 1978.
The Bell, Viking, 1958, Penguin, 1987.
A Severed Head, Viking, 1961.
An Unofficial Rose, Viking, 1962, Penguin, 1987.

The Unicorn, Viking, 1963, Penguin, 1987.
The Italian Girl, Viking, 1964.
The Red and the Green, Viking, 1965, Penguin, 1988.
The Time of the Angels, Viking, 1966, Penguin, 1988.
The Nice and the Good, Viking, 1968.
A Fairly Honorable Defeat, Viking, 1970.
An Accidental Man, Viking, 1971.
Bruno's Dream, Viking, 1973.
The Black Prince, Viking, 1973.
The Sacred and the Profane Love Machine, Viking, 1974.
A Word Child, Viking, 1975.
Henry and Cato, Viking, 1977.
The Sea, The Sea, Viking, 1978.
Nuns and Soldiers, Viking, 1980.
The Philosopher's Pupil, Viking, 1983.
The Good Apprentice, Chatto & Windus, 1985, Viking, 1986.
The Book and the Brotherhood, Chatto & Windus, 1987, Viking, 1988.
The Message to the Planet, Chatto & Windus, 1989, Viking, 1990.

NONFICTION

Sartre: Romantic Rationalist, Yale University Press, 1953, 2nd edition, Barnes & Noble, 1980 (published in England as *Sartre: Romantic Realist,* Harvester Press, 1980).
(Contributor) *The Nature of Metaphysics,* Macmillan, 1957.
(Author of foreword) Wendy Campbell-Purdie and Fenner Brockaway, *Woman against the Desert,* Gollancz, 1964.
The Sovereignty of Good over Other Concepts (Leslie Stephen lecture, 1967), Cambridge University Press, 1967, published with other essays as *The Sovereignty of Good,* Routledge & Kegan Paul, 1970, Schocken, 1971.
The Fire and the Sun: Why Plato Banned the Artists (based on the Romanes lecture, 1976), Claredon Press, 1977.
Reynolds Stone, Warren, 1981.
Acastos: Two Platonic Dialogues, Chatto & Windus, 1986, Penguin, 1987.
Metaphysics as a Guide to Morals, Penguin, 1993.

PLAYS

(With J. B. Priestley) *A Severed Head* (three-act; based on the author's novel of the same title; first produced in London at Royale Theatre, October 28, 1964; produced in New York, 1964), Chatto & Windus, 1964, acting edition, Samuel French, 1964.
(With James Saunders) *The Italian Girl* (based on the author's novel of the same title; first produced at Bristol Old Vic, December, 1967), Samuel French, 1968.

The Servants and the Snow (first produced in London at Greenwich Theatre, September 29, 1970), Chatto & Windus, 1973, Viking, 1974.

The Three Arrows (first produced in Cambridge at Arts Theatre, October 17, 1972), Chatto & Windus, 1973, Viking, 1974.

Art and Eros, produced in London, 1980.

The Servants (opera libretto; adapted from the author's play *The Servants and the Snow*), produced in Cardiff, Wales, 1980.

The Black Prince (based on the author's novel of the same title), produced in London at Aldwych Theatre, 1989.

OTHER

A Year of Birds (poems), Compton Press, 1978.

Contributor to periodicals in United States and Great Britain, including *Listener, Yale Review, Chicago Review, Encounter, New Statesman, Nation,* and *Partisan Review.*

ADAPTATIONS: A Severed Head (based on her novel and play) was filmed by Columbia Pictures, 1971; the film rights to *A Fairly Honourable Defeat* were sold in 1972.

SIDELIGHTS: Described by *Commonweal*'s Linda Kuehl as "a philosopher by trade and temperament," Iris Murdoch is known for her novels full of characters embroiled in philosophical turmoil. Though originally aligned with the existentialist movement, Murdoch's philosophy quickly broadened, and critics now regard her works as "novels of ideas." In addition, her plays and nonfiction works encompass similar philosophical debates and add to her reputation as one of her generation's most prolific and important writers. Murdoch's body of work has proved influential in twentieth-century literature and thought; "she draws eclectically on the English tradition" of Charles Dickens, Jane Austen, and William Thackeray "and at the same time extends it in important ways," writes John Fletcher in *Concise Dictionary of British Literary Biography.*

Though born an only child of Anglo-Irish parents in Ireland, Murdoch grew up in the suburbs of London and earned a scholarship to a private school when she was thirteen. At Somerville College at Oxford, Murdoch was involved in drama and arts when not immersed in her literature and philosophy studies. Her left-wing politics led her to join the Communist party for a brief time in the early 1940s, an affiliation that caused the United States to deny her a visa to study in the country after winning a scholarship several years later. Following her distinguished scholastic career, Murdoch worked at the British Treasury during World War II and later for the United Nations Relief and Rehabilitation Administration. While working for the United Nations, she traveled to Belgium where she met Jean-Paul Sartre as well as the French writer Ray-

mond Quenteau, whose writings greatly influenced her first novel, *Under the Net.* During the 1950s, Murdoch taught philosophy at St. Anne's College at Oxford, and said of the experience to Gill Davie and Leigh Crutchley in a *Publishers Weekly* interview: "I love teaching, and if I were not able to teach philosophy I would happily teach something else."

The existentialist movement, a philosophy that became popular in the 1950s in light of the wide-spread despair caused by World War II, was the impetus for Murdoch's first book. Popularized by such writers as Albert Camus and Jean-Paul Sartre, existentialism proposed that because human existence is meaningless, people must act according to their own free will and may never know the difference between right and wrong. *Sartre: Romantic Rationalist* chronicled the thoughts and influences of one of existentialism's most popular writers. Many critics began to view Murdoch as an emerging theorist of the philosophy, but as she professed to John Russell in the *New York Times:* "I was never a Sartrean, or an existentialist." Focusing on Sartre's influential *Being and Nothingness,* Murdoch examines Sartre's philosophy, and the events in his personal life that led him to his conclusions. Critics commended Murdoch's views; Wallace Fowlie in *Commonweal* calls it "one of the most objective and useful" interpretations of Sartre's works, and Stuart Hampshire in *New Statesman* hails Murdoch as "one who understands the catastrophes of intellectual politics, and who can still take them seriously."

Several critics noted similarities between Sartre and Murdoch. William Van O'Connor writes in *The New University Wits, and the End of Modernism,* that like Sartre, Murdoch views man as a "lonely creature in an absurd world . . . impelled to make moral decisions, the consequences of which are uncertain." Like Sartre, says Warner Berthoff in *Fictions and Events,* Murdoch believes that writing is "above all else a collaboration of author and reader in an act of freedom." Bertoff continues: "Following Sartre she has spoken pointedly of the making of works of art as not only a 'struggle for freedom' but as a 'task which does not come to an end.' "

Though there are similarities, critics note some important differences between the two philosophers. Gail Kmetz writes in *Ms.* that Murdoch "rejected Sartre's emphasis on the isolation and anguish of the individual in a meaningless world . . . because she felt it resulted in a sterile and futile solipsism [a belief that the self is the only existent thing]. She considers the individual always as a part of society, responsible to others as well as to herself or himself; and insists that freedom means respecting the independent being of others, and that subordinating others' freedom to one's own is a denial of freedom itself. Unlike Sartre, Murdoch sees the claims of freedom and love as identical."

Murdoch states in *Chicago Review* that "love is the perception of individuals . . . the extremely difficult realisation that something other than oneself is real," and that only when one is capable of love is one free. Murdoch recently told *CA* that she was critical of Sartre's concept of "a leap into pure freedom" and "his distinction between liberated free persons (intellectuals, artists, wild and courageous, etc.) and the dull, machine-like petty bourgeois [not quite unlike Derrida's later distinction]." But, she adds, "I do not 'follow' Sartre or Derrida."

One of Murdoch's major themes in her fiction is how best to respect the "reality" of others—how best to live "morally." Together with questions of "love" and "freedom," it comprises her major concern. "Miss Murdoch's pervasive theme has been the quest for a passion beyond any center of self," explains *New York Times Book Review* critic David Bromwich. "What her characters seek may go by the name of Love or God or the Good: mere physical love is the perilous and always tempting idol that can become destroyer." "The basic idea," says Joyce Carol Oates in the *New Republic,* "seems to be that centuries of humanism have nourished an unrealistic conception of the powers of the will: we have gradually lost the vision of a reality separate from ourselves. . . . Twentieth-century obsessions with the authority of the individual, the 'existential' significance of subjectivity, are surely misguided, for the individual cannot be (as he thinks of himself, proudly) a detached observer, free to invent or reimagine his life." The consequences of trying to do so are repeatedly explored in Murdoch's fiction, beginning with her first published novel, *Under the Net.*

Based on Austrian philosopher Ludwig Wittgenstein's idea that we each build our own "net" or system for structuring our lives—"the net," Murdoch tells *CA,* "of language under which we may seek for what is real"—*Under the Net* describes the wanderings of Jake Donaghue as he attempts to structure his. However, "planned ways of life are . . . traps," observes James Gindin in *Postwar British Fiction,* "no matter how carefully or rationally the net is woven, and Jake discovers that none of these narrow paths really works." Only after a series of comic misadventures (which change his attitude rather than his circumstances) is Jake able to accept the contingencies of life and the reality of other people. He throws off the net, an act which takes great courage according to Kmetz, "for nothing is more terrifying than freedom." *Under the Net* attracted much critical praise; Davie and Crutchley note that with just one novel to her credit, Murdoch became one of her generation's outstanding English writers.

Though situations vary from book to book, the protagonists in Murdoch's novels generally fashion a "net" of some kind. It may consist of a set of community mores, or a societal role. For Hilary Burde, protagonist of *A Word*

Child, the net is a fixed routine. An unloved, illegitimate child, Hilary becomes a violent juvenile delinquent. When he is befriended by a teacher, he learns that he possesses a remarkable skill with words. In the rigid structure of grammar he seeks shelter from life's randomness. He is awarded a scholarship to Oxford and begins what should be a successful career, However, as *New York Times* critic Bromwich explains, "The structure of things can bear only so much ordering: his university job ends disastrously with an adulterous love affair that is indirectly responsible for two deaths." The story opens twenty years later, when Gunnar—the husband of Hilary's former lover—appears in the government office where Hilary holds a menial job. "The novel's subject," explains Lynne Sharon Schwartz in *Nation,* "is what Hilary will do about his humiliation, his tormenting guilt and his need for forgiveness."

What he does, according to Schwartz, is the worst possible thing. "He attempts to order his friends and his days into the kind of strict system he loves in grammar," she says. "This rigid life is not only penance but protection as well, against chaos, empty time, and the unpredictable impulses of the self. The novel shows the breakdown of the system: people turn up on unexpected days, they refuse—sometimes comically—to act the roles assigned them, and Hilary's dangerous impulses do come forth and insist on playing themselves out." The tragedy of Hilary's early days is repeated. He falls in love with Gunnar's second wife; they meet in secret and are discovered. Once more by accident Hilary commits his original crime.

"At the novel's conclusion," writes *Saturday Review*'s Bruce Allen, "we must consider which is the illusion: the optimist's belief that we can atone for our crimes and outlive them or the nihilist's certainty (Hilary expresses it) that people are doomed, despite their good intentions, to whirl eternally in a muddle of 'penitence, remorse, resentment, violence, and hate.'" David Bromwich interprets the moral issue somewhat differently. "Hilary, the artist-figure without an art," he says, "wants to make the world (word) conform to his every design, and is being guided to the awareness that its resistance to him is a lucky thing. . . . Hilary must consent at last to the arbitrariness of an order imposed on him." Learning to accept the chaos of life without the aid of patterns or categories is a constant struggle for Murdoch's characters.

"I believe we live in a fantasy world, a world of illusion. And the great task in life is to find reality," Murdoch told Rachel Billington in a London *Times* interview. However, the creation of art, she told *Publishers Weekly,* should be the novelist's goal. "I don't think a novel should be a committed statement of political and social criticism," she says. "They should aim at being beautiful. . . . Art holds a mirror to nature, and I think it's a very difficult thing to do," Murdoch continues. The way Murdoch mirrors nature is by creating what she calls "real characters." According to Berthoff in *Fictions and Events,* these are "personages who will be 'more than puppets' and at the same time other than oneself." When asked why these characters are usually male, Murdoch told *CA:* "I find no difficulty in imagining men. . . . I am very much concerned about the (still distant) liberation of women. . . . [but] I do not want to write about 'women's problems' in any narrow, specialized sense. I have female narrators, too. I just identify more with the men."

However, Linda Kuehl explains in *Modern Fiction Studies,* Murdoch fails in her attempt to create these "real characters." Her propensity for nineteenth century characters produces many "types" that populate her novels, and "in each successive novel there emerges a pattern of predictable and predetermined types. These include the enchanter or enchantress—occult, godly, foreign, ancient—who is torn between exhibitionism and introspection, egoism and generosity, cruelty and pity; the observer, trapped between love and fear of the enchanter, who thinks in terms of ghosts, spells, demons and destiny, and imparts an obfuscated view of life; and the accomplice, a peculiar mixture of diabolical intention and bemused charm, who has dealings with the enchanters and power over the observers," analyzes Kuehl. "Though she produces many people," Kuehl continues, "each is tightly controlled in a super-imposed design, each is rigidly cast in a classical Murdochian role."

Lawrence Graver in the *New York Times Book Review* expresses a similar view: "In practice, the more she [talks] about freedom and opaqueness the more over-determined and transparent her novels [seem] to become. . . . Despite the inventiveness of the situations and the brilliance of the design, Miss Murdoch's philosophy has recently seemed to do little more than make her people *theoretically* interesting." Oates mentions this as well in *New Republic,* Murdoch's novels are "structures in which ideas, not things, and certainly not human beings flourish." In *The Novel Now,* Anthony Burgess compares Murdoch to a puppeteer who exerts complete control: "[Murdoch's] characters dress, talk, act like ourselves, but they are caught up in a purely intellectual pattern, a sort of contrived sexual dance in which partners are always changing. They seem to be incapable of free choice."

The Message to the Planet, Murdoch's twenty-fourth novel, published in 1989, encompasses many of Murdoch's familiar themes and conflicts. Marcus Vallar is a somewhat sinister mathematics genius-turned-philosopher; one of " 'pure thought' who pushes his ideas to the point where they might actually kill him through their sheer intensity," says Anatole Broyard in *New York Times Book Review.* A dying man believes Vallar has cursed him. The man sends his friend, Alfred Ludens, in search of Vallar, hoping that Vallar will be able to cure him. Miraculously, Vallar cures the man, and Ludens is so impressed by the event that he becomes Vallar's disciple. The book's other plot involves Luden's friend, Franca. In her quest for perfect love, Franca tolerates her husband's infidelities while she nurses the dying man. After he recovers, she must deal with her husband's affairs, and eventually she consents to letting one of his lovers move in with them.

Though these creatures of an educated middle-class live in a society that Toronto *Globe and Mail* reviewer Phyllis Gotlieb calls "hermetic," they "struggle vividly and convincingly to escape the chaos beneath their frail lives," Gottlieb continues. "The nature of discipleship is a subject Murdoch has made her own," claims Henry Louis Gates, Jr. in a *Village Voice* review of *The Message to the Planet,* "perhaps because it is the most compelling version of one of her great subjects—the character who desperately pursues his fantasy of someone else." Christopher Lehman-Haupt of the *New York Times* adds to a common perception of Murdoch's writing by stating that "Murdoch's characters are paper thin and as contrived as origami decorations." Despite this, Lehman-Haupt continues, "they burn with such moral passion that we watch them with the utmost fascination." He also notes that Murdoch's message is "predictably" that "humans are accidental beings with only love to make life bearable in a random universe."

Murdoch lived for many years in the English countryside (she now lives in the city of Oxford) with her husband, John Bayley, a respected literary critic, and enjoys gardening when she is not writing. She pays little attention to critical reviews of her work, even those that are favorable. Murdoch told *CA* that this is because "articles I have glanced at seem on the whole unperceptive, including the friendly ones." Her writing is deliberate and well thought out; she told *CA* about the process: "I have always made a very careful plan of the whole novel before writing the first sentence. I want to keep the purely inventive stage (plot, characters) open as long as possible." In addition, all of her writing is done longhand. "I don't see how anyone can think with a typewriter," she told Davie and Crutchley. Her most recent novels average more than five hundred pages each; a length that Murdoch insists is necessary because it enables them to encompass "more substance, more thoughts," she told a London *Times* interviewer. The London *Times* also reports that "her enemies are word processors . . . tight, crystalline, first person novels, existentialism, and analytical philosophy."

Despite Murdoch's implication that there is room for improvement in her work, (she confessed to the London *Times* in a 1988 interview that she would "like to understand philosophy, [and] I'm just beginning to now"), many reviewers praise the writing she has done. "She wears her formidable intelligence with a careless swagger," writes *Encounter*'s Jonathan Raban, "and her astonishingly fecund, playful imagination looks as fresh and effortless as ever. . . . Part of the joy of reading Iris Murdoch is the implicit assurance that there will be more to come, that the book in hand is an installment in a continuing work which grows more and more important as each new novel is added to it." Adds Broyard: "We have to keep revising our expectations of what her books are about—usually we find that we must travel farther and over more difficult terrain than we're accustomed to."

For an earlier published interview, see entry in *Contemporary Authors, New Revisions Series,* Volume 8.

BIOGRAPHICAL/CRITICAL SOURCES:

BOOKS

Berthoff, Warner, *Fictions and Events: Essays in Criticism and Literary History,* Dutton, 1971.

Burgess, Anthony, *The Novel Now: A Guide to Contemporary Fiction,* Norton, 1967.

Byatt, Antonia S., *Degrees of Freedom: The Novels of Iris Murdoch,* Barnes & Noble, 1965.

Conradi, P. J., *Iris Murdoch: Work for the Spirit,* Macmillan, 1985.

Concise Dictionary of British Literary Biography, Volume 8, Gale, 1992.

Contemporary Literary Criticism, Gale, Volume 1, 1973, Volume 2, 1974, Volume 3, 1975, Volume 4, 1975, Volume 6, 1976, Volume 8, 1978, Volume 11, 1979, Volume 15, 1980, Volume 22, 1982, Volume 31, 1985, Volume 51, 1989.

Dictionary of Literary Biography, Volume 14: *British Novelists Since 1960,* Gale, 1982.

Dipple, Elizabeth, *Iris Murdoch: Work for the Spirit,* University of Chicago Press, 1981.

Gindin, James, *Postwar British Fiction,* University of California Press, 1962.

O'Connor, William Van, *The New University Wits, and the End of Modernism,* Southern Illinois University Press, 1963.

Rabinowitz, Rubin, *Iris Murdoch,* Columbia University Press, 1968.

Thinkers of the Twentieth Century, St. James, 1987.

Todd, Richard, *Iris Murdoch,* Methuen, 1984.

Wolff, Peter, *The Disciplined Heart: Iris Murdoch and Her Novels,* University of Missouri Press, 1966.

PERIODICALS

Chicago Review, autumn, 1959.

Commonweal, November 5, 1953.

Encounter, July, 1974.

Globe and Mail (Toronto), October 28, 1989.

Modern Fiction Studies, Autumn, 1959.

Ms., July, 1976.

Nation, March 29, 1975; October 11, 1975.

New Republic, November 18, 1978.

New Statesman, January 2, 1954.

New York Times, January 6, 1981; February 22, 1990.

New York Times Book Review, September 13, 1964; February 8, 1970; August 24, 1975; November 20, 1977; December 17, 1978; August 10, 1980; January 4, 1981; March 7, 1982; February 4, 1990.

Publishers Weekly, December 13, 1976.

Saturday Review, October 5, 1974.

Times (London), April 25, 1983; January 23, 1988.

Village Voice, July 17, 1990, p. 73.

—*Sketch by Kathleen Wilson*

N

NASSOUR, Ellis (Michael) 1941-

PERSONAL: Surname is accented on first syllable; born October 25, 1941, in Vicksburg, MS; son of Ellis, Sr. (a grocer) and Mamie (a clothing store manager; maiden name, Webber) Nassour. *Education:* University of Mississippi, B.S., 1964. *Politics:* Republican. *Religion:* Roman Catholic. *Avocational Interests:* Travel, architectural research.

ADDRESSES: Home—61 Horatio St., New York, NY 10014. *Agent*—Walter Gidaly, 750 Third Ave., New York, NY 10017.

CAREER: New York Times, New York City, cultural news writer, 1966-70; Music Corporation of America (MCA), Inc., New York City, manager of artist relations, 1970-72; *New York Daily News,* New York City, entertainment writer, 1978-83; free-lance writer, 1972—. Assistant director and play editor of Blackfriars Guild (Roman Catholic Off-Broadway theatre group), 1966-72.

WRITINGS:

Rock Opera: The Creation of Jesus Christ Superstar, Hawthorn/Dutton, 1973.
Patsy Cline: An Intimate Biography, Tower Books, 1981.
Honky Tonk Angel, The Intimate Story of Patsy Cline, St. Martin's, 1993.

Also author and lyricist of *Nearly Every Damn Spring* (two-act musical), New York City workshop production, fall, 1986, and *Patsy—Honky Tonk Angel,* a two-act biographical musical based on the book, workshop productions in New York City, Allentown, PA, and Tampa, FL, 1989-92. Contributor and music consultant, *American National Biography,* Oxford University Press. Also contributor to periodicals.

WORK IN PROGRESS: Li'l Miss Dynamite, My Story, with Brenda Lee.

SIDELIGHTS: Ellis Nassour once told *CA* that the idea for his book *Rock Opera: The Creation of Jesus Christ Superstar* came while he was working at MCA on *Jesus Christ Superstar.* He decided "the machinations of that production would provide a vehicle to explore the behind-the-scenes record industry and Broadway"—an area that will be further chronicled in his writings.

Nassour added: "I enjoyed Patsy Cline records, but it was my meeting and working with singers Loretta Lynn and Brenda Lee that convinced me what a fascinating woman—innovatively twenty years ahead of her time and the first woman to become a star in the male-dominated country music industry—Cline was. Little archival information existed on the songstress, thus requiring me to obtain more than one hundred oral history interviews in seven states to complete her biography."

Describing himself as a writer who likes "delving into the personal side," Nassour explained that "the secret of collaboration (and it is tough) is to attempt to put yourself into the celebrity's place and examine his or her life—with total honesty."

Nassour also commented: "My goals as a playwright are only now being realized, but I wish to explore such areas as race relations in the South in the 1970s and, in the case of Patsy Cline, to transfer to stage and music her unbelievable drive to become a star against seemingly insurmountable odds."

NATELLA, Arthur A(ristides), Jr. 1941-

PERSONAL: Born November 8, 1941, in Yonkers, NY; son of Arthur A. and Rose Natella. *Education:* Columbia University, B.A., 1963; Syracuse University, M.A., 1965, Ph.D., 1970. *Religion:* Roman Catholic.

CAREER: Syracuse University, Syracuse, NY, instructor in Spanish, 1966-69; University of Maryland, College Park, assistant professor of Spanish and Portuguese, 1969-79; Fordham University, Bronx, NY, assistant professor, 1980-82, associate professor of Spanish, beginning 1982.

MEMBER: Modern Language Association of America, American Association of Teachers of Spanish and Portuguese, American Association of University Professors.

WRITINGS:

The Spanish in America, 1513-1975: A Chronology and Fact Book, Oceana, 1974, revised edition published as *The Spanish in America, 1513-1980,* 1980.

(With David Schoenfeld) *The Consumer and His Dollars,* 3rd edition, Oceana, 1975.

(Contributor) Gladys Zaldivar, editor, *Cinco apre a la narrativa hispanoamericana caontemporanjean* (title means "Five Critical Approaches to Contemporary Latin American Fiction"), Playor, 1976.

(Co-translator) Charles M. Tatum, editor, *Latin American Women Writers: Yesterday and Today,* American Review Press, 1977.

(Contributor) Elias Rivers, editor, *Fabulacion de Eneas,* Ediciones Universal, 1979.

The New Theatre of Peru, Senda Nueva de Ediciones, 1982.

Anacronismos de la nueva literatura hispanoamericana, Editorial Universal, 1990.

Also author of work of fiction, with Y. Natella, *Rendezous.* Contributor to Latin American studies journals.

WORK IN PROGRESS: Contributing a chapter to *Homenaje a Maria Luisa Bombal.**

*   *   *

NEVINS, Francis M(ichael), Jr. 1943-

PERSONAL: Born January 6, 1943, in Bayonne, NJ; son of Francis Michael and Rosemary (Konzelmann) Nevins; married Muriel Walter, June 6, 1966 (divorced 1978); married Patricia Brooks, February 24, 1982. *Education:* St. Peter's College, A.B. (magna cum laude), 1964; New York University, J.D. (cum laude), 1967.

ADDRESSES: Home—7045 Cornell Ave., St. Louis, MO 63130. *Office*—School of Law, St. Louis University, 3700 Lindell Blvd., St. Louis, MO 63108. *Agent*—Maureen Walters, Curtis Brown Ltd., 10 Astor Pl., New York, NY 10003.

CAREER: Admitted to the Bar of New Jersey, 1967; Clark Boardman Ltd., New York City, assistant to editor in chief, 1967; St. Peter's College, Jersey City, NJ, adjunct instructor in government, 1967; Middlesex County Legal Services Corp., New Brunswick, NJ, staff attorney, 1970-71; St. Louis University, School of Law, St. Louis, MO, assistant professor, 1971-75, associate professor, 1975-78, professor of law, 1978—. Advisor to the estate of mystery author Cornell Woolrich, 1970-89. Member of board of directors, St. Louis Volunteer Lawyers for the Arts, 1980-89. Member, Missouri Bar probate code revision subcommittee. *Military service:* U.S. Army Reserve, 1968-70; became captain.

MEMBER: Association of American Law Schools (various offices in Law and the Arts and other sections, 1980—), Mystery Writers of America (chair or member of various committees, 1970—).

AWARDS, HONORS: Edgar Allan Poe Award, Mystery Writers of America, 1975, for *Royal Bloodline: Ellery Queen, Author and Detective,* and 1989, for *Cornell Woolrich: First You Dream, Then You Die.*

WRITINGS:

(With Chris Steinbrunner, Charles Shibuk, Marvin Lachman, and Otto Penzler) *Detectionary,* Hammermill Paper Co., 1971, revised edition, Overlook Press, 1977.

Royal Bloodline: Ellery Queen, Author and Detective, Bowling Green University Popular Press, 1974.

Publish and Perish (novel), Putnam, 1975.

Corrupt and Ensnare (novel), Putnam, 1978.

Missouri Probate Court: Intestacy, Wills and Basic Administration, Harrison Co., 1983.

(With Ray Stanich) *The Sound of Detection: Ellery Queen's Adventures in Radio,* Brownstone, 1983.

The 120-Hour Clock (novel), Walker, 1986.

The Ninety Million Dollar Mouse (novel), Walker, 1987.

Cornell Woolrich: First You Dream, Then You Die, Mysterious Press, 1988.

The Films of Hopalong Cassidy, World of Yesterday, 1988.

Bar-20: The Life of Clarence E. Mulford, Creator of Hopalong Cassidy, McFarland, 1993.

EDITOR

The Mystery Writer's Art, Bowling Green University Popular Press, 1970.

Cornell Woolrich, *Nightwebs,* Harper, 1971, revised edition, Avon, 1974.

Multiplying Villainies: Selected Mystery Criticism of Anthony Boucher, privately printed, 1973.

(With Martin H. Greenberg, Walter Shine, and Jean Shine) John D. MacDonald, *The Good Old Stuff,* Harper, 1982.

(With Greenberg) *Exeunt Murderers: The Best Mystery Stories of Anthony Boucher,* Southern Illinois University Press, 1983.

(With Greenberg) *Buffet for Unwelcome Guests: The Best Short Mystery Stories of Christianna Brand,* Southern Illinois University Press, 1983.

(With Greenberg, W. Shine, and J. Shine) MacDonald, *More Good Old Stuff,* Knopf, 1984.

(With Greenberg) *Carnival of Crime: The Best Mystery Stories of Fredric Brown,* Southern Illinois University Press, 1985.

(With Greenberg) *Leopold's Way: Detective Stories by Edward D. Hoch,* Southern Illinois University Press, 1985.

(With Greenberg) *Darkness at Dawn: Early Suspense Classics by Cornell Woolrich,* Southern Illinois University Press, 1985.

(With Greenberg) *The Best of Ellery Queen,* Beaufort Books, 1985.

(With Greenberg) *Hitchcock in Prime Time,* Avon, 1985.

(With Greenberg) *The Adventures of Henry Turnbuckle: Detective Comedies by Jack Ritchie,* Southern Illinois University Press, 1987.

Better Mousetraps: The Best Mystery Stories of John Lutz, St. Martin's Press, 1988.

(With Greenberg) *Mr. President—Private Eye,* Ballantine, 1988.

(With Greenberg) *Death on Television: The Best of Henry Slesar's Alfred Hitchcock Stories,* Southern Illinois University Press, 1989.

Little Boxes of Bewilderment: Suspense Comedies by Jack Ritchie, St. Martin's Press, 1989.

Edward D. Hoch, *The Night, My Friend: Stories of Crime and Suspense,* Ohio University Press, 1991.

Woolrich, *Schwarz lst die Farbe des Blutes,* Wilhelm Heyne Verlag (Munich), 1993.

OTHER

(Author of foreword) *Private Investigations: The Novels of Dashiell Hammett,* Southern Illinois University Press, 1984.

Contributor to *1001 Midnights,* Arbor House, 1986, and to periodicals, including *New Republic, Journal of Popular Culture, Armchair Detective, Ellery Queen's Mystery Magazine, The Saint Mystery Magazine, Woman's World, Espionage.* Member of editorial board, Bantam Books Collection of Mystery Classics and University of California (San Diego extension) Mystery Library.

SIDELIGHTS: Francis M. Nevins, Jr., once told *CA:* "I was hooked on mystery fiction at the age of thirteen, after

discovering Sherlock Holmes, Charlie Chan, and Perry Mason. Before the end of my first year of high school I was reading and collecting mysteries at a fiendish pace: Ellery Queen, Cornell Woolrich and countless others whom I devoured furiously. It was only after about fifteen years of reading and three or four years of writing occasional reviews and articles about the genre and its practitioners that I took the plunge and tried to write a mystery myself. The eventual discovery that I could sell almost any story I wrote is a shock from which I still haven't recovered."

The literary and legal consultant to the estate of the suspense writer Cornell Woolrich, Nevins, who has edited three volumes of Woolrich's stories, became his biographer in 1988, when he published *Cornell Woolrich: First You Dream, Then You Die.* The book, in which Nevins designates Woolrich "the Poe of the 20th Century and the poet of its shadows," is "a long labor of devotion any author would be grateful to have done on his behalf," *Los Angeles Times Book Review*'s Charles Champlin remarked. Woolrich's work included *The Bride Wore Black, Rear Window,* and *The Night Has a Thousand Eyes.*

BIOGRAPHICAL/CRITICAL SOURCES:

BOOKS

Reilly, John, editor, *Twentieth Century Crime and Mystery Writers,* St. Martin's, 1980, 3rd edition, 1991.
Steinbrunner, Chris, and Otto Penzler, *Encyclopedia of Mystery and Detection,* McGraw, 1976.

PERIODICALS

Los Angeles Times Book Review, November 27, 1988.
New York Times, May 6, 1988.
New York Times Book Review, February 8, 1987, p. 20; March 6, 1988, p. 22; October 9, 1988, pp. 35-36.
Washington Post Book World, September 18, 1988, p. 6.

*   *   *

NICKERSON, Sheila B(unker) 1942-

PERSONAL: Born April 14, 1942, in New York, NY; daughter of Charles Cantine (an investment analyst) and Mavis (McGuire) Bunker; married Martinus Hoffman Nickerson (a traffic engineer), September 5, 1964; children: Helen, Thomas Merriman, Samuel Bunker. *Education:* Bryn Mawr College, B.A. (magna cum laude), 1964; Union Institute, Ph.D., 1985.

ADDRESSES: Home—540 West 10th St., Juneau, AK 99801.

CAREER: Alaska State Council on the Arts, Artists-in-the-Schools Program, writer in residence at schools in Juneau, Petersburg, Skagway, Cordova, Ketchikan, and

Tenakee Springs, 1974-81; University Within Walls (state-wide prison education system), Alaska, editor of prison literary magazine, 1979-82, associate director, instructor, and director of arts program, 1981-82; State of Alaska, Department of Administration, Word Processing Center, proofreader and assistant supervisor, 1983-85, acting supervisor, 1985; editor of *Alaska Fish and Game* (magazine), 1985-92. Free-lance writer. Writer in residence and designer of writing program for the Alaska State Library system, 1979; part-time instructor in English and creative writing for University Within Walls, 1979-81; part-time instructor in creative and technical writing at the University of Alaska, 1979-83, became assistant professor; part-time instructor in technical writing for employees of the State of Alaska, 1979-83; faculty member of Sitka Summer Writers Symposium in Sitka, Alaska, 1984 and 1993. Member of the grants panel for the National Endowment for the Arts literature program, 1980. Has given readings at libraries, bookstores, colleges, and conferences throughout Alaska.

MEMBER: PEN West.

AWARDS, HONORS: Top Hand awards for best book of poetry, 1975, 1980, and 1982; Pushcart Prizes from Pushcart Press, 1976 and 1985-86; publication assistance grant, Alaska State Council on the Arts, 1977; named Alaska's poet laureate, 1977-81; merit and purchase awards for poetry, Alaska State Council on the Arts, 1980; literacy award, Delta Kappa Gamma, 1980.

WRITINGS:

Letter from Alaska and Other Poems, Thorp Springs Press, 1972.

To the Waters and the Wild: Poems of Alaska, Thorp Springs Press, 1975.

In Rooms of Falling Rain (novel), Thorp Springs Press, 1976.

Songs of the Pine-Wife (poetry), Copper Canyon Press, 1980.

(Author of text) *The Enchanted Halibut* (full-length musical play), music by Jack Cannon, first produced in Douglas, Alaska, at Perseverance Theatre, April, 1981.

Waiting for the News of Death (poetry chapbook), Bits Press, 1982.

Writers in the Public Library (nonfiction), Shoe String, 1984.

On Why the Quilt-Maker Became a Dragon (poetry), Vanessa Press, 1985.

Feast of the Animals: An Alaska Bestiary, Volume 1 (poetry), Old Harbor Press, 1987.

In the Compass of Unrest (poetry chapbook), Trout Creek Press, 1988.

Feast of the Animals: An Alaska Bestiary, Volume 2 (poetry), Old Harbor Press, 1991.

Also author of text for *Songs From the Dragon Quilt* (orchestral and choral composition), music by Alice Parker, performed December, 1984, and author of half-hour videotape documentary for educational television, released 1982. Work represented in anthologies, including *The Pushcart Prize: Best of the Small Presses,* Pushcart, 1976, 1985-86; *Wind-flower Almanac,* Windflower Press, 1980; *Hunger and Dreams,* edited by Pat Monoghan, Fireweed Press, 1983; *In the Dreamlight: Twenty-one Alaskan Writers,* Copper Canyon Press, 1984; *Only Morning in Her Shoes,* Utah State University Press, 1990; *Heart of the Flower,* Chicory Blue Press, 1991; and *Reflections from the Island's Edge,* Graywolf, 1993. Contributor of poems to magazines, including *Bits, Crab Creek Review, Croton Review, Hyperion, Ms., New Laurel Review, Permafrost,* and *Tar River Poetry Review.* Co-editor of *Lemon Creek Gold, A Journal of Prison Literature,* 1979-85; co-editor of *JUNEAU 2000 Proceedings,* November, 1982; member of editorial board of *On People and Things Alaskan,* edited by Bridget Smith, Firsthand Press, 1982.

WORK IN PROGRESS: Poetry collections, novels, and nonfiction.

SIDELIGHTS: Sheila B. Nickerson told *CA:* "Although I live in an area of compelling landscape, I am more concerned with inner landscape than outer. On the ferry trip to Juneau, Alaska, in 1971 when I moved there, people asked me, 'Do you think you will like it?' In retrospect I find that a stranger question now than I did at the time. I have written a great deal on Alaska—the land and what the connection with the land has meant to me—but I have come to realize through the years that the place of power is inside, not outside, and that we determine our view of a place by the level of awareness we bring to it. As a writer I work to observe. By observing, I learn to connect with what is there. As I connect, I break through the distractions of the everyday world and find union with the harmony of the universe. The 'Tao of Writing' is my goal—finding in writing the path with a heart, the process that leads us to greater awareness, no matter what the product."

O

OCHS, Michael 1943-

PERSONAL: Surname is pronounced "oaks"; born February 27, 1943, in Austin, TX; son of Jacob (a doctor) and Gertrude (a housewife; maiden name, Phinn) Ochs. *Education:* Ohio State University, B.A., 1966. *Religion:* Jewish.

ADDRESSES: Home and office—524 Victoria Ave., Venice, CA 90291.

CAREER: Worked as a free-lance photographer in Los Angeles, CA, and later as head of publicity for Columbia, Shelter, and ABC record companies for nearly ten years; founder of Michael Ochs Archives (music consultancy and photo leasing business), 1977—; KCRW-Radio, Santa Monica, CA, host of weekly program "Archives Alive," 1985-87. Instructor in history of rock and roll, University of California, Los Angeles, 1992. Member of National Academy of Recording Arts and Sciences Hall of Fame elections committee.

WRITINGS:

Rock Archives: A Photographic Journey Through the First Two Decades of Rock and Roll, Doubleday, 1985.
Marilyn: March 1955, Delta, 1990.
Elvis in Hollywood, Plume, 1990.

Also compiler of recordings *Chords of Fame,* 1976; *Get Right with God,* by the Swan Silvertones, 1989; *A Toast to Those Who Are Gone,* by Phil Ochs, 1989; *There and Now,* by Phil Ochs, 1990; and *Rock and Roll Wedding Songs, Volumes 1 and 2,* 1992.

WORK IN PROGRESS: Other books from the Michael Ochs Archives; *Dead Blondes; Earl Leaf; Best of Living Blues Magazine; Elvis & Miltie;* and *History of Teen Idols.*

SIDELIGHTS: A self-proclaimed "fanatical fan," Michael Ochs once told *CA:* "I began collecting everything I could to document popular music, including records, photographs, program books, and sheet music, while working as head of publicity for a number of record companies beginning in the late 1960s. In 1977, after getting a number of calls from film and television companies wanting my expertise, I decided to make the Michael Ochs Archives into a full-time business, providing music consultancy, props, or photos to all forms of media. I had been leasing photographs to almost every major publisher in the country when Doubleday asked if I would compile and write the definitive photographic history of rock and roll. They made me a financial offer I couldn't refuse, thus I wrote *Rock Archives.* Up to that time, most rock books had more than adequately covered kings and queens of music, but I tried to cover every foot soldier, too—anybody who made at least one important record."

Ochs recently added, "I am now producing five books on popular culture, listed above as works in progress. I am currently writing a one-hour segment of a ten-hour history of rock and roll documentary for Time-Warner. I have purchased the complete photo files of photographers James Kreigsmann, Earl Leaf, and Stephen Paley, as well as the photographic archives of Charlton Publications and Edrei Communications, which include Laufer Publications' files. In my spare time I play with my dog, Doolittle."

*   *   *

ODAGA, Asenath (Bole) 1937-
(Kituomba)

PERSONAL: Born July 5, 1937, in Rarieda, Kenya; daughter of Blasto Akumu Aum (a farmer and catechist) and Patricia Abuya Abok (a farmer); married James Charles Odaga (a manager), January 27, 1957; children:

Odhiambo Odongo, Akelo, Adhiambo, Awnor. *Education:* Attended Kikuyu Teacher Training College, 1955-56; University of Nairobi, B.A. (with honors), 1974, Dip.Ed., 1974, M.A., 1981. *Religion:* Protestant. *Avocational Interests:* Reading, photography, music, cooking, walking, painting, collecting traditional costumes and other artifacts of Kenyan people.

ADDRESSES: Home—P.O. Box 1743, Kisumu, Kenya.

CAREER: Church Missionary Society's Teacher Training College, Ngiya, Kenya, teacher, 1957-58; teacher at Kambare School, 1957-58; Butere Girls School, Kahamega, Kenya, teacher, 1959-60; Nyakach Girls School, Kisumu district, Kenya, headmistress, 1961-63; Kenya Railways, Nairobi, Kenya, assistant secretary, 1964; Kenya Dairy Board, Nairobi, assistant secretary, 1965-68; Kenya Library Services, Nairobi, secretary, 1968; *East African Standard,* Nairobi, advertising assistant, 1969-70; Kerr Downey and Selby Safaris, Nairobi, advertising and office manager, 1969-70; Christian Churches Educational Association, Nairobi, assistant director of curriculum and development program, 1974-75; Institute of African Studies, University of Nairobi, Nairobi, research fellow, 1976-81; free-lance researcher, writer, and editor, 1982—. Manager of Thu Tinda Bookshop, 1982—, and Lake Publishers and Enterprises, 1982—; affiliated with Odaga & Associates (consulting firm), 1984—. Chair of the board of governors of Nyakach Girls High School; member of Museum Management Committee, Kisumu, 1984—, and vice chair, 1984—.

MEMBER: Writers' Association of Kenya (founding member and secretary, 1978-87), Kenya Association of University Women (chair of Kisumu chapter, 1983-87), Kenya Business and Professional Women's Club (past chair), Rarieda Women's Group, Akala Women's Group (patron).

AWARDS, HONORS: Best Story award from *Voice of Women* magazine, 1967, for short story, "The Suitor," and unpublished play, "Three Brides in an Hour."

WRITINGS:

JUVENILE

The Secret of Monkey the Rock, illustrated by William Agutu, Thomas Nelson, 1966.
Jande's Ambition, illustrated by Adrienne Moore, East African Publishing, 1966.
The Diamond Ring, illustrated by A. Moore, East African Publishing, 1967.
The Hare's Blanket and Other Tales, illustrated by A. Moore, East African Publishing, 1967.
The Angry Flames, illustrated by A. Moore, East African Publishing, 1968.

Sweets and Sugar Cane, illustrated by Beryl Moore, East African Publishing, 1969.
The Villager's Son, illustrated by Shyam Varma, Heinemann Educational (London), 1971.
Kip on the Farm, illustrated by B. Moore, East African Publishing, 1972.
(Editor, with David Kirui and David Crippen) *God, Myself, and Others,* Evangel, 1976.
Kip at the Coast, illustrated by Gay Galsworthy, Evans, 1977.
Kip Goes to the City, illustrated by Galsworthy, Evans, 1977.
Poko Nyar Mugumba (title means "Poko Mugumba's Daughter"), illustrated by Sophia Ojienda, Foundation, 1978.
Thu Tinda: Stories from Kenya, Uzima, 1980.
The Two Friends (folktales), illustrated by Barrack Omondi, Bookwise (Nairobi), 1981.
Kenyan Folk Tales, illustrated by Margaret Humphries, Humphries (Caithness, Scotland), 1981.
(With Kenneth Cripwell) *Look and Write Book One,* Thomas Nelson, 1982.
(With Cripwell) *Look and Learn Book Two,* Thomas Nelson, 1982.
My Home Book One, Lake Publishers (Kisumu), 1983.
Odilo Nungo Piny Kirom (title means "Ogilo, the Arms Can't Embrace the Earth's Waist"), illustrated by H. Kiruikoske, Heinemann Educational (London), 1983.
Nyamgondho Whod Ombare (title means " 'Nyamgondho, the Son of Ombare' and Other Stories"), illustrated by Joseph Odaga, Lake Publishers, 1986.
Munde and His Friends, illustrated by Peter Odaga, Lake Publishers, 1987.
The Rag Ball, illustrated by J. Odaga, Lake Publishers, 1987.
Munde Goes to the Market, illustrated by P. Odaga, Lake Publishers, 1987.
Weche Sigendi gi Timbe Luo Moko (title means "Stories and Some Customs of the Luo"), Lake Publishers, 1987.
Story Time (folktales), Lake Publishers, 1987.

OTHER

Nyathini Koa e Nyuolne Nyaka Higni Adek (title means "Your Child from Birth to Age Three"), Evangel, 1976.
"*Miaha*" (five-act play; title means "The Bride"), first produced in Nairobi, 1981.
(With S. Kichamu Akivaga) *Oral Literature: A School Certificate Course,* Heinemann Educational (Nairobi), 1982.
Simbi Nyaima (four-act play; title means "The Sunken Village"; first produced in Kisumu, 1982), Lake Publishers, 1983.

Nyamgondho (four-act play), first produced in Kisumu, 1983.

Yesterday's Today: The Study of Oral Literature, Lake Publishers, 1984.

The Shade Changes (fiction), Lake Publishers, 1984.

The Storm, Lake Publishers, 1985.

Literature for Children and Young People in Kenya, Kenya Literature Bureau (Nairobi), 1985.

Between the Years (fiction), Lake Publishers, 1987.

A Bridge in Time (fiction), Lake Publishers, 1987.

The Silver Cup (fiction), Lake Publishers, 1987.

Riana's Choice (short stories), Lake Publishers, 1987.

A Taste of Life, Lake Publishers, 1988.

Love Potion and Other Stories, Lake Publishers, 1988.

A Reed on the Roof, Block Ten, with Other Stories, Lake Publishers, 1988.

Member of editorial committee of Western Kenya branch of Wildlife Society. Contributor, sometimes under the name Kituomba, to periodicals, including *Women's Mirror* and *Viva.*

WORK IN PROGRESS: A Luo-English, English-Luo dictionary; a book on Juogi beliefs among the Abasuba of Rusinga Island; a book on Luo oral literature.

SIDELIGHTS: Asenath Odaga told *CA:* "I'm basically a storyteller to both children and adults. And like any other artist, I strive to attain perfection through deeper perception and clear insights into the experiences of life and daily events that go on around me, because it's from some of these common banalities that I draw and fashion some of my writing. I realize that together with all those who possess this creative ability, we have in a small way, in all humility, become cocreators with our gods. In the foregoing realization lies my sensitivity (akin to religion) and profound feelings against injustices meted on others through negation of some of the universal human values on account of race (as in the case in South Africa): creed, gender, and culture.

"What I'm driving at is that art (literature) has several functions apart from providing entertainment. At least this has always been the case in most African societies where art, including literature, was never indulged in just for art's sake—or purely for its aesthetic and entertainment values—but always had several other functions in society."

*   *   *

ODEN, Thomas C(lark)   1931-

PERSONAL: Born October 21, 1931, in Altus, OK; son of Waldo T. (an attorney) and Lily (Clark) Oden; married Edrita Pokorny, August 10, 1952; children: Clark, Ed-

ward, Laura. *Education:* University of Oklahoma, B.A. (honors), 1953; Southern Methodist University, Perkins School of Theology, B.D. (highest honors), 1956; Yale University, M.A., 1958, Ph.D., 1960; post-doctoral study at Heidelberg University, 1965-66.

ADDRESSES: Home—6 Loantaka Ter., Madison, NJ 07940. *Office*—Theological School, Drew University, Madison, NJ 07940.

CAREER: Ordained to Methodist ministry, 1956; Yale University, New Haven, CT, assistant instructor in religion, 1957-58; Southern Methodist University, Perkins School of Theology, Dallas, TX, visiting lecturer, 1958-60; Phillips University, Graduate Seminary, Enid, OK, 1960-70, began as associate professor, became professor of theology and ethics; Drew University, Theological School, Madison, NJ, professor of theology and ethics, 1970-81, Henry Anson Buttz Professor of Theology, 1981—.

MEMBER: American Theological Society, American Academy of Religion, Society for Values in Higher Education, Evangelical Theological Society, Fellowship of Catholic Scholars, Wesleyan Theological Society, Phi Beta Kappa, Phi Eta Sigma.

AWARDS, HONORS: LL.D., Ashbury College, 1990.

WRITINGS:

The Crisis of the World and the Word of God, Methodist Student Movement, 1962.

Radical Obedience: The Ethics of Rudolf Bultmann, with a Response by Rudolf Bultmann, Westminster, 1964.

The Community of Celebration: Toward an Ecclesiology for a Renewing Student Movement, Methodist Student Movement, 1964.

Kerygma and Counseling: Toward a Covenant Ontology for Secular Psychotherapy, Westminster, 1966.

Contemporary Theology and Psychotherapy, Westminster, 1967.

The Structure of Awareness, Abingdon, 1969.

The Promise of Barth: The Ethics of Freedom, Lippincott, 1969.

Beyond Revolution: A Response to the Underground Church, Westminster, 1970.

The Intensive Group Experience: The New Pietism, Westminster, 1972.

After Therapy What?: Lay Therapeutic Resources in Religious Perspectives, C. C. Thomas, 1974.

Game Free: The Meaning of Intimacy, Harper, 1974.

TAG: The Transactional Awareness Game, Harper, 1976.

Should Treatment Be Terminated?, Harper, 1976.

(Editor and author of introduction) *The Parables of Kierkegaard,* Princeton University Press, 1978.

Agenda for Theology: Recovering Christian Roots, Harper, 1979.

Guilt Free, Abingdon Press, 1980.
Pastoral Theology, Harper, 1983.
(Editor) John Wesley, *The New Birth,* Harper, 1984.
Care of Souls in the Classic Tradition, Fortress, 1984.
Conscience and Dividends: Churches and the Multinationals, Ethics and Public Policy Center, 1985.
Crisis Ministries, Crossroad, 1986.
The Living God, Harper, 1986.
Becoming a Minister, Crossroad, 1987.
(Editor) *Phoebe Palmer: Selected Writings,* Paulist, 1988.
Doctrinal Standards in the Wesleyan Tradition, Zondervan, 1988.
Ministry Through Word and Sacrament, Crossroad, 1988.
The Word of Life, Harper, 1988.
Pastoral Counsel, Crossroad, 1989.
First and Second Timothy and Titus, Westminister, 1990.
Life in the Spirit, Harper, 1992.
Two Worlds: Notes on the Death of Modernity in America and Russia, IVP, 1992.
The Transforming Power of Grace, Abingdon, 1993.

Contributor of articles to religious periodicals. Senior editor, *Christianity Today,* 1992—.

WORK IN PROGRESS: The Fathers on Christian Doctrine; The Humor of Kierkegaard; Wesley's Teaching.

SIDELIGHTS: Thomas C. Oden explained in *Christian Century* that after nearly thirty years of studying, writing, and teaching, his focus on history, humanity, and theology has changed somewhat since he published his first book, *The Crisis of the World and the Word of God,* in 1962. He wrote: "I now revel in the mazes and mysteries of perennial theopuzzles: Can God be known? Does God care? Why did God become human? Is Jesus the Christ? How could he be tempted yet without sin? If Father, Son and Spirit, how is God one? How does freedom cooperate with grace? How can the community of celebration both express the holiness of the body of Christ in the world and at the same time engage in the radical transformation of the world? How is it possible daily to refract the holiness of God within the history of sin? How shall I live my present life in relation to final judgment? Not a new question on the list, nor a dull one."

BIOGRAPHICAL/CRITICAL SOURCES:

PERIODICALS

Christian Century, December 12, 1990, pp. 28-31, 1164-1168.
Good News, November/December, 1993, pp. 10-16.
Journal of Evangelical Theological Society, July, 1990.

OLIVER, Mary 1935-

PERSONAL: Born September 10, 1935 in Cleveland, OH; daughter of Edward William (a teacher) and Helen M. (Vlasak) Oliver. *Education:* Attended Ohio State University and Vassar College.

ADDRESSES: Home—Box 338, Provincetown, MA 02657. *Agent*—c/o Molly Malone Cook Literary Agency, Box 338, Provincetown, MA 02657.

CAREER: Case Western Reserve University, Cleveland, OH, Mather Visiting Professor, 1980, 1982; Bucknell University, Lewisburg, PA, poet in residence, 1986; University of Cincinnati, Cincinnati, OH, Elliston Visiting Professor, 1986; Sweet Briar College, Sweet Briar, VA, Margaret Banister Writer in Residence, 1991—.

MEMBER: Poetry Society of America, PEN.

AWARDS, HONORS: First prize, Poetry Society of America, 1962, for "No Voyage;" Devil's Advocate Award, 1968, for "Christmas, 1966;" Shelley Memorial Award, 1972; National Endowment for the Arts fellow, 1972-73; Alice Fay di Castagnola Award, 1973; Guggenheim fellow, 1980-81; Award in Literature, American Academy and Institution of Arts and Letters, 1983; Pulitzer Prize, 1984, for *American Primitive;* Christopher Award and L. L. Winship Award, both 1991, both for *House of Light;* National Book Award for Poetry, 1992, for *New and Selected Poems.*

WRITINGS:

No Voyage, and Other Poems, Dent, 1963, expanded edition, Houghton, 1965.
The River Styx, Ohio, and Other Poems, Harcourt, 1972.
The Night Traveler, Bits Press, 1978.
Twelve Moons, Little, Brown, 1978.
Sleeping in the Forest, Ohio Review Chapbook, 1979.
American Primitive, Little, Brown, 1983.
Dream Work, Atlantic Monthly Press, 1986.
Provincetown, Appletree Alley, 1987.
(Author of introduction) Frank Gaspar, *Holyoke,* Northeastern University Press, 1988.
House of Light, Beacon Press, 1990.
New and Selected Poems, Beacon Press, 1992.
A Poetry Handbook, Harcourt, 1994.

Contributor of poetry to periodicals in England and the United States.

SIDELIGHTS: Poet Mary Oliver is an "indefatigable guide to the natural world," writes Maxine Kumin in *Women's Review of Books,* "particularly to its lesser-known aspects." Oliver's verse focuses on the quiet of occurances of nature: industrious hummingbirds, egrets, motionless ponds, "lean owls / hunkering with their lamp-eyes." Kumin notes of the poet: "She stands quite compfortably on the margins of things, on the line between earth and sky, the thin membrane that separates human from what we losely call animal." The power of Oliver's poetry has earned her numerous awards, including 1984's Pulitzer Prize for *American Primitive* and the National Book Award in 1992 for *New and Selected Poems.* Reviewing *Dream Work* for the *Nation,* critic Alicia Ostriker numbers Oliver among America's finest poets, as "visionary as [Ralph Waldo] Emerson."

American Primitive, according to the *New York Times Book Review*'s Bruce Bennet, "insists on the primacy of the physical." Bennet notes that "recurring images of ingestion" figure throughout the volume and he writes that as we joyfully devour "luscious objects and substances . . . we are continually reminded of our involvement in a process in which what consumes will be consumed." Bennet commends Oliver's "distinctive voice and vision" and asserts that the "collection contains a number of powerful, substantial works." Holly Prado of the *Los Angeles Times Book Review* also applauds Oliver's original voice when she writes that *American Primitive* "touches a vitality in the familiar that invests it with a fresh intensity."

Dream Work continues Oliver's search to "understand both the wonder and pain of nature," according to Prado in a later review for *Los Angeles Times Book Review.* Ostriker sounds this note more specifically when she considers Oliver "among the few American poets who can describe and transmit ecstasy, while retaining a practical awareness of the world as one of predators and prey." Colin Lowndes of *Globe & Mail* similarly considers Oliver "a poet of worked-for reconciliations" whose volume deals with thresholds, or the "points at which opposing forces meet." Both Prado and Ostriker praise Oliver's lyrical gift. Ostriker describes Oliver's verse as "intensely lyrical, flute-like, slender and swift. . . . [riding] on vivid phrases," while Prado calls the poetry of *Dream Work* "the best of the real lyrics we have these days." *Dream Work,* for Ostriker, is ultimately a volume in which Oliver moves "from the natural world and its desires, the 'heaven of appetite' . . . into the world of historical and personal suffering." "She confronts as well, steadily," Ostriker continues, "what she cannot change."

The transition from engaging the natural world to engaging the more personal is also evident in *New and Selected Poems.* The volume contains poems from eight of Oliver's previous volumes as well as previously unpublished, newer work. Susan Salter Reynolds in *Los Angeles Times Book Review* notices that Oliver's earliest poems are almost oriented towards nature, occasionally discuss relatives, but seldom examine her own self. In contrast in her later works she appears constantly. This is, as Reynolds notes, a good thing: "This self-consciousness is a rich and graceful addition." Just as the contributor for *Publishers*

Weekly calls particular attention to the pervasive tone of amazement (also the title of a poem) with regard to things seen in Oliver's work, Reynolds finds Oliver's writings to have a "Blake-eyed revelatory quality." Oliver sums up her desire for amazement in her poem "When Death Comes" from *New and Selected Poems:* "When it's over, I want to say: all my life / I was a bride married to amazement. / I was the bridegroom, taking the world into my arms."

BIOGRAPHICAL/CRITICAL SOURCES:

BOOKS

Oliver, Mary, *New and Selected Poems,* Beacon Press, 1992.

PERIODICALS

Globe & Mail, August 23, 1986.
Los Angeles Times Book Review, August 21, 1983, p. 9; February 22, 1987, p. 8; August 30, 1992, p. 6.
Nation, August, 10, 1986, p. 148-150.
New York Times Book Review, July 17, 1983, p. 10, 22; December 13, 1992, p. 12.
Publishers Weekly, May 4, 1990, p. 62; August 10, 1992, 58.
Women's Review of Books, April, 1993.

*   *   *

OLSEN, Tillie 1913-

PERSONAL: Born January 14, 1913, in Omaha, NE; daughter of Samuel (a laborer and Nebraska state secretary of Socialist Party) and Ida Lerner; married Jack Olsen (a printer), 1936; children: Karla, Julie, Katherine Jo, Laurie. *Education:* High school graduate.

ADDRESSES: Home—1435 Laguna #6, San Francisco, CA 94115. *Agent*—Elaine Markson Literary Agency, 44 Greenwich Ave., New York, NY 10011.

CAREER: Worked in industry and as typist-transcriber. Visiting professor, Amherst College, Amherst, MA, 1969-70, and University of Massachusetts, 1974; visiting instructor, Stanford University, Stanford, CA, 1971; writer in residence, Massachusetts Institute of Technology, Cambridge, MA, 1973; visiting lecturer, University of California, San Diego, CA, 1978; regents lecturer, University of California, Berkeley, CA, 1978; International Visiting Scholar, Norway, 1980; writer-in-residence, Kenyon College, Gambier, OH, 1987—.

AWARDS, HONORS: Stanford University creative writing fellowship, 1956-57; Ford grant in literature, 1959; O. Henry Award, best American short story, 1961, for "Tell Me a Riddle"; Radcliffe Institute for Independent Study fellowship, 1962-64; National Endowment for the Arts grant, 1968; Guggenheim fellowship, 1975-76; award in literature, American Academy and National Institute of Arts and Letters, 1975; University of Nebraska, Doctor of Arts and Letters, 1979; Ministry to Women Award, Unitarian Women's Federation, 1980; Litt.D., Knox College, 1982; MacDowell Colony grant.

WRITINGS:

Tell Me a Riddle: A Collection (stories; also see below), Lippincott, 1961, reprinted, Dell, 1989.
(Author of biographical interpretation) Rebecca Harding Davis, *Life in the Iron Mills* (nonfiction), Feminist Press, 1972.
Yonnondio: From the Thirties (novel), Delacorte, 1974, reprinted, Dell, 1989.
Silences (essays), Delacorte, 1978.
I Stand Here Ironing (play), produced New York, 1981, published as "O Yes" in *Tell Me a Riddle*.
(Editor) *Mother to Daughter, Daughter to Mother: A Daybook and Reader,* Feminist Press, 1984.
(Editor with others) *Mothers and Daughters, That Special Quality: An Exploration in Photographs,* Aperture, 1989.

Short stories appear in more than seventy anthologies, including *Best American Short Stories,* 1957, 1961, and 1971, *Fifty Best American Stories, 1915-1965, Prize Stories: The O. Henry Awards, 1961, Norton Introduction to Literature,* 1977, *Elements of Literature,* 1978, and *The Modern Tradition,* 1979. Contributor to *Ms., Harper's, College English,* and *Trellis.*

A collection of Olsen's manuscripts is housed in the Berg Collection at the New York Public Library.

ADAPTATIONS: "Tell Me a Riddle" was adapted for film by Filmways, 1980. Olsen's stories have been recorded by WBAI radio in New York City and by the Lamont Poetry Room at Harvard University. Some stories have been adapted for theatrical presentation.

SIDELIGHTS: Tillie Olsen writes about those people who, because of their class, sex, or race, have been denied the opportunity to express and develop themselves. In a strongly emotional style, she tells of their dreams and failures, of what she calls "the unnatural thwarting of what struggles to come into being but cannot." Olsen has published relatively little, citing her own life circumstances as the cause. She was forced to delay her writing for some twenty years while working at a number of jobs and raising four children. "Although she has said of herself that she 'may have given in too easily to the demands of family,' she followed the rules of her generation, many of which still apply today," writes Lisa See in *Publishers Weekly.* "Few writers have gained such wide respect on

such a small body of published work," Margaret Atwood points out in the *New York Times Book Review.* "Among women writers in the United States, 'respect' is too pale a word: 'reverence' is more like it. This is presumably because women writers, even more than their male counterparts, recognize what a heroic feat it is to have held down a job, raised four children, and still somehow managed to become and to remain a writer."

The daughter of politically active Jewish immigrants, Olsen was influenced by her parents' philosophies about politics and economics: as a young girl she read the *Comrade,* by age ten she was working after school, and at eighteen she joined the Young Communist League. After leaving high school, Olsen worked various jobs as a laborer, had her first baby, and remained involved politically. During this time Olsen was arrested twice for her political activities. Once she was jailed for organizing workers at a packinghouse in Kansas City, which induced her to write about the terrible conditions in the slaughterhouses in Kansas. At about the same time, Olsen was prompted to begin her first book, *Yonnondio: From the Thirties.* She then left the Midwest for California, became involved in the San Francisco Longshoremen's Strike of 1934, and was arrested and jailed again for her union support. In 1936 she married Jack Olsen, also a union supporter. From 1937 on, Olsen became consumed with her family and was not able to complete *Yonnondio* or continue other writings, focusing her energy instead on raising her four daughters and working as a waitress and secretary to help support them.

Olsen did not begin writing again until 1956 when she received a fellowship from Stanford University after taking a creative writing course at San Francisco State University. During this time she completed two short stories and began a third before she had to revert to regular work. Then, in 1959, Olsen received a Ford Foundation grant and completed the O. Henry award winning short story "Tell Me a Riddle." This novella describes the conflict of a Jewish couple, Eva and David, who have endured thirty-seven years of marriage. The wife, suffering from a terminal disease, also suffers from her husband's insensitivity and her inability to remove herself from the situation. Eva has spent her entire life satisfying the needs of her husband and children and continues to do so through her cancerous death. When David's wish to travel supersedes Eva's need for rest and her desire to be in her own home, he sells their house and they travel the United States, visiting their children along the way. Eva finds her only escape from the continuous demands of her husband and children to be hiding herself in a closet and reliving earlier episodes of her life.

"Tell Me a Riddle" received much critical acclaim. "This novella," comments Margaret B. McDowell in *Contempo-*

rary Novelists, "demonstraters [sic] Olsen's artistry in characterization, dialogue, and sensory appeal, and it fully displays, as does all her fiction, her highly rhythmic and metaphorical use of language." The *Los Angeles Times Book Review*'s Elena Brunet praises Olsen's talent for capturing "the modes of speech of characters" regardless of their age. "Tell Me a Riddle," along with several other short stories, was published in a highly praised collection in 1961, also titled *Tell Me a Riddle.* Speaking of *Tell Me a Riddle,* R. M. Elman of *Commonweal* states that "there are stories in this collection which are perfectly realized works of art."

Teaching positions and grants allowed Olsen to continue to develop her work. Eventually this support allowed her to complete her novel *Yonnondio,* almost forty years after its initial inception. Hailed by some critics as one of the best novels of the 1930s, *Yonnondio* details the life of a poor working class family, the Holbrooks, during the Depression. The story is initially narrated by Mazie Holbrook, the young daughter. Mazie details the family's journey to find work, from Wyoming to North Dakota and then to Chicago. Initially hopeful and responsive, Mazie gradually becomes absorbed by the futility of their plight when the family moves to the city. Her father becomes increasingly more ill-tempered and his reliance on alcohol becomes greater while her mother's health diminishes and the physical and verbal abuse her mother withstands escalates. At this point the narrative is taken over by the mother, Anna. Anna endures the same burden of fulfilling the needs of others before herself as Eva, the female protagonist in *Tell Me A Riddle,* experiences. Her life is absorbed by those around her, her children and her spouse. She endures not only oppression by class and economics, but she also endures oppression by gender. Like Eva, Anna finds her escape in avoiding reality; her solution is to breakdown mentally rather than confront the pain of reality.

Yonnondio was well received, although some critics found the story too depressing and hopeless. *Yonnondio* "is the story of real people who are visibly shackled by having no money at all and by the daily insults offered by the world to their pride," writes a contributor to the *New Yorker.* "By the end of the novel . . . pain, rather than building the Holbrook character, has bleached it out" states Susannah Clapp in her review for the *Times Literary Supplement.* "One of the many difficulties in writing about discomfort as a governing routine is that it reduces the possibility of writing convincingly about pleasure." *Village Voice*'s Bell Gale Chevigny also "found the misery at first too unremitting to feel. Overwritten or over-suffered." Chevigny also notes, however, that the author "moves past this. . . . The deepest impression the book leaves—what keeps it painful but not depressing—is of the inti-

mate knowledge the poor and desperate have of happiness because it is so tenuous." *Yonnondio* "puts the reader through much pain without the release that fulfilled art brings," writes *New Republic*'s John Alfred Avant, commenting on the fragmented revision of *Yonnondio.* But Avant also finds that the novel "offers the opportunity to read a flawed but extraordinary early work knowing that its author would later bring her art to completion." And Catherine R. Stimpson, in her review for the *Nation,* notes that although the condition of poverty "seeks to destroy" the characters, "Olsen's compelling gift is her ability to render lyrically the rhythms of consciousness of victims."

Some critics perceive the book as one of the most important works of the 1930s. "*Yonnondio* is one of the most powerful statements to have emerged from the American 'thirties,' " relates Peter Ackroyd in the *Spectator.* "A young woman has pulled out of that uneasy time a living document which is full of the wear and tear of the period, and she has done so without doctrinaire blues, and without falling into the trap of a sentimentality which is, at bottom, self-pity." Likewise the *Washington Post Book World*'s Jack Salzman asserts, "Yonnondio clearly must take its place as the best novel to come out of the so-called proletarian movement of the '30s." Salzman cautions, however, that to limit the meaning of this work to the 1930s would be an error because "Mrs. Olsen's richness of style, her depth of characterization, and her enormous compassion make *Yonnondio* a work which must not—cannot—be restricted by any particular time or period."

Silences, Olsen's subsequent book, is about the difficulties some people have in writing due to economic, social, or familial obligations, as well as from prejudices against color, class, and gender. Because of these difficulties, Olsen contends, some people have written little or nothing; as a result, these voices are never heard, these stories are never told, and they create a void in the world of literature. Olsen supports her viewpoint with examples from her own experience and as well as the struggles of other authors. She includes selections from other writers to illustrate the optimum conditions for writing, then discusses the obstacles that prohibit writers, especially women, from creating. "Tillie Olsen's remarkable power comes from having almost never written at all," observes Helen McNeil in her *Times Literary Supplement* review. "First a silent, then a vocal conscience for American women's writing, Olsen writes with an elegance, compassion, and directness rare in any period." Commenting on Olsen's emotional voice, *Antioch Review*'s Nolan Miller asserts that *Silences* "bears the stamp of a passionate and reasonably angry voice. What is said here needed to be said." Similarly, David Dillon in the *Southwest Review* finds Olsen "angry, sensitive, persistent" but also notes she "remains fresh and compelling." Salzma summarizes,

"Tillie Olsen is one of the greatest prose stylists now writing. One can only think ruefully of what might have been had she not been 'denied full writing life'—had those 40 years been hers."

BIOGRAPHICAL/CRITICAL SOURCES:

BOOKS

Contemporary Literary Criticism, Gale, Volume 4, 1975, pp. 385-87, Volume 13, 1980, pp. 431-33.
Contemporary Novelists, St. James Press/St. Martin's, 1986, pp. 656-57.
Dictionary of Literary Biography, Volume 28: *Twentieth-Century American-Jewish Fiction Writers,* Gale, 1984, pp. 196-203.
Dictionary of Literary Biography Yearbook: 1980, Gale, 1981, pp. 290-97.
Olsen, Tillie, *Silences,* Delacorte, 1978.
Ruddick, Sara, and Pamela Daniels, editors, *Working It Out,* Pantheon, 1977.

PERIODICALS

American Poetry Review, May/June, 1979.
Antioch Review, fall, 1978.
Atlantic, September, 1978.
Chicago Tribune, October 29, 1961.
Christian Science Monitor, November 9, 1961; September 18, 1978.
Commonweal, December 8, 1961.
Los Angeles Times, May 15, 1980.
Los Angeles Times Book Review, January 8, 1989.
Ms., September, 1974.
Nation, April 10, 1972.
New Leader, May 22, 1978.
New Republic, November 13, 1961; March 30, 1974; December 6, 1975; July 29, 1978, pp. 32-34.
New Yorker, March 25, 1974.
New York Herald Tribune Books, December 17, 1961.
New York Times, July 31, 1978.
New York Times Book Review, November 12, 1961; March 31, 1974; July 30, 1978; June 19, 1983.
Publishers Weekly, November 23, 1984, pp. 76, 79.
Southwest Review, winter, 1979, pp. 105-107.
Spectator, December 14, 1974.
Story, Number 1, 1964.
Studies in Short Fiction, fall, 1963.
Time, October 27, 1961.
Times (London), October 26, 1985.
Times Literary Supplement, January 10, 1975, p. 29; November 14, 1980.
Village Voice, May 23, 1974; August 7, 1978.
Virginia Quarterly Review, fall, 1974.
Washington Post, September 11, 1978; March 30, 1980.
Washington Post Book World, April 7, 1974.
Yale Review, winter, 1979.*

OREL, Harold 1926-

PERSONAL: Born March 31, 1926, in Boston, MA; son of Saul and Sarah (Wicker) Orel; married Charlyn Hawkins, May 25, 1951; children: Sara Elinor, Timothy Ralston. *Education:* University of New Hampshire, B.A., 1948; University of Michigan, M.A., 1949, Ph.D., 1952.

ADDRESSES: Home—713 Schwarz Rd., Lawrence, KS 66049. *Office*—Department of English, University of Kansas, Lawrence, KS 66045-2115.

CAREER: University of Maryland, College Park, instructor, 1952-56, instructor in overseas program, 1954-55; General Electric, Evendale, OH, publications specialist, 1957; University of Kansas, Lawrence, associate professor, 1957-62, professor of English, 1962-74, university distinguished professor, 1974—. Lecturer at several universities in Japan and India, and at Westminster Abbey. Consultant, Midwest Research Institute, Kansas City, MO. *Military service:* U.S. Navy, 1944-46.

MEMBER: Modern Language Association of America, American Committee on Irish Studies (vice-president, 1960-70; president, 1970-72; member of executive committee, 1972—), Thomas Hardy Society (vice-president, 1968—).

WRITINGS:

Thomas Hardy's Epic-Drama: A Study of "The Dynasts," University of Kansas Press, 1963.
The Development of William Butler Yeats, 1885-1900, University of Kansas Press, 1968.
English Romantic Poets and the Enlightenment: Nine Essays on a Literary Relationship, Voltaire Foundation, 1973.
The Final Years of Thomas Hardy, 1912-1928, Macmillan, 1976.
Victorian Literary Critics, Macmillan, 1984.
The Literary Achievement of Rebecca West, Macmillan, 1985.
The Victorian Short Story, Cambridge University Press, 1986.
The Unknown Thomas Hardy: Lesser Known Aspects of Hardy's Life and Career, Harvester Press, 1987.
A Kipling Chronology, Macmillan, 1990.
Popular Fiction in England, 1914-1918, Harvester Wheatsheaf Press, 1991.

EDITOR AND CONTRIBUTOR

(With G. J. Worth) *Six Studies in Nineteenth Century English Literature and Thought,* University of Kansas Press, 1962.
(With Worth) *The Nineteenth-Century Writer and His Audience,* University of Kansas Press, 1969.

Irish History and Culture: Aspects of a People's Heritage, Regents Press of Kansas, 1976.

EDITOR

The World of Victorian Humor, Appleton, 1961.

Thomas Hardy's Personal Writings, University of Kansas Press, 1966.

(With Paul Wiley) *British Poetry, 1880-1920: Edwardian Voices,* Appleton, 1969.

Thomas Hardy, *The Dynasts,* Macmillan, 1978.

The Scottish World, Abrams, 1981.

Kipling: Interviews and Recollections (two volumes), Macmillan, 1983.

Victorian Short Stories: An Anthology, Everyman's Library, 1987.

Critical Essays on Rudyard Kipling, G. K. Hall, 1989.

Victorian Short Stories 2: The Trials of Love, Everyman's Library, 1990.

Sir Arthur Conan Doyle: Interviews and Recollections, St. Martin's Press, 1991.

Critical Essays on Sir Arthur Conan Doyle, G. K. Hall, 1992.

Contributor to books, including *Thomas Hardy and the Modern World,* edited by Frank B. Pinion, Thomas Hardy Society, 1974; *The Genius of Thomas Hardy,* edited by Margaret Drabble, Weidenfeld & Nicolson, 1976; and *Budmouth Essays on Thomas Hardy,* edited by Pinion, Thomas Hardy Society, 1976.

SIDELIGHTS: In his several works on British writers of the late nineteenth and early twentieth centuries, Harold Orel writes from the perspective of both the literary historian and the literary critic. For instance, in *The Final Years of Thomas Hardy, 1912-1928,* Orel offers biographical information as well as a poetic analysis of Hardy's later writings, in which the novelist/poet reexamined his own past. Walter Wright, in the *Prairie Schooner,* noted: "Professor Orel's preparation for a new book on Hardy includes his study of Hardy's philosophy in *Thomas Hardy's Epic Drama,* 1963, and the editing of *Thomas Hardy's Personal Writings,* 1966. What he has to say about a given poem or biographical fact is consequently supported by years of immersion in Hardy's life and thought." In addition to discussing Hardy's later work, Orel also captures the noted author's personal feelings about religion and civilization both during and after World War I. Wright concluded, "*The Final Years* achieves the kind of chiaroscuro to which Hardy liked to refer, which renders distinct and at the same time subdued the lineaments of a still searching mind as it reflected upon the long decades of two centuries."

Orel's *Kipling: Interviews and Recollections* is a compilation of stories and anecdotes about English author Rudyard Kipling. "Kipling's fame was global, not confined merely to the English-speaking world," wrote T. J. Binyon in the *Times Literary Supplement.* Bryan Appleyard agreed with this assessment in the London *Times,* where he wrote that Kipling "was a bestseller before the miniseries was invented. He was the voice of every soldier who stoically fulfilled his duties under the Indian sun and the keen moralist of the burdens of empire." Binyon concluded that Kipling was a "public figure, determined to be private: the combination makes [him] an awkward subject for recollection."

Orel attempted to solve the difficulties in chronicling Kipling's life by drawing from a wide range of sources. However, Binyon said that much of the material "has previously been picked over . . . there are no plums left, just an occasional interesting or amusing detail." Appleyard noted that the book contains "dozens of anecdotes, dim recollections and shaky insights from the largely undistinguished types who bumped into Kipling and were at once overwhelmed." Although Binyon found the book lacking in important stories about Kipling, he felt that the "editing of the collection [was] scrupulous." And Appleyard suggested Orel's book "provides fleeting clues to the writer behind the attitudes," and concluded that it reveals Kipling to be "a hearty, hardworking chap who was reluctant to place too much faith in dreams, little realizing that they were the very reality he was pursuing."

With *The Victorian Short Story* Orel once again discusses and analyzes the work of Hardy and Kipling, as well as that of William Carleton, Joseph Sheridan Le Fanu, Charles Dickens, Anthony Trollope, Robert Louis Stevenson, Joseph Conrad and H. G. Wells, but from a new angle—that of the short fiction they produced. Orel argues that the growing popularity of short stories at this time was linked to the flourishing of Victorian periodical presses and a publishing industry interested in offering entertainment as well as more serious scholarship. In the *Times Higher Education Supplement,* reviewer Michael Wheeler described Orel's book as "a pioneering study," and he noted the work combines ". . . two discrete activities— historical/contextual research and critical revaluation." He added, "The book's historical method works most effectively when applied to the relationships between writers and their publishers, editors and reading public. . . ."

Orel once told *CA:* "I am grateful to the generations of critics and scholars who have gone before me, and who have taught me to read literary texts with greater sensitivity than I could have done unaided. I owe them a debt for which all the books I have written, and am yet to write, can provide only a partial repayment."

BIOGRAPHICAL/CRITICAL SOURCES:

PERIODICALS

Contemporary Review (London), November, 1986.
Hudson Review, autumn, 1977.
International Fiction Review, Volume 14, number 1, 1987.
Journal of English and German Philology, October, 1977.
Modern Fiction Studies, summer, 1978.
Prairie Schooner, spring, 1977.

Sewanee Review, April, 1978.
South Atlantic Quarterly, summer, 1977; summer, 1985.
Times (London), August 16, 1984.
Times Higher Education Supplement, October 3, 1986, p. 18.
Times Literary Supplement, May 25, 1984; October 26, 1984.
Victorian Studies, spring, 1978.
Virginia Quarterly Review, spring, 1977.*

P

PARRISH, Michael E(merson) 1942-

PERSONAL: Born March 4, 1942, in Huntington Park, CA; son of Emerson W. and Mabel (Weidemann) Parrish; married Caryl Smith, April, 1963; children: Scott David, Stephanie Lynn. *Education:* University of California, Riverside, B.A. (with high honors), 1964; Yale University, M.A., 1966, Ph.D., 1968. *Politics:* Democrat. *Religion:* Unitarian Universalist.

ADDRESSES: Home—1115 Aloha Dr., Encinitas, CA. *Office*—Department of History, University of California, San Diego, P.O. Box 109, La Jolla, CA 92039.

CAREER: University of California, San Diego, La Jolla, assistant professor, 1968-73, associate professor, 1973-80, professor of history, 1980—.

MEMBER: American Historical Association, Organization of American Historians.

AWARDS, HONORS: Woodrow Wilson fellow, 1964-65.

WRITINGS:

Securities Regulation and the New Deal, Yale University Press, 1970.
(Contributor) Richard Traina and Armin Rappaport, editors, *Source Problems in American History,* Macmillan, 1971.
Mexican Workers, Progressives, and Copper: The Failure of Industrial Democracy in Arizona during the Wilson Years, Chicano Research Publications, University of California (La Jolla), 1979.
Felix Frankfurter and His Times: The Reform Years, Volume I, Macmillan, 1982.
(Editor with David M. Kennedy) *Power and Responsibility: Case Studies in American Leadership,* Harcourt, 1986.

Anxious Decades: America in Prosperity and Depression, 1920-1941, Norton, 1992.

Also contributor to periodicals, including *American Historical Review* and *The Historian.*

WORK IN PROGRESS: Second volume of Felix Frankfurter biography.

SIDELIGHTS: Felix Frankfurter and His Times: The Reform Years, Volume I, the first in a projected two-volume biography of the eminent American jurist, was published in the centennial year of Frankfurter's birth. It also appeared in the wake of two other widely noted books on the same subject—*The Enigma of Felix Frankfurter,* by E. N. Hirsch, which took a psychoanalytic approach toward its subject, and *The Brandeis-Frankfurter Connection,* by Bruce Murphy, which tried to paint Frankfurter—along with his mentor, Louis Brandeis—as corrupt. "Frankfurter's admirers will find considerably more to cheer about in . . . *Felix Frankfurter and His Times,*" asserted David Margolick in the *New York Times.* Parrish's book also received an enthusiastic notice from financial consultant Eliot Janeway, who reviewed the book for the *Los Angeles Times Book Review.* Janeway called Parrish's work "a great book, an indispensable mother lode for all serious students of the era encompassed by the careers of Theodore and Franklin Roosevelt."

Though Parrish effectively uses an approach which Janeway calls "historical sociology" to thoroughly document Frankfurter's rise to fame and importance as a public figure, some reviewers felt that he was less successful in revealing the private Frankfurter. Margolick claimed that Parrish's neglect of Frankfurter's personality and private life produced a less than interesting, if commendably "sober" and "dispassionate," biography. Alan Brinkley, in the *New York Times Book Review,* also expressed a mixture of admiration for the political and legal side of the book's treatment and disappointment with its biographical aspect. Yet Brinkley summarized the book as an "able new study," admittting that the enigmatic nature of Parrish's biography was in no small part a reflection of the subject himself. Margolick, meanwhile, concluded his review with this advice for readers curious about Felix Frankfurter: "by all means read the Parrish book."

BIOGRAPHICAL/CRITICAL SOURCES:

PERIODICALS

Los Angeles Times Book Review, June 13, 1982, p. 2.
New York Times, June 26, 1982.
New York Times Book Review, August 1, 1982, pp. 10, 21.
Washington Post Book World, June 6, 1982, p. 4.*

*   *   *

PATTEN, Brian   1946-

PERSONAL: Born February 7, 1946, in Liverpool, England; son of Ireen Stella Bevan. *Education:* Attended secondary school in Sefton Park, Liverpool, England.

ADDRESSES: c/o Puffin Books, 27 Wrights Lane, London W8 5TZ, England.

CAREER: Writer. Has worked occasionally as a journalist, gardener, and newspaper vendor. University of California, San Diego, Regents Lecturer, 1985.

MEMBER: Chelsea Arts Club.

AWARDS, HONORS: Eric Gregory Award for poetry, 1967; Pernod Poetry Award, 1967; Arts Council Grant, 1969; special award, Mystery Writers of America, 1977, for *Mr. Moon's Last Case.*

WRITINGS:

POETRY

Portraits, privately printed, 1962.
(With Roger McGough and Adrian Henri) *The Mersey Sound: Penguin Modern Poets 10,* Penguin, 1967, revised and enlarged edition, 1974.
Little Johnny's Confession, Allen & Unwin, 1967.
The Home Coming, Turret Books, 1969.
Notes to the Hurrying Man: Poems, Winter '66-Summer '68, Hill & Wang, 1969.
The Irrelevant Song, Sceptre Press, 1970, revised edition, Allen & Unwin, 1975.
At Four O'Clock in the Morning, Sceptre Press, 1971.
The Irrelevant Song and Other Poems, Allen & Unwin, 1971, revised edition, 1980.
Walking Out: The Early Poems of Brian Patten, illustrated by Pamlar Kindred, Transican, 1971.

(Contributor) John Fairfax, editor, *Double Image: Five Poems by Michael Baldwin, John Fairfax and Brian Patten,* Longman, 1972.
The Eminent Professors and the Nature of Poetry as Enacted Out by Members of the Poetry Seminar One Rainy Evening, Poem-of-the-Month Club (London), 1972.
The Unreliable Nightingale, Rota, 1973.
Vanishing Trick, Allen & Unwin, 1976.
Grave Gossip, Allen & Unwin, 1979.
Love Poems, Allen & Unwin, 1981.
(Selector and author of introduction) Eric Robinson, editor, *Clare's Countryside: A Book on John Clare,* illustrated by Ann Arnold, Heinemann, 1981.
(With Henri and McGough) *New Volume,* Penguin, 1983.
Storm Damage, Unwin Hyman, 1988.
Grinning Jack: Selected Poems, Unwin, 1990.

Poetry anthologized in *The Liverpool Scene,* edited by E. L. Smith, Rapp & Carroll, 1967, and in *The Oxford Book of 20th Century English Verse,* edited by Phillip Larkin, 1977. Former editor of *Underdog* (English poetry magazine).

FOR CHILDREN

The Elephant and the Flower: Almost-Fables, illustrated by Meg Rutherford, Allen & Unwin, 1970.
Jumping Mouse (adaptation of American Indian folktale), Allen & Unwin, 1972.
Manchild, Covent Garden Press, 1973.
Two Stories (short stories), Covent Garden Press, 1973.
(Editor with Pat Krett) *The House That Jack Built: Poems for Shelter,* Allen & Unwin, 1973.
The Pig and the Junk Hill (play), first produced at Everyman Theatre, Liverpool, 1975.
Emma's Doll, Allen & Unwin, 1976.
Mr. Moon's Last Case, illustrated by Mary Moore, Allen & Unwin, 1975, Scribner, 1977.
The Sly Cormorant and the Fishes: New Adaptations into Poetry of the Aesop Fables, illustrated by Errol Le Cain, Kestrel, 1977.
(Editor) *Gangsters, Ghosts, and Dragon Flies: A Book of Story Poems,* illustrated by Terry Oakes, Allen & Unwin, 1981.
Gargling with Jelly: A Collection of Poems, illustrated by David Mostyn, Kestrel, 1985, large print edition, Clio, 1990.
Jimmy Tag-along, illustrated by Mostyn, Kestrel, 1988.
Thawing Frozen Frogs, Viking, 1990.
(Editor) *The Puffin Book of Twentieth Century Children's Verse,* illustrated by Michael Foreman, Viking, 1991.
Grizzelda Frizzle and Other Stories, Viking, 1992.

Also author of stage plays *Riddle-me-hights* and *The Tinder Box,* both produced in England, and of a stage adaptation of *Gargling with Jelly.*

OTHER

Author of plays *The Mouth Trap* (with McGough), 1982, and *Blind Love,* British Broadcasting Corporation (BBC), 1983. Regular contributor of programs to BBC.

ADAPTATIONS: Selections from Little Johnny's Confession and Notes to the Hurrying Man and New Poems (recording), Caedmon, 1969; *Vanishing Trick* (recording), Tangent, 1976; *The Sly Cormorant* (recording; read by Patten and Cleo Laine), Argo Records, 1978; *Gargling with Jelly* (audiocassette), HarperCollins, 1993.

SIDELIGHTS: Discussing his works for children, Brian Patten once remarked, "I am interested in fantasy, but always set the fantastic against realistic backgrounds, so that the everyday world is put into different perspective. I feel that this combination helps to develop the imagination. It is also a way of commenting on our hopes and fears. 'Reality' is not constant. Each child and adult creates his own version of it, depending on his needs."

BIOGRAPHICAL/CRITICAL SOURCES:

PERIODICALS

Books and Bookmen, May, 1967; November, 1967; June, 1969.
London Magazine, August, 1968; December, 1969.
New Statesman, April 25, 1969.
Observer, June 18, 1967.
Poetry, autumn, 1968, May, 1971.
Spectator, June 6, 1987.
Times (London), April 28, 1990; November 30, 1991; December 7, 1991.
Times Literary Supplement, July 13, 1967; July 27-August 2, 1990, p. 803; November 22, 91, p. 22.

* * *

PAYNE, Alan
    See JAKES, John (William)

* * *

PERSE, St.-John
    See LEGER, (Marie-Rene Auguste) Alexis Saint-Leger

PIERCY, Marge 1936-

PERSONAL: Born March 31, 1936, in Detroit, MI; daughter of Robert Douglas and Bert Bedoyna (Bunnin) Piercy; married third husband, Ira Wood, June 2, 1982. *Education:* University of Michigan, A.B., 1957; Northwestern University, M.A., 1958. *Politics:* Democrat. *Religion:* Jewish.

ADDRESSES: Home—Box 1473, Wellfleet, MA 02667. *Agent*—Lois Wallace, Wallace Literary Agency, Inc., 177 East 70th St., New York, NY.

CAREER: Writer. Indiana University, Gary, instructor, 1960-62; University of Kansas, Lawrence, poet-in-residence, 1971; Thomas Jefferson College and Grand Valley State College, Allendale, MI, distinguished visiting lecturer, 1975-76, 1978, and 1980; Fine Arts Work Center, Provincetown, MA, staff member, 1976-77; College of the Holy Cross, Worcester, MA, writer-in-residence, 1976; Cazenovia College, NY, Women's Writers Conference, visiting faculty, 1976, 1978, 1980; Purdue University, West Layfeyette, IN, summer write-in, 1977; State University of New York, Buffalo, Butler professor of letters, 1977; Cumberland Valley Writers Conference, Nashville TN, poetry workshop, 1981; Ohio State University, Columbus, fiction writer-in-residence, 1985; University of California at San Jose, poetry and fiction workshops, 1985; University of Cincinnati, Cincinnati, OH, Elliston poetry fellow, 1986; University of Michigan, Ann Arbor, DeRoy distinguished visiting professor, 1992.

Also active in political and civic organizations, including Students for a Democratic Society, 1965-69, and North American Congress on Latin America, 1966-67. Consultant, New York State Council on the Arts, 1971, Lower Cape Women's Center, 1973-76, Massachusetts Foundation for Humanities and Council on the Arts, 1974 and Wesleyan University Press Poetry Program, 1982—; member of boards of directors, Transition House, 1976, Massachusetts Foundation of Humanities and Public Policy, 1978-85, and Coordinating Council of Literary Magazines, 1982-85; advisory board member, National Forum, 1979-83, Massachusetts Foundation for Humanities and Public Policy, 1986—, Massachusetts Council on the Arts and Humanities, 1986-88, Massachusetts Arts Lottery Council, 1988-89, and Israeli Center for the Arts Literature, Israeli Center for the Creative Arts (HILAI), and National Endowment for the Arts, all 1989—; member, Writers Board, 1985-86, International Board, Israeli Center for Creative Arts, 1986-88, and ALEPH, 1993; advisor, Siddur Project, P'nai Or, 1986—; member of artistic advisory board, American Poetry Center, 1988—, and Am-Ha-Yam, 1988—; literary advisory poetry panel, National Endowment for the Arts, 1989; and governor's appointee to Massachusetts Cultural Council, 1990-91.

MEMBER: PEN, National Organization for Women, Authors Guild, Authors League, National Writers Union, Poetry Society of America, National Audubon Society, Massachusetts Audubon Society, New England Poetry Club.

AWARDS, HONORS: Avery and Jule Hopwood Award, University of Michigan, for poetry and fiction, 1956, and for poetry, 1957; Borestone Mountain Poetry Award, 1968 and 1974; literary award, Massachusetts Governor Communication on the Status of Women, 1974; National Endowment for the Arts award, 1978; Faculty Association medal, Rhode Island School of Design, 1985; Carolyn Kizer Poetry Prize, 1986 and 1990; Sheaffer Eaton-PEN New England Award for Literary Excellence, 1989; Golden Rose Poetry Prize, New England Poetry Club (NEPC), 1990; May Sarton Award, NEPC, 1991; Brit ha-Darot Award, Shalom Center, 1992; Barbara Bradley Award, NEPC, 1992; Arthur C. Clarke Award for best science fiction novel in the United Kingdom, 1992; named James B. Angell and Lucinda Goodrich Downs Scholar; Orion Scott Award in Humanities; honorary Litt.D., Bridgewater State College.

WRITINGS:

POETRY

Breaking Camp, Wesleyan University Press, 1968.
Hard Loving, Wesleyan University Press, 1969.
(With Bob Hershon, Emmet Jarrett, and Dick Lourie) *4-Telling,* Crossing Press, 1971.
To Be of Use, Doubleday, 1973.
Living in the Open, Knopf, 1976.
The Twelve-Spoked Wheel Flashing, Knopf, 1978.
The Moon Is Always Female, Knopf, 1980.
Circles on the Water: Selected Poems of Marge Piercy, Knopf, 1982.
Stone, Paper, Knife, Knopf, 1983.
My Mother's Body, edited by Nancy Nicholas, Knopf, 1985.
Available Light, Knopf, 1988.
Mars and Her Children, Knopf, 1992.

NOVELS

Going Down Fast, Trident, 1969.
Dance the Eagle to Sleep, Doubleday, 1970.
Small Changes, Doubleday, 1973.
Woman on the Edge of Time, Knopf, 1976.
The High Cost of Living, Harper, 1978.
Vida, Summit, 1980.
Braided Lives, Summit, 1982.
Fly Away Home, Summit, 1984.
Gone to Soldiers, Summit, 1987.
Summer People, Summit, 1989.

He, She and It, Knopf, 1991, published in England as *Body of Glass,* Michael Joseph, 1992.

RECORDINGS

Marge Piercy: Poems, Radio Free People, 1969.
Laying Down the Tower, Black Box, 1973.
Reclaiming Ourselves, Radio Free People, 1974.
Reading and Thoughts, Everett/Edwards, 1976.
At the Core, Watershed Tapes, 1976.

OTHER

The Grand Coolie Damn, New England Free Press, 1970.
(With Ira Wood) *The Last White Class: A Play about Neighborhood Terror* (produced in Northampton, MA, 1978), Crossing Press, 1979.
Parti-Colored Blocks for a Quilt: Poets on Poetry (essays), University of Michigan Press, 1982.
(Editor) *Early Ripening: American Women Poets Now,* Unwin Hyman, 1988.
The Earth Shines Secretly: A Book of Days, Zoland Books, 1990.

Work represented in over 100 anthologies, including *Best Poems of 1967, New Women, The Fact of Fiction,* and *Psyche: The Feminine Poetic Consciousness.* Contributor of poetry, fiction, essays and reviews to periodicals, including *Paris Review, Transatlantic Review, Mother Jones, New Republic, Village Voice,* and *Prairie Schooner.* Advisory editor for *APHRA,* 1975-77, and *Poetry on the Buses,* 1979-81, and poetry editor for *Tikkun,* 1988—.

Piercy's books have been translated into many foreign languages, including French, Dutch, Italian, Japanese, Hebrew, German, Norwegian, Swedish, Turkish, and Danish.

Piercy's manuscript collection and archives are housed at the University of Michigan Harlan Hatcher Graduate Library.

ADAPTATIONS: *Gone to Soldiers* has been designed for Macintosh Power Books, Voyager Co., 1992.

WORK IN PROGRESS: A novel, *The Longings of Women.*

SIDELIGHTS: Feminist poet/novelist Marge Piercy writes about the oppression of individuals she sees in our society, infusing her works with political statements, autobiographical elements, and realist and utopian perspectives. "Almost alone among her American contemporaries, Marge Piercy is radical and writer simultaneously, her literary identity so indivisible that it is difficult to say where one leaves off and the other begins," writes Elinor Langer in the *New York Times Book Review.* A prominent and sometimes controversial writer, Piercy first became politically active in the 1960s, when she joined the civil rights movement and became an organizer for Students for a Democratic Society (SDS). After a few years, she concluded that the male power structure associated with the mainstream capitalist society was also operating in the anti-war movement and that women were being relegated to subservient work. In 1969, Piercy shifted her allegiance to the fledgling women's movement, where her sympathies have remained.

Piercy openly acknowledges that she wants her writing—particularly some of her poems—to be "useful." "What I mean by useful," she explained in the introduction to *Circles on the Water*, "is simply that readers will find poems that speak to and for them, will take those poems into their lives and say them to each other and put them up on the bathroom wall and remember bits and pieces of them in stressful or quiet moments. That the poems may give voice to something in the experience of a life has been my intention. To find ourselves spoken for in art gives dignity to our pain, our anger, our lust, our losses. We can hear what we hope for and what we most fear in the small release of cadenced utterance."

Piercy's moralistic stance, more typical of nineteenth- than twentieth-century writers, has alienated some critics, producing charges that she is more committed to her politics than to her craft. The notion makes Piercy bristle. "As a known feminist I find critics often naively imagine I am putting my politics directly into the mouth of my protagonist," she told Michael Luzzi in an interview collected in *Parti-Colored Blocks for a Quilt*. "That I could not possibly be amused, ironic, interested in the consonances and dissonances. . . . They notice what I have created and assume I have done so blindly, instead of artfully, and I ask again and again, why? I think reviewers and academics have the fond and foolish notion that they are smarter than writers. They also assume if you are political, you are simpler in your mental apparatus than they are; whereas you may well have the same background in English and American literature they have, but add to it a better grounding in other European and Asian and South American literatures, and a reasonable degree of study of philosophy and political theory." Fellow feminist and poet Erica Jong has sympathized with Piercy's dilemma, writing in the *New York Times Book Review* that Piercy is "an immensely gifted poet and novelist whose range and versatility have made it hard for her talents to be adequately appreciated critically."

Piercy's sense of politics is deep-rooted. She grew up poor and white in a predominantly black section of Detroit. Her mother was a housewife with a tenth-grade education and her father a millwright who repaired and installed machinery. From her surroundings, Piercy learned about the inequities of the capitalist system: "You see class so clearly there," she told Celia Betsky in the *New York Times Book*

Review. "The indifference of the rich, racism, the strength of different groups, the working-class pitted against itself."

By winning a scholarship to the University of Michigan, Piercy became the first person in her family to attend college. She was an enthusiastic student, encouraged in her writing by winning several Hopwood awards. Still, professional success did not come easily. Ten years elapsed before Piercy was able to give up a series of odd jobs and support herself by writing. Her first six novels were rejected, and she suspects that *Going Down Fast* found a publisher largely because of its lack of women's consciousness and its male protagonist.

Despite such resistance, Piercy kept writing political novels featuring female characters, often with backgrounds similar to her own. In 1973, she published *Small Changes,* a novel that *New Republic* contributing critic Diane Schulder calls "one of the first to explore the variety of life-styles that women . . . are adopting in order to give meaning to their personal and political lives." Addressing women's issues head on, this book conveys what *New York Times Book Review* contributing critic Sara Blackburn calls "that particular quality of lost identity and desperation, which, once recognized as common experience, has sparked the rage and solidarity of the women's liberation movement." In an essay she wrote for *Women's Culture: The Women's Renaissance of the Seventies,* Piercy describes the book as "an attempt to produce in fiction the equivalent of a full experience in a consciousness-raising group for many women who would never go through that experience."

To demonstrate the way that female subjugation cuts across social strata, Piercy includes both a working class woman, Beth, and a middle class intellectual, Miriam, as main characters in *Small Changes.* In her depiction of these women, Piercy concentrates on what Catharine R. Stimpson of the *Nation* calls "the creation of a new sexuality and a new psychology, which will permeate and bind a broad genuine equality. So doing, [Piercy] shifts the meaning of small change." Stimpson continues: "The phrase no longer refers to something petty and cheap but to the way in which a New Woman, a New Man, will be generated: one halting step after another. The process of transformation will be as painstaking as the dismantling of electrified barbed wire."

Widely reviewed by established magazines and newspapers, *Small Changes* has received qualified praise. No critics dismiss the novel as unimportant, and most commend Piercy's energy and intelligence, but many object to the rhetoric of the book. "There is not a good, even tolerable man in the whole lot of characters," observes Margaret Ferrari in her *America* review. "While the women in the novel are in search of themselves, the men are mostly out to destroy themselves and anyone who crosses their paths. The three main ones in the novel are, without exception, stereotyped monsters." For this reason, Ferrari describes her reaction to the novel as "ambivalent. The realistic Boston and New York locales are enjoyable. The poetry is alluring and the characters' lives are orchestrated so that shrillness is always relieved. . . . In short, the novel is absorbing despite its political rhetoric." After praising Piercy's "acute" social reportage and her compelling story line, Richard Todd raises a similar objection. "What is absent in this novel is an adequate sense of the oppressor," he writes in the *Atlantic*. "And beyond that a recognition that there are limits to a world view that is organized around sexual warfare. It's hard not to think that Piercy feels this, knows that much of the multiplicity and mystery of life is getting squeezed out of her prose, but her polemical urge wins out."

Piercy challenges the validity of such criticisms. "People tend to define 'political' or 'polemical' in terms of what is not congruent with their ideas," she told Karla Hammond in an interview collected in *Parti-Colored Blocks for a Quilt*. "In other words, your typical white affluent male reviewer does not review a novel by Norman Mailer as if it were political the same way he would review a novel by Kate Millet. Yet both are equally political. The defense of the status quo is as political as an attack on it. A novel which makes assumptions about men and women is just as political if they're patriarchial assumptions as if they're feminist assumptions. Both have a political dimension." And a few reviewers concede their biases. William Archer, for instance, speculates in his *Best Sellers* review that "the special dimension of this book becomes apparent only through a determined suspension of one's preconceptions and a reexamination of their validity."

If *Small Changes* delineates the oppression of women, *Woman on the Edge of Time* affords a glimpse of a better world. The story of a woman committed to a mental hospital and her periodic time travels into the future, the novel juxtaposes the flawed present against a utopian future. "My first intent was to create an image of a good society," writes Piercy in *Women's Culture: The Women's Renaissance of the Seventies*, "one that was not sexist, racist, or imperialist: one that was cooperative, respectful of all living beings, gentle, responsible, loving, and playful. The result of a full feminist revolution." Despite a cool reception by critics, *Woman on the Edge of Time* remains one of Piercy's personal favorites. "It's the best I've done so far," she wrote in 1981.

With *Vida*, her sixth novel, Piercy returns to the real world of the sixties and seventies, cataloging the breakdown of the anti-war movement and focusing on a political fugitive who will not give up the cause. Named for its main character, Davida Asch, the novel cuts back and forth from past to present, tracing Vida's evolution from liberal to activist to a member of a radical group called the Network. Still on the run for her participation in a ten-year-old bombing, Vida must contend with a splintered group that has lost its popular appeal as well as the nagging temptation to slip back into society and resume normal life. "The main action is set in the autumn of 1979," explains Jennifer Uglow in the *Times Literary Supplement*, "as Vida faces divorce from her husband (turned media liberal and family man), her mother's final illness, her sister's imprisonment and the capture of an old colleague and lover. The pain of these separations is balanced against the hope offered by a new lover, Joel." At the story's close, Joel, a draft dodger, is captured by the Federal Bureau of Investigation and Vida, for whom the loss is acute, is not certain she can continue. But she does. "What swept through us and cast us forward is a force that will gather and rise again," she reflects, hunching her shoulders and disappearing into the night.

A former political organizer, Piercy writes from an insider's point of view, and critics contend that this affects the novel. "There is no perspective, there are not even any explanations," notes Langer in the *New York Times Book Review*. "Why we are against the war, who the enemy is, what measures are justified against the state—all these are simply taken for granted." And while a state of "war" may well exist between American capitalists and American radicals, the 1960s revolutionaries are not of the same caliber as the French Resistance workers or the Yugoslav partisans, according to *Village Voice* contributing reviewer Vivian Gornick. "Vida Asch and her comrades are a parody of the Old Left when the Old Left was already a parody of itself," she maintains.

Politics aside, reviewers find much that is praiseworthy in the novel. "The real strength of the book lies not in its historical analysis but in the power with which the loneliness and desolation of the central characters are portrayed," notes Uglow. Lore Dickstein calls it "an extraordinarily poignant statement on what has happened to some of the middle-class children of the Sixties," in the *Saturday Review*. And Langer commends *Vida* as "a fully controlled, tightly structured dramatic narrative of such artful intensity that it leads the reader on at almost every page."

In Piercy's following novel, *Braided Lives*, she "reminds us, growing up female in the 1950s hurt," writes Brina Caplan in a review for the *Nation*. Jill Stuart, the protagonist, relates how difficult it was for women to survive this time period with esteem and independence intact. Jill describes the obstacles and events that challenged young girls coming of age in the 1950s, including attitudes toward sex, career, marriage, rape, abortion, lesbianism, verbal and physical abuse, sexual harassment, and women in general.

Braided Lives affects us by contrast—by distinctions made between then and now, between those who have and have not survived and, most important, between the subtleties of individual development and the more general movement of history," states Caplan.

In the novel, Jill finds life at home almost unbearable; her father is indifferent and her mother is manipulative. Her parents expect that she will follow traditional ways and get married after high school, have children, and be a homemaker. Jill manages to escape this prescribed female role when she receives a scholarship to college. At college she and her friends vow never to end up as their mothers. "I don't know a girl who does not say, 'I don't want to live like my mother,' " Jill asserts in *Braided Lives*. Jill and her female friends enjoy their initial independence at college; they discuss philosophy and politics and engage in sexual experimentation. But these women are ambivalent and unsure of what they really want out of life. "One moment they [the female characters] are declaiming the need for total honesty with men and vowing that they will never end up possessive and dependent like their mothers. The next, they will do something 'castrating' to their boyfriends, in whom they wouldn't dream of confiding their frequent pregnancy scares," points out the *New York Time*'s Katha Pollitt.

"Is it our mothers, ourselves or our men who mold us?" Jill wonders as she watches some of her friends succumb to cultural pressures and follow the path of their mothers. Many of Jill's friends fare poorly under traditional female roles. Donna, her best friend and cousin, is "haunted by a despair that she believes only marriage can alleviate," according to Caplan. She marries a man who later secretly punctures her diaphragm because he thinks she should get pregnant; when Donna does become pregnant, she gets an illegal abortion and bleeds to death. Another friend, Julie, marries and exists discontentedly in domesticity, while Theo is committed to an institution, first by her psychiatrist who raped her and, again, when she is expelled from college for sleeping with another girl. Out of her circle of friends, Jill alone survives with independence and esteem intact, despite the cultural pressures.

Piercy considers *Braided Lives* one of her best and most original works. In general, critics liked the writing too, but some note that the novel deals too excessively with the problems of women. Caplan points out that *Braided Lives* seems "to accommodate almost every humiliation to which women are liable." Similarly, Pollitt finds that Piercy "makes Jill & Company victims of every possible social cruelty and male treachery, usually more than once." Pollitt hails, however, Piercy's representation of female characters as fighters by noting that even those who did not survive the cultural oppression fought against the attitudes of the day. Pollitt concludes that the book "is a

tribute to Piercy's strengths" and "by virtue of her sheer force of conviction, plus a flair for scene writing, she writes thought-provoking, persuasive novels, fiction that is both political and aimed at a popular audience but that is never just a polemic or just a potboiler."

A strong protagonist and an engaging plot are also the components of *Fly Away Home,* Piercy's eighth novel. Thanks to these strengths, this oft-told tale of a woman's coming to awareness because of divorce becomes "something new and appealing: a romance with a vision of domestic life that only a feminist could imagine," says *Ms.* reviewer Ellen Sweet. Though Daria Walker, the main heroine, is a traditional wife in a conventional role, Alane Rollings deems her "a true heroine. Not a liberated woman in the current terms of career-aggressiveness," Rollings continues in the *Chicago Tribune Book World,* "she is a person of 'daily strengths' and big feelings. When we first meet her, she is a success almost in spite of herself, a Julia Child-type TV chef and food writer, but more important to her, a loving wife and mother in a lovely home." Sweet concurs, calling Daria a "Piercy masterpiece."

Not everyone agrees with this assessment. Because Daria's self-awakening is tied to her growing awareness of her husband's villainy, and because Ross, the husband, is a sexist profiteer who exemplifies the inequities of the capitalist system, some critics suggest that "politics sometimes takes precedence over characterization," as Jeanne McManus puts it in the *Washington Post Book World.* "Daria's not only got to get her own life together but also take on a city full of white-collar real estate criminals who are undermining Boston's ethnic minorities. And she's not just a full-figured woman in a society of lean wolfhounds, but also a bleeding heart liberal, a '60s softy, in an age of Reaganomics. It's a pleasure when Piercy lets Daria sit back and just be herself, frustrated, angry or confused." Piercy contends, however, that she does not try to control characters like Daria; the characters write themselves. In an interview with Michael Luzzi, Piercy asserts that her "characters do have their own momentum and I can't force them to do things they won't do. Sometimes in the first draft, they disturb the neat outlines of the previously arranged plot, but mostly I try to understand them well enough before I start to have the plot issue directly out of the characters." And in the eyes of some critics, Piercy succeeds at this task in *Fly Away Home.* As Sweet observes in *Ms.:* "The real plot is in Daria's growing awareness of herself and her social context."

Piercy's 1991 novel, *He, She and It,* again deals with women's roles and participation in society at large. Rather than dealing with contemporary time periods, however, Piercy has events take place in the twenty-first century, also weaving in a myth from the sixteenth century. In the novel, the author creates a Jewish community of the future called Tikva where the scientist Shira has come to stay with her grandmother, Malkah, after losing a custody battle for her son. Malkah has recently helped develop a cyborg named Yod to protect their community from outside warring forces. While working with Yod, Malkah is reminded of an old Yiddish myth about a rabbi who creates a man of clay, a golem, and gives it life and socialization so that it will protect a Jewish enclave from their enemy. The golem saves the city and the Jews, and then is destroyed when he becomes uncontrollable. Like the rabbi, Malkah has given life to Yod and designates Shira the task of socializing him; eventually Shira falls in love with Yod. Yod saves Tikva, assists Shira in rescuing her son, and in the end, destroys himself and the workshop he was produced in so that his prototypes can not be used as weapons against their will. Shira considers recreating a new lover from the remaining data but concludes that, for the importance of free will, all the information should be destroyed.

Piercy's innovative technique in *He, She, It* is hailed by some critics. "Her approach is so lively and imaginative, her people so energetic, her two worlds realized in such stimulating detail that the novel is never a typical sci-fi adventure or a depressing account of disasters," comments Diana O'Hehir in her review for *Belles Lettres*. The distinguishing feature of the novel, according to London *Times Literary Supplement*'s Anne-Marie Conway, "is the way Marge Piercy combines the story of Shira and Yod with the Yiddish myth of the Golem."

He, She and It received mixed reviews overall. Admiring Piercy's creativity, O'Hehir asserts, "I was amazed at the fertility of Piercy's imaginings," but then points out that "what is lacking is an examination of the questions about creativity, science, and destruction that Piercy appears to be raising at the beginning of her book." "Marge Piercy confronts large issues in this novel: the social consequences of creating anthropomorphic cyborgs, the dynamics of programming both humans and machines, the ethical question of our control of machines that might feel as well as think," writes Malcome Bosse in his review for *New York Times Book Review*. He then notes that Piercy's "ambitious new novel is not likely to enhance her reputation." Bosse finds Piercy's futuristic account beyond belief and contends the book "reads more like an extended essay on freedom of conscience than a full-rigged work of fiction." Conway finds, however, that once the novel moves past the heavily detailed opening chapters, "Piercy relaxes and begins to enjoy telling her story."

In addition to her novels, Piercy has published books of poetry, each of which reflects her political sympathies and feminist point of view. "I am not a poet who writes primarily for the approval or attention of other poets," she explains in her introduction to *Circles on the Water*. "Usu-

ally the voice of the poems is mine. Rarely do I speak through a mask or persona," she once told *CA*. "The experiences, however, are not always mine, and although my major impulse to autobiography has played itself out in poems rather than novels, I have never made a distinction in working up my own experience and other people's. I imagine I speak for a constituency, living and dead, and that I give utterance to energy, experience, insight, words flowing from many lives. I have always desired that my poems work for others. 'To Be of Use' is the title of one of my favorite poems and one of my best-known books."

Piercy's poetry recounts not only the injustices of sexism, but also such pleasures of daily life as making love or gardening. "There is always a danger that poems about little occurrences will become poems of little consequence, that poems which deal with current issues and topics will become mere polemic and propaganda, that poems of the everyday will become pedestrian," observes Jean Rosenbaum in *Modern Poetry Studies*. "To a very large extent, however, Marge Piercy avoids these dangers because most of her poetry contributes to and extends a coherent vision of the world as it is now and as it should be." Writing in the *New York Times Book Review*, Margaret Atwood refers to Piercy's perception as "the double vision of the utopian: a view of human possibility—harmony between the sexes, among races and between humankind and nature—that makes the present state of affairs clearly unacceptable by comparison."

In her poems, Piercy's outrage often explodes. "You exiled the Female into blacks and women and colonies," she writes in *To Be of Use*, lashing out at the mechanistic men who rule society. "You became the armed brain and the barbed penis and the club. / You invented agribusiness, leaching the soil to dust, / and pissed mercury in the rivers and shat slag on the plains."

Some critics maintain that Piercy at her angriest is Piercy at her best, but the poet does not limit herself to negativism. She also writes of sensuality, humor, playfulness, and the strength that lies buried in all women and the ways it can be tapped. In *Hard Loving*, Piercy describes the energy in women's bodies as it moves through their hands and their fingers to direct the world, while a verse from *The Moon Is Always Female* contains advice about writing.

In addition to social problems, Piercy's poetry focuses "on her own personal problems," Victor Contoski explains in *Modern Poetry Studies*, "so that tension exists not only between 'us' and 'them,' but between 'us' and 'me.'" Her poetry is both personal—that is, addressed from a particular woman to a particular man—and public, meaning that it is concerned with issues that pertain to all of society. "Doing It Differently," published in *To Be of Use*, stresses that the legal system still maintains laws that treat women as property, demonstrates that even private relationships are tinged by social institutions, and questions the equality between men and women.

Available Light and *Mars and Her Children,* Piercy's subsequent books of poetry, cover a diverse range of topics, including nature, eating fruit, kitchen remodeling, love, and death. In an interview with *Los Angeles Times*'s Jocelyn McClurg, Piercy explains her range and diversity by stating that, "I think I'm somebody who believes there are no poetic subjects, that anything you pay attention to, if you truly pay attention, there's a poem in it. Because poetry is a kind of constant response to being alive." *Booklist*'s Donna Seaman views *Available Light* overall as expressing the confused feelings of growing older but describes *Mars and Her Children* as a "spectrum of moods" dealing with Piercy's love for life. Due to her numerous books of poetry, some critics suggest that Piercy may be too prolific as a writer. Piercy, however, objects to being labeled prolific. In her interview with McClurg, she comments that "I always know the things I don't get to. The novels you don't get to, the poems you don't get to, those evanescent things that get away from you before you have a chance to sit down. Those things that life is too short to get too."

BIOGRAPHICAL/CRITICAL SOURCES:

BOOKS

Contemporary Authors Autobiography Series, Volume 1, Gale, 1984.
Contemporary Literary Criticism, Gale, Volume 3, 1975, Volume 6, 1976, Volume 14, 1980, Volume 18, 1981, Volume 27, 1984.
Kimball, Gayle, editor, *Women's Culture: The Women's Renaissance of the Seventies,* Scarecrow, 1981.
Piercy, Marge, *Hard Loving,* Wesleyan University Press, 1969.
Piercy, *To Be of Use,* Doubleday, 1973.
Piercy, *The Moon Is Always Female,* Knopf, 1980.
Piercy, *Vida,* Summit, 1980.
Piercy, *Braided Lives,* Summit, 1982.
Piercy, *Parti-Colored Blocks for A Quilt: Poets on Poetry,* University of Michigan Press, 1982.
Piercy, *Circles on the Water: Selected Poems of Marge Piercy,* Knopf, 1982.
Walker, Sue and Eugenie Hamner, editors, *Ways of Knowing: Critical Essays on Marge Piercy,* Negative Capability Press, 1984.

PERIODICALS

America, December 29, 1973.
Atlantic, August, 1971; September, 1973.
Belles Lettres, spring, 1992, p. 25.

Booklist, March 15, 1992, p. 1332.
Chicago Tribune, April 10, 1984; April 7, 1985; March 27, 1988.
Chicago Tribune Book World, January 13, 1980; June 8, 1980; February 14, 1982; April 24, 1983; February 26, 1984.
Detroit Free Press, February 28, 1982.
Detroit News, February 24, 1980; March 21, 1982; March 4, 1984.
Library Journal, February 15, 1992, p. 171.
Los Angeles Times, December 15, 1988.
Modern Poetry Studies, Number 3, 1977.
Ms., July, 1978; January, 1980; June, 1982; March, 1984.
Nation, December 7, 1970; November 30, 1974; December 4, 1976; March 6, 1982, pp. 280-82.
New Republic, December 12, 1970; October 27, 1973; February 9, 1980.
New Statesman, May 18, 1979.
New Yorker, April 10, 1971; February 13, 1978; February 22, 1982.
New York Times, October 21, 1969; October 23, 1970; January 19, 1978; January 15, 1980; February 6, 1982; February 2, 1984.
New York Times Book Review, November 9, 1969; August 12, 1973; January 22, 1978; November 26, 1978; February 24, 1980; February 7, 1982, pp. 6-7, 30-31; August 8, 1982; February 5, 1984; December 22, 1991, p. 22.
Poetry, March, 1971.
Prairie Schooner, fall, 1971.
Publishers Weekly, January 18, 1980.
Saturday Review, March 1, 1980, February, 1982.
Times Literary Supplement, March 7, 1980; January 23, 1981; July 23, 1982; June 15, 1984.
Times Literary Supplement, May 29, 1992, p. 21.
Village Voice, February 18, 1980; March 30, 1982.
Washington Post Book World, January 27, 1980; February 7, 1982; May 30, 1982; February 19, 1984.*

* * *

POLLACK, Sandra (Barbara) 1937-

PERSONAL: Born September 20, 1937, in New York, NY; daughter of Morris (an importer of antiques) and Betty (a homemaker; maiden name, Zalesnick) Pollack; married Mahdi Rubaii, January, 1958 (divorced, 1972); domestic partner, Barbara Stopha; children: Munna, Nadia. *Education:* Cornell University, B.S., 1959; State University of New York College at Cortland, M.A.T., 1971; also attended Sagaris Institute and Union Graduate School. *Politics:* Feminist.

ADDRESSES: Home—313 Washington St., Ithaca, NY 14850. *Office*—Tompkins-Cortland Community College, Dryden, NY 13053.

CAREER: New York State Department of Labor, Rochester, NY, employment interviewer, 1959-61; high school English teacher in Cortland, NY, 1969-70; Tompkins-Cortland Community College, Dryden, NY, instructor, 1971-75, assistant professor, 1975-77, associate professor, 1977-84, professor of liberal arts and humanities, 1984—. Antioch University, Women's Studies in Europe, director, 1987, 1993. Summer research intern at Amalgamated Meat Cutters and Butcher Workers Union and New York State Mediation Board; mediator and trainer at Community Dispute Mediation Center, 1984—; adviser at Women and Minority Rights Resource Center. Producer of videotape "Women in Nontraditional Careers"; producer of film *Never Done—The Working Life of Alice Hanson Cook,* 1993.

MEMBER: National Women's Studies Association (regional coordinator, 1976-78; national coordinator of Task Force on Curriculum and Institutional Change, 1977; community college caucus coordinator, 1977-79), National Council of Teachers of English, Modern Language Association of America, American Association of Women in Community and Junior Colleges.

AWARDS, HONORS: Exchange scholar at Moscow State University, received grants for research on working women in Moscow, Kiev, and St. Petersburg, 1983, 1987.

WRITINGS:

(Editor with Charlotte Bunch) *Learning Our Way: Essays in Feminist Education,* Crossing Press, 1983.
(Editor with Jeane Vaughn) *Politics of the Heart: A Lesbian Parenting Anthology,* Firebrand Books, 1987.
(Editor with Denise D. Knight) *Contemporary Lesbian Writers of the United States: A Bio-Bibliographical Critical Sourcebook,* Greenwood Press, 1993.

Contributor to education journals. Editor of *Minority Women's Resource Guide.*

SIDELIGHTS: Sandra Pollack told *CA:* "My work has been strongly influenced by feminist politics. My current work on lesbian authors is the result of a strong belief that the work of lesbian writers has too long been made invisible. My hope is that *Contemporary Lesbian Writers* will be a valuable teaching aide for a broader inclusion of lesbian literature in the classroom."

POTTER, Beverly A(nn) 1944-

PERSONAL: Born March 3, 1944, in Summit, NJ; daughter of Campbell McLeod (a jet pilot) and Alice (a retired radio executive) Potter. *Education:* San Francisco State College (now University), B.A., 1965, M.S., 1968; Stanford University, Ph.D., 1974.

ADDRESSES: Office—P.O. Box 1035, Berkeley, CA 94701.

CAREER: Psychologist, workshop leader, and lecturer. Member of Staff Development Program at Stanford University, 1976—; has worked as a consultant to various corporations, governmental agencies, associations, and colleges, including Hewlett-Packard, GTE (General Telephone and Electronics), Internal Revenue Service, California State Bar Association, and Stanford Medical School.

MEMBER: Northern California Book Publicists Association, Bay Area Organizational Development Network.

AWARDS, HONORS: The Way of the Ronin was named "one of the best business books of 1984" by *Library Journal;* Ford Foundation dissertation fellowship in women's studies.

WRITINGS:

(With Sharon Bower) *Instructor's Manual for Asserting Yourself,* Addison-Wesley, 1976.
Turning Around: The Behavioral Approach to Managing People, AMACOM, 1980, also published as *Changing Performance on the Job: Behavioral Techniques for Managers,* 1984, and as *Turning Around: Keys to Motivation and Productivity,* Ronin Publishing, 1985.
Beating Job Burnout, Putnam, 1980, also published as *Beating Job Burnout: How to Transform Work Pressure into Productivity,* illustrated by Brian Groppe, Ronin Publishing, 1985, 2nd edition, 1993.
The Way of the Ronin: A Guide to Career Strategy, illustrated by Matt Gouig, AMACOM, 1984, also published as *Maverick Career Strategies: The Way of the Ronin,* 1986, and as *The Way of the Ronin: Riding on the Waves of Change at Work,* Ronin Publishing, 1987.
(With Dhyana Bewicke and others) *Chorella: The Emerald Food,* Ronin Publishing, 1985.
Preventing Job Burnout, illustrated by Mary Swetnika, Crisp Publications, 1986.
(With Sebastian Orfali) *Drug Testing at Work: A Guide for Employers and Employees,* Ronin Publishing, 1990.
(With Orfali) *Brain Boosters: Food and Drugs that Make You Smarter,* Ronin Publishing, 1993.
Finding a Path with a Heart: How to Go from Burnout to Bliss, Ronin Publishing, in press.

Contributor to magazines.

SIDELIGHTS: Beverly A. Potter once told *CA:* "I have had a wide and varied career. I have worked in factories, operated elevators, and waited on tables. I have ridden on the beat in police cars, lived as a 'patient' in a mental hospital, been a social worker in the San Francisco men's county jail, taught police officers how to train other officers to handle family fights, been a substitute high school teacher in Oakland ghetto schools, taught administrators, fire and police officers, and psychologists at the graduate level, trained professional managers, saleswomen, and hippies, made educational films, developed counseling models and training programs, supervised interns, and conducted psychotherapy. I consider myself to be a psychologist of work.

"I believe that the workplace of the industrial world is a feudal society that renders workers powerless and promotes burnout and reduced productivity. My mission is to help usher in the coming corporate renaissance. I teach managers at all levels humanistic management techniques that empower employees and increase productivity and job satisfaction. I believe that work should be an adventure in self-development."

*   *   *

PRANCE, Claude A(nnett) 1906-

PERSONAL: Born June 28, 1906, in Portsmouth, England; son of Edgar Henry and Clara (Annett) Prance; married Patricia Dorothy Searle, March 29, 1932; children: Romaine Linnell Temple, Jon. *Education:* Attended private schools in Southsea, England. *Avocational Interests:* Reading and world travel.

ADDRESSES: Home—16 Alleyne Close, Macgregor, Canberra A.C.T. 2615, Australia.

CAREER: Midland Bank Ltd., England and Wales, various positions in branch banking, including head of securities department, 1923-41, 1946-50, manager's assistant in intelligence department, 1950-57, assistant manager in public relations department and bank advertising manager, both 1958-66; full-time writer, 1966—. *Military service:* Royal Air Force, 1941-46; served in England, North Africa, and the Middle East; became flight lieutenant.

MEMBER: Chartered Institute of Bankers (associate), Chartered Institute of Secretaries (associate), Charles Lamb Society (vice-president, 1983), Private Libraries Association, Society for Theatre Research, Selbome Society, Keats-Shelley Association of America, Bookplate Society, Book Collectors Society of Australia.

WRITINGS:

The Peppercorn Papers (essays), Golden Head Press, 1965.
The Laughing Philosopher (essays), Villiers, 1976.
(With Frank P. Riga) *Index to the London Magazine,* Garland Publishing, 1978.
Companion to Charles Lamb, Mansell, 1983.
E. V. Lucas and His Books, Locust Hill Press, 1988.
Essays of a Book Collector, Locust Hill Press, 1989.
The Characters in the Novels of Thomas Love Peacock 1785-1866, Edwin Mellen Press, 1992.

Contributor to *Crowell's Reader's Encyclopaedia of English Literature, British Literary Magazine,* and other periodicals.

SIDELIGHTS: Claude A. Prance's *Peppercorn Papers* and *The Laughing Philosopher* are collections of essays on such diverse subjects as eighteenth-century bookselling, books on cricket, and a host of minor poets and writers. Peter Stockham noted that the "pleasure of [*The Peppercorn Papers*] is its wide variety of essays, all having a gently civilized, nostalgic atmosphere, aimed at a bookish audience one is delighted to know still exists." A *Book Collector* critic recommended *The Laughing Philosopher* as a "bedside book, although the admirable index may keep you awake by leading you from one bit of Mr. Prance's well-stocked mind to another."

A lifelong interest in the study of English literature of the early nineteenth century led Prance to publish *Companion to Charles Lamb* in 1983. The work is a biographical dictionary covering the more than one hundred years that were crucial to the birth, development, and death of Charles Lamb and his sister, Mary. The volume concentrates on Lamb's love of the theatre as well as on critical literature about Lamb and his time. In a *Times Literary Supplement* review, Neil Berry notes that Prance "sets out to enter up in alphabetical order everything and everybody in any way connected with Lamb's life and, as it were, afterlife. If there are any books or bookmen concerned with Lamb not mentioned here, it is probably not from want of zeal on Prance's part." Berry feels the work "has the virtue of showing how widespread the cult of Lamb has been." *Observer* contributor Naomi Lewis writes of *Companion to Charles Lamb:* "With its hundreds of entries, biographies, anecdotes, its maps, charts, and very full chronology, this engaging compendium has the hypnotic attraction of all such manuals."

Prance once told *CA:* "Although [I was] for many years occupied in the world of finance, this love of literature instilled into me at school and at first a spare time, but absorbing, hobby, turned when opportunity permitted into a full time occupation. The desire and compulsion to write about books and things that interested me had always been great and this was further stimulated by the fortunate and life-long habit of frequenting antiquarian booksellers' shops and bookstalls where the material to fan this flame was found. Enthusiasm I consider one of the greatest inducements to work.

"The desire for self-expression is perhaps one of the strongest spurs to my work, which starting as a hobby, naturally took the subject which interested me most, and has led, I believe, to relative stability and contentment of mind.

"Although fashions in writing and style change from time to time, my own admiration is entirely for the writer whose style is simple and clear and whose meaning can in no way be misconstrued. Hard though it is to achieve such a style, it has been my aim, for I have no sympathy or understanding for the writer whose work is obscure, or who writes jargon, however erudite it may appear at first glance. After all the purpose of writing is generally communication to another and this is defeated if the reader is left in doubt as to the meaning.

"*Index to the London Magazine,* published in 1978 and which I wrote jointly with Dr. Frank P. Riga, was the result of ten years' highly dedicated collaboration, and quite a few years of separate research before we found that we were both working on the same subject, one in Europe and the other in the U.S.A. For me the subject followed naturally out of my interest in early nineteenth-century literature, a desire to fill a gap in it and to add to the existing knowledge of the authors of that period.

"I consider writing to be one of the greatest pleasures of my life."

BIOGRAPHICAL/CRITICAL SOURCES:

PERIODICALS

Book Collector, winter, 1977.
British Book News, January, 1977.
New York Review of Books, June 16, 1983.
Observer, June 12, 1983.
Times Literary Supplement, May 27, 1983.

*   *   *

PRINCE, F(rank) T(empleton) 1912-

PERSONAL: Born September 13, 1912, in Kimberley, Cape Province, South Africa; son of Henry (a businessman) and Margaret (a teacher; maiden name, Hetherington) Prince; married Pauline Elizabeth Bush, March 10, 1943; children: Rosanna Mary Prince Salbashian, Caryll Elizabeth Prince Barber. *Education:* Balliol College, Oxford, B.A., 1934. *Politics:* Conservative. *Religion:* Roman Catholic. *Avocational Interests:* Music.

ADDRESSES: Home—32 Brookvale Rd., Southampton, Hampshire, England SO2 1QR.

CAREER: Royal Institute of International Affairs (Chatham House), Study Groups Department, London, England, 1937-40; University of Southampton, Southampton, England, lecturer, 1946-55, reader, 1955-56, professor of English, 1957-74, dean of arts faculty, 1962-65; Cambridge University, Clark Lecturer, 1972-73; University of the West Indies, Mona, Kingston, Jamaica, professor of English, 1975-78; Brandeis University, Waltham, MA, Fannie Hurst Visiting Professor, 1978-80; Washington University, St. Louis, MO, visiting professor, 1980-81; Sana'a University, North Yemen, Arab Republic, visiting professor, 1981-83; Princeton University, Princeton, NJ, visiting fellow, 1935-36; All Souls College, Oxford, visiting fellow, 1968-69; Hollins College, Hollins College, VA, writer in residence, 1984. *Military service:* British Army, Intelligence Corps, 1940-46; became captain.

AWARDS, HONORS: D.Litt., Southampton University, 1981, University of York, 1982; literary award, American Academy and Institute of Arts and Letters, 1982.

WRITINGS:

POETRY

Poems, Faber, 1938, New Directions, 1941.
Soldiers Bathing and Other Poems, Fortune Press, 1954.
The Stolen Heart, Press of the Morning Sun, 1957.
The Doors of Stone: Poems, 1938-1962, Hart-Davis, 1963.
Memoirs in Oxford, Fulcrum Press, 1970.
(With John Heath-Stubbs and Stephen Spender) *Penguin Modern Poets Twenty,* Penguin, 1971.
Drypoints of the Hasidim, Menard Press, 1975.
Afterword on Rupert Brooke, Menard Press, 1976.
Collected Poems, Sheep Meadow Press, 1979.
The Yuan Chen Variations, Sheep Meadow Press, 1981.
Later On (contains "The Yuan Chen Variations," "His Dog and Pilgrim," and "A Byron-Shelley Conversation"), Sheep Meadow Press, 1983.
Fragment Poetry, English Association, 1986.
Walks in Rome, Anvil Press Poetry, 1987.
Collected Poems 1935-1992, Sheep Meadow Press, 1993.

EDITOR

John Milton, *Samson Agonistes,* Oxford University Press, 1957.
The Poems, by William Shakespeare, Harvard University Press, 1960.
Milton, *Paradise Lost, Books I and II,* Oxford University Press, 1962.
Milton, *Comus and Other Poems,* Oxford University Press, 1968.

OTHER

The Italian Element in Milton's Verse (criticism), Clarendon Press, 1954.
(Translator) Sergio Baldi, *Sir Thomas Wyatt,* Longman, 1961.

Also contributor of critical and descriptive essay *William Shakespeare: The Poems* (includes a section on the *Sonnets*) to series *Writers and Their Work,* Longmans, Green, 1963; and contributor to *Milton Encyclopedia,* edited by W. Buckley, University of Texas Press, 1979. Contributor of articles and reviews to periodicals, including *English, Essays and Studies, Review of English Studies, Review of the University of Pietermaritzburg,* and *Times Literary Supplement.*

SIDELIGHTS: The poetry of Roy Campbell, Ezra Pound, T. S. Eliot, William Butler Yeats, and Rimbaud influenced the works of F. T. Prince, a poet and scholar best known for his much-anthologized poem "Soldiers Bathing." Prince grew up in South Africa and later was educated at Oxford, where he became interested in Italian culture and taught himself the language. During World War II, he served six years in the British Army's Intelligence Corps, spending his last six months in uniform as an interpreter in Italian prisoner-of-war camps in England; "Soldiers Bathing" was inspired by his wartime experience. *New York Times Book Review* critic Donald Davie lauded the work as "aside Eliot's 'Four Quartets,' perhaps the finest poem in English to come out of World War II," and E. M. Forster praised it as one of the three most outstanding British books of 1954, according to David Tacium in the *Dictionary of Literary Biography.* A *Choice* review of the 1979 work *Collected Poems* regarded "Soldiers Bathing" as "one of the best wrought, best realized war poems of our time," and hailed Prince's "linguistic and technical virtuosity." Although Richmond Lattimore in *Hudson Review* maintained that Prince "is less well known than his illustrious contemporaries," he declared that the author "is all his own man, he is like no one else, he is a major poet."

Of Prince's 1983 three-poem collection, *Later On, New York Times Book Review* critic A. Poulin, Jr. remarked, "Admirers of . . . his *Collected Poems* (1979) may find much of this new work quirky and frustrating," but he also applauded the included work, "The Yuan Chen Variations," calling it "a beautiful example of Mr. Prince's capacity for moving eloquence." William Scammell in the *Times Literary Supplement* called Prince "a poet of high distinction" and concluded that *Later On* "is a brave and stimulating book."

Prince once told *CA:* "From the beginning it seemed to me that I would have to go my own way. But it takes a long time, and varied experience, to learn what one really thinks and feels—longer if one is a poet, and if one lives in this century. Some of my past work looks strange to me now, but I have kept it because at the very least it can help towards an understanding of the better things."

BIOGRAPHICAL/CRITICAL SOURCES:

BOOKS

Dictionary of Literary Biography, Volume 20: *British Poets, 1914-1945,* Gale, 1983.

PERIODICALS

Choice, September, 1979, p. 836.
Guardian, April 4, 1979.
Hudson Review, autumn, 1979, pp. 441-42.
Listener, June 3, 1976, p. 716.
New York Times Book Review, April 8, 1979, p. 13; September 30, 1984, p. 45.
Observer, June 22, 1975, p. 26; April 29, 1984, p. 22.
Times Literary Supplement, July 26, 1963, p. 557; September 12, 1968, p. 1003; September 11, 1970, p. 994; July 27, 1984, p. 838; June 24, 1988, p. 715.

* * *

PULLEIN-THOMPSON, Josephine (Mary Wedderburn) (Josephine Mann)

PERSONAL: Born in Wimbledon, Surrey, England; daughter of Harold James (an army officer; later secretary to Headmasters' Conference) and Joanna (an author; maiden name, Cannan) Pullein-Thompson. *Education:* Attended Wychwood School. *Religion:* Anglican. *Avocational Interests:* Walking, reading, theatre, travel.

ADDRESSES: *Home*—16 Knivet Rd., London SW6 1JH, England.

CAREER: Writer. Onetime co-owner of two riding schools, competitor in horse shows and hunter trials, and show judge of jumping and dressage events.

MEMBER: Society of Authors, Crime Writers Association, English Centre of International PEN (general secretary, 1976-1993; president, 1994; official delegate of English Centre to PEN International congresses), British Horse Society, Pony Club (visiting commissioner, 1960-68; district commissioner, 1970-76).

AWARDS, HONORS: Ernest Benn Award, 1961, for *All Change;* member of the Order of the British Empire, 1984.

WRITINGS:

ADULT NOVELS

Gin and Murder, Hammond, 1959.
They Died in the Spring, Hammond, 1960.

Murder Strikes Pink, Hammond, 1963.

(Under pseudonym Josephine Mann) *A Place with Two Faces,* Coronet, 1972, Pocket Books, 1974.

JUVENILES

Six Ponies, illustrated by Anne Bullen, Collins, 1946.

(With sisters, Christine Pullein-Thompson and Diana Pullein-Thompson) *It Began with Picotee,* illustrated by Rosemary Robinson, A. & C. Black, 1946.

I Had Two Ponies, illustrated by Bullen, Collins, 1947.

Plenty of Ponies, illustrated by Bullen, Collins, 1949.

Pony Club Team, illustrated by Sheila Rose, Collins, 1950.

The Radney Riding Club, illustrated by Rose, Collins, 1951.

Prince among Ponies, illustrated by Charlotte Hough, Collins, 1952, reprinted, Armada, 1978.

One Day Event, illustrated by Rose, Collins, 1954.

Show Jumping Secret, illustrated by Rose, Collins, 1955, Armada, 1981.

Patrick's Pony, illustrated by Geoffrey Whittam, Brockhampton Press, 1956.

Pony Club Camp, illustrated by Rose, Collins, 1957, Armada, 1980.

The Trick Jumpers, illustrated by Rose, Collins, 1958.

All Change, illustrated by Rose, Benn, 1961, published as *The Hidden Horse,* Armada, 1982.

How Horses Are Trained, Routledge & Kegan Paul, 1961.

Ponies in Colour, with photographs by Nicholas Meyjes, Viking, 1962.

Learn to Ride Well, Routledge & Kegan Paul, 1966.

(Editor) *Horses and Their Owners,* Nelson, 1970.

(Editor) *Proud Riders: Horse and Pony Stories,* Brockhampton Press, 1973.

Ride Better and Better, Blackie, 1974.

(With C. Pullein-Thompson and D. Pullein-Thompson) *Black Beauty's Clan,* Brockhampton Press, 1975, McGraw, 1980.

Star Riders of the Moor, illustrated by Elisabeth Grant, Hodder & Stoughton, 1976.

Race Horse Holiday, Collins, 1977.

(With C. Pullein-Thompson and D. Pullein-Thompson) *Black Beauty's Family,* Hodder & Stoughton, 1978, McGraw, 1980.

Ride to the Rescue, illustrated by Grant, Hodder & Stoughton, 1979.

Fear Treks the Moor, Hodder & Stoughton, 1979.

Black Nightshade, Hodder & Stoughton, 1980.

Ghost Horse on the Moor, illustrated by Eric Rowe, Hodder & Stoughton, 1980.

The No-Good Pony, Severn House, 1981.

Treasure on the Moor, illustrated by Jon Davis, Hodder & Stoughton, 1981.

The Prize Pony, Arrow, 1982.

(With C. Pullein-Thompson and D. Pullein-Thompson) *Black Beauty's Family Two,* Beaver, 1982.

Pony Club Cup, Armada, 1983.

Pony Club Challenge, Fontana, 1984.

Mystery on the Moor, illustrated by Chris Rothero, Hodder & Stoughton, 1984.

Save the Ponies!, Severn House, 1984.

Pony Club Trek, Armada, 1985.

Suspicion Stalks the Moor, illustrated by Glenn Steward, Hodder & Stoughton, 1986.

Black Swift, Cannongate Press, 1991.

A Job with Horses, J. A. Allen, 1994.

OTHER

Contributor to British horse journals.

Q-R

QUIGLEY, Joan 1927-
(Angel Star)

PERSONAL: Born in 1927 in Kansas City, MO; daughter of John B. (a hotelier and prominent Republican) and Zelda (Marks) Quigley. *Education:* Vassar College, B.A. (cum laude), 1947. *Avocational Interests:* Tennis, bridge, art history.

ADDRESSES: Home—1055 California St., San Francisco, CA 94108. *Agent*—Bill Berger Associates, Inc., 44 East 58th St., New York, NY 10022.

CAREER: Astrologer, 1953—.

MEMBER: American Federation of Astrologers, Junior League of San Francisco.

WRITINGS:

(Under pseudonym Angel Star) *Astrology for Teens,* Bantam, 1968.
Astrology for Adults, Holt, 1969.
Astrology for Parents of Children and Teenagers, Prentice-Hall, 1971.
"What Would Joan Say?": My Seven Years as White House Astrologer to Nancy and Ronald Reagan, Birch Lane Press/Carol Publishing Group, 1990.

SIDELIGHTS: Joan Quigley, a San Francisco-based astrologer, came to public attention in May 1988 when former White House Chief of Staff Donald Regan revealed in his memoir, *For The Record,* that Nancy Reagan regularly consulted an astrologer about President Ronald Reagan's schedule. Quigley, as it soon turned out, was the unnamed astrologer. She was introduced to Mrs. Reagan by Merv Griffin in 1973 when she was appearing as a guest on the Merv Griffin Show. She later volunteered astrological advice to the Reagans during the 1980 presidential campaign. In 1981 when Griffin told Mrs. Reagan that Quigley had predicted the assassination attempt on Reagan's life, the First Lady began paying for the astrologer's advice. Though Quigley never spoke with the President directly, Regan reports in *For the Record* that the President kept a color-coded calendar in his office, provided by Quigley, which indicated good and bad days for, among other things, negotiations with foreign powers. Mrs. Reagan continued to use Quigley's services until 1988, when Regan's book prompted her to sever all contact with her astrologer.

In 1989 Mrs. Reagan wrote her own memoir of the Reagan years, *My Turn,* in which she downplayed Quigley's role in the White House schedule. "Joan's recommendations had nothing to do with policy or politics—ever," Reagan avowed. "Her advice was confined to timing." But Quigley disagrees, and says she wrote *"What Would Joan Say?": My Seven Years as a White House Astrologer to Nancy and Ronald Reagan* both to set the record straight on astrology in general and on her role as White House astrologer.

Quigley says she influenced such events as the President's visit to Bitburg, the Geneva summit with Gorbachev, the arrivals and departures of Air Force One, the Reykjavik summit, and the President's cancer surgery, among many others. But Mark A. Stein, in the Los Angeles Times, observes that "contemporary news accounts do not always match her versions of events." Molly Ivins, calling Quigley's book both "dreadful" and "fascinating" in her *New York Times* review, wrote: "If the book consisted solely of this loony list of how Ms. Quigley changed the course of history, it would be no end of fun. Unfortunately she has dedicated her book 'to Astrology'. . . ." Quigley met President Reagan only once, at a 1985 White House dinner where she shook his hand. But, she says, "there is no doubt whatsoever in my mind that the President was fully aware of the contribution I made, the scheduling, my ideas, the problems I solved and the advice I gave."

BIOGRAPHICAL/CRITICAL SOURCES:

BOOKS

Bestsellers '90, number 3, Gale, 1991.
Reagan, Nancy *My Turn,* Random, 1989

PERIODICALS

Chicago Tribune, March 19, 1990.
Library Journal, February 1, 1970, p. 504.
Los Angeles Times, September 15, 1989; March 18, 1990.
Los Angeles Times Book Review, March 25, 1990; March 3, 1991.
Nation, May 21, 1988.
New Statesman, October 14, 1988.
New York Review of Books, June 30, 1988.
New York Times, November 1, 1989.
New York Times Book Review, March 18, 1990.
Time, May 16, 1988.*

* * *

QUINN, Martin
   See SMITH, Martin Cruz

* * *

QUINN, Simon
   See SMITH, Martin Cruz

* * *

RENN, Casey
   See CRIM, Keith R(enn)

* * *

REYNOLDS, Terry S(cott) 1946-

PERSONAL: Born January 15, 1946, in Sioux Falls, SD; son of Ira E. (a machinist) and Therasea (a homemaker; maiden name, Janzen) Reynolds; married Linda Gail Rainwater (a church secretary), June 4, 1967; children: Trent Aaron, Dane Adrian, Brandon Vincent, Derek Vinson. *Education:* Southern State College (now Southern Arkansas University), B.S. (with honors), 1966; University of Kansas, M.A., 1968, Ph.D., 1973. *Politics:* Moderate. *Religion:* "Baptist/Methodist."

ADDRESSES: Home—1209 East 7th Ave., Houghton, MI 49931. *Office*—Department of Social Sciences, Michigan Technological University, Houghton, MI 49931.

CAREER: University of Wisconsin—Madison, assistant professor, 1973-79, associate professor of general engineering and history of science, 1979-83; Michigan Technological University, Houghton, associate professor of science, technology, and society, 1983-87, director of program in science, technology, and society, 1983-87, professor of history, 1987—, head of department of social sciences, 1990—.

MEMBER: Society for the History of Technology (member of steering committee, Technology Studies and Education Division, 1984-87; coordinator of special publication projects, 1985-87; chairperson of Dexter Prize committee, 1986-87; chairperson of awards committee, 1988-89), Society for Industrial Archeology, Technology and Humanities Association, National Association for Science, Technology, and Society.

AWARDS, HONORS: Woodrow Wilson fellow, 1971-72; grant, University of Wisconsin, 1974; Norton Prize, Society for Industrial Archeology, 1985, for article on Sault Ste. Marie, MI, hydroelectric plant; grants, Michigan Department of Education, 1986 and 1987, and National Science Foundation, 1990.

WRITINGS:

Sault Ste. Marie: A Project Report, Government Printing Office, 1982.
75 Years of Progress: A History of the American Institute of Chemical Engineers, 1908-1983, American Institute of Chemical Engineers, 1983.
Stronger Than a Hundred Men: A History of the Vertical Water Wheel, Johns Hopkins University Press, 1983.
(Editor and compiler) *The Machine in the University: Sample Course Syllabi for the History of Technology and Technology Studies,* Society for the History of Technology, 1987.
(Editor and contributor) *The Engineer in America,* University of Chicago Press, 1991.

Also author or consulting author of numerous reports and pamphlets for communities and government agencies, 1978—. Contributor to books, including *The World of the Industrial Revolution: Comparative and International Aspects of Industrialization,* edited by Robert Weible, Museum of American Textile History, 1986; and *Science, Technology and Society Programs,* edited by John Wilkes, Worcester Polytechnic Institute, 1987. Advisory editor and contributor, *Encyclopedia Americana,* 1980—. Contributor to *New Book of Knowledge,* 1986, *Encyclopedia of American Business and Biography,* 1989 and in press, *World Book Encyclopedia,* 1991, *American National Biography,* and to proceedings of professional organizations. Member of advisory board, *Great Engineers and Pioneers of Technology,* St. Martin's Press, 1980-84. Contributor of numerous articles to professional journals, including *En-*

gineering *Design Graphics Journal, Technology and Culture, Engineering Education, Industrial Archeology: The Journal of the Society for Industrial Archeology, Louisiana History,* and *Scientific American.* Referee for numerous professional organizations, periodicals, and publishers. Author of script and selected images for four-projector audio-visual orientation program "Life on the Michigan Iron Ranges," Michigan Iron Industry Museum, 1990.

Stronger Than a Hundred Men: A History of the Vertical Water Wheel has been translated into Japanese.

WORK IN PROGRESS: Research on the history of American engineering education.

SIDELIGHTS: Terry S. Reynolds's *Stronger Than a Hundred Men,* which *Times Literary Supplement* critic Norman Smith describes as "a valuable work of reference," traces the history of the vertical waterwheel from its inception in Greco-Roman times to its gradual demise with the advent of the water turbine. Smith heralds Reynolds's book as "a pioneering effort" and labels it "the definitive compilation . . . on vertical water-wheels." Smith notes that although the book contains careful documentation and illustrations, Reynolds has left some gaps in recounting the waterwheel's two thousand year history. The reviewer believes Reynolds fails to deal conclusively with the origins of waterpower and does not adequately explore the development of the vertical waterwheel in relation to that of the horizontal waterwheel. Despite his concerns about the historical treatment of the waterwheel, Smith applauds the book's readability and observes that it is "likely to appeal to a very wide audience." Smith concludes that *Stronger Than a Hundred Men* is "highly informative about waterpower in general."

BIOGRAPHICAL/CRITICAL SOURCES:

PERIODICALS

Times Literary Supplement, November 25, 1983.

* * *

RICHARDSON, (George) Peter 1935-

PERSONAL: Born January 6, 1935, in Toronto, Ontario, Canada; son of George G. (an accountant) and M. Louise (a teacher; maiden name, Everett) Richardson; married Nancy Jean Cameron (a nurse), December 22, 1959; children: Mary Rebekah, Susan Elizabeth, Jonathan Peter, Ruth Anne. *Education:* University of Toronto, B. Arch. (with honors), 1957, B.D. (with honors), 1962; Clare College, Cambridge, Ph.D., 1965. *Avocational Interests:* Architecture, archaeology, building, preservation of historical sites, photography, travel, antique furniture, art.

ADDRESSES: Home—42 St. Andrews Gardens, Toronto, Ontario, Canada M4W 2E1. *Office*—University College, University of Toronto, 15 Kings College Circle, Toronto, Ontario, Canada M5S 1A1.

CAREER: John B. Parkins Associates (architects), Don Mills, Ontario, designer, 1957-59; campus pastor of Presbyterian church in Toronto, Ontario, 1965-69; Loyola of Montreal (now Concordia University, Loyola Campus), Montreal, Quebec, assistant professor, 1969-72, associate professor of theological studies, 1972-74, coordinator of Loyola Lacolle Centre for Educational Innovation, 1973-74; University of Toronto, Toronto, associate professor of humanities and chairman of humanities, 1974-77, principal of University College, 1977-89, professor of religious studies, 1977—. Member of Council of Ontario Universities, 1983-86; member of senate of Presbyterian College, Montreal, 1969-75; chairperson, Joint Practice Board (for architects and engineers), 1984—; vice-president, Canadian Corporation for Studies in Religion, 1990—; associate editor, Wilfrid Laurier University Press, 1990—.

MEMBER: Canadian Society of Biblical Studies (executive member, 1972-74; chairman of research and publications committee, 1975-78; executive secretary, 1978-82; vice-president, 1983-84; president, 1984-85), Canadian Society for the Study of Religion, Canadian Committee of Scientists and Scholars, American Academy of Religion, American Society for the Study of Religion, Catholic Biblical Association of America, Studiorum Novi Testamenti Societas, Institute for Biblical Research (executive secretary, 1971-77), Society for Biblical Literature.

AWARDS, HONORS: Grants from Connaught Fund, 1976, Wintario, 1977 and 1978, Canada Council, 1979, and Social Science and Humanities Research Council of Canada, 1980-81. Honorary member, Ontario Association of Architects, 1987.

WRITINGS:

Paul's Ethic of Freedom, Westminster, 1979.
(Editor with John C. Hurd) *From Jesus to Paul: Studies in Honour of Francis Wright Beare,* Wilfrid Laurier University Press, 1984.
(Editor with David Granskou) *Anti-Judaism in Early Christianity,* Volume I, Wilfrid Laurier University Press, 1985.
(Co-author, with Stephen Westerholm, A. I. Baumgarten, Michael Pettem, and Cecilia Wassen) *Law in Religious Communities in the Roman Period: The Debate Over Torah and Nomos in Post-Biblical Judaism and Early Christianity,* Wilfrid Laurier University Press, 1991.

Also author of monograph, *Israel in the Apostolic Church*, Cambridge University Press, 1969. Contributor to *The Trial of Jesus: Cambridge Studies in Honour of C. F. D. Moule*, edited by Ernst Brammel, S.C.M. Press, 1970; *Anti-Judaism in Early Christianity*, Volume II, edited by S. G. Wilson, Wilfrid Laurier University Press, 1985; *Gospel Perspectives V: The Jesus Tradition Outside the Gospels*, edited by David Wenham, JSOT Press, 1985; and *Tradition and Interpretation in the New Testament: Studies in Honor of E. E. Ellis*, edited by Gordon Fee, J. C. B. Mohr, 1987. Contributor of articles and reviews to religious studies journals. Member of board of *Crux*, 1966-78; cofounder and member of editorial board of *Arc*, 1973-74; guest editor of *Studies in Religion*, 1984 and 1985; managing editor of *Studies in Religion/ Sciences Religieuses*, 1985—; editor of *Studies in Christianity and Judaism*, 1989—.

WORK IN PROGRESS: Series of imaginary letters to Paul provisionally entitled *Dear Saul;* biographical study of Herod the Great, provisionally entitled *Herod, King of Jews and Friend of Romans;* study on the architecture and religious interests of Herod the Great.

SIDELIGHTS: Peter Richardson told *CA:* "My interests have gradually changed in two directions—towards a joining of my dual background in architecture and religion, and away from straightforward textual studies to writing that is more imaginative and more culturally rooted. My works on both Paul and Herod will be informed by my travel in the Middle East and by my interests in the material culture and the remains of Judea, Galilee, Syria, Turkey, and Greece."

*   *   *

RICHELSON, Jeffrey T(albot) 1949-

PERSONAL: Born December 31, 1949, in New York, NY; son of Herbert H. and Edna (Len) Richelson. *Education:* City College of the City University of New York, B.A., 1970; University of Rochester, M.A., 1974, Ph.D., 1975.

ADDRESSES: Home—5 West Glebe Rd., C-24, Alexandria, VA 22305.

CAREER: University of Texas at Austin, visiting assistant professor of government, 1976-77; Analytical Assessments Corp., Marina del Rey, CA, research associate, 1977-81; University of California, Los Angeles, senior fellow at Center for International and Strategic Affairs, 1981-82; American University, Washington, DC, assistant professor of government and public administration, 1982-87; writer and consultant, 1987—.

MEMBER: Amnesty International, Naval Intelligence Professionals, National Military Intelligence Association, National Association of Science Writers.

WRITINGS:

The U.S. Intelligence Community, Ballinger, 1985, 2nd edition, 1988.
Sword and Shield: The Soviet Intelligence and Security Apparatus, Ballinger, 1985.
(With Desmond Ball) *The Ties that Bind: Intelligence Cooperation between the UKUSA Countries*, Allen & Unwin, 1985.
The Soviet Target: American Espionage and the Cold War, Morrow, 1987.
Foreign Intelligence Organizations, Ballinger, 1988.
America's Secret Eyes in Space, Harper, 1990.

Contributor to economic and political journals.

WORK IN PROGRESS: A Century of Spies: Intelligence in the Twentieth Century.

SIDELIGHTS: Jeffrey T. Richelson told *CA:* "Despite the end of the Cold War, there remains a need for a significant intelligence collection and analysis establishment. In addition to understanding the dynamics of individual countries and regions—from Russia to South Africa—there are a variety of problems such as proliferation of advanced weaponry and international terrorism that will require attention from the U.S. and allied intelligence communities."

BIOGRAPHICAL/CRITICAL SOURCES:

PERIODICALS

Los Angeles Times Book Review, March 17, 1985.
Naval Institute Proceedings Book Review, April, 1991.
Philadelphia Inquirer Book Review, January 28, 1990.

*   *   *

RIDER, J. W.
    See STEVENS, Shane

*   *   *

RIEGLE, Donald W(ayne), Jr. 1938-

PERSONAL: Born February 4, 1938, in Flint, MI; son of Donald Wayne (in sales) and Dorothy (Fitchett) Riegle; married Nancy E. Brandt, 1957; divorced; married Meredith Ann White (a magazine editor), January, 1972; divorced, 1977; married Lori Hansen, May 20, 1978; children: (first marriage) Catherine Anne, Laurie Elizabeth, Donald W. III, (third marriage) one daughter. *Education:* Attended Flint Junior College, 1956-57, and Western

Michigan University, 1957-58; University of Michigan, B.A., 1960; Michigan State University, M.B.A, 1961; further graduate study at Harvard University, 1964-66. *Politics:* Democrat.

ADDRESSES: Office—U.S. Senate, 105 Dirksen Senate Bldg., Washington, DC 20510.

CAREER: International Business Machines Corp. (IBM), senior pricing analyst, 1961-64; Harvard University, Cambridge, MA, member of faculty, 1965-66; Republican member of U.S. House of Representatives from the Seventh District (Michigan), Washington, DC, 1966-73, Democratic member, 1973-76; member of U.S. Senate from Michigan, 1977-93; member of House Appropriations Committee, 1967-73; member of Senate Foreign Affairs Committee, 1974-77; chairman of Committee on Banking, Housing and Urban Affairs, 1989-93; chairman of Subcommittee on Health, Families and the Uninsured, 1989-93. Member of faculty of Michigan State University, 1962, and Boston University, 1965.

AWARDS, HONORS: Named one of America's ten Outstanding Young Men by the United States Junior Chamber of Commerce, 1967; named one of the two best Congressmen of the year by *Nation* magazine, 1967.

WRITINGS:

(With Trevor Armbrister) *O Congress,* Doubleday, 1972.

SIDELIGHTS: Donald Riegle was elected to the U.S. House of Representatives in 1966, when he was just twenty-eight years old. At that time a Republican, he was intensely critical of American involvement in Vietnam, and would frequently challenge Democratic secretary of defense Robert McNamara to justify the presence of U.S. armed forces there. He was considered by many to be the most well-informed congressman on the topic of Vietnam, allowing him to better scrutinize the proposals of his more hawkish colleagues.

As he gained more experience in Congress, Riegle became more and more disillusioned with the Republican party; particularly dissatisfying was the amount of dissention between members of the party. Riegle once wrote: "There are roughly 190 Republicans in the Congress, and maybe ten of them see things as I do. There are about 240 Democrats in the Congress, of whom 160 see things as I do and vote as I would." He documented this slow political transition in his 1972 book *O Congress,* which presents a behind-the-scenes view of Congress between April, 1971, and March, 1972. In 1973 he switched affiliation to the Democratic party, and was quickly elected to the U.S. Senate.

Riegle has spent much of his senatorial career vigorously defending the interests of his home state of Michigan.

That state's fragile economy has often forced Riegle to campaign for federal assistance—usually successfully. He likens his role to that of an army field medic: "I never get out of my operating clothes because I have so many damaged cities, damaged companies, and damaged individuals coming through the door every day." His support for the auto industry—an intrinsic part of Michigan's economy, if not its primary contributor—has earned him the label "the Senator from GM." Ralph Nader once remarked that Riegle's strategy "basically is to champion the auto companies' proposals and to try to get the UAW and the auto companies on the same side on all issues." Still, he has not ignored the Democratic cause; during his presidency, Ronald Reagan often referred to Riegle as "the demagogue from Michigan."

In 1990, Riegle's political reputation suffered what may have been a fatal blow. In the investigation of Charles Keating, a banking mogul whose bankrupt Lincoln Savings & Loan would cost taxpayers more than $2 billion to bail out, Riegle and four other senators were discovered to have received from Keating "campaign contributions" totaling nearly $1.4 million. In addition, several of the senators had accepted vacation-type stays at Arizona and Florida resorts. The ensuing hearings by the Senate Ethics Committee were described by *Time*'s Ed Magnuson as "almost as historic" as the McCarthy and Iran-Contra hearings: "Never before had five Senators faced the judgment of their peers in such a public tribunal." Ethics Committee chairman Howell Heflin explained to the senators—who had been dubbed "the Keating five" by the press—the offenses of which they were accused: "[That] your services were bought by Charles Keating, that you were bribed, that you sold your office."

After fourteen months of investigation, the Senate Ethics Committee found just one of the "Keating five," California senator Alan Cranston, guilty of "impermissible conduct." The relative leniency of the verdict upset some voters, many of whom had considered the hearings an opportunity for congressional reform. Fred Wertheimer, president of the citizen's lobby group Common Cause, commented: "The U.S. Senate remains on the auction block to the Charles Keatings of the world." Though proclaimed innocent by the Ethics Committee, the four other senators faced a political future that was murky at best. This was particularly true of Riegle, who had been accused by the media of being "deceptive and suspiciously forgetful" during the hearings, according to Magnuson. Though Riegle eventually gave back the campaign funds donated to him by Keating, his political reputation remained tarnished; during the hearings, Ethics Committee lawyer Robert Bennett said of the scandal, "There is substantial evidence that Senator Riegle played a much greater role than he now recalls."

In September, 1993, Riegle announced that he was retiring in order to spend more time with his family.

BIOGRAPHICAL/CRITICAL SOURCES:

PERIODICALS

American Spectator, February, 1991, p. 29.
Business Week, February 4, 1991, p. 63.
Meet the Press, January 15, 1989, p. 1.
Nation, December 31, 1990, p. 832.
Time, January 8, 1990, pp. 48-50; October 29, 1990, p. 43;
    November 26, 1990, p. 35; March 11, 1991, p. 69.
Washington Post, September 7, 1982, p. A4.*

—*Sketch by Brandon Trenz*

*   *   *

ROBINSON, Earl (Hawley)   1910-1991

PERSONAL: Born July 2, 1910, in Seattle, WA; died of injuries sustained in a car accident, July 20, 1991, in Seattle, WA; son of Morris John and Hazel Beth (maiden name, Hawley) Robinson; married Helen Wortis, February 17, 1937 (died June 1963); married Ruth Friedman Martin, May 5, 1965 (divorced September 1975); children: (first marriage) Perry, James. *Education:* University of Washington, Seattle, B.Mus. and Normal Diploma, 1933; studied composition privately with Aaron Copland, George Antheil, and Hanns Eisler. *Politics:* Independent. *Religion:* Humanist. *Avocational Interests:* Chess, gardening, psychic reading.

ADDRESSES: Home and office—3701 41st Ave. SW, Seattle, WA 98116.

CAREER: Composer, writer, entertainer, conductor, and teacher. Joined Workers Theatre of Action, 1934, and Works Progress Administration Federal Theatre Project, 1937; wrote music for several shows presented in New York City, 1936-39; conductor, American Peoples' Chorus, 1937-40; composed music for Hollywood films, 1943; director of music and conductor of chorus and orchestra, Elisabeth Irwin High School, 1957-65; University of California, Los Angeles, conductor of Extension Chorus and lecturer, 1967-71; teacher of composition, music theory, and guitar. Composer of orchestral works, cantatas, songs, and music for stage, film, television, and radio; conductor of orchestras (including New York Philharmonic) and choruses in New York, Hollywood, San Francisco, Chicago, Toronto, Berlin, Prague, and other cities; director or conductor of many performances of his own cantatas and of other productions such as Marc Blitzstein's *Cradle Will Rock* and *Words and Music by Bob Dylan.*

MEMBER: American Federation of Musicians, Authors League of America, Dramatists Guild, American Guild of Authors and Composers (alternate council member), Screen Actors Guild, Composers and Lyricists Guild of America, American Society of Composers, Authors and Publishers.

AWARDS, HONORS: Guggenheim fellowship, 1940-41, for musical adaptation of Carl Sandburg's poem "The People, Yes"; Academy Award, Academy of Motion Picture Arts and Sciences, 1946, for short film built around his song *The House I Live In;* Hall of Fame award, National Academy of Recording Arts and Sciences, 1980; U.S. Department of the Treasury Citation for cantata *Battle Hymn;* Award of Merit, Civil War Centennial Commission of Illinois, for cantata *The Lonesome Train.*

WRITINGS:

(Arranger of music and author of notes) *Young Folk Song Book,* introduction by Pete Seeger, Simon & Schuster, 1963.
Folk Guitar in Ten Sessions, Consolidated-Amsco, 1965.
(Editor with Eric Bentley) *Songs of Brecht and Eisler,* Oak, 1967.
(Editor and arranger of music) *Songs of the Great American West,* compiled by Irwin Silber, Macmillan, 1967.
German Folk Songs, Oak, 1968.

ORCHESTRAL WORKS AND CANTATAS

Ballad for Americans, premiered on radio, 1938.
Sing for Your Supper, premiered on radio, 1939.
Illinois People, performed for Illinois Sesquicentennial, 1968.
Piano Concerto, premiered in East Berlin, 1973.
To the Northwest Indians, premiered at World Fair Expo, Spokane, WA, 1974.

SONGS AND SCORES FOR TV PRODUCTIONS

Maybe I'll Come Home in the Spring, American Broadcasting Corp. (ABC), 1971.
Adventures of Huckleberry Finn, ABC, 1975.
The Pumpkin Who Couldn't Smile, Columbia Broadcasting System, 1979.

OTHER

Also composer of orchestral works, *Concerto for Five String Banjo and Orchestra* and *A Country They Call Puget Sound,* cantatas, *Battle Hymn, The Lonesome Train, The People, Yes, The Town Crier, When We Grow Up, Giants in the Land, Preamble to Peace, A Santa Barbara Story, The Strange Unusual Evening, Grand Coulee Dam* and *Ride the Wind* (from musical *Washington Love Story*), stage productions, (with Waldo Salt) *Sandhog, Dark of the Moon, Bouquet for Molly, One Foot in America, Washington Love Story, Earl Robinson's America, David of Sassoun, Listen for the Dolphins,* and *Song of Atlantis,* music for film, *A Walk in the Sun, California, Ro-*

mance of *Rosie Ridge, The House I Live In, Uptight,* and *The Great Man's Whisker's,* and songs, *Hurry Sundown, Free and Equal Blues, Johnny O, Katie O, Abe Lincoln, Joe Hill, Black and White,* and *My Fisherman, My Laddio, My Love.* Also composer of some 450 unpublished songs, including *Spring Song, The Same Boat Brother, Hold Fast to Your Dreams, Four Hugs a Day, Logan's Lament, All the Words Are New, Where It Is, Suppose (They Gave a War, and No One Came), Song of Sassoun, She Always Lights a Candle,* and *Once Upon a Soon Time.* Author of unproduced chamber opera musical entitled *I Been Thinkin' about J. C.*

SIDELIGHTS: Throughout his long career, Earl Robinson relied heavily on major social and political causes for inspiration. Originally intending to study "serious" music after leaving his native Washington for New York City in the early 1930s, Robinson joined the Workers Theatre and became caught up in the labor movement instead. He then began composing what can best be described as folk songs, most notably *Joe Hill,* a tribute to a fallen hero of the radical Industrial Workers of the World, revived by singer Joan Baez in the late 1960s. Other songs from this time, most of them written for guitar, spoke of revolution, the labor movement, and other Old Left causes.

In the 1940s Robinson headed west, spending much of the decade in California composing music for the film industry. His continued support of leftist causes, however, eventually earned him a spot on Hollywood's blacklist during the McCarthy era of the 1950s. "I stayed in the Communist Party too long," Eleanor Blau of the *New York Times* quoted Robinson explaining. "I quietly dropped out in the blacklist days. The party still has something to say, but I'm not sure it has anything worth listening to." *Black and White,* a Robinson composition dating from this same period that was inspired by the anti-desegregation disturbances in the South, became a hit some twenty years later (in 1972) when it was recorded by the group Three Dog Night.

Although the 1960s saw a return to the popularity of Robinson's music due to the growing number of political and social protest movements, the 1970s and 1980s found the composer increasingly interested in psychic phenomena. His opera *David of Sassoun,* for example, resulted from his curiosity about Armenian history combined with several personal psychic experiences. Robinson's children's opera on human-dolphin communication, *Listen for the Dolphin,* stemmed directly from his belief in the psychic powers of non-human creatures.

BIOGRAPHICAL/CRITICAL SOURCES:

PERIODICALS

Santa Barbara News-Press, August 16, 1979.

OBITUARIES:

PERIODICALS

Chicago Tribune, July 23, 1991, section 3, p. 13.
Los Angeles Times, July 23, 1991, p. A22.
New York Times, July 23, 1991, p. B5.
Time, August 5, 1991, p. 61.
Times (London), August 6, 1991, p. 14.
Washington Post, July 23, 1991, p. B6.*

*   *   *

ROGERS, Floyd
See SPENCE, William John Duncan

*   *   *

ROGIN, Michael Paul   1937-

PERSONAL: Born June 29, 1937, in Mount Kisco, NY; son of Lawrence (an educator) and Ethel (a librarian; maiden name, Lurie) Rogin; married Deborah Donohue, November 19, 1959; children: Isabelle Rose, Madeleine Anne. *Education:* Harvard University, B.A. (summa cum laude), 1958; University of Chicago, M.A., 1959, Ph.D., 1962.

ADDRESSES: Office—Department of Political Science, University of California, Berkeley, CA, 94720.

CAREER: University of Chicago, Chicago, IL, assistant professor of political science at Makerere University College (now University), Kampala, Uganda, 1962-63; University of California, Berkeley, assistant professor, 1963-69, associate professor, 1969-75, professor of political science, 1975—. Fulbright lecturer at University of Sussex, 1967-68; visiting fellow at Center for the Humanities, Wesleyan University, autumn, 1975; Christian Gauss seminars, Princeton University, 1984.

MEMBER: Phi Beta Kappa.

AWARDS, HONORS: Albert J. Beveridge Award, American Historical Association, 1968, for *The Intellectuals and McCarthy: The Radical Specter;* Guggenheim fellow, 1972-73; National Endowment for the Humanities fellow, 1979; Pi Sigma Alpha Award, Western Political Science Association, 1980.

WRITINGS:

The Intellectuals and McCarthy: The Radical Specter, M.I.T. Press, 1967.
(With John L. Shover) *Political Change in California: Critical Elections and Social Movements, 1890-1966,* Greenwood Press, 1970.
Fathers and Children: Andrew Jackson and the Subjugation of the American Indian, Knopf, 1975.

Subversive Genealogy: The Politics and Art of Herman Melville, Knopf, 1983.
"Ronald Reagan," The Movie and Other Episodes in Political Demonology, University of California Press, 1987.

Contributor to *National Unity and Regionalism in Eight African States,* edited by Gwendolyn Carter, Cornell University Press, 1966; *Power and Community,* edited by Philip Green and Sanford Levinson, Pantheon, 1970; and *The Transient and the Permanent: Essays in American Politics,* J. David Greenstone, University of Chicago Press, 1982. Also contributor of nearly fifty articles and reviews to political science and sociology journals and to popular magazines, including *Transition, Commonweal, Listener,* and *Partisan Review.*

* * *

ROLAND, Mary
  See LEWIS, Mary (Christianna Milne)

* * *

ROSEN, Dorothy 1916-

PERSONAL: Born August 13, 1916, in Hartford, CT; daughter of Herman and Bella Schack; married Sidney Rosen (a professor); children: David. *Education:* Mount Holyoke College, A.B. (cum laude), 1938; University of Illinois at Urbana-Champaign, M.A., 1971.

ADDRESSES: Home—1417 Mayfair Rd., Champaign, IL 61821.

CAREER: Boston Public Library, Boston, MA, children's librarian, 1947-57; free-lance editor, 1958—. Guest on *Today* television show.

MEMBER: Mystery Writers of America.

WRITINGS:

(With husband, Sidney Rosen) *Death and Blintzes* (mystery novel), Walker & Co., 1985.
The Magician's Apprentice (juvenile historical novel), Carolrhoda Books, 1993.
The Baghdad Mission (juvenile historical novel), Carolrhoda Books, 1993.
A Fire in Her Bones: Mary Lyon, Founder of Mount Holyoke College (juvenile biography), Carolrhoda Books, 1994.

SIDELIGHTS: Dorothy Rosen once told *CA:* "The mystery novel has always been treated as a stepchild in this country, but I feel that one can say as much about the human condition within the parameters of the mystery as

in any other form. Indeed, the thoughtful mystery novel concerns itself above all with the why of human behavior. Another goal in our writing was to present the flavor of the 1930's, a time of less affluence and less conformity, but more hopefulness. And perhaps most important of all was to sustain a mood of playfulness. Is there a better gift the writer can give the reader than humor? A joy that made up for all the rewritings of the book was the moment that Gene Shalit told us, on the *Today* show, that '*Death and Blintzes* is a very funny book . . . a very cheerful detective story.'"

Rosen adds: "My husband and I are devoting our writing to the juvenile field, particularly the category of historical novels. I feel that this is one way that young people can learn history without pain."

* * *

RUTSALA, Vern 1934-

PERSONAL: Born February 5, 1934, in McCall, ID; son of Ray Edwin (in sales) and Virginia (Brady) Rutsala; married Joan Colby, April 6, 1957; children: Matthew, David, Kirsten. *Education:* Reed College, B.A., 1956; State University of Iowa, M.F.A., 1960.

ADDRESSES: Office—English Department, Lewis and Clark College, Portland, OR 92719.

CAREER: Lewis and Clark College, Portland, OR, 1961—, currently professor of English. Visiting professor, University of Minnesota, 1968-69, and Bowling Green State University, 1970; writer in residence, Redlands University, 1979, and University of Idaho, 1988. *Military service:* U.S. Army, 1956-58.

AWARDS, HONORS: National Endowment for the Arts fellow, 1974, 1979; Guggenheim fellow, 1982; Carolyn Kizer Poetry Prize, 1988; Masters fellowship, Oregon Arts Commission, 1990; Hazel Hall Prize, Oregon Book Award, 1992, for *Selected Poems;* Juniper Prize, University of Massachusetts Press, 1994, for *Little-Known Sports.*

WRITINGS:

The Window: Poems, Wesleyan University Press, 1964.
Small Songs: A Sequence (poems), Stone Wall Press, 1969.
The Harmful State, Best Cellar, 1971.
(Editor) *British Poetry 1972,* Baleen Press, 1972.
Laments, New Rivers Press, 1975.
The Journey Begins, University of Georgia Press, 1976.
Paragraphs, Wesleyan University Press, 1978.
The New Life, Trask House, 1978.
Walking Home from the Icehouse, Carnegie Mellon University Press, 1981.
The Mystery of Lost Shoes, Lynx, 1985.
Backtracking, Storyline Press, 1985.

Ruined Cities, Carnegie Mellon University Press, 1987.
Selected Poems, Story Line Press, 1991.

Also author of *Little-Known Sports,* 1994. Contributor to anthologies, including *West of Boston,* edited by G. Stevenson, Qara Press, 1959; *Midland,* edited by Paul Engle and others, Random House, 1961; *A Geography of Poets,* edited by Edward Field, Bantam, 1979; *Rain in the Forest, Light in the Trees,* edited by R. Ives, Owl Creek Press, 1983; *A New Geography of Poets,* University of Arkansas Press, 1992; and *The Carnegie Mellon Anthology of Poetry,* Carnegie Mellon University Press, 1993. Contributor to *Atlantic Monthly, Times Literary Supplement, Paris Review, Nation, Midland, Poetry, New Yorker, Harper's, American Poetry Review,* and other publications. Poetry editor, *December,* 1959-62; editor, *Hubbub* (special British issue), 1985.

WORK IN PROGRESS: Poetry and fiction.

SIDELIGHTS: Of his own work, Rutsala has said, "A poem starts with something I call a kind of buzz or hum of potential. There is rarely any explicit idea—usually it's just a feeling that I've got hold of, the very tip of something, and the first lines are an effort to uncover what that thing may be. Obviously, it has to seem worth pursuing and the pursuit results in a draft which is open to every possibility that bears on that triggering buzz. Form, sense, the niceties of language are not concerns at this point. What is important is the block of words which form the first draft—the kitchen sink draft. The draft is usually set aside for a time—out of the need to earn a living but increasingly by preference—and looked at later with a cold eye. If the buzz is still there then the shaping begins, which may go on for hours, weeks, or months.

"Though we all want them to come across quickly, each poem sets its own agenda. You know the poem may not work out but you take the chance and hope the law of averages is with you. But, as Eliot said, you write with a wastebasket, and that's the only way. Every writer lives with waste, almost extravagantly so. Carefulness and caution strangle the creative impulse. Staying alert and not too anxious keeps it alive."

In *Saturday Review,* R. D. Spector wrote of Rutsala's work that "for all the casual language, there is a precision of metaphor: for all the quietness, a moving force, and for all the commonplace experiences, a genuine significance. . . . Rutsala is a poet of the very real world. . . . It is not merely authenticity but understanding and wisdom that speak out."

BIOGRAPHICAL/CRITICAL SOURCES:

PERIODICALS

Chicago Review, June, 1967.

Saturday Review, February 13, 1965.

*   *   *

RYGA, George   1932-1987

PERSONAL: Born July 27, 1932, in Deep Creek, Alberta, Canada; died November 18, 1987, in Summerland, British Columbia, Canada; son of George (a farmer) and Maria (Kolodka) Ryga; married Norma Lois Campbell; children: Lesley, Tanya, Campbell, Sergei, Jamie. *Education:* "Self-educated." *Politics:* Socialist-humanitarian.

CAREER: Worked in farming, construction, and hotel industry; CFRN, Edmonton, Alberta, radio producer, 1950-54; full-time writer, 1962-87. Guest professor at University of British Columbia, Banff School of Fine Arts, and Simon Fraser University.

MEMBER: Association of Canadian Television and Radio Artists, Writers Guild of America—West, British Columbia Civil Liberties Association (honorary member).

AWARDS, HONORS: Imperial Order Daughters of the Empire Award, 1950 and 1951; Canada Council senior arts grant, 1972; Fringe Frist Award, Edinburgh Festival, 1973; *Ploughmen of the Glacier* won two best play awards in Germany, 1979 and 1980; Governor General's Award nomination, for *A Letter to My Son.*

WRITINGS:

Song of My Hands (poems), National (Edmonton), 1956.
Hungry Hills (novel), Longmans, Green (Toronto), 1963, revised edition, Talonbooks, 1974.
Ballad of a Stone-Picker (novel), Macmillan (Toronto), 1966, revised edition, Talonbooks, 1976.
Night Desk (also see below), Talonbooks, 1976.
Beyond the Crimson Morning: Reflections from a Journal through Contemporary China (travel book), Doubleday, 1979.
In the Shadow of the Vulture, Talonbooks, 1985.
Summerland, Talonbooks, 1992.

PLAYS

Nothing But a Man, produced in Edmonton, Alberta, at Walterdale Playhouse, 1966.
Indian (also see below; produced in Winnipeg, Manitoba, at Manitoba Theatre Centre, 1974), Book Society of Canada, 1967.
The Ecstasy of Rita Joe (two-act; music by Ann Mortifee and Willy Dunn; also see below; produced in Vancouver, British Columbia, at Queen Elizabeth Playhouse, 1967; produced in Washington, DC, 1973), Talonbooks, 1970.
Just an Ordinary Person, produced in Vancouver at Metro Theatre, 1968.

Grass and Wild Strawberries (music by The Collectors; also see below), produced in Vancouver at Queen Elizabeth Playhouse, 1969.

(Author of music and lyrics) *Captives of the Faceless Drummer* (produced in Vancouver at Vancouver Art Gallery, 1971), Talonbooks, 1971.

(Author of music) *Sunrise on Sarah* (produced in Banff, Alberta, at Banff School of Fine Arts, 1972), Talonbooks, 1973.

Portrait of Angelica (also see below) produced in Banff at Banff School of Fine Arts, 1973.

Paracelsus (also see below; published in *Canadian Theatre Review*, fall, 1974), produced in Vancouver at Playhouse Theatre, 1986.

Ploughmen of the Glacier (also see below; produced in Vernon, British Columbia, at Vernon Community Centre, 1976), Talonbooks, 1977.

Seven Hours to Sundown (also see below; produced in Edmonton at University of Alberta Studio Theatre, 1976), Talonbooks, 1977.

The Last of the Gladiators (adapted from *Night Desk*), produced in Summerland, British Columbia, by Giant's Head Theatre Company, 1976.

Jeremiah's Place (children's play), produced in Victoria, British Columbia, 1978.

A Letter to My Son (also see below), produced in North Bay, Ontario, by Kam Theatre Lab, 1981.

One More for the Road, produced in Vancouver at Firehall Theatre, 1985.

RADIO PLAYS

Author of radio plays, including *A Touch of Cruelty,* 1961, *Half-Caste,* 1962, *Masks and Shadows,* 1963, *Bread Route,* 1963, *Departures,* 1963, *Ballad for Bill,* 1963, *The Stone Angel,* 1965, and *Seasons of a Summer Day,* 1975. Also author of scripts for the series, *Miners, Gentlemen, and Other Hard Cases,* 1974-75, and *Advocates of Danger,* 1976.

TELEVISION PLAYS

Author of television plays, including *Indian,* 1962, *The Storm,* 1962, *Bitter Grass,* 1963, *For Want of Something Better to Do,* 1963, *The Tulip Garden,* 1963, *Two Soldiers,* 1963, *The Pear Tree,* 1963, *Man Alive,* 1965, *The Kamloops Incident,* 1965, *A Carpenter by Trade* (documentary), 1967, *Ninth Summer,* 1972, *The Mountains* (documentary), 1973, and *The Ballad of Iwan Lepa* (documentary), 1976. Also author of scripts for the series, *The Manipulators,* 1968, and *The Name of the Game,* 1969.

COLLECTIONS

The Ecstasy of Rita Joe and Other Plays (contains *The Ecstasy of Rita Joe, Indian,* and *Grass and Wild Strawberries*), introduced by Brian Parker, New Press, 1971.

Country and Western (contains *Portrait of Angelica, Ploughmen of the Glacier,* and *Seven Hours to Sundown*), Talonbooks, 1976.

Two Plays (contains *Paracelsus* and *Prometheus Bound*), Turnstone Press, 1982.

Portrait of Angelica [and] *A Letter to My Son,* Turnstone Press, 1984.

The Athabasca Ryga, edited by E. David Gregory, Talonbooks, 1990.

OTHER

A Feast of Thunder (oratorio), music by Morris Surdin, produced in Toronto at Massey Hall, 1973.

Author of other oratorios, including *Twelve Ravens for the Sun,* music by Mikis Theodorakis, 1975. Author of preface, *The Collected Plays of Gwen Pharis Ringwood,* edited by Enid Delgatty Rutland, Borealis, 1982. Also author of short stories, film scripts, and two albums of folk songs. Contributor to periodicals, including *Canadian Theatre Review, Canadian Drama,* and *Canadian Literature.*

A collection of Ryga's papers is housed in the University of Calgary Library. Ryga's work has been translated into other languages, including Ukrainian.

ADAPTATIONS: The Ecstasy of Rita Joe was adapted for ballet and produced by the Royal Winnipeg Ballet, 1971.

SIDELIGHTS: Canadian playwright and novelist George Ryga was a controversial author who used his work as a voice for social change. He was a champion of the underdog whose plays focus on an individual's struggle within a repressive social structure, battling outside forces and feelings of loneliness and isolation. Usually his heroes and heroines are poor, drawn from the working classes. His early experiences—leaving school at thirteen, taking correspondence courses, and working full-time as a manual laborer—helped to form his identification and sympathy with this group. Ryga also perceived the need for a cultural mythology based on the people themselves, not the "official history" of politicians supported by the government. Jerry Wasserman, writing in the *Dictionary of Literary Biography,* noted that Ryga's dramatic works and fiction are "distinguished by a strong consciousness and the attempt to create a folk art using contemporary themes."

Ryga was perhaps best known for his play *The Ecstasy of Rita Joe,* the story of an Native American woman's attempts to become a part of the white world around her, only to be raped and murdered by a gang of white men. *The Ecstasy of Rita Joe* "established that an English-Canadian play could address serious social issues in vernacular language and nonrealistic style and still be commercially appealing, helping make possible the explosion of Canadian drama that occurred in the late 1960s and early 1970s," commented Wasserman. Neil Carson proclaimed in a 1970 *Canadian Literature* article that *The Ecstasy of Rita Joe* "establishes Ryga as the most exciting talent writing for the stage in Canada today."

Ryga's other plays call up characters similar to Rita Joe—alienated individuals in search of something, such as acceptance. In his first novel, *Hungry Hills,* Ryga creates Snit Mandolin on a quest for his origins and a sense of belonging. What Snit discovers is incest, the barren farmlands of northern Alberta, and his indomitable Aunt. His efforts to reestablish a life there fail in the face of the "cowardly greed of these hungry hills." *Hungry Hills* "shows Ryga's interest in the lives of the poor and oppressed as well as his preoccupation with problems of structure," declares Carson in the *Journal of Canadian Fiction.*

"Romeo has tales, and no place to tell them except . . . before the night desk," describes W. H. Rockett, writing in *Saturday Night,* of *Night Desk.* The story of Romeo Kuchmir as narrated by his sole listener, the night man or "kid," *Night Desk* tells the tale of one isolated man. His stage is the night desk, but he is the only character in the "play" of this novel. Rockett believes that Kuchmir "has made what Brian Parker had called a Ryga folk ballad. Words trigger words, responses, new anecdotes, old ideas. Everything weaves back on senseless legs to the same loneliness. . . . Romeo is his own best audience."

Ryga's focus on the individual is at the core of his work. His protagonists are isolated, alienated, and rejected by society. "The sense of spiritual homelessness is common in Ryga's work and many of his characters define themselves by their relationship to a country they have lost or one they never find," comments Carson in *Canadian Litera-* ture. He also notes in the *Journal of Canadian Fiction* that "what impresses in [Ryga's] work is not his social criticism, still less his portrayal of the agents of justice and bureaucracy, but his assertion of individual courage and dignity in the face of those most terrible oppressions—loneliness and death."

BIOGRAPHICAL/CRITICAL SOURCES:

BOOKS

Contemporary Literary Criticism, Volume 14, Gale, 1980.
Dictionary of Literary Biography, Volume 60: *Canadian Writers since 1960, Second Series,* Gale, 1987.
Moore, Mavor, *Four Canadian Playwrights,* Holt, 1973.
New, William H., editor, *Dramatists in Canada: Selected Essays,* University of British Columbia Press, 1972.
Who's Who in Canadian Literature: 1985-86, Reference Press, 1985.

PERIODICALS

Books and Bookmen, February, 1966.
Canadian Forum, January/February, 1979.
Canadian Literature, summer, 1970, pp. 155-62.
Journal of Canadian Fiction, Volume IV, number 4, 1979, pp. 185-87.
Saturday Night, May, 1966; January/February, 1977, pp. 83-84.
Spectator, January, 1966.

OBITUARIES:

PERIODICALS

Times (London), November 28, 1987.*

S

SACASTRU, Martin
See BIOY CASARES, Adolfo

*   *   *

SAMUELS, Ernest 1903-

PERSONAL: Born May 19, 1903, in Chicago, IL; son of Albert (a grocer) and Mary (Kaplan) Samuels; married Jayne Newcomer, August 24, 1938; children: Susanna, Jonathan, Elizabeth. *Education:* University of Chicago, Ph.B., 1923, J.D., 1926, M.A., 1931, Ph.D., 1942. *Politics:* Independent. *Avocational Interests:* Camping, travel.

ADDRESSES: Home—3116 Park Place, Evanston, IL 60201.

CAREER: Admitted to the bar of Texas and of Illinois; attorney at law in El Paso, TX, 1928-30, in Chicago, IL, 1933-37, as partner in Samuels & Samuels; State College of Washington (now Washington State University), Pullman, instructor in English, 1937-39; Northwestern University, Evanston, IL, instructor, 1942-46, assistant professor, 1946-49, associate professor, 1949-54, professor of English, 1954-71, professor emeritus, 1971—, Franklyn Bliss Snyder Professor of English, 1942-71, chairman of department, 1964-66. Visiting associate professor, University of Chicago, 1950; Fulbright lecturer and Inter-University Chair in American studies to the Belgian universities, 1958-59; first holder of the Bing Chair in English and American Literature, University of Southern California, 1966-67. Member of advisory committee for the publication of Henry Adams's papers; member of Commission of Scholars, Illinois Board of Higher Education, 1966-71; member of Council of Scholars, Library of Congress, 1979-80. Served on Pulitzer Prize juries for biography, 1967, 1968, 1972, and for history, 1969.

MEMBER: Modern Language Association, Massachusetts Historical Society.

AWARDS, HONORS: Guggenheim fellowships, 1955-56, and 1972-73; Bancroft Prize, Columbia University, and Francis Parkman Prize, Society of American Historians, both 1959, both for *Henry Adams: The Middle Years;* Pulitzer Prize in biography and Friends of Literature Award, both 1965, both for *Henry Adams: The Major Phase;* American Book Award nomination, 1980, and Carl Sandburg Award, 1981, both for *Bernard Berenson: The Making of a Connoisseur;* English-Speaking Union Books-Across-the Sea Ambassador of Honor Books, 1985.

WRITINGS:

Business English Projects, Prentice-Hall, 1936.
The Young Henry Adams (first in trilogy), Harvard University Press, 1948.
Henry Adams: The Middle Years (second in trilogy), Belknap Press of Harvard University Press, 1958.
Henry Adams: The Major Phase (third in trilogy), Belknap Press of Harvard University Press, 1964.
Bernard Berenson: The Making of a Connoisseur, Belknap Press of Harvard University Press, 1979.
(With wife, Jayne Newcomer Samuels) *Bernard Berenson: The Making of a Legend,* Belknap Press of Harvard University Press, 1987.
Henry Adams (revised and abridged version of the Adams trilogy), Belknap Press of Harvard University Press, 1989.

EDITOR

History of the United States of America During the Administrations of Jefferson and Madison, abridged edition, University of Chicago Press, 1967.
(And author of introduction and notes) *The Education of Henry Adams,* Houghton, 1973.

(With others) *The Letters of Henry Adams, I-III: 1858-1892,* Belknap Press of Harvard University Press, 1982.

(With others) *The Letters of Henry Adams, IV-VI: 1892-1918,* Belknap Press of Harvard University Press, 1988.

Selected Letters, Belknap Press of Harvard University Press, 1992.

OTHER

Also author of introduction to *Mont-Saint-Michel and Chartres,* by Henry Adams, New American Library, 1961; *Democracy,* by Adams, Smith, 1961; *Esther,* by Adams, Smith, 1961; and *Chartres.* Editor of *Writings of Henry Adams,* 1983. Contributor to *Major American Writers,* Harcourt, 1962; *Essays in American and English Literature Presented to Bruce Robert McElderry, Jr.,* edited by Max F. Schulz, William T. Templeman, and Charles R. Metzger, Ohio University Press, 1967. Also contributor of articles to periodicals, including *Quarterly Journal of the Library of Congress, American Quarterly, Nation, American Literature, Christian,* and *Lincoln Herald.* Member of editorial board, *American Literature.*

The Ernest Samuels Papers are in the Northwestern University Archives.

SIDELIGHTS: Trained as a lawyer as well as a literary scholar, Ernest Samuels is known for the exhaustive research that has contributed copious details to his multivolume biographies of author Henry Adams and art historian Bernard Berenson. The first volume of the Adams trilogy, *The Young Henry Adams,* stresses Adams's intellectual development at Harvard and as contributor to and editor of the *North American Review.* Samuels undercuts the previously held misconception that Adams was detached from public events of his time, and analyzes the development of Adams's literary style. *Henry Adams: The Middle Years,* the second volume in Samuels's Adams project, describes the subject's life in Washington, DC, during the 1870s and 1880s, years when Adams was writing the novels *Democracy* and *Esther. Henry Adams: The Major Phase* concentrates on Adams's great later books, *Mont Saint-Michel and Chartres* and *The Education of Henry Adams;* in this volume Samuels makes use of previously unpublished Adams letters.

In general, the trilogy received favorable reviews. Reviewing the third volume, *Henry Adams: The Major Phase,* for the *New York Review of Books,* Alfred Kazin called the trilogy "exemplary" and "so far as any real information is concerned . . . the only biography we have of Henry Adams." Calling attention to Samuels's scholarly detachment, patient, quiet years of research, and avoidance of theorizing, Kazin added: "He will not 'explain' Adams, for he is working in too close detail." Leo Marx, reviewing

the third volume for the *Nation,* maintained that Samuels's trilogy is "definitive," adding, "Professor Samuels fulfills all of his scholarly obligations without smothering his subject. . . . The astonishing result is an engrossing book, with the man in it: cold, arrogant, tough, irascible, egocentric, sentimental, brilliant Henry Adams." When Samuels's one-volume abridgement was issued in 1989, Hugh Brogan in the *New York Times Book Review* announced: "It is a complete success. Nowhere does it seem compressed or unintelligible (except where the fault is Adams's) or skimpy. Rather it seems both economical . . . and ample. . . . It seems to be just the right length for its subject. In all, *Henry Adams* is a remarkable feat of the biographer's art." From the fittingness of the biography at its shortened length, Brogan went on to conclude that Adams's standing was somewhat lower than it had been a generation earlier. Richard Eder, in the *Los Angeles Times,* asserted the three-volume opus is "a classic," but acknowledged approvingly the need for, and success of, the abridgement. Eder also called for a selected edition of the six-volume Adams letters—a volume that Samuels published in 1992. Harold Holzer, in the Chicago *Tribune Books,* considered the abridged biography "a pleasure to read," claiming, "even at his most crotchety . . . Henry Adams himself might not have been able to resist this enthralling book."

While researching Adams, Samuels came upon some letters of Bernard Berenson's, which sparked his interest in his second major biographical subject. He visited the 91-year-old Berenson in Italy in 1956 for the purpose of requesting some of Adams's letters; the eventual result was a request from the Berenson estate that Samuels prepare the authorized two-volume biography of the great art appraiser. *New York Times* reviewer Anatole Broyard said of the first volume, *Bernard Berenson: The Making of a Connoisseur,* "Everybody who was anybody in the art world at the time appears in [it]. . . . The killings in the art market, the quarrels among experts and the convoluted negotiations all make for even better reading than one might anticipate, for at the center of it all, beyond the story of our greatest art critic, is art itself." The second volume, *Bernard Berenson: The Making of a Legend,* was published at a time when Berenson's reputation was increasingly shaky because of widespread accusations of unscrupulous art dealings. Contributor Hilton Kramer reviewed Samuels's book for the *Washington Post Book World* and judged, "There can be no question but that Berenson took full advantage of the opportunities that were offered him. Yet Samuels has acquitted Berenson of the charge of knowingly falsifying his opinions for the purpose of turning a profit. . . . To have established this point beyond question—which I believe Samuels has now done—is in itself a considerable scholarly feat."

BIOGRAPHICAL/CRITICAL SOURCES:

BOOKS

Dictionary of Literary Biography, Volume 111, *American Literary Biographers, Second Series,* Gale, 1992, pp. 233-40.

PERIODICALS

Canadian Forum, March, 1968.
Chicago Sunday Tribune, November 23, 1958.
Globe & Mail (Toronto), July 11, 1987.
Los Angeles Times, December 7, 1989.
Nation, February 15, 1965, pp. 171-72.
New England Quarterly, March, 1959.
New York Review of Books, January 14, 1965, pp. 5-7.
New York Times, May 12, 1979, p. 19; March 24, 1987.
New York Times Book Review, March 29, 1987, pp. 1, 35-38; November 19, 1989, p. 22.
Saturday Review, November 8, 1958.
Time, April 6, 1987, pp. 77-78.
Times Literary Supplement, October 28, 1965, p. 949; June 5, 1987, pp. 595-96.
Tribune Books (Chicago), February 11, 1990, p. 6.
Virginia Quarterly Review, winter, 1965.
Washington Post Book World, May 10, 1987, pp. 4-5.*

* * *

SCAVULLO, Francesco 1929-

PERSONAL: Born January 16, 1929, in Staten Island, NY; son of Angelo Carmelo (in manufacturing) and Margaret (Pavis) Scavullo; married Carol McCallson (a model), 1952 (divorced, 1956). *Education:* Educated in New York, NY. *Religion:* Roman Catholic.

ADDRESSES: Home and office—212 East 63rd St., New York, NY 10021.

CAREER: Vogue Studios, New York City, apprentice photographer with Horst, 1945-48; Scavullo Studio, New York City, proprietor and photographer, 1948—; TC&S (production company), co-owner, 1984—; Scavullo Gallery, New York City, owner, 1988—. Photographer for magazines in New York City, including *Seventeen,* 1948-50, *Town and Country,* 1950, *Harper's Bazaar,* 1960, *Cosmopolitan,* 1965—, and *Vogue,* 1974—. Work is represented in permanent collections of major museums, including Metropolitan Museum of Art; has had exhibitions of his work throughout the United States. Director of television commercials for Shearson Lehman Brothers, Covermark, and Memorex, and film projects, including the *Crystal Gayle Special,* CBS-TV, December, 1979. Actor and visual consultant for motion picture *Lipstick,* 1978.

MEMBER: Directors Guild of America, American Federation of Television and Radio Artists, Screen Actors Guild.

AWARDS, HONORS: Named Photographer of the Year, 1977.

WRITINGS:

Scavullo on Beauty, Random House, 1976.
Scavullo on Men, Random House, 1977.
(With Sean M. Byrnes) *Scavullo Women,* Harper, 1982.
(With Byrnes) *Scavullo: Francesco Scavullo Photographs, 1948-1984,* Harper, 1984.

Photographs have appeared in numerous magazines, including *Oui, Playboy, Viva, People, Good Housekeeping, Ladies' Home Journal, New York, Rolling Stone, Time, Newsweek, Redbook,* and *Glamour;* photographer for motion picture advertisements and album covers.

WORK IN PROGRESS: Two book projects to be published in 1995.

SIDELIGHTS: Acknowledged as the dominant photographic influence on American fashion and beauty, Francesco Scavullo has photographed many of the celebrated luminaries of the latter half of the twentieth century, including Cher, Meryl Streep, Bette Midler, Barbara Walters, Bianca Jagger, Grace Kelly, Elizabeth Taylor, Barbra Streisand, Brooke Shields, Diana Vreeland, Sting, Norman Mailer, Gloria Vanderbilt, Edward Albee, and numerous others. "Scavullo . . . is a magician behind the camera," commented Ruthe Stein in the *San Francisco Chronicle,* adding, "He can make plain woman look glamorous; pretty women, beautiful; and intellectual men, sexy."

One of five children, Scavullo developed an early interest in photography when his grandfather took him to the movies regularly. His father's camera served for his initial photographic efforts, and he convinced his mother to buy him a motion picture camera when he was nine years old. By the time he was in high school, Scavullo knew he wanted to pursue fashion photography as a career. His first real break came when he was hired by *Vogue* magazine, where he worked for three years as apprentice/ assistant to *Vogue* photographer Horst. When he was nineteen years old, *Seventeen* published his first cover photograph, the success of which led to a three-year contract with the magazine.

During the 1950s Scavullo experimented with the lighting techniques that have come to distinguish his work. Preferring a minimalist background, his all-white studio allows him to concentrate on the lighting for his subject. Using natural or artificial light, he frequently diffuses its source through muslin fabric or shades it with white umbrellas.

He also has created innovative techniques for both reflecting and focusing light.

In 1965 *Cosmopolitan* editor Helen Gurley Brown invited him to develop a new look for the magazine's cover, and the "Cosmo girl" was born. Since then, *Cosmopolitan* covers have featured Scavullo's photographs; the beautiful, seductively dressed models reflect the magazine's image of contemporary, successful women. His photographs have also graced the covers of other magazines, including *Harper's Bazaar, Mademoiselle, Glamour, Woman, Rolling Stone,* and *Life.*

Scavullo and his photographic expertise have reputedly influenced career opportunities for some of his subjects. A shampoo advertisement that he photographed with a then relatively unknown Farrah Fawcett led to Scavullo's choosing her for a *Cosmopolitan* cover, and she was shortly thereafter selected as one of "Charlie's Angels" in the television series of the same name. And his controversial shot of a nude Burt Reynolds for a 1971 *Cosmopolitan* centerfold reportedly helped revitalize Reynolds's career.

Scavullo on Beauty, the photographer's first book, was described as "a compendium of beauty hints, celebrity portraits and intimate interviews with 59 women," by Susan Cheever Cowley and Lisa Whitman in *Newsweek.* Blair Sabol, one of the subjects in the book, remarked in *Village Voice* that "it's too bad that the 59 women he used weren't more diverse. Most of them are or were models, movie stars, or socialites (not one bag lady in the bunch)." A subsequent book, *Scavullo Women,* contains photographs of forty-six women, many with before-and-after shots. Nina Hyde asserted in *Washington Post Book World* that "Francesco Scavullo's photos are bold, aggressive. . . . Scavullo seems to go for the jugular—admittedly a beautiful jugular—to create a single, gripping picture of each of the 46 women he photographed for this book."

Scavullo credits much of his photographic success to the rapport he achieves with his subjects. He attempts to draw them out and converse with them prior to and during the actual shooting. About his clients, he explained to Stein: "I really want a performance from them, but I have to put the energy out to spark it. Otherwise, you end up with dead pictures. I do a lot of talking. I don't know how this happens because I'm basically shy, but I just seem to know what to say to bring them out." Warren Wotton wrote in the *Tacoma News Tribune* that "[Scavullo] believes that his art is good only when it's kind to people. When it shows them at their best. When it puts their pain and passion into perspective. And when it gives them all their dignity, whoever they may be."

In assessing Scavullo's work, Wotton further stated that "Scavullo takes the triviality of lights, camera and made-up action and turns it into the photo documents of

deep and sometimes even touching quality." Critics of Scavullo, however, have found fault with what they deem his limited perception of beauty and suggest that his photographs lack a sense of realism and social conscience. His provocative 1983 *Harper's Bazaar* layout featuring a five-year old girl made up to look much older, for instance, was viewed by some observers as child exploitation. Scavullo responded to that charge in a *Los Angeles Herald Examiner* interview with Jeannine Stein: "The reason people got upset is because there *is* a sexuality about her. . . . I'm only trying to show what *we* are doing to the children, not what *I* am doing to them." During the 1970s and 1980s Scavullo began to work in film and television directing. In 1984 he co-founded a production company to film television commercials; his credits include commercials for Memorex and Shearson Lehman Brothers.

BIOGRAPHICAL/CRITICAL SOURCES:

BOOKS

Biography News, Volume 2, Gale, 1975.

PERIODICALS

Los Angeles Herald Examiner, October 22, 1984.
Los Angeles Times Book Review, December 12, 1982.
Newsweek, February 4, 1974; November 22, 1976.
New York, December 16, 1974.
New York Daily Mail, March 30, 1977.
New York Daily News, November 20, 1977.
New York Post, October 20, 1978.
People, May 1, 1980.
Philadelphia Inquirer, January 9, 1975.
San Diego Union, July 30, 1978.
San Francisco Chronicle, October 22, 1985.
San Francisco Examiner, November 23, 1977.
St. Paul Pioneer Press and Dispatch, September 10, 1985.
Tacoma News Tribune, May 9, 1985.
Village Voice, November 1, 1986.
Washington Post Book World, September 11, 1983.

—*Sketch by Michaela Swart Wilson*

* * *

SCHLEIFER, Ronald 1948-

PERSONAL: Born May 10, 1948, in New York, NY; son of Cy and Helen (Szozkida) Schleifer; married Nancy Lou Mergler, January 23, 1982; children: Cyrus Joseph, Benjamin Whitmore. *Education:* Brandeis University, B.A., 1970; Johns Hopkins University, M.A., 1973; Ph.D., 1974.

ADDRESSES: Home—730 Chautauqua Ave., Norman, OK 73069. *Office*—Department of English, University of Oklahoma, Norman, OK 73019.

CAREER: University of Oklahoma, Norman, assistant professor, 1975-82, associate professor of English, 1982—. Emory University, visiting assistant professor, 1974-75; visiting professor at University of Hawaii at Hilo, spring, 1986, and University of Kansas, 1990.

MEMBER: Modern Language Association of America.

AWARDS, HONORS: Woodrow Wilson fellow, 1970-72; grant from American Council of Learned Societies, 1977.

WRITINGS:

(Editor) *The Genres of the Irish Literary Revival,* Wolfhound Press, 1980, Pilgrim Books, 1980.
(Translator with Alan Velie and Daniele MacDowell) A. J. Greimas, *Structural Semantics,* University of Nebraska Press, 1983.
(Editor with Robert Markley) *Kierkegaard and Literature: Irony, Repetition, and Criticism,* University of Oklahoma Press, 1984.
(Editor with Robert Con Davis) *Rhetoric and Form: Deconstruction at Yale,* University of Oklahoma Press, 1985.
A. J. Greimas and the Nature of Meaning: Linguistics, Semiotics, and Discourse Theory, University of Nebraska Press, 1987.
(Editor with Davis) *Contemporary Literary Criticism,* 2nd edition, Longman, 1989.
Rhetoric and Death: The Language of Modernism and Postmodern Discourse Theory, University of Illinois Press, 1990.
(With Davis) *Criticism and Culture: The Role of Critique in Modern Literary Theory,* Longman, 1991.
(With Davis and Nancy Mergler) *Culture and Cognition: The Boundaries of Literary and Scientific Inquiry,* Cornell University Press, 1992.

Editor of *Genre,* 1976—.

*   *   *

SCHWARTZ, Hillel 1948-

PERSONAL: Born April 27, 1948, in Chicago, IL; son of Harry Raymond (a chemist) and Frieda Leah (a nurse; maiden name, Levin) Schwartz. *Education:* Brandeis University, B.A. (summa cum laude), 1969; Yale University, Ph.D., 1974; University of California, Berkeley, M.L.S., 1975. *Religion:* "Amelist."

ADDRESSES: Home—699 North Vulcan, No. 37, Encinitas, CA 92024.

CAREER: University of Florida, Gainesville, adjunct assistant professor of history and humanities, 1975-77; University of California, San Diego, La Jolla, visiting assistant

professor of history and humanities, 1977-78, 1989, 1992; San Diego State University, San Diego, lecturer in English, history, humanities, and religious studies, 1979-82; independent scholar, 1982—. Director of Del Mar Arts Cooperative, 1979-81. Member of board of directors of Yale Cooperative, 1972.

MEMBER: American Historical Association, Society for Values in Higher Education.

AWARDS, HONORS: Abram L. Sachar traveling fellowship, Brandeis University, for study in Europe, 1969-70; Danforth fellow, 1969; named president's scholar by University of Florida, 1977-78; Journalism Award, Catholic Press Association, 1984, for best poetry published in a Catholic periodical; American Council of Learned Societies international travel grant, 1987; Richard Hugo Prize, *Poetry Northwest,* 1988.

WRITINGS:

Knaves, Fools, Madmen, and that Subtitle Effluvium, University Presses of Florida, 1978.
The French Prophets: The History of a Millenarian Group in Eighteenth-Century England, University of California Press, 1980.
(Translator with David G. Roskies) Howard Schwartz and Anthony Rudolf, editors, *Voices within the Ark* (anthology), Avon, 1980.
Phantom Children, State Street Press, 1982.
Never Satisfied: A Cultural History of Diets, Fantasies, and Fat, Free Press, 1986.
Century's End: A Cultural History of the Fin de Siecle from the 1890s through the 1990s, Doubleday, 1990.
Striking Likenesses: The Culture of the Copy in the Modern World, Knopf, 1994.

PLAYS

Animal Park (two-act), produced in Del Mar, CA, 1979.
Krill (one-act), produced in Del Mar, 1980.
Leapghosts (three-act), produced in Del Mar, 1980.

OTHER

Work included in numerous anthologies, including *Anthology of Magazine Verse,* edited by Alan Pater, Monitor Book, 1980; *Amorotica,* edited by Elliot Fried, Deep River Press, 1981; and *Nuke Rebuke,* edited by Morty Sklar, Spirit That Moves Us, 1984. Contributor to books, including *Notebooks in Cultural Analysis,* edited by Cantor and King, Duke University Press, 1985; *Encyclopedia of Religion,* edited by Mircea Eliade, Free Press, 1986; *Fragments for a History of the Human Body,* MIT/Zone, 1989; and *Incorporations,* MIT/Zone, 1992.

Contributor of poetry and fiction to numerous periodicals, including *Beliot Poetry Journal, Boulevard, Centennial Review, Chicago Review, Commonweal, Fiddlehead, Indi-*

ana Review, Michigan Quarterly Review, New Orleans Review, Prairie Schooner, Salmagundi, Threepenny Review, and *Yankee.* Book reviewer, *Journal of Unconventional History.*

WORK IN PROGRESS: *Slipstick,* a screenplay.

*   *   *

SCOTLAND, Jay
    See JAKES, John (William)

*   *   *

SCOTT, Bonnie Kime 1944-

PERSONAL: Born December 28, 1944, in Philadelphia, PA; daughter of Roy Milford (an electrical engineer) and Sheila (a schoolteacher and homemaker; maiden name, Burton) Kime; married Thomas Russell Scott (a professor and neurophysiologist), June 17, 1967; children: Heather, Ethan, Heidi. *Education:* Wellesley College, B.A., 1967; University of North Carolina at Chapel Hill, M.A., 1969, Ph.D., 1973. *Politics:* Democrat. *Avocational Interests:* "I derive personal satisfaction from everyday relationships with my husband, children, students, and colleagues, from international travel, reading, sewing, gardening, and excursions into nature."

ADDRESSES: *Home*—216 Orchard Rd., Newark, DE 19711. *Office*—Department of English, University of Delaware, Newark, DE 19716.

CAREER: University of Delaware, Newark, assistant professor, 1975-80, associate professor, 1980-86, professor of English, 1986—, coordinator of Women's Studies Interdisciplinary Program, 1980-81, acting director of Center for Teaching Effectiveness, 1980-81. Delaware Humanities Council, chairperson of publicity and fundraising.

MEMBER: Modern Language Association of America, American Conference for Irish Studies (founding chairperson of mid-Atlantic region), James Joyce Foundation (founder of Women's Caucus, 1982; member of board of directors, 1990—), Virginia Woolf Society, Phi Beta Kappa.

AWARDS, HONORS: American Philosophical Society grant, 1981; National Endowment for the Humanities grant, 1984; Excellence in Teaching Grant, Mortar Board, 1984; University of Delaware Center for Advanced Study grant, 1991-92.

WRITINGS:

Joyce and Feminism, Indiana University Press, 1984.
James Joyce, Harvester Press, 1987.

New Alliances in Joyce Studies, University of Delaware Press, 1988.
The Gender of Modernism, Indiana University Press, 1990.

Also contributor to scholarly journals and to numerous anthologies of literary criticism, including *Classics of Joyce Criticism,* edited by Janet Egleson Dunleavy, University of Illinois Press, 1991; *Joyce in Context,* edited by Timothy P. Martin and Vincent Cheng, Cambridge University Press, 1992; *Irish Writing: Exile and Subversion,* edited by Paul Hyland and Neil Sammells, Macmillan, 1992; and *The Johns Hopkins Guide to Literary Criticism and Theory,* edited by Michael Groden and Martin Kreiswirth, Johns Hopkins University Press, 1993. Member of editorial board, *Joyce Studies Annual.*

WORK IN PROGRESS: *The Web in the Scaffolding: The Feminist Modernisms of Virginia Woolf, Rebecca West and Djuna Barnes; The Selected Letters of Rebecca West.*

SIDELIGHTS: Bonnie Kime Scott once told *CA:* "As a student I had a bewildering array of profound interests, including astronomy and international politics. I decided that I could be most effective in probing human nature and contexts through literature. The advent of women's studies brought a new archive and a thorough revision of my view of the scope, politics, and possibilities of literature, including my two most valued authors, Virginia Woolf and James Joyce.

"Woolf offers methods of questioning and communicating with readers, of catching the atoms of experience, and of acknowledging the importance of female lives and perceptions. Joyce first attracted me with his rendering of sensual perception and human psychology; he retains my interest with his development of 'polylogue'—his evasion of monological language and philosophy. Modernist problems of disintegration and renewal, brought to the level of language itself, remain central to our postmodern world. The texts are demanding and thus stimulating to mental life, hence my satisfaction at studying and teaching them. Irish literature, which I entered via Joyce, offers other, decentered worlds to the modern imagination and reminds us of the constant merger of the political with the literary."

She later added, "Among the authors I have come to value recently are Rebecca West, for her amazing scope of history, and Djuna Barnes, for her ability to probe pain and sexual marginality. I look forward to better cross-cultural communication via writers such as Toni Morrison and Alice Walker."

BIOGRAPHICAL/CRITICAL SOURCES:

PERIODICALS

Times Literary Supplement, January 11, 1985.

*   *   *

SCOTT, Stephen E. 1948-

PERSONAL: Born April 12, 1948, in Portsmouth, OH; son of Duffy (a factory worker) and Darlene (Patrick) Scott; married Harriet Sauder, June 30, 1973; children: Andrew, Hannah, Catharine. *Education:* Attended Cedarville College and Wright State University. *Religion:* Old Order River Brethren.

ADDRESSES: Home—2778 Ironville Pike, Columbia, PA 17512. *Office*—Good Enterprises, P. O. Box 419, Intercourse, PA 17534.

CAREER: Williams Tool and Machine, Lancaster, PA, chart maker and statistician, 1980-84; Good Enterprises, Intercourse, PA, research, 1984—. Teacher at Mennonite school in Manheim, PA, 1979-80.

MEMBER: Costume Society of America, Carriage Association of America, Brethren in Christ Historical Society, Lancaster Mennonite Historical Society.

WRITINGS:

Plain Buggies, Good Books, 1981.
Why Do They Dress That Way?, Good Books, 1986.
The Amish Wedding, Good Books, 1988.
(With Kenneth Pellman) *Living without Electricity,* Good Books, 1990.
Amish Houses and Barns, Good Books, 1992.
A Guide to the Peace Churches, Good Books, 1993.
An Introduction to Old Order and Conservative Mennonite Groups, Good Books, 1993.

Contributor to periodicals, including *Pennsylvania Mennonite Heritage.*

SIDELIGHTS: Stephen E. Scott told *CA:* "As a teenager in suburban Dayton, OH, I became attracted to the 'Plain People,' those piously dressed folk I saw occasionally during my youth. I read everything I could about these people and eventually visited, worked, and lived with them. At twenty-one years of age I became a member of the Old Order River Brethren Church, which upholds the strong beliefs that Christianity cannot be separated from daily living and that the church should provide scripturally based guidelines on such areas of life as conduct, speech, entertainment, and especially dress. I have a deep respect for the 'Plain People' (Amish, Mennonite, and Brethren), and I wish to share with others their faith, life, and history through my writing."

SCOVILLE, Herbert, Jr. 1915-1985

PERSONAL: Born March 16, 1915, in New York City, died of cancer, July 30, 1985, in Washington, DC; son of Herbert, Sr. and Orlena (Zabriskie) Scoville; married Ann Curtiss, June 26, 1937; children: Anthony Church, Thomas Welch, Nicholas Zabriskie, Mary Curtiss. *Education:* Yale University, B.S., 1937; Cambridge University, graduate work in physical chemistry, 1937-39; University of Rochester, Ph.D., 1942. *Avocational Interests:* Travel and trout fishing.

ADDRESSES: Home and office—6400 Georgetown Pike, McLean, VA 22101.

CAREER: National Defense Research Committee, Washington, DC, began as assistant chemist, became associate chemist, handled a variety of research contracts in chemical warfare in various locations, 1941-45; Atomic Energy Commission, Los Alamos Scientific Laboratory, CA, senior scientist, 1946-48; U.S. Department of Defense, technical director of Armed Forces Special Weapons Project in Virginia, 1948-55; Central Intelligence Agency, Washington, DC, 1955-63, began as assistant director of scientific intelligence, became deputy director for research; U.S. Arms Control and Disarmament Agency, Washington, DC, assistant director for science and technology, 1963-69; Carnegie Endowment for International Peace, New York City, director of arms control program, 1969-71. Member of Killian Committee, Technological Capabilities Panel, 1955; member of U.S. delegation to the Geneva Conference, 1958; chairperson of U.S. delegation to NATO disarmament experts' meetings, 1966-68, and of U.S. delegations to Japan, Australia, and South Africa on the non-proliferation treaty, 1967-68. Consultant to President's Science Advisory Agency, 1969-73.

MEMBER: Arms Control Association (former president), American Association for the Advancement of Science (AAAS; council member, 1979-85), Union of Concerned Scientists (board member, 1980-85), Council for a Livable World (board member, 1979-85), Public Welfare Foundation (board member), Council of Foreign Relations, Sigma Xi, Cosmos Club (Washington, DC), Century Club (New York).

AWARDS, HONORS: Rockefeller Public Service Award, 1981, for promotion of peace.

WRITINGS:

(With Robert Osborn) *Missile Madness,* Houghton, 1970.
Toward a Strategic Arms Limitation Agreement, Carnegie Endowment, 1970.
(Contributor) Boskey and Willrich, editors, *Nuclear Proliferation: Prospects for Control,* Dunellen, 1970.

(With Betty G. Lall and Robert E. Hunter) *The Arms Race: Steps Toward Restraint,* Carnegie Endowment, 1972.

(Contributor) *The Future of the Sea-Based Deterrent,* MIT Press, 1973.

(Contributor) Rhidelander and Willrich, editors, *SALT: The Moscow Agreements and Beyond,* Free Press, 1974.

MX: Prescription for Disaster, MIT Press, 1981.

Contributor to *Verification and SALT* by William C. Potter, Westview Press, 1980. Contributor of articles on national security to *Scientific American, New Republic, Foreign Affairs, Foreign Policy,* and other periodicals.

OBITUARIES:

PERIODICALS

Los Angeles Times, August 1, 1985.
New York Times, July 31, 1985.
Time, August 12, 1985.
Washington Post, July 31, 1985.*

*   *   *

SHACKELFORD, Jean A. 1946-

PERSONAL: Born March 11, 1946, in Lexington, KY; daughter of Thomas B. (a landscape architect) and Delmyre (a teacher; maiden name, Cable) Shackelford; married Ronald J. Brinkman (a computer scientist), June 1, 1975; children: Brian Geoffrey. *Education:* Kansas State University, B.A., 1967; University of Kentucky, M.A., 1968, Ph.D., 1974.

ADDRESSES: Home—610 Maple Street, Lewisburg, PA 17837. *Office*—Department of Economics, Bucknell University, Lewisburg, PA 17837.

CAREER: University of Kentucky, Lexington, teaching assistant, 1967-69, part-time instructor, 1969-70; Top of Alabama Regional Council of Governments, Huntsville, AL, consultant, 1972; University of Alabama, Huntsville, instructor in economics, 1971-73; State University of New York College at Geneseo, assistant professor of economics, 1973-75; Bucknell University, Lewisburg, PA, assistant professor, 1975-81, associate professor of economics, 1982—. Research assistant, Kansas State University, 1967, and Spindletop Research, 1969. Founder and president of Lewisburg Area Child Care Center, Inc. Lecturer on economics and other topics.

MEMBER: International Studies Association, American Economic Association (member of executive committee, 1979-83; chairperson of Eastern Region's Committee on the Status of Women, 1978-83), Eastern Economic Association, Regional Science Association, Omicron Delta Epsilon, Phi Epsilon Delta.

AWARDS, HONORS: McKenna Foundation grant, 1979; Women's Educational Equity Program grant, U.S. Education Department, 1980; RCA Corporation grant, 1981; Exxon Education Foundation grant, 1981; Avon Foundation grant, 1981; Exxon Computer Graphics Project award, 1982; Computer Literacy Project award, Sloan Foundation, 1983.

WRITINGS:

(With Tom Riddell and Steve Stamos) *Economics: A Tool for Understanding Society,* Addison-Wesley, 1979, 4th edition, 1991.
Urban and Regional Economics, Gale, 1980.

Also author of *Overall Economic Development Program,* 1972, and *Women in the Professional and Managerial Workplace,* three volumes, Educational Development Center; also editor with Catherine Blair and Molly Wingate of *Papers and Proceedings of the Second Annual Conference on Peer Tutoring.* Contributor of articles and book reviews to *American Economic Review, Growth and Change,* and other publications.*

*   *   *

SHALOFF, Stanley 1939-

PERSONAL: Born October 10, 1939, in Bronx, NY; son of Isidore and Tolanda (Simon) Shilofsky; married Esther Heber, February 19, 1978; children: Jennifer Yael, Rebecca Irit. *Education:* City College (now City College of the City University of New York), B.A., 1960; Northwestern University, M.A., 1962, Ph.D., 1967. *Politics:* Democrat. *Religion:* Jewish.

ADDRESSES: Home—11407 Fairoak Dr., Silver Spring, MD 20902. *Office*—Office of the Historian, Bureau of Public Affairs, U.S. Department of State, Washington, DC 20520.

CAREER: Wisconsin State University, Oshkosh, instructor, 1964-67, assistant professor, 1967-69, associate professor of history, 1970-75; U.S. Department of State, Bureau of Public Affairs, Office of the Historian, Washington, DC, historian, 1976—. Visiting lecturer in history, University of Ghana, Legon, 1968-69; visiting associate professor of African-American Studies, University of Maryland Baltimore County, 1972-73; visiting associate professor, University of Wisconsin—Madison, 1974-75; associate professorial lecturer, George Washington University, spring, 1977, 1981.

MEMBER: African Studies Association, American Historical Association, Phi Beta Kappa, Phi Alpha Theta.

AWARDS, HONORS: National Endowment for the Humanities Research Fellow, 1969-70.

WRITINGS:

Reform in Leopold's Congo, John Knox, 1970.
(Co-editor) *Foreign Relations of the United States,* Volume XI: *1952-54: Africa and South Asia,* U.S. Government Printing Office, 1983.
(Co-editor) *American Foreign Policy Basic Documents, 1977-1980,* U. S. Department of State, 1983.

Contributor of articles to history journals in Britain, France, Ghana, and the United States. Book reviewer, *Societas: A Review of Social History,* 1971-79.

WORK IN PROGRESS: U.S. Policy Toward Africa, 1950-1960. *

*   *   *

SHANNON, David Allen 1920-

PERSONAL: Born November 30, 1920, in Terre Haute, IN; son of John Raymond and Esther (Allen) Shannon; married Jane Short, August 31, 1940; children: Molly, Sarah. *Education:* Indiana State College (now University), B.S., 1941; University of Wisconsin, M.S., 1946, Ph.D., 1951.

ADDRESSES: Home—Pavilion V, West Lawn, University of Virginia, Charlottesville, VA 22903.

CAREER: Carnegie Institute of Technology, Pittsburgh, PA, instructor of history, 1948-51; Teachers College, Columbia University, New York City, began as assistant professor, became associate professor of history, 1951-57; University of Wisconsin—Madison, began as associate professor, became professor of history, 1957-65; University of Maryland, College Park, lecturer of history and chairman of department, 1965-68; Rutgers University, New Brunswick, NJ, professor of history and chairman of department, 1968-69; University of Virginia, Charlottesville, professor of history and dean of faculty of arts and sciences, 1969-71, vice-president and provost, 1971-1981, Commonwealth Professor of History, 1975—. Instructor, University of California at Berkeley, 1957; lecturer in history, University of Stockholm, 1959, University of Lund, Sweden, 1960, and University of Aix-Marseille (France), 1962-63; Thomas Jefferson visiting fellow, Downing College, Cambridge University, 1976. *Military service:* U.S. Army Air Corps, 1943-45, became staff sergeant.

MEMBER: American Historical Association, Organization of American Historians, Virginia Historical Association (trustee, 1981—).

WRITINGS:

(With Lawrence A. Cremlin) *A History of Teachers College, Columbia University,* Columbia University Press, 1954.
The Socialist Party of America: A History, Macmillan, 1955.
(Editor) *The Great Depression,* Prentice-Hall, 1959.
The Decline of American Communism: A History of the Communist Party of the United States since 1945, Harcourt, 1959.
Twentieth Century America, Rand McNally, 1963.
(Editor) Beatrice Webb, *Beatrice Webb's American Diary, 1898,* University of Wisconsin Press, 1963.
Between the Wars: America, 1919-1941, Houghton, 1965, 2nd edition, 1979.
(Editor) *Progressivism and the Post-War Reaction,* McGraw, 1966.
(Editor) *Southern Business: The Decades Ahead,* with foreword by Rand V. Araskog, Bobbs-Merrill, 1981.

Contributor to various professional journals.

WORK IN PROGRESS: FDR and Congress. *

*   *   *

SHEPHERD, Jack 1937-

PERSONAL: Born December 14, 1937, in Summit, NJ; son of John Edwin (in advertising) and Grace (Anderson) Shepherd; married Kathleen Kessler (special education supervisor), September 3, 1960; children: Kristen, Caleb. *Education:* Haverford College, B.A., 1960; Columbia University, M.S., 1961; Boston University, Ph.D., 1989. *Religion:* Society of Friends (Quaker).

ADDRESSES: Home—Rte. 1, RFD 405, Norwich, VT 05055. *Agent*—Sterling Lord, 1 Madison Ave., New York, NY 10005.

CAREER: Look magazine, New York City, senior editor, 1964-69, assistant managing editor, 1969-70, senior editor in charge of special issues, 1970-71; *Newsweek,* New York City, associate editor, 1971-72; Carnegie Endowment for International Peace, New York City, senior associate, 1974-75, 1984-85; South-North News Service, Hanover, NH, managing editor, 1985-88. Free-lance writer, 1972—. President of Shepherd Associates, Inc., 1968—; professor of war and peace studies and environmental studies, Dartmouth College, 1988-93; director, global security fellows program, Cambridge University, 1993—. *Military service:* U.S. Army Reserve, 1961-62.

AWARDS, HONORS: National Education award, National Education Association, 1966; National Magazine award finalist, 1974; Haverford award, Haverford College, 1978, 1993; University Fellow, Boston University, 1982-83.

WRITINGS:

(With Christopher S. Wren) *Quotations from Chairman LBJ,* Simon & Schuster, 1968.

(With Wren) *The Almanack of Poor Richard Nixon,* World Publishing, 1969.

(Editor) *Earth Day: The Beginning,* Penguin, 1970.

(With Wren) *The Super Summer of Jamie McBride,* Simon & Schuster, 1971.

The Forest Killers, Weybright & Talley, 1975.

The Adams Chronicles, Little, Brown, 1976.

The Politics of Starvation, Carnegie Endowment for International Peace, 1976.

(With Daniel Levinson) *Seasons of a Man's Life,* Knopf, 1978.

(With Bob Glover) *The Runner's Handbook Training Diary,* Penguin, 1978.

Cannibals of the Heart: A Personal Biography of Louisa and John Quincy Adams, McGraw, 1981.

(With Pete Schuder and Glover) *Competitive Runner's Handbook,* Viking, 1983.

(With Glover) *The Runner's Handbook,* Penguin, 1978, revised edition, 1985.

(With Glover) *The Family Fitness Handbook,* Penguin Books, 1989.

SCREENPLAYS

The Acid Trip, Harcourt, 1969.

Black America's West African Heritage, Harcourt, 1970.

OTHER

Also author of television documentary, "Nuclear Power," 1973. Contributor to *The Challenge of Famine,* edited by John O. Field, Kumarian, 1993; *Africa: The Anguished Continent,* Newsweek Resource Unit, 1987; *Scribner Economics,* Scribner Educational Publishers, 1987. Contributor to periodicals, including *Harper's, New York Times Sunday Magazine, Psychology Today, Reader's Digest, Newsweek,* and *Cosmopolitan.*

ADAPTATIONS: The Adams Chronicles was filmed by Indiana University Audio-Visual Center for WNET-TV in New York City, 1976.

SIDELIGHTS: Jack Shepherd has written books on a wide range of topics, including politics, environmentalism, and historical biography. In 1968 he teamed up with fellow *Look* editor Christopher Wren for *Quotations from Chairman LBJ,* the satirical American equivalent of *Quotations From Chairman Mao Tse-tung.* This book of "happy homilies of the Great Society barbecue," as John Quirk of *Commonweal* dubs them, was aimed at the emerging counterculture, but its popularity quickly

broadened as controversy surrounding Johnson's policies grew. With President Johnson's classic quips such as "Hello down there. This is your candidate, Lyndon Johnson," Wren theorizes in *New York Times Book Review* that the book "talks for the silent center."

Shepherd confronts controversy again in *The Forest Killers,* an investigation into the U. S. Forest Service's abuse of the wilderness it was enacted to protect. Anthony Wolff in *Saturday Review* calls Shepherd's exposure of the Forest Service's alliance with the logging industry and its corruption of its multiple-use policy a "saddening, maddening revelation." Environmental activist and writer Edward Abbey, reviewing the book in *New York Times Book Review,* agrees with Shepherd that the U.S. Forest Service has become "a public relations branch of the timber industry, the mining industry and the road-building industry" and suggests that the Forest Service's slogan " 'Land of Many Uses' might appropriately be modified to 'Land of Many Abuses.' "

Shepherd examines the strained relationship and triumphant public life of Louisa Catherine and John Quincy Adams in *Cannibals of the Heart,* an outgrowth of his earlier book and TV series for WNET-TV in New York, *The Adams Chronicles.* Shepherd recounts Louisa's and John's personal tragedies (their hardships in Russia from 1809-18, the deaths of three of their children—including their oldest son's suicide), and their public triumphs (Louisa's relentless campaign that landed John the presidency in 1825, and his subsequent fruitful career in the House of Representatives until his death). Shepherd extols Louisa as an early feminist who struggled with a domineering husband and feelings of inferiority: "an intelligent and forthright woman living under the tyranny of a cold, ambitious husband," according to Laurel Brodsley in the *Los Angeles Times.* Louisa, in addition to her selfless support of John, promoted abolition of slavery in conjunction with women's rights and urged her husband to bring these issues into the forefront during his last years in congress. While Charles Akers comments in *Washington Post Book World* that Shepherd's "creative interpretation" is "uncritical and sometimes dogmatic," Brodsley remarks that Shepherd is "too honest a historian . . . to obscure fact for the sake of an idea."

Jack Shepherd told *CA:* "I am primarily an investigative, curious writer, looking at the new things of the day. Any writer of talent must illuminate society's path, and not trail along as the tailgate rider. I have traveled, as an author and journalist, in 46 of the 50 United States, and throughout Western Europe, the Caribbean, parts of the Far East, and Ghana, Nigeria, Upper Volta, Kenya, Tanzania, and Ethiopia in Africa. To keep fresh ideas flowing, at age 43, I returned to graduate school to finish work on my Ph.D. while continuing to write about things that interest me and are of value to others."

BIOGRAPHICAL/CRITICAL SOURCES:

PERIODICALS

Atlantic, March, 1976.
Intellectual Digest, February, 1973, March, 1974.
Look, August 12, 1969.
Los Angeles Times, April 23, 1981.
New Yorker, April 20, 1981.
New York Times Book Review, March 24, 1968; July 20, 1975.
Saturday Review, September 6, 1975.
Washington Post Book World, April 5, 1981.
Village Voice, January 4, 1968.

*　　*　　*

SHOUP, Laurence H(enry) 1943-

PERSONAL: Born June 10, 1943, in Los Angeles, CA; son of David John (a jeweler) and Edna Ruth (a teacher; maiden name, Jaenke) Shoup; married Suzanne Marie Baker (an archeologist), August 12, 1974; children: Daniel David. *Education:* Glendale College, A.A., 1963; California State College at Los Angeles (now California State University, Los Angeles), B.A., 1966, M.A., 1967; Northwestern University, Ph.D., 1974. *Avocational Interests:* Camping, hiking, fishing, Africa, gold panning, traveling.

ADDRESSES: Home—609 Aileen Street, Oakland, CA 94609.

CAREER: Writer. U.S. Peace Corps, Tigre, Ethiopia, teacher of world history, 1967-69; Northwestern University, Evanston, IL, instructor in U.S. history, 1971-74; University of Illinois, Urbana, assistant professor of U.S. history, 1974-75. Lecturer at University of California, Berkley, 1975 and 1980, and at San Francisco State University, San Francisco, CA, 1976-77. Partner in Archeological/Historical Consultants, Oakland, CA, 1978—. Co-chair of membership committee of Sunset Cooperative Nursery School, 1980-81. Member of steering committee, National Committee for Independent Political Action, 1990—.

WRITINGS:

(With William Minter) *Imperial Brain Trust, The Council on Foreign Relations and U.S. Foreign Policy,* Monthly Review Press, 1977.
The Carter Presidency and Beyond: Power and Politics in the 1980s, Ramparts, 1980.
(With Roberta Greenwood) *Robinson's Ferry/Melones: A History of a Motherlode Town, 1848-1942,* National Park Service, 1984.

(With wife, Suzanne Baker) *Speed, Power, Production and Profit: Railroad Logging in the Goosenest District, Klamath National Forest, 1900-1956,* U.S. Forest Service, 1981.
Cultural Resources Study of the Gibsonville and Bellevue Timber Conglomerate, Sierra and Plumas Counties, Californa, Plumas National Forest, 1985.
Historical Overview of Pacific Gas and Electric Company's Tule River Hydroelectric System and Environs, Tulare County, California, Pacific Gas and Electric Company, 1985.
(With Greenwood and Michael Moratto) *Final Report of the New Melones Archeological Project, California,* Volume 7: *Review and Synthesis of Research at Historical Sites,* Coyote Press, 1987.

Contributor to professional journals.

SIDELIGHTS: In *The Carter Presidency and Beyond,* Laurence H. Shoup explored the forces that make and control the U.S. presidency. In this book he argues that members of the American ruling class—the leading media, the corporate elite, and private policy planning organizations like the Council on Foreign Relations and Trilateral Commission—are the nation's "real power wielders." These "real sources of political power," Shoup contended, control the political parties and elections. He stated that the aim of the ruling class is to enhance its power and influence through selecting and financing favored candidates and controlling the process by which ideology is disseminated. For example, Shoup explained, "a key function of primaries from the point of view of far-sighted ruling class leaders is to determine which of several acceptable candidates can gain broad support from the American people."

Critics Michael Kinsley of the *Washington Post Book World* and Aaron Wildavsky of the *New York Times Book Review* objected to Shoup's definition of the ruling class. "The concept of a ruling class in America is not silly, but Shoup's treatment of it is," commented Kinsley. His version "is flexible enough to cover any contingency." Wildavsky also expressed doubts about some of the author's classifications. He questioned Shoup's statement that the members of the "Eastern establishment control the elite universities of America": "Why has a distinguished member of the Princeton faculty . . . been allowed to write a laudatory introduction to this book attacking the 'ruling class'?"

On the other hand, Harvey Bresler of the *Seattle Times Magazine* found that "the author gives a coherent persuasive account of the damage to the public weal of a Carter administration whose primary concern is healthy company profits." The *Berkley Graduate*'s Marian Kester complimented Shoup's work: "Whatever its theoretical shortcomings, *The Carter Presidency and Beyond* is full of highly useful and sometimes prophetic information." The author, she continued, "accurately predicted, writing in the summer of '79, that a Cold War II would be both the logical extension of administration policy, and a terrorist style 'non-negotiable demand' for Carter's re-election."

Shoup told *CA:* "The aim of my intellectual work is to understand how the U.S. and world power system operates as a first step towards transforming this system into a cooperative commonwealth characterized by respect for nature, nonviolence, equality, economic democracy, world peace, and social justice."

BIOGRAPHICAL/CRITICAL SOURCES:

PERIODICALS

Berkley Graduate, April, 1980.
Le Monde Diplomatique, November, 1980.
New York Times Book Review, April 27, 1980.
Seattle Times Magazine, June 29, 1980.
Washington Post Book World, March 16, 1980.

*   *   *

SHULMAN, Alix Kates 1932-

PERSONAL: Born August 17, 1932, in Cleveland, OH; daughter of Samuel S. (an attorney and labor arbitrator) and Dorothy (Davis) Kates; married Marcus Klein, April 19, 1953 (divorced); married Martin Shulman (a designer), June 19, 1959 (divorced, 1985); married Scott York, April 16, 1989; children: (second marriage) Theodore, Polly. *Education:* Case Western Reserve University, B.A., 1953; graduate study in philosophy at Columbia University, 1953-55; special student in mathematics, New York University, 1960-62; New York University, M.A., 1978.

ADDRESSES: Home—New York City and Long Island, ME. *Office*—c/o Ellen Levine Curtis Brown Ltd., 60 East 56th St., New York, NY 10022. *Agent*—Amanda Urban, ICM Agency, 40 West 57th St., New York, NY 10019.

CAREER: Writer and teacher of creative writing. Editor, *Collier's Encyclopedia*, 1957-61, and *Encyclopedia of Philosophy*, 1963-66. Taught writing workshops at New York University, 1976-84, Yale University, 1979-81, and University of Southern Maine, summers, 1982-84, University of Arizona, 1993. Visiting artist, American Academy in Rome, 1982; visiting writer in residence, University of Colorado, 1984-86, and Ohio State University, 1987; citizen's chair, University of Hawaii, 1991-92. Founding member of New York University Faculty Colloquium on Sex and Gender, fall, 1980—, and Committee for Abortion Rights and Against Sterilization Abuse (CARASA).

Member of advisory boards for New York Feminist Art Institute, 1978-86 and International Festival of Women's Films, 1978-80 and Westbeth Feminist Theater.

MEMBER: PEN (executive board, 1976-91; vice president, 1982 and 1983), Authors Guild, Authors League, National Writers Union, Women's Ink, Women's Institute for Freedom of the Press, The Women's Salon, Feminist Writer's Guild, Columbia University Seminar on Women and Society (executive board, 1980-82), New York Institute for the Humanities Seminar on Sex, Gender, and Consumerism.

AWARDS, HONORS: Outstanding book citation, *New York Times* and *Library Journal*, 1971, for *To the Barricades: The Anarchist Life of Emma Goldman;* MacDowell Colony for the Arts fellow, 1975-77, 1979, 1981; Millay fellow, Millay Colony for the Arts, 1978; DeWitt Wallace/Readers Digest fellow, 1979; outstanding book citation, *New York Times Book Review*, 1981, for *On the Stroll;* Yale University fellow of Saybrook College, 1980—; creative writing grant, National Endowments for the Arts, 1983, Golden Key Honor Society, 1992.

WRITINGS:

NOVELS

Memoirs of an Ex-Prom Queen, Knopf, 1972.
Burning Questions, Knopf, 1978.
On the Stroll, Knopf, 1981.
In Every Woman's Life . . . , Knopf, 1987.

JUVENILE

Bosley on the Number Line, illustrated by Gena, David McKay, 1970.
To the Barricades: The Anarchist Life of Emma Goldman, Crowell, 1971.
Finders Keepers, illustrated by Emily McCully, Bradbury Press, 1971.
Awake or Asleep, illustrated by Frank Bozzo, Addison-Wesley, 1971.

EDITOR

The Traffic in Women and Other Essays by Emma Goldman, Times Change Press, 1970.
Red Emma Speaks: Selected Writings and Speeches by Emma Goldman, Random House, 1972.

OTHER

Author of introduction, Anne Marie Rousseau, *Shopping Bag Ladies*, Pilgrim Press, 1981.
Author of introduction, *Five Sisters: Women Against the Tsar*, edited by Barbara A. Engel and Cliford N. Rosenthal, Knopf, 1975.

Contributor to *Woman in Sexist Society: Studies in Power and Powerlessness,* edited by Vivian Gornick and B. K. Moran, Basic Books, 1971; *Between Women,* edited by Ascher, di Salvo, Ruddick, Beacon Press, 1983, and *Critical Fictions: The Politics of Imaginative Writing,* Bay Press, 1991. Work has been anthologized in *Rediscovery,* Avon, 1982 and *Words on the Page,* Harper and Row, 1990. Contributor of articles, short stories, and reviews to periodicals, including *New York Times, New York Times Book Review, Village Voice, Ms., Atlantic, Redbook, Womansports, Feminist Studies,* and *Socialist Review.* Advisor, *Aurora,* 1979-81 and member of advisory board, *Aphra,* 1978-82.

Shulman's novels have been translated into German, Dutch, Danish, Swedish, French, Hebrew, Spanish, Serbo-Croatian, and Italian.

WORK IN PROGRESS: Drinking the Rain, a memoir.

SIDELIGHTS: Author and teacher Alix Kates Shulman's writings include novels that explore the problems American women faced from the 1950s to the 1980s, children's books that explain the concepts of math and sleep, and nonfiction works that detail the lives of early feminists. Shulman won wide attention and acclaim for her first novel, *Memoirs of an Ex-Prom Queen,* which attained status as a "break-through book," in the words of Lucy Rosenthal in the *Saturday Review,* for the feminist movement of the early 1970s. Shulman describes the book to *CA* as a "comic novel about coming of age in the fifties." Sasha Davis, the protagonist, is "a white, middle-class midwestern girl" continues Shulman, "who grows to womanhood trying to be everything an ideal woman was expected to be before the women's movement—sexy prom queen, beautiful wife, devoted mother. But nothing works out as expected." Rosenthal comments that women, especially, will identify strongly with the issues, but notes that Shulman's "insights bridge the gender gap." Sara Blackburn in the *Washington Post Book World,* however, thinks of the book as "more a memoir of a middle-class Jewish girlhood" rather than a feminist novel per se, and Marilyn Bender, reviewing the novel for the *New York Times Book Review,* expresses mixed feelings, giving the "angry" novel "a bravo as a consciousness-raising attempt."

Burning Questions, Shulman's second novel, is, according to its author, "the story of another kind of woman," Zane IndiAnna, "a self-styled rebel whose political awakening in the late sixties transforms her. At once a political and historical novel, spanning four decades . . . *Burning Questions* attempts to portray the important changes in women's lives and consciousness wrought by contemporary feminism." Structured as Zane's autobiography, the novel includes numerous quotations from real-life feminist writers and a bibliography at the end. Fiction writer

Lynne Sharon Schwartz, writing in *Ms.,* found that *Burning Questions* is really two books: a traditional growing-up novel, in its first half, and a portrayal of the feminist movement, in its second half. Schwartz prefers the second half, saying, "Shulman is at her best when describing with passion the young days of the Movement." Anne Tyler, in the *Washington Post Book World,* expresses reservations about the novel's protagonist, citing Zane's "extreme distance from her own life," conveyed by the habit of mentioning major experiences off-handedly. Tyler admits, however, to being won over in the end by Shulman's "new clear-eyed, steady view" of the 1970s.

Shulman's third novel, *On the Stroll,* departs considerably from her earlier portrayals of middle-class women while retaining her feminist concern for women's lives. "The Stroll" is the slang term for a strip of New York's Eighth Avenue frequented by streetwalkers, runaways, and the homeless. Its main characters are a brief cross-section of local types: Owl, the bag lady, Robin, the 16-year-old runaway, and Prince, the pimp who becomes involved with Robin. *New York Times* reviewer Anatole Broyard calls the novel "selfless, careful and satisfying," and singles out the characterization of Owl as lifting the book "above the level of the well-made novel." Similarly, in the *New York Times Book Review,* Mary Cantwell writes, "In *On the Stroll,* [Shulman] is on new ground, and it has provided her with a far better book than her first two." *Washington Post Book World* reviewer Michelle Slung sounds a similar note, regretting the "gushy earnestness" of Shulman's first two novels and preferring *On the Stroll:* "Shulman plugs into myth to give us a contemporary fable of people on the outside and her empathy sustains the book throughout. . . . She sometimes achieves an almost Dickensian sense of society's underside. *On the Stroll* is an unexpected book, and a worthy one."

Shulman's following novel, 1987's *In Every Woman's Life . . .,* returns to her familiar middle-class setting. The title refers to the premise that every woman, at some point in life, must think about marriage; the novel focuses on how three woman think about it. The three women are Rosemary Streeter, a successful New York professional/wife/mother who, in the author's words, "has made-do" in a long-lasting marriage; Nora Kennedy, something of a foil for Rosemary, a journalist, single, and opposed to marriage but involved in an affair with a married man; and Rosemary's daughter, Daisy, who "must still decide how to live," in Shulman's words. Novelist Meredith Sue Willis, in the *New York Times Book Review,* calls the novel "several books in one," and favors its conventional, family-novel aspect, saying, "A novella-length chapter called 'Beached' fairly bursts off the page with the sensuality of pregnancy and the complex ways in which men and women create the unspoken rules of their marriages." Willis regrets that the novel too often analyzes its characters and themes intellectually rather than letting go emotionally. Grace Lichtenstein, in the *Washington Post Book World,* finds the character of Rosemary to be the book's strength, averring that Shulman explores and resolves Daisy's dilemmas too conveniently. And Chicago *Tribune Books* reviewer Roberta Rubenstein finds that the characters, because of their lack of guilt, are not sympathetic, and faults Shulman for a lack of irony.

Recalling her personal involvement in the feminist movement of the 1960s, Shulman related to *CA:* "Those were heady times: a new generation was ardently questioning traditional social and political values in every quarter of American society. The radical feminist ideas we were developing . . . gave me an understanding of my life and society that fueled my writing and ultimately, by giving me both a subject and an audience, enabled me finally to create a life of my own choosing."

BIOGRAPHICAL/CRITICAL SOURCES:

BOOKS

Brown, Cherly L. and Karen Olsen, editors, *Feminist Criticism: Essays on Theory, Poetry and Prose,* Scarecrow Press (London), 1978.
Contemporary Literary Criticism, Volume 2, Gale, 1974, Volume 10, Gale, 1979.
Cornillon, Susan Koppelman, editor, *Images of Women in Fiction: Feminist Perspectives,* Bowling Green University Press, 1972.
Hendin, Josephine, *Vulnerable People: A View of American Fiction Since 1945,* Oxford University Press, 1978.
Hiatt, Mary P., *The Way Women Write,* Teachers College Press, 1977.

PERIODICALS

Commonweal, May 21, 1971.
Ms., March, 1978, pp. 40-41.
New York Times, April 25, 1972; September 16, 1981.
New York Times Book Review, April 23, 1972, pp. 34, 36; March 26, 1978, p. 12; September 27, 1981; May 31, 1987.
Saturday Review, May 20, 1972, pp. 76-77.
Times Literary Supplement, July 1, 1983.
Tribune Books (Chicago), June 21, 1987.
Village Voice, April 3, 1978.
Washington Post, May 13, 1972.
Washington Post Book World, May 14, 1972, p. 13; March 26, 1978, p. G3; November 1, 1981; May 31, 1987.

SHUMSKY, Zena
SEE COLLIER, Zena

*   *   *

SILBER, Mark 1946-

PERSONAL: Born October 26, 1946, in the U.S.S.R.; immigrated to the United States in 1959; son of Aleksander (an engineer) and Cyla Silber; married Terry S. Brown (an editor), April 26, 1969. *Education:* Harvard University, B.A., 1970.

CAREER: Massachusetts General Hospital, Boston, photographer, 1968; EGC Advertising, Cambridge, MA, partner, 1970; Garland Junior College, Boston, instructor in photography, 1970-72; free-lance photographer, 1972—. Chairman of photography, Harvard Yearbook Co., 1968-69. Has exhibited photographs in one-person and group shows in the United States and England.

AWARDS, HONORS: Bookbuilders Award, 1972, for *Rural Maine.*

WRITINGS:

Rural Maine (photographic essay), Godine, 1972.
(Compiler) Gilbert Wight Tilson and Fred W. Record, *The Family Album: Photographs of the 1890s and 1900s,* Godine, 1973.
(With wife, Terry Silber) *The Complete Book of Everlastings: Growing, Drying and Designing with Dried Flowers,* Knopf, 1987.

OTHER

Contributor of photographs to national and regional magazines, including *Newsweek, Popular Photography, Down East, Atlantic Monthly, Interplay, Audience* and *Boston Review of the Arts.*

WORK IN PROGRESS: Three books; social documentary research and photography.*

*   *   *

SIMON, Paul 1928-

PERSONAL: Born November 29, 1928, in Eugene, OR; son of Martin Paul (a minister and publisher of religious magazines) and Ruth (a missionary; maiden name, Troemel) Simon; married Jeanne Hurley (an attorney), April 21, 1960; children: Sheila, Martin. *Education:* Attended University of Oregon, 1945-46, and Dana College, 1946-48. *Politics:* Democrat. *Religion:* Lutheran. *Avocational Interests:* Music, reading.

ADDRESSES: Home—Carbondale, IL 62901. *Office*—
U.S. Senate, 462 Dirksen Senate Bldg., Washington, DC
20510.

CAREER: Troy Tribune, Troy, IL, publisher, 1948-66;
member of Illinois House of Representatives, 1955-63;
senator in Illinois, 1963-69; lieutenant governor of Illinois,
1969-72; Sangamon State University, Springfield, IL, professor of public affairs, 1973-74; U.S. House of Representatives, Washington, DC, congressman from 24th Illinois
district, 1975-85, serving on House Budget Committee
and chairing the Education and Labor subcommittee on
higher education; U.S. Senator from Illinois, 1985—, serving on Senate Foreign Relations Committee, Labor and
Human Resources Committee, Judiciary Committee, and
Budget Committee; campaigned for U.S. Democratic
presidential nomination, 1987-88. Member of U.S. delegation to the United Nations. Member of board of directors
of Dana College. *Military service:* U.S. Army, Counterin-
telligence Corps, 1951-53.

MEMBER: Lions International, National Association for
the Advancement of Colored People, National Urban
League, American Legion, Veterans of Foreign Wars, Lutheran Human Relations Association, Sigma Delta Chi.

AWARDS, HONORS: Award for distinguished reporting
of state and local government, American Political Science
Association, 1957; thirty-six honorary degrees, including
LL.D. from Dana College, 1965, Concordia Teachers College, 1968, Lincoln Christian College, 1969, and Loyola
University, 1969; D.Litt. from McKendree College, 1965;
and D.C.L. from Greenville College, 1968; John F. Kennedy Institute of Politics fellow at Harvard University,
1973; named best legislator seven times by Independent
Voters of Illinois.

WRITINGS:

Lovejoy: Martyr to Freedom, Concordia, 1964.
*Lincoln's Preparation for Greatness: The Illinois Legisla-
    tive Years,* University of Oklahoma Press, 1965.
A Hungry World, Concordia, 1966.
(With wife, Jeanne Hurley Simon) *Protestant-Catholic
    Marriages Can Succeed,* Association Press, 1967.
*The Ombudsman in Illinois: An Experiment in Govern-
    ment,* Springfield, 1970.
You Want to Change the World? So Change It!, Thomas
    Nelson, 1971.
(With brother, Arthur Simon) *The Politics of World Hun-
    ger: Grass-Roots Politics and World Poverty,* Harper
    Magazine Press, 1973.
*The Tongue-Tied American: Confronting the Foreign Lan-
    guage Crisis,* Continuum, 1980.
The Once and Future Democrats: Strategies for Change,
    Continuum, 1982.

*The Glass House: Politics and Morality in the Nation's
    Capital,* Continuum, 1984.
*Beginnings: Senator Paul Simon Speaks to Young Ameri-
    cans,* Continuum, 1986.
Let's Put America Back to Work, Bonus Books, 1987.
*Winners and Losers: The 1988 Race for the Presidency—
    One Candidate's Perspective,* Continuum, 1989.
*Advice and Consent: Clarence Thomas, Robert Bork, and
    the Intriguing History of the Supreme Court's Nomi-
    nation Battles,* National Press Books, 1992.

Also author of weekly columns "Sidelights from Springfield," distributed to over three hundred newspapers,
1955-72, and "P.S./Washington," 1975—. Contributor of
articles to periodicals including *Harper's, Saturday Review, New Republic,* and *Columbia Journalism Review.*

SIDELIGHTS: Paul Simon's interest in public life began
at an early age. At sixteen he entered the University of Oregon to study journalism. Three years later he left school
to buy a defunct weekly newspaper. With the help of a
$3,600 loan underwritten by the local Lions Club, he pur-
chased the *Troy Tribune,* thus becoming the youngest edi-
tor-publisher in the country. He gradually put together a
group of fourteen weekly newspapers, which he sold in
1966. "Simon proved a gutsy, crusading editor with a
good eye for detail and a knack for self-promotion," Bill
Petersen would later report in the *Washington Post.* "His
paper was outspoken, crisply written and moralistic." He
used his papers to expose prostitution rings and syndicate
gambling connections with government officials in Madison County, Illinois. Because of this work he was called
to testify before the U.S. Senate's Crime Investigating
Committee in 1951.

After two years of Army service in Europe, Simon returned home in 1953, resumed his publishing career, and
in 1954 ran for the Illinois House of Representatives. Here
he became one of a small group of young, idealistic reformers that included state representative and attorney
Jeanne Hurley. They married in 1960, becoming the first
husband-wife team in the history of the Illinois general assembly. During his career as an Illinois representative,
Simon won passage of forty-six major pieces of legislation,
including a law establishing the high school equivalency
(G. E. D.) test in that state, a law creating the Illinois Arts
Council, and the state's first "open meeting" law. He was
also an early supporter of strong civil rights legislation.
Simon earned a reputation as a staunchly ethical crusader,
progressive on social issues but a watchdog on public expenditures. An article he published in *Harper's* in 1964 ex-
posing widespread corruption in the Illinois legislature
earned him the rancor of many of his colleagues, who
voted him a "Benedict Arnold" award.

In 1968 Simon won election as lieutenant governor of Illinois, despite the defeat of his party's gubernatorial candidate. In 1972 he ran for governor with the support of Chicago Mayor Richard Daley's powerful political organization. But in one of the few electoral losses of his life, Simon narrowly lost the primary to an opponent who accused Simon of supporting higher taxes and of selling out to Daley's political machine. Simon briefly left politics, setting up a graduate program in journalism at Sangamon State College and teaching at Harvard's John F. Kennedy School of Government, but in 1973 he successfully campaigned for a seat in the U.S. Congress, representing Illinois's 24th district. In his twelve years in the House he served on the Budget Committee and chaired the Education and Labor subcommittee on higher education, working for college student loan programs, greater aid for handicapped students, and broader foreign exchange and foreign language programs.

In 1984 Simon decided to run for the Senate, taking on Republican incumbent Charles H. Percy in a race that Petersen would later describe as "one of the most vicious in the country." Simon's campaign focused on Percy's character, accusing him of flip-flopping on issues; Percy, Petersen reported, "accused Simon of wanting to raise taxes, being friendly to Iran's Ayatollah Ruhollah Khomeini, and 'kowtowing' to Israeli interests." Despite the powerful coattails of the incumbent Republican president, Ronald Reagan, who that year defeated Democratic candidate Walter Mondale in a landslide, Simon edged out his Republican opponent by a narrow, two-percent margin. During his first two years in the Senate Simon voted against the MX missile, the B1 bomber, and the Strategic Defense ("Star Wars") Initiative, called for reductions in the federal deficit, and opposed the Reagan administration's policies in Central America. Simon's voting record in both the House and the Senate was, on the whole, solidly liberal. Petersen noted, however, a "conservative turn" in 1984, the year in which Simon ran for the Senate. "He voted for litmus-test issues supported by the liberal Americans for Democratic Action 40 percent of the time that year, compared with 70 percent of the time in 1983 and 95 percent in 1985," Petersen observed.

On May 18, 1987, Simon announced his candidacy for the Democratic presidential nomination. In a year in which most Democratic candidates sought to recapture the votes of "Reagan Democrats" by toning down their party's liberal image, Simon unabashedly embraced his party's liberal roots, basing his campaign on classic Democratic slogans of compassion, leadership, and activism in government. His campaign called for increased spending on domestic programs, particularly in education and job-training, coupled with achieving a balanced budget within three years through a combination of military spending cuts, lower interest rates, increased employment, and taxes on luxury items and fuels. "He spins the vision of a nurturing government," Robin Toner reported in the *New York Times*. Political commentators attributed much of Simon's early popularity in the polls to his reputation for honesty and his homespun image as a citizen reformer. He had long presented himself, Toner pointed out, as "a man outside of politics as usual." James Risen, writing in the *Los Angeles Times,* cited the senator's "unpretentious quality personified in his trademark bow-tie and TV emcee Bill Cullen bad looks."

Many observers suggested, however, that Simon's image as a naive and squeaky-clean outsider was somewhat unrealistic. Referring to his hard-hitting senatorial campaign against Charles Percy, Toner commented that his was "not the record of an unworldly man." Petersen described Simon as "hard to pigeonhole," at once "conservative and liberal, or idealistic and pragmatic." He noted the apparent contradiction between Simon's support for a constitutional amendment for a balanced budget and his call for increased spending on social programs, and observed, "the same year (1984) that [Simon] published a book calling for a crackdown on political action committee contributions, his own campaign accepted $904,054 in PAC donations." Simon's rivals for the Democratic nomination—who included Representative Richard Gephardt of Missouri, Senator Albert Gore of Tennessee, the Reverend Jesse Jackson, and Massachusetts Governor Michael Dukakis, who would eventually win the nomination—questioned the feasibility of Simon's economic strategy, claiming that his economic projections were overly optimistic and that his ambitious social programs would require massive tax increases. After a strong early showing in the polls and a primary victory in his home state of Illinois, Simon fared poorly in the other primaries, and on April 7, 1988, he suspended his campaign. But despite speculation by some analysts that Simon's unsuccessful bid for the presidency might cost him his Senate seat, Simon won re-election to the U.S. Senate in 1990.

Senator Simon's writings are closely related to his political concerns. Many of his books have provided detailed discussions of issues he has adopted during his long legislative career. "There is the earnest tone of the social worker or the minister in much of Mr. Simon's writings and deep-voice speeches," wrote Toner, adding that Simon "is enamored of anecdotes." *The Politics of World Hunger,* written in 1973 with his brother, Arthur, a Lutheran minister, discussed the history of U.S. foreign aid programs and the problems of developing nations. *The Tongue-Tied American,* published in 1980, argued for a greater emphasis on teaching foreign languages in American secondary schools and universities. Writing in *Washington Post Book World,* Joseph Nocera found Simon to be "at his polemical best" in showing why the United States' weakness in foreign languages "does matter—a great deal." Roselle M. Lewis, in the *Los Angeles Times,* felt that "Simon's corrective proposals" were "too little too late," but added that "this important survey of our national muteness, full of call-to-action statistics, should be seriously heeded." In *The Once and Future Democrats: Strategies for Change,* which appeared in 1982, Simon called on his party to adhere to its traditional liberal principles, and to avoid being swept towards the right by the apparent conservatism of the electorate following Ronald Reagan's election as president in 1980. *Let's Put America Back to Work,* published in 1987, proposed the formation of a Guaranteed Job Opportunity Program, reminiscent of the New Deal, that would provide minimum-wage jobs and educational programs for the unemployed. This proposal would figure largely in Simon's 1987-88 bid for the Democratic presidential nomination.

Several of Simon's books have examined the American political process itself. In *The Glass House: Politics and Morality in the Nation's Capital,* Simon emphasized the moral implications of political decisions. He also pointed out that the "moral" choice on a complex political issue can be difficult to determine; in some cases, he observed, a "moral stance could bring about an immoral result." *Winners and Losers: The 1988 Race for the Presidency* presented the senator's analysis of the 1988 presidential campaign. A reviewer for the *Los Angeles Times Book Review* remarked that the book was "often less-than-revelatory," but was "brightened by some delightful and insightful stories about [Simon's] fellow candidates." Merle Black, writing in the *Washington Post,* suggested that the book suffered from Simon's "aversion to introspection," but the reviewer found value in the author's "observations about his rival candidates, the problems of the nomination process and the dilemmas facing the Democratic Party in becoming again a realistic contender in presidential elections." Simon's 1992 book, *Advice and Consent,* examined the process of judicial appointments in light of the controversy over the appointment of Clarence Thomas to the Supreme Court and other confirmation controversies. Jon R. Waltz characterized this book as "intermittently helpful" and "evenhanded." In a review in the *Washington Post Book World,* he commended the author's presentation of the "legal and historical background," as well as "Simon's comments on who told the truth at the Thomas hearings and his thoughtful suggestions for reforming the process."

Simon once told *CA:* "One of the problems that has concerned me most during more than two decades in office has been the question of public confidence in elected officials. I have made a complete and detailed disclosure of my personal income, assets, and liabilities every year since 1955, because I think disclosure is the best way to deal with conflict of interest problems that arise during public service. We need stronger disclosure laws at both the federal and state level.

"Another principal issue I've been dealing with for a number of years is the twin problem of world population and hunger. Doing something about overpopulation and scarcity of food is the major problem we face for the remainder of this century. When John F. Kennedy took office in 1961, he set two goals for this nation: putting a man on the moon and wiping hunger from the face of the earth. The more glamorous of the two we have achieved. But we have a long way to go on the more important of the two challenges."

BIOGRAPHICAL/CRITICAL SOURCES:

BOOKS

Simon, Paul. *The Glass House: Politics and Morality in the Nation's Capital,* Continuum, 1984.

PERIODICALS

America, September 29, 1973, p. 221.
Chicago Tribune, January 9, 1988; February 14, 1988; February 21, 1988; February 25, 1988; March 2, 1988; March 13, 1988; March 17, 1988; March 22, 1988; March 31, 1988; April 8, 1988; April 10, 1988; May 15, 1988; July 19, 1988.
Critic, January/February, 1974, p. 80.
Harper's, September, 1964.
Los Angeles Times, December 15, 1980; November 27, 1987; January 27, 1988; February 12, 1988; February 21, 1988; February 25, 1988; March 13, 1988; April 1, 1988; April 8, 1988.
Los Angeles Times Book Review, March 6, 1988, pp. 8-9; February 26, 1989, p. 4.
Nation, May 2, 1987, pp. 584-85.
National Review, November 9, 1973, p. 1256.
New York Times, November 20, 1987; December 9, 1987; December 11, 1987; March 14, 1988; April 5, 1988.
New York Times Book Review, June 24, 1984, p. 23; March 5, 1989, p. 23.
Tribune Books, October 10, 1982, p. 6.
Washington Post, November 20, 1987; November 23, 1987; December 11, 1987; February 25, 1988; March 10, 1988; March 16, 1988; April 8, 1988; April 3, 1989.
Washington Post Book World, November 16, 1980, p. 9; May 16, 1982, p. 4; July 12, 1992, pp. 1, 10.*

—*Sketch by Mary L. Onorato*

SIMONTON, Dean Keith 1948-

PERSONAL: Born January 27, 1948, in Glendale, CA; son of Dean Clarence and Laverne (a nurse; maiden name, Merkobrad) Simonton; married Susan Deborah Youel, June 21, 1971 (divorced, 1982); married Melody Ann Boyer (an academic counselor), December 29, 1984; children: Amanda Leigh Burke (stepdaughter), Sabrina Dee Simonton. *Education:* Occidental College, B.A. (magna cum laude), 1970; Harvard University, M.A., 1973, Ph.D., 1975. *Politics:* Independent. *Religion:* "Define what you mean by God, Soul, Immortality, etc., and I'll tell you whether we are co-religionists."

ADDRESSES: Home—2903 Solito St., Davis, CA 95616. *Office*—Department of Psychology, University of California, Davis, CA 95616.

CAREER: Harvard University, Cambridge, MA, teaching fellow in psychology and social relations, 1970-72; University of Arkansas, Fayetteville, assistant professor of psychology, 1974-76; University of California, Davis, assistant professor, 1976-80, associate professor, 1980-85, professor of psychology, 1985—. Consultant to North Atlantic Treaty Organization, National Defense University (Department of Defense), California Youth Authority, Center for Creative Leadership, and Creative Problem Solving Institute. Lecturer at conferences and universities, including University of Kansas, Carleton College, and University of Southern California.

MEMBER: International Society of Political Psychology, American Psychological Association (fellow; president of Psychology and the Arts Division), American Psychological Society (fellow), American Association for the Advancement of Science, American Association of Allied and Preventative Psychology (fellow), Phi Beta Kappa, Psi Chi, Sigma Xi.

AWARDS, HONORS: Danforth fellow, 1970-74; National Science Foundation fellow, 1970-72; Magnar Ronning Award for Teaching Excellence, 1979; grant, North Atlantic Treaty Organization for University of Goettingen, 1980-81; Award for Excellence, Mensa Education and Research Foundation, 1986.

WRITINGS:

Genius, Creativity, and Leadership: Historiometric Inquiries, Harvard University Press, 1984.
Why Presidents Succeed: A Political Psychology of Leadership, Yale University Press, 1987.
Scientific Genius: A Psychology of Science, Cambridge University Press, 1988.
Psychology, Science, and History: An Introduction to Historiometry, Yale University Press, 1990.
Greatness: The Psychology of Important Personalities and Big Events, Guilford Press, in press.

Member of editorial boards, *Journal of Personality,* 1985—; *Leadership Quarterly,* 1988—; and *Creativity Research Journal,* 1988—. Editor, *Journal of Behavior,* 1993—. Contributor to numerous books, including *Frontiers of Creativity Research: Beyond the Basics,* edited by S. G. Isaksen, Bearly Ltd., 1985; *The Nature of Creativity: Contemporary Psychological Perspectives,* edited by R. J. Sternberg, Cambridge University Press, 1988; *Creativity: The Reality Club IV,* edited by J. Brockman, Simon & Schuster, 1993. Contributor to *Encyclopedic Dictionary of Psychology, International Encyclopedia of Education,* and *Encyclopedia of Human Development and Education.* Also contributor of more than numerous articles and reviews to scholarly journals, including *Journal of Cross-Cultural Psychology, Journal of Personality and Social Psychology, American Psychologist, Journal of Creative Behavior, Journal of Experimental Social Psychology, Creativity Research Journal, The Scientist,* and *Administrative Science Quarterly.*

WORK IN PROGRESS: Gifted Child/Adult Genius: Talent Development Across the Life Span; The Origins of Genius: Psyche, Chance, and Zeitgeist; Genius: Creativity, Leadership, and Talent; articles for books and journals on a wide variety of subjects, including an evolutionary theory of creative genius, the emergence of adult genius from child giftedness, and musical creativity in the symphonies of Beethoven.

SIDELIGHTS: Dean Keith Simonton once told *CA:* "I've always admired a good many geniuses from the past who, in the guise of either creativity or leadership, left a lasting impression for posterity. I most admire the classical composers, notably Beethoven, Bach, Mozart, and Handel. Had I more musical talent, I might have become a composer or, the next best thing, a conductor. Similar obstacles prevent me from turning others I admire into active sources of inspiration, with the exception of such scientists as Galileo, Darwin, and Einstein. Hence, to the extent that my native wit permits, I have devoted my life to the scientific study of genius: to the discovery of the laws that govern the emergence of the most distinguished creators and leaders of history.

"In particular, I have developed the technique called historiometry, whereby mounds of information abstracted from biographies, histories, and original creative products are fed into computers; it is subjected to complex mathematical analysis, with the goal of devising equations that allow us to predict creative or leadership potential. Typically, hundreds, even thousands, of eminent personalities enter these calculations. Besides aiding the prediction and identification of future genius, this method contributes to our understanding and control of the factors that best nourish the emergence of genius. But is it too late to apply these discoveries to my own life?"

BIOGRAPHICAL/CRITICAL SOURCES:

PERIODICALS

Contemporary Psychology, September, 1985; November, 1989.
Harvard, January-February, 1980.
Issues in Science and Technology, summer, 1989.
Los Angeles Times, February 3, 1985; August 21, 1988.
National Enquirer, August 24, 1982.
New Scientist, May 6, 1989.
Newsweek, June 28, 1993.
Science 82, July-August, 1982.
Scientist, November-December, 1991.

* * *

SINCLAIR, James
See STAPLES, Reginald Thomas

* * *

SINGH, G(han Shyam) 1929-

PERSONAL: Born January 24, 1929, in Jaipur, Rajasthan, India; son of Kaloo and Gulab (Kunwar) Singh. *Education:* Rajasthan University, B.A., 1948, M.A. (with first class honors), 1950, Ph.D., 1954; Milan State University, Dott.Lett., 1959; University of Bologna, Dott.Lett., 1962; Birkbeck College, London, Ph.D., 1963.

ADDRESSES: Office—Italian Department, Queen's University, Belfast, Northern Ireland.

CAREER: Muslim University, Aligarh, India, lecturer in English, 1954-56; Institute of Middle East and Far East Studies, Milan, Italy, lecturer in Indian languages and literature, beginning 1958; Universita Commerciale Luigi Bocconi, Milan, reader in English, 1962-65; Queen's University, Belfast, Northern Ireland, professor of Italian and chairman of department, 1965—. Summer lecturer in English, Anglo-American Centre, Mullsjoe, Sweden, 1958-64.

WRITINGS:

Pessimism in Swinburne's Early Poetry (monograph), Raleigh Literary Society, Muslim University (Aligarh), 1956.
Leopardi and the Theory of Poetry, University Press of Kentucky, 1964.
(Compiler and author of introduction) Frank Raymond Leavis, *Essaeyer,* translated by Aake Nylinder, Cavefors (Stockholm), 1966.
(Editor and translator with Ezra Pound) *Le Poesie di Kabir,* Scheiwiller, 1966.
(Author of introduction) Rabindranath Tagor, *Opere,* Le Club degli Editori (Milan), 1966.

(Compiler, translator, and author of introduction) *Contemporary Italian Verse,* London Magazine Editions, 1967.
Leopardi e l'Inghilterra, Le Monnier, 1968.
(Compiler, translator, and author of introduction) *Poesie di Thomas Hardy,* Guanda, 1968.
(Translator from Italian) Eugenio Montale, *The Butterfly of Dinard,* London Magazine Editions, 1970, University Press of Kentucky, 1971.
(Compiler and translator) *Da Swift a Pound: Saggi critici di F. R. Leavis,* Einaudi, 1973.
Eugenio Montale: A Critical Study of His Poetry, Prose, and Criticism, Yale University Press, 1973.
(Author of introduction and commentary) *Eugenio Montale: Selected Poems,* Manchester University Press, 1975.
(Compiler, translator, and author of introduction) *Eugenio Montale: New Poems,* New Directions, 1976.
(Editor, translator, and author of introduction) *Eugenio Montale: Selected Essays,* Carcanet Press, 1978.
The Caged Lion (poems), Proza Press, 1978.
Skuggor baa en rockaerm (poems), translated by Martin Allwood, Eternit Press, 1978.
Ezra Pound, La Nuova Italia, 1979.
(Translator and author of introduction) Montale, *It Depends: A Poet's Notebook* (poems), New Directions, 1980.
(Editor and author of introduction) *F. R. Leavis: The Critic as Anti-Philosopher,* Chatto & Windus, 1982.
(Editor and author of introduction) Q. D. Leavis, *The Englishness of the English Novel,* Cambridge University Press, 1983.
(Editor and author of introduction) Q. D. Leavis, *The American Novel and Reflections on the European Novel,* Cambridge University Press, 1985.
T. S. Eliot: Poeta, drammaturgo e critico, Longo Editore (Ravenna, Italy), 1985.
(Editor and author of introduction) *F. R. Leavis Valuation in Criticism and Other Essays,* Cambridge University Press, 1986.
Neanche un minuto (poetry), preface by Mario Luzi, Campanotto Editore (Udine, Italy), 1986.
(Editor, translator, and author of introduction) *Le Canjoni di Mira,* Edizioni Quattro Venti, 1988.
(Editor and author of introduction) Q. D. Leavis, *The Novel of Religious Controversy,* Cambridge University Press, 1989.
(Editor, translator, and author of introduction) Thomas Hardy, *I Dinasti,* Passigli Editore, 1989.
(Editor and author of introduction) *Ezra Pound Centenary Essays,* Campanotto editore, 1990.
Olga and Pound: Poems, Campanotto editore, 1987.
Leopardi e i poeti inglesi, Transeuropa Lavoro Editoriale, 1990.

Contributor to *Times Literary Supplement, London Magazine, Italian Studies, Forum Italicum,* and *World Literature Today.*

BIOGRAPHICAL/CRITICAL SOURCES:

PERIODICALS

London Magazine, September, 1970.
Times Literary Supplement, October 17, 1968.

*   *   *

SIROF, Harriet   1930-

PERSONAL: Born October 18, 1930, in New York, NY; daughter of Herman (a dress manufacturer) and Lillian (Miller) Hockman; married Sidney Sirof (a psychologist), June 18, 1949; children: Laurie, David, Amy Sirof Bordiuk. *Education:* New School for Social Research, B.A., 1962.

ADDRESSES: Home and office—792 East 21st St., Brooklyn, NY 11210.

CAREER: Remedial reading teacher at elementary schools in Brooklyn, NY, 1962-76; St. John's University, Jamaica, NY, instructor in creative writing, 1978—. Instructor at South Shore Adult Center, 1977-83, Long Island University, 1978-79, and Brooklyn College of the City University of New York, 1980-81, 1984—.

MEMBER: International Women's Writing Guild, Authors Guild, Authors League of America, League of Women Voters (past president of Brooklyn branch).

WRITINGS:

JUVENILE

A New-Fashioned Love Story (novel), Xerox Education Publications, 1977.
The IF Machine (novel), Scholastic, 1978.
The Junior Encyclopedia of Israel, Jonathan David, 1980.
Save the Dam! (novel), Crestwood, 1981.
That Certain Smile (novel), Xerox Education Publications, 1981.
The Real World (novel), F. Watts, 1985.
Anything You Can Do (novel), Weekly Reader Books, 1986.
Because She's My Friend (novel), Atheneum, 1993.
The Road Back: Living With A Physical Disability, Macmillan, 1993.

OTHER

Also author of "Your Child," a column in *Flatbush News,* in *King's Courier,* in *Bay News,* and in *Canarsie Digest,* all 1962-65. Contributor to anthologies, including *Voices of Brooklyn,* edited by Sol Yurick, American Library Association, 1973; *Remember Me and Other Stories,* edited by Mary Verdick, Xerox Education Publications, 1976; and *Triple Action Play Book* (contains "Itchy Feet," a one-act play for children), edited by Jeri Shapiro, Scholastic Book Services, 1979. Contributor of stories and articles to magazines for adults and young people, including *North American Review, Descant, Highlights for Children, Rainbow,* and *Maine Review.*

WORK IN PROGRESS: A young adult novel about a girl who deals with a devastating tragedy in her life by escaping into the past.

SIDELIGHTS: "My life is representative of a generation of women who grew up before the women's movement," Harriet Sirof commented to *CA.* "I learned to read at the age of four and dreamed of being a writer from the time I was seven. At ten, I was dictating stories to my friend Boopsie who planned to be a secretary. But by the time I entered college at seventeen, I was persuaded to train for something practical like teaching English. I married at eighteen, left school to plunge wholeheartedly into domesticity, and soon had three small children. Writing was relegated to the status of an abandoned childhood fantasy.

"Then, driven by the feeling that something was missing in my life, I returned to school, graduated first in my class, and became a reading teacher. Although I wrote educational materials for my students and published some of them, I was still dissatisfied. Next I tried my hand at short stories. Sales to the literary quarterlies and the interest of an agent led me to attempt an adult novel. It took me nearly two years and two thousand discarded pages to discover that it was not for me. Deeply discouraged, I considered giving up writing.

"When I heard that Scholastic was looking for novels for teens with reading problems, it seemed like something I could do. The resulting *The IF Machine* is still selling sixteen years later. It was a short step from *The IF Machine* to young adult novels, and I finally found my niche. I have since published seven novels and two nonfiction books for young adults.

"I like writing for and about teens because adolescence is a time of changing and becoming, and change is always interesting and exciting. YA novels deal with many of the same moral and ethical problems as adult novels in a clearer and simpler form. My books grow out of the current issues in my own life, and as I write I learn as much as I teach. I suspect I am drawn to writing for teens because, like them, I am still asking myself who I am and what I want to be."

SLATER, Robert 1943-

PERSONAL: Born October 1, 1943, in New York, NY; son of Joseph George (a business executive) and Gertrude (a homemaker; maiden name, Levy) Slater; married Elinor Resnik, June 13, 1966; children: Miriam Blessing, Joseph Adam, Rachel Abigail. *Education:* University of Pennsylvania, B.A., 1966; London School of Economics and Political Science, London, M.S., 1967.

ADDRESSES: Home—60 Pal Yam, French Hill, Jerusalem, Israel 97890. *Office*—8 Rabbi Akiva Street, Jerusalem, Israel.

CAREER: Bucks County Courier Times, Levittown, PA, reporter, 1968-70; United Press International, Trenton, NJ, reporter, 1970-71, bureau chief, 1971; Jewish Telegraphic Agency, Jerusalem, Israel, reporter, 1972-73; United Press International, Jerusalem, reporter, 1973-74; *Newsweek,* New York City, reporter in Jerusalem, 1974-76; *Time,* New York City, reporter in Jerusalem, 1976—. *Military Service:* Israel Defense Forces Reserves, 1978—.

MEMBER: Israel Foreign Press Association (chairman, 1987-90).

AWARDS, HONORS: This . . . Is CBS was nominated as a finalist for the 1988 Electronic Media Book of the Year Award for 1988; *Warrior Statesman: The Life of Moshe Dayan* was nominated for the 1992 National Jewish Book Award in the Israel category.

WRITINGS:

Rabin of Israel, Robson Books, 1977, revised edition, 1993.
Golda: The Uncrowned Queen of Israel, Jonathan David, 1981.
Great Jews in Sports, Jonathan David, 1983, revised edition, 1992.
The Titans of the Takeover, Prentice-Hall, 1986.
Portraits in Silicon, MIT Press, 1987.
This . . . Is CBS, Prentice-Hall, 1988.
Warrior Statesman: The Life of Moshe Dayan, St. Martin's, 1991.
The New GE: How Jack Welch Revived an American Institution, Business One, 1992.
The Jewish Child's Book of Sports Heroes, Jonathan David, 1993.

WORK IN PROGRESS: "A book, co-authored with my wife Elinor, on the one hundred most outstanding Jewish women in history, tentatively entitled, *Great Jewish Women.*"

SIDELIGHTS: Robert Slater once told *CA:* "For as long as I can recall, I have loved books: the feel of them, the way they look, and especially what's written inside of them. At the age of twenty-eight, I moved from the United States to Israel to work in journalism. Deep down, I shared the common itch of most reporters—the itch to write a book. My biography of Yitzhak Rabin, *Rabin of Israel,* appeared in October, 1977, shortly after he resigned from the prime ministership under the cloud of a minor scandal.

"Since then, I have written eight more books, including biographies of two other Israeli leaders, Golda Meir and Moshe Dayan. Because my reporting chores for *Time* magazine have absorbed me on a minute-by-minute basis with the Arab-Israeli conflict, I decided to branch out in my bookwriting and work on American-oriented subjects. Hence, I have also written books on American business takeover personalities, computer pioneers, the CBS television network, and General Electric's chairman and CEO, Jack Welch.

"The most peculiar turn of events in my bookwriting career occurred in 1992 when, thanks to Yitzhak Rabin's re-election as Israeli prime minister that year, I was able to publish an updated version of my very first book. Back in 1977, when Rabin left the prime ministership, he could have had little hope of returning to the prime ministership. I also could have had little hope that the biography would ever re-appear in an updated version. On July 13, 1992, the day Rabin presented his new government to the Knesset, I received word from Robson Books, publisher of *Rabin of Israel,* that I should update my book—fifteen years later. What a happy turn of events, I thought, for Rabin and for me!

"My third book, *Great Jews in Sports,* has turned into a perennial seller, and a popular present for 13-year-old boys for their Bar Mitzvahs. My wife Elinor and I hope that our new book, tentatively called *Great Jewish Women,* will likewise become a popular present for 13-year-old girls for their Bat Mitzvahs.

"I am often asked how someone like myself, living as I do in Jerusalem, can write books on American subjects. I am uncomfortable with the question for it assumes that one ought to write only on subjects within one's midst. Thanks to jet planes, computers, and faxes, the world is thankfully getting smaller and smaller. For my American-oriented books, I do all my research in the United States. I do the writing both in the United States and in Israel."

BIOGRAPHICAL/CRITICAL SOURCES:

PERIODICALS

Kirkus Reviews, June 1, 1993.
Library Journal, June 1, 1993.
Los Angeles Times Book Review, January 3, 1982.
Publishers Weekly, May 31, 1993.

SLOAN, Pat(rick Alan) 1908-1978

PERSONAL: Born May 19, 1908, in Gosforth, Newcastle upon Tyne, England; died, December 25, 1978; son of Robert Patrick (a company chairman) and Inda A. L. (Ellis) Sloan; married Margaret Cohen (a nurse), October 23, 1944; children: Duncan, Robert, Daniel, Alan. *Education:* Cambridge University, first class honors in economics tripos, 1929. *Politics:* Communist.

ADDRESSES: Home—1 Bucks Cross Cottages, Chelsfield Village, Orpington, Kent BR6 7RN, England. *Office*—134 Ballards Lane, London N3 2PD, England.

CAREER: University College of Bangor, Wales, assistant lecturer in economics, 1929-31; British Soviet Friendship Society, London, England, general secretary, 1950-59; *British Soviet Friendship* (magazine), London, England, editorial director, beginning 1960; Kwame Nkrumah Ideological Institute, Ghana, senior lecturer, 1964-66; *Labour Monthly* (magazine), London, editor, 1976-78. Lived and worked in Russia, 1931-36, and visited there six times.

WRITINGS:

Soviet Democracy, Gollancz, 1937.
Russia without Illusions, Muller, 1938.
(Editor) *John Cornford: A Memoir,* J. Cape, 1938.
Russia: Friend or Foe?, Muller, 1939.
(Editor) *Russia in Peace and in War,* Pilot Press, 1941.
How the Soviet State Is Run, Lawrence & Wishart, 1941.
Russia Resists, Muller, 1941.
Guide to Economics, African University Press, 1970.
Marx and the Orthodox Economists, Rowman & Littlefield, 1973.

Contributor to periodicals, including *Quarterly Review, Contemporary Review, Humanist, Freethinker,* and *Comment,* and to Soviet periodicals. Editor, *Russia Today,* 1938-41.

SIDELIGHTS: Pat Sloan's books have been issued in India, Spain, and the United States.

*   *   *

SMALL, Kenneth A(lan) 1945-

PERSONAL: Born February 9, 1945, in Sodus, NY; son of Cyril Galloway (in agricultural extension) and Gertrude (Andrews) Small; married Adair Bowman (a nurse), June 8, 1968; children: Gretchen Lenore. *Education:* University of Rochester, B.S., A.B., both 1968; University of California, Berkeley, M.A, 1972, Ph.D., 1976. *Religion:* Unitarian Universalist.

ADDRESSES: Home—Irvine, CA. *Office*—Department of Economics, University of California, Irvine, CA 92717.

CAREER: Princeton University, Princeton, NJ, assistant professor of economics, 1976-83; University of California, Irvine, associate professor of economics, 1983-86, professor, 1986, associate dean of social sciences, 1986-93, chair of economics department, 1992—. Research associate at Brookings Institution, Washington, DC, 1978-79. Visiting professor of economics, Harvard University, 1991-92. Reviewer for the National Academy of Sciences, the U.S. Office of Technology Assessment, and the World Bank. Consultant to New York State Legislative Tax Study Commission, Eco Northwest, and DRI/McGraw-Hill. Member of advisory panels for South Coast Air Quality Management District, 1988-92, Southern California Association of Governments, 1990-91 and National Research Council, 1992—. Speaker and panelist on economic and transportation issues, 1978—.

MEMBER: American Economic Association, Econometric Society, American Real Estate and Urban Economic Association, Royal Economic Society, Transportation Research Board, Regional Science Association International.

AWARDS, HONORS: Received grants from National Science Foundation, 1977-78, 1980-82, 1982-84, 1985-87, Institute of Transportation Studies, University of California, 1984-85, 1985-86, 1986-87, 1987-88, 1988-89, Energy Research Group, University of California, 1985-86, John Randolph Haynes and Dora Haynes Foundation, 1987-88, and University of California Transportation Center, 1988—.

WRITINGS:

(With Katharine L. Bradbury and Anthony Downs) *Futures for a Declining City: Simulations for the Cleveland Area,* Academic Press, 1981.
(With Bradbury and Downs) *Urban Decline and the Future of American Cities,* Brookings Institution, 1982.
(With Clifford Winston and Carol A. Evans) *Road Work: A New Highway Pricing and Investment Policy,* Brookings Institution, 1989.
Urban Transportation Economics, Harwood Academic, 1992.

Contributor to numerous books, including *Policy Options for the Gasoline Shortage,* with Randal J. Pozdena, edited by Joseph Gabarino, University of California, Institute of Business and Economic Research, 1974; *High Energy Costs: Assessing the Burden,* edited by Hans Landsberg, Resources for the Future, 1982; and *Studies in State and Local Public Finance,* with C. Winston, edited by Harvey S. Rosen, University of Chicago Press, 1986. Also contributor of articles and book reviews to periodicals, including *American Economic Review, Econometrica, Journal of Urban Economics, Los Angeles Times, Transportation Research, Urban Development Commentary, Environment and Planning,* and *Journal of Business and Economic Sta-*

tistics. Associate editor, *Regional Science and Urban Economics,* 1987—; co-editor, *Urban Studies,* 1992—; member of editorial boards, *Regional Science and Urban Economics, Journal of Urban Economics, Transportation,* and the book series, *Transportation Research, Economics and Policy,* Kluwer Academic.

WORK IN PROGRESS: Research on transportation, urban economics, econometrics, and land use models.

SIDELIGHTS: Kenneth A. Small once told *CA:* "Academics isn't the easy life many think it to be, but it does have the big rewards of flexibility and variety in one's work. Writing and teaching are what pull together the pieces of knowledge and experience into some kind of coherence."

* * *

SMALLWOOD, Joseph R(oberts) 1900-1991

PERSONAL: Generally known as "Joey" Smallwood; born December 24, 1900, in Gambo, Newfoundland, Canada; died December 17, 1991, in Newfoundland; son of Charles W. (a lumber surveyor and sawmill owner) and Mary "Minnie" (Devannah) Smallwood; married Clara Isobel Oates, November 25, 1925; children: Ramsay, William, Clara. *Education:* Attended Rand School of Social Science, Cooper Union Institute, and the Labor Temple. *Politics:* Liberal. *Religion:* United Church of Canada. *Avocational Interests:* Reading.

ADDRESSES: Home—Box 1, Site 4, R.R.1, Roaches Line, Newfoundland, Canada, A0A 1W0.

CAREER: Apprentice to printer in St. John's, Newfoundland, beginning 1915; *Evening Telegram,* St. John's, reporter, 1918-20, and acting editor, 1919-20; associated with the *Herald,* Halifax, Nova Scotia, 1920; reporter for the Boston *Herald-Traveler,* Boston, MA, c. 1920, and *New York Call,* New York City, c. 1921-25; free-lance writer and Socialist Party speaker, New York City, 1921-25; organizer of Newfoundland trade unions and cooperatives, 1925-1946; free-lance writer in England, 1926-27; editor of *Daily Globe,* St. John's, *Humber Herald* (later merged with *Western Star*), Corner Brook, Newfoundland (founder), and *Watchdog;* broadcast weekly radio show, "The Barrelman," Newfoundland, 1932-39; operator of piggery in Newfoundland; leader of Newfoundland's and Labrador's "Confederation with Canada" movement and member of National Convention of Newfoundland, 1946-49; interim prime minister of province of Newfoundland, 1949, premier, 1949-71, and minister of economic development, 1950-71; member, Newfoundland House of Assembly, 1949-71, 1975-77. Founder and member of Newfoundland Liberal party,

1949-72; leader of Liberal Reform party, 1975-77. Founder and first president of Newfoundland Federation of Labour. Member of Privy Council of Canada, 1967.

MEMBER: Liberal Club, St. John's Club, Masons (York rite, Scottish rite, Shrine; past master).

AWARDS, HONORS: D.C.L., Acadia University, University of Victoria, McGill University, and University of Windsor; LL.D., University of British Columbia, Dalhousie University, University of New Brunswick, St. Dunstan's University, and Waterloo Lutheran University; D.Litt., Memorial University of Newfoundland.

WRITINGS:

The New Newfoundland: An Account of the Revolutionary Developments Which Are Transforming Britain's Oldest Colony from the "Cinderella of the Empire" into One of the Great Small Nations of the World, Macmillan, 1931.
(Editor) *The Book of Newfoundland,* Newfoundland Book Publishers, Volumes 1-2, 1937, Volumes 3-4, 1967, Volumes 5-6, 1975.
Dr. William Carson, the Great Newfoundland Reformer: His Life, Letters, and Speeches—Raw Material for a Biography, 1940, reprinted, Newfoundland Book Publishers, 1978.
Our Case: Premier Smallwood's Statement of Policy (bound with *Newfoundland, the Fortress Isle,* by James Wentworth Day), Brunswick Press, 1960.
Peril and Glory, High Hill Publishing House, 1966.
To You with Affection from Joey: A Short Message from Your Premier, Action for Joey Committee, 1969.
I Chose Canada: The Memoirs of the Honourable Joseph R. "Joey" Smallwood, Macmillan of Canada, 1973, published in the United States in two volumes, New American Library, 1975.
(Editor) *Newfoundland Miscellany,* Volume 1, Newfoundland Book Publishers, 1978.
(Editor) *No Apology from Me: A Book of Startling Surprises about Confederation,* Newfoundland Book Publishers, 1979.
The Time Has Come To Tell, Newfoundland Book Publishers, 1979.
(Editor) *Encyclopedia of Newfoundland and Labrador,* Newfoundland Book Publishers, Volume 1, *A-E,* 1981, Volume 2, *Fac-Hoy,* 1984.

Also author of *Coaker of Newfoundland: The Man Who Led the Deep-Sea Fishermen to Political Power,* 1926; *The New Newfoundland,* 1932; *Newfoundland Hand Book, Gazetteer, and Almanac,* 1940; *Surrogate Robert Carter,* 1940; *Newfoundland, Canada's Happy Province,* 1966; and *The Face of Newfoundland,* 1967. Contributor to magazines and newspapers, including *Saturday Night.*

BIOGRAPHICAL/CRITICAL SOURCES:

BOOKS

Gwyn, Richard J., *Smallwood: The Unlikely Revolutionary*, McClelland & Stewart, revised edition, 1972.

Karsh, Yousuf, *Karsh Canadians*, University of Toronto Press, 1978.

New York Times: Men in the News, Volume 2, Lippincott, 1960.

Young, Ewart, editor, *This Is Newfoundland*, Ryerson, 1949.

PERIODICALS

Maclean's, August 15, 1949; July 2, 1979.
New Liberty, July, 1951.
Pathfinder, March 23, 1949.
Standard, August 27, 1948.
Time, September 22, 1952; February 14, 1972.

OBITUARIES:

PERIODICALS

New York Times, December 19, 1991.*

*   *   *

SMITH, Bradley F. 1931-

PERSONAL: Born October 5, 1931, in Seattle, WA; son of Frederick C. (a professor) and Edna (a teacher; maiden name, Barrie) Smith; married (divorced, 1969); married Jennifer Wilkes, December, 1983; children: Margaret Lynn, Leslie Ann. *Education:* University of California, Berkeley, B.A., 1957, M.A., 1960; also attended University of Washington, Reed College, San Jose State University, and University of Munich.

ADDRESSES: Home—Box 1225, Soquel, CA 95073. *Office*—104 Regents Park Rd., London NW1 8G, England.

CAREER: Cabrillo College, Aptos, CA, instructor in history, 1960-66; Miles College, Birmingham, AL, instructor in history, 1967-69; Cabrillo College, instructor in history, 1969—. Writer of historical studies and biographies. *Military service:* U.S. Air Force, 1950-54.

MEMBER: American Historical Association, Authors Guild, Phi Beta Kappa.

AWARDS, HONORS: Reaching Judgment at Nuremburg was named by the London *Observer* as one of its books of the year, 1977; *The Road to Nuremburg* was a finalist in the *Los Angeles Times* book of the year competition, 1981.

WRITINGS:

Adolph Hitler: His Family, Childhood, and Youth, Hoover Institution, 1967, 7th edition, 1986.

Heinrich Himmler: A Nazi in the Making, 1900-1926, Hoover Institution, 1971, 2nd edition, 1973.

(Editor with Agnes F. Peterson) *Himmler Geheimreden*, [Frankfurt], 1974.

Reaching Judgment at Nuremburg, Basic Books, 1977.

(With Elena Agarossi) *Operation Sunrise: The Secret Surrender*, Basic Books, 1979.

The Road to Nuremburg, Basic Books, 1981.

The American Road to Nuremburg: The Documentary Record, Hoover Institution, 1981.

The Shadow Warriors: O.S.S. and the Origins of the C.I.A., Basic Books, 1983.

The War's Long Shadow: World War II and Its Aftermath, Simon & Schuster, 1986.

O.S.S. Jedburgh Teams I, Garland Publishing, 1989.

O.S.S. Jedburgh Teams II, Garland Publishing, 1989.

The Spy Factory and Secret Intelligence, Garland Publishing, 1989.

The Ultra-Magic Deals and the Most Secret Special Relationship, 1940-1946, Presidio Press, 1993.

Contributor to periodicals, including *Washington Post, American Historical Review, Time Out, German Studies Review, Encounter, Journal of Modern History, New York Review of Books, Journal of Interdisciplinary History, Library Journal, American Historical Association Newsletter, History of Childhood Quarterly, Los Angeles Times, Independent* (London), *Intelligence and National Security*, and *Defence Analysis*.

WORK IN PROGRESS: A series of articles; a large book project on East-West intelligence cooperation in World War II.

SIDELIGHTS: Bradley F. Smith once told *CA:* "I slipped into writing due to my interest in history. Initially, I worked only on narrow research-based projects on the Nazis, depending heavily on obscure German manuscript sources. Over the last ten years I've moved along to broader topics, bigger books, and a more complex style. In consequence, I tend to feel that young writers should first get a hand on something to say and then gradually develop the means to say it. For me this approach has opened up a whole series of interesting projects and given me the pleasure of having my thought and style change and develop."

Smith's first popular book, *Reaching Judgment at Nuremburg*, is about the post-World War II trials of German war criminals. Using the unpublished papers and diaries of Francis Biddle, the senior American judge at Nuremburg, Smith analyzed the verdicts, telling why two defendants were acquitted and why Justice Biddle altered his initial recommendation of a death sentence for Albert Speer. A reviewer for the *New Yorker* wrote that *Reaching Judgment at Nuremburg* "opens up new avenues of inquiry not only into Nuremburg—the morality and legality of which have bothered many people for thirty years—but into the entire question of the accountability for warmaking and the vexed question of 'victor's justice.' "

Smith's next book, *Operation Sunrise: The Secret Surrender,* reconstructed the negotiations between Karl Wolff and Allen Dulles that led to the surrender of the German armies in northern Italy at the end of World War II. According to a *Spectator* review by Patrick Cosgrave, *Operations Sunrise* was an "enthralling and beautifully written book." John Kenneth Galbraith, in the *Washington Post Book World,* stated that Smith and co-author Elena Agarossi told "an extraordinarily good and effective story."

The Shadow Warriors: O.S.S. and the Origins of the C.I.A., published in 1983, documented the role of General William J. "Wild Bill" Donovan in guiding American intelligence efforts during World War II and in training future Central Intelligence Agency (C.I.A.) leaders such as William J. Casey. Assessing the book for the *New York Times Book Review,* Philip Taubman mentioned occasional slowness of pace due to excessive detail. "But these flaws may be forgiven," Taubman added, "because the book offers an honest, lively portrait of an important American and the contributions, good and bad, that he and the O.S.S. made to the American intelligence system." An "unexpected dividend" of the volume, Taubman remarked, is its relevance to contemporary foreign policy issues concerning the use of covert action. In the *New Republic,* Stephen A. Schuker called *The Shadow Warriors* "an outstanding account of the interagency battles in Washington that at times overshadowed the shooting war abroad. . . . [Smith] provides a masterful study of the O.S.S. at war as it appeared to higher officials in the eye of the storm." In the *New York Review of Books,* Thomas Powers praised Smith's archival research but claimed the book was an uninteresting read. As Powers noted, "Smith's *The Shadow Warriors* contains many useful bits from the numerous archives that he consulted, but it is dull to read." In contrast, Thomas F. Troy in *Washington Post Book World* commented that "Smith writes well, forcefully, albeit too glibly at times," and *Los Angeles Times Book Review* writer Otto J. Scott remarked, "Smith's account is engrossing and brilliant."

The year 1986 saw the publication of Smith's *The War's Long Shadow: World War II and Its Aftermath.* Focusing on the origins of the Cold War in the United States, the Soviet Union, China, and Britain, Smith put forth "an audacious and intriguing thesis," according to Arnold R. Isaacs in *Washington Post Book World.* This thesis, Isaacs reported, was "that the dramatic realignment of global politics after the war, and particularly the hardening of the U.S.-Soviet rivalry into the Cold War, did not arise

chiefly from competing ideologies or national ambitions" but from "the wartime experience itself, specifically 'the general mobilizing of production, manpower, and popular will' in each country for the purpose of waging total war." Isaacs faulted the thesis for oversimplification and for Smith's excessive reliance on public-opinion-poll data. Despite serious reservations, however, Isaacs declared that "*The War's Long Shadow* is built around an important idea: that the history of the last four decades, by and large, represents the working-out of issues and forces set in motion by the cataclysm of World War II." *Times Literary Supplement* critic John Lewis Gaddis underplayed the novelty of Smith's thesis, and concentrated instead on the author's strength in synthesizing familiar material. "Smith has managed it admirably," Gaddis wrote. He added, "This brief book is filled with fresh insights: that in 1939 less than 3 percent of Americans paid income taxes; that six other nations had armies larger than that of the United States in 1947. . . . The war had little lasting impact on the birth-rate or population profile of China, but a profound one on those of the Soviet Union."

BIOGRAPHICAL/CRITICAL SOURCES:

PERIODICALS

American Political Science Review, December, 1971.
Los Angeles Times Book Review, September 4, 1983, p. 5.
New Republic, September 19, 1983, pp. 35-39.
New Statesman, July 29, 1977.
New Yorker, February 21, 1977.
New York Review of Books, May 12, 1983, pp. 29-37.
New York Times Book Review, March 14, 1971; April 15, 1979; August 21, 1983, pp. 10-11.
Spectator, January 5, 1980.
Times Literary Supplement, January 13, 1978; May 8, 1987, pp. 479-480.
Washington Post Book World, September 9, 1979; July 31, 1983, p. 8; September 28, 1986, pp. 4-5.

*   *   *

SMITH, Kay Nolte 1932-
(Kay Gillian)

PERSONAL: Born July 4, 1932, in Eveleth, MN; daughter of Clifford Paul (in civil service) and Sigrid (a librarian; maiden name, Johnson) Nolte; married Phillip J. Smith (a professor), May 30, 1958. *Education:* University of Minnesota, B.A. (summa cum laude), 1952; University of Utah, M.A., 1955. *Politics:* Libertarian. *Avocational Interests:* Philosophy, psychology, classical music, nineteenth-century romantic literature.

ADDRESSES: Home—73 Hope Rd., Tinton Falls, NJ 07724. *Agent*—Meredith Bernstein, 2112 Broadway, Suite 503A, New York, NY 10023.

CAREER: Stern Brothers, New York City, copywriter, 1957-59; Fletcher, Richards, Calkins, and Holden, New York City, copywriter, 1959-63; free-lance actress under stage name Kay Gillian, 1963-73; Trenton State College, Trenton, NJ, instructor, 1975-80; Brookdale Community College, Lincroft, NJ, instructor, 1975-82; communications consultant, AT&T Bell Laboratories, 1978—.

MEMBER: Mystery Writers of America, Actors Equity Association, Phi Beta Kappa.

AWARDS, HONORS: Edgar Allan Poe Award from Mystery Writers of America, 1980, for *The Watcher.*

WRITINGS:

The Watcher, Coward, 1980.
Catching Fire, Coward, 1982.
Mindspell, Morrow, 1983.
Elegy for a Soprano, Random House, 1985.
(Translator) Edmond Rostand, *Chantecler,* University Press of America, 1987.
Country of the Heart, Random House, 1988.
A Tale of the Wind, Random House, 1991.

Work represented in numerous anthologies, including *Every Crime in the Book,* Putnam, 1975; *Best Detective Stories of 1975,* Dutton, 1975; *One Hundred Miniature Mysteries,* Taplinger, 1980; *Ellery Queen's Book of First Appearances,* David, 1982; *Suspicious Characters,* Ivy, 1987; and *Shrouds and Pockets,* Davis, 1988. Author of columns appearing in *Objectivist,* 1968-71, and *TV Show-people,* 1973. Contributor of articles to *Vogue, Opera News,* and *American Baby.*

WORK IN PROGRESS: An historical novel about the *Commedia dell'arte* players; another mystery novel.

SIDELIGHTS: Kay Nolte Smith once told *CA:* "The two things I greatly admire in others' work, and try for in my own, are a strong plot and the revelation and/or exploration of some aspect of human psychology. It seems sad, if not criminal, that these two elements, which coexisted happily in the great nineteenth-century works, are now split apart. Today the suspenseful, inventive plots of much 'popular' fiction often have paper-thin people and no real themes; and the 'serious' writers, who otherwise can probe deeply, frequently disdain the very concept of plot. For me the ideal is to have both: a real 'page-turner' that also reaches the heart and mind."

BIOGRAPHICAL/CRITICAL SOURCES:

PERIODICALS

Los Angeles Times, August 2, 1985.

SMITH, Martin
See SMITH, Martin Cruz

*   *   *

SMITH, Martin Cruz   1942-
   (Martin Smith; pseudonyms: Martin Quinn, Simon Quinn; Nick Carter, Jake Logan, house pseudonyms)

PERSONAL: Original name, Martin William Smith; born November 3, 1942, in Reading, PA; son of John Calhoun (a musician) and Louise (a jazz singer and Indian rights leader; maiden name, Lopez) Smith; married Emily Arnold (a chef), June 15, 1968; children: Ellen Irish, Luisa Cruz, Samuel Kip. *Education:* University of Pennsylvania, B.A., 1964.

ADDRESSES: Home—240 Cascade Dr., Mill Valley, CA 94941. *Agent*—Knox Burger Associates Ltd., 39½ Washington Sq. S., New York, NY 10012.

CAREER: Writer. Worked for local television stations, newspapers, and as a correspondent for Associated Press; *Philadelphia Daily News,* Philadelphia, PA, reporter, 1965; Magazine Management, New York City, 1966-69, began as writer, became editor of *For Men Only.*

MEMBER: Authors League of America, Authors Guild.

AWARDS, HONORS: Edgar Award nomination, Mystery Writers of America, 1972, for *Gypsy in Amber,* 1976, for *The Midas Coffin,* 1978, for *Nightwing,* and 1982, for *Gorky Park;* Gold Dagger, Crime Writers Association, 1982.

WRITINGS:

NOVELS

Nightwing (also see below), Norton, 1977.
The Analog Bullet, Belmont-Tower, 1978.
Gorky Park, Random House, 1981.
Stallion Gate, Random House, 1986.
Polar Star, Random House, 1989.
Red Square, Random House, 1992.

NOVELS; UNDER NAME MARTIN SMITH

The Indians Won, Belmont-Tower, 1970, reprinted under name Martin Cruz Smith, Leisure Books, 1981.
Gypsy in Amber, Putnam, 1971.
Canto for a Gypsy, Putnam, 1972, reprinted under name Martin Cruz Smith, Ballantine, 1983.

NOVELS; UNDER PSEUDONYM SIMON QUINN

His Eminence, Death, Dell, 1974.
Nuplex Red, Dell, 1974.
The Devil in Kansas, Dell, 1974.

The Last Time I Saw Hell, Dell, 1974.
The Midas Coffin, Dell, 1975.
Last Rites for the Vulture, Dell, 1975.
The Human Factor (movie novelization), Dell, 1975.

NOVELS; UNDER HOUSE PSEUDONYM JAKE LOGAN

North to Dakota, Playboy Press, 1976.
Ride for Revenge, Playboy Press, 1977.

UNDER PSEUDONYM MARTIN QUINN

The Adventures of the Wilderness Family (movie novelization), Ballantine, 1976.

OTHER

(Under name Martin Cruz Smith, with Steve Shagan and Bud Shrake) *Nightwing* (screenplay; based on novel of same title), Columbia, 1979.

Also author of several other genre novels under various pseudonyms, including Nick Carter. Contributor of stories to *Male, Stag,* and *For Men Only* and of book reviews to *Esquire. Gorky Park* has been translated into Russian.

ADAPTATIONS: Gorky Park, starring William Hurt and Lee Marvin, was released by Orion Pictures, 1983.

SIDELIGHTS: In 1972, a struggling young writer named Martin William Smith approached his publisher, G. P. Putnam's Sons, with an idea for a different sort of mystery. Inspired by a *Newsweek* review of *The Face Finder,* a nonfiction book recounting the efforts of Soviet scientists to reconstruct faces from otherwise unidentifiable human remains, Smith outlined a plot involving a partnership between a Soviet detective and his American counterpart as they attempt to solve an unusual murder. (As the author later revealed in the *Washington Post,* his original inclination was to portray a sort of "Butch Cassidy and the Sundance Kid, but one [partner would be] Russian.") Putnam's liked Smith's proposal and agreed to pay him a $15,000 advance.

For the next five years, Smith eked out a living writing several dozen paperback novels, often under one of his various pseudonyms. ("I didn't want to be associated with those books," he told *Newsweek*'s Peter S. Prescott.) Whenever he had accumulated enough to live on for awhile, he did research for his murder mystery; in 1973, he even managed to make a trip to Moscow where he spent almost a week wandering through the city jotting down notes on how it looked and sketching scenes he hesitated to photograph. Later denied permission for a return visit, Smith instead spent hours pumping various Russian emigres and defectors for details about life in the Soviet Union "on everything from the quality of shoes . . . to whether a ranking policeman would have to be a member of the Communist Party," as Arthur Spiegelman of the *Chicago*

Tribune noted. "I would write a scene and show it to one of my Russian friends," Smith recalled. "If he would say that some Russian must have told me that, then I knew it was OK."

By this time, Smith knew he no longer wanted to write a conventional thriller. "I suddenly realized that I had something," he commented in the *Washington Post.* "This [was] the book that [could] set me free." He abandoned the idea of a partnership between detectives, deciding instead to focus on the challenge of making the Soviet detective his hero. Putnam's, however, was less than enthusiastic about the change in plans, for the publisher doubted that such a book would have much commercial appeal. Smith was urged to stick to more marketable plots—namely, those featuring an American hero.

The year 1977 proved to be a turning point of sorts for Smith; he not only bought back the rights to his novel from Putnam's (after a long and bitter battle) and changed his middle name from William to Cruz (his maternal grandmother's name), he also received approximately a half million dollars when *Nightwing,* his vampire bat horror-thriller, became a surprise success. *Nightwing,* featuring Hopi Indian characters caught up in a vampire bat legend, dealt with Indian attitudes and folklore. In a *Contemporary Authors* interview, Smith discussed his own Pueblo Indian heritage and acknowledged that he "relied on [his] own background and research" for the novel. The following period of financial security enabled Smith to put the finishing touches on his "simple detective story," which by now had grown into a 365-page novel. In 1980, Smith and his agent began negotiating with Random House and Ballantine for the publishing rights. Despite the lack of interest Putnam's had shown in his work, Smith was confident that his book would indeed be published—and at a price *he* would name. As he remarked to Prescott: "Every time I looked at the novel I decided to double the price. When I wrote the last line, I *knew;* I have never been so excited in my life, except for the birth of children, as when I wrote the last line of [that book]. Because I knew it was just right. I had this marvelous book and I was *damned* if I was going to sell it for anything less than a marvelous price. The words 'one million' seemed to come to mind." Before the end of the year, Smith *was* $1 million richer and Random House was preparing to gamble on an unusual 100,000-copy first printing of what soon would become one of the most talked-about books of 1981—*Gorky Park.*

The result of eight years of research and writing, *Gorky Park* chronicles the activities of homicide detective Arkady Renko as he investigates a bizarre murder. Three bullet-riddled bodies—two men and a woman—have been discovered frozen in the snow in Moscow's Gorky Park, their faces skinned and their fingertips cut off to hinder identification. Renko immediately realizes that this is no ordinary murder; his suspicions are confirmed when agents of the KGB arrive on the scene. But instead of taking over the investigation, the KGB suddenly insists that Renko handle the affair. From this point on, the main plot is complicated by an assortment of sub-plots and a large cast of characters, including a greedy American fur-dealer, a visiting New York City police detective who suspects one of the murder victims might be his radical brother, and a dissident Siberian girl with whom Renko falls in love. Before the end of the story, the detective has tracked the killer across two continents and has himself been stalked and harassed by the KGB, the CIA, the FBI, and the New York City police department.

Critics praised the novel for Smith's ability to portray exceptionally vivid Russian scenes and characters. A review by Peter Andrews in the *New York Times Book Review* was typical. "Just when I was beginning to worry that the large-scale adventure novel might be suffering from a terminal case of the Folletts," he wrote, "along comes *Gorky Park* . . . , a book that reminds you just how satisfying a smoothly turned thriller can be." The *Washington Post Book World*'s Peter Osnos compared Smith to John Le Carre, maintaining that "*Gorky Park* is not at all a conventional thriller about Russians. It is to ordinary suspense stories what John Le Carre is to spy novels. The action is gritty, the plot complicated, the overriding quality is intelligence. You have to pay attention or you'll get hopelessly muddled. But staying with this book is easy enough since once one gets going, one doesn't want to stop." Perhaps because he is the protagonist, the character of Arkady Renko seems to have impressed reviewers the most, though Osnos, among others, pointed out that Smith avoids making *any* of his characters into the "sinister stick figures" common in other novels about the Soviets. The *New Republic*'s Tamar Jacoby regarded the detective as an "unusual and winning . . . moral hero without a trace of righteousness, an enigmatic figure as alluring as the mystery he is trying to solve. . . . Smith sees to it that there is nothing easy or superior about the moral insight that Arkady earns."

In 1986, Smith published *Stallion Gate,* setting his fiction among the scientists and military personnel of the Manhattan Project, those men and women who gathered near Los Alamos, New Mexico, to develop and test the first atom bomb. "Where *Gorky Park*'s subject was Russian," wrote Stephen Pickles in the *Spectator,* "in this novel Martin Cruz Smith turns to something very American, taking on one of the 20th century's most crucial historical moments." Yet, even with this more familiar setting, Smith recognized the need to investigate his subject in order to reanimate the now famous scientists and to reconstruct the historical setting. Explained Pickles, Smith "researched the subject for 18 months, interviewing survivors

and anyone who knew or worked with those involved with the Manhattan Project."

Though closer to home, the backdrop for Smith's novel of intrigue gives it an alien quality much as Moscow colored *Gorky Park*. Set in the desert, the novel blends native Indian allusions with modern, even futuristic images of scientists and their work. At the test site are J. Robert Oppenheimer, Edward Teller, Enrico Fermi, Brigadier General Leslie Groves, Harry Gold, and Klaus Fuchs. In a review of *Stallion Gate* for *Time*, R. Z. Sheppard observed that Smith "shapes images that contain haunting affinities: wild horses and Army jeeps; rattlesnakes and coils of electrical cable; the lustrous surfaces of ceremonial pottery and the polished plutonium core of the atom bomb." "Through the Indians, the author develops a magical dimension within the story," added Pickles. Through the chief of security, an army captain who suspects Oppenheimer of passing project secrets to the Soviets, Smith involves his main character and his readers in this story of suspense. Yet, in the view of *New York Review of Books* contributor Thomas R. Edwards, "This is only reluctantly a thriller. Smith, himself part Indian, is interested in the cultural collision between modern science and native beliefs and folkways of New Mexico." For this reason, as Thomas observed, "*Stallion Gate* is crammed with facts about the customs of the various Indian tribes that dwell in New Mexico, and of another tribe, this one composed of scientists." In a *Los Angeles Times Book Review* article on *Stallion Gate,* Tony Hillerman concluded, "Martin Cruz Smith, master-craftsman of the good read, has given us another dandy."

Smith resumed the adventures of *Gorky Park*'s hero, Russian inspector Arkady Renko, in two novels: 1989's *Polar Star,* and *Red Square,* published in 1992. Readers last saw Renko at the end of *Gorky Park* returning from America to his homeland, Russia. Upon his arrival, however, he is imprisoned in a mental hospital, escapes to Siberia, and lands a job as a second-class seaman on the Russian fishing ship *Polar Star,* bound for the Bering Sea. Once out to sea, the fishing nets haul in a dead body identified as crew member Zina Patiashvili. Renko is then ordered to investigate whether Patiashvili's death was suicide or murder.

Reviews of *Polar Star* were largely favorable; Robert Stuart Nathan's comments in the *New York Times Book Review* were typical. "The novel opens with a Conradian evocation of a ship at sea," he proclaimed, "and immediately we are reminded of just how skilled a storyteller Mr. Smith is, how supple and commanding his prose." Reid Beddow, in the *Washington Post Book World,* labeled the characterization of Renko as "terrific," adding that "Martin Cruz Smith writes the most inventive thrillers of anyone in the first rank of thriller-writers." Smith's descriptive settings in *Polar Star* were also singled out for critical acclaim. Although some reviewers noted that the setting has a tendency to overpower the plot, Allen J. Hubin of *Armchair Detective* asserted that the book is "filled with graphic images and cinematic sequences, involving the ship and the frigid, ice-filled expanses of the Bering Sea." Likewise, T. J. Binyon, in the *Times Literary Supplement,* remarked that "Martin Cruz Smith does a magnificent job on the background," calling the work "wholly absorbing."

In Smith's 1992 novel *Red Square,* Renko operates in post-Communist Russia, a Moscow quite different, but every bit as threatening, as that of *Gorky Park.* In *Red Square,* Renko faces a new threat—the corrupt "Chechen" mafia of Moscow. As black markets flourish in this new capitalist atmosphere, Renko seeks to solve the murder of his informant Rudy, who turns out to have had connections with the mob. Reviewers such as Francis X. Clines in *New York Times Book Review* praised the work, focusing on Smith's finely detailed settings: "The great virtue of the book is its narrative rendering of the sleazy, miasmic environment of *fin-de-Communisme* Moscow . . . that slouching, unworkable 'Big Potato,' as its citizens call it." Other reviewers praised Smith's expert characterization. A *Washington Post Book World* critic welcomed back Smith's much-loved hero, Renko, as "an immensely complex and likeable man. Here his qualities stand out even more luminously." The critic added that Martin Cruz Smith's *Red Square* "is as good popular fiction should be, a novel that proceeds on many levels." Reid Beddow in the *Washington Post Book World* pointed to Smith's competence in dealing with varied subjects— everything from American Indians, forensic medicine, police procedures and atomic secrets, to life in Soviet Russia and the Commonwealth of Independent States. The reviewer concluded that "rather than relying on the repetition of a successful formula, [Smith] has constantly sought to freshen his material."

BIOGRAPHICAL/CRITICAL SOURCES:

BOOKS

Smith, Martin Cruz, interview in *Contemporary Authors,* Volume 23, Gale, 1988, pp. 378-384.

PERIODICALS

Armchair Detective, Fall, 1990.
Chicago Tribune, March 25, 1981; July 19, 1992, p. 9.
Chicago Tribune Book World, April 19, 1981; May 11, 1986.
Los Angeles Times Book Review, April 19, 1981; May 11, 1986; June 24, 1990.
Newsweek, April 6, 1981; May 25, 1981; April 14, 1986; September 14, 1992, p. 70.
New Yorker, April 6, 1981.

New York Times, March 19, 1981.
New York Times Book Review, April 5, 1981; May 3, 1981; May 4, 1986; July 16, 1989, pp. 33-34; July 15, 1990, p. 32; October 18, 1992, pp. 45-46.
Time, March 30, 1981; May 12, 1986.
Times Literary Supplement, June 5, 1981; December 8, 1989, p. 1369.
Washington Post Book World, March 29, 1981; April 30, 1986; July 2, 1989, p. 5; November 1, 1992, p. 3.

* * *

SMITH, Rowland (James)   1938-

PERSONAL: Born August 19, 1938, in Johannesburg, South Africa; immigrated to Canada, naturalized citizen; son of John James (a schoolmaster) and Gladys Spencer (Coldrey) Smith; married Catherine Ann Lane, September 22, 1962; children: Russell Claude, Belinda Claire. *Education:* University of Natal, B.A., 1959, Ph.D., 1967; Oxford University, B.A., 1963, M.A., 1967.

ADDRESSES: Home—5683 Inglis Street, Halifax, Nova Scotia, Canada B3H 1K2. *Office*—Department of English, Dalhousie University, Halifax, Nova Scotia, Canada B3H 3J5.

CAREER: University of Natal, Pietermaritzburg, South Africa, junior lecturer in Latin, 1960; University of the Witwatersrand, Johannesburg, South Africa, lecturer in English, 1963-67; Dalhousie University, Halifax, Nova Scotia, assistant professor, 1967-70, associate professor, 1970-77, professor of English, 1977—, McCulloch Professor, 1988—, assistant dean of Arts and Science, 1972-74, director of Centre for African Studies, 1976-77, chair of Department of English, 1977-83, 1985-86, dean of Arts and Social Sciences, 1988-93. Visiting fellow, Dalhousie University, 1965-66; visiting member, Senior Common Room, Lincoln College, Oxford, 1974-75; professor, chercheur associe a l'Institut Pluridisciplinaire d'Etudes Canadiennes, Universite de Rouen, 1994; member of board of governors, Halifax Grammar School, 1972-74, and Neptune Theatre Foundation, 1977-78; 1979-85; member of education committee, Victoria General Hospital, 1986-90; director of publicity and promotion, Nova Scotia Rugby Football Union, 1987-89; chair of Nova Scotia Department of Education-University Liaison Committee, 1990-93; member of board of directors, Canadian Federation for the Humanities, 1992—; member of selection committee and judge for numerous book awards and scholarship programs.

MEMBER: Association of Canadian University Teachers of English (secretary-treasurer, 1968-70; member of professional concerns committee, 1979-81), Canadian Association of Chairmen of English (vice-president, 1981-82; president, 1982-83; executive-member-at-large, 1985-86), Canadian Association for Commonwealth Literature and Language Studies (executive member, 1989-92), Modern Language Association of America (division chair, 1984; member of delegate assembly, 1987-90).

AWARDS, HONORS: Transvaal Rhodes scholar, 1960; Canada Council Leave fellow, 1974-75; Canada Council and Social Sciences and Humanities Research grants; grant to lecture in Scandinavia and "Bank of Two Hundred Days" grant to lecture in France, Department of External Affairs; International Conference Grant.

WRITINGS:

Lyric and Polemic: The Literary Personality of Roy Campbell, McGill-Queen's University Press, 1972.
(Editor) *Exile and Tradition: Studies in African and Caribbean Literature,* Longman, 1976.
(Editor) *Critical Essays on Nadine Gordimer,* G. K. Hall, 1990.

Author of television scripts for Canadian "University of the Air." Contributor to books, including *Aspects of South African Literature,* edited by Christopher Heywood, Heinemann, 1976; *Olive Schreiner and After,* edited by Malvern Van Wyk Smith and Don Maclennan, David Philip, 1983; *Graham Greene: A Revaluation,* edited by Jeffrey Meyers, Macmillan, 1990; *International Literature in English: Essays on the Major Writers,* edited by Robert L. Ross, Garland, 1991; and *The Later Fiction of Nadine Gordimer,* edited by Bruce King, Macmillan, 1993. Also contributor to numerous periodicals, including *Africana Journal, Canadian Literature, Dalhousie Review, English Studies in Africa, Journal of Commonwealth Literature, Journal of Southern African Studies, Malahat Review, Queen's Quarterly,* and *Theoria.* Assistant editor, *English Studies in Africa,* 1964-67; editorial advisory board, *Ariel,* 1991—; and editorial board, *Routledge Encyclopedia of Post-Colonial Literatures in English.*

*   *   *

SMITH, Toby 1946-

PERSONAL: Born June 8, 1946, in New Haven, CT; son of Royall G. (in advertising) and Marie (an artist; maiden name, Tiemann) Smith; married Susan Keil, June 22, 1974; children: Jedediah Royall, Carson Keil. *Education:* University of Missouri, B.J., 1968; New York University, M.A., 1976; attended Harvard University, 1979. *Politics:* Democrat. *Religion:* Presbyterian. *Avocational Interests:* Tennis, long-distance running, hiking, gardening.

ADDRESSES: Home—3813 Inca St. N.E., Albuquerque, NM 87111. *Office—Albuquerque Journal,* P.O. Drawer J, Albuquerque, NM 87103.

CAREER: Norwalk Hour, Norwalk, CT, reporter, 1966-67; *Columbia Missourian,* Columbia, MO, reporter and copy editor, 1967-68; *Guideposts,* New York, NY, associate editor, 1971-76; *Que Pasa,* Albuquerque, NM, editor, 1976; *Albuquerque Journal,* Albuquerque, editor and writer, 1977—. Instructor at University of New Mexico, 1977-83, 1992. *Military service:* U.S. Army, 1968-70, reporter for *Fort Gordon Rambler,* 1969, copy editor for *Stars and Stripes,* Tokyo, Japan, 1970.

MEMBER: Albuquerque Press Club, University of Missouri Alumni Association.

AWARDS, HONORS: Journalism awards from New Mexico Press Association, 1977-93; National Endowment for the Humanities fellow, 1979; award from Religious Public Relations Council, 1980, for religious news reporting; Oscars in Agriculture from University of Illinois, 1984 and 1987, both for best newspaper feature story; award from New Mexico Medical Society, 1984, for excellence in journalism; Women's Sports Foundation Award, 1992; Associated Press Sports Editors awards, 1988-92.

WRITINGS:

(Editor) *Prison Letters,* Fleming Revell, 1975.
(Editor) *Intended for Pleasure,* Fleming Revell, 1977.
Dateline: New Mexico (nonfiction), University of New Mexico Press, 1982.
Pieces of the Promise (nonfiction), McLeod Printing, 1982.
Skyborne (nonfiction), Somesuch Press, 1985.
New Mexico Odyssey (nonfiction), University of New Mexico Press, 1987.
Kid Blackie (nonfiction), Wayfinder Press, 1987.
Stay Awhile (nonfiction), Red Crane Press, 1992.

Work represented in anthologies, including *Son of a Giant Sea Tortoise,* Viking, 1975. Contributor to *Collier's Encyclopedia Yearbook,* 1985-90. Author of "Tennis Talk," a column in *Our Town,* 1974. Also contributor to magazines, including *Sports Illustrated, Ski, McCall's, Ford Times, Outside, Golf Illustrated, Sport, Tennis, New Mexico, New York,* and *Ms.*; and to newspapers, including *Los Angeles Times, Christian Science Monitor, Village Voice, New York Times, Wall Street Journal,* and *Dallas Morning News.*

WORK IN PROGRESS: A nonfiction book on Dawson, New Mexico, a company-run coal mining town that disappeared in 1950.

SIDELIGHTS: Toby Smith told *CA:* "My long-standing writing interest has been people—their hopes, fears, successes, and failures. If a person intrigues me—whether he be a vacuum cleaner salesman or a Fortune 500 vice-president—I have an innate feeling that I can make readers care. And that's why I write—to make someone care.''

*   *   *

SNOWDON
   See ARMSTRONG-JONES, Antony

*   *   *

SOCHEN, June   1937-

PERSONAL: Born November 26, 1937, in Chicago, IL; daughter of Sam (a grocer) and Ruth (Finkelstein) Sochen. *Education:* University of Chicago, B.A., 1958; Northwestern University, M.A., 1960, Ph.D., 1967. *Avocational Interests:* Reading, tennis, writing fiction.

ADDRESSES: Home—6238 North Harding Ave., Chicago, IL 60659. *Office*—Department of History, Northeastern Illinois University, Chicago, IL 60625.

CAREER: Northeastern Illinois University, Chicago, instructor, 1964-67, assistant professor, 1967-69, associate professor, 1969-72, professor of history, 1972—.

MEMBER: American Historical Association, American Studies Association, American Jewish Historical Association.

AWARDS, HONORS: National Endowment for the Humanities grant, 1971; Delta Kappa Gamma Society's Outstanding Educator's Award, for *Cafeteria America;* Distinguished Professor Award, Northeastern Illinois University, 1993-94.

WRITINGS:

The Unbridgeable Gap: Blacks and Their Quest for the American Dream, Rand McNally, 1972.
The New Woman: Feminism in Greenwich Village, 1910-1920, Quadrangle, 1972.
Movers and Shakers: American Women Thinkers and Activists, 1900-1970, Quadrangle, 1973.
Herstory: A Woman's View of American History, Alfred Publishing, 1974, 2nd edition, 1981.
Consecrate Every Day: The Public Lives of Jewish American Women, 1880-1980, State University of New York Press, 1981.
Enduring Values: Women in Popular Culture, Praeger, 1987.
Cafeteria America: New Identities in Contemporary Life, Iowa State University Press, 1988.
Mae West: She Who Laughs, Lasts, H. Davidson, 1992.

EDITOR

The Black Man and the American Dream, 1900-1930, Quadrangle, 1971.
The New Feminism in Twentieth-Century America, Heath, 1971.
(With Duke Frederick and William Howenstine) *Destroy to Create: Interaction with the Environment,* Dryden, 1972.
(And author of introduction) *Women's Comic Visions,* Wayne State University Press, 1991.

OTHER

Also contributor to Martin Jackson and John O'Connor, editors, *American History/American Film,* Ungar, 1979; Daniel Walden, editor, *Studies in American Jewish Literature,* State University of New York Press, 1983; Sarah Blacher Cohen, editor, *From Hester Street to Hollywood,* Indiana University Press, 1983; Jack Fishel and Sanford Pinster, editors, *Jewish-American History and Culture,* 1992; and Darlene Clark Hine, editor, *Black Women in America,* 1993.

WORK IN PROGRESS: A history, *Growing Up in America.*

*   *   *

SPENCE, Bill
   See SPENCE, William John Duncan

*   *   *

SPENCE, Duncan
   See SPENCE, William John Duncan

*   *   *

SPENCE, William John Duncan   1923-
   (Bill Spence, Duncan Spence; Jim Bowden, Hannah Cooper, Kirk Ford, Floyd Rogers, Jessica Blair, pseudonyms)

PERSONAL: Born April 20, 1923, in Middlesbrough, England; son of John Robert (a teacher) and Anne (Payne) Spence; married Joan Mary Rhoda Ludley, September 8, 1944; children: Anne Spence Hudson, Geraldine Spence Jones, Judith Spence Gilbert, Duncan. *Education:* Attended St. Mary's College, Strawberry Hill, England, 1940-42. *Religion:* Roman Catholic.

ADDRESSES: Home—Post Office, Ampleforth College, York YO6 4EZ, England.

CAREER: Teacher in primary school in Middlesbrough, England, 1942; Ampleforth College, York, England, store manager, 1946-77; writer, 1977—. Tutor at writing school. *Military service:* Royal Air Force, Bomber Command, 1942-46.

MEMBER: Society of Authors, Hakluyt Society, Whitby Literary and Philosophical Society.

WRITINGS:

UNDER NAME BILL SPENCE

(With wife, Joan Spence) *Romantic Ryedale,* Ryedale Printing Works, 1977.
Harpooned (nonfiction), Conway Maritime Press, 1980.
(With J. Spence) *The Medieval Monasteries of Yorkshire,* AMBO Publications, 1981, published as *Stories from Yorkshire Monasteries,* Highgate Publications.
Bomber's Moon (war novel), R. Hale, 1981.
Secret Squadron (war novel), R. Hale, 1986.

UNDER NAME DUNCAN SPENCE

Dark Hell (novel), Brown Watson, 1959.

UNDER PSEUDONYM JIM BOWDEN; NOVELS

The Return of the Sheriff, R. Hale, 1960.
Wayman's Ford, R. Hale, 1960.
Two Gun Justice, R. Hale, 1961.
Roaring Valley, R. Hale, 1962.
Revenge in Red Springs, R. Hale, 1962.
Black Water Canyon, R. Hale, 1963.
Arizona Gold, R. Hale, 1963.
Trail of Revenge, R. Hale, 1964.
Brazo Feud, R. Hale, 1965.
Guns along the Brazo, R. Hale, 1967.
Gun Loose, R. Hale, 1969.
Valley of Revenge, R. Hale, 1971.
Trail to Texas, R. Hale, 1973.
Thunder in Montana, R. Hale, 1973.
Showdown in Salt Fork, R. Hale, 1975.
Hired Gun, R. Hale, 1976.
Incident in Bison Creek, R. Hale, 1977.
CAP, R. Hale, 1978.
Dollars of Death, R. Hale, 1979.
Renegade Riders, R. Hale, 1980.
Gunfight at Elm Creek, R. Hale, 1980.
The Shadow of Eagle Rock, R. Hale, 1982.
Pecos Trail, R. Hale, 1983.
Incident at Elm Creek, R. Hale, 1984.
Hangmen's Trail, R. Hale, 1986.
Return of the Gunmen, R. Hale, 1988.
Robbery at Glenrock, R. Hale, 1992.
A Man Called Abe, R. Hale, 1993.

UNDER PSEUDONYM HANNAH COOPER; NOVELS

Time Will Not Wait, R. Hale, 1983.

UNDER PSEUDONYM KIRK FORD; NOVELS

Trail to Sedalia, R. Hale, 1967.
Feud Riders, R. Hale, 1974.

UNDER PSEUDONYM FLOYD ROGERS; NOVELS

The Man from Cheyenne Wells, R. Hale, 1964.
Revenge Rider, R. Hale, 1964.
The Stage Riders, R. Hale, 1967.
Montana Justice, R. Hale, 1973.
Hangman's Gulch, R. Hale, 1974.
Incident at Elk River, R. Hale, 1979.

UNDER PSEUDONYM JESSICA BLAIR; NOVELS

The Red Shawl (historical saga), Piatkus, 1993.
The Distant Harbour (historical saga), Piatkus, 1993.

OTHER

Contributor to Automobile Association/Ordnance Survey leisure guide, *North York Moors.* Contributor of articles and reviews to magazines, including *Country Life, Yorkshire Life, North,* and to newspapers.

WORK IN PROGRESS: Two historical novels, one with 18th-century smuggling as the background, and one set during the War of 1812; research into life in a medieval monastery.

SIDELIGHTS: William John Duncan Spence once commented: "As a peace-loving individual I think that all decisions can be achieved without violent argument, but rather by rational discussion. This tends to be reflected in my latest writing when characters become opposed. Though there may be extreme conflict this does not necessarily result in extreme violence. Maybe this has been worked out of my system in my Westerns! My advice to would-be writers is to have courage and determination. Write, write, write, and go on writing."

*   *   *

SPIERS, Edward M(ichael) 1947-

PERSONAL: Born October 18, 1947, in Edinburgh, Scotland; son of Ronald Arthur (a master mariner) and Margaret C. L. (a teacher; maiden name, Manson) Spiers; married Fiona Elizabeth McLeod (a historical editor), August 21, 1971; children: Robert Edward Andrew, Amanda Louise. *Education:* University of Edinburgh, M.A. (with first class honors), 1970, Ph.D., 1974.

ADDRESSES: Office—University of Leeds, Leeds, West Yorkshire LS2 9JT, England.

CAREER: University of Leeds, Leeds, England, lecturer in defense studies, 1975—, reader, 1987-93, professor of strategic studies, 1993—. Councillor of Edinburgh District Council, 1974; member of British Military History Commission, 1977—.

MEMBER: Royal Historical Society (fellow).

AWARDS, HONORS: Jeremiah Dalziel Prize from Edinburgh University, 1974, for doctoral achievements in British history.

WRITINGS:

Haldane: An Army Reformer, Columbia University Press, 1980.
The Army and Society, 1815-1914, Longman, 1980.
Radical General: Sir George de Lacy Evans, 1787-1870, Manchester University Press, 1983.
Chemical Warfare, Macmillan, 1986.
Chemical Weaponry, Macmillan, 1989.
The Late Victorian Army, 1868-1902, Manchester University Press, 1992.

Contributor to periodicals, including *Journal of Imperial and Commonwealth History, Army Quarterly and Defence Journal, Royal Air Force Quarterly, Journal of the Society for Army Historical Research, British Journal of International Studies, Journal of the Royal United Services Institute for Defence Studies, Journal of Strategic Studies, NATO Review, Yorkshire Post,* and *Times Higher Education Supplement.*

WORK IN PROGRESS: A book on chemical weapon proliferation.

SIDELIGHTS: In *The Army and Society, 1815-1914* Edward M. Spiers examines the relationship between Britain and its army during the years 1815 to 1914. Exploring the conditions that made the army "less than professional"— rank purchasing, inadequate pay, poor living conditions— the author also looks at military reform, especially those broad changes effected by the ministry of Edward Cardwell from 1868 to 1874. Reviewing the book for the *Times Literary Supplement,* Brian Bond noted that Spiers "skillfully depicts changing conditions within the army and the service's popular reputation." While the critic regretted the absence of an introduction and conclusion to the study, he nonetheless found it "an admirable survey which thoroughly exploits the fruits of published and unpublished research of the past twenty years."

Turning again to the subject of military reform in *Haldane: An Army Reformer,* Spiers discusses the achievements of Richard Burdon Haldane, the secretary of state for war who reorganized Britain's regular and auxiliary forces in the years preceding World War I. Unlike his predecessors, Haldane "grasped the essence of army reform," explained Bond; "he could not only implement measures within the narrow parameters set by a peacetime Liberal

administration. . . . Within these limits . . . he fashioned Expeditionary and Territorial Forces which are generally regarded as the most efficient that Britain ever possessed at the start of a major war." The critic concluded that "Spiers's study of Haldane as an army reformer is thoroughly researched, neatly arranged and forcefully presented."

Spiers told *CA:* "I am currently concentrating on strategic studies with a focus partly on chemical warfare and partly on trans-Atlantic relations within NATO."

BIOGRAPHICAL/CRITICAL SOURCES:

PERIODICALS

Times Literary Supplement, August 22, 1980; January 20, 1984.

*   *   *

STAMBAUGH, Sara   1936-

PERSONAL: Surname rhymes with "awe"; born December 4, 1936, in New Holland, PA; daughter of Clarence W. (a truck driver) and Evelyn (a homemaker; maiden name, Hershey) Stambaugh. *Education:* Beaver College, B.A., 1959; University of Minnesota—Twin Cities, M.A., Ph.D., 1969.

ADDRESSES: Home—11630 76th Ave., Edmonton, Alberta, Canada T6G 0K8. *Office*—Department of English, University of Alberta, Edmonton, Alberta, Canada T6G 2E9.

CAREER: University of Minnesota—Twin Cities, Minneapolis, instructor in English, 1963-66; Towson State College (now University), Baltimore, MD, assistant professor, 1966-69; University of Alberta, Edmonton, assistant professor, 1969-74, associate professor, 1974-89, professor, 1989—.

MEMBER: Writers Union of Canada, Authors Guild, Lancaster Mennonite Historical Society, Lancaster Historical Society.

WRITINGS:

I Hear the Reaper's Song (novel), Good Books, 1984.
The Witch and the Goddess in the Stories of Isak Dinesen (criticism), UMI Research Press, 1988.
The Sign of the Fox (novel), Good Books, 1991.

Contributor of articles, stories, and poems to scholarly journals and magazines, including *Nineteenth-Century Fiction, Mosaic, Scandinavica, Descant, Fiddlehead, Event, Festival Quarterly,* and *Liars and Rascals: Mennonite Short Stories.*

WORK IN PROGRESS: "A Pennsylvania novel set in the early decades of the twentieth century—drawn from the other side of the family."

SIDELIGHTS: Sara Stambaugh told *CA:* "I wrote *I Hear the Reaper's Song* as a tribute to my mother's family after I discovered that an 1896 family accident had precipitated a religious revival in the Lancaster County, Pennsylvania, Mennonite community. It struck me that my people had not received much respect from the outside world, and I tried to present them with dignity. Unfortunately, novels are not academically respectable. I wrote the second book to get a promotion and the third (with illness and strain) to satisfy my publishers. I am now writing to please myself and I am anticipating early retirement from an institution I no longer believe in."

*   *   *

STANKIEWICZ, Edward   1920-

PERSONAL: Surname is pronounced Stan-*ke*-vich; born November 17, 1920, in Poland; immigrated to United States, 1950, naturalized citizen, 1956; son of Stefan (a contractor) and Ida (Gruen) Stankiewicz; married Florence Freiser, November 7, 1950; children: Barbara, Steven. *Education:* University of Chicago, M.A., 1951; Harvard University, Ph.D., 1954. *Avocational Interests:* Poetry, painting.

ADDRESSES: Home—30 Fernwood Rd., Hamden, CT 06517. *Office*—Department of Slavic Languages, Yale University, New Haven, CT 06520.

CAREER: Indiana University, Bloomington (now Indiana Univeristy at Bloomington) assistant professor, 1954-59, associate professor of Slavic linguistics, 1959-60; University of Chicago, Chicago, IL, associate professor, 1960-62, professor of Slavic and general linguistics, 1962-71, chairman of department of Slavic languages, 1962-71; Yale University, New Haven, CT, professor of Slavic linguistics, 1971—. Collitz Professor, Linguistic Society of America, 1964; distinguished visiting professor, University of Colorado, summer, 1969; visiting professor at seminar in linguistics, Tokyo, Japan, 1971. Research consultant to U.S. Department of Health, Education, and Welfare, National Science Foundation, and Ford Foundation.

MEMBER: Modern Language Association of America, Linguistic Society of America.

AWARDS, HONORS: Ford Foundation research grant, 1955-56; Social Science Research Council grant to Yugoslavia, 1957; American Council of Learned Societies grant, 1962-63, for research in Yugoslavia; Guggenheim fellowship, 1977.

WRITINGS:

(Editor) Viktor M. Zhirmunskii, *Introduction to Metrics,* Mouton (Netherlands), 1966, Humanities, 1967.

(With D. S. Worth) *Selected Bibliography of Slavic Linguistics,* Volume 1, Mouton (Netherlands), 1966, Humanities, 1967, Volume 2, Mouton (Netherlands), 1970.

Declension and Gradation of Russian Substantives, Mouton (Netherlands), 1968.

(Editor, translator, and author of introduction) *Baudouin de Courtenay Anthology,* Indiana University Press, 1972.

Baudouin de Courtenay and the Foundations of Structural Linguistics, P. de Ridder, 1976.

Studies in Slavic Morphophonemics and Accentology, Michigan Slavic Publications, 1979.

(With Alexander M. Schnenker) *The Slavic Literary Languages: Formation and Development,* Slavica Publishers, 1980.

Grammars and Dictionaries of the Slavic Languages from the Middle Ages up to 1850, Mouton (Hawthorne, NY), 1984.

Baudouin de Courtenay: a podstawy wspolczesnego jezykoznawstwa, Zaklad Narodowy, 1986.

The Slavic Languages: Unity in Diversity, Mouton (Hawthorne, NY), 1986.

The Accentual Patterns of the Slavic Languages, Stanford University Press, 1993.

Co-editor of three volumes, *Current Trends in Linguistics,* for U.S. Department of Health, Education, and Welfare. Contributor of articles to encyclopedias, symposia, and American and foreign journals.

WORK IN PROGRESS: A comprehensive book on Slavic accentuation; a monograph on emotive language; articles on poetics and history of linguistics.

*   *   *

STAPLES, Mary Jane
See STAPLES, Reginald Thomas

*   *   *

STAPLES, Reginald Thomas   1911-
(James Sinclair, Robert Tyler Stevens, Mary Jane Staples)

PERSONAL: Born November 26, 1911, in London, England; son of William George (a naval officer) and Mary Jane (Brady) Staples; married Florence Anne Hume (a company director), June 12, 1937; children: Jeffery

Charles. *Education:* Attended secondary school in London, England. *Politics:* "Distrust modern politics. Distrust all politicians even more." *Religion:* Anglican. *Avocational Interests:* "Spare time pursuits—squash, tennis, badminton, hockey, cricket, golf. Gave them all up in turn, except golf and tennis, to save myself dropping dead while life was still beautiful."

ADDRESSES: Home—52 Dome Hill, Caterham, Surrey CR3 6EB, England. *Office*—Vista Sports Ltd., Sydenham Rd., Croyden, Surrey, England. *Agent*—Sheila Watson, 26 Charing Cross Rd., London WC2, England.

CAREER: Winemaker's apprentice at Pedro Domenecq (winemaking firm), 1928-30; worked in office for Blue Star Shipping Co., 1930-40, 1946-50; assistant editor for Home Publishing Co., 1950-53; Staples & Hancock Ltd., founder, 1953, director, 1953-66; managing director of Town & Country Studios Ltd. (commercial photographers), 1966—. Chairman of board of directors of Fullerton & Lloyd Ltd. (magazine publishers), 1953—, and of Vista Sports Ltd., 1970—. *Military service:* British Army, Royal Artillery, 1940-46; served in the Middle East; became sergeant.

MEMBER: Brevet Flying Club.

WRITINGS:

HISTORICAL NOVELS; UNDER PSEUDONYM JAMES SINCLAIR

Warrior Queen (the story of Boadicea), Souvenir Press, 1977.
Canis the Warrior, Souvenir Press, 1979.

HISTORICAL NOVELS; UNDER PSEUDONYM ROBERT TYLER STEVENS

The Summer Day Is Done, Doubleday, 1976.
Flight from Bucharest, Souvenir Press, 1977.
Appointment in Sarajevo, Souvenir Press, 1978.
The Fields of Yesterday, Hamlyn, 1982.
Shadows in the Afternoon, Hamlyn, 1983.
The Hostage, Severn House, 1985.
Woman in Berlin, Severn House, 1987.
The Professional Gentleman, Severn House, 1988.

UNDER PSEUDONYM MARY JANE STAPLES

Down Lambeth Way, Bantam, 1988.
Our Emily, Bantam, 1989.
King of Camberwell, Bantam, 1990.
Two for Three Farthings, Bantam, 1990.
The Lodger, Bantam, 1991.
Rising Summer, Bantam, 1991.
Pearly Queen, Bantam, 1992.
Sergeant Joe, Bantam, 1992.
On Mother Brown's Doorstep, Bantam, 1993.
The Trap, Bantam, 1993.

SIDELIGHTS: Reginald Thomas Staples once told *CA:* "My spare time pleasure—writing. Wrote millions of words of rubbish over a period of many years. Came down from the mountain of garbage (many) years ago to apply myself more seriously. Still wrote rubbish but it read better. *Woman* magazine had a rush of blood and accepted *The Summer Day Is Done* for serialisation, giving it press and television coverage. Same magazine has [since] serialised *Appointment in Sarajevo,* story based on the assassination of Franz Ferdinand in 1914, and *The Fields of Yesterday.*

"Am also wondering how long it will take publishers to achieve what they seem set on: to offer the public two kinds of books only—hyped novels and the autobiographies of discarded mistresses." Staples added, "They are, today, making excellent progress!"

*   *   *

STAR, Angel
   See QUIGLEY, Joan

*   *   *

STEELE, Elizabeth   1921-

PERSONAL: Born May 27, 1921, in Indianapolis, IN; daughter of George William Eppard (an insurance executive) and Lois Berniece (a novelist; maiden name, Avery) Smith; married Arthur Steele (a professor of history), 1947. *Education:* Butler University, B.A., 1944; University of New Mexico, M.A., 1950; Bowling Green State University, Ph.D., 1967. *Politics:* Democrat. *Religion:* Christian Science. *Avocational Interests:* Music and drama.

ADDRESSES: Home—Kendal Dr., apt. 259, Oberlin, OH 44074.

CAREER: High school English and Spanish teacher in Indiana, 1944-47, and in Ohio, 1957-62; University of Toledo, Toledo, OH, assistant professor, 1968-73, associate professor, 1973-81, professor emerita, 1981—.

MEMBER: Modern Language Association, English Association of Northwestern Ohio (former president), Phi Kappa Phi, Alpha Chi Omega.

WRITINGS:

Hugh Walpole, Twayne, 1972.
Virginia Woolf and Companions, Pageant, 1979.
Virginia Woolf's Literary Sources and Allusions, Garland Publishing, 1983.
Virginia Woolf's Rediscovered Essays, Garland Publishing, 1987.

(Editor with Diane F. Gillespie) *Julia Duckworth Stephen: Stories for Children, Essays for Adults,* Syracuse University Press, 1987.

Contributor to *New Wonder World Encyclopedia, Choice, Journal of Popular Culture, Christian Science Monitor, Colby Quarterly, Studies in Short Fiction,* and *Henry James Review.* Author of four-part play, *Pink Collar,* 1984.

* * *

STEINER, K. Leslie
See DELANY, Samuel R(ay, Jr.)

* * *

STEPHENS, Michael (Gregory) 1946-

PERSONAL: Born March 4, 1946; son of James Stewart (a U.S. customs employee) and Rose (Drew) Stephens. *Education:* City College of New York, B.A., 1975, M.A., 1976; Yale University, School of Drama, M.F.A., 1979.

ADDRESSES: Home—520 West 110th Street, No. 5-C, New York, NY 10025.

CAREER: Novelist, poet, journalist, and playwright; has worked in bookstores, on merchant ships, and as a greenskeeper at various times; Columbia University, New York City, lecturer, 1977-91; Fordham University, writer-in-residence and assistant professor, 1979-85; Princeton University, Princeton, NJ, lecturer, 1986-91; New York University, New York City, lecturer, 1989-91.

MEMBER: PEN, Associated Writing Programs, Royal Asiatic Society.

AWARDS, HONORS: MacDowell Colony fellowship, 1968; Fletcher Pratt prose fellowship, Breadloaf Writers Conference, 1971; Creative Artists Public Service fiction award, 1978; fiction grant, Connecticut Commission on the Arts, 1979; Associated Writing Programs award in creative nonfiction, 1993.

WRITINGS:

PLAYS

A Splendid Occasion in Spring, first produced in New York City at West End Bar, February 9, 1974.
Off-Season Rates, Yale Playwrights Projects, 1978.
Cloud Dream, Yale Playwrights Projects, 1979.
Our Father, first produced in New York City, 1980.
R & R, first produced in New York City, October, 1984.

OTHER

Season at Coole (novel), Dutton, 1972.

Alcohol Poems, Loose Change Press, 1973.
Paragraphs (short stories), Mulch Press, 1974.
Still Life (fiction), Kroesen Books, 1978.
Tangun Legend (poetry), Seamark Press, 1978.
Shipping Out (novel), Apple-wood Books, 1979.
Circles End (poetry and prose), Spuyten Dyvil, 1982.
Translations (Korean poetry), Red Hanrahan, 1984.
The Dramaturgy of Style (nonfiction), Southern Illinois University Press, 1986.
Lost in Seoul: And Other Discoveries on the Korean Peninsula, Random House, 1990.
Jig and Reels (prose), Hanging Loose Press, 1992.
After Asia (poetry), Spuyten Duyvil, 1993.

Contributor of articles, stories, poems, and reviews to over 100 literary magazines and newspapers, including *Nation, Rolling Stone, Village Voice, Tri-Quarterly, New Letters, American Pen, Boston Phoenix,* and *Contemporary Fiction.*

WORK IN PROGRESS: Green Dreams: Essays under the Influence of the Irish, to be published in 1994.

* * *

STERLING, Helen
See WATTS, Helen L. Hoke

* * *

STEVENS, Robert Tyler
See STAPLES, Reginald Thomas

* * *

STEVENS, Shane 1941-
(J. W. Rider)

PERSONAL: Born October 8, 1941, in New York City; son of John and Caroline (Royale) Stevens. *Education:* Columbia University, M.A., 1961.

ADDRESSES: Agent—William Morris Agency, 1350 Avenue of the Americas, New York, NY 10019.

CAREER: Stevens calls his vocation "traveler," having traveled to Mexico, South America, Europe, Asia, and Africa; about the rest he says, "I am very secretive."

MEMBER: Authors Guild, Writers Guild of America, Bread Loaf, Santa Barbara Writers Conference.

WRITINGS:

Go Down Dead, Morrow, 1967.
Way Uptown in Another World, Putnam, 1971.
Dead City, Holt, 1973.

Rat Pack, Seabury, 1974.
By Reason of Insanity (also see below), Simon & Schuster, 1979.
The Anvil Chorus, Delacorte, 1985.

UNDER PSEUDONYM J. W. RIDER

Jersey Tomatoes, Morrow, 1986.
Hot Tickets, Morrow, 1987.

Also author of screenplays *The Me Nobody Knows,* 1975, and *By Reason of Insanity.* Contributor to *New York Times, Washington Post,* and *Life.*

SIDELIGHTS: Shane Stevens told *CA:* "I am a novelist: always, now and forever; nothing I would do could shatter the significance of that. Whatever I have done in my life, I have done with that in mind. The details are of no consequence. . . . I never give interviews, stay in shadow, travel by night. I don't associate with writers, don't do book reviews, don't play politics or give advice. I try not to hurt anyone. I go where I want and write what I want."

BIOGRAPHICAL/CRITICAL SOURCES:

PERIODICALS

New York Times Book Review, January 29, 1967.
Publishers Weekly, October 31, 1966.
Times, February 24, 1967.
Village Voice, August 24, 1967.*

*   *   *

STEWART, Donald Ogden   1894-1980

PERSONAL: Born November 30, 1894, in Columbus, OH; died of heart disease, August 2, 1980, in London, England; son of Gilbert Holland (a lawyer and judge) and Clara (Landon) Stewart; married Beatrice Ames, July 24, 1926 (divorced September 8, 1938); married Ella Winter Steffens (a writer), March 4, 1939; children: (first marriage) Ames Ogden, Donald Ogden, Jr.; Peter Stephens Steffens (stepson). *Education:* Attended Exeter Academy; Yale University, A.B., 1916.

CAREER: Playwright, screenwriter, humorist, and political activist. *Vanity Fair,* New York City, writer, 1921-29. Actor on stage and in films, including *Holiday,* 1928, *Rebound,* 1928, and *Not So Dumb,* 1930. *Military service:* U.S. Naval Reserve Force, 1917-19; instructor in navigation, naval ordnance, and signals; became chief quartermaster.

MEMBER: Screenwriters Guild, League of American Writers (past president), Hollywood Anti-Nazi League (past president).

AWARDS, HONORS: Academy of Motion Picture Arts and Sciences, Academy Award nomination, 1930-31, for

Laughter; Academy Award for best screenplay, 1940, for *The Philadelphia Story.*

WRITINGS:

A Parody Outline of History, Wherein May Be Found a Curiously Irreverent Treatment of American Historical Events, Imagining Them as They Would Be Narrated by America's Most Characteristic Contemporary Authors (humorous parodies), George H. Doran, 1921.
Perfect Behavior: A Parody Outline of Etiquette (satirical anecdotes), George H. Doran, 1922, reprinted, Dover, 1964.
Aunt Polly's Story of Mankind, George H. Doran, 1923.
Mr. and Mrs. Haddock Abroad (novel), George H. Doran, 1924, reprinted, Southern Illinois University Press, 1975, original edition published as *Mr. and Mrs. Haddock in Paris, France,* Harper and Brothers, 1926.
The Crazy Fool, A. & C. Boni, 1925.
Father William: Comedy of Father and Son, Harper and Brothers, 1929.
(Editor) *Fighting Words,* Harcourt, 1940.
By a Stroke of Luck!: An Autobiography, Paddington Press, 1975.

PLAYS

Rebound: A Comedy in Three Acts (produced November, 1928, produced on Broadway, 1930), Samuel French, 1931.
(Author of book) *Fine and Dandy* (musical), produced in New York at Erlanger Theatre, 1930.
How I Wonder, produced Off-Broadway, 1947.
The Kidders, produced on the West End, 1957.
Honor Bright, produced on the West End, 1958.

Also author of play, *Emily Brady.*

SCREENPLAYS

Laughter, Paramount, 1930.
(With John Balderston) *Smiling Through,* Metro-Goldwyn-Mayer, 1932.
White Sister (based on the novel by F. Marion Crawford), Metro-Goldwyn-Mayer, 1933.
Going Hollywood, Metro-Goldwyn-Mayer, 1933.
(With Ernest Vajda and Claudine West) *The Barretts of Wimpole Street,* Metro-Goldwyn-Mayer, 1934.
(With Herman J. Mankiewicz) *Another Language,* Metro-Goldwyn-Mayer, 1935.
(With Horace Jackson) *No More Ladies,* Metro-Goldwyn-Mayer, 1935.
(With Balderston and Wells Root) *Prisoner of Zenda* (based on the novel by Anthony Hope), United Artists, 1938.
(With Sidney Buchman) *Holiday,* Columbia, 1938.
(With Vajda and West) *Marie Antionette,* Metro-Goldwyn-Mayer, 1938.

Night of Nights, Independent, 1939.

(With Delmer Davis) *Love Affair,* RKO Radio Pictures, 1939.

(With Dalton Trumbo) *Kitty Foyle,* RKO Radio Pictures, 1940.

The Philadelphia Story (based on the play by Philip Barry), Metro-Goldwyn-Mayer, 1940.

That Uncertain Feeling, United Artists, 1941.

(With Elliott Paul) *A Woman's Face,* Metro-Goldwyn-Mayer, 1941.

(With others) *Tales of Manhattan,* Twentieth Century-Fox, 1942.

Keeper of the Flame (based on the novel by I. A. R. Wylie), Metro-Goldwyn-Mayer, 1942.

(With others) *Forever and a Day,* RKO Radio Pictures, 1944.

Without Love, Metro-Goldwyn-Mayer, 1945.

Life with Father, Warner Bros., 1947.

(With Sonja Levien) *Cass Timberlaine* (based on the novel by Sinclair Lewis), Metro-Goldwyn-Mayer, 1947.

Edward My Son, Metro-Goldwyn-Mayer, 1949.

Malaya, Metro-Goldwyn-Mayer, 1950.

OTHER

Also editor of and contributor to *Exeter Remembered,* 1965. Contributor to periodicals.

SIDELIGHTS: Donald Ogden Stewart began his literary career in the 1920s as a magazine writer and novelist best known for his parodies of social etiquette and middle-class values. As a member of an elite group of writers in New York City during this time, which included Dorothy Parker and Robert Benchley, he participated in the famous daily "Algonquin Round Table" discussions. He left for Hollywood in the 1930s—as did many of his contemporaries—and became a successful screenwriter, ultimately winning an Academy Award in 1940 for his screenplay for *The Philadelphia Story.* However, because of his membership in the Communist Party in the 1930s, he was blacklisted during the McCarthy era, and soon found himself unemployed. Forced to leave the country in 1951, he relocated to England where he remained until his death in 1980.

Stewart, the son of a successful judge, was born and raised in Columbus, Ohio. After graduating from Yale University in 1916, he attempted a career in business. While working for American Telephone & Telegraph in Minneapolis, Minnesota, he became friends with F. Scott Fitzgerald, who at the time was working on the manuscript for *This Side of Paradise.* Several years later, Fitzgerald moved to New York City and Stewart soon followed, leaving behind his business career in favor of becoming a writer. Fitzgerald introduced Stewart to *Vanity Fair* editor Edmund Wilson, who was impressed by Stewart's par-

odies of famous contemporary writers and offered to publish them in the magazine. Wilson also invited Stewart to join the "Algonquin Round Table" group. Noted for its members' collective wit and often biting humor, the group was the vanguard of its literary generation. Though Stewart acknowledged the influence and wit of the group, he claimed that he "never really [felt] at ease in this company. . . . [T]he atmosphere seemed . . . to be basically unfriendly," according to James C. McNutt in *Dictionary of Literary Biography.*

Stewart's first book established him as one of the country's most popular humorists. "Gentler than [James] Thurber or Parker," writes Calvin Tompkins in *New York Times Book Review,* Stewart "made his mark in a genre of pure nonsense and non sequitur that came to be known as 'crazy humor.' " *A Parody Outline of History, Wherein May Be Found a Curiously Irreverent Treatment of American Historical Events, Imagining Them as They Would Be Narrated by America's Most Characteristic Contemporary Authors* spoofed the writing styles of many popular writers of the day, including H. G. Wells, Edith Wharton, and Eugene O'Neill. The critics varied in their reviews of the historical vignettes; a *Boston Transcript* reviewer wrote that it was "not clever or ingenious in its irreverence," but L. Masson of *New York Times* said that it revealed "the insight of [a] genuine humorist." However, it was popular with readers, and Stewart soon aspired to "be the new Mark Twain, fearless, uncorrupted," quotes McNutt in *Dictionary of Literary Biography.*

Stewart's next book, *Aunt Polly's Story of Mankind,* reached beyond his previous lighthearted humor in its attempt at satirizing religious and middle-class values. As Stewart told the *New York Times:* "I didn't want to use my humor just to get laughs in drawing rooms. . . . I want to have bite, to make people examine themselves." Aunt Polly, a socialite, decides to teach her nieces and nephews the history of the world from her own narrow viewpoint, which sanctifies her middle-class standing. Prompted by her moralistic urging, the children initiate a small-scale war during their school's Armistice Day pageant. According to Ted Thackrey, Jr. in *Los Angeles Times,* Stewart "gradually shaped his work toward a form of humor aimed more generally at deflation of pretention and exposure of hypocrisy." However, *Aunt Polly's Story of Mankind* received silence from critics and readers alike. Greatly disappointed with the lack of attention the book received, Stewart returned to magazine writing. He continued to write lighthearted parodies of manners which proved to be popular, including *Perfect Behavior,* and *Mr. and Mrs. Haddock Abroad.*

Stewart followed many of his contemporaries to Hollywood in the early 1930s, where the large motion picture studios were paying writers top dollar for screenplays. His first script, a light comedy called *The Crazy Fool,* impressed noted director King Vidor. Vidor showed the script to Irving Thalberg at Metro-Goldwyn-Mayer (MGM) and Thalberg hired Stewart. *Laughter,* released in 1930 at the dawn of the sound era, was Stewart's first screenplay to make it to the theaters. Among the first comedies written specifically for the screen and not the stage, *Laughter* provided the formula for the popular screwball comedies of the late 1930s. Stewart continued to augment his salary by writing a syndicated column for the *Chicago Tribune* as well as short pieces for the *New Yorker* during these years.

Stewart soon accumulated an impressive list of screenplay credits, and his scripts were directed by the most notable directors of the day, including George Cukor, King Vidor, and David O. Selznick. The biggest Hollywood names starred in his pictures: Cary Grant, Clark Gable, Joan Crawford, Jimmy Stewart, and Katherine Hepburn. His greatest success came with *The Philadelphia Story,* a love-triangle comedy in which a socialite's marriage plans become tangled by her ex-husband and a reporter who falls in love with her. After winning the Academy Award for best screenplay for his adaptation of *The Philadelphia Story,* Stewart remarked that it was "the easiest award anybody got, because it was a hell of a play. I just got out of the way," quotes Duane Byrge in *Dictionary of Literary Biography.* At the height of his career, Stewart was among the highest paid screenwriters in Hollywood, earning up to $5,000 a week.

Because of his political activities as a member of the Communist party and his support for Soviet dictator Joseph Stalin in the 1930s, Stewart became a target for Senator Joseph McCarthy's House Un-American Activities Committee. Even though he was an active anti-Fascist, Stewart was called upon to testify at the hearings and name other Communists. Stewart refused to indict himself or anyone else, and as a result his career suffered. He was fired by MGM and no other studio would hire him. He relocated to England and collaborated on several other screenplays under pseudonyms. During these years he wrote little besides his autobiography, *By a Stroke of Luck!,* which was published in 1975. A *New Yorker* reviewer noted that *By A Stroke of Luck!* is an "engaging autobiography" in which Stewart's "sole regret in his zigzag career is having believed in Stalin."

BIOGRAPHICAL/CRITICAL SOURCES:

BOOKS

Dictionary of Literary Biography, Gale, Volume 4: *American Writers in Paris, 1920-1939,* 1980, pp. 375-378, Volume 11: *American Humorists, 1800-1950,* 1982, pp. 466-473, Volume 26: *American Screenwriters,* 1984, pp. 304-310.

Stewart, Donald Ogden, *By a Stroke of Luck!: An Autobiography,* Paddington Press, 1975.

PERIODICALS

Boston Transcript, December 28, 1921.
Los Angeles Times, August 4, 1980.
New Yorker, January 5, 1976.
New York Times, December 18, 1921.
New York Times Book Review, December 14, 1975.

OBITUARIES:

PERIODICALS

Chicago Tribune, August 5, 1980.
Newsweek, August 18, 1980, p. 57.
New York Times, August 3, 1980.
Time, August 18, 1980, p. 49.
Washington Post, August 4, 1980.*

—*Sketch by Kathleen Wilson*

*   *   *

STOCK, R(obert) D(ouglas) 1941-

PERSONAL: Born December 2, 1941, in Akron, OH; son of Robert P. (a chemical engineer) and Barbara (Broughton) Stock; married Barbara Jergovich, 1975. *Education:* Kent State University, B.A., 1963; Princeton University, M.A., 1965, Ph.D., 1967. *Politics:* Conservative. *Religion:* Episcopalian.

ADDRESSES: Home—1611 B St., Lincoln, NE 68502. *Office*—Department of English, University of Nebraska, 304 Andrews Hall, Lincoln, NE 68588.

CAREER: University of Nebraska, Lincoln, assistant professor, 1967-72, associate professor, 1972-77, professor of English, 1977—, vice chairman of Department of English, 1987-90.

MEMBER: American Society for Eighteenth-Century Studies.

WRITINGS:

Samuel Johnson and Neoclassical Dramatic Theory, University of Nebraska Press, 1973.
Samuel Johnson's Literary Criticism, University of Nebraska Press, 1974.
The New Humanists in Nebraska, University of Nebraska Press, 1979.
(Contributor) M. Hannay, editor, *As Her Whimsey Took Her,* Kent State University Press, 1979.
The Holy and the Daemonic from Sir Thomas Browne to William Blake, Princeton University Press, 1982.
The Flutes of Dionysus: Daemonic Enthrallment in Literature, University of Nebraska Press, 1989.

WORK IN PROGRESS: Book on the treatment of the un-canny or eerie in fiction, discursive prose, and film (espe-cially silent film).

SIDELIGHTS: R. D. Stock once told *CA:* "I have been especially interested in studying the decline in modern so-ciety of the 'enchanted view,' or a sense of the numi-nous—a phenomenon remarked by such diverse thinkers as Carl Jung, Emile Durkheim, Robert Nisbet. As a writer, consequently, I have been much occupied with the eighteenth century, when the decay of those feelings first became evident in a forcible way, and with those writers since who have endeavored through their philosophical and imaginative works to revive a sense of the uncanny or supernatural world. 'Emancipation' is a word celebrated by many contemporary writers, but the emancipation I should like to proclaim is from the trite and dogmatic ma-terialism to which many of them, it seems, subscribe."

BIOGRAPHICAL/CRITICAL SOURCES:

PERIODICALS

Choice, December, 1973.
Criticism, winter, 1983.
Sewanee Review, July, 1983.
Times Literary Supplement, September 24, 1982.

*   *   *

STONE, Roger D. 1934-

PERSONAL: Born August 4, 1934, in New York, NY; son of Patrick W. (a diplomat) and Kathleen Mary (Davies) Stone; married Florence Smith (an association executive), May 19, 1962; children: Leslie Burnam. *Education:* Yale University, B.A., 1955. *Politics:* Democrat. *Religion:* Epis-copal.

ADDRESSES: Home—3403 O St. N.W., Washington, DC 20007; Deer Hill Rd., Cornwall-on-Hudson, NY 12520. *Office*—ECO, Inc., 1212 New York Ave., Suite 345, Washington, DC 20005.

CAREER: Worked for Time Inc., 1955-70, *Time* maga-zine, New York City, trainee, 1955-56, assistant to the publisher, 1958-60, Time-Life News Service, news corre-spondent in San Francisco, CA, 1961-62, chief of San Francisco bureau, 1962-64, bureau chief in Rio de Janeiro, Brazil, 1964-67, bureau chief in Paris, France, 1967-68, as-sistant to the president of Time Inc., New York City, 1968-70; Chase Manhattan Bank, New York City, vice-president of International Department, 1970-75; Center for Inter-American Relations, New York City, president, 1975-82; World Wildlife Fund—U.S., Washington, DC, vice-president, working in Washington and New York City, 1982-86, Armand G. Erpf Conservation fellow,

1986-89, senior fellow, 1989—; ECO Inc. (publisher), Washington, DC, vice-chairman, 1992—. Council on For-eign Relations, Whitney H. Shepardson fellow, 1990-91, consultant on environmental issues, 1991-92; Sustainable Development Institute, Garrison, NY, director, 1993—. Member of board of directors of Asian Institute of Tech-nology (AIT) Foundation, Caribbean Conservation Cor-poration, Cintas Foundation, and Armand G. Erpf Fund. Has served as member of board of directors of World Wildlife Fund—U.S., University of the Andes Founda-tion, Center of Inter-American Relations, Americas Foundation, Accion International, Near East Emergency Donations, and Arts International. *Military service:* U.S. Navy, aviator, 1956-59.

MEMBER: Americas Society, Council on Foreign Rela-tions, Visual Arts Advisory Board, Century Association.

WRITINGS:

NONFICTION

Dreams of Amazonia, Elisabeth Sifton/Viking, 1985.
The Voyage of the Sanderling, Alfred A. Knopf, 1990.
Wildlands and Human Needs, World Wildlife Fund, 1991.
The Nature of Development: Reports from the Rural Trop-ics on the Quest for Sustainable Economic Growth, Al-fred A. Knopf, 1992.

Also contributor to books, including *Collier's Year Book 1986; People of the Rain Forest,* University of California Press, 1988; *Sea Changes: American Foreign Policy in a World Transformed,* Council on Foreign Relations, 1990; and *Global Economics and Environment: Toward Sustain-able Rural Development in the Third World,* Council on Foreign Relations, 1991. Contributor to periodicals, in-cluding *Time, Life, Fortune, Foreign Affairs, New York Times, Christian Science Monitor, Islands, Oceans, Envi-ronmental Forum, World Wildlife Fund Newsletter, Con-servation Foundation Letter, Wildlife Conversation,* and *ECO.*

WORK IN PROGRESS: Research for a book on interna-tional nature conservation; research on international af-fairs.

SIDELIGHTS: In *Dreams of Amazonia,* Roger D. Stone writes about the Amazon rainforest of Brazil. He charts the history of the region, dating back to the Spanish explo-ration of the Amazon, and recounts the numerous failed attempts by statesmen and private entrepreneurs to de-velop the land for profit. Writing in the *Washington Post Book World,* Mark London noted that what is happening to the Amazon jungle "fits one man's definition of prog-ress—and Stone's definition of ultimate destruction." The author includes interviews with scientists who are "fever-ishly" studying the rainforest before it is spoiled by enterprisers, and Stone writes "deftly and intelligently" about his topic, asserted London. The critic deemed the book "a primer of Amazon history and an articulate warning about its future."

Stone once told *CA:* "I started gathering the material for *Dreams of Amazonia* during my early visits to the region in the 1960s, but the idea of doing the book did not occur to me until I had joined the board of directors of World Wildlife Fund—U.S. (WWF) in 1976 and began thinking about the world in a different way. Reporters tend to concentrate on politics, economics, and security. But WWF, which is concerned about the welfare of all species and does much of its scientific and conservation work in Latin America, provided convincing evidence that biology is a yardstick of fundamental importance.

"The tropical rainforest, I learned, is not just a vast wilderness to be 'conquered,' but rather a valuable and highly vulnerable place that man can quickly destroy through conventional activities. Putting all this together, it occurred to me that a book on the Amazon could shed some new light on the subject and also be more interesting than the usual foreign correspondent accounts of three years in country X. So, I returned to the Amazon a time or two in the late 1970s and began library research and interviews with scientists and conservationists in the United States. By 1980, the project had become a one-hundred-page outline, and, with the help of a six-month sabbatical leave, several further trips to Amazonia, and a wonderful editor, it continued to take shape."

Stone continued: "The reaction to *Dreams* . . . emboldened me to try again to write about economic/environmental intersections. My second effort involved sailing a small boat from Maine to Rio de Janeiro, visiting many coastal regions along the way, and writing about the complexity of eco-political interplay where land meets water. The book, entitled *The Voyage of the Sanderling,* was first published in 1990.

"Returning from this experience, which involved a year aboard the boat, I planned to hunker down for awhile. However, the World Wildlife Fund promptly asked me to embark on a round of worldwide travels leading toward a series of articles about environmentally sound forms of rural economic development in remote places. The 30,000 words I produced for WWF formed the core for the book, *The Nature of Development,* that Knopf published on the eve of the 1992 'Earth Summit' in Rio de Janeiro.

"Currently I am working on a fourth book. It is about the prospects for 'sustainable development' in an affluent part of Long Island, New York, and what these mean to all of us. I seem to be stuck on this kind of subject. But my experience draws me logically to within this 'comfort zone.'

It's easier to write, I find, than to have something to say. So, I try to follow an old rule: talk what you know."

BIOGRAPHICAL/CRITICAL SOURCES:

PERIODICALS

Washington Post Book World, March 24, 1985.

*   *   *

STOVER, Leon E(ugene)   1929-

PERSONAL: Born April 9, 1929, in Lewistown, PA; son of George Franklin (a university professor) and Helen (Haines) Stover; married Takeko Kawai (a college lecturer in Far Eastern history), October 12, 1956; children: (from previous marriage) Laren Elizabeth. *Education:* Western Maryland College, B.A., 1950; graduate study at University of New Mexico, 1950, and Harvard University, 1951; Columbia University, M.A., 1952, Ph.D., 1962.

ADDRESSES: Home—3100 S. Michigan Ave., Apt. 602, Chicago, IL 60616-3825. *Office*—Illinois Institute of Technology, Department of Social Sciences, Chicago, IL 60616.

CAREER: American Museum of Natural History, New York, NY, instructor, 1955-57; Hobart and William Smith Colleges, Geneva, NY, instructor, 1957-63, assistant professor of anthropology, 1963-65; Illinois Institute of Technology, Chicago, IL, associate professor, 1966-74, professor of anthropology, 1974—. Visiting assistant professor of cultural anthropology at University of Tokyo, 1963-66. Founder and chairperson of John W. Campbell Memorial Award, 1972; consultant to the H. G. Wells Travelling Exhibition and Symposium for the state of Illinois, 1986.

MEMBER: Science Fiction Writers of America, Science Fiction Research Association, H. G. Wells Society, Association for Asian Studies, Overseas Chinese Musical and Art Center (director).

AWARDS, HONORS: Human Ecology Fund fellow in Japan, 1963-64; National Institute of Health fellow in Japan, 1964-65; Chris Award and Cine Award, both 1973, for film script "Power and Wheels"; Litt.D., 1980, Western Maryland College.

WRITINGS:

(Contributor) *U.S. Area Army Handbook on Communist China,* U.S. Government Printing Office, 1967.
(Editor with Harry Harrison) *Apeman, Spaceman: Anthropological Science Fiction* (anthology), Doubleday, 1968.
(Contributor) *Orbit 9,* edited by Damon Knight, Putnam, 1971.

(Editor with Willis E. McNelly) *Above the Human Landscape: An Anthology of Social Science Fiction,* Goodyear, 1972.

(With Harry Harrison) *Stonehenge* (a historical novel), Scribner, 1972.

La Science Fiction americaine: Essai d'anthropologie culturelle (title means "American Science-Fiction: An Essay in Cultural Anthropology"), Aubier-Montaigne, 1972.

(With wife, Takeko K. Stover) *The Cultural Ecology of Chinese Civilization: Peasants and Elites in the Last of the Agrarian States,* Universe Books, 1973.

China: An Anthropological Perspective (textbook), Goodyear, 1976.

(With Bruce Kraig) *Stonehenge: The Indo-European Heritage,* Nelson-Hall, 1979.

(Contributor) Jack Williamson, editor, *Teaching Science Fiction,* Owlswick, 1980.

The Shaving of Karl Marx: An Instant Novel of Ideas, After the Manner of Thomas Love Peacock, in which Lenin and H. G. Wells Talk about the Political Meaning of the Scientific Romances (dialogue novel), Chiron, 1982.

Stonehenge: Where Atlantis Died (historical novel), Tor Books, 1983.

The Prophetic Soul: A Reading of H. G. Wells's "Things to Come" (includes film treatment and post-production script), McFarland, 1986.

(Contributor) Curtis C. Smith, editor, *Twentieth-Century Science Fiction Writers,* St. Martin's, 2nd edition, 1986.

Robert A. Heinlein, Twayne, 1987.

Harry Harrison, Twayne, 1990.

Also author of the screenplay, *Power and Wheels: The Automobile in Modern Life,* and other scripts for Encyclopedia Britannica Films; author and on-location narrator of "The Stonehenge Mystery" for Eagle Eye Video Productions. Contributor of short stories and articles to magazines and professional journals. Science editor of *Amazing Stories,* 1967-69.

SIDELIGHTS: Leon E. Stover was an English major at Western Maryland College before he took his Ph.D. in anthropology and China studies at Columbia University, and has written two books in these combined fields. They are *The Cultural Ecology of Chinese Civilization,* a trade book based on his lectures of 1963-65 at Tokyo University, where he was the first non-Japanese to teach in the graduate school, and a textbook, *China: An Anthropological Perspective.* Both works are described by Eric Jones, the economic historian, as theoretical breakthroughs in the historical assessment of Chinese civilization. Stover left Tokyo University in 1965 for a job at the Illinois Institute of Technology, an engineering school where he was

among the first to introduce science fiction studies to the American college curriculum. He edited the first theme anthology of general science fiction collections, *Apeman, Spaceman,* and the first science fiction college textbook, *Above the Human Landscape.* At about the same time, the Sorbonne commissioned him to write a textbook for its American Studies Program, *La Science Fiction Americaine.*

Another of Stover's interests, the remains of Stonehenge, has led him to produce several works. *Stonehenge and the Origins of Western Culture* outlines his own political theory that is now winning acceptance even among astronomers, who once thought of the ruins as a lunar and solar observatory and eclipse computer. Stover first developed his idea in a novel, now revised and expanded under the title, *Stonehenge: Where Atlantis Died.* Later Stover depicted this theory in the TV documentary, "The Stonehenge Mystery."

In the mid 1980s, Stover began to concentrate solely on literary criticism, focusing on the political thought of H. G. Wells. After receiving an honorary Doctor of Letters from his undergraduate alma mater, he declared himself "a born again English major." The first result of this new career was a work of novelized literary criticism, *The Shaving of Karl Marx,* said by an officer of the H. G. Wells Society to be done by an author whose "versatility is little short" of Wells's own. Next came *The Prophetic Soul,* an exhaustive reading of Wells's 1936 film, *Things to Come,* which presented two "lost" documents: the filmmaker's privately printed screenplay for London Films, and the studio's final release script. Stover's 1987 book, *Robert Heinlein,* is the first attempt to treat "the dean of American science fiction writers" as a distinctly American author, not merely a genre writer.

BIOGRAPHICAL/CRITICAL SOURCES:

PERIODICALS

Archaeology, July/August, 1980.
Baltimore Sun, March 16, 1981.
Chicago Tribune, December 17, 1979.
Wellsian, summer, 1983.*

*   *   *

STRICKLAND, Rennard (James) 1940-

PERSONAL: Born September 26, 1940, in St. Louis, MO; son of R. J. (a businessman) and Adell G. (director of senior citizen programs) Strickland. *Education:* Northeastern State College (now University), Tahlequah, OK, B.A., 1962; University of Virginia, J.D., 1965, S.J.D., 1970; University of Arkansas, M.A., 1966.

ADDRESSES: Office—School of Law, University of Tulsa, Tulsa, OK 74104.

CAREER: University of Arkansas, Fayetteville, assistant professor and coordinator of basic speech, 1966; University of West Florida, Pensacola, assistant professor, 1970-71; St. Mary's University of San Antonio, San Antonio, TX, Sylvan Lange Distinguished Visiting Professor, summer, 1972, associate professor, 1972-74, professor of law, 1975, acting dean of law, 1974; University of Washington, Seattle, associate professor of law, 1975-76; University of Tulsa, Tulsa, OK, John W. Shleppey Research Professor of Law, 1976—. Fellow of Doris Duke Foundation, 1970-73, and American Bar Foundation. Member of Prelaw Committee, Law School Admissions Council, 1974-76; visiting professor, University of New Mexico, summers, 1975, 1976, 1977, Harvard University, 1980-81, and University of Florida, 1983. Director, Indian Heritage Association, 1966—. Indian Law Center, visitor, 1974-75, consultant, American Indian law programs, 1975-80.

MEMBER: American Society of Legal History, American Judicare Society, American Society of International Law, Indian Heritage Association, Communications Association of America, Seldon Society, Scribes, Phi Alpha Delta, Phi Delta Phi, Phi Kappa Delta, Delta Sigma Rho, Tau Kappa Alpha, Alpha Chi.

AWARDS, HONORS: Law School Foundation fellow, University of Virginia, 1969-70; American Council of Learned Societies fellow, 1972; Carnegie Corporation research grant, 1977; National Endowment for Humanities grant, 1977-79, 1980-82; Donner Foundation grant, 1978; Pew Foundation grant, 1980-82; award of merit, Association of State and Local History, 1981.

WRITINGS:

(With Donal Stanton and Jimmie N. Rogers) *Sourcebook on Labor Management Relations,* Debate Sourcebook, 1965.
(With Stanton) *Sourcebook on Economic-Military Assistance,* Debate Sourcebook, 1966.
(With Jack Gregory) *Sourcebook on Criminal Investigation,* Debate Sourcebook, 1967.
Sam Houston with the Cherokees, 1829-1833, University of Texas Press, 1967.
(Editor with Gregory) *Starr's History of the Cherokee,* Indian Heritage Association, 1967.
(With Gregory) *Sourcebook on the Draft,* Debate Sourcebook, 1968.
(Editor with Gregory) *Cherokee Cookbook,* Indian Heritage Association, 1968.
(With Gregory) *Cherokee Spirit Tales,* Indian Heritage Association, 1969.
(With Gregory) *Sourcebook on Environmental Policy,* Debate Sourcebook, 1970.

(Editor with Richard Johannesen and Ralph Eubanks) *Language Is Sermonic: Richard M. Weaver on the Nature of Rhetoric,* Louisiana State University Press, 1970.
(With Gregory) *Sourcebook on Judicial Reform,* Debate Sourcebook, 1971.
(With Gregory) *Creek-Seminole Spirit Tales,* Indian Heritage Association, 1971.
(Editor with Gregory) *Hell on the Border: He Hanged Eighty-eight Men,* Indian Heritage Association, 1972.
(With Gregory) *Adventures of an Indian Boy,* Indian Heritage Association, 1972.
(With Gregory) *Choctaw Spirit Tales,* Indian Heritage Association, 1973.
(With Earl Boyd Pierce) *The Cherokee People,* Indian Tribal Series, 1973.
(With Gregory) *American Indian Spirit Tales,* Indian Heritage Association, 1973.
How to Get into Law School, Hawthorn, 1974, revised edition, 1977.
Fire and the Spirits: Cherokee Law from Clan to Court, University of Oklahoma Press, 1975.
Avoiding Teacher Malpractice: A Practical Legal Handbook for the Teaching Professional, Hawthorn, 1976.
The Indians in Oklahoma, University of Oklahoma Press, 1980.
(With Anne Hodges Morgan) *Oklahoma Memories,* University of Oklahoma Press, 1981.
(With Edwin L. Wade) *Magic Images: Contemporary Native American Art,* Philbrook Art Center, University of Oklahoma, 1982.
(With Wade and Carol Haralson) *As in a Vision; Masterworks of American Indian Art: The Elizabeth Cole Butler Collection at Philbrook Art Center,* Philbrook Art Center, University of Oklahoma, 1983.
(Editor with Thomas O. White and Bruce I. Zimmer) *The Right Law School for You,* Law School Admission Council, Law School Admission Services, 1986.
(With Margaret Archuleta) *Shared Visions: Native American Painters and Sculptors in the Twentieth Century,* Heard Museum, 1991.

Also author, with Earl B. Pierce, of *The Cherokee People,* 1973. Contributor to proceedings, and to professional journals. Editor of prelaw handbook, Association of American Law Schools, 1974-80. Project director, *Handbook of Federal Indian Law,* 1975-82.

WORK IN PROGRESS: American Indian Law and Policy; Careers in Law; Law at Dawn; The Creek Way: Law in an Indian Confederacy; Before the Trail of Tears; The Cherokee Removal Debate; Communications in a Changing Society.

STRIEBER, (Louis) Whitley 1945-

PERSONAL: Born June 13, 1945, in San Antonio, TX; son of Karl (a lawyer) and Mary (Drought) Strieber; married Anne Mattocks (a teacher), November 20, 1970; children: Andrew. *Education:* University of Texas, B.A., 1968; London School of Film Technique, certificate, 1968. *Religion:* Roman Catholic. *Avocational Interests:* Strieber has participated in archaeological projects in Central America and has been involved with the attempt to authenticate the "Holy Shroud" that has been undertaken by a scientific group.

ADDRESSES: Office—Wilson & Neff, Inc., 31 Grace Ct., Brooklyn, NY 11201.

CAREER: Novelist. Benton & Bowles Advertising, New York City, media planner, 1968-70; Norman, Craig & Kummel (advertisers), New York City, account supervisor, 1970; Sullivan, Stouffer, Caldwell & Bayless (advertisers), New York City, account supervisor, 1971-74; Cunningham & Walsh Advertising, New York City, management supervisor and vice-president, 1974-77; freelance writer, 1977—.

MEMBER: Authors Guild, Authors League of America, Writers Guild, Science Fiction Writers of America, PEN, Empire State Society, Sons of the American Revolution.

AWARDS, HONORS: Olive Branch Award, Writers and Publishers for Nuclear Disarmament, 1986, for *Warday: And the Journey Onward.*

WRITINGS:

NOVELS

The Wolfen, Morrow, 1978.
The Hunger, Morrow, 1981.
Black Magic, Morrow, 1982.
The Night Church, Simon & Schuster, 1983.
(With James Kunetka) *Warday: And the Journey Onward,* Holt, 1984.
Wolf of Shadows, Sierra Club/Knopf, 1986.
(With Kunetka) *Nature's End: The Consequences of the Twentieth Century,* Warner Books, 1986.
Catmagic, Tor Books, 1987.
Majestic (also see below), Berkley, 1990.
The Wild, Tor Books, 1991.
Billy (also see below), Berkley, 1991.
Unholy Fire, Dutton, 1992.
The Forbidden Zone (also see below), Dutton, 1993.

NONFICTION

Communion: A True Story (also see below), Morrow, 1987.
Transformation: The Breakthrough, Avon, 1990.

SCREENPLAYS

Communion (based on his book), New Line Cinema, 1989.

Also author of the screenplays *Majestic, Billy,* and *The Forbidden Zone,* all based on his novels.

OTHER

(Contributor) *Murder in Manhattan* (stories), Morrow, 1986.

Contributor of short stories to *Omni.* Many of Strieber's works have been released on audiocassette.

ADAPTATIONS: Wolfen was filmed by Orion Pictures in 1981; *The Hunger* was filmed by Metro-Goldwyn-Mayer/United Artists in 1983.

SIDELIGHTS: Whitley Strieber's career has been a strange and unique one. After a decade in the advertising industry, he sold two horror novels—*The Wolfen,* which retold the werewolf legend in modern New York City, and *The Hunger,* which did the same for vampires—both of which were made into movies. During the mid-1980s, Strieber teamed with Robert Oppenheimer biographer James Kunetka to produce a pair of cautionary tales, *Warday* and *Nature's End.* Then, in 1987, Strieber published *Communion: A True Story,* in which he described his own abduction by "visitors" and the experimental procedures to which he was subjected. Almost overnight, *Communion* topped the non-fiction bestseller lists, making Strieber the subject of both praise and ridicule.

The plot of Strieber's first novel, *The Wolfen,* builds upon the traditional legend of the werewolf as portrayed in literature and folklore. The creatures it concerns differ somewhat from the popular concept of werewolves, however. The wolfen, writes Joseph McLellan in the *Washington Post Book World,* "are not human beings who turn into wolves on nights when the moon is full, but wolves who have evolved independently up to a humanoid level." Strieber sets his tale in the South Bronx, where a pack of these creatures lives an organized but hidden existence, venturing out at night to search for the food on which they survive: human beings. When the creatures are discovered by two policemen (who have difficulty persuading the world that the werewolves exist), a battle for survival ensues. While McLellan calls *The Wolfen* "standard adventure fare," Strieber's unique contribution to the genre is captured in the critic's commentary: "The book's real interest lies in its social criticism, its comparison of lupi and human behavior in a whole spectrum that ranges from mating patterns to basic social structures. The book is a howling success."

The Hunger deals with another of horror fiction's classic characters: the vampire. A *Publishers Weekly* reviewer notes that the book's "fast-paced, intriguing plot" laced with "plausible scientific 'findings' skillfully ensnares the readers." The story line of *The Hunger* follows the attempts of the vampire Miriam to find a human companion with whom to share her immortality. Though Miriam's lovers drink the blood of humans in order to survive, they are not true vampires; their lives last a mere two hundred years, after which they rapidly age and expire within a few days. When the vampire's present lover, John Blaylock, reaches the end of his two hundred years, Miriam enters into a relationship with sleep and age researcher Sarah Roberts, with disastrous results.

In an interview with *CA*, Strieber theorized about the popularity of his horror novels: "I believe that people who are happy not only enjoy being frightened but *need* to be frightened from time to time in order to relieve a certain amount of guilt that builds up in any kind of situation. . . . Horror stories can play a rather healthy role in a happy society. It can even be a civilizing role as long as [the stories] don't exploit aggressive or hostile emotions, and I hope mine never do."

Strieber's third and fourth novels, *Black Magic* and *The Night Church,* were also steeped in the macabre, but the former also introduced the author's concern about the possibility of nuclear war—a concern which formed the basis for his 1984 novel, *Warday: And the Journey Onward.* "I feel that the world we live in is, in a certain sense, coming to a climax," Strieber explained to *CA* shortly after the publication of *Warday;* "the amount of tension is so high on so many different levels that we face a very real prospect of an explosive and civilization-destroying war. I don't feel that anyone with communication skills should ignore the problems that we face right now."

Set in 1993, five years after a very limited nuclear skirmish between the United States and the Soviet Union, *Warday* describes humanity's efforts to live on after the disaster. Presenting the novel as a series of journal entries, Strieber and Kunetka cast themselves as reporters who travel across the United States, assessing the damage. Though he warns that *Warday* "sounds ominously as though it were conceived with the movie-rights sale in mind," the *New Republic*'s Gregg Easterbrook finds in the novel "many virtues. . . . The reserved, adult tone of *Warday* is rare in antinuclear writing, and somehow more chilling than anger or outrage—especially when it forces you to think about the sheer practical details of living out your life in a nuclear poverty that could have been prevented by only a few moments' common sense." *Nation*'s Edward Zuckerman, however, complains that "the problem with *Warday* is that it isn't much of a novel. It convincingly evokes a postnuclear-war world, but it is handicapped by not having a plot," and D.G. Myers of the *New York Times Book Review* remarks that *Warday* "would be a marvelously de-

tailed spoof if the co-authors shared a sense of humor. Instead, the book is a ceaseless alarm."

Strieber followed *Warday* with *Wolf of Shadows,* a novel which once again describes the aftermath of a nuclear war—this time from the point of view of a wolf, in order to examine how such a catastrophe would affect animals and the environment. In this way, *Wolf of Shadows* served as a perfect transition to his next novel, *Nature's End: The Consequences of the Twentieth Century.* Again written in collaboration with Kunetka, *Nature's End* presents a world in which the warnings of conservationists have gone unheeded, a world ravaged by overpopulation and complete environmental collapse. To help relieve the overburdened Earth, a powerful political group known as the Depopulationists has suggested that one-third of the planet's inhabitants take a lethal dose of poison. "The characters in *Nature's End* tend toward the well-roundedness of cardboard, and some of the plotting devices verge on the trendy-silly," comments Dennis Drabelle in the *Washington Post Book World.* "But on balance the novel is entertaining and intelligent."

Strieber considered the publication of *Warday* and *Nature's End* to be a turning point in his career, a transition from horror novels to more serious fiction. However, the real turning point—in Strieber's life as well as his career—was close at hand.

On December 26, 1985, Strieber reports that he was awakened to find a figure standing in his bedroom doorway. Stricken with fear, he passed out, reawakening an indeterminable amount of time later naked and unable to move, while three beings transported him to some sort of vessel. While there, Strieber was subjected to a number of experiments, including one in which a long needle was inserted into his brain. He was returned to his home, remembering nothing of the experience; several days later, however, the suppressed memories resurfaced suddenly, along with others—memories which indicated that Strieber had been abducted numerous times over several decades.

Much of *Communion* describes the long psychoanalytical sessions Strieber underwent during 1986, many of which involved hypnosis. These sessions unearthed further details: descriptions of the aliens as small-bodied creatures with large, bald heads and dark, slanted eyes; abductions when Strieber was a child, for years disguised as dreams or hidden behind "screen memories"; even an instance when the aliens informed Strieber, "You are our chosen one." Strieber, a self-described skeptic of the paranormal, says in *People* of his therapy, "I thought I was going crazy in an extremely embarrassing way. I became rather suicidal." Only when he decided to publish his story did Strieber begin to feel a sense of relief.

The publication of *Communion* caused an immediate stir—particularly among literary critics, most of whom expressed serious doubts as to the veracity of Strieber's tale. "I am in every way disposed, by temperament . . . and intellectual proclivity . . . to take seriously this book about extraterrestrial contact," writes *Commonweal's* Michael Zeik. "But I don't." A critic for the *West Coast Review of Books,* too, expressed some reservations: "A best-selling science fiction and horror author suddenly comes out with a supposedly non-fiction book detailing his encounters with apparent extra-terrestrials. Yeah, right, and his house is haunted and he has ESP." By far the most stinging castigation came from the *Nation's* Thomas M. Disch, who devoted nearly eight pages to expressing the opinion that Strieber was lying to his readers, suggesting that following his previous novels with a "non-fiction" work would be "the end of a logical progression." Disch continues: "Perhaps (we ought to at least consider the possibility) [Strieber] is making up the whole story just as if he were writing fiction! Novelists, especially horror novelists, know all kinds of ways to make the implausible seem plausible. It's what they're paid for."

Reviewers were not the only ones to question Strieber's sincerity. *Publishers Weekly* writer Edward Beecher Claflin began a new series on publishing issues with the article "When Is a True Story True?", discussing the wisdom of marketing *Communion* as non-fiction. In that article, Gregory Benford—a physics professor and novelist who had previously described *Communion* in the *New York Times Book Review* as an enjoyable, if problematic, book—berates both Strieber and William Morrow & Co. (the publisher of *Communion*) for their actions. "This book is part of a deplorable trend in publishing," Benford declares. "It is catering to the flagrant irrationalities of the public with tarted-up Potemkin-Village science. The re-emergence of the Shirley MacLaine/Bridey Murphy subgenre is a chastening reminder that we are not, in fact, a deeply rational society in spite of our technology. I regard these people as unwittingly in the same camp as the Fundamentalists."

In order to defend his book, Strieber embarked on a publicity tour that included several appearances on such television talk shows as *The Tonight Show* and *Phil Donahue*. At each stop he reiterated his story, pointing out that he had submitted to a polygraph test to prove that *he,* at least, believed that the story was accurate. He even contributed a page-long essay to *Publishers Weekly,* in response to the article by Claflin. "The suggestion [Claflin had made] was that the nonfiction publication of a book making such outrageous claims was questionable," Strieber points out. "But where are the outrageous claims in *Communion?* They aren't there, unless extracted by out-of-context quotation."

In all of his writings and appearances, Strieber told of the tremendous amount of mail he was receiving from readers who described having similar experiences to those described in his book. "Judging from my reader mail," he writes in *Publishers Weekly,* "*Communion* did well because it asked questions, not because it convinced people that I had met aliens." The book, he goes on, "was written to bring into question the idea of alien abduction. It was intended to enrich speculation about this experience by placing it in historical perspective and—at the same time—acknowledging its power and the startling sense of physical reality that accompanies it." In addition to the support it gave the book, Strieber credits the massive reader response with providing him with emotional support. "It was a great relief to find that others had had the same experience," he told *People.* "It's a very scary thing, but I want to let people know that they can cope if it happens."

Strieber followed *Communion* with two more books addressing the issue of otherworldly visitors: *Transformation: The Breakthrough,* which described his continuing experiences with the beings from *Communion;* and the novel *Majestic,* a fictional account of the government's attempts to cover up evidence of alien contact. Like *Communion* before them, these volumes ignited a conflagration of criticism. "Whitley is back!" announces Disch in the *Nation.* "Those who treasure the more exotic forms of untruth will need no further prompting." Remarking upon Strieber's recounting of how aliens abducted him, his son, and even his cat, Disch muses: "Surely a large part of Whitley's readership approaches his books in a spirit of connoisseurship rather than credulity, relishing the spectacle of his effrontery as one might the penitential tears of Jimmy Swaggert." In a review of *Majestic, Voice Literary Supplement* writer Pagan Kennedy observes that the once-skeptical Strieber "now writes with the fervor of the converted," and Katherine Ramsland of the *New York Times Book Review* considers the book's precarious balance of facts and fabrication to be "engaging as science fiction, unnerving as possible fact," but ultimately "failing to present contact with aliens . . . as an opportunity for enlightenment."

Recently, Strieber has devoted his time once again to pure fiction. 1991's *Billy* tells of a man's obsession with a young boy—an obsession that leads to kidnapping and torture, all in the name of love. The novels *Unholy Fire* and *The Forbidden Zone,* like Strieber's earliest novels, show the author tipping his hat to the masters of the horror genre: *Unholy Fire* is Strieber's contribution to the canon of demonic possession tales, while *The Forbidden Zone* is his homage to the master of gothic/pulp horror, H.P. Lovecraft.

Though he has, in recent days, shelved the issue of alien contact, it remains to be seen whether Strieber can free himself from the label "author of *Communion*" by which he is often cited. As for the future of his writing, he once told *CA:* "Contemporary fiction seems to me to have divided between frenetic commercial brouhaha and arid intellectualism. I wonder if it isn't possible to provide the public with entertainment and prose of value at the same time. To do so is my constant ambition."

For an interview with this author, see *Contemporary Authors New Revision Series,* volume 12.

BIOGRAPHICAL/CRITICAL SOURCES:

PERIODICALS

Commonweal, July 17, 1987, p. 426.
Los Angeles Times, May 31, 1982.
Los Angeles Times Book Review, July 31, 1983; July 30, 1989, p. 10.
Nation, June 23, 1984, p. 771; March 14, 1987, pp. 328-336; November 14, 1988, p. 498.
New Republic, August 6, 1984, p. 40.
New Statesman, March 18, 1988, p. 28.
Newsweek, March 26, 1984, p. 38.
New York Times, November 14, 1983.
New York Times Book Review, April 22, 1984, p. 14; December 1, 1985, p. 39; March 15, 1987, p. 15; August 19, 1990, p. 18.
People, May 11, 1987, pp. 34-39; September 10, 1990, p. 31.
Publishers Weekly, December 12, 1980; August 14, 1987, pp. 23-26; October 2, 1987, p. 72.
Time, March 30, 1987, p. 73.
Times (London), June 6, 1983.
Times Educational Supplement, May 4, 1984, p. 24.
Voice Literary Supplement, June, 1982; November, 1989, p. 8.
Wall Street Journal, June 2, 1987, p. 28; October 30, 1989, p. A8.
Washington Post Book World, October 5, 1978; April 6, 1986, p. 11; July 5, 1987, p. 6; April 5, 1992, p. 12.
West Coast Review of Books, July, 1984, p. 28; number 2, 1987, p. 40; number 5, 1990, p. 27.

—*Sketch by Brandon Trenz*

*   *   *

STUBBS, Jean 1926-

PERSONAL: Born October 23, 1926 in Denton, Lancashire, England; daughter of Joseph and Millis (Darby) Higham; divorced; remarried to Roy Oliver;

children: Gretel Sally, Robin. *Education:* Attended Manchester School of Art, 1944-47. *Avocational Interests:* "My family," the arts, cooking.

ADDRESSES: Home—Trewin, Nancegollan, Helston, Cornwall TR13 OAJ, England. *Agent*—Jennifer Kavanagh, 39 Camden Park Rd., London NW1 9AX, England.

CAREER: Writer, 1960—. Writer-in-residence, Avon, 1984.

MEMBER: PEN, Society of Authors, Society of Women Writers and Journalists, Detection Club, Lancashire Authors Association.

AWARDS, HONORS: Tom Gallon Award, Society of Authors, 1964, for short story "A Child's Four Seasons."

WRITINGS:

NOVELS

The Rose-Grower, Macmillan (London), 1962, St. Martin's, 1963.
The Travellers, St. Martin's, 1963.
Hanrahan's Colony, Macmillan (London), 1964.
The Straw Crown, Macmillan (London), 1966.
My Grand Enemy, Macmillan (London), 1967, Stein & Day, 1968.
The Case of Kitty Ogilvie, Macmillan (London), 1970, Walker, 1971.
Eleanora Duse, Stein & Day, 1970, published in England as *The Passing Star,* Macmillan, 1970.
An Unknown Welshman: A Historical Novel, Stein & Day, 1972.
A Lasting Spring, St. Martin's, 1987.
Like We Used to Be, St. Martin's, 1989.
Light in Summer, St. Martin's, 1991, published in England as *Summer Secrets,* Macmillan, 1990.
Kelly Park, Macmillan (London), 1991, St. Martin's, 1992.

INSPECTOR LINTOTT SERIES

Dear Laura, Stein & Day, 1973.
The Painted Face: An Edwardian Mystery, Stein & Day, 1974.
The Golden Crucible, Stein & Day, 1976.

HOWARTH CHRONICLES

By Our Beginnings, St. Martin's, 1979, published in England as *Kit's Hill,* Macmillan, 1979.
An Imperfect Joy, St. Martin's, 1981, published in England as *The Ironmaster,* Macmillan, 1981.
The Vivian Inheritance, St. Martin's, 1982.
The Northern Correspondent, St. Martin's, 1984.

OTHER

One Hundred Years around the Lizard, Bossiney Books, 1985.
Great Houses of Cornwall, Bossiney Books, 1987.

Short stories appear in collections, including *Winter's Tales,* Macmillan, 1962, 1964, 1967, 1970, and *Winter's Crimes,* Macmillan, 1969, 1971; contributor to magazines including *Good Housekeeping;* author of *Family Christmas,* a play for television, 1965. Reviewer for *Books and Bookmen,* 1966-80.

SIDELIGHTS: Long a popular writer in her native England, Jean Stubbs is known for her historically accurate crime novels which contain meticulous characterizations, particularly strong and complex heroines. Among these are *My Grand Enemy,* a fictionalized account of Mary Blandy, who was hanged in England for her father's murder in 1752. The controversy this case created and which Stubbs explores centers upon whether Mary knowingly poisoned her father, or if she was merely a pawn of her crooked lover. In *The Case of Kitty Ogilvie,* set in eighteenth-century Scotland, Stubbs presents a scrupulously researched tale of a land-owning newlywed couple whose incompatibility quickly leads to licentiousness and murder. However, for several of her mystery novels, Stubbs created the character of Inspector Joseph Lintott, a retired Scotland Yard detective whose pursuit of justice sends him on various adventures. Stubbs, commenting in *Twentieth Century Crime and Mystery Writers* on her preference for devising interesting characters over intricate plots, says she writes "*why-done-its* and not *who-done-its.*"

Stubbs channeled her fascination with the late nineteenth century into the historical biography entitled *Eleanora Duse,* an account of the tumultuous career of the great Italian actress whose fame once rivaled Sarah Bernhardt's. M. Gregory Duffy's review of the novel in *Best Sellers* claims that Stubbs "fails to project the enormous theatrical power" of Duse's performances. Conversely, Bernard Grebanier in *New York Times Book Review* says that "Stubbs has managed the almost impossible feat of writing a fine novel and at the same time an authentic biography. . . . her narrative is admirably paced and shot through with tensely dramatic scenes and poetic insight."

Stubbs told *CA:* "My father was a university lecturer, and I am mainly the product of his teaching: which means I have Edwardian principles and an enquiring mind. I have written ever since I could print words and string them together. As a child I used to write, illustrate and bind my brief dramatic tales. I married young, and when my second child went to school I took a part-time job, and began a story which I wrote on the London Underground [subway] going to work. It developed into my first novel, *The Rose Grower,* which was accepted by Macmillan (London)

in 1961. Around that time my marriage failed, and I decided to supplement my income by writing. I worked freelance as a copy-writer, wrote short stories for magazines, and a variety of novels: straight, historical, crime and biographical. In 1973 I had my first success with *Dear Laura,* a Victorian mystery, and did a publicity tour of the USA, fell in love with San Francisco, and later lived there for a month, basing *The Golden Crucible* on its 1906 earthquake. In 1975 I met my present husband, an engineer who writes poetry. We pulled up our city roots and bought a two-hundred-year-old cottage in Cornwall. This new life and environment marked a change in my writing.

"I planned the 'Howarth Chronicles' as a seven-volume family saga set in Lancashire; my birthplace. I wanted to trace the Industrial Revolution in personal terms, from the rural valley of 1760 to the urban sprawl of 1960; and my husband bought a micro-computer word processor to bank my research and make editing easier. However, I stopped at volume four, feeling the need for change, gave up historical sagas, and began to write in the present century. Period novels *A Lasting Spring* (Lancashire, 1928-1945), and *Like We Used to Be* (London in the 1950s and '60s) were followed by three separate modern novels about Londoners in Cornwall: *Summer Secrets, Kelly Park,* and *Family Games,* which is to be published in 1993 by Macmillan, London, and St. Martin's Press. I notice that I change direction every ten years or so, and I look forward to the next departure.''

BIOGRAPHICAL/CRITICAL SOURCES:

BOOKS

Twentieth Century Crime and Mystery Writers, 3rd edition, St. James, 1988.
Twentieth Century Romance and Historical Writers, 2nd edition, St. James, 1990.

PERIODICALS

Best Sellers, July 15, 1970.
Chicago Tribune, March 17, 1991.
New York Times Book Review, June 7, 1970.
Punch, January 3, 1968.
Sunday Times, February 25, 1973.
Times Literary Supplement, August 28, 1981; December 17, 1982; August 2, 1985.

*   *   *

SUAREZ LYNCH, B.
See BIOY CASARES, Adolfo

SULLIVAN, William M. 1945-

PERSONAL: Born May 2, 1945, in Philadelphia, PA; son of James C. and Iretta (Gorman) Sullivan. *Education:* La Salle College, B.A., 1968; Fordham University, Ph.D., 1971.

ADDRESSES: Home—1420 Locust St., Apt. 23K, Philadelphia, PA 19102. *Office*—Department of Philosophy, La Salle College, Philadelphia, PA 19141.

CAREER: Allentown College, Center Valley, PA, associate professor of philosophy, 1971-82; La Salle College, Philadelphia, PA, associate professor, 1982-86, professor of philosophy, 1987—.

MEMBER: American Philosophical Association.

AWARDS, HONORS: Los Angeles Times award for current interest book, 1985, and Association of Logos Bookstores Book Award for excellence in religious publishing, 1986, both for *Habits of the Heart: Individualism and Commitment in American Life.*

WRITINGS:

(Editor with Paul Rabinow) *Interpretive Social Science: A Reader,* University of California Press, 1979.
Reconstructing Public Philosophy, University of California Press, 1982.
(With Robert N. Bellah, Richard Madsen, Ann Swidler, and Steven M. Tipton) *Habits of the Heart: Individualism and Commitment in American Life,* University of California Press, 1985.
(Co-editor) *Individualism and Commitment in American Life: Readings on the Themes and Habits of the Heart,* Harper, 1987.

WORK IN PROGRESS: The Uncertain Ascendancy, a critical study of the role of the professions in contemporary life, with emphasis on issues of ethics and public service; *The Good Society,* co-author, a continuation of the concerns of *Habits of the Heart* addressing the problem of developing American democracy in the emerging global context.*

*   *   *

SUSSMAN, Henry 1947-

PERSONAL: Born February 10, 1947, in Philadelphia, PA; son of Albert (a cabinetmaker and lumber merchant) and Rosalie (a fundraiser; maiden name, Glickman) Sussman; married Carol Jacobs (a comparatist), September 16, 1972; children: Tamara Jacobs, Nadia Rebecca Jacobs. *Education:* Brandeis University, B.A., 1968; Johns Hopkins University, Ph.D., 1975. *Religion:* Jewish.

ADDRESSES: Home—Williamsville, NY. *Office*—Department of Comparative Literature, State University of New York at Buffalo, Room 638, Clemens Hall, Amherst Campus, Buffalo, NY 14260.

CAREER: John Hopkins University, Baltimore, MD, Mellon scholar in the humanities, 1976-78; State University of New York, Buffalo, assistant professor, 1978-79, associate professor of comparative literature, 1979—, associate dean of arts and letters, 1981—.

MEMBER: Modern Language Association of America.

AWARDS, HONORS: National Endowment for the Humanities fellow, 1980-81, for *The Hegelian Aftermath;* Rockefeller Humanities fellow, 1985-86, for *High Resolution.*

WRITINGS:

Franz Kafka: Geometrician of Metaphor, Coda, 1979.
The Hegelian Aftermath: Readings in Hegel, Kierkegaard, Freud, Proust, and James, Johns Hopkins University Press, 1982.
High Resolution: Critical Theory and the Problem of Literacy, Oxford University Press, 1989.
Afterimages of Modernity: Structure and Indifference in Twentieth-Century Literature, Johns Hopkins University Press, 1990.
Kafka's Unholy Trinity: The Trial, Macmillan, 1993.
Psyche and Text: The Sublime and the Grandiose in Literature, Psychopathology, and Culture, State University of New York, 1993.

Editor, *Modern Language Notes,* 1976-78, and *Glyph: Johns Hopkins Textual Studies,* 1977-80. Contributor of articles to professional journals, including *Publications of the Modern Language Association of America, Modern Language Notes, Glyph, Diacritics,* and *Clio.*

WORK IN PROGRESS: The Esthetic Contract and Other Essays in the Social Dimensions of Literature.

SIDELIGHTS: Henry Sussman once told *CA:* "As the study of what makes written and verbal communication possible, contemporary critical theory touches more than any other field on the mission of higher education, which is to create a population aware of the discrepancies in knowledge as well as the simple correspondences. I attempt to function at the interface between the critiques of representation, logic, and teleology raised by critical theory and the politics of literacy enacted by universities, the media, and other institutions."

SUTTON, Penny
See WOOD, Christopher (Hovelle)

*   *   *

SWEET, Jeffrey 1950-

PERSONAL: Born May 3, 1950, in Boston, MA; son of James Stouder (a writer) and Vivian (a violinist; maiden name, Roe) Sweet; children: Jonathan Brian. *Education:* New York University, B.F.A., 1971. *Avocational Interests:* Reading, playing piano, plays and movies, and "having endless conversations."

ADDRESSES: Home—250 W. 90th St., #15G, New York, NY 10024. *Agent*—Susan Schulman, 165 West End Ave., New York, NY 10023.

CAREER: Playwright and author, 1967—. Editorial assistant with Scholastic Magazines, 1970-71, and with W. W. Norton & Co., Inc., 1974-75; librarian for Russell Sage Foundation, 1977-78; associate writer for TV series, *Another World,* 1981-82; TV writer for Embassy Television, 1983—; lecturer on theater; member of nominating committee for Tony Awards.

MEMBER: Writers Guild of America, Dramatists Guild, New Dramatists, Drama Desk, New York Writer's Bloc (founder).

AWARDS, HONORS: Award for best drama, Society of Midland Authors, 1978, and playwriting fellowship, National Endowment for the Arts, 1989, both for *Porch;* award for best drama, Society of Midland Authors, 1982, and Heideman Award for best one-act play, 1983, both for *The Value of Names;* Outer Critics Circle award, 1984, for *Love.*

WRITINGS:

BOOKS

Something Wonderful Right Away: An Oral History of the Second City and the Compass Players, Limelight, 1978, revised edition, 1987.

PLAYS

Porch (one-act; produced in Washington, DC, 1977), in *Best Short Plays, 1976,* edited by Stanley Richards, Chilton, 1976, revised edition, Samuel French, 1985.
Responsible Parties (three-act; produced in New York City at Actors Studio, 1978), Dramatists Play Service, 1985.
After the Fact (produced in New Haven, CT, 1980), Samuel French, 1981.
Stops Along the Way (one-act; produced in Evanston, IL, 1980) in *Best Short Plays, 1981,* edited by Stanley

Richards, Chilton, 1976, revised edition, Dramatists Play Service, 1981.
Holding Patterns, produced in Chicago, 1981.
Ties (two-act; produced in Chicago at Victory Gardens Theatre, 1981, produced on television by WTTW-TV, Chicago), Dramatists Play Service, 1982.
Routed (produced in Chicago at Victory Gardens Theatre, 1981), Dramatists Play Service, 1982.
The Value of Names (produced in Louisville, KY, 1982), Dramatists Play Service, 1986.
(With Howard Marren and Susan Birkenhead) *Love* (musical adaptation of *Luv* by Murray Schisgal; produced in New York City at Audrey Wood Theater, 1984), Music Theater International, 1984.

OTHER

Contributor of articles and stories to periodicals, including *Chicago Tribune, Los Angeles Times, Newsday, Ellery Queen's Mystery Magazine, Dramatics Magazine,* and *Dramatists Guild Quarterly.*

SIDELIGHTS: Though primarily a playwright, Jeffrey Sweet's first notable work was an account of the improvisational theater movement in 1950s Chicago. *Something Wonderful Right Away* outlines the history of the Compass Players and the later formation of Second City using interviews with the original performers. Sweet told *CA,* "The greatest single influence on my work is the improvisational theater movement, as developed by such figures as Viola Spolin, Paul Sills, David Shepherd, Alan Myerson, Mike Nichols, Elaine May, Del Close, Sheldon Patinkin and others. Watching and/or workshopping with these people over the years has taught me a great deal about the structure and purposes of theater. I cannot recommend any better preparation for a career as a writer, director or actor than to study in an improvisational workshop."

Several of Sweet's early one-act plays take place in small-town, middle America and examine family strife and unmet expectations. *Porch,* a one-act play first produced in 1977, concerns a woman's return from New York City to her Ohio hometown and the strained relationship with her father due to their conflicting lifestyles and values. *New York Times* critic Richard Eder says *Porch* is "written with subtlety and an increasingly compelling emotion." Similarly, *Ties,* a two-act play that presents a college theater director's involvement in a doomed romantic triangle, "grabs hold of an audience with a quietly played story about real human beings in a truly delineated setting," according to *Chicago Times* critic Richard Christiansen. However, in trying to achieve a balance of comedy and drama, "its funny lines sometimes are a little too flip, and [Sweet's] sentimental nature gets the best of him in a pat ending that . . . is just too good to be true," Christiansen says.

Similar ideas are explored in *The Value of Names*, in which an aging comedian comes to terms with the people and events that resulted in his blacklisting during the McCarthy era. Despite its show business and political angles, "its deepest concern," Christiansen states, "is with the primal search for self-worth. . . . a major subject, treated with eloquence and compassion." In *Responsible Parties*, Sweet creates two characters whose philosophical debate concerning the extent of one's responsibility for others is played out against the backdrop of a run-down motel full of somewhat desperate characters. *New York Times* critic Stephen Holden applauds the structure and dialogue of the play, but notes that Sweet "maintains an iron grip on his characters, resolving their ethical debates in pat ironic twists . . . [resulting in] a believable but unmoving sliver of realism that feels smaller than life."

Sweet told *CA*, "I see the primary business of the playwright being not the writing of dialogue but the creation of opportunities for actors to create compelling behavior onstage. Sometimes spoken language is a part of this behavior, sometimes not. (For instance, the part of Helen Keller in William Gibson's *The Miracle Worker* affords the actress playing her brilliant opportunities even though she speaks only a few syllables.) The theater depicts behavior for an audience's evaluation. Of course, as soon as you talk about evaluating behavior, you're talking about ethics. I think that the theater is, by its very nature, an ethical medium. To deal with ethical questions without being didactic is one of the key challenges facing serious dramatic writing today.

"I have a great love for musical theater (I'm a composer-lyricist and have studied with Lehman Engel and Paul Simon), but, Stephen Sondheim and a handful of others aside, see little to be cheery about in the field these days. I hope to get more deeply involved in musical projects in the future."

BIOGRAPHICAL/CRITICAL SOURCES:

PERIODICALS

Chicago Times, January 30, 1981; April 1, 1983; June 17, 1983.
Los Angeles Times, February 20, 1984.
New York Times, November 15, 1978; March 6, 1981; April 16, 1984; October 18, 1984; March 24, 1985.*

*   *   *

SZABO, Denis 1929-

PERSONAL: Born June 4, 1929, in Budapest, Hungary; immigrated to Canada, 1958; Canadian citizen, 1963; son of Denis and Catherine (Zsiga) Szabo; married Sylvie Grotard (a psychologist), June, 1956; children: Catherine, Marianne. *Education:* University of Louvain, Ph.D., 1956; Sorbonne, University of Paris, diploma, 1958.

ADDRESSES: Office—International Centre for Comparative Criminology, University of Montreal, P.O. Box 6128, Montreal, Quebec, Canada H3C 3J7.

CAREER: Lecturer in sociology, University of Paris, Paris, France, and University of Lyon, Lyon, France, 1956-58; University of Montreal, Montreal, Quebec, assistant professor, 1958, associate professor, 1959, founder and director of department of criminology, 1960-70, professor of sociology, 1966—, International Centre for Comparative Criminology, founder and director, 1969-79, president, 1979—. Distinguished professor of jurisprudence, University of Ecuador, Quito, 1984. Visiting professor and lecturer at numerous universities in United States, Europe, Africa, and Asia. Member of numerous committees of various public institutions, including President's Committee on Law Enforcement and Administration of Criminal Justice, and Joint Committee on Correctional Manpower Training.

MEMBER: Societe internationale de criminologie (member of scientific commission, 1961-75; member of board of directors, 1966; vice-president, 1975-78; honorary president, 1979—), Societe internationale de defense sociale (Canadian scientific representative), Association internationale de sociologie, Association internationale de criminologie (president, 1989—), American Society of Criminology (fellow), American Sociological Society (fellow), National Council on Crime and Delinquency (Canadian correspondent), Royal Society of Canada (fellow), Societe canadienne de criminologie (vice-president, 1962-64), Societe canadienne de sociologie et d'anthropologie, Association canadienne des anthropologues, Psychologues sociaux et sociologues de langue francaise, Canadian Association of University Teachers, Hungarian Academy of Science, Association des sociologues de langue francaise, Societe de criminologie du Quebec (secretary-general, 1960-70).

AWARDS, HONORS: Sutherland Award of American Society of Criminology, 1968; Beccaria Medal of Societe Allemande de criminologie, 1970; officer of National Order of the Ivory Coast, 1972; Presidential Citation from American Society of Criminology, for distinguished contributions to Canadian criminology, 1975; Medal of the Council of Europe, 1983; D.H.C., University of Siena (Italy), University of Budapest, 1985, and University d'Aix-Marseille, 1992; recipient of numerous grants.

WRITINGS:

Ordre et changement (title means "Social Order and Social Change"), Les Presses de l'Universite de Montreal, 1959.

Contribution a l'etude de la delinquance sexuelle: Les Delits sexuels des adolescents a Montreal (title means "Contribution to the Study of Sexual Delinquency: Sexual Offences among Adolescents in Montreal"), University of Montreal, 1960.

Crimes et villes: Etude statistique de la criminalite urbaine et rurale en France et en Belgique (title means "Crime and the City: Statistical Study of Urban and Rural Crime in France and Belgium"), Cujas, 1960.

Delinquance sexuelle des adolescents a Montreal (title means "Sexual Delinquency among Adolescents in Montreal"), University of Montreal, 1960.

Delinquance juvenile: Etiologie et prophylaxie (title means "Juvenile Delinquency: Etiology and Treatment"), North Holland Publishing Co., 1963.

Criminologie (title means "Criminology"), Presses de l'Universite de Montreal, 1965.

Criminalite et deviance (title means "Criminality and Deviance"), Colin, 1970.

(With J. L. Beaudouin and J. Fortin) *Le Terrorisme et la justice* (title means "Terrorism and Justice"), Montreal Editions de Jour, 1971.

(With D. Gagne and A. Parizeau) *Face a face: L'Adolescent et la societe* (title means "The Adolescent and Society"), Dessart, 1972.

L'Afrique occidental: Developpement et societe (title means "West Africa: Development and Society"), University of Montreal, 1972.

(With M. Molins-Ysal and Parizeau) *La Theorie de la defense sociale et ses implications empiriques* (title means "The Theory of Social Defence and Its Empiric Implications"), [Quebec], 1972.

Criminalite, planification de la prevention du crime et services de traitement des delinquants: La Cas de l'Afrique de l'Ouest (title means "Criminality, Planning for the Prevention of Crime and Services for the Treatment of Delinquents: The Case of West Africa"), [Quebec], 1973.

La Criminologie: Theorie et Praxis (title means "Criminology: Theory and Practice"), University of Montreal, 1974.

(With Brillon, Tounissoux, and Normandeau) *Attitudes et opinion du public canadien envers l'administration de la justice* (title means "Attitudes and Opinions of the Canadian Public Regarding the Administration of Justice"), International Centre for Comparative Criminology, 1976.

(With Parizeau) *Le Traitement de la criminalite au Canada,* Presses de l'Universite de Montreal, 1977, transla-

tion published as *The Canadian Criminal Justice System,* Lexington Books, 1978.

(With R. D. Crelinsten and D. Laberge-Altmejd) *Terrorism and Criminal Justice: An International Perspective,* Lexington Books, 1978.

Criminologie et politique criminelle, Vrin, 1978, translation published as *Criminology and Crime Policy,* Heath, 1980.

(With Crelinsten) *Hostage Taking,* Lexington Books, 1979.

Offenders and Corrections, Praeger, 1979.

Science et crimes, Vrin, 1985.

De l'anthropologie a la criminologie comparee, Vrin, 1993.

Also author, with others, of *Economic Crimes,* Macmillan (London).

EDITOR

Criminologie en Action: Bilan de la criminologie contemporaine dans ses grands domaines d'applications, Presses de l'Universite de Montreal, 1968.

J. M. Rico and G. Tardif, *Enquete d'opinion publique sur la police au Quebec* (title means "Public Opinion Survey on the Quebec Police"), R. Lefebvre, 1969.

Rico and Tardif, *Enquete d'opinion aupres de cinq services de police du Quebec* (title means "Opinion Survey among Five of the Quebec Police Services"), R. Lefebvre, 1969.

E. A. Fattah and A. Normandeau, *Sondage d'opinion publique sur la justice criminelle au Quebec* (title means "Public Opinion Survey on Criminal Justice in Quebec"), R. Lefebvre, 1970.

J. L. Beaudouin and J. Fortin, *Sondage aupres des criminalistes de Montreal sur la justice criminelle au Quebec* (title means "Survey among Criminal Lawyers on Criminal Justice in Quebec"), R. Lefebvre, 1970.

Fattah and Rico, *Le Role de l'enseignement et de la recherche criminologique dans l'administration de la justice* (title means "The Role of Criminological Education and Research in the Administration of Justice"), R. Lefebvre, 1970.

Fattah, R. Tremblay, and C. Toutant, *L'Alcool chez les jeunes Quebecois* (title means "Alcohol and the Youth of Quebec"), Les Presses de l'Universite Laval, 1970.

P. Dubois, J. Archambault, and R. Boissonneault, *La Satisfaction au travail des policiers municipaux du Quebec* (title means "Work Satisfaction among Quebec Municipal Policemen"), R. Lefebvre, 1970.

Le cout de l'administration de la justice et de la criminalite: Travaux du IIe symposium international de criminologie comparee, Information Canada, 1971.

(With G. Canepa) *Traitement des criminels et proces penal* (title means "The Treatment of Criminals and the Criminal Trial"), [Quebec], 1972.

La Criminalite urbaine et la crise de l'administration de la justice (title means "Urban Crime and the Crisis in the Administration of Justice"), Les Presses de l'Universite de Montreal, 1973.

(With Canepa) *La criminologie clinique: Etat actuel et perspectives futures dans le domaine du traitement et de la recherche,* Tipografia Morandi [Italy], 1973.

Police, culture et societe (title means "The Police, Culture, and Society"), Les Presses de l'Universite de Montreal, 1973.

(With Canepa) *Therapeuthique et recherche* (title means "Therapeutics and Research"), [Quebec], 1973.

(With Canepa) *Diagnostic et pronostic differentiels de l'etat dangereux et traitement de la delinquance juvenile* (title means "Differential Diagnosis and Prognosis on the State of Dangerousness and Treatment of Juvenile Delinquency"), [Quebec], 1974.

(With Canepa) *Homocide, controle et autorite en institution* (title means "Homocide, Institutional Control and Authority"), [Quebec], 1975.

(With Katzenelson) *Offenders and Corrections,* Praeger, 1978.

(With others) *Nigerian Criminal Process: Proceedings of the Second West African Conference in Comparative Criminology,* University of Lagos Press, 1978.

(With LeBlanc) *Traite de criminologie empirique,* Presses de l'universite de Montreal, 1993.

OTHER

Contributor to encyclopedias, including *Encyclopedia Universalis, Encyclopedie medico-chirurgicale, International Encyclopedia of Higher Education,* and *La Psychologie du XXe siecle.* Contributor of articles to publications, including *Criminal Law Quarterly, British Journal of Criminology,* and *Journal of Criminal Law and Criminology. Criminology* (formerly *Acta Criminologica*), founder and editor, 1968-75, currently director; founding member, *Reseaux;* member of editorial committees, *Criminologica* and *Bulletin de medecine legale et de toxicologie.*

SIDELIGHTS: Denis Szabo told *CA:* "Variations and permanent features in deviant and criminal activities of men [are] a basic fact of the history of mankind. Relations between those features and civilizations of diverse types constitute my basic interest.

"The history of mankind goes in cycles. To judge whether it is up or down depends on the criteria we use. Progress for some may be regression for others. As far as I am concerned, I feel that humanity is undergoing a deep crisis which originates mainly in the confusion between the philosophy of skepticism and relativism, proper to scientific endeavor, but unacceptable as a philosophy of life. It requires a commitment to specific values. You can equate two values as a social analyst; you cannot as a man, as a citizen. You must choose—you have to have options. You cannot accept paralyzing compromises."

T

TATE, Eleanora E(laine) 1948-

PERSONAL: Born April 16, 1948, in Canton, MO; daughter of Clifford and Lillie (Douglas) Tate (raised by her grandmother, Corinne E. Johnson); married Zack E. Hamlett III (a photographer), August 19, 1972; children: Gretchen R. *Education:* Drake University, B.A., 1973.

ADDRESSES: Home—1203 Carver St., Myrtle Beach, SC 29577. *Office*—Positive Images, Inc., 1203 Carver St., P.O. Box 483, Myrtle Beach, SC 29578. *Agent*—Charlotte Sheedy, Charlotte Sheedy Literary Agency, 145 West 86th St., New York, NY 10024.

CAREER: Iowa Bystander, West Des Moines, news editor, 1966-68; *Des Moines Register* and *Des Moines Tribune,* Des Moines, IA, staff writer, 1968-76; *Jackson Sun,* Jackson, TN, staff writer, 1976-77; Kreative Koncepts, Inc., Myrtle Beach, SC, writer and researcher, 1979-81; Positive Images, Inc., Myrtle Beach, SC, president and co-owner (with husband, Zack E. Hamlett III), 1983—. Contributor to black history and culture workshops in Des Moines, IA, 1968-76; giver of poetry presentations, including Iowa Arts Council Writers in the Schools program, 1969-76, Rust College, 1973, and Grinnell College, 1975; free-lance writer for *Memphis Tri-State Defender,* 1977; guest author of South Carolina School Librarians Association Conference, 1981 and 1982; writer-in-residence, Elgin, SC, Chester, SC, and the Amana colonies, Middle, IA, all 1986.

MEMBER: National Association of Black Storytellers, Inc. (member of the board, 1988—), Arts in Basic Curriculum Steering Committee, South Carolina Academy of Authors (vice-president of the board of directors, 1988-90; member of the board, 1987—), South Carolina Arts Commission Artists in Education, Concerned Citizens Operation Reach-Out of Horry County, Horry Cultural Arts Council (president of the board of directors, 1990—).

AWARDS, HONORS: Finalist, fifth annual Third World Writing Contest, 1973; Unity Award, Lincoln University, 1974, for educational reporting; Community Lifestyles award, Tennessee Press Association, 1977; Bread Loaf Writer's Conference fellowship, 1981; *Just an Overnight Guest* (film) listed among the "Selected Films for Young Adults 1985" by the Young Adult Committee of the American Library Association; Parents' Choice Award, 1987; Presidential Award, National Association of Negro Business and Professional Women's Clubs, Georgetown chapter, 1988; Grand Strand Press Association Award, Second Place, for Social Responsibilities and Minority Affairs, 1988.

WRITINGS:

(Editor with husband, Zack E. Hamlett III, and contributor) *Eclipsed* (poetry), privately printed, 1975.
(Editor and contributor) *Wanjiru: A Collection of Black-womanworth,* privately printed, 1976.
Just an Overnight Guest, Dial, 1980.
The Secret of Gumbo Grove, F. Watts, 1987.
Thank You, Dr. Martin Luther King, Jr.!, F. Watts, 1990.
Front Porch Stories at the One-Room School, Bantam/Skylark, 1992.

CONTRIBUTOR

Rosa Guy, editor, *Children of Longing,* Bantam, 1970.
Impossible? (juvenile), Houghton, 1972.
Broadside Annual 1972, Broadside Press, 1972.
Communications (juvenile), Heath, 1973.
Off-Beat (juvenile), Macmillan, 1974.
Sprays of Rubies (anthology of poetic prose), Ragnarok, 1975.
Valhalla Four, Ragnarok, 1977.

OTHER

Contributor of poetry and fiction to periodicals, including *Journal of Black Poetry* and *Des Moines Register Picture Magazine.*

ADAPTATIONS: Just an Overnight Guest was adapted as a film starring Fran Robinson, Tiffany Hill, Rosalind Cash, and Richard Roundtree, Phoenix/ B.F.A. Films & Video, 1983.

WORK IN PROGRESS: A Woman for the People, for adults; *Island Girl,* for juveniles.

SIDELIGHTS: Eleanora E. Tate was born in 1948 in Canton, a small town in northeastern Missouri, where during her early childhood legal segregation was still enforced. She attended first grade in 1954 at the town's one-room grade school for African-Americans. The following year her class was integrated into Canton's white school system.

Tate's novels, each focusing on a young African-American girl, are set in places she knows well. Her first novel, *Just an Overnight Guest*—told from the view of nine-year-old Margie Carson—takes place in Nutbrush, Missouri, a small town modeled after Canton. In the story Margie becomes angry when her mother invites Ethel Hardisen, a half-black, half-white four year old, to stay with the family for a night. Ethel, Margie said, "broke stuff, stole candy, threw rocks at people. Once she hit me in the back with a piece of concrete." Ethel's visit is mysteriously extended, despite her bad behavior, and Margie begins to see Ethel as competition for her parents' affection. Only at the end of the book does Margie learn that Ethel had been an abused, neglected child, whose father is Margie's irresponsible Uncle Jake.

Tate once explained that she wrote *Just an Overnight Guest* "to add my voice . . . to the thought that children's childhoods can be happy if they can learn that they can do anything they set their minds to." The book, moreover, drew praise from critics. Merri Rosenberg of the *New York Times Book Review* wrote, "Eleanora Tate does a fine job presenting the emotional complexities of Margie's initiation into adult life's moral ambiguities. . . . If she drives home her point with a slightly heavy hand . . . [she] has imbued the situation with enough realism to make it plausible." In *The Horn Book Magazine* Celia Morris praises Tate for capturing "the nuances of small-town life, the warmth of a Black family struggling with a problem, and the volatile emotions of a young child."

In her second novel, *The Secret of Gumbo Grove* (1987), the setting is similar to Myrtle Beach, South Carolina. The story, explains Tate, is about an eleven-year-old girl, Raisin Stackhouse, who "loves history, but she can't seem to find any positive Black history in her hometown of Gumbo Grove, South Carolina's most famous ocean-side resort, until she stumbles on to an old cemetery owned by her church. . . . The townspeople aren't too happy with her discovery [of the area's history of racial segregation] . . . because they are ashamed with their own families' past." Linda Classen, writing in the *Voice of Youth Advocates,* considers the book important, for it gives "a feeling for life in a black community before blacks had rights, which . . . not many young people today can comprehend." In the *Center for Children's Books Bulletin,* Betsy Hearne calls the ending, when Raisin is given a surprise community service award, "a bit tidy," although she goes on to say that the book "will be satisfying for young readers, who can enjoy this as a leisurely, expansive reading experience."

Also set in Gumbo Grove is Tate's third novel, *Thank You, Dr. Martin Luther King, Jr.!,* a story narrated by nine-year-old Mary Elouise, who is embarrassed about being black and who spends much of her energy trying to please a conceited, blond-haired classmate. She finds it especially embarrassing when her patronizing, uninformed white teacher effusively praises Martin Luther King, Jr. It eventually falls upon the grandmother to help Mary appreciate her black heritage.

Tate approaches this sensitive story with great care. In the *Center for Children's Books Bulletin,* Zena Sutherland, though critical of the book's "repetitive and slow paced" style, praises Tate for not falling prey to racial stereotyping. "One of the strong points of her story," Sutherland says, "is that there is bias in both races, just as there is understanding in both." *Booklist's* Denise Wilms echoes this view: "Tate tackles a sensitive issue, taking pains to keep characters multidimensional and human."

Tate returns to Nutbrush, Missouri, for her next book, *Front Porch Stories at the One-Room School,* the sequel to *Just an Overnight Guest.* At the beginning Margie and Ethel, now three years older, are lying around on a hot summer night, so bored that their "life is duller than dirt." This problem, however, is solved when the father takes them on a walk to an old, one-room building, formerly the grade school for the town's African-American children. The father then begins to tell a number of stories about his childhood, which not only entertain the children but also teach them something important about their heritage. In an afterward to the book, Tate reveals that "most of the stories that [the father] tells . . . are based on my own actual experiences, or on stories I heard and greatly embellished." Although *Publishers Weekly* found the book "somewhat heavy-handed," with a "stilted dialogue that at times borders on the saccharine," it also praised Tate's "evocative language," which "conjures up rural southern life." The book, moreover, points out Tate's special concern for father-daughter relationships. Tate once remarked: "It has been said little black boys need fathers. I believe little black girls need fathers. I emphasize that. It's something that hasn't been played up in recent years. I see it every day with my husband and my daughter."

BIOGRAPHICAL/CRITICAL SOURCES:

BOOKS

Rollock, Barbara T., *Black Authors and Illustrators of Children's Books: A Biographical Dictionary*, Garland, 1988, p. 115.

PERIODICALS

Booklist, April 15, 1990, p. 1636; August, 1992, p. 2014.
Center for Children's Books Bulletin, June, 1987, p. 199; June, 1990, p. 254.
Des Moines Register, March 1, 1981.
Horn Book Magazine, December, 1980, pp. 643-644.
Myrtle Beach Sun News, November 23, 1980.
New York Times Book Review, February 8, 1981, p. 20.
Publishers Weekly, August 10, 1992, p. 71.
Voice of Youth Advocates, August-September, 1987, p. 123.
Washington Post Book World, May 10, 1981.

—*Sketch by Thomas Riggs*

*   *   *

TAYLOR, (Edmund) Dennis 1940-

PERSONAL: Born February 26, 1940, in Baltimore, MD; son of Frank Edmund (a salesman) and Mary (a housewife; maiden name, Sheehan) Taylor; married Mary Brown (a pastoral counselor), August 28, 1966; children: John, Matthew, Kathryn Kwon Yung Soon, Mary Rebecca. *Education:* College of the Holy Cross, B.A., 1960; Yale University, M.A., 1962, Ph.D., 1965. *Politics:* Democrat. *Religion:* Roman Catholic.

ADDRESSES: Home—24 Riverdale Rd., Concord, MA 01742. *Office*—Department of English, Boston College, Chestnut Hill, MA 01742.

CAREER: Bowdoin College, Brunswick, MA, instructor in English, 1962-63; University of California, Santa Barbara, assistant professor of English, 1965-70; Boston College, Chestnut Hill, MA, assistant professor, 1971-74, associate professor, 1974-81, professor of English, 1981—, chairman of department, 1982-87.

MEMBER: Modern Language Association of America, Thomas Hardy Society.

AWARDS, HONORS: Macmillan/Hardy Society Prize, 1990, for *Hardy's Metres and Victorian Prosody.*

WRITINGS:

Hardy's Poetry: 1860-1928, Columbia University Press, 1981.
Hardy's Metres and Victorian Prosody, Clarendon Press, 1988.
Hardy's Literary Language and Victorian Philosophy, Clarendon Press, 1993.

Contributor to journals, including *Victorian Poetry, Wordsworth Circle, English Literary History, Arizona Quarterly,* and *Renascence.* Editor of *Religion, Literature, and the Arts,* 1995—.

WORK IN PROGRESS: From Traditional to Free Verse.

SIDELIGHTS: Dennis Taylor has written three books on the writings of Thomas Hardy. In a *Modern Language Quarterly* review of *Hardy's Poetry: 1860-1928* John Halperin writes that Taylor's book "is one of the most sensitive studies of Hardy's poetry. . . . Taylor's explication of the symbiosis in Hardy's poetry of the inner and the outer lives is utterly unique and totally riveting. . . . This is a rare achievement indeed." Frank R. Giordano, Jr. states in *South Atlantic Quarterly* that Taylor has "devoted about fifteen years to the project, which announces on every page and in its copious notes his conscientious research and critical intelligence. . . . Like the enormous body of poetry it treats, the book succeeds in its striking impressions, its moments of vision."

Writing about Taylor's second book, *Hardy's Metres and Victorian Prosody,* Lloyd Siemens notes in *English Literature in Transition*: "Dennis Taylor is the first Hardy scholar to have tackled at book length the baffling metrical idiosyncrasies at the centre of Hardy's poetry, and the first to have placed these idiosyncrasies convincingly into their historical context. . . . *Hardy's Metres and Victorian Prosody* is a challenging and highly valuable book. It is the kind of book that many serious students of Victorian poetry had meant someday to write and now may wish they had written."

Taylor once told *CA*: "Thomas Hardy's poetry was a second-best topic for me in graduate school, after I decided not to write about the true, the good, and the beautiful. I tried to hammer something publishable out of my thesis; but it would not jell. Then while sitting next to the Pacific Ocean, in the University of California, Santa Barbara, cafeteria, I fell into a musing, and then woke up, having lost count of the time. I suddenly realized that this was a central experience in Hardy's poetry, and was also like what happens to a Darwinian species, which wakes up to find itself changed (sort of). At any rate, this generated years of continued interest in Hardy's poetry long after I was supposed to have gone on to the true, the good, and the beautiful. Eventually I fell into the rabbit hole of prosody (metrical form as the husk of an old awakening) and historical philology (old words asleep over their etymological kernels).

"Meanwhile my marriage and children fell apart, almost, and drove me kicking and screaming into family therapy. Then my second great experience occurred, this time while sitting in a rocking chair next to my living room window (in New England). I kept puzzling over elements of our problem, and suddenly the whole family thing lay out before me, great-grandparents, parents, children, and us. This great awakening became the basis of my interest in the family novel."

Taylor recently added: "I teach a fairly popular course called 'The Literature of Spiritual Quest' (Etty Hillesum, et al.). I am now tiptoeing toward that most verbatim of subjects: how one includes religious or spiritual considerations in critical discourse."

BIOGRAPHICAL/CRITICAL SOURCES:

PERIODICALS

English Literature in Transition, Volume 33, 1990, pp. 332-336.
Modern Language Quarterly, March, 1981, pp. 104-106.
South Atlantic Quarterly, Volume 82, 1983, p. 110.

*   *   *

TAYLOR, Janelle (Diane Williams) 1944-

PERSONAL: Born June 28, 1944, in Athens, GA; daughter of Alton L. Williams (a mechanic) and Frances (a housewife; maiden name, Davis) Edwards; married Michael Howard Taylor (a business manager and accountant), April 8, 1965; children: Angela Michelle, Alisha Melanie. *Education:* Attended Augusta College, 1980-81, and Medical College of Georgia. *Politics:* Republican. *Religion:* Baptist. *Avocational Interests:* Collecting dolls, music boxes, model ships, "sea treasures," souvenir spoons, old books, and book cover art; reading; music; movies (especially old westerns and science fiction films); Indian, American, and English history; sports (football, tennis, fishing, horseback and motorcycle riding, and target practice); chess; exploring the land around her home; working outdoors; traveling around the United States.

ADDRESSES: Home—4366 Deerwood Lane, Evans, GA 30809. *Office*—Janelle Taylor Enterprises, Inc., P.O. Box 211646, Martinez, GA 30917-1646. *Agent*—Acton, Oystel, Leone, Jaffe, Inc., 79 Fifth Ave., 11th floor, New York, NY 10003.

CAREER: Worked as orthodontic nurse in Athens, GA, and Augusta, GA, 1962-72; Medical College of Georgia,

Augusta, medical research assistant, 1977-79. Writer, 1979—. Owner of Janelle Taylor Enterprises, Inc., Augusta, GA; teaches and lectures on romance literature and creative writing at conferences and schools, including Augusta College, 1982—; guest on television and radio programs.

MEMBER: Romance Writers of America, Western Writers of America, Science Fiction Writers of America, Authors Guild, Novelists Inc., Southeastern Writers, Cowboy Hall of Fame, Georgia Romance Writers, Georgia Writers Coalition for Literacy, Augusta Authors Guild.

AWARDS, HONORS: Honored at Sioux National Celebration in South Dakota, 1983, for first five books of "Ecstasy Saga" series; Maggie award for best historical romance, Georgia Romance Writers, 1984, for *First Love, Wild Love;* Reviewers Choice award, *Romantic Times,* 1984, for *Golden Torment;*

Indian Series award, *Romantic Times,* 1985, for first five books of "Ecstasy Saga" series; Golden Pen award, *Affaire de Coeur,* 1986, for *Sweet, Savage Heart;* certificate of merit, American University Women, 1986; reviewer's choice certificate of excellence for Victorian romance, *Romantic Times,* 1992, for *Promise Me Forever;* career achievement certificate of excellence for historical fantasy, *Romantic Times,* 1992.

WRITINGS:

"ECSTASY SAGA" SIOUX HISTORICAL ROMANCE SERIES

Savage Ecstasy, Zebra Books, 1981.
Defiant Ecstasy, Zebra Books, 1982.
Forbidden Ecstasy, Zebra Books, 1982.
Brazen Ecstasy, Zebra Books, 1983.
Tender Ecstasy, Zebra Books, 1983.
Stolen Ecstasy, Zebra Books, 1985.
Bittersweet Ecstasy, Zebra Books, 1987.
Forever Ecstasy, Zebra Books, 1991.

HISTORICAL ROMANCE

Love Me with Fury, Zebra Books, 1983.
First Love, Wild Love, Zebra Books, 1984.
Golden Torment, Zebra Books, 1984.
Savage Conquest, Zebra Books, 1985.
Sweet Savage Heart, Zebra Books, 1986.
Destiny's Temptress, Zebra Books, 1986.
Kiss of the Night Wind, Zebra Books, 1989.
Follow the Wind, Zebra Books, 1990.
Whispered Kisses, Zebra Books, 1990.
Promise Me Forever, Zebra Books, 1991.
Fortune's Flames, Zebra Books, 1991.
Passions Wild and Free, Zebra Books, 1992.
Midnight Secrets, Zebra Books, 1992.
Janelle Taylor Three Novel Collection, Wings Books, 1993.

OTHER

(Contributor) Kathryn Falk, editor, *How to Write a Romance and Get It Published: With Intimate Advice From the World's Most Popular Romantic Writers,* illustrations by Ignatius Sahula, Crown, 1983.

(Contributor) *Candlelight, Romance, and You,* edited by R. Buhrer, P. Moore, and R. Jones, Cookbook Publishers, 1983.

Valley of Fire (contemporary romance), Harlequin, 1984.

(Contributor) *My First Real Romance: Twenty Bestselling Romance Novelists Reveal the Stories of Their Own First Real Romances,* edited by Jerry Biederman and Tom Siberkleit, Stein & Day, 1985.

Moondust and Madness (science fiction romance), Bantam, 1986.

Wild Is My Love (medieval romance), Bantam, 1987.

Wild, Sweet Promise, Bantam, 1989.

Stardust and Shadows, Pinnacle Books, 1992.

Taking Chances, Zebra Books, 1993.

Contributor to *Christmas Rendezvous,* Zebra Books, 1991. Author of short stories and poems; author of newsletter for Janelle Taylor Enterprises, Inc. Contributor of articles and stories to magazines, including *Romantic Times* and *Love Line.*

The "Janelle Taylor Collection" of books, manuscripts, and promotional materials is archived at the University of Georgia Libraries.

SIDELIGHTS: A prolific, best-selling romance novelist, Janelle Taylor is perhaps best known for her historical romance books. Notable among these are the titles comprising the author's immensely popular "Ecstasy Saga" series, which features the ongoing love story between a Sioux warrior and a pioneer woman of English ancestry. The series commences in the northwest territory of the United States during the late 1700s, and the first four novels concentrate on the problems the couple face as a result of their mixed marriage. Later volumes of the series involve their descendants in romantic adventures of their own. Presented against the backdrop of historical events like Custer's defeat at Little Big Horn, the Sioux series explores what Taylor terms in an article for the *Romantic Times* "an in depth look into the life, heart, and mind of the American Indian."

Taylor attributes her interest in Native American culture to her childhood pursuits. She told *CA:* "I think it started off with growing up as a tomboy, with two brothers. We played a lot of cowboys and Indians, and that kind of thing. I read a lot of what used to be called boys' books: [Anna Sewell's] *Black Beauty,* Jack London books like *Call of the Wild* and *White Fang.* I did male things; my brothers taught me to fish and track and hunt and

shoot. . . . And I've watched a lot of westerns and read a lot of western novels—like Louis L'Amour's books."

Taylor reports in the *Romantic Times* that she unearthed a number of "inconsistencies and unknown facts" while researching native North American history for her novels. "It was amazing to me to learn how many customs were attributed to [American Indians] which were actually begun by the white man," Taylor recalls. Focusing on the Sioux tribes in particular, Taylor wants to reveal the native North Americans' struggle to survive and protect their lands against non-native settlers and U. S. Army onslaughts. In addition, she portrays the native North American as victorious, since—as she points out in the *Romantic Times*—"most westerns have the white man as the victor." Taylor further explains to the magazine that native North Americans have been "misunderstood and maligned, and I wanted to reveal their culture and emotions."

It seems that Taylor has touched many readers with the "Ecstasy Saga" series. As Taylor tells *CA:* "I get a great deal of mail from Indians of all tribes telling me how much the series has done for them individually and as a nation. . . . A lot of people write in and say, 'I've always been embarrassed to tell anyone I was an Indian until I read your series.'" Taylor also says her books have inspired many white readers who "have written to the Indians to get more information on Indian culture and religion and things like that. They've said that it's because of reading my books that they've seen things in a different light and developed this interest."

Commenting on the historical aspects of her novels, Taylor states in the *Romantic Times* that she "combined turbulent history with passionate romance," adding, "I tried to intermingle reality with fantasy." Similarly, Taylor incorporates authentic Sioux language into the dialogue of her stories, enhancing what she terms in the *Romantic Times* the "reality, accuracy, and uniqueness" distinguishing her writing. Overall, according to Taylor's synopsis of the "Ecstasy Saga" series, her books provide a balanced account of both the white man's and native North American's motivations while documenting history through a believable love story. In recognition of the realistic depiction of native North Americans and their history and culture presented in her historical romance novels, Taylor was honored at the Sioux National Celebration in Sisseton, South Dakota, in 1983. Two years later she won the Indian Series award given by the *Romantic Times.*

Taylor's literary career began after she saw a television show featuring Kathleen Woodiwiss, a popular historical romance writer. Taylor was inspired by Woodiwiss's observation that many people could be writers if they took time to put on paper the stories that run through their minds. Taylor, who had recently quit her job as a medical research assistant, followed her advice. Reflecting on this decision, she explains to *CA:* "I doubt I could have become a writer before reaching thirty-four, because I hadn't grown enough emotionally or experienced enough of life. When I did begin it was like a dam breaking, and all my pent-up creativity came pouring out very rapidly and intensely. Now I doubt I can ever stop writing—and you have to love writing to do it because it's a lot of work." Taylor wrote her first two manuscripts longhand and says of the experience, "when I had to type my first manuscript and then they told me it still was not in the proper form, my career almost ended then and there. It took me about three-and-one-half months to retype." When business details become overwhelming, Taylor's husband, Michael, steps in to help: "He takes care of all the mail, the government papers, and the tax forms. And he sets up the trips with my publishers, sends most of my public relations stuff out, and takes care of our children and the house. It really helps a lot. I couldn't get as much done as I need to do if I didn't have him to help me."

Being a popular writer has made Taylor a mentor for some of her readers who write asking her either to critique their work or for advice on personal matters. "Mainly people write during hard periods of their life," Taylor tells *CA,* "like after the death of a spouse or the death of a child. . . . People talk about times being so hard now, and that seems to distract them from their present everyday problems." To quell her readers' inquiries, Taylor publishes a newsletter that answers frequently asked questions and updates fans on new novels and characters. "We started the newsletter because so much of the mail that came in would ask basically the same questions: What else have you written? What's it about? When did it come out? What's coming out next? Every time we do a newsletter, we pull about the last ten questions that are asked most frequently by readers. It's so time-consuming to answer mail. Most days, I would say, I get between 150 and 200 letters. It's just impossible to answer those, but you want to. The best way I've found to deal with it is to do a newsletter. It has gone over extremely well."

Taylor aspires to have her books and other romance novels become a respected literary genre and claims that many readers are missing out on worthwhile fiction due to the genre's pigeonholing. In addition, she extols the camaraderie of romance novelists, pointing out to *CA* that "romance writers seem to be one of the most helpful groups of people; they're constantly helping their competition. . . . That's one big thing I've noticed that romance writers have in common, that sense of wanting to help other people." To that end, Taylor teaches writing courses at Augusta College in Georgia and participates in at least four writers conferences a year around the country. "Most people think writing is very easy, and they think about in-

stant fame and fortune. It's very rare, you know, that a first book will be a national best-seller. People don't realize that you've got to pay your dues, to put in years of hard work to get your name known so that you can become a big writer."

While Taylor's courses don't attract many male students, she does notice that a sizeable portion of her readership is male. "When I was doing my signing at the American Booksellers Association Convention, I signed probably 50 percent for men," Taylor tells *CA*. "And a lot of the mail I get is from men. Usually a letter from a man saying, 'My wife (or my girlfriend) said I should read this.' Then they'll ask what else I've done, because they like my style. Because we've been using a romance cover and the books have been in the romance section of the stores, people sometimes don't realize that they're getting about the same thing that they'd get in the mystery and western and other departments. Once they get past the romance image, they realize that they've got a good action-packed book."

Taylor senses a shift away from the more sexually explicit romance novels of recent years. She believes that women want the option of reading "the same thing the man had—books and magazines with different degrees of sensuality," she tells *CA,* but once this interest is fulfilled, women find they prefer stories with an "emphasis on the romance and the relationship between the characters rather than the heavy degree of sensuality." Taylor says this works out well for her, since "one of the things my publisher usually tells me when I turn a book in is that I don't have enough sensuality. My revisions will usually involve adding more. . . . To me, the story is what's important. You don't want the sensuality to overshadow the story."

Giving range to her talents beyond the "Ecstasy Saga" collection, Taylor has written several other historical romances. These include the award-winning national bestsellers, *First Love, Wild Love,* and *Savage Conquest,* which is set in the post-Civil War American South. She also wrote *Love Me with Fury,* an adventure set during the War of 1812, and *Golden Torment*, which takes place in the frozen landscape of the Yukon Territory at the time of the gold rush, as well as *Valley of Fire,* a contemporary romance, and *Moondust and Madness,* the first in a series of Taylor's innovative science fiction romances.

Taylor outlines for *CA* her progress as a writer: "I have matured both as a person and a woman by developing this previously unused talent. Through the extensive research for my books . . . I have discovered good qualities in other people—generosity, kindness, warmth, helpfulness, and understanding. I learned it is never too late to do anything a person wants badly enough. The only drawback to serious, full-time writing and its other requirements—such as publicity and deadlines—is the weighty demand it places upon your energy and time. But would I give up any of it? Never!''

For an interview with this author, see *Contemporary Authors,* Volume 124.

BIOGRAPHICAL/CRITICAL SOURCES:

BOOKS

Contemporary Authors, Volume 124, Gale, 1988.

Kathryn Falk, editor, *How to Write a Romance and Get It Published: With Intimate Advice From the World's Most Popular Romantic Writers,* illustrations by Ignatius Sahula, Crown, 1983.

Twentieth Century Romance & Historical Writers, second edition, St. James Press, 1990.

PERIODICALS

Athens Observer, March 14, 1985.
Augusta Chronicle, April 13, 1981; September 8, 1982; September 21, 1986.
Columbia Sun, October 14, 1986.
Romantic Times, December, 1983.

—*Sketch by Kathleen Wilson*

*   *   *

TERRACE, Herbert S(ydney) 1936-

PERSONAL: Born November 29, 1936, in Brooklyn, NY; son of Morris Abraham and Esther (Marsh) Terrace; married Kathleen A. Frederick, July 26, 1986; children: Gillian Frederick, Jonathan. *Education:* Cornell University, A.B., 1957, M.A., 1958; Harvard University, Ph.D., 1961.

ADDRESSES: Home—460 Riverside Dr., New York, NY 10027. *Office*—418 Schermerhorn Hall, Columbia University, New York, NY 10027.

CAREER: Columbia University, New York City, instructor, 1961-63, assistant professor of psychology, 1963-66, associate professor of psychology, 1966-68, professor of psychology, 1968—. Visiting professor at Harvard University, 1972-73.

MEMBER: American Psychological Association (fellow), American Association for the Advancement of Science, Society for Experimental Analysis of Behavior (president, 1973-75), Eastern Psychological Association (member of board of directors, 1987—).

AWARDS, HONORS: Grants from National Institute of Mental Health, 1962—, National Science Foundation, 1963-81, and W. T. Grant Foundation, 1976-78; J. S. Guggenheim fellowship, 1969-70; H. F. Guggenheim fellowship, 1976-77; Fulbright Senior Research Scholar, 1983-84; All Souls College, Oxford fellowship, 1983-84.

WRITINGS:

(With Scott Parker) *Introduction to Statistics,* Individual Learning Systems, 1971.
(With T. G. Bever) *Psychology and Human Behavior: Prediction and Control in Modern Society,* Warner Publications, 1973.
Nim, Columbia University Press, 1979.
(Editor with C. Locurto and J. Gibbon) *Autoshaping and Conditioning Theory,* Academic Press, 1981.
(Editor with H. L. Roitblat and T. G. Bever) *Animal Cognition,* L. Erlbaum Associates, 1984.
(With P. Marler) *Biology of Learning,* Springer-Verlag, 1984.

Author of introduction, *The Story of Nim: The Chimp Who Learned Language,* by Anna Michel, Knopf, 1979. Associate editor of *Journal of Experimental Analysis Behavior,* 1966-74, *Learning and Motivation,* 1970-72, *Animal Learning and Behavior,* 1971-75, 1984-86, *Behaviorism,* 1972-84, and *Journal of Experimental Psychology: Animal Learning Processes,* 1986—.

SIDELIGHTS: In order to begin Project Nim, Herbert S. Terrace and his associates obtained a baby chimpanzee from the Institute for Primate Studies. Nim Chimpsky (named for linguist Noam Chomsky) was raised in a human home, attended nursery school five days a week at Columbia University, and in under four years learned to use 125 signs of American Sign Language. After the project was completed Nim was returned to his birthplace to live with other chimpanzees.

BIOGRAPHICAL/CRITICAL SOURCES:

PERIODICALS

Washington Post, January 14, 1980.

*   *   *

TERRY, Megan 1932-

PERSONAL: Original name, Marguerite Duffy; born July 22, 1932, in Seattle, WA; daughter of Harold Joseph and Marguerite Cecelia (Henry) Duffy. *Education:* Studied theater at the Seattle Repertory Playhouse under the direction of Florence and Burton James; attended Banff School of Fine Arts, earning certificates in directing, design, and acting, 1950-52, 1956; attended University of Alberta, 1952-53; University of Washington, B.Ed., 1956.

ADDRESSES: Home—2309 Hanscom Blvd., Omaha, NE 68105. *Office*—c/o Omaha Magic Theatre Press, 1417 Farnum St., Omaha, NE 68102. *Agent*—Elisabeth Marton, 96 Fifth Ave., New York, NY 10011.

CAREER: Playwright. Cornish School of Allied Arts, Seattle, WA, drama teacher and director of the Cornish

Players, 1954-56; Open Theatre, New York City, founding member and director of Playwright's Workshop, 1963-68; Omaha Magic Theatre, Omaha, NE, playwright-in-residence and literary manager, 1974—. Yale University, writer-in-residence, 1966-67; New York Theatre Strategy, founding member and vice president, 1971; Women's Theatre Council, founding member, 1971; University of Nebraska at Omaha, adjunct professor of theatre, ending 1977; University of Louisville, Bingham professor of humanities, 1981; University of Minnesota, Hill professor of fine arts, 1983; participant in Nebraska Artist-in-the-Schools program, 1987-; Squaw Valley Community of Writers, member of playwrighting faculty. Appointed to Nebraska Committee for the Humanities 1983-86. Has served on the Theatre Grants Committee for the Ford Foundation, the Nebraska Arts Council, the Bush Foundation, the Ohio Arts Council, the Wisconsin Arts Board, and the Rockefeller Foundation Theatre Panel. Lecturer, director, production consultant, performer and judge of playwrighting competitions in various states.

MEMBER: National Endowment of the Arts (theatre panel, 1975-84; theatre overview panel, 1979, 1981, and 1984; opera/music panel, 1985; advancement panel, 1987), American Theatre Association (co-chair playwrighting program, 1977; chair playwrights project committee, 1978-79; C. Crawford playwrighting award judge, 1987), International Association of Theatre for children and Youth-USA World Theatre Symposium (board of directors, 1986—), Theatre Communications Group (board of directors, 1988—), New Dramatists (alumni, judge national playwrighting competition, 1987-88), Women's Forum (charter member).

AWARDS, HONORS: Stanley Drama Award, 1965, for *Hothouse;* Office of Advanced Drama Research Award, 1965 and 1969; ABC-Yale University fellow, 1966-67; Rockefeller grant, 1968, 1974, and 1987; WGBH (Boston) award, 1968, for *Sanibel and Captiva;* Latin American Festival award, 1969, for *Keep Tightly Closed in a Cool Dry Place;* Obie Award for best new play, *Village Voice,* 1970, for *Approaching Simone;* Earplay Radio Award, 1972, for *American Wedding Ritual,* and 1980, for *Fireworks;* National Endowment for the Arts (NEA) grant, 1972; Creative Artists Public Service fellow, 1973; NEA Literary fellow, 1973 and playwrighting fellow, 1989; Silver Medal, Amoco Oil, 1977, for distinguished contribution to and service in American Theatre; Guggenheim fellow, 1978; annual award for contributions to theatre, Dramatists Guild Committee of Women, 1983; Nebraska Poet Laureate nomination.

WRITINGS:

PLAYS

(And director) *Beach Grass,* produced in Seattle, WA, 1955.
(And director) *Go Out and Move the Car,* produced in Seattle, 1955.
(And director) *Seascape,* produced in Seattle, 1955.
(And director) *The Dirt Boat,* Seattle, broadcast KING-TV, 1955.
New York Comedy: Two, produced in Saratoga, NY, 1961.
When My Girlfriend Was Still All Flowers, produced in New York City by Open Theatre, 1963.
Eat at Joe's, produced in New York City by Open Theatre, 1963.
Ex-Miss Copper Queen on a Set of Pills (one-act; produced Off-Broadway, 1963), published in *Playwrights for Tomorrow: A Collection of Plays,* Volume 1, edited by Arthur H. Ballet, University of Minnesota Press, 1966; published in *The People vs. Ranchman [and] Ex-Miss Copper Queen on a Set of Pills: Two Plays,* Dramatists Play Service, 1968.
Calm Down Mother: A Transformation Play for Three Women (one-act; produced Off-Broadway by Open Theatre with *Keep Tightly Closed in a Cool Dry Place,* 1965), Samuel French, 1966.
Keep Tightly Closed in a Cool Dry Place (one-act; produced Off-Broadway by Open Theatre with *Calm Down Mother,* 1965; also see below), published in *Tulane Drama Review,* 1966.
The Gloaming, Oh My Darling: A Play in One Act (produced in Minneapolis with *Keep Tightly Closed in a Cool Dry Place,* 1965; also see below), Samuel French, 1967.
Comings and Goings: A Theatre Game (produced Off-Broadway by Open Theatre, 1966; also see below), Samuel French, 1967.
(And director with Joseph Chaikin and Peter Feldman) *Viet Rock: A Folk War Movie* (rock musical; three-act; produced Off-Broadway by Open Theatre, 1966; also see below), published in *Tulane Drama Review,* 1966.
The Magic Realists (one-act; produced Off-Broadway by Open Theatre, 1966; also see below), published in *Best One-Act Plays of 1968,* edited by Stanley Richards, Chilton Press, 1969.
The People vs. Ranchman (three-act; produced in Minneapolis, MN, 1967; Off-Broadway, 1968), published in *The People vs. Ranchman [and] Ex-Miss Copper Queen on a Set of Pills: Two Plays,* Dramatists Play Service, 1968.
The Key Is on the Bottom, produced in Los Angeles, 1968.
Jack-Jack (two-act rock musical), produced in Minneapolis, 1968.

Changes, produced Off-Broadway, 1968.

Home: Or Future Soap (three-act; broadcast on *NET-Playhouse,* Public Broadcasting Service, 1968; produced in London at As Theatre, 1974), Samuel French, 1972.

Sanibel and Captiva (also see below), broadcast on WGBH, Boston, 1968.

Massachusetts Trust (produced in Waltham, MA, 1968), published in *The Off-Off Broadway Book,* edited by Albert Poland and Bruce Mailman, Bobbs-Merrill, 1972.

One More Little Drinkie (also see below), broadcast on Public Broadcasting Service, 1969.

(And director) *The Tommy Allen Show* (produced in Los Angeles, 1969), published in *Scripts 2,* December, 1971.

Approaching Simone: A Drama in Two Acts (produced in Boston, 1970; Off-Broadway, 1970; also see below), Samuel French, 1970.

American Wedding Ritual Monitored/Transmitted by the Planet Jupiter (one-act; broadcast on National Public Radio, 1972), published in *Places: A Journal of Theatre,* Volume 1, 1973.

Off Broadway Book, edited by Albert Poland and Bruce Mailman, Bobbs-Merrill, 1972.

Grooving, produced in New York City, 1972.

(With Jo Ann Schmidman) *Choose a Spot on the Floor,* produced in Omaha, NE, 1972.

Susan Perutz at the Manhattan Theatre Club, produced in New York City, 1973.

St. Hydro Clemency; or, A Funhouse of the Lord: An Energizing Event, produced in New York City, 1973.

(With Sam Shepard and Jean-Claude van Itallie) *Nightwalk* (produced in New York City, 1973), published in *Three Works by the Open Theatre,* edited by Karen Malpede, Drama Book Specialists, 1974; Bobbs-Merrill, 1975.

Couplings and Groupings, Riscus Books, 1974.

Babes in the Bighouse: A Documentary Fantasy Musical about Life inside a Women's Prison (produced in Omaha, 1974; also see below), Omaha Magic Theatre Press, 1979.

Women's Prison (musical; produced in Omaha, 1974), Omaha Magic Theatre Press, 1979.

The Pioneer (also see below), produced in Omaha, 1974.

Pro Game; The Pioneer: Two One-Act Plays (produced in New York City, 1974; also see below), *Pro Game* published in *Two One-Act Plays: ProGame and Hothouse* (three-act; produced Off-Off Broadway, 1974), Samuel French, 1975.

Fifteen Million Fifteen Year Olds (musical), Omaha Magic Theatre Press, 1974.

Henna for Endurance, Omaha Magic Theatre Press, 1974.

Hospital Play, Omaha Magic Theatre Press, 1974.

(With others) *All Them Women,* produced in New York City, 1974.

The Narco Linguini Bust, produced in Omaha, 1974.

We Can Feed Everybody Here, produced in New York City, 1974.

Pioneer, Ragnarok Press, 1975.

Women and Law, broadcast on Nebraska Public TV, 1976.

(Editor and contributor) *100,001 Horror Stories of the Plains* (produced in Omaha, 1976), Omaha Magic Theatre Press, 1978.

Lady Rose's Brazil Hide Out, produced in Omaha, 1977.

Brazil Fado: You're Always with Me (produced in Omaha, 1977), Omaha Magic Theatre Press, 1979.

Willie-Willa-Bill's Dope Garden, A Meditation in One-Act on Willa Cather, Ragnarok Press, 1977.

Sleazing toward Athens, Omaha Magic Theatre Press, 1977.

American King's English for Queens (musical; produced in Omaha, 1978; also see below), Omaha Magic Theatre Press, 1978.

Attempted Rescue on Avenue B: A Beat Fifties Comic Opera (produced in Chicago, 1979), Omaha Magic Theatre Press, 1979.

Goona Goona (musical), produced in Omaha, 1979.

Fireworks, broadcast on National Public Radio, 1980.

Advances, Omaha Magic Theatre Press, 1980.

Janis Joplin, published in *Notable American Women: The Modern Period,* edited by Barbara Sicherman and Carol Hurd Green, Harvard University Press, 1980.

The Trees Blew Down, Omaha Magic Theatre Press, 1981.

Flat in Afghanistan, Omaha Magic Theatre Press, 1981.

Katmandu, Omaha Magic Theatre Press, 1981.

Performance Piece, Omaha Magic Theatre Press, 1981.

Winners: The Lives of a Traveling Family Circus and Mother Jones, Omaha Magic Theatre Press, 1981.

(With JoAnne Metcalf) *Mollie Bailey's Traveling Family Circus: Featuring Scenes from the Life of Mother Jones,* Broadway Play, 1983.

Kegger (musical), produced in Washington, DC, 1983.

Amtrak, Omaha Magic Theatre Press, 1988.

Headlights, Omaha Magic Theatre Press, 1988.

Retro, Omaha Magic Theatre Press, 1988.

COLLECTIONS OF PLAYS

Viet Rock and Other Plays (contains *Viet Rock, Comings and Goings, Keep Tightly Closed in a Cool Dry Place,* and *The Gloaming, Oh My Darling*), Simon & Schuster, 1967.

Three One-Act Plays (includes *The Magic Realists, Sanibel and Captiva,* and *One More Little Drinkie*), Samuel French, 1971.

High Energy Musicals from the Omaha Magic Theater (includes *American King's English for Queens,* and *Babes in the Bighouse*), Broadway Play, 1983.
Two By Terry Plus One: An Anthology of Plays by Women (includes *Pro Game, The Pioneer,* and *Walking into the Dawn,* by Rochelle Lynn Holt), I. E. Clark, 1984.

Also author of other plays, including *Avril and Helen,* 1958; *Two Pages a Day,* published by Drama Review; *Dinner's in the Blender; Objective Love; Breakfast Serial; Do You See What I'm Saying?; X-Rayed-Iate* (musical); and *The Snow Queen.* Also author of lyrics for *Thoughts,* a musical by Lamar Alford, produced Off-Broadway, 1973, and *Running Gag,* a musical by Jo Ann Schmidman (produced in Lake Placid, NY, 1980), Broadway Play, 1980. Editor and contributor, *Sea of Forms, Walking through Walls, Babes Unchained, Cancel That Last Thought: Or See the 270 Foot Woman in Spandex, Body Leaks,* and *Sound Fields/Sound Minds.*

Plays represented in numerous anthologies, including *Calm Down Mother* in *Eight Plays from Off-Off Broadway,* edited by M. T. Smith and N. Orzel, Bobbs-Merrill, 1966, and *Plays by and about Women,* edited by V. Sullivan and James Hatch, Vintage Books, 1974; *The Gloaming, Oh My Darling* in *The Norton Introduction to Literature,* edited by Carl E. Bain and others, Norton, 1973; *Sanibel and Captiva* in *Spontaneous Combustion: Eight New American Plays,* edited by Rochelle Owens, Drama Book Specialists, 1973; and *Approaching Simone* in *Women in Drama: An Anthology,* edited by Harriett Kriegel, New American Library, 1975. Contributor to *New York Times, Southwest Review, Drama Review,* and *Valhalla: A Modern Drama Issue.* Contributor of articles to professional journals. Many of Terry's plays have been televised, and her works have been translated into numerous languages.

SIDELIGHTS: Influenced by vaudeville, burlesque and the tutelage of James and Florence Burton, internationally renowned playwright Megan Terry created a new style of writing for her controversial plays on politics, sexual repression, and identity. A proponent of community theater, she is known to go to the streets to find young and old to act in her works. Her philosophy of each participant bringing their "own reality" to the play along with her unique use of space and music are signatures of her productions.

Terry became involved in the theatre at a very young age; when she was seven years old, she attended her first live production and decided theatre would be her career. "I went and I looked at the stage and I fell madly in love," Terry tells Phyllis Jone Rose in the *Dictionary of Literary Biography,* "I knew I wanted to do that, whatever it was." All through school Terry participated in some form of dramatics. She was involved in theatre production

through backyard plays and school productions, not only acting, but writing, directing, and designing and building sets. During her last year in high school, Terry became involved with the Seattle Repertory Playhouse and worked with trained professionals in all aspects of the theatre. Terry attributes much of her current style to the influence of the professionals she worked with there. Director Florence James and actor Burton James' politics contributed to Terry's use of political themes in her plays. Her work with the repertory's set designers helped inspire her view and use of plays as structures. During her college days in Canada, Terry's timing and humor was influenced by Myra Benson, a comedienne she worked with at the University of Edmonton. At this time she also worked behind the scenes as a set designer and a technical director. This work helped Terry decide to become a playwright because she realized she wanted to be "responsible for the entire concept of not only what went on stage, but for the whole environment of the audience," she tells Rose.

After completing college, Terry continued to write and produce. She was initially uncomfortable with her skills and would not take credit for her work. "I was involved in this whole thing of 'women shouldn't be able to do that,'" Terry explains to Rose. "Since I felt that playwrights were the pinnacle of civilization, for me to aspire to that seemed out of reach." Friends of Terry, however, introduced her to an agent and together their enthusiasm for her work helped convince Terry she was a playwright. Terry's innovational styles were evident early on. Her new playwrighting style was combined with a new acting style, based on transformation exercises, and used in her plays at the Open Theatre. The innovative environment at the Open Theatre helped Terry conceive her plays as a series of action blocs rather than sequential scenes. She also began using her scripts as starting points for dialogue and action and allowed the participants to adlib their parts. In the play *Magic Realists,* she uses dream sequences and music to convey her political message about the evils of corporate America.

All of these techniques culminate in Terry's 1966 play *Viet Rock. Viet Rock* was the first rock musical and first play about the Vietnam War; it also became Terry's best known play. *Viet Rock* received mixed reactions to its innovative form and political message. Harold Clurman, writing in the *Nation,* contends, "There is little to indicate that this farrago is propelled by the force of genuine social indignation or understanding. There is hardly any true spontaneity; only untempered ambition and unripe mind." Likewise, Catharine R. Hughes in *America* notes that the play has "numerous faults. The most damaging of them was the sheer amateurishness of its writing and production and the sophomoric quality of its message." In contrast, Al McConagha, quoted in the *Dictionary of Literary Biogra-*

phy, applauds *Viet Rock* as "a provocative, frequently wildly funny, series of theatrical metaphors." In his *New Leader* review of the musical and several of Terry's other plays, Albert Bermel maintains, "What I find most interesting about her plays is their exploitation of the theater as a medium, in particular their accommodation to those unreal and neglected dimensions: stage time and space."

Approaching Simone, which received the 1970 Obie Award for best play, reveals the more serious and reverent qualities of Terry's creative genius. In contrast to her previous work, *Approaching Simone* received wide acclaim from the critics. The play portrays the life of philosopher Simone Weil, who at age thirty-four committed suicide by starvation to protest World War II soldiers starving at the front line. Hughes praises the play in her *America* review for the transformation of "material that at first glance might seem untheatrical—the play, after all, records the journey of a soul—into one of the most powerful and engrossing pieces of theatre to be seen." Jack Kroll writes in his *Newsweek* review, "It is a rare theatrical event for these hysterical and clownish times, a truly serious play, filled with the light, shadow and weight of human life, and the exultant agonies of the ceaseless attempt to create one's humanity."

During the 1970s Terry wrote several plays involving family issues, including *Hothouse, Pioneer, King's English,* and *Goona Goona.* Through scenes of family life, these plays deal with the problems created by parental and social pressure being used to push children into certain roles and decisions. Based on the lives of Terry, her mother, and grandmother, *Hothouse* exposes the contrast of love and pain in their relationships. *Village Voice* contributor Francis Levy criticizes the play for dealing with too much factual information, stating that it would be "enhanced by doing away with the unnecessary material which clouds this powerful portrait of individuals pitted against the predominance of fate." Terry's 1974 play, *The Pioneer,* is about an upper-middle-class mother convincing her daughter to marry. Michael Feingold, quoted in the *Dictionary of Literary Biography,* finds it dealing with themes similar to *Hothouse,* including "the way parents pressure children into certain roles, by instruction and examples; the way society uses this pressure, making the home an horrific training ground for the horrific larger world." Family scenarios are also used in Terry's 1978 play *King's English* to demonstrate the sexism inherent in English language and in the 1979 play *Goona Goona* to illustrate the abuse that occurs in some families.

Terry's love of theatre and prolific writing style have resulted in the production of over fifty musical plays and numerous awards. Explaining her joy of the theatre, Terry was once quoted in the *Dictionary of Literary Biography:* "I remember being on stage and getting that terrific rush

in the frontal lobes every time the audience laughed. I still get it, and that's one of the main reasons I'm still in it. Theatre is profoundly physically rewarding." Applauding her skill in the theatre, Bermel judges Terry as a writer with "prodigious gifts. She threads together many varieties of language, from poetry and lyrical vernacular to senseless, palpitating vocal noises; she sets each one of her multiple scenes economically, without holding up the drama; her lines are rich with buoying rhythms and unforced song; she knows how to make a harsh satirical comment obliquely."

BIOGRAPHICAL/CRITICAL SOURCES:

BOOKS

Contemporary Literary Criticism, Volume 19, Gale, 1981.
Dictionary of Literary Biography, Volume 7: *Twentieth-Century American Dramatists,* Gale, 1981.
Pasolli, Robert, *A Book on the Open Theater,* Bobbs-Merrill, 1970.
van Itallie, Jean-Claude, *Theatre Z: American Theater, 1968-1969,* International Theater Institute, 1970.

PERIODICALS

America, May 20, 1967, pp. 759-61; June 6, 1970, p. 612.
Nation, November 28, 1966, pp. 586-87.
New Leader, September 11, 1967, pp. 23-24.
Newsweek, November 11, 1968, p. 121; March 16, 1970, p. 64.
New York Times, January 14, 1968, p. 17; November 10, 1968, pp. 1, 3.
Time, November 8, 1968, p. 94.
Village Voice, August 22, 1974, p. 66.*

*   *   *

THOMPSON, China
See LEWIS, Mary (Christianna Milne)

*   *   *

THORNTON, Peter (Kai) 1925-

PERSONAL: Born April 8, 1925, in St. Albans, England; son of Sir Gerard (a microbiologist) and Gerda (Noerregaard) Thornton; married Mary Rosamund Helps (a bookbinder), August 22, 1950; children: Emma Bettina, Minna Thecla, Dora Frieda. *Education:* Attended Bryanston School and De Havilland Aeronautical Technical School, 1943-45; Trinity Hall, Cambridge, degree in modern languages, 1950.

ADDRESSES: Home—15 Cheniston Gardens, London W.8, England. *Office*—Sir John Soane's Museum, 13 Lincoln's Inn Fields, London W.C.2, England.

CAREER: Fitzwilliam Museum, Cambridge, England, assistant keeper, 1950-52; National Art-Collections Fund, London, England, joint secretary, 1952-54; Victoria and Albert Museum, London, assistant keeper of textiles, 1954-62, assistant keeper of woodwork, 1962-66, keeper, 1966-84; Sir John Soane's Museum, London, curator, 1984—. *Military service:* British Army, Intelligence Corps, 1945-48; served in Austria.

MEMBER: Furniture History Society (chairman, 1976-84), Society of Antiquaries (fellow).

AWARDS, HONORS: Alice Davis Hitchcock Medallion, Society of Architectural Historians, 1982, for *Seventeenth-Century Interior Decoration*; Sir Bannister Fletcher Medal, Royal Institute of British Architects, 1985, for *Authentic Decor: The Domestic Interior, 1620-1920;* Prix Vasari international de livre d'Art, 1992, for French edition of *The Italian Renaissance Interiors, 1400-1600.*

WRITINGS:

Baroque and Rococo Silks, Faber, 1965.
(Contributor) Helena Hayward, editor, *World Furniture,* Hamlyn, 1965.
Seventeenth-Century Interior Decoration in England, France, and Holland, Yale University Press, 1978.
(With Maurice Tomlin) *The Furnishing and Decoration of Ham House,* Furniture History Society, 1980.
Authentic Decor: The Domestic Interior, 1620-1920, Viking, 1984.
(With Helen Dory) *A Miscellany of Objects from Sir John Soane's Museum,* Abrams, 1992.
The Italian Renaissance Interior, 1400-1600, Abrams, 1991.
Sir John Soane: The Architect as a Collector, Abrams, 1992.

Contributor to periodicals, including *Burlington, Apollo, Antiques, Gazette des Beaux-Arts, Journal of the History of Collections, Furniture History, Pantheon,* and *Times Literary Supplement.*

WORK IN PROGRESS: A book on the history of design in the decorative arts, 1470-1870; a history of the buildings of Sir John Soane's Museum and their contents.

SIDELIGHTS: Peter Thornton's *"Seventeenth-Century Interior Decoration in England, France, and Holland* is a major contribution" to the study of "the relationship between furniture and houses," writes Bruce Boucher in the *Times Literary Supplement.* And E. Pearlman states in *Library Journal* that "Thornton makes a good effort to relate patterns of decoration to social usages." Pearlman concludes that *Seventeenth-Century Interior Decoration in England, France, and Holland* is an "exceedingly valuable book, essential for art and architecture collections."

Thornton once told *CA:* "I have been much concerned with the restoration of historic interiors and country houses; I stress authenticity. I am engaged in conservation work, both technically and politically."

BIOGRAPHICAL/CRITICAL SOURCES:

PERIODICALS

Library Journal, April 1, 1979, p. 820.
Times Literary Supplement, March 21, 1980; January 9, 1981; May 10, 1985.
Washington Post Book World, December 16, 1984.

*   *   *

TINNISWOOD, Peter 1936-

PERSONAL: Born December 21, 1936, in Liverpool, England; son of Thomas Henry Bismarck (a compositor) and May (Broley) Tinniswood; married Patricia Mary Therese Mallen, October 22, 1966; children: Stephen John, Victoria Jane, David Thomas. *Education:* University of Manchester, B.A., 1954. *Avocational Interests:* Ornithology, cricket, music.

ADDRESSES: Home and office—29 Teilo St., Llandaff Fields, Cardiff, Wales. *Agent*—Anthony Sheil Associates Ltd., 43 Doughty St., London WC1N 2LF, England.

CAREER: Worked as insurance clerk in Vienna, Austria; *Sheffield Star* and *Sheffield Telegraph,* Sheffield, England, chief leader and features writer, 1958-62; *Western Mail,* Cardiff, Wales, chief features writer, 1966-67, 1967-68; *Liverpool Daily Post,* Liverpool, England, features writer, 1967; free-lance writer.

MEMBER: Royal Society of Literature (fellow).

AWARDS, HONORS: Authors Club Award, 1969; Winifred Holtby Memorial Prize, Royal Society of Literature, 1974, for *I Didn't Know You Cared;* Welsh Arts Council Prize, 1974.

WRITINGS:

A Touch of Daniel (novel), Doubleday, 1969.
Mog (novel), Hodder & Stoughton, 1970.
The Investiture (play), produced by Bristol Old Vic Company at Bristol Little Theatre, 1971.
I Didn't Know You Cared (novel), Hodder & Stoughton, 1973.
Except You're a Bird (novel), Hodder & Stoughton, 1974, new edition, Arrow Books, 1984.
The Stirk of Stirk (novel), Macmillan (London), 1974.
Shemerelda, Hodder & Stoughton, 1981.
Marketing Decisions, Longman, 1981.
Tales from a Long Room, Arrow Books, 1981.
More Tales from a Long Room, Arrow Books, 1982.

Collected Tales from a Long Room, Hutchinson, 1982.

The Home Front, Granada Publishing, 1982, new edition, Severn House, 1983.

You Should See Us Now (play; produced in London at Greenwich Theatre, 1983), Samuel French, 1983.

The Brigadier Down Under, Macmillan (London), 1983.

The Brigadier in Season, Macmillan (London), 1984.

The Brigadier's Brief Lives (also see below), Pan Books, 1984.

The Brigadier's Tour (also see below), Pan Books, 1985.

Call It a Canary, Macmillan (London), 1985.

Uncle Mort's North Country, illustrated by John Ireland, Pavilion Books, 1986.

The Brigadier's Collection (contains *The Brigadier's Brief Lives* and *The Brigadier's Tour*), Severn House, 1986.

Tales from Witney Scrotum, illustrated by John Lawrence, Pavilion Books, 1987.

Hayballs, Hutchinson, 1989.

Uncle Mort's South Country, Arrow Books, 1990.

Also author of play, *Wilfrid.* Author of radio series, *Hardluck Hall,* and television series, *I Didn't Know You Cared* and *The Home Front,* both based on his novels of the same titles; also author of two television plays, *The Signal Box of Grandpa Hudson* and *The Diaries of Stoker Leishman.* Writer, with David Nobbs, of television scripts for Davis Frost, Fernandel, *That Was the Week That Was,* and other programs.

SIDELIGHTS: Peter Tinniswood once told *CA* that he writes because "it's the nicest way I know of earning money. I write comedies, and all I want to do is make people laugh and more aware of the essential tragi-comic nature of their lives."

Reviewing *A Touch of Daniel,* a *New York Times Book Review* critic claimed, "If you're ready for a good chuckle at the expense of old age, deformity, sickness and death, Mr. Tinniswood, a writer for British TV, is the chap to oblige." A *Punch* writer noted that *Mog* "belongs to the long-established genre which throws together a number of grotesques engaged in some preposterous enterprise and relies heavily on verbal felicities and surprise. The jokes and the language are so pleasing that the wildness of the plot matters less than it should. In other words, Mr. Tinniswood gets away with it." In a London *Times* review of *Hayballs,* Andrew Sinclair praised the author's "terse and lush" descriptive prose which "provokes hiccups of laughter." About Tinniswood, Sinclair added, "Love him or leave him, his is a most particular voice."

In addition to his novels, Tinniswood also writes for television and radio. His series *The Home Front,* about family life, consists of six one-hour television plays. About the first episode, "A Gifted Adult," Bryan Appleyard asserted in the London *Times* that "Tinniswood's achieve-

ment in this first play is to translate a powerful and tragic insight into a delicate and literate comedy." Appleyard concludes, "Television so seldom delivers the real thing that *A Gifted Adult* came as a distinct shock."

BIOGRAPHICAL/CRITICAL SOURCES:

PERIODICALS

Books, June, 1970; October, 1970.

New York Times Book Review, July 20, 1969.

Observer Review, July 26, 1970.

Punch, April 30, 1969; July 29, 1970.

Times (London), February 2, 1983; February 3, 1983; July 26, 1984; July 4, 1985; December 4, 1986; June 1, 1989.*

*   *   *

TITTLER, Jonathan (Paul) 1945-

PERSONAL: Born April 19, 1945, in Brooklyn, NY; son of Herbert (a manufacturer) and Florence (a sales manager; maiden name, Wolin) Tittler; married Susan F. Hill (a teacher), 1978; children: Mara, Ethan. *Education:* Attended New York University program in Spain, 1965-66; Hamilton College, A.A., 1967; attended University of Chicago Law School, 1967-68; Cornell University, Ph.D., 1974.

ADDRESSES: Home—9754 Savercool Rd., Trumansburg, NY 14886. *Office*—Department of Romance Studies, Cornell University, Ithaca, NY 14853.

CAREER: Hamilton College, Clinton, NY, assistant professor of Spanish, 1974-75; Bates College, Lewiston, ME, assistant professor of Spanish, 1975-76; Hamilton College, visiting assistant professor of Spanish, 1976-77; Cornell University, Ithaca, NY, visiting assistant professor, 1977-78, assistant professor, 1978-82, associate professor, 1982-90, professor of Spanish, 1990—. Juror of *Premio Novela Jorge Isaacs,* 1982. Consultant, Advanced Placement Examination in Spanish, Education Testing Service, 1990—, and Fulbright Commission, Andrean and Central American Region, 1992—.

MEMBER: Association of North American Colombianists (vice-president, 1983-85; president, 1985-87), Modern Language Association of America, American Association of Teachers of Spanish and Portuguese, New York State Association of Teachers of Foreign Languages, New York State Latin Americanists, Phi Beta Kappa.

WRITINGS:

(Translator with Susan F. Hill) Adalberto Ortiz, *Juyungo,* Three Continents, 1982.

Narrative Irony in the Contemporary Spanish-American Novel, Cornell University Press, 1984.

(Translator) Manuel Zapata Olivella, *Chambacu: Black Slum,* Latin American Literary Review Press, 1989.
(Translator) Gustavo Alvarez Gardeazaval, *Bazaar of the Idiots,* Latin American Literary Review Press, 1991.
Manuel Puig, Twayne, 1993.

Editor of newsletter of Association of North American Colombianists; member of editorial board, *Diacritic* and *Journal of Colombian Studies.*

WORK IN PROGRESS: A critical anthology of Neo-Colombian literature.

SIDELIGHTS: Jonathan Tittler once told *CA:* "I am, by temperament, primarily an educator and literary critic rather than a scholar. Writing for me is indispensable to understanding my own thinking. Thus far, my work has followed two distinct but related avenues: one playful and another political. Practically all my critical studies on contemporary fiction bear on the notion of irony, perhaps because I have so little of it. If nothing else, delving into irony permits me to work out an enjoyable and fundamental theorizing impulse. The marginalized causes I believe in and quixotically wish to foster—the problems of blacks, homosexuals, the powerless—lead me to the practice of translation. Translation opens channels of communication between Spanish-speaking authors and English-speaking readers, thus enabling the formation of alliances based on comprehension. The various facets of my enterprise are united by the erosion of cultural and linguistic barriers among peoples."

BIOGRAPHICAL/CRITICAL SOURCES:

PERIODICALS

World Literature Today, spring, 1985.

*   *   *

TROUPE, Quincy (Thomas, Jr.) 1943-

PERSONAL: Born July 23, 1943, in New York, NY; son of Quincy, Sr., and Dorothy (Marshall Smith) Troupe; married Margaret Porter; children: Antoinette, Tymme, Quincy, Porter. *Education:* Grambling College (now Grambling State University), B.A., 1963; Los Angeles City College, A.A., 1967.

ADDRESSES: Home—1925 7th Ave., No. 7L, New York, NY 10026. *Office*—Department of Performing and Creative Arts, City University of New York, 130 Stuyvesant Place, Staten Island, NY 10301; and School of the Arts, Writing Division, Columbia University, New York, NY 10027. *Agent*—Marie Brown, 412 West 154th St., No. 2, New York, NY 10032.

CAREER: Watts Writers' Movement, Los Angeles, CA, creative writing teacher, 1966-68; *Shrewd* (magazine), Los

Angeles, associate editor, beginning 1968; University of California, Los Angeles, instructor in creative writing and black literature, 1968; Ohio University, Athens, instructor in creative writing and third world literature, 1969-72; Richmond College, Staten Island, NY, instructor in third world literature, beginning 1972; instructor at institutions including University of California at Berkeley, California State University at Sacramento, and University of Ghana at Legon; College of Staten Island, City University of New York, New York City, associate professor of American and third world literatures and director of poetry center; Columbia University, New York City, member of faculty of Graduate Writing Program, 1985—. Director of Malcolm X Center and John Coltrane Summer Festivals in Los Angeles, summers, 1969 and 1970. Has given poetry readings at various institutions, including Harvard University, New York University, Howard University, Yale University, Princeton University, Louisiana State University, Dartmouth College, Oberlin College, Ohio State University, University of Michigan, and Michigan State University. Presenter of lecture and readings series "Life Forces: A Festival of Black Roots" at the Church of St. John the Divine in New York City.

MEMBER: Poetry Society of America.

AWARDS, HONORS: International Institute of Education grant for travel in Africa, 1972; National Endowment for the Arts Award in poetry, 1978; grant from New York State Council of the Arts, 1979; American Book Award from the Association of American Publishers, 1980, for *Snake-back Solos;* New York Foundation for the Arts fellowship in poetry, 1987.

WRITINGS:

(Editor) *Watts Poets: A Book of New Poetry and Essays,* House of Respect, 1968.
Embryo Poems, 1967-1971 (includes "South African Bloodstone—For Hugh Masekela," "Chicago—For Howlin Wolf," "Profilin, A Rap/Poem—For Leon Damas," "The Scag Ballet," "Midtown Traffic," "Woke Up Crying the Blues," "The Earthquake of Peru; 1970; In 49 Seconds—For Cesar Vallejo, Great Peruvian Poet," "In the Manner of Rabearivello," "Poem From the Third Eye—For Eugene Redmond," and "Black Star, Black Woman"), Barlenmir, 1972, 2nd edition, 1974.
(Editor with Rainer Schulte) *Giant Talk: An Anthology of Third World Writings,* Random House, 1975.
(Author of foreword) Arnold Adoff, editor, *Celebrations: A New Anthology of Black American Poetry,* Follet, 1977.
(With David L. Wolper) *The Inside Story of TV's "Roots,"* Warner Books, 1978.

Snake-back Solos: Selected Poems, 1969-1977 (includes "Springtime Ritual," "The Day Duke Raised," "La Marqueta," "For Miles Davis," "Up Sun South of Alaska," "Today's Subway Ride," "New York Street-walker," "Ghanaian Song—Image," and "Memory"), I. Reed Books, 1978.

Skulls Along the River (poetry), I. Reed Books, 1984.

Soundings, Writers & Readers, 1988.

(Editor) *James Baldwin: The Legacy,* Simon and Schuster, 1989.

(With Miles Davis) *Miles, the Autobiography,* Simon and Schuster, 1989.

Weather Reports: New and Selected Poems, Writers & Readers, 1991.

Also founding editor of *Confrontation: A Journal of Third World Literature* and *American Rag;* guest editor of black poetry and black fiction issues of *Mundus Artium,* 1973; senior editor of *River Styx,* 1983—. Work represented in anthologies, including *The New Black Poetry,* 1969; *We Speak as Liberators,* 1970; *New Black Voices,* 1972; *Black Spirits,* 1972; *Poetry of Black America,* 1973; and *A Rock against the Wind,* 1973. Contributor to periodicals, including *New Directions, Mundus Artium, Iowa Review, Black World, Callaloo, Essence, Antioch Review, Black Creation, Negro American Literature Forum, Umbra, Mediterranean Review, Concerning Poetry, Sumac, Paris Match, Black Review, New York Quarterly,* and *Village Voice.*

SIDELIGHTS: Quincy Troupe is "a poet of great feeling and energy," according to Michael S. Harper, reviewing *Snake-back Solos: Selected Poems, 1969-1977* in the *New York Times Book Review.* Troupe has also founded and edited magazines such as *Confrontation: A Journal of Third World Literature* and *American Rag,* in addition to having a distinguished academic career. He began teaching creative writing for the Watts Writers' Movement in 1966; his other teaching responsibilities have included courses in black literature and third world literature. Troupe was already an established poet and his scholarly interests had led him to compile *Giant Talk: An Anthology of Third World Writings* with Rainer Schulte when, in 1978, he reached a wider audience with *The Inside Story of TV's "Roots."* The book, which Troupe wrote with David L. Wolper, chronicles the production of the highly successful television miniseries about slavery in America, "Roots," which was based on Alex Haley's book of the same title. Troupe's *Inside Story* has sold over one million copies.

Troupe's first poetic publication came in 1964 when *Paris Match* featured his "What Is a Black Man?" Since then he has contributed poetry to many periodicals in addition to having volumes of his poems published in book form. The first of these, *Embryo Poems,* includes poems which

display Troupe's interests in the use of dialect, such as "Profilin, A Rap/Poem—For Leon Damas," and in the area of music, such as "The Scag Ballet," The latter poem depicts the actions of drug addicts as a strange form of dance; another piece likens traffic noises to "black jazz piano." Yet another, "Woke Up Crying the Blues," concerns the assassination of black civil rights leader Martin Luther King, Jr. The sadness the speaker of the poem feels at the loss of "the peaceful man from Atlanta" mingles with the happiness of the news that one of his poems has been accepted for publication, producing a mixture of emotion essential to the singing of a blues song.

Snake-back Solos, Troupe's second volume of poetry, takes its title from a local name—"Snakeback"—for the Mississippi River, recalled from the poet's childhood in St. Louis. Harper cited such poems as "Today's Subway Ride" in praising Troupe's descriptions of "the strange reality of familiar scenes." The subway is painted starkly, its unpleasant atmosphere displayed in "pee smells assaulting nostrils/blood breaking wine stains everywhere." Though Harper faulted the repetition of some of *Snake-back Solos,* including "Up Sun South of Alaska," he lauded "Ghanaian Song—Image" and "Memory" as "striking" and concluded that "the strength and economy" of the poet's "best insights . . . are about people and places he has internalized and often left behind."

Troupe's academic work has also garnered applause from critics. *Giant Talk* was declared "comprehensive" by Jack Slater in the *New York Times Book Review.* The book, which Troupe edited with Rainer Schulte, contains poems, folk tales, short stories, and novel excerpts by black Americans, native Americans, Hispanic Americans, black Africans, and Central and South Americans. According to Slater, the editors define third world writers as "those who identify with the historically exploited segment of mankind, and who confront the establishment on their behalf"; hence the inclusion of U.S.-born authors along with those native to areas more traditionally identified with the third world. Slater hailed the editors' decision to group the anthologized pieces by concept rather than by geographical area or genre. By using categories like "Oppression and Protest" and "Ritual and Magic," Troupe and Schulte "have managed to lessen the unwieldiness of *Giant Talk*'s scope. The uninitiated reader can, therefore, savor with as much ease as possible bits and pieces of longer works . . . as well as enjoy complete works by . . . short-story writers and poets."

James Baldwin: The Legacy, published after Baldwin's death in 1987, is "a sustained fond retrospect," Nicholas Delbanco remarked in a *Tribune Books* review. The book includes tributes and remembrances "studded with remarkable images that attest to the writer's continuing brilliance" from Maya Angelou, Amiri Baraka, Toni Morrison, Chinua Achebe, and others, Charles R. Larson commented in *Washington Post Book World,* and ends with an interview with Baldwin, conducted by Troupe several weeks before the author's death, which is "spirited and funny at times," *Los Angeles Times Book Review* critic Clancy Sigal noted. Delbanco related Troupe's description of the book: " 'It is a celebration of the life, the vision and, yes, the death of our good and great, passionate, genius witness of a brother, James Arthur Baldwin.' "

BIOGRAPHICAL/CRITICAL SOURCES:

BOOKS

Dictionary of Literary Biography, Volume 41: *Afro-American Poets since 1955,* Gale, 1985.
Troupe, Quincy, *Embryo Poems, 1967-1971,* Barlenmir, 1972.
Troupe, Quincy, and Rainer Schulte, *Giant Talk: An Anthology of Third World Writings,* Random House, 1975.
Troupe, Quincy, *Snake-back Solos: Selected Poems, 1969-1977,* I. Reed Books, 1978.

PERIODICALS

Black Scholar, March/April, 1981; summer, 1990.
Freedomways, Volume 10, number 2, 1980.
Los Angeles Times Book Review, April 30, 1989, p. 1.
Mother Jones, December, 1989, p. 42.
Nation, January 29, 1990, p. 139.
New York Times Book Review, November 30, 1975; October 21, 1979; October 15, 1989, p. 97.
Tribune Books (Chicago), March 19, 1989.
Washington Post Book World, April 16, 1989, p. 1.*

* * *

TUSIANI, Joseph 1924-

PERSONAL: Born January 14, 1924, in Foggia, Italy; immigrated to United States in 1947, naturalized citizen, 1956; son of Michael and Maria (Pisone) Tusiani. *Education:* University of Naples, Ph.D. (summa cum laude), 1947. *Religion:* Catholic. *Avocational Interests:* Music, painting.

ADDRESSES: Home—2140 Tomlinson Ave., New York, NY 10461.

CAREER: Liceo Classico, San Severo, Italy, teacher of Latin and Greek, 1944-47; College of Mount Saint Vincent, Riverdale, NY, chairman of Italian department, 1948-71; Hunter College (now Hunter College of the City University of New York), New York City, lecturer in Italian, 1950-63; New York University, New York City, lecturer in Italian literature, 1956-63; Herbert H. Lehman

College of the City University of New York, Bronx, NY, professor of Italian literature, 1971-83.

MEMBER: Poetry Society of America (vice-president, 1958-68), Catholic Poetry Society of America (director, 1956-69), PEN, Dante Society of America, American Association of University Professors.

AWARDS, HONORS: Greenwood Prize, Poetry Society of England, 1956; silver medal for Latin poetry (Rome), 1962; Alice Fay di Castagnola Award, Poetry Society of America, 1968; *Spirit* gold medal, Catholic Poetry Society of America, 1969; College of Mount Saint Vincent, outstanding teacher award, 1969, Litt.D., 1971; Leonard Covello Award, 1980; Leone di San Marco Award, 1982; Congressional Medal of Merit, 1984.

WRITINGS:

(Translator and author of introduction and notes) *The Complete Poems of Michelangelo,* Noonday, 1960.
Rind and All: Fifty Poems, Monastine Press, 1962.
(Translator and author of introduction and notes) *Lust and Liberty: The Poems of Machiavelli,* Obolensky, 1963.
The Fifth Season: Poems, Obolensky, 1964.
Envoy from Heaven (novel), Obolensky, 1965.
Dante's Inferno, as Told for Young People, Obolensky, 1965.
Dante's Purgatorio, as Told for Young People, Obolensky, 1966.
(Translator and author of introduction) Torquato Tasso, *Jerusalem Delivered,* Fairleigh Dickinson University Press, 1970.
(Translator and author of introduction) Boccaccio, *Nymphs of Fiesole,* Fairleigh Dickinson University Press, 1971.
Italian Poets of the Renaissance, Baroque Press, 1971.
(Editor and translator) *From Marino to Marinetti,* Baroque Press, 1972.
(Editor and translator) *The Age of Dante,* Baroque Press, 1972.
(Translator) *Alfieri's America the Free,* Italian-American Center, 1975.
Gente Mia and Other Poems, Italian Cultural Center, 1978.
(Translator) Tasso, *The Creation of the World* (first English translation of *Mondo Creato*), State University of New York Press, 1983.
(Translator) Luigi Pulci, *Morgante,* Indiana University Press, 1994.

IN ITALIAN

Flora (poetry), Caputo, 1947.
Amore e morte (poetry), Caputo, 1948.
Peccato e luce (poetry), Venetian Press, 1949.

La Poesia amorosa di Emily Dickinson, Venetian Press, 1950.

Dante in Licenza (novel), Nigrizia, 1951.

Wordsworthiana, Venetian Press, 1952.

Poesia missionaria in Inghilterra ed America: Storia criticaed antologica, Nigrizia, 1952.

Sonettisti Americani, introduction by Frances Winwar, Clemente Publishing Co., 1954.

L'Italia nell' opera di Frances Win war, [Chicago], 1956.

Lo Speco celeste (poetry), Editrice Ciranna, 1956.

Odi Sacre (poetry), Editrice Ciranna, 1959.

Influenza cristiana nella poesia Negro-Americana, Nigrizia, 1971.

La Parola Difficile, Schena, 1988.

La Parola Nuova (first novel in trilogy), Schena, 1991.

La Parola Antica (second novel in trilogy), Schena, 1992.

Il Ritorno (third novel in trilogy), Schena, 1992.

IN LATIN

Melos Cordia (poems), Venetian Press, 1959.

(Editor) *Viva Camena* (verse anthology), Artemis (Stuttgart), 1961.

Rosa Rosarum, American Classical League, 1984.

In Exilio Rerum, Aubanel (Avignon), 1985.

Confinia Lucis et Umbrae, Peeters (Louvain), 1989.

OTHER

Contributor of essays, reviews, and poetry to numerous periodicals, including *Modern Language Journal, Italica, Catholic World, La Paro la de Popolo, New Yorker, New York Times,* and *Yale Literary Magazine.* Translator of Giacomo Leopardi's *Canti,* published in *Italian Quarterly,* summer, 1989. Associate editor, *Spirit,* 1960-69; poetry editor, *Quccti,* 1976.

WORK IN PROGRESS: Datit's Minor Poems, for Baroque Press.

SIDELIGHTS: In his youth, Joseph Tusiani considered being a painter, then a composer; he passed, he says, "through all the forms of creative restlessness" before realizing that he sought to be a writer. As a child he remembers serving at Mass with Padre Pio, the Italian stigmatic. He arrived in America at the age of twenty-three, with the ability to read, but not speak, the English language. He had mastered the words, but found that was not adequate. He once explained to *CA:* "One must arrive at the point where mastery becomes creative atmosphere. I comforted myself with the thought that poetry had no linguistic barriers and that a poet 'could write in any idiom he has mastered, for language is but a goblet bearing the wine, the ineffable essence which gives universality to his thought and feeling.'" Tusiani's major area of interest is the Renaissance. He once told *CA* that "perhaps [Italian poet Conte Giacomo] Leopardi has influenced me most. He was the

literary god of my childhood. I am considering a verse translation of all his poetry."

Tusiani recently told *CA:* "In the past ten years I have finally published my English translation of Leopardi's *Canti,* and [my translation] of Luigi Pulci's *Morgante.* [*Morgante* is a] fifteenth-century Italian classic (thirty-one thousand lines long), which deeply influenced Lord Byron, who, incidentally, translated the first canto of it. . . . My readers—if I have any—will surely wonder why I write so much Latin in a world where very few know and read it. Who knows, maybe because I firmly believe that the salvation of our education depends on a rediscovery of our classical traditions."

*   *   *

TWITCHELL, James B(uell) 1943-

PERSONAL: Born June 18, 1943, in Burlington, VT; son of Marshal Coleman (a doctor) and Laura (a population specialist; maiden name, Tracy) Twitchell; married Mary Shepperd Poe (a law professor), June 24, 1966; children: Katherine, Elizabeth. *Education:* University of Vermont, B.A., 1962; University of North Carolina at Chapel Hill, M.A., 1966, Ph.D., 1969. *Politics:* Republican. *Religion:* "None yet." *Avocational Interests:* Cooking, racing, high-powered motorcycles.

ADDRESSES: Home—2226 Northwest Second Ave., Gainesville, FL 32603. *Office*—Department of English, 4008 Turlington Hall, University of Florida, Gainesville, FL 32611. *Agent*—Richard Brantley Agency, 708 A Trump Tower, New York, NY.

CAREER: Duke University, Durham, NC, instructor in English, 1969-70; California State College, Bakersfield, assistant professor of English, 1970-73; University of Florida, Gainesville, assistant professor, 1973-75, associate professor, 1975-80, professor of English, 1981—.

MEMBER: Modern Language Association of America, Keats Shelley Association, Wordsworth Circle, South Atlantic Modern Language Association.

AWARDS, HONORS: Ray and Pat Browne Award for best book on an aspect of popular culture, Popular Culture Association, 1985, for *Dreadful Pleasures: An Anatomy of Modern Horror;* National Book Award and National Book Critic's Circle Award nominations, both 1993, both for *Carnival Culture: The Trashing of Taste in America.*

WRITINGS:

The Living Dead: A Study of the Vampire in Romantic Literature, Duke University Press, 1981.

Romantic Horizons: Aspects of the Sublime in English Poetry and Painting, 1770-1850, University of Missouri Press, 1983.

Dreadful Pleasures: An Anatomy of Modern Horror, Oxford University Press, 1985.

Forbidden Partners: The Incest Taboo in Modern Culture, Columbia University Press, 1986.

Preposterous Violence: Fables of Aggression in Modern Culture, Oxford University Press, 1989.

Carnival Culture: The Trashing of Taste in America, Columbia University Press, 1992.

Contributor to *Moto-Cross Annual.* Contributor to literature periodicals, including *Studies in English Literature, Keats-Shelley Journal, Criticism,* and *Georgia Review.*

SIDELIGHTS: James B. Twitchell's *The Living Dead: A Study of the Vampire in Romantic Literature,* hailed by Charles Champlin of the *Los Angeles Times* as a "scholarly but invigorating and unpedantic book," examines literal and figurative vampirism in literature. In addition to the blood-sucking Dracula of Bram Stoker's famous novel, authors have used vampire-like characters to explore such ideas as "greedy love . . . homosexual attraction . . . repressed sexuality . . . and, very often, the process of artistic creation itself, Wilde's 'Dorian Gray' being very vampirical indeed," observed Champlin. The reviewer noted that Twitchell's supporting evidence is "stretched, here and there," but admitted that the author is "the first to say so." In general, Champlin assessed Twitchell's writing as "crisp and readable. If more scholars wrote as well, 'scholarly prose' would cease being a putdown." Champlin concluded, "*The Living Dead,* stretch marks and all, is a fertile, amusing search through the pre-Dracula world of vampires, lamia (female vampires), and dhampires (vampire fighters)."

About *Carnival Culture: The Trashing of Taste in America,* a *Washington Post Book World* critic remarked that Twitchell "understands the genuine and troubling importance of popular culture, and he hasn't many illusions about its aesthetic content." The reviewer found Twitchell "an academic who writes about popular culture, a combination that alone is ample reason to give any reader pause." Discussing the book's content, the reviewer commented on "the tension that is a constant undercurrent in *Carnival Culture* between its author's clear desire to construct a case for mass culture on the one hand and his equally clear distaste for so much of what is has produced on the other." John Sutherland of the *Times Literary Supplement,* however, perceived overt criticism of pop culture in the book, writing "American popular culture, according to James B. Twitchell, has become a perpetual out-of-control Mardi Gras with no Lent to follow," adding, "One suspects that Twitchell knows less than he might about the contents of the movies and texts of which he is so

grandly contemptuous." Sutherland further stated that "*Carnival Culture* is full of apocalyptic factoids which send a chill down the spine, but which are very dubious on close examination." Despite his reservations, Sutherland did commend Twitchell's detailed treatment of the entertainment industry and printing trade, labelling his descriptions "very informative," "admirably concise," and "consistently instructive."

Twitchell once told *CA:* "I have been interested in the relationship of popular culture, adolescence, and violence. I am especially interested in how codes of behavior are transmitted from generation to generation."

BIOGRAPHICAL/CRITICAL SOURCES:

PERIODICALS

Los Angeles Times, January 9, 1981.
New York Review of Books, January 30, 1986.
New York Times Book Review, January 18, 1987, p. 7.
Times Literary Supplement, March 20, 1981; July 31, 1992, p. 16.
Washington Post Book World, January 26, 1986; May 3, 1992.

*　　　*　　　*

TYDEMAN, William (Marcus) 1935-

PERSONAL: Born August 29, 1935, in Maidstone, Kent, England; son of Henry Marcus (a plant breeder) and Elizabeth Mary (a secretary; maiden name, Shepherd) Tydeman; married Jacqueline Barbara Anne Jennison (a teacher), July 29, 1961; children: Josephine Frances, Rosalind Jane. *Education:* University College, Oxford, B.A., 1959, M.Litt., 1965, M.A., 1965. *Religion:* Church of England.

ADDRESSES: Home—22 Llandegai Village, Nr Bangor, Gwynedd LL57 4HU, Wales. *Office*—School of English, University of Wales, Bangor, Gwynedd LL57 2DG, Wales.

CAREER: University of Wales, University College of North Wales, Bangor, assistant lecturer, 1961-64, lecturer, 1964-70, senior lecturer, 1970-83, university reader, 1983-86, professor of English, 1986—, acting head of department, 1983-86, head of department, 1986-92.

WRITINGS:

The Theatre in the Middle Ages: Western European Stage Conditions, circa 800-1576, Cambridge University Press, 1978.
Dr. Faustus: Text and Performance, Macmillan, 1984.
English Medieval Theatre, Routledge & Kegan Paul, 1986.
Henry V, Penguin, 1987.

T. S. Eliot: Murder in the Cathedral and the Cocktail Party, Macmillan Educational, 1988.

(With Vivien Thomas) *The State of the Art: Christopher Marlowe: A Guide through the Critical Maze,* Bristol Press, 1989.

The Bancrofts at the Prince of Wales's Theatre, Chadwyck-Healey, in press.

EDITOR

English Poetry, 1400-1580, Heinemann, 1970.

(With Alun R. Jones) *Wordsworth: Lyrical Ballads* (casebook), Macmillan, 1972.

(With Jones) *Coleridge: The Ancient Mariner and Other Poems* (casebook), Macmillan, 1973.

(With Jones) Joseph Hucks, *A Pedestrian Tour through Wales,* University of Wales Press, 1979.

Plays by Tom Robertson (four dramas), Cambridge University Press, 1982.

Wilde: Comedies (casebook), Macmillan, 1982.

Four Tudor Comedies: Jacke Jugeler, Roister Doister, Gammer Gurton's Nedle, Mother Bombie, Penguin, 1984.

(And contributor) *The Welsh Connection* (essays), Gomer Press, 1985.

Two Tudor Tragedies (contains *Gorboduc* and *The Spanish Tragedy*), Penguin, 1992.

(With Thomas) *The Sources of Marlowe's Plays,* Routledge & Kegan Paul, in press.

WORK IN PROGRESS: English Drama before Shakespeare; with Steven T. Price, *Oscar Wilde: Salome.*

SIDELIGHTS: William Tydeman's 1978 book, *The Theatre in the Middle Ages,* is a "useful publication" that "can be defined as a extensive Forschungbericht, an analytic survey of the various attempts at reconstructing forms of medieval play productions," reported A. M. Nagler in *Theatre Journal.* Nagler commended Tydeman for his "clear presentation of the issues and his urbane treatment of conflicting views" on the development of medieval drama. Writing in *History,* R. B. Dobson described Tydeman as "an obvious enthusiast for his subject," who "is not only exceptionally well-informed but also preserves a very neutral and dispassionate stance towards the many contradictory interpretations of medieval dramatic development advanced in recent years." Several critics praised the author for writing a book that can be enjoyed by both specialists and non-specialists. According to a reviewer in *Antiquaries Journals,* "Mr. Tydeman has produced a readable guide to the whole field of medieval drama." And Stanley Kahrl concluded in *Speculum* that *The Theatre in the Middle Ages* is "certain to become the standard work for nonspecialists and specialists alike."

Tydeman edited and wrote the introduction to *Plays by Tom Robertson,* one volume in the series "British and American Playwrights." Contained in Tydeman's book are four dramas by the Victorian playwright: "Society," "Ours," "Caste," and "School." Julie Hankey wrote in the *Times Literary Supplement* that "Robertson's full stage directions and William Tydeman's theatrically informative introduction" allow the reader to imagine both the plays in production and the middle class Victorian theatrical audience, with whom the playwright's amiable, sentimental pieces—with their staginess and Victorian assumptions about class and character—were extraordinarily popular. Writing in *Notes and Queries,* Peter Mudford described Tydeman's introduction as "informative and well-judged," adding that the author showed a "wide understanding of nineteenth-century theatre, and a clear perceptiveness about the significance of Robertson's contribution to it."

Tydeman told *CA:* "Although I wrote my postgraduate thesis at Oxford on early Tudor poetry, my first love in both the academic and recreational spheres has always been dramatic literature. As a result, nearly all of my future publications are likely to deal in some form with the inter-relationship between the play text on the printed page and its realization on the stage. My book on the theatre in the Middle Ages was the first to attempt a synoptic view of the European stage from the beginnings of liturgical drama to the building of the first custom built playhouses of the sixteenth century. I have now supplemented this general account with a study of five Medieval English plays in performances attempting to reconstruct the probable modes of presentation. I have also a great love for the Victorian theatre, and I plan to develop my study of Robertson into a survey of the gradually emerging taste for realism in nineteenth-century English drama, towards which my monograph on the Bancroft management of the Prince of Wales's Theatre makes a fresh contribution.

Tydeman added: "A large part of the past few years has been taken up with a joint project co-editing the sources of Christopher Marlowe's dramatic works, which we hope will prove helpful in making this rich material readily accessible to general readers and students, as well as critics and scholars."

BIOGRAPHICAL/CRITICAL SOURCES:

PERIODICALS

Antiquaries Journal, Volume 59, number 2, 1979.
History, October, 1980.
Notes and Queries, December, 1980; December, 1984.
Review of English Studies, August, 1980.
Speculum, October, 1980.
Theatre Journal, March, 1980.
Times Literary Supplement, November 23, 1979; August 20, 1982; April 5, 1985.
Washington Post Book World, September 9, 1984.

V-W

VAN ARSDEL, Rosemary T(horstenson) 1926-

PERSONAL: Born September 1, 1926, in Seattle, WA; daughter of Odin (a pharmacist) and Helen (McGregor) Thorstenson; married Paul P. Van Arsdel, Jr. (a physician), July 7, 1950; children: Mary, Andrew. *Education:* University of Washington, Seattle, B.A., 1947, M.A., 1948; Columbia University, Ph.D., 1961. *Religion:* Episcopalian.

ADDRESSES: Home—4702 Northeast 39th St., Seattle, WA 98105. *Office*—Department of English, University of Puget Sound, Tacoma, WA 98416.

CAREER: University of Washington, Seattle, acting instructor in English, 1961, acting assistant professor of literature, 1963; University of Puget Sound, Tacoma, WA, lecturer, 1966-67, assistant professor, 1967-70, associate professor, 1970-77, professor of English, 1977-87, distinguished professor of English emerita, 1987—, chairman of department, 1970-75, adjunct professor in School of Law, 1973-77, director of Writing Institute, 1976-86.

MEMBER: Modern Language Association of America, National Council of Teachers of English, Research Society for Victorian Periodicals (secretary, 1973-77; vice-president, 1977-79; president, 1981-83), Royal Society of Literature, Oxford Bibliographical Society.

WRITINGS:

EDITOR

(With J. Don Vann) *Victorian Periodicals: A Guide to Research,* Modern Language Association of America, Volume 1, 1978, Volume 2, 1988.

(With Gordon S. Haight) *George Eliot: A Centenary Tribute,* Macmillan, 1982.

(With Vann) *Victorian Periodicals and Victorian Society,* University of Toronto Press, 1993.

OTHER

Associate editor and contributor, *The Wellesley Index to Victorian Periodicals, 1824-1900,* five volumes, University of Toronto Press, 1966-88. Contributor to books, including *Papers for the Millions: The New Journalism in Britain, 1850s to 1914,* edited by Joel Wiener, Greenwood Press, 1988, and *Approaches to Teaching George Eliot's Middlemarch,* edited by Kathleen Blake, Modern Language Association of America, 1990. Also contributor to *Dictionary of British Radicals,* Harvester Press, 1976; *Encyclopedia of Victorian Britain,* Garland Publishing, 1988; *Dictionary of Literary Biography,* Volume 106: *British Literary Publishing Houses, 1820-1880,* Gale, 1991; and *The 1890s: An Encyclopedia of British Literature, Art, and Culture,* Garland Publishing, 1992. Contributor to British and American scholarly journals. Member of editorial board, *Union List of Victorian Serials* and *Victorian Review.*

WORK IN PROGRESS: A biography of Florence Fenwick-Miller (1854-1935), "pioneer woman journalist, feminist, and platform speaker"; *Victorian Periodicals and the Nineteenth Century British Empire.*

SIDELIGHTS: Rosemary T. Van Arsdel once commented to *CA:* "My primary scholarly activities include studying British Victorian and Edwardian periodicals, and making them yield their secrets. They offer an unparalleled opportunity for a scholar to re-enter a bygone era.

"Before retirement, I was also very involved with the writing program at the University of Puget Sound, and in the nationwide effort being made to preserve our language. At the university, we offer a senior level Writing Institute, which has had good success in training students to write professionally and enter the job market as writers."

Van Arsdel recently told *CA:* "Now I am a full-time, practicing research scholar and author, free to roam the great libraries of the world and to follow intellectual curiosity to its outer limits."

* * *

van LAWICK-GOODALL, Jane
See GOODALL, Jane

* * *

WALKER, Deward E(dgar), Jr. 1935-

PERSONAL: Born August 3, 1935, in Johnson City, TN; married, 1959. *Education:* Student at Eastern Oregon College, 1953-54, 1956-58, and Mexico City College (now University of the Americas), 1958; University of Oregon, B.A., 1961, Ph.D., 1964; Washington State University, graduate study, 1962.

ADDRESSES: Office—Department of Anthropology, University of Colorado, Boulder, CO 80309.

CAREER: Applied anthropologist, 1963-64; assistant professor of anthropology at George Washington University, Washington, DC, 1964-65, and Washington State University, Pullman, 1965-67; research collaborator at Washington State University at Pullman and Idaho State University at Pocatello, 1967-69; University of Idaho, Moscow, associate professor of sociology and anthropology and chair of department, 1967-69, affiliate faculty member, 1971—; University of Colorado, Boulder, professor of anthropology, 1969—, research associate, Institute of Behavioral Science, 1969-74, associate dean of graduate school, 1973-76; lecturer, Department of Religious Studies, 1982; adjunct professor, Center for the Study of Ethnicity and Race in the Americas, 1990—. Evaluator of various schools, educational laboratory programs, and curriculum innovations concerning problems of Native American education. Expert witness and consultant for the Nez Perce, Umatilla (CTUIR), confederated Salish and Kootenai, Shoshone-Bannock, and Yakima tribes, and to the board of National Missions of United Presbyterian Church, the American Indian Civil Liberties Trust, the advisory board for Indian education of the Northwest Regional Educational Laboratory, and the Native American Rights Fund; member of the technical steering panel of the U.S. Department of Energy's Hanford Environmental Dose Reconstruction Project. *Military service:* U.S. Army, 1954-62; became sergeant.

MEMBER: American Anthropological Association (fellow), American Association for the Advancement of Science, Northwestern Anthropological Conference, Society for Applied Anthropology (fellow; treasurer, 1976-79;

chairman of High Plains Regional Section, 1980-82), American Academy of Political and Social Sciences, Sigma Xi.

AWARDS, HONORS: Grants from National Science Foundation, 1964-65, 1967-68, 1970, National Park Service, 1969-73, National Endowment for the Humanities, 1970-71, and Public Health Service, 1971-75; Sigma Xi Prize for best research contribution at University of Idaho, 1967, 1968; lifetime award from Society for Applied Anthropology, 1982, for contributions to applied anthropology; national award, Bureau of Land Management, 1989, for conservation of natural and cultural resources.

WRITINGS:

A Survey of Nez Perces Religion, Board of National Missions (New York), 1964.

(Contributor) Stuart Levine and Nancy Lurie, editors, *The American Indian Today,* Everett/Edwards, 1966.

An Examination of American Indian Reaction to Proposals of the Commissioner of Indian Affairs for General Legislation, 1967, Department of Anthropology, Washington State University, 1967.

Mutual Cross-Utilization of Economic Resources in the Plateau: An Example from Aboriginal Nez Perce Fishing Practices, Laboratory of Anthropology, Washington State University, 1967.

Conflict and Schism in Nez Perce Acculturation, Washington State University Press, 1968, 2nd edition, with an introduction by Robert Hackenberg, 1985.

(Editor and contributor) *Systems of North American Witchcraft and Sorcery,* University Press of Idaho, 1970.

(Editor and author of introduction) *An Exploration of the Reservation System in North America: A Special Issue,* University of Idaho, 1971.

American Indians of Idaho, University of Idaho, 1971, revised edition published as *Indians of Idaho,* 1978.

Emergent Native Americans: A Reader in Culture Contact, Little, Brown, 1972.

(And translator and editor with Allen P. Slickpoo and Leroy Seth) *Nu-Mee-Pom Tit-Wah-Tit: Nez Perces Legends,* [Lapwai, Idaho], 1972.

(And translator and editor with Slickpoo and others) *Noon Nee-Me-Poo* (title means "We, the Nez Perces"), [Lapwai], 1973.

(And translator and editor with Virginia Beavert and others) *The Way It Was—Anaku Iwacha: Yakima Indian Legends,* Franklin Press, 1974.

(With Sylvester Lahren, Jr.) *Anthropological Guide for the Coulee Dam National Recreation Area,* University of Idaho, 1977.

(Editor and translator) Gonzalo Aguirre Beltran, *Regions of Refuge,* Society for Applied Anthropology, 1978.

Myths of Idaho Indians, illustrated by Gregory Pole, University Press of Idaho, 1980.

(With Haruo Aoki) *Nez Perces Oral Narratives,* University of California Press, 1989.

Witchcraft and Sorcery of the American Native Peoples, preface by David Carrasco, University of Idaho Press, 1989.

Author and editor of special curriculum materials for Native American students. Contributor of articles on Indians of the Northwest and reviews to journals, including *Northwest Anthropological Research Notes, American Antiquity, American Anthropologist, Southwest Journal of Anthropology,* and *Ethnohistory.* Founder and editor with Roderick Sprague, *Northwest Anthropological Research Notes,* 1966—; editor, *Human Organization,* 1970-76; editor, *Plateau Volume: Handbook of North American Indians,* Smithsonian Institution, 1971-92; associate editor, *American Anthropologist,* 1973-74; consulting editor, *Reader's Digest,* 1980—.

*   *   *

WALKER, George F. 1947-

PERSONAL: Born August 23, 1947, in Toronto, Ontario, Canada; son of Malcolm (a laborer) and Florence (Braybrook) Walker; married c. 1965 (marriage ended); married Susan Purdy (an actor); children: Renata, Courtney.

ADDRESSES: Agent—Great North Artists Management, Inc., 350 Dupont St., Toronto, Ontario M5V 1R5, Canada.

CAREER: Playwright. Factory Theatre Lab, Toronto, Ontario, Canada, dramaturge, 1972-73, resident playwright, 1972-76. Has directed productions of his own work, including *Ramona and the White Slaves,* 1976, and *Rumours of Our Death,* 1980.

AWARDS, HONORS: Awarded five grants from Canada Council; Chalmers Award for Distinguished Playwriting nominations, 1977, for *Zastrozzi: The Master of Discipline,* and 1981, for *Theatre of the Film Noir;* Dora Award for directing, 1982, for *Rumours of Our Death;* Chalmers Award for Distinguished Playwrighting, 1985, and Governor General's Literary Award for drama, Canada Council, for *Criminals in Love.*

WRITINGS:

PLAYS

Prince of Naples (produced in Toronto, Ontario, Canada, at Factory Theatre Lab, 1971; produced as a radio play by Canadian Broadcasting Corp. [CBC-Radio], 1973), Playwrights Canada (Toronto), 1973.

Ambush at Tether's End (produced at Factory Theatre Lab, 1971; produced as a radio play by CBC-Radio, 1974), Playwrights Canada, 1974.

Sacktown Rag (produced at Factory Theatre Lab, 1972), Playwrights Canada, 1972.

Bagdad Saloon (produced in London, England, at Bush Theatre, 1973, later produced at Factory Theatre Lab, 1973), Playwrights Canada, 1973.

Demerit, produced at Factory Theatre Lab, 1974.

(And director) *Beyond Mozambique* (produced at Factory Theatre Lab, 1974), Playwrights Co-op, 1975.

(And director) *Ramona and the White Slaves,* produced at Factory Theatre Lab, 1976.

Gossip, produced in Toronto at Toronto Free Theatre, 1977.

Zastrozzi: The Master of Discipline (also known as *Zastrozzi: The Master of Discipline: A Melodrama;* produced at Toronto Free Theatre, 1977; later produced in New York at New York Shakespeare Festival, 1981), Playwrights Canada, 1977, second edition, 1991.

Three Plays by George F. Walker (contains *Bagdad Saloon, Beyond Mozambique,* and *Ramona and the White Slaves*), Coach House Press (Toronto), 1978.

Filthy Rich (produced at Toronto Free Theatre, 1979; later produced in New York City at 47th Street Theatre, 1985), Playwrights Canada, 1979.

(And director) *Rumours of Our Death,* produced at Factory Theatre Lab, 1980.

(And director) *Theatre of the Film Noir,* produced by Factory Theatre Lab at Adelaide Court Theatre, 1981.

Science and Madness, produced in Toronto at Tarragon Theatre, 1982.

(And director) *The Art of War* (also known as *The Art of War: An Adventure;* produced by Factory Theatre Lab at Toronto Workshop Productions, 1983), Playwrights Canada, 1982.

Criminals in Love (also known as *George F. Walker's Criminals in Love;* produced at Factory Theatre [formerly Factory Theatre Lab], 1984), Playwrights Canada, 1984.

The Power Plays (contains *Gossip, Filthy Rich,* and *The Art of War*), Coach House Press, 1984.

Better Living, produced in Toronto at CentreStage, 1986.

Beautiful City, produced at Factory Theatre, c. 1987.

Nothing Sacred: Based on "Fathers and Sons" by Ivan Turgenev, Coach House Press, 1988.

Love and Anger, Coach House Press (Ontario), 1990.

Escape from Happiness, InBook, 1992.

Also author of *The East End Plays,* 1988. Works represented in anthologies, including *Now in Paperback: Canadian Playwrights of the 1970s,* edited by Connie Brissenden, Fineglow Plays (Toronto), 1973, and *The Factory Lab Anthology,* edited by Brissenden, Talonbooks (Vancouver), 1974. Contributor to periodicals, including *Descant.*

FOR TELEVISION

Microdrama, Canadian Broadcasting Corp. (CBC-TV), 1976.
Strike, CBC-TV, 1976.
Sam, Grace, Doug, and the Dog, CBC-TV, 1976.
Overlap, CBC-TV, 1977.
Capital Punishment, CBC-TV, 1977.

FOR RADIO

The Private Man, CBC, 1973.
Quiet Days in Limbo, CBC, 1977.
Desert's Revenge, CBC, 1984.

SIDELIGHTS: George F. Walker is a prominent Canadian playwright whose works are characterized by their emphasis on dark comedy and Walker's satirical, contemporary style, which is influenced by popular culture. His long affiliation with the Factory Theatre (formerly the Factory Theatre Lab), which features innovative productions, has brought many of his acclaimed works to the stage, including *Rumours of Our Death, Theatre of the Film Noir,* and *The Art of War.*

Walker's popular 1984 play *Criminals in Love* was awarded the prestigious Governor General's Literary Award; it follows the lives of two young lovers, Junior Dawson, a shipping clerk, and Gail. Junior and Gail are troubled by a cast of characters, mostly Junior's father, a jailed crook whose criminal habits are eventually forced on Junior and Gail by Junior's Aunt Winerva. Walker, according to *Books in Canada* contributor Richard Plant, described the play as one in which "two kids in love have a dilemma, which becomes a crime, then a revolution." In *Canadian Theatre Review,* Paul Walsh wrote that *Criminals in Love* "speaks with an authenticity that renders even the zaniest improbabilities and cliches acutely real. . . . As we try to make sense of a process that constantly eludes us, we want to believe that things will work out for [Walker's characters] because we have come to care for them." James Harrison, writing in *Theatrum,* noted that "George Walker deserves the recognition [*Criminals in Love* has brought him]. His sharp perceptions, his knowledge of dramatic structuring, and his willingness to tackle intelligent themes indicate his voice will continue to be an exciting one in Canadian literature."

BIOGRAPHICAL/CRITICAL SOURCES:

BOOKS

Wallace, Robert, and Cynthia Zimmerman, *The Work: Conversations with English-Canadian Playwrights,* Coach House Press, 1982, pp. 212-225.

PERIODICALS

Books in Canada, April, 1980, p. 5; April, 1982, p. 10; April, 1985, pp. 11-14; April, 1986, pp. 16-18; March, 1989, p. 28; November, 1992, p. 34.
Canadian Drama/L'Art Dramatique Canadien, Volume 10, number 2, 1984, pp. 195-206; Volume 11, number 1, 1985, pp. 141-49 and 221-25.
Canadian Forum, August/September, 1986, pp. 6-11.
Canadian Literature, summer, 1980, pp. 87-103; winter, 1990, pp. 118, 164.
Canadian Theatre Review, winter, 1985, pp. 144-45.
Globe and Mail (Toronto), November 8, 1984, p. E5.
Los Angeles Times, June 14, 1985.
Performing Arts in Canada, fall, 1981, pp. 43-46.
Scene Changes, October, 1975.
Theatrum, April, 1985, pp. 11-14.
Times (London), July 1, 1983.
University of Toronto Quarterly, summer, 1975; fall, 1986, pp. 65-66.
Variety, December 12, 1984, p. 130.
Village Voice, April 2, 1979.*

*   *   *

WATTS, Helen L. Hoke   1903-1990
(Helen Hoke; Helen Sterling, a pseudonym)

PERSONAL: Born in 1903 in California, PA; died of pneumonia, March 26, 1990, in Bethesda, MD; married John Hoke (an editor); marriage ended; married Franklin Watts (a publisher), May 25, 1945; children: (first marriage) John Lindsay.

ADDRESSES: Home—11 Belgravia House, 2 Halkin Pl., London SW1, England. *Office*—F. Watts Ltd., 1 Vere St., London W1N 9HQ, England.

CAREER: Worked as a teacher and journalist; Franklin Watts, Inc., vice-president and editor-in-chief, beginning 1948, became director of international projects; president of Helen Hoke Associates (consulting and publishing firm), 1956—; author and editor of books for children.

WRITINGS:

UNDER NAME HELEN HOKE

Mr. Sweeney (illustrated by William Wills), Holt, 1940.
(With Richard C. Gill) *Paco Goes to the Fair: A Story of Far-Away Ecuador* (illustrated by Ruth Gannett), Holt, 1940.
(With Gill) *Story of the Other America* (illustrated by Manuel R. Regalado), Houghton, 1941.
(With Miriam Teichner) *The Fuzzy Kitten* (illustrated by Meg Wohlberg), Messner, 1941.
Major and the Kitten (illustrated by Diana Thorne), Holt, 1941.

(With Natalie Fox) *The Wooly Lamb* (illustrated by Sally Tate), Messner, 1942.

The Furry Bear (illustrated by Tate), Messner, 1943.

Doctor, the Puppy Who Learned (illustrated by Thorne), Messner, 1944.

Shep and the Baby (illustrated by Thorne), Messner, 1944.

The Shaggy Pony (illustrated by Dick Hart), Messner, 1944.

Mrs. Silk (illustrated by Thorne), Veritas Press, 1945.

The Fuzzy Puppy (illustrated by Hart), Messner, 1945.

Grocery Kitty (illustrated by Harry Lees), Reynal & Hitchcock, 1946.

Too Many Kittens (illustrated by Lees), McKay, 1947.

Factory Kitty (illustrated by Lees), F. Watts, 1949.

The First Book of Dolls (illustrated by Jean Michener), F. Watts, 1954.

(With Walter Pels) *The First Book of Toys* (illustrated by Michener), F. Watts, 1957.

(With son, John Hoke) *Music Boxes: Their Lore and Lure* (illustrated by Nancy Martin), Hawthorn Books, 1957.

The First Book of Tropical Mammals (illustrated by Helene Carter), F. Watts, 1958.

One Thousand Ways to Make $1,000 in Your Spare Time, Bantam, 1959.

Arctic Mammals (illustrated by Jean Zallinger), F. Watts, 1969.

The Big Dog and the Very Little Cat (illustrated by Thorne), F. Watts, 1969.

Etiquette: Your Ticket to Good Times (illustrated by Carol Wilde), F. Watts, 1970.

Ants (illustrated by Arabelle Wheatley), F. Watts, 1970.

Jokes and Fun (illustrated by Tony Parkhouse), F. Watts, 1972.

(With Valerie Pitt) *Whales* (illustrated by Thomas R. Funderburk), F. Watts, 1973.

Hoke's Jokes, Cartoons, and Funny Things (illustrated by Eric Hill), F. Watts, 1973.

(With Pitt) *Fleas,* F. Watts, 1974.

(With Pitt) *Owls* (illustrated by Robert Jefferson), F. Watts, 1974.

Riddle Giggles (illustrated by Parkhouse), F. Watts, 1975.

(With Oliver Neshamkin) *Jokes, Fun, and Folly,* F. Watts, 1975.

UNDER PSEUDONYM HELEN STERLING

Little Choo Choo (illustrated by Denison Budd), F. Watts, 1944.

The Horse that Takes the Milk around (illustrated by Marjorie Hartwell), F. Watts, 1946.

Little Moo and the Circus (illustrated by Lees), F. Watts, 1945.

The Biggest Family in the Town (illustrated by Vance Locke), McKay, 1947.

EDITOR, UNDER NAME HELEN HOKE

Jokes, Jokes, Jokes (illustrated by Richard Erdoes), F. Watts, 1954.

The Family Book of Humor, Hanover House, 1957.

(With Boris Randolph) *Puns, Puns, Puns* (illustrated by Seymour Nydorf), F. Watts, 1958.

Witches, Witches, Witches (illustrated by W. R. Lohse), F. Watts, 1958.

Alaska, Alaska, Alaska (illustrated by R. M. Six), F. Watts, 1960.

Nurses, Nurses, Nurses, F. Watts, 1961.

Patriotism, Patriotism, Patriotism (illustrated by Leonard E. Fisher), F. Watts, 1963.

More Jokes, Jokes, Jokes (illustrated by Erdoes), F. Watts, 1965.

Spooks, Spooks, Spooks (illustrated by Lohse), F. Watts, 1966.

The Big Book of Jokes (illustrated by Erdoes), F. Watts, 1971.

Dragons, Dragons, Dragons (illustrated by Carol Barker), F. Watts, 1972.

Weirdies, Weirdies, Weirdies (illustrated by Charles Keeping), F. Watts, 1973.

Jokes, Jests, and Jollies (illustrated by True Kelley), Ginn, 1973.

Jokes, Jokes, Jokes, 2 (illustrated by Haro), F. Watts, 1973, published as *Jokes, Jests, and Guffaws,* 1975.

Monsters, Monsters, Monsters (illustrated by Keeping), F. Watts, 1974.

Devils, Devils, Devils (illustrated by Barker), F. Watts, 1976.

More Riddles, Riddles, Riddles (illustrated by Haro), F. Watts, 1976.

Ghosts and Ghastlies (illustrated by Bill Prosser), F. Watts, 1976.

SIDELIGHTS: Helen L. Hoke Watts's early career was marked by her stories for children, written under the name Helen Hoke as well as under her pseudonym, Helen Sterling. *Kirkus Review*'s description of *Factory Kitty* included, "This is perhaps the best of the career kitten stories—from the point of view of text. And the Harry Lees pictures are beguiling, too." The *New York Times* added, "Strong men in action, fascinating machinery, and the engaging calico kitten are dramatized in colorful illustrations which complement the well-told story."

BIOGRAPHICAL/CRITICAL SOURCES:

PERIODICALS

Kirkus Reviews, May 15, 1949.
New York Times, July 17, 1949.
Publishers Weekly, September 1, 1975.

* * *

WEBER, Ronald 1934-

PERSONAL: Born September 21, 1934, in Mason City, IA; son of Harley George and Anne M. (McCauley) Weber; married Patricia Jean Carroll, December 27, 1955; children: Elizabeth, Andrea, Kathryn. *Education:* University of Notre Dame, B.A., 1957; University of Iowa, M.F.A., 1960; University of Minnesota—Twin Cities, Ph.D., 1967.

ADDRESSES: Home—52513 Gumwood Rd., Granger, IN 46530. *Office*—Department of American Studies, University of Notre Dame, Notre Dame, IN 46556.

CAREER: Loras College, Dubuque, IA, instructor in English, 1960-62; University of Notre Dame, Notre Dame, IN, assistant professor, 1963-67, associate professor, 1967-76, professor of American studies, 1976—, chairman of department, 1970-77, chairman of Graduate Program in Communication Arts, 1972-79. University of Coimbra, Fulbright lecturer, 1968-69, senior Fulbright lecturer, 1982.

MEMBER: American Studies Association, Great Lakes American Studies Association (president, 1980-82).

AWARDS, HONORS: National Endowment for the Humanities fellowship, 1972-73; *The Literature of Fact* was included on *Choice*'s outstanding academic book list, 1981-82; Gannett fellow, Columbia University, 1985-86.

WRITINGS:

O Romance Americano (study of the American novel), Livraria Almedina (Coimbra, Portugal), 1969.
(Editor and contributor) *The Reporter as Artist: A Look at the New Journalism Controversy,* Hastings House, 1974.
(Editor with Walter Nicgorski, and contributor) *An Almost Chosen People: The Moral Aspirations of Americans,* University of Notre Dame Press, 1976.
The Literature of Fact: Literary Nonfiction in American Writing, Ohio University Press, 1980.
Seeing Earth: Space Exploration in American Writing, Ohio University Press, 1984.
Company Spook, St. Martin's, 1986.
Troubleshooter, St. Martin's, 1988.
Hemingway's Art of Nonfiction, Macmillan, 1990.

Contributor of more than forty articles to periodicals, including *Cimarron Review, Virginia Quarterly Review, Se-*

wanee Review, South Atlantic Quarterly, Journal of Popular Culture, and *Review of Politics.*

WORK IN PROGRESS: A book on the history of Midwestern literature.

* * *

WEIL, Andrew (Thomas) 1942-

PERSONAL: Surname rhymes with "style"; born June 8, 1942, in Philadelphia, PA; son of Daniel P. (a store owner) and Jenny (a designer of women's hats; maiden name, Silverstein) Weil; married Sabine Charlotte Kremp, March 11, 1990; children: Diana Dakota; stepchildren: three. *Education:* Harvard University, A.B., 1964, M.D., 1968. *Avocational Interests:* Nutrition, gardening, cooking, exercise, yoga, wilderness, and mind-body interaction.

ADDRESSES: Home—1975 West Hunter Rd., Tucson, AZ 85737. *Agent*—International Creative Management, 40 West 57th St., New York, NY 10019.

CAREER: Botanical Museum of Harvard University, Cambridge, MA, research associate in ethnopharmacology, 1971—; private practice as a physician specializing in holistic medicine, Tucson, AZ, 1976—. University of Arizona, College of Medicine, began as lecturer, currently associate director of Division of Social Perspectives in Medicine. Fellow, Institute of Current World Affairs, New York City, 1971-75. *Wartime service:* U.S. Public Health Service, 1969-70; became lieutenant.

MEMBER: Linnean Society of London (fellow), Beneficial Plant Research Association (president), Sigma Xi (Harvard-Radcliffe chapter), Center for Integrative Medicine (president).

AWARDS, HONORS: Fellowship, Institute of Current World Affairs, 1971-75; Norman E. Zinberg Award for Achievement in Medicine and Treatment, 1989; Smart Family Foundation grant for development of an innovative curriculum on preventive health maintenance for children, 1992.

WRITINGS:

The Natural Mind: A New Way of Looking at Drugs and the Higher Consciousness, Houghton, 1972, revised edition published as *The Natural Mind: An Investigation of Drugs and the Higher Consciousness,* 1986.
The Marriage of the Sun and Moon: A Quest for Unity in Consciousness, Houghton, 1980.
(With Winifred Rosen) *Chocolate to Morphine: Understanding Mind-Active Drugs,* Houghton, 1983, revised edition published as *From Chocolate to Morphine: Ev-*

erything You Need to Know About Mind-Altering Drugs, 1993.

Health and Healing: Understanding Conventional and Alternative Medicine, Houghton, 1983.

Natural Health, Natural Medicine: A Comprehensive Guide for Wellness and Self-Care, Houghton, 1990.

Contributor of articles to *Harper's, Psychology Today,* and other periodicals and journals. Member of editorial advisory board, *Journal of Psychoactive Drugs* and *Journal of Ethnopharmacology.*

WORK IN PROGRESS: Research on the medicinal value of plants and other scientific projects; "the creation of a Center for Integrative Medicine at the University of Arizona to train physicians to combine the best ideas and practices of conventional and alternative medicines."

SIDELIGHTS: Andrew Weil's life work, according to James Lardner in the *Washington Post,* is "the study of how and why human beings the world over are forever trying to change what's happening inside their brains." Weil's first three books, *The Natural Mind: A New Way of Looking at Drugs and the Higher Consciousness, The Marriage of the Sun and Moon: A Quest for Unity in Consciousness,* and *Chocolate to Morphine: Understanding Mind-Active Drugs,* concentrate on this much coveted mind-alteration and suggest that this desire is absolutely normal. Reflecting on *The Marriage of the Sun and Moon, New York Times Book Review* contributor Richard Lingeman generalizes that Weil's "objective is the 'high'—a state of altered consciousness to be valued because it promotes a 'fuller use of the nervous system' and 'the emergence of unconscious forces long denied by our culture.'" Consequently, this pioneering doctor who graduated from Harvard Medical School in 1968 has spent years experimenting with a wide variety of mind-altering substances and experiences, from mangos, coca plants, and mushrooms to solar eclipses, magic, and sweat lodges. In *The Marriage of the Sun and Moon,* Lingeman sees Weil as "an explorer of off-the-beaten-track pharmacological and spiritual byways, observing the local flora, fauna and ethnology" of the Americas and East Africa. Psychoactive experiences, Weil explains, are ways in which man can unite the two extremes of his consciousness, ways in which he can wed his rational "solar consciousness" and his intuitive, and often repressed, "lunar consciousness."

Weil's belief that drugs in themselves are neither good nor bad is apparent in his third book, *Chocolate to Morphine.* Written with Winifred Rosen, the book is a consumer's guide to the effects and dangers of both legal and illegal drugs. Knowledge about drugs is one way to prevent addiction, Weil maintains. "Instead of wasting so much time, money and energy fighting the hopeless battle against existing drug abuse," writes Weil, "society must

begin to help people avoid becoming abusers in the first place." Though Weil advocates the altering of one's consciousness, he believes man can satisfy these needs without the use of drugs. Witnessing a solar eclipse is one way of experiencing a nonchemical high because the world is literally seen in a different light, theorizes Weil.

Health and Healing: Understanding Conventional and Alternative Medicine differs from Weil's previous books because it speaks more on healing than on "highs." In *Health and Healing,* the "medical philosopher" Weil, so called by Sandy Rovner in her *Washington Post Book World* review, studies alternative medical treatments, such as homeopathy, acupuncture, and chiropody, as well as traditional medical treatments. Rovner claims that the book is a "call for allopathic medical science to research rather than to reject some of the results of alternative medicine . . . and Weil believes we need these alternative measures because conventional medicine is 'too expensive, too invasive, too dangerous.'"

One fundamental feature of *Health and Healing* is Weil's principle that the mind has healing power in regard to the body. Healing comes from within, not from without, Weil conveys, which is why he believes cancer is a preventable disease. "Weil is so sure the mind can play an active role in healing that he frequently recommends 'visualization' as an adjunct to everything else," notes Jim Spencer in the *Chicago Tribune.* "Meditation-visualization," Weil says, "seems to be one way of suppressing or stimulating the immune system. You visualize healthy cells destroying cancer cells." Ultimately for Rovner, *Health and Healing* "at its deepest level . . . is a warning and a challenge to medical science to open up, to demystify and, probably most important, not to reject the apparent anomalies of alternative medicine out of hand." Weil, invariably seen as an anomaly himself, though respected in his field, employs what Spencer has termed "participatory journalism." "I'm willing to try anything once—if I'm fairly sure it won't kill me," admits Weil in the *Washington Post.*

Weil told *CA:* "I am unusual as a physician with an undergraduate degree in botany, symbolic of my commitment to Nature as the ultimate healer. In my medical work I see patients from all parts of the country and from other countries who are looking for alternatives to the recommendations of conventional medicine. I believe that all healing results from the operation of the body's innate healing mechanisms and that the best treatments are the gentlest, most natural ones that can activate those mechanisms. The kind of medicine I practice is in increasing demand, but the supply of doctors doing it is yet small. For that reason I am trying to train others.

"I enjoy living in the Sonoran desert outside of Tucson, with easy access to spectacular mountains. In recent years

I have been traveling a lot, to lecture and give workshops, as well as to pursue research on medicinal plants. I teach regularly in Japan, lecturing in medical schools there and working to nurture the holistic medical movement, which is just beginning in that country.

"Writing remains for me a principal focus of my work. I learned to do it as an editor of the Harvard *Crimson,* and as editor-in-chief of the *Harvard Review* in the 1960s. In medical school I taught courses in expository writing for Harvard undergraduates. There is so much bad writing in the sciences. Many people think they cannot understand scientific subjects because the content is difficult, when, in fact, the problem is that the writing (and the thinking behind it) is not clear."

BIOGRAPHICAL/CRITICAL SOURCES:

BOOKS

Weil, Andrew, *Chocolate to Morphine: Understanding Mind Active Drugs,* Houghton, 1983.
Weil, *Health and Healing: Understanding Conventional and Alternative Medicine,* Houghton, 1983.
Weil, *The Marriage of the Sun and Moon: A Quest for Unity in Consciousness,* Houghton, 1980.

PERIODICALS

Chicago Tribune, February 20, 1984.
Harper's, November, 1973.
Los Angeles Times Book Review, February 23, 1986.
New York Times Book Review, October 5, 1980.
Psychology Today, July, 1974.
Washington Post, June 5, 1983.
Washington Post Book World, February 18, 1984.

* * *

WELCH, Don(ovan LeRoy) 1932-

PERSONAL: Born June 3, 1932, in Hastings, NE; son of Howard L. (an automobile dealer) and Genevieve B. (Greenslit) Welch; married Marcia Lee Zorn, June 14, 1953; children: Shannon, Timaree, Erin, Kael, Chad, Keir. *Education:* Kearney State College, B.A., 1954; University of Northern Colorado, M.A., 1957; University of Nebraska, Ph.D., 1965.

ADDRESSES: Home—611 West 27th, Kearney, NE 68847. *Office*—Department of English, University of Nebraska at Kearney, 905 West 25th St., Kearney, NE 68849.

CAREER: High school teacher of English and speech in Fort Morgan, CO, 1957-58; high school teacher of English and French in Gothenburg, NE, 1958-59; University of Nebraska at Kearney, Kearney, NE, professor of English,

1959-80, Paul and Calrice Reynolds Distinguished Professor of Poetry, 1989—. Publicity director for American Homing Pigeon Union, 1972; poet-in-the-schools, Nebraska Arts Council, 1975-85. *Military service:* U.S. Army, Counter-Intelligence Corps, 1954-56.

AWARDS, HONORS: Pablo Neruda Prize for poetry, *Nimrod,* 1980, for "The Rarer Game"; first prize in *Blue Unicorn* competition, 1983, for poem "Carved by Obadiah Verity"; first prize in *Pendragon* competition, 1984, for poem "Scene I, Involving You and an Owl"; first prize, *Blue Unicorn* Writing Competition, 1987; first annual prize for poetry, *Nebraska Review,* 1987; teaching excellence award, Board of Trustees of Nebraska State College.

WRITINGS:

POETRY

Dead Horse Table, Wildflower, 1975.
Handwork, Kearney State College Press, 1978.
The Rarer Game, Kearney State College Press, 1980.
The Keeper of Miniature Deer, Juniper Press, 1986.
The Marginalist, Sandhills Press, 1992.
The Platte River, University of Nebraska at Kearney, 1992.
A Day Book, University of Nebraska at Kearney, 1993.
Carved by Obadiah Verity, Press at Colorado College, 1993.

OTHER

Contributor to numerous anthologies, including *Traveling America with Today's Poets,* Macmillan, 1977; *The Wildflower Home Almanac of Poetry,* Wildflower Press, 1980; *Strings,* Bradbury, 1984; *The Poet Dreaming in the Artist's House,* Milkweed Editions, 1984; and *The Decade Dance,* Sandhills Press, 1991.

Also contributor to *Pebble, Georgia Review, Prairie Schooner,* and *Nimrod.*

WORK IN PROGRESS: A manuscript of poems about birds.

SIDELIGHTS: Don Welch once told *CA:* "I came to poetry late, in my early forties, and I began by writing about things I knew, the country things of Nebraska. Because I am a college professor of English, the older, literary world often vied with contemporary subjects. I eventually married the two worlds in poems about animals, imaginary animals. Knowing about history led me into bestiaries of all kinds, and knowing about living animals enabled me to hold onto a realistic base. These poems, which I call 'animalizations,' have preoccupied me for some time and probably will for two or three more years. They are one sign that I am writing about less regional subjects than in the past."

WESTERGAARD, John (Harald) 1927-

PERSONAL: Surname is pronounced "wes-ter-gard" (original Danish pronunciation is "ves-ter-gor"); born October 13, 1927, in London, England; son of Otto (a civil engineer) and Inger (a textiles buyer; maiden name, Nyrop) Westergaard; married Inge Soerensen, August, 1950 (divorced; now deceased); married Anna Hanne Larsen (a studio potter), January, 1975; children: (first marriage) Susan, Niels (deceased), Michael; (second marriage) Camilla. *Education:* London School of Economics and Political Science, B.Sc., 1951. *Politics:* "Left-wing socialist, member of Labour Party." *Religion:* None.

ADDRESSES: Home—39 Rutland Park, Sheffield S10 2PB, England. *Office*—Department of Sociological Studies, University of Sheffield, Sheffield S10 2TN, England.

CAREER: University College, London, England, research assistant, 1951-1955; University of Nottingham, Nottingham, England, research fellow, 1955-56; London School of Economics and Political Science, London, assistant lecturer, 1956-59, lecturer, 1959-66, senior lecturer, 1966-70, reader in sociology, 1970-75, research associate and deputy director of Centre for Urban Studies, 1960-1975; University of Sheffield, Sheffield, England, professor and head of department, 1975-86, emeritus professor of sociology, 1986—. Visiting lecturer at Brown University, 1963-64. Convener, Standing Conference of Arts and Social Sciences in Universities, 1986-92. Member of panels to review academic provision of sociology for University Grants Committee, Council for National Academic Awards, and University of Copenhagen, 1987-89. Has served as committee member of Britain's Social Science Research Council, Council for National Academic Awards, Council for Academic Freedom and Democracy, and British Sociological Association. Co-director of studies for the Economic and Social Research Council.

MEMBER: British Association for the Advancement of Science (president of Section N [sociology], 1987-88), British Sociological Association (president, 1991-93).

AWARDS, HONORS: Litt.D., University of Sheffield, 1993.

WRITINGS:

(With Ruth Glass) *London's Housing Needs,* Centre for Urban Studies, University of London, 1965.

Scandinavian Urbanism, Institute for Organization and Industrial Sociology (Copenhagen), 1968.

(With Glass) *Housing in Camden,* London Borough of Camden, 1969.

(With Anne Weymen and Paul Wiles) *Modern British Society: A Bibliography,* Frances Pinter, 1974, revised edition, 1977.

(With Henrietta Resler) *Class in a Capitalist Society: A Study of Contemporary Britain,* Basic Books, 1975.

(With Iain Noble and Alan Walker) *After Redundancy,* Polity Press, 1988.

Also contributor to books, including *London: Aspects of Change,* MacGibbon & Kee, 1964; *Towards Socialism,* Perry Anderson and Robin Blackburn, editors, Cornell University Press, 1965; *Social Objectives in Educational Planning,* Organisation for Economic Cooperation and Development, 1967; *The Socialist Register 1970,* R. Miliband and J. Saville, editors, Merlin Press (London), 1970; *Family, Class, and Education,* M. Craft, editor, Longmans, Green, 1970; *Ideology in Social Science,* R. Blackburn, editor, Fontana, 1973; *Approaches to Sociology,* J. Rex, editor, Routledge & Kegan Paul, 1974; *Working Class Images of Society,* Routledge & Kegan Paul, 1975; *Inequalities, Conflict, and Change,* A. Blowers and G. Thompson, editors, Open University Press, 1976; *Mass Communication and Society,* James Curran and others, editors, Edward Arnold, 1977; *Class and Class Structure,* A. Hunt, editor, Lawrence and Wishart, 1977; *Problems of Modern Society,* 2nd edition (Westergaard was not associated with earlier edition), P. Worsley, editor, Penguin Books, 1978; *The Socialist Register 1978,* Miliband and Saville, editors, Merlin Press, 1978; *Socialist Arguments,* D. Coates and G. Johnston, editors, Martin Robertson, 1983; *Approaches to Welfare,* P. Bean and S. MacPherson, editors, Routledge & Kegan Paul, 1983; *The Future of the Left,* J. Curran, editor, Polity Press, 1984; *Social Stratification and Economic Decline,* D. Rose, editor, Hutchinson, 1988; and *John H. Goldthorpe,* J. Clark, C. Madgil, and S. Modgil, editors, Falmer Press, 1990. Contributor to professional journals.

WORK IN PROGRESS: Who Gets What? for Polity Press; *Class in Britain since 1979,* for Aoki Publishers (Tokyo); continuing research on various aspects of contemporary class structure and public policy relevant to inequality.

SIDELIGHTS: John Westergaard told *CA:* "My central interests—academic but also political—are in class inequality, change and continuity, and in their relations with economic structures and public policy. These interests are reflected in most of my publications, especially since the mid-1960s, and find reflection also in my current work. I have also been much concerned with recent developments in British higher education and have written, for the Standing Conference of Arts and Social Sciences, a number of papers questioning government policies in this field."

WHITE, Patricia (Ann) 1937-

PERSONAL: Born April 7, 1937, in Bristol, England; daughter of Reginald Arthur (a garage mechanic) and Lilian Marion (a shop assistant; maiden name, Weaver) Middle; married John Peter White (a university teacher), August 3, 1962; children: Louise Bridget. *Education:* University of Bristol, B.A., 1958, Postgraduate Certificate of Education, 1959; University of London, Diploma in Education (with distinction), 1964, M.A., 1966.

ADDRESSES: Office—Department of History, Humanities and Philosophy, Institute of Education, University of London, Bedford Way, London WC1H 0AL, England.

CAREER: German teacher at schools in Worcester, England, 1959-62, and London, England, 1962-65; University of London, Institute of Education, London, lecturer, 1965-74, senior lecturer in philosophy of education, 1974-91, research fellow in philosophy of education, 1991—.

MEMBER: Philosophy of Education Society of Great Britain (chair, 1993-96), American Philosophy of Education Society, Women in Philosophy.

WRITINGS:

Beyond Domination: An Essay in the Political Philosophy of Education, Routledge & Kegan Paul, 1983.
(Editor) *Personal and Social Education: Philosophical Perspectives,* Kogan Page, 1989.
(Co-editor) *Beyond Liberal Education: Essays in Honour of Paul H. Hirst,* Routledge & Kegan Paul, 1993.

WORK IN PROGRESS: "Research on the personal qualities which underpin democratic societies and the institutional structures (particularly educational ones) which might encourage these."

SIDELIGHTS: Patricia White told *CA:* "In *Beyond Domination* I argued that democracy was basically concerned with equal participation in the exercise, or control, of power. This had the implication that, wherever possible, people should participate, on equal terms, in the decision-making bodies of organizations—political, work-related, or whatever—of which they were members. This in turn had certain implications for the organization of schools for education for citizenship.

"In the time since I wrote that book I have become aware of the immense importance in the life of democratic societies of the personal dispositions of the citizens of those societies. Ultimately, the kind of society we have depends on the kind of people we are. Having well-designed institutional structures is only one part of what is required for a flourishing democratic society. I have therefore been working on the nature of qualities like honesty, candor, courage, hope, confidence, self-esteem, trust, [and] friend-

ship, and their place in the life of a democratic society. In particular, in the book which I am currently finishing, I am concerned with how education might foster these.

"This work has relevance to the democratic aspirations of formerly totalitarian countries which will need not just new institutions but new kinds of citizens if they are to become robust democracies.

"In my work on these dispositions I have been very much influenced by the writings of philosophers like Annette Baier, John Kekes, Mary Midgley, Martha Nussbaum, Amelie Oksenberg Rorty, and Bernard Williams."

*   *   *

WHITE, Patrick (Victor Martindale) 1912-1990 (Patrick Victor Martindale)

PERSONAL: Born May 28, 1912, in London, England; died after a long illness, September 30, 1990, in Sydney, Australia; son of Victor Martindale and Ruth (Withycombe) White. *Education:* King's College, Cambridge, B.A., 1935. *Avocational Interests:* Cooking, gardening, music.

CAREER: Novelist, playwright, memoirist, short story writer, and poet. *Military service:* Royal Air Force, 1940-45, intelligence officer.

AWARDS, HONORS: Australian Literary Society gold medal, 1940, for *Happy Valley,* and 1956, for *The Tree of Life;* Miles Franklin Award, 1958, for *Voss,* and 1962, for *Riders in the Chariot;* W. H. Smith & Son Literary Award, 1959, for *Voss;* brotherhood award, National Conference of Christians and Jews, 1962, for *Riders in the Chariot;* Nobel Prize for literature, 1973.

WRITINGS:

POETRY

(Under pseudonym Patrick Victor Martindale) *Thirteen Poems,* [privately printed], 1930.
The Ploughman and Other Poems, Beacon Press, 1935.
Poems, Soft Press, 1974.

NOVELS

Happy Valley, Harrap, 1939, Viking, 1940.
The Living and the Dead, Viking, 1941.
The Aunt's Story, Viking, 1948.
The Tree of Man, Viking, 1955.
Voss, Viking, 1957.
Riders in the Chariot, Viking, 1961.
The Solid Mandala, Viking, 1966.
The Vivisector, Viking, 1970.
The Eye of the Storm, J. Cape, 1973, Viking, 1974.
A Fringe of Leaves, J. Cape, 1976, Viking, 1977.

The Twyborn Affair, Viking, 1980.
Memoirs of Many in One, by Alex Xenophon Demirjian Gray, Viking, 1986.

SHORT STORY COLLECTIONS

The Burnt Ones, Viking, 1964.
The Cockatoos: Shorter Novels and Stories, J. Cape, 1974, Viking, 1975.
Three Uneasy Pieces, J. Cape, 1988, Random House, 1989.

PLAYS

Return to Abyssinia, produced in London, 1947.
Four Plays (contains *The Ham Funeral,* produced in Adelaide, 1961; *The Season at Sarsaparilla,* produced in Adelaide, 1962; *A Cheery Soul,* produced in Melbourne, 1963; *Night on Bald Mountain,* produced in Adelaide, 1964), Eyre & Spottiswoode, 1965, Viking, 1966.

Also author of plays, *Big Toys,* 1977, *Netherwood,* 1983, *Signal Driver,* 1983, and *Shepherd on the Rocks,* 1987.

OTHER

The Night of the Prowler (screenplay; based on White's short story), Chariot/International Harmony, 1979.
Flaws in the Glass: A Self-Portrait (autobiography), Viking, 1981.
Patrick White Speaks (speeches), J. Cape, 1990.

Contributor to *Australian Letters,* Volume 1, 1958. Also contributor to periodicals.

ADAPTATIONS: The film rights to *Voss* have been purchased.

SIDELIGHTS: Patrick White's novels are recognized for their structural and thematic complexity. Although most critics acknowledge White's talent and genius, several have written of the difficulty in reading his novels because of the multiplicity of symbols, myths, and allegories: William Walsh discussed White's "choking thickets of imagery" in his book, *Patrick White's Fiction;* in *Commonweal* Robert Phillips called reading White "a bit like overindulgence in chocolate *mousse*"; and Bruce Allen wrote in *Saturday Review* of White's "stylistic crudeness." However, Harry Heseltine in *Quadrant* asserted that "whether we like it or not, White's style is neither a cover over a hole nor an impediment in the way of full display of his powers. It is in fact a direct function of his deepest response to life." Describing White's use of language, Walsh also remarked, "This is of such an individual sort that it stamps the work indelibly with the writer's personality and it is a form of that characteristic domination of his material which this artist invariably exhibits."

While he has never claimed a large popular audience, critical understanding and appreciation of White's work

evolved over time. The publication of each successive novel afforded a new opportunity to observe his stylistic and thematic concerns in a slightly different context. As it became more clear that White was voicing a genuine, unique artistic vision, the reservations voiced concerning his earlier novels were supplanted by fuller, more appreciative readings. White's 1973 Nobel Prize for literature was acknowledgment of his status as a major figure in contemporary literature. The Nobel committee's citation spoke of his "authentic voice that carries across the world." By the time of this death in 1990, a writer for the London *Times* was able to affirm that "without doubt *The Tree of Man, Voss,* and *The Solid Mandala* are among the most important novels of the century in any language; and as whole his tormented *oeuvre* is that of a great and essentially modern writer."

White's basic orientation was religious and he took from a variety of religious attitudes the philosophies he needed to explore his overriding concern: man's search for meaning in an apparently meaningless society. Inherent in White's consideration of spirituality in a mechanical and materialistic world was the concept of man's isolation in a crowded society. In *Newsweek,* Peter S. Prescott compared White to a medical pathologist, saying the novelist posed the questions, "What pox, what gangrene have we here? What rot will be extruded from this pustule?" Even within the most basic societal structures man is alienated, alone; man's need for meaning is ultimately to be found in the interior world, the world of the imagination and the soul. Robert Phillips said, "White's thesis . . . is simply this: We are all alone in a chaotic world and only we ourselves can help ourselves during our brief tenure." Often White's theory of the duality of man was exhibited through characters decayed in body but spiritually whole. George Steiner wrote, "Incontinence, the worn skin, the sour odors of senility, the toothless appetites and spasms of the old . . . lay bare the ignoble, perhaps accidental fact that the spirit is so meanly housed." White, himself, when asked in an interview if there was any continuing theme running through his work, told Andrew Clark in the *New York Times Book Review* that his "dominant obsession" was the search for "some meaning and design" in what he described as "the tragic farce of life—to find reason in apparent unreason, and how to accept a supernatural force which on the one hand blesses and on the other destroys."

White's frequent use of the isolation theme in his fiction was rooted in his personal feelings of alienation and nonacceptance by his fellow countrymen. Several periods of expatriation preceded his ultimate return to Australia, as he explained to Ingmar Bjoerksten in *Patrick White: A General Introduction:* "It was eighteen years before I dared to come back to Australia for the third time. . . . I couldn't do without the countryside out here. I don't believe in a final break with the place one originates from. Only a temporary break . . . to get perspective. You are shaped by the place you have your roots in; it has become part of you. Outside places don't shape you in the same way. This has nothing to do with nationalism. People are always the same. This is what my compatriots find so difficult to understand." Bjoerksten explored another possible cause of White's feelings of alienation: "For a long time he was dismissed as peculiar, pretentious, and irrelevant by his countrymen, whose restricted vision and whose limited experience of what human life has to offer he exposes time after time, while simultaneously attacking the holy cow that they so deeply revere: an uncritical materialism that never questions itself." White's 1973 Nobel Prize has gained him greater acceptance among Australians, although he is still more widely read in other countries.

In expressing his theories of alienation and individual spirituality, White often used Jungian archetypes of the collective unconscious and symbols of religions such as Buddhism and Christianity. A recurring concept involved the mandala, a motif of Buddhist origin. Mandala is the "Sanskrit word for 'magic ring,' " according to Bjoerksten, who also explained that "the mandala represents the Buddhist concept of the universe, of completeness in the form of a square with circles inside or outside of it." White most often used the Jungian explanation of the mandala motif to express man's own divinity, with man at the circle's center rather than God, according to Bjoerksten. In a 1973 letter, White himself acknowledged both his early indebtedness to Jung and his more recent belief in the possibility of the existence of God: "I have great admiration for [Jung] and his findings, but I also have a belief in a supernatural power of which I have been given inklings from time to time; there have been incidents and coincidences which have shown me that there is a design behind the haphazardness."

Although the obscurity of White's novels has resulted in some critics' continuing to label him "unreadable," a majority have received his efforts with warm acceptance. Writing in *Beyond All This Fiddle: Essays, 1955-1967,* A. Alvarez described White's isolation "an image of great beauty." In the *New York Times Book Review,* Shirley Hazzard spoke of his "rich, distinctive language, now stately, now mercurial, always borne on the civilizing tide of irony." D. Keith Mano remarked in the *National Review:* "It's as easy to be irked or bloody bored by Patrick White as it is to be astonished by him. If you cooperate, magnificence can be tedious, or tedium magnificent. White is, without conditional clause, brilliant. And exasperating."

White's very productive career as a novelist spanned almost exactly a half century and produced twelve novels, three collections of shorter fiction, three volumes of po-

etry, several plays, and a provocative autobiography. Several of the major stylistic and thematic elements that have characterized all of White's work were present even in his earlier novels: stream of consciousness narrative, frequent and complex flashbacks, the use of unusual syntax and esoteric vocabulary, and the exploration of dreams and states of madness. Although he attracted positive critical attention with the publication of his first novel, *Happy Valley,* which won a gold medal from the Australian Literary Society in 1940, it was White's fourth novel, *The Tree of Man,* which brought him international attention. In his book, *Vision and Style in Patrick White,* Rodney Stenning Edgecombe identified a "radical break" in stylistic assurance between White's third novel, *The Aunt's Story,* and *The Tree of Man.* The first three novels, he suggested, "seem to have been promoted more by an urge to be a writer per se than by an impulse to communicate a vision."

The Tree of Man related the experiences of a couple, Stan and Amy Parker, who struggled to establish a dairy farm at the turn of the century. White had this to say to Clark concerning his aims in *The Tree of Man:* "Because the void I had to fill was so immense, I wanted to suggest in this book every possible aspect of life, through the lives of an ordinary man and woman. But at the same time I wanted to discover the extraordinary behind the ordinary, the mystery and poetry, which alone make bearable the lives of such people." The achievements of *The Tree of Man,* according to John B. Beston in *Australian Literary Studies,* "lie in [the book's] depiction of the marital relationship between Stan and Amy; in its portrayal of Amy . . . ; and above all in its depiction of dreams that reveal deep longings and fears." "It is his presentation of fantasy," Beston noted, "that is White's chief contribution to the English novel."

Voss, which followed *The Tree of Man* by two years, was loosely based on the experiences of German explorer Ludwig Leichardt, who disappeared while leading an expedition to penetrate the Australian Outback in the 1840s. The narration drifted between Voss's expedition and Laura Trevelyan, a young woman living in Sydney with whom Voss shared a telepathic connection. This unique connection between his two main characters allowed White to explore one of his continuing themes. As John Coates explained in the *Australian Literary Studies:* "Voss and Laura, in conflict with each other, are halves of the original spiritual androgyny. They are also incarnations of man's double fall: through pride in the case of Voss and through inability to imagine spirituality or sustain a high spiritual state, in the case of Laura." *Voss* represented White's extended treatment of what Laurence Steven characterized in his *Dissociation and Wholeness in Patrick White's Fiction* as "the dualisms which are everywhere apparent in White: mind/body, spirit/flesh, individual/society, permanence/flux, abstract/concrete, deformity/health, and so on."

Riders in the Chariot brought to the fore White's satiric view of modern society in general, and Australian middle-class society and culture in particular. It added fuel to the already hostile attitude toward White which was then prevalent in his home country. The novel intertwined the stories of four eccentrics all living in an imagined Sydney suburb christened Sarsparilla. White has written about this novel, "What I want to emphasize through my four 'Riders'—an orthodox refugee intellectual Jew, a mad *Erdgeist* of an Australian spinster, an evangelical laundress, and a half-caste Aboriginal painter—is that all faiths, whether religious, humanistic, instinctive, or the creative artist's act of praise, are in fact one."

A Solid Mandala was set in the same Sarsaparilla suburb. An updated version of the Cain and Abel story, it portrayed the troubled relations between Arthur and Waldo Brown, elderly twin brothers. Some critics who felt that White had been too mechanical or programmatic in working out his thematic ends in *Riders in the Chariot* praised his mastery of the same material in the newer novel. A number of writers pointed to a new, more autobiographical element in White's work, suggesting that Arthur and Waldo represented the emotional and intellectual sides of the artist's personality.

The Vivisector, published in 1970, was described by the London *Times* as "a sort of imaginative autobiography of White's internal life: an adopted child becomes a painter, and becomes lost in his own mysticism." With this novel, numerous critics began to take note of an increasing bleakness in White's vision and an implied darkening of the novelist's view of his own efforts. (Vivisection is the practice of cutting into or dissecting the body of a living organism.) Steven described *The Vivisector* as "a sustained criticism of the solipsistic quest for significance." Although White's preoccupations remained, following *The Vivisector* he seemed less concerned with questions of resolution or transcendence and more interested in the myriad fashions in which his themes played themselves out in life. Shortly after the publication of *The Vivisector* he told Thelma Herring and G. A. Wilkins in an interview published in Peter Wolfe's *Critical Essays on Patrick White* that he did not see himself as a moralist: "I say what I have to say through the juxtaposition of images and situations and the emotional exchanges of human beings."

The Eye of the Storm and *A Fringe of Leaves* represent a return to a slightly more realistic narrative manner than the novels that had come before them. The former novel narrated the last year and extensive recollections of a rich old woman in Sydney and the power struggle between her

son and daughter who have returned to claim her fortune in order to carry on their lives of artistic and social pretension in Europe. One among many of the dying woman's memories was a treasured period of tranquility while she was temporarily stranded on an island fifteen years earlier. This episode was based on a true account of a woman who was shipwrecked off the Great Barrier Reef in 1836. White returned to this same subject in *A Fringe of Leaves,* which told of a proper Englishwoman who survived a shipwreck, was enslaved by a tribe of aborigines who have murdered her husband, and became a participant in cannibalism and Dionysian rites.

The Twyborn Affair was in part a modern rendering of the Tiresias myth. The novel was divided into three sections, each a separate narrative. In the first part, an Australian matron travelling in pre-World War I France was sexually attracted to Eudoxia, the beautiful, young "wife" of an aged, dissolute, slightly mad Greek. Part two narrates the return to Australia of Eddie, a decorated veteran, following the war. There, he abandoned his parents' comfortable urban life and acquaintances (including the matron in the first section) and sought his identity as a ranch hand in the Outback. The third part leaped to London just before the beginning of the Second World War, where Eadith Trist presided over a sophisticated brothel catering to the most eccentric desires of the British aristocracy. *The Twyborn Affair* was sufficiently ambiguous and allusive that more than one of the first reviewers was oblivious to the fact that Eudoxia, Eddie, and Eadith were one and the same person. Many critics were impressed with White's achievement in finding new expression of a longtime major theme—the infinite possibilities of a single personality. Betty Falkenberg remarked in *New Leader:* "It is no news that 'Things are seldom what they seem.' But White was saying more: Precisely through their disguises shall we come to know them, and they, themselves. Where surfaces blur, the result is not so much confusion as illumination." Reviewing the novel for the *Times Literary Supplement,* William Walsh wrote, "The novel is impressive in its conception, astonishing in its concreteness, sharp in its sardonic social discriminations, and rich in its use of the resources of language." Falkenberg described *The Twyborn Affair* as "an extraordinary novel of quest, an odyssey through place, time, and especially gender—all three of which, by virtue of their boundaries delimit and even alienate the individual from his possible selves." Writing in the *New York Times Book Review,* Benjamin DeMott characterized the book as "a case study of sexual proteanism and the thematic core is the mystery of human identity." He tempered his enthusiasm, however, and explained that "the problem is the book's too unremitting scorn of human attachment."

After accustoming readers to mammoth novels of 400 or more pages, Patrick White performed a surprising about-face with his next novel and produced a slim 192-page volume. The narrative design of this book, however, was even more audacious than *The Twyborn Affair*. *Memoirs of Many in One, by Alex Xenophon Demirjian Gray* was constructed on the conceit that these are the memoirs of the aging Alex Gray edited by her close friend Patrick White. Novelist Patrick White himself appeared as one of the major characters in the memoirs, as well as the writer of interspersed editor's notes. In this novel there was no certainty whatever which of Alex Gray's multiple remembered personae—ranging from a Greek nun to a provincial Shakespearean actress—were real and which creatures of her imagination. The book's main character, Patrick White, contributed an additional layer of confusion when, after Alex's death, lying across her bed he mused, "I suppose I had encouraged her to cultivate [her saints and demons] as an extension of my own creations." Once again, a number of critics noted White's apparent bleak view of his own achievements. As she neared death, Alex discovered that her nurse has never heard of White. "He'd appreciate that," she said. "He's sick of himself. Literature, as they call it, is a millstone around his neck."

Three Uneasy Pieces, White's last published book, has been alternately described as three short stories, a novel, or three autobiographical essays. Despite the narrator's warnings about "the distance between life and literature," it appeared that White had completely dissolved the last boundaries between life and fiction in this work. From the perspective of a long life, the narrator reflected on the present as "a tireless dance," which was always "a variation of the same theme." In these last uneasy pieces, although he recognized that he was honored and admired by others, the narrator only saw himself as "a stuffed turkey at banquets." He contrasted himself with two men—perhaps his alter egos, perhaps his spiritual twins. One of these, identified only as M., was the "sweet reason" to the narrator's "un-reason." M. was assumed by most to be Manoly Lascaris, Patrick White's companion for over forty years. The other man, Blue Platt, was a former schoolmate of the narrator. Blue's various adult experiences included living as a mystic among the Aborigines, rescuing victims during the London blitz, helping Japanese prisoners of war to survive the horrors of captivity, and nursing the victims of the Hiroshima bombing. At the end of the third piece the narrator, then a patient in a geriatric ward, awaited Blue, whom he described as "a part of me I've always aspired to. My unlikely twin, who got away." On the last page his twin may have arrived or he may be the dream-product of an injection. On this ambiguous note, the narrator ends: "It is we who hold the secret of existence."

Morris Philipson wrote in the *Chicago Tribune Book World* that Penelope Mortimer has suggested that the writer with whom Patrick White most deserved comparison is Leo Tolstoy, "for the profundity of his psychological insights and the breadth of his epic powers." Philipson expanded on that comparison in his article, and noted the "capacity for human sympathy" which distinguish both writers. He concluded, "The great variety of characters in the range of White's fiction are not characterized by wanting something they can't have or by dissatisfaction with what it is they have so much as they are characterized by being what they are." White's artistry, he affirmed "is in the service of appreciating what is uniquely human with an indifference to time and place that makes his books of universal significance."

BIOGRAPHICAL/CRITICAL SOURCES:

BOOKS

Alvarez, A., *Beyond All This Fiddle: Essays, 1955-1967*, Random House, 1969.

Beatson, Peter, *The Eye in the Mandala*, Peter Elek, 1976.

Bjoerksten, Ingmar, *Patrick White: A General Introduction*, University of Queensland Press, 1976.

Colmer, John, *Patrick White*, Methuen, 1984.

Contemporary Literary Criticism, Gale, Volume 3, 1975, Volume 4, 1975, Volume 5, 1976, Volume 7, 1977, Volume 9, 1978, Volume 18, 1981, Volume 65, 1991, Volume 69, 1992.

Dyce, J. R., *Patrick White as Playwright*, University of Queensland Press, 1974.

Edgecombe, Roger Stenning, *Vision and Style in Patrick White*, University of Alabama Press, 1989.

Finch, Janette, *A Bibliography of Patrick White*, Libraries Board of South Australia, 1966.

Joyce, Clayton, editor, *Patrick White: A Tribute*, Angus & Robertson, 1991.

Kiernan, Brian, *Patrick White*, St. Martin's, 1980.

Marr, David, *Patrick White: A Life*, J. Cape, 1991.

Morley, Patricia A., *The Mystery of Unity, Theme, and Technique in the Novels of Patrick White*, McGill-Queen's University Press, 1972.

Steven, Laurence, *Dissociation and Wholeness in Patrick White's Fiction*, Wilfred Laurier University Press, 1989.

Walsh, William, *Patrick White's Fiction*, Rowman & Littlefield, 1977.

Weigel, John A., *Patrick White*, Twayne, 1983.

White, Patrick, *Flaws in the Glass: A Self-Portrait* (autobiography), Viking, 1981.

White, Patrick, *Memoirs of Many in One, by Alex Xenophon Demirjian Gray*, Viking, 1986.

White, Patrick, *Three Uneasy Pieces*, J. Cape, 1988, Random House, 1989.

Wolfe, Peter, *Critical Essays on Patrick White*, G. K. Hall, 1990.

PERIODICALS

Atlantic Monthly, May, 1980, p. 102.
Australian Literary Studies, October, 1973, pp. 152-166; May 1979, pp. 119-122.
Books Abroad, summer, 1974.
Chicago Tribune, April 6, 1980, Section 7, p. 1; December 21, 1986, p. 3.
Chicago Tribune Book World, February 26, 1983, pp. 33-34.
Christian Science Monitor, November 12, 1964, p. 11.
Commonweal, November 13, 1964, pp. 241-242; May 17, 1974, p. 269.
Globe & Mail (Toronto), October 25, 1986; March 18, 1989.
Harper's, September, 1970.
Hudson Review, summer, 1974.
Los Angeles Times Book Review, May 18, 1980, p. 4; February 4, 1982.
Listener, November 5, 1970.
National Review, February 15, 1974, p. 3579.
New Leader, September 7, 1970; January 21, 1974; June 2, 1980, pp. 17-18.
New Republic, January 5, 1974; January 12, 1974; March 22, 1975; May 3, 1980, pp. 37-38.
New Statesman and Society, September 7, 1973; July 5, 1974; July 27, 1990, p. 46.
Newsweek, January 21, 1974; March 1, 1982, pp. 71-72.
New York, January 21, 1974.
New Yorker, March 4, 1974.
New York Review of Books, April 4, 1974.
New York Times, April 11, 1980.
New York Times Book Review, January 6, 1974, p. 1; January 19, 1975; April 27, 1980, p. 32; February 7, 1982, p. 9; October 26, 1986, p. 12.
Prairie Schooner, fall, 1974.
Quadrant, winter, 1963.
Saturday Review, January 25, 1975, p. 34.
Sewanee Review, spring, 1974; summer, 1975.
Spectator, June 22, 1974; April 12, 1986, pp. 32-33.
Times Literary Supplement, September 21, 1973; November 30, 1979, p. 77; November 20, 1981, p. 1373; April 4, 1986, p. 357; December 2-8, 1988, p. 1350.
Tribune Books (Chicago), April 6, 1980, Section 7, p. 1; December 21, 1986, p. 3.
Variety, July 22, 1970.
Village Voice, February 7, 1974.
Washington Post Book World, May 18, 1980, p. 3; November 16, 1986, p. 10.

OBITUARIES:

PERIODICALS

Chicago Tribune, October, 1, 1990.
Los Angeles Times, October 1, 1990.
New York Times, October 1, 1990, p. B11.
Times (London), October 1, 1990.
Washington Post, October 1, 1990.*

—*Sidelights by Theodore Knight*

*   *   *

WHITE, Phyllis Dorothy James 1920-
(P. D. James)

PERSONAL: Born August 3, 1920, in Oxford, England; daughter of Sidney Victor (a tax officer) and Dorothy May Amelia (Hone) James; married Ernest Conner Bantry White (a medical practitioner), August 8, 1941 (died, 1964); children: Clare, Jane. *Education:* Attended Cambridge High School for Girls, 1931-37. *Politics:* "I belong to no political party." *Religion:* Church of England. *Avocational Interests:* Exploring churches, walking by the sea.

ADDRESSES: Agent—Elaine Greene Ltd., 37a Goldhawk Rd., London W12 8QQ, England.

CAREER: Festival Theatre, Cambridge, England, assistant stage manager prior to World War II; worked as a Red Cross nurse and at the Ministry of Food during World War II; North West Regional Hospital Board, London, England, became principal administrative assistant, 1949-68; Department of Home Affairs, London, principal administrative assistant in Police Department, 1968-72, and in Criminal Policy Department, 1972-79; full-time writer, 1979—. Associate fellow, Downing College, Cambridge, 1986; British Broadcasting Corp. (BBC) General Advisory Council, 1987-88, member of Arts Council of Great Britain, 1988-92, and of British Council, 1988-93; governor, BBC, 1988-93. Magistrate, 1979-84.

MEMBER: Royal Society of Literature (fellow), Royal Society of Arts (fellow), Society of Authors (chair, 1985-87), Crime Writers Association, Detection Club, Institute of Hospital Administration (fellow).

AWARDS, HONORS: First prize, Crime Writers Association contest, 1967, for short story, "Moment of Power"; Order of the British Empire, 1983; created Life Peer of United Kingdom (Baroness James of Holland Park), 1991; Diamond Dagger Award, Crime Writers Association for services to crime writing; Silver Dagger Awards, Crime Writers Association, for *Shroud for a Nightingale* and *The Black Tower;* Edgar Award, Mystery Writers of America, for *Shroud for a Nightingale;* Scroll Award, Mystery Writers of America, for *An Unsuitable Job for a*

Woman; Litt. D., University of Buckingham, 1992; Doctor of Literature, University of London, 1993.

WRITINGS:

MYSTERY NOVELS, UNDER NAME P. D. JAMES

Cover Her Face, Faber, 1962, Scribner, 1966.
A Mind to Murder, Faber, 1963, Scribner, 1967.
Unnatural Causes, Scribner, 1967.
Shroud for a Nightingale, Scribner, 1971.
An Unsuitable Job for a Woman, Faber, 1972, Scribner, 1973.
The Black Tower, Scribner, 1975.
Death of an Expert Witness, Scribner, 1977.
Innocent Blood (Book-of-the-Month Club selection), Scribner, 1980.
The Skull beneath the Skin, Scribner, 1982.
A Taste for Death, Faber, 1985, Knopf, 1986.
Devices and Desires, Faber, 1989, Random House, 1990.
The Children of Men, Faber, 1992, Knopf, 1993.

OMNIBUS VOLUMES, UNDER NAME P. D. JAMES

Crime Times Three (includes *Cover Her Face, A Mind to Murder, and Shroud for a Nightingale*) Scribner, 1979.
Murder in Triplicate (includes *Unnatural Causes, An Unsuitable Job for a Woman,* and *The Black Tower*), Scribner, 1982.
Trilogy of Death, Scribner, 1984.
P. D. James: Three Complete Novels, Crown, 1987.
An Omnibus P. D. James (includes *Death of an Expert Witness, Innocent Blood,* and *An Unsuitable Job for a Woman*), Faber, 1990.
A Dalgliesh Trilogy (includes *The Black Tower, Death of an Expert Witness,* and *Shroud for a Nightingale*), Penguin/Faber, 1991.

CONTRIBUTOR, UNDER NAME P. D. JAMES

Ellery Queen's Murder Menu, World Publishing, 1969.
Virginian Whitaker, editor, *Winter's Crimes 5,* Macmillan (London), 1973.
Ellery Queen's Masters of Mystery, Davis Publications, 1975.
Hilary Watson, editor, *Winter's Crimes 8,* Macmillan (London), 1976.
Dilys Wynn, editor, *Murder Ink: The Mystery Reader's Companion,* Workman Publishing, 1977.
Crime Writers, BBC Publications, 1978.
Julian Symons, editor, *Verdict of Thirteen,* Harper, 1979.
George Hardinge, *Winter's Crimes 15,* St. Martin's Press, 1983.

OTHER, UNDER NAME P. D. JAMES

(With Thomas A. Critchley) *The Maul and the Pear Tree: The Ratcliffe Highway Murders, 1811,* Constable, 1971.
"A Private Treason" (play), first produced in the West End at the Palace Theatre, March 12, 1985.

The writings of P. D. James have been translated into several languages, including twelve European languages and Japanese.

ADAPTATIONS: Cover Her Face, Unnatural Causes, The Black Tower, A Taste for Death, Devices and Desires, Death of an Expert Witness (1985) and *Shroud for a Nightingale* (1986) have been adapted as television miniseries and broadcast by the Public Broadcasting System (PBS).

SIDELIGHTS: As P. D. James, a name she chose because it is short and gender-neutral, Phyllis Dorothy James White has established herself as one of England's most prominent mystery writers. Often ranked with such masters of the genre as Agatha Christie, Dorothy L. Sayers, and Margery Allingham, James is critically acclaimed for her ability to combine complex and puzzling plots with psychologically believable characters, particularly in her novels featuring Commander Adam Dalgliesh of Scotland Yard. Her "keen, cunning mind and a positively bloody imagination" make her "one of the finest and most successful mystery writers in the world," Peter Gorner writes in the *Chicago Tribune.*

James began her writing career relatively late in life. When her husband returned from World War II suffering from mental illness, James needed to support her family on her own. For nineteen years she worked as a hospital administrator and then, following her husband's death, entered the British Department of Home Affairs as a civil servant in the criminal department. Although she had wanted to write for many years, James was not able to devote time to this pursuit until the late 1950s. Then, as she tells David Lehman and Tony Clifton in *Newsweek,* "I realized that if I didn't make the effort and settle down to begin that first book, eventually I would be saying to my grandchildren, 'Of course I really wanted to be a novelist.' There never was going to be a convenient time." While working in a hospital she began her first novel, *Cover Her Face.* Over a three-year period James wrote for two hours every morning before going to work, composing her story in longhand on notepaper, a method she still prefers. Once completed, the novel was accepted by the first publisher to whom it was sent and James's career as a mystery writer was launched. Since then she has published ten more mystery novels in addition to a novel about a twenty-first century dystopia, *The Children of Men,* and a work of nonfiction, *The Maul and the Pear Tree.* The latter book, written with Thomas A. Critchley, investigates a particularly gruesome murder committed in London in 1811. James has been a full-time writer since her retirement from government service in 1979.

Despite the difficulty of juggling two careers and her family responsibilities, James says she does not regret the long delay in becoming a full-time writer. "As a woman writer, I feel having a working life provided all sorts of experience that I wouldn't have got if I had just been living at home," she told Connie Lauerman in an interview for the *Chicago Tribune.* Her work as a hospital administrator and in the police and criminal policy departments has provided much of the background for her mystery novels, set in such places as a police forensic laboratory, a nurses' training school, and a home for the disabled.

There is an old-fashioned quality to James's mystery novels that puts them squarely in the tradition of classic English detective fiction as practiced by Agatha Christie and similar writers. The character of Adam Dalgliesh, Scotland Yard detective and published poet, for example, follows the familiar pattern of the gentleman detective popularized by such earlier writers as Dorothy L. Sayers and Ngaio Marsh. James's plots are puzzles which, she tells Wayne Warga of the *Los Angeles Times,* follow the traditional formula. "You have a murder, which is a mystery," she explains. "There is a closed circle of suspects. . . . You have, in my case, a professional detective. He finds clues and information which, as he discovers them, are also available to the reader. And at the end of the story there is a credible and satisfactory resolution that the reader could have arrived at as well." James's style, too, writes Thomas Lask in the *New York Times,* "is what we think of as typically British. Her writing is ample, leisurely, and full of loving description of house and countryside." And like that of a number of other mystery writers, states Norma Siebenheller in her study *P. D. James,* James's "work is literate, tightly constructed, and civilized. Her people are genteel and polite."

Yet, while conforming to many of the expectations of the genre, James goes beyond its limitations. For instance, where other writers have concentrated almost entirely on the puzzles in their books to the detriment of such things as characterization, James has not. Although she creates a puzzle for her readers, she focuses her attention on writing realistic mysteries with fully rounded characters. "The classic English mystery, as practiced by many of its female creators," Siebenheller explains, "is basically a puzzle-solving exercise. . . . One never gets over the feeling, when reading these books, that they are all make-believe. . . . James departs from that tradition. . . . The worlds she creates are peopled with varied and interesting characters whose actions spring from believable motivations and whose reactions are true to their complex personalities." As James tells Carla Heffner in the *Washing-*

ton Post, her frequent comparison to Agatha Christie "amazes me. . . . Hers [is] the stereotype English crime novel which is set in the small English village where everyone knows their place. . . . I don't set my novels in that never-never land."

James's concern for realism is reflected in her creation of Adam Dalgliesh, a complex character who is, Siebenheller believes, "a far cry from the almost comical characters who served Christie and Sayers as sleuths." Dalgliesh is an introspective, serious figure—intensely devoted to solving the case at hand—who suppresses his personal feelings. His personality has been shaped by one tragic event many years before: the death of his wife and son during childbirth. It is this painful memory, and the essential chaos it implies, that has formed Dalgliesh's "vision of the world," as Erlene Hubly states in *Clues: A Journal of Detection.* Because of this memory, Dalgliesh is a "Byronic hero," Hubly argues, unable "to adjust to or accept society." Yet, because of his fear of chaos and death, he enforces the rules of society, convinced that they are all humanity has with which to create order. Dalgliesh tries, writes Hubly, "to bring order out of chaos: if he cannot stop death he can at least catch and punish those who inflict it on others."

While Dalgliesh is her most popular character, James's secondary characters are equally realistic. All of her books, Julian Symons notes in the *New York Times Book Review,* "are marked by powerful and sympathetic characterizations." Perhaps her most fully realized character after Dalgliesh is Cordelia Gray, a female private detective who appears in *An Unsuitable Job for a Woman* and *The Skull beneath the Skin.* As James relates in the first of these two novels, Gray was raised in a series of foster homes she found "very interesting." Despite her past misfortunes, Gray is "a totally positive person," Siebenheller relates. "Not only is she optimistic, capable, and clever, she is good-natured as well. . . . This is not to say Cordelia is a Pollyanna. She fully acknowledges the rougher edges of life." She and Dalgliesh enjoy a cordial rivalry whenever they meet on a murder case.

Many of James's other characters are from the respectable English middle class. Educated and humanistic, they find themselves "consumed by jealousy, hatred, lust, sexual fears, and ambition," Gorner states. James explores her characters' labyrinthine emotional and psychological states with a penetrating and compassionate eye. Heffner, for example, sees James as someone "passionately curious about people and their peculiarities." Lask believes that James's work, despite its veneer of traditional English fiction, "is modern in the ambiguous makeup of her characters, their complex motives and the shrewd psychological touches of the relationship between the police and the criminals they pursue."

Moved by a deep moral concern, James sees mystery writing as an important expression of basic human values. Mystery novels, she tells Heffner, "are like twentieth-century morality plays; the values are basic and unambiguous. Murder is wrong. In an age in which gratuitous violence and arbitrary death have become common, these values need no apology." The "corrosive, destructive aspect of crime," Siebenheller maintains, is one of James's major themes. She traces the effects of crime not only on the victim and criminal, but on their family and friends as well. James's concern is obvious, too, in the values she gives her characters. Comparing Adam Dalgliesh to James herself, Warga describes him as "a man who is a realistic moralist much like his creator."

The success of James's novels can be attributed to their popularity among two different audiences, Heffner argues, "the lovers of a good 'whodunit' who read her novels for their action and intricate plots; and the literary world that admires the books for their character and motivation." In the words of Christopher Lehmann-Haupt, writing in the *New York Times,* this wide acceptance has made James "one of the most esteemed practitioners of the [mystery] genre in the English-speaking world."

BIOGRAPHICAL/CRITICAL SOURCES:

BOOKS

Contemporary Literary Criticism, Gale, Volume 18, 1981, pp. 272-77, Volume 46, 1988, pp. 204-211.

James, P. D., *An Unsuitable Job for a Woman,* Faber, 1972, Scribner, 1973.

Siebenheller, Norma, *P. D. James,* Ungar, 1981.

Wynn, Dilys, editor, *Murder Ink,* Workman Publishing, 1977.

Wynn, Dilys, editor, *Murderess Ink,* Workman Publishing, 1977.

PERIODICALS

Atlantic, June, 1980.

Chicago Tribune, June 10, 1980; November 6, 1986; November 16, 1986; February 4, 1990, pp. 1, 4.

Chicago Tribune Book World, May 18, 1980; September 19, 1982.

Christian Science Monitor, June 25, 1980.

Clues: A Journal of Detection, fall/winter, 1982; spring/summer, 1985.

Globe and Mail (Toronto), May 10, 1986; November 8, 1986; February 3, 1990, p. C8.

Listener, June 5, 1975.

Los Angeles Times, June 6, 1980; November 6, 1986; January 21, 1987.

Los Angeles Times Book Review, June 22, 1980; November 30, 1986, p. 6; February 25, 1990, pp. 1, 11.

Maclean's, June 30, 1980.

Ms., April, 1974; August, 1979.

New Republic, July 31, 1976; November 26, 1977.

Newsweek, January 23, 1978; May 12, 1980; September 13, 1982; October 20, 1986, pp. 81-83; February 19, 1990, p. 66.

New Yorker, March 11, 1976; March 6, 1978; June 23, 1980.

New York Review of Books, July 17, 1980.

New York Times, December 11, 1977; July 18, 1979; February 8, 1980; April 27, 1980; May 7, 1980; March 11, 1986; October 5, 1986; October 23, 1986; January 25, 1990, p. C22.

New York Times Book Review, July 24, 1966; January 16, 1972; April 22, 1973; November 23, 1975; April 27, 1980; September 12, 1982; April 6, 1986; November 2, 1986, p. 9; January 28, 1990, pp. 1, 31; April 26, 1990, p. 35.

New York Times Magazine, October 5, 1986.

People, December 8, 1986.

Publishers Weekly, January 5, 1976, pp. 8-9; October 25, 1985; December 1, 1989, p. 48.

Spectator, December 23, 1972; June 12, 1976; September 19, 1992, p. 31.

Time, April 17, 1978; May 26, 1980; March 31, 1986; October 27, 1986, p. 98.

Times (London), March 27, 1980; May 14, 1982; March 9, 1985; March 22, 1985; December 12, 1987.

Times Literary Supplement, October 22, 1971; December 13, 1974; March 21, 1980; October 29, 1982; June 27, 1986, p. 711.

Tribune Books (Chicago), February 4, 1990.

Village Voice, December 15, 1975; December 18, 1978.

Voice Literary Supplement, October, 1982; April, 1990, p. 10.

Washington Post, April 30, 1980; November 10, 1986.

Washington Post Book World, April 15, 1977; April 27, 1980; September 19, 1982; April 20, 1986; November 9, 1986, pp. 5-6; January 21, 1990, p. 7.

*   *   *

WHORTON, M. Donald   1946-

PERSONAL: Born January 25, 1946, in Las Vegas, NM; son of R. H. (in business) and Rachel (in business; maiden name, Siegal) Whorton; married Diana Obrinsky (a physician), April 9, 1972; children: Matthew, Laura. *Education:* Attended U.S. Naval Academy, 1961-62, and New Mexico Highlands University, 1962-64; University of New Mexico, M.D. (with honors), 1968; Johns Hopkins University, M.P.H., 1973.

ADDRESSES: Home—5960 Ascot Dr., Oakland, CA 94611. *Office*—ENSR Health Sciences, 1320 Harbor Bay

Pkwy., Ste. 210, Alameda, CA 94501. *Agent*—John Brockman Associates, Inc., 2307 Broadway, New York, NY 10024.

CAREER: Boston City Hospital, Boston, MA, intern, 1968-69; University of New Mexico, Albuquerque, NM, resident in pathology, 1969-71, instructor in anatomy, 1970-71; Baltimore City Hospitals, Baltimore, MD, resident in medicine, 1972-74, associate director of Division of Emergency Medicine, 1974-75; University of California, Berkeley, lecturer, 1975-79, associate clinical professor of occupational medicine, 1979-87, medical director of Labor Occupational Health Program at Institute of Industrial Relations, Center for Labor Research and Education, 1975-79; ENSR Health Sciences, Alameda, CA, chief medical scientist, 1988—.

Staff physician at Family Planning Clinic, Washington, DC, 1971-72; member of general medical staff of internal medicine at Alta Bates Hospital, 1977-85; principal and senior occupational physician of Environmental Health Associates, Inc., 1978-88. Instructor at Johns Hopkins University, 1973-75; clinical assistant professor at University of California, San Francisco, 1975-77. Advisory Committee for Hazard Evaluation Service and Information Systems, Department of Industrial Relations, State of California, member of committee, 1978-90, chairperson, 1979-86; member of Institute of Medicine, National Academy of Sciences, 1983—, and Permanent Commission on Occupational Health, 1983—.

MEMBER: International Association on Occupational Health, American Public Health Association, Society for Occupational and Environmental Health, American College of Occupational and Environmental Medicine (fellow), American Association for the Advancement of Science, American College of Epidemiology (fellow), California Medical Association, Alameda-Contra Costa County Medical Association, Alpha Omega Alpha.

AWARDS, HONORS: Upjohn Achievement Award, University of New Mexico; clinical scholar of Robert Wood Johnson Foundation, 1972-74.

WRITINGS:

(With others) *A Manual for Floor Covering Apprentices,* Labor Occupational Health Program, University of California, Berkeley, 1976.
(With others) *A Manual for Foundry Workers,* Labor Occupational Health Program, University of California, Berkeley, 1976.
Toxic Substances Regulated by OSHA: A Guide to Their Properties and Hazards, Labor Occupational Health Program, University of California, Berkeley, 1978.
(With others) *Occupational Hazards of Construction: A Manual for Building Trade Apprentices,* Labor Occu-

pational Health Program, University of California, Berkeley, 1979.
(With Eric Skjei) *Of Mice and Molecules: Technology and Human Survival,* Dial, 1983.

Contributor to books, including *Environmental and Occupational Medicine,* edited by W. N. Rom and others, Little, Brown, 1982; *Environmental Influences on Fertility, Pregnancy and Development: Strategies for Measurement and Evaluation,* edited by Marvin S. Legator and others, Alan Liss, 1984; and *Environmental and Occupational Medicine,* 2nd edition, edited by W. N. Rom and others, Little, Brown, 1992. Contributor to proceedings of conferences and workshops. Contributor of about sixty articles to medical journals, including *Journal of Occupational Medicine, Johns Hopkins Medical Journal, Lancet, American Journal of Epidemiology, Journal of the American College of Emergency Physicians, Allergy and Clinical Immunology,* and *Western Journal of Medicine.* Member of editorial board, *American Journal of Public Health,* 1981—.

* * *

WILDE, D. Gunther
See HURWOOD, Bernhardt J.

* * *

WILSON, (Anthony) David 1927-

PERSONAL: Born May 20, 1927, in Rugby, England; son of Donald (an engineer) and Tessie (a teacher; maiden name, Scanlon) Wilson; married Elizabeth Mary Ewins, January 21, 1956 (deceased); children: Clare Wilson Poulter, Andrew, Hatty, James. *Education:* Pembroke College, Cambridge, B.A., 1949, M.A., 1952. *Avocational Interests:* "I hate travel and the theatre; I enjoy opera and old English churches."

ADDRESSES: Home—49 St. James's Ave., Hampton Hill, Middlesex TW12 1HL, England. *Agent:* Michael Sissons, A. D. Peters & Co. Ltd., 10 Buckingham St., London WC2N 6BU, England.

CAREER: Birmingham Post and *Birmingham Mail,* Birmingham, England, reporter, 1952-56; British Broadcasting Corporation (BBC), London, 1956—, began as science correspondent, became manager of Telitext, 1982—.

AWARDS, HONORS: Glasco Travelling Fellowship, 1972; Technology Writers Award, 1978.

WRITINGS:

Body and Antibody, Knopf, 1971, published in England as *The Science of Self,* Penguin, 1971.

The New Archaeology, Knopf, 1976, published in England as *Atoms of Time Past,* Allen Lane, 1976, published as *Science and Archaeology,* Penguin, 1978.

In Search of Penicillin, Knopf, 1976, published in England as *Penicillin in Perspective,* Faber, 1976.

The Colder the Better, Atheneum, 1979, published in England as *Supercold,* Faber, 1979.

Rutherford: Simple Genius, M.I.T. Press, 1983.

SIDELIGHTS: David Wilson's biography, *Rutherford: Simple Genius,* highlights the life of Nobel Prize winner, Ernest Rutherford. The laboratory scientist unlocked the secret of the atom when he became the first person to actually split an atom. In his review of *Rutherford: Simple Genius,* John Campbell writes in the London *Times:* "[David] Wilson was for twenty years science correspondent of the BBC, and his strength lies in expounding Rutherford's work to the layman. Here, his enthusiasm matches, and captures Rutherford's. However effective he may have been in other spheres, Rutherford's genius lay in the laboratory, and genius it unquestionably was, consisting in an infinite capacity for taking pains (he was above all an *experimental* scientist) informed by an extraordinary intuitive sense, an ability to 'see' the necessary structure of the invisible atom and to 'know' what the answer must be before he could prove it."

Philip Morrison comments in a *Scientific American* review of *Rutherford: Simple Genius:* "This full-length biography of Rutherford gathers and orders the many excellent personal accounts already given by many of his colleagues, full of color and scientific appraisal. It makes good use of several interesting studies we owe to professional historians of modern science." Morrison goes on to remark that "this is an honest and comprehensive study of the life and mind of a man who was a genius of the laboratory, although not a simple one, in spite of the catchy subtitle." And finally, Harold Shanee states in the *Library Journal* that in *Rutherford: Simple Genius* "Wilson has given us an excellent biography of one of the scientific giants of the 20th century. . . . This carefully documented book does full justice to a great man."

Wilson explained to *CA* how his background reflects his writings: "I am a journalist. Since I had undergraduate training in science I have found a pleasant 'ecological niche' in science journalism. I earn my living by doing what scientists, on the whole, fail to do; that is by telling people what scientists do and what their results mean in scientific and social terms. I find writing books a delightful relaxation from the strict disciplines of television."

BIOGRAPHICAL/CRITICAL SOURCES:

PERIODICALS

Library Journal, October 15, 1983, p. 1958.

Scientific American, June, 1984, p. 42.
Times (London), February 23, 1984.*

*   *   *

WINCHESTER, Jack
See FREEMANTLE, Brian (Harry)

*   *   *

WINDHAM, Douglas M(acArthur) 1943-

PERSONAL: Born September 5, 1943, in St. Petersburg, FL; son of Hoyt and Ruby (Hattaway) Windham; married Jeanette Poirer, April 27, 1963; children: Karen Adele, Douglas, Jr. *Education:* Florida State University, B.A. (cum laude), 1964, M.A., 1967, Ph.D., 1969.

ADDRESSES: Home—171 Williamsburg Ct., Albany, NY 12203. *Office*—Department of Educational Administration, 1400 Washington Ave., State University of New York at Albany, Albany, NY 12222.

CAREER: Florida A & M University, Tallahassee, part-time assistant professor, 1967-68, assistant professor of economics, 1968-69; University of North Carolina, Greensboro, assistant professor of economics, 1969-72; North Carolina Council on Economic Education, executive director, 1971-72; project specialist in Malaysia, Ford Foundation, 1972-74; University of Chicago, Chicago, IL, associate professor of education and member of department of economics, 1974-79; State University of New York at Albany, professor, Department of Educational Administration, 1979—. Institutional coordinator, USAID-IEES Project, Albany and Washington, DC, 1984—. Consultant on economics education to North Carolina State Department of Public Instruction, 1970, Entrance Examination Board, 1970-71, Greensboro Tax Study Commission, 1971, and World Bank, 1985.

MEMBER: International Society of Educational Planners, American Economic Association, American Educational Research Association, Comparative and International Education Society, Southern Economic Association, Phi Beta Kappa.

AWARDS, HONORS: Spencer Foundation Fellow, 1971.

WRITINGS:

(With Marshall Rudolph Colberg) *The Oyster-Based Economy of Franklin County, Florida,* U.S. Department of Health, Education, and Welfare, 1965.

(With Colberg and T. Stanton Dietrich) *The Social and Economic Values of Apalachicola Bay, Florida,* Federal Water Pollution Control Administration, 1968.

Redistributive Effects of Public Higher Education in Florida (monograph), Department of Economics and

Business Administration, University of North Carolina, Greensboro, 1969.

Education, Equality, and Income Redistribution: A Study of Public Higher Education, Heath, 1970.

Incentive Analysis and Higher Educational Planning, International Institute for Educational Planning, 1978.

Economic Dimensions of Education, National Academy of Education, 1979.

(Editor with Charles E. Bidwell) *Issues in Macroanalysis,* Ballinger, 1980.

(With Lascelles Anderson) *Education and Development: Issues in the Analysis and Planning of Postcolonial Societies,* Lexington Books, 1982.

(With Henry M. Levin) *Accelerating the Progress of All Students,* Institute of Government, State University of New York, 1991.

Also contributor to numerous books. Contributor of articles of journals and periodicals, including *Rivista Internazionale di Scienze Economiche e Commerciali, Journal of Political Economy,* and *Mississippi Valley Journal of Business and Economics.* Member of editorial board, *Economics of Education Review,* 1982—.

WORK IN PROGRESS: Books on the economics of educational financing, the economics of student aid, and state/local tax reorganization.*

*   *   *

WOLFF, Geoffrey (Ansell) 1937-

PERSONAL: Born November 5, 1937, in Los Angeles, CA; son of Arthur Samuels (an aeronautical engineer) and Rosemary (a secretary; maiden name, Loftus) Wolff; married Priscilla Porter (a teacher), August 21, 1965; children: Nicholas Hinckley, Justin Porter. *Education:* Princeton University, A.B. (summa cum laude), 1961; attended Churchill College, Cambridge, 1963-64. *Politics:* Independent. *Religion:* None. *Avocational Interests:* Sailing, listening to jazz.

ADDRESSES: Home—175 Narragansett Ave., Jamestown, RI 02835. *Agent*—Amanda Urban, ICM, 40 West 57th St., New York, NY 10019.

CAREER: Novelist, biographer, essayist. Robert College, Istanbul, Turkey, lecturer in comparative literature, 1961-63; Istanbul University, Istanbul, lecturer and chairman of department of American civilization, 1962-63; *Washington Post,* Washington, DC, 1964-69, began as reporter, became book editor; Maryland Institute, College of Art, Baltimore, lecturer in aesthetics, 1965-69; Corcoran School of Art, Washington, DC, lecturer, 1968-69; *Newsweek,* New York City, books editor, 1969-71; Princeton University, Princeton, NJ, visiting lecturer in creative

arts, 1970-74; Middlebury College, Middlebury, VT, adjunct associate professor, 1977-78; Fannie Hurst Visiting Lecturer, Washington University, 1978; William Jovonovich Lecturer in Fiction, Graduate Writing Program, Columbia University, New York City, 1979; Ferris Professor of Journalism, Princeton University, 1980, 1992; visiting professor, Brown University, 1980-81, 1988, Graduate Writing Program, Boston University, 1982; Brandeis University, Waltham, MA, writer in residence, 1982—. Faculty member, Bread Loaf Writers' Conference, 1976-80, 1985, and Warren Wilson College MFA Program for Writers, Swammanoa, NC, 1982-84, 1993; member of board of trustees, Warren Wilson College Program for Writers, 1981-84; Policy Panel in Literature, National Endowment for the Arts, 1982-85.

AWARDS, HONORS: Woodrow Wilson fellow, 1961-62, 1963-64; Fulbright scholar, 1963-64; Guggenheim fellow in creative writing, 1971-72, 1977-78; National Endowment for the Humanities senior fellow, 1974-75; National Endowment for the Arts fellow, 1979, 1987; nominee for Pulitzer Prize in biography, 1980; American Council of Learned Societies fellow in biographical research, 1984; Distinguished Visiting Scholar, University of Rhode Island, 1987; Rhode Island Governor's Arts Award, 1992; Lila Wallace-*Reader's Digest* fellow, 1992.

WRITINGS:

Bad Debts (novel), Simon & Schuster, 1969.

The Sightseer (novel), Random House, 1974.

Black Sun: The Brief Transit and Violent Eclipse of Harry Crosby (biography), Random House, 1976.

Inklings (novel), Random House, 1977.

The Duke of Deception: Memories of My Father (biography), Random House, 1979.

(Editor and author of introduction) *The Edward Hoagland Reader,* Random House, 1979.

Providence (novel), Viking, 1986.

(Guest editor and author of introductory essay) *The Best American Essays, 1989,* Ticknor & Fields, 1989.

The Final Club (novel), Knopf, 1990.

A Day at the Beach: Recollections (personal essays), Knopf, 1992.

The Age of Consent (novel), Knopf, forthcoming.

Contributor of essay to *Telling Lives: The Biographer's Art,* edited by Marc Pachter, New Republic Books, 1979; contributor of stories, essays and profiles to *American Scholar, New Leader, New Republic, Esquire, Atlantic, Paris Review, Saturday Review,* and other periodicals. Literary critic, *New Times,* 1974-79; contributing editor, *Esquire,* 1979-84, literary editor, 1979; literary critic and contributing editor, *New England Monthly,* 1986-89.

ADAPTATIONS: The Duke of Deception has been purchased by Warner Brothers for a movie; *Providence* has been optioned by Warner Brothers for a movie.

SIDELIGHTS: Essayist, biographer and novelist Geoffrey Wolff is known for his incisive, often satiric characterizations, his ear for dialogue, and his skillful manipulation of style. Two of his books are autobiographical memoirs, and several of his novels also contain a strong autobiographical element.

The main character of Wolff's first novel, *Bad Debts,* is loosely modeled on the author's father, a consummate con artist who would be portrayed directly ten years later in *The Duke of Deception. Bad Debts* follows the misadventures of Benjamin Freeman, a spendthrift who lies and cheats to cover up his misbehavior, and those of his wife and son, who are equally degenerate. According to *New York Times* reviewer John Leonard, the novel "deals wittily with a collection of people . . . whose possibilities appear to have been poisoned at the source, as though birth itself were a fatal wound. Looking at them through Mr. Wolff's savage eye is like being trapped at a disastrous dinner party, or being one among a dozen conscripts in a malfunctioning elevator." The scenes of confrontation between the characters "are in the same league with the best bitterly comic writing of recent years," remarks Richard P. Brickner in the *New York Times Book Review.* "Even though it ends up failing for lack of emotional thrust," the critic comments, "*Bad Debts* is a novel with honest-to-God touchstones in it, a novel to be recommended for virtues rare enough that one is grateful for even their qualified appearance." Writing in the *Yale Review,* Paul Edward Gray calls *Bad Debts* "a rigorously moral novel without a clear moral focus," adding that "it is also, improbable as this may sound, extremely funny, and its appearance provides promising evidence of a new comic talent."

Penned between two less successful novels, Wolff's biography *Black Sun: The Brief Transit and Violent Eclipse of Harry Crosby,* "is a timely document," notes James Atlas in the *Village Voice,* "unsentimental about the '20s and determined not to elevate the importance of his subject." Harry Crosby, the rich and privileged nephew of J. P. Morgan, Jr., shocked his family and Boston society by eloping with a married woman, devoting himself to poetry, and finally committing double suicide with one of his many lovers. *New Republic* contributor J. M. Edelstein describes the biography as "a good story, with all the elements of a spellbinder: the passionate rich, Paris in the '20s, sex, sometimes kinky, scandal in high society and the foreordained ending of tragedy. Geoffrey Wolff makes the most of these exciting elements, writing in a cool and skillful way."

Nevertheless, Edelstein faults *Black Sun* as "a story which has lost its point in the telling, and for that reason it is troubling." The critic explains that "Wolff doesn't claim anything for Harry Crosby; he knows that Harry was not a poet and that his life was neither Art nor artful. As a result, this long and dramatically written book has about as much meaning as most of Harry Crosby's own writing." But D. Keith Mano, writing in the *National Review,* believes that *Black Sun* "is engrossing, chiefly because of those notables who intersect, or were paid to intersect, with Harry Crosby's stupid and selfish brief transit." The *New York Times*'s Christopher Lehmann-Haupt praises Wolff's use of "literary anecdotes, the best of which are very good indeed," as well as his "intelligent social commentaries on Paris in the 1920s and the effects of World War I on its literary generation" and his "detached and ironic prose." The critic concludes that "whatever else he may have been, Harry Crosby was symptomatic of something about his times. They were interesting times, and Mr. Wolff has caught them."

Wolff returned to biography with *The Duke of Deception: Memories of My Father,* an intimate portrait of the man who drifted through various jobs, debts, and scams and left his son with affectionate if ambivalent memories. "A Jewish doctor's son, expelled from a series of boarding schools and rejected by the Army for dental problems," Wolff's father, notes Francine Prose in the *New York Times Magazine,* "reinvented himself as Arthur Saunders Wolff, an Episcopalian, a Yale alumnus, member of the secret society Skull & Bones, an R.A.F. fighter pilot and O.S.S. man who'd served with both the Yugoslavian and the French resistance." When Geoffrey was twelve, Arthur Wolff and his wife separated; Geoffrey stayed with his father while his younger brother Tobias remained with their mother. (Tobias Wolff's own memoir of growing up, *This Boy's Life,* appeared in 1990.)

"To write about one's father—anyone's father—is apt to be an oedipal act," comments Harold Beaver in the *Times Literary Supplement,* "a bid at working him out of the system." Recalling Wolff's earlier, fictionalized treatment of his father in *Bad Debts,* the critic asserts that "ten years later, [Wolff has] come to terms with his [father's] ghost. His second try is triumphant." In telling the story of the man who produced such conflicting emotions in him, "Wolff writes with care and craft, and also with a certain exhilaration, as if this were a story he had wanted to tell for a good long while," observes an *Atlantic* reviewer. "I wrote the book primarily for my sons," the author told Stella Dong in a *Publishers Weekly* interview. "I wanted to show them that even though in the eyes of the world their grandfather might be considered a 'bad' man, that he was not a bad father to me. I had no identity of my own to hang onto when I was growing up, and I wanted to give them as clear a record as possible." Wolff added that "in a way, I realized that I was the connector between my father and my sons."

Although stories of "confidence men" are common in biography and literature, *Time* contributor Paul Gray finds that "Wolff's account of this misspent life is absorbing throughout. It is not just the story of 'a wreck of a desperado,' as he calls the Duke at one point; it is an engrossing, often moving search for the troubled bond between sons and fathers that is known as love." This bond is illustrated throughout the author's narrative, for as John Irving explains in the *New York Times Book Review*, *The Duke of Deception* "is a book abundant with the complexities and contradictions of family sympathy. Keenly perceptive of family ties and family shame, Geoffrey Wolff has succeeded in being true to his emotionally complicated subject while also being divinely easy to read." The critic adds that "in the delicate telling of his father's story, the son manages to bring all versions of 'Duke' Wolff to light." Lehmann-Haupt echoes this assessment, claiming that "without apologizing for any of his father's shortcomings, Wolff also makes us understand the enormous appeal of the man—his erratic genius for self-creation." "Each of us has experienced the feeling of having been deceived by a father or mother or older brother," states Tim O'Brien in the *Saturday Review*. "And this is what gives Geoffrey Wolff's story, with its extreme litany of deception followed by eroding fatherly images, such power and universal truth." Concludes the reviewer: "*The Duke of Deception* awakens us to our own emotions, enlivens our own memories, and compels us to examine our own familial histories."

Several reviewers have also remarked on Wolff's ability to avoid the pitfalls inherent in portraying difficult family relationships. "The problem in writing this book was a problem of tone," claims Donald Hall in the *National Review*, explaining that "if we see the old man through the mature Geoffrey, we see him through the mature Geoffrey watching the young Geoffrey, necessarily a distorting lens." Despite this hazard, Hall believes that Wolff "handles this problem with delicacy, restraint, and intelligence, so that we are able to feel compassion for the old man while the young man rages, at the same time as we feel compassion for the young man saddled with this impossible father." *Los Angeles Times Book Review* contributor Herbert Gold praises in particular Wolff's ability to portray his father "with neither vengefulness and hatred nor false unction. That must have been a task difficult far beyond the normal one of setting down a bizarre account." "This book, in its honesty and lucidity, affirms the son's faithfulness to the father," asserts O'Brien. "It does not condescend, nor judge harshly, nor forgive gratuitously; it does not ignore the father's failings but neither does it

wallow in them. Indeed, in many instances, Geoffrey Wolff celebrates his father's gutty audacity, his flair, his enormous capacity for the outlandish and outlawish." Concludes a *New Yorker* critic: "In this extraordinary memoir—both biography and autobiography—Mr. Wolff recalls, examines, depicts, reaches toward understanding, and brings to the full complexity of life a most exceptional man. . . . It is an achievement of a high order."

When Wolff wrote *The Duke of Deception*, "I wasn't just writing because I was a writer anymore," he told David Remnick of the *Washington Post*. "I wrote it out of need." The author told Remnick that a comparable need inspired *Providence*, a novel that grew out of Wolff's experience with a burglary at his own Providence, Rhode Island, home. *Providence* relates the troubles of Adam Dwyer, a criminal lawyer whose house is robbed shortly after he learns he is dying of leukemia; also appearing are Baby and Skippy, the two hoods who rob Adam, Skippy's girlfriend Lisa, and a cop who becomes involved with both Lisa and the local mob. "In this, his fourth novel, [Wolff] has taken the sense of drama and irony that made [his previous] works so stunningly effective and fused it onto a well-plotted sociological/psychological/moral tale," writes M. George Stevenson in the *Village Voice*. "It is difficult to describe exactly *how* artfully everything is interconnected." While this "might lead you to believe that *Providence* is a humorless, arcane and stultifying 'high art' novel," the critic continues, "it ain't." Writing in the *New York Times Book Review*, James Carroll calls *Providence* "a novel to be read for pleasure, for pure enjoyment, because it brings a supremely light touch to its heavy subject. With unfailing irony and profound affection for all his characters, Mr. Wolff presents their awful story as if he thinks it is funny." "There is a sense of pure reality to these passages," comments Bruce Cook in the *Chicago Tribune Book World*. "Wolff creates the feeling that this is truly the way a man like Adam Dwyer would react."

Many critics draw attention to Wolff's skillful manipulation of style in the novel. "Mr. Wolff has an ear for the way the nuances of English tease one another," Carroll observes. "His paragraphs sparkle because he is a writer at play. Thus each of the five wildly different characters has a distinct voice that is in its way hilarious." In telling the story of the corruption of these characters, "Wolff has deliberately employed a wacky, loose and often wonderful style that breaks most of the rules of grammar known to man," states Ross Thomas in the *Washington Post Book World*. "Yet the style serves the story well, for Wolff is writing largely about civic rot and decay and the various maggots that dwell therein." And a *Time* reviewer remarks that "the atmosphere is entertainingly breezy and sleazy, with a wise-cracking, side-of-the-mouth narrator and some of the tightest, meanest dialogue this side of El-more Leonard."

Lehmann-Haupt, on the other hand, maintains that Wolff's language "is sometimes too dazzling—to the point that it overshadows the people and behavior it purports to be describing. . . . Paradoxically, what purports to be the way people talk sometimes becomes mere literary conceit." Cook similarly finds it distracting that Wolff "programmatically interrupts his narrative with lectures on the social history of Providence and on the structure of organized crime there." "Fortunately, Mr. Wolff's vision of corruption is too powerful and amusing to be undermined by his infatuation with language," concludes Lehmann-Haupt. One aspect of this vision of corruption, according to Celia McGee, is "a reckoning with old-fashioned providence—divine foreknowledge and unavoidable destiny," the critic writes in the *New Republic*. "But Wolff goes one, modern, step further. He positions himself as the all-seeing, all-knowing force behind the story, wielding the power of foresight and informed distance that only storytellers have. This novel," continues McGee, "shows him relishing the role, playing games with genre . . . , creating and destroying lives, speaking in Providence's many different voices." "*Providence* is distinguished both in conception and execution," claims Stevenson. "As a narrative, an essay in novelistic effect, a meditation on degeneration, or a stylistic tour de force, there is little in recent fiction that can equal it."

An autobiographical element is also clearly present in Wolff's next novel, *The Final Club,* which deals with a young man's education at Princeton and two decades of his subsequent career. "Those familiar with [*The Duke of Deception*] will recall that [Wolff], like his hero Nathaniel, attended Princeton in the late 1950s. Indeed, a reading of that memoir and this novel affords glimpses of the human miracle: transmuting the raw material of life into the relatively finished product called art," writes John Meredith Hill in *America*.

As the novel begins, states Arthur Salm in the *San Diego Tribune,* "young Nathaniel Clay, descendant of blue blood on his father's side and immigrant Jewish roughnecks on his mother's, heads east from Seattle for Princeton University" to join the class of 1960. Before he arrives, he witnesses the exclusion by other passengers of a young black man travelling on the same train. Discrimination, both good and bad, and the need to discriminate between the two, emerge as central concerns of the novel as Nathaniel vies for acceptance by Princeton's exclusive "eating clubs" even as he comes to despise himself for buying into the mentality they embody. Nathaniel is eventually accepted by one of the most prestigious clubs, but only after an article appears in the *New York Times* suggesting that the clubs have been systematically excluding Prince-

ton's handful of Jewish students. The latter third of the novel traces Nathaniel's subsequent career through his twentieth college reunion and his own son's application to attend Princeton.

Reviewing *The Final Club* in the *Voice Literary Supplement,* Alberto Mobilio praises Wolff's insight into the workings of class consciousness in America. "Wolff deftly captures our lifelong anxieties about Getting In, although the obsession with gatekeeping wears thin," the critic finds. "Fortunately," he adds, "an energetic sense of irony keeps the ball in play." Similarly, in a *Boston Globe* review, Gail Caldwell admires the way in which, "by focusing on the elite facade and inner sanctum of the class of '60, *The Final Club* exquisitely captures the wider world within its shadowy but hallowed halls." Particularly effective, she finds, is Nathaniel's "uneasy collusion with the things he hates most about Princeton"—his classmates' snobbery and preoccupation with group acceptance. "It is all of a piece, this bone-deep ambivalence, and with Nathaniel, Wolff depicts all the brutality and need that sustain the emotional underpinnings of privilege." *The Final Club,* Mobilio concludes, manages to "impart a sense of real drama to the social rites of young men and women too fortunate to know all clubs are fragile, their members sapped by the price of admission."

Lehmann-Haupt is critical of Wolff's writing in the novel, finding both dialogue and narrative language "too precious." Moreover, he complains, "The plot goes out of control. The ending is too melodramatic." Nonetheless, he concedes, "what's right about *The Final Club* is that somehow it never loses its hold on the reader." Mobilio, on the other hand, praises the author's writing as "muscular" and "telegraphic," while Caldwell finds the second half of the novel particularly effective. The first section, she suggests, is marred somewhat by the narrator's "cheeky tone . . . that too closely mirrors the invincibility of Princeton's chosen." But the second half, she maintains, is "beautifully handled," and "unfolds with poise and sadness, and all the surprise that comes with unsurprising endings."

The Final Club was followed by another memoir, a book of essays entitled *A Day at the Beach.* The nine essays in this collection constitute an episodic autobiography, touching on the author's early enchantment with literature; his teaching days at a boy's school in Istanbul and his apprenticeship as an obituary writer, cub reporter, and finally book editor at the *Washington Post;* a failed friendship and a bout with the bottle; open-heart surgery and subsequent adventures in mountaineering and ocean sailing. The title essay recounts the episode that provided the impetus for Wolff's writing of the memoir: a nightmarish vacation on the Caribbean island of Sint Maarten in 1985 that culminated in a near-fatal heart attack.

As always, Wolff's writing style commands a large portion of critical attention. "Style," suggest Lehmann-Haupt, "is the hero of these essays. Style is what makes them stand or fall." And style, he suggests, is the weapon that enabled the author to survive his tumultuous upbringing and that continues to serve him in dealing with the vicissitudes of adulthood. "At times, Mr. Wolff's relentless grasping for style can pall, particularly when he pays the price of archness to avoid common parlance," the critic claims. Nonetheless, he pronounces the collection on the whole "sparkling." Critiquing *A Day at the Beach* in the *Washington Post Book World*, Mordechai Richler comments that Wolff's "prose is literate, yet enriched by a finely tuned colloquial bounce. He manages to be tender while eschewing sentimentality. His insights into family flow effortlessly through this memoir, never demanding that attention be paid." Richler finds fault only with the final essay, an account of a family sailing trip that he judges overly long and overly technical. "Wolff is as always a dream to read," writes Judith Levine in the *Village Voice*. "He plays his anecdotes like a romantic pianist, rubato, cuts his cameos like a Venetian, and dashes into neologism like an Olympic skater, stopping short safely this side of cute."

Levine suggests that Wolff's essays are weakest when he tries to apply his considerable powers of analysis to his own behavior. "Perceptive as Wolff is about others," she writes, "he misses the mark most regularly when he's introspecting." Nonetheless, she continues, "Even when Wolff misses the mark, . . .he does so with elan, intelligence, and wit." "What emerges from *A Day at the Beach*," writes Emily White in *L. A. Weekly*, "is not the voice of authority or even the voice of reason. . . . Wolff is simply getting his life on paper because he finds it to be wondrous, strange, and because his heart is thundering in his chest." "In these highly stylish and witty pieces," Martha Liebrum states in the *Houston Post*, Wolff "proves himself both a consummate social critic and a great survivor."

BIOGRAPHICAL/CRITICAL SOURCES:

BOOKS

Contemporary Literary Criticism, Volume 41, Gale, 1987, pp. 454-62.

PERIODICALS

America, May 18, 1991.
Atlantic, May, 1974; September, 1979; February, 1986, pp. 86-87.
Book World, November 23, 1969.
Boston Globe, September 16, 1990, pp. B43-B44.
Brick, winter, 1991, 57-59.

Chicago Tribune Book World, August 26, 1979; March 2, 1986.
Detroit Free Press, October 28, 1990.
Detroit News, August 19, 1979.
Houston Post, April 5, 1992.
Kansas City Star, December 9, 1990, p. 1-9.
L. A. Weekly, April 10-16, 1992, p. 34.
Los Angeles Times Book Review, July 8, 1979.
Nation, November 3, 1979.
National Review, November 12, 1976; October 26, 1979.
New Republic, April 27, 1974; November 6, 1976; March 11, 1978; August 18, 1979; June 16, 1986.
Newsweek, November 17, 1969; February 18, 1974; September 6, 1976; August 27, 1979.
New York Daily News, September 30, 1990.
New Yorker, October 8, 1979; May 5, 1986.
New York Newsday, December 16, 1990; March 29, 1992.
New York Review of Books, February 26, 1970; February 17, 1977.
New York Times, November 12, 1969; February 11, 1974; September 6, 1976; September 24, 1976; January 2, 1978; August 13, 1979; February 10, 1986; September 10, 1990.
New York Times Book Review, February 1, 1970; March 3, 1974; August 22, 1976; January 8, 1978; August 12, 1979; February 16, 1986; March 1, 1987.
New York Times Magazine, February 5, 1989, pp. 22-26.
People, May 18, 1992.
Publishers Weekly, September 3, 1979.
Rhode Island Monthly, October, 1990, pp. 52-54, 84.
St. Louis Post-Dispatch, June 14, 1992.
San Diego Tribune, September 12, 1990.
Saturday Review, January 21, 1978; September 29, 1979.
Time, January 5, 1970; September 6, 1976; August 13, 1979; July 7, 1986.
Times (London), June 26, 1980.
Times Literary Supplement, June 11, 1970; August 31, 1974; January 14, 1977; July 4, 1980; November 28, 1986.
Village Voice, November 12, 1976; September 17, 1979; March 18, 1986; April 28, 1992.
Voice Literary Supplement, October, 1990.
Washington Post, January 29, 1978; March 22, 1986.
Washington Post Book World, February 10, 1974; August 8, 1976; August 12, 1979; December 2, 1979; February 23, 1986; September 16, 1990; March 22, 1992, pp. 1-2.
Washington Times, December 31, 1990.
Yale Review, March, 1970.

WOOD, Christopher (Hovelle) 1935-
(Rosie Dixon, Oliver Grape, Timothy Lea, Penny Sutton)

PERSONAL: Born November 5, 1935, in London, England; son of Walter Leonard and Audrey (Hovelle) Wood; married Jane Caroline Patrick, July 21, 1962; children: Caroline Sarah, Adam Sebastian Hovelle, Benjamin Nicholas Hamilton. *Education:* Cambridge University, M.A., 1960. *Politics:* "Pink Conservative." *Religion:* Church of England.

ADDRESSES: Home—The Limes, Meldreth, Cambridgeshire, England. *Office*—Masius Wynne Williams, 2 St. James Sq., London SW1, England. *Agent*—Deborah Rogers, 29 Goodge St., London W1P 12D, England.

CAREER: British Colonial Office, plebiscite organizer in Southern Cameroons, West Africa, 1960-61; Masius Wynne Williams, London, England, account executive, 1961—. *Military service:* British Army, Royal Artillery, served in Cyprus; became second lieutenant.

MEMBER: Institute of Practitioners in Advertising, Royston Rugby Club.

WRITINGS:

Make It Happen to Me, Constable, 1969, published as *Kiss Off,* Sphere Books, 1970.
'Terrible Hard,' Says Alice (novel), Constable, 1970.
John Adam, Samurai, Arlington Books, 1971.
John Adam in Eden, Sphere Books, 1973.
The Further Adventures of Barry Lyndon by Himself, Futura Publications, 1976.
James Bond: The Spy Who Loved Me, J. Cape, 1977.
Fire Mountain, M. Joseph, 1979.
North to Rabaul (novel), Arbor House, 1979.
Moonraker (screenplay), United Artists, 1979, novelization of screenplay published as *James Bond and Moonraker,* Jove, 1979.
Dead Centre, Futura Publications, 1980.
Taiwan, Viking, 1981.
A Dove against Death, Viking, 1983.
Kago, Holt, 1986.

UNDER PSEUDONYM ROSIE DIXON

Confessions of a Gym Mistress, Futura Publications, 1974.
Confessions of a Night Nurse, Futura Publications, 1974.
Confessions from a Package Tour, Futura Publications, 1975.
Confessions of a Lady Courier, Futura Publications, 1975.
Confessions from an Escort Agency, Futura Publications, 1975.
Confessions of a Babysitter, Futura Publications, 1975.
Confessions of a Personal Secretary, Futura Publications, 1976.

UNDER PSEUDONYM OLIVER GRAPE

Crumpet Voluntary, Futura Publications, 1974.
It's a Knock-Up!, Futura Publications, 1975.

UNDER PSEUDONYM TIMOTHY LEA

Confessions of a Window Cleaner, Sphere Books, 1971.
Confessions from a Holiday Camp, Sphere Books, 1972.
Confessions of a Driving Instructor, Sphere Books, 1972.
Confessions from a Hotel, Sphere Books, 1973.
Confessions from the Clink, Sphere Books, 1973.
Confessions of a Film Extra, Sphere Books, 1973.
Confessions of a Travelling Salesman, Futura Publications, 1973.
Confessions from a Health Farm, Futura Publications, 1974.
Confessions from the Pop Scene, Futura Publications, 1974, published as *Confessions of a Pop Performer,* 1975.
Confessions of a Private Soldier, Sphere Books, 1974.
Confessions from the Shop Floor, Futura Publications, 1975.
Confessions of a Long Distance Lorry Driver, Futura Publications, 1975.
Confessions of a Plumber's Mate, Futura Publications, 1975.
Confessions of a Private Dick, Futura Publications, 1975.
Confessions from a Luxury Liner, Futura Publications, 1976.
Confessions from a Nudist Colony, Futura Publications, 1976.

UNDER PSEUDONYM PENNY SUTTON

The Stewardesses, Sphere Books, 1973.
The Stewardesses Down Under, Sphere Books, 1973.
The Jumbo Jet Girls, Futura Publications, 1974.
I'm Penny, Fly Me, Futura Publications, 1975.*

*   *   *

WOOD, Phyllis Anderson 1923-

PERSONAL: Born October 24, 1923, in Palo Alto, CA; daughter of Carl Arthur (a high school principal) and Beulah (Davidson) Anderson; married Roger Holmes Wood (a certified financial planner), December 26, 1947; children: Stephen Holmes, David Anderson, Elizabeth Satterlee. *Education:* University of California, Berkeley, A.B., 1944; Stanford University, teaching certificate, 1946; San Francisco State University, M.A., 1977. *Religion:* Presbyterian.

ADDRESSES: Home—65 Capay Circle, South San Francisco, CA 94080.

CAREER: Teacher of speech, drama, and English in high schools in California, 1944-49; Jefferson High School District, Daly City, CA, teacher of reading and English-as-a-second-language, 1965-90. Volunteer tutor for adult literacy program, Project Read.

MEMBER: Society of Children's Book Writers, Authors Guild, California Writers Club.

AWARDS, HONORS: Helen Keating Ott Award, Church and Synagogue Library Association, 1981.

WRITINGS:

FOR YOUNG ADULTS

Andy, Westminster, 1971, published as *The Night Summer Began,* Scholastic Book Services, 1976.

Your Bird Is Here, Tom Thompson, Westminster, 1972.

I've Missed a Sunset or Three, Westminster, 1973.

Song of the Shaggy Canary, Westminster, 1974.

A Five-Color Buick and a Blue-Eyed Cat, Westminster, 1975.

I Think This Is Where We Came In, Westminster, 1976.

Win Me and You Lose, Westminster, 1977.

The Novels of Phyllis Anderson Wood: A Teacher's Guide, New American Library, 1977.

Get a Little Lost, Tia, Westminster, 1978.

This Time Count Me In, Westminster, 1980.

Pass Me a Pine Cone, Westminster, 1980.

Meet Me in the Park, Angie, Westminster, 1983.

Then I'll Be Home Free, Dodd, 1986.

The Revolving Door Stops Here, Dutton, 1990.

SIDELIGHTS: Phyllis Anderson Wood once told *CA:* "I began writing for young adults because as a teacher of high school reading classes I was continually hampered by the lack of books that appealed to students who hadn't yet formed a reading habit. For the past seven years, through the publication of eight novels, my students have been both my soundest critics and my warmest fans. Having had to decide, initially, whether I would write to please the students or the critics, and having opted for the students' enthusiasm, I now am pleased to be getting positive support from both groups."

*   *   *

WOOD, Robert Coldwell 1923-

PERSONAL: Born September 16, 1923, in St. Louis, MO; son of Thomas Frank and Mary (Bradshaw) Wood; married Margaret Byers, March 22, 1952; children: Frances, Margaret, Frank. *Education:* Princeton University, A.B. (summa cum laude), 1946; Harvard University, M.P.A., 1948, M.A., 1949, Ph.D., 1950. *Politics:* Democrat. *Religion:* Episcopalian.

ADDRESSES: Home—85 East India Row, Boston, MA 02110.

CAREER: Florida Legislative Bureau, Tallahassee, associate director, 1949-51; Bureau of the Budget, Washington, DC, office of management, 1951-54; U.S. Department of Housing and Urban Development (HUD), Washington, DC, undersecretary, 1966-68, secretary, 1968-69; Massachusetts Bay Transportation Authority, Boston, MA, chairman, 1969-70; Boston Public Schools, superintendent, 1978-80. Harvard University, Cambridge, MA, assistant professor, 1954-57; Massachusetts Institute of Technology (MIT), Cambridge, MA, assistant professor, 1957-59, associate professor, 1959-62, professor of political science, 1962-66, head of political science department, 1965-66, 1969-70; Harvard University-MIT Joint Center for Urban Studies, Cambridge, MA, director, 1969-70; University of Massachusetts at Boston, president, 1970-77, professor of political science, 1981-83, director of urban studies, 1981-83; Wesleyan University, Middletown, CT, Henry Luce Professor of Democratic Institutions and the Social Order, 1983-93, John E. Andrus Professor of Government, 1992-93; Luce Professor Emeritus, 1993—. Trustee, College Board; trustee, Boston Museum of Science; director, Lincoln Institute of Land Policy; member, advisory committee for area development; member, committee for economic development, 1961; chair, president's task force on urban and metropolitan problems, 1964-65; chair, Literacy Coalition, 1986-89; chair, urban policy committee, National Association of State Universities and Land Grant Colleges, 1990-91. Visiting professor of political science, Massachusetts Institute of Technology, 1980-81; visiting professor of education, Harvard University, 1980-81. *Military service:* U.S. Army, 1943-46; served in World War II, became sergeant, three battle citations.

MEMBER: American Academy of Arts and Sciences (fellow), American Political Science Association, American Society of Public Administration, American Antiquarian Society, National Municipal League, New England Political Science Association (president, 1989-90), Cosmos Club (Washington, DC), University Club (New York City), Phi Beta Kappa.

AWARDS, HONORS: Fruin Colnon Award in urban affairs, National Municipal League, 1960; public administrator of the year, Massachusetts chapter, American Society for Public Administration, 1969; Mayor's Jubilee Bostonian Award in education, 1980; Hubert Humphrey Award, American Political Science Association (APSA), 1985; Literacy Volunteers of Connecticut award, 1986; career achievement award, APSA, 1989; Humphrey Award, Public Policy Association, 1991.

WRITINGS:

Suburbia: Its People and Their Politics, Houghton, 1959.

Metropolis against Itself, Committee for Economic Development, 1959.

(With V. V. Almendinger) *1400 Governments: The Political Economy of the New York Region,* Harvard University Press, 1961.

(Co-author) *Schoolmen and Politics: A Study of State Aid to Education in the Northeast,* Syracuse University Press, 1962.

(Co-author) *Politics and Government in the United States,* Harcourt, 1965.

The Necessary Majority: Middle America and the Urban Crisis, Columbia University Press, 1972.

(Editor) *Remedial Law: When Courts become Administrators,* University of Massachusetts Press, 1990.

Whatever Possessed the President? Academic Experts and Presidential Policy, 1960-1988, University of Massachusetts Press, 1993.

Contributor to *The Suburban Community,* Putnam, 1958; *Area and Power,* Free Press, 1959; *Urban Life and Form,* Holt, 1962; *Man and the Modern City,* University of Pittsburgh Press, 1963; *Scientists and National Policy Making,* Columbia University Press, 1964; *Parish in the Heart of the City,* 1976; *Suburbia Re-Examined,* edited by Barbara M. Kelly, Greenwood Press, 1988; and *Neighborhood Policy and Programs,* edited by Naomi Carmon, Macmillan (London), 1990. Author of articles for journals, including *Journal of Policy Analysis and Management, New England Journal of Public Policy, Economic Development Quarterly* and *Journal of Public Affairs.*

*   *   *

WOODS, P. F.
See BAYLEY, Barrington J(ohn)

*   *   *

WOODS, William 1916-

PERSONAL: Born in 1916, in New York; married Kato Havas (a violinist), May 17, 1940 (divorced, 1961); married Kit Pharaoh (a teacher), March 4, 1966 (divorced, 1983); children: Susanna Woods Egan, Pamela Woods Thomas, Catherine, Alison, Jonathan, Jason, Thomasin. *Education:* University of North Carolina, B.A., 1936; University of Iowa, M.A., 1939. *Politics:* "Left." *Religion:* None.

ADDRESSES: Home—Yat, Glascwm, Llandrindod Wells, Powys, Wales. *Agent*—Curtis Brown Ltd., 575 Madison Ave., New York, NY 10022.

CAREER: Writer. *Military service:* U.S. Army, Infantry, 1942.

MEMBER: Royal Society of Literature (fellow), Savage Club (London).

WRITINGS:

The Edge of Darkness (novel), Lippincott, 1942.

The Street of Seven Monks (novel), Little, Brown, 1948.

Riot at Gravesend, Duell, Sloan & Pearce, 1952.

Manuela (novel), Hill & Wang, 1957.

A Yugoslav Adventure, Loudin, 1957.

The Mask (novel), Hill & Wang, 1960.

A Mermaid in Nikoli (novel), Hill & Wang, 1967.

Poland: Eagle in the East, Hill & Wang, 1969.

A History of the Devil, Putnam, 1973.

(Editor) *A Casebook of Witchcraft,* Putnam, 1974.

England in the Age of Chaucer, Stein & Day, 1976.

Also author of *Thunder on Saturday,* 1952. Author of more than fifty television plays and six filmscripts.

Woods's work has been translated into German, Spanish, Danish, Swedish, Norwegian, and Slovenian.

WORK IN PROGRESS: A history of female revolutionists.

SIDELIGHTS: William Woods once told *CA:* "Nothing any author says about his own motivation is of the slightest value. And nothing he may feel about liberty, justice, truth, or the eternal verities can possibly be condensed into a paragraph. I have travelled America, Europe, and parts of Africa. I speak German, Slovenian, French, some Polish. I know something of the Middle Ages and intend to know more. I love women, whisky, and literary history, not in any particular order of preference. I possess the best library of English poetry I know of in private hands. I enjoy life more than most, and if I were to drop dead tomorrow would consider I had been well served by my creator."

BIOGRAPHICAL/CRITICAL SOURCES:

PERIODICALS

Times Literary Supplement, July 17, 1969.*

*   *   *

WOOTTERS, John (Henry, Jr.) 1928-

PERSONAL: Born February 9, 1928, in Houston, TX; son of John Henry (a surgeon) and Mary (Spence) Wootters; married Jeanne Claire McRae, April 21, 1951. *Education:* Attended Baylor University, 1946-49. *Politics:* Conservative. *Avocational Interests:* Shooting, hunting, reloading, whitetail deer management on his ranch near Laredo, TX, public speaking on wildlife management, archaeology, herpetology.

ADDRESSES: 206 Walnut Bend Lane, Houston, TX 77042.

CAREER: Texas Medical Center, M. D. Anderson Hospital and Tumor Clinic, Houston, staff writer for *Cancer Bulletin,* 1949-51; McCann-Erickson Advertising Agency, Houston, copywriter, 1951-53; Hayes, Wootters & Troxell Advertising Agency, Houston, partner and creative director, 1953-58; free-lance writer, 1958-77; Petersen Publishing Co., Los Angeles, CA, executive editor of *Hunting,* 1977—. Public speaker. *Military service:* U.S. Army, 1953-55; served in Korea; became sergeant.

MEMBER: Safari Club International (past president of Houston chapter; past member of national board of directors), National Rifle Association (member of board of directors, 1979—), Exotic Wildlife Association (associate member), Texas Trophy Hunters Association (life member), Texas Outdoor Writers Association, Texas Army (colonel), Greater Houston Sportsmen's Coalition (founding chair), Buckhorn Hunting Club, Bayou Rifles.

AWARDS, HONORS: Named Distinguished Rifleman, National Rifle Association, 1945.

WRITINGS:

Complete Guide to Practical Handloading, Winchester Press, 1976.
Hunting Trophy Deer, Winchester Press, 1977.
A Guide to Hunting in Texas, Gulf Publishing, 1979.
(With Jerry Smith) *Wildlife Images,* Petersen Publishing, 1981.
(Author of foreword) J. D. Clayton, *Ruger Number One,* Blacksmith Press, 1983.
The Complete Handloader, Stackpole, 1988.

Contributor to *The American Sportsman Treasury,* edited by Jerry Matson, Knopf, 1971; *Hunting Moments of Truth,* edited by George Peper and James Rikhoff, Winchester Press, 1973; *Hunting America's Game Animals and Birds,* edited by Robert Elman and Peper, Winchester Press, 1975; *All About Waterfowling in America,* edited by Jerome Knap, Winchester Press, 1976; *All About Small-Game Hunting in America,* edited by Russell Tinsley, Winchester Press, 1976; *The Experts' Book of Big-Game Hunting in North America,* edited by D. E. Petzal, Simon & Schuster, 1976; *All About Rifle Hunting and Shooting in America* edited by Steve Ferber, Winchester Press, 1977; and *The Professionals' Guide to Whitetail,* edited by Robert Rogers, Texas Hunting Services, 1984. Also contributor to magazines, including *Handloader's Digest, Outdoor Life, Sports Afield,* and *True.*

WORK IN PROGRESS: A book on whitetail deer, tentatively titled *Wootters on Whitetails.*

SIDELIGHTS: John Wootters was named Distinguished Rifleman by the National Rifle Association when he was seventeen years old. With the 8th Army Small Arms Team in Seoul, Korea, he was rated expert with all infantry weapons. He also competed in skeet and trap shooting, with the silhouette rifle, benchrest, and blackpowder rifle and pistol.

Wootters has hunted big game, small game, birds, and what he calls "varmints" in North America, Central America, South America, and Africa. His writing specialties include ballistics, handloading ammunition, technical firearms, shooting and hunting, wildlife management, wildlife photography and nature study, fresh and salt water angling, knives, and the politics of gun control.

Wootters once told *CA:* "I write for several reasons. I take immense pleasure and satisfaction in the act of writing, and I do not believe in spending my life at any sort of job I do not enjoy. I particularly enjoy sharing my knowledge and experience with others—teaching, if you wish to put it that way. The topics about which I write are also my avocations, so writing about them permits a more extensive involvement and participation.

"Above all, I write to make a living. I am a professional, not a dilettante, not an 'artiste,' and not a person who supports his writing habit with income from other sources. I take great pride in being a professional, as well as in using the language well.

"I have published well in excess of two-and-a-half million words and have long since grown weary of the snobbery of people who feel that only novels, poetry, and such constitute 'real' or 'serious' writing, especially when the majority of them couldn't make a day-in, day-out living from writing if their lives depended on it.

"My work will neither alter the course of literary history nor yield stunning new insights into the fundamental nature of mankind. I flatter myself, however, that it does interpret some aspects of nature for my readers and may help, in a small way, to improve their understanding and appreciation of the real world in which we live, and the role of mankind in it. I believe that's worth doing.

"My book, *Hunting Trophy Deer,* deserves a few words. I am informed it has now become the best-selling book on its topic ever written. It is the only book ever to be a main selection of the Outdoor Life Book Club and and an alternate selection of the Field and Stream Book Club in the same year. It has been called 'an instant classic' and a 'landmark,' and is said by some to represent a turning point in the attitudes of American hunters toward quality deer management in particular and big game management in general. It seems to have become a sort of holy scripture to an emerging cult of whitetail deer worshippers and to have made me one of the gurus of that cult. Far more important, however, it appears to be having a noticeable impact on the thinking of hunters (about themselves, the environment, and the whitetail deer) to the ultimate benefit of this particular wildlife resource. If so, that is a real and worthwhile contribution to society in which I shall take pride.

"The point is that I am one of the relatively few working writers in this country (outside the newspaper field) who fill the white space up every month, but from whose work nobody will ever make a top-grossing movie . . . and with whom that happens to be okay. We writers are famous mostly within our own rather narrow, vertical fields, and we will surely have little impact on American letters. Some of us are very good writers, however, and we do what we do with pride and professionalism. We write more out of discipline than inspiration, but we may influence more readers per year than all the novelists in America, which is a responsibility not to be taken lightly."

BIOGRAPHICAL/CRITICAL SOURCES:

PERIODICALS

Deer and Deer Hunting, July/August, 1984.
North American Whitetail, December, 1983.
Texas Sportsman, December, 1982.*

*   *   *

WORSWICK, Clark 1940-

PERSONAL: Born September 16, 1940, in Berkeley, CA; son of Wallace Burdette and Elizabeth (Benedict) Worswick; married Joan Mitchell (a teacher), September 19, 1970; children: Lucia, Nicholas. *Education:* Attended Visva Bharati, 1959, and Harvard University, 1966-70.

ADDRESSES: Home and office—Oak Summit Rd., Millbrook, NY 12545.

CAREER: Film director, 1960-86; Asia Society Gallery, guest director, 1975—; Japan Society Gallery, guest director, 1978-79.

AWARDS, HONORS: Indo-American fellowship, Smithsonian Institution, 1979.

WRITINGS:

The Last Empire: Photographs of British India, Aperture, 1976.
Imperial China: Photographs 1850-1911, Crown, 1978.
An Edwardian Observer, Crown, 1978.
Japan: Photographs, 1854-1904, Knopf, 1979.
Princely India, Knopf, 1980.

The Camera and the Tribe, Knopf, 1982.

DOCUMENTARY FILM SCRIPTS

Changing Rains, 1965.
California, 1968.
Kotah, 1970.

FEATURE FILM SCRIPTS

Family Honor, Cinerama/Abc Films, 1973.
(With Louis Pastore) *Agent on Ice,* Shapiro Entertainment, 1985.
The Second Raven, 1986.
A.N.T., 1986.

SIDELIGHTS: Worswick writes: "When I was eighteen I went to India to university. At a certain moment in time I calculated that I had traveled seventy thousand miles on Indian third-class trains—some sort of grotesque record, seeing the 'remains' of British India, archaeological sites, and tribal groups. Living in the Salvation Army hostels and the ashrams of the Maha Bodi society during the period I stayed in India affected me most as an artist; it was the last moment the 'white man' was held in (almost) universal esteem in Asia, the Middle East, and Africa. From the time I was eighteen until I was twenty-eight, over a ten-year period, I traveled more or less constantly in Asia, Africa, and the Middle East. I supported myself by doing free-lance photography and films.

"Somewhere along the way I discovered the work of nineteenth-century photographers working in the same areas I was working in, and I brought together a collection of work done in India during the nineteenth century that resulted in an exhibition and a book, *The Last Empire.* It has always amazed me that photography managed, at the penultimate moment in Asia and the Middle East, to document the way traditional cultures were before they were radically, irrevocably changed by the onslaught of the European industrial revolution. This change has been so complete that at this moment Tehran is very similar to Tokyo in looks, Bombay looks like Rio, et cetera."*

*   *   *

WYNN, D(ale) Richard 1918-

PERSONAL: Born November 20, 1918, in Derry, PA; son of Colonel Elsworth and Cora (Jarrett) Wynn; married Helen Louise Specht, August 21, 1941 (divorced, March 15, 1970); married Joanne Lindsay, December 1, 1970; children: (first marriage) Sherry Lindsay Mendelson, Leeanne Snook; (second marriage) Rachel Lindsay. *Education:* Bucknell University, B.S., 1939, M.S., 1946; Columbia University, Ed.D., 1952. *Avocational Interests:* Painting, flying, photography, playing the organ.

ADDRESSES: Home—4514 Bucktail Dr., Allison Park, PA 15101. *Office*—School of Education, University of Pittsburgh, PA 15260.

CAREER: Stoystown High School, Stoystown, PA, teacher, 1940-43; Forbes Joint Schools, Kantner, PA, superintendent, 1946-51; Columbia University, Teachers College, New York City, began as assistant professor, became associate professor, 1952-60, project associate, Cooperative Program in Educational Administration, 1952-55, associate coordinator, Cooperative Center for Educational Administration, 1955-59; University of Pittsburgh, Pittsburgh, PA, professor of education, 1960—, associate dean, 1960-65, chairman of educational administration, 1967-74. President, Associated Educational Consultants, Inc., 1966-69; executive secretary, Tri-State Area School Study Council, 1973-80. Member of board of education, Norwood (NJ) schools, 1956-60. Professor, National Academy for School Executives. Private pilot. *Military service:* U.S. Army Air Forces, 1942-45, held in and escaped from a German prisoner of war camp; became first lieutenant; awarded Air Medal with oak leaf cluster, Purple Heart.

MEMBER: American Association of School Administrators, American Education Research Association, National Association of Elementary School Principals, National Conference of Professors of Educational Administration (secretary-treasurer, 1955-58), National Society for Study of Education, Pennsylvania Council for Educational Administration (member of board of directors, 1981-84), Phi Delta Kappa, Kappa Phi Kappa, Sigma Phi Epsilon.

AWARDS, HONORS: American Education, 5th edition, was cited by Enoch Pratt Library as an outstanding book on education, 1964, and by American Institute of Graphic Arts as one of the textbooks illustrating the best in graphic arts; distinguished achievement award for excellence in educational journalism, Educational Press Association of America, 1982.

WRITINGS:

Careers in Education, McGraw, 1960.
American Education, McGraw, 1960, 7th edition (with wife, Joanne Wynn and C. DeYoung), 1972, 9th edition, C. E. Merrill, 1990.
(With others) *Organizing Schools for Effective Education,* Interstate, 1961.
Organization of Public Schools, Center for Applied Research in Education, 1964.
(With Willard Elsbree and Harold McNally) *Elementary School Administration and Supervision,* 3rd edition, American Book Co., 1967.
Unconventional Methods: Materials for Preparing Educational Administrators, University Council for Educational Administration, 1972.
The Administrative Team: Theory and Practice, American Association of School Administrators, 1973.
Administrative Response to Conflict, University of Pittsburgh, 1973.
Administrative Team: Leadership by Consensus, C. E. Merrill, 1984.

Also contributor to numerous books, including *Administrative Behavior in Education,* Harper, 1957; and *Changes in Teacher Education: An Appraisal,* Yearbook, 1963. Contributor to *Encyclopedia International* and to professional journals.

SIDELIGHTS: D. Richard Wynn told *CA:* "I am now writing short stories based on experiences of mine and others in combat flying and POW camps in Europe in World War II. I want to record human interest aspects of the war—courage, fear, triumphs, tragedies, grim humor, etc."

Y

YACOWAR, Maurice 1942-

PERSONAL: Born March 25, 1942, in Prelate, Saskatchewan, Canada; son of Samuel and Sophie (Gitterman) Yacowar; children: Margaret Mia, Sam Jason Eric. *Education:* University of Calgary, B.A., 1962; University of Alberta, M.A., 1965; University of Birmingham, Ph.D., 1968.

ADDRESSES: Office—1399 Johnston St., Vancouver, British Columbia V6H 3R9 Canada.

CAREER: Lethbridge Junior College, England, lecturer, 1964-66; Brock University, St. Catharines, Ontario, Canada, assistant professor, 1968-72, associate professor, 1972-78, professor of drama and English, 1978-89, chairperson of department of drama, 1972-75, dean of humanities, 1980-87; Emily Carr College of Art and Design, Vancouver, British Columbia, Canada, dean of academic affairs, 1989—. Film reviewer for *St. Catherines Standard,* 1974-89.

WRITINGS:

No Use Shutting the Door (poetry), Fiddlehead, 1971.
Hitchcock's British Films, Archon Books, 1976.
Tennessee Williams and Film, Ungar, 1977.
I Found It at the Movies, Revisionist Press, 1977.
Loser Take All: The Comic Art of Woody Allen, Ungar, 1979, expanded edition, Continuum, 1991.
Method in Madness: The Comic Art of Mel Brooks, St. Martin's, 1981, expanded edition, W. H. Allen, 1982.
The Films of Paul Morrissey, Cambridge University Press, 1993.

YATES, Richard 1926-1992

PERSONAL: Born February 3, 1926, in Yonkers, NY; died of emphysema and complications from minor surgery, November 7, 1992, in Birmingham, AL; son of Vincent M. (a sales executive) and Ruth (Maurer) Yates; married Sheila Bryant, 1948 (divorced, 1959); married Martha Speer, 1968 (divorced, 1974); children: Sharon, Monica, Gina.

CAREER: United Press Association, New York City, financial reporter, 1946-48; Remington Rand, Inc., New York City, publicity writer, 1948-50; free-lance public relations writer, 1953-60; New School for Social Research, New York City, teacher of creative writing, 1959-62; Columbia University, New York City, teacher of creative writing, 1960-62; United Artists, Hollywood, screenwriter, 1962; U.S. Attorney General Robert Kennedy, Washington, DC, speech writer, 1963; University of Iowa, Iowa City, lecturer, 1964-65, assistant professor of English, 1966-92; Columbia Pictures, Hollywood, screenwriter, 1965-66; Wichita State University, writer in residence, 1971-72; has taught at Harvard Extension, Columbia University and Boston University. *Military service:* U.S. Army, 1944-46.

AWARDS, HONORS: Atlantic Firsts award, 1953; National Book Award nomination for *Revolutionary Road;* Guggenheim fellowship, 1962, 1981; American Academy Grant, 1963; National Institute of Arts and Letters grant, 1963 and 1975; Creative Arts Award, Brandeis University, 1964; National Endowment for the Arts grant, 1966, and award, 1984; Rockefeller grant, 1967; Rosenthal Foundation award, 1976; National Magazine Award for Fiction, 1978, for "Oh, Joseph, I'm So Tired."

WRITINGS:

NOVELS

Revolutionary Road, Atlantic-Little, Brown, 1961.
A Special Providence, Knopf, 1969.
Disturbing the Peace, Delacorte, 1975.
The Easter Parade, Delacorte, 1976.
A Good School, Delacorte, 1978.
Young Hearts Crying, Delacorte, 1984.
Cold Spring Harbor, Delacorte, 1986.

SHORT STORIES

Eleven Kinds of Loneliness (collection), Atlantic-Little, Brown, 1962.
Liars in Love (collection), Delacorte, 1981.

Also contributor of short stories to *Prize Stories 1967: The O. Henry Awards,* edited by William Abrahams, Doubleday, 1967, and to periodicals, including *North American Review, Esquire,* and *Saturday Evening Post.*

OTHER

(Editor) *Stories for the Sixties,* Bantam, 1963.
William Styron's Lie Down in Darkness: A Screenplay, Ploughshares, 1985.

Also author of screenplay *The Bridge at Remagen* with William Roberts and Roger Hirson, 1969.

SIDELIGHTS: "If it's true that wisdom comes through suffering, then Richard Yates' characters are the wisest of men and women," *Chicago Tribune Book Review*'s James Kaufmann noted. In stories of thwarted dreams and lives spent yearning for something better, Yates employs a writing style that is both honest and illuminating. James Atlas of *Atlantic* commented, "Yates accomplishes what [F. Scottï Fitzgerald did at his best: an evocation of life's unbearable poignance, the way it has of nurturing hope and denying it, often in the same instant." "Yates treatment of ordinary life . . .," Joyce Carol Oates stated in *Nation,* "stresses the dullness, the lack of pattern, the lack of personal imaginative fulfillment. . . . A sad, gray, deathly world—dreams without substance—aging without maturity; this Yates's world, and it is a disturbing one." "Yates's work is characterized," Jerome Klinkowitz wrote in *Dictionary of Literary Biography,* "by a profound sadness. . . . Yates presents a picture of unrelieved sadness, redeemed only by his excellent literary style."

This portrayal of sadness was first seen in *Revolutionary Road,* Yates's first and best known novel. The book tells the story of Frank Wheeler, a suburban salesman whose marriage is falling apart. "But its true subject," claimed F. J. Warnke of *Yale Review,* "is neither the horrors of suburbia nor the futility of modern marriage. The novel is really about the inadequacy of human beings to fulfill

their own aspirations and its target is not America but existence." *Hudson Review*'s William H. Pritchard saw Yates as "a master at dramatizing how things go wrong in American marriages, how with the best of intentions people, particularly men, destroy what they've built." Gene Lyons of the *New York Times Book Review* viewed *Revolutionary Road* as a "brilliantly chilling and understated first novel about self-pity, pseudo-intellectual despair, and early death." Atlas described it as "one of the few novels I know that could be called flawless."

Fred Chappell found the book's honesty in dealing with its characters to be a crucial factor in its success. He wrote in *Rediscoveries* that *Revolutionary Road* "is so relentlessly honest and so embarrassingly personal that any critic who tries to take the customary view-from-above, the 'superior' stance . . . , has got to feel hypocritical and obtuse. You see yourself here. When you have an argument with your wife, or with someone who is a bit less articulate than you, or with someone over whom you imagine yourself to have a slight edge socially or economically, you begin to hear Frank Wheeler standing inside your voice, expostulating with false earnestness." Similarly, Theodore Solotaroff argued in *The Red Hot Vacuum* that "what makes *Revolutionary Road* as good as it is is mainly Yates's ability to tell the truth—both about the little, summary moments of work and marriage today and—though less clearly—about the larger social issues which the behavior and fate of the Wheelers express. Passage after passage has the ring of authenticity. . . . Yates has the superior novelist's instinct for the nuances by which people give themselves away."

In subsequent novels, Yates continued to earn critical respect for his writing. John Thompson of *Harper's* admired the clear prose with which Yates presents his stories. "Nothing intervenes between the author's knowledge and the reader's understanding," he said of *A Special Providence,* "but simple English that transmits that knowledge." Speaking of *The Easter Parade,* Paul Gray wrote in *Time* that "Yates can make reading about hum-drum pathos—the slow smashup of befuddled lives—invigorating and even gripping. He knows how to pace his material for maximum interest—when to summarize, when to show a scene in full. . . . In his descriptive prose every word works quietly to inspire the illusion that things are happening by themselves."

Another theme that can be traced through each of Yates's novels is that of "madness or suicide and the profession which purports to treat them," *Contemporary Novelists* contributor Carol Simpson Stern commented, pointing to April Wheeler in *Revolutionary Road,* Emily Grimes and her sister Sarah in *The Easter Parade,* John Wilder in *Disturbing the Peace,* and Bob Prentice in *A Special Providence* as examples of characters whose lives are invaded by mental illness, abuse, and death. "The protagonist of *Young Hearts Crying,*" Stern noted, "divides his life after his divorce into two periods: pre-Bellevue and post-Bellevue. He is the victim of several psychotic breakdowns; his daughter, a hippie in the early 1960s, also suffers from drugs and psychosis. Both figures scoff at Freud and psychology. In *Cold Spring Harbor* both the protagonist's mother and his mother-in-law are studies in alcoholism and mental instability."

In *Young Hearts Crying* the author exhibits a "deep understanding of ambition and the tangled web of relationships and makes no attempt to deny the jagged edges of his character's lives" and endows his characters with a credibility uncommon in modern writing, Peter Ross wrote in the *Detroit News. Washington Post Book World*'s Jonathan Yardley, however, criticized the story as familiar but less skillful than Yates's other novels. "*Young Hearts Crying* means to be a sensitive and affectionate account of the lives of its characters, but ends up being mostly bitter—for them and toward them," he remarked. Anatole Broyard also found fault with the book in the *New York Times Book Review*: "*Young Hearts Crying* fails for the most fundamental of reasons: because [the protagonist] Michael Davenport is not an interesting or appealing man. He is so self-pitying that there is no room for our pity. He has few ideas, and he explains them too much—to himself and to us. . . . as his second wife, Sarah, says, he lets his rhetoric run away with him—and it runs away with the book as well." Yet *Los Angeles Times Book Review* contributor Brian Stonehill declared, "Yates, it seems to me, is writing at the top of his form." Noting the author's description of the book's characters as people who " 'can make difficult things look easy,' " Stonehill speculates that the reader should apply that idea to the book itself: "Yates does indeed make it seem effortless—to tell the story of the ordinary daily lives of ordinary but intriguing characters in an interesting way. He succeeds in making the quotidian quotable." *Time* reviewer Jay Cocks concluded, "*Young Hearts Crying* slips seamlessly into the group of Yates novels that includes *Revolutionary Road, Disturbing the Peace* and *The Easter Parade*. All chart the kind of loss, loneliness and irony that are lastingly contemporary. He is just the writer that Michael Davenport always wanted to be."

Yates's final work, *Cold Spring Harbor,* is "an accomplished and somber novel of human hopes and disappointments" centered on another set of sorrowful lives, Frank Howard Mosher noted in *Washington Post Book World.* Mosher found that although the subject matter is dreary, *Cold Spring Harbor* "is so consistently well-written, just, unsentimental and sympathetic that the intertwined lives of the Shepards and Drakes are every bit as fascinating as they are grim." Elaine Kendall, writing in the *Los Angeles Times,* found *Cold Spring Harbor* a "meticulously crafted novel," and noted, "Against all odds, Yates has managed to show that chronic misery can be as much an art form as acute agony." Mosher concluded, "Anyone who's ever had a dream go awry, for whatever reason, should be grateful to Richard Yates for this well-crafted and convincing novel."

Several critics have pointed out that in all his work Yates wrote traditional stories in a conventional manner, avoiding the pyrotechnics of the avant-garde. Gray found Yates to be "a traditionalist in the strictest sense: he is a writer who feels duty-bound to tell familiar stories in conventional ways." "It is this skill in mining the commonplace, forever turning up marks of character and mainsprings of plot, that distinguishes Yates," Jonathan Penner of *New Republic* observed. "Few other writers dare trust themselves for so long with everyday life."

An important consequence of this traditional approach is Yates's constant use of ordinary characters in his stories. "The people in Yates," Penner believed, "are frail rather than strong and good. . . . They are persistently unremarkable." Klinkowitz saw Yates's achievement in his ability "to take characters so average that they tend to be flat and uninteresting and—by his management of imagery and style—capture the truth of their lives, all in a manner which makes the writing itself interesting and optimistic to read, at the same time that the materials described are not."

In a career that began with a book lauded by playwright Tennessee Williams and continued through seven novels of angst-ridden lives which garnered praise from such distinguished figures as publisher Seymour Lawrence and novelists William Styron, John Updike, and Kurt Vonnegut, Yates received less popular renown than he deserved. As critic and novelist Carolyn See wrote in 1981, " 'He's not going to get the recognition he truly deserves because to read Yates is as painful as getting all your teeth filled down to the gum with no anesthetic,' " *Times* staffer Elizabeth Venant noted.

At the time of his death, Yates was working on a book entitled "Uncertain Times," based on his experiences as a speech writer for Attorney General Robert Kennedy in 1963. A *New York Times* obituary noted that Lawrence, Yates's longtime publisher, was unsure whether the manuscript would be published.

BIOGRAPHICAL/CRITICAL SOURCES:

BOOKS

Contemporary Literary Criticism, Gale, Volume 7, 1977, pp. 553-556, Volume 8, 1978, pp. 555-556, Volume 23, 1983, pp. 479-484.

Contemporary Novelists, St. James Press, 1991, pp. 972-974.

Dictionary of Literary Biography, Volume 2: *American Novelists since World War II,* Gale, 1978, pp. 549-551.

Dictionary of Literary Biography Yearbook: 1981, Gale, 1982, pp. 133-136.

Madden, David, editor, *Rediscoveries,* Crown, 1971.

Solotaroff, Theodore, *The Red Hot Vacuum,* Atheneum, 1970.

PERIODICALS

Atlantic, April, 1961; October, 1975; November, 1981.
Chicago Tribune Book World, September 7, 1986.
Christian Century, May 3, 1961.
Commonweal, September 24, 1976.
Detroit News, December 9, 1984.
Harper's, November, 1969.
Hudson Review, spring, 1976.
Los Angeles Times, September 19, 1986; July 9, 1989.
Los Angeles Times Book Review, November 18, 1984, p. 2.
Nation, November 10, 1969.
National Observer, January 12, 1970.
New Republic, May 22, 1961; November 4, 1978.
Newsweek, September 15, 1975; September 25, 1978; September 1, 1986, p. 82.
New York Times, September 7, 1976; December 8, 1978; October 15, 1981; April 25, 1983; October 15, 1984; September 27, 1986.
New York Times Book Review, March 5, 1961; October 5, 1975; September 19, 1976; October 28, 1984, p. 3; October 5, 1986, p. 14.
Ploughshares, December, 1972.
Saturday Review, March 25, 1961.
Time, August 30, 1976; August 21, 1978; October 15, 1984, pp. 104, 106.
Times (London), July 16, 1987.
Times Literary Supplement, August 14, 1987, p. 873.
Yale Review, summer, 1961.
Washington Post Book World, April 3, 1983; October 7, 1984, p. 3; September 28, 1986, p. 6.

OBITUARIES:

PERIODICALS

New York Times, November 9, 1992, p. B9.*

*   *   *

YEHOSHUA, A(braham) B. 1936-

PERSONAL: Given name sometimes is spelled Avraham; born December 9, 1936, in Jerusalem; son of Yakov (an Orientalist) and Malka (Rosilio) Yehoshua; married Rivka Kirsninski (a psychoanalyst), June 14, 1960; children: Sivan, Gideon, Naum. *Education:* Hebrew University of Jerusalem, B.A., 1961; graduate of Teachers College, 1962. *Politics:* Labor. *Religion:* Jewish.

ADDRESSES: Home—102A Sea Rd., Haifa, 34746, Israel. *Office*—Department of Literature, Haifa University, Haifa, Israel.

CAREER: Hebrew University of Jerusalem High School, Jerusalem, Israel, teacher, 1961-63; Israeli School, Paris, France, director, 1963-64; World Union of Jewish Students, Paris, secretary-general, 1964-67; Haifa University, Haifa, Israel, dean of students, 1967-71, senior lecturer, 1971-77, professor of literature, 1977—. Lecturer on tour of American college and university campuses, 1969; visiting fellow, St. Cross College, Oxford, 1975-76; visiting professor, Harvard University, 1977, University of Chicago, 1988, and Princeton University, 1992. Member of board of art, Haifa Municipal Theatre. Adviser to drama editorial board, Israeli Television Network. *Military service:* Israel Army, paratrooper in Nachal unit, 1954-57.

AWARDS, HONORS: Akum Prize, 1961; second prize in Kol-Yisrael Competition, 1964, for radio script, *The Professor's Secret;* Municipality of Ramat-Gan Prize, 1968, for short story collection, *Mul ha-ye'arot;* University of Iowa fellowship in international literature program, 1969; Prime Minister Prize, 1972; Brener Prize, 1982; Alterman Prize, 1986; Bialik Prize, 1988; National Jewish Book Award, 1990 and 1993.

WRITINGS:

FICTION

Three Days and a Child (short stories), translation by Miriam Arad, Doubleday, 1970.
Early in the Summer of 1970 (novella), Schocken, 1972, originally published as *Bi-tehilat kayits—1970.*
Until Winter (short story collection), Hakibbutz, 1974.
The Lover (novel), translation by Philip Simpson, Doubleday, 1977, originally published as *Me'ahev.*
Gerushim me'uharim (novel), ha-Kibuts ha-me'uhad (Tel Aviv), 1982, translation by Hillel Halkin, published as *A Late Divorce,* Doubleday, 1984.
Molkho (novel), ha-Kibuts ha-me'uhad, 1987, translation by Halkin, published as *Five Seasons,* Doubleday, 1989.
The Continuing Silence of a Poet: The Collected Short Stories of A. B. Yehoshua, Penguin, 1991.
Mr. Mani (novel), translation by Halkin, Doubleday, 1992, originally published as *Mar Mani,* 1990.

PLAYS

Two Plays: A Night in May and Last Treatments (A Night in May was produced in Tel Aviv by Bimot Theatre,

1969 and *Last Treatments* was produced by Haifa Theatre), Schocken, 1974.

Hafatsim (title means "Possessions"), produced by Haifa Theatre, Shoken (Jerusalem), 1986.

NONFICTION

Bi-zekhut ha-normaliyut, Shoken (Jerusalem), 1980, translation by Arnold Schwartz published as *Between Right and Right,* Doubleday, 1981.

Israel, photos by Frederic Brenner, translation by Simpson, Harper & Row, 1988.

Hakir V-H-Har (title means "The Wall and the Mountain"; collection of political essays), Zmora Bitan, 1989.

OTHER

Also author of short story collections, including *Mot ha-zaken,* title means "The Death of an Old Man," 1962, and *Mul ha-ye'arot,* title means "Over against the Woods," 1968. Author of the plays *Israeli Babies,* 1991, and *Night's Babies,* Habima National Theatre, and radio script *The Professor's Secret. Three Days and a Child* and *Early in the Summer of 1970* have been produced as films, and *Three Days and a Child* was chosen to represent Israel at the Cannes Film Festival. Member of editorial board, *Keshet,* 1965-72, *Siman Kria,* 1973—, and *Tel Aviv Review,* 1987—.

Yehoshua's short stories, which have been appearing in journals and newspapers since 1957, have been included in anthologies published in Hebrew, English, French, Danish, Spanish, and Norwegian. Yehoshua's works have also been translated into fourteen languages, including Korean, Japanese, and Swedish.

SIDELIGHTS: One of Israel's foremost contemporary writers, Yehoshua deals in fictional form with the political and moral questions that have arisen out of Zionism, the Jewish Diaspora, and the Arab-Israeli conflict. His early short stories were in many cases surrealistic and allegorical. In a review of *Early in the Summer of 1970,* the *New York Times*'s Anatole Broyard calls Yehoshua's stories "a brilliant evocation of one face of life in Israel," namely, the tension between the generation of Israelis that was born in Europe and fled from Nazism and the generation which, like Yehoshua himself, was born in the state of Israel.

Yehoshua's first novel, *The Lover,* was controversial in Israel because of its criticisms of Israeli society—its "disappointment with the dream's implementation," in the words of *Midstream* contributor Nili Wachtel. One of the novel's main characters, the old woman Veducha, suffering in a hospital from degenerative diseases, symbolizes the distortion of Zionism by "messianic" aims, according to Wachtel. He summarizes: "Yehoshua's greatest disap-

pointment . . . [is] that it [Israeli society] lives in Zion like a lover from afar."

A Late Divorce, Yehoshua's second novel, examines questions about the Diaspora, the worldwide Jewish exile. The main character, Yehuda Kaminka, is an Israeli intellectual who had moved to Minneapolis. He must return to Israel briefly to obtain his wife's consent to a divorce so that he can marry his pregnant American girlfriend. Kaminka's nine-day return is narrated in Faulknerian style by a series of different relatives, in-laws, and by Kaminka himself. Harold Bloom, in the *New York Times Book Review,* notes that *A Late Divorce* is "authentic storytelling, acutely representative of current social realities in Israel and marked by extraordinary psychological insight throughout." In the *New Republic,* Leon Wieseltier praises the ambitious scale and subject of the novel and calls the series of monologues "brilliant," commenting that the only ingredient the novel lacks is "transcendence."

In *Five Seasons,* Yehoshua explores the life of his main character, Molkho, in five chapters, each of which is set in a specific season and concerns Molkho's psychological relationship with a woman. Beginning with the death of Molkho's wife from cancer in autumn, it ends as his mother-in-law is dying in a later autumn. Tova Reich, in *Washington Post Book World,* observes that "the novel comes together in Molkho's struggle to snatch some illumination and release from death." Reich asserts that Yehoshua's effort is "a wonderfully engaging, exquisitely controlled, luminous work." Bryan Cheyette, in the *Times Literary Supplement,* maintains that the novel is "a series of delightful set-pieces" that because of its facile comedy, could not, in the reviewer's opinion, sustain its more ambitious themes.

Mr. Mani, Yehoshua's next novel, covers six generations of Jewish history, from 1848 to 1982, through the medium of five separate conversations that go backward chronologically. It "spirals in upon the origins of Israel's current malaise, offering a kaleidoscopic view of Jewish history filtered through the events of one family," in the words of *New York Times Book Review*'s Jay Parini. Explaining his method in an interview with the *New York Times Book Review*'s Laurel Graeber, Yehoshua states that the novel is "intergenerational psychoanalysis," adding, "I wanted to understand the present by digging through the layers of the past." Mark Miller, in the Chicago *Tribune Books,* declares that Mr. Mani "takes on serious issues of Judaism, understanding it as more than a trial run for Zionism."

In his native Israel, Yehoshua's short stories are as well known as his novels. His collected works first appeared in English in 1991 in *The Continuing Silence of a Poet: The*

Collected Stories of A. B. Yehoshua. Francine Prose, reviewing the book for the *New York Times Book Review,* notes that she is "struck by its daring absence of authorial vanity and self-protection." She divides the stories into two genres—realistic stories of urban Israelis, and "parablelike fictions with metaphysical and political overtones." "At its best," Prose concludes, "*The Continuing Silence of a Poet* makes us feel we are seeing ourselves at the first moment of awakening, before we've had time to reinvent the face we show to the world."

BIOGRAPHICAL/CRITICAL SOURCES:

BOOKS

Contemporary Literary Criticism, Gale, Volume 13, 1980, pp. 616-619; Volume 31, 1985, pp. 466-476.

PERIODICALS

Books Abroad, spring, 1971.
Midstream, August-September, Volume 25, number 7, 1979, pp. 48-54.
New Republic, March 12, 1984, pp. 38-40.
New York Times, February 4, 1977.
New York Times Book Review, February 19, 1984, pp. 1, 31; May 26, 1991; March 1, 1992, p. 3.
Times Literary Supplement, May 3, 1985; August 26, 1988, p. 928; October 6, 1989, p. 1103.
Tribune Books (Chicago), March 1, 1992, Sec. 14, pp. 7, 11.
Washington Post Book World, February 5, 1989; March 8, 1992, p. 4.

*   *   *

YU, Ying-shih 1930-

PERSONAL: Born January 22, 1930, in Tientsin, China; son of Hsieh-chung (a professor) and Ya-Yen (Yew) Yu; married Monica Shu-ping Chen (a lecturer in Chinese), June 6, 1964; children: Sylvia Po-wei, Judy Chung-heng. *Education:* Attended Yenching University, 1948-50; Chinese University of Hong Kong, B.A., 1952; Harvard University, Ph.D., 1962. *Avocational Interests:* Go ("Oriental chess, the most intellectual of all games").

ADDRESSES: Home—4588 Province Line Rd., Princeton, NJ 08544. *Office*—Princeton University, 211 Jones Hall, Princeton, NJ 08554.

CAREER: Chinese University of Hong Kong, New Asia College, Hong Kong, instructor in Chinese history, 1954-55; Harvard University, Cambridge, MA, instructor in Chinese history, 1962; University of Michigan, Ann Arbor, assistant professor of Chinese history and language, 1962-66; Harvard University, visiting lecturer,

1966-67, associate professor, 1967-69, professor of Chinese history, 1969-77; Yale University, New Haven, CT, Charles Seymour Professor of History, 1977-87; Princeton University, Princeton, NJ, Michael Henry Strater Professor, 1987—. Chinese University of Hong Kong, pro-vice-chancellor, president of New Asia College, both 1973-75. Overseas consultant, Project of Confucian Ethics, 1983—.

MEMBER: Association of Asian Studies, Academia Sinica.

AWARDS, HONORS: LL.D., Chinese University of Hong Kong, 1977; Litt.D., Middlebury College, 1984.

WRITINGS:

Essays on Philosophy of Civilization, Highland Press (Hong Kong), 1955.
(With Robert Irick and Kwang-ching Liu) *American-Chinese Relations, 1784-1941,* Harvard University Press, 1960.
Trade and Expansion in Han China, University of California Press, 1967.
Fang I-chin: His Last Years and His Death, New Asia Research Institute, Chinese University of Hong Kong, 1972.
Tai Chen and Chang Hsueh-ch'eng: A Study in Mid-Ch'ing Intellectual History, Lung-men Book Store (Hong Kong), 1975.
History and Thought, Linking Publishers, 1976.
(Contributor) *Food in Chinese Culture,* Yale University Press, 1977.
The Two Worlds of the Red Chamber Dream, Linking Publishers, 1978.
Chung-kuo chih shih chieh ts'eng shih lun, Lien ching ch'un pan shih yeh kung ssu (Taipei), 1980.
(Editor) *Early Chinese History in the People's Republic of China: The Report of the Han Dynasty Studies Delegation, October-November, 1978,* University of Washington Press, 1981.
Shih hsueh yu Ch'uan t'ung, Shih pao wen hua ch'u pan shih yeh yu hsien kung ssu (Taipei), 1982.

Also author of *Li shih yu ssu hsiang,* 1976, *Lun Tai Chen Yu Chang Hsueh-ch'eng,* 1976, *Hung lou meng ti liang ko shih chieh,* 1978, *Min chu ko ming lun,* 1979, and *Wen ming lun heng,* 1979. Contributor of articles to professional journals. Editor, *Harvard Journal of Asiatic Studies.*

WORK IN PROGRESS: The Rise of Confucian Intellectualism in Ch'ing China.

BIOGRAPHICAL/CRITICAL SOURCES:

PERIODICALS

American Historical Review, October, 1968.
Archaeology, May, 1981.
English Historical Review, January, 1969.

Journal of Asian Studies, May, 1968.*